a Wolters Kluwer business

# 2007 Accounting Desk Book

*by Lois Ruffner Plank, Donald Morris, Bryan R. Plank, and Christie Plank Ciraulo*

## Highlights

The *2007 Accounting Desk Book* is a practical working tool that provides quick, authoritative, and up-to-date answers for CPAs and Financial Services Professionals applying relevant accounting principles and standards as well as tax rules. It contains all of the important pronouncements from the FASB, GASB, and IASB; financial reporting presentation requirements; required and recommended disclosures; and specialized accounting topics needed to field a client's questions, brush up on the proper treatment of a transaction, or consider an engagement in a new area of practice.

Guidelines, illustrations, and step-by-step instructions simplify complex accounting issues and give public and private accountants quick answers to accounting application questions.

## 2007 Edition

Most chapters have been updated or revised to reflect new guidance or standards on accounting and tax matters. Improvements in coverage have been made throughout. Chapter 2 contains a more complete explanation of earnings per share. Chapter 3 provides a new description of the statement of changes in stockholders' equity, including a sample format. Information on the statement of cash flows from other chapters has now been centralized in Chapter 4. FASB 131 requires that a company provide for each reportable segment, quantitative disclosure of two basic items—total assets and a measure of profit or loss. The content of Chapter 5 has been clarified and expanded to explain this important guidance more fully.

Chapter 10 on not-for-profits contains significant new changes made in this area in 2006 tax legislation. Many small not-for-profits that were formally exempt from reporting to the IRS are now required to file an annual information return with the IRS. Another major change for not-for-profits that generate unrelated business taxable income requires public disclosure of their form 990-T. Additionally, the rules regarding valuation of donations of charitable items have received modification and expansion.

Chapters 11 and 12 dealing with international accounting issues reflect changes during the past year, especially those reflecting the convergence of the international reporting rules with GAAP. In Chapter 12, the revised ISA 230 on audit documentation, a new IES on the competency requirements for auditors and a description of the finalized code of ethics have been added.

Chapter 15 on changes in accounting methods, which previously dealt primarily with IRS requirements, has been updated to include a summary of FASB 154 "Accounting Changes and Error Corrections." Information on tax depreciation, especially section 179, has been updated in Chapters 42-43. Several items in Chapters 31 and 29, dealing with debt and equity securities respectively, have been clarified and given expanded treatment.

In addition to the general updates described above, below lists specific details on several of the key chapters in the book.

- Chapter 6, "Actions of the Financial Accounting Standards Board" — with four new Standards: FASB 158, *Employers' Accounting for Defined Benefit Pension and Other Postretirement Plans—an amendment of FASB Statements No. 87, 88, 106, and 132(R)*, FASB Statement 157, *Fair Value Measurements*, FASB 156, *Accounting for Servicing of Financial Assets*, and FASB 155, *Accounting for Hybrid Instruments*, this chapter covers discussion of several topics even before on-going projects are considered. These include two Exposure Drafts intended to improve the accounting and disclosures for mergers and acquisitions (M&A) by not-for-profit organizations; an exposure draft, *Accounting for Postretirement Benefits, Including Pensions,* which is the second phase of the issues not covered in FASB 158; an ED to provide companies with the option to report selected financial assets and liabilities at fair value; a project to reconsider the current accounting standards for leases; and an Invitation to Comment (ITC) on the potential bifurcation of insurance and reinsurance contracts into insurance components and financing components. The chapter also discusses some of the cooperative efforts of the FASB with the IASB, AICPA, constituents, and other organizations.

- Chapter 8, "Governmental Accounting" — discusses several projects of the GASB including Statement No. 48, *Sales and Pledges of Receivables and Future Revenues and Intra-Entity Transfers of Assets and Future Revenues* which establishes criteria that governments will use to ascertain whether certain transactions should be regarded as a sale or a collateralized borrowing; a PV, *Accounting and Financial Reporting for Derivatives* to improve the accounting and financial reporting of derivatives by state and local governments; and a white paper emphasizing the sometimes-misunderstood point that those who are interested in the financial performance of state and local governments have substantially different information needs than those who follow the financial performance of for-profit entities. This last item is also discussed in more detail in Chapter 9, "Governmental Fund Accounting." As a part of its mission to develop literature that guides and educates the public about its standards, the GASB has published the 2006–2007 edition of its *Comprehensive Implementation Guide*. This guide consolidates and updates previously issued guides to individual standards. It also provides current guidance on standards for which no stand-alone guides have been published. The 2006–2007 edition includes for the first time the new freestanding Implementation Guide to Statement 44 on the Statistical Section and the Implementation Guide to Statements 43 and 45 on Other Postemployment Benefits (OPEB) that are also discussed in this chapter.

- Chapter 17, "Taxpayer Rights" — The National Taxpayer Advocate delivers two reports to Congress each year. The first, delivered in June identifies the priority issues the Office of the Taxpayer Advocate will address in the coming fiscal year. This report is submitted to the House Committee on Ways and Means; the second goes to the Senate Committee on Finance. The statute requires that both reports be submitted directly to the Committees without any prior review or comment from the Commissioner of Internal Revenue, the Secretary of the Treasury, the IRS Oversight Board, or any other officer or employee of the Department of the Treasury or the Office of Management and Budget. The second report, due on December 31 of each year, is required to identify at least 20 of the most serious problems encountered by taxpayers, discuss the 10 tax issues most frequently litigated the prior year, and make administrative and legislative recommendations to resolve taxpayer problems. Many of these topics and some from the 2006-2007 Priority Guidance Plan's 264 projects are discussed in the chapter.

- Chapter 18, "Practicing Before the IRS and the Power of Attorney" — ensuring that tax professionals adhere to professional standards and follow the law is one of the top four enforcement goals for the IRS.

The Treasury Department and the IRS believe that a proposed revision of Circular 230, rules that govern practice before the agency, issued in February 2006, plays a critical part in achieving that goal. The amendments to the provisions relate to various non-shelter items and go back several years. These proposed revisions are the result of a thorough review of the public comments received in 2002 and are related to the amendments to section 330 of title 31 made by the American Jobs Creation Act of 2004. (It is important to remember that until final rulings are issued, the requirements remain the same.) A discussion of the proposed revisions is discussed in the chapter. During 2006, Thomson Prometric, a global testing firm was selected by the IRS to develop and administer a computer-based version of the Special Enrollment Examination (SEE). Those who pass the SEE also undergo an additional background check before enrollment. There are currently about 42,000 active Enrolled Agents. A description of the provisions of the new examination is outlined in the chapter.

- Chapter 20, "E-commerce and E-Communication"—was supposed to grow by leaps and bounds. The forecasts were overblown. Such growth could not be sustained, but e-commerce is decidedly an important facet of personal and business activities today. Considering the impressive growth in retail sales in 2006 over 2005, as shown by the retail e-commerce figures in this chapter, it is fairly obvious that many are finding that buying online is the way to go. The term "e-commerce" has already been superseded by the term "e-business." E-commerce can be described as obtaining and distributing goods and services over the Internet using digital technology. Even though many use the terms interchangeably, the more encompassing term "e-business" can be defined as including all activities conducted by a business over the Internet. This definition for e-business extends beyond the definition of e-commerce by covering a digital approach to the whole enterprise, including other parts of the IT system and other non-transactional activities, such as recruiting employees through the Internet. The chapter discusses some of these uses.

- Chapter 21, "Insurance Accounting"—considers the attention of regulators, standard setters, trade associations, and Congress upon the insurance industry as a result of the accounting machinations of AIG, General Re, PricewaterhouseCooper, and/or their officials. For its part, the SEC pointed out that the problem was not about a violation of "technical accounting rules," but an attempt to fashion transactions expressly for the purpose of providing a specific false accounting effect in the issuer's financial statement. This chapter discusses some of the measures the FASB is considering to try to prevent such irregularities, including an Invitation to Comment (ITC) to determine whether or not to issue an ED on the potential bifurcation of insurance and reinsurance contracts into insurance components and finance components, and a project to consider issuing an ED on the accounting for financial guarantee contracts issued by insurance companies that are *not* accounted for as derivative contracts. The chapter also contains discussions of measures being taken by the National Association of Insurance Commissions to develop improved disclosure requirements in financial reporting by insurance companies.

- Chapter 27, "Public Company Accounting Oversight Board" — discusses Securities and Exchange Commission plans for improving the implementation of the Sarbanes-Oxley investor protection law by moving closer to issuing guidance for management that has been lacking since the law was enacted in 2002. The SEC has learned that issuers, auditors, investors, and others feel that while Section 404 has produced benefits, its implementation has been unduly costly. The Commission has also received specific feedback about issues that remain to be addressed, and actions that the SEC and the Public Company Accounting Oversight Board could, and are planning to take to make the internal control assessment and auditing more efficient and more effective. The intent is for the guidance to be flexible and scalable, so that it will assist companies of all sizes. The SEC has felt since the review of the first year of operating under SOX that registered accounting firms and their smaller clients have been overly cautious in applying the requirements of Section 404 in particular. Other discussions involve actions taken in 2006 including: Auditing Standard No. 4, *Reporting on Whether a Previously Reported Material Weakness Continues to Exist,* proposed revisions to Auditing Standard No. 2, *An Audit of Internal Control Over Financial Reporting Performed in Conjunction with an Audit of Financial Statements,* and relief from Section 404 for smaller companies and many foreign private investors.

- Chapter 36, "Derivatives" — As long as there are derivatives, there will be a continuing need for guidance and revisions of the rules. With FASB Statement No. 133, *Accounting for Derivatives and Hedging Activities,* on the books, there was, at least, a basis from which to work; however, that was only the beginning. This chapter discusses two new Standards related to derivatives issued in 2006. Statement No. 156, *Accounting for Servicing of Financial Assets*, concerns the recognition and measurement of separately recognized servicing assets and liabilities and an approach to simplify efforts to obtain hedge-like (offset) accounting. Statement No. 155, *Accounting for Hybrid Instruments*, is designed to improve the financial reporting of certain hybrid financial instruments by requiring more consistent accounting that eliminates exemptions and provides a means to simplify the accounting for these instruments. The FASB seems always to have several on-going questions to be considered. Among those being considered at present is guidance that relates to the "shortcut method" described in paragraph 68 of the FASB 133. The GASB is also interested in improving the accounting and financial reporting of derivatives—by state and local governments. There are often-complex financial arrangements that governments are entering into. However, these derivatives are rarely reported in the financial statements of governments and the public knows little about them, or with the risks associated with them. This chapter discusses the Preliminary Views (PV) document, *Accounting and Financial Reporting for Derivatives*, issued by the GASB proposing changes that could have a significant impact on the way state and local governments account for derivatives.

- Chapter 38, "Saving for a Higher Education"—the Hope and Lifetime Learning Credits, 529 education funds, Pell Grants, QTPs, Coverdell ESAs, student loans, U. S. Education Savings Bonds, business deductions for work-related education, state prepaid tuition plans, and just plain old-fashioned scholarships—it's a jungle out there. With more than 40 plans sold nationwide by individual states, they include an ever-changing array of state tax implications, a wide range of fees, and everything from an average portfolio with conservative returns to high-risk mutual fund investments. Federally, the IRS delineates education-related adjustments to income related to various plans. The guidelines are fairly clear. However, which to use, when and whether you can use multiple adjustments, is not. This is mostly because each individual and the circumstances are different and the amounts, limits and conditions change annually. A family's accountant/financial advisor can find some ideas to explore in this chapter.

- Chapter 46, "Tip Income"—has been reported much more accurately since the introduction in 1993 of the Tip Rate Determination/Education Program (TRD/EP). It was first promoted in the gaming industry (casino industry) in Las Vegas, Nevada, and has spread to the food and beverage industry. The employer has the option to enter into one of two arrangements under this program: the Tip Rate Determination Agreement (TRDA) or the Tip Reporting Alternative Commitment (TRAC) created in June 1995. Because of the success of these programs, an additional program discussed in this chapter has been introduced. The new Attributed Tip Income Program (ATIP) expands the existing IRS tip reporting and education program by offering employers in the food and beverage industry another option for reporting tip income. ATIP reduces industry recordkeeping burdens, has simple enrollment requirements and promotes reporting tips on Federal income tax returns.

## CCH Learning Center

CCH's goal is to provide you with the clearest, most concise, and up-to-date accounting and auditing information to help further your professional development, as well as a convenient method to help you satisfy your continuing professional education requirements. The CCH Learning Center* offers a complete line of self-study courses covering complex and constantly evolving accounting and auditing issues. We are continually adding new courses to the library to help you stay current on all the latest developments. The CCH Learning Center courses are available 24 hours a day, seven days a week. You'll get immediate exam results and certification. To view our complete accounting and auditing course catalog, go to: **http://cch.learningcenter.com**.

---

*CCH is registered with the National Association of State Boards of Accountancy (NASBA) as a sponsor of continuing professional education on the National Registry of CPE Sponsors. State boards of accountancy have final authority on the acceptance of individual courses for CPE credit. Complaints regarding registered sponsors may be addressed to the National Registry of CPE Sponsors, 150 Fourth Avenue North, Nashville, TN 37219-2417.

*CCH is registered with the National Association of State Boards of Accountancy as a Quality Assurance Service (QAS) sponsor of continuing professional education. Participating state boards of accountancy have final authority on the acceptance of individual courses for CPE credit. Complaints regarding QAS program sponsors may be addressed to NASBA, 150 Fourth Avenue North, Suite 700, Nashville, TN 37219-2417.

# Accounting Research Manager<sup>TM</sup>

**Accounting Research Manager** is the most comprehensive, up-to-date and objective online database of financial reporting literature. It includes all authoritative and proposed accounting, auditing, and SEC literature, plus independent, expert-written interpretive guidance.

Our Weekly Summary e-mail newsletter highlights the key developments of the week, giving you the assurance that you have the most current information. It provides links to new FASB, AICPA, SEC, PCAOB, EITF, and IASB authoritative and proposal-stage literature, plus insightful guidance from financial reporting experts.

Our outstanding team of content experts take pride in updating the system on a daily basis, so you stay as current as possible. You'll learn of newly released literature and deliberations of current financial reporting projects as soon they occur! Plus, you benefit from their easy-to-understand technical translations.

With **Accounting Research Manager**, you maximize the efficiency of your research time while enhancing your results. Learn more about our content, our experts, and how you can request a FREE trial by visiting us at **http://www.accountingresearchmanager.com**.

**12/06**

# 2007
# ACCOUNTING
# DESK BOOK

# 2007
# ACCOUNTING
# DESK BOOK

## The Accountant's Everyday Instant Answer Book

LOIS RUFFNER PLANK
DONALD MORRIS
BRYAN R. PLANK
CHRISTIE PLANK CIRAULO

CCH
a Wolters Kluwer business

This publication is designed to provide accurate and authoritative information in regard to the subject matter covered. It is sold with the understanding that the publisher is not engaged in rendering legal, accounting, or other professional services. If legal advice or other professional assistance is required, the services of a competent professional person should be sought.

ISBN 13: 978-0-8080-1584-0
       10: 0-8080-1582-2

No claim is made to original government works; however, within this Product or Publication, the following are subject to CCH's copyright: (1) the gathering, compilation, and arrangement of such government materials; (2) the magnetic translation and digital conversion of data, if applicable; (3) the historical, statutory and other notes and references; and (4) the commentary and other materials.

# About the Authors

**Lois Ruffner Plank** received her B.A. degree in Public Administration and International Relations from Miami University in Oxford, Ohio, with additional work in investments at the University of California at Los Angeles and at the University of Illinois.

Mrs. Plank is the co-editor of the *Encyclopedia of Accounting Systems* and co-author of several of the supplements to the *Accounting Desk Book*. She has been involved in budgeting and financial management with a government agency in Washington, D.C., and instituted a public relations and marketing program for a suburban Chicago school district.

She is an editor of professional publications and books and is a public relations consultant. Additional experience includes newspaper reporting and chief copy consultant for a national magazine.

**Donald Morris** CPA, Ph.D. has extensive accounting and tax experience in both the business and academic worlds. Dr. Morris managed his own accounting firm in Chicago for more than a decade before selling the practice and taking a position as professor of accounting first at Eastern New Mexico University and now at the University of Illinois at Springfield. With publications in accounting, tax, finance, management and business ethics journals Dr. Morris brings a wide perspective to issues relevant to accountants. In addition to being a Certified Public Accountant he is also a Certified Fraud Examiner and Certified Financial Planner. His newest book, *Opportunity: Optimizing Life's Chances* (Prometheus Books) was released in 2006. Dr. Morris has a Masters in Taxation from DePaul University and earned his Ph.D. in philosophy from Southern Illinois University Carbondale. He is a member of the American Institute of CPAs, the American Accounting Association and both the New Mexico and Illinois CPA Societies. He is also a member of the Society for Business Ethics and the American Philosophical Association. He has received recognition from *Who's Who Among America's Teachers* and *Who's Who in Finance and Industry*.

**Bryan R. Plank** is a wealth management advisor and resident director at a large securities firm. In addition, he holds numerous licenses, certifications, and credentials in securities, insurance, and real estate. Mr.Plank is serving on the NASD committee for the Los Angeles district.

He has 20 years of experience in training and development in the securities industry and is a frequent guest speaker at many San Diego area colleges and universities. Mr. Plank earned university degrees from the University of Southern California and California State Polytechnic University, Pomona, with additional postgraduate work at Claremont Graduate School.

**Christie Plank Ciraulo** has a B.S. in journalism and an MPR in Public Relations from the University of Southern California, with additional studies at the University of Geneva, Switzerland, and the University of California, Los Angeles.

Her work experience in writing includes major Los Angeles hospital and healthcare newsletters and annual reports, as well as media appearances. For 12 years she was owner of a graphic design and writing firm that produced professional and trade publications. As research editor and author, she has been instrumental in the development, research, writing, and editing of the *Accounting Desk Book* and *The Encyclopedia of Accounting Systems*.

# Contents

## TAX MATTERS

## APPENDICES

# Preface

Accounting information is complex, mirroring the complexity of the business, government, and non-profit activities it measures. It is difficult for those practicing the profession to be specialists in more than a few limited areas, let a alone understand it all. Overlaying this problem is the growing influence of the international accounting community and its pursuit of convergence of accounting standards, which could lead to uniform reporting around the world. In this complex and changing environment, it is essential that the accounting practitioner have at least a glancing knowledge of many areas, if only to know what he or she does not know or needs to study.

In auditing in particular, but also in tax and other areas of accounting, the accountant must understand the industry in which his or her client operates including its regulatory environment. One of the goals of the *Accounting Desk Book* is to bring together in one source, changes and updates to areas of accounting and tax compliance from across the business spectrum. While it is difficult for anyone to be an expert in all areas of accounting, it is certainly possible to be aware of recent changes across a wide range of accounting and tax issues. From recent FASB pronouncements, to the implementation of Sarbanes-Oxley, to significant recent tax legislation, this book provides information and guidance on what is occurring on the margins. It is not a textbook or a detailed reference on a niche within accounting. Rather, it spans traditional boundaries in accounting providing current information on financial accounting, tax, cost accounting, non-profit, governmental, and international accounting as well as related information on investments, e-commerce, ethics, the Securities and Exchange Commission, insurance accounting and much more.

Because of its breadth of coverage, this work serves to introduce and update many topics. Nevertheless, in the case of other topics, on which comprehensive information is not always available, such as the treatment of independent contractors and tip income, its coverage is substantial. For many practitioners, the book proves most useful by offering a quick background update on an unfamiliar topic or area in which they have not practiced for a number of years.

It is imperative that all accountants and auditors keep pace with new laws, regulations, official pronouncements and industry guidance affecting their practice. The *Accounting Desk Book* assists the accountant in his or her effort to understand and comply with both new and existing accounting rules and regulations. The importance of current information cannot be overemphasized. Coverage of topics, applications, examples, and definitions of terms is the goal of this volume. It avoids abstract theory, technical jargon, complex "legalese" and textbook-type prose, which can needlessly complicate discussion of the rules and procedures. All topics are covered in straightforward, plain English. Discussions throughout the *Accounting Desk Book* are mostly self-contained. A review of the topics does not require reference to other sources. The table of contents clearly sets forth the subjects discussed and the index helps locate needed information rapidly.

# PART I

## FINANCIAL REPORTING

# Chapter 1
# Principles of Financial Statements, Disclosure, Analysis, and Interpretation

## CONTENTS

## ¶1000  OVERVIEW

The general objective of financial reporting is to provide reliable information on resources, obligations and progress. The information should be useful for comparability, completeness and understandability. The basic features involved in financial accounting are the individual accounting entity, the use of approximation and the preparation of fundamentally related financial statements.

The financial statements—balance sheet, income statement, change in stockholders' equity and statement of cash flows, as well as segment reports and interim reports—will summarize a firm's operations and ending financial position. Analysts, investors, creditors and potential investors and creditors will analyze these documents in their decision-making processes.

## ¶1001  FAIR PRESENTATION IN CONFORMITY WITH GAAP

Fair presentation in conformity with GAAP requires that the following four criteria be met:

1. GAAP applicable in the circumstances have been applied in accumulating and processing the accounting information.
2. Changes from period to period in GAAP have been properly disclosed.
3. The information in the *underlying* records is properly *reflected* and *described* in the financial statements in conformity with GAAP.
4. A proper balance has been achieved between the conflicting needs to:
   a. Disclose the important aspects of financial position and results of operation in conformity with conventional concepts, and
   b. Summarize the voluminous underlying data with a limited number of financial statement captions and supporting notes.

## ¶1003  12 PRINCIPLES OF FINANCIAL STATEMENT PRESENTATION

1. *Basic Financial Statements*. At minimum, these statements must include:
   a. Balance Sheet
   b. Statement of Income
   c. Statement of Changes in Stockholders' Equity
   d. Statement of Cash Flows
   e. Disclosure of Accounting Policies
   f. Full disclosure in Related Notes
   Information is usually presented for two or more periods. Other information also may be presented, and in some cases required, as supplemental information (e.g., price-level statements, information about operations in

different industries, foreign operations and export sales, and major customers (segment reporting)).

2. *The Balance Sheet.* A complete balance sheet must include:
   a. All assets
   b. All liabilities
   c. All classes of stockholders' equity

3. *The Income Statement.* A complete income statement must include:
   a. All revenues
   b. All expenses

4. *The Statement of Cash Flow.* A complete statement of cash flow includes and describes all important aspects of the company's operating, financing and investing activities.

5. *Accounting Period.* The basic time period is one year. An interim statement is for less than one year.

6. *Consolidated Financial Statements.* In the context of a parent company and its subsidiaries statements are presumed to be more meaningful than separate statements of the component legal entities. They are *usually* necessary when one of the group owns (directly or indirectly) *over 50 percent* of the outstanding voting stock. The information is presented as if it were a *single enterprise*.

7. *The Equity Basis.* For unconsolidated subsidiaries (consolidated is used where over 50 percent is owned) where ownership is between 20 percent and 50 percent of the voting stock and the investor has significant influence over investees, the equity method is used to report the amount of the investment on the investor's balance sheet. The investor's share of the net income reported by the investee is picked up (debited if income, credited if loss) and shown as investment income and an adjustment of the investment account is made for all earnings subsequent to the acquisition. Dividends are treated as an adjustment (credit) to the investment account.

8. *Translation of Foreign Branches.* Data are translated into U.S. Dollars by conventional translation procedures involving foreign exchange rates.

9. *Classification and Segregation.* These important components must be disclosed separately:
   a. Income Statement—Sales (or other source of revenue); Cost of Sales; Depreciation; Selling Administration Expenses; Interest Expense; Income Taxes.
   b. Balance Sheet—Cash; Receivables; Inventories; Plant and Equipment; Payables; and Categories of Stockholder's Equity:
      • Par or stated amount of capital stock; Additional paid-in capital
      • Retained earnings affected by:
        —Net income or loss,

¶1003

   —Prior period adjustments,

   —Dividends, or

   —Transfers to other categories of equity.

- Working capital—current assets and current liabilities should be classified as such to be able to determine working capital—useful for enterprises in manufacturing, trading and some service enterprises.
- Current assets—cash and other that can reasonably be expected to be realized in cash in one year or a shorter business cycle.
- Current liabilities—liabilities expected to be satisfied by the use of those assets shown as current; by the creation of other current liabilities; or in one year.
- Assets and liabilities—should *not* be offset against each other unless a legal right to do so exists, which is a rare exception.
- Gains and losses—arise from disposals of other than products or services and may be combined and shown as one item. Examples are the sale of equipment used in operations, gains and losses on temporary investments, non-monetary transactions and currency devaluations.
- Extraordinary items or gain or loss—should be shown separately under its own title. Items distinguished by unusual nature and infrequent occurrence should be shown net of taxes.
- Net income—should be separately disclosed and clearly identified on the income statement.
- Earnings per share information is shown for net income and for individual components of net income.

10. *Other disclosures (Accounting policies and notes)*. These include:

   a. Customary or routine disclosures:
   - Measurement bases of important assets
   - Restrictions on assets
   - Restriction on owners' equity
   - Contingent liabilities
   - Contingent assets
   - Important long-term commitments not in the body of the statements
   - Information on terms of equity of owners
   - Information on terms of long-term debt
   - Other disclosures required by the AICPA

   b. Disclosure of changes in accounting policies

   c. Disclosure of important subsequent events—between balance sheet date and date of the opinion

     d. Disclosure of accounting policies ("Summary of Significant Account-
       ing Policies")

11. *Form of Financial Statement Presentation. No* particular form is presumed
    better than all others for all purposes. Several are used.

12. *Earnings Per Share.* This information must be disclosed on *the face of the
    Income Statement* and should be disclosed for:

    a. Income before extraordinary items

    b. Net Income

Disclosure should consider:

    a. Changes in number of shares outstanding

    b. Contingent changes

    c. Possible dilution from potential conversion of:

      • Preferred stock

      • Options

      • Warrants

This information is disclosed both for basic earnings per share and for
fully-diluted earnings per share which adjusts the denominator for potentially
dilutive shares arising from possible exercise of stock options, conversion of
convertible debt to stock and the like.

# ¶1005 MATERIALITY

Financial statements are subject to the constraint of materiality. There
have been attempts by authoritative rule-making bodies, scholars of accounting, users of financial statements, and others to develop quantitative criteria for
determining the materiality of items in the financial statements. They postulate
that if Item A is X percent of a total, Item A is material. If Item B is Y percent
of a total, then Item B is material, but . . . All efforts have proved fruitless,
and there are no accepted quantitative standards that can be wholly relied
upon for an unquestioned determination of whether an item is material or
immaterial (and thus can be omitted from the financial statements or notes
thereto).

    The courts to some extent have helped. However, it should be cautioned
that different jurisdictions in different geographic areas of the country have
established many opinions and definitions of materiality. For example, the
Tenth Circuit Court of Appeals ruled that information is material if ". . . the
trading judgment of reasonable investors would not have been left untouched
upon receipt of such information." (*Mitchell v. Texas Gulf Sulphur Co.*) In the
"landmark" *Bar Chris* case the judge said that a material fact is one ". . . which
if it had been correctly stated or disclosed would have deterred or tended to deter

the average prudent investor from purchasing the securities in question" (*Escott et al. v. Bar Chris Construction Corporation et al.*).

Principally because the U.S. Supreme Court defined materiality in the *TSC Industries Inc. v. Northway Inc.* case, the following statement of the Court is considered to be an authoritative basis upon which to render a judgment of materiality:

> "An omitted fact is material if there is a substantial likelihood that a reasonable shareholder would consider it important in deciding how to vote. This standard is fully consistent with the general description of materiality as a requirement that the defect have a significant *propensity* to affect the voting process."

> [Note: This decision dealt with omissions of material information.]

> "The Securities and Exchange Commission defines *material information:* 'The term material when used to qualify a requirement for the furnishing of information as to any subject, limits the information required to those matters as to which an average prudent investor ought reasonably to be informed.'"

## .01 What's Material?

The accountant must decide precisely what information requires disclosure. To do this, the accountant must exercise judgment according to the circumstances and facts concerning material matters and their conformity with Generally Accepted Accounting Principles. A few examples of material matters are:

1. The form and content of financial statements.
2. Notes to the statements.
3. The terminology used in the statements.
4. The classification of items in the statements.
5. Amount of detail furnished.
6. The bases of the amounts presented (e.g., for inventories, plants, liabilities).
7. The existence of affiliated or controlling interests.

A clear distinction between materiality and disclosure should be noted. Material information involves both quantitative (data) and qualitative information. Additionally, the information must be disclosed in a manner that enables a person of "average" comprehension and experience to understand and apply it to an investment decision. Contra speaking, information disclosed in a manner that only an "expert" can evaluate is not considered within the meaning and intent of disclosure requirements.

¶1005.01

Materiality should be thought of as an abstract concept. Many efforts to define the term can be found in the literature (e.g., accounting and auditing books, law books, and Regulation S-X). Nevertheless, in the final analysis, judgments with respect to what is material resulting from court decisions, SEC actions, accountants' interpretations, and corporate and financial officers' judgments have ultimately evolved into the subjective judgment of individuals (accountants and management) responsible for deciding what is and is not material.

## ¶1007  DISCLOSURES REQUIRED IN FINANCIAL STATEMENTS

Following is an overview of the most important disclosures required in financial statements with a brief comment on the substance of each requirement.

### .01  Accounting Policies

Accounting Principles Board Opinion 22 (APB 22), *Disclosure of Accounting Policies*, is the applicable GAAP. (See the discussion at the end of this chapter.) The disclosure should set forth the accounting principles underlying the statements that materially affect the determination of financial position, changes in financial position, and results of operations. Also included are the accounting principles relating to recognition of revenue, allocation of asset costs to current and future periods, the selection from existing acceptable alternatives, such as the inventory method chosen, and any accounting principles and methods unique to the industry of the reporting entity.

As a general rule, the preferred position of the review of accounting policies is footnote No. 1, but a section summarizing the policies preceding the footnotes is acceptable.

### .03  Who Decides What Information Is Material?

This decision is the responsibility of management working with the company's accountant. As a generalization, the *causes* for material changes in financial statement items must be noted to the extent necessary for users to understand the business as a whole. This requirement applies to all financial statements, not just to the income statement. The following items are considered material and *must* be recognized.

1. Sales and revenues. Increases or decreases in sales and revenues that are temporary or nonrecurring and their causes.
2. Unusually increased costs.
3. Informative generalizations with respect to each important expense category.

4. Financial expenses. Changes in interest expenses (and interest income); changes in the company's cost of borrowing; changes in the borrowing mix (e.g., long-term vs. short-term).

5. Other income and expense items. These may include dividend income from investees; the equity in the income or losses of investees or of unconsolidated subsidiaries.

6. Income taxes. The effective tax rate paid by corporations should be reconciled to the statutory rates. The reconciliation provides the basis for a description of the reasons for year-to-year variations in the effective tax rate to which a business is subject. Changes caused by the adoption of new or altered policies of tax-deferred accounting are considered material.

7. Material changes in the relative profitability of lines of business.

8. Material changes in advertising, research and development, new services, or other discretionary costs.

9. The acquisition or disposition of a material asset.

10. Material and unusual charges or gains, including credits or charges associated with discontinuance of operations.

11. Material changes in assumptions underlying deferred costs and the plan for the amortization of such costs.

12. The cost of goods sold, where applicable. The gross margin of an enterprise can be affected by important changes in sales volume, price, unit costs, mix of products or services sold, and inventory profits and losses. The composition of cost among fixed, semi-variable and variable elements influences profitability. Changes in gross margins by an analysis of the interplay between selling prices, costs, and volume should be explained.

13. Cash flow information.

14. Dilution of earnings per share.

15. Segmental reporting.

16. Rental expense under leases.

17. Receivables from officers and stockholders.

## ¶1009   FULL DISCLOSURE

*Full Disclosure* is an attempt to present all essential information about a company in the following reports:

1. Balance Sheet
2. Income Statement
3. Statement of Changes in Stockholders' Equity

4. Statement of Cash Flows
5. Accompanying Footnotes

The objectives of financial reporting are set forth in *FASB Concepts Statement 1*. The financial statements, notes to the financial statements, and necessary supplementary information are governed by FASB standards. Financial reporting includes other types of information, such as *Management's Discussion and Analysis*, letters to stockholders, order backlogs, statistical data, and the like, commonly included in reports to shareholders.

## .01  The Full Disclosure Principle

Financial facts significant enough to influence the judgment of an informed person should be disclosed. The financial statements, notes to the financial statements, summary of accounting policies, should disclose the information necessary to prevent the statements from being misleading. The information in the statements should be disclosed in a manner that the intended meaning of the information is apparent to a reasonably informed user of the statements.

## ¶1011  DISCLOSURE IN FINANCIAL REPORTING

### .01  Disclosure

The heart of the compilation and disclosure of financial information is *accounting*. Yet, the idea of "adequate disclosure" stands alone as the one concept in accounting that involves all of the good things and all of the dangers inherent in the professional practice of accounting and auditing. Probably the use of the colloquialism "disclosure" best describes the all-embracing nature of the concept. That is to say, *disclosure is the name of the financial reporting game*.

For decades the profession has been inundated with disclosure literature, rules, regulations, statements, government agencies' accounting regulations, court decisions, tax decisions, intellectualizing by academics, books and seminars, all concerning what disclosure is all about.

Yet nobody has answered precisely what continues to remain the essential question: Disclosure of *what*, by *whom*, for *whom?*

The lack of definitive qualitative and quantitative criteria for what information must or need not be disclosed forces upon the independent accountant the responsibility to decide what constitutes a matter requiring disclosure, requiring an exercise of judgment in light of the circumstances and facts available at the time. The *accountant's* responsibility is confined to the expression of an opinion based upon an examination. The representations made through the statements are *management's* responsibility.

What is a material fact, and for whom does a disclosed fact have material significance? What substantive standards of disclosure must the accountant maintain? Who is to promulgate these standards? The profession? One or all of the governmental regulatory agencies? A federal board of accounting? The courts? The Congress?

One conclusion is clear, however. There is an unmistakable trend toward increasing demands upon the accounting profession for more financial information. What better evidence can be cited than the conclusion of the AICPA Study Group on the Objectives of Financial Statements? The group's report said that ". . . financial statements should meet the needs of those with *LEAST* ability to obtain information."

The confusion between what is and is not *material* is caused by a widely held concept—different facts have different meanings for the individual user of financial information. Information that is important to one user may be insignificant to another.

> "All information must adapt *itself* to the perception of those towards whom the information is intended."
>
> -Anonymous

It is neither possible nor economically feasible, however, for an accountant to cover in the statements every single small detail concerning a client's business. Where should the accountant draw the line? (Not many years ago, a large accounting firm had to defend a lawsuit up to the U.S. Supreme Court at a cost of several million dollars because the accountant did not question the company's chief executive officer's policy that he, alone, open the company's mail.)

Recent trends in financial reporting reflect an increase in the amount of disclosure found in financial statements. The information is communicated in the footnotes, which are an integral part of the financial statements. Although the footnotes are usually drafted in somewhat technical language, they are the accountant's means of amplifying or explaining the items present in the main body of the statements. Footnote information can generally be classified as follows:

1. *Disclosure of Accounting Policies Applied.* This information is required in order to inform the user of the statements of the accounting methods used in preparing the information that appears in statements.
2. *Disclosure of Gain or Loss Contingencies.* Because many contingent gains or losses are not properly included in the accounts, their disclosure in the footnotes provides relevant information to financial statement users.
3. *Examination of Credit Claims.* A liability, such as a bank loan, may have numerous covenants that are not conveniently disclosed in the liability section of the balance sheet.

4. *Claims of Equity Holders*. The rights of various equity security issues along with certain unique features that may apply to certain issues are commonly disclosed in footnotes to the statements.

5. *Executory Commitments*. These refer to contract obligations undertaken by the company that have not been performed, or have been only partially performed at the statement date.

In some cases a company is faced with a sensitive issue that requires disclosure in a footnote. Some examples are:

1. Related party transactions
2. Errors
3. Irregularities
4. Illegal acts

# ¶1013 DISCLOSURES ITEMIZED

Following is an alphabetical listing of items requiring disclosure including short comments if applicable:

Accelerated Depreciation Methods—when methods are adopted.

Accounting Policies—(see the discussion of APB 22 at the end of this chapter.)

Allowances (depreciation, depletion, bad debts)—deduct from asset with disclosure.

Amortization of Intangibles—disclose method and period.

Amounts Available for Distribution—note the needs for any holdback retention of earnings.

Arrangements with Reorganized Debtor—disclose if a subsequent event.

Arrears on Cumulative Preferred Stock—the rights of senior securities must be disclosed on the face of balance sheet or in the notes.

Assets (interim changes in)—only significant changes required for interims.

Business Segments.

Cash-Basis Statements—fact must be disclosed in the opinion with delineation of what would have been had accrual basis been used, its significant variance.

Change in Stockholders' Equity Accounts—in a separate schedule. This does not include the changes in retained earnings statement, which is also a basic requirement.

Change to Declining Balance Method—disclose change in method and effect of it.

Changes, Accounting.

Commitments, Long-Term—disclose unused letters of credit, assets pledged as security for loans, pension plans, plant expansion or acquisition; obligations to reduce debt, maintain working capital or restrict dividend.

Commitments to Complete Contracts—only the extraordinary ones.

Consolidation Policy—method used.

Construction Type Contracts—method used.

Contingencies—disclose when reasonable possibility of a loss, the nature of, and estimated loss. Threats of expropriation, debtor bankruptcy if actual. Those contingencies which might result in gains, but not misleading as to realization. Disclosure of uninsured risks is advised, but not required. Gain contingencies should be disclosed, but not reflected in the accounts.

Contingencies in Business Combinations—disclose escrow items for contingencies in the notes.

Control of Board of Directors—disclose any stock options existing.

Corporate Officer Importance—disclose if a major sales or income factor to the company.

Current Liabilities—disclose why, if any, omitted (in notes).

Dating (Readjusted) Earned Surplus—no more than 10 years is the term now required.

Deferred Taxes—disclose and also see Timing Differences in this text.

Depreciation and Depreciable Assets—disclose the following:

1. Depreciation expense for the period.
2. Balances of major classes of depreciable assets by nature or function.
3. Accumulated depreciation by classes, or in total.
4. A general description of the methods used in computing depreciation.

Development Stage Enterprises—are required to use the same basic financial statements as other enterprises, with certain additional disclosures required. Special type statements are not permissible.

Discontinued Operations—disclose separately below continuing-operating income, net of tax, but before extraordinary items. Show separate EPS.

Diversified Company's Foreign Operations.

Earnings per share—see discussion in this text, but the following is also required in addition to the data stated there (does not apply to nonpublic enterprises):

1. Restatement for a prior period adjustment.
2. Dividend preference.

¶1013

3. Liquidation preference.

4. Participation rights.

5. Call prices and dates.

6. Conversion rates and dates.

7. Exercise prices and dates.

8. Sinking fund requirements.

9. Unusual voting rights.

10. Bases upon which primary and fully diluted earnings per share were calculated.

11. Issues that are common stock equivalents.

12. Issues that are potentially dilutive securities.

13. Assumptions and adjustments made for earnings per share data.

14. Shares issued upon conversion, exercise, and conditions met for contingent issuances.

15. Recapitalization occurring during the period or before the statements are issued.

16. Stock dividends, stock splits or reverse splits occurring after the close of the period before the statements are issued.

17. Claims of senior securities entering earnings per share computations.

18. Dividends declared by the constituents in a pooling.

19. Basis of presentation of dividends in a pooling on other than a historical basis.

20. Per share and aggregate amount of cumulative preferred dividends in arrears.

Equity Method—as follows:

1. Financial statements of the investor should disclose in the notes, separate statements or schedules, or parenthetically:

   a. The name of each investee and percent of ownership,

   b. The accounting policies of the investor, disclosing if, and why, any over 20 percent holdings are not under the equity method,

   c. Any difference between the carrying value and the underlying equity of the investment, and the accounting treatment thereof;

2. Disclose any investments which have quoted market prices (common stocks) showing same—do not write down;

3. Present summary balance sheet and operating information when equity investments are material;

4. Same as above for any unconsolidated subsidiaries where ownership is majority;

5. Disclose material effects of contingent issuances.

¶1013

Extinguishment (Early) of Debt—gains or losses should be described, telling source of funds for payoff, income tax effect, per share amount.

Extraordinary Items—describe on face of income statement (or in notes), show effect net of tax after income from continuing operations, also after business disposals if any, show EPS separately for extraordinary item. May aggregate immaterial items.

Fiscal Period Differences (in Consolidating)—disclose intervening material.

Fiscal Year Change—disclose effect only.

Foreign Items—Assets, must disclose any significant ones included in U.S. statements; gains or losses shown in body of U.S. statement; disclose significant "subsequent event" rate changes; operations, adequate disclosure to be made of all pertinent dollar information, regardless of whether consolidating or not (for foreign subsidiaries).

Headings and Captions—may be necessary to explain.

Income Taxes (and Deferred Taxes)—(see Timing Differences in this text.)

Income Taxes of Sole Proprietor or Partnership—may be necessary to disclose personal taxes to be paid if the money will come from and put a drain on the firm's cash position.

Infrequent Events—show as separate component of income and disclose nature of them.

Interim Statements—(see discussion in Appendix E.)

Inventories—disclose pricing policies and flow of cost assumption in "Summary of Significant Accounting Policies"; disclose changes in method and effect on income. Dollar effect based upon a change should be shown separately from ordinary cost of sales items.

Investment Tax Credits—disclose method used, with amounts if material. Also, disclose substantial carryback or carryforward credits.

Leases.

Legal Restrictions on Dividend Payments—put in notes.

Liability for Tax Penalties—if significant, disclose in notes. May have to take exception in opinion.

Market Value of Investments in Marketable Securities—should be written down to market value and up again, but not to exceed cost for entire portfolio per classification.

Noncumulative Preferred Stock—should disclose that no provision has been made because it is noncumulative.

Obligations (Short-Term)—disclose in notes reason any short-term obligations not displayed as current liabilities.

Partnerships, Limited—disclose fact that it's a limited partnership.

Patent Income—disclose if income is ending.

¶1013

Pension Plans—must disclose the following:
1. Describe and identify employee groups covered by plan.
2. The accounting and funding policy.
3. The provision for pension cost for the period.
4. Excess, if any, of vested benefits over fund total; any balance sheet deferrals, accruals, prepays.
5. Any significant matters affecting comparability of periods presented.

Political Contributions—must disclose if material or not deductible for taxes, or if they are beneficial to an officer.

Price-Level Restatements.

Prior Period Adjustments—must disclose with tax effects. Must disclose in interim reports.

Purchase Commitment Losses—should be separately disclosed in dollars in income statement.

Purchase Option Cancellation Costs—yes, disclose.

Real and Personal Property Taxes—disclose if using estimates, and if substantial. All adjustments for prior year estimates should be made through the current income statement.

Real Estate Appraisal Value—for development companies, footnote disclosure might be useful.

Receivables, Affiliated Companies, Officers and Employees—should be segregated and shown separately from trade receivables.

Redemption Call of Preferred Stock—disclose in the equity section.

Renegotiation Possibilities—use dollars if estimable or disclose inability to estimate.

Research and Development Costs—disclosure must be made in the financial statements of the total research and development costs charged to expenses in each period for which an income statement is presented. Government-regulated enterprises should disclose the accounting policy for amortization and the totals expensed and deferred, but not the confidential details of specific projects, patents, new products, processes or company research philosophy. Applies the above provision for disclosure to business combinations.

Restricted Stock Issued to Employee—disclose circumstance and the restrictions.

Retained Earnings Transferred to Capital Stock—arises usually with "splitups effected as dividends" and with stock dividends; must disclose and include schedule showing transfers from retained earnings to capital stock. Also, must disclose number of shares for EPS; must show subsequent event effects.

¶1013

Sale and Leaseback.

Seasonal Business (Interim Statements)—must disclose, and advisable to include 12-month period, present and past.

Stock Dividends, Split-up—must disclose even if a subsequent event and use as if made for and during all periods presented.

Stock Options—disclose status. Has effect on EPS.

Stockholders Buy/Sell Stock Agreements—disclose.

Subleases.

Termination Claims (War and Defense Contracts)—shown as current receivable, unless extended delay indicated; usually shown separately and disclosed if material, in income statement.

Treasury Stock—Shown in body of balance sheet (equity section ordinarily); should, in notes, indicate any legal restrictions.

Unconsolidated Subsidiaries—if using cost method, should also give independent summary information about position and operations.

Undistributed Earnings of Subsidiaries.

Unearned Compensation.

Unremitted Taxes—disclose only if going concern concept is no longer valid.

## ¶1015  RESTATEMENTS

The following alphabetical listing indicates those areas that *require* a restatement (with disclosure) for all prior periods presented in the comparative financial statements:

Appropriations of Retained Earnings—any change made for the reporting of contingencies requires retroactive adjustment.

Changes in Accounting Principle Requiring Restatement:
1. Change from LIFO to another method.
2. Change in long-term construction method.
3. Change to or from "full cost" method in the extractive industries.
4. Must show effect on both net income and EPS for all periods presented.

Change in Reporting Entity—must restate.

Contingencies—restate for the cumulative effect applying the rules for contingencies.

Earnings Per Share—the effect of all restatements must be shown on EPS, separating as to EPS from continuing operations, EPS from disposals, EPS from extraordinary items and EPS from net income.

Equity Method—restatement required when first applying the method, even though it was not required before.

Extraordinary Items—if a similar one in prior period was not classified as extraordinary but is now, reclassify now for comparison.

Foreign Currency Translations—restate to conform with adoption of standards; if indeterminable, use the cumulative method. Disclose nature of restatement and effect (or cumulative effect) on income before extraordinary items, on net income, and on related per share amounts.

Income Taxes (Equity Method)—restate to comply.

Interim Financial Statements—restate for changes in accounting principle and for prior period adjustments. If it's a cumulative type change, the first interim period should show the entire effect; if in later period, full effect should be applied to the first period and restated for other periods.

Leases.

Prior Period Adjustments—must restate the details affected for all periods presented, disclose and adjust opening retained earnings. Must also do it for interim reports.

Refinancing Short-Term Obligations—restatement is permitted, but not required.

Research and Development Costs—In conforming with standards, apply retroactively as a prior period adjustment. (*No* retroactive recapitalization of costs is permissible. Applies to *purchase* combinations also. Basic rule: expense as incurred.)

Revision based on FASB Opinions—retroactive restatement is not required *unless* the new standard *specifically* states that it is required. (Note that restatements are *not* required for a change from FIFO to LIFO, nor for a change in the method of handling investment tax credits.)

Statistical Summaries (e.g., 5 years, 10 years)—restate all prior years involved in prior period adjustments.

Stock Dividends and Splits—must restate earnings per share figures and number of shares to give effect to stock dividends and splits *including* those occurring after close of period being reported on (for all periods presented).

# ¶1017   PERMANENT AND TIMING DIFFERENCES—INCOME TAX

## .01   Permanent Differences

Those that will not reverse or "turn around" in other periods:

1. Specific revenues exempt from taxability (examples):
   Interest on tax-exempt securities
   Officer life insurance proceeds
   Unrealized gains on marketable securities

Unrealized gains on foreign currency translations

Tax benefits arising from stock-option compensatory plans (when booked as Income)

2. Expenses that are not tax deductible:

Depreciation taken on appraisal increases or donated property

Interest expense paid to carry tax-exempt securities

Premiums on officer life insurance

Tax penalties and fines

Unrealized losses on marketable securities

Unrealized losses on securities or currency translations

Impairment losses not recognized for tax

Federal income taxes paid

3. Those expenses that are predicated upon different bases for financial and tax purposes:

Depreciation on trade-ins

Statutory depletion vs. cost depletion

Amortization of good will for tax purposes

Dividends received deduction

Domestic production deduction

## ¶1019  TIMING DIFFERENCES

Those that *will* turn around or reverse in one or more subsequent periods. Four broad categories:

1. Income—for Accounting NOW—for Taxes LATER
2. Expenses—for Accounting NOW—for Taxes LATER
3. Income—for Accounting LATER—for Taxes NOW
4. Expenses—for Accounting LATER—for Taxes NOW

Below is an explanation of these four categories:

1. Items of *income* included for accounting financial statement purposes NOW not taken on the tax return until a LATER time (examples):
   a. Gross profit on installment method date of sale/when collected on tax return.
   b. Percentage of completion method books/completed contract method for tax return.
   c. Leasing rentals on books under financing method/actual rent less depreciation for tax return.
   d. Subsidiary earnings reported now/as received for tax return.

2. Items of *expense* taken on financial statements NOW, not taken on tax returns until LATER (examples):

   a. Accelerated depreciation used for financials/not for tax return.

   b. Contributions on financials over 10 percent limit/carried over for taxes.

   c. Deferred compensation accruals/taken when paid on tax return.

   d. Estimated costs of various kinds/taken when cost or loss becomes actual and known, such as guarantees, product warranties, inventory losses, legal settlements, segment disposals and major repairs.

   e. Depreciation based on shorter life for books than for tax return.

   f. Organization costs taken now/amortized for tax return.

   g. Capital losses now for financial later for tax.

3. Items of *income* taken into financial books LATER, but reported as income NOW on tax returns:

   a. Rents and royalties deferred until earned/reported when collected for tax return.

   b. Deferred fees, dues, services contracts/reported when collected for tax returns.

   c. Intercompany consolidation gains and losses/taxed now if filing separate return.

   d. Leaseback gains, amortized gains over lease-term/date of sale for tax return.

4. Items of *expense* taken into financial books LATER, but taken NOW on tax returns:

   a. Depreciation; shorter lives used for tax purposes accelerated rates on tax return/straight-line on books; certain emergency facility amortization taken on tax returns/later on books.

   b. Bond discount, premium costs taken on return/amortized on books.

   c. Certain costs that are taken for tax purposes/but deferred for financial purposes, as:

   d. Incidental costs of property acquisitions.

   e. Preoperating costs.

   f. Certain research and development costs (deferred for financial purposes).

## .01  Other Considerations Regarding Income Taxes

Interperiod tax allocation should be followed under the deferred method. Timing differences may be considered individually or grouped by similarity. Tax carryback losses (including investment tax credit carrybacks) should be recognized in the loss period in which the carryback originated. Carryforwards

¶1019.01

should not be recognized until realized (then shown as *extraordinary* item) unless there is no doubt of realization (then shown as part of operating profit or loss).

## .03  Balance Sheet Presentation of Income Taxes

Tax accounts on the balance sheet should be classified separately as to:

1.  Taxes estimated to be paid currently.
2.  *Net* amount of current deferred charges and deferred credits related to timing differences.
3.  *Net* amount of noncurrent deferred taxes related to timing differences.
4.  Receivables for carryback losses.
5.  When realization is beyond doubt, show an asset for the benefit to be derived from a carryforward of losses.
6.  Deferred investment credits, when this method is employed.

## .05  Income Statement Presentation of Income Taxes

All taxes based on income, including foreign, federal, state and local, should be reflected in income tax expense in the income statement.

The following components should be disclosed separately and put on the income statement before extraordinary items and prior period adjustments:

1.  Taxes estimated to be payable.
2.  Tax effects of timing differences.
3.  Tax effects of operating losses.

In addition, the following general disclosures are required:

1.  Amounts of any operating loss carryforwards not recognized in the loss period, with expiration dates and effect on deferred tax accounts.
2.  Significant amounts of any other unused tax deductions or credits, with expiration dates.
3.  Any reasons for significant differences between taxable income and pretax accounting income.
4.  Deferred income taxes related to an asset or liability are classified the same as the related asset or liability. A deferred tax charge or credit is related to an asset or liability if reduction of the asset or liability would cause the underlying timing difference to reverse. Deferred income taxes that are not related to an asset or liability are classified according to the expected reversal date of the timing difference.

## ¶1021  FINANCIAL STATEMENT ANALYSIS AND INTERPRETATION

Analysis techniques applied to financial statements are of interest to the corporate financial officer of any entity for a number of reasons. For one thing, that particular company's financial statements will be subject to analysis by creditors, credit grantors, and investors. Furthermore, the financial officer will want to analyze the company's statements for internal management use as well as analyze other companies' financial statements for credit purposes and perhaps for investment purposes (where an acquisition is being considered).

The financial statements are a systematic and convenient presentation of the financial position and operating performance of a business entity. The question is: What can be learned by analyzing and interpreting the information available in the statements?

There is much valuable information to be learned, as ratio analysis answers questions concerning the financial facts of a business:

1.  GAAP permits a variety of accounting procedures and practices that significantly affect the results of operation reported in the statements. Statement analysis helps to evaluate the choices of alternative accounting decisions.
2.  The statements for a number of successive years can be compared by the use of ratios and unusual trends and changes can be noted.
3.  A company's statements can be compared with those of other similar companies in the same industry.
4.  Statement analysis is the basis for estimating, or projecting, potential operating results by the development of pro forma statements.
5.  The effects of external economic developments on a company's business can be applied to results as shown in the statements.
6.  The balance sheet valuations can be related to the operating results disclosed in the income statement, since the balance sheet is the link between successive income statements.
7.  Since ratios are index numbers obtained by relating data to each other, they make comparisons more meaningful than using the raw numbers without relating an absolute dollar figure to another statement item.

## ¶1023  FOUR GROUPS OF RATIOS

Ratios are usually classified into four groups:

1.  *Liquidity Ratios:* Measures of the ability of the enterprise to pay its short-term obligations.

2. *Profitability Ratios:* Measures of the profits (losses) over a specified period of time.
3. *Coverage Ratios:* Measures of the protection for the interest and principal payments to long-term creditors and investors.
4. *Activity Ratios:* Measures of how efficiently the company is employing its assets.

The ratios in the following discussion are those most commonly applied to measure the operating efficiency and profitability of a company. (There are hundreds of possible relationships that can be computed and trends identified.) The discussion includes an explanation of the answers that each ratio provides; each ratio's application to a specific area of a business will be noted.

## ¶1025    THE ACCOUNTANT'S RESPONSIBILITY

*In evaluating the ratios, the accountant must be mindful that the ratios are simply a measuring tool,* not the final answers nor the end in themselves. They are one of the tools for evaluating the *past* performance and providing an indication of the future performance of the company. Ratios are a *control* technique and should be thought of as furnishing management with a "red flag" when a ratio has deviated from an established norm, or average, or predetermined standard.

Accordingly, ratio analysis is meaningless without an *adequate feedback* system by which management is promptly informed of a problem demanding immediate attention and correction.

While accountants are concerned primarily with the *construction* of the financial statements, particularly their technical accuracy and validity, the accountant is also relied upon by the many different users of the statements for assistance in the interpretation of the financial information. The accountant must use experience and technical skill to evaluate information and to contribute to management decisions that will maximize the optimum allocation of an organization's economic resources.

## .01    Basic Analysis Techniques

Much of the analytical data obtained from the statements is expressed in terms of ratios and percentages. (Carrying calculations to one decimal place is sufficient for most analysis purposes.) The basic analysis technique is to use these ratios and percentages in either a *horizontal* or *vertical* analysis, or both.

*Horizontal Analysis.*    Here, similar figures from several years' financial statements are compared. For example, it may be useful to run down two years' balance sheets and compare such items as the current assets, plant assets, current liabilities and long-term liabilities on one balance sheet with the similar items on the other and to note the amount and percentage increases or decreases for each item. Of course, the comparison can be for more than two years. A number of years may be used, each year being compared with the base year or the immediate preceding year.

*Vertical Analysis.*   Here, component parts are compared to the totals in a single statement. For example, it can be determined what percentage each item of expense on the income statement is of the total net sales, or, what percentage of the total assets the current assets comprise.

*Ratios.*   Customarily, the *numerator* of the equation is expressed first, then the denominator. For example, fixed assets to equity means fixed assets *divided by* equity. Also, whenever the numerator is the larger figure, there is a tendency to use the word "turnover" for the result.

As indicated above, these techniques are widely used, generally in the course of one analysis.

## ¶1027  BALANCE SHEET ANALYSIS

The significance of the balance sheet is that it shows relationships between classes of assets and liabilities. From long experience, businesspeople have learned that certain relationships indicate the company is in actual or potential trouble or is in good financial shape. For example, these relationships may indicate that the business is short of working capital, is undercapitalized generally, or has a bad balance between short- and long-term debt.

It must be emphasized that there are no fixed rules concerning the relationships. There are wide variations between industries and even within a single industry. It is often more valuable to measure these relationships against the past history of the same company than to use them in comparison with other businesses. If sharp disparities do show, however, it is usually wise not to ignore them. Many of the so-called "excesses" that in the past have led to recessions often show up in the balance sheets of individual companies. The most important balance sheet ratios and their implications for the business are discussed below.

## .01  Ratio of Current Assets to Current Liabilities

The *current ratio* is probably the most widely used measure of liquidity (i.e., a company's ability to pay its bills). It measures the ability of the business to meet its current liabilities. The current ratio indicates the extent to which the current liabilities are covered. For example, if current assets total $400,000 and current liabilities are $100,000, the current ratio is 4 to 1.

Good current ratios will range from about 2 to almost 4 to 1. However, the ratio will vary widely in different industries. For example, companies that collect quickly on their accounts and do not have to carry very large inventories can usually operate with a lower current ratio than those companies whose collections are slower and inventories larger.

If current liabilities are subtracted from current assets, the resulting figure is the *working capital* of the company; in other words, the amount of free capital that is immediately available for use in the business. One of the most significant reasons for the failure of small businesses is the lack of working capital, which makes it difficult or impossible for the business to cope with sudden changes in worsening economic conditions. Conversely, lack of a comfortable amount of working capital may prevent a small business from taking advantage of opportunities to expand in a growing economy.

The details of working capital flow are presented in the two-year comparative Statement of Cash Flows, a mandatory part of the financial statements.

An important feature of the ratios to remember is that when both factors are decreased by the same amount, the ratio is increased:

|  | Old | Change | New |
|---|---|---|---|
| Current Assets | $100,000 | $(25,000) | $75,000 |
| Current Liabilities | 50,000 | (25,000) | 25,000 |
| Working Capital | 50,000 | 0 | 50,000 |
| Ratio | 2 to 1 | | 3 to 1 |

By paying off $25,000 worth of liabilities (depleting Cash), you have increased the ratio from 2 to 1 to 3 to 1. Note that the *dollar* amount of *working capital* remains the same $50,000.

Conversely, should you borrow $50,000 on short-terms (increasing Cash and Current Liabilities), you would *reduce* the ratio to *1½ to 1* ($150,000/100,000), again with the dollar amount of working capital remaining at $50,000.

A variation of the current ratio is the *acid test*. This is the ratio of *quick assets* (cash, marketable securities, and accounts receivable) to *current liabilities*. This ratio eliminates the inventory from the calculation, since inventory may not be readily convertible to cash.

## .03   Acid-Test Ratio

The current ratio does not disclose the fact that a portion of the current assets may be tied up in slow-moving inventories, which leaves the question of how long it will take to transform the inventories into finished product and how much will be realized on the sale of the merchandise. Elimination of inventories and prepaid expenses from the current assets will give better information for short-term creditors. A *quick* or *acid-test ratio* relates total current liabilities to cash, marketable securities, and receivables. If this total is $150 divided by current liabilities of $100, the acid-test ratio is 1½ to 1, which is low compared to an industry average of 3 to 1. This means a company would have difficulty meeting its short-term obligations and would have to obtain additional current assets from other sources.

## .05  Defensive-Interval Ratio

The defensive-interval ratio is computed by dividing defensive assets—cash, marketable securities, and receivables—by projected daily expenditures from operations. This ratio measures the time span a firm can operate with present liquid assets without resorting to revenues from next year's sources. Projected daily expenditures are computed by dividing cost of goods sold plus selling and administrative expenses and other ordinary expenses by 365 days. Assuming a company has a defensive-interval measure of 150 days and an industry average of 75 days, the 150 days provides a company with a high degree of protection, and can offset the weakness indicated by low current and acid-test ratios that a company might have.

## .07  Ratio of Current Liabilities to Stockholders' Equity

This ratio measures the relationship between the short-term creditors of the business and the owners. Excessive short-term debt is frequently a danger sign, since it means that the short-term creditors are providing much or all of the company's working capital. If anything happens to concern the short-term creditors, they will demand immediate repayment and create the risk of insolvency. Short-term creditors are most often suppliers of the business, and the company's obligation to them is listed under accounts payable. However, short-term creditors may also include short-term lenders.

A general rule occasionally cited for this ratio is that for a business with a tangible capital and earnings (net worth) of less than $250,000, current liabilities should not exceed two-thirds of this tangible net worth. For companies having a tangible net worth over $250,000, current liabilities should not exceed three-fourths of tangible net worth.

*Tangible* net worth is used instead of total net worth because intangible assets (such as patents and copyrights) may have no actual market value if the company is forced to offer them in distress selling.

## .09  Ratio of Total Liabilities to Stockholders' Equity

The ratio differs from the preceding one in that it includes only long-term liabilities. Since the long-term creditors of a company are normally not in a position to demand immediate payment, as are short-term creditors, this ratio may be moderately greater than the preceding one without creating any danger for the company. However, the ratio should never exceed 100 percent in an industrial company. If it did, this would mean that the company's creditors have a larger stake in the enterprise than the owners themselves. Under such circumstances, it is very likely that credit would not be renewed when the existing debts matured. Utilities and financial companies can operate safely with much higher ratios because more of their liabilities are long-term.

## .11    Ratio of Fixed Assets to Stockholders' Equity

The purpose of this ratio is to measure the relationship between fixed and current assets. The ratio is obtained by dividing the book value of the fixed assets by the tangible value of stockholders' equity. A rule sometimes used is that if tangible net worth is under $250,000, fixed assets should not exceed two-thirds of tangible net worth. If tangible net worth is over $250,000, fixed assets should not exceed three-fourths of tangible net worth.

## .13    Ratio of Fixed Assets to Long-Term Liabilities

Since long-term notes and bonds are often secured by mortgages on fixed assets, a comparison of the fixed assets with the long-term liabilities reveals what "coverage" the note or bondholders have—that is, how much protection they have for their loans by way of security. Furthermore, where the fixed assets exceed the long-term liabilities by a substantial margin, there is room for borrowing additional long-term funds on the strength of the fixed asset position.

## .15    Ratio of Cost of Goods Sold to Inventory— Inventory Turnover

One of the most frequent causes of business failure is lack of inventory control. A firm that is optimistic about future business may build up its inventory to greater than usual amounts. Then, if the expected business does not materialize, the company will be forced to stop further buying and may also have difficulty paying its creditors. In addition, if a company is not selling off its inventory regularly, that item, or part of it, is not really a *current* asset. Additionally, there may be a considerable amount of unsalable inventory included in the total. For all these reasons, a business is interested in knowing how often the inventory "turns over" during the year. In other words, how long will the current inventory be on the shelves, and how soon will it be turned into money?

To find out how often inventory turns over, the average inventory is compared to the cost of goods sold shown on the income statement. (Typically, average is computed by adding opening and closing inventories and dividing the total by two.) For example, if average inventory is $2 million and cost of goods sold adds up to $6 million, during the course of the year, the company has paid for three times the average inventory. Therefore, it can be said that the inventory turned over three times, and at year-end there remained about a four months' supply of inventory on hand.

Because information about cost of goods sold and average inventory may not be readily available in published reports, another way to measure the same results is by using the ratio of net sales to inventory. In this ratio, net sales is substituted for cost of goods sold. Since net sales will always be a larger figure (because it includes the business's profit margin), the resulting inventory turn-over will be a higher figure.

How large an inventory should a company carry? That depends upon many factors within a particular business or industry. What may be large or small may vary with the type of business or the time of year. An automobile dealer with a large inventory at the beginning or middle of a model year will be in a strong position. A large inventory at the end of the season places him in a weak financial position.

## .17   Ratio of Inventory to Working Capital

This is another ratio to measure over- or under-inventory. Working capital is current assets minus current liabilities. If inventory is too high a proportion of working capital, the business is short on quick assets—cash and accounts receivable. A general rule for this ratio is that businesses of tangible net worth of less than $250,000 should not have an inventory which is more than three-fourths of net working capital. For a business with tangible net worth in excess of $250,000, inventory should not exceed net working capital. The larger-size business can tolerate a condition where there are no quick assets because its larger inventory can be borrowed against; in addition, it presumably has fixed assets which can be mortgaged if necessary.

Inventory as a percentage of current assets may indicate a significant relationship when comparison is made between companies in the same industry, but not between different types of companies because of other variables.

## .19   Receivables Turnover

An important consideration for any business is the length of time it takes to collect its accounts receivable. The longer accounts receivable are outstanding, the greater the need for the business to raise working capital from other sources. In addition, a longer collection period increases the risk of bad debts. A general rule for measuring the collection period is that it should not be more than one-third greater than the net selling terms offered by the company. For example, if goods are sold on terms of 30 days net, the average collection period should be about 40 days, though this varies from industry to industry. Special rules apply in the case of installment selling.

Another way of measuring the collection rate of accounts receivable is to divide the net sales from the income statement by the average accounts receivable. This gives the accounts receivable turnover—that is, how many times during the year the average accounts receivable were collected. A comparison with prior years reveals whether the company's collection experience is getting better or worse. The faster the turnover, the more reliable the current and acid-test ratios are for financial analytical purposes.

## .21 Asset Turnover

This ratio indicates how efficiently a company utilizes its assets. If the turnover rate is high, the indication is that a company is using its assets efficiently to generate sales. If the turnover ratio is low, a company either has to use its assets more efficiently or dispose of them. The asset turnover ratio is affected by the depreciation method used. If an accelerated method of depreciation is used, the results would be a higher turnover rate than if the straight-line method is used, all other factors being equal.

## .23 Book Value of the Securities

This figure represents the value of the outstanding securities according to the values shown on the company's books. This may have little relationship to market value—especially in the case of common stock. Profitable companies often show a low net book value but report very substantial earnings. Railroads, on the other hand, may show a high book value for their common stock but have such low or irregular earnings that the stock's market price is much less than the book value. Insurance companies, banks and investment companies are exceptions. Since most of their assets are liquid—cash, accounts receivable, marketable securities—the book value of their common stock may well present a fair approximation of the market value.

Nevertheless, book value is an important test of financial strength. It is computed by simply subtracting all liabilities from total assets. The remaining sum represents the book value of the equity interest in the business. In computing this figure, it is a good idea to include only tangible assets, such as land, machinery and inventory. A patent right or other intangible may be given a large dollar value on the balance sheet, but in the event of liquidation may not be salable at all. The theory underlying the measurement of book value is that it is a good measure of how much cash and credit the company may be able to raise if it comes upon bad times. Book value is usually expressed per share outstanding.

Book value is also an important measure for the bondholders of the company. For them, the value has the significance of telling them how many dollars per bond outstanding the company has in available assets. Since they have a call on the company's assets before either the preferred stockholders or the common stockholders, a substantial book value per bond in excess of the face amount of the bond offers relative assurance of the safety of the bond—assurance that funds will be available to pay off the bonds when they become due. To find the book value of the bonds, add together the total stockholders' equity and the amount of the bonds outstanding.

For example, stockholders' equity totals $5 million. Bonded indebtedness is $2 million. From this $7 million total we subtract $1 million of intangibles. That leaves $6 million of net tangible assets. This represents a coverage of three times the total bond indebtedness, usually a fairly substantial coverage.

## ¶1029  INCOME STATEMENT ANALYSIS

Just as with the balance sheet, most of the figures obtained from the income statement acquire real meaning only by comparison with other figures, either with similar figures of previous years of the same company or with the corresponding figures of other companies in the same or similar business.

For example, comparisons can be made between each significant item of expense and cost and net sales to get a percentage of net sales (vertical analysis) which can then be compared with other companies. Percentages are more meaningful to compare than absolute dollar amounts, since the volume of business done by one company in the same industry may vary substantially from the volume of another company.

Comparison can also be made of each of the significant figures on the income statement with the same figures for prior years (horizontal analysis). Here, too, comparisons of percentages rather than absolute dollar amounts might be more meaningful if the volume of sales has varied substantially from year to year.

Other significant comparisons are covered in the following paragraphs.

## .01  Ratio of Long-Term Debt to Equity

This ratio measures the leverage potential of the business; that is, the varying effects which changes in operating profits will have on net profits. The rule is that the higher the debt ratio, the greater will be the effect on the common stock of changes in earnings because of increased interest expenses.

Many security analysts feel that in an industrial company equity should equal at least half the total of all equity and debt outstanding. Railroads and utilities, however, are likely to have more debt (and preferred stock) than common stock because of the heavy investments in fixed assets, much of which is financed by the use of debt and preferred stock.

A stock is considered to have high leverage if the issuing company has a high percentage of bonds and preferred stock outstanding in relation to the amount of common stock. In good years, this will mean that after bond interest and preferred stock dividends are paid, there will be an impressive earnings per share figure because of the small amount of common stock outstanding.

On the other hand, that same high leverage situation could cause real difficulty with even a moderate decline in earnings. Not only would the decline eliminate any dividends for the common stock, but also could even necessitate drawing from accumulated earnings to cover the full interest on its bonds.

## .03 Earnings per Share

Probably, the most important ratio used today is the earnings per share (EPS) figure. It is a *mandatory* disclosure on all annual financial (income) statements (for public companies) and mandatory for all interim statements (though unaudited) for public companies. Moreover, the EPS must be broken out separately for extraordinary items. The standards of calculation are quite complex where preferred stock, options and convertibility are involved.

## .05 Exposure Draft to Amend FASB 128

In December 2003, the FASB issued an Exposure Draft to amend computational guidance in Statement 128, *Earnings per Share*. The salient points of the ED include:

- Guidance for calculating the number of incremental shares included in diluted shares when applying the treasury stock method.
- Elimination of the provisions of FASB 128 that allow an entry to rebut the presumption that contracts with the option of settling in either cash or stock will be settled in stock.
- A requirement that shares that will be issued upon conversion of a mandatorily convertible security be included in the weighted average number of ordinary shares outstanding used in computing basic earnings per share from the date when conversion becomes mandatory.

In October 2002, the FASB and the IASB undertook a joint project to achieve more comparability in cross-border financial reporting through convergence to a single set of high-quality accounting standards. Each Board reviewed its pronouncements for areas of its generally accepted accounting principles (GAAP) that could be improved by converging with the other board's GAAP.

Since then, the IASB has reexamined IAS 33 and proposed changes to enhance its occupational guidance. Therefore, EPS was identified as an area in which the FASB and the IASB could further improve accounting by converging their standards.

The Board also pointed out that this proposed statement would reaffirm the Board's conclusion in FASB 128 that "... financial statements could be improved by simplifying the existing computational guidance, ... and increasing the comparability of ESP data on an international basis."

The Board also noted that under the IASB approach, the denominator for year-to-date computations of EPS will not be affected by the frequency of interim reporting. If adopted, this proposed Statement would enhance the comparability of financial statements prepared under U.S. GAAP and those prepared under the proposed International Financial Reporting Standards in accordance with the Board's oft-stated goal of promoting the international convergence of accounting standards concurrent with improving the quality of financial reporting.

## .07  FASB 128, *Earnings per Share*

FASB 128 established new standards for computing and presenting earning per share and applies to entities with publicly held common stock or potential common stock.

It simplifies the admittedly complicated methods used for computing earnings per share previously found in APB 15, *Earnings Per Share*, and makes the requirements comparable to new international EPS standards adopted recently. In doing this, FASB 128 replaces the presentation of primary EPS with a presentation of basic EPS. It also requires dual presentation of basic and diluted EPS on the face of the income statement for all entities with complex capital structures and requires a reconciliation of the numerator and denominator of the basic EPS computation to the numerator and denominator of the diluted EPS computation.

The two EPS figures required under FASB 128 follow:

1. Basic Earnings Per Share is computed by dividing income available to stockholders by the weighted average number of common shares outstanding during the period. Shares issued during the period and shares reacquired during the period should be weighted for the portion of the period they were outstanding. The formula would be: (Net income minus preferred dividends) divided by common stock.

2. Diluted EPS reflects the potential dilution that could occur if securities or other contracts to issue common stock were exercised or converted into common stock or resulted in the issuance of common stock that would then share in the earnings of the entity. It is figured in a similar manner to basic EPS after adjusting the numerator and denominator for the possible dilution. Since it is, therefore, computed in a similar manner to fully diluted EPS under APB 15, it will produce a similar earnings per share figure.

*Equity Valuation Unchanged.*   The new standard did not change U.S. equity valuations because:

1. Even though basic earnings per share show a higher figure than primary earnings per share, informed investors do not use basic earnings per share anyway for companies with complex capital structures because it does not take into account the potential dilutive effect of convertibles, options, warrants, and the like.
2. Most entities' dilutive earnings per share are substantially the same as their fully diluted earnings per share had been.

*Resulting Changes.*   Of course, the most important change introduced by the FASB 128 is the elimination of the complicated calculations necessary to arrive at primary earnings per share and replace them with the simpler calculations necessary to obtain basic earnings per share for disclosure.

In addition, diluted EPS is somewhat different from "fully diluted earnings per share." Not only is "fully" dropped, but the calculation of the figure is changed in several ways:

1. Elimination of the provision that the diluted earnings per share need not be given if the potential dilution is less than three percent.
2. Elimination of the use of the end of period stock price in the treasury stock method calculation to determine maximum dilution.
3. Elimination of the modified treasury stock method that was used to calculate potential dilution in cases when an unusually large number of options or warrants were outstanding.
4. Use of the earnings from continuing operations as the "control figure" to determine if a security or contingent issuance is antidilutive in certain situations.

The new statement not only supersedes APB 15 and AICPA Accounting Interpretation 1-102 of APB 15, it also supersedes or amends other accounting pronouncements scattered throughout accounting literature. The provisions in this Statement are substantially the same as those in International Accounting Standard 33, *Earnings per Share*, issued by the International Accounting Standards Committee at the same time.

## .09   Sales Growth

The raw element of profit growth is an increase in sales (or revenues when the company's business is services). While merely increasing sales is no guarantee that higher profits will follow, it is usually the first vital step; therefore, in analyzing a company, the sales figures for the past four or five years are important. If they have been rising and there is no reason to believe the company's markets are near the saturation point, it is reasonable to assume that the rise will continue.

When a company's sales have jumped by the acquisition of another firm, it is important to find out if the acquisition was accomplished by the issuance of additional common stock, by the assumption of additional debt, or for cash. If the company was paid for by common stock and if the acquired firm's earnings are the same on a per-share basis as those of the acquiring firm, the profit picture remains exactly as it was before. The additional sales growth is balanced by the *dilution of the equity*—that is, the larger number of shares now sharing in the earnings.

The situation is quite different if the purchase was for cash or in exchange of bonds or preferred stock. Here, no dilution of the common stock has occurred. The entire profits of the new firm (minus the interest which must be paid on the new debt or the interest formerly earned on the cash) benefit the existing shareholders.

In any event, acquisitions of new companies often require a period of consolidation and adjustment, frequently followed by a decreased rate of sales growth.

Consideration should be given to the effect of inflation on sales. A situation can exist where the increase in sales may be caused by the increase in prices. The result may be that unit sales have dropped in relation to the previous year's, but the dollar sales have increased. Comparing unit sales may be a better method of ascertaining the sales increase under certain circumstances.

## .11  Computing Operating Profit

A company's costs of operations fall into two groups: *cost of goods sold* and *cost of operations*. The first relates to all the costs of producing the goods or services matched to the revenues produced by those costs. The second includes all other costs not directly associated with the production costs, such as selling and administrative costs (usually called period expenses).

Subtracting both of these groups of costs from sales leaves *operating profit*. Various special costs and special forms of income are then added or subtracted from operating income to get *net income before taxes*. After deducting state and federal income taxes, the final figure (which is commonly used for computing the profit per share) is *net income*. When analyzing a company, however, you will often be most interested in the operating profit figure, since this reflects the real earning capacity of the company.

The best way to look at cost figures is as a percentage of sales. Thus, a company may spend 90 cents out of every dollar in operating costs. We say its cost percentage is 90 percent or, more commonly, its *operating profit margin* is

10 percent. Profit margins vary a great deal among industries, running anywhere from 1 percent to 20 percent of sales; thus comparisons should not be made between companies in different industries. The trend of the operating profit margin for a particular company, however, will give an excellent picture of how well management is able to control costs. If sales increases are obtained only by cutting prices, this will immediately show as a decrease in the margin of profit. In introducing a new product it is sometimes necessary to incur special costs to make initial market penetration, but this should be only temporary.

The most used, examined and discussed ratio within a company is the *gross profit ratio*. More significance is probably attached to this ratio than to any other because increases usually indicate improved performance (more sales, more efficient production) and decreases indicate weaknesses (poor selling effort, waste in production, weak inventory controls).

When comparing a company with others in the same field, if the company's profit margin is low by comparison, it signals troubles ahead; if it is high, the company appears to be a worthy competitor.

The terminology in the gross profit percentages is sometimes confusing and misinterpreted, especially when the word "markup" is used. As an example:

|  | $ | % |
|---|---|---|
| Sales | $100 | 100% |
| Cost of Sales | 80 | 80% |
| Gross Profit | $ 20 | 20% |

In conventional usage, there is a 20 percent gross profit or margin on the sale (20/100). However, to determine the *markup*, the cost of sales is the denominator and the gross profit is the numerator (20/80 equals a 25 percent markup).

Starting with gross profit *percentage desired*, to gross 20 percent, what should the selling price be? (The only known factor is cost.)

|  | % | Known | As calculated |
|---|---|---|---|
| Selling price | 100% | ? | $150 |
| Cost | 80% | $120 | 120 |
| Gross Profit | 20% | ? | $ 30 |

Selling price is always 100 percent. If cost is $120 and is equal to 80 percent of the selling price (it must be 80 percent because a gross of 20 percent was set), divide $120 by 80 percent to get the 100 percent selling price of $150.

**¶1029.11**

## .13  Ratio of Net Sales to Stockholders' Equity

A company acquires assets in order to produce sales which yield a profit. If tangible assets yield too few sales, the company is suffering from underselling (the underutilization of its assets). On the other hand, the company may suffer from overtrading (too many sales in proportion to its tangible net worth). In other words, there is too heavy a reliance on borrowed funds to generate sales.

Another way of measuring the effective utilization of assets is to determine the ratio of net sales to total assets (excluding long-term investments).

In either case, comparisons of these ratios with similar ratios of other companies in the same industry can indicate the relative efficiency in utilization of assets of the company being analyzed.

## .15  Ratio of Net Sales to Working Capital

This is similar to the preceding ratio, since it measures the relationship between sales and assets. In this case, however, the ratio measures whether the company has sufficient net current assets to support the volume of its sales or, on the other hand, if the capital invested in working capital is working hard enough to produce sales.

## .17  Profit Margin on Sales

The profit margin on sales is obtained by dividing net income by net sales for the period. A ratio of 7.5 percent compared to an industry average of 4.6 percent indicates a company is achieving an above-average rate of profits on each sales dollar received.

The profit margin on sales does not indicate how profitable a company is for a given period of time. Only by determining how many times the total assets turned over during a period of time is it possible to ascertain the amount of net income earned on total assets. The rate of return on assets is computed by using net income as the numerator and average total assets as a denominator. An average of 6.2 percent compared to an industry average of 4.9 percent is above the average of an industry and results from a high profit margin on sales.

## .19  Rate of Return on Common Stock Equity

This ratio is defined as net income after interest, taxes, and preferred stock dividends (if any) divided by average common stock-holders' equity. When the rate of return on common stock equity is higher than the rate of return on total assets, the company is considered to be trading on the equity. Trading on the equity increases a company's financial risk, but it increases a company's earnings.

¶1029.19

## .21 Dividend Yield

The dividend yield is the cash dividend per share divided by the market price of the stock at the time the yield is determined. This ratio gives the rate of return that an investor will receive at the time on an investment in a stock or bond.

## .23 Times Interest Earned

This ratio is computed by dividing income before interest charges and taxes by the interest charge. The ratio indicates the safety of a bondholder's investment. A company that has an interest earned ratio of 5 to 1 shows a significantly safer position for meeting its bond interest obligations than a company with a lower ratio.

## ¶1031 STATEMENT OF CHANGES IN STOCKHOLDERS' EQUITY

This statement presents an equity analysis of changes from year to year in each shareholder's account, records any additional shares issued, foreign currency translation gains/losses, dividends per share (if paid), retained earnings. This last figure indicates how well the company itself is doing by revealing how much of the profits it can retain to finance further growth opportunities. In an era of corporate raiding and takeovers, management may be wise to be sure that retained earnings are not too high, but are put to good use in increasing total earnings per share for the benefit of current stockholders.

## .01 Return on Equity

This ratio is another method of determining earning power. Here, the opening equity (capital stock plus retained earnings, plus or minus any other equity section items) is divided into the net income for the year to give the percentage earned on that year's investment.

## .03 Return to Investors

This is a relatively new ratio used mostly by financial publications, primarily for comparison of many companies in similar industries. The opening equity is divided into the sum of the dividends paid plus the market price appreciation of the period. In addition, the ratio is sometimes extended to cover five years, ten years or more.

## .05 Dividend Payout Ratio

The *dividend* per common share is divided by the *earnings* per common share to get the *percentage* of dividend payout.

The dividends on common stock will vary with the profitability of the company, but other considerations also affect the percent of payout:

1. The relative stability of the earnings
2. The need for new capital
3. The directors' judgment concerning the outlook for earnings
4. The general views of management relating to the advisability of:
   a. Plowing back a large part of earnings into the business
   b. Raising additional funds from outside sources

Dividends on the preferred stock are not subject to a year-to-year fluctuation. If the fixed dividend on *cumulative* preferred stock for any year cannot be met, the payments would accumulate and be paid before any dividends could be declared on the common stock.

## ¶1033   FASB 130, *Reporting Comprehensive Income*

FASB 130 began in conjunction with the Exposure Draft (ED) on derivatives and hedging. However, since there is much less in it to cause prolonged cotroversy, this Standard was issued requiring reporting and display of comprehensive income effective in 1998, while the new derivatives standard became effective on June 15, 2000. Financial statements from previous periods used for comparison must be reclassified in line with the provisions of Statement 130.

At the time the EDs were issued, U.S. GAAP did not use a comprehensive income concept. The idea was to issue the two EDs simultaneously in anticipation of employing the concept in connection with the derivative and other future standards.

All of the items that are required to be recognized under accounting standards as components of comprehensive income must now be reported in a financial statement that is displayed with the same degree of prominence as other financial statements.

## .01   Comprehensive Income Defined

Comprehensive income is defined in FASB Concepts Statement 6, *Elements of Financial Statements*, as "... the change in equity (net assets) of a business enterprise during a period from transactions and other events and circumstances from non-owner sources. It includes all changes in equity during a period except those resulting from investments by owners and distributions to owners."

FASB 130 considers that comprehensive income consists of two major components—net income and "other comprehensive income." The latter refers to revenues, expenses, gains and losses that, according to GAAP, are included in comprehensive income but excluded from net income. They are direct debits or credits to owners' equity that do not involve transactions with owners, such as foreign currency translation gains and losses, unrealized gains or losses on marketable securities classified as available-for-sale, and minimum pension liability adjustments. Thus, comprehensive income is the total of net income plus the revenue, expense, gain and loss changes in equity during a period which now is not included in net income.

## .03 Equity Valuation Not Affected

This new display and related disclosures will not influence equity valuations, nor is any new or additional information disclosed. It merely repackages existing disclosed data in a new format. FASB 130 may not be of particular interest to sophisticated investors, creditors, and securities firms, but it should be of interest to accountants who have the task of implementing the new format. However, this should not be a particularly onerous job since it is largely a matter of displaying known financial data rather than calculating additional figures that would change recognition of income.

On the other hand, the FASB does appear to believe that, used in conjunction with related disclosures and other information in the financial statements, the comprehensive income information could help the knowledgeable user in assessing an entity's activities, and the timing and extent of future cash flows. Further, the Board emphasizes that while a total comprehensive income figure is useful, information about its components may give more insight into an enterprise's activities.

## .05 Format for Presentation of Comprehensive Income

One aspect for the accountant to consider is the best way to use this new display to inform, but not confuse, the less sophisticated user of financial statements. Since the Statement does not require a specific financial statement format for the display of comprehensive income and its components, the accountant may be expected to make some choices.

1. The requirement to report a new "income" figure for the quarter may be displayed as *either* a performance measurement or a change in equity. Which to choose?

2. Companies are permitted to display total comprehensive income and its components in either an income statement type format or in a statement of changes in equity format. Would it be better to preserve the current income statement as a separate display and show a company's net income figure as the bottom line? Or not? (With the equity format, a statement of changes in equity must be displayed as a primary financial statement.)

3.  The Standard permits companies to report only a total for comprehensive income in condensed interim financial statements issued to shareholders. Would it be less confusing to show total comprehensive income as a part of a complete display of the calculations every time rather than as a single figure?

## .07 Application of Requirements

FASB 130 applies to all companies that present a full set of general-purpose financial statements. Investment companies, defined benefit pension plans, and other employee benefit plans that are exempt from the requirement to provide a statement of cash flows by FASB 102, *Statement of Cash Flows— Exemption of Certain Enterprises and Certification of Cash Flows from Certain Securities Acquired for Resale*, are not exempt from requirements of FASB 130 if it applies in all other respects. However, it does not apply to organizations that have no items of comprehensive income in any period presented, or to not-for-profit organizations that are covered by FASB 117, *Financial Statements of Not-for-Profit Organizations*.

As mentioned above, the Statement suggests how to report and display comprehensive income and its components but does not provide guidance on items that are to be included. For this guidance, the existing and future accounting standards mentioned earlier will need to be consulted.

## .09 Components of Comprehensive Income

At this time, eight items qualify, according to GAAP, as components of other comprehensive income that, under prior standards, bypassed the income statement and had to be reported as a balance within a separate component of equity in a statement of financial position.

1.  Foreign currency translation adjustments.
2.  Gains and losses on foreign currency transactions that are designated as, and are effective as, economic hedges of a net investment in a foreign entity, commencing as of the designation date.
3.  Gains and losses on intercompany foreign currency transactions that are of a long-term-investment nature (i.e., settlement is not planned or anticipated in the foreseeable future), when the entities to the transaction are consolidated, combined, or accounted for by the equity method in the reporting enterprise's financial statements.
4.  A change in the market value of a futures contract that qualifies as a hedge of an asset reported at fair value according to FASB 115, *Accounting for Certain Investments in Debt and Equity Securities*.
5.  A net loss recognized under FASB 87, *Employers' Accounting for Pensions*, as an additional pension liability not yet recognized as net periodic pension cost.

¶1033.09

6. Unrealized holding gains and losses on available-for-sale securities.
7. Unrealized holding gains and losses that result from a debt security being transferred into the available-for-sale category from the held-to-maturity category.
8. Subsequent decreases (if not an other-than-temporary impairment) or increases in the fair value of available for-sale securities previously written down as impaired.

(This list will be expanded now that the derivatives and hedging standard is promulgated. Some gains and/or losses from those transactions will be included as part of other comprehensive income.)

## .11  Terminology

The Statement does not require that the descriptive terms "comprehensive income," "total comprehensive income," or "other comprehensive income" be used in financial statements. It permits companies to use equivalent terms, such as "total non-owner changes in equity," "comprehensive loss" or other appropriate descriptive labels. It may be that most entities will choose to use alternative terms since "comprehensive income" still has a rather hollow ring to it.

## .13  Cash Flow and Equity Valuation Not Affected

Inasmuch as all of the items included in other comprehensive income are noncash items, the FASB decided that indirect-method cash flow statement presentation would continue to begin with net income as required by FASB 95, *Statement of Cash Flows.*

FASB 130 should clarify the extent to which revenue, expense, gain and loss items are being taken directly to owners' equity, but, as mentioned above, the display of comprehensive income and its components will not affect equity valuation. Unlike the requirements in FASB 131, *Disclosures About Segments of an Enterprise and Related Information*, which calls for greatly expanded reporting on segments, the requirements of FASB 130 call for no new data. Since informed investors have always examined owners' equity to evaluate the material now collected under the other comprehensive income items, the new display should have little impact on the public's conception of a company's financial condition.

## ¶1035  APB OPINION 22, *DISCLOSURE OF ACCOUNTING POLICIES*

APB 22 covers *Disclosure of Accounting Policies*. A description of all significant accounting policies of the reporting entity should be included as an integral part of all financial statements. Whether these statements are issued in presenting the entity's financial position, changes in the financial position, or in showing results of operations in accordance with GAAP, a description of all significant accounting policies, methods and practices of the reporting entity should be included as an integral part of all financial statements. When it is appropriate to issue one or more basic financial statements without the others, these statements should also comprise the pertinent accounting policies. Not-for-profit entities should also present details of their accounting policies as an integral part of their financial statements.

## .01  Content and Format of Disclosures

1. Disclosure of accounting policies should identify and describe the accounting principles employed by the reporting business and the methods of applying those principles which are important in the determination of financial position, changes in financial position, or results of operations. The disclosure should include decisions concerning applicability of principles relating to recognition of revenue and allocation of asset costs to current and future periods. The disclosure statement should comprise all the reasoning behind the choice of, or an explanation of, the accounting principles and methods employed that involve any of the following:

   a. Selection of one practice over another from existing acceptable alternatives.

   b. Principles and methods peculiar to the industry of the reporting firm, even when such principles and methods are characteristically followed in that industry.

   c. Unusual or innovative applications of generally accepted accounting principles or of practices and methods peculiar to that industry.

2. Examples of disclosures commonly required in regard to accounting policies include those relating to basis of consolidation, depreciation methods, amortization of intangibles, inventory pricing, accounting for research and development costs and the basis for amortization thereof, translation of foreign currencies, recognition of profit on long-term construction-type contracts, recognition of revenue from franchising and leasing operations, and any other items deemed pertinent to give a complete picture of a firm's financial status.

3. The format follows a plan of having a separate *Summary of Significant Accounting Policies* preceding the notes to the financial statements or, in some cases, as the initial note of the statement.

## ¶1037  Present Value Computation and Application

The procedure of computing interest on principal *and interest on interest* underlies the concept of *compounding*. There are a number of accounting procedures (accounting for bonds, accounts receivable, accounts payable, and leases, for example) to which the compound interest formula (and variations) can be applied:

- The *future value* of a sum of money. If $1,000 (the principal $P$) is deposited in a bank today, what will be the balance ($S$) in the account in *n years* (or *periods*) if the bank accumulates interest at the rate of $i$ percent per year (or *period*)?
- The *present value* of a sum of money due at the end of a period of time. What is the value *today* of the amount owed if $1,000 has to be paid, say to a creditor, *n* years from today?
- The *future value of an annuity*, which is a series of *equal* payments made at *equal* intervals. If $1,000 a year is deposited for *n* years, how much will have accumulated at the end of the *n*-years period if the deposits earn interest at the rate of $i$ percent per year?
- The *present value of an annuity*, which is a series of *equal* payments made at *equal* intervals. If we are to be paid $1,000 a year for *n* years, how much is this annuity worth today, given $i$ percent rate of interest?

The formula for the future value of a sum of money is the familiar compound interest formula. In the four examples to follow, let:

$S$ = The future worth of a sum of money invested today.
$P$ = Principal, or the sum of money that will accumulate to $S$ amount of money.
$i$ = The rate of interest ($r$ may be substituted).
$n$ = Number of periods of time.

It is important to understand that a "period of time" is not necessarily one year, even though rates of interest in the United States are always understood to mean the rate for a period of one year. A period can be any length of time (e.g., day, week, month, year, second, minute, hour). Time is a *continuous*, not a *discrete*, function.

With compound interest the total amount accumulated ($S$ in the formula) at the end of one period earns interest during the subsequent period, or "interest on interest." The formula is:

$$S = P(1 + i)^n$$

At this point, it should be emphasized that the user no longer must do the arithmetic. Not only can the problem types be solved by the use of tables, but hand calculators and software programs will perform the computations and give the answers. The user has simply only to enter the numbers that represent the letters in the formula. With respect to the arithmetic, however, three of the variables in the equation are always known quantities; therefore, finding the value of the fourth and *un*known variable follows.

¶1037

A *Word of Caution.*    Computational errors caused by entering the wrong value for *n* are not uncommon. If *i* = 12% and the compounding period is every six months, *n* in the formula is 2(semi-annual) and the interest rate *i* is 6%, the annual rate divided by 2. If the compounding period is quarterly *n* is 4 and the interest rate *i* is 3%, the annual rate divided by 4. Thus since the nominal interest rate is for a one year period if more compounding periods are involved the number of these periods = *n* and the nominal annual interest rate is divided by the number of compounding periods in a year to get the interest rate *i* needed for the calculation. If the compounding period is daily (as is the case in many financial institutions savings policies) *n* becomes *i*/360—360 days in the year are applied in this country for interest calculations instead of 365. This is because the smaller the denominator, the bit more interest the *lender* collects. However, if the formula applies to a problem involving U.S. Government bonds, a 365-day year must be assumed because it enables the government to borrow a bit cheaper, relatively.

## .01  Annuities

The previous discussion considers the accumulation of interest on a *single* payment, however the single payment may be invested. *Annuities* apply to problems that involve a series of *equal payments* (or investments or savings) made at *equal intervals* of time. The period of time between payments is called the *payment period.* The period of time between computation of the interest accumulation is called the *interest-conversion period.* When the payment period exactly equals the interest-conversion period, the annuity is an *ordinary annuity.* The equal payments are termed rents, which are spread over equal periods of time, the first rent payment made at the *start* of the annuity, and the last payment made at the *end* of the annuity.

The *future worth* of the annuity is the sum of the future worths of each of the separate rents. Assuming $100 invested we have $100 at time 1. At time 2 we have the $100 invested that day, plus the $100 invested at time 1, plus the interest earned during the period between time 1 and time 2. At time 3 another $100 is deposited; we now have the $100 deposited that day, the $100 deposited at time 2 plus the interest earned for one period, and the $100 deposited at time 1 plus the interest earned during the period between time 1 and time 2.

The formula for the future worth of an annuity of $1 is:

$$S = \frac{(1+i)^n - 1}{i}$$

Note that the formula for the accumulation of interest on an ordinary annuity has the same variables as the compounding formula for a single payment.

To obtain *S* for any amount more than $1, multiply both sides of the equation by the amount invested, by *P*. In this case multiply both sides of the equation by 100. As above the amount for $1 can be found in tables (or by the use of a hand calculator).

The *present worth* of an annuity concerns the same question as the present worth of a single payment for *n years at i rate of interest*. How much would we pay today for an annuity in order to receive a given number of equal payments at equal intervals for a given number of periods in the future?

The formula for $1 is:

$$S = \frac{1 - (1+i)^{-n}}{i}$$

The method for accounting for the premium or discount on bonds payable are compound interest procedures. The resultant interest charges are the product of the net balance of bonds payable and the effective interest rate at the time the bonds were issued. For bonds issued at a premium, the computed interest charges will *decrease* each year as the bonds approach maturity because the net balance of the liability decreases each year due to the amortization of the premium. Conversely, for bonds issued at a discount, the computed interest charges will *increase* each year as the bonds approach maturity because of the accumulation of the discount when interest is material the effective interest method is used to amortize either the premium or the discount (see below).

When interest is not material straight-line method is used for the amortization of premiums or accumulation of discounts which involves simply dividing the original premium or discount by the number of years until maturity to determine the constant annual amount of amortization or accumulation.

The most frequent application of the above formula for accounting procedures is the present value formula. For example, when a company issues bonds, cash is debited for the proceeds of the bond issue and a liability account is credited for the amount. The entries will be the present value of the bonds. Assume a bond issue sold at a premium, or for more than the typical $1,000 par value, the present value of which we assume to be $1,200. The entries at the time of the sale of the bonds are:

| | | |
|---|---|---|
| Cash | $1,200 | |
| Bonds Payable | | $1,200 |

An alternative treatment is permissible by rule:

| | | |
|---|---|---|
| Cash | $1,200 | |
| Bonds Payable | | $1,000 (par) |
| Premium on Bonds | | 200 |

**¶1037.01**

The Premium Account is an adjunct account (an addition) to Bonds Payable. The interest charge each year is computed by multiplying the bond liability *at the end of each year* by the effective rate of interest (see the definition). The adjunct account at the end of each period is debited for the amount of interest which reduces the liability each period. *The interest charge calculation is computed on the reduced amount of the liability that occurs each year as the adjunct account is debited.* At maturity the Premium Account has a zero balance and the liability will be reduced to the maturity, or face amount (the par value of $1,000) of the bond.

Assume the bond is sold at a $200 *discount,* that is, $200 less than the $1,000 par value. The journal entry is:

| | | |
|---|---|---|
| Cash | $800 | |
| Bond Discount | 200 | |
| Bonds Payable | | $1,000 |

The Bond Discount account is a *contra* account to bonds payable with the liability at time of issue $800. Again, for an amount deposited for the annuity of more than $1 multiply both sides of the equation by that amount. Also, again note the same variables as in the compound interest formula.

# Chapter 2
# Revenue and Expenses

## CONTENTS

## ¶2000 OVERVIEW

It has been the Financial Accounting Standards Board's (FASB) intention for some time to develop a comprehensive statement on revenue recognition that is conceptually based and framed in terms of principles. This is being done in partnership with the International Accounting Standards Board (IASB). As a joint project, the FASB and the IASB are sharing staff resources and research and are working to coordinate the eventual issuance of Exposure Drafts and final standards. The Boards are also coordinating the timing of their deliberations of the issues within the joint project, but they deliberate and vote on those issues individually. As a result, at any given time there may be some issues for which the FASB has reached a tentative conclusion but for which the IASB has not yet deliberated, and vice-versa.

As conceived at present, the revenue recognition Statement will:

- Eliminate the inconsistencies in the existing authoritative literature and accepted practices.
- Fill the voids that have emerged in revenue recognition guidance in recent years.
- Provide guidance for addressing issues that arise in the future.

Although the FASB plans that a revenue recognition Statement should apply to business entities generally, it has been suggested that later it will decide to exclude certain transactions or industries requiring additional study. In developing this Statement, the FASB decided to reconsider the guidance pertinent to revenue recognition in its Concepts Statements. Conflicts can arise between the conceptual guidance on revenues in FASB Concepts Statement 5, *Recognition and Measurement in Financial Statements of Business Enterprises*, and FASB Concepts Statement 6, *Elements of Financial Statements*. Those conflicts can arise because revenues are defined in Concepts Statement 6 in terms of changes in assets and liabilities, but the revenue recognition criteria in Concepts Statement 5 do not focus on changes in assets and liabilities.

At an August 2003 Board meeting, the staff presented the FASB with an inventory of the existing guidance related to revenue recognition and described the various revenue recognition conventions that are used in practice. The staff also described a possible approach to addressing a comprehensive standard on revenue recognition. The Board is taking into consideration the following aspects of the suggested approach:

- Scope of the standard: possible removal of financial instruments from consideration.
- Balancing principles-based guidance and rules-based guidance: a standard incorporating broad principles with clear, concise implementation guidance.
- Transition from existing guidance: consideration of existing literature individually for retention, modification, or elimination.

Until such time as a new, comprehensive standard is issued by the FASB, the existing rules, regulations, staff bulletins, and other literature remain in effect.

¶2000

## ¶2001   PROGRESS IN FORMULATING COMPREHENSIVE STATEMENT ON REVENUE RECOGNITION

The pace may appear to be relatively slow, but because of the amount of damage that can be and has been caused by firms manipulating revenue recognition in financial statements, any standard covering the topic should certainly be given careful thought and due process.

At its May 2005 meeting, the Board discussed whether the objective and scope of the Revenue Recognition project should be changed and, if so, how. The Board affirmed its past decision to develop a standard for revenue recognition based on recognized changes in assets and liabilities (consistent with the definition of revenues in FASB Concepts Statement No. 6, *Elements of Financial Statements*) that would not be overridden by additional recognition criteria such as realization and the completion of an earnings process (as described in FASB Concepts Statement No. 5, *Recognition and Measurement in Financial Statements of Business Enterprises*). The Board expects that the "realized or realizable" and "earned" criteria in Concepts Statement 5 will be eliminated and the definition of revenues in Concepts Statement 6 will be refined to more clearly distinguish revenues from gains.

The Board also affirmed that its goal is to develop a comprehensive standard on revenue recognition that would apply broadly to *all* revenue arrangements. In connection with that decision, the Board agreed to pursue an approach under which performance obligations would be measured by allocating the customer consideration rather than at the fair value of the obligation (that is, the amount the reporting entity would be required to pay to transfer the performance obligation to a willing third party of comparable credit standing).

The Board plans to continue discussing principles for revenue recognition as well as the implications of measuring performance obligations based on the customer consideration amount. The Board's decision to use the customer consideration amount for measuring performance obligations has not yet been reflected in certain sections of this project update.

## .01   General Approach to the Project

1. The Board is pursuing an approach that focuses on changes in assets and liabilities (consistent with the definition of revenues in Concepts Statement 6) and is not overridden by tests based on the notions of realization and completion of an earnings process presented in Concepts Statement 5. The Board chose the assets and liabilities approach rather than the realization and earnings approach for a number of reasons, including the following:

    a. Applying the realization and earnings approach to revenue recognition in Concepts Statement 5 can lead to conflicts with the definitions of assets and liabilities in Concepts Statement 6. That is because, in certain instances, the realization and earnings approach involves the recognition of deferred debits and deferred credits that do not meet the definitions of assets and liabilities. The definitions of assets and liabilities are the cornerstones of the elements definitions in the conceptual framework, as evidenced by the defining of revenues and expenses in terms of changes in assets and liabilities.

    b. Earning and realization have yet to be (and may be impossible to be) defined precisely and in a manner that can be applied consistently across a range of industries and transactions.

    c. It is difficult to identify consistently when earning or realization occurs under multiple-element revenue-generating arrangements.

## .03   Expectations for Completed Project

The Revenue Recognition Project is expected to result in three levels of guidance:

1. Revision and expansion of Concepts Statements 5 and 6. Concepts Statement 6 defines revenue in terms of assets and liabilities; Concepts Statement 5 describes recognition criteria unique to revenue.

2. A general standard on revenue recognition to replace various literature such as APB Opinion No. 29, *Accounting for Nonmonetary Transactions,* FASB Statement No. 48, *Revenue Recognition When Right of Return Exists,* EITF Issue No. 00-21, *Revenue Arrangements with Multiple Deliverables,* and SEC Staff Accounting Bulletin No. 104, *Revenue Recognition.* Revisions of the Concepts Statement are also expected to provide high-level guidance.

3. Specific application guidance for three types of revenue-generating activities: Rights of Use, Services, and Products. It will also identify the old guidance that is superseded by the new application guidance.

## ¶2003   SEC REVENUE RECOGNITION MEASURES AID FASB PROJECT

SEC sought to fill the gap in the accounting literature with SAB No. 101, *Revenue Recognition in Financial Statements,* which was issued in December 1999, and the companion document, *Revenue Recognition in Financial Statements Frequently Asked Questions and Answers,* which was issued in October 2000. SAB 101 was superceded by SAB 104, *Revenue Recognition,* in December 2003. SAB 104 states that if a transaction falls within the scope of specific authoritative literature on revenue recognition, that guidance should be followed; in the absence of such guidance, the revenue recognition criteria in

Concepts Statement 5 (namely, that revenue should not be recognized until it is (a) *realized or realizable* and (b) *earned*) should be followed. However, SAB 104 is more specific, stating additional requirements for meeting those criteria, and reflects the SEC staff's view that the four basic criteria for revenue recognition in AICPA SOP 97-2, *Software Revenue Recognition,* should be a foundation for all basic revenue recognition principles. Those criteria are:

- Persuasive evidence of an arrangement exists.
- Delivery has occurred.
- Collectibility is probable.
- Fixed or determinable fee.

Some criticized SAB 101 on the basis that the criteria in SOP 97-2 were developed for a particular industry and that broader application of those criteria was neither contemplated nor intended. They asserted that that guidance might not be appropriate for certain recognition issues, including some that the EITF has considered. Others noted that a SAB is designed to provide the SEC staff's interpretive responses and not to change generally accepted accounting principles (GAAP). For that reason, SABs are issued without an invitation for comment. Critics argued that SAB 101 had in fact changed GAAP by promulgating changes in industry practice without the full due process and deliberation that characterize the FASB's decision-making process. Even though the SEC guidance for revenue recognition applies only to SEC registrants, the FASB considers that the work done in developing and implementing SAB 101 has focused attention on revenue recognition issues and is useful in their project toward adopting a standard.

## .01 Staff Accounting Bulletin No. 104

Staff Accounting Bulletin No. 104, *Revenue Recognition,* supersedes SAB 101. It was adopted primarily to rescind accounting guidance contained in SAB 101 related to *multiple element revenue arrangements,* superseded as a result of the issuance of EITF 00-21. Additionally, SAB 104 rescinds the SEC's Revenue Recognition in Financial Statements Frequently Asked Questions issued with SAB 101 that had been codified in SEC Topic 13, Revenue Recognition. Selected portions of the FAQ have been incorporated into SAB 104. Although the wording of SAB 104 has changed to reflect the issuance of EITF 00-21, the revenue recognition principles of SAB 101 remain largely unchanged by the issuance of SAB 104.

## .03 Revenue Recognition in Topic 13

Because the accounting literature on revenue recognition includes both broad conceptual discussions and certain industry-specific guidance, the SEC has stated that if a transaction is within the scope of specific authoritative literature that provides revenue recognition guidance, that literature should be applied. However, in the absence of authoritative literature addressing a specific arrangement or a specific industry, the staff will consider the existing authoritative accounting standards as well as the broad revenue recognition criteria specified in the FASB's conceptual framework that contain basic guidelines for revenue recognition.

Based on these guidelines, revenue should not be recognized until it is realized or realizable and earned. Concepts Statement 5, paragraph 83(b) states that "an entity's revenue-earning activities involve delivering or producing goods, rendering services, or other activities that constitute its ongoing major or central operations, and revenues are considered to have been earned when the entity has substantially accomplished what it must do to be entitled to the benefits represented by the revenues." Paragraph 84(a) continues, "the two conditions (being realized or realizable and being earned) are usually met by the time product or merchandise is delivered or services are rendered to customers, and revenues from manufacturing and selling activities and gains and losses from sales of other assets are commonly recognized at time of sale (usually meaning delivery)." In addition, paragraph 84(d) states that "If services are rendered or rights to use assets extend continuously over time (for example, interest or rent), reliable measures based on contractual prices established in advance are commonly available, and revenues may be recognized as earned as time passes."

The staff believes that revenue generally is realized or realizable and earned when all of the following criteria are met:

- Persuasive evidence of an arrangement exists.
- Delivery has occurred or services have been rendered.
- The seller's price to the buyer is fixed or determinable.
- Collectibility is reasonably assured.

Some revenue arrangements contain multiple revenue-generating activities. The staff believes that the determination of the units of accounting within an arrangement should be made prior to the application of the guidance in this SAB Topic by reference to the applicable accounting literature.


## ¶2005   CAUTIONS FOR ACCOUNTANTS, AUDITORS, INVESTORS

When it comes to imaginative accounting, apparently nothing lends itself more readily to myriad forms of skullduggery than revenue recognition. As has been quite evident over the last few years, accounting has faced more criticism than ever before. As a result what was formerly a self-regulatory profession has been deluged with rules and regulations. However, not all of these rules have managed to prevent willing companies from painting a rosier picture of revenues than is warranted. So, forewarned is forearmed. The following may help users of financial statements avoid being fooled.

## .01    Different Materiality Focus

The task of accountants, auditors, and investors is difficult enough without becoming overly concerned about immaterial items. This may be a reasonable position to take, but, as a large investment company cautions, the CPA/PFS and investors focusing on revenue growth should constantly be aware that they must adopt a view of what is or is not "material" that differs from that often adopted by auditors and general practice accountants.

In the interest of his or her clients, a financial advisor needs to measure materiality against the change in revenues because their revenue-multiple valuation metric is driven by *revenue growth rates*. In contrast, auditors and accountants tend to focus on the *total revenue figure* when thinking of materiality. These different perspectives can lead to different materiality assessments. What is immaterial to accountants and auditors may be quite material to investors and their advisors. The reverse is seldom, if ever, true. To think as an investor, the PFS must measure revenue materiality against the *change or trend in revenues*.

## .03    Avoiding Revenue Growth Traps

Because revenue growth is the primary driver of sustained profit growth, unusual revenue growth can be an indication of a costly trap for investors if it is the result of accounting fraud, manipulation, or excessively aggressive accounting practices. The 50 percent of the Securities and Exchange Commission accounting enforcement actions that involve revenue recognition are ample testimony to this fact. In a majority of these cases, investors suffered significant losses because they were overly impressed by a company's glowing revenue-growth story, which in the end turned out to be inflated.

In order to avoid revenue growth traps, investors need to know:

- How to measure materiality correctly.
- The common forms of revenue recognition manipulation.
- How to detect the common forms of revenue manipulation.
- The extent to which they can rely on auditor opinions and other forms of assurance, such as management certifications.

¶2005.03

## .05   Revenue Manipulations

Revenue misstatements come in a remarkable variety of frequently occurring practices. Auditors, accountants, financial advisors, and their clients should be aware of any number of questionable practices that may be used to paint a rosier picture than the facts warrant. The user of financial statements has a better chance of avoiding problems if he or she is aware of some of the more imaginative practices.

Common forms of revenue manipulations encompass:

1. Including in the current period revenue on products delivered and services rendered after the end of the period's cut-off date.
2. Convincing a company being acquired to slow down their selling activity in the period prior to their acquisition so that the deferred sales can be recognized after the company has been acquired.
3. Including inappropriate items in revenue, such as gains, financial income, and other items that are peripheral, incidental, or unrelated to the company's *major or central operations*.
4. Undisclosed side-letters between the seller and buyer, such as generous no-penalty return privileges that actually modify the sales arrangements.
5. Improper allocation of revenue to the various components of sales arrangements involving multiple deliverables over time, with the result that excessive revenue is recognized upfront.
6. Shipments to fictitious customers.
7. Recognizing revenues from contracts that are in essence consignment-type arrangements, such as:
   a. Bill-and-hold arrangements.
   b. Unusual deferred-payment schedules.
   c. Delivery to customer storage facilities paid for by the seller.
8. The buyer and seller enter into an underhanded reciprocal arrangement to boost revenue in which both parties record revenue or one party records revenue and the other an investment.
9. The seller is actually an agent but recognizes the full transaction value rather than just the agent's fees.
10. Net revenues are overstated because of inadequate provisions for deductions from gross revenues, such as provisions for returns and allowances.

Although revenue manipulation can be difficult to spot, it is often used in conjunction with other accounting schemes by a company bent on showing greater profit from year to year. It is sometimes easier to locate signs of other income manipulation schemes that may be part of a concerted effort to project better than actual operating results.

Two procedures that might have tipped the investor off in many of the famous revenue-inflating schemes of the past (as well as other income manipulation schemes) are formal analytical procedures simple to perform using an electronic spreadsheet—vertical analysis and horizontal analysis. Such analysis involves placing the items of income and expense from the company's most recent income statements (preferably at least five years) in a spreadsheet. The horizontal analysis is accomplished by determining the incremental difference from each year to the next for each item on the income statement and expressing this amount as a percent. Thus if commission expense increased from $10,000 last year to $12,000 this year the $2,000 increase is shown as 20%. This amount of change can then be compared with the percent change for this account in prior years or with changes in sales or payroll or other relevant accounts to see if the change is in proportion. Horizontal analysis will highlight increases or deceases in percentage for each line item on the income statement from year to year making it easy to spot trends that are out of line with expectations and require further investigation.

Vertical analysis begins with computing, for each year, what percentage each item on the income statement is of gross revenue—for example: gross profit, selling expense, and depreciation. Each item is then compared across time noting any changes in the percent that a given statement item is to the gross revenue. As a general rule, the percentages should change little from year to year unless there is a compelling reason. If revenues are increasing from year to year, there is normally no *prima facie* reason that the gross profit or other expense items should decrease or fluctuate erratically. Vertical and horizontal analyses are typically used in tandem to spot items requiring further explanation. Horizontal analysis shows the percent of change within an account and vertical analysis shows the relative percent each account is to gross revenue.

If a particular expense item is decreasing across the spreadsheet, it could be an indication of greater efficiency, *or* it could indicate that certain expenses are being capitalized that were previously written off. This occurs frequently in attempts to show a greater profit. Manipulation of cost of goods sold, deferral of operating expenses, and other schemes may be highlighted using this spreadsheet technique. Although spotting other income manipulation schemes does not directly imply that revenue is being inflated, the existence of these schemes are warning flags prompting further investigation of revenue recognition procedures in use.

# ¶2007  REVENUE [INCOME]

The principles upon which net income is determined derive from the pervasive measurement principles, such as realization, recognition, matching, and conservatism.

The entire process of income determination and recognition consists of identifying, measuring, and relating revenue and expenses for an accounting period. Revenue is usually determined by applying the realization principle in conjunction with a measure of the earnings process. Realization refers to the process of converting noncash resources into cash or rights to cash. Revenue is generally recognized when it is both realized and the earning process is essentially complete—when the company has completed what it must do to be entitled to the new assets or other benefits—the ends for which its work was performed. Revenue arises from three general activities:

1. Selling products.
2. Rendering services.
3. Letting others use owned resources, resulting in interest or rent.

Revenue (as a reporting category on the income statement) does not include proceeds from the sale of assets or other resources not part of the company's normal business operations (for example, proceeds producing a gain or loss on disposal of equipment formerly used in the earnings process—such items are reported as other income or expense). Revenue also does not include proceeds from the sale of a company's stock, whether original issuance or treasury stock, and prior period adjustments reflecting income earned but incorrectly reported in a prior period.

Revenue, in the balance sheet sense, is a gross increase in assets or a gross decrease in liabilities recognized and measured in conformity with generally accepted accounting principles (GAAP), which results from those profit-directed activities that can change owners' equity.

Revenue is considered *realized* when:

• The earning process is complete or virtually complete, and
• An exchange has taken place.

The objectives of accounting determination of income are not always the same as the objectives used for tax purposes.

There are various acceptable ways of determining income:

1. *Revenue* (see three general activities above):
   a. Accrual method—this is financial accounting and GAAP.
   b. Cash method—this is *not* considered financial accounting, and not GAAP, because one of the characteristics of GAAP is the *accrual* of appropriate items. Note: Tax accounting also requires accrual accounting procedures in a number of situations even for an otherwise cash basis taxpayer such as when a business has inventory and its sales are a material income producing factor.
   c. Installment sales method—generally for retail stores.

¶2007

    d. Completion of production method—used for precious metals.

    e. For long-term construction contracts:

       (1) Completed contract method.

       (2) Percentage-of-completion method.

    f. For leasing activities:

       (1) The direct financing method.

       (2) The operating method.

       (3) The sales method.

    g. The cost recovery method (used for installment sales).

    h. Consolidation method—for majority-owned subsidiaries (more than 50 percent).

    i. Equity method—for non-consolidated subsidiaries and for controlled non-subsidiaries (generally when more than 20 percent of stock is owned.

2. *Other* types of income requiring special determination:

    a. Extraordinary items of income.

    b. Unrealized income arising from:

       (1) Foreign currency holdings or transactions.

       (2) Ownership of marketable securities shown as current assets. Note: If marketable securities are shown as current assets and management intends to hold them only a short time they are referred to as "available for sale securities" and their unrealized income is reported currently as realized on the income statement. If management intends to sell the securities in the current operating cycle but not immediately they are referred to as "available for sale securities" and the unrealized income from these items is reflected in the equity section of the balance sheet as part of "comprehensive income."

A *shareholder* in a corporation does *not* have income when that corporation earns income (except for a Sub-S corporation). The shareholder has, and reports for tax purposes, income only upon *distribution* of that income in the form of dividends. Generally, distributions of stock—stock dividends and stock splits— are *not* income to the shareholder, but merely an adjustment of the number of shares he holds (for the same original cost plus token costs, if any). However, there are some situations which call for the stockholder to report stock dividends as income.

If a buyer has a right of return to the seller, revenue is recognized if *all* of the following criteria are met:

- Buyer is obligated to pay (and not contingent upon resale of the product) or has paid the seller;

¶2007

- Buyer's obligation would not be changed by theft, damage, or destruction of the product;
- Seller does not have any significant obligation to buyer related to resale of the product by the buyer; and
- Buyer's business must have economic substance separate from the seller's business.

If these criteria are met, sales revenue and cost of sales reported in the income statement are reduced to reflect estimated returns; expected losses are accrued.

There are important differences in revenue recognition between GAAP and accrual basis tax accounting. Numerous items such as installment sales, prepaid rent, estimates, and items reportable as income for financial purposes that are exempt from tax cause the necessity of carefully reconciling GAAP income to accrual basis taxable income.

## ¶2009  EXPENSES

Expenses are one of the six basic elements of financial accounting, along with assets, liabilities, owners' equity, revenue and net income. Expenses are determined by applying the expense recognition principles on the basis of relationships, between acquisition costs [the term "cost" is commonly used to refer to the amount at which assets are initially recorded, regardless of how determined], and either the independently determined revenue or accounting periods. Since the point in time at which revenue and expenses are recognized is also the time at which changes in amounts of net assets are recorded, income determination is interrelated with asset valuation.

All costs are not expenses. Some costs are related to later periods, will provide benefits for later periods, and are carried forward as assets on the balance sheet. Other costs are incurred and provide no future benefit, having expired in terms of usefulness or applicability—these expired costs are called "expenses." All expenses, therefore, are part of the broader term "cost." These expired costs are not assets and are shown as deductions from revenue to determine net income.

Expenses are gross decreases in assets or gross increases in liabilities recognized and measured in conformity with GAAP that result from those types of profit-directed activities that can change an owner's equity.

### .01  Recognizing Expenses

Three pervasive principles form the basis for recognizing expenses to be deducted from revenue to arrive at net income or loss:

1. Associating cause and effect ("matching")—For example, manufacturing cost of goods sold is measured and matched to the *sale* of the product.

Assumptions must be made as to how these costs attach to the product—whether on machine hours, space used, or labor expended. Assumptions must also be made as to how the costs flow out (LIFO, FIFO, average costs).

2. Systematic and rational allocation—When there is no direct way to associate cause and effect and certain costs are known (or presumed) to have provided benefits during the accounting period, these costs are allocated to that period in a systematic and rational manner and to appear so to an unbiased observer. The methods of allocation should be consistent and systematic, though methods may vary for different types of costs. Examples are depreciation of fixed assets, amortization of intangibles and interperiod allocation of rent or interest. The allocation referred to here is not the allocation of expired manufacturing costs with the "cost" area to determine unit or job costs; it is rather the broader area of allocation to the manufacturing area from the unexpired asset account: Depreciation on factory building, rather than overhead-depreciation on Product A, B, or C.

3. Immediate recognition (period expenses)—Costs are expensed during an accounting period because:

   a. They cannot be associated on a cause-and-effect basis with revenue, yet no useful purpose would be achieved by delaying recognition to a future period,

   b. They provide no discernible future benefits, or

   c. They were recorded as assets in a prior period and now no longer provide discernible future benefits.

Examples are officers' salaries, advertising expenses, most selling expenses, legal fees (unless associated with acquisition or defense of certain intangible assets such as patents), and most general and administrative expenses.

## ¶2011   OTHER REVENUES (AND EXPENSE)

*Gains and Losses.*   Expenses and revenue from *other* than sales of products, merchandise, or services should be separated from (operating) revenue and disclosed separately under Other Revenue and (Expense).

*Unusual Items.*   Unusual items of expense or income not meeting the criteria of "extraordinary" should be shown as a separate component of income from continuing operations.

*Extraordinary Items.*   Extraordinary items are discussed elsewhere in this book. They should be shown separately—net of applicable taxes—*after* net income from continuing operations. Any disposals of business segments should be shown immediately prior to extraordinary items—also with tax effect.

¶2011

## ¶2013  IMPUTED INTEREST ON NOTES RECEIVABLE OR PAYABLE

### .01  Accounting Considerations

The American Institute of Certified Public Accountants (AICPA) sets forth the appropriate accounting when the face amount of certain receivables or payables ("notes") does not reasonably represent the present value of the consideration given or received in certain exchanges. The objective of these rules is to prevent the form of the transaction from prevailing over its economic substance. (*Present value* is the sum of future payments, discounted to the present date at an appropriate rate of interest.)

Accounting Principles Board (APB) Opinion 21 states that:

1. When a note is received or issued solely for cash, the note is presumed to have a present value equal to the cash received. If it is issued for cash equal to its face amount, it is presumed to earn the stated rate of interest.

2. When a note is received for cash and some other rights or privileges, the value of the rights or privileges should be given accounting recognition by establishing a note discount or premium account, with the offsetting amount treated as appropriate. An example is a five-year noninterest-bearing loan made to a supplier in partial consideration for a purchase of products at lower than prevailing market prices. Under such circumstances, the difference between the present value of the receivable and the cash lent to the supplier is regarded as (a) an additional cost of the purchased goods, and (b) interest income, amortized over the life of the note.

3. When a note is exchanged for property, goods, or services and (a) interest is not stated, or (b) it is stated but is unreasonable, or (c) the stated face amount of the note is materially different from the current cash sale price of goods (or services), the note, the sales price, and the cost of the property (goods or services) should be recorded at their fair value, or at an amount that reasonably approximates the market value of the note, whichever is more clearly determinable.

Any resulting discount or premium should be regarded as interest expense or income and be amortized over the life of the note, in such a way as to result in a constant effective rate of interest when applied to the amount outstanding at the beginning of any given period.

Opinion 21 also provides some general guides for determining an "appropriate" interest rate and the manner of amortization for financial reporting purposes.

IMPUTED INTEREST: When a sale is made for an amount that is collectible at a future time giving rise to an account receivable, the amount is regarded as consisting of a sales price *and* a charge for interest for the period of the payment deferral. APB Opinion 21 requires that in the absence of a stated rate of interest, the present value of the receivable should be determined by reducing the face amount of the receivable by an interest rate that is approximated under the circumstances for the period that payment is deferred.

This rate is the *imputed rate*. It is determined by approximating the rate the supplier pays for financing receivables, or by determining the buyer's credit standing and applying the rate the borrower would have to pay if borrowing the sum from, say, a bank.

The process of arriving at the present value of the receivable is referred to as *discounting* the sum. If the total present value of the receivable (face amount plus the imputed interest) is less than the face amount, the difference between the face value of the receivable and its present value is recognized as a discount. If the present value exceeds the face amount of the receivable, the difference is recognized as a premium.

The sale is recorded as a debit to a receivable account, a credit to a discount on the receivable, and a credit to sales at the present value as reported for the receivable. The discount is amortized as a credit to interest income over the life of the receivable. On the balance sheet any unamortized discount at the end of the accounting period is reported as a direct subtraction from the *face amount* of the receivable.

**Example:** A seller ships merchandise totaling $10,000 to a customer with payment deferred for five years. Seller and customer agree to impute an interest charge of 10 percent for the $10,000. The journal entries follow.

| | | |
|---|---|---|
| Accounts Receivable | 10,000 | |
| Sales (Present value at 10%) | | 6,209 |
| Unamortized Discount | | 3,791 |
| (To record the sale of merchandise at the present value of the receivable) | | |

The *interest method* is applied to amortize the discount.

| | | |
|---|---|---|
| End of Year 1 | | |
| Unamortized Discount | 620.90 | |
| Interest Income | | 620.90 |
| (10% of $6,209.00) | | |
| End of Year 2 | | |
| Unamortized Discount | 682.99 | |
| Interest Income | | 682.99 |
| (10% of $6,829.90) | | |

| | | |
|---|---|---|
| End of Year 3 | | |
| Unamortized Discount | 751.29 | |
| Interest Income | | 751.29 |
| (10% of $7,512.89) | | |
| End of Year 4 | | |
| Unamortized Discount | 826.42 | |
| Interest Income | | 826.42 |
| (10% of $8,264.18) | | |
| Unamortized Discount | 909.06 | |
| End of Year 5 | | |
| Unamortized Discount | 909.06 | |
| Interest Income | | 909.06 |
| (10% of $9,090.60) | | |

At the end of five years full amortization of the discount has been recorded and the face amount of the receivable results. (*Note:* Opinion 21 does not require the imputed interest method when ". . . receivables and payables arising from transactions with customers or suppliers in the normal course of business which are due in customary trade terms not exceeding approximately one year.")

## ¶2015 CLASSIFYING AND REPORTING EXTRAORDINARY ITEMS

Income statement presentation requires that the results of *ordinary operations* be reported first, and applicable provision for income taxes provided for. In order, the following should then be shown:

1. Results of discontinued operations:
   a. Income or loss from the operations discontinued for the portion of the period until discontinuance—shown net of tax, with the tax shown parenthetically;
   b. Loss (or gain) on disposal of the business segments, including provision for phase-out operating losses—also shown net of tax parenthetically.
2. Extraordinary items—Should be segregated and shown as the last factor used in arriving at net income for the period. Here, the caption is shown net of applicable income taxes, which are shown parenthetically. Note that extraordinary items do *not* include disposal of business segments as such, because they are segregated and shown separately prior thereto (as above).

An example of the reporting of the above:

| | 2002 | | 2001 |
|---|---|---|---|
| Income from continuing operations | | | |
| before income taxes | $ xxx | | $ xxx |
| Provision for income taxes | xx | | xx |
| Income from continuing operations | | $ xxx | xxx |
| Discontinued operations (Note): | | | |
| Income from operations of discontinued | | | |
| Division B (less applicable taxes of $xx) | $ xx | | |
| | 2002 | | 2001 |
| Loss on disposal of Division B, including provision for phase-out operating losses of $xx (less applicable income taxes of $xx) | xx | xx | |
| Income before extraordinary items | | xxx | |
| Extraordinary items (less applicable income taxes of $xx) (Note) | | xx | |
| Net Income | | $ xxx | $ xxx |
| Earnings per share: | | | |
| Income from continuing operations | | $ x.00 | $ x.00 |
| Discontinued operations | | x.00 | x.00 |
| Extraordinary items | | x.00 | x.00 |
| Net Income | | $ x.00 | $ x.00 |

Note that earnings per share should be broken out separately for the factors of discontinued operations and extraordinary items, as well as for income from (continuing) operations.

The criteria for classifying a transaction or event as an "extraordinary item" are as follows:

Extraordinaryitems are events and transactions that are distinguished by their unusual nature *and* by the infrequency of their occurrence. Thus, *both* of the following criteria should be met to classify an event or transaction as an extraordinary item:

1. *Unusual nature.* The underlying event or transaction should possess a high degree of abnormality and be of a type clearly unrelated to, or only incidentally related to, the ordinary and typical activities of the entity, taking into account the environment in which the entity operates.

¶2015

2. *Infrequency of occurrence.* The underlying event or transaction should be of a type that would not reasonably be expected to recur in the foreseeable future, taking into account the environment in which the entity operates.

Items that are *not* to be reported as extraordinary, because they may recur or are not unusual, are:

- Write-downs of receivables, inventories, intangibles, or leased equipment.
- Effects of strikes.
- Gains or losses on foreign currency translations.
- Adjustment of accruals on long-term contracts.
- Gains or losses on disposal of business segments.
- Gains or losses from abandonment or sale of property, plant or equipment used in the business.

Note that some highly unusual occurrence might cause one of the above types of gains or losses and should be considered extraordinary, such as those resulting from major casualties (earthquake), expropriations and legal restrictions. Miscellaneous data pertaining to extraordinary items:

- Bargain sales of stock to stockholders are *not* extraordinary items, but they should be shown separately.
- A gain or a loss on sale of coin collections by a bank is *not* an extraordinary item.

## ¶2017  EARNINGS PER SHARE

According to FASB Statement No. 128 a GAAP presentation of income requires that earnings per share (EPS) be calculated along with net income. There are two separate calculations of EPS, one is the basic calculation using the weighted number of common shares outstanding for the year. The other is a "fully diluted" earnings per share, where the number of common shares used in the denominator of the calculation reflects potential dilution caused by the possible exercise of stock options, conversions of convertible bonds, conversions of convertible preferred stock or other stock transactions which could produce either more shares of common stock or less income into which the shares are divided.

***Simple or basic EPS***    The calculation of basic EPS involves first modifying income if there are preferred shares of stock outstanding for the dividends to be paid on these shares. This reflects the fact that preferred shareholders are to be paid dividends prior to common shareholders and that once the preferred dividends have been paid, there will be fewer resources available to pay the common shareholders. Thus, although income itself is not actually reduced by the payment of preferred dividends, the net income figure used to compute EPS is reduced by subtracting the dividends on preferred shares. If the preferred stock is cumulative, the dividends are subtracted whether they have been declared for the year or not. When there are additional shares of common stock issued or repurchased during the year, the weighted average number of shares used in the denominator is computed by determining the effective number of shares outstanding for the periods before and after the issuance or repurchase of shares. Finally, if there is a stock split or stock dividend issued during the year, the number of common shares outstanding is retroactively increased back to the start of the year (or if prior years are being included in the financial statements, back to the beginning of those periods).

*Fully diluted EPS*    The computation of fully diluted earnings per share can become complex depending on the contingent shares a corporation may be committed to issuing. If a corporation has incentive stock options, for example, the total number of shares that could arise through the exercise of the options and the subsequent issuance of additional shares must be computed. These shares are only added to the denominator if their overall effect is dilutive. Here a procedure referred to as the "treasury stock method" is used to determine potential dilution. This requires a calculation of the hypothetical proceeds resulting from the exercise of the stock options and the application of the proceeds received by the company from these options to the purchase of the company's own stock at its current market price on the date the options are exercised. This calculation will result in both an increase in the potential number of common shares outstanding from the exercise of the stock options and a decrease due to the hypothetical repurchase of treasury shares using the proceeds from the exercise of the options.

On September 30, 2005 the FASB issued an exposure draft amending FASB 128 which would alter the "treasury stock method" by requiring the number of incremental shares included in year-to-date diluted EPS be computed using the average market price of common shares for the year-to-date period independent of the quarterly computations required by the existing statement. In addition, the proposed changes would clarify earnings per share computations involving certain instruments, such as mandatorily convertible instruments and contractual obligations that may be settled with cash or by issuing shares.

# ¶2019   SAB 101, *Revenue Recognition in Financial Statements*

This Staff Accounting Bulletin (SAB) summarizes certain of the Securities and Exchange Commission staff's views in applying GAAP to revenue recognition in financial statements. At present, it should be considered the key revenue recognition standard. The staff is providing this rather specific guidance due, in part, to the large number of revenue recognition issues that registrants encounter. For example, a March, 1999 report entitled *Fraudulent Financial Reporting 1987–1997: An Analysis of U. S. Public Companies,* sponsored by the Committee of Sponsoring Organizations (COSO) of the Treadway Commission, indicated that more than half of financial reporting frauds in the study involved overstating revenue. At this point, it would be almost impossible to "fix" a figure for the number of fraudulent cases of overstated revenue.

## .01 The Effect of SAB 101

Among other responses to the SEC's SAB 101, some companies will find it necessary to:

1. Exclude from revenues and/or improve the disclosure of amounts collected by the company acting as an agent. One facet of this will involve assessing whether revenue (if recognized) should be reported gross with separate display of cost of sales to arrive at gross profit or on a net basis. In their appraisal, the SEC staff considers whether the registrant:

   a. Acts as principal in the transaction.

   b. Takes title to the products.

   c. Has risks and rewards of ownership, such as the risk of loss for collection, delivery, or returns.

   d. Acts as an agent or broker (including performing services, in substance, as an agent or broker) with compensation on a commission or fee basis.

   If the company performs as an agent or broker without assuming the risks and rewards of ownership of the goods, sales should be reported on a net basis.

2. Not recognize revenue from "channel stuffing" and other transactions that make it difficult to estimate product returns.

   Registrants and their auditors should carefully analyze all factors, including trends in historical data, that may affect registrants' ability to make reasonable and reliable estimates of product returns.

   The staff believes that the following additional factors, among others, may affect or preclude the ability to make reasonable and reliable estimates of product returns:

   a. Significant increases in or excess levels of inventory in a distribution channel (sometimes referred to as "channel stuffing").

   b. Lack of "visibility" into, or the inability to determine or observe the levels of inventory in, a distribution channel and the current level of sales to end users.

   c. Expected introductions of new products that may result in the technological obsolescence of and larger than expected returns of current products.

    d. The significance of a particular distributor to the registrant's business, sales and marketing.

    e. The newness of a product.

    f. The introduction of competitors' products with superior technology or greater expected market acceptance, and other factors that affect market demand and changing trends in that demand for the registrant's products.

3. Exclude from revenue consignment-like transactions. Products delivered to a consignee pursuant to a consignment arrangement are not sales and do not qualify for revenue recognition until a sale occurs. The staff believes that revenue recognition is not appropriate because the seller retains the risks and rewards of ownership of the product and title usually does not pass to the consignee.

Other situations may exist where title to delivered products passes to a buyer, but the substance of the transaction is that of a *consignment or a financing*. Such arrangements require a careful analysis of the facts and circumstances of the transaction, as well as an understanding of the rights and obligations of the parties, and the seller's customary business practices in such arrangements.

The staff believes that the presence of one or more of the following characteristics in a transaction precludes revenue recognition even if title to the product has passed to the buyer, but the buyer has the right to return the product and:

    a. The buyer does not pay the seller at the time of sale, nor is the buyer obligated to pay the seller at a specified date or dates.

    b. The buyer does not pay the seller at the time of sale but rather is obligated to pay at a specified date or dates, but the buyer's obligation to pay is contractually or implicitly excused until the buyer resells the product or subsequently consumes or uses the product.

    c. The buyer's obligation to the seller would be changed (e.g., the seller would forgive the obligation or grant a refund) in the event of theft or physical destruction or damage of the product.

    d. The buyer acquiring the product for resale does not have economic substance apart from that provided by the seller.

    e. The seller has significant obligations for future performance to directly bring about resale of the product by the buyer.

Purchase order and sale agreement documentation practices vary widely between customers, companies, and industries. The SEC appears to be willing to accept that there is *persuasive evidence* of an agreement shown by these varied practices *as long as* there is some form of written or electronic evidence that a binding final customer purchase authorization, including the terms of sale, is in the hands of the seller.

¶2019.01

4. Include in revenue only those sales backed up by a binding written sales agreement. Typically, revenue is recognized when *delivery has occurred* and the customer has taken title and assumed the risks and rewards of ownership of the goods specified in the customer's purchase order or sales agreement. If revenue is recognized before delivery has occurred, such as in a "bill and hold" transaction, the following criteria must be met:

   a. The risks of ownership must have passed to the buyer.

   b. The customer must have made a fixed commitment to purchase the goods, preferably in written documentation.

   c. The buyer, not the seller, must request that the transaction be on a bill and hold basis. In these instances, the buyer must have a substantial business purpose for ordering the goods on a bill and hold basis.

   d. A fixed schedule for delivery of the goods must have been established. The date for delivery must be reasonable and must be consistent with the buyer's business purpose (e.g., storage periods are customary in the industry).

   e. The seller must not have retained any specific performance obligations to the extent that the earning process is not complete.

   f. The ordered goods must have been segregated from the seller's inventory and not be subject to use to fill other orders.

   g. The equipment (product) must be complete and ready for shipment.

   h. In applying the above criteria, the following should be considered even if the above criteria are all satisfied:

      (i)    The date by which the seller expects payment, and whether the seller has modified its normal billing and credit terms for this buyer.

      (ii)   The seller's past experiences with and pattern of bill and hold transactions.

      (iii)  Whether the buyer has the expected risk of loss in the event of a decline in the market value of goods.

      (iv)   Whether the seller's custodial risks are insurable and insured.

      (v)    Whether extended procedures are necessary in order to assure that there are no exceptions to the buyer's commitment to accept and pay for the goods sold (i.e., that the business reasons for the bill and hold have not introduced a contingency to the buyer's commitment).

5. Exclude from sales all shipments where the customer has not taken title to the goods and thereby not assumed the risks and rewards of ownership.

6. Defer revenue recognition of up-front fees until the related earnings process is completed. The staff believes that up-front fees, even if nonre

fundable, are normally earned as the products and services are delivered or performed over the term of the arrangement or the expected period of performance. Therefore, they should generally be deferred and recognized systematically over the periods that the fees are earned.

7. Defer recognition of revenue from refundable membership sales until the end of the refund period, except in limited circumstances when certain rigorous and demanding criteria have been met.

   Because reasonable people hold different views about the application of the accounting literature in this regard, pending further action in this area by the FASB, the SEC staff will not object to the recognition of refundable membership fees, net of estimated refunds, as earned revenue over the membership term in the limited circumstances where *all* of the following criteria have been met:

   a. The estimates of terminations or cancellations and refunded revenues are being made for a large pool of homogeneous items (e.g., membership or other service transactions with the same characteristics, such as terms, periods, class of customers, or nature of service).

   b. Reliable estimates of the expected refunds can be made on a timely basis. Either of the following two items would be considered indicative of an inability to make reliable estimates: (1) recurring, significant differences between actual experience and estimated cancellation or termination rates (e.g., an actual cancellation rate of 40 percent versus an estimated rate of 25 percent) even if the impact of the difference on the amount of estimated refunds is not material to the consolidated financial statements; or (2) recurring variances between the actual and estimated amount of refunds that are material to either revenue or net income in quarterly or annual financial statements. In addition, the staff believes that an estimate, for purposes of meeting this criterion, would not be reliable unless it is remote that material adjustments (both individually and in the aggregate) to previously recognized revenue would be required. The staff presumes that reliable estimates cannot be made if the customer's termination or cancellation and refund privileges exceed one year.

   c. There is a sufficient company-specific historical basis upon which to estimate the refunds, and the company believes that such experience is predictive of future events. In assessing these items, the staff believes that estimates of future refunds should take into consideration, among other things, such factors as historical experience by service type and class of customer, changing trends in historical experience and the basis thereof (e.g., economic conditions), the impact or introduction of competing services or products, and changes in the customers' "accessibility" to the refund (i.e., how easy it is for customers to obtain the refund).

¶2019.01

   d. The amount of the membership fee specified agreement at the outset of the arrangement is fixed, other customer's right to request a refund.

8. End the practice of including the fair value of free services included as part of a sale transaction as revenue.

9. Additional observations made by the SEC staff on the subject of *delivery and performance* before revenue should be recognized included:

   a. Delivery is not considered to have occurred unless the product has been delivered to the customer's place of business.

   b. If uncertainty exists about a customer's acceptance of a product or service, revenue should not be recognized even if the product is delivered or the service performed.

   c. Revenue should not be recognized until the seller has substantially completed or fulfilled the terms specified *in the* purchase order or sales agreement.

   d. In licensing and similar arrangements, delivery does not occur for revenue recognition purposes until the license term begins.

## .03  Revenue Recognition Accounting Literature

The accounting literature on revenue recognition includes both broad conceptual discussions as well as certain industry-specific guidance. Examples of existing literature on revenue recognition in December 1999, when SAB 101 was issued, included:

- FASB Statements of Financial Accounting Standards: 13, *Accounting for Leases*; 45, *Accounting for Franchise Fee Revenue*; 48, *Revenue Recognition When Right of Return Exists*; 49, *Accounting for Product Financing Arrangements*; 50, *Financial Reporting in the Record and Music Industry*; 51, *Financial Reporting by Cable Television Companies*, and 66, *Accounting for Sales of Real Estate*.

- APB Opinion 10, *Omnibus Opinion*—1966.

- Accounting Research Bulletins (ARB) 43 and 45, *Long-Term Construction-Type Contracts*.

- AICPA Statements of Position (SOP) 81-1, *Accounting for Performance of Construction-Type and Certain Production-Type Contracts*, and 97-2, *Software Revenue Recognition*.

- Emerging Issues Task Force (EITF) Issue 88-18, *Sales of Future Revenues*; 91-9, *Revenue and Expense Recognition for Freight Services in Process*; 95-1, *Revenue Recognition on Sales with a Guaranteed Minimum Resale Value*, and 95-4, *Revenue Recognition on Equipment Sold and Subsequently Repurchased Subject to an Operating Lease*.

- FASB Statement of Financial Accounting Concepts (SFAC) 5, *Recognition and Measurement in Financial Statements of Business Enterprises.*

If a transaction is within the scope of specific authoritative literature that provides revenue recognition guidance, that literature should be applied. However, in the absence of authoritative literature addressing a specific arrangement or a specific industry, the staff will consider the existing authoritative accounting standards as well as the broad revenue recognition criteria specified in the FASB's conceptual framework that contain basic guidelines for revenue recognition.

Based on these guidelines, revenue should not be recognized until it is realized or realizable and earned. SFAC 5 states that "an entity's revenue-earning activities involve delivering or producing goods, rendering services, or other activities that constitute its ongoing major or central operations, and revenues are considered to have been earned when the entity has substantially accomplished what it must do to be entitled to the benefits represented by the revenues." It continues "the two conditions (being realized or realizable and being earned) are usually met by the time product or merchandise is delivered or services are rendered to customers, and revenues from manufacturing and selling activities and gains and losses from sales of other assets are commonly recognized at time of sale (usually meaning delivery)."

If services are rendered or rights to use assets extend continuously over time (for example, interest or rent), reliable measures based on contractual prices established in advance are commonly available, and revenues may be recognized as earned as time passes.

The staff believes that revenue generally is realized or realizable and earned when all of the following criteria are met:

- Persuasive evidence of an arrangement exists.
- Delivery has occurred or services have been rendered.
- The seller's price to the buyer is fixed or determinable.
- Collection of the sale proceeds is reasonably assured.

## .05 Disclosures for Revenue Recognition

Disclosures relating to the recognition of revenue are covered in several different areas of the accounting literature:

- A registrant should disclose its accounting policy for the recognition of revenue in line with APB Opinion 22, *Disclosure of Accounting Policies*, which states, "... the disclosure should encompass important judgments as to appropriateness of principles relating to recognition of revenue ..."

Because revenue recognition generally involves some level of judgment, the staff believes that a registrant should always disclose its revenue recognition policy. If a company has different policies for different types of revenue transactions, including barter sales, the policy for each material type of transaction should be disclosed.

- If sales transactions have multiple elements, such as a product *and* service, the accounting policy should clearly state the accounting policy for each element as well as how multiple elements are determined and valued. In addition, the staff believes that changes in estimated returns recognized in accordance with FASB 48 should be disclosed, if material (e.g., a change in estimate from 2% of sales to 1% of sales).

- Regulation S-X requires that revenue from the sales of products, services, and other products each be separately disclosed on the face of the income statement. The SEC staff believes that costs relating to each type of revenue similarly should be reported separately on the face of the income statement.

- Management's Discussion and Analysis (MD&A), included in SEC filings, requires a discussion of liquidity, capital resources, results of operations and other information necessary to an understanding of a registrant's financial condition, changes in financial condition, and results of operations.

Changes in revenue should not be evaluated solely in terms of volume and price changes, but should also include an analysis of the reasons and factors contributing to the increase or decrease. To go beyond evaluation in terms of volume and price changes, the Commission stated in Financial Reporting Release (FRR) 36 that MD&A should "give investors an opportunity to look at the registrant through the eyes of management by providing a historical and prospective analysis of the registrant's financial condition and results of operations, with a particular emphasis on the registrant's prospects for the future."

Examples of such revenue transactions or events that the staff has asked to be disclosed and discussed in accordance with FRR 36 are:

- Shipments of product at the end of a reporting period that significantly reduce customer backlog and might be expected to result in lower shipments and revenue in the next period.

- Granting of extended payment terms that will result in a longer collection period for accounts receivable and slower cash inflows from operations, and the effect on liquidity and capital resources.

- Changing trends in shipments into, and sales from, a sales channel or separate class of customer that could be expected to have a significant effect on future sales or sales returns.

¶2019.05

- An increasing trend toward sales to a different class of customer, such as a reseller distribution channel with a lower gross profit margin than existing sales to end users.
- Increasing service revenue that has a higher profit margin than product sales.
- Seasonal trends or variations in sales.
- Gain or loss from the sale of an asset(s).

# Chapter 3

# Stockholders' Equity

## CONTENTS

## ¶3000   OVERVIEW

"Stockholders' equity" is the most commonly used term to describe the section of the balance sheet encompassing the corporation's capital and retained earnings. Other terms used are "net worth" or "capital and surplus" though the latter term is strongly discouraged by GAAP and is losing currency. Stockholders' equity consists of three broad source classifications:

1. Investments made by owners: Capital Stock (Common and/or Preferred)— at par value (legal value) or stated amount. Additional Paid-In Capital— "In Excess of Par," "Capital Surplus," etc.
2. Income (loss) generated by operations: Retained Earnings—the accumulated undistributed annual profits (losses), after taxes and dividends
3. Appraisal Capital—resulting from the revaluation of assets over historical cost (not in conformity with GAAP)

*Changes* in shareholders' equity, primarily in retained earnings, are caused by:

1. Periodic net income (loss) after taxes
2. Dividends declared
3. Prior period adjustments of retained earnings
4. Contingency reserves (appropriations of retained earnings)
5. Recapitalizations:
   a. Stock dividends and split-ups
   b. Changing par or stated value
   c. Reducing capital
   d. Quasi-reorganizations
   e. Stock reclassifications
   f. Substituting debt for stock
6. Treasury stock dealings
7. Business combinations
8. Certain unrealized gains and losses

## ¶3001  CAPITAL STOCK

Capital stock is the capital contributed by the stockholders to the corporation.

### .01  Common Stock

The common stockholders are the residual owners of the corporation; that is, they own whatever is left after all preceding claims are paid off in a liquidation. By definition, common stock is "a stock which is subordinate to all other stocks of the issuer."

When a corporation has a single class of stock, it is often called "capital stock" instead of "common stock." The three aspects of stock ownership are (1) dividends, (2) claims against assets on liquidation, and (3) shares in management (i.e. voting rights). As to these aspects of ownership, common stockholders have the following rights: (1) The amount of any/all dividend payments depends upon the profitability of the company. (2) Common stockholders have no fixed rights but, on the other hand, are limited to no maximum payment. (3) Their claim against the assets of the corporation on liquidation is last in the order of priority, following all creditors and all other equity interests. (4) The common stockholders, by statute, must have a (voting) voice in management. Their voice is often to the exclusion of all other equity interests, but they may also share their management rights with other classes of stock.

Common stock may be classified as par and no-par stock or class stock according to state law.

*Par and No-Par Stock.* Par stock is stock with a stated, legal dollar value, whereas no-par stock lacks such a given value. The distinction today is largely an academic one. However, state laws regarding stock dividends and split-ups and the adjustments of par value may affect the accounting treatment of such dividends.

*Classes of Common Stock.* Common stock may be divided into separate classes, such as class A or class B. Usually, the class distinction deals with the right to vote for separate directors, or one class may have the right to vote and one class may not. Class stock is a typical technique used where a minority group wishes to maintain control.

The equity section of a corporation's balance sheet must contain information on the number of shares of stock **authorized** under state law (stipulated in the articles of incorporation). In addition the number of shares **issued** must be stated as well as the number of shares **outstanding**. The number of shares issued includes those that have been purchased back by the company as treasury stock, as long as the shares have not been cancelled. Thus the number of shares outstanding refers only to those shares that are in the hands of stockholders, not including the shares owned by the company in its treasury.

## .03 Preferred Stock

The second major type of capital stock is preferred stock, that which has some preference with regard to dividend payments or distribution of assets on liquidation. In the usual situation, preferred stock will have a preferer liquidation, to the extent of the par value of the stock. In addition, it dividends depends on whether it is classified as participating or non right, convertible, or cumulative or noncumulative.

*Participating and Nonparticipating Right.* If the pr a fixed dividend each year (assuming a dividend is declar to share in any additional dividends over and abov nonparticipating preferred. If it is entitled to a share of any dividends over and above those to which it has priority, it is called participating. For example, a preferred may have the right to a 5 percent (of par) annual dividend and then share equally with the common stock in dividends after a dividend (equal to the preferred per-share dividend) has been paid to the common stockholders.

*Cumulative and Noncumulative.* A corporation that lacks earnings and profits, either current or accumulated, cannot pay dividends on its preferred on common stock. In that case, the question arises whether the past dividend must be paid in future years. If past dividends do accumulate and must be paid off, the stock is cumulative; otherwise, noncumulative.

The preferred may share voting rights equally with the common stock; it may lack voting rights under any circumstances; or it may have the right to vote only if either one or more dividend is passed. In the latter case, the preferred may have the exclusive right to vote for a certain number of directors to be sure that its interests as a class are protected.

Dividends are only accrued when declared by the board of directors. Care should be taken when computing earnings per share to reduce the earnings available for common dividends by the amount of dividends allocated to preferred stock including the current year's undeclared dividends on cumulative preferred stock.

*Convertible Preferred Stock.* Convertible preferred is stock that may, at the holder's option, be exchanged for common. The terms of the exchange and the conversion period are set forth on the preferred certificate. Thus one share of $100 par preferred may be convertible beginning one year after issue into two shares of common. The preferred stockholder who converts will own two shares of common at a cost of $50 per share (this assumes the purchase of the preferred at par). A company will issue a convertible security at a time when it needs funds but for one reason or another cannot or does not wish to issue common stock. For example, in a weak stock market, common may be poorly received while a convertible preferred can be privately placed with a large institutional investor. The conversion privilege, from the point of view of the purchaser, is a "sweetener" since it affords the opportunity to take a full equity position in the future if the company prospers. The issuer may be quite satisfied to give the conversion privilege because it means that (assuming earnings rise) the preferred stock, with a prior and fixed dividend claim, will gradually be eliminated in exchange for common shares.

Accounting for a convertible preferred issue follows the usual rules. That is, when the preferred is first issued, a separate capital account will be set up, to which will be credited the par value of the outstanding stock. When conversion takes place, an amount equal to the par of the converted stock is debited to the preferred account. The common stock account will be credited with an amount equal to the par or stated value of the shares issued in exchange for the preferred. Any excess will go to capital surplus.

Both participating (1) and convertible (2) preferred stocks above must be taken into consideration when computing earnings per share.

## .05  Par Value, Stated Capital, and Capital Stock Accounts

The money a corporation receives for its stock is in a unique category. It is variously referred to as "a cushion for creditors," "a trust fund," and similar expressions. The point is that in a corporation which gives its stockholders limited liability, the only funds to which the creditors of the corporation can look for repayment of their debts in the event the corporation suffers losses is the money received for stock, which constitutes the stated capital account. Consequently, most state corporation statutes require a number of steps to be taken before a corporation can reduce its stated capital. These steps include approval by the stockholders and the filing of a certificate with the proper state officer, so that creditors may be put on notice of the reduction in capital.

Stated capital is actually divided into separate accounts, each account for a particular class of stock. Thus, a corporation may have outstanding a class A common, a class B common, a first preferred, and a second preferred. Each class would have its own account, which would show the number of shares of the class authorized by the certificate of incorporation, the number actually issued and the consideration received by the corporation.

It is at this point that the distinction between par and no-par stock becomes important. Par stock is rarely sold for less than its par value, although it may be sold for more. In many states, it is illegal to sell stock at a discount from par, and even when not illegal, there may be a residual stockholder liability for that original discount to the creditors. In any case, an amount equal to the par value of the stock must be credited to its capital account, with any excess going into a surplus account.

In the case of no-par stock, the corporation, either through its board of directors or at a stockholders' meeting, assigns part of the consideration received as stated capital for the stock and treats the rest as a additiional paid in capital. Treating part of the consideration received as stated capital is the equivalent of giving the stock a par value.

## .07  Capital Stock Issued for Property

Where capital stock is issued for property in a non-cash *
surement of owners' investment is usually determined by usin

value of the assets received (and/or the discounted present value of any liabilities transferred).

When the fair value of the assets transferred cannot be measured, the market value of the stock issued may be used instead for establishing the value of the property received.

When the acquisition is an entire business, the principle of "fair value" is extended to cover each and every asset acquired (other than goodwill). If the fair value of the *whole* business is considered to be *more* than the individual values, that excess is considered to be goodwill.

The difference between fair value put on the assets received and the *par value* (stated) of the stock issued goes to the Capital-in-Excess of Par Value account (or Additional Paid-in Capital, etc.) as either a positive or negative (discount) amount. Note that this does *not* pertain to any "negative" goodwill which might have been created; said negative goodwill, if any, should be used to reduce, immediately, the noncurrent assets (except investment securities) proportionately to zero.

## .09   Capital in Excess of Par or Stated Value

The term "capital surplus" is rarely used and its use is discouraged by GAAP as misleading to shareholders; the preferred terminology is "capital in excess of par" or "additional paid-in capital."

The capital in excess of par account is credited with capital received by the corporation which is not part of par value or stated capital. It is primarily the excess of consideration received over par value or the amount of consideration received for no-par stock which is not assigned as stated capital.

In addition, donations of capital to the corporation are credited to this account. If stated capital is ever reduced as permitted by law, the transfer is from the capital stock account to this capital in excess of par account.

This account is also credited for the excess of market value over par value for stock dividends (which are not split-ups) and for the granting of certain stock options and rights.

## ¶3003   Retained Earnings

Terminology bulletins do not have authoritative status; however, they are issued as useful guides. Accounting Terminology Bulletin No. 1 recommended that:

1. The term "surplus" be abandoned.
2. The term "earned surplus" be replaced with such terms that indicate the source, such as:

a. Retained Earnings,
b. Retained Income,
c. Accumulated Earnings, or
d. Earnings Retained for Use in the Business.

Retained earnings are the accumulated undistributed past and current years' earnings, net of taxes and dividends paid and declared.

Portions of retained earnings may be set aside for certain contingencies, appropriated for such purposes as possible future inventory losses, sinking funds, etc. A Statement of Changes in Retained Earnings is one of the basic financial statements *required* for fair presentation of results of operation and financial condition to conform with GAAP. It shows net income, dividends, prior period adjustments. A Statement of Changes in Stockholders' Equity shows additional investments by owners, retirements of owners' interests and similar events (if these are few and simple, they may be put in the notes).

Regardless of how a company displays its undistributed earnings, or the disclosures thereof, for tax purposes, the actual earnings and profits which could have been or are still subject to distribution as "dividends" *under IRS regulations* may, under some circumstances, retain that characteristic for the purpose of ordinary income taxation to the ultimate recipient. GAAP reporting does not require disclosure of IRS earnings and profits calculations which determine the tax status of dividends.

## ¶3005   PRIOR PERIOD ADJUSTMENTS

Only the following rare types of items should be treated as prior period adjustments and *not* be included in the determination of current period net income:

1. Correction of an error (material) in prior financial statements; and
2. Realization of income tax pre-acquisition operating loss benefits of *purchased* subsidiaries.

Corrections of errors are *not* changes in accounting *estimates*. Error corrections are those resulting from:

1. Mathematical errors;
2. Erroneous application of accounting principles; and
3. Misuse of, or oversight of, facts existing at a prior statement period.

Changes in accounting *estimates* result from *new* information or developments, which sharpen and improve judgment.

Litigation settlements and income tax adjustments *no longer* meet the definition of prior period adjustments. However, for *interim periods only* (of the current fiscal year), material items of this nature should be treated as prior interim adjustments to the identifiable period of related business activity.

Goodwill cannot be written off as a prior period adjustment.

Retroactive adjustment should be made of all comparative periods presented, reflecting changes to particular items, net income and retained earnings balances. The tax effects should also be reflected and shown. Disclosure of the effects of the restatement should be made.

Prior period adjustments must be charged or credited to the opening balance of retained earnings. They cannot be included in the determination of net income for the current period. For income tax purposes such changes must be disclosed in Schedule M-2 of form 1120.

| | | |
|---|---|---|
| Beginning Retained Earnings | | $1,000 |
| Correction Depreciation Error | | |
| $300 × .50 (net of tax) | | 150 |
| Adjustment Beginning Retained Earnings | | 1,150 |
| Net Income | | 400 |
| Ending — Retained Earnings | | $1,550 |
| Accumulated Depreciation | $300 | |
| Taxes Payable | | 150 |
| Retained Earnings | | 150 |

## ¶3007  CONTINGENCY

A "contingency" is defined as "an existing condition, situation, or set of circumstances involving uncertainty as to possible gain or loss to an enterprise that will ultimately be resolved when one or more events occur or fail to occur." Loss contingencies fall into three categories:

1. Probable
2. Reasonably possible
3. Remote

In deciding whether to accrue the estimated loss by charging income or setting aside an appropriation of retained earnings, or merely to make a disclosure of the contingency in the notes to the financial statement, the following standards have been set:

A charge is accrued to income if *both* of the following conditions are met at the date of the financial statements:

1. Information available *before* the issuance of the financial statements indicates that probably the asset will be impaired or a liability incurred; and

2. A *reasonable* estimate of the loss *can* be made.

   (When a contingent loss is probable but the reasonable estimate of the loss can only be made in terms of a range, the amount shall be accrued for the loss. When some amount within the range appears at the time to be a better estimate than any other amount within the range, that amount shall be accrued. When no amount within the range is a better estimate than any other amount, the minimum amount in the range shall be accrued.)

   If discovery of the above impairment occurs *after* the date of the statements, but before their issuance disclosure should be made and pro-forma supplementary financial data presented giving effect to the occurrence as of the balance sheet date.

   When a contingent loss is only *reasonably possible* or the probable loss cannot be estimated, an estimate of the *range* of loss should be made or a narrative description given to indicate that *no* estimate was possible. Disclosure should be made; but no accrual.

   When the contingency is *remote*, disclosure should be made when it is in the nature of a guarantee. Other remote contingencies are not required to be disclosed, but they may be, if desired, for more significant reporting.

   General reserves for unspecified business risks are not to be accrued and no disclosure is required.

   Appropriations for loss contingencies from retained earnings must be shown with the stockholders' equity section of the balance sheet, and clearly identified as such.

   Examples of loss contingencies are:

1. Collectibility of receivables.
2. Obligations related to product warranties and product defects.
3. Risk of loss or damage of enterprise property by fire, explosion, or other hazards.
4. Threat of expropriation of assets.
5. Pending or threatened litigation.
6. Actual or possible claims and assessments.
7. Risk of loss from catastrophes assumed by property and casualty insurance companies including reinsurance companies.
8. Guarantees of indebtedness of others.
9. Obligations of commercial banks under "standby letters of credit."
10. Agreements to repurchase receivables (or to repurchase the related property) that have been sold.

¶3007

Handling of these loss contingencies depends upon the nature of the loss probability and the reasonableness of estimating the loss. (Gain contingencies are not booked, only footnoted.)

## ¶3009   RECAPITALIZATIONS

Essentially, a recapitalization means changing the structure of the capital accounts. It can also mean a reshuffling between equity and debt. A recapitalization may be done voluntarily by the corporation; or it may be part of a reorganization proceeding in a court, pursuant to a bankruptcy or a reorganization petition filed by the corporation or its creditors.

In almost all cases of recapitalizations, stockholder approval is required at some point during the process. This is because a recapitalization may affect the amount of stated capital of the corporation or change the relationships between the stockholders and the corporation or between classes of stockholders. The different categories of recapitalizations are discussed in the following paragraphs.

### .01   Stock Split-Ups

A split-up involves dividing the outstanding shares into a larger number, as, for example, two for one in which each stockholder receives a certificate for additional shares equal to the amount of shares already held. The split-up is reflected in the corporate books by reducing the par value or the stated value of the outstanding shares. Thus if shares with a par value of $10 are split two for one, the new par becomes $5. No entry is necessary, other than a memo entry. The stockholder adjusts his or her basis for the unit number of shares.

Reverse split. The opposite of a split-up is a reverse split, which results in a lesser number of outstanding shares. Stockholders turn in their old certificates and receive a new certificate for one-half, for example, of former holdings. The par value or stated value is adjusted to show the higher price per share. A reverse split is sometimes used in order to increase the price of the stock immediately on the open market.

### .03   Stock Dividends

As far as the stockholder is concerned, a stock dividend is the same as the stock split; the stockholder receives additional shares, merely changing the unit-basis of holding. But the effect is quite different from the point of view of the corporation. A stock dividend requires a transfer from retained earnings of the *market value* of the shares. Capital stock is credited for the par value and capital in excess of par value is credited for the excess of market price over par. (The stockholder who has the option of receiving cash must report the dividend as ordinary income.)

## .05 Stock Split-Up Effected in the Form of a Dividend

Usually, a stock distribution is either a dividend or a split-up. However, there is another type of distribution, which, because of certain state legal requirements pertaining to the minimum requirements for or the changing of par value, necessitates a different nomenclature.

In those instances where the stock dividend materially reduces the market value, it is by nature and AICPA definition a "split-up." However, because certain states require that retained earnings must be capitalized in order to maintain par value, those types of transactions should be described by the corporation as a "split-up effected in the form of a dividend." The entry would then be a reduction of retained earnings and an increase in capital stock for the *par value* of the distribution. For income tax purposes, the corporation may be required to show this reduction of retained earnings as a Schedule M adjustment and may technically still have to consider it as available for ordinary rate ultimate distribution.

## ¶3011 CHANGING PAR OR STATED VALUE OF STOCK

This type of recapitalization involves changing from par to no-par or vice versa. This is usually done in conjunction with a reduction of stated capital. A corporation, for example, may decide to change its stock from par stock to no-par stock in order to take advantage of lower franchise fees and transfer taxes. Or no-par shares may be changed to shares having par value to solve legal problems existing under particular state statutes. A par value stock which is selling in the market at a price lower than its par must be changed if the corporation intends to issue new stock. This is necessary because of some state laws which prohibit a corporation from selling its par value stock for less than par value. In such a case, the corporation may reduce par value or may change the par to no-par; thereby, the new stock can be given a stated value equivalent to the price it can bring in the open market.

## ¶3013 QUASI-REORGANIZATIONS

Current or future years' charges should be made to the income accounts instead of to capital surplus. An exception to this rule (called "readjustment") occurs when a corporation elects to restate its assets, capital stock and retained earnings and thus avail itself of permission to relieve its future income account or retained earnings account of charges which would otherwise be made. In such an event, the corporation should make a clear report to its shareholders of the restatements proposed to be made, and obtain their formal consent. It should present a fair balance sheet as at the date of the readjustment, in which the readjustments of the carrying amounts are reasonably complete, in order that there may be no continuation of the circumstances which justify charges to capital surplus.

As an example of how this readjustment might occur, suppose that a company has a deficit in its retained earnings (earned surplus) of $100,000. By revaluing its assets upward, it is possible for this company to create a capital surplus account for the write-up to fair value, then write off the deficit in retained earnings to that account. From then on, a new retained earnings account should be established and the fact be disclosed for ten years.

## ¶3015  STOCK RECLASSIFICATIONS

Another category of stock recapitalization involves reclassifying the existing stock. This means that outstanding stock of a particular class is exchanged for stock of another class. For example, several outstanding issues of preferred stock may be consolidated into a single issue. Or, common stock may be exchanged for preferred stock, or vice versa. The objective in this type of reclassification is to simplify the capital structure, which in many cases is necessary in order to make a public offering or sometimes to eliminate dividend arrearages on preferred stock by offering a new issue of stock in exchange for canceling such arrearages.

## ¶3017  SUBSTITUTING DEBT FOR STOCK

One form of recapitalization that has become popular in some areas involves substituting bonds for stock. The advantage to the corporation is the substitution of tax-deductible interest on bonds for nondeductible dividends on preferred stock. Of course, where dealing with a closely held corporation, substituting debt for stock in a manner to give the common stockholders a pro rata portion of the debt may be interpreted for tax purposes as "thin" capitalization, and the bonds may be treated as stock, regardless.

Also, to attract new money into the corporation, it is advantageous to consider the issuance of convertible debt securities bonds—to which are attached the rights (warrants) to buy common stock of the company at a specified price. The advantages of this type of security are:

1. An interest rate that is lower than the issuer could establish for nonconvertible debt;

2. An initial conversion price greater than the market value of the common stock; and

3. A conversion price that does not decrease.

The portion of proceeds from these securities that can be applied to the warrants should be credited to paid-in capital (based on fair value of both securities) and discounts or premiums should be treated as they would be under conventional bond issuance.

## ¶3019  TREASURY STOCK

Treasury stock is stock that has previously been issued by a corporation but is no longer outstanding. It has been reacquired by the corporation and, as its name implies, held in its treasury. Treasury stock is not canceled because cancellation reduces the authorized issue of corporation stock. In some circumstances, it is permissible to show treasury stock as an asset if adequately disclosed.

### .01  Treasury Stock Shown at Cost

When a corporation acquires its own stock to be held for future sale or possible use in connection with stock options, or with no plans or uncertainty as to future retirement of that stock, the cost of the acquired stock can be shown separately as a deduction from the total of capital stock, capital surplus and retained earnings. Gains on subsequent sales (over the acquired-cost price) should be credited to additional paid-in capital or additional capital in excess of par and losses (to the extent of prior gains) should be charged to that same account, with excess losses going to retained earnings. State law should be followed if in contravention.

Although extremely rare, if adequately disclosed, it is permissible in some circumstances to show stock of a corporation held in its own treasury as an asset. For example, pursuant to a corporation's bonus arrangement with certain employees, treasury stock may be used to pay the bonus, and, in accordance with the concept of a current asset satisfying a current liability, that applicable treasury stock might be shown as current asset. However, dividends on such stock should not be treated as income while the corporation holds the stock. Furthermore, it should also be noted that even though it is permissible, it is not according to GAAP to report treasury stock as an asset.

Treasury stock has neither voting rights nor the right to receive dividends. (Note: treasury stock remains *issued* stock, but not *outstanding* stock). Treasury stock can either be retired or resold. Treasury stock is an owners' equity account and is deducted from the stockholders' equity on the balance sheet.

---

When a company buys its own stock:
| | | |
|---|---|---|
| Treasury Stock | XXX | |
| Cash | | XXX |

If the stock is resold:
| | | |
|---|---|---|
| Cash | XXX | |
| Treasury Stock | | XXX |

(The credit is the amount paid for the
stock when purchased by the corporation)

---

If there is a difference between the corporation's acquisition of the stock and the resale price, the difference is debited or credited to an account Paid-In Capital from Treasury Stock Transactions for the amount of the difference between the proceeds of the resale and the amount paid by the corporation.

Under the cost method, treasury stock is shown as the last item before arriving at stockholders' equity, while under the par value method treasury stock reduces the common stock account directly under the capital stock section of stockholders' equity.

***Statement of Changes in Stockholders' Equity*** As noted above, A Statement of Retained Earnings shows the factors that caused retained earnings to increase or decrease during the period. An alternative, and more comprehensive presentation, is provided by a Statement of Changes in Stockholders' Equity. While it is not required that GAAP financial statements contain a Statement of Changes in Stockholders' Equity, many corporations prepare this statement as a means of disclosing in one place information about changes in all aspects of shareholders' equity, not merely retained earnings. Formal disclosure is required for changes in different classes of common stock, additional paid-in capital, dividends paid, retained earnings, prior period adjustments, treasury stock, and other comprehensive income. If the Statement of Changes in Stockholders' Equity is prepared, it replaces the Statement of Retained Earnings and eliminates the need to separately disclose in notes or parenthetically the other changes that occurred within stockholders' equity. If a corporation chooses to include a Statement of Changes in Stockholders' Equity, containing comprehensive income as well as changes in stock issuance, it must display this statement as a major financial statement.

In preparing a Statement of Changes in Stockholders' Equity the corporation will list separately columns for the number of common shares and their par or stated value (or if more than one class of common exists, a column for each), a column for the number and par value of preferred stock if any, columns showing additional paid-in capital for common, treasury, and preferred stock, a column for treasury stock, as well as columns for retained earnings and other comprehensive income. The notations to the left indicate the causes or sources of changes in each of these categories.

The topic of other comprehensive income is discussed in Chapter 2. It represents elements of income or expense not reported in the Income Statement but representing changes in the corporation's equity. Other comprehensive income includes items requiring revaluation of assets or liabilities resulting in balance sheet changes not currently reflected in the income statement. These include, for example, changes in the valuation account for available-for-sale securities or translation adjustments from converting the financial statements of a company's foreign operations to U. S. dollars. See Chapter 2 for a full discussion of this topic.

### Sample format for Statement of Changes in Stockholders' Equity

| Statement of Changes in Stockholders' Equity For the Year Ended 12/31/XX | Common Shares Issued | Stock Shares Amount | Additional Capital Common Stock | Paid-in Treasury Stock | Retained Earnings | Accumulated Other Comprehensive Income | Treasury Stock |
|---|---|---|---|---|---|---|---|
| Balances, 1/1/XX | 1,000 | $2,000 | $15,000 | $50 | $125,000 | $4,000 | ($200) |
| Issued for cash | 500 | 1,000 | 10,000 | | | | |
| Unrealized increase in value of available-for-sale securities | | | | | | 700 | |
| Treasury stock acquired | | | | | | | (300) |
| Net income | | | | | 35,000 | | |
| Cash dividends | | | | | (6000) | | |
| Conversion debt to stock | | 25 | 50 | 250 | | | |
| Stock options exercised | | 10 | 20 | 100 | | | |
| Balances 12/31/XX | 1,535 | $3,070 | $25,350 | $50 | $154,000 | $4,700 | ($500) |

## .03 Treasury Stock Shown at Par or Stated Value

When treasury stock is acquired for the purpose of *retirement* (or constructive retirement), the stock should be shown at par value or stated value as a reduction in the equity section; the excess of purchase cost over par (stated) value should be charged to capital surplus to the extent of prior gains booked for the same issue, together with pro-rata portions applicable to that stock arising from prior stock dividends, splits, etc. Any remaining excess may be applied pro-rata to either common stock or to retained earnings.

# Chapter 4

# Statement of Cash Flows

## CONTENTS

## ¶4000 OVERVIEW

The term "cash flow" refers to a variety of concepts, but its most common meaning in financial literature is the same as "funds derived from operations." The *concept* of cash flow can be used effectively as one of the major factors in judging the ability to meet debt retirement requirements, to maintain regular dividends, and to maintain regular dividends, and to finance replacement and expansion costs.

Assessing a company's cash flow is a valuable tool in evaluating the quality of earnings reported on the income statement. A statement of cash flow, one of the four statements required by GAAP, provides an analysis of the amount and source of cash flow, whether from operating, investing, or financing activities.

## ¶4001  IMPORTANCE OF CASH FLOW

The concept of cash flow was originated by security analysts. It has been stated that in evaluating the investment value of a company, cash flow is frequently regarded as more meaningful to them than net income.

Cash flow from operations data in financial summaries shows the liquid or near-liquid resources generated from operations that may be available for the discretionary use of management. Analysts have suggested that this is a useful measure of the ability of the entity to accept new investment opportunities, to maintain its current productive capacity by replacement of fixed assets, and to make distributions to shareholders without drawing on new external sources of capital.

While information about cash flow from operating activities is useful, it should be considered carefully within the framework of the complete statement of cash flows. This statement reflects management's decisions as to the use of these cash flows and the external sources of capital used relating to investing and financing activities. The implication of considering or analyzing only the cash flows generated from the operations portion of a cash flows statement is that its use is entirely at the discretion of management. In fact, certain obligations (e.g., mortgage payments) may exist even if replacement of nondepreciating assets is considered unnecessary.

In using cash flow as an analytic tool, care is required. For example, Corporation X has been capitalized with straight common stock. Corporation Y, the same size as Corporation X and comparable in other respects, has been capitalized 25 percent with common stock and 75 percent with debt. A cash flow equivalent to, say, 20 percent of each corporation's gross sales will seem to be four times as large in relation to Corporation Y's stock when compared with the common stock of Corporation X. Cash flow as a meaningful tool, therefore,

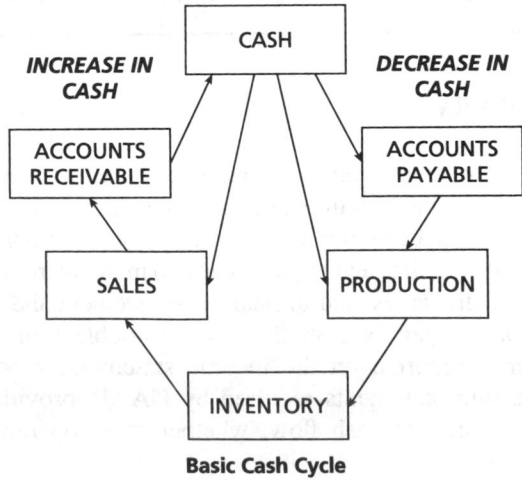

**Basic Cash Cycle**

will have more significance when related to industries and companies in which long-term debt is limited.

For industries where depreciation represents a material expense on the income statement, the cash flow statement accentuates the potential difference between a company's earnings and its cash flow from operations. Since depreciation is an expense that reduces income but does not use cash, the greater the amount of depreciation the greater will be the discrepancy between net income and cash flow from operations.

High cash flow is also the reason that some companies with meager earnings per share are able to pay cash dividends, sometimes in excess of earnings. The SEC has noted situations where investors were misled by these cash distributions in excess of net income when not accompanied by disclosure indicating clearly that part of the distribution represented a return of capital.

In the extractive industries such as oil, coal and other natural resources, the depletion allowance and amortization of development costs, in addition to depreciation, are responsible for increasing the extent of cash flow relative to net income.

Cash flow also helps analysts judge whether debt commitments can be met without refinancing, whether the regular cash dividend can be maintained despite ailing earnings, whether the extractive industries (i.e., oils and mining) will be able to continue exploration without raising additional capital, or whether additional facilities can be acquired without increasing debt or present capital.

Relative cash flow is an important factor in deciding whether to buy or lease. But it is not necessarily true that owning property creates funds for use in expansion. The cash made available to a corporation through operations will be similar whether the business property is owned or leased. Owned property acquired by borrowed capital will require periodic payments on the debt which will have to be met before funds are available for expansion.

## ¶4003   FASB STATEMENT 95, *STATEMENT OF CASH FLOWS*

Statement 95 was issued in November, 1987. The Statement establishes the standards for reporting cash flows in the financial statements. It supersedes APB Opinion 19, *Reporting Changes in Financial Position*, and supersedes or amends prior pronouncements. Specifically, the Statement requires disclosure of cash flows to be included in the full set of financial statements.

Business enterprises are encouraged to report cash flows from operating activities *directly* by disclosing the major sources of operating cash receipts and disbursements (the *direct* method). Enterprises can elect not to show operating cash receipts and disbursements, but will be required to disclose the same amount of net cash flow from operating activities *indirectly* by adjusting net income to reconcile the net cash flow from operating activities (the *indirect reconciliation method*) by eliminating the effects of:

- All deferrals of past operating cash receipts and payments.
- All accruals of expected future operating cash receipts and payments.
- All items that are included in net income that do *not* affect operating cash receipts and payments.

It should be noted that if the direct method is applied, a reconciliation of net income and net cash flow from operating activities is required to be provided in a separate schedule.

If a reporting company has foreign business operations, the cash flows statement must disclose the currency equivalent of foreign currency cash flows, applying the current exchange rate at the time of the cash flow. The effect of changes in the exchange rates is disclosed as a separate item in the reconciliation of beginning and ending balances of cash and cash equivalents.

Information about investing and financing activities not resulting in cash receipts or payments is to be disclosed separately.

## .01   Terminology

Precise definitions to clarify the meaning of the terms related specifically to FASB 95 can be helpful to an understanding of the requirements.

*Cash*. Includes currency on hand, demand deposits with banks, and accounts with financial institutions that have the general characteristics of demand deposits; e.g., a depository that accepts deposits and permits withdrawals without prior notice or penalty.

*Cash Equivalent*. Short-term, highly liquid investments that are 1) readily convertible into known amounts of cash, and 2) near enough to maturity (see *Original Maturity*) that a change in the interest rate structure presents an insignificant risk of changes in the value of the investment.

*Cash Flow*. Cash receipts and cash payments resulting from investing, financing, or operating activities.

*Direct Method*. Shows the principal components to be operating cash receipts and payments; e.g., cash received from accounts receivable; cash paid to suppliers.

*Financing Activities*. Issuing stock; repurchasing stock; paying dividends; borrowing money; paying borrowings; long-term credit. In general, transactions to acquire and repay capital.

*Indirect Method*. Computation starts with net income that is adjusted for revenue and expense items *not* resulting from operating cash transactions (e.g., noncash transactions) to reconcile to net cash flow from operating activities. This method does not disclose operating cash receipts and payments.

*Investing Activities*. Making loans; collecting loans; acquiring and disposing of debt; acquiring and disposing of equity; acquiring and disposing of productive assets (e.g., plant and equipment).

*Net Cash Flow*. The arithmetic sum of gross cash receipts and gross cash payments which results in the net cash flow from operating activities.

*Noncash and Investing Activities*. Investing and financing activities that affect assets or liabilities, but do not result in cash receipts or cash payments.

*Operating Activities*. All transactions and other events that are not defined as investing or financing activities. Cash flows from activities which generally result from transactions and other events that enter into the determination of net income.

*Original Maturity*. An investment *purchased* three months from the maturity date.

NOTE: An investment *purchased more than three months from maturity is not* a cash equivalent, even though its remaining maturity on financial statement date is within the three months' rule.

## .03 Summary

The summary that follows brings together in columnar format the significant requirements of the Statement that are scattered throughout the FASB manual.

1. The objective of FASB 95 is to provide detailed information about the cash receipts and cash payments of an enterprise during a specified accounting period.

2. The statement of cash flows reports the cash effects of any enterprise's operations, investing transactions and financing transactions.

3. Related disclosures detail the effects of investing and financing transactions that affect an enterprise's financial position, but do not directly affect cash flows.

4. Net income and net cash flow from operating activities are reconciled to provide information about the *net* effects of operating transactions, other events, and financial activities.

5. The cash flows statement should explain the change during specified accounting period in cash and cash equivalents.

6. FASB 95 requires enterprises with foreign currency transactions (e.g., cash receipts and payments) to report the currency equivalent of foreign currency cash flows applying the exchange rates in effect at the time of the cash flows. (A weighted average exchange rate for the period for translation is permissible as specified in FASB 52, Para. 12.)

7. Noncash transactions have a significant effect on the cash flows of a company and should be disclosed. (Reference APB Opinion 29, *Accounting for Nonmonetary Transactions*.)

## ¶4005  CLASSIFICATION OF CASH RECEIPTS AND CASH PAYMENTS

### .01  Resulting from Operating Activities

| *Cash Inflows* | *Cash Outflows* |
|---|---|
| Receipts from sale of goods and services. | Payments to suppliers. |
| Collections on accounts. | Payments on accounts. |
| Collections on short- and long-term notes and other credit arrangements. | Principal payments on short-and long-term payables. |
| Interest and dividend receipts. | Interest payments. |
| Other cash receipts that do not originate from investment or financing activities. | Other cash payments that do not originate from investment or financing activities. |
| Generally, the cash effects of transactions that enter into the determination of net income. | Payments to employees, tax payments, etc. |

## .03 Resulting from Investing Activities

| *Cash Inflows* | *Cash Outflows* |
|---|---|
| *Principal* collections on loans | Loans made. Payment for debt instruments of subsidiaries. |
| Sale of equity securities of other enterprises. | Purchases of equity securities of other enterprises. |
| Sale of plant, equipment, property, and other productive assets. | Purchases of plant, equipment, property, and other productive assets. |

## .05 Resulting from Financing Activities

| *Cash Inflows* | *Cash Outflows* |
|---|---|
| Proceeds from new securities issues. | Repurchase of enterprise's equity securities. |
| Bonds, mortgages, notes, and other indebtedness. | Debt repayments; dividend payments. |

## ¶4007 DIRECT METHOD—DISCUSSION AND ILLUSTRATION

Two methods for preparing the statement of cash flows are provided by FASB 95, the direct method and the indirect method. While the direct method is preferred by the FASB, the indirect method is more widely used in practice. The direct method requires reporting the three major classes of gross cash receipts and gross cash payments, as well as their arithmetic sum to disclose the *net cash flow* from operating activities.

The Rule allows reporting entities to detail cash receipts and payments to any extent considered to be meaningful. For example, payments to suppliers might be divided between raw material purchases and other major supplies used in the business. Wage and salary payments might be divided between manufacturing, selling, and administrative expenses. Sales receipts could be divided among different sources, with an "other" operating cash receipts, if any.

The reconciliation of net income to net cash flow from operating activities must be provided in a separate schedule.

## Statement of Cash Flows
### Increase (Decrease) in Cash and Cash Equivalents

---

(Direct Method)
Year Ended December 31, 20xx

Cash flows from *operating* activities:

| | | |
|---|--:|--:|
| Cash received from customers | $ 435,000 | |
| Interest received | 5,000 | |
| Cash provided by operations | | 440,000 |
| Cash paid to employees and suppliers | (382,000) | |
| Interest paid | (13,000) | |
| Taxes paid | (20,000) | |
| Cash disbursed by operations | | (415,000) |
| Net cash flow from operations | | $ 25,000 |

Cash flows from *investing* activities:

| | | |
|---|--:|--:|
| Marketable securities purchases | $(32,500) | |
| Proceeds—marketable securities sales | 20,000 | |
| Loans made | (8,500) | |
| Loan collections | 6,000 | |
| Plant purchase | (80,000) | |
| Proceeds—sale of plant assets | 37,500 | |
| Net cash used in investing activities | | $(57,500) |

Cash flows from *financing* activities:

| | | |
|---|--:|--:|
| Loan proceeds | $ 22,500 | |
| Debt repayment | (27,500) | |
| Proceeds—Bond issue | 50,000 | |
| Proceeds—Common Stock issue | 25,000 | |
| Dividends paid | (20,000) | |
| Net cash provided by financing activities | | $ 50,000 |
| Net increase (decrease) in cash | | $ 17,500 |

---

The following is a more comprehensive Statement of Cash Flow from operations applying the *direct* method. This approach includes the disclosure of noncash transactions in a separate schedule formatted beneath the statement.

¶4007

## Statement of Cash Flows
### Increase (Decrease) in Cash and Cash Equivalents

(Direct Method)
Year Ended December 31, 20xx

Cash flow from operations:

| | | |
|---|---:|---:|
| Cash from receivables | $10,000,000 | |
| Dividend receipts | 700,000 | |
| Cash provided | | 10,700,000 |
| Cash paid to suppliers | 2,000,000 | |
| Wage and salary payments | 4,000,000 | |
| Interest payments | 750,000 | |
| Taxes | 1,000,000 | |
| Cash disbursed | | 7,750,000 |
| Net cash flow from operations | | $ 2,950,000 |

Cash flow from investing activities:

| | | |
|---|---:|---:|
| Property and plant purchases | (4,000,000) | |
| Proceeds from sale of equipment | 2,500,000 | |
| Acquisition of Corporation X | (900,000) | |
| Securities purchases | (4,700,000) | |
| Securities sales | 5,000,000 | |
| Borrowings | (7,500,000) | |
| Collections on notes receivable | 5,800,000 | |
| Net cash outflow from investments | | $(3,800,000) |

Cash flow from financing activities:

| | | |
|---|---:|---:|
| Increase in customer deposits | 1,100,000 | |
| Short-term borrowings (increase) | 75,000 | |
| Short-term debt payments | (300,000) | |
| Long-term debt proceeds | 1,250,000 | |
| Lease payments | (125,000) | |
| Common stock issue | 500,000 | |
| Dividends to shareholders | (450,000) | |
| Net cash provided by financing | | $ 2,050,000 |
| Foreign exchange rate change | | 100,000 |
| Net increase (decrease) in cash | | $ 1,300,000 |

Schedule—Noncash Investing and Financing Activities:

| | | |
|---|---:|---:|
| Incurred lease obligation | $ | 750,000 |
| Acquisition of Corporation X: | | |
| Working capital acquired (except cash) | (100,000) | |
| Property and plant acquired | 3,000,000 | |

(Direct Method) *Cont'd*
Year Ended December 31, 20xx

| | |
|---|---:|
| Assumed long-term debt | (2,000,000) |
| Cash paid for acquisition | $   900,000 |
| Common stock issued in payment of long-term debt | $   250,000 |

## ¶4009   INDIRECT METHOD—DISCUSSION AND ILLUSTRATION

The indirect method (also termed the *reconciliation method*) requires *net cash flow* to be reported indirectly with an adjustment of net income to reconcile it to net cash flow from operating activities. The adjustment requires:

1. The removal from net income of the effects of all deferrals of past operating cash receipts and payments.
2. The removal from net income of the effects of all accruals of expected future operating cash receipts and payments.
3. The removal from net income of the effects of items of all investing and financing cash flows.

The reconciliation can be reported *either* within the statement of cash flows *or* in a separate schedule, with the statement of cash flows reporting only the net cash flow from operating activities. However, if the reconciliation is disclosed in the cash flow statement, the adjustments to net income must be identified as reconciling items.

### Statement of Cash Flows
### Increase (Decrease) in Cash and Cash Equivalents

(Indirect Method)
Year Ended December 31, 20xx

| | | |
|---|---:|---:|
| Cash flows from *operating* activities: | | |
| Net cash flow from operating activities | | $ 25,000 |
| Cash flows from *investing* activities: | | |
| Marketable securities purchases | $(32,500) | |
| Proceeds—marketable securities sales | 20,000 | |
| Loans made | (8,500) | |
| Loan collections | 6,000 | |
| Plant purchase | (80,000) | |
| Proceeds—sale of plant assets | 37,500 | |
| Net cash used in investing activities | | $(57,500) |

(Indirect Method) *Cont'd*
Year Ended December 31, 20xx

Cash flows from *financing* activities:

| | |
|---|---:|
| Loan proceeds | $ 22,500 |
| Debt repayment | (27,500) |
| Proceeds—Bond issue | 50,000 |
| Proceeds—Common Stock issue | 25,000 |
| Dividends paid | (20,000) |
| Net cash provided by financing activities | $ 50,000 |
| Net increase (decrease) in cash | $ 17,500 |

The following is a more comprehensive Statement of Cash Flow from operations applying the *indirect* method. This approach includes the disclosure of noncash transactions in a separate schedule formatted beneath the statement.

## Statements of Cash Flows

(Indirect Method)
Year Ended December 31, 20xx

| | | |
|---|---:|---:|
| Net cash flow from operations | | $ 2,950,000 |
| Cash flow from investing activities: | | |
| Property and plant purchases | (4,000,000) | |
| Proceeds from sale of equipment | 2,500,000 | |
| Acquisition of Corporation X | (900,000) | |
| Securities purchases | (4,700,000) | |
| Securities sales | 5,000,000 | |
| Borrowings | (7,500,000) | |
| Collections on notes receivable | 5,800,000 | |
| Net cash outflow from investments | | $ (3,800,000) |
| Cash flow from financing activities: | | |
| Increase in customer deposits | 1,100,000 | |
| Short-term borrowings (increase) | 75,000 | |
| Short-term debt payments | (300,000) | |
| Long-term debt proceeds | 1,250,000 | |
| Lease payments | (125,000) | |
| Common stock issue | (500,000) | |
| Dividends to shareholders | (450,000) | |
| Net cash provided by financing | | $ 2,050,000 |
| Foreign exchange rate change | | 100,000 |
| Net increase (decrease) in cash | | $ 1,300,000 |

¶4009

(Indirect Method) *Cont'd*
Year Ended December 31, 20xx

Schedule—Earnings to net cash flow
reconciliation from operations:

| | | |
|---|---:|---:|
| Net income | $ 3,000,000 | |
| Noncash expenses, revenues, losses, and gains included in income: | | |
|     Depreciation and amortization | 1,500,000 | |
|     Deferred taxes | 150,000 | |
|     Net increase in receivables | (350,000) | |
|     Net increase in payables | (200,000) | |
|     Net increase in inventory | (300,000) | |
|     Accrued interest earned | (350,000) | |
|     Accrued interest payable | 100,000 | |
|     Gain on sale of equipment | (600,000) | |
| Net cash flow from operations | | $2,950,000 |

Schedule of noncash investing and
financing activities:

| | |
|---|---:|
| Incurred lease obligation | $ 750,000 |
| | |
| Acquisition of Corporation X: | |
|     Working capital acquired (except cash) | $ (100,000) |
|     Property and plant acquired | 3,000,000 |
|     Assumed long-term debt | (2,000,000) |
| Cash paid for acquisition | $ 900,000 |
| | |
| Common stock issued in payment of long-term debt | $ 250,000 |

The preparation of the statement of cash flows using the indirect method requires computing the change in each account from the beginning of the year to the end. These differences form the basis for an analysis of the resulting effect on cash flows. The differences among current assets including inventory and accounts receivable as well as between current liabilities including accounts payable and accrued expenses represent either increases or decreases in cash flow relative to operating income. If accounts receivable have increased during the year, for example, this means that more revenue has been recorded during the year than can be accounted for by the receipt of cash. On the statement of cash flows this change is represented as use or reduction in cash relative to income; the difference is thus subtracted from net income in arriving at cash flow from operating activities.

Particular care must be exercised in analyzing changes in fixed asset and investment accounts. Here the change from the beginning of the year to the end may represent a netting of increases and decreases. For example an overall increase in a fixed asset account, upon analysis, may include the disposal of some assets and the acquisition of others. These changes must be segregated as

¶4009

the disposals will be shown as sources of cash flow from investing activities while acquisitions will be shown as uses of cash from investing activities. In addition, any gains or losses resulting from the disposal of fixed assets or other investments must be shown in the changes in operating section of the cash flow statement since they represent increases or decreases to income that produced no corresponding increase or decrease in cash—the cash resulting from or used in the transaction has already been shown in the changes in investing activities.

## ¶4011   BANKERS' USE OF FINANCIAL STATEMENTS

The accountant needs to know how financial information is used and interpreted by different kinds of statement users who have different needs for credit information. The following review concerns accountants' relationships with banker clients and specific items in financial statements that bankers emphasize in their analysis of financial statements that accompany loan applications.

Of specific concern to a banker are the *trends*, both short-term and long-term, in the prospective borrower's operating results. Sales, liquidity, earnings, and the equity accounts give significant evidence of a company's operating performance since it has been in business and in the near-term trends in those indicators. Banks lend money; a business has inherent risks. The more complete, accurate, and timely the financial statements of the borrower are, the more acceptable are the borrower's statements in a risk-evaluation examination by a banker.

In the case of audited financial statements, the acceptability of financial statements and the verifiability of the information in the financial reports that accountants attest give the banker confidence in a borrower's accountant and in the integrity of the financial information furnished by the borrower. The audit report should be an unqualified opinion. There should be no violations of accounting principles (GAAP), no AICPA or SEC disclosure deficiencies, and no lack of accuracy and consistency with previous years' reports.

## .01   Evaluation of Financial Ratios

While most ratios are valuable in measuring the financial excellence of a business, certain ratios, such as the current ratio, are emphasized for particular purposes. The following discussion covers the more common purposes for which ratios are used by bankers.

With respect to those commonly used by bankers, no one ratio can be said to be the most important, as they are all related to one another. For bank loan officers *the current ratio* is important because the nature of the banking business—deposits available upon demand—requires bank lending activity to be concerned predominantly with furnishing short-term loans, i.e., working capital loans. Banks as creditors attach importance to the *debt-to-net-worth ratio* and the borrower's ability to generate sufficient cash flow to service any current debt load.

## .03    Management Evaluation

Management's primary interest is efficient use of the company's assets. Management is particularly interested in the turnover ratios, such as the inventory turnover and the relationship of working capital to total sales. To the extent that assets are not being used efficiently, the company is overinvesting and realizing a smaller return than possible on its equity. On the other hand, excessive turnover is dangerous because it puts the company in a vulnerable position. Bankers are also particularly interested in trend relationships shown in the income statements for the past years. Excessive selling expenses may indicate that commissions or other payments are out of line with the market. Bank creditors will also make a comparison between a loan applicant and its competitors in all areas to indicate where improvements in operations should be expected.

## .05    Short-Term Creditors

As was stated earlier, a loan officer making short-term loans is particularly interested in the current ratio, since this is a measure of the borrower's working capital and ability to meet current debt obligations. Also discussed was the importance of the net-worth-to-debt ratio, which shows the relationship of the stockholders' investments to funds furnished by trade creditors and others, and shows a borrower's ability to stand up under pressure of debt. The sales-to-receivables ratio (net annual sales divided by outstanding trade receivables) shows the relationship of sales volume to uncollected receivables and indicates the liquidity of the receivables on the balance sheet. Another ratio important to a short-term lender is cost of sales to inventory, which shows how many times a company turns over its inventory, which shows whether inventories are fresh and salable and helps evaluate its liquidating value.

## .07    Long-Term Creditors

Since the long-term lender is looking far into the future, a banker wants to be convinced that the company's earnings will continue at least at the current level. In addition, a lending officer will study the various working capital ratios to determine if the company will have sufficient cash when needed to amortize the debt. The ratio of total liabilities to the stockholders' equity is important because the long-term lender wants to be sure that the shareholders have a sufficient stake in the business. One ratio which is used by long-term lenders is the number of times fixed charges are earned. Fixed charges represent the interest payments on the lender's debt as well as any debt which has priority over it. When total earnings of the company are divided by total fixed charges (including preferred stock dividends, if any) the resulting figure represents the number of times fixed charges are earned.

# ¶4013  FASB STATEMENTS AMENDING THE CASH FLOW STATEMENT

## .01  FASB 102, *Statement of Cash Flows—Exemption of Certain Enterprises and Classification of Cash Flows from Certain Securities Acquired for Resale*

This amendment of FASB 95 exempts certain entities from the requirement to provide a cash flow statement. Entities that are not required to provide a cash flow statement are as follows:

1. A pension plan classified as a defined benefit plan covered by FASB 35, *Accounting and Reporting by Defined Benefit Pension Plans*, as well as employee benefit plans (other than defined benefit pension plans).
2. Highly liquid investment companies meeting the requirements of the Investment Company Act of 1940, as well as the four conditions listed below, or an investment company that is similar to one that meets these requirements.
3. A fund maintained by an administrator, guardian, or trustee, such as a bank, for the purpose of investing and reinvesting money on a collective basis that meets the four conditions listed below. These could include a trust fund or a variable annuity fund.

An investment company, described in 2 or 3, above, must meet all of the following conditions to be exempt from providing a cash flow statement.

1. Significantly all of the investments held by the company during the accounting period are liquid.
2. Significantly all of the investments held by the company are reported at market value or the lower of cost or market value.
3. As related to average total assets, the company had little, if any, debt. Average outstanding debt is used for the comparison.
4. A statement of changes in net assets is provided by the company.

## .03  FASB 104, *Statement of Cash Flows—Net Reporting of Certain Cash Receipts and Cash Payments and Classification of Cash Flows from Hedging Transactions*

This amendment of FASB 95, exempts savings institutions, credit unions, and banks from reporting gross cash flows related to customer loans, time deposits, and deposits with other financial institutions.

It also amends FASB 95 to permit cash flows resulting from futures contracts, option contracts, forward contracts, or swap contracts that are accounted for as hedges of identifiable transactions, or events to be classified in the same category as the cash flows from the items being hedged, provided that accounting policy is disclosed.

# Chapter 5

# Segment Reporting

## CONTENTS

## ¶5000  OVERVIEW

Continuing the newfound path of developing Standards with other standard setting bodies, the FASB issued Statement 131, *Disclosures About Segments of an Enterprise and Related Information* in conjunction with the Accounting Standards Board (AcSB) of the Canadian Institute of Chartered Accountants. Simultaneously, the two bodies published almost identical statements that became effective in 1998. FASB 131 supersedes FASB 14, *Financial Reporting for Segments of a Business Enterprise.*

## ¶5001   FASB Statement 131, *Disclosures About Segments of an Enterprise and Related Information*

At the same time as the U.S. and Canadian groups were working together, the International Accounting Standards Committee (IASC) was also working closely with them to revise International Accounting Standard (IAS)14, *Reporting Financial Information by Segment*. However, after the many discussions to minimize differences that did effectively reduce the gap, the international organization still decided to publish its own Standard. That group declined to go as far in requiring increased disclosure in IAS 14 (rev.), *Segment Reporting*, as the U.S. and Canadian pronouncements required. Subsequently the International Accounting Standards Board (IASB) issued an exposure draft, ED 8 *Operating Segments*, with a comment period ending May 19, 2006. If the exposure draft is adapted as a replacement to IAS 14 it is effective for annual financial statements for periods beginning on or after January 1, 2007.

## .01   Reporting Requirements

Public corporations preparing consolidated financial statements are given guidance on the proper extent of reporting on the business segments aggregated to form the consolidated business.

FASB 131 sets forth stricter requirements than previously for the way a business reports financial and related information about reportable operating segments in annual and interim reports. The Statement does not apply to non-public business enterprises nor to not-for-profit organizations.

The requirements went into effect for the first annual statement after December 15, 1997, but quarterly interim statements were not due until after the first annual disclosure. Thus, the interim statements did not begin until 1999. Then, comparative information for interim periods in the first year was to be reported in financial statements for the second year.

Reporting financial information under FASB 131 is based on the *management approach* in contrast to the *industry approach* that was used in FASB 14. While this Standard required reporting of information about major customers, and some data was provided on related product and service groups, it was felt that the industry approach was too subjective. So much discretion was left to the reporting company in the application of FASB 14 that unfavorable earnings figures could be hidden (by switching industry groupings around, for example).

Generally, this Standard requires that the information be reported on the same basis as the enterprise uses *internally* for evaluating segment performance and deciding how to allocate resources to segments. This leads to new data being disclosed by companies and should be useful to investment analysts and informed investors. They become privy to much of the operations information that goes to upper management to assist them in their decision making.

## .03  Objectives of the Standard

It would appear that the FASB considers this a refinement of the general principles of good general-purpose financial reporting. The Board apparently feels that providing the required segment information will better the financial statement user's ability to:

- Understand the enterprise's performance.
- Estimate the enterprise's prospects relating to future cash flows.
- Arrive at better informed judgments about the enterprise as a whole.

## .05  Operating Segment Disclosure Requirements

FASB 131 establishes new standards for related financial and other disclosures in relation to:

- Products and services.
- Geographical areas.
- Major customers.

This information must be reported whether the business actually uses it in making operating decisions or not—unless preparing information that is not used internally would be impracticable. The enterprise must also:

1. Provide background information about the manner in which the operating segments were established.
2. Describe the particular products and/or services provided by each segment.
3. Explain any differences between the measurements used in reporting segment information and those used in their general-purpose financial statements.
4. Explain any changes in the measurement of segments from one reporting period to another.
5. Indicate shifts in a company's sources of profits, geographical risk, and investment requirements.

FASB 131 requires that a company provide for each reportable segment quantitative disclosure of two basic items—total assets and a measure of profit or loss. The newer standard defines neither segment profit (loss) not assets. Instead as stated above, management is required to determine what is reportable based on how they operate their business. In addition, the company-wide disclosure must include the following for each segment, but only if management includes them in measuring segment profit or loss:

1. A measure of profit or loss and total assets for each segment reported.
2. Revenues from external customers allocated between those arising from the enterprise's country of domicile and those from foreign sources.
3. Interest revenue and interest expense.
4. Depreciation, depletion, and amortization and other significant non-cash items.
5. Income tax benefit or expense.
6. Extraordinary items and information on disposal of a segment.
7. Information about the extent of the enterprise's dependence on major customers—defined as customers providing 10 percent or more of the enterprise's revenues. It is not necessary to report the name of a major customer but it is required that such customer be associated with a particular segment.
8. Equity in net income of equity method investees.

## .07 Management Approach

The management approach is based on the way management organizes the segments within a company for making operating decisions and assessing performance. Because of this, the segments should be evident from the structure of the company's organization. Therefore, financial statement preparers should be able to provide the additional required information without a great amount of additional time and effort.

The management approach should result in consistent descriptions of a company in its annual report since it focuses on financial information that an enterprise's decision makers have been using to make their decisions regarding company operations. The components that management establishes for that purpose are referred to in FASB 131 as operating segments.

According to the FASB, if management were to change the internal structure of their organization to the extent that the operating segment lines were altered, the changed reporting may be handled in one of two ways:

1. By restating segment information for earlier periods, including interim periods.
2. By disclosing segment information for the current period under both the old and the new bases of segmentation unless it is impracticable to do so.

## .09 IASC's Revised Segment Reporting Standard

As mentioned, the release of the IASC's revised Standard on segment reporting was delayed while efforts were made to synchronize it with the new segment disclosure Standards developed by the FASB and Canadian standard setters. The original IAS 14 was revised to bring it into line with the common disaggregated disclosure requirements agreed upon by the IASC and the FASB, and embodied in FASB 131.

The IASC went along with the FASB/Canadian measures as far as to adopt the management approach in which a company's internal structure and its system of internal financial reporting to senior management is normally the basis for identifying reportable segments and, thus, for its segment disclosures. Unlike the two North American standards, IAS 14 (rev.) does allow management under some circumstances to depart from the management approach.

It also differs from them in another respect. The IASC Standard requires that segment data disclosures be prepared using the accounting policies adopted for the company's consolidated financial statements. In contrast, FASB 131 requires the same accounting as management uses internally to be used in its segment data disclosures.

In its 2006 exposure draft ED 8 *Operating Segments*, the IASB is attempting to complete the process of bringing the IAS 14 standards into congruence with SFAS 131. The draft adopts the management approach to segment reporting and its wording is the same as that of SFAS 131 except for changes necessary to make the terminology consistent with that of other IFRSs.

## .11   Operating Segments Defined

FASB 131 defines an operating segment as a component of an enterprise:

* That engages in business activities from which it may earn revenues and incur expenses.
* Whose operating results are regularly reviewed by the enterprise's chief operating decision maker regarding decisions about resources to be allocated to the segment and to assess its performance.
* For which discrete financial information is available.

(The term "chief operating decision maker" identifies a function, not a person with that title. The person's or persons' function is to allocate resources to and assess the performance of the company's segments. A chief operating decision maker is frequently a company's chief executive officer or chief operating officer, but it also could be a group of decision makers, for example, the company's president, executive vice presidents and others.)

## .13   No More Secrets

As with other recent exposure drafts and standards, there was a storm of protest raised about the requirements. Most of the complaints were leveled at the increased disclosure requirements that respondents felt would result in competitive harm. They felt that the specificity of the required reporting would place them at a disadvantage by giving competitors and suppliers sufficient information to figure out their profit margins on particular products.

Strangely enough, when the SEC requested comment on whether the proposed revisions, if adopted, would have an adverse effect on competition, or would impose a burden on competition that was neither necessary nor appropriate in furthering the purposes of the Securities Act and the Exchange Act, no commenter addressed the issue. Therefore, based upon this apparent lack of concern and further study, the Commission determined that there would be no adverse effect on competition, and that the rule changes would not impose any unnecessary burden on competition that is not appropriate in furthering the purposes of the federal securities laws.

## .15   Segment Quantitative Thresholds

In accordance with FASB 131, except as indicated below, a company must report separately information about an operating segment that meets any of the following quantitative thresholds:

1. Its reported revenue, including both sales to external customers and inter-segment sales or transfers, is 10 percent or more of the combined revenue, internal and external, of all reported operating segments. (The *revenue* test.)
2. The absolute amount of its reported profit or loss is 10 percent or more of the greater, in absolute amount, of one of the following:
   a. The combined reported profit of all operating segments that did not report a loss.
   b. The combined reported loss of all operating segments that did report a loss. (The *profitability* test.)
3. Its assets are 10 percent or more of the combined assets of all operating segments. (The *asset* test.)

Information about operating segments that do not meet any of the quantitative thresholds may be disclosed separately.

FASB 131 permits combining information about operating segments that do not meet the quantitative thresholds with information about other operating segments that do not meet the quantitative thresholds to produce a reportable segment only if the operating segments have similar economic characteristics and share a majority of the following aggregation criteria:

- The nature of the products and services.
- The nature of the production process.
- The type or class of customers for their products and services.
- The methods used to distribute their products or provide their services.

- If applicable, the nature of the regulatory environment (banking, insurance, or public utilities, for example).

If the total of external revenue reported by operating segments is less than 75 percent of the enterprise's total consolidated revenue, additional operating segments must be identified as reportable segments. This must be done even if the segments do not meet the quantitative threshold criteria until at least 75 percent of total consolidated revenue is included in reportable segments. That is, once the 10 percent tests have been completed as above, if the external revenues of the segments thus identified do not constitute a substantial portion of the company's total operations (substantial portion being defined as 75 percent of its consolidated revenues), the difference must be made up with segments representing less than 10 percent of revenue, profitability, or assets, until the total of the original segments identified plus these smaller segments reaches 75 percent of the company's consolidated revenue.

Finally, an "all other" category is to be set up for disclosure about other business activities and operating segments that are not reportable under the previously mentioned quantitative threshold criteria. Sources of the revenue included in this category must be revealed.

## .17  Rules for Single Segment Entities

FASB 131 includes disaggregated disclosure requirements for companies that have a single reportable segment and whose business activities are not organized on the basis of differences in related products and services or differences in geographical areas of operations. Disclosures about products and services, geographical areas, and major customers are required of these companies. As a result:

1. The expanded disclosure of operating segment income statements and asset data should enhance investors' understanding of an operating segment's performance, cash flows, and investment requirements.
2. The operating segment data presentation should be more consistent with other parts of a company's annual report.

## .19  Other Aspects

Under FASB 131, the following take effect.

1. Disclosures about different parts of a business are required, but the basic income statement and balance sheet are not changed.
2. Entities may no longer claim that their business consists of only one segment if, in fact, it does not.

¶5001.19

3. Operating segment data will be reported quarterly.
4. Reporting geographic operating data by countries should aid in the evaluation of performance and risk resulting from the global nature of present day business and commerce. The cultural, economic, political, and social data resulting from this disclosure and reporting should better serve top management as well as creditors and investors in evaluating a company as a whole—not just particular segments.
5. The FASB has taken the first big step in its consolidations projects. Consolidations policy and procedure, and unconsolidated entities are still to come.

In the final analysis, FASB 131 attempts to provide information for the user of financial statements about the different types of business activity in which a company engages, the different environments in which it operates, and the nature of its client base.

## ¶5003  SECURITY AND EXCHANGE COMMISSION RESPONSE TO FASB 131

As a result of the promulgation of FASB 131, the Security and Exchange Commission adopted technical amendments to Regulations S-X, S-K, and Schedule 14A in order to bring SEC reporting requirements in line with new disclosures relating to a business enterprise's operating segments. These steps also required consistent changes to Form 20-F and a section of the Codification of Financial Reporting Policies (CFRP).

Since FASB 14 had required corporations to disclose certain financial information by "industry segment" as defined in that statement and by geographic area, the SEC had adopted amendments to their rules to integrate that information to be furnished under FASB 14 with the narrative and financial disclosures required in various SEC disclosure forms.

The SEC agreed to adopt the rules in FASB 131 essentially as proposed. They believe that this is in keeping with their long-standing policy to rely upon the private sector for the promulgation of generally accepted accounting principles (GAAP). The Commission felt this step was also in line with their goal of integrating existing accounting information into the narrative disclosure in documents mandated by the federal securities laws. However, as frequently happens, the SEC retains some of their more stringent requirements while adopting the FASB rules.

### .01  Description of Business—Item 101

In the past, SEC Regulation S-K had required issuers to disclose in the "business description" sections of documents that they filed with the Commission, pertinent financial information based on GAAP's old "industry segment" standard. Now, registrants report segment information in accordance with GAAP's operating segment standard.

*Principal Products or Services.*    Historically, the SEC has required a discussion, by segment, of the principal markets for and methods of distribution of each segment's products and services. On the other hand, GAAP required, and continues to require, only disclosure of the types of products and services from which each segment derives its revenues, without reference to principle markets and distribution methods. The SEC continues to believe such information is also useful to investors; consequently, the provision is retained in their rules.

The SEC also requires registrants to disclose the amounts of revenues from each class of similar products and services based on quantitative thresholds. Specifically, the issuer must state the amount or percentage of total revenue contributed by any class of similar products or services that accounted for 10 percent or more of consolidated revenue in any of the last three fiscal years, or if total revenue did not exceed $50 million during any of those three fiscal years, 15 percent or more of consolidated revenue. The Commission amended their rules to conform with FASB 131 requirements, but retained some of their own previous provisions.

FASB 131 requires disclosure of revenues from external customers for each product and service or each group of similar products and services, regardless of amount, unless it is impracticable to do so. It appears, then, to require more disclosure than SEC rules. FASB 131 provisions result in *disclosure of a range of amounts of products and services, depending upon how a company defines a class of related products or services.* In fact, the SEC decided that Statement 131 could well require disclosure of amounts below the existing 10% threshold of SEC requirements.

However, the Commission believes that a clearly stated minimum threshold for disclosure is desirable. Such a measure should eliminate any possible ambiguity resulting from attempts to apply an unwritten materiality threshold to small amounts of reportable revenues. The SEC, therefore, decided to retain the thresholds.

*Retroactive Restatement of Information.*    The SEC has required issuers to restate retroactively previously reported financial information when there has been a material change in the way they group products or services into industry segments and that change affects the reported segment information. FASB 131 provides that if an issuer changes the structure of its internal organization in a manner that causes the composition of its reportable segments to change, the issuer must restate the corresponding information for earlier periods unless it is impracticable to do so. In their final rule, the SEC conforms the language of Item 101 with the language of FASB 131 regarding when a company must restate information.

¶5003.01

## .03   Property—Item 102

Regulation S-K Item 102 requires descriptions of an issuer's principal plants, mines, and other "materially important" physical properties. Companies must identify the industry segment(s) that use the described properties. An updating of the item reflects FASB 131 financial statement reporting requirements.

# .05   Management's Discussion and Analysis

Regulation S-K Item 303, which requires management to include a discussion and analysis of an issuer's financial condition and results of operations, provides:

"Where in the registrant's judgment a discussion of segment information or other subdivisions of the registrant's business would be appropriate to an understanding of such business, the discussion shall focus on each relevant, reportable segment or other subdivision of the business and on the registrant as a whole."

The Commission has in the past relied on the FASB's definition for segment disclosure in Management's Discussion and Analysis (MD&A), and intends to continue to rely on the FASB's standards, thereby allowing issuers to use the management approach under FASB 131. No rule change is necessary.

Under the language in Item 303, a multi-segment registrant preparing a full fiscal year MD&A should analyze revenues, profitability (or losses) and total assets of each significant segment in formulating a judgment as to whether a discussion of segment information is necessary to an understanding of the business.

Although the SEC did not adopt changes to the language of Item 303, they did amend the CFRP which provides informal guidance about MD&A. (See later in this chapter.) The revisions in Item 303 conform the Codification's language with that of FASB 131, and add a new footnote, that reads:

"Where consistent with the registrant's internal management reports, FASB 131 permits measures of segment profitability that differ from consolidated operating profit as defined by GAAP, or that exclude items included in the determination of the registrant's net income. Under FASB 131, a registrant also must reconcile key segment amounts to the corresponding items reported in the consolidated financial statements in a note to the financial statements. Similarly, the Commission expects that the discussion of a segment whose profitability is determined on a basis that differs from consolidated operating profit as defined by GAAP or that excludes the effects of items attributable to the segment also will address the applicable reconciling items in Management's Discussion and Analysis.

"For example, if a material charge for restructuring or impairment included in management's measure of the segment's operating profit or loss, registrants would be expected to discuss in Management's Discussion and Analysis the applicable portion of the charge, the segment to which it relates and the circumstances of its incurrence. Likewise, the Commission expects that the effects of management's use of non-GAAP measures, either on a consolidated or segment basis, will be explained in a balanced and informative manner, and the disclosure will include a discussion of how that segment's performance has affected the registrant's GAAP financial statements."

In short, SEC wants to make it clear that they expect a narrative discussion in MD&A of items that affect the operating results of a segment but that are not included in segment operating profit defined by management.

Where consistent with the registrant's internal management reports, FASB 131 permits measures of segment profitability that differ from consolidated operating profit as defined by GAAP, or that exclude items included in the determination of the registrant's net income. Under FASB 131, a registrant also must reconcile key segment amounts to the corresponding items reported in the consolidated financial statements in a note to the financial statements.

Similarly, the Commission expects that the discussion of a segment whose profitability is determined on a basis that differs from consolidated operating profit as defined by GAAP, or that excludes the effects of items attributable to the segment, will also explain the applicable reconciling items in MD&A.

For example, if a material charge for restructuring or impairment relates to a specific segment, but is not included in management's measure of the segment's operating profit or loss, registrants would be expected to discuss in MD&A:

- The applicable portion of the charge.
- The segment to which it relates.
- The circumstances relating to how and why the charge was incurred.

The Commission expects that the effects of management's use of non-GAAP measures, either on a consolidated or segment basis, will be explained in a balanced and informative manner, and the disclosure will include a discussion of how that segment's performance has affected the registrant's GAAP financial statements.

## .07   Form 20-F

Form 20-F is the registration statement and annual report for foreign private issuers promulgated under the Securities Exchange Act of 1934. Form 20-F has permitted a foreign registrant that presents financial statements according to United States GAAP to omit FASB 14 disclosures if it provides the information required by Item 1 of the form. A reference to FASB 131 replaces that to FASB 14.

¶5003.07

Much of the material required by the FASB Standards is supplied in Item 1, which requires registrants to disclose sales and revenues by categories of activity and geographical areas, as well as to discuss each category of activities that provides a disproportionate contribution to total "operating profit" of the registrant.

## .09 Other Reporting Requirements

*Geographic Areas.*    Now companies must disclose revenues from external customers deriving from:

- Their country of domicile.
- All foreign countries in total from which the company derives revenues.
- An individual foreign country, if material.

A company must also disclose the basis for attributing revenues from external customers to individual countries.

The Standard requires an issuer to disclose long-lived assets other than financial instruments, long-term customer relationships of a financial institution, mortgage and other servicing rights, and deferred policy acquisition costs. It is also necessary to include deferred tax assets located in its country of domicile and in all foreign countries, in total, in which the enterprise holds assets. If assets in an individual foreign country are material, an issuer must disclose those assets separately.

Even those companies whose segments were defined by geography, continue to report designated information based on geographic areas, unless the information is already provided as part of the reportable operating segment information required by the accounting standards. Consistent with FASB 131, rules no longer will require companies to disclose geographic information relating to profitability, unless their segments are defined by geographic areas, or export sales.

*Majors Customers.*    Since the adoption of FASB 14, GAAP has required disclosure of revenues from major customers. FASB 131 now requires issuers to disclose the amount of revenues from each external customer that amounts to 10 percent or more of an enterprise's revenue as well as the identity of the segment(s) reporting the revenues.

The accounting standards had never before required issuers to identify major customers. On the other hand, the SEC has historically required naming a major customer if sales to that customer equal 10 percent or more of the issuer's consolidated revenues and if the loss of the customer would have a material adverse effect on the issuer and its subsidiaries. The Commission believes that the identity of major customers is material information to investors.

¶5003.09

This disclosure improves a reader's ability to assess risks associated with a particular customer. Additionally, material concentrations of revenues related to a particular customer may be judged more accurately. Consequently, the SEC continues to require this information.

## ¶5005   SEGMENT INFORMATION ADDED TO INTERIM REPORTS

GAAP historically has not required segment reporting in interim financial statements. In FASB 131, the FASB changed its position. Under the new accounting standards, issuers must include in condensed financial statements for interim periods the following information about each reportable segment:

1.  Revenues from external customers.
2.  Intersegment revenues.
3.  A measure of segment profit or loss.
4.  Total assets for which there has been a material change from the amount disclosed in the last annual report.
5.  A description of differences from the last annual report in the basis of segmentation or in the basis of measurement of segment profit or loss.
6.  A reconciliation of the total of the reportable segments measures of profit or loss to the enterprise's consolidated income before income taxes, extraordinary items, discontinued operations, and the cumulative effect of changes in accounting principles.

Thus, issuers must now disclose in interim financial statements, including those filed with the Commission, condensed financial information about the segments identified as reportable segments for purposes of their annual reports.

## ¶5007   CODIFICATION UPDATE, REVISED SECTION 501.06

The Codification of Financial Reporting Policies (CFRP) contains current Commission interpretive guidance relating to financial reporting and is updated whenever it is deemed necessary. In this case the new guidance information results from the technical amendments to Regulations S-X and S-K.

### .01   Segment Analysis

In formulating a judgment as to whether a discussion of segment information is necessary to an understanding of the business, a multi-segment SEC registrant preparing a full fiscal year MD&A should analyze revenues, profitability, and the cash needs of its significant segments.

To the extent any segment contributes in a *materially disproportionate* way to those items, or where discussion on a consolidated basis would present an incomplete and misleading picture of the enterprise, *segment discussion* should be included.

Examples could include:

1. When there are legal or other restrictions upon the free flow of funds from one segment, subsidiary, or division of the registrant to others.
2. When known trends, demands, commitments, events, or uncertainties within a segment are reasonably likely to have a material effect on the business as a whole.
3. When the ability to dispose of identified assets of a segment may be relevant to the financial flexibility of the registrant.
4. Other circumstances in which the registrant concludes that segment analysis is appropriate to an understanding of its business.

## .03   Financial Information About Segments

Each segment must report, as defined by GAAP, revenues from external customers, a measure of profit or loss and total assets. A registrant must report this information for each of the last three fiscal years or for as long as it has been in business, whichever period is shorter. If the information provided in response to *this* paragraph conforms with GAAP, a registrant may include in its financial statements a cross reference to this data instead of presenting duplicate information in the financial statements; conversely, a registrant may cross reference to the financial statements.

If a registrant changes the structure of its internal organization in a manner that causes the composition of its reportable segments to change, the registrant must restate the corresponding information for earlier periods, including interim periods, unless it is impracticable to do so.

Following a change in the composition of its reportable segments, a registrant must disclose whether it has restated the corresponding items of segment information for earlier periods. If it has not restated the items from earlier periods, the registrant is to disclose, in the year in which the change occurs, the segment information for the current period under both the old basis and the new basis of segmentation, unless it is impracticable to do so.

## .05   Financial Information About Geographic Areas

1. The SEC registrant must state the following for the last three fiscal years, or for each fiscal year the registrant has been engaged in business, whichever period is shorter:

a. Revenues from external customers attributed to:
- The registrant's country of domicile.
- All foreign countries, in total, from which the registrant derives revenues.
- Any individual foreign country, if material. The registrant must disclose the basis for attributing revenues from external customers to individual countries.

b. Long-lived assets, other than financial instruments, long-term customer relationships of a financial institution, mortgage and other servicing-rights, deferred policy acquisition costs, and deferred tax assets, located in:
- The registrant's country of domicile.
- All foreign countries, in total, in which the registrant holds assets.
- Any individual foreign country, if material.

2. A registrant must report the amounts based on the financial information that it uses to produce the general-purpose financial statements. If providing the geographic information is impracticable, the registrant must disclose that fact. A registrant may wish to provide, in addition to the information required by this Section, subtotals of geographic information about groups of countries. If the disclosed information conforms with GAAP, the registrant may include a cross reference to this data instead of presenting duplicate data that is in its financial statements; conversely, a registrant may cross-reference to the financial statements.

3. A registrant is required to describe any risks attendant to the foreign operations and any dependence on one or more of the registrant's segments upon its foreign operations. Or the registrant might consider it more appropriate to discuss this information in connection with one or more of the segments in an individual foreign country.

## ¶5009    THE SEC QUESTIONS REGISTRANTS' APPLICATION OF AGGREGATION POLICIES

*Segment disclosures,* or disclosure of disaggregated information, have long been a source of pain for registrants, auditors, Commission staff, and standard-setters. The Securities and Exchange Commission points out that the disclosures have also been a source of pain for users who should be benefiting from them. The SEC realizes that users are rarely united in terms of *what* information they would like to see in filings of public companies, but they do know that they want segment data. The FASB's progress with Statement 131, *Disclosures About Segments of an Enterprise and Related Information*, has increased the volume of segment data, but, as with standards in other areas, perhaps the follow-through from the preparers has not gone as far as the FASB had intended.

## .01 Specific Provisions for Segment Aggregation

Members of the SEC's Chief Accountant's office consider that one of the reasons for this is that there are many companies that take advantage of FASB 131's provisions that allow for aggregation of operating segments. Although aggregation of immaterial segments is easy to understand and accept, it is more difficult for users to accept aggregation that occurs primarily because a company contends that material operating segments are so similar that they should be combined.

If the SEC registrant is following the *intent* of FASB 131, specifically paragraph 17, aggregation can occur only if each of the operating segments unquestionably meets certain requirements. Two or more operating segments may be aggregated into a single operating segment if:

1. Aggregation is consistent with the objective and basic principles of the Statement.
2. The segments have similar economic characteristics.
3. The segments are similar in each of the following areas:
   - The nature of the products and services.
   - The nature of the production processes.
   - The type or class of customer for their products and services.
   - The methods used to distribute their products or provide their services.
4. The segments sell their products or services in similar regulatory environments, for example, banking, insurance, or public utilities.

With all of these caveats, it would appear that this should be a high hurdle to aggregation. The FASB makes clear in the basis for conclusions to Statement 131 that aggregation is acceptable in certain situations because "separate reporting of segment information *will not add significantly* to an investor's understanding of an enterprise if its operating segments have characteristics so similar that they can be expected to have essentially the same future prospects." To put it bluntly, aggregation is permissible if presenting the information separately *would not provide the users with any additional useful information.*

## .03 SEC Concerned About Unwarranted Aggregation

When the SEC has queried registrants about *why* the company aggregated segment data, the answer *has not* focused on whether the additional information would be useful to users or whether aggregation in the particular instance is consistent with the objectives and principles of FASB 131. Instead, the discussions have all revolved around whether each of the six objective criteria has been met and how the evaluation of similar economic characteristics should be performed. In addition, registrants often cite a complaint that they had made when segment disclosure was being debated before the adoption of Statement 131—the competitive harm that would befall the company if it disclosed additional information. It would appear that the registrant is more concerned about maintaining secrecy from its competitors than in gaining the respect of users or their financial statement for the *full and complete disclosure* of the financial condition of the entity.

## ¶5011   FASB PROVIDES ADDITIONAL SEGMENT GUIDANCE

It is important to point out that FASB 131 is not being amended, superceded, or even expanded. The provisions are being reiterated, emphasized, and reemphasized. This is largely an attempt to convince management, chief operating decision makers, preparers of financials, and those who decide whether to aggregate, to be very careful to follow the mandates of the SEC and the FASB in making the decision.

The SEC feels that better and more honest application of FASB 131 would allow aggregation *only* when providing the more detailed information would, in fact, not add *anything* to a user's understanding of the company's financial results and prospects. Evidently, the FASB is of like mind because the Board is planning to issue further guidance on this and related problems in an FASB Staff Position (FSP). Leading up to this FSP, The Emergency Issues Task Force has wrestled with specific problems in: EITF Issue No. 04-10, and EITF Issue No. 04-E.

## .01   To Aggregate the Segments or Not

In an attempt to solve some of the problems related to aggregation the Emerging Issues Task Force published Issue No. 04-10, *Determining Whether to Aggregate Operating Segments That Do Not Meet the Quantitative Thresholds.* FASB 131, *Disclosures about Segments of an Enterprise and Related Information,* requires that a public business enterprise report financial and descriptive information about its reportable operating segments. Operating segments are components of an enterprise about which separate financial information is available that is evaluated regularly by the chief operating decision maker in deciding how to allocate resources and in assessing performance. Generally, financial information is required to be reported on the basis that it is used internally for evaluating segment performance and deciding how to allocate resources to segments. This particular issue is how an enterprise should evaluate the aggregation criteria in paragraph 17 of FASB 131 when determining whether operating segments that do not meet the quantitative thresholds may be aggregated in accordance with paragraph 19 of FASB 131.

In late November 2004, the FASB Board ratified a decision by the EITF Task Force that because the issues are interrelated, the effective date of this Issue should coincide with the effective date of the anticipated FSP. However, early application is permitted.

In addition, the FASB staff notes that public companies may still be required to disclose the effects of this consensus in financial statements issued before the effective date to comply with SEC Staff Accounting Bulletin No. 74, *Disclosures by Registrant When an Accounting Standard Has Been Issued But Not Yet Adopted.*

## .03 "Similar Economic Characteristics"

Issue No. 04-E, *The Meaning of Similar Economic Characteristics,* refers to Paragraph 17 of FASB Statement 131, which allows two or more operating segments to be aggregated if, among other things, "they have similar economic characteristics." Significant diversity exists as to what is meant by "similar economic characteristics." The particular issue in this instance is whether it is possible for two operating segments to have different long-term and future expected financial results and still have similar economic characteristics. The Task Force agreed to remove this Issue from the agenda, but asked the FASB staff to provide guidance on it in the anticipated FSP.

The consensus states that operating segments that do not meet the quantitative thresholds can be aggregated only if aggregation is consistent with the *objective* and *basic principles* of FASB Statement 131, *Disclosures about Segments of an Enterprise and Related Information,* the segments have similar economic characteristics, and the segments share a majority of the aggregation criteria listed in paragraph 17 of Statement 131.

## .05 Both Qualitative and Quantitative Factors Should be Considered

In March 2005, the FASB staff did issue the proposed FSP, 131-a, *Determining Whether Operating Segments Have "Similar Economic Characteristics,"* under Paragraph 17 of FASB Statement 131, *Disclosures About Segments of an Enterprise and Related Information,* to address the questions discussed earlier.

The proposal states that *both quantitative* and *qualitative* factors should be considered for purposes of determining whether the economic characteristics of two or more operating segments are similar. The factors to be considered should be based on the primary factors that the chief operating decision maker uses in allocating resources to individual segments:

- Quantitative factors—Could include performance measures such as gross margins, trends in sales growth, returns on assets employed, and operating cash flows.
- Qualitative factors—Could include nonperformance measures such as competitive and operating risks, currency risks, and economic and political conditions associated with each segment.

The proposed FSP indicates that the quantitative and qualitative factors should be similar in order to conclude that the operating segments have similar economic characteristics. The evaluation of whether economic characteristics are similar is a matter of judgment and must depend upon the specific facts and circumstances.

An enterprise is permitted to aggregate two or more operating segments into a single operating segment *only* if the operating segments meet *all of the criteria* in paragraph 17 of Statement 131, which states: "Operating segments often exhibit similar long-term financial performance if they have similar economic characteristics." For example, similar long-term average gross margins for two operating segments would be expected if their economic characteristics were similar. FSP 131-a reiterates the list of characteristics (listed above) to consider.

In reaching its decision to permit aggregation of some operating segments, the Board believed that separate reporting of segment information would not add significantly to an investor's understanding of an enterprise if the enterprise's operating segments have characteristics so similar that they can be expected to *have essentially the same future prospects*. In those circumstances, the Board concluded that although information about each of those segments is available, the benefit would be insufficient to justify individual disclosure.

## .07 Frequently Asked Questions

Evidently the FASB anticipates some questions are still going to ask regardless of how basically the requirements are spelled out.

**Q1:** Should both quantitative and qualitative factors be considered for purposes of determining whether the economic characteristics of two or more operating segments are similar?

**A1:** The FASB staff believes both quantitative and qualitative factors should be considered for purposes of determining whether the economic characteristics of two or more operating segments are similar. Even if the qualitative factors (including those listed in paragraph 17 of Statement 131) are virtually identical, the FASB staff believes it is still, necessary to evaluate the quantitative factors to determine whether the segments have similar economic characteristics. Quantitative factors could include performance measures such as gross margins, trends in sales growth, returns on assets employed, and operating cash flows. Qualitative factors could include nonperformance measures such as competitive and operating risks, currency risks, and economic and political conditions associated with each segment.

**Q2:** How should an enterprise identify the factors to consider for purposes of determining whether two or more operating segments have similar economic characteristics?

**A2:** The FASB staff believes that the factors that should be considered for purposes of determining whether operating segments have similar economic characteristics should be based on the primary factors that the chief operating decision maker (CODM) uses in allocating resources to individual segments. For example, if the CODM primarily uses gross margin, sales volume, and expected future sales growth to allocate resources to individual operating segments, those are the quantitative factors that should be considered for purposes of determining whether the operating segments have similar economic characteristics. The FASB staff would expect the quantitative and qualitative factors to be similar in order to conclude that the operating segments have similar economic characteristics; however, evaluating whether economic characteristics are similar is a matter of judgment that depends on specific facts and circumstances.

# PART II

---

## STANDARDS

# Chapter 6

# Actions of the Financial Accounting Standards Board

## CONTENTS

# ¶6000  OVERVIEW

In response to the Securities and Exchange Commission "Study on Off-Balance Sheet Arrangements" as required by Section 401(c) of the Sarbanes-Oxley Act, and a desire to work with the International Accounting Standards Board in bringing about convergence of international standards and GAAP, the Financial Accounting Standards Board has many projects in various stages of development and has also approved new Statements, Interpretations and FSPs

As chronicled previously, with the designation of the FASB as the official standard-setter for the U.S. by the SEC, also pursuant to Sarbox, the FASB has reaffirmed its commitment to improving transparency and usefulness of financial reporting to better serve investors and the capital markets. The Board considers reducing complexity and improving transparency and overall usefulness of financial statements as key challenges facing the financial reporting system.

**¶6000**

In response to the SEC Report, the Board provides an update on their activities and projects intended to address and improve outdated, overly complex accounting standards. The areas include:

- Accounting for leases.
- Accounting for pensions and other post employment benefits.
- Consolidation policies.
- Accounting for financial instruments.
- Accounting for intangible assets.
- Conceptual and disclosure frameworks.

The FASB has also undertaken several initiatives aimed at improving the understandability, consistency, and overall usability of existing accounting literature by:

- Codification of existing standards and rulings.
- Attempting to stem the proliferation of new pronouncements emanating from multiple sources.
- Developing new standards in a "principles-based" or "objectives-oriented" approach.

The FASB reiterates its commitment to protecting the interests of investors and the capital markets by developing accounting standards that, if faithfully followed, provide relevant, reliable and useful financial information. The Board remains concerned about the basic causes and the effects that complexity continues to have on the financial reporting system and believes that concerted and coordinated action by the SEC, the FASB, and the PCAOB, together with other parties in the financial reporting system, is critical.

## ¶6001    FASB 158 TO IMPROVE ACCOUNTING FOR PENSION PLANS

In another step to deal with the extensive problems involving retirement plans, the Financial Accounting Standards Board adopted a standard in September 2006 that requires employers to recognize fully the obligations associated with single-employer defined benefit pension, retiree healthcare, and other postretirement plans in their financial statements. The Standard is expected to make it easier for investors, employees, retirees, donors, and other financial statement users to understand and assess an employer's financial position and its ability to fulfill the obligations under its benefit plans.

In existing regulations, the funded status of an employer's postretirement benefit plan (i.e., the difference between the plan assets and obligations) was not always completely reported in the balance sheet. In fact, employers almost always reported an asset or liability quite different from the plan's funded status because the accounting standards allowed them to delay recognition of certain changes in plan assets and obligations that affected the costs of providing such benefits. Further, past standards only required an employer to disclose the complete funded status of its plans in the notes to the financial statements.

## .01  Reporting Requirements

The issuance of this Statement, FASB 158, *Employers' Accounting for Defined Benefit Pension and Other Postretirement Plans—an amendment of FASB Statements No. 87, 88, 106, and 132(R)*, completes the first phase of the Board's comprehensive project to improve the accounting and reporting for defined benefit pension and other postretirement plans. A second, broader phase of the project will be a comprehensive consideration of the remaining issues, as discussed later in this chapter. The Board expects to collaborate with the International Accounting Standards Board on that phase.

The completion of this phase requires an employer that is a business entity and sponsors one or more single-employer defined benefit plans to:

1. Recognize the funded status of a benefit plan—measured as the difference between plan assets at fair value (with limited exceptions) and the benefit obligation—in its statement of financial position. For a pension plan, the benefit obligation is the projected benefit obligation; for any other post-retirement benefit plan, such as a retiree health care plan, the benefit obligation is the accumulated postretirement benefit obligation.

2. Recognize as a component of other comprehensive income, net of tax, the gains or losses and prior service costs or credits that arise during the period but are not recognized as components of net periodic benefit cost pursuant to FASB Statement No. 87, *Employers' Accounting for Pensions*, or No. 106, *Employers' Accounting for Postretirement Benefits Other Than Pensions*. Amounts recognized in accumulated other comprehensive income, including the gains or losses, prior service costs or credits, and the transition asset or obligation remaining from the initial application of Statements 87 and 106, are adjusted as they are subsequently recognized as components of net periodic benefit cost pursuant to the recognition and amortization provisions of those Statements.

3. Measure defined benefit plan assets and obligations as of the date of the employer's fiscal year-end statement of financial position (with limited exceptions).

4. Disclose in the notes to financial statements additional information about certain effects on net periodic benefit cost for the next fiscal year that arise from delayed recognition of the gains or losses, prior service costs or credits, and transition asset or obligation.

The Statement applies to plan sponsors that are public and private companies and nongovernmental not-for-profit organizations that do not report other comprehensive income. For a not-for-profit organization those changes will be reported in changes in net assets. (The reporting requirements were tailored with this sector in mind.)

## .03  Amends Portions of Previous Standards

It is important to remember that FASB 158 amends, but does not altogether supersede, FASB 87, *Employers' Accounting for Pensions*, FASB 88, *Employers' Accounting for Settlements and Curtailments of Defined Benefit Pension Plans and for Termination Benefits*, FASB 106, *Employers' Accounting for Postretirement Benefits Other Than Pensions*, and FASB 132 (revised 2003), *Employers' Disclosures about Pensions and Other Postretirement Benefits*, and other related accounting literature. Upon initial application of this Statement and subsequently, an employer should continue to apply the provisions in Statements 87, 88, and 106 in measuring plan assets and benefit obligations as of the date of its statement of financial position and in determining the amount of net periodic benefit cost.

## .05  Constituents Request Improvement

The Standard was developed in direct response to concerns expressed by numerous FASB constituents who believed that past standards of accounting for postretirement benefit plans needed to be revisited to improve the transparency and usefulness of the information reported about them. Among the Board's constituents calling for change were many members of the investment community, the Financial Accounting Standards Advisory Council, the User Advisory Council, the SEC staff and others.

Thus, the Statement was formulated to address their concerns that prior standards on employers' accounting for defined benefit postretirement plans failed to communicate the funded status of those plans in a complete, understandable, and adequate way. Earlier standards did not require an employer to report the overfunded or underfunded status of a defined benefit postretirement plan in its statement of financial position. Nor did they require an employer to recognize completely in earnings or other comprehensive income the financial effects of certain events affecting the plan's funded status when those events occurred. Furthermore, they could even "hide" the complete funded status of the plans in the notes to the financial statements. No more!

## .07  Effective Dates

The requirement to recognize the funded status of a benefit plan and the disclosure requirements are effective as of the end of the fiscal year ending after

December 15, 2006, for entities with publicly traded equity securities, and at the end of the fiscal year ending after June 15, 2007, for all other entities. The requirement to measure plan assets and benefit obligations as of the date of the employer's fiscal year-end statement of financial position is effective for fiscal years ending after December 15, 2008.

## ¶6003    FASB 157 PROVIDES ENHANCED GUIDANCE FOR FAIR VALUE MEASUREMENTS

In September 2006, the FASB issued FASB Statement 157, *Fair Value Measurements* that provides enhanced guidance for using fair value to measure assets and liabilities. The standard also responds to investors' requests for expanded information about:

- The extent to which companies measure assets and liabilities at fair value.
- The information used to measure fair value.
- The effect of fair value measurements on earnings.

The standard applies whenever other standards require (or permit) assets or liabilities to be measured at fair value.

### .01    Confusion Added to Confusion!

The Board pointed out that over 40 current accounting standards within GAAP require or permit entities to measure assets and liabilities at fair value. For a number of years, various new statements have provided slightly different guidance until it became difficult to decide just how to treat fair value.

And just what does "fair value" mean? There have been different definitions of fair value and limited guidance for applying those definitions in GAAP. Moreover, the guidance was dispersed among the many accounting pronouncements that require fair value measurements. Differences in the guidance created inconsistencies that added to the complexity. The diversity had become so widespread that it would be difficult to decide if/when/how/why . . . until even those who were committed to fair value measurement were having difficulty defending its use.

And the methods for measuring fair value had become particularly diverse and inconsistent for items that are not actively traded. In the case of derivatives (which are complicated enough without adding further confusion), the Board consulted with investors, who generally supported fair value even when market prices are not available. They also favored increased disclosure of the methods used, and the effect upon earnings. The standard clarifies that for items that are not actively traded, including certain kinds of derivatives, fair value should reflect the price in a transaction with a market participant, not just the company's mark-to-model value. The standard also requires expanded disclosure of the effect on earnings for items measured using unobservable data.

## .03   Fair Value Defined and Guidance Enhanced

Under this Standard, fair value refers to the price that would be received to sell an asset or paid to transfer a liability in an orderly transaction between market participants in the pertinent market.

FASB 157 also clarifies and emphasizes the principle that fair value measurement *should be based on the assumptions market participants would use when pricing the asset or liability.* In support of the latter, the Standard establishes a fair value hierarchy that prioritizes the information used to develop those assumptions. The fair value hierarchy gives the highest priority to quoted prices in active markets (sources independent of the reporting entity); the lowest priority is assigned to unobservable data inputs (for example, the reporting entity's own data). Under the Standard, fair value measurements would be separately disclosed by level within the fair value hierarchy.

The Statement establishes a market-based framework for measuring assets and liabilities at fair value if/when a particular accounting standard calls for it. The Board believes that by requiring companies to provide expanded information about the assets and liabilities measured at fair value, investors and other financial statement users will be able to make more informed decisions about the potential effect of those measurements on an entity's financial performance.

## .05   Effective Date

FASB 157 is effective for financial statements issued for fiscal years beginning after November 15, 2007, and interim periods within those fiscal years. Early adoption is encouraged provided that the reporting entity has not yet issued financial statements for that fiscal year, including any financial statements for an interim period within that fiscal year.

Additionally, prospective application of the provisions is required as of the beginning of the fiscal year in which it is initially applied, except when certain circumstances require retrospective application.

## .07   Convergence with IASB

In line with the commitment to international convergence of accounting standards, the International Accounting Standards Board (IASB) intends to issue this statement to its constituents in the form of a preliminary views document.

¶6003.07

## ¶6005    STANDARDS AIMED AT SIMPLIFYING ACCOUNTING FOR DERIVATIVES

These Standards represent two more attempts to make less onerous some of the complicated accounting for derivatives. Both are amendments to FASB Standard 133, *Accounting for Derivative Instruments and Hedging Activities*, the much maligned initial reaction to the scandal resulting from Orange County, California's misuse of derivatives, and FASB 140, *Accounting for Transfers and Servicing of Financial Assets and Extinguishments of Liabilities—a Replacement of FASB Statement 125.*

## .01    FASB 156 to Account for Separately Recognized Servicing Assets and Liabilities

The FASB issued Statement 156, *Accounting for Servicing of Financial Assets*, in March 2006. The Standard, which is an amendment to FASB140, will simplify the accounting for servicing assets and liabilities, such as those common with mortgage securitization activities.

Specifically, the Standard addresses the recognition and measurement of separately recognized servicing assets and liabilities and provides an approach to simplifying efforts to obtain hedge-like (offset) accounting.

The standard also:

1.  Clarifies when an obligation to service financial assets should be separately recognized as a servicing asset or a servicing liability.
2.  Requires that a separately recognized servicing asset or servicing liability be initially measured at fair value, if practicable.
3.  Permits an entity with a separately recognized servicing asset or servicing liability to choose either of the following methods for subsequent measurement:
    a.  Amortization Method
    b.  Fair Value Method

FASB 156 permits a servicer that uses derivative financial instruments to offset risks on servicing to report both the derivative financial instrument and related servicing asset or liability by using a consistent measurement attribute – fair value.

The Board specifically designed this Statement to simplify and encourage more consistent accounting in the area. It is the latest step in a series of somewhat similar projects aimed at reducing complexity while providing an approach that allows hedge-like accounting without having to deal with the complicated rules of FASB 133.

The Statement is effective for all separately recognized servicing assets and liabilities acquired or issued after the beginning of an entity's fiscal year begun after September 15, 2006.

## .03 FASB 155 Simplifies Accounting for Hybrid Financial Instruments

The FASB issued a final standard in February 2006 that improves the financial reporting of certain hybrid financial instruments by requiring more consistent accounting that eliminates exemptions and provides a means to simplify the accounting for these instruments.

This standard, FASB 155, *Accounting for Hybrid Instruments,* also amends FASB Statements 133 and 140 and reflects constituent comments provided to the FASB in 2005.

Specifically, the standard allows financial instruments that have embedded derivatives to be accounted for as a whole (eliminating the need to bifurcate the derivative from its host) if the holder elects to account for the whole instrument on a fair value basis.

The standard also:

1. Clarifies which interest-only strips and principal-only strips are not subject to the requirements of Statement 133
2. Establishes a requirement to evaluate interests in securitized financial assets to identify interests that are freestanding derivatives or that are hybrid financial instruments that contain an embedded derivative requiring bifurcation
3. Clarifies that concentrations of credit risk in the form of subordination are not embedded derivatives
4. Amends Statement 140 to eliminate the prohibition on a qualifying special-purpose entity (QSPE) from holding a derivative financial instrument that pertains to a beneficial interest other than another derivative financial instrument.

The FASB believes the standard improves financial reporting by reducing complexity through the elimination of unnecessary exemptions and by providing ways to make the overall accounting simpler.

The statement became effective for all financial instruments acquired or issued after the beginning of an entity's first fiscal year beginning after September 15, 2006

## ¶6007 FASB CLARIFIES EXISTING RULINGS

The Financial Accounting Standards Board sometimes finds it less time consuming and more efficient to issue other forms of rules and regulations and/or explain and amplify the provisions of some of the more complicated Statements than to amend them. This has been the case in the last year or two. Interpretations and FSPs may not appear to be as authoritative as Standards, but they certainly do have their place.

## .01    Interpretation 48 Reduces Diversity in Reporting of Income Taxes

The FASB issued Interpretation 48 in mid-July 2006 to increase the relevancy and comparability of financial reporting by clarifying the manner in which companies account for uncertainty in income taxes. Currently, the accounting for uncertainty in income taxes, which is based upon validity of a tax position, is subject to significant and varied interpretations that have resulted in widely diverse and inconsistent accounting practices and measurements.

Therefore, this Interpretation of FASB Statement No. 109, *Accounting for Income Taxes* prescribes a consistent recognition threshold and measurement attribute, as well as clear criteria for subsequently recognizing, derecognizing, and measuring such tax positions for financial statement purposes. The Interpretation also requires expanded disclosure with respect to the uncertainty in income taxes.

The Board expects this Interpretation will result in increased relevance and comparability in financial reporting of income taxes because all tax positions accounted for in accordance with Statement 109 will be evaluated for recognition, derecognition, and measurement using consistent criteria. In addition, the disclosure provisions of Interpretation 48 are expected to provide more information about the uncertainty in income tax assets and liabilities.

Any differences that occur between tax positions taken in a tax return and amounts recognized in the financial statements will generally result in one of the following:

1. An increase in a liability for income taxes payable or a reduction of an income tax refund receivable
2. A reduction in a deferred tax asset or an increase in a deferred tax liability
3. Both (1) and (2).

The Interpretation, which incorporates comments received from FASB constituents, as well as views expressed during a public roundtable, is effective for fiscal years beginning after December 15, 2006.

## .03    FSP To Require Recalculation of Leveraged Leases If Timing of Tax Benefits Affect Cash Flows

The FASB issued an FSP in July 2006 to require companies to recalculate their leveraged leases if there is a change, or projected change, in the timing of cash flows relating to income taxes generated by the leveraged lease. This FSP is being issued concurrently with the interpretation of FASB 109, *Accounting for Income Taxes*, discussed above.

Leveraged leases can provide significant tax benefits to the lessor, and the timing of tax benefits provided to the lessor can significantly influence the accounting for such transactions. Changes in the timing and/or amount of these tax benefits may have a material effect on the cash flows of the transaction.

The FSP reflects the FASB's belief that accounting should fully reflect the economics of a transaction. Therefore, any change in either the timing or the amount of the cash flows associated with these leveraged lease transactions must be properly reflected in the financial statements.

The guidance in this FSP applies to fiscal years after December 15, 2006

## ¶6009   VARIED PROJECTS COVER WIDE RANGE OF ISSUES

The FASB has a multitude of tasks lined up for consideration and action, none of which appears to be particularly easily handled, issued, and on-to-the-next. In fact one of the latest agenda items to be added to the list is a reconsideration of accounting for leases, which is second to pension accounting as the most pressing problem needing their attention. It, too, is on the agenda. Additionally, insurance and derivatives are receiving considerable attention because of various instances of malfeasance related to them.

### .01   Two EDs to Improve M&A Accounting Guidance for Not-For-Profit-Organizations

The FASB issued two Exposure Drafts in October 2006 intended to improve the accounting and disclosures for mergers and acquisitions (M&A) by not-for-profit organizations. This is another step in the Board's continuing effort to meet the specific reporting needs of the not-for-profit sector and to ensure that financial statement users have access to decision-useful information.

Recent studies indicate that the total asset base of the not-for-profit sector in this country would make it the sixth largest economy in the world. Similar studies estimate that the number of not-for-profit entities reporting financial results grew by 68% between 1993 and 2003, representing approximately 9% of the U.S. gross domestic product (GDP).

The FASB points out that these figures show that the not-for-profit-sector makes up a sizable portion of reporting entities and GDP in the U.S. and the accounting for M&A activity can have a significant impact on the reported financial position of these entities. However, there has been limited accounting guidance for not-for-profits relating to M&A activity. That limited guidance has often led to different financial statement results for similar economic transactions and events.

The EDs relate to these concerns by proposing accounting standards that would produce financial information that is more consistent, comparable, and faithfully representative of the underlying economics of M&A events.

*Method of Accounting Specified*    Specifically, the proposal, *Not-for-Profit Organizations: Mergers and Acquisitions,* would eliminate the use of the pooling-of-interests method of accounting by not-for-profit organizations, in which assets acquired and liabilities assumed are recorded at "carryover" amounts recorded on the books of acquired organizations. This proposal would instead require the application of the acquisition method to all mergers and acquisitions by a not-for-profit organization.

In applying the acquisition method, the proposal generally would require that not-for-profit organizations:

1. Recognize the identifiable assets acquired and liabilities assumed that compose the business or nonprofit activity acquired in a merger or acquisition.
2. Measure those assets and liabilities at their fair values as of the acquisition date.
3. Recognize either goodwill of the acquired business or nonprofit activity or the contribution inherent in the merger or acquisition as a residual based on the value of the identifiable assets acquired, liabilities assumed, and the consideration transferred (if any).
4. Disclose information to enable users of the financial statements to evaluate the nature and financial effects of the merger or acquisition.

*Guidance for Intangible Assets*    *Not-for-Profit Organizations: Goodwill and Other Intangible Assets Acquired in a Merger or Acquisition,* proposes accounting guidance for those intangible assets after a merger or acquisition. The proposed guidance is consistent with the accounting for all other acquired intangible assets-whether purchased or donated, or whether acquired individually or as part of a group.

Under this proposal, not-for-profit organizations would be required to provide:

1. Consistent and comparable information about identifiable intangible assets acquired by not-for-profit organizations in a merger or acquisition.
2. More faithfully representative and relevant information about events resulting in impairments of goodwill that a not-for-profit organization has acquired.

These provisions, similar to the current measures included in the accounting for business combinations in the for-profit sector, as well as those proposed in the June 2005 Exposure Draft, will provide financial statement users with more consistent and comparable information. The Board expects that the result should more reliably portray the underlying economics of M&A transactions by not-for-profit organizations.

## .03 FASB Adds Project to Reconsider Lease Accounting

The FASB formally added a project to its agenda in July 2006 to reconsider the current accounting standards for leases. The goal of that project is to insure that investors and other users of financial statements are provided useful, transparent, and complete information in those financial statements about leasing transactions. The decision to add a leasing project, which will be conducted jointly with the International Accounting Standards Board, reflects the Board's concern that the current accounting in this area *does not* clearly portray the resources and obligations arising from lease transactions.

Before assuming this task, the FASB consulted with its constituents, including the FASB's Financial Accounting Standards Advisory Council (FASAC), its User Advisory Council (UAC), and the SEC staff. Many of those constituents urged the Board to undertake such a project. All expressed the view that current lease accounting standards fail to provide complete and transparent information. In fact, the SEC staff formally raised issues with, and recommended improvements to, this area as part of its June 2005 report to Congress on off-balance sheet arrangements as required by the Sarbanes-Oxley Act of 2002.

***Basic Lease Standard Outdated***   Written in 1976, FASB 13, *Accounting for Leases,* defines all leases as either capital leases or operating leases. When a company is financing an asset purchase via a capital lease, it records the asset and lease payments on the balance sheet. In contrast, a rental contract—an operating lease—requires neither the asset nor the payment obligation to be recorded on the balance sheet.

Leases serve a vital role in businesses around the world. FASB 13 represented a significant improvement at the time, but lease arrangements have evolved considerably over the past 30 years and the standards are outdated. Today, leasing arrangements can vary from simple rentals of equipment to complex, tax-motivated arrangements involving real estate and other types of assets. Moreover, the current accounting standards in this area are complex and rules-based, which makes it possible to structure transactions to achieve desired creative accounting outcomes, as was demonstrated by the Enron fiasco.

The Board has been asked to reconsider the accounting standards on leasing for varied reasons:

1.  Investors are concerned that existing standards do not require balance sheet recognition of significant assets and liabilities arising from leases.

2. Current accounting guidance in this area is rules-basedand voluminous. Accordingly, the goal of this project is to develop principles that would faithfully represent lease transactions in the financial statements of lessees and lessors and would reflect similarities and differences in the wide variety of leasing arrangements prevalent in today's business environment.
3. In the June 2005 report to Congress as part of the Sarbanes-Oxley Act, the SEC staff pointed out that lease-accounting standards should be rewritten. They estimated that the standards allow publicly traded companies to keep an undiscounted $1.25 trillion in future cash obligations off their balance sheets.

*Time Frame for Project*    One of the initial steps will be to form a working group made up of interested parties with knowledge and expertise about a wide range of leasing arrangements, and coordinating that effort with the IASB. The FASB will also continue to seek input from their advisory councils and Investor Task Force. This seems to be a rather long, drawn out process. It is being suggested that the updated rule will actually be issued three years from now. The timeline for amending FASB 13, *Accounting for Leases*, is as follows:

1. In 2006, the FASB and IASB staffs will meet to develop issues to be considered.
2. In 2007, the two boards will deliberate the issues and request public comment.
3. A Preliminary Views document, summarizing the views of both boards will be published preliminary views will be issued for constituent comment in 2008.
4. Sometime in 2009, an amended FASB 13 could be issued.

## .05  Board Invites Comments on Project to Improve Financial Reporting for Insurance Accounting

As part of a broader initiative to improve financial reporting for insurance accounting, the FASB in May 2006 issued an Invitation to Comment (ITC) on the potential bifurcation of insurance and reinsurance contracts into insurance components and financing components.

This step reflects the Board's concern about a possible lack of transparency in the financial statements of both policyholders and (re)insurance companies relating to the depiction of insurance risk associated with contracts that include terms or features that significantly limit the actual amount of risk transferred. Such contracts are frequently referred to as finite risk contracts. However, this ITC is not limited to concern about finite risk contracts.

Current accounting standards provide guidance for insurance accounting address financial reporting by insurance and reinsurance companies, particularly.

However, these standards provide only limited guidance on how to account for insurance contracts by policyholders. Moreover, insurance and reinsurance contracts often have both insurance components and financing components that are combined and accounted for simply as "insurance contracts."

***Bifurcation Given Consideration*** Accordingly, the Board plans to gather information about whether bifurcation would improve financial reporting by providing users of financial statements with better information about the economic substance of insurance arrangements.

Bifurcation would divide some or all of such contracts into two main components for financial reporting purposes:

1. Components of those contracts that transfer significant insurance risk would be accounted for under existing insurance accounting guidance and generally provide an income statement benefit (recovery) in the period of an insured loss.
2. Financing components that are accounted for as deposits would be recorded as an asset by the policyholder. Any recovery from an insured event would reduce the deposit and not have a significant income statement benefit.

***Board Seeks Wide Input*** The Invitation to Comment requests specific information from buyers and sellers of insurance and reinsurance contracts and the users of their financial statements.

The FASB is encouraging the active participation of all constituents in this process; however, the organization is particularly interested in hearing from noninsurance company policyholders—including small and private companies. Bifurcation could have a significant impact on the way some insurance contracts are accounted for. The Board wants to ensure that all parties have an opportunity to consider all sides of these issues and have the opportunity to express their points of view.

## .07   Phase II to Improve Accounting For Postretirement Benefit Plans

The FASB issued an exposure draft at the end of March 2006, *Accounting for Postretirement Benefits, Including Pensions*. The aim was to improve the transparency and completeness of financial statements related to employment benefits, thus providing shareholders, creditors, employees, retirees, donors, and other users of the reports with a much better picture of the condition of the plans.

The ED applied to all plan sponsors including public and private companies and nongovernmental not-for-profit organizations. The exposure draft was the result of the first phase of a previously announced comprehensive project to reconsider guidance in Statement No. 87, *Employers' Accounting for Pensions*,

Statement No. 106, *Employers' Accounting for Postretirement Benefits Other Than Pensions*, and 123(R), *Share-Based Payment*.

The first phase of this ED has been completed; a second, broader phase of the project will be a comprehensive consideration of the issues not covered in that first phase — FASB 158 (discussed at the beginning of this Chapter). The Board expects to collaborate on this phase with the International Accounting Standards Board, as well as other standard setters. In addition, they will seek the views of other parties, including the Department of Labor and the Pension Benefit Guaranty Corporation that are currently involved in independent reviews of the pension system.

This more complex, broader phase will cover the entire retiree-benefit accounting system, including health benefits as well as pensions. It is expected to cover:

- How best to recognize and display in earnings and other comprehensive income, the various elements that affect the cost of providing postretirement benefits.
- How best to measure obligations, in particular those obligations falling under plans with lump-sum settlement options.
- Whether more, or different, guidance should be provided regarding measurement assumptions.
- Whether postretirement benefit trusts should be consolidated by the plan sponsor.

When rumors about possible problems facing pension plans and retirement savings became media fodder, investors, creditors, the SEC, as well as the FASB voiced concern. The difficulty in assessing an employer's financial position because of incomplete, rather opaque accounting came at a time when the accounting profession could ill afford adverse publicity. The completion of Phase I, by requiring sponsoring employers to reflect the current overfunded or underfunded positions of postretirement benefit plans in the balance sheet as a corporate asset or liability, makes the basic financial statements more complete, useful, and transparent, and clarifies the likelihood of the organization's ability to meet the obligations of the plans.

***Little Opposition from Financial Executives***    From the very beginning, there appears to have been little opposition to the project. In a recent survey, around 70 percent of a group of financial executives agreed that companies should be required to account for pension-plans in a manner such as that outlined in the ED.

Reasons for their lack of objection may be because:

- Corporate pension information is actually disclosed even if only in the footnotes to the financial statements.

- There has been a shift away from corporate defined benefit plans to defined contribution retirement programs like 401(k) and 403(b) plans, which will not be affected by the FASB proposal.
- It should be tougher for bankrupt companies to dump their pension obligations on to the Pension Benefit Guaranty Corporation. (Executives of healthy firms are understandably angered when, in effect, they are forced to subsidize seriously underfunded plans.)
- A majority of those surveyed believe that the quality of financial reporting has improved since the passage of Sarbanes-Oxley; however, a much larger percent felt that there is still a need for greater transparency in financial reporting.

## .09 ED to Reduce Complexity in Accounting for Financial Instruments

The FASB issued an Exposure Draft in January 2006 to provide companies with the option to report selected financial assets and liabilities at fair value. Under the option, any changes in fair value would be included in earnings. The proposed standard is an attempt to reduce both complexity in accounting and volatility in earnings resulting from differences in the existing accounting rules.

Current GAAP uses different measurement attributes for different assets and liabilities, leading to earnings volatility. The standard would help to mitigate this type of accounting-induced volatility by enabling companies to achieve a more consistent accounting for changes in the fair value of related assets and liabilities without their having to apply complex hedge accounting provisions.

Under this proposal, entities would be able to measure at fair value financial assets and liabilities selected on a contract-by-contract basis. They would be required to display those values separately from those measured under different attributes on the face of the balance sheet. Furthermore, the proposal would require companies to provide additional information that would help investors and other users of financial statements to understand the effect on earnings more readily.

The Board feels that the option to measure related financial instruments at fair value should simplify accounting and encourage the display of more relevant and understandable information for investors and other users of financial statements. In addition, this is another step in the effort to achieve further convergence with the IASB, which previously adopted a fair value option for financial instruments.

## .11 FASB Issues Revised Proposal to Improve Reporting of EPS

The FASB issued a revised Exposure Draft in September 2005 of a proposed standard that would make targeted improvements to the reporting of earnings per share (EPS). Specifically, the proposed changes would clarify earnings per share computations involving certain instruments, such as mandatorily convertible instruments and contractual obligations that may be settled with cash or by issuing shares. The ED is a revision of the December 2003 proposed Statement, *Earnings per Share*, which was issued as part of the Board's ongoing efforts with the IASB to bring about convergence between U.S. and international accounting standards.

The FASB feels this proposal improves the reporting of EPS in several ways by:

- Simplifying the existing guidance.
- Producing similar earnings per share results for economically similar situations.
- Enhancing the comparability of financial reporting internationally by eliminating differences between FASB 128 and comparable International Financial Reporting Standards

The proposed Statement would be effective for interim and annual periods ending after June 15, 2006.

## .13    ED to Account for Transfer of Financial Assets

Of the three Exposure Documents issued together in August 2005, only one remains; the other two became FASB Standards 155 and 156, The remaining one, *Accounting for Transfers of Financial Assets,* is directed toward clarifying the derecognition requirements for financial assets that were developed initially in FASB Statement No. 125, *Accounting for Transfers and Servicing of Financial Assets and Extinguishments of Liabilities,* and revised in Statement 140, and to change and simplify the initial measurement of interests related to transferred financial assets that are held by a transferor. The proposed changes principally apply to securitizations and loan participations.

This particular issue appears to have a rather long history. The current ED is a revision of the June 2003 one, *Qualifying Special-Purpose Entities and Isolation of Transferred Assets.* The revised Exposure Draft reflects what the Board learned from constituents' comments in the earlier effort and deals with some new issues.

Specifically, this proposed Statement seeks to:

1. Clearly specify the circumstances that require the use of a qualifying special-purpose entity (SPE) in order to derecognize all or a portion of financial assets.
2. Provide additional guidance on permitted activities of qualifying SPEs.

3. Eliminate the prohibition on a qualifying SPE's ability to hold passive derivative financial instruments that pertain to beneficial interests held by a transferor.

## .15 IASB and FASB Publish EDs – First Joint Proposals on Business Combinations

The International Accounting Standards Board (IASB) and the FASB each published an Exposure Draft containing joint proposals to improve and align the accounting for business combinations in June 2005. The proposals include a draft standard that the Boards developed in their first major joint project. The objective of the project is to develop a single high-quality standard for accounting for business combinations that could be used for both domestic and cross-border financial reporting. The proposed standard would replace the existing requirements of the IASB's IFRS3 *Business Combinations* and the FASB's Statement No. 141, *Business Combinations.* (For a discussion of their plans, please refer to the section, "FASB and IASB on Flexible Path to Convergence."

## ¶6011 FASB Issues Final Statement on Accounting for Share-Based Payment

In December 2004 the FASB published Statement 123 (revised 2004), *Share-Based Payment.* This Statement is designed to provide investors and other users of financial statements with more complete and neutral financial information by requiring that the compensation cost relating to share-based payment transactions be recognized in financial statements. That cost will be measured based on the fair value of the equity or liability instruments issued. The Statement is the result of a two-year effort to respond to requests from investors and other users for improvement in accounting for share-based payment arrangements with employees. It became fairly obvious that the cost of share-based payments in the financial statements was necessary to improve the relevance, reliability, and comparability of the financial information. This additional information should help users of the financial statements to understand better the economic transactions affecting an entity.

## .01 Scope of FASB Provisions

FASB 123(R) covers a wide range of share-based compensation arrangements including:

- Share options.
- Restricted share plans.

- Performance-based awards.
- Share appreciation rights.
- Employee share purchase plans.

In addition to the accounting standard that sets forth the financial reporting objectives and related accounting principles, FASB 123(R) includes an appendix of implementation guidance that provides expanded guidance on measuring the fair value of share-based payment awards. In developing that guidance, the FASB included several special measurement provisions for private companies designed to ease implementation. The implementation guidance also includes numerous examples illustrating the accounting for common types of share-based payment arrangements.

Statement 123(R) replaces FASB Statement No. 123, *Accounting for Stock-Based Compensation*, and supersedes APB Opinion No. 25, *Accounting for Stock Issued to Employees*. Statement 123, as originally issued in 1995, established as preferable a fair-value-based method of accounting for share-based payment transactions with employees. However, that Statement permitted entities the option of continuing to apply the guidance in Opinion 25, as long as the footnotes to financial statements disclosed what net income would have been had the preferable fair-value-based method been used. Although those disclosures helped to mitigate the problems associated with accounting under Opinion 25, many investors and other users of financial statements emphasized the fact that the failure to include employee compensation costs in the income statement impaired the transparency, comparability, and credibility of financial statements.

## .03   Gradual Steps to Stock Option Expensing

At the time of the adoption of 123R, approximately 750 public companies in the United States had voluntarily applied Statement 123's fair-value-based method of accounting for share-based payments or had announced plans to do so. The International Accounting Standards Board and the Canadian Accounting Standards Board had previously issued accounting standards requiring entities in their respective jurisdictions to recognize the cost of employee services received in share-based payment transactions in financial statements.

After adding the project to its agenda in March 2003, the FASB held 60 public meetings, conducted field visits with companies and employee benefit consultants, held public roundtables, consulted with numerous valuation experts, companies, auditors, and many others, and reviewed thousands of comment letters from interested parties.

The FASB obviously recognized the high level of interest in this subject ever since 123 was passed as a compromise after extensive political pressure basically forced the Board to settle for an either/or solution. Therefore, this Statement is the outcome of a careful, extensive due process.

## ¶6012 THE SEC TAKES STEPS TO AID IN IMPLEMENTATION OF STATEMENT 123R

Realizing that this accounting Standard requires the use of assumptions and estimates about future events and that some of the inputs to valuation models require considerable judgment, the SEC evidently decided to provide additional time and guidance to make the process go more smoothly.

The Commission has acknowledged that in applying the Standard, preparers, auditors, and those assisting in valuing equity-based awards are required to use their best judgment. It is anticipated that assumptions and estimates of fair value related to employee stock options will improve as companies gain experience. The agency realizes that, for many companies which had continued with the guidance of Opinion 25, their best estimates under the new Standard will differ from those previously used in footnote disclosures. Indications are that the SEC staff will take this into consideration in evaluating implementation of the new requirements.

## .01 SEC Chief Accountant's Comments on FASB 123R

Apparently to put a stop to rumors that the SEC might fold under tremendous pressure by antiexpensing forces, the Chief Accountant's office has indicated that it is supportive of the Standard, and the FASB has contributed Herculean efforts to provide a forum for all sides to air their views.

The Commission has emphasized that Statement 123R is expected to result in more transparent, complete, and comparable information in financial statements provided to the investors that is, after all, the function of the Securities and Exchange Commission.

Comments issued pointed out that Statement 123R requires that the cost of all employee stock options, as well as other equity-based compensation arrangements, be reflected in the body of the financial statements based on the estimated fair value of the awards. Thus, it will provide complete information and will make it easier for investors to compare financial results among entities regardless of whether they use fixed or variable stock options or other forms of employee compensation.

Stock options have been a valuable and important tool used by many companies, particularly in the high-tech sectors, as a means to motivate employees and to promote business growth. Statement 123R requires that the value of these arrangements be measured and recognized in the financial statements.

Now that Statement 123R has been issued, companies are expected to focus on implementation.

## .03 SEC Provides Additional Time for Options Expensing

The SEC had encouraged early adoption of Statement123R by those companies that were able to and who choose to do so; however, realizing the difficulties just cited, the Commission members voted to delay the effective date of 123R for treating employee stock options as expenses.

The decision means that companies that report earnings on a calendar year were provided with an additional six months before they must start treating options as expenses. The delay provided companies until the start of their first fiscal year after June 15, 2005. Under the FASB's rule, expensing would have started with the first fiscal quarter after that date.

Feedback from public companies, accounting firms, and others indicated that implementing Statement 123R in a period other than the first quarter of a fiscal year could potentially make compliance more complicated. For example, comparisons of quarterly reports would be more difficult, according to the chief accountant of the SEC. Concerns were also raised because the accounting staffs at companies and accounting firms had already been stretched thin by other compliance responsibilities, such as the internal controls reporting.

Therefore, implementing the new standard at the beginning of a fiscal year allows companies to change their accounting systems in a more orderly fashion, and should allow auditors to conduct more consistent audit and review procedures.

## .05 SEC Issues SAB 107 Guidance for FASB 123R

In March 2005 the U.S. Securities and Exchange released Staff Accounting Bulletin relating to the FASB's accounting standard for stock options and other share-based payments. The interpretations in Staff Accounting Bulletin No. 107, *Share-Based Payment* (SAB 107), express views of the SEC staff regarding the application of Statement 123 (revised 2004), *Share-Based Payment* (Statement 123R).

Among other elements, SAB 107 provides interpretive guidance related to the interaction between Statement 123R and certain SEC rules and regulations, as well as providing the staff's views regarding the valuation of share-based payment arrangements for public companies. SAB 107 also reminds public companies of the importance of including disclosures within their filings made with the SEC relating to the accounting for share-based payment transactions, particularly during the transition to Statement 123R.

The SEC staff believes that the interpretive guidance in SAB 107 will assist both the FASB and the SEC in applying the provisions of Statement 123R as well as assisting investors and other users of financial statements in analyzing the information provided under that Statement.

## .07 FSPs Make Applying Provisions Easier

Several FASB Staff Position (FSP) have been issued to amend positions or address specific questions raised in implementing 123R which is not surprising in that this Standard is based upon rules that have been amended, revised, modified and interpreted.

## ¶6013 FASB 151, 153, AND 154 FURTHER CONVERGENCE WITH IASB

In line with the FASB's continuing effort to improve the comparability of cross-border financial reporting through working with the International Accounting Standards Board (IASB) to eliminate differing requirements, the Board approved three of the four Exposure Drafts that were issued in December 2004. These three Standards erase moderate differences between U.S. GAAP and International Standards.

## .01 FASB 154 Improves Financial Reporting

The FASB issued Statement No. 154, *Accounting Changes and Error Corrections*, a replacement of APB Opinion No. 20 and FASB Statement No. 3, in June 2005. The Statement applies to all voluntary changes in accounting principles and changes the requirements for accounting for and reporting of a change in accounting principles.

Statement 154 requires retrospective application to prior periods' financial statements of a voluntary change in accounting principle unless it is impracticable. Opinion 20 previously required that most voluntary changes in accounting principles be recognized by including in net income of the period of the change the cumulative effect of changing to the new accounting principle.

Statement 154 requires that a change in method of depreciation, amortization, or depletion for long-lived, nonfinancial assets be accounted for as a change in accounting estimate that is brought about by a change in accounting principle. Opinion 20 previously required that such a change be reported as a change in accounting principle.

The Board pointed out that this is an example of instances in which the Board concluded that the IASB requirements result in better financial reporting than U.S. GAAP. Thus, the measure improves financial reporting because its requirements enhance the consistency of financial information between periods, and it also furthers convergence with international standards.

In keeping with the goal of simplifying U.S.GAAP, the Board decided to completely replace Opinion 20 and Statement 3 with one Statement rather than amending both. Therefore, Statement 154 carries forward many provisions of Opinion 20 without change, including:

- The provisions related to the reporting of a change in accounting estimate.
- A change in the reporting entity.
- The correction of an error.

FASB 154 also carries forward the provisions of FASB 3 that govern reporting accounting changes in interim financial statements.

Statement 154 was effective for accounting changes and corrections of errors made in fiscal years beginning after December 15, 2005.

## .03   FASB 153 Amends APB 29

The FASB issued FASB 153, *Exchanges of Nonmonetary Assets*, as an amendment of APB Opinion No. 29, *Accounting for Nonmonetary Transaction*, in December 2004. The amendments made by Statement 153 are based on the principle that exchanges of nonmonetary assets should be measured based on the fair value of the assets exchanged.

Further, the amendments eliminate the narrow exception for nonmonetary exchanges of similar productive assets and replace it with a broader exception for exchanges of nonmonetary assets that do not have commercial substance. Previously, Opinion 29 required that the accounting for an exchange of a productive asset for a similar productive asset or an equivalent interest in the same or similar productive asset should be based on the recorded amount of the asset relinquished.

FASB 153 is the result of a broader effort by the FASB to improve the comparability of cross-border financial reporting by working with the IASB toward development of a single set of high-quality accounting standards. Opinion 29 provided an exception to its basic measurement principle (fair value) for exchanges of similar productive assets. The Board believes that that particular exception required that some nonmonetary exchanges, although commercially substantive, be recorded on a carryover basis. By focusing the exception on exchanges that lack commercial substance, the Board believes this Statement produces financial reporting that more faithfully represents the economics of the transactions. Language similar to that used in the IASB's IAS 16, *Property, Plant, and Equipment,* was used to promote consistent application of the requirements of those standards.

The Statement became effective for nonmonetary asset exchanges occurring in fiscal periods beginning after June 15, 2005.

## .05   FASB Issues Statement 151 on Inventory Costs

The FASB issued FASB Statement 151, *Inventory Costs*, an amendment of ARB No. 43, Chapter 4, in November 2004. The amendments made by Statement 151 are aimed at improving financial reporting by clarifying the position that abnormal amounts of idle facility expense, freight, handling costs, and wasted materials (spoilage) should be recognized as current-period charges regardless of whether they meet the criterion of "so-called abnormal," as stated in the previous guidance. The provisions also require the allocation of fixed production overheads to inventory based on the normal capacity of the production facilities.

As noted above, Statement 151 is one facet of a broad effort by the FASB to improve comparability of cross-border financial reporting systems by working with the International Accounting Standards Board (IASB) toward development of a single set of high-quality accounting standards. The FASB and the IASB noted that ARB 43, Chapter 4, and IAS 2, *Inventories*, are both based on the principle that the primary basis of accounting for inventory is cost. Both of those accounting standards also require that abnormal amounts of idle freight, handling costs, and wasted materials be recognized as period costs; however, the Boards noted that differences in the wording of the two standards could lead to inconsistent application of those similar requirements. The FASB concluded that clarifying the existing requirements in ARB 43 by adopting language similar to that used in IAS 2 is consistent with its goals of improving financial reporting in the United States and promoting convergence of accounting standards internationally.

The guidance was effective for inventory costs incurred during fiscal years beginning after June 15, 2005.

## ¶6014   FASB 152 TO IMPROVE ACCOUNTING AND REPORTING OF TIME-SHARING TRANSACTIONS

FASB 152, *Accounting for Real Estate Time-Sharing Transactions*, amends FASB 66, *Accounting for the Sales of Real Estate*, and FASB 67, *Accounting for Costs and Initial Rental Operations of Real Estate Projects*, in association with the issuance of AICPA Statement of Position (SOP) 04-2, *Accounting for Real Estate Time-Sharing Transactions*.

The Accounting Standards Executive Committee of the American Institute of Certified Public Accountants issued SOP 04-2 to address the diversity in practice caused by a lack of guidance specific to real estate time-sharing transactions. FASB 152 and SOP 04-2 are designed to fill the gap left by previous standards. These actions should improve the accounting and reporting of these types of transactions.

The guidance became effective for financial statements for fiscal years beginning after June 15, 2005.

## ¶6015 FASB AND IASB ON FLEXIBLE PATH TO CONVERGENCE

The FASB and IASB have agreed that convergence of their standards is a primary objective of both standard setters. In line with this goal, the Board has reached certain conclusions: in relation to several short-term goals. They are also working on other, more complicated, far-reaching projects, some of which are discussed below.

## .01 Short-Term Projects on Path to Global Standards (H-2)

The FASB is aware of several areas in which the international position is preferable to current U.S. GAAP, and others in which the two bodies could easily and quickly resolve any differences. Among conclusions reached by the FASB are the following:

1. To agree with the IASB position that a voluntary change in accounting principle should be accounted for retrospectively. Prior periods should be restated as if this accounting policy had always been used, except when retroactive application is impracticable. This occurs only when:
   a. The effects of retroactive application are indeterminable.
   b. Retroactive application requires assumptions about management's intent in a prior period.
   c. Retroactive application requires significant management estimates as of a prior period.
2. A change in accounting resulting from a new pronouncement would be reported using the guidance for voluntary changes in accounting principles, unless the transition provisions require a different method.
3. Nonmonetary exchanges of productive assets should be accounted for at fair value unless:
   a. Neither the asset received nor that surrendered has a fair value determinable within reasonable limits.
   b. The transaction lacks commercial substance.
4. To adopt the IASB position that a long-term financial liability to be settled within 12 months of the balance sheet date should be classified as a current liability, unless an agreement to refinance the liability on a long-term basis is completed on or before the balance sheet date. It would no longer be permissible to classify as current a financing agreement completed after the balance sheet date but before the financial statements are authorized for issue.

5. That a long-term financial liability that is payable on demand at the balance sheet date because the entity breached a condition of its loan agreement should be classified as current, unless:

   a. The lender has agreed on or before the balance sheet date to demand payment as a consequence of the breach (convergent with the IASB position), or

   b. The lender has agreed on or before the balance sheet date not to provide a period of grace during which the obligation is not callable, and within which an entity can rectify the breach, and either:

      (i)   The entity rectifies the breach within the period of grace, or

      (ii)  At the time that the financial statements are issued, it is probable that the breach will be rectified within the period of grace. (This is consistent with U.S. GAAP.)

6. To converge with the IASB position that a change in depreciation method is a change in accounting estimate that is affected by a change in accounting principle. As a result, a change in depreciation method would be accounted for in:

   a. The period of change if the change affects that period only.

   b. The period of change and also the future periods if the change affects both.

If the FASB and the IASB can continue their flexibility along the convergence route, the idea of one set of global accounting rules should not be dismissed lightly. Both Boards have much to gain, and lose. U.S. Standards can certainly not be considered inviolate; however, they are the most complete and have been the basis of an economy that is second to none. This present accord may be an early step in a successful attack on the short-term convergence project launched by the two standard setters. As noted above the FASB has issued a series of four EDs aimed toward convergence. Among other projects in about 20 areas relative to which they hope to achieve convergence are accounting for research and development, interim financial reporting, proportionate consolidation, construction contracts, financial performance, pension plan disclosure, and income taxes.

## .02  FASB and IASB Issue Memorandum

Because of the burgeoning global activity and trade, it becomes even more important to bring about convergence of U.S. generally accepted accounting principles (GAAP), and the International Accounting Standards Board's International financial Reporting Standards (IFRSs). The FASB and IASB are taking active steps to reaffirm their commitments to bring about consistency, comparability, and efficiency in global capital markets.

Together, the two Boards published a Memorandum of Understanding (MOU) in February 2006 to reaffirm the Boards' shared objective of developing high quality, common accounting standards for use in the world's capital markets. Both Boards believe that a common set of high quality accounting standards will enhance the consistency, comparability and efficiency of financial statements, enabling global markets to move with less friction.

The MOU is a further elaboration of the objectives and principles first described in the Boards' Norwalk Agreement published in October 2002 (see the Chapter. International Standards: Accounting). While the document does not represent a *change* in the Boards' convergence work program, it does, however, reflect the context of the 'roadmap' for the removal of the reconciliation with GAAP requirement for non-US companies that use IFRSs and are registered in the United States. It also reflects the work undertaken by the Committee of European Securities Regulators (CESR) to identify areas for improvement of accounting standards.

The FASB considers that the document underscores the organization's strong commitment to continue to work with the IASB to bring about a common set of accounting standards to enhance the quality, comparability and consistency of global financial reporting.

On their part, the IASB considers the memorandum another significant step in the partnership with the FASB to reach a global set of accounting standards. The organization feels that the pragmatic approach in the MOU provides stability for companies using IFRSs in the near term, while taking advantage of an opportunity to contribute to removing the need for reconciliation requirements. At the same time, the IASB plans to continue its work on other areas not in the MOU and on topics that arise concerning the implementation and interpretation of IFRSs.

Both the FASB and the IASB note that removing the current reconciliation requirements will require continued progress on the Boards' convergence program. Accordingly, the MOU sets out milestones that the FASB and the IASB believe are achievable.

The roadmap also addresses auditing and enforcement, topics that are not accounting standard-setting issues and will require the co-operation of regulators and auditors. In developing the MOU, representatives of the Boards continue to hold discussions with representatives of the European Commission and the SEC staff, with the Boards' respective advisory councils, and with other interested parties.

The Boards agree that trying to eliminate differences between standards that are both in need of significant improvement is not the best use of resources; instead, new common standards should be developed. Consistent with that principle, convergence work continues to proceed on the following two tracks:

- First, the Boards will reach a conclusion about whether major differences in focused areas should be eliminated through one or more short-term

¶6015.02

standard-setting projects; if so, the goal is to complete or substantially complete work in those areas by 2008.

- Second, the FASB and the IASB seek to make progress in other areas identified by both Boards where accounting practices under U.S. GAAP and IFRSs are in need of improvement.

The Boards point out that their work programs are not limited to the items listed in the MOU. The FASB and the IASB will follow their normal due process when adding items to their agendas.

## .03  International Group to Advise on Lease Accounting

In July 2006, the IASB and the FASB added a joint project on leasing to their respective agendas (see above and in the Chapter, International Standards: Accounting). The project's scope includes a reconsideration of existing standards of accounting for both lessees and lessors. The current project plan envisages, as a first step, the publication of a joint discussion paper.

The IASB and the FASB have formed an international group to serve both Boards inasmuch as the leasing project is a joint project between them. The composition of the working group will reflect the diversity and breadth of interest in this area, and will ensure that there is a satisfactory balance of perspectives. The group will be comprised of individuals from a variety of backgrounds—preparers, auditors, and users of financial statements, subject-matter experts, and others.

The membership of the group is expected to include:

- Preparers of financial statements that are lessors of various asset types such as equipment, other property, and real estate (including real estate investment companies).
- Preparers of financial statements that lease various asset types such as equipment, other property, and real estate.
- Knowledgeable investors, investment analysts, and other users of financial statements.
- Auditors of financial statements.

The role of the working group is to provide views and practical advice on the concepts, ideas, and proposals developed by the Boards and their staff, not to develop proposals. Consequently, the group will not vote on proposals brought to it by the staff; that is, their role is to provide information and practical insights from their own perspectives. The staff will turn to working group members during the life of the project, as they need input. As the staff initially identifies issues to be addressed, researches issues, and develops its analysis of possible alternative approaches, they may find it advantageous to ask for help from the

¶6015.03

working group. Members serve not only as a source of information for the staff, but also as a sounding board for the staff and the Boards. Input from the working group will be sought in a variety of ways, through e-mails, video conferences, and face-to-face meetings. At the Boards' invitation, regulators may also be called upon to participate in the working group.

Members of the working group should be willing to set aside their existing views or practices in favor of working toward improved financial reporting. The Boards can learn from national or industry practice, but will not be constrained by it. The Boards are interested in developing a workable standard that is conceptually grounded, principles-based, and convergent. The Boards are seeking a broad cross-section of nominees, preferably with global as well as regional expertise. Fluency in English is necessary since all correspondence, documents, and discussions will be in English.

## .05    FASB and IASB Publish First Draft Chapters of Joint Conceptual Framework

The FASB and the IASB today each published for public comment a consultative document setting out their preliminary views on the first two chapters of an enhanced conceptual framework. The draft chapters define the objective of financial reporting, and the qualitative characteristics of decision-useful financial information.

The document is the first to result from the boards' joint project on the conceptual framework. This project was described in their Memorandum of Understanding (discussed above), which laid out a joint program of work for the two Boards. The work on the conceptual framework will cover their efforts to achieve the objectives described in the MOU.

At present, their respective framework guides each Board. These differ from each other in various respects, are incomplete, and are not up to date. The publication of their joint preliminary views reflects their shared commitment to build upon, improve and achieve the convergence of their existing conceptual frameworks. The boards believe that a common conceptual framework will improve the foundation and concepts that underlie global financial reporting and serve as a more effective guide in developing global financial reporting standards.

The preliminary views restate the existing frameworks' definition of the objective of general purpose external financial reporting as providing information that is useful to present and potential investors and creditors and others in making investment, credit and similar resource allocation decisions. The document also identifies relevance, faithful representation, comparability (including consistency) and understandability among the characteristics of financial information that make it decision-useful.

A member of the FASB pointed out that a common goal of the Boards and their constituents is for standards to be based on consistent principles rooted in fundamental concepts, rather than a collection of conventions. To achieve this, they need to affirm even the most basic building blocks of financial reporting, from which all other concepts will flow, in this case, what is financial information intended to do?

On the part of the IASB, they believe that the ideas set out in the document are some of the most fundamental in accounting. They look forward to obtaining views on these proposed enhancements as they work toward establishing a more effective and sound foundation to guide them in the development of future accounting and reporting standards.

## .07   IASB and FASB Joint Proposals on Business Combinations

The International Accounting Standards Board (IASB) and the FASB each published an Exposure Draft containing joint proposals to improve and align the accounting for business combinations in June 2005. The proposals include a draft standard that the Boards developed in their first major joint project. The objective of the project is to develop a single high-quality standard for accounting for business combinations that could be used for both domestic and cross-border financial reporting. The proposed standard would replace the existing requirements of the IASB's IFRS3 *Business Combinations* and the FASB's Statement No. 141, *Business Combinations*

The IASB believes that the work to develop a single standard demonstrates the ability of the IASB and the FASB to work together. By focusing on fundamental principles and avoiding exceptions, the proposals aim to eliminate many of the inconsistencies in the existing guidance for accounting for business combinations.

The FASB agrees that a common Standard on the very important area of accounting for business combinations will help users and preparers by improving the comparability of financial information reported by companies around the world that issue financial statements in accordance with either International Financial Reporting Standards or U.S. GAAP.

The proposals in the Exposure Drafts retain the fundamental requirement of IFRS 3 and Statement 141 to account for all business combinations using a single method—where one party is always identified as acquiring the other. The principal changes being proposed include a requirement to measure the business acquired at fair value and to recognize the goodwill attributable to any noncontrolling interests (previously referred to as minority interests) rather than just the portion attributable to the acquirer. The proposals would also result in fewer exceptions to the principle of measuring assets acquired and liabilities assumed in a business combination at fair value. Additionally, the proposals would result in payments to third parties for consulting, legal, audit, and similar services associated with an acquisition being recognized generally as expenses when incurred rather than capitalized as part of the business combination.

At the same time, the IASB and the FASB today also published Exposure Drafts that propose that noncontrolling interests be classified as equity within the consolidated financial statements and that acquisitions of noncontrolling interests be accounted for as equity transactions.

## ¶6017    PURCHASE METHOD PROCEDURES

The FASB is nearing completion of a broad reconsideration of existing purchase accounting guidance.

The Board believes the project was necessary, since some current purchase accounting rules and practices do not provide transparent information to users and are sometimes inconsistent with the Conceptual Framework.

The Board joined with the International Accounting Standards Board on the project. As a joint project, the FASB and IASB shared staff resources and research and work toward issuance of exposure drafts and final standards. Although the Boards will also coordinate the timing of deliberation on issues within the joint project, each will individually deliberate (and vote) on the issues.

The joint project broadly reconsiders aspects of the purchase method of accounting, excluding most areas deliberated by the Board in FASBs 141, *Business Combinations*, and 142, *Goodwill and Other Intangible Assets*. These areas include:

- Measuring the value of the business combination.
- Recognition and measurement of identifiable assets and liabilities (including such issues and contingencies and liabilities for terminating activities of an acquired entity).

### .01    Summary of Tentative Decisions

FASB members reached a tentative agreement on the following working principles for recording a business combination. The accounting for a business combination is based on the assumption that the transaction is an exchange of equal values; the total amount to be recognized should be measured based on the fair value of the consideration paid or the fair value of the net assets acquired, whichever is more clearly evident. If the consideration paid is cash or other assets (or liabilities incurred) of the acquiring entity, the fair value of the consideration paid determines the total amount to be recognized in the financial statements of the acquiring entity. If the consideration is in the form of equity instruments, the fair value of the equity instruments ordinarily is more clearly evident than the fair value of the net assets acquired and, thus, will determine the total amount to be recognized by the acquiring entity.

In a business combination, the acquiring entity obtains control over the acquired entity and is, therefore, responsible for the assets and liabilities of the acquired entity. An amount equal to the fair value, on the date control is obtained, should be assigned to the identifiable assets acquired and liabilities assumed. If the total fair value exchanged in the purchase transaction exceeds the amounts recognized for identifiable net assets, that amount is the *implied fair value* of goodwill. If the total fair value exchanged in the purchase transaction is less than the amounts recognized for identifiable net assets, that amount should be recognized as a gain in the income statement.

Other decisions reached are discussed below.

## .03  Contingent Consideration in a Business Combination

Contingent consideration issued in a business combination is an obligation of the acquirer as of the acquisition date and, therefore, should be recognized as part of the purchase price on that date. Consistent with the working principle, the initial measurement of contingent consideration should be at fair value.

Some contingent consideration arrangements obligate the acquirer to deliver its equity securities if specified future events occur. Classification of these instruments as either equity or as a liability depends on existing U.S. GAAP. Presuming that the Board issues a standard on accounting for financial instruments with the characteristics of liabilities, equity, or both, prior to the issuance of guidance in this project, the guidance in that standard would apply to contingent consideration arrangements.

An exception in FASB 133, *Accounting for Derivative Instruments and Hedging Activities*, should be eliminated in order that contingent consideration arrangements that otherwise meet the definition of a derivative would be subject to the requirements of Statement 133.

Subsequent remeasurement (after the acquisition date) of contingent consideration liabilities does not result in a change to the purchase price of the business combination. These amounts, therefore, should be recorded in the income statement.

## .05  Other Measurement Issues Related to the Acquired Business

Equity securities issued, as consideration in a business combination, should be measured on the acquisition date. The description of the acquisition date in FASB 141 should be modified to clarify that the acquisition date is the date that the acquirer gains control over the target entity.

## .07  Recognition and Measurement of Identifiable Assets and Liabilities

In the acquisition of less than 100 percent of the acquired entity, the identifiable assets and liabilities of the acquired entity should be recorded at full fair value. The current practice of considering the subsidiaries' carryover basis to the extent of the noncontrolling interest should be eliminated.

If negative goodwill is present in a business combination, the acquiring entity should review the procedures used to identify and measure the net assets of the subsidiary; however, no asset acquired should be measured at an amount that is known to be less than its fair value, nor should any liability assumed or incurred be measured at an amount known to be higher than its fair value. If negative goodwill remains, the acquiring entity should recognize the amount in the income statement (recognized as an extraordinary item under FASB 141).

Preacquisition contingencies of the acquired entity that are assets or liabilities should be recognized and should be initially measured at fair value. The Board agreed to eliminate the alternative described in Statement 141 that allows for recognition under an approach consistent with FASB 5, *Accounting for Contingencies*. The issue of measuring preacquisition contingencies subsequent to the acquisition date will be addressed in the project at a later date.

The period of time permitted to recognize and measure all assets acquired and liabilities assumed (referred to as the "allocation period") ends at the earlier of one year from the acquisition date or when the acquiring entity is no longer waiting for information that it has arranged to obtain and that is known to be available or obtainable. The objective of obtaining information during the allocation period is to measure the assets acquired and liabilities assumed at their fair values as of the acquisition date. Therefore, the only information that should be considered in recording assets acquired and liabilities assumed in a business combination is information that would affect the determination of their fair values as of the acquisition date. For example, discovery during the allocation period of the need for an adjustment to the measurement of an acquired asset for an event that had not occurred as of the acquisition date would not be reflected in the purchase price allocation but would result in a *charge to earnings*.

## ¶6019   POTPOURRI OF BOARD PROJECTS

The current Board appears not only to be a very active one with a well-stocked agenda, but also one that is heeding the Sarbanes-Oxley Act and the SEC's suggestions to pursue the idea of convergence of GAAP and international standards as well as to do all things in a timely manner.

The nature of many of the changes and plans appears to stem from the failures of U.S. GAAP, highlighted by the collapse of Enron Corporation and the abusive accounting practices employed by certain telecommunications and high-tech companies. A few of the many projects under way are mentioned below.

## .01  Principle-Based Standards

The FASB had earlier initiated an evaluation of whether or not and, if so, how to adopt a *principles-based approach to standard setting.* The Sarbanes-Oxley Act *requires* the Securities and Exchange Commission to study the adoption of a principles-based accounting system by the U.S. financial reporting system. The FASB and SEC are working together on this effort.

The principles-based accounting standards with emphasis on detailed rules has obviously not worked too well in recent years, perhaps because the U.S. approach has:

- Been too complex for many financial report users to understand.
- Been difficult and sometimes costly to implement causing rules to be ignored, overlooked, or subverted.
- Failed to reveal the economic substance of transactions, even when the preparer "followed" the detailed rules.
- Allowed Enron (and other companies) to use the "specifics" of GAAP and various rules and regulations as a starting point for figuring out just what they could get away with, despite knowing full well the principle behind the rule.

To date, the FASB has stated its support for a principles-based approach and has issued for public comment a proposal discussing a possible approach to principle-based standards. As this proposal indicates, standards developed under this approach would:

- Apply broadly to transactions other than the events covered by the standards; accounting principles would continue to be developed from the FASB's conceptual framework.
- Contain few, if any, exceptions to the principles.
- Provide less interpretive and implementation guidance for applying standards.

The FASB is exploring the International Accounting Standard Board's principle-based approach to standard setting inasmuch as many countries will be adopting the IASB's Standards.

There are some who question whether it is wise to expect the necessary degree of good judgment and moral fortitude required of CEOs, CFOs, auditors, and other decision makers in light of recent financial reporting scandals. Those holding this view believe a principles-based approach to standard setting may not be workable. On the other hand, the prescriptive type seems not to have worked in quite a number of cases, either.

## .03    Financial Performance Reporting

The FASB's Financial Performance Reporting by Business Enterprises project may change the form and content, classifications and aggregations, and display of specified items and summarized amounts on the face of all basic financial statements. The important result of this project could well be the elimination of net income as an income statement item. It would be replaced by *comprehensive income*. Currently, comprehensive income plays little, if any, role in equity valuations.

The project's goal is twofold:

1. Improve the quality of information displayed in financial statements so statement users can better evaluate an enterprise's performance.
2. Ensure that sufficient information is contained in financial statements to permit calculation of key financial measures used by investors and creditors.

The FASB is working closely on the project with the IASB, which has a similar project under way with the United Kingdom's Accounting Standards Board.

*Comprehensive Income Defined.*    The FASB's Concept Statement No. 6 defines comprehensive income as the change in equity of a business enterprise during a period from transactions and other events and circumstances from nonowner sources. It includes all changes in equity during a period except those resulting from investments by owners and distributions to owners.

FASB 130, *Comprehensive Income*, required companies to display in their financial statements total comprehensive income and its components in either an income statement-type format or in a changes in equity format. Most companies chose to use the changes in equity format.

The operational definition of comprehensive income in FASB 130 is net income plus other comprehensive income. Other comprehensive income is made up of the accounting items that are direct debits or credits to owners' equity in U.S. GAAP that do not involve transactions with owners, such as foreign currency translation gains and losses and unrealized gains or losses on marketable securities classified as available-for-sale.

## ¶6023    FASB EMPHASIZING CO-OPERATIVE EFFORT WITH CONSTITUENTS AND OTHER ORGANIZATIONS

As the on-going projects and obligations of the Board multiply, it seems only natural to turn to those individuals and groups most directly affected by their decisions. And so they have! As discussed above, the FASB and the IASB have combined efforts in many directions. Several of the other Board projects described above involve committees or working groups of those affected by their rulings. And now small business and private entities are invited to provide input on accounting issues related to their condition.

## .01  Small Business Advisory Group Formed

In an effort to increase involvement by the small business community in developing U.S. accounting standards, the FASB established a Small Business Advisory Committee in March 2004. Committee members are a resource to the FASB in providing additional and ongoing input on accounting issues before the Board. Possibly the impetus for this move is the belief that smaller companies have been disproportionately hit by the added costs of complying with new auditing and accounting regulations. Membership of this group add breadth and represent diverse perspectives and experiences.

Although the FASB has met with members of small business in the past as part of its due process procedures, establishment of a formal committee that provides the perspectives of this group will offer greater opportunity to share ideas, knowledge, and experience with the Board as well as with the other group members.

The Committee is composed of lenders; investors and analysts; preparers of financial statements from a broad range of businesses, including controllers and chief financial officers; and auditors from the small business community.

## .03  FASB and AICPA Consider Joint Advisory Committee

In June 2006, the FASB and AICPA issued a joint initiative requesting constituent feedback on proposed improvement in the FASB's standard-setting procedures that would determine whether the Board should consider differences in accounting standards for private companies within Generally Accepted Accounting Principles (GAAP).

Under the proposal, the organization would implement certain measures to:

- Improve the financial reporting for those constituents.
- At the same time, enhance the transparency of its standard setting process for these entities.
- Sponsor and fund a joint committee to serve as an additional resource to the FASB to ensure that the views of private company constituents are incorporated into the standard-setting process.

FASB and the AICPA are encouraging everyone who plays a role in private company financial reporting – bank lenders, sureties/bonding companies, investors, owners and preparers, and practitioners – to review the proposal and comment on it.

¶6023.03

The two organizations point out that since the private companies are a vital force in the economy, this joint proposal is another step in the effort to get input from, and the participation of that sector in improving the standard setting process relating to them. The importance of non-issuers to the capital market system is obvious when considering the fact that about 17,000 companies are registered with the SEC, compared to over 20 million privately held entities creating jobs, products and services.

## ¶6025   FASB 150, ACCOUNTING FOR FINANCIAL INSTRUMENTS WITH CHARACTERISTICS OF BOTH LIABILITIES AND EQUITY

The FASB issued Statement 150 in May 2003 to improve the accounting for certain financial instruments that, under previous guidance, issuers could account for as equity. The Statement requires that those instruments now be classified as liabilities in statements of financial position.

FASB 150 affects the issuer's accounting for three types of freestanding financial instruments:

1.  Mandatorily redeemable shares, which the issuing company is obligated to buy back in exchange for cash or other assets. This is an unconditional obligation requiring the issuer to redeem it by transferring its assets at a specified or determinable date (or dates) or upon an event that is certain to occur.

2.  Put options and forward purchase contracts, which involve instruments that do or may require the issuer to buy back some of its shares in exchange for cash or other assets. This is an instrument, other than an outstanding share, that from the very beginning embodies an obligation to repurchase the issuer's equity shares, or is indexed to such an obligation. It requires, or may require, the issuer to settle the obligation by a transfer of assets (e.g., a forward purchase contract or written put option on the issuer's equity shares that is to be physically settled or net cash settled).

3.  A financial instrument that embodies an unconditional obligation, or a financial instrument other than an outstanding share that embodies a conditional obligation, that the issuer must or may settle by issuing a variable number of its equity shares, if, at inception, the monetary value of the obligation is based solely or predominantly on any of the following:

    a.  A fixed monetary amount known at inception (e.g., a payable that can be settled with a variable number of the issuer's equity shares).

    b.  Variations in something other than the fair value of the issuer's equity shares (e.g., a financial instrument indexed to the S&P 500 and that can be settled with a variable number of the issuer's equity shares).

    c.  Variations inversely related to changes in the fair value of the issuer's equity shares (e.g., a written put option that could be settled with net share).

FASB 150 does not apply to features embedded in a financial instrument that is not a derivative in its entirety.

Financial instruments involving the potential issuance of common stock classified as liabilities under SFAS 150 are excluded from the computation of basic and diluted earnings per share.

Most of the provisions of the Statement are consistent with the existing definition of *liabilities* in FASB Concepts Statement 6, *Elements of Financial Statements*. The remaining provisions are consistent with the Board's proposal to revise that definition to encompass certain obligations that a reporting entity can or must settle by issuing its own equity shares, depending on the nature of the relationship established between holder and issuer. That revision is scheduled as part of a second phase of the Board's project on liabilities and equity. In that phase, the plans are to address the accounting for convertible bonds, putable stock, and other instruments with embedded features characteristic of both liability and equity that are not in the scope of FASB 150.

In addition to its requirements for the classification and measurement of financial instruments in its scope, this subsequent Statement also requires disclosures about alternative ways of settling the instruments and the capital structure of entities, all of whose shares are mandatorily redeemable.

## .01   Phase 2 of the Project Under Way

With the issuance of FASB 150, the Board continued with phase 2 of the liabilities and equity project. In this phase, the Board considers the following issues:

* Separating compound financial instruments with characteristics of both liabilities and equity (including convertible debt, conditionally redeemable stock, and dual-indexed obligations to issue shares) into their liability and equity components.
* The definition of ownership relationship.
* The definition of liabilities in Concepts Statement 6.

Several FSPs have been issued as a result of the need for guidance and/or interpretation related to the Standard.

## ¶6027   FASB 149, AMENDMENT OF STATEMENT 133 ON DERIVATIVE INSTRUMENTS AND HEDGING ACTIVITIES

The FASB issued Statement 149 to amend and clarify accounting for derivatives, including certain derivative instruments embedded in other contracts, and for hedging activities under Statement 133 in April 2003.

The amendments set forth in FASB 149 improve financial reporting by requiring that contracts with comparable characteristics be accounted for similarly. It clarifies under what circumstances a contract with an initial net investment meets the characteristic of a derivative described in Statement 133. In addition, it clarifies *when* a derivative contains a financing component that calls for special reporting in the statement of cash flows.

Statement 149 also amends certain other existing pronouncements. Those changes will result in more consistent reporting of contracts that are derivatives in their entirety or that contain embedded derivatives that warrant separate accounting.

Questions were answered regarding implementation issues raised in relation to the application of the **definition of a derivative**, particularly in regard to the meaning of an underlying instrument and the characteristics of a derivative that contains financing components. The language now conforms to that used in the definition of an underlying instrument in FASB Interpretation 45, *Guarantor's Accounting and Disclosure Requirements for Guarantees, Including Indirect Guarantees of Indebtedness of Others.*

## ¶6029    FASB 148, *ACCOUNTING FOR STOCK–BASED COMPENSATION — TRANSITION AND DISCLOSURE — AN AMENDMENT OF FASB 123*

This Statement, adopted in December 2002, amends FASB 123, *Accounting for Stock-Based Compensation*, to provide alternative methods of transition for a voluntary change to the fair value method of accounting for stock-based employee compensation. In addition, FASB 148 amends the disclosure requirements of Statement 123 to require prominent disclosures in both annual and interim financial statements about the method of accounting for stock-based employee compensation and the effect of the method used on reported results.

### .01    Reasons for Issuing the Statement

In light of all the scandals and lack of openness in financial reporting, a number of companies have adopted the fair value method of accounting for stock-based employee compensation of their own volition. This Statement requires new disclosures about the effect of stock-based employee compensation on reported results. The Statement also requires that those effects be disclosed more prominently by specifying the form, content, and location of those disclosures.

## .03   Improvement in Financial Reporting

In the absence of a single accounting method for stock-based employee compensation, this Statement requires disclosure of comparable information for *all* companies, regardless of whether, when, or how an entity adopts the preferable, fair value method of accounting. This Statement improves the prominence and clarity of the pro forma disclosures required by Statement 123 by prescribing a specific tabular format and by requiring disclosure in the "Summary of Significant Accounting Policies" or its equivalent. In addition, this Statement improves the timeliness of those disclosures by requiring their inclusion in financial reports for interim periods as well as the annual report.

## ¶6031   FIN 44, ACCOUNTING FOR CERTAIN TRANSACTIONS INVOLVING STOCK COMPENSATION

This FASB stock option ruling in Interpretation 44, *Accounting for Certain Transactions Involving Stock Compensation*, is an interpretation of APB Opinion 25, *Accounting for Stock Issued to Employees*.

Accounting for stock options is governed by FASB 123, *Accounting for Stock-Based Compensation*, which allows companies to select one of two approaches to accounting and reporting of stock-based employee compensation plans. It was this "compromise" from requirements of a *fair value method only* standard that finally led to the adoption of FASB 123. Now, it is either intrinsic value method or fair value method.

The FASB encourages companies to adopt the fair value method, but it is not required. It is acceptable to use the intrinsic value method prescribed in APB Opinion 25, *Accounting for Stock Issued to Employees*, which is the pre-FASB 123 Standard dealing with stock-based compensation plans. If a company continues to use the Opinion 25 approach, the entity must disclose the pro forma impact on income and earnings per share of using the fair value method.

In the case of stock options, the fair value is determined using an option pricing model. Once the fair value is determined at the grant date, it is not subsequently adjusted for:

*   Changes in the price of the underlying stock.
*   The volatility of the stock.
*   The life of the option.
*   Dividends on the stock.
*   The risk free interest rate.

## .01 Delineation of Requirements

The Interpretation requires the following:

1. Compensation in the form of stock options granted to independent contractors or other providers of services and goods, who are not employees, are to be accounted for using the *fair value method*. The principal consequence of this Interpretation is that the granting company must record a stock compensation cost based on the option's fair value at the grant date over the option's life for a transaction. Previously, this may not have resulted in a stock compensation cost.

2. Nonemployee board members are considered to be employees for stock option compensation accounting purposes. As a result, under the stock option plans of most companies, the practice will continue that no compensation cost will be recognized for stock options granted to nonemployee directors.

3. If the exercise price of a fixed option award is reduced or repriced, the modified stock options must be accounted for as a variable option plan from the date of modification to the date the award is exercised, forfeited, or expires unexercised. The consequence for the grantor is:

   a. Very few fixed option plans will lead to a stock compensation cost.

   b. If the company's stock price exceeds the option's strike price during the stock option's life, variable option plans may result in a stock compensation cost.

4. A modification to a fixed stock option to add a reload feature requires the modified award be accounted for as a variable plan award regardless of the method used to determine the terms of the reload grant. Therefore, a reload feature provides for the automatic grant of a new option at the current market price in exchange for each previously owned share tendered by an employee in a stock-for-stock exercise.

   Most reload grants awarded as modifications of a fixed plan will now result in a compensation cost if the company's stock price exceeds the reload option's strike price during the stock option's life.

5. There is no accounting consequence for changes in the exercise price or the number of shares of a stock option award as the result of an exchange of fixed stock option awards in a business combination accounted for as a pooling of interests as long as two criteria are met:

   a. The aggregate intrinsic value of the options immediately *after* the exchange is no greater than the aggregate intrinsic value of the options immediately *before* the exchange.

   b. The ratio of the exercise price per option to the market value per share is not reduced.

(This is a very important facet of the requirements. If these two criteria are not met, a new measurement of compensation is *required*.)

6. A modification to a fixed stock option award that does *not* affect the life of the award, the exercise price, or the number of shares to be issued does not have an accounting consequence.

7. A modification that either renews a fixed award or extends the award's life requires a new measurement of compensation cost as if the award were newly granted. As a result, a compensation cost would be recognized in the case of:

a. An employee fixed plan award over the life of the award for any significant difference between the current stock price and the stock price at the modification date.

b. A nonemployee stock grant at the fair value of the stock option at the modification date.

8. Any modification increasing the number of shares to be issued under a fixed stock option plan requires that the award be accounted for as a variable plan award from the modification date to the date the award is exercised, forfeited, or expires. The accounting consequence is that if the stock price exceeds the award's strike price during the stock option's life, after the award date a stock compensation cost will be recognized.

A fixed option award that is canceled and replaced with a new award that results in a lower option price must be accounted for as a variable plan if the replacement award is made within six months of the cancellation date.

## .03  Possible Results of the Interpretation

Repercussions of FIN may lead to the following:

- It potentially increases the cost of acquiring nonemployee services paid for with stock options.
- It discourages the repricing of options.
- It encourages companies, as an alternative to repricing, to grant new stock option awards at the current market price to employees whose existing stock option award's strike prices are below the current market price.

## ¶6033   FASB 147, *Acquisitions of Certain Financial Institutions*

The FASB issued Statement 147, *Acquisitions of Certain Financial Institutions*, on October 1, 2002. The Statement provides guidance on the accounting for the acquisition of a financial institution. It applies to all acquisitions except those between two or more mutual enterprises. (The Board has a separate project on its agenda that will provide this guidance.)

Statement 147 contains the following provisions:

- The excess of the fair value of liabilities assumed over the fair value of tangible and identifiable intangible assets acquired in a business combination represents goodwill that should be accounted for under FASB 142, *Goodwill and Other Intangible Assets.*

- The specialized accounting guidance in paragraph 5 of FASB 72, *Accounting for Certain Acquisitions of Banking or Thrift Institutions*, does not apply after September 30, 2002. If certain criteria in Statement 147 are met, the amount of the unidentifiable intangible asset will be reclassified to goodwill upon adoption of the new Statement.

- Financial institutions meeting conditions outlined in FASB 147 are required to restate previously issued financial statements. The objective of the restatement requirement is to present the balance sheet and income statement as if the amount accounted for under FASB 72 as an unidentifiable intangible asset had been reclassified to goodwill as of the date FASB 142 was initially applied. The transition provisions were effective on October 1, 2002.

- The scope of FASB 144, *Accounting for the Impairment or Disposal of Long-Lived Assets*, has been amended to include long-term customer-relationship intangible assets, such as depositor- and borrower-relationship intangible assets and credit cardholder intangible assets.

## ¶6035   FASB 146, Accounting for Costs Associated with Exit or Disposal Activities

In July 2002, the FASB issued Statement 146, *Accounting for Costs Associated with Exit or Disposal Activities.* The Standard requires companies to recognize costs associated with exit or disposal activities *when they are incurred* rather than at the date of a commitment to an exit or disposal plan. Examples of costs covered by the standard include lease termination costs and certain employee severance costs that are associated with a restructuring, discontinued operation, plant closing, or other exit or disposal activity.

Commenting on the standard, the FASB stated that liabilities represent present obligations to others. Because a commitment to a plan, by itself, does not create a present obligation to others, the principal effect of applying Statement 146 will be on the *timing of recognition of costs* associated with exit or disposal activities. In many cases, those costs will be recognized as liabilities in periods following a commitment to a plan, not at the date of the commitment.

**¶6035**

## ¶6037  FASB 145, RESCISSION OF FASB STATEMENTS 4, 44, AND 64, AMENDMENT OF FASB STATEMENT 13, AND TECHNICAL CORRECTIONS

In April 2002, the FASB issued Statement 145, *Rescission of FASB Statements No. 4, 44, and 64, Amendment of FASB Statement No. 13, and Technical Corrections*, which updates, clarifies and simplifies existing accounting pronouncements.

FASB 145 rescinds FASB 4, which required all gains and losses from extinguishment of debt to be aggregated and, if material, classified as an extraordinary item, net of related income tax effect. As a result, the criteria in APB Opinion 30 will now be used to classify those gains and losses.

FASB 64 amended FASB 4, and is no longer necessary since FASB 4 is no more.

FASB 44 was issued to establish accounting requirements for the effects of transition to the provisions of the Motor Carrier Act of 1980. Because the transition has been completed, Statement 44 is no longer necessary.

FASB 145 amends FASB 13 to require that certain lease modifications that have economic effects similar to sale-leaseback transactions is accounted for in the same manner as sale-leaseback transactions. This amendment is consistent with the FASB's goal of requiring similar accounting treatment for transactions that have similar economic effects.

This Statement also makes technical corrections to existing pronouncements. While those corrections are not substantive in nature, in some instances, they may change accounting practice. Thus, FASB 145 appears to have taken care of a multitude of housekeeping chores.

## ¶6039  FASB 144, ACCOUNTING FOR THE IMPAIRMENT OR DISPOSAL OF LONG–LIVED ASSETS

The FASB issued Standard 144, in August 2000, governing the financial accounting and reporting for the impairment or disposal of long-lived assets individually or as asset groups that include long-lived assets. An impaired long-lived asset or asset group is one whose carrying amount exceeds its fair value. This Statement:

- Supersedes FASB 121, *Accounting for the Impairment of Long-Lived Assets and for Long-Lived Assets to Be Disposed Of.*
- Supersedes the accounting and reporting provisions of Accounting Principles Board (APB) Opinion 30, *Reporting the Results of Operations — Reporting the Effects of Disposal of a Segment of a Business, and Extraordinary, Unusual and Infrequently Occurring Events and Transactions*, for

the disposal of a segment of a business (as previously defined in that Opinion).

- Amends ARB 51, *Consolidated Financial Statements*, to eliminate the exception to consolidation for a subsidiary for which control is likely to be temporary.

## .01 Caution from the Securities and Exchange Commission

The Securities and Exchange Commission warned companies that it expects impaired assets to be written down to their *net realizable value*. The SEC's warning was motivated by the economic slowdown and the historical reluctance of managers to recognize asset impairment losses in a timely manner.

## .03 Reasons for Issuing This Statement

Because FASB 121 did not address the accounting for a segment of a business accounted for as a discontinued operation under ARB 30, two accounting models were in use for long-lived assets to be disposed of. The Board decided to establish a single accounting model, based on the framework established in FASB 121, for long-lived assets to be disposed of by sale. The Board also decided to resolve significant implementation issues related to it.

## .05 Long-Lived Assets to Be Held and Used

FASB 144 retains the requirements of FASB 121 relating to when an impairment loss must be recognized for a long-lived asset or asset group to be held and used. Two test conditions apply. First, an impairment loss is recognized only if the carrying amount of the long-lived asset is *not recoverable* from its undiscounted cash flows. A long-lived asset or asset group's carrying amount is not recoverable if it exceeds the sum of the undiscounted cash flows expected to result from the use and eventual disposal of the long-lived asset or asset group. The estimates of future cash flows should be based on the existing service potential of the long-lived asset or asset group and include only those cash flows necessary to maintain the existing service potential. Second, an impairment loss is measured as the difference between the carrying amount and fair value of the asset when the carrying amount exceeds its fair value. A long-lived asset's cash flows should be based on the existing service potential of the long-lived asset or asset group and include only those cash flows necessary to maintain the existing service potential.

If a long-lived asset or asset group fails the first test, its fair value must be determined using the best information available. Suggested procedures include:

- Using quoted market prices to determine fair value. The wording of FASB 144 expresses a preference for this technique but also recognizes that these may not always be available.
- Using a present-value-based valuation technique based on assumptions marketplace participants would consider an acceptable alternative. This is the next choice the Standard suggests.
- If market-based assumptions are unavailable, management can use its own assumptions.

To resolve implementation issues, FASB 144:

- Removes goodwill from its scope and therefore eliminates the requirement of FASB 121 to allocate goodwill to long-lived assets to be tested for impairment.
- Describes a probability-weighted cash flow estimation approach to deal with situations in which alternative courses of action to recover the carrying amount of a long-lived asset are under consideration or a range is estimated for the amount of possible future cash flows.
- Establishes a primary-asset approach to determine the cash flow estimation period for a group of assets and liabilities that represents the unit of accounting for a long-lived asset to be held and used.

## .07  Long-Lived Assets to Be Disposed of by Sale

The accounting model for long-lived assets to be disposed of by sale is used for all long-lived assets, whether previously held and used or newly acquired. That accounting model retains the requirement of Statement 121 to measure a long-lived asset classified as held for sale at the lower of its carrying amount or fair value less cost to sell and to cease depreciation (amortization). *Therefore, discontinued operations are no longer measured on a net realizable value basis, and future operating losses are no longer recognized before they occur.*

If the fair value less cost to sell of an asset or asset group held for sale is lower than its carrying amount, the carrying amount is written down to its fair value less cost to sell and an operating loss is recognized for the write-down. The loss is included in the measurement of operating income, unless the long-lived asset or asset group is deemed for the purpose of the new standard to be a component of an entity.

If subsequently the fair value less cost to sell increases, the carrying amount is increased by the increase in fair value less cost to sell to the extent of previously recognized write-downs and a gain is recognized in operating income. (Any loss or gain adjustments are made only to the carrying amount of the long-lived asset whether classified as held for sale individually or as part of a group of assets.)

Long-lived assets held for sale should not be depreciated or amortized; however, interest on liabilities attributable to an asset or asset group held for sale must continue to be accrued.

Long-lived assets or asset groups held for sale should be presented separately on the balance sheet or in the notes on a gross basis. (Any gain or loss resulting from the eventual sale is recognized at the time of sale.)

In such cases, this Statement retains the basic provisions of *Opinion 30* for the presentation of discontinued operations in the income statement but broadens that presentation to include *a component of an entity* rather than *a segment of a business.*

A component of an entity comprises operations and cash flows that can be clearly distinguished, operationally and for financial reporting purposes, from the rest of the entity. A component of an entity that is classified as held for sale or that has been disposed of is presented as a discontinued operation *if* the operations and cash flows of the component will be (or have been) eliminated from the ongoing operations of the entity and the entity will not have any significant continuing involvement in the operations of the component.

***Important Features of Implementation.***   To resolve implementation issues, FASB 144:

1. Establishes criteria beyond that previously specified in Statement 121 to determine when a long-lived asset is held for sale, including a group of assets and liabilities that represents the unit of accounting for a long-lived asset classified as held for sale. Among other things, those criteria specify that:
   a. The asset must be available for immediate sale in its present condition subject only to terms that are usual and customary for sales of such assets.
   b. The sale of the asset must be probable, and its transfer expected to qualify for recognition as a completed sale, within one year, with certain exceptions.
2. Provides guidance on the accounting for a long-lived asset if the criteria for classification as held for sale is met *after* the balance sheet date but *before* issuance of the financial statements. That guidance prohibits retroactive reclassification of the asset as held for sale at the balance sheet date.

¶6039.07

3. Provides guidance on the accounting for a long-lived asset classified as held for sale if the asset is reclassified as held and used. The reclassified asset is measured at the *lower* of its:

   a. Carrying amount before being classified as held for sale, adjusted for any depreciation (amortization) expense that would have been recognized had the asset been continuously classified as held and used.

   b. Fair value at the date the asset is reclassified as held and used.

## .09  Long-Lived Assets to Be Disposed of Other Than by Sale

Long-lived assets or asset groups to be disposed of other than by sale, such as by abandonment, should be classified as *held for use* until the disposal date. When the disposal date is earlier than the asset's previously estimated useful life, future depreciation estimates are to be revised to reflect the new shorter useful life.

If long-lived assets or asset groups are to be exchanged for similar productive assets, or if distributed to owners in a spin-off are tested for recoverability before the exchange or distribution date, the cash flows used in the recoverability test should be based on the assumption that the exchange or disposal will not occur. At the exchange or disposal date, a loss should be recognized for any excess of carrying amount over the fair value of the long-lived asset or asset group exchanged or disposed of.

In summary, FASB 144 applies to a long-lived asset that is scheduled to be:

- Abandoned.
- Exchanged for a similar productive asset.
- Distributed to owners in a spin-off. (In such a case, it must then be considered held and used until it is disposed of.)

The effects from other literature upon these portions of the Statement are twofold. The requirement that the depreciable life of a long-lived asset to be abandoned is revised in accordance with APB Opinion 20, *Accounting Changes.* In addition, the amendment of APB Opinion 29, *Accounting for Nonmonetary Transactions*, to require that an impairment loss be recognized at the date a long-lived asset, as mentioned above, is exchanged for a similar productive asset or distributed to owners in a spin-off when the carrying amount of the asset exceeds its fair value.

## .11  Discontinued Operations

If long-lived assets or asset groups are disposed of and are deemed for the purposes of FASB 144 to be a component of an entity, they should be reported in financial statements as discontinued operations. A component of an entity consists of those operations and cash flows that for financial reporting purposes are clearly distinguishable from the rest of the entity. In practice, a component of an entity may be:

- A reportable or operating segment presented in the business segment disclosures included in financial statements.
- A reporting unit to which goodwill has been assigned for goodwill testing purposes.
- A subsidiary, or the lowest level of a group of long-lived assets and their related other assets and liabilities for which associated identifiable cash flows are largely independent of the cash flows of other groups of assets and liabilities.

The results of operations of a component of an entity either disposed of or classified as held for sale should be classified as discontinued operations if after the disposal transaction:

- The component's cash flows and operations have been or will be eliminated from the ongoing cash flows of the company.
- The company will not have any significant continuing involvement in the component.

## .13   Relation to FASB Conceptual Framework

In reconsidering the use of a measurement approach based on net realizable value, and the accrual of future operating losses required under that approach, the Financial Accounting Standards Board used the definition of a liability in FASB Concepts Statement 6, *Elements of Financial Statements*. The Board determined that *future operating losses* do not meet the definition of a liability.

In considering changes to FASB 121, the Board focused on the qualitative characteristics discussed in FASB Concepts Statement 2, *Qualitative Characteristics of Accounting Information*. In particular, the Board determined that:

- Broadening the presentation of discontinued operations to include more disposal transactions provides investors, creditors, and others with decision-useful information that is relevant in assessing the effects of disposal transactions on the ongoing operations of an entity.
- Eliminating inconsistencies resulting from two accounting models for long-lived assets to be disposed of by sale improves comparability in

financial reporting among entities. Thus, it enables users to identify similarities in and differences between two sets of economic events.

FASB 144 also incorporates the guidance in FASB Concepts Statement 7, *Using Cash Flow Information and Present Value in Accounting Measurements*, for using present value techniques to measure fair value.

## ¶6041   FASB 143, ACCOUNTING FOR ASSET RETIREMENT OBLIGATIONS

The Board concluded deliberations and unanimously voted to issue Statement 143, *Accounting for Asset Retirement Obligations*. Initiated in 1994 as a project to account for the costs of nuclear decommissioning, the Board soon expanded the scope to include similar closure or removal-type costs in other industries. These include oil and gas production facilities, landfills, mines, and environmental cleanups. The existing financial reporting practices had been inconsistent and, in some cases, misleading.

The Standard requires entities to record the fair value of a liability for an asset retirement obligation in the period in which it is incurred. When the liability is initially recorded, the entity capitalizes a cost by increasing the carrying amount of the related long-lived asset. Over time, the liability is accreted to its present value each period, and the capitalized cost is depreciated over the useful life of the related asset. Upon settlement of the liability, an entity either settles the obligation for its recorded amount or incurs a gain or loss upon settlement.

### .01   Objective of the Project

The aim of the asset retirement obligations (ARO) project has been to provide accounting requirements for retirement obligations associated with these tangible long-lived assets. The obligations included within the scope of the project are those that an entity cannot avoid as a result of either the acquisition, construction, or normal operation of a long-lived asset.

The obligation must result from a long-lived asset's acquisition, construction, or normal use. The "asset" may be a functional group of assets or a component part of a group of long-lived assets for which there are separable, identifiable asset retirement obligations.

In the case of leased long-lived assets, the standard applies to a lessee's long-lived leased assets accounted for as a capital lease. It applies to the lessor if the lease is an operating lease.

### .03   Capitalization

The Board decided that an asset retirement cost should be capitalized as part of the cost of the related long-lived asset. That capitalized asset retirement cost should then be allocated to expense by using a systematic and rational method. An entity is not precluded from using an allocation method that would have the effect of capitalizing and allocating to expense the same amount of cost in the same accounting period.

## .05   Requirements

The standard requires:

- Recognition of a long-lived tangible asset retirement obligation liability and an offsetting increase in the amount of the related long-lived asset.
- The obligation be measured at its fair value.
- Allocation of the asset retirement cost in the form of additional depreciation to expense over the related asset's useful life.
- Changes in the amount of the obligation liability subsequent to initial recognition be recognized if they arise from the passage of time and revisions to either the timing or amount of the related estimated cash flows.
- Recognition of an interest-type charge related to the obligation.

## .07   Change in Fair Value Methodology

The Board decided that the objective for initial measurement of an ARO liability should be use of the fair value method using a valuation technique, such as expected present value, to estimate fair value.

The methodology to determine fair value under this Standard represents a departure from past practice. The FASB now believes when the timing or amount of estimated cash flow related to an obligation is uncertain and in the absence of quoted market prices in active markets or prices for similar liabilities, fair value should be determined using an expected present value technique.

"Expected present value" refers to the sum of probability-weighted present values in a range of estimated cash flows, all discounted using the same interest rate convention. For purposes of measuring an ARO liability, an entity is required to use a discount rate that equates to a risk-free rate adjusted for the effect of its credit standing (credit-adjusted risk-free rate).

FASB's traditional present value approach used a single estimate of future cash flows, and the Board still believes the traditional approach is appropriate for measuring the fair value of assets and liabilities with contractual cash flows.

## .09   Recognition

An asset retirement obligation must be recognized when three requirements are met:

1. The obligation meets the definition of a liability.
2. A future transfer of assets associated with the obligation is probable.
3. The amount of the liability can be reasonably measured.

In order to meet the definition of a liability—the first test—the three characteristics of a liability must be satisfied:

1. The company has a present duty or responsibility to one or more other entities that entails settlement by probable future transfer or use of assets.
2. The company has little or no discretion to avoid a future transfer of use of assets.
3. An obligating event has already happened.

## .11 Obligating Events

The Standard deals with obligations arising under three circumstances:

1. Obligations incurred upon acquisition, construction, or development of an asset.
2. Obligations incurred during the operating life of an asset, either ratably or nonratably.
3. Obligations incurred any time during the life of an asset because of a newly enacted law or statute, or a change in contract provisions, or because an entity has otherwise incurred a duty or responsibility to one or more other entities.

Obligations incurred upon acquisition, construction, or development of an asset should be recognized when the cost of the long-lived asset is recognized. Those incurred during the operating life of an asset should be recognized concurrent with the events creating the obligation.

## .13 Subsequent Measurement of an ARO Liability

The Board decided that an entity should be required to use an allocation approach for subsequent measurement of an ARO liability. Under that approach, an entity is not required to remeasure an ARO liability at fair value each period. Instead, it is required to recognize changes in an ARO liability resulting from the passage of time and revisions in cash flow estimates. Those changes are then incorporated into a remeasurement of an ARO liability. The rate used to record accretion of the liability and revisions in cash flow estimates is the credit-adjusted risk-free rate applied when an ARO liability was initially measured.

## .15    Disclosures

An entity should disclose the following information in its financial statements:

- A general description of the asset retirement obligations and of the associated long-lived assets.
- The fair value of assets that are legally restricted for purposes of settling asset retirement liabilities.
- If any significant change occurs in the components of an asset retirement obligation, a reconciliation of the beginning and ending aggregate carrying amount of the liability showing separately the changes attributable to:
- —The liability incurred in the current period.
- —The liability settled in the current period.
- —Accretion expense.
- —Revisions in expected cash flows.

## ¶6042    FASB Issues Interpretation on Accounting For Conditional Asset Retirement Obligations

In March 2005 the FASB published FASB Interpretation No. 47, Accounting for Conditional Asset Retirement Obligations. The Board expects Interpretation 47 to result in:

1. More consistent recognition of liabilities relating to asset retirement obligations.
2. More information about expected future cash outflows associated with those obligations.
3. More information about investments in long-lived assets because additional asset retirement costs are recognized as part of the carrying amounts of the assets.

Interpretation 47 clarifies that the term conditional asset retirement obligation, as used in FASB 143, Accounting for Asset Retirement Obligations, refers to a legal obligation to perform an asset retirement activity in which the timing and (or) method of settlement are conditional on a future event that may not be within the control of the entity. The obligation to perform the asset retirement activity is unconditional even though uncertainty exists about the timing and (or) method of settlement. Uncertainty about the timing and (or) method of settlement of a conditional asset retirement obligation should be factored into the measurement of the liability when sufficient information exists. Interpretation 47 also clarifies when an entity would have sufficient information to estimate reasonably the fair value of an asset retirement obligation.

**¶6041.15**

## ¶6043    FASB 141 AND 142, BUSINESS COMBINATIONS AND GOODWILL AND OTHER INTANGIBLE ASSETS

In August, 1996, the Board added to its agenda a project on business combinations to reconsider APB Opinions 16, *Business Combinations*, and 17, *Intangible Assets*. The project was an attempt to improve the transparency of the accounting for business combinations presumably to give the user of the financial statement a clearer picture of the financial health of the new entity.

The project focused on the accounting for goodwill and other purchased intangible assets and the fundamental issues related to the methods of accounting for business combinations, including whether there is a need for two separate and distinct methods (purchase method and pooling-of-interests method).

The project did not address how to account for in-process research and development (IPR&D) costs.

## .01    FASBs 141 and 142 Approved

In June 29, 2001, the Board members unanimously voted in favor of two measures: Statement 141, *Business Combinations*, and Statement 142, *Goodwill and Other Intangible Assets*.

The Statements changed the accounting for business combinations and goodwill in two significant ways. Statement 141 requires that the purchase method of accounting be used for all business combinations initiated after June 30, 2001. Use of the pooling-of-interest method is prohibited.

Application of the purchase method requires identification of the acquiring enterprise. To determine which enterprise is the acquiring enterprise, all pertinent facts need to be considered, particularly the relative voting rights in the combined enterprise after the combination, the composition of the board of directors, the senior management of the combined enterprise, and which enterprise received a premium.

The Board decided that the definition of financial asset used in FASB Statement 141, *Business Combinations*, should be based on the definition of financial instrument in FASB Statement 107, *Disclosures about Fair Value of Financial Instruments*.

FASB 142 changes the accounting for goodwill from an amortization method to an impairment-only approach. The Statement requires that an impairment loss recognized in the year of initial application for nonamortized intangible assets should be recognized in the same manner as goodwill; that is, as the effect of a change in accounting principle. Intangible assets that will no longer be amortized should be tested for impairment in the first interim period in which the Statement is initially applied.

Acquired intangibles other than goodwill will be amortized over their useful life, which may extend beyond the current 40-year maximum amortization period. An intangible asset that is being amortized and is subsequently determined to have an indefinite useful life should stop being amortized and be accounted for in the same manner as other intangible assets deemed to have an indefinite useful life.

In January 2000, the Board began discussions on a closely related project to consider purchase method procedures and new basis accounting.

The Board believes that comment letters received in the first phase of the business combinations project indicated the necessity to address the purchase method procedures. The project is reconsidering purchase method guidance that was not reconsidered as part of Statements 141 and 142.

Tentatively, the project is focusing on purchase method guidance in the following areas:

1. Accounting for noncontrolling interests.
2. Determining the cost of an acquisition, and accounting for contingent consideration.
3. Recognizing assets acquired and liabilities assumed.
4. Accounting for pre-acquisition contingencies.

The Canadian Accounting Standards Board is adopting identical Standards to those adopted by the FASB with the goal of converging North American accounting standards related to business combinations.

## ¶6045   FASB 140, *Accounting for Transfers and Servicing of Financial Assets and Extinguishments of Liabilities — A Replacement of FASB Statement 125*

FASB 140 replaces FASB 125, *Accounting for Transfers and Servicing of Financial Assets and Extinguishments of Liabilities*, and revises the standards for accounting for securitizations and other transfers of financial assets and collateral. It also requires certain disclosures, but it carries over most of Statement 125's provisions without reconsideration.

It provides accounting and reporting standards for transfers and servicing of financial assets and extinguishments of liabilities. Those standards are based on consistent application of a *financial-components approach* that focuses on control. Under that approach, after a transfer of financial assets, an entity:

- Recognizes the financial and servicing assets it controls and the liabilities it has incurred.
- Derecognizes financial assets when control has been surrendered.
- Derecognizes liabilities when extinguished.

The Statement provides consistent standards for distinguishing transfers of financial assets that are sales from transfers that are secured borrowings.

## .01 Assets Accounted for as a Sale

A transfer of financial assets in which the transferor surrenders control over those assets is accounted for as a sale to the extent that consideration other than beneficial interests in the transferred assets is received in exchange. The transferor has surrendered control over transferred assets if and only if all three of the following conditions are met:

1. The transferred assets have been isolated from the transferor—put presumptively beyond the reach of the transferor and its creditors, even in bankruptcy or other receivership.
2. Each transferee (or, if the transferee is a qualifying special-purpose entity [SPE], each holder of its beneficial interests) has the right to pledge or exchange the assets (or beneficial interests) it received. In addition, nothing prevents the transferee (or holder) from taking advantage of its right to pledge or exchange or provide more than a trivial benefit to the transferor.
3. The transferor does not maintain effective control over the transferred assets through either:
   a. An agreement that both entitles and obligates the transferor to repurchase or redeem them before their maturity, or
   b. The ability to unilaterally cause the holder to return specific assets, other than through a cleanup call.

## .03 Measurement of Assets and Liabilities

This Statement requires that liabilities and derivatives incurred or obtained by transferors as part of a transfer of financial assets be initially measured at fair value, if practicable. It also requires that servicing assets and other retained interests in the transferred assets be measured by allocating the previous carrying amount between the assets sold, if any, and retained interests, if any, based on their relative fair values at the date of the transfer.

This Statement requires that servicing assets and liabilities be subsequently measured by:

- Amortization in proportion to and over the period of estimated net servicing income or loss.
- Assessment for asset impairment or increased obligation based on their fair values.

¶6045.03

FASB 140 requires that a liability be derecognized if and only if either:

- The debtor pays the creditor and is relieved of its obligation for the liability, or
- The debtor is legally released from being the primary obligor under the liability either judicially or by the creditor. Therefore, a liability is not considered extinguished by an in-substance defeasance.

## .05   Implementation Guidance Provided

FASB 140 provides implementation guidance for:

- Assessing isolation of transferred assets.
- Conditions that constrain a transferee.
- Conditions for an entity to be a qualifying SPE.
- Accounting for transfers of partial interests.
- Measurement of retained interests.
- Servicing of financial assets.
- Securitizations.
- Transfers of sales-type and direct financing lease receivables.
- Securities lending transactions.
- Repurchase agreements including "dollar rolls," "wash sales," loan syndications, and participations.
- Risk participations in bankers' acceptances.
- Factoring arrangements.
- Transfers of receivables with recourse.
- Extinguishments of liabilities.

In addition to all of that, the Statement also provides guidance about whether a transferor has retained effective control over assets transferred to qualifying SPEs through removal-of-accounts provisions, liquidation provisions, or other arrangements.

It requires a debtor to:

1. Reclassify financial assets pledged as collateral and report those assets in its statement of financial position separately from other assets not so encumbered, if the secured party has the right by contract or custom to sell or repledge the collateral.

2. Disclose assets pledged as collateral that have not been reclassified and separately reported in the statement of financial position.

## .07 Additional Disclosures

FASB 140 also requires a secured party to disclose information about collateral that it has accepted and is permitted by contract or custom to sell or re-pledge. The required disclosure includes the fair value at the end of the period of that collateral, and of the portion of that collateral that it has sold or repledged, and information about the sources and uses of that collateral.

The Statement requires an entity that has securitized financial assets to disclose information about accounting policies, volume, cash flows, key assumptions made in determining fair values of retained interests, and sensitivity of those fair values to changes in key assumptions.

It also requires that entities that securitize assets disclose for the securitized assets and any other financial assets it manages together with them:

- The total principal amount outstanding, the portion that has been derecognized, and the portion that continues to be recognized in each category reported in the statement of financial position, at the end of the period.
- Delinquencies at the end of the period.
- Credit losses during the period.

## ¶6047 FASB ISSUES FIN 45 TO EXPAND DISCLOSURE REQUIREMENTS FOR GUARANTEES

In the hope of improving disclosures about loan guarantees, the FASB issued Interpretation 45, *Guarantor's Accounting and Disclosure Requirements for Guarantees, Including Indirect Guarantees of Indebtedness of Others*, in November 2002.

The Interpretation clarifies and expands existing disclosure requirements for guarantees, including loan guarantees. It also requires that when a company issues a guarantee, the company must recognize a liability for the fair value, or market value, of its obligations under that guarantee. An improved disclosure and accounting treatment should provide a more faithful picture of a company's financial position and the risk it has assumed.

The Interpretation does not address the subsequent measurement of the guarantor's recognized liability over the term of the guarantee. It also incorporates, without change, the guidance in FASB Interpretation 34, *Disclosure of Indirect Guarantees of Indebtedness of Others.*

This guidance would not apply to:

- Guarantee contracts issued by insurance companies.
- A lessee's residual value guarantee embedded in a capital lease.
- Contingent rents and price rebates.

The provisions related to recognizing a liability at inception for the fair value of the guarantor's obligations would not apply to product warranties or to guarantees accounted for as derivatives.

# Chapter 7

# Consolidation of Variable Interest Entities

## CONTENTS

## ¶7000  OVERVIEW

Just as derivatives received much of the blame for questionable accounting practices during the 1990s, special-purpose entities (SPEs) appear now to be getting much of the blame for the accounting profession's fall from grace. Yet both of these vehicles can serve, and have served, a useful and legitimate purpose. However, as is often suggested, as long as there is someone who is determined to show a profit regardless of what is right or wrong, a way will be found. The more legitimate appearing, the better to subvert! Measures have been taken to see that derivatives are properly regulated; the ones used to sort out special-purpose entities are variable interest entities (VIEs), and assorted off- balance-sheet vehicles.

## ¶7001    IMPROVING FINANCIAL REPORTING FOR VARIOUS ENTITIES

In an effort to end the abusive accounting for, to restore the legitimacy of, and to expand upon and strengthen existing accounting guidance on special-purpose entities, the Financial Accounting Standards Board (FASB) issued Interpretation 46 (FIN 46), *Consolidation of Variable Interest Entities* . The Interpretation addresses when a company should include the assets, liabilities, and activities of these entities in its financial statements.

Although many variable interest entities have commonly been referred to as special-purpose entities or off-balance-sheet structures, the guidance applies to a *larger group* of entities. The FASB explains that, in general, a variable interest entity is a corporation, partnership, trust, or any other *legal* structure used for business purposes that either:

- Does not have equity investors with voting rights; or
- Has equity investors that do not provide sufficient financial resources for the entity to support its activities.

A variable interest entity often holds financial assets, including loans or receivables, real estate, or other property. A VIE may be essentially passive or it may engage in research and development or other activities on behalf of another company. As pointed out, these types of entities can be put to perfectly legitimate use. Therefore, the Board's objective in FIN 46 is not to restrict the use of variable interest entities, but to improve financial reporting by companies involved with them.

Until now, one company generally has included another entity in its consolidated financial statements *only* if it controlled the entity through voting interests. However, the Board believes that if a business enterprise actually has a controlling *financial* interest (regardless of method of determination) in a variable interest entity, the assets, liabilities, and results of the activities of that variable interest entity should be included in consolidated financial statements with those of the business enterprise. Thus, FIN 46 changes present use by requiring a variable interest entity to be consolidated by a company if that company is subject to a majority of the risk of loss from the variable interest entity's activities or entitled to receive a majority of the entity's residual returns, or both.

## .01    Impetus for FIN 46

According to various reports, the failure of Enron was due largely to losses it incurred in connection with its financial guarantees and interests in off-balance-sheet partnerships (or SPEs). In Enron's case, the company's significant interests and obligations relating to those partnerships were not fairly or adequately reported in its financial statements. Therefore, this rule was drafted primarily in response to the financial failure of Enron with the hope that such disasters could be prevented in the future.

In a project begun early in 2002 to clarify the rules regarding the circumstances in which a business enterprise must consolidate an off-balance-sheet entity, the Board acknowledged that very little accounting literature addressed the topic. It also acknowledged that the need for such guidance had become critical because transactions involving SPEs (which had previously raised concerns) had become increasingly common in recent years. But, what is the cause of the current number of references to VIEs when so much of the Enron debacle was blamed on the part played by SPEs?

## .03   FASB Coins a New Term

Leading up to FIN 46's final form, the FASB made several significant changes to the draft rule relating to the Interpretation. During a meeting in mid-October 2002, the Board agreed to discontinue the use of the term "special-purpose entities" in favor of the term "variable interest entities." The new term coined by the FASB includes many, but not all, of the entities that were referred to in the past as special-purpose entities or off-balance-sheet structures, as well as additional entities.

FIN 46 began as an interpretation of FASB Accounting Research Bulletin (ARB) 51, *Consolidated Financial Statements*, which addresses consolidation by business enterprises of variable interest entities. The Exposure Draft that preceded this Interpretation referred to the entities being covered by its requirements as special-purpose entities. Because some entities that have been commonly referred to as SPEs may not be subject to this Interpretation, and other entities that have not commonly been referred to as SPEs may be subject to the Interpretation, the FASB decided to use the term "variable interest entity."

## .05   VIEs and Exceptions Defined

The new term is used for those entities having at least one of the following characteristics:

- The equity investment at risk is not sufficient to permit the entity to finance its activities without additional subordinated financial support from other parties. This is provided through other interests that are to absorb some or all of the expected losses of the entity.
- The equity investors lack one or more of the following essential characteristics of a controlling financial interest:
  - The direct or indirect ability to make decisions about the entity's activities through voting rights or similar rights.

—The obligation to absorb the expected losses of the entity if they occur, which makes it possible for the entity to finance its activities.

—The right to receive the expected residual returns of the entity if they occur, which is the compensation for the risk of absorbing the expected losses.

*Exceptions.*   With only a few exceptions, the Interpretation applies to any business enterprise that has an ownership interest, contractual relationship, or other relationship to a VIE. Those that should not consolidate include:

- Not-for-profit organizations, unless they are used by business enterprises in an attempt to circumvent the provisions of the Interpretation. The FASB explains that the Interpretation generally applies to business enterprises and the arrangements used by them. ARB 51 refers to "companies," and FASB 94, *Consolidation of All Majority-Owned Subsidiaries*, which amends ARB 51, refers only to "business enterprises." The Board considered it inappropriate to extend the requirements of this Interpretation to not-for-profit organizations because the document being interpreted does not apply specifically to them. The Board is aware that some of the requirements in ARB 51 are applied in modified forms to certain not-for-profit organizations and does not intend this Interpretation to cause a change in those practices.
- Employee benefit plans covered by the provisions of FASB 87, *Employers' Accounting for Pensions;* FASB 106, *Employers' Accounting for Post-retirement Benefits Other Than Pensions;* and FASB 112, *Employers' Accounting for Postemployment Benefits.*
- Registered investment companies subject to the Investment Company Act of 1940.
- Separate accounts of life insurance enterprises covered in the *AICPA Auditing and Accounting Guide: Life and Health Insurance Entities* . Existing accounting standards specifically require life insurance enterprises to recognize these accounts and the Board considered it unwise to change them without more extensive reconsideration of insurance accounting.
- An enterprise subject to SEC Regulation S-X Rule 6-03(c)(1) should not consolidate any entity that is not also subject to that same rule.
- A transferor of financial assets or their affiliates should not consolidate a qualifying SPE or grandfathered qualifying SPE covered by FASB 140, *Accounting for Transfers and Servicing of Financial Assets and Extinguishments of Liabilities* . They are not required to consolidate those entities used to transfer assets, as long as the transferor of assets has no rights or obligations that would prevent it under existing accounting

rules from derecognizing the assets. The transferor is, however, required to report its rights and obligations related to the particular qualifying special-purpose entity according to the requirements of FASB 140.

This prohibition was specifically intended to exclude those special-purpose entities from ongoing and future Board decisions about consolidations. The derecognition requirements in Statement 140 are based on control of assets. Reporting of an enterprise's rights and obligations related to financial assets that have been transferred and derecognized is based on a *financial components approach* . Because a qualifying SPE has such limited decision-making abilities, the Board decided that retention of the financial components approach for parties involved with a qualifying SPE entity was more appropriate than consolidation based on variable interests. Therefore, this Interpretation does not change that requirement.

*Importance of Exempting Transferors of Assets from Consolidating SPEs Covered by FASB 140.*     This is an important exemption, because many asset-backed security issuance structures involve a qualifying SPE. FASB 140 defines a qualifying SPE as a trust or other legal vehicle that meets certain conditions. The principal conditions are:

1.  It is demonstrably distinct from the transferor.
2.  Its permitted activities:
    a.  Are significantly limited.
    b.  Were entirely specified in the legal documents that established the SPE or created the beneficial interests in the transferred assets that it holds.
    c.  May be significantly changed only with the approval of the holders of at least a majority of the beneficial interests held by entities other than any transferor, its affiliates, and its agents.
3.  It may hold only:
    a.  Financial assets transferred to it that are passive in nature.
    b.  Passive derivative financial instruments that pertain to beneficial interests.
    c.  Financial assets that would reimburse it if others were to fail to adequately service financial assets transferred to it or to timely pay obligations due to it and that it entered into at one of these points:
        (1) When it was established.
        (2) When assets were transferred to it.
        (3) When beneficial interests (other than derivative financial instruments) were issued by the SPE.
    d.  Servicing rights related to financial assets that it holds.

    e. Temporarily, nonfinancial assets obtained in connection with the collection of financial assets that it holds.

    f. Cash collected from assets that it holds and investments purchased with that cash pending distribution to holders of beneficial interests that are appropriate for that purpose (that is, money-market or other relatively risk-free instruments without options and with maturities no later than the expected distribution date).

4. If it can sell or otherwise dispose of noncash financial assets, it can do so in automatic response to conditions specified in FASB 140.

In the case of nonqualifying SPEs, a transferor that holds a subordinated retained interest in the transferred assets may be considered to be a variable interest holder.

## ¶7003   Specific Provisions of FIN 46

The FASB divided entities into two classes in the determination of which entities should be consolidated in the financial statements of another entity:

1. Those for which the consolidation decision is based on the controlling equity interests in the entity.
2. Those where the consolidation decision is based on interests *other than* controlling equity interests. (These are the interests now referred to as variable interests. Thus, these are the entities in which consolidation is subject to the nature of these variable interests. It is these, in particular, that are the subject of the Interpretation.)

FIN 46 addresses consolidation by business enterprises where equity investors do *not* bear the residual economic risks and rewards. These entities have been commonly referred to as special-purpose entities.

The underlying principle behind the new Interpretation is that, if a business enterprise has the majority financial interest in an entity (defined in the guidance as a variable interest entity), the assets, liabilities, and results of the activities of the variable interest entity should be included in consolidated financial statements with those of the business enterprise.

Majority-owned subsidiaries are entities separate from their parents that are subject to this Interpretation and may be VIEs.

The Interpretation explains how to identify variable interest entities. It also explains how an enterprise should assess its interest in an entity when deciding whether or not to consolidate that entity and include the assets, liabilities, noncontrolling interests, cash flows, and results of operations of a particular VIE in its consolidated financial statements.

## .01   Determination of Status

The initial determination of whether an entity is a VIE and thus subject to the Interpretation is made at the time when an enterprise becomes involved with the entity through ownership, a contractual interest, or other pecuniary interest (i.e., the determination date). These interests can change with the entity's net asset value and may take a variety of forms, including but not limited to guarantees, options to acquire assets, purchase contracts, management or other service contracts, credit enhancements, leases, or subordinated loans. Equity interests with or without voting rights are considered variable interests if the entity is a VIE.

Also at the determination date, the enterprise should determine whether its investments or other interests will absorb any portions of the VIE's expected losses or receive any portions of the entity's expected residual returns. If so, they are indeed variable interests and subject to the Interpretation. VIEs whose variable interests effectively disperse risk among the parties involved need not be consolidated by any of the parties.

A company that consolidates a VIE is called the *primary beneficiary* of that entity. The FASB believes consolidation by a primary beneficiary of the assets, liabilities, and results of activities of VIEs will provide more complete information about the resources, obligations, risks, and opportunities of the consolidated company. To further assist financial statement users in assessing a company's risks, FIN 46 also requires disclosures about VIEs that a company is *not* required to consolidate but in which it has a significant variable interest.

## .03   Difference between FIN 46 and Previous Practice

In the past, two enterprises generally have been included in consolidated financial statements because one enterprise controlled the other through voting interests. FIN 46 explains other methods of identifying variable interest entities and then indicates how an enterprise assesses its particular interests in a VIE to decide whether or not to consolidate that entity. FIN 46 requires existing unconsolidated variable interest entities to be consolidated by their *primary beneficiaries* if the entities do not effectively disperse risks among parties involved. The variable interest entities that do effectively disperse risks will not be consolidated, unless a single party holds an interest or combination of interests that effectively recombines risks that had previously been dispersed.

The ability to make decisions is not a variable interest, but it is an indication that the decision maker should carefully consider whether it holds sufficient variable interests to be the primary beneficiary. An enterprise with a variable interest in a VIE must consider variable interests of related parties and de facto agents as its own in determining whether it is the primary beneficiary of the entity.

## .05 Measurement

Assets, liabilities, and noncontrolling interests of newly consolidated VIEs generally will be initially measured at their fair values except for assets and liabilities transferred to a variable interest entity by its primary beneficiary, which will continue to be measured as if they had not been transferred. If recognizing those assets, liabilities, and noncontrolling interests at their fair values results in a *loss* to the consolidated enterprise, that loss will be reported immediately as an extraordinary item. On the other hand, if recognizing those assets, liabilities, and noncontrolling interests at their fair values results in a *gain* to the consolidated enterprise, that amount will be allocated to reduce the amounts assigned to assets in the same manner as if consolidation resulted from a business combination.

However, assets, liabilities, and noncontrolling interests of newly consolidated variable interest entities that are under common control with the primary beneficiary are measured at the amounts at which they are carried in the consolidated financial statements of the enterprise that controls them (or would be carried if the controlling entity prepared financial statements) at the date the enterprise becomes the primary beneficiary. After initial measurement, the assets, liabilities, and noncontrolling interests of a consolidated variable interest entity will be accounted for as if the entity were consolidated based on voting interests. In some circumstances, earnings of the variable interest entity attributed to the primary beneficiary arise from sources other than investments in equity of the entity.

## .07 Disclosure Requirements

An enterprise that holds significant variable interests in a variable interest entity but *is not the primary beneficiary* is required to disclose:

- The nature, purpose, size, and activities of the variable interest entity.
- The nature of its involvement with the entity and date when the involvement began.
- Its maximum exposure to loss as a result of involvement with the VIE.

The *primary beneficiary* of a variable interest entity is required to disclose the following, unless it also holds a majority voting interest in the VIE:

- The nature, purpose, size, and activities of the variable interest entity.
- The carrying amount and classification of consolidated assets that are collateral for the variable interest entity's obligations.

¶7003.05

- Any lack of recourse by creditors (or beneficial interest holders) of a consolidated variable interest entity to the general credit of the primary beneficiary.

The primary beneficiary must, in addition, disclose all information that may be required by other standards. It is also important for a primary beneficiary to reconsider its status from time to time, particularly if:

- The VIE's governing documents or contractual arrangements among the involved parties change.
- The primary beneficiary sells or otherwise disposes of all or part of its interest to other parties.

A holder of beneficial interests that is *not a primary beneficiary* should also reconsider its status if the enterprise acquires newly issued interests in the entity or part of the primary beneficiary's interest in the VIE.

A cautionary note about disclosure: disclosures required by FASB 140 about a variable interest entity must be included in the same note to the financial statements as the information required by FIN 46. Information about VIEs may be reported in the aggregate for similar entities if separate reporting would not add material information.

## ¶7005  What Constitutes a Variable Interest?

An entity is a VIE and, therefore, subject to consolidation according to the provisions of FIN 46 if, by the way it is structured, either of two conditions exists:

1. The total equity investment as reported as equity in the entity's statements at risk is not sufficient to permit the entity to finance its activities without additional subordinated financial support from other parties. That is, the equity investment at risk is not greater than the expected losses of the entity. For this purpose, the total equity investment at risk:
    a. Includes only equity investments in the entity that participate significantly in profits and losses, even if those investments do not carry voting rights.
    b. Does not include equity interests that the entity issued in exchange for subordinated interests in other VIEs.
    c. Does not include amounts provided to the equity investor by the entity or other parties involved with the entity (such as fees, charitable contributions, or other payments), unless the provider is a parent, subsidiary, or affiliate of the investor required to be included in the same set of consolidated financial statements as the investor.

    d. Does not include amounts financed for the equity investor (for example, by loans or guarantees of loans) directly by the entity or by other parties involved with the entity, unless that party is a parent, subsidiary, or affiliate of the investor that is required to be included in the same set of financial statements of the investor.

2. As a group, the holders of the equity investment at risk lack any one of the following three characteristics of a controlling financial interest:

    a. The direct or indirect ability to make decisions about an entity's activities through voting rights or similar rights. The investors do not have that ability through voting rights or similar rights if no owners hold voting rights or similar rights (such as those of a common shareholder in a corporation or a general partner in a partnership). In addition, the equity investors as a group also are considered to lack the characteristic of this condition if:

      (1) The voting rights of some investors are not proportional to their obligations to absorb the expected losses of the entity, to receive the expected residual returns of the entity, or both.

      (2) Substantially all of the entity's activities (for example, providing financing or buying assets) either involve or are conducted on behalf of an investor and any related parties of the investor that have disproportionately few voting rights. According to FIN 46, this provision is necessary to prevent a primary beneficiary from avoiding consolidation of a VIE by organizing the entity with non-substantive voting interests.

    b. The obligation to absorb the expected losses of the entity if they occur. Investor or investors do not have that obligation if they are directly or indirectly protected from the expected losses or are guaranteed a return by the entity itself or by other parties involved with the entity.

    c. The right to receive the expected residual returns of the entity if they occur. The investors do not have that right if their return is capped by the entity's governing documents or arrangements with other variable interest holders or with the entity.

Several of these provisions have been included in an attempt to forestall methods of circumventing the intent of the various rulings to provide a true financial picture for the benefit of the financial statement user in general and the investor in particular.

## .01 Equity Investment at Risk

The determination of the total amount of equity investment at risk that is necessary to permit an entity to finance its activities is a matter of judgment.

FIN 46 offers guidance, but each case must be determined based on its facts and circumstances. A VIE's expected losses and expected residual returns include:

- The expected variability in the entity's net income or loss.
- The expected variability in the fair value of the entity's assets (except as explained below in "Specified Assets" ), if it is not included in net income or loss.
- Fees to the decision maker (if there is one).
- Fees to providers of guarantees of the values of all or substantially all of the entity's assets (including writers of put options and other instruments with similar results) and providers of guarantees that all or substantially all of the entity's liabilities will be paid.

## .03   Ten Percent Guideline

An equity investment of *less than 10 percent* of the entity's total assets is *not* to be considered sufficient to permit the entity to finance its activities without subordinated financial support in addition to the equity investment *unless* the equity investment can be demonstrated to be sufficient in at least one of three ways:

1. The entity has demonstrated that it can actually finance its activities without additional subordinated financial support.
2. The entity has at least as much equity invested as other entities that hold only similar assets of similar quality in similar amounts and operate with no additional subordinated financial support. (This comparison should be very carefully researched and considered, not merely an attempt to validate a questionable decision.)
3. The amount of equity invested in the entity exceeds the estimate of the entity's expected losses based on reasonable quantitative evidence.

FIN 46 points out that some entities may require an equity investment greater than 10 percent of their assets to finance their activities. This is particularly true if they engage in high-risk activities, hold high-risk assets, or have exposure to risks that has not been adequately shown in the reported amounts of their assets or liabilities. It is unquestionably the responsibility of the enterprise to determine whether a particular entity with which it is involved needs an equity investment *greater than 10 percent* of its assets in order to finance its activities without subordinated financial support in addition to the equity investment. At the time of the Enron fiasco, the guideline was only 3 percent, and even this was not observed. Auditors and management must move very cautiously when deciding whether or not an entity must be consolidated.

## .05 Specified Assets

A variable interest can be in the VIE or specified assets of the VIE, such as a guarantee or subordinated residual value.

A variable interest in specific assets of a VIE are considered to be a variable interest in the VIE only if:

- The fair value of the specific asset is more than 50 percent of the fair value of the VIE's total assets.
- The holder has another variable interest in the VIE as a whole, except where those other interests are insignificant or have little or no variability.

If an enterprise has a variable interest in specified assets that are essentially the only source of payment for specified liabilities or other specified interests of the VIE, the enterprise should treat that portion of the entity as a separate VIE. If this is the case and the holder is required to consolidate only this discrete piece of the VIE, the holders of other variable interests need not consider that portion to be part of the larger VIE.

## ¶7007 WHO SHOULD CONSOLIDATE WHOM AND WHEN?

The consolidation policy rule appears on the surface, and from all the provisos, to be very complicated. However, once everything has been considered, it is relatively simple. An enterprise must consolidate a VIE if that enterprise has a variable interest (or a combination of variable interests) that will:

- Absorb a majority of the VIE's expected losses, if they occur.
- Receive a majority of the VIE's expected residual returns if they occur.
- Both.

In the situation where one enterprise will absorb the majority of the expected losses and another enterprise will absorb the majority of the expected residual returns, the enterprise absorbing the losses must consolidate the VIE.

The consolidating entity is called the primary beneficiary in the Interpretation. The determination of primary beneficiary status is made at the time the enterprise becomes involved in the VIE.

## .01 Decisions Relating to Variable Interests

The initial determination of whether an entity is a variable interest entity needs to be *reconsidered* only if one or more of the following occur:

- The entity's governing documents or the contractual arrangements among the parties involved change.

- The equity investment or some part thereof is returned to the investors, and other parties become exposed to expected losses.
- The entity undertakes additional activities or acquires additional assets that increase the entity's expected losses.

## .03 Determination Date

The initial determination of whether an entity is a variable interest entity is to be made on the date at which an enterprise becomes involved with the entity through ownership, a contractual interest, or other pecuniary interest. Such determination should be based on the circumstances occurring on that date, including future changes that are required in existing governing documents and existing contractual arrangements. An enterprise is not required to determine whether an entity with which it is involved is a variable interest entity if it is apparent that the enterprise's interest would not be a significant variable interest and if the enterprise, its related parties, and its de facto agents were not involved in forming the entity.

Any entity that previously did not require consolidation does not become subject to the Interpretation because it loses more than its "expected losses," resulting in a reduction of the equity investment.

## .05 Related Parties

An enterprise's variable interest in a VIE includes the variable interests of any related parties in the same VIE. For the purposes of the Interpretation, related parties as identified in FASB 57, *Related Parties*, and certain other de facto agents of the variable interest holder are considered to be related parties. FASB 57 identifies related parties as:

- A parent company and its subsidiaries.
- Subsidiaries of a common parent.
- An enterprise or trust for the benefit of employees that is managed by or under the trusteeship of the enterprise's management.
- An enterprise and its principal owners, management, or members of their immediate families.
- Affiliates.

FIN 46 considers the following to be de facto agents of an enterprise:

- A party that cannot finance its operations without subordinated financial support from the enterprise (e.g., another VIE of which the enterprise is the primary beneficiary).
- A party that received its interests as a contribution or loan from the enterprise.

- An officer, employee, or member of the governing board of the enterprise.
- A party that has:
  — An agreement that it cannot sell, transfer, or encumber its interests in the entity without the prior approval of the enterprise.
  — A close business relationship like that between a professional service provider and one of its significant clients.

If two or more related parties hold variable interests in the same VIE, the following guidelines should be used to determine which is the primary beneficiary:

- If two or more parties with variable interests have an agency relationship, the principal is the primary beneficiary.
- If the relationship is not that of a principal and an agent, the party with activities that are most closely associated with the entity is the primary beneficiary.

## .07  Fair Value Measurement

A primary beneficiary initially measures the assets, liabilities, and non-consolidated interests in a VIE at their *fair value* upon consolidation. There are two exceptions to this rule. Assets and liabilities transferred by a primary beneficiary to a newly consolidated VIE are measured at the same amount they would have been measured at if no transfer had occurred. If the primary beneficiary and the VIE are under common control, assets and liabilities transferred to the VIE are measured at their carrying amounts on the financial statements of the enterprise that controls the VIE. After the initial measurement, the assets, liabilities, and noncontrolling interests of a consolidated VIE are accounted for based on voting interests.

## ¶7009  Expected Results of FIN 46 Implementation

The effects of FIN 46 could hasten possibly more significant changes in consolidation policy. In November 2001, the FASB decided to defer consideration of changes in the consolidation policy rules, including its proposal requiring consolidation of all controlled entities, irrespective of the level of equity ownership, to concentrate effort on developing the VIE Interpretation. With this project completed, the FASB is again considering the broader consolidation issues. Indications from the earlier proposals are that the changes in consolidation accounting could be far more encompassing than those resulting from the new *rulings* .

FIN 46 is a reaction to the flouting of honest accounting for off-balance-sheet entities by Enron and others. FASB's earlier proposal, on the other hand, is a proactive initiative to improve the relevance, comparability, consistency, and completeness of consolidated statements. The proposals would also bring U.S. consolidation practices more in line with non-U.S. accounting practices and International Accounting Standards. Both the Sarbanes-Oxley Act and the Securities and Exchange Commission indicate the growing desire to close the gaps between FASB and the International Accounting Standards Board standards.

## .01 FASB Defers Implementation Date

At its October 2003 Board meeting, the FASB decided to defer to the fourth quarter from the third quarter the implementation date for FIN 46. This deferral applies only to variable interest entities that existed prior to February 1, 2003. The FASB believes that additional time is needed for companies and

## ¶7011 INTERPRETATION AND GUIDANCE FOR FIN 46

In March 2003, the Board decided that the appropriate way to provide implementation guidance for FIN 46, as needed, was through FASB Staff Positions and routine technical inquiries. The Board also directed the staff to begin work on other aspects of the consolidations project. The four issues to be addressed are:

1. Consolidation without a majority voting interest.
2. Effect on consolidation of minority shareholder rights.
3. Possible consolidation because of ownership of convertible debt, options, or other means of obtaining a voting interest.
4. Related parties and de facto agents.

## .01 Guidance Provided on Questions Raised by Users

Guidance in several areas was provided in July 2003 through five FASB Staff Positions (FSPs). The guidance in each of the FSPs was effective immediately for VIEs to which the requirements of the Interpretation had already been applied. The guidance is applied to other variable interest entities as a part of the adoption of FIN 46. If the guidance results in changes to previously reported information, the cumulative effect of the accounting change should be reported in the first period ending after July 24, 2003.

These FSPs may be applied by restating previously issued financial statements for one or more years with a cumulative-effect adjustment as of the beginning of the first year restated.

Regardless of specific language used in FIN 46 that caused some readers to question whether a distinction was being drawn regarding certain types of health care organizations, this was not the intention. All not-for-profit organizations as defined in FASB 117, *Financial Statements of Not-for-Profit Organizations,* including health care organizations subject to the AICPA *Audit Guide,* are included within the scope of the exemption for not-for-profits. To make this perfectly clear, the Board has agreed that the not-for-profit organization scope exception to Interpretation 46 will be clarified in a forthcoming technical amendment to the Interpretation. However, FIN 46 does point out that not-for-profit organizations may be related parties for purposes of applying certain portions of the Interpretation. In addition, as emphasized earlier in this chapter, a not-for- profit entity used by a business enterprise in a manner similar to a VIE in an effort to circumvent the provisions of Interpretation 46 is subject to the Interpretation.

A specified asset (or group of assets) of a variable interest entity and a related liability secured only by the specified asset or group are not treated as a separate VIE if other parties have rights or obligations related to the specified asset or to residual cash flows from the specified asset. The FSP explains that this is considered so because a separate VIE is deemed to exist for accounting purposes only if essentially all of the assets, liabilities, and equity of the deemed entity are separate from the overall entity and specifically identifiable. It is further explained that, essentially none of the returns of the assets of the deemed entity can be used by the remaining variable interest entity, and essentially none of the liabilities of the deemed entity are payable from the assets of the remaining VIE.

Transition requirements for initial application of FIN 46 provide that both of the following determinations should be made as of the date the enterprise became involved with the entity unless events requiring reconsideration of the entity's status or the status of its variable interest holders have occurred:

1. Whether an entity is a VIE.
2. Which enterprise, if any, is a VIE's primary beneficiary.

If a reconsideration event has occurred, each determination should be made as of the most recent date at which the Interpretation would have required consideration. However, if, at transition, it is impracticable for an enterprise to obtain the information necessary to make such a determination (as of the date the enterprise became involved with an entity or at the most recent reconsideration date), the enterprise should make the determination as of the date on which FIN 46 is first applied. If the VIE and primary beneficiary determinations are made in accordance with these conditions, then the primary beneficiary must measure the assets, liabilities, and noncontrolling interests of the VIE at fair value as of the date on which the Interpretation is first applied.

The two remaining June 2003 FSPs deal with the term "expected losses" . The phrase "expected losses of the entity" as used in the Interpretation, is based

**¶7011.01**

on the variability in the entity's net income or loss and not on the amount of the net income or loss. Procedures in FIN 46 and Appendix A require that the outcomes used to calculate expected losses include (1) the expected unfavorable variability in the entity's net income or loss and (2) expected unfavorable variability in the fair value of the entity's assets, if it is not included in the net income or loss. (Even an entity that expects to be profitable will have expected losses when this criterion for determining expected losses is considered.) Detailed instructions for calculating expected losses are also provided.

## ¶7013   FIN 46(R)

As pointed out above, the "derivatives problem" has not been easily solved, nor has the SPE/VIE fiasco. Will it take a headline grabber like Orange County or Enron to furnish the FASB sufficient clout to require effective accounting for the costs of stock options? The FASB was not unaware of possible problems arising from the growing use of off-balance sheet vehicles before Enron succeeded in utilizing them in their creative accounting. Numerous Standards and other rulings had obviously failed to control the situation or were too easily subverted.

Interpretation 46 was a big step toward preventing misuse of SPEs. As noted above, the Board realized immediately that implementation guidance and additional interpretation would be necessary. Thus, in the summer of 2003, the several staff positions were published to help clarify the requirements. But after almost a year of working with it, financial statement preparers were still not interpreting FIN 46 as the Board had intended. If this were not such a high profile "case," this might be an ideal time to try out the principles-based approach to standard setting.

FIN 46 (R) adopted in December 2003 is the next step in trying to make everything perfectly clear. Provisions re-emphasize those entities that are subject to consolidation as well as those that are not. It appears that, to make sure that they did not run into trouble, too many organizations were consolidating off- balance sheet entities erroneously. Therefore, the revision reiterates and emphasizes the types of organizations that are not required to consolidate, and spells out other exceptions to the scope of the Interpretation in the following manner:

- An enterprise with an interest in a variable interest entity or potential variable interest entity created before December 31, 2003, is not required to apply this Interpretation to that entity if the enterprise, after making an exhaustive effort, is unable to obtain the necessary information.
- An entity that is deemed to be a business (as defined in this Interpretation) need not be evaluated to determine if it is a variable interest entity unless one of the following conditions exists:
  —The reporting enterprise, its related parties, or both participated significantly in the design or redesign of the entity, and the entity is neither a joint venture nor a franchisee.

—The entity is designed so that substantially all of its activities either involve or are conducted on behalf of the reporting enterprise and its related parties.

—The reporting enterprise and its related parties provide more than half of the total of the equity, subordinated debt, and other forms of subordinated financial support to the entity based on an analysis of the fair values of the interests in the entity.

—The activities of the entity are primarily related to securitizations, other forms of asset-backed financings, or single-lessee leasing arrangements.

• An enterprise is not required to consolidate a governmental organization and is not required to consolidate a financing entity established by a governmental organization unless the financing entity:

—Is not a governmental organization.

—Is used by the business enterprise in a manner similar to a variable interest entity in an effort to circumvent the provisions of this Interpretation.

## .01  FASB's Explanation for the Revision

It would appear that FIN 46(R) is not so much a "revision" as a reemphasis of FIN 46. As mentioned above, many VIEs may have been consolidated that should not necessarily have been. On the other hand, users of financial reports would probably prefer this condition to one in which they are not, and, thus, information relating to them is more difficult to ascertain. It is because transactions involving variable interest entities have become increasingly common, and the relevant accounting literature is so fragmented and incomplete that the FASB has found it necessary to issue the Interpretation. The Board has pointed out that ARB 51 requires that an enterprise's consolidated financial statements include subsidiaries in which the enterprise has a controlling financial or voting interest. As has become evident, the voting interest approach is not effective in identifying controlling financial interests in entities that are not controllable through voting interests or in which the equity investors do not bear the residual economic risks.

Thus, the objective of the Interpretation is not to restrict the use of variable interest entities but to improve financial reporting by enterprises involved with variable interest entities. The Board believes that if a business enterprise has a controlling financial interest in a variable interest entity, the assets, liabilities, and results of the activities of the variable interest entity should be included in consolidated financial statements with those of the business enterprise.

## .03  Relationship of FIN 46(R) to the Conceptual Framework

The Board evidently felt that after pulling together much of the diverse scattered rulings related to various forms of off-balance-sheet entities and

¶7013.01

attempting to control their financial reporting with Interpretations, it was important to tie the requirements to their roots. Thus, references to the appropriate Concepts Statements:

FASB Concepts Statement No. 1, *Objectives of Financial Reporting by Business Enterprises*, states that financial reporting should provide information that is useful in making business and economic decisions. Including variable interest entities in consolidated financial statements with the primary beneficiary will help achieve that objective by providing information that helps in assessing the amounts, timing, and uncertainty of prospective net cash flows of the consolidated entity.

Completeness is identified in FASB Concepts Statement No. 2, *Qualitative Characteristics of Accounting Information*, as an essential element of representational faithfulness and relevance. Thus, to represent faithfully the total assets that an enterprise controls and liabilities for which an enterprise is responsible, assets and liabilities of variable interest entities for which the enterprise is the primary beneficiary must be included in the enterprise's consolidated financial statements.

FASB Concepts Statement No. 6, *Elements of Financial Statements*, defines assets, in part, as probable future economic benefits obtained or controlled by a particular entity and defines liabilities, in part, as obligations of a particular entity to make probable future sacrifices of economic benefits. The relationship between a variable interest entity and its primary beneficiary results in control by the primary beneficiary of future benefits from the assets of the variable interest entity even though the primary beneficiary may not have the direct ability to make decisions about the uses of the assets. Because the liabilities of the variable interest entity will require sacrificing consolidated assets, those liabilities are obligations of the primary beneficiary even though the creditors of the variable interest entity may have no recourse to the general credit of the primary beneficiary.

## .05   Effective Date of FIN 46(R)

Special provisions applied to enterprises that had fully or partially applied Interpretation 46 prior to issuance of the revision. Otherwise, application was required in financial statements of public entities that had interests in VIEs or potential VIEs for periods ending after December 15, 2003. Application by public entities (other than small business issuers) for all other types of entities was required in financial statements for periods ending after March 15, 2004. Application by small business issuers to entities other than special-purpose entities and by nonpublic entities to all types of entities is required at various dates in 2004 and 2005. In some instances, enterprises have the option of applying or continuing to apply FIN 46 for a short period of time before applying FIN 46(R).

# Chapter 8

# Governmental Accounting

## CONTENTS

## ¶8000  OVERVIEW

Indications are that the Governmental Accounting Standards Board is seriously following up on the aim of GASB 34, *Basic Financial Statements— and Management's Discussion and Analysis—for State and Local Governments*, to present usable, easily understood, business-like financial statements for the general public as well as for the investor. The Board appears to indicate through the content of the recently adopted standards that the many and varied governmental bodies' financial condition is of interest to the average citizen as well as to the purchaser of the entity's debt obligations. To a great extent, the new Standards and Interpretations are a result of the Board's systematic review and updating of some of the older Standards.

All levels of state and local governments have now begun functioning under that all-encompassing Standard. At the same time, the Board continues to do everything it can to make the transition of all entities to this "new" governmental accounting model as painless and error-free as possible by providing implementation guides and how-to-manuals. These publications, including a new one entitled, *What Else You Should Know about a Government's Finances: A Guide to Notes to the Financial Statements and Supporting Information,* are described at the end of the chapter.

A brief description of the requirements of new Standards, Exposure Drafts, and other relevant pronouncements issued since its adoption precede the discussion of the salient features of GASB 34; GASB 35, which expanded the new requirements to public colleges and universities; and GASB 33 which goes hand-in-hand with GASB 34 and GASB 35.

## ¶8001   GASB Begins Work on New Five-Year Plan

The Governmental Accounting Standards Board has released its new five-year strategic plan, which begins with a series of sweeping surveys of the Board's standing with its constituency as well as a barometer of its progress. The Board is issuing the first items in the planned survey series, which involves establishing a baseline on such issues as:

1. The percentages of governments that prepare financial statements in accordance with GASB Standards.
2. Auditors who are satisfied with the quality of those standards.
3. Users of government financial information who are satisfied with the information they receive.

The new plan, which will guide the Board until 2009, offers nothing radically different from past years, but it includes a shift to an increased emphasis upon communication. Inasmuch as the effectiveness of communication is difficult to measure, the Board will use the surveys to track and measure results. Separate polls will go to government financial officers, auditors, citizens, and constituent groups using governmental financial statements. (Concept Statement No. 3, discussed later in the chapter, provides a conceptual basis for selecting communication methods.)

### .01   GASB Doing Its Part

The members of the GASB decided that because they, too, are in the accountability business—involving encouraging others to be more open and transparent and to communicate more effectively about their performance, service efforts and accomplishments—they should do likewise.

The Board's previous strategic plans specified directions but lacked specific outcomes and performance measures. Currently, the Board does not know what percentage of the country's approximately 87,500 government units are actually reporting under GASB Standards. The Board members feel that whatever the number is, it is not high enough. Therefore, they need to confirm that their communication efforts over the next few years do actually encourage more governments to use generally accepted accounting principles (GAAP), and use them effectively.

## .03   GASB Issues White Paper

With FASB 34 and other of the subsequent standards, governments may truly be run "more like a business," but as a recent document points out—not in every way. In March 2006, the GASB released a white paper emphasizing the sometimes-misunderstood point that those who are interested in the financial performance of state and local governments have substantially different information needs than those who follow the financial performance of for-profit entities.

As mentioned above, these different and diverse needs result from basic differences between these types of entities: governments and businesses. The white paper cites several crucial differences that generate user demand for unique information. (For a discussion of the white paper, please see the Governmental Fund Chapter.)

## ¶8002    STATEMENT TO CLARIFY GUIDANCE ON ACCOUNTING FOR SALES AND PLEDGES OF RECEIVABLES AND FUTURE REVENUES

In September 2006, the Governmental Accounting Standards Board (GASB) issued Statement No. 48, *Sales and Pledges of Receivables and Future Revenues and Intra-Entity Transfers of Assets and Future Revenues.* This Statement establishes criteria that governments will use to ascertain whether certain transactions should be regarded as a sale or a collateralized borrowing. Such transactions are likely to comprise the sale of delinquent taxes, certain mortgages, student loans, or future revenues such as those arising from tobacco settlement agreements.

This Statement also includes a provision that stipulates that governments should not revalue assets that are transferred between financial reporting entity components. Guidance for reporting the effects of such transactions in governmental financial statements have been provided in several standards or, in certain cases, has not been authoritatively addressed. This has resulted in considerable diversity in practice in the manner that such transactions have been reported.

In addition to clarifying guidance on accounting for sales and pledges of receivables and future revenues, the Statement:

- Requires enhanced disclosures pertaining to future revenues that have been pledged or sold

- Provides guidance on sales of receivables and future revenues within the same financial reporting entity
- Provides guidance on recognizing other assets and liabilities arising from the sale of specific receivables or future revenues.

According to the Board, Statement 48 is intended to clarify accounting by establishing clear criteria for determining whether proceeds received from a given transaction should be reported as revenue or as a liability. In addition, the Standard's enhanced disclosure requirements are expected to improve the usefulness of financial reporting by enabling the public to become better informed about the status of future revenues that may have been pledged or sold.

In response to feedback, from individuals and constituent organizations in response to the Exposure Draft of the proposed standards, FASB 48 contains several modifications from the ED, including the following:

- Statement 48 supersedes guidance regarding future revenue sales provided in Technical Bulletin 2004-1, *Tobacco Settlement Recognition and Financial Reporting Entity Issues.* However, in response to concerns expressed by several respondents to the 2005 exposure draft, the Statement transition provisions were modified to allow for prospective, rather than retroactive, application of the requirements that pertain to sales of future revenues.
- The criteria for distinguishing a borrowing transaction from a sale transaction were clarified for both receivables and future revenues.
- The definition of active involvement was sharpened. Active involvement is a key consideration in determining whether a transaction transferring the right to a future revenue stream could qualify as a sale.
- The detailed accounting and reporting guidance proposed in the Exposure Draft was expanded and enhanced, especially for governmental funds.
- The requirements for disclosures about pledged revenues were clarified and an exemption from those disclosure requirements was granted for legally separate entities that report as stand-alone business-type activities whose operations are financed primarily by a single major revenue source.

The requirements of this Statement became effective for financial statements for periods beginning after December 15, 2006.

## ¶8003 PROPOSAL TO PROVIDE ADDITIONAL INFORMATION ON PENSION PLANS

The GASB added a project in August 2006 to its technical agenda intended to require state and local governments to provide enhanced disclosures and supplementary information about their pension plans to users of governmental financial statements. Like the FASB, the GASB has been very busy finalizing projects and quickly bringing others to a climax. This project, which is expected to be completed quickly, is designed to bring current pension disclosure requirements for governments in line with those recently required for other post-employment benefits, or OPEB.

Separately, in accordance with the GASB's strategic plan, the Board is conducting a concurrent research project to determine the effectiveness of existing governmental accounting standards in the area. Based upon constituent feedback received during that research, the Board then plans to determine whether further change to current governmental accounting standards for pensions is necessary.

Both projects reflect the GASB's commitment to help ensure that users of governmental financial statements have access to the highest quality information available to make their decisions. The Board points out that accounting standards do not, and cannot require funding of such pension plans. The information they provide enhances constituent knowledge *about how well the obligations are being met*. The short-term project is intended to address certain shortfalls in pension disclosures that were first identified during the development of the OPEB standards; this pension research project is expected to enable the Board to determine if even greater steps need to be taken.

Disclosure requirements previously adopted by the Board in regard to OPEB that potentially would be required for pensions as a result of GASB's short-term project include:

1. Disclosure of the current funded status of the plan as of the most recent actuarial valuation date in the notes to the financial statements of pension plans and certain employers.
2. Note disclosure of funded status and a multi-year schedule of funding progress using the entry age actuarial cost method as a surrogate when the aggregate actuarial cost method has been used to determine annual required contributions and annual pension cost.
3. Additional note disclosures about actuarial methods and assumptions used in valuations on which reported information about the annual required contribution (ARC) and funded status of the plan is based.
4. Disclosure by cost-sharing employees of how the contractually required contribution rate is determined.
5. Presentation of the required schedules for a cost-sharing plan in which an employer participates in the employer's report, if the plan does not issue a GAAP-compliant report that includes required supplementary information (RSI) or the plan is not included in the financial report of another entity.

A formal exposure draft on this initiative is expected before the end of 2007.

¶8003

## ¶8004  PROPOSED CONCEPT STATEMENT NO. 4

The GASB proposed its fourth Concepts Statement, *Elements of Financial Statement*, in August 2006 defining the seven elements of governmental financial statements. When considered collectively, Concepts Statements form the GASB's conceptual framework that provides a foundation to guide the Board's development of accounting and financial reporting standards.

In order to develop a conceptual framework appropriate for the government environment, the Board needs to define even the most basic building blocks of financial reporting. A central feature of each of the proposed definitions of elements is a *resource,* which is an item with a present capacity to provide service. Accordingly, this proposal defines the elements of *statements of financial position* as:

- *Assets*—resources the entity presently controls
- *Liabilities*—present obligations to sacrifice resources or future resources that the entity has little or no discretion to avoid
- A *deferred outflow of resources*—a consumption of net resources by the entity that is applicable to a future reporting period
- A *deferred inflow of resources*—an acquisition of net resources by the entity that is applicable to a future reporting period
- *Net assets*—the residual of all other elements presented in a statement of financial position.

Today's proposal also defines elements of *resource flows statements* as:

- *Outflow of resources*—a consumption of net resources by the entity that is applicable to the reporting period
- *Inflow of resources*—an acquisition of net resources by the entity that is applicable to the reporting period.

## .01  Board Gradually Establishing Concept Statements

These proposals reflect the Board's ongoing commitment to develop a conceptual framework that to guide the Board in its decision making, promote high-quality accounting standards, and make the process for developing those standards more consistent. An improved framework will also aid financial statement preparers and auditors as they evaluate transactions for which there are no existing standards, according to the Board. The proposed Concepts Statement would be the GASB's fourth to date.

- In May 1987, the Board issued Concepts Statement No. 1, *Objectives of Financial Reporting.*

- In April 1994, GASB issued Concepts Statement No. 2, *Service Efforts and Accomplishments Reporting*.
- In April 2005, GASB issued Concepts Statement No. 3, *Communication Methods in General Purpose External Financial Reports That Contain Basic Financial Statements*. (See below.)

The Board expects to begin work soon on a fifth Concept Statement focusing on recognition and measurement attributes.

## ¶8005   CONCEPTS STATEMENT NO. 3 ON COMMUNICATION METHODS

In April 2005, GASB issued Concepts Statement No. 3, *Communication Methods in General Purpose External Financial Reports That Contain Basic Financial Statements*. The purpose of the Concepts Statement is to provide a conceptual basis for selecting communication methods to present items of information within the general-purpose external financial reports containing the basic financial statements. These communication methods include:

1. Recognition in basic financial statements.
2. Disclosure in notes to basic financial statements.
3. Presentation as required supplementary (RSI).
4. Presentation as supplementary information.

The Concepts Statement:

1. Defines the communication methods commonly used in general-purpose external financial reports.
2. Develops criteria for each communication method.
3. Provides a hierarchy for their use.

The definitions, criteria, and hierarchy should help the GASB and preparers of financial reports determine the appropriate methods to use to communicate an item of information. Greater consistency in the communication and reporting methods used by various governmental units should make comparisons more meaningful. This, in turn, should lead to more efficient and effective use of governmental financial reports.

## ¶8007   REPORTING ON POLLUTION REMEDIATION OBLIGATIONS

In March 2005, the GASB released a Preliminary Views (PV) document, *Accounting and Financial Reporting for Pollution Remediation Obligations*.

Its purpose is to highlight the Board's preliminary views concerning accounting and financial reporting standards for pollution remediation obligations to address the current or potential detrimental effects of existing pollution. The aim is to bring about participation in pollution remediation activities such as site assessments and cleanups.

The PV proposes that, once any one of five specified obligating events occurs, governments would be required to estimate the components of expected pollution remediation outlays using an "expected cash flow" measurement technique. They should then determine whether future outlays for those components should be accrued as a liability or, in limited instances, capitalized when goods and services are acquired.

## .01 Obligating Events

The Board had considered requiring recognition of all legal liabilities or moral obligations to perform pollution remediation but, instead, decided that recognition should not be considered until an obligating event occurs. Therefore, when a governmental unit knows, or can reasonably assume, that a site is polluted, the entity should determine whether one or more components of a pollution remediation obligation might be a liability. A liability should be recognized when any of these events occurs:

1. Pollution creates an imminent endangerment to public health or welfare or to the environment to the extent that it compels the government to take pollution remediation action.
2. The government is in violation of a pollution prevention-related permit or license, such as a Resource Conservation and Recovery Act permit.
3. The government is named, or is aware of evidence indicating that it will be named, by a regulator as a responsible party or potentially responsible party (PRP) 1 for remediation.
4. The government is actually named, or is aware of evidence indicating that it will be named, in a lawsuit to compel the entity to participate in remediation.
5. The government commences, or obligates itself to commence cleanup activities, or monitoring and/or operation and maintenance of the remediation effort. If these activities are voluntarily commenced and no other events have occurred relative to the entire site, the amount recognized should be based on the portion of the remediation project that the government has initiated and is legally required to complete.

## .05 Recognition Benchmarks

This PV proposes a series of steps in the remediation process that governments should consider in determining when components of pollution remediation liabilities are reasonably estimable. These benchmarks would require evaluation of recognition of certain liability components no later than when the benchmarks occur.

Most pollution remediation outlays should be accrued as a liability and expenditure or expense, as appropriate, when a range of expected outlays is reasonably estimable. In some cases, a government should be able to estimate reasonably a range of all components of its liability early in the process if the site situation is similar to previously handled pollution situations. In such cases, the entire liability should be recognized in the beginning. In other cases, however, the government may have insufficient information to estimate reasonably the ranges of all components of its liability. If a government cannot reasonably estimate the range of all components of the liability, it should recognize the liability when the range of each component (for example, legal services, site investigation, or required postremediation monitoring) could be reasonably estimated. The PV proposes a series of recognition benchmarks "steps in the remediation process," which governments should consider in determining when the components of pollution remediation liabilities are reasonably estimable.

The range of an estimated remediation liability often will be defined, and periodically redefined, as necessary, as different stages in the remediation process occur. Certain stages of a remediation effort or process and of responsible party or PRP involvement provide benchmarks that should be considered when evaluating the extent to which a range of potential outlays for a remediation effort or process is reasonably estimable.

Benchmarks should not, however, be applied in a manner that would delay recognition beyond the point at which a reasonable estimate of the range of a component of a liability can be made. The following are recognition benchmarks that typically apply to pollution remediation obligations that are not common or similar to situations at other sites with which the government has experience. At a minimum, the estimate of a pollution remediation liability should be evaluated as each of these benchmarks occurs.

Recognition benchmarks include:

- Participation in a site assessment.
- Completion of a corrective measures feasibility study.
- Issuance of an authorization to proceed.

These are essentially the same recognition benchmarks found in SOP 96-1, modified to make them more broadly applicable to governments as well as corporations, for example. AICPA Statement of Position (SOP) 96-1, Environmental Remediation Liabilities, covers auditing and accounting topics dealing with environmental issues. It details the responsibilities of corporations involved in environmental cleanup, and responsibilities of corporations to avoid

**¶8007.05**

environmental destruction. SOP 96-1 is a comprehensive environmental issues guide.

Because the provisions in this PV fill a gap in the accounting guidance for state and local governments, if adopted, they should result in pollution remediation liabilities being reported more completely and consistently.

The provisions of the PV would be applied retroactively. Provisions for an effective date will be provided if and when the PV is issued as an Exposure Draft.

## .06 New Exposure Draft Proposal Identifies Five Key Circumstances Under Which Accounting for Pollution Remediation is Required

The proposal, issued by GASB in January 2006, reflects the Board's intention to ensure that certain costs and long-term obligations not specifically addressed by current governmental accounting standards will be included in financial reports.

The proposed standards build on a Preliminary Views draft that was released for public comment in March 2005. Specifically, the proposal sets forth the key circumstances under which a government would be required to report a liability related to pollution remediation. According to the proposal, a government would have to estimate its expected outlays for pollution remediation if any of the following occur:

1. Pollution poses an imminent danger to the public or environment and a government has little or no discretion to avoid fixing the problem
2. A government has violated a pollution prevention-related permit or license
3. A regulator has identified (or evidence indicates a regulator will do so) a government as responsible (or potentially responsible) for cleaning up pollution, or for paying all or some of the cost of the clean up
4. A government is named in a lawsuit (or evidence indicates that it will be) to compel it to address the pollution
5. A government begins to clean up pollution or conducts related remediation activities (or the government legally obligates itself to do so).

In addition to the liabilities, expenses, and expenditures which would be estimated using an "expected cash flows" measurement technique and be reported in the financial statements, the proposed standard would require governments to disclose information about their pollution clean up efforts in the notes to the financial statements. The requirements of this proposed Statement would be effective for financial statements for periods beginning after June 15, 2007.

## ¶8008   GASB COMPLETES ACCOUNTING STANDARDS FOR TERMINATION BENEFITS—STATEMENT NO. 47

In issuing its Statement No. 47, effective for financial statements covering periods beginning after June 15, 2005, the GASB addresses the issue of the proper accounting for termination benefits. The statement provides accounting and disclosure benchmarks for state and local governments that offer benefits such as early retirement incentives or severance pay to employees who are involuntarily terminated. Statement 47 specifies when governments should recognize the cost of termination benefits they offer in accrual basis financial statements, Benefits provided for involuntary terminations should be accounted for in the period in which a government becomes obligated to provide benefits to terminated employees, which is not necessarily the same period in which the benefits are actually provided. The cost of such benefits must be recognized when the termination offer is accepted by the employee.

The Statement provides an exception to the general recognition requirements for termination benefits that affect defined benefit postemployment benefits, such as pensions or retiree healthcare. Those termination benefits should be accounted for in the same manner as defined benefit pensions or other postemployment benefits, although any increase in an actuarially accrued liability associated with a termination benefit is required to be disclosed separately. For termination benefits that affect defined benefit postemployment benefits other than pensions, governments should implement Statement 47 simultaneously with Statement No. 45, *Accounting and Financial Reporting by Employers for Postemployment Benefits Other Than Pensions*.

## ¶8009   GASB CLARIFIES REPORTING OF NET ASSETS

The Governmental Accounting Standards Board issued Statement 46, *Net Assets Restricted by Enabling Legislation*, as an amendment of GASB Statement 34 in December 2004. The purpose is to determine when net assets have been restricted to a particular use by the passage of enabling legislation and to specify how those net assets should be reported in financial statements when there are changes in the circumstances surrounding that legislation.

A government's net assets should be reported as restricted when the purpose for, or manner in which they can be used, is limited by:

*   An external party.
*   A constitutional provision.
*   Enabling legislation.

*Enabling legislation* is a specific type of legislation that both authorizes the raising of new resources and imposes legally enforceable limits on how they may be used.

## .01    Reasons for Enacting this Standard

Statement 46 is intended to alleviate difficulties in identifying enabling legislation restrictions by clarifying that "legally enforceable" means that an external party "such as citizens, public interest groups, or the judiciary" can compel a government to use resources only for the purposes stipulated by the enabling legislation.

GASB 46 confirms that the determination of legal enforceability is a matter of professional judgment, which may entail reviewing the legislation and determinations made in relation to similar legislation, as well as obtaining the advice of legal counsel. The Statement indicates that governments should review the legal enforceability of enabling legislation restrictions when new enabling legislation has been enacted to replace existing legislation, and when resources are used for purposes not specified by the enabling legislation.

The Statement also requires governments to disclose in the notes to the financial statements the amount of net assets restricted by enabling legislation as of the end of the reporting period. Statement 46 is effective for periods beginning after June 15, 2005.

## ¶8013    TECH BULLETIN CLARIFIES ACCOUNTING FOR EMPLOYERS' CONTRIBUTIONS TO COST-SHARING PENSION AND OPEB PLANS

The GASB was quite busy at the end of 2004 publishing a staff Technical Bulletin, *Recognition of Pension and Other Postemployment Benefit (OPEB) Expenditures/Expense and Liabilities by Cost-Sharing Employers*. The Technical Bulletin clarifies the application of requirements regarding accounting for employers' contractually required contributions to cost-sharing pension and OPEB plans issued in GASB 27, *Accounting for Pensions by State and Local Governmental Employers*, and GASB 45, *Accounting and Financial Reporting by Employers for Postemployment Benefits Other Than Pensions*, respectively. The Technical Bulletin was issued to address questions raised and to foster a comparable application of the recognition requirements of those Statements by cost-sharing employers.

In a cost-sharing pension or OPEB, the participating employers pool their benefit obligations and assets. In addition to providing administrative services, the plan assumes from the individual employers the responsibility of funding the promised benefits. In exchange, the individual cost-sharing employers incur liabilities to the plan for the contractually required contributions assessed to them by the plan as their share of the aggregate funding requirements for specified periods.

The Technical Bulletin clarifies that a cost-sharing employer should recognize the contractually required contributions assessed for the employer's financial reporting period as expenditures of that period. They should also recognize any unpaid contributions assessed for that period as liabilities in governmental fund financial statements prepared on the modified accrual basis of accounting. Because the employer's liability for unpaid contractually required contributions for the period is a matured liability, no reconciling item generally will be required between the amount recognized as expenditures and the amount recognized as expense in government-wide financial statements prepared on the accrual basis of accounting.

The Technical Bulletin is effective for financial statements for periods ending after December 15, 2004, with respect to pension transactions (earlier application is encouraged) and should be applied simultaneously with the implementation of GASB 45 with respect to OPEB transactions.

## ¶8017 GASB STATEMENT 44, ECONOMIC CONDITION REPORTING: THE STATISTICAL SECTION

In June 2004, GASB issued Statement 44, *Economic Condition Reporting: The Statistical Section*. This Statement amends the portions of NCGA Statement 1, *Governmental Accounting and Financial Reporting Principles* that guide the preparation of the statistical section. The new requirements enhance and update the statistical section that accompanies a state or local government's basic financial statements by reflecting the significant changes that have taken place in government finance, including the more comprehensive government- wide financial information required by GASB 34. The added requirements are intended to provide financial statement users with information necessary to assess an entity's financial well-being.

The Board expects to improve the understandability and usefulness of statistical section information by addressing problems identified since the NCGA Statement was issued in 1979:

- Statement 1 presented a list of 15 required schedules with no additional explanation of the nature of the information they were to contain. As a result, some governments prepared their statistical sections differently from others, thus, reducing the usability and comparability of the information.
- The requirements were oriented specifically toward general-purpose local governments, leaving other types of governments with little guidance on adapting the requirements to their particular circumstances. The result has been incomplete and inconsistent application of the standards with little thought to the value of the material to the user or to a basis for comparison with like entities.
- Finally and obviously, the 1979 requirements for the statistical section did not cover the new information governmental bodies are required to present in their financial statements under GASB 34.

The statistical section is made up of schedules presenting the required information. In order to clarify that the requirements are applicable to all types of state and local governmental entities that prepare a statistical section, this Statement establishes the objectives of the statistical section and the five categories of information it is expected to contain:

1. Financial trends information.
2. Revenue capacity information.
3. Debt capacity information.
4. Demographic and economic information.
5. Operating information.

Not only does GASB 44 establish new requirements for the statistical section, but it also attempts to clarify and update some of the previous requirements. The NCGA requirements included a schedule of "miscellaneous statistics." The new Statement specifies that a statistical section should include 10-year trends in three types of operating information: government employment levels, operating statistics, and capital asset information.

This Statement also clarifies certain features of previously required information, such as which governmental funds to include in information about trends in changes in fund balances. It also updates the schedules to include requirements for governments to report the many types of debt they now issue in addition to general obligation bonds that were previously reported. In addition, it replaces prior requirements, which were oriented toward general-purpose local governments. These clearer, more meaningful guidelines can be implemented by any type of governmental body.

With a nod to the average citizen and the less sophisticated investor, the understandability and usefulness of statistical section information is further improved by requiring governments to include notes regarding sources, methodologies, and assumptions, and narrative explanations of:

- The objectives of statistical section information.
- Unfamiliar concepts.
- Relationships between information in the statistical section and elsewhere in the financial report.
- Atypical trends and anomalous data that users would not otherwise understand.

The most significant new information added to the statistical section is the government-wide, accrual-based information required by Statement 34. The statistical section will include 10-year trend information about net assets and changes in net assets. The debt information presented in the statistical section will also be more comprehensive as a result of the requirement to include information from the government-wide financial statements and notes.

It is important to note that the statistical section is a required part of a comprehensive annual financial report (CAFR) if the body does, in fact, present the basic financial statements within a CAFR. Although governments are not required to prepare a statistical section, if they do include one in their basic financial statements, it must now meet the requirements of GASB 44.

Statement 44 is effective for periods beginning after June 15, 2005.

## .01 Implementation Guide to Statement 44 on the Statistical Section

In December 2005 GASB published a *Guide to Implementation of GASB Statement 44 on the Statistical Section.* The guide was prepared by GASB staff to assist preparers and auditors of governmental financial statements as they implement the updated and expanded statistical section. The statistical section is the part of a state or local government's comprehensive annual financial report (CAFR) that presents trend information for the last ten years about a government's financial results, major revenue sources, outstanding debt, economic and demographic indicators, and operating activities. The Implementation Guide contains over 120 questions and answers on important aspects of Statement 44.

The questions and answers are accompanied by more than 160 illustrations, including complete sample statistical sections, alternative formats, and optional schedules for nine types of governments—local, county, and state general purpose governments, a school district, a library district, a public university, a water and sewer authority, an airport, and a retirement system. The Guide also includes a glossary, topical index, and the Standards section of Statement 44.

## ¶8019   GASB Issues Statement 43 to Improve Postemployment Benefit Plan Reporting

In May 2004, the GASB issued Statement No. 43, *Financial Reporting for Postemployment Benefit Plans Other Than Pension Plans.* In addition to pensions, many state and local governmental employers provide other postemployment benefits (OPEB) as part of the total compensation offered to attract and retain the services of qualified employees. OPEB includes postemployment healthcare as well as other forms of postemployment benefits (e.g., life insurance) when provided separately from a pension plan.

GASB 43 establishes uniform financial reporting standards for OPEB plans and supersedes the interim guidance included in Statement No. 26, *Financial Reporting for Postemployment Healthcare Plans Administered by Defined Benefit Pension Plans.* The approach in this Statement generally is consistent with the approach adopted in Statement No. 25, *Financial Reporting for Defined Benefit Pension Plans and Note Disclosures for Defined Contribution Plans,* with modifications to reflect differences between pension plans and OPEB plans.

The Statement covers requirements in financial reports for:

- OPEB trust funds included in the financial reports of plan sponsors or employers.
- The stand-alone financial reports of OPEB plans.
- The public employee retirement systems.
- Third parties that administer retirement systems.
- OPEB funds reported by administrators of multiple-employer OPEB plans, in which the fund used to accumulate assets and pay benefits or premiums when they are due is not a trust fund.

The Board believes that GASB 43 provides a framework for transparent financial reporting by governmental entities that have fiduciary responsibility for OPEB plan assets regarding their stewardship of plan assets, the funded status and funding progress of the plan, and employer contributions to the plan. Very explicit requirements have been specified for the different types of plans that require close attention to the details relating to the financial reporting framework and measurement of the various plans.

To further cover this area, the Board has drafted an additional standard: *Accounting and Financial Reporting by Employers for Postemployment Benefits Other Than Pensions*, issued as GASB 45. GASB 45, referred to as "the related Statement," addresses standards for the measurement, recognition, and display of employers' OPEB expense/expenditures and related liabilities (assets); note disclosures; and, if applicable, required supplementary information (RSI).

The measurement and disclosure requirements of the two Statements (GASBs 43 and 45) are related, and disclosure requirements are coordinated to avoid duplication when an OPEB plan is included as a trust or agency fund in an employer's financial report. In addition, reduced disclosures are acceptable for OPEB trust or agency funds when a stand-alone plan financial report is publicly available and contains all of the information required in this Statement.

## .01 Plans Administered as Trusts (or Equivalent Arrangements)

The financial reporting framework for defined benefit OPEB plans that are administered as trusts or equivalent arrangements includes two financial statements and two multiyear schedules that are required to be presented as RSI (required supplementary information) immediately following the notes to the financial statements. The financial statements focus on reporting current financial information about plan net assets held in trust for OPEB and financial activities related to the administration of the trust. The statement of plan net assets provides information about the fair value and composition of plan assets, plan liabilities, and plan net assets held in trust for OPEB. The statement of changes in plan net assets provides information about the year-to-year changes in plan net assets, including additions from employer, member, and other contributions and net investment income and deductions for benefits and refunds paid, or due and payable, and plan administrative expenses.

Required notes to the financial statements include a brief plan description, a summary of significant accounting policies, and information about contributions and legally required reserves. In addition, OPEB plans are required to disclose information about the current funded status of the plan as of the most recent actuarial valuation date, and actuarial methods and assumptions used in the valuation.

The required schedules (RSI) provide actuarially determined historical trend information from a long-term perspective. A minimum of three valuations is required relating to: (1) the funded status of the plan, (2) the progress being made in accumulating sufficient assets to pay benefits when due, and (3) employer contributions to the plan.

The schedule of funding progress reports the actuarial value of assets, the actuarial accrued liability, and the relationship between the two over time. The schedule of employer contributions reports the annual required contributions of the employer(s) (ARC) and the percentage of ARC recognized by the plan as contributions. Notes regarding factors that significantly affect the identification of trends in the amounts reported accompany the required schedules.

## .03 Plans Not Administered as Trusts or Equivalent Arrangements

Multiple-employer defined benefit OPEB plans that are not administered as trusts or equivalent arrangements should be reported as agency funds. Any assets accumulated in excess of liabilities to pay premiums or benefits, or for investment or administrative expenses, should be offset by liabilities to participating employers. Required notes to the financial statements include a brief plan description, a summary of significant accounting policies, and information about contributions.

## .05 Defined Contribution Plans

Defined contribution plans that provide OPEB are required to follow the requirements for financial reporting by fiduciary funds generally, and by component units that are fiduciary in nature, set forth in Statement 34 and the disclosure requirements set forth in paragraph 41 of Statement 25.

## .07 Effective Dates and Transition

The requirements of GASB 43 for OPEB plan reporting are effective one year prior to the effective date of GASB 45 for the employer (single-employer plan) or for the largest participating employer in the plan (multiple-employer plan). The requirements of the related Statement are effective in three phases based on a government's total annual revenues, as defined in that Statement, in the first fiscal year ending after June 15, 1999—the same criterion used to determine a government's phase for implementation of Statement No. 34, *Basic Financial Statements—and Management's Discussion and Analysis—for State and Local Governments:*

1. The sole or largest participating employer is a phase 1 government (those with total annual revenues of $100 million or more). Phase 1 entities are required to implement this Statement in financial statements for periods beginning after December 15, 2005.
2. The sole or largest participating employer is a phase 2 government (total annual revenues of $10 million or more but less than $100 million). They are required to implement this Statement in financial statements for periods beginning after December 15, 2006.
3. The sole or largest participating employer is a phase 3 government (total annual revenues of less than $10 million). This group is required to implement the Statement in financial statements for periods beginning after December 15, 2007.

If comparative financial statements are presented, restatement of the prior-year financial statements is required. Early implementation of this Statement is encouraged.

## ¶8020   GASB 45 Addresses Employer Reporting of OPEB

GASB 45, *Accounting and Financial Reporting by Employers for Post-employment Benefits Other Than Pensions*, adopted in August 2004, addresses how state and local governments should account for and report their costs and obligations related to postemployment healthcare and other nonpension benefits. Collectively, these benefits are commonly referred to as *other postemployment benefits,* or *OPEB.*

The statement generally requires that state and local governmental employers account for and report the annual cost of OPEB and the outstanding obligations and commitments related to OPEB in essentially the same manner as they currently do for pensions. Annual OPEB cost for most employers will be based on actuarially determined amounts that, if paid on an ongoing basis, generally would provide sufficient resources to pay benefits as they come due.

### .01   Application and Implementation of the Provisions

The provisions of Statement 45 may be applied prospectively and do not require governments to fund their OPEB plans. An employer may establish its OPEB liability at zero as of the beginning of the initial year of implementation; however, the unfunded actuarial liability is required to be amortized over future periods.

Statement 45 also establishes disclosure requirements:

1. Information about the plans in which an employer participates.
2. The funding policy followed.
3. Actuarial valuation process and assumptions.
4. For certain employers, the extent to which the plan has been funded over time.

When implemented, GASB 45 will provide those who use government financial reports with:

1. Improved information about the cost of providing postemployment benefits.
2. The commitments that governments have made related to those benefits.
3. The extent to which those commitments have been funded.

Statement 45 is effective in three phases based on a government's total annual revenues. These phases are:

1. The largest employers would be required to implement the requirements of Statement 45 for periods beginning after December 15, 2006.
2. Medium-sized employers have one additional year to implement the standards.
3. The smallest employers have two additional years.

Earlier implementation is encouraged.

## .03   Implementation Guide to Statements 43 and 45

In August 2005, GASB published an *Implementation Guide to Statements 43 and 45 on Postemployment Benefits Other Than Pensions*. The guide was prepared by GASB staff primarily to assist prepares and auditors of governmental financial statements and those that advise them as they implement the GASB's recently issued standards on accounting and reporting for healthcare and other non-pension benefits provided to retirees.

Guidance is provided to over 250 questions on implementation of the new standards. In addition, the guide includes questions and answers and expanded illustrations related to the option provided for certain employers and plans with small plan memberships, allowing them to apply an alternative measurement method to estimate liabilities and expenses associated with their other postemployment benefits (OPEBs).

## ¶8021   GASB 42, ACCOUNTING AND FINANCIAL REPORTING FOR IMPAIRMENT OF CAPITAL ASSETS AND FOR INSURANCE RECOVERIES

In November 2003, the GASB published Statement 42, *Accounting and Financial Reporting for Impairment of Capital Assets and for Insurance*

*Recoveries*, that requires governments to report the effects of capital asset impairment in their financial statements when loss of service utility occurs, rather than as a part of the ongoing depreciation expense or upon disposal of the capital asset. The guidance also enhances comparability of financial statements by requiring all governments to account for insurance recoveries in the same manner.

Because capital assets are long-lived, they are exposed to various risks. Governments are required to evaluate prominent events or changes in circumstances affecting capital assets to determine whether impairment of a capital asset has actually occurred. Events or changes in circumstances that may indicate impairment include:

- Evidence of physical damage
- Enactment or approval of laws or regulations
- Changes in environmental factors
- Technological changes
- Evidence of obsolescence
- Changes in the manner or duration of use of a capital asset
- Construction stoppage.

A capital asset generally should be considered impaired if both the decline in service utility of the capital asset is large in magnitude and the event or change in circumstance is outside the normal life cycle of the capital asset. The statement defines "impairment" as a significant unexpected decline in the service utility of an asset. "Significant" refers to the relative financial impact of the decline in value of the asset. "Unexpected" refers to something that management did not expect when it acquired the asset. The Board has indicated that they are well aware that what is significant for a small entity could have no significance whatsoever for a much larger entity.

Although the FASB has dealt effectively with the problem in the private sector, there has been little, if any, formal guidance on reporting the effects of impairment, and for insurance recoveries on impaired capital assets in the public sector. GASB 42 explicitly and succinctly delineates the how and why of accounting for impaired capital assets:

- Impaired capital assets that will no longer be used by the government should be reported at the lower of carrying value or fair value. Impairment losses on capital assets that will continue to be used by the government should be measured using the method that best reflects the diminished service utility of the capital asset.
- Impairment of capital assets with physical damage generally should be measured using a restoration cost approach, an approach that uses the estimated cost to restore the capital asset to identify the portion of the historical cost of the capital asset that should be written off.

¶8021

- Impairment of capital assets that are affected by enactment or approval of laws or regulations or other changes in environmental factors or are subject to technological changes or obsolescence generally should be measured using a service units approach, an approach that compares the service units provided by the capital asset before and after the impairment event or change in circumstance.

- Impairment of capital assets that are subject to a change in manner or duration of use generally should be measured using a service units approach, as described above, or using deflated depreciated replacement cost, an approach that quantifies the cost of the service currently being provided by the capital asset and converts that cost to historical cost.

- Impaired capital assets that are idle should be disclosed, regardless of whether the impairment is considered permanent or temporary.

Losses are to be reported in accordance with the guidance in pertinent sections of Statement No. 34, *Basic Financial Statements—and Management's Discussion and Analysis—for State and Local Governments*, and Accounting Principles Board Opinion No. 30, *Reporting the Results of Operations—Reporting the Effects of Disposal of a Segment of a Business, and Extraordinary, Unusual and Infrequently Occurring Events and Transactions*.

The Statement includes several new disclosure requirements designed to help the users of financial statements understand the nature and impact of impairment. Disclosures are required for losses and insurance recoveries that are not readily evident on the face of financial reports, and for impaired assets that are idle. If not otherwise apparent from the face of the statements, the description, amount, and financial statement classification of impairment losses should be disclosed in the notes to the financial statements. If evidence is available to demonstrate that the impairment will be temporary, the capital asset should not be written down.

GASB collaborated with the International Federation of Accountants' Public Sector Committee during the research and development of Statement, as that organization has been developing a similar project for an international standard. According to IFAC, the GASB statement and the Exposure Draft issued by the federation's international public sector accounting standard are compatible, but not identical. The principle and approach are compatible; however, the GASB uses a strictly historical cost basis of accounting while IFAC does not.

GASB 42 improves the comparability of financial statements between governments by requiring all governments to account for insurance recoveries in the same manner. An insurance recovery associated with events or changes in circumstances resulting in impairment of a capital asset should be netted with the impairment loss. Restoration or replacement of the capital asset using the insurance recovery is to be reported as a separate transaction. Insurance

¶8021

recoveries are to be disclosed if not apparent from the face of the financial statements. Insurance recoveries for circumstances other than impairment of capital assets are reported in the same manner.

The provisions of this Statement are effective for fiscal periods beginning after December 15, 2004. Earlier application is encouraged.

## ¶8023  TOBACCO SETTLEMENTS TECHNICAL BULLETIN

In May 2003, the FASB issued its Technical Bulletin No. 2004-1, *Tobacco Settlement Recognition and Financial Reporting Entity Issues*, which addresses accounting by state and local governments in connection with settlements made by U.S. tobacco companies.

The Board pointed out that in 1998, the U.S. tobacco industry reached an agreement, known as the Master Settlement Agreement, with state governments releasing tobacco companies from present and future smoking-related claims that had been, or potentially could be, filed by the states. In exchange, the tobacco companies agreed to make annual payments in perpetuity to the states, subject to certain conditions and adjustments.

This technical bulletin clarifies accounting authority that is created to obtain the rights to all or a portion of future tobacco settlement resources as a component unit of the government that created it. In addition, the Technical Bulletin clarifies recognition guidance for these transactions and for payments made to settling governments in line with the Master Settlement Agreement. The Board believes that the guidance provided by the Technical Bulletin is needed to provide users of financial statements comparable information on these significant transactions.

The GASB's proposed Technical Bulletin clarifies accounting guidance on whether a Tobacco Settlement Authority that is created to obtain the rights to all or a portion of future tobacco settlement resources is a component unit of the government that created it. In addition, the proposed Technical Bulletin clarifies asset and revenue recognition guidance for these transactions for the settling governments and the Tobacco Settlement Authorities.

## ¶8025  BUSINESS-LIKE ACCOUNTING COMES TO STATE AND LOCAL GOVERNMENT: GASB 34

The Governmental Accounting Standards Board unanimously adopted the long-awaited comprehensive changes for state and local government financial reporting throughout the country in June 1999. GASB 34, *Basic Financial Statements—and Management's Discussion and Analysis—for State and Local Governments*, provides a new look and focus in reporting public finance in the U.S. The Board's action may have been a response to the oft-voiced complaint, ". . . if only they'd run the government more like a business!" Now "they" must, at least from an accounting standpoint. Many big "businesses" and even more mid-size and small "businesses" — states, cities, counties, towns — adding up to a total of 87,000 in 1999, according to the GASB, are adopting the new measures.

## .01   The GASB Gains Stature

GASB 34 can certainly be considered the most significant change in the history of governmental accounting and should signal the "coming of age" of the GASB. It represents a dramatic shift in the manner and comprehensiveness in which state and local governments present financial information to the public. When fully implemented, it will create new information and will restructure much of the fund information that governments have presented in the past.

The new requirements were developed to make annual reports more comprehensive and easier to understand and use. Now, anyone with an interest (vested or otherwise) in public finance — citizens, the media, bond raters, creditors, investors, legislators, investment bankers and others — will have readily available information about the respective governmental bodies.

Thousands of preparers, auditors, academics, and users of governmental financial statements participated during a decade and a half in the research, consideration, and deliberations that preceded the publication of GASB 34. Members of various task forces began work on this and related projects as early as 1985.

## .03   Provisions of GASB 34

Among the major innovations of Statement 34, governments are required to:

1. Report on the *overall* state of the government's financial health, not just its individual funds as has been the case.
2. Provide the most complete information ever made available about the cost of providing services to the citizens.
3. Prepare an introductory narrative section (the Management's Discussion and Analysis — MD&A) to the basic report analyzing the government's financial performance.
4. Provide enhanced fund reporting.
5. Include information about the government's public infrastructure assets. The Statement explains these assets as long-lived assets that are normally stationary and capable of being preserved longer than most capital assets. Bridges, roads, storm sewers, tunnels, drainage systems, dams, lighting systems, and swimming pools are among those mentioned. (This is certainly the most innovative requirement introduced to governmental financial reporting.)

## .05  Background Information

The GASB's first concepts Statement, *Objectives of Financial Reporting*, issued in 1987, identified what the Board believed were the most important objectives of financial reporting by governments. Some of those objectives reaffirm the importance of information that governmental units have historically included in their annual reports. To cover more of the original objectives, the Board felt it necessary to provide for a much broader range of information.

As a result, Statement 34 is a dual-perspective report requiring governmental bodies to retain much of the information they currently report, but also requiring them to go further in revealing their operations. The first perspective focuses on the traditional funds with some additional information required for major funds. The second perspective is government-wide to provide an entirely new look at a government's financial activities.

The Board feels that adding new material will result in reports that accomplish more of the objectives emphasized in the original concepts Statement.

## .07  The Time for Accountability Is Now

According to the GASB, state and local governments in the U.S. invest approximately $140–$150 billion annually in the construction, improvement, and rehabilitation of capital assets, including infrastructure assets like bridges, highways, and sewers. Since these expenditures represent more than 10% of the monies spent by those governments, it would appear quite natural for them to be accounted for in financial documents readily available to the public.

The majority of this infrastructure investment is financed by borrowing—selling municipal bonds and using the proceeds to pay for construction. (Enter the investor.)

The need for public accountability arises when such sums are spent and when current and future generations are committed to repay such debts. The public should know how much governments spend on infrastructure construction and how much they borrow to finance it. (Enter the taxpayer.)

The public also wants to know if government officials subsequently are caring for the infrastructure they have built with public resources. (Enter the voter.)

Although the need for information about infrastructure should be fairly obvious, the primary instruments for demonstrating fiscal accountability (the government's annual financial statements) have not previously been required to provide this information. The accounting method for preparing state and local government financial statements has focused on short-term financial resources like cash and investments. Infrastructures have been left off the balance sheet and no charge was included on the income statement for the cost of using the infrastructure assets to provide services. Because of the significant share of government spending devoted to capital assets, this has been a major omission. But with the advent of GASB 34, all of that is changing.

## .09   Retention of Fund Accounting

Annual reports currently provide information about funds. Most funds are established by governing bodies (such as state legislatures, city councils, or school boards) to show restrictions on the planned use of resources or to measure, *in the short term*, the revenues and expenditures arising from certain activities. GASB 1 noted that annual reports should allow users to assess a government's accountability by assisting them in determining compliance with finance-related laws, rules, and regulations.

This new Statement requires governments to continue to present financial statements that provide fund information. The focus of these statements has been sharpened to require governments to report information about their major funds, including the general fund. In previous annual reports, fund information was reported in the aggregate by fund type. This often made it difficult for users to assess accountability of any "public servants."

Fund statements continue to measure and report the "operating results" of many funds by measuring cash on hand and other assets that can be easily converted to cash. These statements show the performance, in the short term, of individual funds using the same measures that many governments use when financing their current operations. The Board points out that if a government issues fifteen-year debt to build a school, it does not collect taxes in the first year sufficient to repay the *entire* debt; it levies and collects what is needed to make that year's required payments. On the other hand, when governments charge a fee to users for services—as is done for most water or electric utilities—fund information continues to be based on accrual accounting to ensure all costs of providing services are being measured.

## .11   The All-Important Governmental Budget

Showing budgetary compliance is an important component of government's accountability. (At the national level, with which GASB 34 has no connection, of course, THE BUDGET is undoubtedly the most widely recognized financial document.) At the state and local levels, diverse citizen groups, special interest groups, and individuals participate in the process of establishing the original annual operating budgets of the particular body.

Governments will be required to continue to provide budgetary comparison information in their annual reports. An important change that should certainly make the comparison more meaningful is the requirement to add the government's *original* budget to that comparison. Many governments revise their original budgets during the year for various reasons. Requiring governments to report that original document in addition to their *revised* budget adds a new analytical dimension and should increase the usefulness of the budgetary comparison.

## .12  Required Supplementary Information

To demonstrate whether resources were obtained and used in accordance with the government's legally adopted budget, RSI should include budgetary comparison schedules for the general fund and for each major special revenue fund that has a legally adopted annual budget.
The budgetary comparison schedules should include:

1. The original budget.
2. The final appropriated budgets for the reporting period.
3. Actual inflows, outflows, and balances, stated on the government's budgetary basis.

As pointed out above, the Statement also requires certain disclosures in RSI for governments that use the modified approach for reporting infrastructure assets and data currently required by earlier Statements.

Presumably, the original budget was the "best thought" of the adopting body at the time. Subsequent "revised" budgets could be the result of political pressures or personal preferences. The GASB concedes that budgetary changes are not necessarily undesirable. However, the Board decided that in the interest of accountability to those who were aware of, and may have made decisions based upon the original budget, inclusion of its contents could deter ill-considered changes. The comparison also gives the user a look at any changes that have been made. The Board suggested that this is an additional method of assessing the governmental body's ability to estimate and manage its general resources—without too many detours.

Thus, the original budget, the final appropriated budgets and the actual inflows, outflows and balances stated on the government's budgetary basis are mandated as required supplemental information (RSI) for the general fund and for each major special revenue fund that has a legally adopted annual budget. Rather than include this information in RSI, a government may elect to report these comparisons in a budgetary comparison statement as part of the basic financial statements.

## .13  New Information Is Readily Available

For the first time, government financial managers are required to introduce the financial report by sharing their attitude toward and understanding of the transactions, events, and conditions reflected in the government's report and of the fiscal policies that govern its operations. The required management's discussion and analysis (MD&A) should give the users an easily readable analysis of the government's *financial* performance for the year. Users thus have information they need to help them gauge the government's state of financial health as a result of the year's operations.

Additionally, financial managers themselves are in a better position to provide this analysis because, for the first time, the annual report also includes new government-wide financial statements prepared using accrual accounting for all of the government's activities. Most governmental utilities and private-sector companies use accrual accounting. With GASB 34, state and local governments join most of the rest of the world in using it. The reason for the change is that accrual accounting measures not just current assets and liabilities, but also long-term assets and liabilities (such as capital assets, including infrastructure, and general obligation debt). It also reports all revenues and *all* costs of providing services each year, not just those received or paid in the current year or soon after year-end. After all, government is an ongoing endeavor; officials elected or appointed come and go.

## .15   Users Benefit

These government wide financial statements undoubtedly will help users:

1. Assess the finances of a government in its entirety, including the year's operating results.
2. Determine whether a government's overall financial position improved or deteriorated.
3. Evaluate whether a government's current-year revenues were sufficient to pay for current-year services.
4. Be aware of the cost of providing services to the citizenry.
5. Become cognizant of the way in which a government finances its programs— through user fees and other program revenues, or general tax revenues.
6. Understand the extent to which a government has invested in capital assets, including roads, bridges, and other infrastructure assets.
7. Make better comparisons between governments.

## .17   Required Information and Format

GASB 34 sets financial reporting standards for state and local governments, including states, cities, towns, villages, and special-purpose governments such as school districts and public utilities. It establishes that the basic financial statements and required supplementary information for general purpose governments should consist of:

1. *Management's Discussion and Analysis.* MD&A introduces the basic financial statements and provides an analytical overview of the government's financial activities. Although it is required supplementary information and one would expect to find it in the final portion of the report,

governments are required to present MD&A *before* the basic financial statements. Presumably the belief is that a clearly written—plain English, perhaps—introduction provides a link between the two perspectives (fund and government-wide) to prepare the reader for a better understanding of the financial statements.

2. ***Basic Financial Statements.*** The basic financial statements must include:

   a. *Government-wide financial statements*, consisting of a statement of net assets and a statement of activities. Prepared using the economic resources measurement focus and the accrual basis of accounting, these statements should report all of the assets, liabilities, revenues, expenses, and gains and losses of the government. Each statement should distinguish between the *governmental* and *business-type activities* of the primary government and between the total primary government and the separately presented component units by reporting each in separate columns. (*Fiduciary activities*, with resources not available to finance the government's programs, are not included in the government-wide statements.)

   b. *Fund financial statements* consisting of a series of statements that focus on information about the government's major governmental and enterprise funds, including blended component units. Fund financial statements also should report information about a government's fiduciary funds and component units that are fiduciary in nature.

   c. *Governmental* fund financial statements (including financial data for the general fund and special revenue, capital projects, debt service, and permanent funds). These are to be prepared using the current financial resources measurement focus and the modified accrual basis of accounting.

   d. *Proprietary* fund financial statements (including financial data for enterprise and internal service funds) and *fiduciary* fund financial statements (including financial data for fiduciary funds and similar component units). This group is to be prepared using the economic resources measurement focus and the accrual basis of accounting.

   e. *Notes to the financial statements* are notes and explanations that provide information which is *essential* to a user's understanding of the basic financial statements.

3. ***Required Supplementary Information (RSI).*** In addition to MD&A, this Statement requires *budgetary comparison schedules* to be presented as RSI along with other types of data as required by previous GASB pronouncements. This Statement also requires RSI for governments that use the modified approach for reporting infrastructure assets.

Special-purpose governments engaged in only governmental activities (such as some library districts) or engaged in both governmental and business-type activities (such as some school districts) should normally be reported in the same manner as general purpose governments. Special-purpose governments engaged

¶8025.17

only in business-type activities (such as utilities) should present the financial statements required for enterprise funds, including MD&A and other RSI.

## .19 Content of MD&A

MD&A should provide an objective and easily readable analysis of the government's financial activities based on currently known facts, decisions, or conditions. It should be emphasized that this section is a preparation for the casual reader who is less skilled in reading financial statements as well as for the more experienced "user" to understand fully the implications of the basic report.

MD&A should include:

1. Comparisons of the current year to the prior year based on the government-wide information.
2. An analysis of the government's overall financial position and results of operations to assist users in assessing whether that financial position has improved or deteriorated as a result of the year's activities.
3. An analysis of balances and transactions of individual funds and significant budget variances.
4. A description of capital asset and long-term debt activity during the period.
5. A conclusion with a description of currently known facts, decisions, or conditions that could be expected to have a significant effect upon the financial position or results of operations.

## .21 Government-Wide Financial Statements

The new annual reports contain much more comprehensive financial information. Government-wide statements now display information about the reporting government as a whole, except for its fiduciary activities. These statements include separate columns for the governmental and business-type activities of the primary government and its component parts. Government-wide statements are prepared using the economic resources measurement focus and the accrual basis of accounting. This latter requirement is a fairly dramatic step forward since heretofore governmental accounting followed only the modified-accrual basis. The statement must include a statement of net assets as well as all of the government's activities, not just those that cover costs by charging a fee for services, as currently required.

Governments should report all *capital assets*, including infrastructure assets, in the government-wide statement of net assets and generally should report depreciation expenses in the statement of activities. Infrastructure assets that are part of a network or subsystem of a network are not required to be depreciated as long as the government manages those assets using an asset management system that has certain characteristics and the government can document that the assets are being preserved approximately at (or above) a condition level established and disclosed by the government in the RSI.

To qualify for a qualified asset management system, the government must:

1. Have an up-to-date inventory of the eligible infrastructure assets.
2. Perform condition assessments of the eligible assets and summarize the results using a measurement scale.
3. Estimate each year the annual amounts necessary to maintain and preserve the assets at the established and disclosed condition level. Condition assessments are to be documented so that they can be replicated. The assessments may be performed by the government itself or by contract with an outside source.

The net assets of a government should be reported in three categories— *invested in capital assets net of related debt, restricted, and unrestricted.* Net assets are considered "restricted" when constraints are placed on their use by:

1. External sources such as creditors, grantors or contributors.
2. Laws or regulations of other governments.
3. Legal or constitutional provisions or enabling legislation.

Permanent endowments or permanent fund principal amounts included in restricted net assets should be displayed in two additional components— *expendable and nonexpendable.*

The government-wide *statement of activities* should be presented in a format that reports expenses minus program revenues, to obtain a measurement of "net (expense) revenue" for each of the government's functions. Program expenses should include all direct expenses. General revenues, such as taxes, and special and extraordinary items should be reported separately to arrive at the change in net assets for the period.

*Special and extraordinary items* are both significant transactions or other events, either unusual or infrequent, over which management has control. Both types should be reported separately at the bottom of the statement of activities with special items listed prior to any extraordinary items. These types of transactions or events over which a government does not have control should be disclosed in the notes to financial statements.

## .23   Fund Financial Statements

To report additional and detailed information about the primary government, separate fund financial statements should be presented for each fund category: governmental, proprietary and fiduciary.

1. *Governmental funds* report on the basic activities of the government, including general fund accounts and special revenue, capital projects, debt service, and permanent funds.

2. *Proprietary funds* cover activities that are generally financed and operated like private businesses such as enterprise (fees charged to outside users) and internal service funds.

3. *Fiduciary funds* include pension and other employee benefit and private purpose trust funds that cannot be used to support the government's own programs.

Required *governmental fund* statements are:

1. A balance sheet.
2. A statement of revenues, expenditures, and changes in fund balances.

Required *proprietary fund* statements are:

1. A statement of net assets.
2. A statement of revenues, expenses, and changes in fund net assets.
3. A statement of cash flows.

To allow users to assess the relationship between fund and government-wide financial statements, governments should present a summary reconciliation to the government-wide financial statements at the bottom of the fund financial statements or in an accompanying schedule.

Each of the fund statements should report separate columns for the *general fund* and for *other major governmental and enterprise funds*.

1. *Major funds* are funds in which revenues, expenditures/expenses, assets, or liabilities (excluding extraordinary items) are at least 10% of corresponding totals for all governmental or enterprise funds and at least 5% of the aggregate amount for all governmental and enterprise funds. Any other fund may be reported as a major fund if the government's officials consider it to be particularly important to financial statement users.

2. *Nonmajor funds* should be reported in the aggregate in a separate column.

3. *Internal service funds* also should be reported in the aggregate in a separate column on the proprietary fund statements.

Fund balances for governmental funds should also be segregated into *reserved* and *unreserved* categories. Proprietary fund net assets should be reported in the same categories required for the government-wide financial statements. Proprietary fund statements of net assets should distinguish between current and noncurrent assets and liabilities and should display restricted assets.

Proprietary fund statements of revenues, expenses, and changes in fund net assets should distinguish between operating and nonoperating revenues and expenses. These statements should also report capital contributions, contributions to permanent and term endowments, special and extraordinary items, and transfers separately at the bottom of the statement to arrive at the all-inclusive change in fund net assets. Cash flow statements should be prepared using the direct method.

Separate fiduciary fund statements (including component units that are fiduciary in nature) also should be presented as part of the fund financial statements. Fiduciary funds should be used to report assets that are held in a trustee or agency capacity for others and that cannot be used to support the government's own programs.

Required *fiduciary fund* statements are:

1. A statement of fiduciary net assets.
2. A statement of changes in fiduciary net assets.

Interfund activity includes interfund loans, interfund services provided and used, and interfund transfers. This activity should be reported separately in the fund financial statements and generally should be eliminated in the aggregated government-wide financial statements.

## .27 Interpretation Relating to Modified Accrual Standards

The Board decided this Interpretation was necessary to shore up usage of modified accrual accounting used in governmental fund accounting retained by GASB 34.

Interpretation 6, *Recognition and Measurement of Certain Liabilities and Expenditures in Governmental Fund Financial Statements*, addresses concerns about the interpretation and application of existing *modified accrual standards*. The purpose of modified accrual accounting is to measure flows of current financial resources in governmental *fund financial statements*.

This Interpretation clarifies the application of existing standards for distinguishing between the portions of certain types of liabilities that should be reported as:

1. Governmental fund liabilities and expenditures.
2. General long-term liabilities of the government.

GASB 34, *Basic Financial Statements—and Management's Discussion and Analysis—for State and Local Governments*, carried forward the requirement that governmental fund financial statements be prepared using the existing financial resources measurement focus and the modified accrual basis of accounting. This traditional measurement focus and basis of accounting provides useful information related to a government's fiscal accountability, as part of the new financial reporting model. In addition, the new model provides useful information related to a government's operational accountability, including government-wide financial statements prepared on the *accrual basis* of accounting.

Concerns had been raised, however, about the interpretation and application of *existing modified accrual standards*. These concerns included:

1. Lack of comparability in the application of standards for recognition of certain fund liabilities and expenditures.
2. Perceived subjectivity of some interpretations and applications.
3. Potential circularity of the criteria for recognition of revenues and expenditures.

The objective of Interpretation 6 is to improve the comparability, consistency, and objectivity of financial reporting in governmental fund financial statements by providing a common, internally consistent interpretation of standards in areas where practice differences have occurred or could occur.

The effective date of this Interpretation was designed to coincide with the effective date of Statement 34 for the particular reporting government.

## ¶8026 GUIDES TO GASB 34

After the adoption of Governmental Accounting Standard Board Statement 34, *Basic Financial Statements—and Management's Discussion and Analysis—for State and Local Governments*, the Board was concerned about helping the accountants, auditors, and state and local officials "get it right" in adopting the new accounting model. Because GASB 34 is such a comprehensive overhauling of state and local government financial reporting, those involved needed helpful input to meet the requirements.

Acknowledgement of this is demonstrated by the Board's publication of:

1. An *Implementation Guide* for accountants.
2. Two *What You Should Know* guides.
3. A more sophisticated analyst's guide.
4. Three *Quick Guides*.

## .01  A Guide for Implementing New Financial Statements

For those accountants faced with the daunting task of putting Statement 34 into practice, the GASB issued an *Implementation Guide* to help the preparers and auditors of state and local government financial statements understand and apply the provisions. The provisions are detailed later in this chapter.

The guide includes nearly 300 questions and answers developed by the GASB staff with the assistance of a 36-member advisory group. In addition to the question-and-answer section, the guide also includes:

1. More than 50 illustrative financial statement exhibits.
2. How-to exercises on ten of the more difficult requirements.
3. The complete standards section of Statement 34.
4. A sample financial statement for a state government.
5. A sample financial statement for a municipal government, including a complete illustrative MD&A and selected note disclosures.
6. A sample financial statement for an independent school district.

*In-Depth Instructions for Compliance.*  The "Exercises" section furnishes step-by-step suggestions on how to comply with some of the requirements of Statement 34, including:

1. Calculating composite depreciation rates.
2. Applying group depreciation to infrastructure assets at transition and in subsequent years.
3. Calculating net asset balances for governmental activities.
4. Reporting internal service fund balances and results.
5. Determining major funds.
6. Reconciling fund financial statements to government-wide financial statements.
7. Indirectly determining direct-method cash flows.
8. Estimating historical cost using current replacement cost.
9. Calculating weighted-average age of infrastructure assets at transition.
10. Determining major general infrastructure assets.

## .03  A Guide to Local Government Financial Statements

The guide, *What You Should Know About Your Local Government's Finances: A Guide to Financial Statements*, is the GASB's first publication written specifically for citizens, taxpayers, legislators, researchers, and other people who use government financial information. The specific purpose is to highlight for financial statement users the information contained in the annual reports of local governments.

The guide is intended not only for those accustomed to using financial statements but also as a resource for auditors and government finance officers who need to explain financial statements to elected officials, citizens, and clients.

***Providing a Pathway to Information.*** The guide emphasizes how information in the financial statements of counties, cities, and other local governments may be used to aid in the decision-making process. This publication should be of value to a varied group of people including:

1. Entrepreneurs considering where to locate a business.
2. Investors deciding whether to buy a particular government's bonds.
3. Real estate agents developing information for a "sales pitch."
4. Developers determining a viable location for construction of a shopping mall or condominium complex.

The guide is designed to be suitable for use by a newcomer to the world of government finance as well as by the the long-time government manager or official.

It contains graphics as well as text to enhance its readability and usefulness, such as:

1. Figures and tables, including an annotated set of illustrative financial statements (complete with management's discussion and analysis) for a local government.
2. A running story that makes it easier for the reader to understand the concepts by relating them to personal financial decisions.
3. Boxes and sidebars that:
   a. Explore the issues raised in the text.
   b. Provide more detailed definitions and explanations.
   c. Offer tips on using financial statement information.
4. Easy identification of key terms that are defined in a glossary that accompanies the text.
5. An appendix containing an overview of the basics of governmental accounting and financial reporting.
6. A second appendix that explains some basic financial ratios that may be used to analyze government financial statements.

The guide covers the history-making changes in the preparation of state and local government financial statements brought about by the issuance of GASB Statement 34.

¶8026.03

This guide should give the preparer as well as the user of financial statements an overview of governmental accounting with particular emphasis on GASB 34's new "business" approach to accountability.

## .05 A Guide to a School District's Financial Statements

*What You Should Know About Your School District's Finances: A Guide to Financial Statements* is the second in the series of guides developed specifically for persons who use public sector financial information. It is aimed at educating readers about the information that can be found in the financial statements of public school district.

The school district guide is designed to help anyone from public finance novices to long-time public sector managers understand school district financial statements. For the users of public school financial information (school board members, parents, taxpayers, financial analysts, and others) the guide provides insight into how the information in financial statements can be used as a basis for decision making. The guide is also a handy reference for school district finance officers and certified public accountants seeking to understand the usefulness of the new financial statements and to explain them to citizens, elected officials, and clients.

***Unlocking the Key to a School District's Fiscal Condition.*** Those charged with or interested in the fiscal health of public school systems should be able to use this guide to learn something about how to judge a school district's fiscal health. The GASB believes that this guide serve a double purpose: it may help the public use financial statements to hold school districts accountable; on the other hand, it may assist the districts in demonstrating their accountability to the public they serve.

The guide provides important insights into a broad range of issues, including:

1. The comparative fiscal health of a given school district in relation to previous years, as well as to similarly situated districts.
2. The reasons for a district's improved or degenerating financial condition.
3. What a school district owns and how much it owes.
4. Whether a school system will be able to pay its bills and repay its debts.
5. Looming issues that may affect a district's future finances.

Among the features contained in the school guide, which encompasses the sweeping changes the Board made to state and local government financial statements with the issuance of GASB 34, are:

1. Nearly two dozen figures and tables, including a set of annotated sample financial statements for a fictional school district.

¶8026.05

2. Boxes and sidebars that help to explain and simplify financial statement information.

3. Clear identification of important terms and an extensive glossary.

4. Two appendices that introduce the basics of financial statement analysis and school district accounting.

## .07 A Guide for Financial Analysts

The new publication, *An Analyst's Guide to Government Financial Statements*, introduces the financial statements that governments prepare under GASB Statement 34.

The analyst's guide was developed specifically for regular and intensive users of public sector financial statements, including:

1. Mutual fund analysts.

2. Rating agencies.

3. Institutional investors.

4. Bond insurers.

5. Research organizations.

6. Taxpayer groups.

*The Greater Depth of Information in the New Statements.* This historic Standard was actually developed to provide analysts as well as other financial statement users with the more comprehensive and comprehensible data they require to assess government finances. The Board's goal in developing this guide is to help analysts more effectively assimilate the information from the new and expanded governmental financial statements into their analytical and decision-making processes.

For years the complaint about any given level of government has been, "Why can't they run it more like a business?" With the Statement, *Basic Financial Statements—and Management's Discussion and Analysis—for State and Local Governments*, establishing new requirements for state and local governments, this may happen. These requirements appear to be headed in the direction of a more businesslike approach, at least from an accountant's point of view. Governmental units must now prepare their financial reports according to GAAP. The new rules substantially change the appearance and content of government financial statements, which had previously been solely involved with fund accounts.

*An Analyst's Guide to Government Financial Statements* is written in an easy-to-understand style, but is more comprehensive in coverage than the two *What You Should Know* guides. It presents nearly 80 illustrations of financial statements for states, localities, school districts, public colleges and universities, and other special-purpose types of governments.

## ¶8027   GASB 35 COMES TO PUBLIC COLLEGES AND UNIVERSITIES

After an earlier decision by the Governmental Accounting Standards Board not to require a separate financial reporting model for public colleges and universities in order to make it easier for state and local governments to include these institutions in their financial statements, the GASB issued a proposal in July, 1999 to provide accounting and financial reporting guidance for public colleges and universities in their separately issued financial statements. That proposal became GASB 35.

This Statement amends GASB 34, *Basic Financial Statements—and Management's Discussion and Analysis—for State and Local Governments*, to include public colleges and universities within its guidance for general purpose external financial reporting.

It is anticipated that this step will make it easier to compare public institutions and their private counterparts. Such a step had been requested by GASB constituents.

Under the new guidance, public colleges and universities can report their finances as public institutions:

1. Engaged only in business-type activities.
2. Engaged only in governmental activities.
3. Engaged in both governmental and business-type activities.

A public institution is also required to include the following in separately issued financial reports, regardless of whether or not they are legally separate entities:

1. Management's discussion and analysis (MD&A).
2. Basic financial statements, as appropriate for the category of special-purpose government reporting.
3. Notes to the financial statements.
4. Required supplementary information other than MD&A.

The requirements of the Statement are effective in three phases for public institutions that are not part of another reporting entity, beginning with fiscal years beginning after June 15, 2001. All public institutions that are part of (or are component units of) a primary government were required to implement this standard at least by the same time as its primary government, regardless of the phase-in guidance contained in GASB 34.

Public colleges and universities are required to report infrastructure assets as follows:

1.  Public institutions that are not part of another primary government and report as either special-purpose governments engaged only in governmental activities or engaged in both governmental and business-type activities must report infrastructure in accordance with the phase-in guidance of GASB 34 beginning with fiscal years ending after June 15, 2005.

2.  Public institutions that report as special-purpose governments engaged only in business-type activities are required to report infrastructure upon implementation, without regard to the phase-in periods included in Statement 34.

## ¶8029   GASB 33 ON NONEXCHANGE TRANSACTIONS

Late in 1998, the Governmental Accounting Standards Board issued GASB Statement 33, *Accounting and Financial Reporting for Nonexchange Transactions*, which specifies the accounting and reporting for nonexchange transactions involving financial or capital resources. These transactions include most taxes, grants, and donations. The Statement became effective for periods beginning after June 15, 2000.

In a nonexchange transaction, the government gives or receives value without directly receiving or giving equal value in exchange. When there isn't an exchange, it can be difficult to decide *when* a transaction should be recognized in the financial statements. Statement 33 attempts to simplify the problem.

The timing of financial statement recognition will depend on the nature of the nonexchange transaction as well as the basis of accounting (accrual or modified accrual). The GASB has identified four classes of nonexchange transactions:

1.  Derived tax revenues, such as sales and income taxes. These will be recognized when the underlying exchange on which the government imposes the tax actually occurs. An example would be when a customer buys a washing machine or refrigerator that is subject to a sales tax.

2.  Imposed nonexchange revenues, such as property taxes and fines. These are to be recognized as assets when the government has an enforceable legal claim. For example, property taxes receivable generally will be recognized on the lien date, even though a lien may not be formally placed on the property at that date. Revenues will be recognized in the period in which the resources are required to be used.

3.  Government-mandated nonexchange transactions, such as federal or state programs that state or local governments are required to provide. These will be recognized when all eligibility requirements are met, as specified in Statement 33. For example, when a recipient is required to incur allowable

costs before reimbursement is made, the incurring of allowable costs is an eligibility requirement.

4. Voluntary nonexchange transactions, such as most grants, appropriations, donations, and endowments. These will also be recognized when the Statement 33 eligibility requirements are met. These requirements include contingencies. For example, to qualify for a grant, a recipient may be required to provide matching resources.

For revenue recognition on the modified accrual basis, resources also should be "available," as defined in existing standards. Statement 33 goes hand in hand with the Board's standards on the governmental and the college and university financial reporting models under GASB 34. The Board feels that GASB 33 will improve consistency in how governments report nonexchange transactions.

## ¶8031  GASB 41 PROVIDES GUIDANCE ON BUDGETARY COMPARISONS

The GASB issued Statement 41, *Budgetary Comparison Schedule—Perspective Differences*, in May 2003 to clarify existing guidance on budgetary comparisons in GASB 34, *Basic Financial Statements—and Management's Discussion and Analysis—for State and Local Governments*. This amendment applies to governments whose budgetary structures (for example, certain program-based budgets) prevent them from presenting budgetary comparison information for their general funds and major special revenue funds, as currently required by GASB 34. Under GASB 41, these governments will present their budgetary comparison schedules as required supplementary information (RSI) based on the fund, organization, or program structure that that particular government uses for its legally adopted budget. Generally, governments should present budgetary comparisons for the activities that are reported in the general fund and each major special revenue fund.

The requirements were effective for financial statements for periods beginning after June 15, 2002. Unless otherwise specified, pronouncements of the GASB apply to financial reports of all state and local governmental entities, including general-purpose governments; public benefit corporations and authorities; public employee retirement systems; public utilities, hospitals, and other health care providers; and colleges and universities.

## ¶8033  GASB 40, *DEPOSIT AND INVESTMENT RISK DISCLOSURES—AN AMENDMENT OF GASB STATEMENT NO. 3*

In March 2003, the GASB issued GASB 40, *Deposit and Investment Risk Disclosures—an Amendment of GASB Statement No. 3*, to consider the deposits and investments of state and local governments that are exposed to risks that have the potential to result in losses. This Statement addresses common deposit and investment risks related to credit risk, concentration of credit risk, interest rate risk, and foreign currency risk. As an element of interest rate risk, this Statement requires certain disclosures of investments that have fair values that are highly sensitive to changes in interest rates. Deposit and investment policies related to the risks identified in this Statement should also be disclosed.

The Board reconsidered the disclosures required by GASB 3, *Deposits with Financial Institutions, Investments (including Repurchase Agreements), and Reverse Repurchase Agreements.* Portions of that Statement are modified or eliminated. The custodial credit risk disclosures of GASB 3 are modified to limit required disclosures to:

- Deposits that are not covered by depository insurance and are:
  — Uncollateralized.
  — Collateralized with securities held by the pledging financial institution.
  — Collateralized with securities held by the pledging financial institution's trust department or agent but not in the depositor-government's name.
- Uninsured investment securities that are not registered in the name of the government and are held by either:
  — The counterparty.
  — The counterparty's trust department or agent but not in the government's name.

GASB 3 disclosures generally referred to as category 1 and 2 deposits and investments are eliminated. However, GASB 40 does not change the required disclosure of authorized investments or the requirements for reporting certain repurchase agreements and reverse repurchase agreements, and it maintains, with modification, the level-of-detail disclosure requirements of GASB 3.

The provisions of GASB 40 are effective for financial statements for periods beginning after June 15, 2004. Earlier application is encouraged.

## .01 How the Changes in This Statement Improve Financial Reporting

Deposit and investment resources often represent significant assets of governmental, proprietary, and fiduciary funds. These resources are necessary for the delivery of governmental services and programs or to carry out fiduciary responsibilities. GASB 40 is designed to inform financial statement users about deposit and investment risks that could affect a government's ability to provide services and meet its obligations as they become due. The Board believes that there are risks inherent in all deposits and investments, and it believes that the disclosures required by this Statement provide users of governmental financial statements with information to assess common risks inherent in deposit and investment transactions.

The Board adopted fair value accounting for most investments in GASB 31, *Accounting and Financial Reporting for Certain Investments and for External Investment Pools*. Fair value portrays the market's estimate of the net future cash flows of investments, discounted to reflect both time value and risk. In order to understand the measurement of investments at fair value, the timing of cash flows (including investment time horizons) and investment risks need to be communicated.

In the Exposure Draft (ED), the Board had pointed out that all investments carry some form of risk and the public should be made aware of any risks in financial statements. Deposit and investment resources often represent the largest assets of governmental and fiduciary funds. Proprietary funds also report significant deposit and investment balances. These resources are critical to delivering governmental services and programs.

Financial statement disclosures would cover deposit and investment risks. Among these would be:

- Credit risk disclosures, including credit quality information issued by rating agencies.
- Interest rate disclosures, including investment maturity information, such as weighted average maturities or specification identification of the securities.
- For investments that are highly sensitive to changes in interest rates (e.g., inverse floaters, enhanced variable-rate investments, and certain asset-backed securities), disclosures that indicate the basis for their sensitivity.
- Disclosure of foreign investment disclosures would indicate the foreign investment's denomination.
- Deposit and investment policies related to risks.

GASB 40 results from the Board's formal reviews of its existing standards. These reviews—part of the Board's strategic plan—are designed to evaluate the continuing usefulness of current requirements. The reduction of existing custodial credit risk disclosures follows from federal banking reforms adopted since the release of GASB 3.

## ¶8035  TECHNICAL BULLETIN TO IMPROVE DISCLOSURES ABOUT DERIVATIVES

In an effort to improve disclosures about the risks associated with derivative contracts, the GASB issued accounting guidance in June 2003 that provides more consistent and comprehensive reporting by state and local governments. The Technical Bulletin, *Disclosure Requirements for Derivatives Not Presented at Fair Value on the Statement of Net Assets*, is designed to increase the public's understanding of the significance of derivatives to a government's net assets and to provide key information about the potential effects on future cash flows. It will also provide the users of financial statements with better information about the risks assumed in derivative contracts. Derivatives are often used by governments as a means to potentially reduce borrowing costs. Although derivatives may support financing needs, the lower costs come with additional risks. The objectives and terms of derivative contracts, their risk, and the fair value of the contracts had generally not been specified in financial reports.

This Technical Bulletin is designed to increase the public's understanding of the significance of derivatives to a government's financial position and provide key information about their potential effects on future cash flows.

GASB pointed out that even estimating the notional amounts of outstanding derivatives in this market based on information that has been readily available is difficult. Estimates of notional value range from $200 billion to $400 billion. Under this guidance, state and local governments are *required* to disclose such information.

One GASB official agreed that GASB's own research indicated that it often has been difficult to understand how governments have been accounting for derivatives. These disclosures should clear up the mystery surrounding the transactions. It should now be possible to see what a government has done, why it has done it, the fair value of the derivative, and the risks that have been assumed. Governments will be required to disclose information in their financial statements about risks that relate to credit, interest rates, basis, termination dates, rollovers, and market access.

Whereas state and local governments use an array of increasingly complex derivative instruments to manage debt and investments, they may, at the same time, be assuming significant risks. Governments are expected to communicate those risks to financial statement users and the public. The proposed Technical Bulletin's purpose is to clarify existing accounting guidance so that more consistent disclosures can be made across all governments.

The GASB is aware that the market for derivative instruments has expanded for state and local governments, which find themselves in a dismal budgetary environment. Some derivative contracts may pose substantial risks; therefore, the Board's aim is to help officials better explain those risks in their financial statements.

This Technical Bulletin requires that governments disclose the derivative's:

- Objectives,
- Terms,

- Fair value, and
- Risks.

The proposed accounting guidance requires the governments to disclose in their financial statements what is faced in terms of:

- Credit risk,
- Interest rate risk,
- Basis risk,
- Termination risk,
- Rollover risk, and
- Market access risk.

## ¶8036  PROPOSAL TO PROVIDE UNDERSTANDING OF DERIVATIVE RISK

The GASB is still working to provide more and better information about the use of derivatives with a Preliminary Views document. In April 2006, the GASB voted unanimously to issue a PV, *Accounting and Financial Reporting for Derivatives* to improve the accounting and financial reporting of derivatives by state and local governments.

While derivatives were possibly the number one buzzword of the FASB and the financial sector for most of the '90s, there has also been a substantial increase in both the number and dollar amounts of governmental derivative contracts. The GASB believes the public needs more and better information about the risks these transactions pose and the impact they can have upon government financial positions.

The proposal requires that the fair value of derivatives be reported in the financial statements, as well as the change in that fair value. If, however, a derivative is effectively hedging (reducing) the risk it was created to address, then the annual changes in the derivative's fair value is deferred and reported in a government's balance sheet. In addition, governments must disclose additional information about their derivatives in the notes to the financial statements.

The GASB believes that the public needs to understand the nature of these transactions to enable them to evaluate the inherent risks better. After all, it was Orange County California's misuse of derivatives that brought to widespread attention the danger that derivatives potentially pose to the financial health of governments. The PV is intended to make the reporting of derivatives and disclosure of related risks more transparent.

The Preliminary Views document is accompanied by a plain-language supplement that summarizes the standards for financial statement users and others without an accounting background.

## ¶8037 FINANCIAL REPORTING GUIDANCE FOR FUND-RAISING FOUNDATIONS AND SIMILAR ORGANIZATIONS UNDER GASB 39

Statement 39, *Determining Whether Certain Organizations Are Component Units, an Amendment of GASB Statement 14*, clarifies existing accounting guidance and provides greater consistency in accounting for organizations that are closely related to a primary government. The standard provides criteria for determining whether certain organizations, such as not-for-profit foundations related to public universities and school districts, should be reported as component units based on the nature and significance of their relationship to a state or local government.

Under this ruling, state and local governments that have qualifying fund-raising foundations would be required to include, through discrete presentations, the financial activities of those foundations in their financial statements. Previously, there was no consistency in dealing with their financial matters:

1. Some entities had included the balances and transactions of their related fund-raising organizations in their financial statements.
2. Others disclosed limited information in the notes.
3. Still others provided no information at all.

GASB 39 should bring a greater level of comparability to state and local financial reporting. It amends Statement 14 to provide additional guidance to determine whether certain organizations for which the primary government is not financially accountable should be reported as component units based on the nature and significance of their relationship with a primary government.

The standard sets forth criteria on which a government is required to provide a discrete presentation that includes financial information about its own activities as well as those of the affiliated organization.

Generally, a legally separate, tax-exempt, fund-raising organization whose primary purpose is to raise or hold significant resources for the benefit of a specific governmental unit should be included as a component unit of that governmental unit's financial reporting entity.

## ¶8039 GASB 38, *CERTAIN FINANCIAL STATEMENT NOTE DISCLOSURES*

Statement 38 modifies, adds, and deletes various note disclosure requirements. The requirements cover such areas as:

1. Revenue recognition policies.
2. Actions taken in response to legal violations.
3. Debt service requirements.

4. Variable-rate debt.
5. Receivable and payable balances.
6. Interfund transfers and balances.
7. Short-term debt.

The new requirements are an additional attempt to address the needs of users of financial statements as determined through ongoing Board research. In discussing the benefits to users, the Board considered that with respect to interfund transfers, users of financial statements will, for the first time, be able to trace transfers from the source fund to the receiving fund and to understand why the government uses transfers.

Now users will also be able to see the purpose and extent of the use of short-term debt, which is especially important for debt issued and redeemed within the government's fiscal year.

Statement 38 is the result of the GASB's intention to ensure the continuing effectiveness of existing standards. The Board reaffirmed that most note disclosure requirements are still relevant.

## ¶8041  GASB 37, BASIC FINANCIAL STATEMENTS—AND MANAGEMENT'S DISCUSSION AND ANALYSIS—FOR STATE AND LOCAL GOVERNMENTS: OMNIBUS—AN AMENDMENT OF GASB STATEMENTS 21 AND 34

GASB 37, which was adopted in June 2001, amends GASB 21, *Accounting for Escheat Property*, and GASB 34, *Basic Financial Statements—and Management's Discussion and Analysis—for State and Local Governments*.

The amendments to Statement 21 are necessary because of the changes to the fiduciary fund structure required by Statement 34. Generally, escheat property that was previously reported in an *expendable trust fund* should now be reported in a *private-purpose trust fund* under Statement 34. Statement 37 explains the effects of that change.

The amendments to GASB 34 either:

1. Clarify certain provisions that, in retrospect, may not be sufficiently clear for consistent application, or
2. Modify other provisions that the Board believes may have unintended consequences in some circumstances.

The provisions aimed at *clarifying* previous provisions are not new but may have been unclear or confusing for the user. They include:

1. *Management's Discussion and Analysis (MD&A) requirements*—Governments should confine the topics discussed in MD&A to those listed

in Statement 34 rather than consider those topics as "minimum requirements."

2. *Modified approach*—Adopting the modified approach for infrastructure assets that have previously been depreciated is considered a change in an *accounting estimate*. The effect of the change is accounted for prospectively rather than as a restatement of prior periods.

3. *Program revenue classifications*—Fines and forfeitures should be included in the broad *charges for services* category. Also, additional guidance is provided to aid in determining to which function certain program revenues pertain.

4. *Major fund criteria*—Major fund reporting requirements apply to a governmental or enterprise fund if the *same* element (for example, revenues) exceeds *both* the 10 percent *and* 5 percent criteria.

The provisions, which are modifications of the requirements of Statement 34, include:

1. Eliminating the requirement to capitalize construction-period interest for governmental activities.

2. Changing the minimum level of detail required for business-type activities in the statement of activities from *segments* to *different identifiable activities*.

The Board believed that GASB 37 would help governments implement Statement 34 and improve the usefulness of state and local governments' financial statements under the far-reaching new reporting model. Statement 38 was implemented to provide users with new information and eliminate some disclosures that the Board found were no longer needed.

The provisions of Statement 37 were to be simultaneously implemented with Statement 34. For governments that had already implemented GASB 34 prior to the issuance of GASB 37, the requirements were effective for financial statements for periods beginning after June 15, 2000.

## ¶8043   GASB 36 ON SYMMETRY BETWEEN RECIPIENTS AND PROVIDERS IN ACCOUNTING FOR CERTAIN SHARED REVENUES

GASB 36 amends GASB 33, *Accounting and Financial Reporting for Non-exchange Transactions*, which required recipients of shared derived tax or imposed nonexchange revenue to account for it differently from the provider government. This practice could have resulted in the two governments recognizing the sharing at different times.

The Statement provides symmetrical accounting treatment for both the giver and receiver of the shared revenue. Statement 36 eliminates the timing difference by requiring recipients to account for the sharing in the same way as provider governments.

## ¶8045 COMPREHENSIVE IMPLEMENTATION GUIDE, 2006-2007

As a part of its mission to develop literature that guides and educates the public about its standards, the GASB has published the 2006–2007 edition of its *Comprehensive Implementation Guide*. This guide consolidates and updates previously issued guides to individual standards. It also provides current guidance on standards for which no stand-alone guides have been published. The 2006–2007 edition includes for the first time the freestanding *Implementation Guide to Statement 44 on the Statistical Section and the Implementation Guide to Statements 43 and 45 on Other Postemployment Benefits (OPEB)*.

This guide has been reorganized to better accommodate the addition of new questions and employs a new numbering system designed to make it easier to follow changes from year to year, according to the GASB. It provides the answers to new questions about OPEB and a variety of other topics, including:

- Compensated absences.
- The modified approach for reporting infrastructure assets.
- Asset impairment.
- Reporting net assets.
- Termination benefits.

In addition, the guide revises existing questions and deletes obsolete questions. It also features a new chapter that brings together questions on pronouncements not covered in other chapters that are devoted to a particular pronouncement or subject.

## ¶8047 GASB PUBLISHES ADDITION TO USER GUIDE SERIES

In June 2005, the GASB published a new volume in its User Guide Series. Written for nonaccountants, *What Else You Should Know about a Government's Finances: A Guide to Notes to the Financial Statements and Supporting Information* is a plain-language introduction to the information that accompanies a state or local government's annual financial statements.

### .01    Subjects Covered in Citizen's Guide to Understanding a Government's Financial Statement

This guide comprehensively discusses all of the notes to the financial statements required by generally accepted accounting principles. The guide also covers required supplementary information, such as MD & A, and infrastructure condition reporting, as well as the information presented in a comprehensive annual financial report, such as combining statements and the recently revised statistical section.

*What Else You Should Know about a Government's Finances* includes chapters devoted to notes and supporting information regarding:

1. Assets, such as receivables, investments, and infrastructure.
2. Liabilities, such as long-term debt, derivatives, pensions, and other postemployment benefits.
3. Revenues, expenses, and expenditures.
4. Net assets and fund balances.
5. Specific parts of a government, such as component units and transfers between funds.
6. Other issues, such as subsequent events and significant violations.

Like the GASB's other User Guides, this guide focuses on the value of the information found in a government's audited financial report and how it can be used to understand and assess the financial health of a government. The guide contains more than 80 annotated illustrations, a detailed alphabetical index, and an exhaustive glossary.

### ¶8049    "CLIFFIES" FOR GOVERNMENT FINANCIAL STATEMENTS

The GASB has also published three *Quick Guides*—one each for state governments, local governments, and school districts. In an attempt to reach more of its constituents, the GASB has issued this series of "pocket" guides to assist users in understanding the financial statements that state and local governments prepare once they have fully implemented GASB Statement 34. The *Quick Guides* provide a summarized overview of the thorough introduction to government financial statements presented in the GASB's first three user guides.

They provide "need-to-know" information in brief and easy-to-read style delineating the major features of the new financial statements. They also highlight the ways in which government financial statement information may be useful to decision makers such as legislators, taxpayers, citizen groups, parents, public employees, financial analysts-even interested, involved citizens and voters.

The *Quick Guides* are directed toward school board members, legislators, and other elected officials who need a short and understandable explanation of government financial statements-and don't have the time or inclination for an in-depth indoctrination.

They are the perfect companion to the larger user guides, which are useful resources to government finance officers, accountants, and auditors who need to understand how financial statement information is used and are looking for help in explaining the new financial statements to their elected officials or clients.

# Chapter 9

# Governmental Fund Accounting

## CONTENTS

## ¶9000 OVERVIEW

The Government Accounting Board Statement 34, *Basic Financial Statements—and Management's Discussion and Analysis—for State and Local Governments* establishes new financial reporting requirements for state and local governments. However, these entities are to continue to present financial statements that provide fund information. The focus of these fund statements has been sharpened to require governments to report information about their major funds, including the general fund. In current annual reports, fund information is reported in the aggregate by fund type. This has often made it difficult for users to assess accountability.

Fund statements will continue to measure and report the "operating results" of many funds by measuring cash on hand and other assets that can easily be converted to cash. These statements show the performance, in the short-term, of individual funds using the same measures that governments use when financing their current operations.

## ¶9001    DIFFERENCES BETWEEN GOVERNMENTAL AND COMMERCIAL ACCOUNTING

While both types of entities use double-entry bookkeeping procedures and either cash or accrual methods, and both prepare balance sheets and operating statements, there are many differences between commercial and governmental systems.

Governmental accounting is associated with: (1) an absence of a profit; (2) compliance with statutory and/or legal requirements; (3) a fundamental difference in the treatment of net worth. Commercial accounting provides accounting for preferred and common stock and retained earnings, with a paid-in capital account where appropriate. Governmental accounting treats "net worth" under account classifications *Reserve for Encumbrances or Unappropriated Surplus;* (4) characteristically, government accounts will include a *Reserve for Contingencies* account since the projected (budgeted) reserve may not materialize as the accounting year progresses.

Governmental Accounting, specifically accounting for state and local governments, is in a transitional stage. These entities have been adding more "business-like" requirements to their financial reporting. At the same time, the government accountant will still need to draw upon his or her knowledge of fund accounting.

## .01    GASB Issues White Paper

In March 2006, the GASB released a white paper emphasizing this point that those who are interested in the financial performance of state and local governments have substantially different information needs than those who follow the financial performance of for-profit entities.

As mentioned above, these different and diverse needs result from basic differences between these types of entities: governments and businesses.

- The primary purpose of governments is to enhance or maintain the well-being of citizens by providing services in accordance with public policy goals.
- In contrast, for-profit business enterprises focus primarily on wealth creation, interacting principally with those segments of society that fulfill their mission of generating a financial return on investment for shareholders.

The white paper cites several other crucial differences that generate user demand for unique information:

- Governments serve a broader group of stakeholders, including taxpayers, citizens, elected representatives, oversight groups, bondholders, and others in the financial community.
- Most government revenues are raised through involuntary taxes rather than a willing exchange of comparable value between two parties in a typical business transaction.
- Monitoring actual compliance with budgeted public policy priorities is central to government public accountability reporting.
- Governments exist longer than for-profit businesses and are not typically subject to bankruptcy and dissolution.

The paper points out that the significant differences, and the important role that state and local governments play in the U.S. economy, are the primary reasons that separate accounting and financial reporting standards for governments are needed. According to Federal data presented in this white paper:

- Revenue collected by state and local governments totaled $1.8 trillion or 20 percent of the 2002 U.S. gross domestic product.

The state and local governments account for 12 percent of total U.S. employment.

## ¶9002 GASB INVITES PUBLIC COMMENT ON ACCOUNTING ISSUES RELATED TO FUND BALANCE REPORTING AND GOVERNMENTAL FUND TYPE DEFINITIONS

In October 2006, as Invitation to Comment (ITC) was issued by the GASB seeking constituent comments and perspectives on issues currently being addressed in the Board's project on fund balance reporting and governmental fund type definitions.

Fund balance is the difference between assets and liabilities in governmental funds. It is among the most universally used metrics in state and local government external financial reports. Ideally, this information allows financial statement users to identify resources that are available to finance the governmental entities' activities, programs, or projects relating to:

- Making debt service payments.
- Reducing taxes.

- Beginning a new service.
- Expanding an existing service.

However, GASB research has discovered that there may be several issues that could significantly diminish the usefulness of the fund balance information being reported to the users of governmental financial statements, including:

- The actions taken to set aside fund balance for specific purposes vary from government to government making it difficult to assess the likelihood that resources will actually be used for the purposes that are reported.
- Some governments transfer resources from the general fund to other governmental funds without an intention to use the resources in the receiving fund—a practice that may mislead financial statement users regarding the amount of available resources and the purposes for which those resources can be used.
- Some governments report fund balance as reserved for specific purposes when, in fact, it should be unreserved, perhaps because the current standards are not sufficiently clear.
- Because the reporting of designations of unreserved fund balance is optional, it is difficult to compare—if not impossible, to compare information reported by governments that designate fund balance with those that do not.

As a part of the search for input on fund accounting, the GASB included a list of 14 questions in this ITC for interested users to answer and e-mail or mail to the Board.

## ¶9003  Legal Provisions

In governmental accounting, legal provisions relate to budgeting and to the disposition of assets. The preparation and implementation of the projected budget and related accounting procedures are governed by certain legal provisions expressed specifically in legislation (statutory) or restrictions imposed by a nonlegislative (regulatory) authority. The accounting system must have built-in safeguards that expenditures will comply with both types of restrictions. Governmental accounting must also include revenue and expense data which facilitates the preparation of budgets for the future.

As will be seen, certain *funds* are considered less flexible in their accounting treatment. The least flexible type is the one created by a state constitution or by legislation, because the accountant must keep the books as determined by law. The most flexible is the type established by executive authority, since such authority can make changes in a fund without prior legislative approval.

In fund accounting *estimated and actual revenues* and *expenditures* are compared on an ongoing basis, e.g., reviewed by the governing bodies approving the initial budget and the appropriation for the fund. Comparisons reveal the extent to which the "actuals" are in line with the estimates (the budget) and will show significant deviations, if any, during the fiscal year of actual revenues and expenditures from the budgeted amounts.

*Assets and liabilities* incurred by a fund are similar to those in a commercial enterprise. Asset accounts, for example, will include cash, accounts receivable, etc., while liabilities will show accounts or vouchers payable, notes payable, bonds payable, etc.

A separate *general ledger* must be maintained for each fund related to the governmental entity's budget. Each general ledger has a self-balancing account that brings the revenue and appropriation accounts into balance at the end of the fiscal year.

As a general rule independent auditors will insist on the entity using an *accrual* system, unless the financial authorities for that specific fund can demonstrate that the financial reports would not *materially* differ if a cash accounting system is used.

## ¶9005    Is Governmental Accounting Complex? No!

While fund accounting is perceived to be complicated, it is not any more difficult than commercial accounting. Why then is it thought to be complicated? The answer is for the same reason that we initially think any totally new and unfamiliar discipline appears difficult—the *terminology* is the culprit. It is well-settled that learning the terminology of a new discipline is 50% or more of the learning battle of anything new that one endeavors to learn. Governmental accounting terminology is indeed entirely different from commercial accounting terminology; it has a vocabulary that is totally unique to governmental accounting; no governmental accounting term can be found in any other system of accounting, whether commercial, industrial, or otherwise.

The first step, then, to acquire an understanding of fund accounting procedures is to review and become familiar with the terms. The following list of definitions will enable the user to easily apply the accounting methods for the various types of funds which are covered in the material following the definitions.

## ¶9007    Terminology

Here is a listing of definitions applicable only to fund accounting:

**Abatement.** Cancellation of amounts levied or of charges made for services.

**Accrued Assets.** Assets arising from revenues earned but not yet due.

**Accrued Expenses.** Expenses resulting in liabilities which are either due or are not payable until some future time.

**Accrued Revenues.** Levies made or other revenue earned and not collected.

**Allotment Ledger.** A subsidiary ledger which contains an account for each allotment showing the amount allotted, expenditures, encumbrances, the net balance, and other related information.

**Appropriation.** An authorization granted by the legislative body to make expenditures and to incur obligations for specific purposes.

**Appropriation Expenditure.** An expenditure chargeable to an appropriation.

**Appropriation Ledger.** A subsidiary ledger containing an account with each appropriation.

**Assessment.** The process of making an official valuation of property for the purpose of taxation.

**Authority Bonds.** Bonds payable from the revenues of a specific public authority.

**Betterment.** An addition or change made in a fixed asset which prolongs its life or increases its efficiency.

**Budget.** A plan of financial operation embodying an estimate of proposed expenditures for a given period or purpose, and the proposed means of financing them.

**Budgetary Accounts.** The accounts necessary to reflect budget operations and condition, such as estimated revenues, appropriations, and encumbrances.

**Capital Budget.** An improvement program and the methods for the financing.

**Clearing Account.** An account used to accumulate total charges or credits for the purpose of distributing them among the accounts to which they are allocable, or for the purpose of transferring the net difference to the proper account.

**Current Special Assessment.** Assessments levied and due during the current fiscal period.

**Current Taxes.** Taxes levied and becoming due during the current fiscal period—from the time the amount of the tax levy is first established, to the date on which a penalty for nonpayment is attached.

**Debt Limit.** The maximum amount of gross or net debt legally permitted.

**Debt Service Requirement.** The amount of money necessary periodically to pay the interest on the outstanding debt and the principal of maturing bonded debt not payable from a sinking fund.

¶9007

**Deficit.** The excess of the liabilities of a fund over its assets.

**Delinquent Taxes.** Taxes remaining unpaid on and after the date on which a penalty for nonpayment is attached.

**Direct Debt.** The debt which a governmental unit has incurred in its own name, or assumed through the annexation of territory.

**Encumbrances.** Obligations in the form of purchase orders, contracts, or salary commitments which are chargeable to an appropriation, and for which a part of the appropriation is reserved.

**Endowment Fund.** A fund whose principal must be maintained inviolate, but whose income may be expended.

**Expendable Fund.** A fund whose resources, including both principal and earnings, may be expended.

**Expenditures.** If the fund accounts are kept on the accrual basis, expenditures are the total charges incurred, whether paid or unpaid, including expenses, provision for retirement of debt not reported as a liability of the fund from which retired, and capital outlays.

**Franchise.** A special privilege granted by a government permitting the continuing use of public property.

**Full Faith and Credit.** A pledge of the general taxing body for the payment of obligations.

**Fund Accounts.** All accounts necessary to set forth the financial operations and financial condition of a fund.

**Fund Group.** A group of related funds.

**Governmental Accounting.** The preparation, reporting, and interpretation of accounts for governmental bodies.

**Grant.** A contribution by one governmental unit to another unit.

**Gross Bonded Debt.** The total amount of direct debt of a governmental unit, represented by outstanding bonds before deduction of sinking fund assets.

**Indeterminate Appropriation.** An appropriation which is not limited either to any definite period of time, or to any definite amount, or to both time and amount.

**Inter-Fund Accounts.** Accounts in which transactions between funds are reflected.

**Inter-Fund Loans.** Loans made by one fund to another fund.

**Inter-Fund Transfers.** Amounts transferred from one fund to another.

**Judgment.** An amount to be paid or collected by a governmental unit as the result of a court decision, including a condemnation award in payment for private property taken for public use.

**Lapse.** As applied to appropriations, this term denotes the automatic termination of an appropriation.

**Levy.** To impose taxes or special assessments.

**Lump-Sum Appropriation.** An appropriation made for a stated purpose, or for a named department, without specifying further the amounts that can be spent for specific activities or for particular expenditures.

**Municipal.** An adjective applying to any governmental unit below or subordinate to the state.

**Municipal Corporation.** A body or corporate politic established pursuant to state authorization, as evidenced by a charter.

**Net Bonded Debt.** Gross bonded debt less applicable cash or other assets.

**Non-Expendable Fund.** A fund the principal, and sometimes the earnings, of which may not be expended.

**Non-Operating Income.** Income of municipal utilities and other governmental enterprises of a business character, which is not derived from the operation of such enterprise.

**Operating Expenses.** As used in the accounts of municipal utilities and other governmental enterprises of a business character, the term means the costs necessary to the maintenance of the enterprise, or the rendering of services for which the enterprise is operated.

**Operating Revenues.** Revenues derived from the operation of municipal utilities or other governmental enterprises of a business character.

**Operating Statement.** A statement summarizing the financial operations of a municipality.

**Ordinance.** A bylaw of a municipality enacted by the governing body of the governmental entity.

**Overlapping Debt.** The proportionate share of the debts of local governmental units, located wholly or in part within the limits of the reporting government, which must be borne by property within such government.

**Prepaid Taxes.** The deposit of money with a governmental unit on condition that the amount deposited is to be applied against the tax liability of the taxpayer.

**Proprietary Accounts.** Accounts which show actual financial condition and operations such as actual assets, liabilities, reserves, surplus, revenues, and expenditures as distinguished from budgetary accounts.

**Public Authority.** A public agency created to perform a single function, which is financed from tolls or fees charged those using the facilities operated by the agency.

**Public Trust Fund.** A trust fund whose principal, earnings, or both, must be used for a public purpose.

**Quasi-Municipal Corporation.** An agency established by the state primarily for the purpose of helping the state to carry out its functions.

**Refunding Bonds.** Bonds issued to retire bonds already outstanding. The refunding bonds may be sold for cash and outstanding bonds redeemed in cash, or the refunding bonds may be exchanged with holders of outstanding bonds.

**Related Funds.** Funds of a similar character which are brought together for administrative and reporting purposes.

**Reserve for Encumbrances.** A reserve representing the segregation of surplus to provide for unliquidated encumbrances.

**Revenue Bonds.** Bonds the principal and interest on which are to be paid solely from earnings, usually the earnings of a municipally owned utility or other public service enterprise.

**Revolving Fund.** A fund provided to carry out a cycle of operations.

**Special Assessment.** A compulsory levy made by a local government against certain properties, to defray part or all of the cost of a specific improvement or service, which is presumed to be of general benefit to the public and of special benefit to the owners of such properties.

**Special District Bonds.** Bonds of a local taxing district, which has been organized for a special purpose—such as road, sewer, and other special districts—to render unique services to the public.

**Suspense Account.** An account which carries charges or credits temporarily pending the determination of the proper account or accounts to which they are to be posted.

**Tax Anticipation Notes.** Notes issued in anticipation of collection of taxes, usually retired only from tax collections as they come due.

**Tax Levy.** An ordinance or resolution by means of which taxes are levied.

**Tax Liens.** Claims which governmental units have upon properties until taxes levied against them have been paid.

**Tax Rate.** The amount of tax stated in terms of a unit of the tax base.

**Trust Fund.** A fund consisting of resources received and held by the governmental unit as trustee, to be expended or invested in accordance with the conditions of the trust.

**Unencumbered Appropriation.** An appropriation or allotment, or a part thereof, not yet expended or encumbered.

**Utility Fund.** A fund established to finance the construction, operation, and maintenance of municipally owned utilities.

**Warrant.** An order drawn by a legislative body, or an officer of a governmental unit, upon its treasurer, directing the treasurer to pay a specified amount to the person named, or to the bearer.

## ¶9009    GOVERNMENTAL ACCOUNTING SYSTEMS

### .01    Governmental Accounting Standards Board (GASB)

The GASB was established in 1984, under the oversight of the Financial Accounting Foundation which, in turn, oversees the Financial Accounting Standards Board (FASB). Before the establishment of the GASB, the reports of governmental entities were criticized by the accounting community because they could not be interpreted in a manner consistent with the financial reports of private business organizations. The primary purpose of the GASB is to develop standards of reporting for state and local government entities; its organizational and operational structure is similar to that of the FASB, and its objective is to make the combined general purpose financial reports of governmental entities as comparable as possible to those of private business.

As a general rule the GASB will promulgate standards that parallel GAAP. However, there are instances that require a governmental entity to comply with a state law or regulatory accounting requirement that is in non-compliance with GAAP. Such reports are classified as *Special Reports or Supplemental Schedules*, which are not a part of the general purpose statements. In these cases governmental units can publish two sets of statements, one in compliance with legal requirements and one in compliance with GAAP. (An example of this problem is that it is not uncommon for some governmental entities to be required by law to apply the cash basis of accounting.)

Governmental accounting systems are developed on a *fund basis*. A fund is defined as an independent fiscal and accounting entity with a self-balancing set of accounts recording cash and other resources together with all related liabilities, obligations, reserves, and equities that are segregated for the purpose of carrying on specific activities or attaining specified objectives in accordance with applicable regulations, restrictions, and other statutory and regulatory limitations.

In addition to each fund's transactions within the fund itself, each fund in a governmental unit can have financial transactions with other funds in the same entity. The financial statements must reflect interfund transactions which result from services rendered by one fund to another.

The accrual basis of accounting is recommended for matching revenues and expenditures during a designated period of time which refers specifically to the time when revenues and expenditures are recorded as such in the accounting records.

Governmental revenues should be classified by fund and source. Expenditures should be classified by fund, function, organization unit, activity, character, and principal classes of objectives in accordance with standard recognized classifications. Common terminology and classifications should be used consistently throughout (1) the budget; (2) the accounts; and (3) the financial reports. These three elements of governmental financial administration are inseparable

**¶9009.01**

and can be thought of as the "cycle" of governmental financial transactions and final product of the accounting system.

## .03 Seven Types of Funds

1. The *General Fund* which accounts for all transactions not accounted for in any other fund.
2. *Special Revenue Fund* which accounts for revenues from specific sources or to finance specific projects.
3. *Debt Service Fund* which accounts for the payment of interest and principal on longterm debt.
4. *Capital Project Fund* which accounts for the receipt and disbursement of funds used for the acquisition of capital facilities.
5. *Enterprise Funds* which account for the financing of services to the public paid for by the users of the services.
6. *Fiduciary Funds: Trust and Agency Funds* which account for assets held by a governmental unit as trustee or agent for individuals, private organizations, or other governmental units.
7. *Internal Service Funds* which account for the financing of special projects and services performed by one governmental entity for an organization unit within the same governmental entity.

The accountant should:

- Maintain complete and adequate files for the initial documentation which established or restricted the fund, together with any special reporting requirements demanded.
- Keep separate detailed books of entry for each fund, separate bank account for that fund, separate identification of all property and securities.
- Under *no* circumstances should assets of separate funds be commingled. Transfers between funds should not be permitted without documentary authorization, and inter-fund receivables and payables should, in contra-effect, be equal and clearly identified, always maintaining the original integrity of each fund.
- Interest accruals, cooperative-share funding (example: government 80%— college 20% in Work Study Program), expense allowances or allocations—all should be made timely.
- Federal, state and local reporting requirements should be studied, met and reported as due to avoid stringent penalties, interest and possible loss of tax-exempt status. Options may exist regarding the handling of payroll and unemployment taxes; they should be studied and explored for money-saving possibilities.

¶9009.03

- Independently audited annual financial statements by fund are usually required both by organizational charter and governmental departments (especially where grant-participation is involved). Publication of the availability of these statements is sometimes mandatory (foundations).

- One area of discussion and dispute is the "compliance" feature of audits involving certain governmental agency grants. Here, the independent auditor is called upon to measure the agency's compliance with certain non-accounting rules, such as eligibility of money-recipients, internal controls and other matters not ordinarily associated with a financial audit. The integrity of the auditor's financial opinion should never be compromised by peripheral compliance requirements. In most cases, the auditor should qualify any opinion indicating the results and *extent of tests* made for compliance. The AICPA, to some extent, has spelled out guidelines for "compliance" opinions in Section 9641 of its "Statements on Auditing Standards."

- Municipal accounting techniques, procedures, format and demands are not discussed here. Their overall application involves the use of fund accounting. The main distinction is the entering of the budget—the anticipated revenues and the appropriations thereof—directly on and as part of the books of account. Progress reports then show how actual compares with anticipated. The estimates are then zeroed out at yearend. The meaning and use of "encumbrances" should also be understood. Reports for some local subdivisions, such as school boards, usually involve a strict accounting of each receipt and disbursement, including the detailing of outstanding checks.

*Accounting for the General Fund (GF).*    The General Fund is the type most frequently used as it accounts for revenues not allocated to specified activities by law or by contract. Every governmental entity *must* have a General Fund; none of the other types of funds are required, but are established as needed.

Entries in the GF system originally are made to Estimated Revenues and Appropriations and simultaneously a debit or credit, whichever is the case, is recorded in the Fund Balance account. For proper controls the encumbrance system is used with entries recorded when commitments are made or orders placed. This procedure has the effect of setting aside the money for the payment of future purchase orders and payment vouchers. When a purchase is actually made, the entries to an Encumbrances and Reserve for Encumbrances are reversed and those accounts cleared. (The later expenditure is not always the same as the encumbrance.) Simultaneously, the actual expenditure is recorded by a Debit to an Expenditures account and a credit to Vouchers Payable.

Taxes and service charges are budgeted in a Taxes-Receivable—Current Account. The estimated amounts should be recorded after the estimate and posting of uncollectibles, so the entries are a credit to Revenues and a credit to Estimated Uncollectible Taxes. When collections are actually received during the fiscal year, they are recorded with a debit to cash and a credit to Taxes Receivable—Current. Subsequently, it is determined that a certain amount of taxes will become delinquent as the year progresses. These amounts are recorded in a Taxes Receivable—Delinquent account (debit) and a credit to Taxes Receivable-Current. At this point an Interest and Penalties account should be opened for fees, penalties and other charges associated with the collection of delinquent taxes.

| | | |
|---|---|---|
| Taxes Receivable—Delinquent | xxx | |
| Estimated Uncollectible Current Taxes | xxx | |
|    Taxes Receivable—Current | | xxx |
|    Estimated Uncollectible Delinquent Taxes | | xxx |
| Interest and Penalties | xxx | |
|    Estimated Uncollectible Interest and Penalties | | xxx |

At the end of the fiscal year, the accounts of the General Fund are closed out. Any differences are recorded for or against the Fund Balance.

***Accounting for Special Revenue Funds (SRF).***    Special Revenue Funds account for revenues obtained via specific taxes or other designated revenue sources. They are usually mandated by statute, charter, or local ordinance to fund specific functions or activities. Examples are parks, museums, highway construction, street maintenance, business licensing.

Revenue Funds resources cannot be used for any purpose other than the purpose for which the bonds were sold.

| | | |
|---|---|---|
| Journal entries: | | |
|   Encumbrances | xxx | |
|     Reserve for Encumbrances | | xxx |
|   Reserve for Encumbrances | xxx | |
|     Encumbrances | | xxx |
|   Expenditures | xxx | |
|     Vouchers Payable | | xxx |
|   Vouchers Payable | xxx | |
|     Cash | | xxx |

Taxes and service charges are budgeted in a Taxes-Receivable—Current account. The estimated amounts should be recorded after the estimate and posting of uncollectibles, so the entries are a credit to Revenues and a credit to Estimated Uncollectible Taxes; e.g.,

| | | |
|---|---|---|
| Taxes Receivable—Current | xxx | |
| Estimated Uncollectible Current Taxes | | xxx |
| Revenues | | xxx |

When collections are actually received during the fiscal year they are recorded with a debit to Cash and a credit to Taxes Receivable—Current.

***Accounting for Debt Service Funds (DSF).*** Debt Service Fund accounts for the payment of interest and principal on long-term debt resulting from the sale of general obligation bonds. This fund does not include the accounting for special assessments and service debts of governmental enterprises.

There are three types of long-term debt:

- Term or sinking fund bonds.
- Serial bonds.
- Notes and time warrants having a maturity of *more than one year* after issuance.

The first entry in the accounting cycle for a bond fund is to record the bond authorization:

| | | |
|---|---|---|
| Bonds Authorized—unissued | xxx | |
| Appropriations | | xxx |
| The bonds are sold: | | |
| Cash | xxx | |
| Bonds Authorized—unissued | | xxx |

If the bonds are sold at a premium, a Premium on Bonds account is credited. If sold at a discount, a Discount on Bonds account is debited.

***Accounting for the Capital Projects Fund (CPF).*** Capital Projects Funds are a set of accounts for all resources used to acquire *capital* facilities (except funds financed by special assessment and enterprise funds). There must be Capital Project Funds for each authorized project to ensure that the proceeds of a bond issue, for example, are expended only as authorized. There is also a separate budget for the CPF, usually labeled the Capital Budget.

The accounting process begins with project authorization which is in memorandum form; no entry is necessary. Assuming the project is financed by the proceeds of a bond issue (as most projects are), the proceeds of the borrowing is an entry to the Cash account and a credit to Revenues for the *par value* of the bonds. If the bonds were sold at a premium, there is a credit to a Premium on Bonds account for the amount of the premium. Since GAAP requires bond premiums to be treated as an adjustment to the interest costs, the premiums are transferred *to* the Debt Service Fund established to service the debt. The entry to record the transfer is:

| | | |
|---|---|---|
| Premium on Bonds | xxx | |
| Cash | | xxx |

If the bonds are sold at a discount, the discount is eliminated by a transfer of the amount of the discount *from* the Debt Service Fund *to* the Capital Projects Fund.

*Accounting for Enterprise Funds (EF).*    Enterprise Funds finance self-supporting (not taxpayers') activities of governmental units that render services on a user charge basis to the general public. Common enterprises are water companies, electricity, natural gas, airports, transportation systems, hospitals, port authority, and a variety of recreational facilities.

In most jurisdictions, utilities and other enterprises are required to adopt and operate under budgets in the same manner as non-enterprise operations of governmental units. A budget is essential for control of each enterprise's operating results and to ensure that the resources of one enterprise are not illegally or improperly utilized by another.

The accrual basis of accounting is the required method for Enterprise Funds. As customers are billed, Accounts Receivable accounts are debited and revenue accounts *by sources* are credited.

Four financial statements are required to disclose fully the financial position and results of operations of an Enterprise Fund:

- Balance Sheet
- Revenue and Expenses
- Changes in Financial Position
- Analysis of Changes in Retained Earnings

*Accounting for Trust and Agency Funds (TAF).*    Trust and Agency Funds are similar; the primary difference is that a Trust Fund is usually in existence for a long period of time, even permanently. Both have fiduciary responsibilities for funds and assets that are not owned outright by the funds.

¶9009.03

There are two types of Trust Funds, i.e., expendable and nonexpendable funds. The former allows the principal and income to be spent on designated operations, while nonexpendable funds must be preserved intact. Pension and various retirement funds are examples of expendable funds; a loan fund from which loans are made for specific purposes and must be paid back, which requires maintaining the *original amount* of the fund, is a nonexpendable fund.

Trust Funds are operated as required by statutes and governmental regulations established for their existence. Accounting for Trust Funds consists primarily of the proper recording of receipts and disbursements. Additions are credited directly to the Fund Balance account and expenditures charged directly against the Fund Balance.

An Agency Fund can be thought of as sort of a clearinghouse fund established to account for assets received for and paid to others; the main asset is cash which is held only for a brief period of time, so is seldom invested because cash is usually paid out shortly after receipt.

An Agency Fund simplifies the complexities that can result from the use of numerous fund accounting entities; e.g., instances in which a single transaction affects several different funds. All Agency Fund assets are owed to another fund, a person, or an organization. The entries for receipts and disbursements in Agency Funds are easy:

| | | |
|---|---|---|
| Upon receipt: | | |
| Cash | xxx | |
| Fund Balance | | xxx |
| Upon disbursement: | | |
| Fund Balance | xxx | |
| Cash | | xxx |

*Accounting for Intergovernmental Service Funds (ISF).* ISF, also referenced as Working Capital Funds and Internal Service Funds, finances and provides accountability for services and commodities provided by a designated agency of a governmental unit to other departments, agencies, etc., of the same governmental entity. Examples are motor pools, centralized garages, central purchasing, storage, facilities, and central printing services.

Funds for the establishment of ISF usually originate from three sources:

• Contributions from another operating fund—e.g., the General Fund or an Enterprise Fund.

• The sale of general obligation bonds.

• Long-term advances from other funds, which are to be repaid over a specific period of time from the earnings of a revolving fund.

As cash is expended for the benefit of other fund-users, the users are charged with the cost of the materials or services furnished by the ISF and the ISF is then reimbursed by interdepartmental cash transfers from the departments of other funds to which materials or services have been furnished.

The accounting for ISF should include all accounts necessary to compile an accurate statement of the outcome of its financial operations, and of its financial position at any given time. These accounts will usually include the fixed assets owned by the fund, accounts for buildings financed from capital Project Funds, depreciation recorded on fixed assets to obtain an accurate computation of costs and to preclude depletion of the fund's capital. The accrual basis must be used for all ISF accounting, with all charges to departments of various funds billed at the time materials or services are rendered and expenditures are recorded when incurred. Encumbrances may or may not be formally recorded in the books of account; if they are the entries would be:

| | | |
|---|---|---|
| Encumbrances | xxx | |
| Reserve for Encumbrances | | xxx |

If encumbrances are not recorded in the accounts, memorandum records of orders and commitments should be maintained to preclude over-obligation of cash and other fund resources.

When an ISF is established, the entry to be made will depend upon the service the fund is to provide. If the fund's capital is obtained from the General Fund, the entry would be:

| | | |
|---|---|---|
| Cash | xxx | |
| Contribution from General Fund | | xxx |

If a general obligation bond issue is a source of the fund's capital:

| | | |
|---|---|---|
| Cash | xxx | |
| Contribution from | | xxx |
| General Obligation Bonds | | |

If fund capital is obtained from another fund of the same governmental unit the entry is:

| | | |
|---|---|---|
| Cash | xxx | |
| Advance from (name of fund) | | xxx |

¶9009.03

*Accounting for the General Fixed Assets Account Group (GFA).* The fixed asset accounts are maintained on the basis of original cost, or the estimated cost if the original cost is not available, as in the case of gifts. The appraised value at the time of receipt of the asset is an acceptible valuation. Otherwise, initial costs of fixed assets are obtainable from contracts, purchase vouchers, and other transaction documents generated at the time of acquisition or construction.

Depreciation on fixed assets should not be recorded in the general accounting records. Depreciation charges are computed for unit cost purposes, provided such charges are recorded in memorandum form and do not appear in the fund accounts.

Different from depreciation accounting for commercial enterprises, the depreciation of fixed assets is not recorded as an expense because there is no purpose in doing so. Property records should be kept, however, for each piece of property and equipment owned by the fund. The sum of the cost value of the properties—buildings, improvements, machinery, and equipment—should equal the corresponding balances of those accounts carried in the general ledger.

*Accounting for the Long-Term Debt Group (LTD).* General Obligation Bonds and other types of long-term debt supported by general revenues are obligations of the governmental unit as a whole, not of any of the entity's constituent funds individually. Additionally, the monies from such debt can be expended on facilities that are used in the operation of several funds. Accordingly, the total of long-term indebtedness backed by the "full faith and credit" of the government should be recorded and accounted for in a separate self-balancing group of accounts titled General Long-Term Debt Group of Accounts. Included in this debt group are general obligation bonds, time warrants, and notes that have a maturity date of *more than one year* from the date of issuance.

Long-term debt is recorded in the self-balancing accounts, so do not affect the liabilities of any other fund. The reason for these accounts is to record a governmental unit's long-term debt at any point in time from the date the debt is incurred until it is finally paid. Under GAAP the proper valuation for the long-term debt liability is the sum of (1) the present discounted value of the principal payable at the stipulated maturity date in the future and (2) the present discounted value of the periodic interest payments to the maturity date.

The entries to be made at the time the bonds are sold are:

| | | |
|---|---|---|
| Amounts to be Provided for the Payment of Term Bonds | xxx | |
| Term Bonds Payable | | xxx |

The proceeds of the bond issue are entered in a Capital Projects Fund account to be expended as authorized in the Authorized Capital Outlay account.

(Note: Not-for-profit accounting for other than governmental entities uses the accrual basis of accounting—e.g., colleges and universities, voluntary hospitals, health and welfare organizations, and so on.)

## ¶9011  OBJECTIVES OF FINANCIAL REPORTING BY NONBUSINESS ORGANIZATIONS

The main distinguishing characteristics of nonbusiness organizations include:

1. Receipts of significant amounts of resources from resource providers who do not expect to receive either repayment or economic benefits commensurate with the resources provided.
2. Operating purposes for objectives other than to provide goods or services at a profit.
3. Absence of defined ownership interests that can be sold, transferred, or redeemed, or that convey entitlement to a share of a residual distribution of resources in the event of liquidation of the organization.

These characteristics result in certain types of transactions that are largely, although not entirely, absent in business enterprises, such as contributions and grants, and in the absence of transactions with owners, such as issuing and redeeming stock and paying dividends. General purpose financial reporting by nonbusiness organizations does not attempt to meet all the information needed by those interested parties or to furnish all of the different types of information that financial reporting can provide. It is not intended to meet specialized needs of regulatory bodies, donors or grantors, or others having the authority to obtain the information they need. The most important users in the nonbusiness environment are resource providers, such as members, taxpayers, contributors, and creditors. A full set of financial statements for a period should show:

1. Financial position at the end of the period.
2. Earnings for the period.
3. Comprehensive income for the period.
4. Cash flows during the period.
5. Investments by and distributions to owners during the period.

Financial statements result from simplifying, condensing, and aggregating masses of data. As a result, they convey information that would be obscured if great detail were provided.

# Chapter 10

# Not-for-Profit or Exempt Organizations

## CONTENTS

## ¶10,000 OVERVIEW

Accounting for nonbusiness organizations such as not-for-profit and exempt organizations has many of the same characteristics as accounting for business entities; however, there are also wide differences. Among the foremost of these are differing objectives of financial reporting by nonbusiness entities.

## ¶10,001 CHARACTERISTICS OF NONBUSINESS ORGANIZATIONS

The main distinguishing characteristics of nonbusiness organizations include:

1. Receipts of significant amounts of resources from resource providers who do not expect to receive either repayment or economic benefits commensurate with the resources provided.
2. Operating purposes for objectives other than to provide goods or services at a profit.
3. Absence of defined ownership interests that can be sold, transferred, or redeemed, or that convey entitlement to a share of a residual distribution of resources in the event of liquidation of the organization.

These characteristics result in certain types of transactions that are largely, although not entirely, absent in business enterprises, such as contributions and grants, and in the absence of transactions with owners, such as issuing and redeeming stock and paying dividends. General purpose financial reporting by nonbusiness organizations does not attempt to meet all the information needed by those interested parties or to furnish all of the different types of information that financial reporting can provide. It is not intended to meet specialized needs of regulatory bodies, donors or grantors, or others having the authority to obtain the information they need. The most important users in the nonbusiness environment are resource providers, such as members, tax-payers, contributors, and creditors. A full set of financial statements for a period should show:

1. Financial position at the end of the period.
2. Earnings for the period.
3. Comprehensive income for the period.

**¶10,000**

4.  Cash flows during the period.
5.  Investments by and distributions to owners during the period.

Financial statements result from simplifying, condensing, and aggregating masses of data. As a result, they convey information that would be obscured if great detail were provided.

## ¶10,003   NOT-FOR-PROFITS UNDER SCRUTINY

Not-for-profit organizations have not escaped their share of the recently exposed scam artists. At this point, it appears to be Congress and the IRS that are leading the attack to preserve the integrity of the charitable donation system. As a result, the IRS will be allotted increased funds to step up its auditing inspection and enforcement efforts based upon the existing laws. Congress is also considering additional legislation in several areas including increased disclosure, increased number of independent, outside directors, and more frequent application to the IRS for tax exemption status.

### .01   Tax Exempt Compensation Initiative

As a result of an aggressive new Tax Exempt Compensation Initiative about to be launched by the Internal Revenue Service, nonprofit foundations that give "excessive compensation" to insiders—and the accountants who wink at such tax scams—are coming under intense federal scrutiny henceforth.

In outlining plans for the crackdown in testimony before the Senate Finance Committee, the IRS told Congress that the tax service will be demanding "detailed information and supporting documents" on compensation practices at hundreds of private foundations, as well as "public charities of various sizes."

The initiative, which the IRS launched during the summer of 2004, is part of a broader drive by the agency to respond to growing congressional concern that tax-exempt charities are being abused by greedy taxpayers in the U.S. and manipulated to fund terrorist organizations abroad. The agency believes that if abuses are left unchecked, there is the risk that Americans not only will lose faith in and reduce support for charitable organizations but that the integrity of the tax system will be compromised.

Under the nonprofit compensation initiative being developed by the IRS, charitable groups will be asked to provide investigators with "details concerning the independence of the governing body that approved the compensation, and details of the duties and responsibilities of these managers." During subsequent stages of the initiative, the IRS plans to examine a variety of "insider transactions" by nonprofits, including loans or sales to officers of the organization.

During congressional hearings concerning the new compensation initiative, a parade of witnesses told horror stories of abusive tax avoidance schemes involving charities and other nonprofit organizations.

## .03  That Old "Beater"

The growth of the donations of unused or extra cars to charities has grown dramatically as anyone who ever listens to a radio or turns on a TV will attest. However, as the IRS can attest, the process has taken place without taxpayers and charities always understanding their obligations under tax law. Therefore, the IRS makes available two publications, which were written in conjunction with state charity officials, as part of an ongoing effort by state and federal officials to work together to educate taxpayers and charities:

1. "Guide to Car Donations," provides descriptions of several different car donation programs, filing and disclosure requirements for charities operating these programs, and related information. Included among the description of vehicle donation programs is an example of an arrangement that would fail to preserve the deductibility of a contribution.
2. Publication 4303, "A Donor's Guide to Car Donations," reminds taxpayers that they need to make sure they are donating their vehicle to a qualified organization, receive a written acknowledgment from the charity, keep records, and properly assess the fair market value of their vehicle.

Both publications are intended to assist individual taxpayers and those operating car donation programs to comply with tax law.

## .05  Tougher Rules for Donating Vehicles

The 2004 tax law changes the method for valuing a vehicle donated to charity and claimed as an itemized deduction in 2005 and beyond. Not without reason, the IRS believed that too many taxpayers had taken advantage of the system by "over estimating" the value of their donated cars. A charity is now required to send taxpayers receipts showing how much the cars they donated sold for at an auction. That will be the amount allowable as a deduction.

In addition, new penalties are imposed by the IRS on donee organizations that provide a false or fraudulent acknowledgment of a vehicle contribution or fail to furnish the proper acknowledgment.

## .07  Varied Improper Usage of Not-for-Profits

It is not surprising that some governmental agency or body should begin investigating the ins and outs of "donations to earn you cash and reduce your

¶10,003.03

taxes." Someone or some group must be profiting from the process if they can afford the myriad TV and radio pleas for the contribution of your old, worthless (?) car.

The IRS is targeting some of the more complicated ways to avoid paying taxes. Areas in which considerable sums may have been avoided are through the above-mentioned compensation deals, and another area discussed below—real estate easement deductions. Additional areas of concern are:

- Evaluation of donated items other than cars, such as patents, fine art, musical instruments, jewelry, and land.
- Scam not-for-profit credit counselors, debt managers, and financial managers who are more concerned with adding funds to their coffers than to solving the problems of their clients.
- Donated assets that appear to be benefiting the donor as much as or more than the recipient.

## .09  Improper Deductions for Conservation Easement Donations

The Treasury Department and the Internal Revenue Service issued a notice in June 2004 to advise taxpayers that the IRS intends to disallow improper charitable contribution deductions for transfers of easements on real property to charitable organizations and for transfers of easements in connection with purchases of real property from charitable organizations. Taxpayers claiming improper charitable contribution deductions for such transfers may be subject to accuracy-related penalties. This action results from the IRS having uncovered numerous instances where the tax benefits of preserving open spaces and historic buildings have been twisted for inappropriate individual benefit. The IRS is aware that some taxpayers are claiming inappropriate charitable contribution deductions for easement transfers that do not qualify as qualified conservation contributions, or are claiming deductions for amounts that exceed the fair market value of the donated easement.

In addition, some taxpayers are claiming inappropriate charitable contribution deductions for cash payments or easement transfers to charitable organizations in connection with the taxpayers' purchases of real property. The IRS may impose penalties on promoters, appraisers and other persons involved in these transactions. In appropriate cases, the IRS may challenge the tax-exempt status of the charitable organization, based on the organization's operation for a substantial nonexempt purpose or impermissible private benefit.

One of the agency's four service-wide enforcement priorities is to discourage and deter noncompliance within tax-exempt and government entities and the misuse of such entities by third parties for tax avoidance and other unintended purposes.

## .13    New Reporting Requirements for Controlling Entities

Within the tax legislation signed into law in 2006 (sec. 1205(b) of the Pension Protection Act of 2006) is a provision requiring certain exempt organizations to disclose information about controlled organizations. The information is formally referred to as the "IRC Section 6033(h) Reporting Requirement." If an organization is a controlling organization within the meaning of IRC sec. 512(b)(13) and files either a form 990, 990-EZ or 990-PF, then the following information must be included on its 2005 return (only if the due date for the return (excluding extensions) is after August 17, 2006.

For each controlled entity, include 1) the name of the controlled entity 2) Income description for each item of interest, annuities, royalties, or rents received 3) the amounts of each form of income 4) a list of any loans made to the controlled entity 5) descriptions and amounts of each transfer between controlling entity and controlled entity. If the organization files electronically, this information should be included in the "General Explanation Attachment."

## .15    New Transparency for Exempt Organization Reporting

The Pension Protection Act of 2006 has placed taxpayers, contributors and others interested in analyzing the operations of exempt organizations on a level playing field with those scrutinizing publicly traded companies. Just as the financial statements and SEC Forms 10-K are available for public inspection through the SEC, exempt entities, in particular 501(c)(3) organizations are now required to provide access not only the tax exempt portion of their operations through public disclosure of Form 990 but also to the taxpaying portion—the operations generating unrelated business taxable income (UBTI)—through public disclosure of Form 990-T. This is a major step for monitoring the operations and corporate governance of exempt organizations and for the first time will allow outsiders to view the whole picture necessary to evaluate an exempt organization's performance.

Accounting scandals, CEO compensation issues and corporate governance have demanded their share of headlines in recent years; transparency is now the clarion call of accounting. Sarbanes-Oxley was Congress' response to the problems plaguing the accounting profession and corporate accountability. But the private sector is not alone in its concern over accounting abuse. In an effort to deflect criticism aimed at abuse of their tax-exempt status by some 501(c)(3) organizations Congress in 1996 enacted IRC sec. 6104(d) requiring these organizations to make their annual information returns and "tax exempt status application materials" available to the public. This provision was added to the law in part because of the proliferation of tax exempt organizations during the last 30 years.

The Form 990 disclosure rules were finally effective in 1999 with the completion of IRS regulations. Since that time interested parties have been able to request, or view on the organization's website, the Form 990 (or 990-PF) filed by the organization with the IRS as well a copies of its exempt status application—Form 1023 or determination letter. The disclosure requirement includes the availability of Schedule A and those parts of the return that show the compensation paid to "specific persons."

How exempt organizations spend their exempt revenue is an important aspect of the government oversight of this large and growing component of the U. S. economy. The importance of this issue was re-addressed in the new legislation mandating fuller public transparency with respect to federally tax exempt organizations. The new law amended IRC sec. 6104(d)(1) to include the requirement that form 990-T be brought within the public disclosure requirements already applicable to Forms 990. The change is effective for 990-T returns filed after August 17, 2006.

An important reason for the requirement of more transparency for tax exempt organizations (especially when the organization is a 501(c)(3) entity) is to allow the public to see how exempt organizations allocate their scarce resources. Of particular interest in this regard is the amount of compensation paid to the top executives. Unfortunately, the Taxpayer Bill of Rights 2 (1996) did not go far enough in providing this information because it neglected an organization's UBTI (Form 990-T).

The instructions for Form 990 state, "Report on form 990 . . . items of income and expense that are also reported on Form 990-T when the organization is required to file both forms." But because the 990-T was not required to be disclosed to the public, the total amount of income and expense items allocated to the taxable portion of the organization's revenue was hidden from view. The public therefore had no means for gauging how total executive compensation, for example, is allotted between the tax exempt and the taxable operations of the organization.

The ability to combine the operations reported on form 990 with those on 990-T will allow significant opportunity for increased analytic review. Expenses that are subject to allocation between the tax exempt and the taxable portion of the organization can now be determined in total and subject to analysis. The results will give reviewers of the organization's returns empirical data regarding the allocation of expenses either to the tax exempt or taxable revenue. This, in turn, will aid interested parties in evaluating an organization's effectiveness in meeting the objectives of its exempt purpose.

## .17  New Reporting for Entities Exempt from Form 990 Filing

In an apparent effort to keep better track of smaller exempt organizations the new law mandates information returns for exempt organizations with gross receipts of under $25,000. Though these entities are still excused from filing Form 990 they are now required to check-in with the IRS on an annual basis.

¶10,003.17

Reporting is to be done electronically. The information requested is the legal name of the organization, any assumed name or dba, its mailing address and Internet website (if any), the taxpayer ID number, the name and address of a principal officer and evidence of the organization's continuing basis for its exemption from the 990 filing requirements—a statement of its gross receipts for the year. If the organization terminates its existence, the IRS must be notified as well.

Hefty penalties are awaiting organizations ignoring the new reporting law. If an organization fails to provide the required notice for three consecutive years, the organization will lose its tax exempt status. The new reporting requirements take place for annual accounting periods starting after 2006.

## .19 Donations Not Used for Exempt Purpose

When a deductible donation to an exempt organization is made and the value of the donation is more than $5,000 the 2006 law requires the organization to track the use of the donated property for three years. If during those three year the property is not put to use for the exempt organization's exempt purpose but is disposed or, not only must the organization report this fact to the IRS, the taxpayer making the donation must now recapture (take into income) the deduction taken for the item. The law change applies to tangible personal property donated after September 1, 2006. Prior law had required tracking of the donation's use for only two years and reporting to the IRS but no recapture of the deduction.

## ¶10,005 ABUSIVE PRACTICES BY TEOs AND CHARITIES

The Internal Revenue Service continues to be concerned about abusive practices by tax-exempt organizations (TEOs) and charities as well as the individual taxpayers who aid, abet, and cooperate with them in various and sundry schemes. On the other hand, as the Commissioner of the IRS and other representatives reported to Congress, with abuse becoming increasingly present in the nonprofit sector, too many charities "are wantonly abusing" the generosity and faith of other members of the public who want to help those in need.

Among items on the list of concerns are:

1. Schemes designed to channel excessive compensation to executives at tax-exempt organizations.
2. The suspicion that growing numbers of charities and other TEOs facilitate the marketers of abusive tax shelters by serving as "tax-indifferent parties." However the IRS has also made it clear that the Service is well aware that charities are not just innocent dupes of shelter promoters, but are often knowing participants in the schemes.

3. The evident need to step up scrutiny of charities with foreign connections in order to reduce the likelihood that these organizations are channeling funds to terrorist organizations.

4. The sharp increase in the size, complexity, and value of the assets of the nonprofit sector, along with inadequate enforcement by the IRS as the result of insufficient resources to police the segment.

5. The fact that no serious evaluation of the law for tax-exempt organizations has been carried out since 1969. However, it was pointed out at the April 2005 hearing before the Senate Finance Committee that most of the abuses uncovered in 2004, prompting stepped-up surveillance by the IRS were already illegal.

## .01 Excessive Compensation

This past year, the IRS implemented a comprehensive enforcement project investigating what the IRS Commissioner called "the seemingly high compensation paid to individuals associated with some exempt organizations."

Although they are seldom enforced, penalties for charities that overcompensate their officers and directors can be severe. In addition to stripping nonprofits of their tax-exempt status, the IRS may also impose an excise tax on employees of charities and social welfare organizations who receive more than their due.

The tax service's aggressive new enforcement initiative is aimed at awakening the nonprofit sector to the fact that need to clean up their act by "creating positive tension for organizations as they decide on compensation arrangements" for their officers and directors. As part of this new enforcement crackdown, the Service is in the process of contacting nearly 2,000 public charities and private foundations to obtain supporting documents on their compensation practices and procedures.

The Internal Revenue Service has published its annual listing of notorious tax scams, the "Dirty Dozen." It is interesting to note the items mentioned in the introduction of the announcement: The 'Dirty Dozen' for 2005 includes several new scams that either manipulate laws governing charitable groups, abuse credit-counseling services or rely on refuted arguments to claim tax exemptions. The announcement also cautions: "Involvement with tax schemes can lead to imprisonment and fines. The IRS routinely pursues and shuts down promoters of these scams. But taxpayers should also remember that anyone pulled into these schemes could face repayment of taxes plus interest and penalties."

The IRS is placing special attention on organizations that did not provide complete compensation information on their Form 990 filings. The agency ordered those organizations to submit any missing information immediately. One example of devious attempts to hide excessive compensation payments is by spreading compensation among several affiliated organizations to decrease transparency.

¶10,005.01

## .03 Questionable "Contributions"

The IRS has observed an increase in the use of tax-exempt organizations to shield income or assets from taxation improperly. This can occur, for example, when a taxpayer moves assets or income to a tax-exempt supporting organization or donor-advised fund but maintains control over the assets or income, thereby obtaining a tax deduction without transferring a commensurate benefit to charity.

A "contribution" of a historic facade easement to a tax-exempt conservation organization is another example. In many cases, local historic preservation laws already prohibit alteration of the home's facade, making the contributed easement superfluous. Even if the facade could be altered, the deduction claimed for the easement contribution may far exceed the easement's impact on the value of the property.

## .05 Suspect Foreign Activities

The IRS plans to step up scrutiny of charities with foreign connections in order to reduce the likelihood that these organizations are channeling funds to terrorist organizations.

Recently, the IRS revised its Form 1023 to require more specific information on foreign activities by nonprofits, and a soon-to-be-announced revision of the Form 990 is expected to require similar information. The Service is planning to require better baseline information about the practices of organizations that make grants to foreign entities and the level of oversight the organizations exercise over the use of the funds abroad.

## .07 Credit Counseling Agency Scams

The IRS Tax Exempt and Government Entities Division has made auditing credit counseling organizations a priority in their investigations because some of these tax-exempt organizations, which are intended to provide education to low-income customers with debt problems, are charging debtors large fees while providing little or no counseling.

## .09 Number, Assets of NFPs Outstrip IRS Resources

The number of tax-exempt entities listed by the IRS has increased by nearly 500,000 since 1995, to 1.8 million. The value of the assets held by these organizations has grown even faster, rising 50 percent, from $2 trillion in 1998 to $3 trillion in 2002.

At the same time, the IRS resources assigned to policing this segment failed to keep pace with this growth. Although there was a 40 percent increase in the number of exempt organization tax returns filed between 1995 and 2003, the number of IRS personnel assigned to this area actually declined by nearly one-third during the period.

## ¶10,007   FASB Plans to Issue Exposure Draft on Not-for-Profit Organizations

It would appear that features are about to be "finalized" in the FASB's continuing plans for combinations of not-for-profit organizations. In the second and third quarters of 2005, the Board planned to address all remaining issues in the project and begin drafting the first Exposure Draft (ED).

The Board plans to issue an ED in the third quarter of 2005, after it issues its ED for the "Business Combinations: Purchase Method Procedures" project. A few of the issues and some of the decisions reached by the Board in its project on combinations of not-for-profits are discussed below.

### .01   Questions Remaining to Be Settled

The remaining follow-up items from previous deliberations include:

1. The narrative and extent of pro forma information about a combination that should be disclosed by not-for-profit organizations (if any), and whether such requirements should be applied to all or just certain organizations

2. The type of guidance, if any, which should be provided for measuring the fair value of the acquired organization in the absence of market transactions.

### .03   Approach to the NFP Standard

The project has been conducted following an approach that presumed that FASB 141, Business Combinations (as revised by the Purchase Method Procedures project) should apply to combinations of not-for-profit organizations unless a circumstance unique to those combinations is identified that would justify a different accounting treatment. That approach is referred to as the *differences-based approach*.

Among the guidelines along the way have been the decision that the definition of a not-for-profit organization in FASB 116, *Accounting for Contributions Received and Contributions Made,* be used and that the proposed Statement was to provide general guidance to describe the accounting for an acquisition of assets subject to certain liabilities.

The project was to cover:

1. Combinations between two or more not-for-profit organizations.
2. The acquisition of a for-profit business enterprise by a not-for-profit organization. (The acquisition of a not-for-profit organization by a business enterprise is within the scope of FASB 141.)
3. Combinations in which no combining entity dominates the process of selecting a voting majority of the combined entity's governing board (transactions which are sometimes referred to as mergers of equals).

However, the scope of the proposed Statement excluded the following transactions:

1. The formation of a joint venture under joint control.
2. A transfer of net assets or exchange of equity interests between entities under common control.

## ¶10,009   FASB Plans for Combinations of NFPs in 2004

Nearing the end of their deliberations in the project on combinations of not-for-profit organizations, the FASB addressed the following items:

1. Whether to provide guidance for postacquisition accounting for goodwill when a reporting unit no longer qualifies for:
   a. The Statement 142 impairment test, because it ceases to be primarily supported by fees, or
   b. The trigger-based approach to impairment testing of goodwill because fees have primarily support it.
2. The narrative and extent of pro forma information about a combination that should be disclosed by not-for-profit organizations (if any) and whether such requirements should be applied to all or just certain organizations.
3. The type of guidance, if any, which should be provided for measuring the fair value of the organization in the absence of market transactions.

### .01   Background

In November 1999, the FASB affirmed its earlier decision to undertake a project on combinations of not-for-profit organizations that was separate from its business combinations project. As a result of that decision, combinations of NFP organizations were excluded from the scope of Part I of the September 1999 FASB Exposure Draft, *Business Combinations and Intangible Assets*.

**¶10,009**

The objective of this project to develop guidance on the accounting and reporting for *combinations* of NFP organizations. The following paragraphs describe the reasons for the Board deciding to undertake this separate project.

## .03  Diversity in Current Practice

Some combinations between NFP organizations have characteristics that distinguish them from business combinations. For example:

1.  Some combinations do not include the exchange of cash or other assets as consideration.
2.  There are differing interpretations of the application of the provisions of APB Opinion 16, *Business Combinations*, to be applied to combinations of NFP organizations.
3.  This divergence occurs particularly in treating those combinations in which there is no exchange of consideration.

These differing interpretations have led to wide diversity in practice.

## .05  The Effect of Elimination of Pooling-of-Interests

Statement 141, *Business Combinations*, eliminated the pooling-of-interests method. At present, many combinations of NFP organizations are accounted for in a manner similar to the pooling method. This project is needed to provide guidance to NFP organizations in light of the Board's prohibition of the use of that method.

## ¶10,011  BOARD DELIBERATIONS

### .01  Tentative Decisions Relating to Intangibles

The decisions reached by the Board to date in its project on combinations of NFP organizations are:

1.  The project will be conducted following an approach that presumes that Statement 141 should apply to combinations of NFP organizations, unless a circumstance unique to such combinations is identified that calls for a different accounting treatment. This approach is being referred to as the *differences-based approach*.
2.  The definition of *not-for-profit organization* in Statement 116 will be used for this project.
3.  The scope of this project includes:

a. Combinations between two or more NFP organizations.

b. The acquisition of a for-profit business enterprise by an NFP organization. (The acquisition of an NFP organization by a business enterprise is within the scope of FASB 141.)

## ¶10,013   THE METHOD OF ACCOUNTING FOR A COMBINATION OF NFP ORGANIZATIONS

The facts and circumstances of each combination of two or more NFP organizations should be reviewed to determine the extent to which the combination is a *contribution* or a *bargained exchange*. The proposed Statement is likely to include guidance describing the types of facts and circumstances that should be considered in making that determination:

1. A combination of NFP organizations in which no consideration is exchanged should be presumed to be a nonreciprocal transfer and accounted for in a manner similar to a contribution under Statement 116.

2. A combination that includes the exchange of consideration should be presumed to be a bargained exchange and accounted for in accordance with Statement 141.

3. When the facts and circumstances provide evidence that the combination is in part an exchange and in part a contribution, the contribution inherent in that transaction should be recognized by the acquiring organization in accordance with Statement 116.

If the acquired entity is an NFP organization, the contribution recognized by the *acquiring* organization would be measured as the excess of the sum of the fair values of the identifiable assets acquired and the liabilities assumed over the fair value of the assets transferred as consideration (if any).

In the rare cases in which the sum of the fair values of the liabilities assumed exceeds the sum of the fair values of the identifiable assets acquired, the acquiring organization should initially recognize that excess as an unidentifiable intangible asset (goodwill).

If the acquired entity is a business enterprise, the contribution inherent in a combination should be measured as the excess of the fair value of the acquired business enterprise over the cost of that business enterprise.

### .01  Combinations That Include the Exchange of Cash or Other Assets As Consideration

The Board made the following decisions regarding the accounting for a combination of NFP organizations in which cash or other assets are exchanged as consideration. The decisions apply to both combinations between two or more NFP organizations and the acquisition of a business enterprise by a not-for-profit organization:

1. The following are examples of facts and circumstances that provide evidence that the combination is one that is in part an exchange and in part a contribution:

   a. The sum of the fair values of the assets acquired and liabilities assumed exceeds the fair value of the consideration exchanged (the excess), particularly if the amount of that excess is substantial in relation to the fair value of the net assets acquired, and no unstated rights or privileges are involved.

   b. A review of the facts and circumstances surrounding the combination, including careful study of the negotiations, provides evidence that the participants were acting as a donor and a donee and as a buyer and a seller.

2. Organizations should be provided with the following list of examples of facts and circumstances that indicate a combination is a bargained exchange:

   a. The organization or business enterprise is acquired through a competitive bidding process involving multiple potential acquirers.

   b. The amount of consideration offered by the acquiring organization was developed in consultation with acquisition advisors, was based on an estimate of the acquired entity's fair value, or both. That estimate of the acquired entity's fair value may have been developed internally by the acquiring organization or by independent valuation experts.

   c. The acquired entity's former parent or predecessor board of directors retained outside specialists to assist in negotiating the combination, used estimates of the organization's fair value to evaluate the adequacy of the offers received, or both.

   d. One or both parties to the combination retained consultants to provide an opinion on the fairness of the transaction.

   e. The provisions of NFP corporation law or involvement on the part of a state attorney general or other regulatory body influenced the terms or structure of the combination transaction.

3. In general, assets transferred (or liabilities incurred) by the acquiring organization as a requirement of a combination should be accounted for as consideration paid for the acquired entity unless the acquiring organization retains control over the future economic benefits of the transferred assets. If control over the future economic benefits of the transferred assets is retained by the acquiring organization, the asset transfer should be

reported as an asset-for-asset exchange. Examples of conditions that would result in the acquiring organization retaining control over the future economic benefit or the transferred assets include:

a. The asset transfer is repayable or refundable.

b. The assets are transferred to a recipient that is controlled by the acquiring organization.

c. The assets are transferred with the stipulation that they be used on behalf of, or for the benefit of, the acquired organization, the acquiring organization, or its affiliates.

4. An acquiring NFP organization should account for a regulatory required asset transfer as consideration paid for the acquired organization.

5. Communities neither own nor control NFP organizations and, therefore, a community's relationship with an NFP organization should have no effect on the method of accounting for a combination of NFP organizations.

6. Contingent consideration in a combination should be accounted for in accordance with the guidance in FASB 141.

## .03  Identifying the Acquiring Organization

There is no question but that the FASB wants to make it perfectly clear that the acquiring organization should be identified beyond a shadow of a doubt.

The Board made the following decisions regarding how the acquiring organization in a combination between NFP organizations should be identified:

1. The following general principle should be used as a guide in the process of identifying the acquirer in a combination between NFP organizations: In determining which organization is the acquiring organization in a combination of NFP organizations involving two or more organizations, all pertinent facts and circumstances should be considered, particularly whether one of the combining organizations has the ability to dominate the process of selecting a voting majority of the combined organization's initial governing body.

   To determine this, consideration should be given to the existence of rights to appoint members to the combined organization's governing body provided by:

   a. The combined organization's articles of incorporation.

   b. Its bylaws.

   c. Provisions in the combination agreement.

   d. Other means.

2. The FASB suggests that an appendix of implementation guidance should be provided that lists the following factors to consider in identifying the acquiring organization:

   a. Do the combined organization's articles of incorporation or bylaws state that the members of the governing body are appointed? Does one of the combining organizations have the right to appoint a voting majority of the governing body?

   b. Is the combined organization's governing body self-perpetuating?

   c. If so, has one of the combining organizations negotiated the right to select a voting majority of the combined initial governing body as part of the combination agreement?

   d. Or, does one of the combining organizations have the ability to dominate the selection of a voting majority of the governing body through means other than negotiated appointment rights, such as through disproportionate representation on the committee that selects nominees for that body?

   e. If the initial governing body is elected by the combining organizations' members, what are the relative voting rights of the combining organizations in the combined organization?

   f. Are there any other rights to appoint or designate members of the combined organization's governing body, either as of the combination date or in the near future (such as upon the expiration of the terms of some or all of the initial members)?

   g. What are the powers of any sponsoring organizations and corporate members and the composition of those sponsors and members? If sponsors and corporate members have limited powers, what is the effect of those limited powers on the ability of one of the combining organizations to control the combined organization?

   h. If positions on the governing body are designated positions, what is the effect of those designated positions on the ability of a combining organization to appoint a voting majority of the combined organization's governing body?

   i. If the governing body delegates corporate powers to committees, what is the nature of those delegated powers? The composition of the committees?

   j. What is the effect of voting requirements (such as supermajority voting requirements) on the ability of one organization to appoint or dominate the selection of a supermajority of the governing body?

   k. What is the composition of senior management? What factors are considered by the combining organizations in selecting that management team?

## .05 Collection Acquired in a Combination of NFP Organizations

The Board decided that the requirements of Statement 116 would continue to be used to account for collection items that are contributed to, or purchased by, an NFP organization and added to its inexhaustible collection. They agreed that when collection items are acquired in connection with a combination of NFP organizations, the acquirer should follow the guidance in Statement 116 to account for items acquired to be added to its collection.

## .07 Identification of Intangible Assets

The criteria in FASB 141 for recognizing identifiable intangible assets should be applied in the recording of combinations of NFP organizations.

## ¶10,015 FASB 136, *Transfers of Assets to a Not-for-Profit Organization or Charitable Trust That Raises or Holds Contributions for Others*

FASB Stantement 136, the most recent FASB pronouncement on not-for-profit organizations (NPOs) establishes standards for transactions in which a donor makes a contribution by transferring assets to a not-for-profit organization or charitable trust—the recipient organization.

The not-for-profit organization accepts the assets from the donor and agrees to do one of the following:

1. Use those assets on behalf of a beneficiary specified by the donor.
2. Transfer those assets to said beneficiary.
3. Transfer the return on investment of those assets to that beneficiary.
4. Transfer both the assets and the return on investments to the specified beneficiary.

It also establishes standards for transactions that take place in a similar manner but are not contributions because the transfers are any of the following:

1. Revocable.
2. Repayable.
3. Reciprocal.

It follows that the Statement requires a recipient organization that is willing to accept cash or other financial assets from a donor and to agree to abide by the stipulations spelled out above in the interest of that specified unaffiliated beneficiary. In doing so, it also agrees to recognize the fair value of those assets as a liability to the specified beneficiary concurrent with recognition of the assets received from the donor.

However, if the donor explicitly grants the recipient organization variance power, or if the recipient organization and the specified beneficiary are financially *interrelated* organizations, the recipient organization is required to recognize the fair value of any assets it receives as a contribution received.

Not-for-profit organizations are financially interrelated if:

1. One organization has the ability to influence the operating and financial decisions of the other.
2. One organization has an ongoing economic interest in the net assets of the other.

The Statement does not establish standards for a trustee's reporting of assets held on behalf of specified beneficiaries, but it does establish standards for a beneficiary's reporting of its rights to assets held in a charitable trust.

Further, it requires that a specified beneficiary recognize its rights to the assets held by a recipient organization as an asset unless the donor has explicitly granted the recipient organization variance power. Those rights are one of the following:

1. An interest in the net assets of the recipient organization.
2. A beneficial interest.
3. A receivable.

If the beneficiary and the recipient organization are financially interrelated organizations, the beneficiary is required to recognize its interest in the net assets of the recipient organization and adjust that interest for its share of the change in net assets of the recipient organization.

If the beneficiary has an unconditional right to receive all or a portion of the specified cash flows from a charitable trust or other identifiable pool of assets, the beneficiary is required to recognize that beneficial interest, measuring and subsequently remeasuring it at fair value, using a valuation technique such as the present value of the estimated expected future cash flows.

If the recipient organization is explicitly granted variance power, the specified beneficiary does not recognize its potential for future distributions from the assets held by the recipient organization. In all other cases, a beneficiary recognizes its rights as a receivable.

FASB 136 covers four conditions under which a transfer of assets to a recipient organization is accounted for as *a liability* by the recipient organization and as *an asset* by the resource provider because the transfer is revocable or reciprocal.

The four circumstances occur when:

1. The transfer is subject to the resource provider's unilateral right to redirect the use of the assets to another beneficiary.
2. The transfer is accompanied by the resource provider's conditional promise to give or is otherwise revocable or repayable.
3. The resource provider controls the recipient organization and specifies an unaffiliated beneficiary.
4. The resource provider specifies itself or its affiliate as the beneficiary and the *transfer is not an equity transaction.*
   - When the transfer is an equity transaction and the resource provider specifies itself as beneficiary, it records an interest in the net assets of the recipient organization (or an increase in a previously recognized interest).
   - When the resource provider specifies an affiliate as beneficiary, the resource provider records an equity transaction as a separate line item in its statement of activities, and the affiliate named as beneficiary records an interest in the net assets of the recipient organization. The recipient organization records an equity transaction as a separate line item in its statement of activities.

Certain disclosures are required when a not-for-profit organization transfers assets to a recipient organization and specifies itself or its affiliate as the beneficiary or if it includes in its financial statements a ratio of fundraising expenses to amounts raised.

The Statement incorporates without reconsideration the guidance in FASB Interpretation 42, *Accounting for Transfers of Assets in Which a Not-for-Profit Organization Is Granted Variance Power*, and supersedes that Interpretation. (It states that an NPO should be considered both a *donee* and a *donor* when it receives assets from a resource provider, *and* has received explicit unilateral authority to redistribute the assets and income from the assets to a beneficiary.)

FASB 136 became effective for financial statements issued for fiscal periods beginning after December 15, 1999, except for the provisions incorporated from Interpretation 42, which continue to be effective for fiscal years ending after September 15, 1996. Earlier application was encouraged. This Statement was applicable either by restating the financial statements of all years presented or by recognizing the cumulative effect of the change in accounting principle in the year of the change.

# ¶10,017   IRS RULINGS AND LEGISLATION RELATING TO DISCLOSURE

At the same time that the Financial Accounting Standards Board was adopting FASB 136, the Internal Revenue Service was issuing new rulings relating to the availability to the public of financial documents revealing the details of the operations of not-for-profit (or in the parlance of the IRS, *exempt*) organizations. The new regulations increase the disclosure burden of exempt organizations—and their accountants.

These exempt organizations are entities described in Sections 501(c) and 501(d) of the Internal Revenue Code and exempt from taxation under Section 501(a). They include charitable, educational, scientific, literary, and medical organizations, trade and professional associations, sports leagues, social welfare organizations, public radio and television stations, trade and professional associations, social clubs, cemeteries, and fraternal beneficiary societies. The rules do not apply to disclosure requirements of private foundations.

## .01  Other Disclosure Requirements

Considering the huge sums of money that many of these NPOs handle, it is not surprising that in addition to other FASB Standards discussed later in this chapter, Congress has seen fit to set up some rules relating to disclosure by not-for-profits. Legislation has included the Omnibus Budget Reconciliation Act of 1987 and the Taxpayer Bill of Rights 2, passed in 1996.

The former requires exempt organizations, including public foundations, to provide access for public inspection of their tax exemption applications. It also required that they (other than private foundations) allow public inspection at their principal offices of the last three years' annual reports. The Taxpayer Bill of Rights 2 provided for additional public disclosures which have been finalized in these IRS rulings.

## .03  Specific Documents for Inspection

Not only do the most recent rulings specify *what* should be disclosed, but they are very specific about *how* and *where* applicable documents are made available by the exempt organization (other than a private foundation).

The documents that must be available upon request for inspection if they apply to the particular organization include:

1. Form 990, *Return of Organization Exempt from Income Tax.*
2. Form 990BL, *Information and Initial Excise Tax Return for Black Lung Benefit Trusts and Certain Related Persons.*
3. Form 990EZ, *Short Form Return for Organization Exempt from Income Tax.*
4. Form 1023, *Application for Recognition of Exemption Under Section 501(c)(3) of the Internal Revenue Code.*
5. Form 1024, *Application for Recognition of Exemption Under Section 501(a) for Determination Under Section 120 of the Internal Revenue Code.*
6. Form 1065, *U.S. Partnership Return of Income.*

In addition to the documents themselves, other relevant information must also be made available:

For Forms 1023 or 1024, all supporting documents filed by, or on behalf of the organization in connection with that application, as well as any correspondence with the IRS should be available. If the application was filed before July 15, 1987, the organization need not supply the document unless the organization possessed a copy of the application on that date.

For Forms 990, 990-EZ, 990-BL or Form 1065, including all schedules and attachments filed with the IRS, the organization must make available its three most recent returns. However, in the interest of confidentiality, the organization should *not* including the portions of the returns that give the names and addresses of contributors.

The exempt organization must also copy documents, or portions thereof, when requested either in writing or in person.

## .05 Procedures

The ruling is quite specific about establishing the various procedures for making these documents available for public inspection.

1. It specifies the amount of fees for copying and postage the organization may charge. The organization may charge a reasonable amount for copying and mailing as long as it does not exceed the IRS fees for copies of documents (currently $1 for the first page and 15 cents for each subsequent page). They can charge for the actual cost of postage.
2. It gives instructions on *where* the documents must be available for inspection. In general, the documents must be made available at the organization's principal office, and at larger regional or district offices.
3. It sets limitations an organization may put on requests for copies of documents. Copies of documents should normally be available upon personal request the same day at the place where the documents are available for inspection. Under unusual circumstances, the organization may respond on the next business day, or on the business day following the day the unusual circumstances occurred, as long as the delay does not exceed 5 business days. Written requests must be honored within 30 days of receipt.
4. It outlines how an organization can avoid having to respond to individual requests for copies. Rather than furnish copies, an organization may put the documents on its Web page or another Internet site where there is a database of similar information. Placing the specified documents on the Internet covers the requirement to provide copies, but the organization must still allow public inspection. The regulations specify a number of criteria for posting documents on the Internet.

a. The documents must be posted so that the public can view, download, and print them in the same format as the original document.

b. The documents must be accessible without a fee and without having any specialized computer hardware or software.

5. It furnishes guidance to organizations that believe they are the victims of harassment campaigns. If an exempt organization has sufficient cause based on facts and circumstances to believe it is the victim of a harassment campaign, it may take certain steps:

   a. Demonstrate that a group of apparently unreasonable requests aims to disrupt the organization's operations rather than to obtain information.

   b. Refuse to respond to those requests.

   c. Request the IRS district director for a determination.

   d. While a determination is pending, the organization need not respond to the apparently frivolous requests.

   e. Comply on a timely basis with any seemingly valid requests.

## .07  Noncompliance

The IRS has set rather stiff penalties for noncompliance:

1. An *individual* whose duty it is to make the required disclosures, but fails to comply without reasonable cause with his or her obligations on behalf of the exempt organization is subject to a penalty of $20 per return or exemption application for each day the failure continues. The maximum penalty for failure to disclose is $10,000 per return. No maximum is specified for the exemption application.

2. An exempt *organization* that willfully fails to comply with the requirement to allow public inspection or to provide copies of returns or exemption applications upon proper request is liable for a $5,000 penalty (per return or application).

3. Criminal penalties may be applied to any person or exempt organization that willfully furnishes false or fraudulent information.

## ¶10,021  FASB STATEMENT 116, *ACCOUNTING FOR CONTRIBUTIONS RECEIVED AND CONTRIBUTIONS MADE* AND FASB STATEMENT 117, *FINANCIAL STATEMENTS OF NOT-FOR-PROFIT ORGANIZATIONS*

In the past, differing requirements, or deficient guidelines, have led divergent forms of not-for-profit enterprises to abide by various rulings promulgated for their particular type of organization, to follow lines of least resistance, or merely to perpetuate custom. This was true whether or not the organization or the external users were gaining insightful information from the various accounting and reporting procedures. The new rules supersede any/all inconsistencies or discrepancies with previous guides, announcements, or statements.

Statement 116 specifically addresses accounting standards for contributions of cash, assets, services or unconditional promises to provide these at some future time, made or received by any organization, whether it be a not-for-profit or a for-profit business concern:

1. Contributions *received*, including unconditional promises to give, are recognized at fair market value in the period received.
2. Contributions *made*, including unconditional promises to give, are recognized as expenses at fair market value in the period when given.
3. Conditional promises to give (whether received or made) are appropriately recognized when the conditions are substantially met.

This Statement acts to tighten some of the provisions relating to measurement and recognition of volunteer services and their relevancy. It specifies that before these services can be included in revenue, they must create or enhance nonfinancial assets, be of a specialized nature, and be provided by skilled individuals contributing services that would otherwise be purchased. Therefore, the services requiring little skill or training provided by the average volunteer will not be considered as revenue or gains. On the other hand, volunteer work by trained professionals and tradesmen, such as nurses, teachers, carpenters, plumbers may be measured at fair value and recognized in the financial report with explanatory notes describing the value of service rendered to various aspects of particular programs. Recognition of these services must also be deemed to be clearly relevant and clearly measurable. If practicable, the fair value of the ordinary volunteer services contributed but not recognized as revenue should also be disclosed even though not recognized as revenue.

Both Statements 116 and 117 take into consideration three classes of contributions:

1. Permanently restricted net assets.
2. Temporarily restricted net assets.
3. Unrestricted net assets.

Statement 116 also requires accounting for the expiration of donor-imposed restrictions if/when said restrictions expire. It also establishes standards for accounting for disclosures relating to works of art, historical treasures, rare books and manuscripts—collections whether capitalized or not.

¶10,021

To be considered a "collection," the assets must be:

1. For the purpose of public exhibition, education or research, not an investment for financial gain.
2. Conserved, cared for, and remain unencumbered.
3. Protected by an organizational policy requiring that proceeds from the sale of any collection items be used to acquire other items for collections.

An organization is not required to recognize contributions if they are added to collections which meet the above criteria. However, when applying FASB 116, organizations are encouraged to capitalize previously acquired collections retroactively or to capitalize them on a prospective basis. One stipulation is that capitalization of selected collections or items is *not* permitted. If capitalized retroactively, these assets may be stated at their cost, at fair value at the time of acquisition, current cost or current market value.

When collections have been capitalized, additional contributed items are to be recognized as revenue or gains; if the collections have not been capitalized, these items are not recognized. There is, however, additional disclosure information required for them and for collections which have been capitalized prospectively.

1. On the face of the statement of activities, apart from revenues, expenses, gains and losses an organization that has not capitalized must report the cost of items purchased as a decrease in the appropriate class of net assets; or proceeds resulting from the sale of items; or from insurance recoveries as an increase in the appropriate class of net assets.
2. An organization that capitalizes prospectively must report proceeds from sales or insurance recoveries of items not previously capitalized separately.
3. Both those organizations that do not capitalize, or do so prospectively, must describe the collections and their significance, and the accounting conservatorship policies relating to them.
4. They must also describe and report the fair value of items lost or removed from collections for whatever reason.
5. A line in the body of the financial statement must refer directly to the note on collections.

In addition to the accounting functions which these stipulations provide, they would appear to help ensure the integrity of important collections.

The intent and purpose of FASB 117 is to begin to bring a measure of uniformity to the financial statements of NPOs, particularly for the benefit of external users. Emphasis is upon relevance and significance of the information provided, the ease with which it can be understood and interpreted, and the readiness with which financial reports can be compared with those of other not-for-profit entities.

¶10,021

FASB 117 stipulates that three financial statements with appropriate notes be included in all NPO financial reports:

1. Statement of financial position.
2. Statement of activities.
3. Statement of cash flows.

This latter requirement is new for not-for-profit entities and thus amends FASB 95, *Statement of Cash Flows*, in which the requirements had previously applied only to business entities. Statement 117 also *requires* Voluntary Health and Welfare Organizations (*encourages* other NPOs) to prepare an additional financial statement showing expenses in natural classifications as well as the functional classifications required of all NPOs. Organizations may continue to present other financial reports if they have found them to be beneficial in demonstrating the handling of the service aspects of the particular type of NPO.

Most organizations probably found that their accounting and reporting activities had not become more complicated and restrictive, but simplified, and at the same time, more meaningful once the initial changeover had been completed. This is particularly true if the organization carried fund accounting to the extreme and attempted to fit everything into the pattern whether or not this proved to be appropriate or useful. Statement 117 does not tamper with fund accounting *per se* but does require that the emphasis on financial reporting be placed on the entity as a whole. Thus, organizations may continue to prepare their statement of financial position showing fund groups, but the groups must be aggregated into net asset classes.

In line with the aim to give a clear picture of an NPO's liquidity, FASB 117 requires that an organization must break down its net assets into the three classes mentioned above. Further, information about the amounts and/or conditions of the two restricted categories can be made in the statement itself if this is deemed sufficient, or it may be necessary to give detailed explanations in the notes. The latter could be more frequently necessary than not, since the restrictions could range from a wealthy donor's desire to aid a "pet project" to a government grant funding a Congressional bill.

Much of the impetus for these statements was to bring about more readily usable full disclosure. Requirements will now make it more important than ever to distinguish between program and support activities and expenses. FASB 117 separates the latter into three classes:

1. Managements and general.
2. Fund-raising.
3. Membership development.

It is important for the preparer of the financial statement to be reminded that the focus should be on the *service* aspect of the NPO and how well this is being accomplished. Since it is doubtful if this information can be conveyed adequately in the body of the financial statement, the accompanying notes will be of particular relevance.

Below are some important points to keep in mind relating to the purpose of the three basic financial reports of not-for-profit entities.

## .01 Statement of Financial Position

- Present assets, liabilities and net asset figures for the organization as a whole.
- Demonstrate credit status, liquidity, ability to meet service and financial obligations, need for outside financial aid.
- Distinguish between permanently restricted assets, temporarily restricted assets, unrestricted assets.
- Disclose donor-imposed restrictions and internally imposed restrictions relating to both time and purpose.

## .03 Statement of Activities (Operating Statement for NPOs)

- Report the changes in total net assets (equities).
- Present the changes in each of the three net asset classes (not fund balances): permanently restricted, temporarily restricted, unrestricted.
- Indicate total changes in net assets.
- Disclose expenditures by functional and/or natural classification as required/recommended for a particular type of NPO.

## .05 Statement of Cash Flows

- Amends FASB 95 to require *all* NPOs to include a cash flow statement in their external financial reports.
- Present changes in cash and cash equivalents including certain donor-restricted cash used on a long-term basis.
- Present cash flow information utilizing either direct or indirect method.

## ¶10,023    FASB STATEMENT 124, *ACCOUNTING FOR CERTAIN INVESTMENTS HELD BY NOT-FOR-PROFIT ORGANIZATIONS*

FASB 124 is another step in the process of bringing reason, conformity, consistency, and comparability in accounting and financial reporting to the world of not-for-profit entities.

This statement is reminiscent of FASB 115, *Accounting for Certain Investments in Debt and Equity Securities*, to the extent that it covers the same securities; however, accounting treatment for NPOs is markedly different from that applied to for-profit businesses.

## .01 Fair Value Requirements

Statement 124 requires that certain equity securities and all investments in debt securities be reported at fair value. The specific equity securities are those with readily determined fair value which are not accounted for by the equity method or as investments in consolidated subsidiaries. Gains and losses are to be reported in the statement of activities. This Statement also requires specific disclosures about all investments, including the return on the investments.

*Readily determinable* fair value of an equity security is considered to have been met if one of the following criteria applies:

1. Sale prices or bid or asked quotations are available on an SEC registered exchange.
2. Sales prices or bid or asked prices on OTC markets if they are reported by NASDAQ or the National Quotation Bureau.
3. If the equity security is traded only on a foreign market, that market is comparable to one of those given above.
4. If a mutual fund investment, fair value per share or unit has been determined and published as the basis for ongoing transactions.

Although many NPOs have been reporting all of their investments at fair value, it has not been required; therefore, there has been a considerable degree of diversity in the various organizations' accounting and financial reporting. The FASB believes that fair value will give a truer picture of the resources available for the further growth of the program of a not-for-profit organization. In addition, not only the staff and administrators, but also the donors will have improved information to assist them in allocating their efforts and resources.

## .03 Accounting Procedures

Application of this Statement may be made in either of two ways:

1. Restating of all financial statements presented for prior years.
2. Recognizing the cumulative effect of the change in the year of adoption.

Accounting and reporting for investments by various types of not-for-profit organizations has heretofore been provided by several AICPA guides.

Any guidance in those sources which is inconsistent with the provisions of FASB 124 are superseded by these new requirements in this Statement.

In addition to the accounting principles set forth in this pronouncement, any additional disclosure and accounting requirements not discussed here but included in other Statements may apply to investments held by not-for-profit entities as well as to for-profit companies. They are:

1. FASB 107, *Disclosure about Fair Value of Financial Instruments* (amended).
2. FASB 133, *Accounting for Derivative Instruments and Hedging Activities.*

## .05  Disclosure and Reporting

The Statement of Activities for each reporting period for an NPO must include the following specific items:

1. Investment income from dividends, interest, etc.
2. Net gains or losses on investments reported at other than fair value.
3. Net gains or losses on those reported at fair value.
4. Reconciliation of investment return if separated into operating and non-operating amounts.
5. Description of the policy used to decide what items should be included in determining operating costs.
6. Discussion for so doing if there is a change in that policy.

The Statement of Financial Position for each reporting period for an NPO must include the following:

1. Aggregate carrying amount of investments by major type.
2. Basis on which carrying amounts were determined for investments other than equity securities with readily determinable fair value and all debt securities.
3. Procedures used in determining fair values of investments other than financial instruments if carried at fair value. (Financial instruments are covered by the same requirement in FASB 107.)
4. Aggregate amount of any deficiencies in donor-related funds in which fair value of the assets has fallen below the level necessary to abide by donor stipulation or legal requirements.

For the most recent period, a not-for-profit organization must disclose in the Statement of Financial Position the nature of and carrying amount of any investments that represent a significant concentration of market risk.

¶10,023.05

## ¶10,025 IRS E-FILE FOR CHARITIES AND NONPROFITS

The 990 series of forms are used by tax-exempt organizations including charities, private foundations, and other tax-exempt organizations to provide information about their programs and activities to verify that they are operating in accordance with their stated tax-exempt purpose. Information on these returns may be disclosed to the public as provided by law.

In February 2004, the IRS released new electronic forms for tax-exempt organizations in partnership with software developers, tax professionals, and state charity officials. The February 2004 release of forms included

- Form 990, "Return of Organization Exempt from Income Tax"
- Form 990-EZ, "Short Return of Organization Exempt from Income Tax"
- Form 1120-POL, "U.S. Income Tax Return of Political Organizations"
- Form 8868, "Application for Extension of Time To File an Exempt Organization Return"

Form 990-PF, "Return of Private Foundation," became available in January 2005.

## .01 Who Can Participate

Any exempt organization can participate in this program by electronically filing their returns through an *Approved IRS 990-efile Provider*. This Web page also contains links to companies that offer 990 e-file. The providers' page is updated as new companies are added.

## .03 How to Participate

Tax professionals who plan to file Forms 990, 990-EZ, 990-PF, or 1120-POL electronically must submit a new or revised electronic IRS e-file application using the electronic e-Services application. This is a one-time registration process and application must be made at least 45 days prior to filing electronically.

## .05 Benefits of Electronic Filing

The IRS points out that e-file takes much of the hassle and worry out of the filing:

- No more preparing paper returns or buying stamps.
- Eliminates returns being lost in the mail.

**¶10,025**

- Virtually eliminates late filing fees and penalties.
- Filers receive fast electronic acknowledgment that Form 990 has been received for processing.
- Tax preparation is automated with return preparation software that performs calculations, and highlights needed forms and schedules.
- Easily understood error messages.
- Information is quickly available to IRS Customer Service sites.
- Quick processing time.
- Fewer risks of transcription errors.
- Higher accuracy rates.
- Tax information is secure.
- Only authorized users have access to the system.

## ¶10,027  NEW IRS E-FILE REQUIREMENTS FOR LARGE TAX-EXEMPT ORGANIZATIONS

On January 12, 2005, the IRS released regulations that require certain tax-exempt organizations to file annual exempt organization returns electronically beginning in 2006. For tax year 2005 returns due in 2006, the regulations require organizations with total assets of $100 million or more to file electronically.

The electronic filing requirements apply only to entities that file at least 250 returns, including income tax, excise tax, employment tax, and information returns, during a calendar year. Example: If an organization has 245 employees, it must file Form 990 or Form 990-PF electronically, because each Form W-2 and quarterly Form 941 is considered a separate return; therefore, the organization files a total of 250 returns (245 W-2's, four 941's, and one 990/990-PF).

Beginning in 2007, private foundations and charitable trusts will be required to file Form 990-PF electronically regardless of their asset size, if they file at least 250 returns.

# Chapter 11

# International Standards: Accounting

## CONTENTS

## ¶11,000   OVERVIEW

During the current evolutionary period for global markets, the unification of accounting practices has lagged behind the market forces driving business globalization. Opportunities for business expansion could not wait for the accounting profession to recognize and implement the needed international accounting standards. Advances in information technology, transportation, and communication, including the Internet, have served as catalysts, allowing businesses to seek new customers and new markets in the international arena. The rapid pace of cross-border business growth has arisen in spite of the fact that accounting practices differed from country to country. Individual accounting practices in each country were the natural result of diverse economic policies, legal frameworks, social factors, and cultural traditions. The imminent standardization of accounting practices, however, is clearly visible upon the horizon.

## ¶11,001   THE NATURE OF INTERNATIONAL ACCOUNTING

One of the central goals of the movement to unify international accounting practices is the need for financial reporting comparability. Whereas U.S. GAAP seeks meaningful comparison in financial reporting among companies in the same industry, the impetus in international accounting is to avoid reporting that produces different income statement results for the same company during the same period, when the reports are prepared in one country rather than another.

To accommodate relevant differences between countries, one of the principles underlying the desire to unify international accounting practices is to allow reporting flexibility without producing distortion. Since the goal of international accounting, like that of U.S. GAAP accounting, is to produce general-purpose financial statements, it is not necessary to impose a strict standardization. Rather, a coordination or harmonization of reporting that leaves room for legitimate differences but still produces meaningful financial reporting is the desired result.

The Financial Accounting Standards Board (FASB) believes the ideal outcome of cooperative international accounting standard-setting efforts will be the worldwide use of a single set of high-quality accounting standards for both U.S. and cross-border financial reporting. The FASB's objective is to increase the international comparability and the quality of standards used in the United States. Here, domestic firms that are registrants with the Securities and Exchange Commission (SEC) must file financial reports using U.S. generally accepted accounting principles. Foreign firms filing with the SEC can use U.S. GAAP, their home country GAAP, or international standards. However, if they use their home country GAAP or international standards, foreign issuers must provide reconciliation to U.S. GAAP. As international standards and U.S. GAAP converge the reconciliation will become easier and involve fewer substantive issues.

In 2002 the FASB and the International Accounting Standards Board (IASB) announced the issuance of a memorandum of understanding, the "Norwalk Agreement." The Agreement was a significant step toward formalizing their commitment to the convergence of U.S. and international accounting standards. At their joint meeting in Norwalk, Connecticut, the FASB and the IASB each acknowledged their commitment to the development of high-quality, compatible accounting standards that can be used for both domestic and cross-boarder financial reporting. At that meeting, both the FASB and IASB pledged to use their best efforts to (a) make their existing financial reporting standards fully compatible as soon as practicable and (b) to coordinate their future work programs to ensure that once achieved, compatibility is maintained.

To achieve compatibility, the FASB and IASB agreed, as a matter of high priority, to the following:

- Undertake a short-term project aimed at removing a variety of individual differences between U.S.GAAP and International Financial Reporting Standards (IFRSs).

- Remove other differences between IFRSs and U.S.GAAP that will remain at January 1, 2005, through coordination of their future work programs; that is, through the mutual undertaking of discrete, substantial projects, which both Boards will address concurrently.

- Continue progress on the joint projects that they are currently undertaking.

- Encourage their respective interpretative bodies to coordinate their activities.

## ¶11,003  2005 REPORTING STANDARDS FOR LISTED PUBLIC COMPANIES IN THE EU

Starting January 1, 2005, listed public companies in European Union (EU) are required to report financial results using International Accounting Standards (IASs) and IFRSs. There will be a temporary exception for companies that are currently traded in the United States and use U.S.GAAP and for companies that have issued debt instruments but not equity instruments. Those companies will be required to comply with international standards by January 1, 2007.

In a concerted effort to hasten the congruity between International Accounting Standards (IASs) and U.S. GAAP, 15 of 40 existing International Accounting Standards were revised between December 2003 and March 2004. One new IAS was added as well (No. 41, *Agriculture*). Five IFRSs have also been implemented.

## ¶11,005  EXEMPTIONS FOR SMALL AND MEDIUM-SIZED ENTITIES

Those responsible for establishing International Accounting Standards recognize the disparity in size between large entities and medium-sized or smaller entities. In the U.S. the issue of "big GAAP" and "little GAAP" has been around for long time. The central question regards the relative financial reporting responsibility of entities whose stock is traded on public markets as opposed to privately held entities. The initial measures addressing this concern in the arena of international accounting sought to establish by number of employees, balance sheet or revenue measures, eligibility requirements for small or medium-sized entities to report on a more modest basis.

The IASB has begun addressing the question of small and medium-sized entities (SMEs) in relation to its standards. The result has been a statement of the Board's preliminary views through May 7, 2004, which include the following:

1. The objectives of financial reporting stated in IASB framework are appropriate for SMEs. Therefore, according to the Board, full IFRSs should be regarded as suitable for all entities.

2. The IASB has determined to allow the use of the SME standards *without a specific size test*. National jurisdiction should determine whether all entities that meet the IASB's characteristics, or only some, should be required or permitted to use the IASB Standards for SMEs.

3. Public accountability is the overriding characteristic that distinguishes SMEs from other entities. An entity has public accountability if, according to the Board "there is a high degree of outside interest in the entity from nonmanagement investors or other stakeholders, and those stakeholders depend primarily on external financial reporting as their only means of obtaining financial information about the entity; or the entity has an essential public service responsibility because of the nature of its operations."

4. The test of public accountability is based on meeting any one of the following criteria:
   a. The entity "has filed, or it is in the process of filing, its financial statements with a securities commission or other regulatory organization for the purpose of issuing any class of instruments in a public market;
   b. It holds assets in a fiduciary capacity for a broad group of outsiders, such as a bank, insurance company, securities broker/dealer, pension fund, mutual fund, or investment banking entity;
   c. It is a public utility or similar entity that provides an essential public service; or
   d. It is economically significant in its home country based on criteria such as total assets, total revenue, number of employees, degree of market dominance, and nature and extent of external borrowings."

5. The IASB will develop a set of financial reporting standards suitable to entities that do not have public reporting responsibilities.

6. SMEs using the modified standards must disclose this in the basis of presentation as well as in the auditor's report.

7. IASB reporting rules for SMEs will provide a single set of high-quality, understandable, and enforceable accounting standards.

¶11,005

8. The IASB focus in preparing the SME standards is on the needs of users of SME financial statements.
9. The foundation for these standards will be the same conceptual framework as that used for the IFRSs.
10. The IASB's goal is to reduce the financial reporting burden on SMEs that want to use global standards.
11. For those SMEs that subsequently become publicly accountable, the transition from the SME standards to the full IFRSs should involve minimal inconvenience.
12. An entity will be regarded as not having public accountability only if all of the holders of its shares, including those not otherwise entitled to vote, have been informed about, and do not object to, the entity preparing its financial statements on the basis of IASB Standards for SMEs rather than on the basis of full IFRSs.
13. A subsidiary, joint venture, or associate of an entity with public accountability should comply with full IFRSs, not IASB Standards for SMEs, in its separate financial statements if it prepares financial information in accordance with full IFRSs to meet the requirements of the parent, venturer, or investors.

## ¶11,007 INTERNATIONAL ACCOUNTING STANDARDS CHANGES

The International Accounting Standards Board (IASB) adopted the Standards issued by its predecessor body, the International Accounting Standards Committee (IASC). It is now in the process of reviewing and, where necessary, making changes to those standards. Those pronouncements continue to be designated "International Accounting Standards." Following are lists of the IASs currently in force, previously issued and withdrawn, and those proposed. They represent the core group of international standards necessary for cross-border reporting. The IASB Standards updating project was undertaken with 15 of the existing pronouncements. The Board has completed its work in time for them to be used by companies adopting them for the first time in 2005. The full Standards should be consulted for specific guidance on technical issues.

Several standards remain unchanged:

- IAS 7, *Cash Flow Statements*
- IAS 11, *Construction Contracts*
- IAS 12, *Income Taxes*
- IAS 18, *Revenue*—The standard is applicable for annual periods beginning on or after January 1, 2005. No change.
- IAS 20, *Accounting for Government Grants and Disclosure of Government Assistance*
- IAS 23, *Borrowing Costs*

- IAS 26, *Accounting and Reporting by Retirement Benefit Plans*
- IAS 29, *Financial Reporting in Hyperinflationary Economies*
- IAS 30, *Disclosures in the Financial Statements of Banks and Similar Financial Institutions*
- IAS 34, *Interim Financial Reporting*
- IAS 37, *Provisions, Contingent Liabilities, and Contingent Assets*

The standards that have been withdrawn are:

- IAS 15, *Information Reflecting Effects of Changing Prices*
- IAS 22, Business Combinations (replaced by IFRS 3, *Business Combinations*)

Proposed amendments issued are:

- IAS 19, *Employee Benefits—Actuarial Gains and Losses, Group Plans and Disclosures* (proposed amendments issued)

The revised standards are discussed below; they were revised December 2003 through March 2004.

## .01   IAS 1, *Presentation of Financial Statements*

The revised Standard is applicable for annual periods beginning on or after January 1, 2005. Critical judgments made by management in applying accounting policies must be disclosed (par. IN12). Disclosure is also required for management's assumptions that are important in determining accounting estimates and could cause material adjustment to the carrying amounts of assets and liabilities (par. IN12) the Standard does not apply to interim financial statements (IAS 34, *Interim Financial Reporting*). The financial statement is to consist of a balance sheet, an income statement, a statement of changes in equity, and a cash flow statement, as well as notes comprising a summary of significant accounting policies, and other explanatory disclosures.

The following specific requirements are mandated:

- Accrual basis accounting.
- Going concern basis.
- Consistent classification schemes from one period to the next.
- Related assets and liabilities are not offset.
- Presentation of comparative information.
- Separate statement of current and noncurrent assets and liabilities.

¶11,007.01

## .03 IAS 2, *Inventories*

The revised Standard is applicable for annual periods beginning on or after January 1, 2005. The cost of inventories, other than those for which specific identification of cost are used, is assigned using first-in, first-out (FIFO) or a weighted average cost flow method. LIFO (last-in, first-out) inventory valuation method sometimes used in the U.S. and elsewhere has been removed (par. IN13). Inventories are measured at the lower of cost or net realizable value. Net realizable value is the estimated selling price in the ordinary course of business less the estimated costs of completion and the estimated costs necessary to sell. The amount of any write-down of inventories to net realizable value is recognized as an expense in the period the write-down or loss occurs.

## .05 IAS 8, *Accounting Policies, Changes in Accounting Estimates, and Errors*

The revised Standard is applicable for annual periods beginning on or after January 1, 2005. Retrospective application of voluntary changes in accounting policies and retrospective restatement to correct all material prior-period errors are now required. This means a change in accounting policy is applied retrospectively to all periods presented in the financial statements as if the new accounting policy had always been applied.

A material prior-period error is corrected retrospectively in the first set of financial statements after its discovery. The comparative amounts for the prior periods presented in which the error occurred are restated. Before this change IAS 8 contained an alternative for both changes and errors that allowed including the resultant effects in the profit or loss for the current period. When this alternative was applied, comparative information was not amended. Under the improved Standard comparatives are restated (pars. IN8–IN9). An entity should change an accounting policy only if the change is required by an IFRS or if the change results in the financial statements providing more relevant and reliable information.

The Standard specifies the following hierarchy of guidance, which management uses when selecting accounting policies:

1. Requirements of Standards and Interpretations dealing with similar matters.
2. The definitions, recognition criteria, and measurement concepts for assets, liabilities, income, and expenses in the *Framework for the Preparation and Presentation of Financial Statements.*
3. The most recent pronouncements of other standard-setting bodies that use a similar conceptual framework, other accounting literature, and accepted industry practices, to the extent that these do not conflict with IFRSs and the Framework.

The effect of a change in an *accounting estimate* is recognized prospectively in profit or loss in the period of change and in profit or loss in future periods if the change affects both periods.

## .07  IAS 10, *Events After the Balance Sheet Date*

The revised Standard is applicable for annual periods beginning on or after January 1, 2005. Events after the balance sheet date are those events that occur between the balance sheet date and the date when the financial statements are authorized for issue. The Standard requires an entity to adjust the amounts recognized in the financial statements to reflect adjusting events after the balance sheet date. Adjusting events are those that provide evidence of *conditions that existed at the balance sheet date*. These include, but are not limited to, the settlement of a court case after the balance sheet date that confirms that the entity had a present obligation at the balance sheet date or a customer's filing for bankruptcy thereby confirming the amount of loss at the balance sheet date. Nonadjusting events are not used to adjust the financial statements at the balance sheet date. These are events that occurred after the balance sheet date, but have no reference to the balance-sheet-date values.

## .09  IAS 16, *Property, Plant, and Equipment*

The revised Standard is applicable for annual periods beginning on or after January 1, 2005. An entity is required to measure an item of property, plant, and equipment at fair value when acquired in exchange for a nonmonetary asset or assets, or a combination of monetary and nonmonetary assets. An exception is allowed if the exchange transaction lacks commercial substance (par. IN8).

Property, plant and equipment are initially recognized at cost. Subsequently, the carrying amount is:

- Cost, less accumulated depreciation, and any accumulated impairment losses, or
- Revalued amount, less subsequent accumulated depreciation, and any accumulated impairment losses. The revalued amount is the fair value at the date of revaluation. The choice of measurement is applied consistently to an entire class of property, plant, and equipment. Any revaluation increase is credited directly to the revaluation surplus in equity, unless it reverses a revaluation decrease previously recognized in profit or loss.

## .11  IAS 17, *Leases*

The revised Standard is applicable for annual periods beginning on or after January 1, 2005. Initial direct finance costs for lessors can no longer be charged as expenses as incurred. Rather, they are included in the carrying amount of the leased asset and recognized as an expense over the term of the lease. Manufacturer-dealer lessors recognize costs of this type as an expense when the selling profit is recognized (par. IN12).

A lease is classified as a finance or operating lease at its inception. Finance leases are those that transfer substantially all of the risks and rewards incident to ownership to the lessee. At the inception of a finance lease, an asset and liability are recognized. The asset is recorded at the lower of the fair value of the leased asset or the present value of the minimum lease payments.

On the books of the lessor, a finance lease is recorded as a receivable at an amount equal to the net investment in the lease. This amount is the present value of the minimum lease payments with any unguaranteed residual value accruing to the lessor. Operating lease income is recognized on a straight-line basis over the lease term.

## .13   IAS 19, *Employee Benefits: Amendment*

In its June 2005 IASB reported in its newsletter that its staff had presented a paper proposing a basis for distinguishing between defined benefit and defined contribution plans. The key to the distinction relates to the existence of an employer obligation and related risk to the employer in connection with providing specified future benefits. At its September 2005 meeting the discussion of IAS 19 was continued. Discussed was the extent to which a minimum funding requirement (MFR) imposed by law might restrict recognition of a net asset that otherwise would be recognized. In December 2004 IAS 19, dealing with several issues in the highly technical defined benefit plan reporting area, was amended to allow reporting in full of actuarial gains and losses, outside profit or loss, in a statement of recognized income and expense.

## .15   IAS 21, *The Effects of Changes in Foreign Exchange Rates*

The revised Standard is applicable for annual periods beginning on or after January 1, 2005. Capitalization of exchange differences resulting from severe devaluation or depreciation of a currency against which there is no means of hedging is no longer permitted (par. IN10).

A foreign currency transaction is recorded initially in the functional currency (the currency of the primary economic environment in which the entity operates), by applying to the foreign currency amount the spot exchange rate between the functional currency and the foreign currency at the date of the transaction. For practical reasons, a rate that approximates the actual rate at the date of the transaction is often used (e.g., an average weekly or monthly rate).

At each balance sheet date:

1. Foreign currency monetary items are translated using the closing rate.
2. Nonmonetary items that are measured in terms of historical cost in a foreign currency are translated using the exchange rate at the date of the transaction.
3. Nonmonetary items that are measured at fair value in a foreign currency are translated using the exchange rates at the date when the fair value was determined.

When translating a foreign operation for inclusion in the reporting entity's financial statements, assets and liabilities are translated at the closing rate. Income and expenses are translated at exchange rates at the dates of the transactions.

In 2005, a technical correction was proposed to IAS 21 relating to a monetary item denominated in a currency other than the functional currency of either the reporting entity or the foreign operation. The change requires that in such a situation an exchange difference does occur in the reporting entity's separate financial statements and in the foreign operation's individual operations.

## .17  IAS 24, *Related Party Disclosures*

The revised Standard is applicable for annual periods beginning on or after January 1, 2005. The definition of related parties and the disclosure requirement for related parties have both been expanded by adding parties (including joint ventures and postemployment benefit plans) and by requiring the disclosure of transactions, balances, terms and conditions, and details of guarantees (pars. IN8 and IN11-IN13). Entities are also now required to disclose the compensation of key management personnel (par. IN5).

A party is related to an entity if it:

- Directly or indirectly controls, is controlled by, or is under common control with the entity.
- Has significant influence over the entity.
- Has joint control over the entity.
- Is a close member of the family of any individual who controls, or has significant influence or joint control over the entity.
- Is an associate of the entity.
- Is a joint venturer with the entity.
- Is a member of the key management (or close family member) of the entity or its parent.

- Is a postemployment benefit plan for the benefit of employees of the entity, or of any of its related parties.

The Standard prescribes specific disclosure requirements including the nature of the relationships, names of entities, compensation of key management personnel and the nature of the transactions.

## .19  IAS 27, *Consolidated and Separate Financial Statements*

The revised Standard is applicable for annual periods beginning on or after January 1, 2005. Entities are required to present minority interests on the consolidated balance sheet within the equity section separately from the parent shareholders' equity (par. IN12). If consolidation is required, it is so required regardless of the nature of the parent entity. Thus, the requirement to consolidate controlled subsidiaries applies to parent entities that are venture capital organizations, mutual funds, and unit trusts (par. IN8).

The requirement for entities such as venture capital companies to consolidate controlled entities was already in force. However, it contained an exception when a subsidiary is acquired and held exclusively with a view to its subsequent disposal in the near future. The meaning of *near future* has now been clarified, however, to mean within twelve months. When the entity elects to present separate financial statements for investments in subsidiaries, jointly controlled entities, and associates, they are to be accounted for at cost or in accordance with IAS 39.

## .21  IAS 28, *Investments in Associates*

The revised Standard is applicable for annual periods beginning on or after January 1, 2005. An associate is an entity over which the investor has significant influence and is neither a subsidiary nor an interest in a joint venture. An investment in an associated is generally accounted for using the equity method. However, the equity method is not used when:

- The investment is classified as held for sale in accordance with IFRS 5, *Non-Current Assets Held for Sale and Discontinued Operations*; or
- The investor is itself a subsidiary, its owners do not object to the equity method not being applied, and its debt and equity securities are not publicly traded. In this case, the investor's parent must present consolidated financial statement that comply with IFRSs.

When financial statements of an associate are used in preparing the financial statements of an investor entity using the equity method of valuation, and the period ended is different from that of the investor, the difference must be no greater than three months (par. IN12). Investors must consider the carrying amount of the investment in the equity of an associate and its other long-term interests in the associate when recognizing its share of losses of that associate (par. IN14).

An investor discontinues the equity method from the date that it ceases to have significant influence over the associate. "Significant influence" is the power to participate in financial and operating policy decisions of the investee, but is not control or joint control over those policies.

## .23  IAS 31, *Interests in Joint Ventures*

The revised Standard is applicable for annual periods beginning on or after January 1, 2005. The Standard applies in accounting for interests in joint ventures and the reporting of joint venture assets, liabilities, income, and expenses in the financial statements of a venturer.

A joint venture is a contractual arrangement whereby two or more parties undertake an economic activity that is subject to joint control. Joint ventures are of three types:

1.  Jointly controlled operations.
2.  Jointly controlled assets.
3.  Jointly controlled entities.

Joint control exists only when the strategic financial and operating decisions relating to the economic activity require the unanimous consent of the parties sharing control. The Standard prescribes the method for recognizing each form of joint venture in the financial statements.

IAS 31 does not apply to interests in jointly controlled entities held by:

*   Venture capital organizations, or
*   Mutual funds, unit trusts, and similar entities, including investment-linked insurance funds that upon initial recognition are designated at fair value through profit or loss or are classified as held for trading and accounted for in accordance with IAS 39, *Financial Instruments: Recognition and Measurement.*

## .25  IAS 32, *Financial Instruments: Disclosure and Presentation*

The revised Standard is applicable for annual periods beginning on or after January 1, 2005. This Standard deals with the disclosure and presentation of financial instruments in the financial statements. (IAS 39 deals with measurement and recognition requirements.) The Standard applies to all companies reporting under International Financial Reporting Standards. It requires disclosure of information to increase users understanding of why particular financial instruments are used by businesses and the associated risks. The required disclosures include:

*   The risks associated with the entity's financial instruments.
*   Management's policies for controlling those risks.
*   The accounting policies applied to the instruments.
*   The nature and extent of an entity's use of the financial instruments.
*   The business purposes they serve.

The Standard is intended to enhance financial statement users' understanding of the significance of financial instruments to an entity's financial position, performance, and cash flows.

Financial instruments are classified, from the perspective of the issuer, as financial assets, financial liabilities, and equity instruments. Compound financial instruments may contain both a liability and an equity component.

IAS 32 applies to all types of financial instruments except:

*   Those interests in subsidiaries, associates, and joint ventures that are consolidated or are accounted for using the equity method or proportionate consolidation in accordance with IAS 27, *Consolidated and Separate Financial Statements*; IAS 28, *Investment in Associates*; or IAS 31, *Interests in Joint Ventures*.
*   Employers' rights and obligations under employee benefit plans (IAS 19, *Employee Benefits*).
*   Contracts for contingent consideration in a business combination (IFRS 3, *Business Combinations*).
*   Insurance contracts as defined by IFRS 4, *Insurance Contracts.*
*   Financial instruments that are within the scope of IFRS 4, *Insurance Contracts* because they contain a discretionary participation feature.
*   Financial instruments, contracts, and obligations under share-based payment transactions (IFRS 2, *Share-Based Payment*).

At its June 2005 meeting, IFRIC considered a possible amendment to IAS 32. The specific proposal set forth was that for classification purposes only, a fixed amount of foreign currency is considered to be a fixed amount of cash. This change was expected to result in such instruments receiving classification as equity.

### .27 IAS 33, *Earnings per Share*

The revised Standard is applicable for annual periods beginning on or after January 1, 2005. Additional guidance and illustrative examples have been provided on the following selected complex matters related to earnings per share:

- Contingently issuable shares.
- Potential ordinary shares of subsidiaries, joint ventures or associates.
- Participating equity instruments.
- Written put options.
- Purchased put and call options.
- Mandatorily convertible instruments.

The Standard applies to entities whose ordinary shares are publicly traded or entities in the process of issuing shares to be publicly traded.

Basic earning per share is calculated by dividing profit or loss attributable to ordinary equity holders of the parent entity by the weighted average number of ordinary shares outstanding during the period.

Diluted earnings per share is calculated by adjusting the profit or loss attributable to ordinary equity holders of the parent entity, and the weighted average number of ordinary shares outstanding for the effects of all potentially dilutive shares. Shares are treated as potentially dilutive when their conversion to ordinary shares would decrease earnings per share or increase loss per share from continuing operations. Dilutive shares include options, warrants, convertible instruments, and contingently issuable shares.

## .28 IAS 34, Interim Financial Reporting

In its August 2005 newsletter, IFRIC considered a possible inconsistency between IAS 34, IAS 36, *Impairment of Assets* and IAS 39 *Financial Instruments: Recognition and Measurement*. The committee's concern relates to the nature of certain events reported in the full-year financial statements and how or to what extent those items must be reported in interim financial statements. The requirements for interim reporting in IAS 34 were also considered in light of financial reporting guidelines contained in IAS 16, *Property, Plant and Equipment*, IAS 38 *Intangible Assets*, IAS 40 *Investment Properties*, IAS 19 *Employee Benefits* and IAS 37 *Provisions, Contingent Liabilities and Contingent Assets*.

### .29 IAS 36, *Impairment of Assets*

The revised Standard is applicable to goodwill and intangible assets acquired in business combinations after March 31, 2004, and to all other assets for annual periods beginning on or after March 31 2004. IFRS 3, *Business Combinations* requires goodwill to be tested for impairment annually, or more frequently if events or changes in circumstances indicate a possible impairment. Goodwill impairment is not reversed, nor is goodwill amortized.

The Standard prescribes the procedures that an entity applies to ensure that its assets are carried at no more than their recoverable amount. It does not apply to inventories; assets arising from construction contracts; deferred tax assets, assets arising from employee benefits; financial assets within the scope of IAS 39, *Financial Instruments: Recognition and Measurement;*, investment property measured at fair value; biological assets related to agricultural activity; deferred acquisition costs; and intangible assets and noncurrent assets classified as held for sale in accordance with IFRS 5, *Non-Current Assets Held for Sale and Discontinued Operations.*

The recoverable amount of an asset is measured whenever there is an indication that the asset may be impaired, but at least annually. The recoverable amount is determined for an individual asset or the smallest identifiable group of assets that generates cash inflows that are largely independent of the cash inflows from other assets or groups of assets.

An impairment loss, calculated as the carrying amount of an asset less its recoverable amount, is recognized immediately in profit or loss. If the asset is revalued in accordance with another standard, the impairment loss is treated as a revaluation decrease in accordance with that other standard.

An impairment loss recognized in prior periods is reversed if there is a change in the estimates used to determine the asset's recoverable amount since the last impairment loss was recognized. If this has occurred, the carrying amount of the asset is increased to its recoverable amount, but not to exceed the carrying amount of the asset that would have been determined had no impairment loss been recognized in prior years.

## .31   IAS 38, *Intangible Assets*

This Standard is applied to the accounting for intangible assets acquired in business combinations after March 31, 2004. IFRS 3, *Business Combinations*, requires goodwill to be tested for impairment annually, or more frequently if events or changes in circumstances indicate a possible impairment. It prohibits the reversal of impairment losses for goodwill as well as prohibiting the amortization of goodwill.

An intangible asset is initially recognized at cost if *all* the following criteria are met:

- The asset is identifiable and controlled by the entity.
- It is probable that future economic benefits that are attributable to the asset will flow to the entity.
- The cost of the asset can be reliably measured.

For an intangible item that does not meet the criteria for recognition as an asset, such as internally generated goodwill, brands, and customer lists, the expenditure is recognized as an expense when incurred.

Subsequent to initial recognition, an intangible asset is carried at one of the following:

- Cost, less any accumulated amortization and any accumulated impairment losses; or
- Revalued amount (only if there is an active market), less any subsequent accumulated amortization an any accumulated impairment losses. The revalued amount is fair value at the date of revaluation and is determined by reference to an active market

An entity assesses whether the useful life of an intangible asset is finite or indefinite. For assets with finite lives, the asset is amortized on a systematic basis over its useful life. If the life is indefinite, there is no foreseeable limit to the period over which the asset is expected to generate net cash flows, and there is no amortization.

In June 2005 IFRIC continued discussion of an amendment aimed at reporting emission rights that are traded on an active market at their fair value with gains and losses arising from changes in the fair value recognized in profit or loss.

## .33  IAS 39, *Financial Instruments: Recognition and Measurement – The Fair Value Option*

The revised Standard is applicable for annual periods beginning on or after January 1, 2005. This Standard deals with the measurement of financial instruments and with their recognition—when they should be included in the financial statements and how they should be valued. (IAS 32 deals with disclosure and presentation requirements.) The Standard applies to all companies reporting under International Financial Reporting Standards. It requires derivatives to be reported at their fair or market value rather than at cost. This overcomes the problem that the cost of such instruments may be very small in relation to their market value, resulting in distortions when cost is used. The revised Standard now tracks the equivalent U.S. GAAP standard.

The Standard divides financial assets and financial liabilities into five classes with three different accounting treatments; the treatments mirror those for U.S.GAAP, classifying instruments into trading, held to maturity, or available for sale:

1. Trading assets and liabilities, including all derivatives that are not hedges, are measured at fair value. Their gains or losses are recognized currently in profit or loss as they occur.

2. Loans and receivables are accounted for at amortized cost.
3. Held-to-maturity investments are accounted for at amortized cost.
4. Financial liabilities that are not held for trading are amortized using the effective interest method.
5. All other financial assets are ordinarily classified as available for sale and measured at fair value, with all gains and losses taken into equity.

On disposal, gains and losses previously taken into equity are reclassified to profit or loss.

The Standard describes two forms of hedging relationship and their respective accounting treatments:

1. In the case of a fair value hedge, defined as a hedge in which the fair value of the item being hedged changes as market prices change, both the changes in the fair value of the hedging instrument and the hedged item are reported in profit or loss.
2. In a cash flow hedge, one where the cash flows of the item being hedged change as market prices change, the changes in the fair value of the hedging instrument are initially reported in equity and reclassified to profit or loss to match the recognition of the offsetting gains and losses on the hedged transaction.

Another aspect of asset valuation occurs whenever there is evidence of impairment. With respect to when and how losses should be recognized, the Standard clarifies that:

- Impairment should take into account only losses that have already been incurred and not those likely to occur in the future; and
- Impairment losses on available-for-sale assets are reclassified from equity and recognized in profit or loss. For equity investments, objective evidence of impairment may include significant adverse changes in the issuer's market position, or a significant or prolonged decline in the fair value of the investment.

## .35  IAS 40, *Investment Property*

The revised Standard is applicable for annual periods beginning on or after January 1, 2005. Entities are permitted to account for a property interest held under an operating lease as investment property if certain criteria are met and the lessee accounts for the lease as if it were a finance lease and measures the resulting lease at fair value (par. IN5).

Investment property is initially recognized at cost. Subsequently, investment property is carried either at:

- Cost, less accumulated depreciation and any accumulated impairment losses, as prescribed by IAS 16 *Property, Plant, and Equipment*, or
- Fair value. Changes in fair value are recognized immediately in profit or loss.

The investment model is applied consistently to all investment property. However, an entity may choose either the fair value model or the cost model for investment property backing liabilities that pay a return linked directly to the fair value of specified assets including that investment property. This is regardless of the model chosen for all other investment property.

## .37  IAS 41, *Agriculture*

This Standard is applicable for periods beginning on or after January 1, 2003. A biological asset is a living animal or plant. The Standard prescribes the accounting treatment, financial statement presentation, and disclosures related to agricultural activity. It applies to biological assets, agricultural produce at the point of harvest, and government grants related to biological assets.

IAS 41 does not apply to:

- Land related to agricultural activity (IAS 16, *Property, Plant and Equipment*).
- Intangible assets related to agricultural activity (IAS 38, *Intangible Assets*).
- The processing of agricultural produce after harvest (IAS 2, *Inventories*).

A biological asset is measured at its fair value less estimated point-of-sale costs, on initial recognition and at each subsequent balance sheet date. Agricultural produce harvested from an entity's biological assets is measured at its fair value less estimated point-of-sale costs at the point of harvest. Point-of-sales costs include commissions, levies, and transfer duties and taxes. A gain or loss arising on initial recognition at fair value less point-of-sale costs and from a change in fair value less point-of-sale costs is included in profit or loss.

An unconditional government grant related to a biological asset is recognized as income when the grant becomes receivable; a conditional government grant is recognized when the conditions attaching to the grant are met.

IAS 41 specifies required disclosures related to agricultural activity.

## ¶11,009  INTERNATIONAL FINANCIAL REPORTING STANDARDS

The IASB publishes its financial reporting standards in a series of pronouncements called *International Financial Reporting Standards* (IFRSs). It has also adopted the body of Standards issued by its predecessor, the Board of the International Accounting Standards Committee (IASC). Those pronouncements continue to be designated "International Accounting Standards."

### .01  IFRS 1, *First–Time Adoption of International Financial Reporting Standards*

Following recent decisions by several additional jurisdictions to adopt IFRSs, more than 90 countries plan either to require or to permit their use in the next few years. Thousands of companies worldwide are making a transition in financial reporting by expanding beyond national practices and changing to accounting standards established by the IASB. To help companies make this change as smoothly as possible, and to enable users of company reports to understand the effect of applying a new set of accounting standards, the IASB issued IFRS 1, *First-Time Adoption of International Financial Reporting Standards*, in June 2003. The Standard explains how the transition is made to IFRSs from another basis of accounting.

Through IFRS 1, the IASB has sought to address the demand of investors to have transparent information that is comparable over all periods presented. IFRS 1 is also fashioned to give reporting entities a suitable starting point for their accounting under IFRSs.

IFRS 1 requires an entity to comply with every IASB Standard in force in the first year when the entity first adopts IFRSs. However, after consideration of the cost of full compliance some specific exceptions are permitted (see below.) Under IFRS 1, entities must explain how the transition to IASB Standards affects their reported financial position, financial performance, and cash flow.

IFRS 1 applies to entities whose first IFRS financial statements are for a period beginning on or after January 1, 2004. It also applies to each interim financial report, if any, that the entity presents under IAS 34, *Interim Financial Reporting*, for part of the period covered by its first IFRS financial statements.

Adoption of international reporting standards may not be done piecemeal, an entity must adhere to all requirements as set out in the IFRS. In particular an entity's opening balance sheet must:

• Recognize all assets and liabilities required by IFRSs.

• Not recognize items as assets or liabilities if IFRSs do not permit such recognition.

- Reclassify items that were recognized under previous GAAP as one type of asset, liability, or component of equity but that should be classified by IFRS as a different type of asset, liability, or component of equity.
- Apply IFRSs in measuring all recognized assets and liabilities. The transition provisions in other IFRSs do not apply to a first-time adopter's transition to IFRSs

IFRS 1 grants limited exemptions from these requirements in specified areas. where the cost of complying would be likely to exceed the benefits to users of financial statements. Such exemptions are available for:

- Business combinations.
- Fair value or revaluation as deemed cost for certain noncurrent assets.
- Defined benefit employee benefit plans.
- Cumulative translation differences.
- Compound financial instruments.
- Assets and liabilities of subsidiaries, associates and joint ventures.
- Designation of previously recognized financial instruments.
- Share-based payment transactions.
- Insurance contracts.

The IFRS also prohibits retrospective application of IFRSs in some cases, particularly where retrospective application would require judgments by management about past conditions after the outcome of a particular transaction is already known.

IFRS 1 requires disclosures that explain how the transition from previous GAAP to IFRSs affected the entity's reported financial position, financial performance, and cash flows.

## .03   IFRS 2, Share–Based Payment

IFRS 2 *Share-Based Payment* was issued in February 2004 and applies to annual accounting periods beginning on or after January 1, 2005. Its application is retrospectively for liabilities arising from share-based payment transactions existing at the effective date.

The Standard prescribes the financial reporting by an entity when it undertakes a share-based payment transaction. It applies to grants of shares, share options, or other equity instruments made after November 7, 2002, that had not yet vested at the effective date of the IFRS.

When share options are granted to employees, IFRS 2 requires an entity to reflect such payments in its profit or loss and financial position, including expenses associated with share options granted.

¶11,009.03

The valuation of the transaction for equity-settled, share-based payment transactions with employees (and others providing similar services) is based on the fair value of the equity instruments granted. Fair value is measured at the date of grant. The valuation focuses on the specific terms and conditions of a grant of shares or share options. In general, vesting conditions are not taken into account in the grant date valuation but the number of equity instruments included in the measurement of the transaction amount is adjusted so that, ultimately, the transaction amount is based on the number of equity instruments that vest.

If the terms and conditions of an option or share grant are modified or if a grant is cancelled, repurchased, or replaced with another grant of equity instruments, the IFRS provides guidance. The Standard also contains requirements for equity-settled transactions with parties other than employees and those providing similar services.

For cash-settled transactions, the good or services received and the liability incurred are measured at the fair value of the liability. The liability is remeasured to fair value at each reporting date and at the date of settlement, with changes in fair value recognized in profit or loss.

IFRS 2 also specifies requirements for transactions in which the terms of the arrangement provide either the entity or the supplier of goods or services with a choice of whether the entity settles the transaction in cash (or other assets) or by issuing equity instruments. Disclosure requirements are also specified.

In January 2006 IFRIC issued an interpretation of IRRS 2—IFRIC 8 *Scope of IFRS 2*. According to the chairman of IFRIC "This interpretation should assist preparers in those parts of the world where, for public policy or other reasons, companies give their shares or rights to shares to individuals, organizations or groups that have not provided goods or services to the company. IFRIC 8 confirms that these arrangements fall within the scope of IFRS 2."

## .05 IFRS 3, *Business Combinations*

This Standard, issued in March 2004, is applicable for business combinations for which the agreement date is on or after March 31, 2004. *It requires the purchase method of accounting and prohibits the pooling method.* The Standard replaces IAS 22, *Business Combinations*.

The Standard prescribes the financial reporting for an entity when involved in a business combination. A business combination is the combining of separate entities or businesses into one reporting unit.

IFRS 3 does *not* apply to:

- Joint ventures.
- Business combinations involving entities or businesses under common control.
- Business combinations involving two or more mutual entities.

- Business combinations in which separate entities or businesses are brought together to form a reporting entity by contract alone without the obtaining of an ownership interest.

All business combinations are required to apply the purchase method of accounting, which views the business combination from the perspective of the acquirer. The acquirer is the combining entity that obtains control of the other combining entities or businesses. This change mirrors a similar reform in U.S.GAAP with the institution of FASB 141, *Business Combinations*.

The new rules require the acquirer to measure the cost of a business combination as the aggregate of:

- The fair values, at the date of exchange, of assets given, liabilities incurred or assumed, and equity instruments issued by the acquirer, in exchange for control of the acquiree.
- Any costs directly attributable to the business combination.

Any adjustment to the cost of the combination that is contingent on future events, is included in the cost of the combination at the acquisition date if the adjustment is probable and can be reliably measured.

The acquiring entity is required to allocate the cost of the business combination by recognizing the acquired entity's identifiable assets, liabilities, and contingent liabilities at their fair value at the date of acquisition. An exception is made for noncurrent assets that are classified as held for sale in accordance with IFRS 5, *Non-Current Assets Held for Sale and Discontinued Operations*. Such assets are recognized at fair value less costs to sell.

Goodwill is recognized as an asset and subsequently carried at cost less any accumulated impairment losses in accordance with IAS 36, *Impairment of Assets*. Goodwill is defined as the excess of the cost over the acquirer's interest in the net fair value of the identifiable assets, liabilities, and contingent liabilities at the date of acquisition. Goodwill and other intangible assets with indefinite useful lives are no longer amortized. Instead they are to be tested annually for impairment. Reversal of impairment losses, once recognized, is not allowed.

Intangible assets acquired in a combination must be segregated from goodwill if they meet the definition of an asset and their fair value can be separately measured.

If the acquirer's interest in the net fair value of the identifiable assets, liabilities, and contingent liabilities exceeds the cost of the combination (badwill), the acquirer:

- Should reassess the identification and measurement of the acquiree's identifiable assets, liabilities and contingent liabilities and the measurement of the cost of the combination, associating the difference between fair value and cost to specific assets or liabilities where possible.

¶11,009.05

- Recognize immediately in profit or loss any excess remaining after that reassessment.

This treatment of goodwill closely parallels U.S. GAAP changes in goodwill reporting as set forth in FASB 142.

IFRS 3 specifies the accounting treatment:

- For business combinations that are achieved in stages.
- Where fair values can be determined only provisionally in the period of acquisition.
- Where deferred tax assets are recognized after the accounting for the acquisition is complete.
- For previously recognized goodwill, negative goodwill, and intangible assets.

The disclosure requirements for business combinations and related goodwill issues are also addressed in this Standard.

## .07  IFRS 4, *Insurance Contracts*

This Standard was issued in March, 2004, and is applicable for annual periods beginning on or after January 1, 2005. It prescribes the financial reporting for insurance contracts by any entity that issues such contracts.

It applies to:

- Insurance contracts issued.
- Reinsurance contracts held.
- Financial instruments issued with a discretionary participation feature.

It does *not* apply to:

- Product warranties issued directly by a manufacturer, dealer or retailer (IAS 18, *Revenue*, and IAS 37, *Provisions, Contingent Liabilities, and Contingent Assets*).
- Employers' assets and liabilities under employee benefit plans (IAS 19 *Employee Benefits*) and retirement benefit obligations reported by defined benefit retirement plans (IAS 26, *Accounting and Reporting by Retirement Benefit Plans*).
- Contractual rights or obligations that are contingent on the future use of or right to use a nonfinancial item, as well as lessee's residual value guarantees on finance leases (IAS 17, *Leases;* IAS 18, *Revenue* and IAS 38 *Intangible Assets*).
- Financial guarantees entered into or retained on transferring financial assets or financial liabilities within the scope of IAS 39.

¶11,009.07

- Contingent consideration payable or receivable in a business combination (IFRS 3, *Business Combinations*).
- Direct insurance contracts that an entity holds as a policyholder.

An entity need not apply some aspects of IFRS 4 to comparative information that relates to annual periods beginning before January 1, 2005.

IFRS 4 is phase one of the IASB's project on insurance contracts. An entity is temporarily exempt from some requirements of other IFRSs, including the requirement in IAS 8 to consider the Framework in selecting accounting policies for insurance contracts. However, IFRS 4:

- Prohibits the recognition of provisions for possible future claims under insurance contracts that are not in existence at the reporting date (e.g., catastrophe provisions and equalization provisions) as liabilities.
- Requires assessment of the adequacy of recognized insurance liabilities and recognition of any impairment of reinsurance assets.
- Requires an entity to keep insurance liabilities in its balance sheet until they are discharged or cancelled, or expire, and to present insurance liabilities without offsetting them against related reinsurance assets.

An entity may change its accounting policies for insurance contracts only if the result is financial statements that are more relevant and no less reliable, or financial statements that are more reliable and no less relevant. In particular, an entity must not introduce any of the following practices, although it may continue using accounting policies that involve them:

- Measuring insurance liabilities on an undiscounted basis.
- Measuring contractual rights to future investment management fees at an amount that exceeds their fair value as implied by a comparison with current fees charged by other market participants for similar services.
- Using nonuniform accounting policies for the insurance contracts of subsidiaries
- Measuring insurance liabilities with excessive prudence.

There is a rebuttable presumption that an insurer's financial statements will become less relevant and reliable if the presentation introduces an accounting policy that reflects future investment margins in the measurement of insurance contracts. When an insurer changes its accounting policies for insurance liabilities, it may reclassify some or all financial assets as "at fair value through profit or loss."

The Standard also specifies the following:

- An entity need not account for an embedded derivative separately at fair value if the embedded derivative meets the definition of an insurance contract.

¶11,009.07

- An entity is required to unbundle deposit components of some insurance contracts and account for them separately.
- An entity may apply "shadow accounting" (i.e., account for both realized and unrealized gains or losses on assets in the same way relative to measurement of insurance liabilities).
- Discretionary participation features contained in insurance contracts or financial instruments may be recognized separately from the guaranteed element and classified as a liability or as a separate component of equity.

Disclosure requirements include (1) the amounts in the entity's financial statements that arise from insurance contracts and (2) the amount, timing, and uncertainty of future cash flows from insurance contracts.

## .09   IFRS 5, Non–Current Assets Held for Sale and Discontinued Operations

The Standard is applicable for annual periods beginning on or after January 1, 2005. This Standard prescribes the accounting for assets held for sale and the presentation and disclosure of discontinued operations. The measurement provisions of IFRS 5 apply to all noncurrent assets and disposal groups, except for:

- Deferred tax assets (IAS 12, *Income Taxes*).
- Assets arising from employee benefits (IAS 19, *Employee Benefits*).
- Financial assets within the scope of IAS 39, *Financial Instruments. Recognition and Measurement.*
- Noncurrent assets that are accounted for in accordance with the fair value model in IAS 40, *Investment Property.*
- Noncurrent assets that are measured at fair value less estimated point-of-sale costs in accordance with IAS 41, *Agriculture.*
- Contractual rights under insurance contracts as defined in IFRS 4, *Insurance Contracts.*

*Assets Held for Sale.*    An asset held for sale is one available for immediate sale when its sale is highly probable. A noncurrent asset (or disposal group) is classified as held for sale if its carrying amount will be recovered principally through a sale transaction, rather than through continuing use. A noncurrent asset (or group of assets) classified as held for sale is measured at the lower of fair value less costs to sell and its carrying amount.

Any impairment loss on write-down of an asset (or disposal group) to fair value less costs to sell is recognized currently in profit or loss. Any gain on subsequent increase in fair value less costs to sell is also recognized in profit or

**¶11,009.09**

loss, but not in excess of the cumulative impairment loss already recognized on the asset either in accordance with IFRS 5 or IAS 36 *Impairment of Assets.*

*Discontinued Operations.*    A discontinued operation is a component of an entity that either has been disposed of, or is held for sale. It may be a subsidiary, a major line of business, or geographical area. It will have been a cash-generating unit (or group of cash-generating units) as defined in IAS 36, *Impairment of Assets.*

Disclosures of discontinued operations include:

* Analysis of the post-tax profit or loss into revenue, expenses, pre-tax profit or loss, and the related income tax expense.
* The gain or loss recognized on measurement to fair value less costs to sell or on disposal, and the related income tax expense.
* Net cash flows attributable to operating, investing and financing activities.
* Assets held for sale separately from all other assets.
* Liabilities of a disposal group held for sale separately from all other liabilities.

## .11   IFRS 6, *Exploration for and Evaluation of Mineral Resources*

In December 2004 a new reporting standard was issued for the specialized area extractive activities. It is effective for periods beginning on or after January 1, 2006. Industries affected include mining, oil and gas.

## .15   IFRS 7, Financial Instruments: Disclosures

In its announcement of IFRS 7 in August 2005 the Board stated its belief that the new guidance will lead to greater transparency about the risks that entities confront from the use of financial instruments. The standard applies to all risks arising from all financial instruments unless an instrument is already covered by a more specific standard. IFRS 7 applies to all entities but the nature and extent of required disclosure will depend on the extent of the entity's use of financial instruments and its exposure to risk.

## ¶11,011   THE IASB CONCEPTUAL FRAMEWORK

The IASB employs a conceptual framework underlying its financial reporting Standards and Interpretations. *The Framework for the Preparation and Presentation of Financial Statements* (the Framework) sets out the concepts that underlie the preparation and presentation of financial statements for external users. The Framework serves to assist the IASB in the development of future International Accounting Standards and in reviewing and evaluating existing standards.

The Framework supports the interests of better reporting through convergence of the IASB with the best accounting practices from around the world. It removed a number of options contained in IASs, whose existence had caused uncertainty and reduced comparability. The completion of these improved standards brings the IASB closer to its commitment to have a platform of high-quality, improved standards.

The primary means of publishing International Financial Reporting Standards is now by electronic format through IASB's subscriber Web site IASB.org.

The Framework specifies:

- The objectives of financial statements.
- The qualitative characteristics used to determine the usefulness of information reported in financial statements.
- The definition, recognition, and measurement of the elements used in preparing financial statements.
- The concepts of capital and capital maintenance.

The Framework endorses the objective of financial statements as general purpose, as does U.S. GAAP. The purpose of financial statements is to provide information about the financial position at a given date, performance during a period, as well as changes in financial position during that period. More specifically, financial statements should provide useful information about an entity's economic resources, financial structure, liquidity, and solvency.

The Framework is based on fundamental assumptions, similar to U.S.GAAP—the use of the accrual basis of accounting and the presumption that an entity is a going concern. Qualitative characteristics of financial statements include: understandability, relevance (including materiality), reliability (faithful representation, substance over form, neutrality, prudence, completeness) and comparability. The elements of financial statements include: financial position (assets, liabilities, equity), performance, income, and expenses.

In 2005, it was announced that the IASB and the FASB had begun a joint project to revisit their conceptual frameworks for financial accounting and reporting. The goal of the joint project are to build on the respective Boards' existing frameworks by refining, updating and converging them to form a common framework to be used by both Boards in formulating new and revising existing accounting standards.

An overriding goal of both the IASB and the FASB is to ground their standards on principles rather than a collection of conventions. The coherency and integrity of a set of financial standards begins with a set of common and agreed-upon fundamental concepts. Using a common framework as a basis for developing a set of financial accounting standards helps insure coherence and internal consistency among the standards.

¶11,011

In developing a conceptual framework, the intention is not only to assist standard setters but also the preparers of financial statements. The IASB and FASB Boards have been pursuing a number of projects that are aimed at achieving short-term convergence on specific issues, as well as several extensive projects aimed at the goal of full convergence. But to achieve the ultimate goal of full convergence of standards it is necessary that the conceptual frameworks first achieve convergence.

The project is simplified by the fact that the existing conceptual frameworks are similar in emphasis. Both stress the need for standards to be useful in:

In 2005, it was announced that the IASB and the FASB had begun a joint project to revisit their conceptual frameworks for financial accounting and reporting. The goal of the joint project are to build on the respective Boards' existing frameworks by refining, updating and converging them to form a common framework to be used by both Boards in formulating new and revising existing accounting standards.

An overriding goal of both the IASB and the FASB is to ground their standards on principles rather than a collection of conventions. The coherency and integrity of a set of financial standards begins with a set of common and agreed-upon fundamental concepts. Using a common framework as a basis for developing a set of financial accounting standards helps insure coherence and internal consistency among the standards.

In developing a conceptual framework, the intention is not only to assist standard setters but also the preparers of financial statements. The IASB and FASB Boards have been pursuing a number of projects that are aimed at achieving short-term convergence on specific issues, as well as several extensive projects aimed at the goal of full convergence. But to achieve the ultimate goal of full convergence of standards it is necessary that the conceptual frameworks first achieve convergence.

The project is simplified by the fact that the existing conceptual frameworks are similar in emphasis. Both stress the need for standards to be useful in:

- Making economic decisions
- Assessing cash flow prospects
- Assessing resources and claims against those resources
- Measuring changes in financial resources

A central issue to be addressed in the course of the project includes providing definitive definitions of such fundamental concepts as asset, liability, equity, revenue recognition, measurement (historical cost, fair value, current cost), and reporting entity.

## ¶11,013    INTERPRETATIONS OF INTERNATIONAL ACCOUNTING STANDARDS

The IASC, in 1977 began publishing Interpretations of International Accounting Standards developed by the Standing Interpretations Committee (SICs). This responsibility now falls on the IASB International Financial Reporting Interpretations Committee (IFRIC). Final Interpretations are numbered SIC-1, SIC-2, and so on. Because of the great number of recent changes to the IASs, care should be exercised in consulting the SICs, because they may reflect interpretations that were only reliable until a specific date. Summaries of SICs are available on the IASC web site for those indicated with an asterisk(*); all those listed without an asterisk are superceded.

The following is a list of the SICs:

| | |
|---|---|
| SIC-1 | Consistence—Different Cost Formulas for Inventories |
| SIC-2 | Consistence—Capitalization of Borrowing Costs |
| SIC-3 | Elimination of Unrealized Profits and Losses on Transactions with Associates |
| SIC-5 | Classification of Financial Instruments—Contingent Settlement Provisions |
| SIC-6 | Cost of Modifying Existing Software |
| SIC-7* | Introduction of the Euro |
| SIC-8 | First-Time Application of IASs as the Primary Basis of Accounting |
| SIC-9 | Business Combinations—Classification Either as Acquisitions or Uniting of Interests |
| SIC-10* | Government Assistance—No Specific Relation to Operating Activities |
| SIC-11 | Foreign Exchange—Capitalization of Losses Resulting from Severe Currency Devaluations |
| SIC-12* | Consolidation—Special-Purpose Entities |
| SIC-13* | Jointly Controlled Entities—Non-Monetary Contributions by Venturers |
| SIC-14 | Property, Plant and Equipment—Compensation for the Impairment or Loss of Items |
| SIC-15* | Operating Leases—Incentives |
| SIC-16 | Presentation of Treasury Shares |
| SIC-17 | Equity—Costs of an Equity Transaction |
| SIC-18 | Consistency—Alternative Methods |
| SIC-19 | Reporting Currency—Measurement and Presentation of Financial Statements Under IAS 21 and IAS 29 |
| SIC-20 | Equity Accounting Method—Recognition of Losses |
| SIC-21* | Income Taxes—Recovery of Revalued Non-Depreciable Assets |

| SIC-22 | Business Combinations—Subsequent Adjustment of Fair Values and Goodwill Initially Reported |
|---|---|
| SIC-23 | Property, Plant, and Equipment—Major Inspection or Overhaul Costs |
| SIC-24 | Earnings per Share—Financial Instruments That May Be Settled in Shares |
| SIC-25* | Income Taxes—Changes in the Tax Status of an Enterprise or its Shareholders |
| SIC-27* | Evaluating the Substance of Transactions Involving the Legal Form of a Lease |
| SIC-28 | Business Combinations—Measurement of Shares Issued as Purchase Consideration |
| SIC-29* | Disclosure—Service Concession Agreements |
| SIC-30 | Reporting Currency—Translation from Measurement Currency to Presentation Currency |
| SIC-31* | Revenue—Barter Transactions Involving Advertising Services |
| SIC-32* | Intangible Assets—Web Site Costs |
| SIC-33 | Consolidation and Equity Method—Potential Voting Rights |

## ¶11,015 THE INTERNATIONAL ORGANIZATION OF SECURITIES COMMISSIONS

According to the International Accounting Standards Committee Foundation, The International Organization of Securities Commissions (IOSCO) is the representative body of the world's securities markets regulators. Members include the Australian Securities and Investments Commission, the French Commission des Operations des Bourse (COB), the Italian Commissione Nazionale per le Societ e la Borsa (CONSOB), the members of the Canadian Securities Administrators (CSA), the UK's Financial Services Authority (FSA) and the United States Securities and Exchange Commission (SEC).

High-quality financial information is vital to the operation of efficient capital markets, and differences in the quality of the accounting policies and their enforcement between countries leads to inefficiencies between markets. IOSCO has been active in encouraging and promoting the improvement and quality of IASs and IFRSs for more than 10 years. This commitment was evidenced by the agreement between IASC and IOSCO to work on a program of "core standards," which could be used by publicly listed entities when offering securities in foreign jurisdictions. The Core Standards project resulted in 15 new or revised IASs that were completed in 1999 with the issuance of IAS 39, *Financial Instruments: Recognition and Measurement.* IOSCO spent a year reviewing the results of the project and released a report in May 2000 which recommended to all of its members that they allow multinational issuers to use

IASC Standards, as supplemented by reconciliation, disclosure, and interpretation, where necessary, to address outstanding substantive issues at a national or regional level. IASB staff and IOSCO continue to work together to resolve outstanding issues and to identify areas where new IASB Standards are needed. IOSCO representatives sit as observers on the International Financial Reporting Interpretations Committee.

# Chapter 12

# International Standards: Auditing, Ethics, Public Sector

## CONTENTS

## ¶12,000  OVERVIEW

As the movement to produce a unified international accounting profession evolved, two authoritative bodies emerged as leaders, the International Federation of Accountants (IFAC) and the International Accounting Standards Board (IASB), formerly the International Accounting Standards Committee (IASC). By 1982, it became obvious to the leadership of the IFAC and the IASC that their particular bailiwicks needed to be clearly established in order to avoid confusion concerning their respective roles. It was agreed that the IASC (now IASB) should be the sole international body to set *financial accounting and reporting standards*. At the same time, IASC agreed to IFAC's role as the worldwide *organization for the accountancy profession*.

## ¶12,001  THE INTERNATIONAL FEDERATION OF ACCOUNTANTS

The Board of the IFAC considered the following to be among the organization's most important tasks:

1. Develop auditing initiatives;
2. Develop guidance and standards relating to education, ethics, management accounting, information technology, and the public sector;
3. Give consideration to such professional issues as accountant's liability and the liberalization of professional services;
4. Act as primary spokesperson on professional accountancy issues.

Founded in 1977, the International Federation of Accountants with headquarters in New York, now consists of 163 member organizations from 119 countries with 2.5 million members in public practice, education, government service, industry, and commerce. Individual accountants are represented through their membership in their national accountancy organization. IFAC emphasizes that the international accountancy profession be considered to have two primary standard-setting bodies: IFAC and the IASC.

*Associate* members of IFAC are national organizations whose members work in a support role to the accountancy professions and newly formed accountancy bodies that have not yet met the full membership criteria.

*Affiliate* members of IFAC are international organizations that represent a particular area of interest or a group of professionals who frequently interact with accountants.

There is considerable mutual support for one another's objectives. IFAC member bodies, in addition to their responsibility to promote and use IFAC guidance, are committed to promote and implement IASB pronouncements. There is also regular contact and coordination between the two organizations at the leadership level.

This arrangement has been working successfully. In addition, both organizations appear to believe that it provides, on the one hand, the necessary degree of independence for the IASB Board to set accounting standards, but also ensures the accountancy profession's commitment to help in seeing that these standards are actually implemented in international practice.

IFAC's overall mission is to "serve the public interest, strengthen the world-wide accountancy profession, and contribute to the development of strong international economies by establishing and promoting adherence to high-quality professional standards. The organization realizes that public confidence in financial information is vital to capital market growth and economic development." As a result in 2002 IFAC began the process of establishing the foundation for major reforms necessary to (re)build trust in the financial reporting process.

This process has continued through the creation of a Monitoring Group, launching of an IFAC Leadership Group, and (in March 2005) the IFAC announced the formation of its Public Interest Oversight Board (PIOB). The Board will oversee the work of IFAC's auditing, ethics and education standard-setting committees. The objective of the board is to ensure that IFAC's standard-setting activities reflect the public interest and are fully transparent to those affected by the standards.

The Monitoring Group (MG) comprises international regulators and representatives of related organizations. The MG will update the Public Oversight Board regarding significant events in the regulatory environment, and among other charges, act as the vehicle for dialogue between regulators and the international accountancy profession.

The IFAC Leadership Group includes the IFAC President, Deputy President, Chief Executive, the Chairs of the IAASB, the Transitional Auditors Committee, the Form of Firms, and up to four other members designated by the IFAC Board. It will work with the MG and address issues related to the regulation of the profession.

## ¶12,003 INTERNATIONAL PUBLIC SECTOR ACCOUNTING STANDARDS

International Public Sector (Governmental) Accounting Standards (IPSASs) set out the requirements for financial reporting by governments and other public sector organizations with the ultimate objective of enhancing the accountability and financial management of governments worldwide. The International Public Sector Accounting Standards Board (IPSASB) receives funding from:

1. The World Bank.
2. United Nations Development Program.
3. Asian Development Bank.
4. International Monetary Fund.

Thus far, the Board has developed 21 IPSASs as part of its *comprehensive* Standards Project to assist governments in reporting comparable, relevant, and understandable financial information.

## .01 The Public Sector Board (IPSASB)

The Public Sector Board is charged with servicing the needs of those involved in public sector financial reporting, accounting, and auditing on a worldwide scope. "Public sector" refers to national governments, regional governments (e.g., state, provincial, and territorial), local governments (e.g., city and town) and related governmental entities (e.g., agencies, boards, commissions, and enterprises). The Committee has been given the authority to issue International Public Sector Accounting Standards (IPSASs).

The objective of the Board is to develop programs aimed at improving public sector financial management and accountability, including developing accounting standards and promoting their acceptance.

The problem in international public sector accounting arises from the fact that governments and other public sector entities follow diverse financial reporting practices and, in many countries, there are no authoritative standards for the public sector. In some countries where standards do exist, the body of standards may be either at an early stage of development or limited in application to specific types of entities in the public sector.

The Public Sector Board issues a range of publications, including Standards, Guidelines, Studies and Occasional Papers. The Standards are the authoritative requirements established by the Board to improve the quality of financial reporting in the public sector around the world.

## .03 Synopsis of IPSASs

- IPSAS 1—*Presentation of Financial Statements*. This Standard sets out the overall considerations for the presentation of financial statements, guidance for the structure of those statements and minimum requirements for their content under the accrual basis of accounting.
- IPSAS 2—*Cash Flow Statements*. This Standard requires the provision of information about the changes in cash and cash equivalents during the period from operating, investing and financing activities.
- IPSAS 3—*Net Surplus or Deficit for the Period, Fundamental Errors and Changes in Accounting Policies*. This Standard specifies the accounting treatment for changes in accounting estimates, changes in accounting policies, and the correction of fundamental errors; defines extraordinary items; and requires the separate disclosure of certain items in the financial statements.
- IPSAS 4—*The Effect of Changes in Foreign Exchange Rates*. This Standard deals with accounting for foreign currency transactions and foreign

operations. It sets the requirements for determining which exchange rate to use for the recognition of certain transactions and balances, and how to recognize in the financial statements the financial effect of changes in exchange rates.

- IPSAS 5—*Borrowing Costs.* This Standard prescribes the accounting treatment for borrowing costs and requires either the immediate expensing of borrowing costs or, as an allowed alternative treatment, the capitalization of borrowing costs that are directly attributable to the acquisition, construction, or production of a qualifying asset.

- IPSAS 6—*Consolidated Financial Statements and Accounting for Controlled Entities.* This Standard requires all controlling entities to prepare consolidated financial statements that consolidate all controlled entities on a line-by-line basis. The Standard also contains a detailed discussion of the concept of control, as it applies in the public sector, and guidance on determining whether control exists for financial reporting purposes.

- IPSAS 7—*Accounting for Investments in Associates.* This Standard requires all investments in associates to be accounted for in the consolidated financial statements using the equity method of accounting. However, when the investment is acquired and held exclusively with a view to its disposal in the near future, the cost method is required.

- IPSAS 8—*Financial Reporting of Interests in Joint Ventures.* This Standard requires proportionate consolidation to be adopted as the benchmark treatment for accounting for such joint ventures entered into by public sector entities. However, IPSAS 8 also permits, as an alternative, joint ventures to be accounted for using the equity method of accounting.

- IPSAS 9—*Revenue from Exchange Transactions.* This Standard establishes the conditions for the recognition of revenue arising from exchange transactions, requires such revenue to be measured at the fair value of the consideration received or receivable, and includes disclosure requirements.

- IPSAS 10—*Financial Reporting in Hyperinflationary Economies.* This Standard describes the characteristics of a hyperinflationary economy and requires financial statements of entities that operate in such economies to be restated.

- IPSAS 11—*Construction Contracts.* This Standard defines construction contracts, establishes requirements for the recognition of revenues and expenses arising from such contracts, and identifies certain disclosure requirements.

- IPSAS 12—*Inventories.* This Standard defines inventories, establishes measurement requirements for inventories (including those inventories held for distribution at no or nominal charge) under the historical cost system and includes disclosure requirements.

- IPSAS 13—*Leases*. This Standard prescribes for both lessees and lessors the appropriate accounting policies and disclosures to apply in relation to finance and operating leases. It includes guidance on the classification of leases, disclosures to be made in the financial statements of lessees and lessors, and accounting for sale and leaseback transactions.

- IPSAS 14—*Events After the Reporting Date*. This Standard prescribes when an entity should adjust its financial statements for events that occur after the reporting date and the disclosures that it should make about other "nonadjusting" events that occur after the reporting date.

- IPSAS 15—*Financial Instruments: Disclosure and Presentation*. This Standard prescribes how financial instruments are to be classified and identifies disclosures to be made in general-purpose financial statements.

- IPSAS 16—*Investment Property*. This Standard prescribes requirements for accounting for investment property, including the initial and subsequent measurement and disclosure of such property by governments and their agencies.

- IPSAS 17—*Property, Plant and Equipment*. This Standard prescribes requirements for the initial recognition and measurement of property, plant, and equipment. It also deals with subsequent measurement, depreciation, and disclosures about these assets. The Standard provides a transitional period to support the orderly implementation of its requirements and allows but does not require heritage assets to be recognized in general-purpose financial statements.

- IPSAS 18—*Segment Reporting*. This Standard establishes principles for reporting financial information about distinguishable activities of a government or other public sector entity appropriate for:
  - Evaluating the entity's past performance in achieving its objectives.
  - Identifying the resources allocated to support the major activities of the entity.
  - Making decisions about the future allocation of resources.

- IPSAS 19—*Provisions, Contingent Liabilities, and Contingent Assets*. The objective of this Standard is to define provisions, contingent liabilities, and contingent assets and to identify the circumstances in which provisions should be recognized, how they should be measured, and the disclosures that should be made about them. The Standard also requires that certain information be disclosed about contingent liabilities and contingent assets in the notes to the financial statements to enable users to understand their nature, timing, and amount.

- IPSAS 20—*Related Party Disclosures*. The objective of this Standard is to require the disclosure of the existence of related party relationships where control exists, and the disclosure of information about transactions between the entity and its related parties in certain circumstances. This information is required for accountability purposes and to facilitate a better understanding of the financial position and performance of the reporting entity. The principal issues in disclosing information about related parties are identifying which parties control or significantly influence the reporting entity, and determining what information should be disclosed about transactions with those parties. These IPSASs are to be applied when the accrual basis of accounting is adopted.

• IPSAS 21–*Impairment of Non-Cash Generating Assets*. The objective of this Standard, issued December 23, 2004, is to prescribe the foundation on which an entity determines whether noncash-generating assets are impaired and, if so, under what conditions a loss should be recognized. Strict guidance on impairment "is a key element in ensuring that property, plant and equipment and certain other assets of public sector entities are not carried at an amount in excess of their service capacity," according to Philippe Adhémar, IPSASB Chair.

Governments and other public sector entities that prepare general-purpose financial statements under the accrual basis of accounting are the focus of this standard. It requires that an asset not be carried at an amount in excess of its recoverable service amount. If conditions indicate, a determination must be made whether there is an impairment of noncash-generating assets on the balance sheet. If there is such an indication, the entity is required to estimate the recoverable service amount of the asset and to determine whether an impairment loss should be recognized.

The Standard includes:

• Definitions of cash-generating assets and impairment.
• Guidance on identifying an asset that may be impaired.
• Measuring an asset's recoverable service amount.
• Measuring an impairment loss.
• Requirements for the recognition, and reversal of an impairment loss.

All Standards have been developed to improve the quality of financial reporting in the public sector worldwide. An important goal is to achieve convergence of these Standards where possible.

## .05 Other Pronouncements

In February 2005 the International Public Sector Accounting Standards Board (IPSASB) of the International Federation of Accountants (IFAC) issued an Exposure Draft (ED) for a proposed new International Public Sector Accounting Standard (IPSAS). This proposed Standard is directed at enhancing the transparency and relevance of disclosures about the receipt and use of external financial assistance by governments and other public-sector, cash-basis reporting entities. The proposed Standard, which will apply to those entities which adopt the cash basis of accounting is entitled *Proposed International Public Sector Accounting Standard: Financial Reporting Under the Cash Basis of Accounting–Disclosure Requirements for Recipients of External Assistance.*

Recipients may receive assistance from a number of external providers who require the disclosure of information using different accounting practices and reporting methods. Adoption of the proposed requirements by the international donor community provides a mechanism to reduce the costs of compliance imposed on recipients.

The proposed standard would apply to all entities that receive external assistance and prepare their general purpose financial statements under the cash basis of accounting, the system of accounts used by many recipients of external assistance. It should be read in conjunction with the International Public Sector Accounting Standards (IPSASB), *Cash Basis IPSAS: Financial Reporting Under The Cash Basis of Accounting.*

The Public Sector Committee has also released Study 14, *Transition to the Accrual Basis of Accounting: Guidance for Governments and Government Entities.* This study identifies key issues to be addressed in the transfer from the cash to the accrual basis of accounting and alternative approaches that can be adopted when implementing the accrual basis in an efficient and effective manner in the public sector.

It also identifies key requirements of IPSASs and other relevant sources of guidance to assist in the transition from the cash basis to the accrual basis. The Committee believes that governments and governmental entities will find Study 14 a useful tool in dealing with complex issues necessary to implement an accrual system. IFAC refers to the study as a "living document" that will be updated periodically as further IPSASs are issued, and additional implementation issues and experiences are identified.

The new study contributes to the ongoing body of guidance being developed by the Public Sector Committee to enhance the accountability and financial management of governments worldwide.

Other recent exposure drafts issued include:

- ED 24 Financial Reporting Under the Cash Basis of Accounting—Disclosure, Requirements for Recipients of External Assistance (2005)
- ED 25 Proposed Amendment to the Preface to the International Public Sector Accounting Standards—Equal Authority of Paragraphs in IPSASs (2005)
- ED 26 Improvements to International Public Sector Accounting Standards (2005)
- ED 27 Presentation of Budget Information in General Purpose Financial Statements (2005)

- ED 28 Disclosure of Financial Information about the General Government Sector (2005)
- ED 29 Revenue from Non-Exchange Transactions (Including Taxes and Transfers)

## ¶12,005  DEVELOPMENT OF IPSASs

Initially, these Standards (the IPSASs) are being developed through adapting International Accounting Standards issued by the International Accounting Standards Committee (IASC) to a public sector context. In this process, the Committee attempts, wherever possible, to maintain the accounting treatment and original text of the IASs unless there is a significant public sector issue that warrants a departure. The work of the IASC has been turned over to the International Accounting Standards Board and IASs are being updated and revised and supplemented through the issuance of IFRSs.

The Committee is also engaged in projects dealing with:

- Accounting for Development Assistance.
- Accounting for Social Policies of Governments.
- Budget Reporting.
- Harmonization of Government Financial Reporting.
- Revenue from Non-Exchange Transactions.
- Improvements to Existing IPSASs in line with the IASB's General Improvements Project.

In its ongoing work program the Committee also intends to develop IPSASs dealing with financial reporting issues in the public sector that are either not comprehensively dealt with in existing IASs or for which IASs have not been developed by the IASC (succeeded by IASB).

The Committee is developing a set of IPSASs that will include Standards applying to the accrual basis and a separate IPSAS that will specify the requirements for the cash basis.

To ensure maximum worldwide standards coordination, in developing its standards (IPSASs) the Committee utilizes pronouncements issued by the IASB, national regulatory authorities; professional accounting bodies, and other organizations interested in financial reporting, accounting, and auditing in the public sector.

In the fulfillment of its mission, the IFAC follows the IASB's *Framework for the Preparation and Presentation of Financial Statements*. Thus, most IPSASs are based on IASs. Accordingly, financial statements issued for users who are unable to demand financial information to meet their specific information needs are referred to as *general-purpose financial statements*.

When the accrual basis of accounting is used in the preparation of the financial statements, the financial statements are required to include the statement of financial position, the statement of financial performance, the cash flow statement and the statement of changes in net assets/equity. When the cash basis of accounting is used in the preparation of the financial statements, the primary financial statement is the cash flow statement. IPSASs apply to the published financial statements of public sector entities other than Government Business Enterprises.

In addition to preparing general-purpose financial statements, an entity may prepare tailored financial statements to meet the specific needs of governing bodies, the legislature, and other parties who perform an oversight function. Such statements are referred to as *special purpose financial statements*. The Committee encourages the use of IPSASs in the preparation of special purpose financial statements where appropriate.

According to the Committee "some entities in the process of moving from cash accounting to accrual accounting may wish to adopt the requirements of particular accrual-based IPSASs during this process. An entity may voluntarily adopt the relevant disclosure provisions in an accrual-based IPSAS, although its core financial statements will nonetheless be prepared according to the IPSAS dealing with financial reporting under the cash basis of accounting." IPSAS 1, *Presentation of Financial Statements*, requires disclosure of the extent to which the entity has applied any transitional provisions.

Whenever an audit opinion is expressed on public sector financial statements, the same audit principles apply regardless of the nature of the entity, because users of audited financial statements are entitled to a uniform quality of audit performance. Because ISAs set out the basic audit principles and related practices and procedures, they apply to audits of the financial statements of governments and other public sector entities as well. However, the application of certain ISAs may need to be clarified or supplemented to accommodate the public sector circumstances and perspective of individual jurisdictions. The nature of potential matters for clarification or supplementation is identified in the "Public Sector Perspective" included at the end of each ISA.

## ¶12,007    Auditing Update

During 2003, the International Auditing and Assurance Standards Board (IAASB) worked to revise and develop auditing standards for historical financial statements and on insuring greater transparency with respect to the standards-setting process. The standards considered deal with the following four concerns:

1. The overall performance of the audit,
2. How auditors report and communicate their responsibilities and findings,

3. Considerations and procedures in areas of highest audit risk, and

4. Quality control at both the firm level and the individual engagement level.

IAASB pronouncements to date include the following International Standards on Auditing (ISAs):

- ISA 120 (withdrawn 2004).
- ISA 200, *Objective and General Principles Governing an Audit of Financial Statements* (conforming amendments effective June 15, 2006).
- ISA 210, *Terms of Audit Engagements* (conforming amendments effective December 15, 2004).
- ISA 220 (revised), *Quality Control for Audit Work.*
- ISA 230 (revised September 2005), *Audit Documentation* (conforming amendments effective December 15, 2004).
- ISA 240, *The Auditor's Responsibility to Consider Fraud in an Audit of Financial Statements.*
- ISA 250, *Consideration of Laws and Regulations in an Audit of Financial Statements* (conforming amendments effective December 15, 2004).
- ISA 260 (revision pending), *Communications of Audit Matters with Those Charged with Governance* (conforming amendments effective December 15, 2004).
- ISA 300 (revised), *Planning an Audit of Financial Statements.*
- ISA 310 (withdrawn 2004).
- ISA 315, *Understanding the Entity and Its Environment and Assessing the Risks of Material Misstatement.*
- ISA 320 (revision pending), *Audit Materiality* (conforming amendments effective December 15, 2004).
- ISA 330, *The Auditor's Procedures in Response to Assessed Risks* (conforming amendments effective June 15, 2006).
- ISA 400 (withdrawn 2004).
- ISA 401 (withdrawn 2004).
- ISA 402, *Audit Considerations Relating to Entities Using Service Organizations* (conforming amendments effective December 15, 2004).
- ISA 500, *Audit Evidence.*
- ISA 501, *Audit Evidence—Additional Considerations for Specific Items* (conforming amendments effective December 15, 2004).
- ISA 505, *External Considerations* (conforming amendments effective December 15, 2004).
- ISA 510, *Initial Engagements—Opening Balances* (conforming amendments effective December 15, 2004).

- ISA 520, *Analytical Procedures* (conforming amendments effective December 15, 2004).
- ISA 530, *Audit Sampling and Other Means of Testing.*
- ISA 540 (revision pending), *Audit of Accounting Estimates.*
- ISA 545, *Auditing Fair Value Measurements and Disclosures.*
- ISA 550, *Related Parties.*
- ISA 560, *Subsequent Events.*
- ISA 570, *Going Concern.*
- IAS 580, *Management Representations.*
- ISA 600 (revision pending), *Using the Work of Another Auditor.*
- ISA 610, *Considering the Work of Internal Auditing.*
- ISA 620, *Using the Work of an Expert.*
- ISA 700 (revised), *The Independent Auditor's Report on a Complete Set of General Purpose Financial Statements.*
- ISA 701, *Modifications to the Independent Auditor's Report.*
- ISA 705 (Exposure Draft), *Modifications to the Opinion in the Independent Auditor's Report.*
- ISA 706 (Exposure Draft), *Emphasis on Matter Paragraphs and Other Matters Paragraphs in the Independent Auditor's Report.*
- ISA 710, *Comparatives.*
- ISA 720, *Other Information in Documents Containing Audited Financial Statements.*
- ISA 800, *The Independent Auditor's Report on Special Purpose Audit Engagements.*

Exposure drafts (EDs) for pending revisions to existing guidance

- ISA 230, *Audit Documentation* and amendments to ISA 330, *The Auditor's Procedures in Response to Assessed Risks* and ISQC 1, *Quality Control for Firms that Perform Audits and Reviews of Historical Financial and Other Assurance and Related Service Engagements.* Comment period ended January 31, 2005.
- ISA 260, *The Auditor's Communication with Those Charged with Governance.* Comment period ended July 31, 2005.
- ISA 320, *Materiality in the Identification and Evaluation of Misstatements.* Comment period ended April 30, 2005.
- ISA 540, *Auditing Accounting Estimates and Related Disclosures* (Other than Those Involving Fair Value Measurements and Disclosures). Comment period ended April 30, 2005.
- ISA 550 (revised) Related Parties.

**¶12,007**

- ISA 600 (revised), *The Work of Related Auditors and Other Auditors* in the Audit of Group Financial Statements and IAPS, The Audit of Group Financial Statements. Comment period ended March 31, 2004.
- ISA 701 The Independent Auditor's Report on Other Historical Financial Information.
- ISA 705, *Modifications to the Opinion in the Independent Auditor's Report.* Comment period ended July 31, 2005.
- ISA 706, *Emphasis on Matter Paragraphs and Other Matters Paragraphs in the Independent Auditor's Report* (derived from ISA 701). Comment period ended July 31, 2005.
- ISA 800 The Independent Auditor's Report on Summary Audited Financial Statements.

## .01    Discussion of (revised) ISA 300

The revised ISA 300, *Planning an Audit of Financial Statements*, was released on July 12, 2004, requiring auditors to be more rigorous in the planning of their audits. The revised ISA builds on the new audit risk standards issued in 2003 and requires the auditor to plan audits so that engagements will be performed in an effective manner. The continual nature of planning is emphasized by the standard. It stresses the auditor's responsibility throughout the engagement to be cognizant of unexpected events, changes in conditions, or other circumstances that may lead the auditor to reevaluate the planned audit procedures.

The standard, effective for audits of financial statements for periods beginning on or after December 15, 2004, requires the auditor to establish the overall strategy for the audit that sets the scope, timing, and direction for the audit.

## .03    Discussion of (revised) ISA 700

International Standard on Auditing (ISA) 700 was issued in revised form on December 28, 2004. It establishes a new form of auditor's report designed to enhance the transparency and comparability of auditor's reports across international borders. The updated standard, *The Independent Auditor's Report on a Complete Set of General Purpose Financial Statements*, sets out a framework to separate audit reporting requirements in connection with an ISA audit from additional supplementary reporting responsibilities required in some jurisdictions.

In those circumstances when an audit is conducted in accordance with both ISAs and the auditing standards of a specific jurisdiction, guidance is provided to the auditor—in particular, on preparing an auditor's report to meet both the report structure required by the national jurisdiction and the requirements of the

ISA. According to IAASB Chairman John Kellas, "The European Commission asked the IAASB to look at this project as a matter of urgency to contribute to harmonized audit reporting within the EU. Many EU and other countries require the auditor to report on additional matters to the financial statements, but these requirements differ between countries. Our solution is to require a two-part report: the first deals with the financial statements, and should be essentially the same for all audits conducted in accordance with ISAs; the second deals with any further matters that may be required by local regulations. We thereby require comparability where it matters, while allowing appropriate flexibility to deal with local circumstances."

The new wording for the auditor's report includes:

- Better explanations of the respective responsibilities of management and the auditor;
- An updated description of the audit process to reflect the new IAASB Audit Risk Standards; and
- Clarification of the scope of the auditor's responsibilities with respect to internal control.

The new form of the report is to be applied for auditor's reports dated on or after December 31, 2006. Conforming amendments to other ISAs are applicable for audits of financial statements for periods beginning on or after December 15, 2005. To prevent confusion that might arise if both the old and new forms of report were being used at the same time, the IAASB has not allowed for early application of the new report wording.

## .05 Discussion of ISA 240

Issued in 2004, ISA 240, *The Auditor's Responsibility to Consider Fraud in an Audit of Financial Statements*, is effective for audits of financial statements for periods beginning on or after December 15, 2004. "The purpose of this ISA is to establish basic principles and essential procedures and to provide guidance on the auditor's responsibility to consider fraud in an audit of financial statements." The Standard tracks the U.S. Statement on Auditing Standards (SAS) 99, *Consideration of Fraud in a Financial Statement Audit*. The Standard makes two important preliminary distinctions: between fraud and error, and between fraud resulting from misappropriation of assets and fraud from fraudulent financial reporting. Fraud is distinguished from error primarily on the basis of *intention to defraud*:

The term "error" refers to an unintentional misstatement in financial statements, including the omission of an amount or a disclosure. . . . The term "fraud" refers to an intentional act by one or more individuals among management [management fraud], those charged with governance, employees [employee fraud], or third parties, involving the use of deception to obtain an unjust or illegal advantage.

The Standard requires the auditor to maintain an attitude of professional skepticism throughout the audit "notwithstanding the auditor's past experience with the entity about the honesty and integrity of management and those charged with governance." It further requires the members of the audit engagement team to "discuss the susceptibility of the entity's financial statements to material misstatement due to fraud."

In designing the audit procedures auditors are required by the Standard to respond to the risk of management override of controls. But *"auditors do not make legal determination of whether fraud has actually occurred."*

*Why Fraud Occurs.* ISA 240 points out the importance of understanding why fraud occurs. For example "fraudulent financial reporting can be caused by the efforts of management to manage earnings." In general terms, the Standard makes reference, without attribution, to the "fraud triangle" concept pioneered by criminologist Donald Cressey. Fraud involves a need, incentive, or pressure. In addition, there must be a perceived opportunity and the ability of the perpetrator to rationalize the need to commit the fraud. In the case of an individual, the need or incentive often involves someone living beyond their means, excess debt, or a drug or gambling problem. Fraudulent financial reporting may be committed because management is being pressured to achieve a certain (and perhaps unrealistic) earnings target. Someone in a position of trust or who knows of specific weaknesses in internal control may, for example, perceive opportunity for fraudulent financial reporting or misappropriation of assets. The process of rationalization consists of contriving reasons why the act of fraud is justified, such as "everyone does it" or "the company owes me a raise."

*Management Responsibility.* ISA 240 indicates that the primary responsibility for detection and prevention of fraud rests with management. By placing a strong emphasis on fraud prevention, management may reduce opportunities for fraud to take place; by emphasizing fraud deterrence, management could persuade individuals not to commit fraud because of the likelihood of detection and punishment.

Unfortunately the risk of not detecting *fraud* is higher than the risk of not detecting *error*, "because fraud may involve sophisticated and carefully organized schemes designed to conceal it." In addition, the auditor is less likely to detect fraud perpetrated by management than by employees because management is in a position to directly or indirectly manipulate accounting records and present fraudulent financial information.

In discussing the possibility of audit, the members of the audit team set aside any beliefs that management and those charged with governance are honest and have integrity and must adopt a questioning mind-set. The discussion should take the form of an exchange of ideas and a consideration of the circumstances, known external and internal factors that may create an incentive to commit fraud, and any unusual or unexplained changes in behavior or lifestyle of management or employees that have come to the attention of the engagement team.

*Risk Assessment Procedures.*   The risk assessment procedures to be carried out in the audit include consideration of any unusual or unexpected relationships that have been identified in performing analytic review procedures. In addition, the auditor should make inquiries of "management, internal audit, and others within the entity as appropriate, to determine whether they have knowledge of any actual, suspected, or alleged fraud affecting the entity." The "others" includes those charged with governance, including the board of directors. During the course of the audit, the auditor should also obtain an understanding of the business rationale for significant transactions that are outside of the normal course business for the entity or unusual given the auditor's understanding of the entity and its environment and other information obtained during the audit.

Care should be taken to consider the consequences of performing analytical procedures during the year as well as at year-end. Trends noted during either timeframe should be compared with the other and reconciled if they diverge. It should not be assumed that the year-end results are the only proper data for analysis. Among the reasons for this is that large and unusual amounts of revenue, for example, may be recorded at the end of the year in order to bring significant ratios into normal range. "Determining which particular trends and relationships may indicate a risk of material misstatement due to fraud requires professional judgment." Thus meta-analytical procedures—analysis of both interim and year-end financial statements against each other as well as against comparable prior periods—are required.

*Extent of Auditor's Responsibility.*   Although the Standard indicates that the auditor is not responsible for making the legal determination that fraud has occurred, paragraph 93 speaks of the auditor identifying fraud in the context of communications with management. "If the auditor has identified a fraud or has obtained information that indicates that a fraud may exist, the auditor should communicate these matters as soon as practicable to the appropriate level of management." This is a stronger statement than the comparable paragraph in U.S. SAS 99.

The Standard requires the auditor to document his or her understanding of the entity and its environment as well as the risks of material misstatement. This should include "The significant decisions reached during the discussion among the engagement team regarding the susceptibility of the entity's financial statements to material misstatement due to fraud; and the identified and assessed risk of material misstatement due to fraud at the financial statement level and at the assertion level."

¶12,007.05

## .06  Discussion of ISA 230 (revised) Audit Documentation

Issued in September 2005, the purpose of this ISA is to establish standards and provide guidance on audit documentation. Audit documentation refers to the record of audit procedures performed, the audit evidence obtained as well as the conclusions reached by the auditor. The audit documentation may be recorded on paper or on electronic or other media. Included in audit documentation are audit programs, records of analytic procedures performed, memoranda, summaries of significant matters, confirmation letters and representations, checklists and correspondence (including emails).

In preparing audit documentation, the overriding goal is to provide documentation that would provide an experienced auditor, having no previous experience with the audit, to understand the nature, timing, and extent of audit procedures performed, to evaluate the audit evidence performed as well as the conclusions reached upon completion of the audit. As part of the documentation, the auditor may prepare a summary memorandum describing the significant matters identified during the audit and how they were addressed. The memo may also include cross-references to other relevant supporting audit documentation. During the audit, the auditor frequently discusses matters of significance with management or others. Such discussions should be documented in a timely manner.

An integral aspect of audit documentation is the identification of the auditor performing the work and the date the work was performed. ISQC 1 requires audit firms to establish policies and procedures for the retention of audit documentation. For an audit engagement, the retention period for records is at least five years from the date auditor s report.

## .07  Discussion of ISA 545, *Auditing Fair Value Measurements and Disclosures*

In August 2002, to address the increasing number of complex accounting pronouncements containing measurement and disclosure provisions based on fair value, IFAC's International Auditing and Assurance Standards Board (IAASB) announced development of a new International Standard on Auditing entitled *Auditing Fair Value Measurements and Disclosures*. ISA 545 addresses audit considerations relating to the valuation, measurement, presentation and disclosure for material assets, liabilities and specific components of equity presented or disclosed at fair value in financial statements. Specifically, the ISA provides information on:

1.  Understanding the entity's process for determining fair value measurements and disclosures and relevant control procedures.
2.  Assessing the appropriateness of fair value measurements and disclosures.
3.  Using the work of an expert.

4. Testing the entity's fair value measurements and disclosures.
5. Evaluating the results of audit procedures.
6. Management's process for determining fair value and management representations.
7. Communication with those charged with governance.

The appendix to the ISA discusses fair value measurements and disclosures under different financial reporting frameworks.

The organization emphasizes that it is important that auditors obtain sufficient audit evidence that fair value measurements and disclosures are in accordance with the entity's identified financial reporting framework as changes in fair value measurements that occur over time may be treated in different ways under different financial reporting frameworks.

This ISA is effective for audits of financial statements for periods ending on or after December 31, 2003. Recognizing the important need for guidance in this area, the United States used this ISA as its basis in issuing an Exposure Draft on the same subject within the United States.

## ¶12,009   INTERNATIONAL AUDITING PRACTICE STATEMENTS (IAPSs)

Statements in this category provide guidance from the IAASB in specialized areas of auditing.

IAPS 1000, *Inter-Bank Confirmation Procedures*

IAPS 1004, *The relationship Between Banking Supervisors and Banks' External Auditors*

IAPS 1005, *The Special Considerations in the Audit of Small Entities*

IAPS 1006, *Audits of the Financial Statements of Banks*

IAPS 1010, *The Consideration of Environmental Matters in the Audit of Financial Statements*

IAPS 1012, *Auditing Derivative Financial Instruments*

IAPS 1013, *Electronic Commerce — Effect on the Audit of Financial Statements*

IAPS 1014, *Reporting by Auditors on Compliance with International Financial Reporting Standards*

### .01   IAPSs Withdrawn

At its meeting in December 2004 the IAASB announced the withdrawal of the following IAPSs, indicating they were rendered obsolete by technological advances.

¶12,009

- IAPS 1001, *IT Environments – Stand-Alone Computers*
- IAPS 1002, *IT Environments – On-Line Computer Systems*
- IAPS 1003, *Environments – Database Systems*
- IAPS 1007, *Communication with Management*
- IAPS 1008, *Risk Assessments and Internal Control – CIS*
- IAPS 1009, *Computer-Assisted Audit Techniques*
- IAPS 1011, *Implications for Auditors and Managers*

## ¶12,011   GUIDANCE ON DERIVATIVES

The IAPS 10125, *Auditing Derivative Financial Instruments*, provides guidance to the auditor in planning and performing auditing procedures for assertions about derivative financial instruments. The focus of the practice statement is on auditing derivatives held by end users, including banks and other financial sector entities when they are the users.

In addition to addressing auditor responsibilities with respect to assertions about derivatives, the statement also addresses:

1. Responsibility of management and those charged with governance.
2. The key financial risks.
3. Risk assessment and internal control, including the role of internal auditing.
4. Various types of substantive procedures and when they should be used.

## ¶12,013   ETHICS–REVISIONS TO CODE OF ETHICS ISSUED

In October 2004 the Ethics Committee released an exposure draft for the Revised Code of Ethics for Professional Accountants, clarifying independence requirements for professional accountants in public practice who perform assurance engagements. The finalized version of the Code has now been issued and is effective as of January 1, 2006. The 100 plus page document deals specifically with the five fundamental principles of professional ethics: 1) integrity, 2) objectivity, 3) professional competence and due care, 4) confidentiality, and 5) professional behavior.

The changes are designed to conform the Code to the *International Framework for Assurance Engagements,* issued by the International Auditing and Assurance Standards Board; and definitions contained in *International Standard on Quality Control (ISQC) 1, Quality Control for Firms that Perform Audits and Reviews of Historical Financial Information, and Other Assurance Related Services Engagements.*

This international Code is intended to serve as a model on which to base national ethical guidance for accountants. The Code includes principles that are applicable to all professional accountants and distinguishes between those that affect professional accountants in public practice and those that are applicable to other accountants employed in business and industry.

Although the accountancy profession throughout the world operates in an environment with different cultures and regulatory requirements, it is vital that all accountants share a commitment to a strong code of ethics. The IFAC Code states the fundamental principles that should be observed by professional accountants to meet their responsibility in protecting the public's interests.

The introduction to the Code notes that a distinguishing mark of the accountancy profession is its acceptance of the responsibility to act in the public interest. The organization of the Code includes the fundamental principles of professional ethics including their conceptual framework. Following the statement of general principles the Code provides examples of their application to specific situations noting that is impossible to define every situation that creates ethical concerns for professional accountants.

## ¶12,015  INTERNATIONAL EDUCATION STANDARDS FOR PROFESSIONAL ACCOUNTANTS

The Education Committee of the International Federation of Accountants (IFAC) is responsible for establishing educational requirements for all professional accountants. In general these standards apply to all professional accountants, irrespective of specialty or branch of accounting (auditing, management accounting, financial reporting), area of employment (public sector, public practice, corporate environment).

### .01  IES8 Competence Requirements fun Audit Professionals

In 2005 the committee proposed new guidance, in the form of an exposure draft (ED), intended to assist specifically audit professionals in the performance of their public interest responsibilities. The exposure draft led to the issuance of a new International Education Standard (IES), entitled *Competence Requirements for Audit Professionals,* which applies to all professional accountants who have a substantial involvement in the audit area and who are responsible for making significant judgment decisions contributing to the overall audit opinion.

According to the IES exposure draft, "The aim of the proposed standard is to require professional accountants to acquire the specific capabilities (i.e. professional knowledge, professional skills and professional values, ethics, and attitudes) they need to carry out their work as competent audit professionals." The Standard applies not only to auditors but also to those who have a substantial involvement in the audit assignment and are responsible for making

¶12,015

significant judgment decisions contributing to the overall audit opinion. Among its changes, the new standard defines the term *audit professional*, limiting its meaning to a professional accountant, specifically, an individual who is a member of an IFAC body. Its application, therefore, is to accountants who already meet requirements of existing IESs.

This is considered a landmark document because it is the first time the Education Committee has developed education requirements for a specific area of the accountancy profession according to the Education Committee Chair. Because of the reliance placed on the audits of financial statements, the committee felt it was vital to provide direction to IFAC member bodies and professional accountants worldwide on the specialized knowledge and skills required to perform competently in the audit field.

The minimum competency requirements for audit professionals include 1) knowledge content, 2) professional skills, 3) professional values, ethics and attitudes, 4) practical experience, 5) continuing professional experience, and 6) assessment of progress in items 1-5 listed. IES 8 prescribes requirements for professional accountants assuming the role of audit professionals and having responsibility for significant judgments in an audit of historical financial information. IFAC member bodies need to establish policies and procedures that will allow members to satisfy the requirements of this IES before they take on the role of an audit professional. The need for specific requirements for audit professionals, according to the IES is the fact that accountants need to specialize, not only to be competitive in the industry, but also in order to be competent professionals. No one professional accountant can master all areas of accountancy. Auditing is one of the recognized professional specialties.

The knowledge content of the audit of historical financial statements should include the best practices of the auditing profession including current issues and developments and International Standards on Auditing (IASs) and International Auditing Practice Statements (IAPSs).

According to the new standard the professional skills requirement within the development program for auditors should include

- Identifying and solving problems
- Undertaking technical research
- Gathering and evaluating evidence
- Working effectively in teams
- Presenting, discussing, and defending views effectively through formal, informal, written, and spoken communication

In the advanced development of professional auditors, the standard requires demonstrating professional skepticism, withstanding and resolving conflicts and demonstrating capacity for inquiry, abstract logical thought, and critical analysis.

¶**12,015.01**

In specifying the nature of the practical experience required the IES states that such practical experience would normally be not less than three years, of which at least two years should be spent in the area of audits of historical financial statements under the supervision and guidance of an engagement partner.

The new standard, in addition to establishing guidance for auditors generally, also addresses the need for further specialization within the profession. For example, the IES discusses the need for more specialized development for those doing "transnational audits." These are audits that are or may be relied upon outside the entity s jurisdiction.

Finally, IES 8 gives direction to the measurement of competence in the case of the engagement partner. At this level of the audit, the engagement partner requires the development of additional professional knowledge, professional skills and professional values, ethics and attitudes. Also important at this level are leadership responsibilities and the ability to form conclusions on compliance with applicable independence requirements.

IES 8 is effective from July 1, 2008.

## .03    Ensuring Qualifications of New Professional Accountants

A critical area for the accounting profession is ensuring that new entrants to the profession are qualified to meet the responsibilities they will face. To address this challenge, in December 2004 the IFAC Education Committee released International Education Paper (IEP) 3, *Assessment Methods,* which presents a detailed discussion of assessment techniques to help national accountancy organizations ensure that candidates are appropriately qualified before being admitted to membership of their associations.

According to the IFAC Education Committee the paper is intended to help member bodies meet this obligation and comply with the International Education Standard, IES 6, *Assessment of Professional Capabilities and Competence*, issued in October 2003. Various techniques are used to assess candidates throughout the education process, and many of the member bodies use a wide range of these techniques. The paper is intended to help member bodies consider their current approach to assessment and select techniques which suit their environment and circumstances. It also includes two practical tools: a series of questions designed to assist member bodies when reviewing their assessment methods, and secondly, a list of electronically accessible reference materials available through the Education Committee section of the IFAC web site.

## .05    Prior International Education Standards

From 2003 to 2004 the IFAC issued seven International Education Standards (IESs) intended to promote consistency and convergence in the accounting education process throughout the world. The standards are designed to promote greater global mobility of competent professional accountants and contribute to mutual recognition cooperation among professional accountancy bodies.

The goal of accounting education and practical experience is to produce competent professional accountants capable of making a positive contribution over their lifetimes to the profession and society in which they work.

Increasingly, today's professional accountants need to be technical experts with excellent communication skills; they need to be able to meet the reporting and information needs of the new knowledge economy. At the same time, professional values, ethics and attitudes are integral to being a professional accountant.

IESs for professional accountants are intended to advance the profession of accountancy by establishing benchmarks for the minimum learning requirements of qualified accountants, including education, practical experience, and continuing professional development.

IESs prescribe standards of generally accepted "good practice" in the education and development of professional accountants. These Standards express the benchmarks that member bodies are expected to meet in the preparation and continual development of professional accountants. They establish the essential elements of the content and process of education and development at a level that is aimed at gaining international recognition, acceptance, and application. The gray-letter paragraphs within the Standards are intended to help explain the prescriptions within the black-letter, standard paragraphs.

The pronouncements on education issued by the Education Committee include:

- IES 1, *Entry Requirements to a Program of Professional Accounting Education.*
- IES 2, *Content of Professional Accounting Education Programs.*
- IES 3, *Professional Skills.*
- IES 4, *Professional Values, Ethics and Attitudes.*
- IES 5, *Practical Experience Requirements.*
- IES 6, *Assessment of Professional Capabilities and Competence.*
- IES 7, *Continuing Professional Development.*

The Education Committee has also issued International Education Guideline (IEG) 11, *Information Technology for Professional Accountants.* IESs are an important part of IFAC's overall efforts to ensure high-quality performance by professional accountants worldwide by providing the basis for achieving convergence of technical and practical standards. Members are expected to comply with the new standards beginning in January 2005.

All IFAC member bodies are expected to comply with IES, and the Standards are directed primarily at IFAC member bodies rather than individuals. Member bodies are expected to use their best endeavors to:

- Work toward implementation of all IES and other statements developed by the IFAC Education Committee; and
- Incorporate in their education programs the essential elements of the content and process of education on which IES are based or, where responsibility for the education program lies with third parties, persuade those responsible for the educational requirements for the accountancy profession to incorporate the essential elements into that program.

Increased emphasis needs to be placed on a set of professional knowledge, professional skills, and professional values, ethics, and attitudes broad enough to enable adaptation to constant change. Individuals who become professional accountants should have a constant desire to learn and apply what is new.

Accountancy is a profession that plays an important role in all societies. As the world moves toward global market economies, and with investments and operations crossing borders to an ever greater extent, professional accountants need a broad global outlook to understand the context in which businesses and other organizations operate.

Professional education prepares accountants to be able to maintain competence throughout their professional careers. Professional education may be pursued at academic institutions or through the programs of professional bodies or both.

Rapid change has been the main characteristic of the environment in which professional accountants work. Pressures for change are coming from many sources including globalization, information, and communication technologies and the expansion of stakeholder groups, including regulators and oversight boards. Professional accountants are now expected to serve the needs not only of investors and creditors but also the information needs of many other users of financial and nonfinancial information.

Businesses and other organizations are engaging in ever more complex arrangements and transactions:

- Risk management has become more important.
- Information technology continues to advance at a rapid pace
- The Internet has revolutionized global communications.
- Trade and commerce have become more transnational.
- Privatization has become an increasingly important trend in many countries.
- Legal action has become more usual in many societies, while in others it is the legal framework that defines the profession's responsibilities.
- Concern for the environment and sustainable development has grown.

¶12,015.05

These trends lead to the need for greater accountability and, as a result, in all cultures demands on the profession are high and continue to rise. It is the profession's capacity to satisfy these demands that determines its value to society.

The overall goal is to produce competent professional accountants by combining the parts of an education program in a suitable fashion. The exact combination of parts may vary as long as this goal is achieved. Different combinations exist in various parts of the world.

# ¶12,017 INFORMATION TECHNOLOGY COMMITTEE (ITC)

This group is charged with keeping the worldwide accounting community abreast of the latest developments and applications relating to information technology (IT). It encourages member bodies to keep up-to-date on available hardware and software and the relationship between IT and the accounting profession.

At a recent international meeting, the committee focused on the use of IT in developing countries and approved a research program and budget. Research will involve determination of the current usage of IT in these countries and identification of the type and level of assistance which would be appropriate in developing economies.

The IFAC *Handbook of International Information Technology Guidelines* includes five Information Technology Guidelines developed by IFAC's IT Committee: *Technology Planning for Business Impact; Managing Information Technology Planning for Business Impact; Managing Security of Information; Acquiring Information Technology;* and *IT Delivery and Support.*

# ¶12,019 INFORMATION TECHNOLOGY – THE IFAC JOINS THE XBRL CONSORTIUM

## .01 Value of XBRL

The XML-based language automatically and transparently tags each segment of computerized business information with an identification code or marker. These markers remain with the information regardless of how the information is formatted or rearranged by a browser or within software applications.

Before XBRL, no generally accepted format for reporting business data existed. The labor-intensive task of entering and reentering data into computer applications results in substantial costs and the all-too-likely risk of data entry errors. The use of XBRL streamlines this process, potentially lowering costs while helping to ensure the integrity and quality of the data.

With XBRL, once financial information is created and formatted the first time, the data can be rendered in any form; for example:

- A printed financial statement.
- An HTML document.
- A regulatory filing document.
- A raw HML file.
- Credit reports.
- Loan applications.

All of these applications can be created without manually keying information in a second time or reformatting the data.

XBRL does not change existing accounting standards, nor does it require companies to disclose additional information. Instead, it simply enhances the accessibility and usability of the financial information that companies are required to report, according to IFAC.

## .03   XBRL Leads to Better Dissemination of Information

By providing easier access to accurate company financial data and more efficient analysis capabilities, XBRL will add value for anyone who creates or accesses an organization's business data. Ultimately, XBRL benefits all users in the financial information supply chain:

- Public and private companies.
- The accounting profession.
- Regulators.
- Analysts.
- The investment community.
- Capital markets.
- Lenders.
- Key third parties—software developers and data aggregators.

IFAC believes that by providing accurate and reliable information, XBRL gives industry leaders access to better information available. Ultimately, it will enable company management to more quickly access information stored in different places within the organization and to move that information both within the company and externally to their shareholders.

With less time spent on translation and data entry, financial advisors and investors, large and small, can devote more time to analysis and can perhaps screen more companies for investment opportunities. This can benefit those companies in the investment community that typically might not make it onto the investor's radar screen.

XBRL should help financial services companies to collect and update information about borrowers, automate reports to regulators and distribute or collect information related to loan portfolio sales and purchases.

Accountancy institutes worldwide consider the development of XBRL as a natural next step in the clarification and development of the fundamental language of business and a vital tool for enhancing the access and breadth of financial information available to the investing public. Additionally, XBRL will help to position accountants as valued knowledge providers and financial advisors for their clients or firms. By helping businesses leverage their use of emerging technologies such as XBRL, accountants can expand their professional opportunities and value in the marketplace, IFAC contends.

## ¶12,021  NEW BUSINESS PLANNING GUIDE FOR SMEs

In May 2006, IFAC issued an informational paper entitled "Business Planning Guide: Practical Application for SMEs." The eighty plus page guide should be a valuable resource for any small or start-up business as it systematically outlines the necessary thought process needed to effectively develop a business plan and an overview of the business and its future. The guide deals with such foundational concepts as the vision and mission statements, corporate values, business goals and objectives as well as risk management and succession planning.

In a section devoted to the organization and organizational structure of a business, the guide outlines the need to present a company s management capabilities and core organizational competencies. A helpful section is devoted to marketing including the crucial processes of identifying a target market and analyzing the competition.

The construction of specific financial statements is clearly outlined including: the income statement, statement of cash flow, and balance sheet. The process of financial budgeting is also discussed.

Perhaps most valuable for many small businesses is the sample business plan and an accompanying business plan checklist presented in the appendix.

## ¶12,023  MANAGEMENT ACCOUNTING—VALUE TO AN ORGANIZATION

A major study released by IFAC's Financial and Management Accounting Committee in June 2002, presents a global, best-practice perspective on management accounting. Contemporary management accounting is an integral part of the management process focused on the effective use of resources in ongoing value creation by organizations. The study highlights the competences related to best practice in management accounting and the competences required of those taking key roles in this field of management.

Entitled *Competency Profiles for Management Accounting Practice and Practitioners*, the study builds on competency standards developed by IFAC member bodies and expands on the groundbreaking International Management Accounting Practice Statement 1, *Management Accounting Concepts*.

The study elaborates competency standards and related assessment methodologies for both management accounting practice and management accounting practitioners. The competency standards are illustrated by profiling contemporary issues related to:

1. Management practices in organizations.
2. Membership of professional associations.
3. Preparatory and continuing education associated with management practice and professional membership.

## .01  Those Toward Whom the Study Is Directed

Those who can benefit from the study and the benchmark competency standards it illustrates include:

1. Organizations seeking to move toward best practice in management accounting.
2. Professional accountants seeking to focus their work or develop their careers in the sphere of management accounting.
3. Educators, as they seek to focus and develop curricula that will contribute to the preparation of persons seeking to work in this domain of management.
4. IFAC member bodies in establishing required competences and profiling the developmental needs of their members in this sphere of management.

Study 12 provides both a benchmark and a resource for the development of practice in a range of contexts around the world. Beyond this, it is likely to open up and stimulate discussion internationally about a critical and distinctive dimension of management work.

## .03  Management Accountancy Faces a Changing Environment

A publication issued in April 2001 by the Financial and Management Accounting Committee (FMAC) presents a global perspective on the transformation of the accounting profession to a management profession. The study, entitled *A Profession Transforming: From Accounting to Management*, investigates both the causes and effects of the movement by presenting the perspectives and experiences of a dozen professional associations from around the world.

One goal of the publication is to bring to the surface the problems and solutions professional associations of accountants face in trying to understand and cope with the changes. It takes a look at the impact of the past decade of change on both the present and the future.

Such information can be useful to a wide group, including educators preparing the next generation of accountants, employers of management accountants, and professional associations that serve an increasing number of members not employed in public practice.

Currently, IFAC membership totals approximately 2.5 million accountants. More than 60% of them are employed in business. This percentage is rising steadily. The study is important for many of them who are coping with a new and still developing business environment. IFAC points out that the changed environment is one that requires new skills, increasing flexibility, and an unprecedented ability to manage change.

The study also points out that two parallel movements seem to be driving change in the accounting profession:

1.  A movement to reform corporate governance as the underpinning of global capital markets, with consequent changes in financial reporting, auditing standards, and processes for institutional oversight and assurance.
2.  A less visible but equally strong movement for accounting work to be absorbed into the management process of organizations. This development not only alters the competencies expected of practitioners but also makes such work accessible to those who are not accountants.

Features of the study include:

1.  Twelve distinct perspectives on the changes in the profession. They were contributed by twelve professional associations in Australia, Canada, Italy, Malaysia, the UK, and U.S. chapters.
2.  An introductory chapter summarizes key trends, and highlights threats and opportunities facing the management accounting profession and the associations that serve it. This overview also points out how the associations are attempting to meet the challenges.

## ¶12,025   IFAC MOVES AGAINST MONEY LAUNDERING

At the new year, 2002, IFAC urged the world's accountants to participate in efforts to combat money laundering. IFAC's Board approved the release of a white paper on anti-money laundering for dissemination to its 156 member organizations and their 2.4 million accountants and is widely disseminating the document through its Web site.

The paper explores the role of all accountants—whether they act as independent auditors, accountants in management positions, or in any other professional capacity—in ongoing public-and private-sector efforts to safeguard against money laundering. It also is designed to highlight potential indications of money laundering and to increase awareness of how professional obligations with respect to money laundering relate to and interact with corruption and transparency, privacy and consumer protection and the professional services provided by accountants. The paper draws attention to numerous risks that could lead to or reveal money-laundering situations and provides best practices to help accountants address those risks.

## .01   Accountants Asked to Play Larger Role in Detection

The IFAC emphasized the fact that, until relatively recently, the battle against money laundering and related financial crime was the exclusive domain of law enforcement. Approximately 15 years ago, forensic accountants started to join forces with law enforcement to contribute their skills in detecting possible money-laundering activity buried in the books and records of victimized financial institutions.

Specifically, since 9/11, and the U.S. Patriot Act, even the general public in this country is well aware of money laundering per se and as a method of funneling money to terrorists in particular. However, this awareness is not limited to the American public. Governments and businesses worldwide increasingly look to the accounting profession to:

1. Aid in their monitoring and detection efforts.
2. Establish and strengthen controls and safeguards against money laundering.
3. Identify its perpetrators since they are in a good position to do so.
4. Identify the perpetrators' accomplices in organized financial crime when they become aware of them.

This white paper is part of a series of IFAC initiatives to assist the world's accountants in protecting the public interest as well as their own. In recent years, IFAC has strengthened its standard-setting role with International Standards on Auditing and Public Sector Accounting Standards. It is also in the process of establishing a global self-regulatory regime for the international profession.

## ¶12,027   IFAC's Task Forces

From time to time, IFAC's Council appoints special task forces to address significant issues that warrant focused attention:

**¶12,025.01**

- Developing Nations Permanent Task Force
- Small and Medium Practices Permanent Task Force
- Task Force on Rebuilding Public Confidence in Financial Reporting

## .01   Developing Nations

In March 2004 the IFAC Board established the Developing Nations Permanent Task Force to support the development of the accountancy profession in all regions of the world. The purposes of the Task Force include:

- Working with standard-setting committees to ensure they are aware of issues relevant to the profession in developing nations.
- Monitoring the work of other IFAC committees to provide support and input when necessary.
- Working with the IFAC compliance program to respond to the needs of developing nations, including accessing resources within the IFAC membership and donor agencies.

The Task Force met in 2004 to set priorities; it was scheduled to meet again in June 2005 in Uruguay.

## .03   Small and Medium Practices Task Force

The Small and Medium Practices Task Force investigates ways in which IFAC can respond to the needs of members operating in small and medium-sized practices and small and medium-sized enterprises. The Task Force studies issues relevant to SMPs, develops papers on topics of global concern, and provides input on the work of other IFAC committees where appropriate. It also plans to set out proposals for IFAC's future involvement in the SMP/ SME area for presentation to the IFAC Board.

The Task Force issued a study, *An Assessment of International Needs and Analysis of the Activities Offered within Seven Member Bodies* to address the needs of SMPs and provide recommendations for action at the international level. The report includes descriptions of current national initiatives based on an analysis of programs and initiatives currently in place in IFAC member organizations in Canada, India, Italy, Israel, the UK, and the U.S.:

- Service to members, including such things as educational courses and training, marketing support, technical aids, web-related services, and networking support.
- Participation of SMPs in standard setting, including their presence on standard-setting committees and on governing bodies of the profession.

- Innovative service areas that can help SMPs grow their businesses and meet expanding client needs.
- Advocacy and alliances, including contacts with public authorities, governmental agencies, and regulators; advertising and promotion; and placement services.

## .05  Rebuilding Public Confidence in Financial Reporting

IFAC introduced an Internet resource center for the public in March 2003 entitled: *Viewpoints: Governance, Accountability and the Public Trust.* This section on the IFAC web site has been developed to support IFAC's Task Force on Rebuilding Credibility in Financial Reporting. The task force is charged with identifying and analyzing the causes of the loss of credibility in financial reporting. It is considering alternative courses of action to restore credibility. The final report will include recommendations on principles of best practices in the areas of financial reporting, corporate governance, corporate disclosure, and auditor performance.

In carrying out its work, the task force is considering:

- The large volume of work already undertaken by IFAC member bodies and others at a national level in addressing the loss of credibility.
- Cross-national variation in the extent of the loss of credibility and its causes.
- The emerging patterns of convergence in such areas as financial reporting and corporate governance.

*Categories Deal with Varied Areas.*    As part of its ongoing work, the task force has assembled numerous materials on various aspects of governance and financial reporting from around the world. This information is posted on the web site as a service to IFAC member bodies and their members, those involved in governance processes, and investors and other stakeholders interested in obtaining additional information on this topic. The information is posted in six categories:

1. *Global perspectives.* Information on a wide range of governance issues categorized by country.
2. *Public policy and regulation.* Statements and positions submitted by regulatory and policy-making bodies from around the world.
3. *The governance process.* Roles and Responsibilities—Papers and speeches on the roles of corporate management, boards of directors, audit committees, and auditors and others involved in the governance process.

4. *Financial reporting.* Research and other materials on the financial reporting model and specific principles and rules.

5. *Auditing issues.* Papers and commentaries on the changing role of auditors and key audit issues, such as scope of services, will be found in this section.

6. *Ethics.* Best practices for codes of ethics for professional accountants and commentaries on ethics in business.

# PART III

## ACCOUNTING PROCEDURES

# Chapter 13
## Cost Accounting

## CONTENTS

## ¶13,001 WHAT IS COST ACCOUNTING?

The cost accounting function in an organization is a system broadly defined in terms of procedures: the gathering, sorting, classifying, resorting, reclassifying, processing (computations), summarizing, reporting and filing of information relevant to a company's costs—largely in the form of data (numbers). It measures all costs associated with doing business and providing a service.

Often, cost accounting is thought of only in terms of manufacturing operations. However, many of the concepts can be useful in other areas of a small business or a service enterprise.

What is the function of a cost accounting system? Primarily, the system accepts disorganized, meaningless raw data (input) from the environment and processes (transforms) the data into understandable form. The information then leaves the system (output) in an organized form of reports required by management to account for the production costs of a business.

Specifically, cost accounting explicitly sets forth data that relate to the costs associated with the business. This includes the assignment of costs to a particular product, process, operation, or service, in the case of a service business.

## .01   The Objective of a Cost Accounting System

The primary objective of cost accounting is to provide information management can use to make the decisions necessary for the successful operation of the business. To achieve this objective, the system should be designed to provide information concerning the efficiency and effectiveness of production and service processes. The aim then, is cost reduction and increased profits.

An analysis of accurate cost data is the essence of profit planning:

1. What should be produced?
2. How much should be produced?
3. When does the law of diminishing returns kick in?
4. What price should be charged?
5. Should a particular product be discontinued?
6. Should a new product be given a "break" when dividing overhead?
7. Are costs in line with what they should be?

Management should expect cost reports to show the results of past operations in terms of costs per unit of product, costs per unit of production in each operating department, or costs per unit of service in the case of a service organization. The system should provide immediate feedback information on changes in costs from accounting period to accounting period and on *comparisons of costs with predetermined estimates or norms*. With the proper cost information, management can adjust operations quickly to changing economic and competitive conditions.

## .03   Developing a Cost System

The task of developing a cost accounting system is to determine the specific needs of management and the extent to which it is economically feasible to add detailed procedures to a basic system. The system must be easily understood by all individuals in the organization who are involved in the use of control procedures, and it must be flexible in its application. The system should be simple—that is, it must not include procedures that accumulate information that might be interesting but not particularly useful. (A common pitfall is a cost system that, itself, is more expensive than the costs to be saved.) In addition, the cost system must provide useful information in the most efficient manner. *Accurate* accounting records are particularly significant.

The cost accounting system also must be flexible, because businesspeople are often required to adapt their operations to meet changes in:

- The needs and desires of customers.
- Production methods caused by improved technology.
- The economic and social environment in which the business operates.
- Governmental regulations.

Likewise, most business ventures hope to grow and become larger. All business ventures hope to make substantial profits. New cost accounting control requirements will appear as a result of the nature of the growth process. Any system should be planned to meet changing needs with the least possible alteration of the existing system.

Fundamental cost control methods apply to most businesses and include principles applicable to an individual business. The type of production, the number of products manufactured, the size of the business, the types of costs associated with the business and the desires, capabilities and attitudes of the individuals involved in the business will all have a part in determining the structure of the cost control system.

Personnel responsible for the procedures relating to the accounting and control techniques must be constantly aware of the unique characteristics of the particular business.

## .05 Alternative Approaches

It is a rare instance that there is just one obviously right answer to any business problem. Certainly, alternative choices for the allocation of an enterprise's limited resource confront the business manager every day. Information for selecting the "right" choice is provided by a cost accounting system:

- Is the product profitable?
- Is the product priced to yield a predetermined profit margin?
- What are the per-unit costs of the product?
- Could it profitably be sold at a lower, more competitive price?

- Should production be expanded, reduced, discontinued?
- Are costs out of line?
- What are the controllable costs?
- What are the uncontrollable costs?

These are only a few items of significant information that are furnished by a well-developed cost accounting system.

## ¶13,003   FOUNDATION OF A COST ACCOUNTING SYSTEM

What input does a cost accounting system accept? An infinite amount of data within the business environment can be entered into the system. It should be emphasized that the choice of data to be entered is not random. Chance or guesswork are not acceptable determinants of data input. Rather, data selection is performed within a carefully designed framework of the information *needed* to provide the required output (reports), with the framework continually subject to modification by a feedback system. The framework is governed by a set of controls to ensure compliance with the procedures, policies and objectives the system has been designed to carry out.

The elements of the framework for a set of books to track costs are briefly described as follows:

1. The system is for a specific organization and accepts data relating only to that organization.
2. Precautions should be taken against superfluous (and expensive) input.
3. The system accepts information about transactions generated by events that have actually occurred—a purchase, for example.
4. The system accepts information that has numbers assigned to it, with dollars and cents the most common measurement.
5. The system accepts only information that has been predetermined to meet the needs of the users of the information.
6. Information entered into the system should be completely free of bias; only absolutely objective information is acceptable.
7. Information must be verifiable. Verifiability means transactions that are recorded in the same way by two or more qualified personnel acting independently of each other.
8. Information entered into the system must be consistent. Consistency prevents manipulation of data in the accounts and makes the financial information comparable from one period of time to another.

## .01   Four Group Classifications

The production activities of most businesses (of any size) can be classified into one of the following four groups:

1. **Jobbing Plants**—Jobbing plants specialize in products that are made to order and therefore not conducive to a repetitive operation. Some examples are machine shops, custom cabinet shops, builders of custom homes, printers and repair shops of all kinds—generally, custom-made products of any kind. Certain service providers, including engineers, architects and various consultants, use some job order techniques to track specific costs of a project (further explanation is given in item 4 below.)

2. **Continuous Processing Plants**—Continuous processing is used for products that are made for inventory and sale at a later date, instead of ordered in advance. The significant aspect of continuous processing is that the production process is a repetitive operation involving sequential steps in the conversion of raw materials into finished products, all the units of which are the same. Mass production techniques apply. Examples are shoe, glass, soap, paper, textile and automobile manufacturers and food processors.

3. **Assembly Plants**—Products are made up of many component parts, either manufactured by the assembler or purchased from other manufacturers. Aircraft manufacturers are one of the best examples; they subcontract various parts of the aircraft to literally hundreds of subcontractors. Automobile production is an example of both continuous processing and assembling, as many parts for automobiles are purchased from other manufacturing suppliers.

4. **Service Establishments**—Service establishments include businesses that provide various services to the public rather than manufactured products. Medical, legal, accounting, architectural, transportation, food and recreational services are examples of service businesses.

## ¶13,005   ITEMS FOR CONSIDERATION IN DEVELOPING COST CONTROL SYSTEMS

Because the cost control problems are different for each of the groups listed above, control and cost procedures must be designed for each type as well as for individual businesses within a group. Certainly not all of the items listed below will apply in every situation; however, careful consideration of this general outline should provide the basis for an effective system for any business.

## Cost Accounting System—An Outline

### Job Order Costs
Need for a job order cost system.
Use of journals and ledgers.
Cost control reports.
Recording job costs.

### Process Costs
Need for a process cost system.
Advantages of a process cost system.
Accuracy of data provided by the
    system.
Characteristics of a process cost
    system.
Production controls.
Flow assumptions (first-in, first-out
    [FIFO] or alternatives).
Conversion cost components.
Per-unit cost information.
Spoilage problems, shrinkage,
    breakage, theft and
    defective units.
Units of production.

### Accounting for Raw Materials
Determining raw materials
    requirements.
Purchasing.
Recording materials costs.
Counting and pricing materials.
Accounting for materials used.
Materials control procedures—for
    example, storing and issuing.

### Accounting for Labor Costs
Labor and payroll records.
Purpose for accounting for labor costs.
Timekeeping.
Allocating labor costs.
By-products.
Joint products.
Distribution costs.
Transfer pricing.
Payroll preparation.
Recording payrolls.

Paying the payroll.
Individual employee earnings' record.
Salaried employees payroll records.
Fringe benefits.

### Responsibility Accounting
Cost centers.
Profit centers.

### Accounting for Overhead Costs
What is overhead? Manufacturing
    overhead? Administrative overhead?
Overhead costs and tight control systems
    are important.
Allocating overhead costs.
Overhead budgets (determining
    overhead rates).
Administrative (nonmanufacturing)
    overhead, such as accounting and
    other support functions.

### Cost Targets
Predetermined costs.
Determining cost estimates
    (the cost standards).
Use of the standards in ledger
    accounts.
Analyzing cost deviations from the
    standards.
Standard costs for a job system.
Standard costs for a process system.

### Break-Even Analysis
Cost-price-volume relationships.
Fixed costs.
Variable costs.
Production capacity levels.
Effects of changes in product price.
Effects of changes in product costs.
Unit costs.
Total costs.
Graphic method.
Incremental costs.
Single or multiproduct firms.

¶13,005

---

### Cost Accounting System—An Outline

---

**Budgeting and Profit Planning**

Various types of budgets
  (operating and capital
  budgets).

Cash flow planning.

Cash budget.

**Cost Allocation Techniques**

Direct costing and contribution
  approach.

Absorption costing.

Contribution approach.

**Ratio Analysis for Control**

The most commonly applied ratios,
  with the emphasis on the ratios for
  the expense elements of the income
  statement.

How to interpret and apply the
  ratios to business decisions.

Ratios as warning signals (red flags).

**Summary of Operations**

Promptness.

Accuracy.

Comparative reports—with
  current vs. past trends highlighted.

Cost trends highlighted and explained.

Cost reports for areas of specific
  responsibility.

Report contents:
  Direct labor hours and costs.
  Indirect labor hours and costs.
  Direct materials used.
  Production overhead applied.
  Actual overhead expense.
  Variances.
  Idle time costs, if any.
  Overtime costs.
  Spoilage costs.
  Maintenance hours and costs.
  Scrap costs.
  Inventory status report.
  New order book.
    Orders shipped during the period.
    New order bookings.
  Interim expense and income
    statements (for predetermined
    periods of time—week, month;
    actual versus budgeted costs for
    the period. Comparisons with
    prior determined periods of time;
    year-to-date totals and
    comparisons with prior years).

---

## ¶13,007  COST ACCOUNTING TERMINOLOGY FOR QUICK REFERENCE

Following are some brief definitions of various types of costs:

1. Alternative—estimated for decision areas.
2. Controllable—subject to direct control at some level of supervision.
3. Departmental—production and service, for cost distributions.
4. Differential—changes in cost that result from variation in operations.
5. Direct—obviously traceable to a unit of output or a segment of business operations.
6. Discretionary—are avoidable and not essential to an objective.
7. Estimated—are predetermined.

8. Fixed—do not change in the total as the rate of output varies.
9. Future—are expected to be incurred at a later date.
10. Historical—are measured by actual cash payments or their equivalent at the time of outlay.
11. Imputed—never involve cash outlays or appear in financial records. Imputed costs involve a foregoing on the part of the person whose costs are being calculated.
12. Incremental—are the costs that are added or eliminated if segments were expanded or discontinued.
13. Indirect—are not obviously traceable to a unit of output or to a segment of business operations.
14. Joint—exist when from any one unit source, material or process come products having different unit values.
15. Noncontrollable—are not subject to control at some level of supervision.
16. Opportunity—are those for which measurable advantage is foregone as a result of the rejection of alternative uses of resources, whether of materials, labor or facilities.
17. Out of pocket—necessitate cash expenditure.
18. Period—are associated with the income of a time period.
19. Postponable—may be shifted to future period without affecting efficiency.
20. Prime—are labor and material costs that are directly traceable to a unit of output.
21. Product—are associated with units of output.
22. Replacement—are considered for depreciation significance.
23. Standard—are scientifically predetermined.
24. Sunk—are historical and unrecoverable in a given situation.
25. Variable—do change with changes in rate of output.

## ¶13,009  HISTORICAL AND STANDARD COST SYSTEMS

Cost accounting systems vary with the type of cost used—present or future. When present costs are used, the cost system is called an historical or actual cost system. When future costs are used, the cost system is called a standard cost system. In practice, combinations of these costs are used even in actual or standard systems. Where there is an intentional use of both types of costs, it is sometimes referred to as a hybrid cost system.

### .01  Actual Cost Systems

Because an actual cost system uses costs already incurred, the system determines costs only after manufacturing operations have been performed. Under this system, the product is charged with the actual cost of materials, the actual cost of labor, and an estimated portion of overhead (overhead costs represent the future cost element in an actual cost system).

## .03  Standard Cost Systems

A standard system is based on estimated or predetermined costs. Although both estimated and standard costs are "predetermined" costs, estimated costs are based on average past experience, and standard costs are based on scientific facts that consider past experience and controlled experiments. Arriving at standard costs involves:

- Careful selection of the exact amount of raw material and subassemblies required.
- An engineering study of equipment and manufacturing facilities.
- Time and motion studies.

In either system, adjustment must be made at the financial statement date to the closing inventory so that it is shown at actual cost or reasonably approximate actual cost, or at market if lower.

Also, the inventory must bear its share of the burden of overhead. The exclusion of all overheads from inventory costs does not constitute an accepted accounting procedure.

For interim statements, estimated gross profit rates may be used to determine cost of goods sold during the interim, but this fact must be disclosed.

It must be emphasized that whatever cost accounting method is chosen by a company, its purpose is primarily an internal management tool directed at:

- Controlling costs.
- Setting production goals.
- Measuring efficiencies and variances.
- Providing incentives.
- Identifying production problems.
- Establishing realistic relationships between unit costs, selling prices and gross margins.
- Correcting manufacturing difficulties/errors.

Regardless of costing methods used, generally accepted accounting procedures (GAAP) must be followed for the preparation of the financial statements, wherein the valuation must be cost or market, whichever is lower.

In addition, the FIFO or last-in, first-out (LIFO) methods (or the average method) may be used under any cost system. These methods pertain to the assumption of the flow of costs, not to the actual costs themselves. Note that both methods may be used within one inventory, as long as the method is applied to that portion of the inventory consistently from period to period. Disclosures should be made of any change in method.

## .05 Elements of Cost

Production costs consist of three elements: direct materials, direct labor, and manufacturing (overhead) expenses. Direct materials are those materials that can be identified with specific units of the product. Direct labor likewise can be identified with specific units of the product. Manufacturing expenses (overhead) are costs (including indirect material or labor) that cannot be identified with specific units of the product. These costs represent expenses for the factory and other facilities that permit the labor to be applied to the materials to manufacture a product. Sometimes, overhead is further subdivided into direct overhead (manufacturing costs, other than for material and direct labor, that specifically apply to production and require no allocation from other expense areas) and indirect overhead (expenses that have been allocated into the manufacturing expense area from other more general areas). For financial statement purposes, overhead should not include selling expenses or general administrative expenses.

## .07 Integrating a Cost System

It is not essential to integrate a cost system with the rest of the accounting system, but it is highly desirable. A cost system is actually an extension of the regular system. With an integrated system, entries in the inventory account in the general ledger should represent the sums of figures taken from the cost accounting data. The general-ledger inventory accounts (e.g., finished goods, work in process and raw materials) are the control accounts and they should tie in with the amounts of physical inventories actually on hand. Discrepancies may result from errors, spoilage or thievery.

## ¶13,011 Job Order or Process Cost Systems

There are distinctions between cost systems other than the use of present or future costs. A job order system compiles costs for a specific quantity of a product as it moves through the production process. This means that material, labor, and overhead costs of a specific number or lot of the product (usually identifiable with a customer's order or a specific quantity being produced for stock) are recorded as the lot moves through the production cycle.

A process system compiles costs as they relate to specific processes or operations for a period of time. To find the unit cost, these figures are averaged for a specified period and spread over the number of units that go through each process. Process costing is used when large numbers of identical products are manufactured, usually in assembly-line fashion.

Keep in mind that actual or estimated costs can be used with either a job order or process cost system.

## .01   Benefits and Drawbacks

Whether the job order or process system is used depends on the type of operation. The job order system is rarely used in mass production industries. It is invariably used when products are custom made. Process costing is used when production is in a continuous state of operation, as for baking and making paper, steel, glass, rubber, sugar or chemicals.

Following are some of the relative merits and shortcomings of each method.

---

### ADVANTAGES

| *Job Order System* | *Process System* |
|---|---|
| Appropriate for custom-made goods | It is usually only necessary |
| Appropriate for increasing finished | to calculate costs each month |
| goods inventory in desired | A minimum of clerical work |
| quantities | is required |
| Adequate for inventory pricing | If there is only one type of |
| Permits estimation of future costs | product cost, computation is |
| Satisfies cost-plus contract requisites | relatively simple |

### DISADVANTAGES

| *Job Order System* | *Process System* |
|---|---|
| Expensive to use—a good deal | Use of average costs ignores |
| of clerical work is required | any variance in product cost |
| Difficult to make sure that all | Involves calculating the stage |
| materials are accurately charged | of a specific job in process |
| to each equivalent | and the use of units |
| Difficult to determine cost of goods | |
| sold when partial shipments are | |
| made | |
| before completion | |

---

¶**13,011.01**

## ¶13,013  How to Use Standard Costs

Smith Company manufactures only one product, glubs—a household article made out of a certain type of plastic. Glubs are made from D raw material, which goes through a single process. Glubs are turned out from D material in a fraction of a day. Smith Company has a process-type cost setup integrated with its other financial records. D material is charged to work in process through requisitions based on actual cost. Direct labor is charged to work in process based on payroll. Manufacturing expense is charged to work in process based on the number of payroll hours. Each day, a record of the number of glubs manufactured is kept. This is the responsibility of the production department.

This is the way the Smith Company process cost system operates: Every month, total figures are worked up for raw material, payroll and factory expenses. Each of these figures is then divided by the total number of glubs produced for that month to arrive at a unit cost per glub.

Following is what the unit cost accumulation for the first four months of operation shows (this example assumes no work-in-process inventory and no equivalent units):

UNIT COST PER GLUB MANUFACTURED

|  | First Month | Second Month | Third Month | Fourth Month | Weighted Average |
|---|---|---|---|---|---|
| Material D | $ .94 | $ .91 | $ .97 | $1.10 | $ .95 |
| Direct Labor | 1.18 | 1.22 | 2.00 | .70 | 1.29 |
| Manufacturing Expense | 1.22 | 1.47 | 2.11 | .82 | 1.42 |
|  | $3.34 | $3.60 | $5.08 | $2.62 | $3.66 |

Right now, glubs are being sold at $4.30, and the present profit appears sufficient. T. O. Smith, the president and major stockholder of the corporation, feels that if glubs were sold at $3.30 each, four times as many could be sold. He also reports that he has learned that Glubco, Inc., Smith's competitor, is going to market glubs for $3.60. Smith thinks that $3.30 is a good sales price since the cost records indicate that glubs were manufactured for as low as $2.62 in the fourth month.

Smith Company's accountant says the president is incorrect. He points out that, on the basis of the cost records for six months, the average cost is somewhere in the area of $3.55 to $3.80. Selling glubs for $3.30 would create losses. The factory foreman says that during the third and fourth months there was an error in calculating the number of glubs put into finished goods inventory. From the figures for the fourth month, it appears that the foreman is correct. The unit cost per glub is unusually low. Mr. Smith wants to know the lowest at which he can sell glubs and still make a reasonable profit. The accountant suggests setting up a cost system based on standard costs and the following information is then determined:

1. Purchasing department records indicate that material D should cost no more than 15¢ per pound. (According to the chief engineer, it takes approximately two pounds of D to produce one glub.) The 15¢ figure takes future market conditions into account.
2. A time study of half a dozen workers who produce glubs is made. The average time it takes each of these six workers to produce one glub is one-sixth of an hour. The average hourly wage of these workers is $6.
3. Based on reasonable levels of production for the following year, a departmental manufacturing expense or overhead is estimated to be 100 percent of direct labor.

Based on the preceding determinations, the standard cost per glub is $2.30. It is calculated as follows:

| | |
|---|---|
| Raw Material D: two pounds at 15¢ per pound | $ .30 |
| Direct Labor: 1/6 hour at $6.00 per hour | 1.00 |
| Manufacturing Expense: 100% of direct labor | 1.00 |
| Total | 2.30 |

In order to produce glubs at this cost, the following points are agreed upon:

1. When more than 15¢ a pound is paid for raw material D, the excess is to be charged to a special variance account instead of the raw material account. These excesses are to be explained periodically by the purchasing department.
2. Requisitions for raw material D are to be limited to two pounds of D for each glub to be manufactured. If more than two pounds per glub is issued to meet scheduled production, the excess over two pounds is to be charged to a separate variance account. The reason for any excess will also have to be explained.
3. The daily number of direct labor hours spent making glubs is to be multiplied by six. This should equal the number of glubs produced that day. Any discrepancy here is probably due to inefficiency. The number of inefficient hours at the standard $6 rate times the 100 percent manufacturing expense rate is to be charged to a special variance account.
4. Payroll over $6 an hour is to be charged to a variance account. Only $6 an hour is to be charged to the work-in-process account. The factory supervisor will have to explain hourly labor figures over $6 periodically.
5. Departmental variations in the 100 percent of direct labor manufacturing expense burden are to be charged or credited to separate variance accounts. This is what happened each month after this system was instituted:

| Variance Accounts | Fifth Month | Sixth Month | Seventh Month | Eighth Month | Ninth Month |
|---|---|---|---|---|---|
| 1. Material D Price | $ 2,100 | $ 300 | $ 750 | $ 0 | $ 0 |
| 2. Material Usage | 19,500 | 13,000 | 5,000 | 500 | 400 |
| 3. Labor Efficiency | 8,000 | 5,050 | 800 | 700 | 300 |
| 4. Labor Rate | 400 | 150 | (50) | 400 | 100 |
| 5. Manufacturing Expense | 0 | 5,000 | 1,000 | 300 | (100) |
| | $30,000 | $23,500 | $ 7,500 | $1,900 | $ 700 |
| Unit Manufactured | 48,000 | 48,500 | 48,000 | 48,000 | 48,000 |
| Variance per Unit | .63 | .49 | .16 | .04 | .01 |
| Standard Unit Cost | 2.30 | 2.30 | 2.30 | 2.30 | 2.30 |
| Actual Cost | $ 2.93 | $ 2.79 | $ 2.46 | $ 2.34 | $ 2.31 |

Where there were variances, this is what was elicited from discussion with the persons responsible for the different variance accounts:

1. The purchase price for raw material D exceeded 15¢ per pound mainly because of the distance of Smith Company from where D is obtained in the South. The head of purchasing feels that D could be purchased for no more than 15¢ if there could be a small office in the South with one assistant who would remain there. It was decided to go ahead and provide the office and the additional employee.

2. The factory supervisor, together with the chief engineer, has been going over the requisitions of raw material D. More D was needed because some of the glubs had air holes in them and were not usable. It seems that the pressure used to extrude them was insufficient. The chief engineer says that he can replace the present air die channels with larger ones so that these defects do not reoccur. The supervisor knew that some glubs were scrapped in the past, but it was not until this switch to standard costs that he knew how much waste there really was.

3. The supervisor and the industrial engineer who performed the time-and-motion study discussed the labor efficiency loss. It was their opinion that:

   a. There were more factory employees than needed to carry out various operations to convert D into finished glubs.

   b. Some employees needed additional training.

   c. Some workers were overskilled for their particular functions.

   d. Other workers were not producing at reasonable levels for some as yet unknown reason.

   Both the supervisor and engineer felt that a training program instructing employees in the efficient use of available tools would increase production. Further time-and-motion studies on every phase of the production process were initiated.

¶13,013

4. There was not much variance in labor rate, but it was hoped that the training program would release more technically skilled and higher-paid employees for use in the more complicated production steps.

At the end of the seventh month, it was obvious that the steps taken were beginning to pay off. The additional costs incurred in carrying out these steps (for example, the additional employee in purchasing and the southern office) created a manufacturing overhead variance where none had existed before; but the success in other areas outweighed this.

At the end of the ninth month, everyone agreed that the switch to standard costs had exceeded expectations. The new lower production cost would help expand the market for glubs. Smith Company was also in a good competitive position compared with Glubco since it probably could now undersell it.

This illustration shows the advantages of standard costs:

- Control and reduction of costs.
- Promotion and measurement of efficiencies.
- Calculation and setting of selling prices.
- Evaluation of inventories.
- Simplification of cost procedures.

## ¶13,015   DIRECT COSTING

Another type of cost accounting that is used for internal purposes, but not for financial or tax reporting purposes, is direct costing. This is a method in which only those costs that are a consequence of production of the product are assigned to the product—direct material cost, direct labor cost and only variable manufacturing overhead. All fixed manufacturing costs are treated as expenses of the period.

The methods of recording costs for direct material and direct labor are similar under direct costing and conventional costing. It is in the method of reflecting manufacturing overhead that the systems differ:

1. In conventional costing, only one overhead control account is used.

2. In a direct costing system, overhead costs are classified as fixed or variable.

Two control accounts are used—a direct overhead account and an indirect overhead account. The *direct overhead account* is for variable expenses—those that vary with the volume of production. Under direct costing, direct labor, direct material and overhead costs that vary with production find their way into the inventory. The other manufacturing overhead expenses are charged off currently against income. The important reason behind direct costing is not to value inventories but to segregate expenses.

The *indirect overhead account* is for fixed expenses—those that do not vary with production. These are charged as expenses of the period rather than as costs of the finished product. Research costs, some advertising costs, and costs incurred to keep manufacturing and non-manufacturing facilities ready for use are considered expenses of the period.

## .01    The Effect of Direct Costing on Financial Statements

Direct costing, if used on the financial statements (for internal use), would produce the following results:

1. Where the inventory of manufactured goods does not fluctuate from one accounting period to the next, there should be no difference between net income using direct costing or net income using conventional costing.
2. Where the inventory does fluctuate and is increased, net income under direct costing will be lower. This is because fixed overhead costs under direct costing will have been charged to the current period instead of deferred by increasing the value of inventory. Under conventional costing, the value of the ending inventory will have been increased by these fixed overhead costs.
3. Where inventory decreases, net income under direct costing will be higher than conventional costing. The reason is that fixed overhead costs included in the value of the inventory under conventional costing will now increase the cost of goods sold, thereby reducing income.

## ¶13,017   SUMMARY

When a business enterprise becomes as operationally and financially complex as even most small and medium-sized companies are today, fairly sophisticated control and evaluation techniques must be developed to ensure an adequate level of operational efficiency and financial stability.

The historical essence of cost accounting systems has been the flow of financial resources into, through, and out of the business. It cannot be overemphasized that the ultimate objective of cost accounting is to provide relevant, valid and timely information of the cost of manufactured products or of the cost of services provided by service organizations. It is important to remember that the cost accounting process is a tool, not an end unto itself.

# Chapter 14

# Budgeting for Profit Planning and Budgetary Control

## CONTENTS

## ¶14,000 OVERVIEW

A budget in its simplest terms is an estimate of future events. A budget is not a purely random guess, but a forecast which is computed from historical data that has been verified and assumed with some degree of credibility. The volume of sales for the following year, for example, may be estimated by using data from past experience, present-day market conditions, buying power of the consumer and other related factors.

Merely preparing the annual budget, then leaving it unaltered for the remainder of the budget period, is not the purpose. Preparation is only the first step. The second step is for management to control the operations of the firm and to adhere to the budget. Budgetary control is the tool of management for carrying out and controlling business operations. It establishes predetermined objectives and provides bases for measuring performance against these objectives. If variations between performance and objective arise, management should alter the situation by either correcting the weakness in performance or modifying the budget. Firms that adopt budgetary control have a better control of operations and are better able to modify them to meet expectations.

In addition to a review of the rolling budgets based on previous years' expenditures and operations, two management tools related to budgeting will also be discussed: break-even analysis (BE) and zero-base budgeting (ZBB).

The objective of break-even analysis is to determine an approximation as close as possible to the changes in costs generated by changes in the volume of production. Determining the BE point is a technique that can be applied to the control of costs, in the evaluation of alternatives, in the allocations of a firm's resources, and in making decisions in virtually every phase of a company's business.

The value to budgeting in break-even analysis is that the approach can be applied to sales, profits, costs, and selling prices, to help make sound decisions for the utilization of idle plant capacity, for proposed advertising expenditures, and for proposed expansion in production levels.

ZBB is a logical process, combining many elements of management. The key components of ZBB are:

1. Identifying objectives.
2. Determining value of accomplishing each activity.
3. Evaluating alternative funding levels.
4. Establishing priorities.
5. Evaluating workload and performance measures.

ZBB recognizes that the budgeting process is a management process, a decision-making process, and a driving force.

## ¶14,001   TYPES OF BUDGETS

There are two principal types of annual profit budgets: the operating or earnings budget and the financial or cash budget. The earnings budget, as its name implies, is an attempt to forecast the earnings of a company for a future period. To make such forecast, other estimates must be made. Consequently, organizations have sales budgets, production budgets (which include labor budgets, materials budgets, manufacturing expense budgets), capital expenditure budgets, administrative expense budgets, distribution expense budgets and appropriation-type budgets (e.g., advertising, research). The accuracy of each of these budgets determines the accuracy of the earnings forecast.

The cash budget, on the other hand, tries to forecast the utilization of the company's cash resources. It estimates the company's anticipated cash expenditures and resources for a period of operation. Cash budget forecasts, like the earnings forecast, depend heavily on sales forecasts. The amount of sales determines the amount of cash the company has for purposes of its operation.

## ¶14,003  THE SALES BUDGET

The foundation of the entire budget program is the sales budget. If anticipated sales of a particular product (or project) do not exceed the cost to produce and market it by an amount sufficient to reward the investors and to compensate for the risks involved, the product (project) should not be undertaken. Sales forecasting must be continuous. Conditions change rapidly; in order to direct one's efforts into the most profitable channels, there must be a continuous review and revision of the methods employed.

### .01  Forecasting Sales

A sales forecast represents the revenue side of the earnings forecast. It is a prediction as to the sales quantity and sales revenue. Sales forecasts are made for both short and long periods.

Forecasting sales with any degree of accuracy is not an easy task. For example, a firm which estimates sales with the expectation that a patent which it holds will not become obsolete may be disappointed.

In general, the business forecaster has two situations: (1) those which he or she can to some extent control and (2) those where conditions created by others can only be observed, recorded, interpreted, and applied to his or her own situation. A firm that has a monopoly due to an important patent which it owns is an example of a company which controls the situation. Forecasts made by such a company may be very accurate. In most cases, however, a company has no such control. It must attempt to interpret general conditions, the situation in its own industry, and future sales of its particular company before making forecasts.

Making the forecast is the responsibility of the sales manager, who, with the help of the district managers and the individual salespersons, determines the primary sales objectives for the year. Corrections of the forecast are made by the heads of the firm so that sales estimates will better reflect expected economic conditions. Before an estimate of sales is made, there must be a reasonable expectation that the projection is attainable. It must be based on the best evidence available. As conditions change, the forecast is revised.

If a firm desires to sell more than in the past, an analysis of past sales performances must be supplemented by other analyses. Consideration must be given to general business conditions. The effects of political and economic changes throughout the world are quickly reflected on individual business communities. Some of these factors which affect sales are wars, government regulations, and technological developments. This information should be used in appraising the probable effect of these changes on the sales of the firm for the budget period.

## .03  Market Analysis

A sales manager needs to know if the firm is getting its full share of potential customer demand as indicated by a market analysis.

The questionnaire is a popular method of reaching consumers, retailers and jobbers. Data collected give the firm valuable information, essential in arriving at a forecast of sales possibilities.

A market analysis at a given time gives a picture of the present and potential consumption of a product. This picture provides only half the significant information. The other half can be obtained by continuing the survey over a period of time to discover market trends.

## .05  Pricing Policy

The sales budget is not complete until the firm decides on a practical policy as to what price can be secured for its products. Generally, estimates should be made to conform with the market prices during the budget period.

The next step is to formulate the sales policies of the firm. These policies should be established relative to such considerations as territorial expansion and selection, customer selection, types and quality of products and service, prices, terms of sales, and sales organization and responsibility.

Only after a firm has thoroughly analyzed past sales experience, general business conditions, market potentials, the product to be sold, determined the prices to be charged and formulated its sales policies is it ready to develop the sales program.

## .07  Measuring Individual Performance

As a basis for measuring individual performance, a rewarding-merit sales standard could be established. A sales standard is an opinion of the best qualified judgment of performance which may reasonably be achieved under ideal conditions. By comparing this standard with the budget estimate (the figure expected) under normal conditions, management has provided the most important tool of sales control.

An example of how a comparison between the standard and budget estimate may serve as a basis for reward is the following: A saleswoman may be told to produce sales of $150,000 (standard), but the firm may expect her to produce sales of only $125,000 (budget estimate). The saleswoman does not have to be told what the firm's budget figures are. In an endeavor to reach $150,000, she is trying to better what she believes is the budget figure. Depending on how close she comes to the $150,000, the firm may devise a method of rewarding her. It should be kept in mind, however, that the standard should not be set too high, since it may have a reverse effect if the sales personnel feel it is unreachable.

# ¶14,005   THE PRODUCTION BUDGET

After the sales budget has been prepared, the next step is to prepare the production budget, which specifies the quantity and timing of production requirements.

While the sales budget is prepared in anticipation of seasonal fluctuations, the production budget endeavors to smooth out the fluctuations and thus make most effective use of productive capacity. This is accomplished by manufacturing for stock over the slow periods and using the stock to cover sales during busy periods.

There are different problems for a firm that sells stock products and one that produces special-order goods. The objective for a stock-order-type firm is to coordinate sales and production to prevent excessive inventories, but at the same time to have enough stock to meet sales. A forecast of production in such a firm should enable the executive to arrange to lay out the factory so as to handle the anticipated volume most conveniently. Production in such a firm must be as evenly distributed as possible over the year. It is uneconomical to manufacture the whole period's requirements within a relatively short time at the beginning of the budget period. This involves unduly heavy capital costs of carrying the large inventory. Also, distributing the work over the entire period spreads the labor costs.

With special-order items, the production department must be prepared at all times to manufacture the goods as soon as possible after receiving the order. Production in this case has to be arranged for the best possible utilization of equipment and labor, so that idle time is reduced to a minimum.

## .01   Budgeting Production Costs

Production budgets should be rigid as long as conditions remain the same, but they should be capable of prompt adjustment when circumstances change. For example, if a company operates at 70 percent of capacity in a period and the budget was based on a production volume of 80 percent, the budget is of little use. The budget will have to be altered to show what production costs will be at the 70 percent level. It is prudent when planning production at a particular anticipated percentage level to indicate in the budget the estimates of possible production costs at different levels.

## .03  Preparing the Production Budget

The production budget period may vary in length. However, it is common practice among large corporations to use what is known as a "product year." As an example, the automobile industry will usually start with the introduction of new models. The budget year should include at least one complete cycle of operations so that money tied up in raw materials and work-in-process materials may undergo one complete liquidation. Another factor influencing the budget period is the stability of general business conditions. It is more difficult to budget operations during an unstable period, and it is advisable at these times to shorten the budget period.

The production budget should be expressed in terms of physical units. To compute the physical quantities is simple. For example, a simple computation to estimate production required is:

|  | Units |
|---|---|
| Estimated sales | 250,000 |
| Less opening inventory | 150,000 |
| Total requirements | 100,000 |
| Add: Closing inventory | 100,000 |
| Production required | 200,000 |

Before computing the quantity to be produced, it is necessary to decide quantities to be in the inventory at the end of the period. This decision should be based on factors such as:

1. Adequate inventory to meet sales demands
2. Evenly distributed production to prevent shortage of material and labor
3. Danger of obsolescence
4. High costs of storing large inventories.

*Available Facilities.*    The production program must conform with the plant facilities available and should determine the most economical use of these facilities. The capacity of the plant is measured in two ways: optimum plant capacity and normal plant capacity. All other measurements are in percentages of optimum or normal capacity. Optimum capacity of course, can never actually be attained. There are many unavoidable interruptions, such as waiting for setup of machines; time to repair machines; lack of help, tools, materials; holidays; inefficiency; etc. However, these interruptions should be looked into to determine how they can be minimized.

Management should also consider whether additional equipment is needed just to meet temporary sales demands. Later, such equipment may be idle. The replacement of old machinery with new high-speed equipment should also be considered. A careful study should help determine which step would be more profitable in the long run.

Records for each product showing the manufacturing operations necessary and a record of each machine's capability and capacity, should be maintained. Estimates must be made of material to be used, number of labor hours and quantities of service (power) required for each product. These estimates are called "standards of production performance." The establishment of these standards is an engineering rather than an accounting task. In this respect, these standards are similar to those used in standard cost accounting.

*Cost of Production.*    The following illustrates how cost of production is determined: Assume a concern has a normal capacity of 100 units of product. Current production budget calls for 80 units. Only one product is made; and its production requires two operations, A and B. The standard costs are: variable costs per unit of product, one unit of direct material, $2; operation A (direct labor and overhead), $3; operation B (direct labor and overhead), $5; total $10. Fixed production costs for the budget period are $500, or $5 per unit based on normal capacity. This production cost budget would then be expressed as follows:

| | |
|---|---:|
| Variable cost (80 units @ $10) | $    800 |
| Fixed costs (80 units @ $5) | 400 |
| Costs chargeable to production | 1,200 |
| Cost of idle capacity (500 less 400) | 100 |
| Total budgeted costs | $  1,300 |

There is a tie-in here between estimated costs, standard costs, and production budgets.

# ¶14,007   THE LABOR BUDGET

The labor budget deals only with direct labor. Indirect labor is included in the manufacturing expense budget. (The manufacturing expense budget includes the group of expenses in addition to indirect labor, expenses such as indirect material, repairs and maintenance, depreciation and insurance.)

The purpose of the labor budget is to ascertain the number and kind of workers needed to execute the production program during the budget period. The labor budget should indicate the necessary worker-hours and the cost of labor required for the manufacture of the products in the quantities shown by the production budget.

## .01   Preparation of the Labor Budget

The preparation of a labor budget begins with an estimate of the number of labor hours required for the anticipated quantity of products. Before this can be done, it is necessary to know the quantity of items to be produced, as in the production budget. If the products are uniform and standard labor time allowances have been established, it is just a matter of multiplying the production called for by the standards to determine the labor hours required. If the products are *not* uniform but there is uniformity of operations, it is first necessary to translate production into operation requirements. Operation standards then should be established in terms of worker- or machine-hours to ascertain the quantity of labor required. The next step in preparing the labor budget is to estimate the cost of direct labor. These estimates are computed by multiplying the number of units to be produced by the labor costs per unit. The problem then is to predetermine the unit labor costs. Some of the methods of determining these costs are:

• Day rate system.
• Piece rate system.
• Bonus system.

In firms where standard labor costs have been established for the products manufactured, it is necessary only to multiply the units of the product called for in the production budget by the standard labor costs.

A detailed analysis should frequently be made of the differences between actual and estimated labor costs to determine whether they are justified. An investigation may reveal inefficient workers, wasted time, defective materials, idle time, poor working conditions, high-priced workers, etc. Responsibility must be definitely placed and immediate action taken to correct those factors which are capable of being controlled.

The budgets for direct labor and manufacturing expenses are not complete until schedules of the final estimates are prepared. The form will vary, depending on the needs of the firm. The following is an example of a schedule of estimated direct labor costs where estimates are shown for each department of the firm:

### X Corporation

### Estimated Direct Labor Costs for the Period 1/1/xx to 12/31/xx

| Dept. | Quantity to be Produced | Standard Labor Cost Per Unit | Total Estimated Labor Cost |
|---|---|---|---|
| 1 ............... | 127,600 | $.90 | $115,000 |
| 2 ............... | 127,600 | 1.60 | 204,000 |
| 3 ............... | 127,600 | 1.12 | 143,000 |
| | | $3.62 | $462,000 |

## ¶14,009   MATERIALS BUDGET

The purpose of the materials budget is to be sure that there are sufficient materials to meet the requirements of the production budget. This budget deals with the purchase of raw materials and finished parts and controls the inventory. How to estimate the material required depends on the nature of the individual company. A company manufacturing standard articles can estimate fairly accurately the amount of raw materials and the purchases required for the production program. Even where the articles are not standard, there is usually a reliable relationship between the volume of business handled and the requirements for the principal raw materials.

## .01   Tie-In to Standard Costs

In the preparation of the material budget, there is a tie-in to standard costs. Here is an example of how purchase requirements are computed:

| | |
|---|---|
| Quantity required for production | 300,000 units |
| Desired inventory at end of budget period | 75,000 units |
| Total requirements | 375,000 units |
| Less: Inventory at beginning of period | 80,000 units |
| Purchase requirements | 295,000 units |

The next step is to express material requirements in terms of prices. Some firms establish standard prices based on what are considered normal prices. Differences between standard and actual purchase prices are recorded as price variance.

## .03  Factors Affecting Policy

These are:

1. The time it takes the material to be delivered after the purchase order is issued.
2. The rate of consumption of material as indicated by the production budget.
3. The amount of stock that should be on hand to cover possible delays in inventory of raw materials.

On the basis of these factors, the purchasing department working with the production department can establish figures of minimum stocks and order quantities of raw materials and parts for each product handled. Purchases in large quantities are advisable if price advantages can be obtained. Bulk purchases are advisable during periods of rising prices but not during periods of declining prices. The unavoidable time lag between order and delivery of the material is also a reason to buy in advance.

Buying in advance does not necessarily involve immediate delivery. The deliveries may be spread over the budget period in order to coordinate purchases with production and to control inventory. To control inventory, it is desirable to establish minimum and maximum quantities for each material to be carried. The lower limit is the smallest amount which can be carried without risk of production delays. If materials can be obtained quickly, the inventory can be held near the lower limit. The advantage of keeping inventory at this lower limit is that it minimizes the cost of storage and possible obsolescence. If materials cannot be obtained quickly, there is the possibility of a rise in prices, as well as an unforeseen delay in delivery which could hold up production and so it is advisable to carry more than minimum inventory.

## .05  Goods in Process

The time it takes for material to enter the factory and emerge as a finished product is frequently much longer than necessary for efficient production. Comparisons with other companies may reveal that a firm allows its goods to remain in process much longer than other firms. Investigations should be made to determine the causes of such delays and formulate remedies. These investigations are usually made in connection with the production budget.

## .07  Finished Goods

The budget of finished goods inventory is based on the sales budget. For example, if 100 units of an item are expected to be sold during the budget period, the problem is to determine how much must be kept in stock to support such a sales program. Since it is difficult to determine the exact quantity customers will demand each day, the finished goods inventory must maintain a margin of safety so that satisfactory deliveries can be made. Once this margin is established, the production and purchasing programs can be developed to replenish the stock as needed.

## ¶14,011  MANUFACTURING EXPENSE BUDGET

In preparing the manufacturing expense budget, estimates and probable expenses should be prepared by persons responsible to authorize expenditures. The general responsibility for variable expenses lies with the production manager. But the immediate responsibility for many of these expenses lies with the supervisors of the several departments. Generally, expenses are estimated by those who control them. Each person who prepares a portion of the manufacturing expense budget is furnished with data of prior periods and any plans for the budget period which may affect the amount of expenses. With these data decisions can be made about:

1.  Which, if any, present expenses can be eliminated.
2.  Probable effect of the sales and production forecasts on those expenses which must be incurred.

No plans for the elimination or reduction of variable expenses should be made unless it is certain that the plan can be enforced.

The responsibility for many fixed manufacturing expenses is with the general executives. Such fixed expenses include long-term leases, pension plans, patents, amortization, salaries of major production executives, etc.

In preparing the budget estimates of manufacturing expenses, a common practice is to use percentages. Each expense is taken as a percent of sales or production costs. For example, if a certain expense is estimated to be 5 percent of sales, this percentage is applied to the sales estimate to obtain the amount of this expense. The fallacy with this method is that all expenses do not vary proportionately with sales or production. A sounder method of estimating manufacturing expenses is to give individual expenses separate treatment.

In estimating the indirect labor expense, it is important to first analyze the expense for the period preceding the budget period. The requirements for additional help, or the possibility of eliminating some of the help, should be considered along with plans for increasing or decreasing any rates of compensation. Detailed schedules should be prepared, showing the nature of each job and the amount to be paid. By summarizing these schedules, an aggregate estimate can be determined.

Indirect materials expense should be estimated by first analyzing the amount consumed in prior periods. This, together with the production budget showing the proposed volume for the budget period, serves as a basis for estimating the quantities of the indirect material requirements. The probable cost of such requirements estimated by the purchasing department is the amount to be shown in the manufacturing expense budget.

Repairs and maintenance estimates are based on past experience data, supplemented by a report on the condition of the present equipment. If any additional equipment is to be installed during the budget period, recognition must be given to the prospect of additional repairs and maintenance charges. Electric power expense is in direct proportion to the production volume. The charges for depreciation of equipment can be estimated with considerable accuracy.

Insurance expense for the budget period is estimated on the basis of the insurance in force charged to production with adjustments made for contemplated changes in equipment, inventories, or coverage of hazard incident to manufacturing.

To budget manufacturing expenses effectively it is important to establish standard overhead rates.

At frequent intervals during the budget period, comparison should be made between the actual expenses in each department and the amount estimated to be spent for actual production during the period. Variations should be investigated and steps taken to correct weaknesses in the production program.

A distinction should be made between controllable and uncontrollable expenses so that the responsibility of individuals can be more closely determined. To facilitate the estimating of expenses, a further distinction is made between fixed and variable expenses. Fixed expenses are those which remain the same regardless of the variations in sales or production. Variable expenses are those which increase or decrease proportionally with changes in volume, sales or production. Maintenance is seldom treated in a separate budget. It is usually regarded as part of the manufacturing expense budget.

¶14,011

Following is an example of a Schedule of Estimated Manufacturing Expenses for each operation of a particular product:

### Y Corporation for the Year Ended 12/31/xx

|  | Total | Operation 1 | Operation 2 | Operation 3 |
|---|---|---|---|---|
| Variable expenses: |  |  |  |  |
| Indirect materials | $ 20,000 | $ 5,000 | $ 10,000 | $ 5,000 |
| Indirect labor | 100,000 | 10,000 | 15,000 | 75,000 |
| Light and power | 30,000 | 5,000 | 13,000 | 12,000 |
| Telephone | 5,000 | 3,000 | —0— | 2,000 |
| Fixed and semi-variable: |  |  |  |  |
| Factory rent | 50,000 | 14,000 | 18,000 | 18,000 |
| Superintendence | 100,000 | 30,000 | 35,000 | 35,000 |
| Depreciation | 100,000 | 20,000 | 20,000 | 60,000 |
| General and |  |  |  |  |
| administrative expense | 50,000 | 12,000 | 17,000 | 21,000 |
| Total | $455,000 | $ 99,000 | $168,000 | $188,000 |

After estimates of materials, direct labor and manufacturing expenses have been prepared, a Schedule of Estimated Cost of Production may be prepared as follows:

### Z Corporation for the Year Ended 12/31/xx

|  | Total | Product A | Product B | Product C |
|---|---|---|---|---|
| Cost Element: |  |  |  |  |
| Materials | $200,000 | $ 80,000 | $ 50,000 | $ 70,000 |
| Labor | 340,000 | 100,000 | 80,000 | 160,000 |
| Manufacturing expenses | 70,000 | 30,000 | 30,000 | 10,000 |
| Total | $610,000 | $210,000 | $160,000 | $240,000 |

## ¶14,013  CAPITAL EXPENDITURES BUDGET

Since capital expenditures represent a large part of the total investment of a manufacturing concern, the capital expense budget is of great importance. Unwise capital expenditures can seldom be corrected without serious loss to stockholders. The purpose of the capital expenditures budget is to subject such expenditures to careful examination and so avoid mistakes that cannot easily be corrected.

A carefully prepared capital expenditures budget should point out the effect of such expenditures on the cash position of the company and on future earnings. For example, too large a portion of total assets invested in fixed plant and equipment sooner or later may result in an unhealthy financial condition because of the lack of necessary working capital.

## .01    Preparation of Capital Expenditures Budget

In preparing the capital expenditures budget, the following information is recorded:

1. The amount of machinery, equipment, etc., on hand at the beginning of the budget period;
2. Additions planned for the period;
3. Withdrawals expected for the period;
4. The amount of machinery, equipment, etc., expected at the end of the budget period.

Consideration should be given to estimates of additions planned for the period. Additions will be justified if they increase the volume of production and earnings, will reduce unit costs, and the money needed can be spared. Consideration should also be given to the percentage of investment for fixed assets as compared with net worth of the firm for a number of years. Various business authorities have realized that an active business enterprise with a tangible net worth between $50,000 and $250,000 should have as a maximum not more than two-thirds of its tangible net worth in fixed assets. Where the tangible net worth is in excess of $250,000, not more than 75 percent of the tangible net worth should be represented by fixed assets. When these percentages are greatly exceeded, annual depreciation charges tend to be too heavy, the net working capital too moderate, and liabilities expand too rapidly for the good health of the business; alternative leasing should be considered.

The capital expenditures budget should include estimates not only for the budget period, but long-range estimates covering a period of many years. The ideal situation occurs when machinery is purchased at a time when prices are low. A long-range capital expenditures budget will indicate what machinery will be of use in the future; then, machinery may be acquired when prices are considered low. Inefficient or obsolete machines can sometimes be made into satisfactory units by rebuilding. If it is estimated that gains derived from rebuilding machinery will exceed the costs, then provision should be made in the capital expenditures budget to incur these expenses. Such expenditures are frequently called betterments and prolong the useful life of the machines. The preparation of detailed and accurate records is an essential part of the capital expenditures budget. The following information should be included in such a record:

1. Description of machines;
2. Date of requisition;
3. Cost for depreciation rate.

From the above information, it is a simple matter to complete the depreciation for the budget period.

As with other budgets, actual expenditures should be compared with the estimates, and any variation should be analyzed. In addition, a statement should be prepared showing the extent to which actual results obtained from the use of certain capital expenditures are in line with expectations. This is particularly important where substantial investments are made in labor-saving equipment, new processes or new machines.

## ¶14,015  The Cash Budget

The cash budget is a composite reflection of all the operating budgets in terms of cash receipts and disbursements. Its purpose is to determine the cash resources that will be available during the entire budget program so that the company will know in advance whether it can carry out its program without borrowing or obtaining new capital or whether it will need to obtain additional capital from these sources. Thus, the company can arrange in advance for any necessary borrowing, avoiding emergencies and, more important, a cash crisis caused by a shortage.

A knowledgeable financial person goes into the market to borrow money when there is the cheapest rate. The cash budget will tell the manager when there is the need to borrow so he or she can plan accordingly. In a like manner, the manager can foresee when there will be sufficient funds to repay loans.

A cash budget is very important to a firm which does installment selling. Installment selling ties up cash resources, and a careful analysis of estimated future collections is needed to forecast the cash position of the company.

Other purposes of the cash budget are: (1) to provide for seasonal fluctuations in business which make heavy demands on funds to carry large inventories and receivables; (2) to assist the financial executive in having funds available to meet maturing obligations; (3) to aid in securing credit from commercial banks (a bank is more likely to lend funds for a definite plan that has been prepared, indicating when and how the funds will be repaid) and 4) to indicate the amount of funds available for investments, when available and for what duration.

## .01   Preparation of the Cash Budget

The main difference between a cash budget and other budgets is that in the cash budget all estimates are based on the dates when it is expected cash will be received or paid. Other budgets are prepared on the basis of the accrual of the different items (for accrual-basis companies). Therefore, in the cash budget, the budget executive cannot base the estimate of cash receipts directly on the sales budget for the obvious reason that all the cash will not be received from such sales in the same month in which they are billed. This is not true in the case of a business on a strictly cash basis.

Depreciation is another item handled differently in the cash budget. Depreciation is a cost of doing business; it increases expenses and reduces net income for financial reporting purposes. It is not, however, a cash item and is ignored in preparing the cash budget, but the amount paid for a new plant or equipment in a single year or budget period is included in full in the cash budget.

Cash receipts of a typical firm come from cash sales, collections on accounts and notes receivable, interest, dividends, rent, sale of capital assets and loans. The cash sale estimate is taken from the sales budget. The estimate of collections on accounts should be based on the sales budget and company experience in making collections. With concerns whose sales are made largely on account, the collection experience should be ascertained with considerable care. As an illustration, assume the March account sales have actually been collected as follows:

| Month | % |
|---|---|
| March | 6.4 |
| April | 80.1 |
| May | 8.5 |
| June | 3.6 |
| Cash Discount Taken | 1.1 |
| Bad Debts Loss | .3 |
| Total | 100.00 |

If the same experience is recorded for each month of the year, it is possible to resolve the sales estimates into a collection budget. It is sometimes desirable to develop the experience separately for different classes of customers for different geographical areas. Once these figures are ascertained, they should be tested from time to time.

Cash disbursements in a typical firm are made for payroll, materials, operating expenses, taxes, interest, purchases of equipment, repayment of loans, payment of dividends, and other like items. With a complete operating budget on hand, there is little difficulty in estimating the amount of cash that will be required and when it will be required. Wages and salaries are usually paid in cash and on definite dates. For purchases of material (from the materials budget), the purchasing department can readily indicate the time allowed for payments. Operating expenses must be considered individually. Some items, such as insurance, are prepaid. Others, such as commissions, are accrued. So, cash payments may not coincide with charges on the operating budget.

## ¶14,017   Zero-Base Budgeting

A different approach to budgeting adopted by some industrial organizations as well as not-for-profit entities and governmental units is appropriately termed *Zero-Base Budgeting*. Whether adopted wholeheartedly on a yearly basis, as a review every few years, or merely as a mind-set tool, its precepts can be of value in the budgeting process.

Expenses for industrial organizations can be divided into two categories:

1. Direct manufacturing expense, for materials, labor, and overhead.
2. Support expense, for everything else.

It is the "everything else" that causes problems at budget time, when, for example, management is beset by rising costs and must decide between decreasing the budgetary allocation for a research and development project or cutting funds for executive development. Traditionally, problems like these boil down to one question: How should the company shift its allocations around? Rather than tinker with their existing budget, many companies have implemented this budgeting method that starts at base-zero.

This approach requires that the company view all of its discretionary activities and priorities afresh, and create a different and hopefully better set of allocations for the ensuring budget year. The base-zero procedure gives management a firm grip on support allocations of all kinds, a procedure for describing all support expense minutely, classifying the alternatives to each, and sorting them all according to their importance and priority.

This technique in budgeting differentiates between the basic and necessary operations and those of a more discretionary character, thus enabling management to focus specific attention on the optional group. The basic steps for effective zero-base budgeting require justification of every dollar spent on discretionary costs, and a prescribed order of approach to the final allocation of funds:

1. Describe each optional activity in a "decision" package.
2. Evaluate and rank these decision packages by cost/benefit analysis.
3. Allocate resources based on this analysis.

## .01 Where to Use Zero-Base Budgeting

Zero-base budgeting (ZBB) is best applied to service and support areas of company activity rather than to the basic manufacturing operation. Since a corporation's level of manufacturing activity is determined by its sales volume, the production level, in turn, determines how much the company should spend on labor, materials, and overhead. Hence, there is not the same simple relationship between costs and benefits here as there is in the service and support areas where management can trade off a level of expenditures on a given project against the direct returns on investment. Cost benefit analysis, which is crucial to zero-base budgeting, cannot be applied directly to decisions to increase or decrease expenditures in the manufacturing areas.

The main use of zero-base budgeting occurs when management has discretion to choose between different activities having different direct costs and benefits. Such areas normally include marketing, finance, quality control, personnel, engineering and other non-production areas of company activity.

## .03 Decision Package Concept

When implementing ZBB, a company must explain the "decision package concept" to all levels of management and then present guidelines for the individual manager to use in breaking the specific activities into workable packages. Next, higher management must establish a ranking, consolidation and elimination process. The decision package is the document that identifies and describes a specific activity in such a manner that management can (1) evaluate and rank that activity against other activities competing for limited resources, (2) decide whether to approve or disapprove expenditures in that area.

The specifications in each package must provide management with the information needed to evaluate the activity. Included should be (1) a statement of the goals of the activity; (2) the program by which the goals are to be attained; (3) the benefits expected from the program and methods of determining whether they have been attained; (4) suggested alternatives to the program; (5) possible consequences of not approving the package and expenditure of funds; (6) designation of personnel required to carry out the program.

There are two basic types of decision packages:

1. Mutually exclusive packages identify alternative means of performing the same function. The best alternative is chosen and the other packages are discarded.

2. Incremental packages reflect different levels of effort that may be expended on a specific function or program. One package, the "base package," may establish a minimum level of activity, and others identify increased activity or expenditure levels.

A logical starting point for determining next year's needs is the current year's operations. Each ground level manager who has the ultimate responsibility takes the areas's forecasted expense level for the current year, identifies the activities creating this expense, and calculates the cost for each activity. At this stage, the manager identifies each activity at its current level and method of operation and does not attempt to identify alternatives or increments.

After current operations have been separated into preliminary decision packages, the manager looks at requirements for the upcoming year. To aid in specifying these requirements, upper management should issue a formal set of assumptions on the activity levels, billings, and wage and salary increases for the upcoming year. These formal assumptions provide all managers with uniform benchmarks for estimating purposes.

At the conclusion of the formulation stage, the manager will have identified all of the proposed activities as follows:

1. Business-as-usual packages.
2. Decision packages for other ongoing activities.
3. Decision packages for new activities.

The ranking process forces management to face squarely the most basic decision: How much money is available and where should it be spent to obtain the greatest good? Management arrives at the decisions by listing, and then studying all the packages identified in order of decreasing benefit to the company, and eliminating those of least value.

It is possible for one ranking of decision packages to be obtained for an entire company and judged by its top management. While this one, single ranking would identify the best allocation of resources, ranking and judging the high volume of packages created by describing all of the activities of a large company would result in an unwieldy task for top management.

This problem can be resolved by grouping decision units which may correspond to a budget unit in organizations with detailed cost-center structures, or they can be defined on a project basis.

The initial ranking should occur at the cost-center or project level so that each manager can evaluate the relative importance of the segments and rank the packages accordingly.

The manager at the next level up the ladder then reviews these rankings with the appropriate managers and uses the resulting rankings as guides to produce a single consolidated ranking for all packages presented from below.

At higher levels of a large organization, the expertise necessary to rank packages is best obtained by committee. The committee membership should consist of all managers whose packages are being ranked with their supervisor serving as chairperson.

¶14,017.03

Each committee produces its consolidated ranking by voting on the decision packages presented by its members. As at the cost-center level, the most beneficial packages are ranked highest and the least important ranked lowest.

It is best to establish the cutoff line at the highest consolidation level first, and then for the lower levels. The most effective way to establish the first cutoff is for management at the highest consolidation level to estimate the expense that will be approved at the top level and then to set the cutoff line far enough below to allow trading off between the divisions whose packages are being ranked.

The ability to achieve a list of ranked packages at any given organization level allows management to evaluate the desirability of various expenditure levels throughout the budgeting process. This ranked list also provides management with a reference point to be used during the year to identify activities to be reduced or expanded if allowable expenditure levels change.

Zero-base budgeting can be a flexible and useful tool in simplifying the budgeting process and in bringing about better resource allocation by forcing meaningful consideration of varying priorities for available funds.

## ¶14,019   BREAK-EVEN POINT ANALYSIS

The break-even point (BE) is that amount of sales necessary to yield neither income nor loss. If sales should be less than indicated by the BE point, a loss results. If the total cost of goods sold and other expenses is less than sales, and if this total varied in direct proportion to sales, operations would result in net income. BE analysis is not a budget, in itself, but is an approach in the budgeting process for dealing intelligently with the uncertainty of estimates for future operations that are based on statistical data. Breakeven analysis can be applied to sales, profit, costs, and selling price problems, and it can be used to help make sound decisions for employing idle plant capacity, planning advertising, granting credit, and expanding production. BE is a tool, and a useful one, with which to begin to approach decision problems.

BE Analysis, is an inexpensive method for analyzing the possible effects of decisions. Discounted cash flow techniques require large amounts of data expensive to develop. BE can help with the decision whether or not it is worthwhile to do more intensive, costly analysis.

BE provides a means for designing product specifications, which permits a comparison of different designs and their costs before the specifications for a specific product are accepted as the best choice cost-wise. For example, a new product with an uncertain volume is considered to be feasible if it's made with hand tools rather than with expensive capital equipment. The first method typically has higher variable costs, but lower fixed costs. This often results in a lower breakeven point for the project, and lower risks and potential profits. The fixed capital equipment approach raises the BE, but also raises the risks and profit potential for the manufacturer. BE helps to examine these trade-offs.

**¶14,019**

An important factor when using BE analysis is the nature of the user's cost structure. Some firms have a flexible labor force and standard cost analysis works well. In other businesses, however, management must treat labor costs differently. Certain skilled workers cannot be laid off when business is slow. BE analysis assumes a realistic definition of costs, both in amount and type. While fixed costs will not change with changes in revenue, variable and semi-variable costs do change with changes in sales, up or down. Product pricing can be significantly aided by using variations of breakeven analysis.

*Break-Even Chart.*    A break-even chart presents a visual representation of sales volume, capacity, or output when expenses and revenues are equal, i.e., a volume level at which income equals expenses. A BE chart provides a projection of the impact of output upon expenses, income, and profits which makes the chart a useful tool for profit planning and control.

The BE chart assumes that selling prices do not change, total fixed expenses remain the same at all levels of output, and variable costs increase or decrease in direct proportion to sales. The N line remains the same regardless of sales volume; the point B on the chart is the total of the fixed and variable expenses on the list on the vertical axis. The area between line M and the fixed expense line N is the amount of variable expenses at different volumes of sales. The area between line M and the horizontal axis represents the total costs at various levels of sales. Line M can be considered a total cost line, since total costs for various volumes of sales can be readily determined from it. This can be done by starting at any point on the horizontal scale and measuring upward to line M and across to the vertical scale.

The income line P starts at zero and extends through point C, which is the point at which total sales and total income are shown on both scales, about $1,200. The profit area lies to the right of break-even point D where the revenue line P crosses the total cost line M. Revenue is greater than costs above—i.e., to the right—of the break-even point D; the loss area is below—i.e., to the left—of the break-even point D.

*Break-Even Technique.*    Break-Even is an inexpensive technique to determine whether or not it would be advisable to do more intensive and costly analysis of a proposed project. It provides a method for designing product specifications. Each design has costs which affect price and marketing feasibility by providing comparison of possible designs before the specifications are frozen by cash commitments. BE serves as a substitute for estimating an unknown factor in making project decisions. In deciding whether to go ahead with a project or to disband it, there are always variables to be considered such as costs, price, demand, and other miscellaneous factors. When most expenses associated with a proposed project can be determined, only two variables need be considered as variable items—profits (cash flow) and demand (sales). Demand is usually more difficult to estimate. By deciding that profit must at

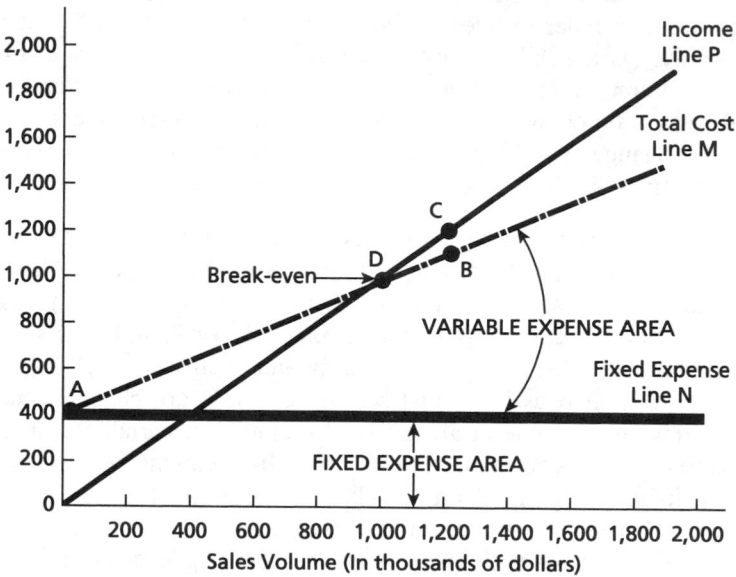

CONVENTIONAL BREAK-EVEN CHART

least be zero, the BE point, the demand is more easily estimated by determining what sales levels are needed to make the project a worthwhile undertaking. BE provides a way to attack uncertainty, to at least develop marketing targets for desired levels of income. One of the major problems of BE analysis is that no product exists in isolation; there are always alternative uses for an organization's funds. BE analysis helps decision makers to consider not only the value of an individual project, but how it compares to other uses of the funds and facilities.

Another problem is that BE analysis does not permit proper examination of cash flows. In considering financial commitments, the appropriate way to make investment or capital decisions is to consider the value of a proposed project's anticipated cash flows. If the discounted value of the cash flows exceeds the required investment outlay in cash, the project is acceptable. BE analysis makes restrictive assumptions about cost-revenue relationships; it is basically a negative technique defining constraints rather than looking at benefits; it is essentially a static tool for analyzing income and outflow for a single period of time.

The BE technique requires a realistic definition of costs, both in amount and type. A BE approach, therefore, should not be considered a technique to be used to make *final* investment decisions. It is a supplemental tool among the many factors a business decision maker must consider; it is an approach helpful to apply at the beginning of an analysis of a proposed solution of a business problem.

¶14,019

Although a complete and adequate budget may be developed without using a break-even analysis, its use adds to the understanding of estimates as shown in the following example.

Where the total cost of goods sold and other expenses is less than sales and if this total varied in direct proportion to sales, operations would always result in net income. For example, in a company in which the cost of goods sold and expenses amount to $1.80 per unit sold and the sale price is $2, on the first unit there would be net income of 20¢. On a million items, the net income would amount to $200,000.

As a practical matter, the simple example cited above is not realistic. Although some expenses may vary with volume of sales (e.g., salesperson's commissions, traveling expenses, advertising, telephone, delivery costs, postage, supplies, etc.), there are many other types of expenses which are not affected by the variations in sales. These expenses are the fixed expenses. Examples are depreciation, rent, insurance, heat, and so on.

If, going back to the above illustration, it is assumed that fixed costs and expenses amount to $40,000, at least $40,000 of costs and expenses are incurred before even one unit is sold. If a million units are sold, however, income before deducting fixed expenses is $200,000. After fixed expenses, net income is $160,000. So, the income picture goes from a loss of $40,000 (where no units are produced) to a profit of $160,000 (where one million units are produced). Somewhere between these, however, is a point represented by a certain number of units at which there will be neither income nor loss—the break-even point.

## .01  How to Compute the Break-Even Point

To determine the break-even point, let S equal the sales at the break-even point. Since sales at this point are equal to the total fixed costs and expenses ($40,000) plus variable costs and expenses ($1.80 per unit or 90 percent of sales):

$$S = \$40,000 + .9S$$
$$S - .9S = \$40,000$$
$$.1S = \$40,000$$
$$S = \$400,000$$

Even the above illustration oversimplifies the problem. It makes the assumption that all costs and expenses can be classified as either fixed or *variable*. However, in actual operations, expenses classified as fixed expenses may become variable where sales increase beyond a certain point, and some variable expenses may not vary in direct proportion to the sales.

¶14,019.01

Rent expense, for example, may not always be a fixed expense. A substantial increase in sales may create a need for additional showroom or salesroom space or, perhaps, expenses for salesperson's offices, or salesper-son's commissions may rise unexpectedly when they have gone above a certain quota.

Then, there are types of hybrid expenses which may be classified as *semifixed*. For example, executives' salaries, association dues, subscriptions to periodicals and many other expenses are not in proportion to sales. Another unreality in the above problem is that as sales increase, there is a likelihood that sale prices will decrease because of larger orders. Now let's take a look at another situation:

| | | |
|---|---|---|
| Net sales | | $ 2,500,000 |
| Costs and expenses: | | |
| Fixed | $    250,000 | |
| Variable | $ 1,500,000 | 1,750,000 |
| Net income | | $    750,000 |

This company currently has under consideration an investment in a new plant which will cause an increase in its fixed expenses of $200,000.

The present break-even point is as follows:

$$S = \$250,000 + .6S$$
$$S - .6S = \$250,000$$
$$.4S = \$250,000$$
$$S = \$625,000$$

If the company builds the plant, the break-even calculation will be:

$$S = \$450,000 + .6S$$
$$S - .6S = \$450,000$$
$$.4S = \$450,000$$
$$S = \$125,000$$

If the plant expansion is undertaken, then the sales must be increased by $500,000 for the company to maintain its net income of $750,000, as follows:

$$S = \$450,000 + .6S + \$750,000$$
$$S - .6S = \$1,200,000$$
$$.4S = \$1,200,000$$
$$S = \$3,000,000$$
Increase $= \$500,000$ ($\$3,000,000$ less $\$2,500,000$)

**¶14,019.01**

The situation can be analyzed using two alternatives. The maximum production with the present plant is 1,500,000 units. At an average sale price of $2 per unit, sales would be $3,000,000. With the new plant, sales are estimated to hit $5,000,000 (2,500,000 units @ $2 per unit).

|  | Without New Plant | With New Plant |
|---|---|---|
| Net Sales | $3,000,000 | $5,000,000 |
| Less: Fixed costs and expenses | 250,000 | 450,000 |
|  | 2,750,000 | 4,550,000 |
| Less: Variable costs and expenses (60% of sales) | 1,800,000 | 3,000,000 |
| Net income | $ 950,000 | $1,550,000 |

If sales do not increase, the increase in fixed costs and expenses of $200,000 would cut the net income to $550,000. The break-even point will have been boosted $500,000, and the sales will have to be increased by this amount to produce the current $750,000 of income. Alternatively, the net income can be increased by $600,000 if the sales figure is increased by $2,000,000. Although these figures are based on an assumption that all costs and expenses are fixed or variable, the break-even analysis focuses attention on the factors involved in costs and income and provides a basis for consideration of various problems.

# Chapter 15

# Change in Accounting Methods and Consideration of Accounting Periods

## CONTENTS

## ¶15,000   OVERVIEW

Changes in accounting procedures can take several forms and be prompted by different needs of the organization. For financial accounting as well as tax accounting changes require appropriate justification because, in the case of financial accounting, change can lessen comparability of financial statements and in the case of tax accounting, can lead to a change in tax liability. Changes in accounting include, but are not limited to, changes in methods used to value inventory, changes in estimates regarding assets and liabilities and overall changes of method such as cash method to accrual method. This chapter addresses both the financial reporting of changes as mandated by the FASB and tax reporting of changes under the rules administered by the IRS. Changes in accounting periods are also addressed primarily from the tax accounting standpoint—since it is the tax law that places formidable restrictions on proposed changes in fiscal reporting periods.

The issues related to accounting changes are treated separately for financial accounting and tax accounting because the sources of authority and their diverse goals require very different measures to accomplish similar ends.

## ¶15,001   RECENT DEVELOPMENTS IN TREATMENT OF ACCOUNTING CHANGES

The release of FASB 154 "Accounting Changes and Error Corrections" In 2005 marked a major adjustment in the treatment of changes in accounting principles for financial accounting. An overview of this FASB is presented in Chapter 6. The change was from the longstanding treatment of a change in accounting principle cumulatively as a separate line item on the income statement to a retrospective approach—requiring the restatement of prior financial statements as if the new principle had been employed in previous reporting periods—and an adjustment to beginning retained earnings of the earliest period being reported to "catch-up" the income or expense difference from prior years.

The FASB issued Statement No. 154 as a replacement of APB Opinion No. 20 and FASB Statement No. 3, in June 2005. The Statement applies to all voluntary changes in accounting principles and dramatically changes the requirements for accounting for and reporting of a change in accounting principles. Opinion 20 previously required that most voluntary changes in accounting

¶15,000

principles be recognized by including in net income of the period of the change the cumulative effect of changing to the new accounting principle. Statement 154 requires that a change in method of depreciation, amortization, or depletion for long-lived, nonfinancial assets be accounted for as a change in accounting estimate that is brought about by a change in accounting principle. Opinion 20 previously required that such a change be reported as a change in accounting principle.

The Board pointed out that this is an example of instances in which the Board concluded that the IASB requirements result in better financial reporting than U.S. GAAP. Thus, the measure improves financial reporting because its requirements enhance the consistency of financial information between periods, and it also furthers convergence with international standards.

In keeping with the goal of simplifying U.S.GAAP, the Board decided to completely replace Opinion 20 and Statement 3 with one Statement rather than amending both. Therefore, Statement 154 carries forward many provisions of Opinion 20 without change, including:

- The provisions related to the reporting of a change in accounting estimate.
- A change in the reporting entity.
- The correction of an error.

For financial accounting purposes a change in accounting estimate, such as a change in the estimated lives of depreciable assets, is treated prospectively. The change is assumed to be the result of new information or additional experience. In the year the estimate is changed the new estimate is used and no attempt is made to correct past amounts reported. Since an estimate by definition is subject to correction, the change is simply applied in the current year and carried forward. Examples of items subject to estimate that may require revision include obsolete inventory, an allowance for doubtful accounts, periods to be benefited by deferred costs and estimated costs for future warranty agreements.

An example of a change in reporting entity is a change in the subsidiaries that are consolidated in the preparation of consolidated financial statements. In such a case the proper reporting requires the restatement of prior period financial statements that are being presented for comparison with the current year.

The correction of a material error is treated as a prior period adjustment to beginning retained earnings. This includes mathematical errors, errors in applying accounting principles and errors of omission.

FASB 154 also carries forward the provisions of FASB 3 that govern reporting accounting changes in interim financial statements.

Statement 154 is effective for accounting changes and corrections of errors made in fiscal years beginning after December 15, 2005. Earlier application is permitted for accounting changes and corrections of errors made occurring in fiscal years beginning after June 1, 2005. The Statement does not change the transition provisions of any existing accounting pronouncements, including those that are in a transition phase as of the effective date of this Statement.

¶15,001

## ¶15,002  NEW IRS AUTOMATIC APPROVAL PROCEDURES FOR ACCOUNTING PERIOD CHANGES

Notices 2001-34 and 2001-35 had indicated the IRS thinking in regard to changes in accounting periods. Revenue Procedure 2002-35 finalized the guidance in Notice 2001-35 regarding automatic approval procedures for accounting periods for partnerships, S corporations, electing S corporations and professional service corporations.

Rev. Proc. 2002-39 is the result of guidance outlined in Notice 2001-34 relating to requests for changes in accounting periods. Rev. Proc. 2002-37, issued at the same time, provides automatic approval procedures for corporations.

### .01  Revenue Procedure 2002-37

Rev. Proc. 2002-37 outlines the procedures that certain corporations are required to follow to be regarded as having automatic approval for a change in their annual accounting period. A corporation complying with the new procedures will be deemed to have established a sufficient business purpose and to have obtained IRS approval for the change.

The revenue procedure states that it is the exclusive procedure to be used by corporations within its scope and then specifies the types of corporations covered or excluded. The final guidance:

1. Provides more flexibility for changing to or from a 52–53-week tax year and for changes to, or retention of, a natural business year by a corporation that satisfies the 25 percent gross receipts test.
2. Shortens from 6 years to 48 months, the required time between a requested change and a prior accounting period change. It also adds to the list of changes that will not be considered prior changes for purposes of the new 48-month rule.
3. Adds to the list of corporations outside of the scope of the procedure in the areas of interests in a pass-through entity, controlled foreign corporations, foreign personal holding companies and corporations with a required tax year.
4. Provides additional guidance for exceptions to the record-keeping/bookkeeping conformity rule and the prevention of the carryback of capital losses generated in the short period resulting from the accounting period change.

### .03  Revenue Procedure 2002-38

Rev. Proc. 2002-38 provides the exclusive procedures for certain partnerships, S corporations, electing S corporations and personal service corporations, to obtain automatic approval to adopt, change or retain an annual accounting period.

Consistent with the changes for corporations promulgated in Rev. Proc. 2002-37, this procedure also provides more flexibility in changing to or from a 52–53-week tax year, changes to a required or natural business year satisfying the 25 percent gross receipts test, the new 48-month period between the requested change and the prior accounting period change and the restrictions on the carryback of capital losses from the short period. In addition, it provides:

1.  Guidance relating to changes to a year corresponding to the ownership.
2.  Guidance specifying that, under certain circumstances, a partnership can retain its current tax year for one year, even though a minor percentage change in ownership would have otherwise required a change in the tax year.
3.  That a professional service corporation may automatically change its tax year even if it makes an S corporation election for the tax year immediately following the short period.
4.  Restrictions that prevent using the guidance to change an annual accounting period while under examination.
5.  Guidance that permits S corporations and electing S corporations to disregard the ownership interests of certain tax exempt entities when determining their tax year.

Except in specified circumstances, the entities that are subject to Rev. Proc. 2002-38 will be required to compute their income and keep their books and records (including financial statements) on the basis of the requested tax year. The guidance also extends the due date for filing a Form 1128 to the due date of the taxpayer's federal income tax return (including extensions) for the first effective year, and provides audit protection for accounting period changes made within the scope of the procedure.

## .05  Revenue Procedure 2002-39

In contrast to the automatic procedures for corporations and pass-through entities that are covered in Rev. Procs. 2002-37 and 2002-38, Rev. Proc. 2002-39 provides guidance to all taxpayers when obtaining IRS approval to adopt, change or retain an annual accounting period and for establishing a business purpose for the change.

The business purpose requirement is a facts-and-circumstances test, although a business purpose is deemed satisfied for an accounting period that corresponds to the taxpayer's required tax year, ownership tax year, or natural business year. The natural business year again is based on the 25 percent gross receipts test.

Safe harbors are provided in connection with annual business cycles and seasonal businesses. The revenue procedure states that the safe harbors are designed to require reliance on a facts-and-circumstances test only in rare situations. Excepted from the scope of this general guidance are, on the one hand,

¶15,002.05

requests for automatic approval and, on the other, requests in which the taxpayer is under examination or where the accounting period is already an issue in a proceeding.

In the earlier exception, the IRS advised taxpayers to check the rules for automatic approval before filing a request with the IRS for a change.

## .07    Effective Date

The effective date for all three Revenue Procedures—2002-37, -38 and -39—is generally for applications filed on or after May 10, 2002. All three provide for similar elections of retroactive application.

Previously, to simplify the procedures to obtain IRS consent for taxpayers to change methods of accounting for federal income tax purposes, the IRS had modified and/or eliminated a number of the complicated rules governing changes in these accounting methods. The purpose of the new procedures is to provide incentives to encourage prompt, voluntary compliance with proper tax accounting principles. Under this approach, a taxpayer usually receives more favorable terms and conditions by filing a request for a change in method before the IRS contacts the taxpayer for an examination. A taxpayer who is contacted for an examination and required by the IRS to change his or her method of accounting generally receives less favorable terms and conditions and may also be subject to penalties.

## ¶15,003   Significant Tax Changes

Probably the single most important change for the taxpayer was that Form 3115 requesting a change in method may now be filed any time during the year. Other new rules reduce or eliminate many of the complex provisions of the previous procedure including:

1. The Category A and Category B, and Designated A and Designated B have been eliminated.
2. The 90-day window at the *beginning* of an examination has been eliminated.
3. The 30-day window for taxpayers under *continuous examination* has been increased to 90 days.
4. The number of consecutive months the taxpayer is required to be under examination has been reduced from 18 to 12.
5. The definition of "under examination" has been clarified.
6. The consent requirement for taxpayers before an appeals officer or a federal court has been replaced with a notification procedure.

7. The various adjustment periods have been replaced with a single 4-year adjustment period for both positive and negative adjustments.

8. Several of the terms and conditions relating to the adjustment have been eliminated.

## ¶15,005  CHANGE IN METHOD OF ACCOUNTING DEFINED

A change in method of accounting includes a change in the overall plan of accounting for gross income or deductions, or a change in the treatment of any material item. A *material item* is any item that involves the proper time for the inclusion of the item in income or the taking of the item as a deduction.

In determining whether a taxpayer's accounting practice for an item involves timing, the relevant question is whether the practice permanently changes the amount of the taxpayer's lifetime income. If the practice does not permanently affect the taxpayer's lifetime income, but does or could change the taxable year in which income is reported, it involves timing and is, therefore, a method of accounting.

*Consistency:* Although a method of accounting may exist under this definition without a pattern of consistent treatment of an item, a method of accounting is not adopted in most instances without consistent treatment. The treatment of a material item in the same way in determining the gross income or deductions in two or more consecutively filed tax returns, without regard to any change in status of the method as permissible or not permissible, represents consistent treatment of that item. If a taxpayer treats an item properly in the first return that reflects the item, however, it is not necessary for the taxpayer to treat the item consistently in two or more consecutive tax returns to have adopted a method of accounting. If a taxpayer has adopted a method of accounting under the rules, the taxpayer cannot change the method by amending prior income tax returns.

*Classification:* A change in the classification of an item can constitute a change in the method of accounting if the change has the effect of shifting income from one period to another. A change in method of accounting does not include correction of mathematical or posting errors, or errors in the computation of a tax liability.

## ¶15,007  FILING FORM 3115

Except as otherwise provided, a taxpayer must secure the consent of the Commissioner before changing a method of accounting for federal income tax purposes. In order to obtain the Commissioner's consent for a method change, a taxpayer must file a Form 3115, *Application for Change in Accounting Method* during the taxable year in which the taxpayer wants to make the proposed change.

The Commissioner can prescribe administrative procedures setting forth the limitations, terms, and conditions deemed necessary to permit a taxpayer to obtain consent to change a method of accounting. The terms and conditions the Commissioner can prescribe include the year of change, whether the change is to be made with an adjustment or on a cutoff basis, and the adjustment period.

Unless specifically authorized by the Commissioner, a taxpayer cannot request, or otherwise make, a retroactive change in method, regardless of whether the change is from a permissible or an impermissible method.

## ¶15,009   METHOD CHANGE WITH ADJUSTMENT

Adjustments necessary to prevent amounts from being duplicated or omitted must be taken into account when the taxpayer's taxable income is computed under a method of accounting different from the method used to compute taxable income of the preceding tax year. When a change in method is applied, income for the taxable year preceding the year of change must be determined under the method of accounting that was then employed. Income for the year of change and the following taxable years must be determined under the new method as if the new method had always been used.

Required adjustments can be taken into account in determining taxable income in the manner and subject to the conditions agreed to by the Commissioner and the taxpayer. In the absence of an agreement, the adjustment is taken into account completely in the year of change, which limits the amount of tax where the adjustment is substantial. However, under the Commissioner's authority to prescribe terms and conditions for changes in method, specific adjustment periods are permitted that are intended to achieve an appropriate balance between mitigating distortions of income that result from accounting method changes and providing appropriate incentives for voluntary compliance.

## ¶15,011   METHOD CHANGE USING A CUTOFF METHOD

Certain changes can be made in a method and without an adjustment, using a cutoff method. Under a cutoff method, only the items arising on or after the beginning of the year of change are accounted for under the new method. Certain changes, such as changes in the last-in first-out (LIFO) inventory method, *must* be made using the cutoff method. Any items arising before the year of change or other operative date continue to be accounted for under the taxpayer's former method of accounting. Because no items are duplicated or omitted from income when a cutoff method is used to make a change, no adjustment is necessary.

## ¶15,013  Initial Method

A taxpayer can generally choose any permitted accounting method when filing the first tax return. IRS approval is not needed for the choice of the method. The method chosen must be used consistently from year to year and clearly show the taxpayer's income. A change in an accounting method includes a change not only in an overall system of accounting, but also in the treatment of any material item. Although an accounting method can exist without treating an item the same all the time, an accounting method is not established for an item, in most cases, unless the item is treated the same every time.

## ¶15,015  IRS Approval

After a taxpayer's first return has been filed, the taxpayer must get IRS approval to change the accounting method. If the current method clearly shows the income, the IRS will consider the need for consistency when evaluating the reason for changing the method used. The following changes require IRS approval:

1. A change from the cash method to an accrual method or vice versa unless this is an automatic change to an accrual method.
2. A change in the method or basis used to value inventory.
3. A change in the method of figuring depreciation, except certain permitted changes to the straight-line method for property placed in service before 1981.

Approval is not required in the following instances:

1. Correction of a math or posting error.
2. Correction of an error in computing tax liability.
3. An adjustment of any item of income or deduction that does not involve the proper time for including it in income or deducting it.
4. An adjustment in the useful life of a depreciable asset.

## ¶15,017  Reflections of Income

The important point to remember is that methods of accounting should clearly reflect income on a continuing basis, and that the IRS exercises its discretion and in a manner that generally minimizes distortion of income across taxable years on an annual basis. Therefore, if a taxpayer asks to change from a method of accounting that clearly reflects income, the IRS, in determining whether to consent to the taxpayer's request, will weigh the need for consistency against the taxpayer's reason for desiring to change the method of accounting.

## ¶15,019 NEED FOR ADJUSTMENT

The adjustment period is the applicable period for taking into account an adjustment, whether positive (an increase in income) or negative (a decrease in income), required for the change in method of accounting. Adjustments necessary to prevent amounts from being duplicated or omitted are taken into account when the taxpayer's taxable income is computed under a method of accounting different from the method used to compute taxable income for the preceding taxable year. When there is a change in method of accounting, income for the year preceding the year of change must be determined under the method of accounting that was then employed, and income for the year of change and the following years must be determined under the new method of accounting.

## ¶15,021 NEW FLEXIBILITY FOR ACCRUAL BASIS TAXPAYERS

In regulations issued in 2004 (1.263(a)-4 and -5) the IRS liberalized the rules for accrual basis taxpayers allowing deduction for certain prepaid expenses, bringing them in line with cash basis deduction rules. However, the rules were buried in the regulations and not widely known or publicized, so the IRS extended the deadline for making the election to change to this alternate method of accounting until the filing of 2005 tax returns in 2006 (Rev. Rule 2005-9).

When a business using the accrual method incurs an expense—such as an annual casualty insurance premium—during the year, the accrual method generally requires the capitalization of the portion of the premium that extends to the following year, expensing only the portion representing an expense for the current year. Thus the accrual-basis financial statements will reflect an asset account for prepaid or unexpired insurance. Until the recent IRS rule change the same treatment would be applicable for tax accounting as well. But the new accounting method allows a current deduction of certain prepaid expenses if the benefit received from so doing does not extend past the earlier of 12 months or beyond the end of the following tax year. If the prepayment is made on the last day of the business' fiscal year, therefore, both periods would overlap and end on the same day. In addition to insurance, the new method may also be beneficial to businesses in deducting taxes, warranty costs, rebates and refunds, worker's compensation awards, and service contracts.

To qualify for this new accounting method for prepaid expenses it is necessary for taxpayers to complete IRS Form 3115 (under Reg. 263(a)-4(f)) using "Automatic Change Request 78." The Form 3115 should list each kind of expense for which the change from prepaid to immediate write-off is elected. The completed Form 3115 is attached to the taxpayer's 2005 tax return and a copy is also sent to the IRS in Washington D.C. (See Form 3115 instructions.)

As with any accounting method change, it is necessary to compute the amount of any adjustment to current income (under Internal Revenue Code section 481(a)) for beginning balances in prepaid expense accounts. The instructions for Form 3115 should be consulted. (See earlier ¶15,007, Filing Form 3115, and ¶15,009, Method Change with Adjustment.)

The same procedure also enables the taxpayer to adopt the "recurring item exception" contained in Reg. 1.461-5. If not previously adopted, this will allow the current accrual and deduction of amounts that are to be paid by the time the tax return is filed or within 8½ months after the business' year-end. The election should indicate which specific expense items constitute recurring items and many or all of these may be the same as for the election relating to prepaid expenses. The flexibility provided by this new rule allows businesses to smooth out the deduction of certain recurring expenses without compromising cash flow during a lean year. In the case of the casualty insurance deduction noted earlier, it will now be possible to accrue the unpaid expense in some years and take a current deduction, or prepay it in other years receiving the same deduction.

It should be noted that accrual basis taxpayers can only take advantage of the new prepaid expensing election for expenses which have also met the "economic performance" rules set out in Reg. 1.461-4. Not all expenses can meet the economic performance test just by being paid; generally what is being paid for must also have been received. However, in the case of insurance, taxes, service contracts, awards, rebates or refunds, and worker's compensation award liabilities, economic performance is evidenced by the payment of the expense. On the other hand, rent and interest do not qualify for the economic performance test but can only be deducted by an accrual basis taxpayer with the passage of time.

## ¶15,023   90-DAY AND 120-DAY WINDOW PERIODS

A taxpayer under examination cannot file a Form 3115 to request a change in accounting methods except as provided in the 90-day window and 120-day window periods, and the consent of the district director. A taxpayer filing a Form 3115 beyond the time periods provided by the 90-day and 120-day windows will not be granted an extension of time to file except in unusual and compelling circumstances.

A taxpayer can file a Form 3115 during the first 90 days of any taxable year if the taxpayer has been under examination for at least 12 consecutive months as of the first day of the taxable year. The 90-day window is not available if the method of accounting the taxpayer is requesting to change is an issue under consideration at the time the Form 3115 is filed, or is an issue the examining agent has placed in suspense at the time.

A taxpayer requesting a change under the 90-day window must provide a copy of the Form 3115 to the examining agent at the same time the original form is filed with the IRS. The form must contain the name and telephone number of the examining agent, and the taxpayer must attach to the form a separate statement signed by the taxpayer certifying that, to the best of his or her knowledge, the same method of accounting is not an issue under consideration or an issue placed in suspense by the examining agent.

A taxpayer can file a Form 3115 to request a change in accounting method during the 120-day period following the date an examination ends regardless of whether a subsequent examination has commenced. The 120-day window is not available if the method of accounting the taxpayer is requesting to change is an issue under consideration at the time the form is filed or is an issue the examining agent has placed in suspense at the time of the filing.

A taxpayer requesting a change under the 120-day window rule must provide a copy of the Form 3115 to the examining agent for any examination that is in process at the same time the original form is filed with the IRS. The form must contain the name and telephone number of the examining agent, and must have a separate signed statement attached certifying that, to the best of the taxpayer's knowledge, the same method of accounting is not an issue under consideration or an issue placed in suspense by the examining agent.

## ¶15,025 UNDER EXAMINATION

A taxpayer is "under examination" if the taxpayer has been contacted in any manner by a representative of the IRS for the purpose of scheduling any type of examination of any of its federal income tax returns. If a consolidated return is being examined, each member of the consolidated group will be considered under examination for purposes of the accounting method change requirements.

However, according to the 1997 ruling, on the date a new subsidiary becomes affiliated with a consolidated group, a 90-day window period can be provided within which the parent of the group may request a method change on behalf of the new member, unless the subsidiary itself is already under examination. Previously, if a consolidated group was being examined, each member of the consolidated group was considered under examination regardless of the tax year under examination.

An examination of a taxpayer, or consolidated group of which the taxpayer is a member, is considered to end at the earliest of the date:

1. The taxpayer or consolidated group of which the taxpayer is a member receives a "no-change" letter.
2. The taxpayer or consolidated group of which the taxpayer is a member pays the deficiency—or proposed deficiency.
3. The taxpayer or consolidated group requests consideration by an appeals officer.

¶15,025

4. The taxpayer requests consideration by a federal court.
5. The date on which a deficiency, jeopardy, termination, bankruptcy, or receivership assessment is made.

A taxpayer under examination cannot ask to change an impermissible method of accounting if under examination for the year in which the taxpayer adopted the method, and it was an impermissible method of accounting in the year of adoption. A taxpayer under examination cannot ask to change a method to which it changed without permission if under examination for the year in which the unauthorized change was made. Under any other circumstance, a taxpayer under examination can change an accounting method only if the taxpayer requests the change under the applicable procedures, terms, and conditions set forth in the regulation.

## ¶15,027   APPLICATION PROCEDURES

The IRS can decline to process any Form 3115 filed in situations in which it would not be in the best interest of sound tax administration to permit the requested change. In this regard, the IRS will consider whether the change in method of accounting would clearly and directly interfere with compliance efforts of the IRS to administer the income tax laws.

A change in the method of accounting filed must be made pursuant to the terms and conditions provided in the regulations. The rule notwithstanding, the IRS can determine, based on the unique facts of a particular case, terms and conditions more appropriate for a change different from the changes provided in the regulations.

In processing an application for a change in an accounting method, the IRS will consider all the facts and circumstances, including whether:

1. The method of accounting requested is consistent with the Tax Code regulations, revenue rulings, revenue procedures, and decisions of the United States Supreme Court.
2. The use of the method requested will clearly reflect income.
3. The present method of accounting clearly reflects income.
4. The request meets the need for consistency in the accounting area.
5. The taxpayer's reasons for the change are valid.
6. The tax effect of the adjustment is appropriate.
7. The taxpayer's books and records and financial statements will conform to the proposed method of accounting.
8. The taxpayer previously requested a change in the method of accounting for the same item but did not make the change.

¶15,027

If the taxpayer has changed the method of accounting for the same item within the four taxable years preceding the year of requesting a change for that item, an explanation must be furnished stating why the taxpayer is again requesting a change in the method for the same item. The IRS will consider the explanation in determining whether the subsequent request for change in method will be granted.

## ¶15,029  CONSOLIDATED GROUPS

Separate methods of accounting can be used by each member of a consolidated group. In considering whether to grant accounting method changes to group members, the IRS will consider the effects of the changes on the income of the group. A parent requesting a change in method on behalf of the consolidated group must submit any information necessary to permit the IRS to evaluate the effect of the requested change on the income of the consolidated group. A Form 3115 must be submitted for each member of the group for which a change in accounting method is requested. A parent can request an identical accounting method change on a single Form 3115 for more than one member of a consolidated group.

## ¶15,031  SEPARATE TRADES OR BUSINESSES

When a taxpayer has two or more separate and distinct trades or businesses, a different method of accounting may be used for each trade or business, provided the method of accounting used for each trade or business clearly reflects the overall income of the taxpayer as well as that of each particular trade or business. No trade or business is separate and distinct unless a complete and separate set of books and records is kept for that trade or business. If the reason for maintaining different methods of accounting creates or shifts profits or losses between the trades or businesses of the taxpayer so that income is not clearly reflected, the trades or businesses of the taxpayer are not separate and distinct.

## ¶15,033  RESOLVING TIMING ISSUES: APPEALS AND COUNSEL DISCRETION

An appeals officer or counsel for the government may resolve a timing issue when it is in the interest of the government to do so. To reflect the hazards of litigation, they are authorized to resolve a timing issue by changing the taxpayer's method of accounting using compromise terms and conditions or they may use a nonaccounting method change basis using either an alternative-timing or a time-value-of-money resolution.

## .01 Requirement to Apply the Law to the Facts

An appeals officer or counsel for the government resolving a timing issue must treat the issue as a change in method of accounting. The law must be applied without taking into account the hazards of litigation when determining the new method of accounting. An appeals officer or government official can change a taxpayer's method of accounting by agreeing to terms and conditions that differ from those applicable to an "examination-initiated" accounting method change.

The appeals officer may compromise on several points:

1. The year of change (by agreeing to a later year of change).
2. The amount of the adjustment (a reduced adjustment).
3. The adjustment period (a longer adjustment period).

If an appeals officer agrees to compromise the *amount* of an adjustment, the agreement must be in writing.

A change in a taxpayer's method of accounting ordinarily will *not defer the year of change* to later than the most recent taxable year under examination on the date of the agreement finalizing the change, and in no event will the year of change be deferred to later than the taxable year that includes the date of the agreement finalizing the change.

## .03 Alternative Timing

An appeals officer can resolve a timing issue by not changing the taxpayer's method of accounting, and by the IRS and the taxpayer agreeing to alternative timing for all or some of the items arising during/prior to and during, the taxable years before appeals or a federal court. The resolution of a timing issue on an alternative-timing basis for certain items will not affect the taxpayer's method of accounting for any items not covered by the resolution.

## .05 Time-Value-of-Money

An appeals officer or government counsel may resolve a timing issue by not changing the taxpayer's method of accounting, and by the IRS and the taxpayer agreeing that the taxpayer will pay the government a specified amount that approximates the time-value-of-money benefit the taxpayer derived from using its method of accounting for the taxable years before appeals or a federal court. This approach is instead of the method of accounting determined by the appeals officer to be the proper method of accounting. The "specified amount" is reduced by an appropriate factor to reflect the expense of litigation. The specified amount is not interest and cannot be deducted or capitalized under any provision of the law. An appeals officer may use any reasonable manner to compute the specified amount.

¶15,033.05

## .07  Taxpayer's Advantage

As outlined above, these IRS requirements, which are part of the "new" IRS image, cover timing problems that have been resolved by the IRS on a nonaccounting-method change basis. They provide terms and conditions for IRS-initiated changes that are intended to encourage taxpayers to *voluntarily request a change from an impermissible method of accounting* rather than being contacted by an agent for examination. Under this approach, a taxpayer who is contacted for *examination* and required to change methods of accounting by the IRS generally receives less favorable terms and conditions than if the taxpayer had filed a request to change before being contacted for examination.

The new regulations may be consistent with the policy of encouraging prompt voluntary compliance with proper tax accounting principles, but they appear to have some limitations. It is now easier for the taxpayer to change an accounting method, but the IRS ordinarily will not initiate an accounting method change if the change will place the taxpayer in a more favorable position than if the taxpayer had been contacted for examination. An examining agent will not initiate a change from an impermissible method that results in a negative adjustment. If the IRS declines to initiate such an accounting method change, the district director will consent to the taxpayer requesting a voluntary change.

## ¶15,035  RESOLVING TIMING ISSUES: DISCRETION OF EXAMINING AGENT

An examining agent proposing an adjustment on a timing issue will treat the issue as a change in method of accounting. In changing the taxpayer's method of accounting, the agent will properly apply the law to the facts without taking into account the hazards of litigation when determining the new method of accounting. An examining agent changing a taxpayer's method of accounting will impose an adjustment.

The change can be made using a cutoff method only in rare and unusual circumstances when the examining agent determines that the taxpayer's books and records do not contain sufficient information to compute the adjustment and the adjustment is not susceptible to reasonable estimation. An examining agent changing a taxpayer's method of accounting will effect the change in the earliest taxable year under examination (or, if later, the first taxable year the method is considered impermissible) with a one-year adjustment period.

## ¶15,037  METHOD CHANGES INITIATED BY THE IRS

If a taxpayer does not regularly employ a method of accounting that clearly reflects his or her income, the computation of taxable income must be made in a manner that, in the opinion of the Commissioner, does clearly reflect income. The Commissioner has broad discretion in determining whether a taxpayer's method of accounting clearly reflects income, and the Commissioner's determination must be upheld unless it is clearly unlawful.

The Commissioner has broad discretion in selecting a method of accounting that properly reflects the income of a taxpayer once it has been determined that the taxpayer's method of accounting does not clearly reflect income. The selection can be challenged only upon showing an abuse of discretion by the Commissioner.

The Commissioner has the discretion to change a method of accounting even though the IRS had previously changed the taxpayer to that method if it is determined that the method of accounting does not clearly reflect the taxpayer's income. The discretionary power does not extend to requiring a taxpayer to change from a method of accounting that clearly reflects income to a method that, in the Commissioner's view, more clearly reflects income.

The accounting method of a taxpayer that is under examination, before an appeals office, or before a federal court, can be changed except as otherwise provided in published guidance. The service is generally precluded from changing a taxpayer's method of accounting for an item for prior taxable years if the taxpayer timely files a request to change the method of accounting for the item.

## .01 Retroactive Method Change

Although the Commissioner is authorized to consent to a retroactive accounting method change, the taxpayer does not have a right to a retroactive change, regardless of whether the change is from a permissible or impermissible method.

Except under unusual circumstances, if a taxpayer who changes the method of accounting is subsequently required to change or modify that method of accounting, the required change or modification will not be applied retroactively provided that:

1. The taxpayer complied with all the applicable provisions of the consent agreement.
2. There has been no misstatement nor omission of material facts.
3. There has been no change in the material facts on which the consent was based.
4. There has been no change in the applicable law.
5. The taxpayer to whom consent was granted acted in good faith in relying on the consent, and applying the change or modification retroactively would be to the taxpayer's detriment.

## .03 New Method Established

An IRS-initiated change that is final establishes a new method of accounting. As a result, a taxpayer is required to use the new method of accounting for the year of change and for all subsequent taxable years unless the taxpayer obtains the consent of the commissioner to change from the new method or the IRS changes the taxpayer from the new method on subsequent examination. As indicated above, the IRS is not precluded from changing a taxpayer from the new method of accounting if the IRS determined that the new method does not clearly reflect the taxpayer's income. A taxpayer who executes a closing agreement finalizing an IRS initiated accounting method change will not be required to change or modify the new method for any taxable year for which a federal income tax return has been filed as of the date of the closing agreement, provided that:

1. The taxpayer has complied with all the applicable provisions of the closing agreement.
2. There has been no taxpayer fraud, malfeasance, or misrepresentation of a material fact.
3. There has been no change in the material facts on which the closing agreement was based.
4. There has been no change in the applicable law on which the closing agreement was based.

## .05 Required Change or Modification of New Method

The IRS may require a taxpayer to change or modify the new method in the earliest open taxable year if the taxpayer fails to comply with the applicable provisions of the closing agreement, or upon a showing of taxpayer's fraud, malfeasance, or misrepresentation of a material fact. The taxpayer can be required to change or modify the new method in the earliest open taxable year in which the material facts have changed, and can also be required to change or modify the new method in the earliest open taxable year in which the applicable law has changed. For this purpose, a change in the applicable law includes:

1. A decision of the U.S. Supreme Court.
2. The enactment of legislation.
3. The issuance of temporary or final regulations.
4. The issuance of a revenue ruling, revenue procedure, notice, or other guidance published in the Internal Revenue Bulletin.

Except in rare and unusual circumstances, a retroactive change in applicable law is deemed to occur when one of the events described in the preceding sentence occurs and not when the change in law is effective.

¶15,037.03

# ¶15,039  Accounting Periods

Taxable income must be figured on the basis of a tax year. A *tax year* is an annual accounting period for keeping records and reporting income and expenses. The tax years usable are:

1. A calendar year.
2. A fiscal year.

The tax year is adopted in the first year that an income tax return is filed. The tax year must be adopted by the due date, not including extensions, for filing a return for that year. The due date for individual and partnership returns is the 15th day of the 4th month after the end of the tax year. "Individuals" include sole proprietorships, partners, and S corporation shareholders. The due date for filing returns for corporations and S corporations is the 15th day of the 3rd month after the end of the tax year. If the 15th day of the month falls on a Saturday, Sunday, or legal holiday, the due date is the next business day.

## .01  Calendar Year

If a calendar year is chosen, the taxpayer must maintain books and records and report income and expenses from January 1 through December 31 of each year. If the first tax return uses the calendar year and the taxpayer later begins business as a sole proprietor, becomes a partner in a partnership, or becomes a shareholder in an S corporation, the calendar year must continue to be used unless the IRS approves a change. Anyone can adopt the calendar year. However, if any of the following apply, the calendar year must be used:

1. The taxpayer does not keep adequate records.
2. The taxpayer has no annual accounting period.
3. The taxpayer's tax year does not qualify as a fiscal year.

## .03  Fiscal Year

A fiscal year is 12 consecutive months ending on the last day of any month except December. A 52–53-week tax year is a fiscal year that varies from 52 to 53 weeks. If a fiscal year is adopted, books and records must be maintained, and income and expenses reported using the same tax year.

A 52–53-week tax year may be elected if books and records are kept, and income and expenses are reported on that basis. If this election is chosen, the tax year will be 52 or 53 weeks long, and will always end on the same day of the week. The tax year can end only on the same day of the week that:

1. Last occurs in a particular month.

2. Occurs nearest to the last day of a particular calendar month.

To make the choice, a statement with the following information is attached to the tax return for the 52–53-week tax year:

1. The month in which the new 52–53-week tax year ends.
2. The day of the week on which the tax year always ends.
3. The date the tax year ends. It can be either of the following dates on which the chosen day:
   a. Last occurs in the month in (1).
   b. Occurs nearest to the last day of the month in (1).

When depreciation or amortization is figured, a 52–53-week tax year is considered a year of 12 calendar months unless another practice is consistently used. To determine an effective date, or apply provisions of any law, expressed in terms of tax years beginning, including, or ending on the first or last day of a specified calendar month, a 52–53-week tax year is considered to:

1. Begin on the first day of the calendar month beginning nearest to the first day of the 52–53-week tax year.
2. End on the last day of the calendar month ending nearest to the last day of the 52–53-week tax year.

If the month in which a 52–53-week tax year ends is changed, a return must be filed for the short tax year if it covers more than 6 but less than 359 days. If the short period created by the change is 359 days or more, it should be treated as a full tax year. If the short period created is 6 days or less, it is not a separate tax year. It is to be treated as part of the following year.

A corporation figures tax for a short year under the general rules described for individuals. There is no adjustment for personal exemptions.

## .05 Improper Tax Year

A calendar year is a tax year of 12 months that ends on December 31, and a fiscal year is a tax year of 12 months that ends on the last day of any month except December, including a 52–53-week tax year. If business operations start on a day other than the last day of a calendar month and adopt a tax year of exactly 12 months from the date operations began, the taxpayer has adopted an *improper* tax year. The requirements for a calendar or fiscal tax year, including a 52–53-week tax year, have not been met. To change to a proper tax year, one of the following requirements must be met:

1. An amended tax return should be based on a calendar year.

¶15,039.05

2. IRS approval should be sought to change to a tax year, other than a calendar year.

## .07  Business Purpose Tax Year

A business purpose tax year is an accounting period that has a substantial business purpose for its existence.

In considering whether there is a business purpose for a tax year, significant weight is given to tax factors. A prime consideration is whether the change would create a substantial distortion of income. The following are examples of distortions of income:

1. Deferring substantial income or shifting substantial deductions from one year to another to reduce tax liability.
2. Causing a similar deferral or shifting for any other person, such as a partner or shareholder.
3. Creating a short period in which there is a substantial net operating loss.

The following nontax factors, based on convenience for the taxpayer, are generally not sufficient to establish a business purpose for a particular year:

1. Using a particular year for regulatory or financial accounting purposes.
2. Using a particular pattern, such as typically hiring staff during certain times of the year.
3. Using a particular year for administration purposes, such as:
   a. Admission or retirement of partners or shareholders.
   b. Promotion of staff.
   c. Compensation or retirement arrangements with staff, partners, or shareholders.
4. Using a price list, model year, or other item that changes on an annual basis.
5. Deferring income to partners or shareholders.

## .09  Natural Business Year

One nontax factor that may be sufficient to establish a business purpose for a tax year is an annual cycle of business, called a "natural business year." A natural business year exists when business has a peak and a nonpeak period. The natural business year is considered to end at or soon after the end of the peak period. A business whose income is steady from month-to-month all year would not have a natural business year as such. A natural business year is considered a substantial business purpose for an entity changing its accounting period. The IRS will ordinarily approve this change unless it results in a substantial deferral of income or another tax advantage.

The IRS provides a procedure for a partnership, an S corporation, or a personal service corporation to retain or automatically change to a natural business year as determined by the 25 percent test. It also allows an S corporation to adopt, retain, or change to a fiscal year that satisfies the "ownership tax year test." The 25 percent test uses the method of accounting used for the tax returns for each year involved. To figure the 25 percent test:

1. The gross sales and services receipts for the most recent 12-month period that includes the last month of the requested fiscal year are totaled for the 12-month period that ends before the filing of the request. Gross sales and services receipts for the last 2 months of that 12-month period are then totaled.
2. The percentage of the receipts for the 2-month period is then determined by dividing the total of the 2-month period by the total for the 12-month period. The percentage should be carried to two decimal places.
3. The percentage following steps 1 and 2 should then be figured for the two 12-month periods just preceding the 12-month period used in 1.

If the percentage determined for each of the three years equals or exceeds 25 percent, the requested fiscal year is the *natural business year*. If the partnership, S corporation, or personal service corporation qualifies for more than one natural business year, the fiscal year producing the higher average of the three percentages is the natural business year. If the partnership, S corporation, or personal service corporation does not have at least 47 months of gross receipts—which may include a predecessor organization's gross receipts—it cannot use this automatic procedure to obtain permission to use a fiscal year.

If the requested tax year is a 52–53-week tax year, the calendar month ending nearest the last day of the 52–53-week tax year is treated as the last month of the requested tax year for purposes of computing the 25 percent test.

An S corporation or corporation electing to be an S corporation qualifies for automatic approval if it meets the ownership tax year test. The test is met if the corporation is adopting, retaining, or changing to a tax year and shareholders holding more than 50 percent of the issued and outstanding shares of stock on the first day of the requested tax year have, or are all changing to, the same tax year.

## .11  Change in Tax Year

A tax year change must be approved by the IRS. A current Form 1128 must be filed by the 15th day of the end calendar month after the close of the short tax year to get IRS approval. The *short tax year* begins on the first day after

¶15,039.11

the end of the present tax year and ends on the day before the first day of the new tax year. If the short tax year required to effect a change in tax years is a year in which the taxpayer has a net operating loss (NOL), the NOL must be deducted ratably over a 6-year period from the first tax year after the short period.

A husband and wife who have different tax years cannot file a joint return. There is an exception to this rule if their tax years began on the same date and ended on different dates because of the death of either or both. If a husband and wife want to use the same tax year so they can file a joint return, the method of changing a tax year depends on whether they are newly married. A newly married husband and wife with different tax years who wish to file a joint return can change the tax year of one spouse without first getting IRS approval.

The correct user fee must be included, if any. The IRS charges a user fee for certain requests to change an accounting period or method, certain tax rulings, and determination letters. The fee is reduced in certain situations and for certain requests, such as a request for substantially identical rulings for related entities.

## .13  Year of Change

While this heading and the one above are similar, the connotation is somewhat different. The year of change is the taxable year for which a change in the method of accounting is effective, that is, the first taxable year the new method is used even if no affected items are taken into account for that year. The year of change is also the first taxable year for taking an adjustment and complying with all the terms and conditions accompanying the change.

## .15  Partnership

A partnership must conform its tax year to its partners' tax years unless the partnership can establish a business purpose for a different period. The rules for the required tax year for partnerships are:

1. If one or more partners having the same tax year own a majority interest— more than 5 percent—in partnership profits and capital, the partnership must use the tax year of those partners.
2. If there is no majority interest tax year, the partnership must use the tax year of its principal partners. A principal partner is one who has a 5 percent or more interest in the profits or capital of the partnership.
3. If there is no majority interest tax year and the principal partners do not have the same tax year, the partnership generally must use a tax year that results in the least aggregate deferral of income to the partners.

If a partnership changes to a required tax year because of these rules, the change is considered to be initiated by the partnership with IRS approval. No formal application for change in the tax year is needed. Any partnership that changes to a required tax year must notify the IRS by writing at the top of the first page of its tax return for its first required tax year: *Filed Under Section 806 of the Tax Reform Act of 1986.*

The tax year that results in the least aggregate deferral of income is determined by:

1. Figuring the number of months of deferral for each partner using one partner's tax year. The months of deferral are found by counting the months from the end of that tax year forward to the end of each other partner's tax year.
2. Each partner's months of deferral figured in step (1) are multiplied by that partner's share of interest in the partnership profits for the year used in step (1).
3. The amounts in step (2) are added to get the aggregate (total) deferral for the tax year used in step (1).
4. Steps (1) through (3) are repeated for each partner's tax year that is different from the other partners' years.

The partners' tax year that results in the lowest aggregate—total—number is the tax year that must be used by the partnership. If more than one year qualifies as the tax year that has the least aggregate deferral of income, the partnership can choose any year that qualifies. If one of the tax years that qualifies is the partnership's existing tax year, the partnership must retain that tax year.

## .17   S Corporations

If a business meets the requirements of a small business corporation, it can elect to be an S corporation. All S corporations, regardless of when they became an S corporation, must use a *permitted tax year*. A permitted tax year is the calendar year or any other tax year for which the corporation establishes a business purpose.

## .19   Personal Service Corporations

A personal service corporation must use a calendar year unless it can establish a business purpose for a different period or it makes a Section 444 election (discussed below). For this purpose, a corporation is a personal service corporation if all of the following conditions are met:

1. The corporation is a C corporation.

2. The corporation's principal activity during the testing period is the performance of personal services.
3. Employee-owners of the corporation perform a substantial part of the services during the testing period.
4. Employee-owners own more than 10 percent of the corporation's stock on the last day of the testing period.

The principal activity of a corporation is considered to be the performance of personal services if, during the testing period, the corporation's compensation costs for personal service activities is more than 50 percent of its total compensation costs.

Generally, the *testing period for a tax year is the prior tax year.* The testing period for the first tax year of a new corporation starts with the first day of the tax year and ends on the earlier of the following dates:

1. The last day of its tax year.
2. The last day of the calendar year in which the tax year begins.

The *performance of personal services* involves any activity in the fields of health, veterinary services, law, engineering, architecture, accounting, actuarial science, performing arts, or certain consulting services.

An employee-owner of a corporation is a person who:

1. Is an employee of the corporation on any day of the testing period.
2. Owns any outstanding stock of the corporation on any day of the testing period.

A further clarification of the definition of an independent contractor by the 1997 Act states, "A person who owns any outstanding stock of the corporation and who performs personal services for or on behalf of the corporation is treated as an *employee* of the corporation. This rule applies even if the legal form of the person's relationship to the corporation is such that the person would be considered an independent contractor for other purposes."

## .21  Section 444 Election

A partnership, S corporation, or personal service corporation can elect under Section 444 of the Internal Revenue Code to use a tax year different from its required tax year. Certain restrictions apply to the election. In addition, a partnership or S corporation may have to make a payment for the deferral period. The Section 444 election does not apply to any partnership, S corporation, or personal service corporation that establishes a business purpose for a different period.

¶15,039.21

A partnership, S corporation, or personal service corporation can make a Section 444 election if it meets all the following requirements:

1. It is not a member of a tiered structure.
2. It has not previously had a Section 444 election in effect.
3. It elects a year that meets the deferral period requirement.

The determination of the *deferral period* depends on whether the partnership, corporation, or personal service corporation is retaining its current tax year or adopting or changing its tax year with a Section 444 election.

A partnership, S corporation, or personal service corporation can make a Section 444 election to *retain* its tax year only if the deferral period of the new tax year is three months or less. The deferral period is the number of months between the beginning of the retained year and the close of the first required tax year.

If the partnership, S corporation, or personal service corporation is *changing* to a tax year other than its required year, the deferral period is the number of months from the end of the new tax year to the end of the required tax year. The IRS will allow a Section 444 election only if the deferral period of the new tax year is less than the shorter of:

1. Three months.
2. The deferral period of the tax year being changed. This is the tax year for which the partnership, S corporation, or personal service corporation wishes to make the Section 444 election.

If the tax year is the same as the required tax year, the deferral period is zero.

A Section 444 election is made by filing a form with the IRS by the earlier of:

1. The due date of the income tax return resulting from the 444 election.
2. The 15th day of the 6th month of the tax year for which the election will be effective. For this purpose, the month in which the tax year begins is counted, even if it begins after the first day of that month. The Section 444 election stays in effect until it is terminated. If the election is terminated, another Section 444 election cannot be made for any tax year. The election ends when any of the three corporations does any of the following:

1. Changes its tax year to a required tax year.
2. Liquidates.
3. Willfully fails to comply with the required payments or distributions.
4. Becomes a member of a tiered structure.

¶15,039.21

The election also ends if:

1. An S corporation's election is terminated. However, if the S corporation immediately becomes a personal service corporation, it can continue the Section 444 election of the S corporation.
2. A personal service corporation ceases to be a personal service corporation. If the personal service corporation elects to be an S corporation, it can continue the election of the personal service corporation.

## .23  Corporations

A new corporation establishes its tax year when it files its first return. A newly reactivated corporation that has been inactive for a number of years is treated as a new taxpayer for the purpose of adopting a tax year. A corporation other than an S corporation, a personal service corporation, or a domestic international sales corporation (C-DISC) can change its tax year without getting IRS approval if all the following conditions are met:

1. It must not have changed its tax year within the 10 calendar years ending with the calendar year in which the short tax year resulting from the change begins.
2. Its short tax year must not be a tax year in which it has a net operating loss.
3. Its taxable income for the whole tax year, if figured on an annual basis, is 80 percent or more of its taxable income for the tax year before the short tax year.
4. If a corporation is one of the following for either the short tax year or the tax year before the short tax year, it must have the same status for both the short tax year and the prior tax year.
   a. Personal holding company.
   b. Foreign personal holding company.
   c. Exempt organization.
   d. Foreign corporation not engaged in a trade or business within the United States.
5. It must not apply to become an S corporation for the tax year that would immediately follow the short tax year required to effect the change.

The corporation must file a statement with the IRS office where it files its tax return. The statement must be filed by the due date for the short tax year required by the change. It must indicate the corporation is changing its annual accounting period, and show that all the preceding conditions have been met. If the corporation does not meet all the conditions because of later adjustments in establishing tax liability, the statement will be considered a timely application to

¶15,039.23

change the corporation's annual accounting period to the tax year indicated in the statement.

The IRS will waive conditions (1) and (5) above, as well as conditions (2) and (3)(c) outlining automatic approval criteria for a corporation that:

1. Meets all the other conditions.
2. Elected to be an S corporation for the tax year beginning January 1, 1997.
3. It must:
   a. Write "Filed" at the top of the forms required.
   b. Write "Attention, Entity Control" on the envelope.
   c. Mail the forms to the IRS where the corporation files its return.

Corporations can automatically change their tax year if it cannot meet the five conditions and has not changed its annual accounting period within 6 calendar years or in any of the calendar years of existence, and if the corporation is *not any of the following:*

1. A member of a partnership.
2. A beneficiary of a trust or an estate.
3. An S corporation.
4. An interest-charging DISC or a foreign sales corporation (FSC).
5. A personal service corporation.
6. A controlled foreign corporation.
7. A cooperative association.
8. Certain tax-exempt organizations.

## ¶15,041   CHANGES DURING THE TAX YEAR

A corporation, other than an S corporation, a personal service corporation, or a domestic international sales corporation (IC-DISC) can change its tax year without getting IRS approval if all the following conditions are met:

1. It must not have changed its tax year within the 10 calendar years in which the short tax year resulting from the change begins.
2. Its short tax year must not be a tax year in which it has a net operating loss (NOL).
3. Its taxable income for the short tax year, when figured on an annual basis, annualized, is 80 percent or more of its taxable income for the tax year before the short tax year.

4. If a corporation is one of the following for either the short tax year or the tax year before the short tax year, it must have the same status for both the short tax and the prior tax year.

5. It must not apply to become an S corporation for the tax year that would immediately follow the short tax year required to effect the change.

The corporation must file a statement with the IRS office where it files its tax return. The statement must be filed by the due date, including extensions, for the short tax year required by the change. It must indicate the corporation is changing its annual accounting period, and that all the preceding conditions have been met.

Certain corporations can *automatically* change their tax year by meeting all the following criteria:

1. It cannot meet the conditions listed earlier.

2. It has not changed its annual accounting period within six calendar years of existence, or in any of the calendar years of existence, if less than six years.

# Chapter 16

# Auditor Independence and the Audit Committee

## CONTENTS

## ¶16,000 OVERVIEW

The new Public Company Accounting Oversight Board (PCAOB) is just one important step toward restoring investor confidence in auditors and, more generally, in the capital markets. The new rules regarding independence standards for public company auditors that the Securities and Exchange Commission (SEC) adopted in January 2003 are viewed by the agency as another important step.

The Commission points out that with the accusatory headlines pointing at the accounting profession, it is perceived as no longer acting in a manner that puts investors first. Whether that assertion is true or not really does not matter anymore, according to the SEC. The perception is so strong in the minds of so many people that it has been affecting business activities, investment decisions, and the markets.

## ¶16,001 IMPORTANCE OF AUDIT COMMITTEE EMPHASIZED BY NEW RULINGS

New rules have been adopted that are aimed at addressing an auditor's independence for the registrant it audits *in both fact and appearance*. The independence and importance of the independent auditor and audit committee were forcibly emphasized again when the Commission adopted rules in April 2003, directing the national securities exchanges and national securities associations (self-regulatory organizations) to prohibit the listing of any security of an issuer that is not in compliance with the audit committee requirements established by The Sarbanes-Oxley Act of 2002. These rules and amendments implement the requirements of the Securities Exchange Act of 1934, as added by section 301 of the Sarbanes-Oxley Act.

## ¶16,003 REQUIREMENTS FOR AUDIT COMMITTEE

Under these rules, national securities exchanges and national securities associations are prohibited from listing any security of an issuer that is not in compliance with the following requirements:

- Each member of the audit committee of the issuer must be independent, according to the specified criteria in section 10A(m).
- The audit committee must be directly responsible for the appointment, compensation, retention, and oversight of the work of any registered

public accounting firm engaged for the purpose of preparing or issuing an audit report or performing other audit, review, or attest services for the issuer, and the registered public accounting firm must report directly to the audit committee.

- The audit committee must establish procedures for the receipt, retention, and treatment of complaints regarding accounting, internal accounting controls, or auditing matters, including procedures for the confidential, anonymous submission by employees of concerns regarding questionable accounting or auditing matters.
- The audit committee must have the authority to engage independent counsel and other advisors, as it determines necessary to carry out its duties.
- The issuer must provide appropriate funding for the audit committee.

## .01    Criteria for Committee Members

The rules established two criteria for audit committee member independence:

1. Audit committee members must be barred from accepting any consulting, advisory, or compensatory fee from the issuer or any subsidiary, other than in the member's capacity as a member of the Board or any Board committee.
2. An audit committee member must not be an affiliated person of the issuer or any subsidiary apart from capacity as a member of the Board or any Board committee.

## .03    Specific Rules for Foreign Issuers

The rules apply to both domestic and foreign listed issuers. It is important to note that, based on significant input from, and dialogue with, foreign regulators and foreign issuers and their advisers, several provisions, applicable only to foreign private issuers, have been included that seek to address the special circumstances of particular foreign jurisdictions. These provisions include:

- Allowing nonmanagement employees to serve as audit committee members, consistent with "co-determination" and similar requirements in some countries.
- Permitting shareholders to select or ratify the selection of auditors, also consistent with requirements in many foreign countries.
- Allowing alternative structures, such as boards of auditors, to perform auditor oversight functions where such structures are provided for under local law.

- Addressing the issue of foreign government shareholder representation on audit committees.

The rules also make several updates to the Commission's disclosure requirements regarding audit committees, including updates to the audit committee financial expert disclosure requirements for foreign private issuers.

The release also provides guidance on the provision of nonaudit services by foreign accounting firms, including the treatment of legal services and tax advice. The SEC also stands ready to work with other regulatory bodies on these issues.

The Commission established two sets of implementation dates for listed issuers. Generally, listed issuers are required to comply with the new listing rules by the date of their first annual shareholders meetings after January 15, 2004, but in any event no later than October 31, 2004. Foreign private issuers and small business issuers are required to comply by July 31, 2005.

## ¶16,005   STRICTER REQUIREMENTS REGARDING AUDITOR INDEPENDENCE

The SEC adopted amendments to its existing requirements regarding auditor independence to enhance the independence of accountants who audit and review financial statements and prepare attestation reports filed with the SEC. The final rules emphasize the critical role played by audit committees in the financial reporting process and the unique position of audit committees in ensuring auditor independence.

Consistent with the directions in the Sarbanes-Oxley Act, the SEC adopted rules to:

- Revise the Commission's regulations related to the nonaudit services that, if provided to an audit client, would impair an accounting firm's independence.
- Require an issuer's audit committee to preapprove all audit and nonaudit services provided to the issuer by the auditor of an issuer's financial statements.
- Prohibit certain partners on the audit engagement team from providing audit services to the issuer for more than five or seven consecutive years, depending on the partner's involvement in the audit, except that certain small accounting firms may be exempted from this requirement. The rules provide that firms with fewer than five audit clients and fewer than ten partners may be exempt from the partner rotation and compensation provisions, provided each of these engagements is subject to a special review by the PCAOB at least every three years.
- Prohibit an accounting firm from auditing an issuer's financial statements if certain members of management of that issuer had been members of the

accounting firm's audit engagement team within the one-year period preceding the commencement of audit procedures.

- Require that the auditor of an issuer's financial statements report certain matters to the issuer's audit committee, including "critical" accounting policies used by the issuer.
- Require disclosures to investors of information related to audit and nonaudit services provided by, and fees paid to, the auditor of the issuer's financial statements.
- In addition, an accountant would not be independent from an audit client if the audit partner received compensation based on selling engagements to that client for services other than audit, review, and attest services.

These rules also have an impact on foreign accounting firms that conduct audits of foreign subsidiaries and affiliates of U.S. issuers as well as of foreign private issuers. Many of the modifications to the proposed rules, such as those limiting the scope of partner rotation and personnel subject to the "cooling off period," have the added benefit of addressing particular concerns raised about the international implications of these requirements. Additional time is being afforded to foreign accounting firms with respect to compliance with rotation requirements. Guidance on the provision of nonaudit services by foreign accounting firms, including the treatment of legal services and tax services is provided in the final rule.

## .01 Transition Period Provided

The effective date was May 6, 2003; however, a transition period was also provided. If the following relationships did not impair the accountant's independence under preexisting requirements of the Commission, the Independence Standards Board, or the accounting profession in the United States, an accountant's independence is not deemed to be impaired:

- By employment relationships described that commenced at the issuer prior to May 6, 2003.
- By certain compensation earned or received during the accounting firm's fiscal year that includes May 6, 2003.
- Until May 6, 2004, by the provision of certain services described *provided* those services are pursuant to contracts in existence on May 6, 2003.
- Until May 6, 2003, by the provision of services that have not been preapproved by an audit committee as now required.
- Until the first day of the issuer's fiscal year beginning after May 6, 2003, by a "lead" partner and other audit partner (other than the "concurring" partner) providing services in excess of those permitted under section 210.2-01(c)(6).

¶16,005.01

- Until the first day of the issuer's fiscal year beginning after May 6, 2004, by a "concurring" partner providing services in excess of those permitted under section 210.2-01(c)(6).

## ¶16,007  BACKGROUND FOR AMENDMENTS TO AUDITOR INDEPENDENCE

Title II of the Sarbanes-Oxley Act, entitled "Auditor Independence," required the Commission to adopt, by January 26, 2003, final rules under which certain nonaudit services are prohibited, conflict of interest standards are strengthened, auditor partner rotation and second partner review requirements are also strengthened, and the relationship between the independent auditor and the audit committee are clarified and enhanced.

These rules are amendments to current SEC rules regarding auditor independence. The final rules advance the SEC's policy goal of protecting the millions of people who invest in securities markets in reliance on financial statements that are prepared by public companies and other issuers and that, as required by Congress, are audited by independent auditors. The final rules were an attempt at striking a reasonable balance among commenters' differing views about the proposals while achieving the Commission's public policy goals.

As directed by the Sarbanes-Oxley Act, the rules focus on key aspects of auditor independence:

- The provision of certain nonaudit services.
- The unique ability and responsibility of the audit committee to insulate the auditor from the pressures that may be exerted by management.
- The potential conflict of interest that can be created when a former member of the audit engagement team accepts a key management position with the audit client.
- The need for effective communication between the auditor and audit committee.

In addition, under the final rules, an accountant would not be independent from an audit client if any audit partner received compensation based directly on selling engagements to that client for services other than audit, review, and attest services.

## .01  Additions to the Securities Exchange Act of 1934

Title II of the Sarbanes-Oxley Act adds new subsections (g) through (l) to section 10A of the Securities Exchange Act of 1934 as follows:

- Section 201 adds subsection (g), which specifies that a number of nonaudit services are prohibited. Many of these services were previously prohibited by the Commission's independence standards adopted in November 2000 (with some exceptions and qualifications). The rules amend the Commission's existing rules on auditor independence and clarify the meaning and scope of the prohibited services under the Sarbanes-Oxley Act.

- Section 201 also adds subsection (h), which requires that nonaudit services that are *not* prohibited under the Sarbanes-Oxley Act and the Commission's rules be subject to preapproval by the registrant's audit committee. These rules specify the requirements for obtaining such preapproval from the registrant's audit committee.

- Section 202 adds subsection (i), which requires an audit committee to preapprove allowable nonaudit services and specifies certain exceptions to the requirement to obtain preapproval. These rules specify the requirements of the registrant's audit committee for preapproving nonaudit services by the auditor of the registrant's financial statements.

- Section 203 adds subsection (j), which establishes mandatory rotation of the lead partner and the concurring partner every five years. These rules expand the number of engagement personnel covered by the rotation requirement and clarify the "time out" period.

- Section 204 adds subsection (k), which requires that the auditor report on a timely basis certain information to the audit committee. In particular, the Sarbanes-Oxley Act requires that the auditor report to the audit committee on a timely basis:

  — Alternative accounting treatments that have been discussed with management along with the potential ramifications of using those alternatives.

  — Other written communications provided by the auditor to management, including a schedule of unadjusted audit differences. These rules strengthen the relationship between the audit committee and the auditor.

- Section 206 adds subsection (l), which addresses certain conflict-of-interest provisions. The Sarbanes-Oxley Act prohibits an accounting firm from performing audit services for a registrant if certain key members of management have recently been employed in an audit capacity by the audit firm. These rules clarify which members of management are covered by these conflict-of-interest rules.

- Under the final rules, an accountant would not be independent of an audit client if the audit partner received compensation based on selling engagements to that client for services other than audit, review, and attest services.

As noted above, the rules establish and clarify the important roles and responsibilities of registrant audit committees as well as the registrant's independent accountant.

The SEC also adopted a separate rule under the Exchange Act to implement the Sarbanes-Oxley Act and clarify that the rules implementing Title II of Sarbanes-Oxley not only define conduct that impairs independence but also

¶16,007.01

constitute separate violations under the Exchange Act. In addition, it adopted rules (except for the proxy disclosure changes) as part of Regulation S-X, and placed them among the current auditor independence provisions.

## ¶16,009  CONFLICTS OF INTEREST RESULTING FROM EMPLOYMENT RELATIONSHIPS

The Commission's previous rules deem an accounting firm to be not independent with respect to an audit client if a former partner, principal, shareholder, or professional employee of an accounting firm accepts employment with a client if he or she has a continuing financial interest in the accounting firm or is in a position to influence the firm's operations or financial policies. The 2003 rules do not change that existing requirement, but they do add other restrictions.

### .01  "Cooling Off" Period Provided

In line with section 206 of the Sarbanes-Oxley Act, the SEC added a restriction on employment with audit clients by former employees of the accounting firm. The Act specifies that an accounting firm cannot perform an audit for a registrant if its chief executive officer, controller, chief financial officer, chief accounting officer, or any person serving in an equivalent position for the issuer was employed by that registered independent public accounting firm and *participated in any capacity in the audit* of that issuer during the one-year period preceding the date of the initiation of the audit.

Admittedly, the passage of time is an additional safeguard to reduce the perceived loss of independence for the audit firm caused by the acceptance of employment by specified members of the engagement team with an audit client. However, the SEC believes that the Act is clear that the cooling off period should apply more broadly.

The Commission decided that, when the lead partner, the concurring partner, or any other member of the audit engagement team who provides more than 10 hours of audit, review, or attest services for the issuer accepts a position with the issuer in a "financial reporting oversight role" within the one-year period preceding the commencement of audit procedures for the year that included employment by the issuer of the former member of the audit engagement team, the accounting firm is not independent with respect to that registrant. The rule applies to all members of the audit engagement team unless specifically exempted, as discussed later. (The term "financial reporting oversight role" refers to any individual who has direct responsibility for oversight over those who prepare the registrant's financial statements and related information (e.g., management's discussion and analysis) that are included in filings with the Commission.)

The Commission recognizes that, in certain instances, there are individuals who meet the definition of engagement team members while spending a relatively small amount of time on audit-related matters of the issuer. For example, a staff member may be asked to spend one day of time to observe inventory. Although the input may have been important to resolving specific aspects of the audit, the staff member likely has not had significant interaction with the audit engagement team or management of the issuer. However, it is likely that those who spent more than a de minimis amount of time on the engagement team *did* participate in a meaningful audit capacity. Because of their roles in the engagement, the lead and concurring partner are *always* considered to have participated in a meaningful audit capacity, regardless of the number of hours spent on the engagement. In order to provide useful guidance, the SEC decided that the rule on conflicts of interest resulting from employment relationships should specify that, other than the lead and concurring partner, an individual must provide more than 10 hours of service during the annual audit period as a member of the engagement team to have participated in an audit capacity.

The rules relating to the cooling off period and to employment relationships entered into between members of the audit engagement team also apply to "any person serving in an equivalent position for the issuer."

*Few Exemptions Provided.*     Because the Sarbanes-Oxley Act and the Commission view the auditor independence issue as being vitally important in the effort to regain investor confidence in the veracity of financial statements, few exceptions to the rules have been permitted. They include:

- Those who provided *10 or fewer hours* of audit, review, or attest services.
- Conflicts that are created through merger or acquisition, unless the employment was taken in contemplation of the combination. The individual or the issuer could not be expected to know that his or her employment decision would result in a conflict. Thus, as long as the audit committee is aware of this conflict, the audit firm would continue to be independent under these rules.
- Emergency or unusual circumstances, which should be invoked very rarely. Because in certain foreign jurisdictions, it may be extremely difficult or costly to comply with these requirements, the Commission decided upon an additional exemption. For a company to avail itself of this exemption, the audit committee must determine that doing so is in the best interests of investors.
- Difficulties when there is, potentially, a different applicable date for each member of the engagement team. For that reason, the final rule adopted a uniform date for all members of the engagement team. For purposes of this rule, audit procedures are deemed to have commenced for the current audit engagement period the day after the prior year's periodic annual report (e.g., Form 10-K, 10-KSB, 20-F, or 40-F) is filed with the Commission. The audit engagement period for the current year is deemed to conclude the day the current year's periodic annual report (e.g., Form 10-K, 10-KSB, 20-F, or 40-F) is filed with the Commission.

¶16,009.01

The Sarbanes-Oxley Act specifies that the cooling off period must be one year. Under Commission rules, the prohibition would require the accounting firm to have completed one annual audit subsequent to when an individual was a member of the audit engagement team. As previously discussed, the measurement period is based upon the dates the issuer filed its annual financial information with the Commission.

With respect to investment companies, the employment of a former audit engagement team member in a financial reporting oversight role at any entity in the same investment company complex during the one-year period after the completion of the last audit would impair the independence of the accounting firm with respect to the audit client. The rule was designed to prevent a former audit engagement team member from taking a position in an investment company complex where he or she could influence the preparation of the financial statements or the conduct of the audit.

The rule recognizes that certain positions exist at an entity in the investment company complex that would be considered financial reporting or oversight positions but that have no direct influence in the financial reporting or operations of an investment company in the investment company complex. In these instances, the SEC believes tailoring the focus of this rule will not harm investor interests.

To provide for orderly transition, the rules are effective only for employment relationships with the issuer that commence after the effective date of the rules.

## ¶16,011    SCOPE OF SERVICES PROVIDED BY AUDITORS

Section 201(a) of the Sarbanes-Oxley Act adds a new section to the Securities Exchange Act of 1934. Except as discussed below, this section states that it is unlawful for a registered public accounting firm that performs an audit of an issuer's financial statements (and any person associated with such a firm) to provide to that issuer, contemporaneously with the audit, any nonaudit services, including the nine categories of services set forth in the Act. In addition, the Act states that any nonaudit service, including tax services, that is not described as a prohibited service can be provided by the auditor without impairing the auditor's independence only if the service has been *preapproved* by the issuer's audit committee. The categories of prohibited nonaudit services included in the Act are:

- Bookkeeping or other services related to the accounting records or financial statements of the audit client.
- Financial information systems design and implementation.
- Appraisal or valuation services, fairness opinions, or contribution-in-kind reports.

- Actuarial services.
- Internal audit outsourcing services.
- Management functions or human resources.
- Broker or dealer, investment adviser, or investment banking services.
- Legal services and expert services unrelated to the audit.
- Any other service that the Board determines, by regulation, is impermissible.

The Commission's principles of independence with respect to services provided by auditors are largely predicated on three basic principles, violations of which would impair the auditor's independence. An auditor cannot:

- Function in the role of management.
- Audit his or her own work.
- Serve in an advocacy role for his or her client.

The Commission adopted rules related to the scope of services that independent accountants *can* provide to their audit clients. In adopting these rules, the Commission is clarifying the scope of the prohibited services. The prohibited services contained in these rules apply only to nonaudit services provided by independent accountants to their audit clients. These rules do not limit the scope of nonaudit services provided by an accounting firm to a nonaudit client. Under the Act, the responsibility falls on the audit committee to preapprove all audit and nonaudit services provided by the accountant.

## .01 Bookkeeping or Other Services Related to Financial Statement Preparation

Previously, an auditor's independence was impaired if the auditor provided bookkeeping services to an audit client, except in limited situations, such as in an emergency or where the services are provided in a foreign jurisdiction and certain conditions were met. The current rule continues the prohibition on bookkeeping, but the SEC eliminated the limited situations where bookkeeping services could have been provided under the previous rules.

Citing the principle that an auditor cannot audit his or her own work and maintain his or her independence, the SEC pointed out that when an accounting firm provides bookkeeping services for an audit client, the firm may be put in the position of later auditing the accounting firm's own work. If, during an audit, an accountant must audit the bookkeeping work performed by his or her accounting firm, it is questionable that the accountant could (or that a reasonable investor would believe that the accountant could) remain objective and impartial. If the accountant found an error in the bookkeeping, the accountant could well be under pressure not to raise the issue with the client. Raising the issue could jeopardize the firm's contract with the client for bookkeeping services or result in heightened litigation risk for the firm. In addition, keeping the books is a *management function*, which also is prohibited. Therefore, the SEC determined that all bookkeeping services would cause the auditor to lack independence unless it is reasonable to conclude that the results will not be subject to audit procedures. (This proviso applies to all of the services discussed.) The final rules strongly emphasize the responsibility of the accounting firm in making a determination that these services, if provided, will *not* be subject to audit procedures, as further discussed below.

**Definition of Bookkeeping or Other Services Used in SEC Rules.** The rules utilize the previous definition of bookkeeping or other services, which focuses on the provision of services involving:

- Maintaining or preparing the audit client's accounting records.
- Preparing financial statements that are filed with the Commission or the information that forms the basis of financial statements filed with the Commission.
- Preparing or originating source data underlying the audit client's financial statements.

This definition demonstrates that the concept of bookkeeping and other services is well understood in practice. Accountants are sometimes asked to prepare statutory financial statements for foreign companies, and these are not filed with the SEC. Consistent with the Commission's previous rules, an accountant's independence would be impaired where the accountant prepared the statutory financial statements if those statements form the basis of the financial statements that are filed with the Commission. Under these circumstances, an accountant or accounting firm that has prepared the statutory financial statements of an audit client is put in the position of auditing its own work when auditing the resultant U.S. GAAP financial statements.

With respect to the prohibitions on bookkeeping; financial information systems design and implementation; appraisal, valuation, fairness opinions, or contribution-in-kind reports; actuarial services; and internal audit outsourcing, the rules state that the service may not be provided "unless it is reasonable to conclude that the results of these services will not be subject to audit procedures during an audit of the audit client's financial statements."

As proposed, for bookkeeping, appraisal or valuation, and actuarial services, the provision was "where it is reasonably likely that the results of these services will be subject to audit procedures during an audit of the audit client's financial statements," whereas for the other two services, there was no such wording. The Commission added the new wording to all five services to provide

¶16,011.01

consistency in application. In addition, the change from "reasonably likely..." to "unless it is reasonable to conclude" is intended to narrow the circumstances in which that condition can be invoked to justify the provision of such services.

## .03 Financial Information Systems Design and Implementation

Currently, there are certain information technology services that, if provided to an audit client, impair the accountant's independence. The proposed rules identified information technology services that would impair the auditor's independence.

The Commission adopted rules, consistent with previous rules, that prohibit an accounting firm from providing any service related to the audit client's information system. These rules do not preclude an accounting firm from working on hardware or software systems that are unrelated to the audit client's financial statements or accounting records, as long as those services are preapproved by the audit committee.

The rule does prohibit the accountant from designing or implementing a hardware or software system that aggregates source data or generates information that is significant to the financial statements taken as a whole. In this context, information would be "significant" if it is reasonably likely to be material to the financial statements of the audit client. Because materiality determinations may not be complete before financial statements are generated, the audit client and accounting firm by necessity will need to evaluate the general nature of the information as well as system output during the period of the audit engagement. An accountant, for example, would not be independent of an audit client for which it designed an integrated Enterprise Resource Planning or similar system, as the system would serve as the basis for the audit client's financial reporting system.

Designing, implementing, or operating systems affecting the financial statements may place the accountant in a management role, or result in the accountant auditing his or her own work or attesting to the effectiveness of internal control systems designed or implemented by that accountant. This prohibition does not, however, preclude the accountant from evaluating the internal controls of a system as it is being designed, implemented, or operated—either as part of an audit or as part of an attest service—and making recommendations to management. Likewise, the accountant would not be precluded from making recommendations on internal control matters to management or other service providers in conjunction with the design and installation of a system by another service provider.

## .05 Appraisal or Valuation Services

The SEC's previous independence rules stated that an accountant is deemed to lack independence when providing appraisal or valuation services, fairness opinions, or contribution-in-kind reports for audit clients. However, the previous rules contained certain exemptions that have been eliminated.

Appraisal and valuation services include a process of valuing assets, both tangible and intangible, or liabilities. They include valuing, among other things, in-process research and development, financial instruments, assets and liabilities acquired in a merger, and real estate. Fairness opinions and contribution-in-kind reports are opinions and reports in which the firm provides its opinion on the adequacy of consideration in a transaction. When it is time to audit the financial statements, it is likely that the accountant would review his or her own work, including key assumptions or variables that underlie an entry in the financial statements. Moreover, if the appraisal methodology involves a projection of future results of operations and cash flows, the accountant who prepares the projection may be unable to evaluate skeptically and without bias the accuracy of that valuation or appraisal. Therefore, the rules prohibit the accountant from providing *any* appraisal service, valuation service, or any service involving a fairness opinion or contribution-in-kind report for an audit client.

The rules do not prohibit an accounting firm from providing such services for non-financial reporting (e.g., transfer pricing studies, cost segregation studies, and other tax-only valuations) purposes. Similarly, the rules do not prohibit an accounting firm from utilizing its own valuation specialist to review the work performed by the audit client itself or an independent, third-party specialist employed by the audit client, provided that specialist (and not the specialist used by the accounting firm) provides the technical expertise that its client used in determining the required amounts recorded in the client's financial statements.

In those instances, the accountant will not be auditing his or her own work, because a third party or the audit client is the source of the financial information subject to the audit. In fact, the quality of the audit may be improved where specialists are utilized in such situations.

Because a strict application of these rules related to contribution-in-kind reports may create conflicts in certain foreign jurisdictions, the SEC will continue to work with other regulatory agencies in solving this type of problem.

## .07    Actuarial Services

The previous rules generally barred auditors from providing actuarial services related only to insurance company policy reserves and related accounts. However, the SEC believes that when the accountant provides actuarial services for the client, he or she is placed in a position of auditing his or her own work. Accordingly, the current rules prohibit an accountant from providing an audit client any actuarially oriented advisory service involving the determination of amounts recorded in the financial statements and related accounts for the audit client. It is permissible to assist a client in *understanding* the methods, models, assumptions, and inputs used in computing an amount.

¶16,011.07

Nevertheless, the Commission believes that it is appropriate to *advise* the client on the appropriate actuarial methods and assumptions that will be used in the actuarial valuations. It is not appropriate for the accountant to provide the actuarial valuations for the audit client. The rules also provide that the accountant may utilize his or her own actuaries to assist in conducting the audit provided the audit client uses its own actuaries or third-party actuaries to provide management with its actuarial capabilities.

## .09  Internal Audit Outsourcing

The previous rules on internal audit outsourcing allowed a company to outsource part of its internal audit function to the independent audit firm subject to certain exemptions. For example, smaller businesses were exempt from the internal audit outsourcing prohibition because there had been concerns about the potentially disproportionate impact on such companies.

Some companies outsource internal audit functions by contracting with an outside source to perform, among other things, all or part of their audits of internal controls. As emphasized by the Committee of Sponsoring Organizations, internal auditors play an important role in evaluating and monitoring a company's internal control system. As a result, some argue that internal auditors are, in effect, part of a company's system of internal accounting control.

Because the external auditor typically will rely, at least to some extent, on the existence of an internal audit function and consider its impact on the internal control system when conducting the audit of the financial statements, the accountant may be placed in the position of auditing his or her firm as part of the internal control system. In other words, if the internal audit function is outsourced to an accountant, the accountant assumes a management responsibility and becomes part of the company's control system.

The rules adopted prohibit the accountant from providing to the audit client internal audit outsourcing services. This prohibition includes any internal audit service that has been outsourced by the audit client and that relates to the audit client's internal accounting controls, financial systems, or financial statements.

When conducting the audit in accordance with generally accepted auditing standards (GAAS) or when providing attest services related to internal controls, the auditor evaluates the company's internal controls and, as a result, may make recommendations for improvements to the controls. Doing so is a part of the accountant's responsibilities under GAAS or applicable attestation standards and therefore does not constitute an internal audit outsourcing engagement.

Along those lines, this prohibition on outsourcing does not preclude engaging the accountant to perform nonrecurring evaluations of discrete items or other programs that are not, in substance, the outsourcing of the internal audit function. For example, the company may engage the accountant, subject to the audit committee preapproval requirements, to conduct "agreed-upon procedures" engagements related to the company's internal controls. It is understood that management takes responsibility for the scope and assertions in those engagements. The prohibition also does not preclude the accountant from performing operational internal audits unrelated to the internal accounting controls, financial systems, or financial statements.

## .11  Management Functions

No significant changes were made to the previous rule on management functions. The rules prohibit the accountant from acting, temporarily or permanently, as a director, officer, or employee of an audit client, or performing any decision-making, supervisory, or ongoing monitoring function for the audit client.

However, those types of services in connection with the *assessment* of internal accounting and risk management controls, as well as providing recommendations for improvements, do not impair an accountant's independence. Accountants must gain an understanding of their audit clients' systems of internal controls when conducting an audit in accordance with GAAS. With this insight, accountants often become involved in diagnosing, assessing, and recommending, to audit committees and management, ways in which their audit client's internal controls can be improved or strengthened. The resulting improvements in the audit client's controls not only result in improved financial reporting to investors but also can facilitate the performance of high-quality audits. For these reasons, the rules continue to allow accountants to assess the effectiveness of an audit client's internal controls and to recommend improvements in the design and implementation of internal controls and risk management controls.

Designing and implementing internal accounting and risk management controls is considered to be fundamentally different from obtaining an understanding of the controls and testing the operation of the controls, which is an integral part of any audit of the financial statements of a company. Likewise, design and implementation of these controls involves decision making and therefore is different from *recommending improvements* in the internal accounting and risk management controls of an audit client (which is permissible, if preapproved by the audit committee).

The SEC believes that designing and implementing internal accounting and risk management controls impair the accountant's independence because they place the accountant in the role of management. Conversely, obtaining an understanding of, assessing the effectiveness of, and recommending improvements to the internal accounting and risk management controls are fundamental to the audit process and do not impair the accountant's independence. Furthermore, the accountant may be engaged by the company, subject to the audit committee preapproval requirements, to conduct an agreed-upon procedures engagement related to the company's internal controls or to provide attest services related to the company's internal controls without impairing his or her independence.

¶16,011.11

## .13  Human Resources

The previous rules deemed an accountant to lack independence when performing certain human resources functions. The rules provided that an accountant's independence is impaired with respect to an audit client when the accountant searches for or seeks out prospective candidates for managerial, executive, or director positions; acts as negotiator on the audit client's behalf, such as determining position, status, compensation, fringe benefits, or other conditions of employment; or undertakes reference checks of prospective candidates. Under the current rule, an accountant's independence is also impaired when the accountant engages in psychological testing or other formal testing or evaluation programs, or recommends or advises the audit client to hire a specific candidate for a specific job.

Assisting management in human resource selection or development could place the accountant in the position of having an interest in the success of those employees the accountant has selected, tested, or evaluated.

## .15  Broker-Dealer, Investment Adviser, Investment Banking Services

Previous rules deemed an accountant to lack independence when performing brokerage or investment advising services for an audit client. The newer rules add serving as an unregistered broker-dealer to the rules that prohibit serving as a promoter or underwriter, making investment decisions on behalf of the audit client or otherwise having discretionary authority over an audit client's investments, executing a transaction to buy or sell an audit client's investment, or having custody of assets of the audit client. The rule is substantially the same as the Commission's previous rule related to the provision of these types of services to audit clients. However, unregistered broker-dealers are added to the scope of the rules because the nature of the threat to independence is unchanged whether the entity is or is not a registered broker-dealer.

The SEC explains that selling—directly or indirectly—an audit client's securities is incompatible with the accountant's responsibility of assuring the public that the company's financial condition is fairly presented. When an accountant, in any capacity, recommends to anyone (including nonaudit clients) that they buy or sell the securities of an audit client or an affiliate of the audit client, the accountant has an interest in whether those recommendations were correct. That interest could affect the audit of the client whose securities, or whose affiliate's securities, were recommended. These concepts are echoed in the "simple principles" included in the legislative history to the Sarbanes-Oxley Act. In such a situation, if an accountant uncovers an accounting error in a client's financial statements, and the accountant, in an investment adviser capacity, had recommended that client's securities to investment clients, the accountant performing the audit may be reluctant to recommend changes to the client's

¶16,011.15

financial statements if the changes could negatively affect the value of the securities recommended by the accountant to its investment adviser clients.

Broker-dealers often give advice and recommendations on investments and investment strategies. The value of that advice is measured principally by the performance of a customer's securities portfolio. When the customer is an audit client, the accountant has an interest in the value of the audit client's securities portfolio, even as the accountant must determine whether management has properly valued the portfolio as part of an audit. Thus, the accountant would be placed in a position of auditing his or her own work. Furthermore, the accountant is placed in a position of acting as an advocate on behalf of the client.

## .17   Legal Services

The previous rule stated that an accountant is deemed to lack independence when he or she provides legal services to an audit client. The SEC believes that a lawyer's core professional obligation is to advance clients' interests. Rules of professional conduct in the U.S. require the lawyer to "represent a client zealously and diligently within the bounds of the law." The lawyer must "take whatever lawful and ethical measures are required to vindicate a client's cause or endeavor....In the exercise of professional judgment, a lawyer should always act in a manner consistent with the best interests of the client."

The Commission maintains that an individual cannot be both a zealous legal advocate for management or the client company, and maintain the objectivity and impartiality that are necessary for an audit. The Supreme Court has also expressed this view. In *United States v. Arthur Young*, the Supreme Court emphasized, "If investors were to view the accountant as an advocate for the corporate client, the value of the audit function itself might well be lost."

The final rule is that an accountant is prohibited from providing to an audit client any service that, under circumstances in which the service is provided, could be provided only by someone licensed, admitted, or otherwise qualified to practice law in the jurisdiction in which the service is provided.

There may be implications for some foreign registrants from this rule. For example, in some jurisdictions it is mandatory that someone licensed to practice law perform tax work, and that an accounting firm providing such services, therefore, would be deemed to be providing legal services. As a general matter, SEC rules are not intended to prohibit foreign accounting firms from providing services that an accounting firm in the United States may provide. In determining whether or not a service would impair the accountant's independence solely because the service is labeled a legal service in a foreign jurisdiction, the Commission will consider whether the provision of the service would be prohibited in the United States as well as in the foreign jurisdiction.

Evaluating and determining whether services are permissible may require a comprehensive analysis of the facts and circumstances. The SEC is aware of these issues, and encourages accounting firms and foreign regulators to consult with the SEC staff to address such issues.

## .19  Expert Services

The Sarbanes-Oxley Act includes expert services in the list of nonaudit services an accountant is prohibited from performing for an audit client. As discussed earlier, the legislative history related to expert services is focused on the accountant's role when serving in an advocacy capacity.

Clients retain experts to lend authority to their contentions in various proceedings by virtue of the expert's specialized knowledge and experience. In situations involving advocacy, the provision of expert services by the accountant makes the accountant part of the team that has been assembled to advance or defend the client's interests. The appearance of advocacy created by providing such expert services is sufficient to deem the accountant's independence impaired. The prohibition on providing expert services included in this rule covers engagements that are intended to result in the accounting firm's specialized knowledge, experience, and expertise being used to support the audit client's positions in various adversarial proceedings.

The rules now adopted prohibit an accountant from providing expert opinions or other services to an audit client (or the client's legal representative) to advocate that client's interests in litigation and regulatory or administrative proceedings. For example, under this rule an auditor's independence would be impaired if the auditor were engaged to provide forensic accounting services to the audit client's legal representative in connection with the defense of an investigation by the Commission's Division of Enforcement. An accountant's independence likewise would be impaired if the audit client's legal counsel, in order to acquire the requisite expertise, engaged the accountant to provide such services in connection with a litigation, proceeding, or investigation.

The SEC rules do not, however, preclude an audit committee or its legal counsel from engaging the accountant to perform internal investigations or fact-finding engagements. These types of engagements may include, among others, forensic or other fact-finding work that results in the issuance of a report to the audit client. The involvement by the accountant in this capacity generally requires performing procedures that are consistent with, but more detailed or more comprehensive than, those required by GAAS. Performing such procedures *is consistent* with the role of the independent auditor and should improve audit quality. If, subsequent to the completion of such an engagement, a proceeding or investigation is initiated, the accountant may allow its work product to be utilized by the audit client and its legal counsel without impairing the accountant's independence. The accountant, however, may not then provide additional services, but may provide factual accounts or testimony about the work that had previously been performed.

Therefore, the rules do not prohibit an accountant from assisting the audit committee in fulfilling its responsibilities to conduct its own investigation of a potential accounting impropriety. For example, if the audit committee is concerned about the accuracy of the inventory accounts at a subsidiary, it may engage the auditor to conduct a thorough inspection and analysis of the accounts, the physical inventory, and related matters without impairing the auditor's independence.

The auditors already have obligations under the Exchange Act and GAAS to search for fraud that is material to an issuer's financial statements and to make sure the audit committee and others are informed of their findings. Auditors should conduct these procedures whether they become aware of a potential illegal act as a result of audit, review, or attestation procedures or of the audit committee's expressing concerns about a part of the company's financial reporting system. In these situations, the auditor may conduct the procedures, with the approval of the audit committee, and provide the reports that the auditor deems appropriate. If litigation arises while the auditors are conducting such procedures, the SEC would not consider the completion of these procedures to be prohibited, as long as the auditor remains in control of his or her work. The work may not become subject to the direction or influence of legal counsel for the issuer.

Furthermore, under this rule, an accountant's independence is not considered to be impaired when an accountant provides factual accounts or testimony describing work he or she had previously performed. Nor will it be deemed impaired if the individual explains the positions taken or conclusions reached during the performance of any service provided for the audit client.

## .21  Tax Services Permitted

Since the Commission issued its auditor independence proposal, there has been considerable debate regarding whether an accountant's provision of tax services for an audit client can impair the accountant's independence. Tax services are unique among nonaudit services for a variety of reasons. Detailed tax laws must be consistently applied, and the Internal Revenue Service has discretion to audit any tax return. In addition, accounting firms have historically provided a broad range of tax services to their audit clients.

The Commission reiterates its long-standing position that an accounting firm can provide tax services to its audit clients without impairing the firm's independence. Accordingly, accountants may continue to provide tax services such as tax compliance, tax planning, and tax advice to audit clients, subject to the normal audit committee preapproval requirements. However, the rules require registrants to *disclose the amount of fees* paid to the accounting firm for tax services. The rules are consistent with the Act, which states that:

> Merely labeling a service as a "tax service" will not necessarily eliminate its potential to impair independence under Rule 2-01(b). Audit committees and

accountants should understand that providing certain tax services to an audit client would, or could, in certain circumstances, impair the independence of the accountant. Specifically, accountants would impair their independence by representing an audit client before a tax court, district court, or federal court of claims. In addition, audit committees also should carefully scrutinize the retention of an accountant in a transaction initially recommended by the accountant, the sole business purpose of which may be tax avoidance and the tax treatment of which may be not supported in the Internal Revenue Code and related regulations.

At about the time that these rules were being adopted, the Commission had reason to be concerned about having given auditors *any* right to offer tax services to their audit clients. Some very unorthodox and downright illegal shenanigans between major accounting firms and clients regarding tax shelters were being brought to light. Therefore, audit committees should be doubly careful about their preapproval considerations regarding any tax service being provided.

## ¶16,013   DEFINITION AND EXTENT OF AUDIT COMMITTEE

The definition of "audit committee" used in the SEC independence rules is the same as that given in section 205 of the Sarbanes-Oxley Act:

> A committee (or equivalent body) established by and amongst the Board of directors of an issuer for the purpose of overseeing the accounting and financial reporting processes of the issuer and audits of the financial statements of the issuer.

The Act further stipulates that if no such committee exists, the audit committee is the entire Board of directors.

The audit committee serves as an important body, acting in the interests of investors to help ensure that the registrant and its accountants fulfill their responsibilities under the securities laws. Because the definition of an audit committee can include the entire Board of directors if no such committee of the Board exists, these rules do not require registrants to establish audit committees. Likewise, the auditor independence rules do not require the committee to be composed of independent members of the Board. Some entities do not have Boards of directors and therefore do not have audit committees. For example, some limited liability companies and limited partnerships that do not have a corporate general partner may not have an oversight body that is the equivalent of an audit committee.

Nevertheless, the Commission is not exempting these entities from the requirements. Such an issuer is expected to scan through each general partner of the successive limited partnerships until a corporate general partner or an individual general partner is reached. With respect to a corporate general partner, the registrant should consider the audit committee of the corporate general partner or to the full Board of directors as fulfilling the role of the audit committee. With respect to an individual general partner, the Commission expects the registrant to consider the individual as fulfilling the role of the audit committee.

The rules, however, do exempt asset-backed issuers and unit investment trusts from this requirement. Because of the nature of the entity, these issuers are subject to substantially different reporting requirements. Most significantly, asset-backed issuers are not required to file financial statements, as are other companies. Similarly, unit investment trusts are not required to provide shareholder reports containing audited financial statements. Such entities are, typically, passively managed pools of assets. Therefore, the requirements related to audit committees in these rules do not apply to such entities.

## ¶16,015  Retention of Records Relevant to Audits

On the same day in January that it approved the above-mentioned rules, the SEC also approved the adoption of Rule 2-06 of Regulation S-X to implement section 802 of the Sarbanes-Oxley Act. This rule requires that accounting firms retain records relevant to the audits or reviews of issuers' and registered investment companies' financial statements, including workpapers and other documents that form the basis of the audit or review and memoranda, correspondence, communications, other documents, and records (including electronic records) that are created, sent, or received in connection with the audit or review and that contain conclusions, opinions, analyses, or financial data related to the audit or review.

These records must be retained for seven years after the auditor concludes the audit or review of the financial statements, instead of the proposed period of five years from the end of the fiscal period in which an audit or review was concluded. This change coordinated the Commission's rule with the expected auditing standards from the PCAOB that are scheduled to require the retention of audit documentation for seven years.

The rule defines the term "workpapers" to be those documents that record the audit or review procedures performed, the evidence obtained, and the conclusions reached by the auditor. The definition recognizes that the PCAOB may establish auditing standards further defining the term.

The rule also spells out a requirement to keep records that either support the auditor's final conclusions or contain information or data, relating to a significant matter, that is inconsistent with the final conclusions of the auditor on that matter or on the audit or review. The rule also states that the documents and records to be retained include, but are not limited to, those documenting consultations on, or resolutions of, differences in professional judgment.

The compliance date for these rules is October 31, 2003.

¶16,015

## ¶16,017  DISCLOSURE REQUIREMENTS TO IMPLEMENT THE SARBANES-OXLEY ACT

The Commission voted to adopt rules implementing sections 406 and 407 of the Sarbanes-Oxley Act of 2002. These rules require public companies to disclose information about corporate codes of ethics and audit committee financial experts. They require a company subject to the reporting requirements of the Securities Exchange Act of 1934 to include the following two new types of disclosures in their Exchange Act filings:

1. Pursuant to section 407, a company will be required to disclose annually whether it has at least one "audit committee financial expert" on its audit committee. If so, the company is to supply the name of said financial expert and whether he or she is independent of management. If the company does not have an audit committee financial expert, it is required to explain why it has no such expert.

2. Pursuant to section 406, a company is required to disclose annually whether the company has adopted a code of ethics for the company's principal executive officer, principal financial officer, principal accounting officer or controller, or persons performing similar functions. If not, the company is required to explain why it has not. The rules also require a company to disclose on a current basis amendments to, and waivers from, the code of ethics relating to any of those officers.

## .01  Audit Committee Financial Experts

The rules expand the proposed definition of the term "financial expert" and also substitute the designation "audit committee financial expert" for "financial expert." The rules define "audit committee financial expert" to mean a person who has the following attributes:

- An understanding of financial statements and generally accepted accounting principles.
- An ability to assess the general application of such principles in connection with the accounting for estimates, accruals, and reserves.
- Experience preparing, auditing, analyzing, or evaluating financial statements that present a breadth and level of complexity of accounting issues that are generally comparable to the breadth and complexity of issues that can reasonably be expected to be raised by the registrant's financial statements, or he or she may have experience actively supervising one or more persons engaged in such activities.
- An understanding of internal controls and procedures for financial reporting.
- An understanding of audit committee functions.

**¶16,017.01**

A person can acquire such attributes through any one or more of the following means:

- Education and experience as a principal financial officer, principal accounting officer, controller, public accountant, or auditor or experience in one or more positions that involve the performance of similar functions.
- Experience actively supervising a principal financial officer, principal accounting officer, controller, public accountant, auditor, or person performing similar functions or experience overseeing or assessing the performance of companies or public accountants with respect to the preparation, auditing, or evaluation of financial statements.
- Other relevant experience.

An individual must possess all of the attributes listed in the above definition to qualify as an audit committee financial expert.

The rules also provide a safe harbor to make clear that an audit committee financial expert is not to be deemed an "expert" for any purpose, including for purposes of section 11 of the Securities Act of 1933. The designation of a person as an "audit committee financial expert" does not impose any duties, obligations, or liability on the person that are greater than those imposed on such a person as a member of the audit committee in the absence of such designation, nor does it affect the duties, obligations, or liability of any other member of the audit committee or Board of directors.

## .03   Codes of Ethics

Under the rules, a company is required to disclose in its annual report whether it has a code of ethics that applies to the company's principal executive officer, principal financial officer, principal accounting officer or controller, or persons performing similar functions. The rules define a code of ethics as written standards that are reasonably necessary to deter wrongdoing and to promote:

- Honest and ethical conduct, including the ethical handling of actual or apparent conflicts of interest between personal and professional relationships.
- Full, fair, accurate, timely, and understandable disclosure in reports and documents that a company files with, or submits to, the Commission and in other public communications made by the company.
- Compliance with applicable governmental laws, rules, and regulations.
- The prompt internal reporting of code violations to an appropriate person or persons identified in the code.
- Accountability for adherence to the code.

A company is required to make available to the public a copy of its code of ethics, or portion of the code that applies to the company's principal executive officer, principal financial officer, principal accounting officer or controller, or persons performing similar functions. The code of ethics may be made available to the public by filing it as an exhibit to its annual report, providing it on the company's Internet Web site, or as otherwise set forth in the final rule.

A company, other than a foreign private issuer or registered investment company, is also required to disclose any changes to, or waivers of, the code of ethics within five business days, to the extent that the change or waiver applies to the company's principal executive officer or senior financial officers. A company can provide this disclosure on Form 8-K or on its Internet Web site. Foreign private issuers and registered investment companies are required to disclose changes to, and waivers of, such codes of ethics in their periodic reports or on their Internet Web sites.

Companies were required to provide the new disclosures in annual reports for fiscal years ending on or after July 15, 2003. Small business issuers are required to provide the new audit committee financial expert disclosure in annual reports for fiscal years ending on or after December 15, 2003.

## ¶16,019    THE SEC'S 2002 RULES GOVERNING INDEPENDENCE OF AUDITORS

After extensive prodding and action by the SEC, auditor independence and financial disclosure about audit committees came to the foreground in concerns relating to independence and the openness of the auditing and accounting professions.

The rather lengthy lead time, punctuated by considerable negative pressure from Congress (bipartisan and bicameral), the American Institute of Certified Public Accountants (AICPS), three of the Big Five firms and the American Bar Association, to single out only a few, ended with the Security and Exchange Commissioners voting unanimously on November 15, 2000, to adopt new rules that modernize the requirements for auditor independence. Obviously, the measures were too little, too late to protect the investors in Enron. Until additional restrictions and guidelines are officially adopted and put in place, the measures adopted at that time are still in effect.

The three areas covered are:

1. Investments by auditors or their family members in audit clients.
2. Employment relationships between auditors or their family members and audit clients.
3. The third area—the scope of services provided by audit firms to their audit clients—has been superseded by the newer rules delineated above.

The new rules reflect the Commission's consideration of comments received on the rules it proposed in June 2000.

## .01   Principal Provisions

Significant features of the new rules include:

1. Reduction of the number of audit firm employees and their family members whose investments in, or employment with, audit clients would impair an auditor's independence.
2. Identification of certain nonaudit services that, if provided to an audit client, would impair an auditor's independence. (The rules do not extend to services provided to nonaudit clients.)
3. Disclosure in their annual proxy statements of certain information about nonaudit services provided by the company's auditors during the last fiscal year.

## .03   Four Principles

A preliminary note to the new rules identifies four principles by which to measure an auditor's independence. An accountant is not independent when the accountant:

1. Has a mutual or conflicting interest with the audit client.
2. Audits his or her own firm's work.
3. Functions as management or an employee of the audit client.
4. Acts as an advocate for the audit client.

## .05   Financial Relationships

Compared to the previous rules, the newly adopted rules narrow significantly the number of people whose investments trigger independence concerns. Under previous rules, many partners that did not work on the audit of a client, as well as their spouses and families, were restricted from investment in a firm's audit clients. The new rules limit restrictions principally to those who work on the audit or can influence the audit.

## .07   Employment Relationships

The employment relationship rules narrow the scope of people within audit firms whose families will be affected by the employment restrictions necessary to maintain independence. The rules also identify the positions in which a person *can* influence the audit client's accounting records or financial statements. These are positions that could impair an auditor's independence if held by a close family member of that auditor.

**¶16,019.01**

## .09  Business Relationships

Consistent with existing rules, independence will be impaired if the accountant or any covered person has a direct or material indirect business relationship with the audit client, other than providing professional services.

## .11  A General Standard for Auditor Independence

This SEC rule is based on the widely endorsed principle that an auditor must be independent both *in fact* and *in appearance*. The new rule specifies that an auditor's independence is impaired either when the accountant is not independent *in fact* or when a "reasonable investor," after considering all relevant facts and circumstances, would conclude that the auditor would not be capable of acting without bias. The reasonable investor standard is a common construct in securities laws.

## .13  Affiliate Provisions

When it was first proposed in June 2000, the rule contained a definition of an "affiliate of an accounting firm" that many commenters felt might affect accounting firms' joint ventures with companies that are not their audit clients and the continuation of small firm alliances. These types of relationships traditionally have not been thought to impair an accountant's independence. After considering these comments, the SEC decided that it would continue to analyze these situations under existing guidance.

An "affiliate of an audit client" continues to be defined as any entity that can significantly influence, or is significantly influenced by, the audit client, provided the equity investment is material to the entity or the audit client. "Significant influence" generally is presumed when the investor owns 20 percent or more of the voting stock of the investee. The significant influence test is used because under GAAP it is the trigger that causes the earnings and losses of one company to be reflected in the financial statements of another company.

## .15  Contingent Fee Arrangements

The rules reiterate that an accountant cannot provide any service to an audit client that involves a contingent fee.

## .17  Quality Controls

The rules provide a limited exception from independence violations to the accounting firm if certain factors are present:

1. The individual did not know the circumstances giving rise to his or her violation.

¶16,019.17

2. The violation was corrected promptly once the violation became apparent.
3. The firm has quality controls in place that provide reasonable assurance that the firm and its employees maintain their independence.
4. For the largest public accounting firms, the basic controls must include among others:
   a. Written independence policies and procedures.
   b. Automated systems to identify financial relationships that may impair independence.
   c. Training, internal inspection, and testing.
   d. Disciplinary mechanism for enforcement.

## .19 Proxy Disclosure Requirement

Companies must disclose in their annual proxy statements the fees for audit, IT consulting, and all other services provided by their auditors during the last fiscal year.

Companies must also state whether the audit committee has considered whether the provision of the nonaudit services is compatible with maintaining the auditor's independence.

Finally, the registrant is required to disclose the percentage hours worked on the audit engagement by persons other than the accountant's full-time employees, if that figure exceeded 50 percent. This requirement is in answer to recent actions taken by some accounting firms to sell their practices to financial services companies. The partners or employees often, in turn, become employees of the financial services firm. The accounting firm then leases assets, namely auditors, back from those companies to complete audit engagements. In such cases, most of the auditors who work on an audit are employed elsewhere without the public, investors, or the client being aware of the situation.

## ¶16,021 APPLICATION OF REVISED RULES ON AUDITOR INDEPENDENCE

Since the adoption of the Commission's Revised Rules on Auditor Independence, the SEC staff has received questions regarding the implementation and interpretation of the rules. They encourage these questions and related correspondence regarding auditor independence as they do to all of the rulings which may be difficult to interpret.

### .01 Frequently Asked Questions

Publications of staff responses to certain questions received are referred to as Frequently Asked Questions (FAQs). Many of the questions are rather technical, referring to a specific item on a specific schedule. Others have a more general and widespread application and give the preparer a better feel for what the SEC staff is looking for in the reports. Following is a sample of the latter variety.

### Question 6

**Q:** Should the fees billed in prior years be disclosed so investors may compare trends in audit, information technology, and other non-audit fees?

**A:** The rule does not require comparative disclosures. Registrants may include such information voluntarily.

### Question 7

**Q:** In situations where other auditors are involved in the delivery of services, to what extent should the fees from the other auditors be included in the required fee disclosures?

**A:** Only the fees billed by the principal accountant need to be disclosed. See Question 8 regarding the definition of "principal accountant." If the principal accountant's billings or expected billings include fees for the work performed by others (such as where the principal accountant hires someone else to perform part of the work), then such fees should be included in the fees disclosed for the principal accountant.

In some foreign jurisdictions, a registrant may be required to have a joint audit requiring both accountants to issue an audit report for the same fiscal year. In these circumstances, fees for each accountant should be separately disclosed as they are both "principal accountants."

### Question 8

**Q:** Does the term "principal accountant" in the ruling include associated or affiliated organizations?

**A:** Yes. "Principal accountant" has the meaning given to it in the auditing literature. In determining what services rendered by the principal accountant must be disclosed, all entities that comprise the accountant, as defined, should be included. This term includes not only the person or entity who furnishes reports or other documents that the registrant files with the Commission, but also all of the person's or entity's departments, divisions, parents, subsidiaries, and associated entities, including those located outside of the United States.

### Question 15

**Q:** Does the restriction on the independent accountant providing legal services to an audit client apply only to litigation services?

**A:** No. The Commission's rule provides that an auditor's and firm's independence would be impaired if an auditor provides to its audit client a service for which the person providing the service must be admitted to practice before the courts of a U.S. jurisdiction. This standard includes all legal services. The rule does not apply only to appearance in court or solely to litigators. The only circumstances excluded by the rule are those in which local U.S. law allows certain limited activities without admission to the bar (generally confined to advice concerning the law of foreign jurisdictions).

Additionally, as discussed in the adopting release, some firms may be providing legal services outside of the United States to registrants when those services are not precluded by local law and are routine and ministerial or relate to matters that are not material to the consolidated financial statements. Such services raise serious independence concerns under circumstances other than those meeting at least those minimum criteria.

### Question 17

**Q:** The final rule did not define an affiliate of an accounting firm. Does the lack of a definition signal a change in the Commission's approach to this issue?

**A:** No. The final rule's definition of an "accounting firm" includes the accounting firm's "associated entities." As noted in the adopting release, the Commission used this phrase to reflect the staff's current practice of addressing these questions in light of all relevant facts and circumstances, and of looking to the factors identified in our previous guidance on this subject. Much of this guidance is cited in footnotes of the adopting release. The staff is available for consultations on this issue.

### Question 18

**Q:** Did the final rule change the Commission's guidance with respect to business relationships?

**A:** No. The final rule is consistent with the Commission's prior guidance on business relationships. The basic standard of the Commission's prior guidance has now been codified in the rule. In addition, as the adopting release notes, much of the Commission's previous guidance has been retained and continues to apply. For example, joint ventures, limited partnerships, investments in supplier or customer companies, certain leasing interest and sales by the accountant of items other than professional services are examples of business relationships that may impair an accountant's independence.

The SEC further explained its position in a letter to an accounting firm. The Commission stated:

"The Commission has recognized that certain situations, including those in which accountants and their audit clients have joined together in a profit-sharing venture, create a unity of interest between the accountant and client. In such cases, both the revenue accruing to each party...and the existence of the relationship itself create a situation in which to some degree the auditor's interest is wedded to that of its client. That interdependence impairs the auditor's independence, irrespective of whether the audit was in fact performed in an objective, critical fashion. Where such a unity of interests exists, there is an appearance that the auditor has lost the objectivity and skepticism necessary to take a critical second look at management's representations in the financial statements. The consequence is a loss of confidence in the integrity of the financial statements."

***Question 21***

**Q:** The new rule permits the auditor to continue to provide certain internal audit and financial information systems design and implementation services provided certain criteria are met. Do these criteria for internal audit apply to all internal audit engagements? What are the responsibilities of management pursuant to these criteria?

**A:** The six criteria for internal audit services apply to all internal audit services the auditor provides to its audit client, including those services related to operational audits or for companies with less than $200 million in assets.

All of the specified criteria must be met for both internal audit and financial information systems design and implementation to ensure that management not only takes responsibility for the services and projects performed by the auditor, but also makes the required management decisions. An audit client that merely signs a letter acknowledging responsibility for the services or project, without actually meeting each of the specified conditions, is not sufficient to ensure the auditor's independence.

## ¶16,023   WHERE THERE'S A WILL, THERE MAY BE A WAY

Needless to say, all of this activity relating to auditor independence, audit committees, and related financial disclosure did not come about without some very strong impetus. When the public and average investors begin to question truthfulness as well as the usefulness of business "checks and balances," someone will take action.

## ¶16,025   THE BLUE RIBBON PANEL'S TEN COMMANDMENTS

Although described as "recommendations," the report of the Blue Ribbon Panel on Improving the Effectiveness of Corporate Audit Committees made it quite clear that not only the average investor but also a distinguished group of those "in the know" had questions about the effectiveness of the "independent" audit process. The group comprising the Panel was formed by the New York Stock Exchange (NYSE) and the National Association of Securities Dealers (NASD or NASDAQ) in September 1998, after the SEC Chairman had publicly expressed grave concern about the "independence" of the audit process. During the deliberations of the group consisting of business, accounting, and securities professionals, testimony was provided by two dozen organizations, including the AICPA, the Financial Executives International, the Independence Standards Board, and the Institute of Management Accountants.

The panel's 71-page report listed ten recommendations for strengthening the independence of the audit committee and increasing its importance and effectiveness. These recommendations were:

1. The NYSE and NASD adopt strict definitions of independence for directors serving on audit committees of listed companies.
2. The NYSE and NASD require larger companies to have audit committees composed entirely of independent directors.
3. The NYSE and NASD require larger companies to have "financially literate" directors on their audit committees.
4. The NYSE and NASD require each company to adopt a formal audit committee charter and to review its adequacy annually.
5. The SEC requires each company to disclose in its proxy statement whether it has adopted an audit committee charter as well as other information.
6. Each NYSE and NASD listed company state in the audit committee charter that the outside auditor is ultimately accountable to the board of directors and the audit committee.
7. All NYSE and NASD listed companies ensure their charters mandate that their audit committee does communicate with the outside auditors about independence issues in accordance with Independent Standards Board regulations.
8. Generally accepted auditing rules require that the outside auditor discuss with the audit committee the quality and suitability, not just the acceptability, of the accounting principles used.
9. The SEC require the annual report include a letter from the audit committee clarifying that it has reviewed the audited financial statements with management as well as performed other tasks.
10. The SEC require the outside auditor to perform an interim review under Statement on Auditing Standards (SAS) SAS-71, *Interim Financial Information*, before a company files its form 10-Q.

## ¶16,027  NEW RULES FOR AUDIT COMMITTEES AND REVIEWS OF INTERIM FINANCIAL STATEMENTS

On December 15, 1999, the Securities and Exchange Commission adopted new rules aimed at improving public disclosure about the functioning of corporate audit committees and enhancing both the reliability and credibility of financial statements of public companies. These SEC rules build upon new rules adopted by the NYSE, the American Stock Exchange (AMEX), and the NASD that govern audit committees of listed companies.

The new rules also coincide with the issuance of Statement of Auditing Standard 90 by the AICPA's Auditing Standards Board. This ASB Standard requires independent auditors to discuss with the audit committee the auditor's judgment about the *quality,* and not just the *acceptability* under generally accepted accounting principles, of the company's own accounting principles as applied in its financial reporting.

Much of this activity results from the grave concern ably and loudly voiced by the SEC (particularly by the Chairman) which, in turn, led to the appointment of the Blue Ribbon Panel on Audit Effectiveness.

## .01    SEC Rules Relating to the Interim Statement

The Commission's rules require that:

1. Companies' interim financial statements must be reviewed by independent auditors before they are filed on Forms 10-Q or 10-QSB with the Commission.
2. Companies, other than small business issuers filing on small business forms, must supplement their annual financial information with disclosures of selected quarterly financial data under Item 302(a) of Regulation S-K.
3. Companies must disclose in their proxy statements whether the audit committee reviewed and discussed certain matters relating to:
   a. The ASB's Statements of Auditing Standards 61 concerning the accounting methods used in the financial statements.
   b. The Independence Standard Board's Standard 1 (concerning matters that may affect the auditor's independence) with management and the auditors.
   c. Possible recommendation to the Board that the audited financial statements be included in the Annual Report on Form 10-K or 10-KSB for filings with the Commission.
4. Companies must disclose in their proxy statements whether the audit committee has a written charter, and file a copy of their charter every three years.
5. Companies whose securities are listed on the NYSE or AMEX or are quoted on NASDAQ must disclose certain information in their proxy statements about any audit committee member who is not "independent." All companies must disclose, if they have an audit committee, whether the members are "independent." (Independence is defined in the listing standards of the NYSE, AMEX, and NASD.)

Under the new rules, timely interim auditor reviews were required beginning with the first fiscal quarter ended after March 15, 2000. Compliance with the other new requirements is required in filings after December 15, 2000.

Foreign private issuers are exempt from requirements of the new rules. The new rules include a "safe harbor" for the disclosures.

¶**16,027.01**

## .03 Blue Ribbon Reminders

In their final report in August, 2000, the Blue Ribbon Panel on Audit Effectiveness recommended that, among other things audit committees:

1. Obtain annual reports from management assessing the company's internal controls.
2. Specify in their charters that the outside auditor is ultimately accountable to the board of directors and audit committee.
3. Inquire about time pressures on the auditor.
4. Preapprove nonaudit services provided by the auditor.

## .05 Criteria for Gauging Appropriateness

The Panel, more specifically, provided guidance that an audit committee can use to determine the appropriateness of a service. This guidance includes:

1. Whether the service is being performed principally for the audit committee.
2. The effects of the service, if any, on audit effectiveness, or on the quality and timeliness of the entity's financial reporting process. For example, what is the effect, if any, upon the technology specialists who ordinarily also provide recurring audit support?
3. Whether the service would be performed by audit personnel, and if so, whether it will enhance their knowledge of the entity's business and operations.
4. Whether the role of those performing the service would be inconsistent with the auditor's role (e.g., a role where neutrality, impartiality, and auditor skepticism are likely to be subverted).
5. Whether the audit firm personnel would be assuming a management role or creating a mutual or conflicting interest with management.
6. Whether the auditors, in effect, would be "auditing their own numbers."
7. Whether the project must be started and completed very quickly.
8. Whether the audit firm has unique expertise in the service.
9. The size of the fee(s) for the nonaudit service(s).

# Chapter 17

# Taxpayer Rights

## CONTENTS

# ¶17,000   OVERVIEW

The National Taxpayer Advocate delivered a report to Congress in June that identifies the priority issues the Office of the Taxpayer Advocate will address in the coming fiscal year. This is the first of two reports required by statute that the Advocate Office must submit to Congress annually. This report is submitted to the House Committee on Ways and Means; the second goes to the Senate Committee on Finance.

The statute requires that both reports be submitted directly to the Committees without any prior review or comment from the Commissioner of Internal Revenue, the Secretary of the Treasury, the IRS Oversight Board, or any other officer or employee of the Department of the Treasury or the Office of Management and Budget. The first report, due on June 30 of each year, must identify the objectives of the Office of the Taxpayer Advocate for the fiscal year beginning in that calendar year.

The second report, due on December 31 of each year, is required to:

1. Identify at least 20 of the most serious problems encountered by taxpayers.
2. Discuss the 10 tax issues most frequently litigated in the courts during the prior year.
3. Make administrative and legislative recommendations to resolve taxpayer problems.

# ¶17,001   REPORT TO HOUSE WAYS AND MEANS COMMITTEE

The issues in the June 30, 2006, report to the House Committee include:

1. The rules governing the use or disclosure of tax return information by return preparers.
2. A recently imposed requirement that taxpayers submitting lump-sum offers in compromise make a down payment of 20 percent of the amount of the offer.
3. IRS guidelines in evaluating "non-hardship effective tax administration" offers.
4. The importance of safeguarding taxpayer rights as the IRS rolls out its private debt collection initiative.

The office also released a report, presented as Volume II, that examines the role the IRS plays in facilitating the refund anticipation loan (RAL) industry, and makes recommendations to improve refund delivery to taxpayers, including the "unbanked."

The required report notes that the IRS is under significant pressure both to reduce the tax gap and to maintain and improve taxpayer services. The report commends the IRS for adopting a more strategic approach to these objectives. However, the Advocate's Office is concerned, that the IRS is approaching its taxpayer service and enforcement initiatives on almost entirely separate tracks. In the IRS today, enforcement employees concentrate on enforcement initiatives and taxpayer service employees consider taxpayer service initiatives, with little, if any, contact between the two. The offer in compromise is cited as an example of an instance in which the one does lead to the other: incorporating high quality service within enforcement initiatives will ultimately help bring noncompliant taxpayers into compliance and thus reduce the tax gap.

## .01    Issues to be addressed in FY 2007

The report sets out the objectives of the Office of the Taxpayer Advocate for the upcoming fiscal year and provides substantive analysis of issues as well as statistical information. The report identifies four areas for particular emphasis in FY 2007:

1. Rules Governing the Use or Disclosure of Tax Return Information by Return Preparers. The statute and regulations governing what tax preparers may do with confidential tax return information they receive from their clients were written in the 1970s. To make the rules more applicable to e-filing and other changes that have occurred over the past 30 years, the IRS issued proposed regulations late last year. The Taxpayer Advocate believes that the proposed regulations provide more protection to taxpayers than the existing regulations. Some improvements to the proposed rules may be needed, and the suggestion is that limiting the use and disclosure of tax return information solely to instances where it is necessary for tax-administration purposes would be advisable.

2. New Partial Payment Requirement with Submissions of Offers in Compromise. A taxpayer who is unable to pay his or her tax liability in full may seek to compromise the debt by submitting an "offer in compromise." The offer program is a good deal for both the government and the taxpayer. The government benefits because it frequently collects more than it would in the absence of the program and the taxpayer is induced to pay taxes on time and in full in the future; a taxpayer whose offer is accepted must remain fully compliant for 5 years into the future or face reinstatement of the full amount of the compromised tax debt. The taxpayer benefits because he or she is able to make a fresh start. Legislation enacted this year will require taxpayers who submit "lump-sum" offers to make a down payment of 20 percent of the amount of the offer with the submission. (See discussion below.) The Advocate's Office believes that this requirement:

   a. Will reduce the number of viable offers the IRS receives.

¶17,001.01

  b. Increase the number of accounts not resolved.

  c. Reduce the amount of revenue collected.

  The office is working with the IRS and the Treasury Department to implement the requirement, and intends to make a legislative recommendation to repeal the requirement in the year-end report to Congress.

3. Guidance on Non-Hardship Effective Tax Administration Offers. In 1998, Congress expanded the authority of the IRS to compromise tax debts by directing it to consider equity, public policy, and hardship in cases where doing so would promote effective administration of the tax laws. The Advocate has criticized the IRS in prior reports for reading this authorization too narrowly. In 2004, the IRS developed unsigned and unpublished internal guidance that it has been using to evaluate non-hardship offers. The Advocate writes that the IRS should make this guidance public to assist taxpayers and their representatives in determining whether they may qualify for relief and to make clear what standards they need to meet. The Advocate also believes that this guidance should be made more widely available within the IRS. This year, the office will push within the IRS for broader dissemination of the guidance.

4. Private Debt Collection Initiative. In 2004, Congress granted IRS the authority to use private debt collectors to collect certain tax debts, and the IRS is now working actively to implement the initiative in the coming months. The Advocate has expressed opposition to this initiative, citing risks to taxpayer privacy and confidence in the federal tax system. In FY 2007, the office will monitor the initiative closely – with respect to both specific cases and systemic issues – and will immediately share any significant observations or concerns with the IRS and Congress. The office will also try to track the amount of "re-work" the initiative creates for the IRS and taxpayers to help facilitate comprehensive and accurate return-on-investment calculations to assist in evaluating the program.

## .03    Refund Anticipation Loans criticized in Volume II

In Volume II of the report, the office states that the IRS facilitates the refund anticipation loans (RALs), which can be very detrimental for the low-income taxpayer by:

1. Not conducting sufficient oversight of Electronic Return Originators (EROs) that retail RALs,

2. Not promulgating stricter protections for taxpayer privacy with respect to the Debt Indicator,

3. Failing to develop a fast, secure, and free refund delivery option for "unbanked" taxpayers.

¶17,001.03

Moreover, the Advocate states that the IRS's rule permitting an ERO to purchase up to a 49 percent ownership interest in RALs creates a conflict between the ERO's and the taxpayer's financial interests. It should also be noted that too few taxpayers realize that there are ways to obtain speedy refunds from the IRS and avoid the high interest rates charged by most RALs.

## ¶17,003   IRS Revamps Offer in Compromise Program

The Internal Revenue Service announced that under a new federal law, taxpayers submitting new offers in compromise must, in many cases, make a 20 percent nonrefundable, up-front payment.

The Tax Increase Prevention and Reconciliation Act of 2005 (TIPRA) made major changes to the offer in compromise (OIC) program, tightening the rules for lump-sum offers and periodic-payment offers. These changes became effective for all offers received by the IRS starting July 2006.

An offer in compromise is an agreement between a taxpayer and the IRS that resolves the taxpayer's tax debt. The IRS has the authority to settle, or "compromise," federal tax liabilities by accepting less than full payment in certain circumstances.

Under the new law, taxpayers submitting requests for lump-sum OICs must include a payment equal to 20 percent of the offer amount. The payment is nonrefundable; that is, it will not be returned if the OIC request is later rejected. A lump-sum OIC refers to any offer of payments made in five or fewer installments. As noted above, the National Taxpayer Advocate intends to make a legislative recommendation to repeal the requirement in the year-end report to Congress because the belief is that the measure will result in less tax money being collected.

Taxpayers submitting requests for periodic-payment OICs must include the first proposed installment payment with their application. A periodic payment OIC is any offer of payments made in six or more installments. The taxpayer is required to pay additional installments while the IRS is evaluating the offer. All installment payments are nonrefundable.

Under the law, taxpayers qualifying as low-income or filing an offer based solely on doubt as to liability qualify for a waiver of the new partial payment requirements. If the IRS cannot make a determination on an OIC within two years, then the offer will be deemed accepted. If a liability included in the offer amount is disputed in any court proceeding, that time period is omitted from calculating the two-year timeframe.

OIC requests are submitted using Form 656, Offer in Compromise. The form provides detailed instructions for completing an offer and includes all of the necessary financial forms. When submitting Form 656, taxpayers must include an application fee of $150 unless they qualify for the low-income exemption or are filing a doubt-as-to-liability offer.

## ¶17,005  ADVOCATES REPORT FOR 2006 EMPHASIZED NEED FOR TAX SIMPLIFICATION

The National Taxpayer Advocate urged Congress to enact fundamental tax simplification in the report issued to the Senate Finance committee in January 2006. The Office pointed out that the tax code has grown so complex that it creates opportunities for taxpayers to make inadvertent mistakes as well as to game the system. As taxpayers become confused and make mistakes, or deliberately "push the envelope," the IRS understandably responds with increased enforcement actions. The exploitation of "loopholes" leads to calls for new legislation to crack down on abuses, which in turn makes the tax law more complex. And the vicious cycle goes on and on.

### .01  Core Principles Suggested

This cycle can only be broken by true tax simplification, followed by ongoing legislative and administrative discipline to avoid "complexity creep," according to the Advocate Office. They believe that the Code should be revised to incorporate six core principles:

1. It should not "entrap" taxpayers.
2. It should be simple enough so that taxpayers can prepare their own returns without professional help, simple enough so that taxpayers can compute their tax liabilities on a single form, and simple enough so that IRS telephone assistors can fully and accurately answer taxpayers' questions.
3. It should be written in a way that anticipates the largest areas of noncompliance and minimizes the opportunities for such noncompliance.
4. It should provide some choices, but not too many choices.
5. It should not necessarily avoid refundable credits but, if it includes them, it should design them in a way that is administrable.
6. It should require a periodic review of its provisions – in short, a sanity check.

### .03  Additional Legislation Recommended

At the same time, the report makes legislative recommendations to cover a wide variety of topics, while avoiding complexity. Among the suggestions:

1. Reduce noncompliance in the "cash economy."
2. Simplify the Code's family-status provisions.
3. Revamp the rules governing joint-and-several liability on joint returns as well as community property in the collection of tax.

¶17,005

4. Require brokers to track and report cost basis for stocks and mutual funds to both investors and the IRS.

5. Lessen the burdens of tracking the cost basis of stocks and mutual funds if the current-law step-up in basis on death is eliminated as scheduled in 2010.

6. Restructure and reform the Code's collection due process (CDP) provisions.

## .05  Not 20 Questions, But 20 Problems

By statute, the National Taxpayer Advocate is required to identify at least 20 of the most serious problems encountered by taxpayers.

1. This year's report identifies trends in taxpayer service as the most serious problem. While expressing support for a strong IRS enforcement presence, the Office questions whether the IRS is expanding enforcement at the expense of taxpayer service. The report states that the IRS:

   • Has eliminated TeleFile.

   • Significantly reduced the number of returns IRS personnel prepare for taxpayers who seek IRS assistance.

   • Reduced the percentage of taxpayer calls IRS telephone assisters answer as compared with FY 2004.

   • Substantially reduced its taxpayer education function for small businesses.

   • Has taken these actions without any empirical evidence that the reductions will not harm taxpayers and not result in decreased compliance.

2. The report cites Criminal Investigation (CI) refund freezes as the second most serious problem facing taxpayers. The report states that CI places "freezes" on hundreds of thousands of refunds each year because of a suspicion of fraud under the Questionable Refund Program (QRP). The Service then makes a "determination" whether the returns are, in fact, fraudulent without notifying taxpayers that their claims are under review or giving them an opportunity to present evidence supporting their positions. (See IRS response below.)

   In FY 2004, more than 28,000 taxpayers whose refunds had been frozen sought assistance from the Taxpayer Advocate Service (TAS). The TAS research function studied a statistically representative sample of these cases and found that, with TAS assistance, taxpayers ultimately received the full amount of the refund they had claimed in 66 percent of the frozen-refund cases and a portion of the refund they had claimed in an additional 14 percent of the cases.

   The Office urges the IRS to implement procedures to notify taxpayers promptly that their refunds have been frozen, provide taxpayers with an opportunity to submit supporting documentation, and bring cases to a quicker resolution. The TAS research study is published as Volume II of the report.

3. Other problems catalogued by the Advocate's Office in their list of 20 that the IRS should deal with include:

   • Developing a comprehensive strategy to address noncompliance in the "cash economy."

   • Making sure of the adequacy of training for private debt collection employees as the IRS begins the Private Debt Collection (PDC) initiative.

   • Preventing delays and related problems in examining returns that claim the earned income tax credit (EITC).

## .07  Steps to Improve Questionable Refund Program

The Internal Revenue Service wasted no time in responding to the second most serious problem faced by taxpayers as cited by the National Taxpayer Advocate The IRS announced new steps to improve the Questionable Refund Program (QRP) and reduce the number of taxpayers subject to frozen refunds.

The changes include notifying taxpayers when a tax refund has been frozen. Other new procedures will result in a more timely release of frozen tax refunds for those cases that do not warrant further review.

The actions constitute significant improvements of an important program. The Service plans to improve the screening procedures and notify all taxpayers whose refunds are held. The IRS is attempting to reach a balance between taxpayer rights and enforcement of the law.

Highlights of the changes:

1. Improvements to screening procedures. The IRS will improve and refine the accuracy of filters in the program to reduce the initial number of valid refund claims that are held.
2. Notification to taxpayers. The IRS will notify all taxpayers whose refunds are frozen.
3. Earlier release of refunds. The IRS will expedite the review of returns to provide for an earlier release of refunds.

Notification procedures will be implemented this filing season. Improvements to the screening and review processes will be implemented as soon as possible in the coming months. The IRS will also continue to identify and implement other areas for improvement.

This review occurred following delivery of the report discussed above. After receiving the Taxpayer Advocate's report, members of Congress also questioned the length of delay and lack of notification for refund claims. The IRS then developed the new procedures in consultation with the NTA.

¶17,005.07

The IRS had established the Questionable Refund Program to deal with the serious problem of refund fraud, which has increased significantly in recent years. The IRS estimates that fraudulent refund claims now exceed a half-billion dollars a year. Congress has held a number of hearings urging the IRS to devote additional resources and improve its detection and prevention of fraudulent refunds, particularly those involving prisoners.

The typical fraudulent refund claim involves false income and withholding. A significant portion includes false Earned Income Tax Credit claims of up to $4,400 per return.

According to the IRS, each year it receives more than 130 million individual income tax returns and issues over 100 million refunds totaling over $200 billion. The QRP holds up for further scrutiny less than 1 percent of refund returns. Of the refund claims held beyond the normal refund cycle, about 200,000 or 0.2 percent of all refund claims are held longer than one week, and many refunds are held for a period of months or even years. These are customarily those refunds held because the returns are subject to additional, possibly criminal, investigation.

## ¶17,007  IRS JOINS NATIONAL TAXPAYER ADVOCATE TO AID TAXPAYERS

In June 2006, the Internal Revenue Service announced plans to survey nearly 50,000 taxpayers on two quite different surveys in line with their continuing aim to improve the manner in which it provides taxpayer services. The National Taxpayer Advocate and the IRS Oversight Board are collaborating on the larger project to address questions about taxpayers' service preferences and needs.

Both the TAB Opinion Survey of Taxpayer Resources and Services and the Media & Publications External Customer Satisfaction Survey are designed to provide IRS with greater and more accurate understanding of taxpayer service needs, preferences, and behavior. Both surveys will be repeated in future years, to allow the IRS to refine and improve taxpayer services continually based on taxpayer preferences and needs

### .01  Customer Service Operations

The larger of the two is the Opinion Survey of Taxpayer Resources and Services sent to 40,000 taxpayers as part of the Taxpayer Assistance Blueprint (TAB), a multi-year effort by the IRS to review its customer service operations and develop plans for continued improvements.

The agency has been attempting to work out a balanced program of quality service and equitable enforcement of the law by providing effective taxpayer services within available resources. The agency believes their Blueprint will provide a solid foundation on which to base decisions about these taxpayer services.

The IRS, the National Taxpayer Advocate and the IRS Oversight Board are collaborating on the TAB Project to address questions about taxpayers' service preferences and needs. The IRS currently delivers services to taxpayers electronically, through third parties such as tax practitioners or volunteer preparers, by mail, telephone, or through face-to-face assistance.

Taxpayers, chosen at random, will be asked 25 questions about how they presently use IRS services and how they would like to use them. An IRS-approved contractor will mail the questionnaire to the taxpayers. The survey does not ask for any financial or personal information nor should the respondents provide any. Individual responses will remain confidential.

## .03   Effectiveness of IRS Forms and Publications

The other survey of 10,000 taxpayers is designed to help the IRS determine the effectiveness of its forms and publications. Because clarity and effectiveness of forms, publications, and instructions are vital if the IRS is to provide quality taxpayer service, Media & Publications is surveying approximately 10,000 individual and business taxpayers, tax preparers and community-based partners to obtain their perspective on this aspect of IRS service.

The Media & Publications External Customer Satisfaction Survey will measure how satisfied those who respond are with the information they get from the IRS and how well it equips them to understand and meet their obligations under federal tax laws. Questions will address the content, usefulness, format, graphics and delivery of IRS forms and publications. Customers will have the option of taking the survey by telephone or via the Internet.

## ¶17,009   INDUSTRY ISSUE RESOLUTION PROGRAM

Business taxpayers and associations may seek resolution of problematic tax issues through the Internal Revenue Service's Industry Issue Resolution (IIR) Program. They may submit business tax issues for consideration where the tax treatment has been uncertain, unclear, frequently disputed, or seemingly unnecessarily burdensome or costly. Submissions may be made at any time, but the IRS reviews them semi-annually after March 31st and August 31st.

The objective of the IIR program is to resolve business tax issues common to *significant numbers* of taxpayers through new guidance. In past years, associations and others representing both small and large business taxpayers have submitted issues that have resulted in tax guidance affecting thousands of business taxpayers engaged in a variety of industries. Recent results of the IIR program include:

- Providing a safe harbor accounting method that heavy equipment dealers can use to calculate heavy equipment parts inventories more simply using standard price lists. (Rev Proc 2006-14)
- Allowing companies to reduce administrative burden by signing employment tax returns by facsimile. (Rev Proc 2005-39)

For each issue selected, an IIR team of IRS and Treasury industry specific personnel gather relevant facts from taxpayers or other interested parties affected by the issue. The goal is to recommend guidance to resolve the issue. This goal is accomplished by providing clear (Plain English ?) guidance that business taxpayers can use. Thus, both taxpayers and the IRS benefit by saving time and expense that would otherwise be expended on resolving the issue through examinations.

## .01   Business Tax Issues Appropriate for IIR

The IIR program is available to all business taxpayers served by the Small Business and Self-Employed Division (SB/SE) and Large and Mid-Size Business Division (LMSB). Business tax issues appropriate for the IIR program must have at least two of these characteristics:

- The proper tax treatment of a common factual situation is uncertain.
- The uncertainty results in frequent, and often repetitive, examinations of the same issue.
- The uncertainty results in taxpayer burden.
- The issue is significant and impacts a large number of taxpayers, either within an industry or across industry lines.
- The issue requires extensive factual development. Learning about industry practices and views concerning the issue would assist the Service in determining the proper tax treatment.

## .03   Issues Not Appropriate for IIR Treatment

The IIR Program is *not appropriate* for resolving the following types of business tax issues:

- Issues unique to one or a small number of taxpayers.
- Issues that are primarily under the jurisdiction of the Operating Divisions of the Service other than the LMSB and SB/SE Divisions.

¶17,009.03

- Issues that involve transactions that lack a bona fide business purpose, or transactions with a significant purpose of improperly reducing or avoiding federal taxes.
- Issues involving transfer pricing or international tax treaties.

## .05   How the IIR Process Works

The Industry Issue Resolution Program resolves frequently disputed or burdensome tax issues that affect a significant number of business taxpayers through the issuance of guidance. The IRS solicits suggestions for issues from taxpayers, representatives and associations for the IIR Program. For each issue selected for the program, a resolution team is assembled to gather and analyze relevant information for the issue and develop and recommend guidance. To summarize:

- Business taxpayers, industry associations, and other interested parties may submit issues for resolution at any time.
- Typically team members consisting of representatives from LMSB, SB/SE, Appeals, Chief Counsel and Treasury screen, evaluate and select the issues semi-annually.
- Factors considered include the appropriateness of the issue for the program and whether the requested guidance promotes sound tax administration.
- Issues reviewed and IIR projects selected are announced publicly.
- An IIR team is formed for each issue selected.
- The team's role includes fact-finding, evaluating input, and recommending guidance to resolve the particular issue.
- For issues selected, the role of submitters and other interested parties may include meeting with the team and providing the team additional information, including the opportunity to review books and records to assist in the development of the issue.
- Resolution of an issue is generally through IRS published guidance; typically a revenue ruling and/or revenue procedure covers the matter. However, resolution may include administrative guidance.

## ¶17,011   PRIORITY GUIDANCE PLAN 2006-2007

In August, the Department of the Treasury and the IRS released the 2006 - 2007 Priority Guidance Plan covering 264 projects listed under 15 topics ranging from "Consolidated Returns" to "Tax Exempt Bonds." These projects include final regulations, guidance in a multitude of areas, revisions, and proposed regulations.

¶17,009.05

The Plan also includes an appendix, which lists regularly scheduled publications. Among them are monthly publications like the Bureau of Labor Statistics' price indexes, which department stores may use in valuing inventory. The list also includes many periodically or annually published reports including the revenue procedure under section 1 and other sections of the Code regarding the inflation adjusted items for 2007.

## .01  Guidance Focused on User Need

Because of the importance of public input to formulate a Priority Guidance Plan that focuses resources on guidance items that are most important to taxpayers and tax administration, it is based on solicited suggestions from all interested parties, including taxpayers, tax practitioners, and industry groups.

Beginning in 2002, updates to the Priority Guidance Plan were issued during the plan year as user needs arise. The IRS intends to update and republish the Priority Guidance Plan periodically again this year to reflect additional guidance they intend to publish during the year to help the users navigate the tax system.

The IRS explains that the periodic updates allow flexibility throughout the plan year to consider comments received from taxpayers and tax practitioners relating to additional projects and to respond to developments that arise.They updated the 2005 - 2006 Priority Guidance Plan to reflect the publication of substantial guidance providing relief relating to the year's hurricanes, the announcement of a global tax shelter settlement initiative and an announcement describing the Compliance Assurance Process pilot program.

## .03  Something for Everyone

With all of the attention being given to the problems with employee benefits, it would not be surprising if there is updating related to the effect that the new pension law will have on taxes related to them. To begin the year, under the heading "Employee Benefits," 37 projects are divided between "A. Retirement Benefits," and "B. Executive Benefits, Health Care and Other Benefits, and Employment Taxes." The Tax Accounting section contains 21 entries including guidance items, and several changes in method of accounting.

The potpourri of items includes such varied projects as guidelines for estimating stock basis in reorganizations, guidance regarding the transfer of treasury stock to a corporation controlled by the transferor, guidance on Health Savings Accounts, tax shelter standards for covered opinions and other written advice. regulations regarding the income forecast method, guidance on mergers involving foreign corporations, revenue procedure regarding arbitration procedures for Appeals, guidance on when to treat costs of qualified film and television productions as an expense, final regulations regarding solid waste

¶17,011.03

disposal facilities, the replacement period for livestock sold because of drought, flood, or other weather related conditions, guidance on political activities for non-profit organizations.

## ¶17,013  NEW IMAGE FOR THE IRS

The *IRS Restructuring Reform Act of 1998* contains the Taxpayer Bill of Rights 3. It preserves the balance between safeguarding the rights of the individual taxpayers and enabling the Internal Revenue Service to administer the tax laws efficiently, fairly, and with the least amount of burden to the taxpayer.

Under this bill, taxpayer rights have been expanded in several areas:

1. The burden of proof will shift to the IRS in certain court proceedings.
2. In certain cases, taxpayers may be awarded damages and fees, and get liens released.
3. Penalties will be eased when the IRS exceeds specified time limits between when a return is filed and when the taxpayer is notified of a tax liability.
4. Interest will be eliminated in certain cases involving federally-declared disaster areas.
5. There are new rules for collection actions by levy.
6. Innocent spouse relief provisions have been strengthened.
7. In certain situations, taxpayer-requested installment agreements must be accepted. Taxpayers will get annual status reports of their installment agreements.

Included are requirements that IRS employees are now required to be more polite and responsive. For example, any IRS correspondence not computer generated must include the name and telephone number of an employee whom a taxpayer can contact. The new law also established a nine-member board to oversee the general administration of the agency. And to assure that key decision making is not confined to the self-protecting hands of IRS career employees, six of the board's members must be "outsiders." Many of these provisions are contained in the material that follows.

## ¶17,015  DECLARATION OF TAXPAYER RIGHTS

The first part of this discussion explains some of a taxpayer's most important rights. The second part explains the examination, appeal, collection, and refund procedures.

I. *Protection of a Taxpayer's Rights*. IRS employees will explain and protect a taxpayer's rights throughout his or her contact with the IRS.

II. *Privacy and Confidentiality.* The IRS will not disclose to anyone the information given to the IRS, except as authorized by law.

III. *Professional and Courteous Service.* If a taxpayer believes an IRS employee has not treated him or her in a professional, fair, and courteous manner, the employee's supervisor should be told. If the supervisor's response is not satisfactory, the taxpayer should write to the IRS District Director or Service Center Director.

IV. *Representation.* A taxpayer can either represent himself or herself or, with proper written authorization, have someone else as a representative. The taxpayer's representative must be a person allowed to practice before the IRS, such as an attorney, certified public accountant, or enrolled agent.

If a taxpayer is in an interview and asks to consult such a person, then the IRS must stop and reschedule the interview in most cases. Someone may accompany the taxpayer to an interview, and make recordings of any meetings with the IRS examining agent, appeal or collection personnel, provided the taxpayer tells the IRS in writing 10 days before the meeting.

V. *Payment of Only the Correct Amount of Tax.* Taxpayers are responsible for paying the correct amount of tax due under the law—no more, no less. If a responsible taxpayer cannot pay all of his or her tax when it is due, it may be possible to make monthly installment payments. Arrangements for payments are made with the IRS.

VI. *Help with Unresolved Tax Problems.* The National Taxpayer Advocate's Problem Resolution Program can help a taxpayer who has tried unsuccessfully to resolve a problem with the IRS. A local Taxpayer Advocate can offer special help for a significant hardship as a result of a tax problem. The taxpayer may call toll-free or write to the Taxpayer Advocate at the IRS office that last contacted him or her.

VII. *Appeals and Judicial Review.* If a taxpayer disagrees with the IRS about the amount of a tax liability or certain collection actions, it is the taxpayer's right to ask the Appeals Office to review the case. The taxpayer also has the right to ask a court to review the case.

VIII. *Relief from Certain Penalties and Interest.* The IRS will waive penalties when allowed by law if a taxpayer can show he or she has acted reasonably and in good faith or relied on the incorrect advice of an IRS employee. The IRS will waive interest that is the result of certain errors or delays caused by an IRS employee.

## ¶17,017 EXAMINATIONS, APPEALS, COLLECTIONS, AND REFUNDS

*Examinations (Audits).* The IRS accepts most taxpayers' returns as filed. If the IRS inquires about a return or selects it for examination, it does not suggest the taxpayer is dishonest. The inquiry or examination may or may not result in more tax. A case can be closed without change, or the taxpayer may receive a refund.

The process of selecting a return for examination usually begins in one of two ways:

1.  Computer programs are used to identify returns that may have incorrect amounts. These programs may be based on:
    a.  Information returns, such as Forms 1099 and W-2.
    b.  Studies of past examinations.
    c.  Certain issues identified by compliance projects.
2.  Information is used from outside sources that indicate that a return has incorrect amounts. These sources include:
    a.  Newspapers.
    b.  Public records.
    c.  Individuals.

If it is determined that the information is accurate and reliable, this information may be used to select a particular tax return for examination.

***Examinations by Mail.***   The IRS processes many examinations and inquiries by mail. They will send a letter to a taxpayer with either a request for more information or a reason the IRS believes a change in a return may be needed. The taxpayer can respond by mail or can request a personal interview with an examiner. If the taxpayer mails the requested information or provides an explanation, the IRS may or may not agree with the taxpayer's explanation, and will explain the reasons for any changes. The IRS urges taxpayers not to hesitate to write about anything they do not understand.

***Examination by Interview.***   If the IRS notifies a taxpayer that they will conduct an examination through a personal interview, or the taxpayer requests such an interview, the taxpayer has the right to ask that the examination take place at a reasonable time and place that is convenient for both the taxpayer and the IRS. If an examiner proposes any changes to a return, the examination will make clear the reasons for the changes. If the taxpayer does not agree with these changes, he or she can meet with the examiner's supervisor.

***Repeat Examinations.***   If the IRS examined a return for the same items in either of the two previous years and proposed no change to the taxpayer's tax liability, he or she should contact the IRS as soon as possible so that the IRS can determine if the current examination should be discontinued.

***Appeals.***   If a taxpayer does not agree with an examiner's proposed changes, he or she can appeal them to the Appeals Office of the IRS. Most

¶17,017

differences can be settled without expensive and time-consuming court trials. If the taxpayer does not want to use the Appeals Office or disagrees with its finding, the case can be taken to the U.S. Tax Court, U.S. Court of Federal Claims, or the U.S. District Court where the taxpayer lives. If a case is taken to court, the IRS will have the burden of proving certain facts. These would include whether the taxpayer:

- Kept audit records to show the tax liability.
- Cooperated fully with the IRS.
- Met certain other conditions.

If the court agrees with the taxpayer on most issues in a case, and finds that the IRS position was largely unjustified, the taxpayer may be able to recover some of the administrative and litigation costs. However, the taxpayer cannot recover these costs unless he or she tried to resolve a case administratively, including going through the appeals system, and giving the IRS the information necessary to resolve the case.

*Innocent Spouse Relief.*    Generally, both spouses are responsible, jointly and individually, for paying the full amount of any tax, interest, or penalties due on their joint return. However, one spouse may not have to pay the tax, interest, and penalties related to the other spouse or former spouse.

Tax law changes make it easier to qualify for innocent spouse relief and add two other ways to get relief through ''separation of liability'' and ''equitable relief.'' Thus, there are now three types of relief available:

1. Innocent spouse relief which applies to all joint filers.
2. Separation of liability, which applies to joint filers who are divorced, widowed, legally separated, or have not lived together for the past 12 months.
3. Equitable relief, which applies to all joint filers and married couples filing separate returns in community property states.

Innocent spouse relief and separation of liability apply only to items incorrectly reported on the return. If a spouse does not qualify for innocent spouse relief or separation of liability, the IRS may grant equitable relief.

*Refunds.*    A taxpayer can file a claim for a refund if he or she thinks too much tax was levied. The claim must generally be filed within three years from the date the original return was filed, or two years from the date the tax was paid, whichever is later. The law generally provides for interest on a refund if it is not paid within 45 days of the date the return was filed or the refund was claimed.

¶17,017

## ¶17,019  THE IRS COLLECTION PROCESS

There are steps the IRS can take to collect overdue taxes. The information in this discussion applies to all taxpayers—for individuals who owe income taxes and employers who owe employment tax. Special rules that apply only to employers are given at the end of this discussion.

By law, taxpayers have the right to be treated professionally, fairly, promptly, and courteously by IRS employees. Some of those rights are to:

- Disagree with claims on the tax bill.
- Meet with an IRS manager if the taxpayer disagrees with the IRS employee who handles the tax case.
- Appeal most IRS collection actions.
- Transfer a case to a different IRS office.
- Be represented by someone when dealing with IRS matters.
- Receive a receipt for any payment he or she makes.

***Disagreement with an IRS Decision.***  If a taxpayer disagrees with a decision of an IRS employee at any time during the collection process, the taxpayer can ask the employee's manager to review the case. The employee will then refer the taxpayer to a manager who will either speak with the taxpayer then or return a call by the next work day.

If the taxpayer disagrees with a manager's decision, the taxpayer has the right to file an appeal which enables him or her to appeal most collection actions taken by the IRS, including filing a lien, placing a levy on the taxpayer's wages or bank account, or seizing a taxpayer's property.

***Someone to Represent a Taxpayer.***  When dealing with the IRS, a taxpayer can choose to represent himself or herself, or can have an attorney, a certified public accountant, an enrolled agent, or any person enrolled to practice before the IRS as a representative.

***Problem Resolution Program.***  This program ensures that taxpayers' problems are handled promptly and properly. If repeated attempts have been made to sort out a tax problem with the IRS, but have been unsuccessful, then the taxpayer can first ask any IRS employee or manager for help. If the problem continues, the taxpayer may ask for an appointment with the Taxpayer Advocate in the local IRS office. The Taxpayer Advocate determines whether the taxpayer qualifies for the Problem Resolution Program.

***IRS Sharing Information.***  By law the IRS can share a taxpayer's information with city and state tax agencies and, in some cases, with the Department of Justice, other federal agencies, and with people the taxpayer authorizes to receive that information. Such information can also be shared with certain foreign governments under tax treaty provisions.

The IRS can contact other sources, such as neighbors, banks, employers or employees, to investigate a case. However, after January 18, 1999, the law provides that before contacting other persons, the IRS must notify the individual that, in examining or collecting tax liability, they may contact third parties. In addition, the law requires the Service to provide a list of persons who were questioned. This information is to be provided periodically and upon request.

The notification provision does not apply in the following circumstances:

- Pending criminal investigations.
- When providing notice would jeopardize collection of any tax liability.
- Where providing notice may result in reprisal against any person.
- When the taxpayer authorized the contact.

If a taxpayer is involved in a bankruptcy proceeding, the proceeding may not eliminate the tax debt, but it may temporarily stop IRS enforcement action from collecting a debt related to the bankruptcy.

*If a Taxpayer Owes Child Support.*    If a taxpayer is entitled to a federal or state tax refund while still owing unpaid taxes or child support, the IRS can apply the refund toward the debt and send the taxpayer the remaining balance, if there is any.

*When a Taxpayer Can't Pay.*    When a tax return is filed, the IRS checks to see if the mathematics is accurate and if the taxpayer has paid the correct amount. If the taxpayer has not paid all that is owed, the IRS will send a bill called a *Notice of Tax Due and Demand for Payment.* The bill will include the taxes, plus penalties and interest, and the IRS encourages a taxpayer to pay the tax bill by check or money order as quickly as possible.

If the taxpayer has received a bill for unpaid taxes, the entire amount should be paid, or the IRS should be notified why the taxpayer cannot pay. If the taxpayer does not pay the taxes owed and makes no effort to pay them, the IRS can ask the taxpayer to take action to pay by selling or mortgaging any assets, or getting a loan. If the taxpayer still makes no effort to pay the taxes owed or to work out a payment plan, the IRS can also take more serious action, such as seizing the taxpayer's bank, levying his or her wages, or taking other income or assets.

*If a Taxpayer Believes the Bill Is Wrong.*    If a taxpayer believes a bill is wrong, the IRS should be contacted as soon as possible by:

- Calling the number on the bill.
- Writing to the IRS office that sent the bill.
- Visiting the local IRS office.

¶17,019

To help IRS consideration of the problem, the taxpayer should send a copy of the bill along with copies (not originals) of any records, tax returns, and canceled checks that will help the IRS understand why the taxpayer believes the bill to be wrong. When writing to the IRS, the taxpayer should state clearly why he or she believes the bill is wrong. If the IRS finds the taxpayer is correct, the account will be adjusted, and, if necessary, the taxpayer will be sent a corrected bill.

If the total amount owed cannot be paid immediately, as much as possible should be paid. By paying that portion, the amount of interest and penalty will be reduced. The taxpayer should call, write, or visit the nearest IRS office to explain the situation. The IRS will ask for a completed form, *Collection Information Statement*, to help them consider the amount the taxpayer can pay based upon the taxpayer's monthly income and expenses. The IRS will then help to figure out a payment plan that fits the situation. The IRS will work with the taxpayer to consider several different ways to pay what is owed:

- The taxpayer may be able to make monthly payments through an installment agreement.
- The taxpayer may be able to apply for an offer in compromise.
- The taxpayer may qualify for a temporary delay, or the case may be considered a significant hardship.

***An Installment Agreement.***    Installment agreements allow the full payment of taxes in smaller, equal monthly payments. The amount of each installment payment is based on the amount of tax owed and the taxpayer's ability to pay that amount within the time available to the IRS to collect the tax debt.

Previously, the IRS did not have to agree to accept the payment of taxes in installments. However, as of July 22, 1998, they must enter into an installment agreement for the payment of income tax if the taxpayer meets all of the following conditions on the date he or she offers to enter into the agreement:

1. The total income tax owed is not more than $10,000.
2. In the last five years, the taxpayer (and spouse if the liability relates to a joint return) has:
   a. Filed all required income tax returns.
   b. Paid all taxes shown on the returns filed.
   c. Not entered into an installment agreement to pay any income tax.
3. The taxpayer shows (and the IRS agrees) that the individual cannot pay the income tax in full when due.
4. The taxpayer agrees to pay the tax in full in three years or less.
5. The taxpayer agrees to comply with the tax laws while the agreement is in effect.

¶17,019

An installment agreement is a reasonable payment option for some taxpayers, but they should be aware that an installment agreement is more costly than paying all the tax owed and may be more costly than borrowing funds to pay the full amount. Why? Because the IRS charges interest and *penalties* on the tax owed and also charges interest on the unpaid penalties and interest that have been charged to the taxpayer's account. This means that while the taxpayer is making payments on his or her tax debt through an installment agreement, the IRS continues to charge interest and penalties on the unpaid portion of that debt.

The interest rate on a bank loan or on a cash advance on a credit card may be lower than the combination of penalties and interest the IRS charges. There is also another cost associated with an installment agreement. To set up the payment program, the IRS charges a $43 user fee.

If a taxpayer owes combined tax, penalties, and interest of $25,000, the taxpayer can call the number on the tax bill to set up a plan. The IRS will inform the taxpayer what has to be done to begin immediately.

If more than $25,000 is owed, the IRS may still be able to set up an installment agreement with the taxpayer based on the completed form, *Collection Information Statement*. Even though a taxpayer agrees to an installment plan, the IRS can still file a *Notice of Federal Tax Lien* to secure the government's interest until the taxpayer makes the final payment.

However, the IRS cannot levy against the taxpayer's property:

- While a request for an installment agreement is being considered.
- While an agreement is in effect.
- For 30 days after the request for an agreement has been rejected.
- For any period while an appeal of the rejection is being evaluated by the IRS.

If an installment agreement is arranged, the taxpayer can pay with personal or business checks, money orders, certified funds, or payroll deductions the employer takes from the taxpayer's salary and regularly sends to the IRS, or by electronic transfers from the employee's bank account or other means.

An installment agreement is based on the taxpayer's financial situation. If a change in the financial situation makes it necessary to change the terms of the installment agreement, the IRS will inform the taxpayer by letter 30 days before changing the established plan. The payments on an installment agreement must be paid on time; if a payment cannot be made, the IRS should be informed immediately. The IRS can end an agreement if the taxpayer does not furnish updated financial information when the IRS requests it, or if the taxpayer fails to meet the terms of the agreement.

An agreement could end if the taxpayer misses a payment, or does not file or pay all required tax returns. In that case, the IRS can take enforced collection action. In some cases, the IRS will accept an offer in compromise. On the other hand, if taxes are not paid when they are due, the taxpayer may be subject to a failure-to-pay penalty of 5 percent of the unpaid taxes for each month they are not paid. But if a return was filed on time, the penalty will be reduced to 2.5 percent for any month beginning after 1999 in which the taxpayer has an installment agreement in effect.

*Offer in Compromise.*    In some cases, the IRS may accept an Offer in Compromise to settle an unpaid tax account, including any interest and penalties. With such an arrangement, they can accept less than the amount owed when it is doubtful that they would be able to collect all of the taxpayer's debt any time in the near future.

*Temporary Delay.*    If the IRS determines that the taxpayer cannot pay *any* of a tax debt, they may temporarily delay collection until the taxpayer's financial condition improves. If the IRS does delay collection, the debt will increase because penalties and interest are charged until the full amount is paid. During a temporary delay, the IRS will review the individual's ability to pay, and may file a *Notice of Federal Tax Lien* to protect the government's interest in the taxpayer's assets.

*A Significant Hardship.*    The IRS can consider whether a significant hardship exists for a taxpayer to pay a tax liability. It would be judged a significant hardship if the taxpayer cannot afford to maintain even the necessities to live day to day (adequate food, clothing, shelter, transportation, and medical treatment). Other cases that can be considered as significant hardship by law:

- An immediate threat of adverse action.
- Delay of more than 30 days in resolving taxpayer account problems.
- Incurring significant costs (including fees for professional representation) if relief is not granted.
- Irreparable injury to, or long-term adverse impact on, the taxpayer if relief is not granted.

A taxpayer may apply for emergency relief if facing a significant hardship. He or she should call the toll-free IRS Taxpayer Assistant number or visit the district's Taxpayer Advocate. A qualifying taxpayer will be assisted in filling out the form, *Application for Taxpayer Assistance Order.*

## ¶17,021    EMPLOYMENT TAXES FOR EMPLOYERS

To encourage prompt payment of withheld income and employment taxes, including Social Security taxes, railroad retirement taxes, or collected excise taxes, Congress passed a law that provides for the trust fund recovery penalty. (These taxes are called *trust fund taxes* because the employer actually holds the employee's money in trust until making a federal tax deposit in that amount.)

¶17,021

If the IRS plans to assess an employer for the trust fund recovery penalty, they will send a letter stating that the employer is the *responsible* person. An employer has 60 days after receiving the letter to appeal the IRS proposal. If the employer does not respond to the letter, the IRS will assess the penalty and send a *Notice and Demand for Payment*. The IRS can apply this penalty even if the employer has gone out of business.

*Responsible Person.*    A responsible person is a person or group of people having the duty to perform and the power to direct the collecting, accounting, and paying of trust fund taxes. This person may be:

- An officer or an employee of a corporation.
- A member or employee of a partnership.
- A corporate director or shareholder.
- A member of a board of trustees of a nonprofit organization.
- Another person with authority and control over funds to direct their disbursement.

*Assessing the Trust Fund Recovery Penalty.*    The IRS may assess the penalty against anyone who:

- Is responsible for collecting or paying withheld income and employment taxes, or for paying collected excise taxes.
- Willfully fails to collect or pay them.

For *willfulness* to exist, the responsible person must:

- Have known about the unpaid taxes.
- Have used the funds to keep the business going or allowed available funds to be paid to other creditors.

*Employment Taxes.*    Employment taxes include the amount the employer should *withhold* from employees for both income and Social Security tax, plus the amount of Social Security tax paid on behalf of each employee.

If the employer fails to pay employment taxes on time, or if required to but did not include payment with the return, the IRS will charge interest and penalties on any unpaid balance. They may charge penalties of up to 15 percent of the amount not deposited, depending on how many days late the payment is.

If withheld trust fund taxes are not paid, the IRS may take additional collection action. They may require the employer to:

- File and pay the employee's taxes monthly rather than quarterly, or
- Open a special bank account for the withheld amounts, under penalty of prosecution.

¶17,021

# ¶17,023    AWARD OF ADMINISTRATIVE COSTS

Rules for awarding reasonable administrative costs and certain fees incurred after January 18, 1999 include:

*Qualified Offer Rule.*    The taxpayer can receive reasonable costs and fees as a prevailing party in a civil action or proceeding when all of the following occur:

- The taxpayer makes a qualified offer to the IRS to settle the case.
- The IRS rejects that offer.
- The tax liability (not including interest) later determined by the Court is not more than the qualified offer.

The Court can consider the IRS not to be the prevailing party in a civil action or proceeding based on the fact that the IRS has lost in other courts of appeal on substantially similar issues.

*Qualified Offer.*    This is a written offer made by the taxpayer during the qualified offer period. It must specify both of the following:

- The amount of the taxpayer's liability (not including interest).
- That it is a qualified offer when made.

It must remain open until the earliest of the following dates:

- The date the offer is rejected.
- The date the trial begins.
- Ninety days from the date of the offer.

The qualified offer period is the period beginning with the date that the 30-day letter is mailed by the IRS to the taxpayer and ending on the date that is 30 days before the date the case is first set for trial.

Administrative costs can be awarded for costs incurred after the earliest of the following dates:

- The date of the notice of deficiency.
- The date the first letter of proposed deficiency is sent that allows an opportunity to request administrative review in the IRS Office of Appeals.
- The date the taxpayer receives the IRS Office of Appeals' decision.

*Attorney Fees.*    The basic rate of an award for attorney fees in 2005 was set at $150 per hour and it can be higher in certain circumstances. Those circumstances now include the difficulty level of the issues in the case and the availability of tax expertise locally. The basic rate is subject to adjustment each year.

Attorney fees now include the fees paid for the services of anyone who is authorized to practice before the Tax Court or before the IRS. In addition, attorney fees can be awarded in civil actions taken for unauthorized inspection or disclosure of the taxpayer's tax return or return information.

Fees can be awarded in excess of the actual amount charged if all of the following apply:

- The fees are charged at less than the $125 basic rate.
- The taxpayer is represented for no fee, or for a nominal fee, as a pro bono service.
- The award is paid to the taxpayer's representative or to the representative's employer.

## ¶17,025  EXPLANATION OF CLAIM FOR REFUND DISALLOWANCE

The IRS has the obligation to explain the specific reasons that a claim for refund is disallowed or partially disallowed. Claims for refund can be disallowed based on a preliminary review or on examination by a revenue agent. This means that the taxpayer must receive one of the following:

1. A form explaining that the claim is disallowed for one of the following reasons:
   a. The claim was filed late.
   b. It was based solely on the unconstitutionality of the revenue acts.
   c. It was waived as part of a settlement.
   d. It covered a tax year or issues that were part of a closing agreement or an offer in compromise.
   e. It was related to a return closed by a final court order.
2. A revenue agent's report explaining the reasons that the claim is disallowed.

## ¶17,027  TAX COURT PROCEEDINGS

*Burden of Proof.* Generally, for court proceedings resulting from examinations started after July 22, 1998, the IRS has the burden of proving any factual issue if the taxpayer has introduced credible evidence relating to the issue. However, the taxpayer must also have done all of the following:

- Complied with all substantiation requirements of the Internal Revenue Code.

- Maintained all records required by the Internal Revenue Code.
- Cooperated with all reasonable requests by the IRS for information regarding the preparation and related tax treatment of any item reported on a tax return.
- Had a net worth of $7 million or less at the time the tax liability is contested in any court proceeding if the tax return is for a corporation, partnership, or trust.

*Use of Statistical Information.*   The IRS has the burden of proof in court proceedings that are based on any reconstruction of an individual's income solely through the use of statistical information on unrelated taxpayers.

*Penalties.*   The IRS has the burden of proof in court proceedings with respect to the liability of any individual taxpayer for any penalty, addition to tax, or additional amount imposed by the tax laws.

*Refund or Credit of Overpayments Before Final Decision.*   Beginning July 22, 1998, any court with proper jurisdiction, including the Tax Court, has the authority to order the IRS to refund any part of a tax deficiency that the IRS collects from the taxpayer during a period when the IRS is not permitted to assess, levy, or engage in any court proceeding to collect that tax deficiency. In addition, the court can order a refund of any part of a tax deficiency that is not at issue in a taxpayer's appeal to the court. The court can order these refunds before its decision on the case is final. Generally, the IRS is not permitted to take action on a tax deficiency during the following periods.

1.  The 90-day (or 150-day if outside of the United States) period that the taxpayer has to petition a notice of deficiency to the Tax Court.
2.  The period that the case is under appeal.

Under prior law, no authority existed for ordering the IRS to refund any amount collected during an Impermissible period, or to refund any amount that was not at issue in an appeal, before the final decision of the Tax Court.

*Small Case Procedures.*   For proceedings beginning after July 22, 1998, small tax case procedures are available for disputes that involve $50,000 or less. Under prior law, small tax case procedures were limited to disputes involving $10,000 or less. Small tax case procedures can be used, at the taxpayer's request and with the Tax Court's concurrence, for income, estate, gift, certain employment, and certain excise taxes. The proceedings are conducted as informally as possible. Neither briefs nor oral arguments are required. Most taxpayers represent themselves, although they may be represented by anyone admitted to practice before the Tax Court.

¶17,027

# PART IV

---

## NICHE ACCOUNTING

# Chapter 18

## Practice Before the IRS and the Power of Attorney

### CONTENTS

# ¶18,000   OVERVIEW

Regulations relating to practice before the Internal Revenue Service were adopted after considering the need to take into account legal developments, professional integrity, and fairness to practitioners, taxpayer service, and sound tax administration.

Ensuring that tax professionals adhere to professional standards and follow the law is one of the top four enforcement goals for the Service. The Treasury Department and the IRS believe that a proposed revision of Circular 230, rules that govern practice before the agency, issued in February 2006, plays a critical part in achieving that goal.

# ¶18,001   PROPOSED AMENDMENTS TO CIRCULAR 230

These amendments to the provisions of Circular 230 relate to various non-shelter items and go back several years. In December 2002, the Treasury Department and the IRS issued an advance notice of proposed rulemaking . (2002 ANPRM) requesting comments on a similar list of amendments to the regulations relating to the Office of Professional Responsibility: unenrolled practice, eligibility for enrollment, sanctions and disciplinary proceedings, contingent fees and confidentiality agreements. These proposed revisions are the result of a thorough review of the extensive public comments received in response to the 2002 ANPRM and reflecting amendments to section 330 of title 31 made by the American Jobs Creation Act of 2004.(It is important to remember that until final rulings are issued, the requirements remain the same.)

The revisions to Circular 230 are designed to modify:

1. The definition of practice.
2. Eligibility for enrollment.
3. Unenrolled practice.
4. The rules concerning:
   a. Affidavits and other papers.
   b. Appeals.
   c. Conflicts of interest.
   d. Contingent fees.
   e. Expedited suspension.
   f. Hearings and discovery.
   g. Incompetence and Disreputable Conduct.
   h. Publicity of disciplinary actions.
   i. Standards with respect to tax returns and documents.
   j. Sanctions.

k. Supplemental Charges.

l. Other rules.

In December 2004, in a business arena strongly influenced by repercussions from Enron, Arthur Anderson, and widely publicized abusive tax shelters, the Internal Revenue Service issued final regulations relating to Circular 230. These rules cover accountants, attorneys, enrolled agents and enrolled actuaries.

The proposed regulations also include conforming amendments to reflect the final regulations relating to best practices, covered opinions and other written advice published as TD 9165 on December 20, 2004 and as TD 9201 on May 19, 2005. However, they do not address the standards for written tax advice that were the subject of final amendments to these measures.

## ¶18,001 EXPANDING THE CONFIDENTIALITY PRIVILEGE

The confidentiality protection for communications between a taxpayer and attorney has been expanded to communications involving tax advice between a taxpayer and any *federally authorized tax practitioners*. These tax practitioners include attorneys, certified public accountants, enrolled agents, enrolled actuaries, and certain other individuals allowed to practice before the Internal Revenue Service. This provision became effective for communications occurring after July 21, 1998.

This protection applies only to the advice given to the taxpayer by any of these individuals. Tax advice is considered to be advice in regard to a matter that is within the scope of the practitioner's authority to practice. The confidentiality protection is applied to communications that would be privileged if between the taxpayer and an attorney, and that relate to noncriminal tax matters or to tax proceedings brought in federal court by or against the United States.

This protection of tax advice communications does not apply to certain written communications between a federally authorized tax practitioner and a director, shareholder, officer, employee, agent, or representative of a corporation. It does not apply if the communication involves the promotion of the direct or indirect participation of the corporation in any tax shelter.

## ¶18,003 OVERVIEW OF BASIC REGULATIONS GOVERNING PRACTICE BEFORE THE IRS

The basic regulations became effective July 26, 2002. They modify the general standards of practice affecting those individuals who are eligible to practice before the Internal Revenue Service. The rules require that:

- An enrolled agent maintain records and educational materials regarding his or her satisfaction of the qualifying continuing professional education credit.

- Sponsors of qualifying continuing professional education programs maintain records and educational material concerning these programs and those who attended them. (The collection of this material helps to ensure that individuals enrolled to practice before the IRS are informed of the newest developments in federal tax practice.)
- A practitioner obtain and retain for a reasonable period written consents to representation whenever such representation conflicts with the interests of the practitioner or the interests of another client of the practitioner. The consents are to be obtained after full disclosure of the conflict is provided to each party.
- A practitioner retain for a reasonable period any communication and the list of persons to whom that communication was provided with respect to public dissemination of fee information. (The collection of consents to representation and communications concerning practitioner fees protects the practitioner against claims of impropriety and ensures the integrity of the tax administration system.)
- An agency not conduct or sponsor, and a person not respond to, a collection of information unless it displays a valid control number.
- Books or records relating to a collection of information be retained as long as their contents might become material in the administration of any internal revenue law. Generally, tax returns and tax return information are confidential, as required by 26 U.S.C. 6103.

## ¶18,005   PRACTICING BEFORE THE IRS

A person is practicing before the IRS if he or she:

1. Communicates with the IRS for a taxpayer regarding taxpayer's rights, privileges, or liabilities under laws and regulations administered by the IRS.
2. Represents a taxpayer at conferences, hearings, or meetings with the IRS.
3. Prepares and files necessary documents with the IRS for a taxpayer.

Just preparing a tax return, furnishing information at the request of the IRS, or appearing as a witness for a taxpayer, does not constitute practicing before the IRS.

## ¶18,007   BECOMING A RECOGNIZED REPRESENTATIVE

Any of the following individuals can practice before the IRS. However, any individual who is recognized to practice—a recognized representative—must file a written declaration with the IRS that he or she is qualified and authorized to represent a taxpayer.

Those individuals include:

1. Any attorney who is not currently under suspension or disbarment from practice before the IRS and who is a member in good standing of the bar at the highest court of any state, possession, territory, commonwealth, or in the District of Columbia.

2. Any Certified Public Accountant who is not currently under suspension or disbarment from practice before the IRS and who is qualified to practice as a CPA in any state, possession, territory, commonwealth, or in the District of Columbia.

3. Any enrolled agent.

4. Any individual who is enrolled as an actuary by the Joint Board for the Enrollment of Actuaries. The practice of enrolled actuaries is limited to certain Internal Revenue Code sections that relate to their area of expertise, principally those sections governing employee retirement plans.

5. Any individual other than an attorney, CPA, enrolled agent, or enrolled actuary who prepares a return and signs it as the return preparer is an unenrolled return preparer. Also, any individual who prepares a return and is not required to sign it as the preparer is considered to be an unenrolled preparer.

   These individuals are limited in their practice. They can represent a taxpayer concerning the tax liability only for the year or period covered by the return that he or she prepared. Also, an unenrolled return preparer is permitted to represent taxpayers only before the Examination Division of the IRS and is not permitted to represent taxpayers before the Appeals, Collection, or any other division of the IRS.

   Unenrolled return preparers cannot perform the following activities for another taxpayer:

   a. Sign claims for a refund.

   b. Receive refund checks.

   c. Sign consents to extend the statutory period for assessment for or collection of tax.

   d. Sign closing agreements regarding a tax liability.

   e. Sign waivers of restriction on assessment or collection of a tax deficiency.

6. Because of their special relationship with a taxpayer, the following unenrolled individuals can represent the specified taxpayers before the IRS, provided they present satisfactory identification and proof of authority to represent.

   a. An individual can represent himself or herself before the IRS and does not have to file a written declaration of qualification and authority.

¶18,007

b. An individual family member can represent members of his or her immediate family. Family members include a spouse, child, parent, brother, or sister of the individual.

c. A *bona fide* officer of a corporation (including parents subsidiaries, or affiliated corporation), association, organized group, or, in the course of his or her other official duties, an officer of a governmental unit, agency, or authority can represent the organization of which he or she is an officer.

d. A trustee, receiver, guardian, personal representative, or executor can represent a trust or estate.

e. A regular full-time employee can represent his or her employer. An employer can be, but is not limited to, an individual, partnership, corporation (including parents, subsidiaries, or affiliated corporations), association, trust, receivership, guardianship, estate, organized group, governmental unit, agency, or authority.

An unenrolled individual can represent any individual or entity before IRS personnel who are outside the United States.

## .01   Denial of Right to Limited Practice

The IRS Director of Practice, after giving notice and an opportunity for a conference, can deny eligibility for limited practice before the IRS to any unenrolled preparer or other unenrolled individual who has engaged in disreputable conduct. This conduct includes, but is not limited to, the list of items under Disreputable Conduct.

## .03   Authorization for Special Appearance

An individual can be authorized to practice before the IRS or represent another person in a particular matter. The prospective representative must request this authorization in writing from the Director of Practice. It is granted only when extremely compelling circumstances exist. If granted, the IRS will issue a letter that details the conditions related to the appearance and the particular tax matter for which the authorization is granted.

The authorization letter should not be confused with a letter from an IRS service center advising an individual that he or she has been assigned a *Centralized Authorization File* number which identifies an assigned representative. The issuance of a number does not indicate that a person is either recognized or authorized to practice before the IRS. It merely confirms that a centralized file for authorizations has been established for the representative under that number.

¶18,007.01

## .05  Who Cannot Practice

Individuals cannot practice before the IRS either because they are not eligible to practice, or because they have lost the privilege as a result of certain actions. The following individuals generally cannot practice before the IRS:

1. Individuals convicted of any criminal offense under the revenue laws of the U.S.
2. Individuals convicted of any offense involving dishonesty or breach of trust.
3. Individuals under disbarment or suspension from practicing as attorneys, CPAs, public accountants, or actuaries in any state, possession, territory, commonwealth, or in the District of Columbia, or before any federal court, or any body or board of any federal agency.
4. Individuals who are disbarred or suspended from practice before the IRS because they refuse or have refused to comply with the regulations governing practice before the IRS.

## ¶18,009  METHODS OF ENROLLMENT

The Director of Practice can grant an enrollment to practice before the IRS to an applicant who has demonstrated special competence in tax matters by passing a written examination. Enrollment also can be granted to an applicant who qualifies because of past service and technical experience in the IRS. In either case certain application forms must be filed. An applicant must never have engaged in any conduct that would justify suspension or disbarment by the IRS.

An *enrollment card* will be issued to each individual whose application is approved. The individual is enrolled until the expiration date shown on the enrollment card. To continue practicing beyond the expiration date, the individual must request renewal of the enrollment.

## .01  New Provisions for the Special Enrollment Examination

Thomson Prometric, a global testing firm was selected in 2006 by the IRS to develop and administer a computer-based version of the Special Enrollment Examination (SEE).

In general, passing the Special Enrollment Examination enables an individual to become an enrolled agent through demonstrating special competence in tax matters. An Enrolled Agent is a person who has earned the privilege of practicing before the IRS. Enrolled agents, like attorneys and certified public accountants (CPAs), can represent taxpayers in both examinations and collection matters. Those who pass the SEE also undergo an additional background check before enrollment. There are currently about 42,000 active Enrolled Agents.

The revised exam consists of three parts:

- Part 1 – Individuals
- Part 2 – Businesses
- Part 3 – Representation, Practice and Procedures

Each part of the exam will have about 100 questions, but candidates will not be required to take all parts in one sitting. Candidates will take the examination at a computer terminal at approximately 300 testing centers operated by Thomson Prometric. Previously, the IRS offered testing at about 90 locations.

## .03   Transition Rules

Under previous rules, subject to certain restrictions, some candidates who did not pass all four parts of the old IRS Special Enrollment Examination could carry over scores for the sections they passed. For the new format of the exam, the following transition rules will be in effect. Subject to the conditions noted below, candidates who were eligible to carry over passing scores under the IRS four part format will not be required to take the corresponding part of the Thomson Prometric three-part examination.

| Thomson Prometic | Corresponding IRS SEE Parts |
|---|---|
| Part 1 - Individuals | Part 1 - Individuals |
| Part 2 - Businesses | Part 2 - Sole Proprietorships and Partnerships AND Part 3 Corporations, Fiduciaries, Estate and Gift Tax and Trusts |
| Part 3 - Representation, Practice and Procedure | Part 4 -Ethics, Recordkeeping Procedures, Appeal Procedures, etc. |

Candidates who passed only part two or only part three under the old format must retake part two under the new exam format.

The above transition carryover rules are subject to the following restrictions:

- In order to carryover scores from the IRS format to the Thomson Prometric format, candidates must meet prior minimum retention rules for carryover; specifically the candidates must have been notified by the IRS that they could carryover scores for the parts passed.

¶18,009.03

- Candidates applying carryover scores from the IRS format to the Thomson Prometric format may only do so through December 31, 2007. Consequently, individuals who passed part(s) of the 2003, 2004 or 2005 exams (and met prior minimum retention rules for carryover) would have until December 31, 2007 to pass the remaining part(s) of the exam.
- Candidates who passed parts of the 2002 exam or earlier exams may not carryover their scores. They have used up all remaining attempts to pass the exam under the former rules.

The application form to take the Special Enrollment Examination, as well as information about the examination can be found on the Thomson Prometrics website at prometric.com/irs.

## .05   Fees for the Examination, Enrollment, and Renewal

Candidates sitting for the Special Enrollment Examination in 2007 will pay $97 for each part of the examination that they take. This cost includes an $86 examination fee to Thomson Prometric and the $11 user fee relating to the cost of oversight of the examination process. In addition, the fee for renewal and enrollment has increased to $125. Enrolled agents applying for renewal during the November 1, 2006 - January 31, 2007 renewal period will pay this renewal fee.The fee for candidates applying for enrollment has also increased to $125.

## .07   Renewal of Enrollment

These revisions set forth the conditions and process for renewal of enrollment to practice before the Internal Revenue Service. One condition for renewal of enrollment is that the enrolled agent complete a minimum number of hours of continuing professional education (CPE) in programs comprising current subject matter in federal taxation or federal-tax-related matters. It incorporates a system of rolling renewals for enrollment. The year in which enrolled agents will be required to apply for renewal of enrollment will vary based on the last digit of the enrolled agent's social security number. This change is made in order to balance the workflow involved in processing renewals. (The schedule for renewal and details of the CPE requirements are detailed later in this Chapter.)

The final regulations clarify that enrollment and the renewal of enrollment of *actuaries* is also governed by the regulations of the Joint Board for the Enrollment of Actuaries.

## .09   Unenrolled Practice

The final regulations preserve the scope of unenrolled practice as it has existed and make only nonsubstantive changes in nomenclature that are necessitated by the organizational restructuring of the Internal Revenue Service.

¶18,009.09

## .11 Expansion of Issues Authorized for the Enrolled Actuary

The regulations also expanded the list of issues with respect to which an *enrolled actuary* is authorized to represent a taxpayer in limited practice before the Internal Revenue Service. The list is expanded to include issues involving:

- Treatment of funded welfare benefits.
- Transfers of excess pension assets to retiree health accounts.
- Tax on nondeductible contributions to qualified employer plans.
- Taxes with respect to funded welfare benefit plans.
- Tax on reversion of qualified plan assets to employer.

## ¶18,011 RULES OF PRACTICE

An attorney, CPA, enrolled agent, or enrolled actuary authorized to practice before the IRS who is referred to as a practitioner has the duty to perform certain acts and is restricted from performing other acts. Any practitioner who does not comply with the rules of practice or engages in disreputable conduct is subject to disciplinary action. Also, unenrolled preparers must comply with most of these rules of practice and conduct to exercise the privilege of limited practice before the IRS.

Practitioners must promptly submit records or information requested by officers or employees of the IRS. When the IRS requests information concerning possible violations of the regulations by other parties, the practitioner must provide it and be prepared to testify in disbarment or suspension proceedings. A practitioner can be exempt from these rules if he or she believes in good faith and on reasonable grounds that the information requested is privileged or that the request is of doubtful legality.

A practitioner who knows that his or her client has not complied with the revenue laws, or has made an error in or omission from any return, document, affidavit, or other required paper has the responsibility to advise the client promptly of the noncompliance error or omission.

### .01 Required Due Diligence

A practitioner must exercise due diligence when performing the following duties:

1. Preparing or assisting in the preparation, approving, and filing of returns, documents, affidavits, and other papers relating to IRS matters.

2. Determining the correctness of oral or written representations made by him or her to the Department of the Treasury.

3. Determining the correctness of oral or written presentations made by him or her to clients with reference to any matter administered by the IRS.

## .03  Restrictions

Practitioners are restricted from engaging in certain practices:

1. A practitioner must not unreasonably delay the prompt disposition of any matter before the IRS.

2. A practitioner must not knowingly, directly or indirectly, employ or accept assistance from any person who is under disbarment or suspension from practice before the IRS.

3. He or she must not accept employment as an associate, correspondent, or subagent from, or share fees with, any person under disbarment or suspension by the IRS.

4. He or she must not accept assistance from any former government employee where provisions of these regulations or any federal law would be violated.

5. If a practitioner is a notary public and is employed as counsel, attorney, or agent in a matter before the IRS, or has a material interest in the matter, he or she must not engage in any notary activities relative to that matter.

6. A partner of an officer or employee of the executive branch of the U.S. Government, or of an independent agency of the U.S. or of the District of Columbia, cannot represent anyone in a matter before the IRS in which the officer or employee has or had a personal or substantial interest as a government employee. There are similar and additional restrictions on former government employees.

## .05  Disreputable Conduct

Disreputable conduct by a practitioner includes such things as:

1. Committing any criminal offense under the revenue laws, or committing any offense involving dishonesty or breach of trust.

2. Knowingly giving or participating in the giving of false or misleading information in connection with federal tax matters.

3. Willful failure to file a tax return, evading or attempting to evade any federal tax or payment, or participating in such actions.

4. Misappropriating, or failing properly and promptly remit funds received from clients for payment of taxes.

¶18,011.05

5. Directly or indirectly attempting to influence the official action of IRS employees by the use of threats, false accusations, duress, or coercion, or by offering gifts, favors, or any special inducements.

6. Being disbarred or suspended by the District of Columbia or by any state, possession, territory, commonwealth, or any federal court, or any body or board of any federal agency.

7. Knowingly aiding and abetting another person to practice before the IRS during a period of suspension, disbarment, or ineligibility, or maintaining a partnership so that a suspended or disbarred person can continue to practice before the IRS.

8. Contemptuous conduct in connection with practice before the IRS, including the use of abusive language, making false accusations and statements, or circulating or publishing malicious or libelous matter.

9. Giving a false opinion knowingly, or recklessly, or through gross incompetence, or following a pattern of providing incompetent opinions in questions arising under the federal tax laws.

10. Soliciting employment by prohibited means.

## ¶18,013 INFORMATION TO BE FURNISHED

This ruling requires a practitioner to respond promptly to a proper and lawful request for records and information, unless the practitioner believes in good faith and on reasonable grounds that the records or information are privileged. The right and ability of practitioners to resist efforts that the practitioner believes to be of doubtful legality is preserved.

The final regulations adopt, with amendment and clarification, the requirement that a practitioner provide information regarding the identity of persons the practitioner reasonably believes may have possession or control of requested documents. The requirement applies only when requested records or information are not in the possession or control of the practitioner or the practitioner's client. The practitioner's duty is limited only to making reasonable inquiry of the practitioner's client and there exists no obligation on the practitioner to make inquiry of any other person or to independently verify information provided by a client.

## ¶18,015 KNOWLEDGE OF CLIENT'S OMISSION

IRS Circular 230 has historically required a practitioner to advise a client promptly of any noncompliance, error, or omission. These final regulations modify this preexisting duty by simply requiring that, in addition to notifying the client of the fact of the noncompliance, error, or omission, the practitioner advise the client of the consequences as provided under the Code and regulations of the noncompliance, error, or omission. This change requires practitioners to provide information that taxpayers who consult tax professionals typically *expect to receive*.

### .01   Diligence as to Accuracy

The final regulations adopt the proposed clarification that a practitioner is presumed to have exercised due diligence if the practitioner relies on the work product of another person and the practitioner uses reasonable care in engaging, supervising, training, and evaluating such person, taking proper account of the relationship between the practitioner and the person. It is expected that practitioners will use common sense and experience in guiding their conduct under this section. The section applies both in the *context of a firm* and in circumstances involving a practitioner's engagement of an *outside practitioner*.

For example, in circumstances in which a practitioner must hire another practitioner for a specialized or complicated matter, the practitioner's duty under the section will be more focused on the reasonable care taken in the engagement of the specialist. Supervising and training are not part of a practitioner's engagement of a specialist. Conversely, in the context of a firm, the section's application will focus more on supervising and training, if there is an issue with regard to a supervisory practitioner's reliance on a subordinate.

## ¶18,017   CONTINGENT FEES

The final regulations adopt clarification governing the prohibition on contingent fees in connection with advice rendered in connection with a position taken or to be taken on an original tax return. The Department of the Treasury and the Internal Revenue Service *remain concerned* regarding the use of contingent fees and intend to give the matter further consideration.

## ¶18,019   RETURN OF CLIENT'S RECORDS

The final regulations adopt, with substantial changes, a proposed requirement that a practitioner return a client's records upon the client's request, regardless of a fee dispute. This section is restricted to the extent that the client's records that are necessary for the client to comply with his or her federal tax obligations. Further, the term "records of the client" is defined to exclude such items as returns or other documents prepared by the practitioner that the practitioner is withholding pending the client's payment of fees for those documents. These changes are incorporated to protect practitioners from being disadvantaged or compromised by clients seeking to obtain an unfair advantage under this section.

In consideration of various state laws that may permit liens on a client's records in favor of practitioners during the course of fee disputes, the regulations provide that a practitioner must return only those records that must be attached to the client's return if a fee dispute has triggered an applicable state lien provision. The practitioner, however, must provide the client access to review and copy any of the records retained by the practitioner under law that are necessary for the client to comply with federal tax obligations.

## ¶18,021 CONFLICTING INTERESTS

A client must give informed consent, confirmed in writing, to representation by a practitioner when the representation of one client will be directly adverse to another client or there is a significant risk that the representation of one or more clients will be materially limited by the practitioner's responsibilities to another client, a former client, or a third person or by a personal interest of the practitioner. The adoption of this requirement results in parallel application to conflicts with another client and conflicts with the practitioner's own interest. The section requires a practitioner to retain the written consent for at least 36 months after the conclusion of the representation and to provide the written consents to the IRS, if requested to do so.

## ¶18,023 SOLICITATION

Under the final regulations, a practitioner is prohibited from making written and oral solicitations of employment in matters related to the IRS if such solicitations would violate federal or state statutes or other rules applicable to the practitioner regarding the uninvited solicitation of prospective clients.

For example, if an attorney is prohibited under that attorney's governing state bar's rules from making a certain type of uninvited solicitation, the attorney's uninvited solicitation with respect to a matter related to the IRS will constitute a violation of rules. Conversely, if such a solicitation is permissible under the relevant state bar rule, the making of the solicitation with respect to a matter related to the IRS is permissible.

This rule also expands the prohibition of deceptive and other improper solicitation practices to cover private, as well as public, solicitations. It provides that a practitioner may not, in matters related to the IRS, assist, or accept assistance from, any person or entity that, to the knowledge of the practitioner, obtains clients or otherwise practices in a manner forbidden under this section.

## ¶18,025  SANCTIONS

The final regulations adopt the additional sanction of *censure*, which is defined as a public reprimand. The sanction of censure has not been used previously. The final regulations are modified to clarify that suspended representatives may be subject to conditions and the conditions placed upon suspended or censured practitioners may only be imposed for a period that is reasonable in light of the gravity of a practitioner's violations.

## .01  Disciplinary Proceedings

The regulations have been modified to specifically provide that the standard of proof in Circular 230 proceedings is that of a *preponderance of the evidence*, if the sanction sought by the Director of Practice is censure or a suspension of less than six months' duration. If the Director of Practice seeks a sanction of disbarment or a suspension of six months or longer or the disqualification of an appraiser, the standard of proof is *clear and convincing evidence*. The Treasury Department and IRS conclude that the preponderance of evidence standard is justified in the case of the less severe sanctions of censure and suspension of a short duration.

When the Director of Practice seeks a more significant sanction, the clear and convincing evidence standard is adopted to protect the interests of the practitioner.

## ¶18,027  REQUIREMENTS FOR ENROLLMENT RENEWAL

As noted above, these regulations became effective on July 26, 2002. To maintain active enrollment to practice before the Internal Revenue Service, each individual enrolled is required to have his or her enrollment renewed. Failure by an individual to receive notification from the Director of Practice of the renewal requirement *will not* be justification for the failure to satisfy this requirement. It should be noted that the cycle will continue and applications for renewal will be required between November 1 and January 31 of every subsequent third year as specified below.

The timing for the new renewal schedule is provided below:

- All individuals licensed to practice before the IRS who have a social security number or tax identification number that ends with the numbers 0, 1, 2, or 3, except for those individuals who received their initial enrollment after November 1, 2003, must apply for renewal between November 1, 2003, and January 31, 2004. The renewal will be effective April 1, 2004.
- All individuals licensed to practice before the IRS who have a social security number or tax identification number that ends with the numbers

4, 5, or 6, except for those who received their initial enrollment after November 1, 2004, must apply for renewal between November 1, 2004, and January 31, 2005. The renewal will be effective April 1, 2005.

- All individuals licensed to practice before the IRS who have a social security number or tax identification number that ends with the numbers 7, 8, or 9, except for those individuals who received their initial enrollment after November 1, 2005, must apply for renewal between November 1, 2005, and January 31, 2006. The renewal will be effective April 1, 2006.

- Thereafter, applications for renewal will be required between November 1 and January 31 of every subsequent third year as specified above. Those individuals who receive initial enrollment after November 1 and before April 2 of the applicable renewal period will not be required to renew their enrollment before the first full renewal period following the receipt of their initial enrollment.

- The Director of Practice will notify the individual of his or her renewal of enrollment and will issue the individual a card evidencing enrollment.

- The final regulations establish a separate $125 user fee for processing the renewal of enrollment.

- Forms required for renewal may be obtained from the Director of Practice, Internal Revenue Service, 1111 Constitution Avenue, NW, Washington, DC 20224.

## .01 Condition for Renewal: Continuing Professional Education

To qualify for renewal of enrollment, an individual enrolled to practice before the Internal Revenue Service must certify, on the application for renewal form that he or she has satisfied the following continuing professional education requirements:

1. For renewed enrollment effective after March 31, 2004, a minimum of 16 hours of continuing education credit must be completed during each calendar year in the enrollment term.

2. For renewed enrollment effective after April 1, 2007:

   a. A minimum of 72 hours of continuing education credit must be completed during each three-year period as described below. (Each three-year period is known as an enrollment cycle.)

   b. A minimum of 16 hours of continuing education credit, including 2 hours of ethics or professional conduct, must be completed in each year of an enrollment cycle.

   c. An individual who receives initial enrollment during an enrollment cycle must complete 2 hours of qualifying continuing education credit for each month enrolled during the enrollment cycle. Enrollment for any part of a month is considered enrollment for the entire month.

## .03 Qualifying Continuing Education

In general, to qualify for continuing education credit, a course of learning must be a qualifying program designed to enhance professional knowledge in federal taxation or federal-tax-related matters (i.e., programs comprising current subject matter in federal taxation or federal-tax-related matters, including accounting, tax preparation software, and taxation or ethics) or must be conducted by a qualifying sponsor.

A formal program qualifies as continuing education programs if it:

- Requires attendance that must be validated by the program sponsor providing each attendee with a certificate of attendance.
- Requires that the program be conducted by a qualified instructor, discussion leader, or speaker (i.e., a person whose background, training, education, and experience is appropriate for instructing or leading a discussion on the subject matter of the particular program).
- Provides or requires a written outline, textbook, or suitable electronic educational materials.

Correspondence or individual study programs (including taped programs) qualify for CPE credit if they are conducted by qualifying sponsors and completed on an individual basis by the enrolled individual. The allowable credit hours for such programs will be measured on a basis comparable to the measurement of a seminar or course for credit in an accredited educational institution. Such programs qualify as continuing education programs if they:

- Require registration of the participants by the sponsor.
- Provide a means for measuring completion by the participants (e.g., a written examination), including the issuance of a certificate of completion by the sponsor.
- Provide a written outline, textbook, or suitable electronic educational materials.

An instructor, discussion leader, or speaker receives one hour of CPE credit for each contact hour completed as an instructor, discussion leader, or speaker at an educational program that meets the continuing education requirements of this section. Two hours of CPE credit are awarded for actual subject preparation time for each contact hour completed as an instructor, discussion leader, or speaker at such programs; it is the responsibility of the individual claiming such credit to maintain records to verify preparation time. The maximum credit for instruction and preparation, however, may not exceed 50 percent of the continuing education requirement for an enrollment cycle. An instructor, discussion leader, or speaker who makes more than one presentation on the same subject matter during an enrollment cycle, will receive continuing education credit for only one such presentation for the enrollment cycle.

Credit for published articles and books will be awarded for publications on federal taxation or federal-tax-related matters, including accounting, financial management, tax preparation software, and taxation, provided the content of such publications is current and designed for the enhancement of the professional knowledge of an individual enrolled to practice before the Internal Revenue Service.

The credit allowed will be on the basis of one-hour credit for each hour of preparation time for the material. It is the responsibility of the person claiming the credit to maintain records to verify preparation time. The maximum credit for publications may not exceed 25 percent of the continuing education requirement of any enrollment cycle.

Individuals may establish eligibility for renewal of enrollment for any enrollment cycle by achieving a passing score on each part of the Special Enrollment Examination administered during the three-year period prior to renewal or by completing a minimum of 16 hours of qualifying continuing education during the last year of an enrollment cycle. (Courses designed to help an applicant prepare for the examination are considered basic in nature and are not qualifying continuing education.)

## ¶18,029   RENEWAL OF ENROLLMENT FOR ACTUARIES

An individual who is enrolled as an actuary by the Joint Board for the Enrollment of Actuaries may practice before the IRS. The practice of enrolled actuaries is limited to certain Internal Revenue Code sections that relate to their area of expertise, principally those sections governing employee retirement plans.

An Enrolled Actuary's enrollment to practice is renewable every three years. To qualify for renewal of enrollment an Enrolled Actuary must certify that he/she has satisfied the continuing professional education (CPE) requirements specified in the Joint Board Regulations. In addition, an Enrolled Actuary must submit a completed Form 5434-A (Joint Board for the Enrollment of Actuaries Application for Renewal of Enrollment) and a filing fee of $25.00.

### .01   Current Enrollment Cycle Information

The current enrollment cycle ends March 31, 2008. The next enrollment cycle begins April 1, 2008. To renew enrollment an enrolled actuary must complete a minimum of 36 hours of continuing professional education (CPE) credits during the period January 1,2005 to December 31, 2007. Of the 36 hours at least 18 must be comprised of core subject matter; the remainder may be of a non-core nature. CPE courses must be taken from a qualifying sponsor as described in the Joint Board Regulations.

Form 5434-A (Joint Board for the Enrollment of Actuaries Application for Renewal of Enrollment) will be mailed in October 2007. However, it is each Enrolled Actuary's responsibility to make sure that he/she has timely renewed and completed the appropriate number of CPE credits.

## ¶18,030  THE POWER OF ATTORNEY

A power of attorney is a taxpayer's written authorization for an individual to act for him or her in tax matters. If the authorization is not limited, the individual can generally perform all acts that a taxpayer can perform. The authority granted to an unenrolled preparer cannot exceed that shown under the special rules of limited practice.

Any representative, other than an unenrolled preparer, can usually perform the following acts:

1. Represent the taxpayer before any office of the IRS.
2. Record the interview.
3. Sign an offer or a waiver of restriction on assessment or collection of a tax deficiency, or a waiver of notice of disallowance of claim for credit or refunds.
4. Sign a consent to extend the statutory time period for assessment or collection of a tax.
5. Sign a closing agreement.
6. Receive, but not endorse or cash, a refund check drawn on the U.S. Treasury. The taxpayer must specifically sign a form showing the name of the individual designated to receive the refund check.

The representative named under a power of attorney is not permitted to sign the taxpayer's income tax return unless the signature is permitted under the Internal Revenue Code and the related regulations of the Tax Regulations. The taxpayer can authorize this in the taxpayer's power of attorney.

The regulation permits a representative to sign a client's income tax return if the client is unable to make the return for any of the following reasons:

1. Disease or injury.
2. Continuous absence from the United States for a period of at least 60 days prior to the date required by law for filing the return.

3. Other good cause if specific permission is requested of and granted by the IRS.

If a taxpayer wants a representative to receive a refund check, the taxpayer must specifically so authorize it in the power of attorney. However, if the representative is an income tax return preparer, the representative cannot be authorized to endorse or otherwise cash the client's check related to income taxes.

The appointed representative can substitute a representative or delegate authority to a new representative only if this is specifically authorized under the power of attorney. A power of attorney is generally terminated if the client becomes incapacitated or incompetent. The power of attorney can continue, however, in the case of the taxpayer's incapacity or incompetency if the taxpayer had previously authorized that it be continued.

## .01   When a Power of Attorney Is Required

A taxpayer should submit a power of attorney when he or she wants to authorize an individual to represent him or her before the IRS, whether or not the representative performs any of the other acts discussed earlier. A power of attorney is most often required when a taxpayer wants to authorize another individual to perform at least one of the following acts on his or her behalf:

1. Represent the taxpayer at a conference with the IRS.
2. Prepare and file a written response to the IRS.

A taxpayer can appoint an unenrolled return preparer as his or her representative. The preparer can represent the taxpayer only before revenue agents and examining officers. Also, the preparer can represent a taxpayer concerning his or her tax liability only for the period covered by a return prepared by the preparer.

The IRS will accept a non-IRS power of attorney, but a transmittal form must be attached in order for the power of attorney to be entered into the *Centralized Authorization File*. If a power of attorney document other than the required transmittal form is used, it must contain the following information:

1. The taxpayer's name and mailing address, Social Security number, and/or employer identification number.
2. An employee plan number, if applicable.
3. The name and mailing address of the taxpayer's representative.
4. The types of tax involved.
5. The federal tax form number.

6. The specific years or periods involved.
7. For estate tax matters, the decedent's date of death.
8. A clear expression of the taxpayer's intention concerning the scope of authority granted to his or her representative.
9. The taxpayer's signature and date.

The taxpayer must also attach to the non-IRS power of attorney a signed and dated statement made by the taxpayer's representative. This statement, which is referred to as the *Declaration of Representative* is included with the transmittal form filed.

## .03    Filing a Power of Attorney

The power of attorney is filed with each IRS office with which the taxpayer deals. If the power of attorney is filed for a matter currently pending before an office of the IRS, it should be filed with that office. Otherwise, the power should be filed with the service center where the related return was, or will be, filed.

## .05    Third-Party Designee

The authority given to a designee was expanded in 2004 and is now revocable. Designees are now able to exchange information with the IRS. They may also request and receive written tax information relating to the tax return, including copies of notices, correspondence, and account transcripts. The designee may be any individual (including a spouse), corporation, firm, organization, or partnership. To name a designee, the taxpayer should check the Yes box in the Third-Party Designee area of the return. This new provision results in change regarding when a power of attorney is not required as indicated below.

## .07    When a Power of Attorney Is Not Required

A power of attorney is not required in some situations when dealing with the IRS, such as when:

- Providing information to the IRS.
- Authorizing the disclosure of tax return information through Form 21.
- Allowing the IRS to discuss return information with a third-party designee.
- Allowing a tax matters partner or person (TMP) to perform acts for the partnership.

¶18,030.07

- Allowing the IRS to discuss return information with a fiduciary.
- Representing a taxpayer through a nonwritten consent.

## .09   The Tax Matters Partner or Person (TMP)

A TMP is authorized by law to perform various acts on behalf of a partnership or Subchapter S corporation. This includes the power to delegate authority to represent the TMP and to sign documents in that capacity, but certain acts performed by the TMP cannot be delegated.

## .11   The Fiduciary

A fiduciary, trustee, executor, administrator, receiver, or guardian, stands in the position of the taxpayer and acts as the taxpayer. Therefore, a fiduciary does not act as a representative and should not file a power of attorney. A fiduciary should file Form 56, *Notice Concerning Fiduciary Relationship*, to notify the IRS of the fiduciary relationship.

## .13   Completed Documents

A power of attorney will be recognized after the Form 56 is received, reviewed, and determined by the IRS to contain the required information. However, until a power of attorney is entered into the Centralized Authorized File (CAF), IRS personnel, other than the individual to whom the form is submitted, may be unaware of the authority of the taxpayer's representative and request an additional copy.

When the IRS receives a complete and valid power of attorney, the IRS will take action to recognize the representative. This involves processing the document into the CAF system. The power of attorney is not considered valid until all required information is entered on the document. The individual named as representative will not be recognized to practice before the IRS until the document is complete and accepted by the IRS.

In most instances, the recognition involves processing the document by recording the information on the CAF which enables the IRS to automatically direct copies of mailings to an authorized representative and to instantly recognize the scope of authority granted.

After the power of attorney is filed, the IRS will recognize the taxpayer's representative. However, if it appears the representative is responsible for unreasonably delaying or hindering the prompt disposition of an IRS matter by failing to furnish, after repeated requests, nonprivileged information, the IRS can bypass the representative and contact the taxpayer directly.

## .15   Revoking a Power of Attorney

If a taxpayers wants to revoke an existing power of attorney and does not want to name a new representative, there are two ways to do it:

1. By sending a *revocation copy* of a previous appointment form to each office of the IRS where forms were originally filed.
2. By sending a *revocation statement* to the service center where a return was filed that was covered by the power of attorney.

Unless a taxpayer wants to revoke a power of attorney for which no form was filed, a letter can be written requesting the revocation with a copy of the power of attorney to be revoked. The letter should be signed and dated and sent to each office of the IRS where the taxpayer originally filed the non-IRS power of attorney.

Unless a taxpayer specifies otherwise, a newly filed power of attorney concerning the same matter will revoke a previously filed power of attorney, but not a previously filed tax authorization. A newly filed tax information authorization will revoke a previously filed tax authorization concerning the same matter, but will not revoke a power of attorney concerning that matter.

# Chapter 19

# Internet Accounting

## CONTENTS

# ¶19,000   OVERVIEW

With anything new, many and varied practices spring up. Some variations are a result of different people attempting to explain a similar situation in as logical a manner as possible. Other variations have arisen as a result of less fair-minded individuals attempting to show a situation to the best advantage for themselves. Or it may be that the variations stem from mere ineptitude to downright chicanery.

This phenomenon is as true of Internet business accounting practices as it is of any other innovation. Who better to try to bring order to a rather chaotic state of development than the Chief Accountant's Office of the Security and Exchange Commission?

The SEC's stated purpose is to protect the investor. How companies recognize revenue for the goods and services they offer and, in turn, how this appears on their financial report have become increasingly important issues. Some investors have been known to value Internet-based companies on a multiple of revenues, rather than a multiple of gross profit or earnings. Such a valuation may be satisfactory for a while, but may lead to dismay down the road.

The last few years have borne out this concern. Many Internet company stocks that were once $100, $200, or even $300-level stocks ended trading at penny stock levels. Their previous lofty price levels had been based upon earnings expectations that never would have existed had shareholders' investment practices conformed to conventional beliefs related to balance sheets, financial statements, and other commonly accepted accounting standards.

# ¶19,001   ISSUES RELATED TO INTERNET ACCOUNTING

Late in 1999, the Chief Accountant of the SEC sent a letter to the Director of Research and Technical Activities of the Financial Accounting Standards Board. He suggested that the Emerging Issues Task Force (or another standard-setting body) should deal with a list of issues that had arisen in Internet businesses.

Attached to the letter was a list of 20 accounting issues developed by the SEC staff. The list included those issues they believed warranted consideration by a standard-setting body with suggested priority levels for addressing each of the issues (priority levels 1-3). However, they expected that all of the issues should eventually be addressed.

The staff agreed that several issues could best be addressed by staff announcements.

¶19,000

## ¶19,003  TARGETED AREAS IN ACCOUNTING FOR INTERNET ACTIVITIES

The list comprises accounting on issues the SEC staff had dealt with in registrant filings, as well as issues identified through input from accounting firms. One or more of the following applies to all of these issues:

1. There appears to be a diversity in practice.
2. The situation does not appear to be addressed in existing accounting literature.
3. The SEC staff is concerned that the developing practice may be inappropriate under generally accepted accounting principles (GAAP).

Some of the issues arise because of the new business models used in Internet operations, while others are issues that also exist in businesses with no Internet operations. It was pointed out that advertising partnerships, coupon and rebate programs, and complex equity instruments, while perhaps more common in Internet businesses, were in use long before the Internet. As a general rule, the SEC staff believes that Internet companies engaging in transactions that are similar to transactions entered into by traditional companies should follow the already established accounting models for those transactions.

The SEC believes that all of the issues discussed deserved further consideration by the accounting and financial reporting community. Each issue represents an area in which investors benefit from improved financial information and consistency as a result of providing additional guidance on the issue. In order to maximize the benefits of providing such guidance, the Commission believes it is important that guidance address not only recognition and measurement questions, but also classification and disclosures.

For each issue, the SEC staff added comments regarding the issue, and an assessment of the priority for addressing the issue.

## ¶19,005  QUALITY ACCOUNTING NEEDED

After careful consideration of the "call to accountability" letter from the SEC's chief accountant, it would appear that the Task Force (and the SEC, for that matter) really believe that the new economy is not so much in need of "new accounting," as of *quality* accounting. Basically, the Emerging Issues Task Force (EITF) has resolved many of the issues by reference to interpretations and guidance found in existing accounting pronouncements. Regardless of the rather complex list of perceived abuses and inconsistencies referred to, the solutions do not appear to require radical changes to traditional accounting models.

## ¶19,007   EITF 01-9, *Accounting for Considerations from Vendor to Retailer*

In attempting to bring a little more organization to various aspects of accounting for vendor/customer/reseller transactions, EITF Issue 01-9, *Accounting for Consideration Given by a Vendor to a Customer or a Reseller of the Vendor's Products,* brings together three EITF Issues on the topic. This might almost be called a "vendor's omnibus issue."

Issues 00-14, *Accounting for Certain Sales Incentives;* 00-22, *Accounting for "Points" and Certain Other Time-Based or Volume-Based Sales Incentive Offers, and Offers for Free Products or Services to be Delivered in the Future;* and 00-25, *Vendor Income Statement Characterization of Consideration from a Vendor to a Retailer,* have addressed various aspects of the accounting for consideration given by a vendor to a customer or a reseller of the vendor's products. Issue 01-9 is an effort to codify and reconcile the Task Force consensuses on those varied but related Issues. It also identifies other related interpretive issues that resulted from this codification.

Issues 1 and 2 are basically concerned with income statement treatment of cash consideration, including sales incentives. The Task Force reached a consensus requiring a *reduction in revenue* for cash consideration (including sales incentives) given by vendors unless *both* of the following conditions are true:

1.  The vendor has received, or will receive, a benefit that is sufficiently separable from the customer's purchase of products and services from the vendor.

2.  A reasonable estimate of the fair value of this benefit is available.

*When these conditions are met, the consideration is to be treated as a cost.* The excess of consideration paid over the fair value of the benefit received must be reported as a *reduction in revenue.*

Vendors must also treat as cost any "free" products or services given to customers. Although the EITF did not reach a consensus on the income statement display of such costs, the SEC staff considers such costs to be *components of cost of sales.* Slotting fees and other similar product development or placement fees are to be reported as *reductions in revenue.* Because this EITF applies to both intermediate and final resellers, their cooperative advertising and marketing programs are subject to this consensus.

*Issue 1.*    Issue 1 considers how a vendor should account for an offer to a customer (in connection with a current revenue transaction) for free or discounted products or services from the vendor that is redeemable by the customer at a future date without a further exchange transaction with the vendor. The Task

¶19,007

Force reached a consensus that transactions that involve offers by a vendor to a customer for free or discounted products or services are multiple deliverable transactions. This issue refers to Issue 00-21 for further evaluation. (See sections in this chapter on problem 11 and "Updated Status of EITF 00-22 Relating to Various Incentives.")

*Issue 2.* Issue 2 covers how to clarify the scope and application of paragraph 16 of EITF 00-25, which addresses vendor consideration at the inception of the relationship with a customer or reseller. The Task Force reached a consensus that paragraph 16 of Issue 00-25:

1. Applies to variable consideration, including equity instruments accounted for in accordance with Issue 96-18, for which a measurement date has not yet occurred.
2. Precludes a vendor from recharacterizing as an expense consideration that otherwise meets the conditions in paragraph 16 that permits expense characterization, if a portion of that consideration is not immediately recognized in the income statement. This also applies if, by the time that consideration is recognized in the income statement, there is cumulative revenue from the reseller.
3. Does not preclude a vendor from characterizing as an expense that portion of consideration that a vendor remits, or is obligated to remit, at the beginning of the overall relationship with a reseller that exceeds the amount of probable future revenue to be received from the reseller.

The Task Force also agreed that a purchase commitment or exclusive arrangement is not necessary to conclude that future revenues are probable. Financial statements for annual or interim periods beginning after December 15, 2001, must reflect these consensuses.

*Issue 3.* Issue 3 considers whether the consensus on Issue 2 of Issue 00-14 (regarding when to recognize and how to measure a sales incentive when there is a loss on the sale) should apply to arrangements within the scope of Issue 00-25. This applies to arrangements for which the sum of the consideration from the vendor and the vendor's estimated cost of sales are expected to exceed the estimated revenues from the reseller.

The Task Force reached a consensus that Issue 2 of Issue 00-14 should not apply to arrangements within the scope of Issue 00-25.

*Issue 4.* Issues 4, 5, and 6 are particularly concerned with:

- The timing—when to recognize the transaction.
- How to measure the cost of the incentive.

In Issue 4, relating to sales incentive offered without charge to the customer and voluntarily by the vendor, the Task Force reached a consensus requiring the recognition of the cost of such incentives at the later of the following:

- The date at which the related revenue is recognized by the vendor.
- The date at which the sales incentive is offered.

This consensus was to be applied no later than in financial statements for annual or interim periods beginning after December 15, 2001. Additionally, Issue 4 is concerned with how the impact of changes in estimates (or other factors based on the guidance in paragraphs 14-17 of Issue 00-25 that result in fluctuations in negative revenue during multiple financial reporting periods) should be presented in the income statement.

The Task Force reached a consensus that for the purposes of applying the guidance in paragraphs 14 through 17 of Issue 00-25, each financial reporting period must stand on its own. If an amount is classified as an expense in one period, amounts presented in the income statement for that period must not be reclassified later, even if that approach results in a credit to expense in a later period.

*Issue 5.*    Issue 5 deals with whether the Issue 00-25 income statement characterization applies to the amortization of an exclusive arrangement that is valued in a purchase business combination.

The Task Force reached a consensus that the Issue 00-25 income statement characterization model does not apply to the amortization of an exclusive arrangement acquired and recognized as an intangible asset in a business combination. The Task Force also noted that this issue is more closely related to Issue 01-3 than to Issue 01-9. Accordingly, this issue will be moved to Issue 01-3.

*Issue 6.*    Issue 6 asks whether the consensus on Issue 2 of Issue 00-25 applies to consideration that consists of other than cash or equity instruments, or whether consideration that consists of other than cash or equity instruments should always be characterized as an expense when recognized in the income statement.

The Task Force reached a consensus that consideration that is not in the form of cash, equity instruments, or "credits" (that the reseller can apply against trade amounts owed to the vendor) should always be characterized as an expense in the income statement. There were those Task Force members who observed that ultimately the form of the consideration should unquestionably dictate the accounting based on this consensus.

*Not the Last Word.*    Elsewhere in this chapter, Problem 3 is related to EITF 00-14 and 00-25 and Problems 5 and 14 are related to EITF 00-14.

Previously, an "inactive issue," 02-E became Issue No. 02-16, *Accounting by a Customer (Including a Reseller) for Certain Consideration Received from a Vendor.*

¶19,007

**EITF Issue No. 01-9,** *Accounting for Consideration Given by a Vendor to a Customer (Including a Reseller of the Vendor's Products),* requires consideration *given by a vendor* to a customer to be characterized as a reduction of revenue unless certain conditions are met. However, Issue 01-9 or any other authoritative literature does not address the customer's accounting for consideration *received from a vendor.* Therefore, the issue, here, is how the customer should account for consideration received from a vendor.

**Status**: At the November 21, 2002, meeting, the Task Force reached a consensus that cash consideration received by a customer from a vendor is presumed to be a reduction of the prices of the vendor's products or services and should, therefore, be characterized as a reduction of cost of sales when recognized in the customer's income statement. That presumption is overcome when the consideration is either:

1.  A reimbursement of costs incurred by the customer to sell the vendor's products, in which case the cash consideration should be characterized as a reduction of that cost when recognized in the customer's income statement; or

2.  A payment for assets or services delivered to the vendor, in which case the cash consideration should be characterized as revenue when recognized in the customer's income statement.

The Task Force also reached a consensus that a rebate or refund of a specified amount of cash consideration that is payable only if the customer completes a specified cumulative level of purchases or remains a customer for a specified time period should be recognized as a reduction of the cost of sales based on a systematic and rational allocation of the cash consideration offered to each of the underlying transactions that results in progress by the customer toward earning the rebate or refund, provided the amounts are reasonably estimable.

The Task Force agreed to discontinue consideration of whether up-front nonrefundable cash consideration given by a vendor to a customer results in a liability or whether that consideration should be recognized immediately in the customer's income statement due to the broad, general nature of the related questions.

At the January 23, 2003 meeting, the Task Force rescinded the transition guidance provided on Issue 1 at the November 21, 2002 meeting. The Task Force concluded that the consensus on Issue 1 should be applied to new arrangements, including modifications of existing arrangements, entered into after December 31, 2002. If determinable, pro forma disclosure of the impact of the consensus on prior periods presented is encouraged. Early application of the consensus is permitted as of the beginning of periods for which financial statements have not been issued.

At the March 20, 2003 meeting, the Task Force reconsidered the transition for the consensus in Issue 1 and clarified that an entity would not be precluded from recasting prior-period financial statements provided it does not result in a change to previously reported net income. Also, the Task Force concluded that entities should be permitted to report the change in accounting as a cumulative effect adjustment in accordance with APB Opinion No. 20, *Accounting Changes*, and FASB Statement No. 3, *Reporting Accounting Changes in Interim Financial Statements*.

**Issue No. 03-10,** *Application of EITF Issue No. 02-16, 'Accounting by a Customer (Including a Reseller) for Certain Consideration Received from a Vendor,' by Resellers to Sales Incentives Offered to Consumers by Manufacturers.* Under Issue 1 of Issue 02-16, cash consideration received by a customer from a vendor is presumed to be a price reduction of the vendor's products or services and should, therefore, be characterized as a reduction of cost of sales when recognized in the income statement of the customer.

That presumption may be overcome if the cash received represents:

- A payment for assets or services delivered to the vendor (in which case the cash received would be characterized as revenue); or
- A reimbursement of a specific, incremental, identifiable cost incurred by the customer in selling the vendor's products or services (in which case the cash would be characterized as a reduction of that cost).

The issue is whether consideration received by a reseller in the form of a reimbursement by the vendor for honoring the vendor's sales incentives offered directly to consumers (for example, coupons) should be recorded as revenue or as a reduction of the cost of the reseller's purchases from the vendor under the guidance to be followed in Issue 02-16. The Issue will also consider whether any aspects of EITF Issue No. 01-9, *Accounting for Consideration Given by a Vendor to a Customer (Including a Reseller of the Vendor's Products)*, will be affected.

**Status:** At the November 12-13, 2003 EITF meeting, the Task Force confirmed as a consensus its previously reached tentative conclusion, which was presented in a draft abstract for Task Force members' review, with certain revisions to paragraph 5(c). The Board ratified the consensus at its November 25, 2003 meeting.

Several years have passed, but EITF Issue No.01-9 is still an important milestone in Internet accounting as demonstrated by the first issue in 2006 Issue No. 06-1, "Accounting for Consideration Given by a Service Provider to Manufacturers or Resellers of Equipment Necessary for an End-Customer to Receive Service from the Service Provider."

A vendor (service provider) may provide services that require its customers to purchase special equipment. That equipment may be manufactured, distributed, and sold through a third party manufacture (including producers of components used by the manufacture—such as manufacturers of computer chips) and retailers/resellers of the equipment without the direct involvement of the service provider (that is, the service provider does not manufacture or purchase and directly sell the required equipment to the purchasers of its services but, rather, relies on other enterprises to conduct those activities). If the retail price of the specialty equipment is cost prohibitive to the end customer, a service provider may provide certain incentives to reduce the cost of the equipment to stimulate end customer demand for the equipment and, accordingly, the service provider's service.

The issue is whether the provisions of EITF Issue No. 01-9, "Accounting for Consideration Given by a Vendor to a Customer (Including a Reseller of the Vendor's Products)," should be applied to payments made by a service provider to manufacturers and/or retailers/resellers of specialized equipment that is necessary for a customer to receive a service from the service provider when the manufacturers and/or retailers/resellers of that equipment are not involved in the service provider's distribution chain.

**Status:** At the September 7, 2006 EITF meeting, the Task Force affirmed as a consensus the tentative conclusion that if the consideration given by a service provider to a manufacturer or reseller (that is not a customer of the service provider) can be linked contractually to the benefit received by the service provider's customer, a service provider should account for the characterization of the consideration in accordance with Issue 01-9.

The service provider should characterize the consideration given to a third-party manufacturer or reseller based on the form of consideration directed by the service provider to be provided to the service provider's customer. If the form of the consideration is stipulated to be anything other than "cash consideration" (as defined in Issue 01-9), then the form of the consideration should be characterized as "other than cash" consideration for purposes of applying Issue 01-9.

If the service provider does not control the form of the consideration provided to the service provider's customer, the consideration should be characterized as "other than cash" consideration for purposes of applying Issue 01-9. In reaching that conclusion, Task Force members observed that consideration paid by a service provider that results in a customer receiving a reduced price on equipment purchased from a manufacturer or reseller should be characterized as "other than cash" consideration for purposes of applying Issue 01-9. The Board will consider the ratification of this consensus at its September 20, 2006 meeting.

**Dates discussed:** March 16, 2006; June 15, 2006;September 7, 2006.

## ¶19,009  GROSS VERSUS NET

Some of the more significant issues facing Internet businesses surround whether to present grossed-up revenues and cost of sales, or merely report the net profit as revenues, similar to a commission. The significance is greater because of the importance often placed on the revenue line in the valuation of Internet stocks.

¶19,009

## .01  Problem 1

The question of gross versus net revenue and cost display has arisen several times in connection with an Internet company that distributes or resells third-party products or services. Because the Internet is a new distribution channel and can be used in the distribution of tangible assets, intangible assets, and services, the existing practices used for making this determination are not always sufficient. (Priority level 1.)

## .03  Status of Problem 1

The FASB's Emerging Issues Task Force reached a consensus on this first issue in EITF 99-19, "Reporting Revenue Gross as a Principal versus Net as an Agent" at the July, 2000 meeting. The issue addressed was *when* a vendor should report revenue as the gross amount billed to a customer rather than the net amount earned by the vendor in the transaction. At the July meeting, the EITF affirmed as a consensus the tentative conclusion reached at the May 2000 meeting, with minor modifications to the indicators.

Consensus is that none of the indicators should be considered presumptive or determinative. However, the relative strength of each indicator should be considered. The members of the Task Force believe that the primary obligor, general inventory risk, and pricing latitude are the strongest indicators that would point to recording revenue gross. They also amended the consensus to allow transition to mirror the required implementation in SAB 101, *Revenue Recognition in Financial Statements*.

This attempt to reach consensus on when it is appropriate for a company to record revenue on a gross basis when acting as a principal versus on a net basis when acting as an agent has not been easy. For example, during EITF's May meeting, the EITF observed that an Internet retailer who had only credit and inventory risk during the time period goods were in transit would not qualify for gross revenue recognition.

Materials prepared by the FASB staff for the EITF's May 2000 meeting discussion of gross versus net revenue recognition indicate the variety of issues considered. The staff made the following suggestions to the EITF's members:

- The answer to the question of when it is appropriate to recognize and report gross revenues turns on the risks assumed by the vendor in an exchange of goods and services with a customer.
- Indicators taken alone or in combination that gross revenue recognition may be appropriate include that the vendor, from the customer's perspective, is the primary obligor; the vendor is primarily responsible for the fulfillment of the ordered product or service; the vendor has a credit loss risk; the vendor has an inventory loss risk; the vendor adds significant

value to the products or services ordered by a customer; and the vendor has complete latitude to set prices of products or services ordered.

- Some gross revenue recognition indicators are more persuasive than others. For example, taking title to inventory before a customer orders is more to the point than taking title to inventory after the customer orders.
- No one indicator necessarily dictates gross revenue recognition. For example, while a vendor's failure to take title for the goods sold to a customer may be a strong indicator of net revenue recognition, taking title alone may not be enough to justify gross revenue recognition.
- Some sale transactions and industry revenue recognition practices may be beyond the scope of the EITF consensus because of existing accounting standards. These include sale of financial assets, lending transactions, insurance and reinsurance transactions, and revenue recognition practices in airline, casino, construction contractor, and investment companies.

## .05  Problem 2

The staff pointed out that a number of press articles had commented on the following issue: Many Internet companies enter into advertising barter transactions with each other in which they exchange rights to place advertisements on each others' Web sites. There has been diversity in practice in accounting for these transactions. The staff believes a prerequisite to reflecting these transactions in the accounting records is that the value of the transaction must be reliably measurable. In addition, the staff believes registrants should be making transparent disclosure that will clearly convey to investors the accounting being used. (Priority level 1.)

## .07  Status of Problem 2

The Emerging Issues Task Force reached consensus in EITF 99-17 that the fair value of bartered advertising transactions can be included in revenue (with an offsetting amount charged to revenue) so long as the recording entity has a history of receiving cash in a similar advertising deal transacted during the last six months. If not, the company cannot book the cash.

A "cash" transaction can serve as support for revenue recognition of advertising barter transactions only up to the dollar amount of the cash transaction. Once that dollar amount has been reached, the "cash" transaction cannot serve as evidence of fair value for any other barter transaction. In other words, a cash transaction cannot support more than its original value or quantity in barter transactions. The following disclosures are required for advertising barter transactions, for each income statement period that is presented:

- Disclosure of the amount of revenue and expense recorded from advertising barter transactions.

- If the fair value of the advertising barter transactions is not determinable, information must be provided that clearly explains the volume and type of advertising surrendered and received, such as the number of pages or minutes or the overall percentage of advertising volume.
- The EITF intends the barrier to recording barter transaction revenue at its fair value to be high. The evidence must be persuasive to overcome the presumption that the barter transaction should be recorded at zero or its historical cost. Reciprocal cash transactions between counterparties are considered to be barter transactions (i.e., each company places advertising with the other for a cash payment). The fair value of barter transactions must be disclosed in a footnote.

This EITF ruling was effective for transactions occurring after January 20, 2000.

## .09    Problem 3

Internet service providers (ISPs) and personal computer (PC) retailers at times offer a rather substantial rebate to purchasers of new PCs who contract for a given period of Internet service. It appears that:

- Most of the rebate cost is borne by the ISP while a portion is borne by the PC retailer.
- The retailer provides advertising and marketing for the arrangement.
- The rebate, or a portion thereof, must be returned by the consumer to the ISP if the consumer breaks the contract with the ISP.

Some ISPs and retailers believe their portion of the cost of the rebate should be a marketing expense, as opposed to a reduction of revenues. The SEC staff generally believes that such rebates should be considered a reduction of revenues.

## .11    Status of Problem 3

The SEC staff felt that a staff announcement indicating that discounts like these should be accounted for as reductions of revenue was appropriate and adequate. The Task Force thought otherwise. Two of the EITFs, 00-14 and 00-25, deal with this to some extent, and to related issues. (For provisions included in Issue 00-14, *Accounting for Certain Sales Incentives,* please see Problem 5, which seems to have been solved by this consensus.) A discussion of EITF 00-25, *Accounting for Consideration from a Vendor to a Retailer in Connection with the Purchase or Promotion of the Vendor's Products,* follows:

Since the EITF reached a consensus on EITF 00-14, questions have been raised about the income statement characterization of consideration (other than that directly addressed in Issue 00-14) from a vendor to an entity that resells the vendor's products.

The term "vendor" is used to represent a product seller, such as a manufacturer or distributor, who sells to an entity that resells the vendor's products. The term "retailer" is used to represent that reseller entity, whether that entity is another distributor, a conventional retailer, or another type of reseller.

Examples of arrangements within the scope of this Issue include, but are not limited to, arrangements labeled as follows:

- "Slotting fees." A vendor pays or agrees to pay a fee to a retailer to obtain space for the vendor's products on the retailer's store shelves.
- Cooperative advertising arrangements. A vendor agrees to reimburse a retailer for a portion of the costs incurred by the retailer to advertise the vendor's products.
- "Buydowns." A vendor agrees to reimburse a retailer up to a specified amount for shortfalls in the sales price received by the retailer for the vendor's products over a specified period of time.

Although many of the arrangements within the scope of this Issue (in particular, slotting fees) result in cash payments by a vendor to the retailer, the form of the consideration may be "credits" that the retailer can apply against trade amounts owed to the vendor, or against equity instruments of the vendor. Measurement of consideration in the form of vendor equity instruments is outside the scope of this Issue.

Guidance currently exists in:

- EITF 96-18, *Accounting for Equity Instruments That Are Issued to Other Than Employees for Acquiring, or in Conjunction with Selling, Goods or Services*, which requires that equity instruments issued be recognized in the same period and in the same manner as if cash were paid.
- Issue 00-14, which requires that a reduction in or refund of the selling price of the product or service resulting in a sales incentive be classified in the issuer's financial statements as a reduction of revenue.

*EITF 00-25 Progress.*   However, the issues requiring attention from the Working Group considering EITF 00-25 are:

- *Issue 1:* For nonrefundable consideration from a vendor to a retailer to obtain shelf space for the vendor's products, the period(s) and manner in which the vendor should recognize the consideration.
- *Issue 2:* Whether consideration from a vendor to a retailer is: (i) Adjustment of the selling prices of the vendor's products to the retailer and,

therefore, should be deducted from revenue when recognized in the vendor's income statement; or (ii) A cost incurred by the vendor for assets or services provided by the retailer to the vendor and, therefore, should be included as a cost or expense when recognized in the vendor's income statement.

- *Issue 3(a):* The period(s) and manner (that is, capitalize versus expense) in which the entity should recognize the measured cost of nonrefundable up-front consideration paid to a counterparty if future specific performance (by providing or purchasing goods or services) is not required by the counterparty in order to earn the consideration.
- *Issue 3(b):* Whether a cost that is evaluated to be an asset under Issue 1, above, should be recognized in a different manner (classified as contra-equity) if the consideration paid is equity instruments of the entity.
- *Issue 4:* If consideration from a vendor to a retailer results in negative revenue, whether the negative revenue amount should be included within revenues or expenses in the statement of operations.

In January 2001, the Task Force reached a tentative conclusion on Issue 2 that consideration from a vendor to any downstream purchaser of the vendor's products, even when that purchaser is not a direct customer of the vendor, is presumed to be a reduction to the selling prices of the vendor's products and, therefore, should be characterized as a reduction of revenue when recognized in the vendor's income statement.

That presumption is overcome and the consideration should be characterized as a cost incurred if, and to the extent that, a benefit is received from the retailer that meets both of the following:

1. The vendor receives, or will receive, an identifiable benefit (goods or services) from the retailer in return for the consideration. In order to meet this condition, the identified benefit must be sufficiently separable from the vendor's arrangement to sell its goods or services such that the vendor would have entered into an exchange transaction with parties other than a retailer customer in order to receive that benefit.
2. The vendor has sufficient, objective, and reliable evidence to estimate the fair value of the benefit. For example, if the benefit received from the retailer is advertising and the benefit's fair value estimate is based on the cost of "similar" advertising, that advertising must have characteristics reasonably similar to the advertising received from the retailer with respect to:
   a. Circulation, exposure, or saturation within an intended market.
   b. Timing (time of day, day of week, daily, weekly, 24 hours a day/7 days a week, and season of the year).

**¶19,009.11**

c. Prominence (page on Web site, section of periodical, location on page, and size of advertisement that relates to vendor's brands or products).

d. Demographics of readers, viewers, or customers.

e. Duration (length of time advertising will be displayed).

If the amount of consideration exceeds the estimated fair value of the benefit received, that excess amount should be characterized as a reduction of revenue when recognized in the vendor's income statement.

The Task Force did not discuss Issues 1, 3, or 4; therefore, further discussion is expected at a future meeting.

## .13  Problem 4

Shipping and handling costs are a major expense for Internet product sellers. Most sellers charge customers for shipping and handling in amounts that are not a direct pass-through of costs. Some display the charges to customers as revenues and the costs as selling expenses, while others net the costs and revenues.

In either situation, the staff noted that Internet companies generally do not provide any separate disclosure of shipping revenues and costs (e.g., by reporting shipping revenue and costs as separate line items, or by providing footnote disclosure of the gross shipping revenues and costs).

The staff noted that there was diversity in practice that should be eliminated, but that the issue related to a smaller portion of revenues and costs than some of the other items. (Priority level 2.)

## .15  Status of Problem 4

There are two questions here: (1) how a seller of goods should classify in the income statement amounts billed to a customer for shipping and handling, and (2) how the seller should classify in the income statement costs incurred for shipping and handling. The Task Force reached a consensus in EITF 00-10 in the first instance that all amounts billed to a customer in a sale transaction related to shipping and handling, if any, represent revenues earned for the goods provided and should be classified as revenue.

In the second, they decided that the classification of shipping and handling costs is an accounting policy decision that should be disclosed pursuant to Opinion 22, *Disclosure of Accounting Policies*. A company may adopt a policy of including shipping and handling costs in cost of sales. If shipping costs or handling costs are significant, and are not included in cost of sales (that is, if those costs are accounted for together or separately on other income statement line items), a company should disclose both the amount(s) of such costs and the line item(s) on the income statement that include them.

¶19,009.15

## .17   Problem 5

Some Internet companies have concluded that a free or heavily discounted product or service, as is provided in introductory offers (e.g. a free month of service, six CDs for a penny) should be accounted for as a sale at full price, with the recognition of marketing expense for the discount. The staff notes that an AICPA Technical Practice Aid Section relating to "One-Cent Sales"addresses this issue, concluding that, "The practice of crediting sales and charging advertising expense for the difference between the normal sales price and the 'bargain day' sales price of merchandise is not acceptable for financial reporting."

The SEC staff believes that a staff announcement indicating that discounts like these should be accounted for as reductions of revenue is appropriate. Here, again, the EITF thought otherwise. (Much of their thinking is contained in Issue 00-14.)

## .19   Status of Problem 5

*Issue 1.*   A sales incentive is offered voluntarily by a vendor and without charge to customers. This incentive can be used by a customer as a result of a single exchange transaction; it will not result in a loss on the sale of a product or service. The issue is when to recognize and how to measure the cost of the sales incentive. (Here the term "vendor" includes a manufacturer that sells its products to retailers or other distributors.)

Consensus: The Task Force reached consensus on Issue 1 that for a sales incentive that will not result in a loss on the sale of a product or service, a vendor should recognize the "cost" of the sales incentive at the latter of the following:

- The date at which the related revenue is recorded by the vendor.
- The date at which the sales incentive is offered (which would be the case when the sales incentive offer is made after the vendor has recognized revenue; for example, when a manufacturer issues coupons offering discounts on a product that it already has sold to retailers).

Certain sales incentives entitle a customer to receive a reduction in the price of a product or service by submitting a form or claim for a refund or rebate of a specified amount of a prior purchase price charged to the customer at the point of sale (for example, mail-in rebates and certain manufacturer coupons). The Task Force reached consensus that a vendor should recognize a liability (or "deferred revenue") for those sales incentives at the latter of (a) or (b), above, based on the estimated amount of refunds or rebates that will be claimed by customers. However, if the amount of future rebates or refunds cannot be reasonably and reliably estimated, a liability (or "deferred revenue") should be

¶19,009.17

recognized for the maximum potential amount of the refund or rebate (that is, no reduction for "breakage" should be made). The ability to make a reasonable and reliable estimate of the amount of future rebates or refunds depends on many factors and circumstances that will vary from case to case. However, the Task Force reached consensus that the following factors may impair a vendor's ability to make a reasonable and reliable estimate:

- Relatively long time periods in which a particular rebate or refund may be claimed.
- The absence of historical experience with similar types of sales incentive programs with similar products, or the inability to apply such experience because of changing circumstances.
- The absence of a large volume of relatively homogeneous transactions.

*Issue 2.*    A sales incentive is offered voluntarily by a vendor and without charge to customers. This incentive can be used by a customer as a result of a single exchange transaction; it will result in a loss on the sale of a product or service. The issue is when to recognize and how to measure the cost of the sales incentive.

Consensus: For sales incentives within the scope of this Issue that will result in a loss on the sale of a product or service (Issue 2), the Task Force reached consensus that a vendor should not recognize a liability for the sales incentive prior to the date at which the related revenue is recognized by the vendor. However, the Task Force observed that the offer of a sales incentive that will result in a loss on the sale of a product may indicate an impairment of existing inventory under ARB 43.

*Issue 3.*    A sales incentive is offered voluntarily by a vendor and without charge to customers. This incentive can be used by a customer as a result of a single exchange transaction. The issue is how the cost of the sales incentive should be classified in the income statement.

Consensus: For Issue 3, the Task Force reached consensus that when recognized, the reduction in or refund of the selling price of the product or service resulting from any cash sales incentive should be classified as a reduction of revenue. However, if the sales incentive is a free product or service delivered at the time of sale (for example, a gift certificate or free airline ticket that will be honored by another, unrelated entity), the cost of the free product or service should be classified as an expense (as opposed to a reduction of revenues). That is, the free item is an element in the exchange transaction and not a refund or rebate of a portion of the amount charged to the customer.

While the Task Force did not reach consensus on the classification of the expense associated with free products, the SEC Observer indicated that the SEC staff believes that the expense associated with a free product or service delivered at the time of sale of another product or service should be classified as cost of sales. The Task Force observed that sales incentives in the form of options or warrants to purchase stock or the issuance of shares of stock of the vendor are multiple-element transactions that are outside the scope of this Issue.

Companies should have applied the consensuses no later than in (a) annual financial statements for the fiscal year beginning after December 15, 1999, or (b) financial statements for the fiscal quarter beginning after March 15, 2001, whichever is later. Earlier adoption was encouraged.

## .21   Problem 6

Several Internet-based businesses have experienced service outages. Related costs may include:

- Refunds to customers/members.
- Costs to correct the problem that caused the outage.
- Damage claims.

The facts and circumstances surrounding these situations are likely to be very diverse, making the development of general guidance difficult. They add that issues could include:

- When to accrue the refunds and costs.
- Whether refunds that are not required but are given as a gesture of good-will are reductions of revenues, or a marketing expense, or "other."
- The "other" could be imaginative; therefore, the SEC staff decided upon a Priority level 3 for this item.

## .23   Status of Problem 6

The staff indicated that the diversity of facts, circumstances, and causes surrounding the outages and handling could make general guidance difficult. Thus far, the issue is not being discussed. Although some indication may be drawn from 00-14.

## ¶19,011   Definition of Software

The SEC noted several issues that relate to whether Web sites themselves and files or information available on Web sites should be considered software, and therefore be subject to the provisions of SOPs 97-2, *Software Revenue Recognition,* and 98-1, *Accounting for the Costs of Computer Software Developed or*

*Obtained for Internal Use,* and/or FASB 86, *Accounting for the Costs of Computer Software to Be Sold, Leased, or Otherwise Marketed.*

## .01  Problem 7

In EITF Issue 96-6, the SEC staff expressed its view that the costs of software products that include film elements should be accounted for under the provisions of FASB 86. As such, revenue from the sale of such products should be accounted for under the provisions of SOP 97-2. By analogy, the staff believes that guidance should be applied to software with other embedded elements, such as music. However, EITF 96-6 did not discuss accounting for the costs of computer files that are essentially films (e.g., MPEG, RealVideo), music (e.g., MP3), or other content. A number of questions may arise relating to these files, including whether a company purchasing the rights to distribute music in the MP3 format should account for those costs under FASB 50, *Financial Reporting in the Record and Music Industry,* or FASB 86. Similarly, it is not clear whether the revenue from the sales of MP3 files falls under SOP 97-2.

The staff indicated that as the areas of software, film, music, and so on continue to converge, it is important to be able to identify which accounting models apply to various transactions. In addition, resolving this Issue may be necessary in order to resolve Issue 8. (Priority level 2.)

## .03  Status of Problem 7

This item is on the agenda of the Task Force, but has not yet been discussed, as noted in Issue 00-X1 at the end of this chapter.

Although these two issues do not deal directly with the problem as posed by the SEC, they do concern both directly and indirectly issues relating to software and might be of interest in dealing with the accounting questions.

Issue 02-G, *Recognition of Revenue from Licensing Arrangements on Intellectual Property.* Licensing arrangements can take many forms, such as arrangements with a specific term or those with an unlimited term. The accounting for licensing arrangements varies in practice. Some may view the licensing of intellectual property as indistinguishable from a lease of a physical asset in which the total arrangement fee should be recognized over the contract term, while others may view such licensing arrangements as indistinguishable from the licensing of software or motion picture rights in which revenue is recognized once the license has been conveyed and the seller has no further obligations. The latter group believes their approach is fully consistent with the guidance in AICPA SOP 97-2, *Software Revenue Recognition,* and SOP 00-2, *Accounting by Producers or Distributors of Films.* The issue is when to recognize revenue from licensing arrangements on intellectual property.

**Status:** To be discussed at a future meeting.

¶19,011.03

Related to the Issue above is Issue 00-20, which has been considered a possible answer to some of the questions raised relating to the accounting for the costs of computer files that are essentially films, music, or other content.

Issue 00-20, *Accounting for Costs Incurred to Acquire or Originate Information for Database Content and Other Collections of Information.* Some companies derive revenues from making databases and other collections of information available to users. Those collections of information may be made available electronically or otherwise. The Issue is how the costs of developing or acquiring those collections of information should be accounted for (that is, capitalized and amortized or charged to expense as incurred).

**Status:** At the November 21, 2002, meeting, the Task Force agreed to remove this Issue from its agenda because it involves a fundamental question regarding the definition of an asset and therefore would more appropriately be addressed by the FASB. It had last been discussed at the September 20-21, 2000, meeting. (This notation is also made toward the end of this Chapter, where there is a listing of Issues that have been removed from the EITF agenda for a variety of reasons, particularly in relation to several of the FASB's projects.)

## .05   Problem 8

Costs of developing a Web site, including the costs of developing services that are offered to visitors (chat rooms, search engines, e-mail, calendars, etc.) are significant costs for many Internet businesses. In fact, the staff concluded that it is the largest cost for many of them. The SEC staff believes that a large portion of such costs should be accounted for as software developed for internal use in accordance with SOP 98-1, *Accounting for the Costs of Computer Software Developed or Obtained for Internal Use.* The staff notes that SOP 98-1 states, "If software is used by the vendor in providing the service but the customer does not acquire the software or the future right to use it, the software is covered by this SOP."

A letter to the FASB noted the staff view that a large portion of Web site development costs should be accounted for in accordance with this SOP, as software developed for internal use. However, at that time some companies were not following the requirements of SOP 98-1 for such costs.

The letter pointed out that even during the development of 98-1, some participants had questioned the wisdom of capitalizing software development costs. However, an answer was reached after significant comment and debate that requires capitalization when certain conditions have been met. (Priority level 1.)

## .07   Status of Problem 8

The Task Force reached consensus in EITF 00-2, on Web site development costs, effective for quarters beginning after June 30, 2000.

Organizations thinking about or in the process of developing a Web site must be aware of accounting guidance covering various stages of development and use (i.e., the planning stage, the development stage and the operating stage):

- Costs incurred during the planning stage are to be expensed as incurred. This includes developing a project plan, determining functions and technology, identifying needed hardware, Web applications, and graphics, choosing vendors and software packages — any and all necessary planning aspects.

- Costs related to acquiring or developing software that operates a Web site should be accounted for under SOP 98-1 and should generally be capitalized if the entity does not intend to market the software externally. This includes developing software and graphics, obtaining and registering a domain name, developing HTML Web pages or templates, installing applications on servers, creating initial hypertext links, and testing Web applications.

  If at the time the software is being developed, the organization that owns the site has, or is developing, a plan to market the software externally, the organization should account for the software under FASB 86. Accounting for related computer hardware and Web site content (the information on the Web site) is not addressed in EITF 00-2. This will be discussed as a separate EITF issue.

  Fees incurred for Web site hosting should be expensed over the period of benefit. Data input costs should be expensed as incurred. Software acquired or developed to integrate a database with a Web site should usually be capitalized.

- Costs incurred at the operating stage are generally expensed as incurred. Such costs include training employees, administration, maintenance, registering the Web site with Internet search engines, updating graphics, creating new links, and performing security reviews.

  However, costs that add additional functions or features to the Web site (including graphics) should be accounted for as new software following the guidance in SOP 98-1 for upgrades and enhancements if the new software will not be marketed externally.

## ¶19,013    REVENUE RECOGNITION

As with any new business model, issues exist regarding the recognition of revenue for various types of Internet activities.

### .01    Problem 9

Auction sites usually charge both up-front (listing) fees and back-end (transaction-based) fees. The staff understands that the listing fees are being recognized as revenue when the item is originally listed, despite the requirement for the auction site to maintain the listing for the duration of the auction.

In addition, some auction sites recognize the back-end fees as revenue at the end of the auction, despite the fact that the seller is entitled to a refund of the fee if the transaction between the buyer and seller doesn't close. (Note: The auction house is merely a facilitator and takes no part in assisting in closing the transaction.) Given that many popular sites have recently started up auction services, this issue may become more prevalent.

The SEC staff comments relating to the front-end stated that a staff announcement indicating that fees like this should be recognized over the listing period (the period of performance) is appropriate.

The comments relating to the back-end indicated that the staff believes the facts and circumstances of the agreements among the auction site, the buyers, and the sellers may vary significantly, making it difficult to provide applicable guidance. (Priority level 3.)

## .03   Status of Problem 9

The issue relating to auction sites is on the agenda of the EITF but has not been discussed. (See Issue 00-X2 at the end of this chapter.)

## .05   Problem 10

Some purchasers of software do not actually receive the software. Rather, the software application resides on the vendor's or a third party's server, and the customer accesses the software on an as-needed basis over the Internet. The customer is paying for two elements — the right to use the software, and the storage of the software on someone else's hardware. The latter service is often referred to as "hosting." When the vendor also provides the hosting, several revenue recognition issues may arise. For example, there may be transactions structured in the form of a service agreement providing Internet access to the specified site, without a corresponding software license. In such instances, it may not be clear how to apply SOP 97-2. In addition, when the transaction is viewed as a software license with a service element, it is not clear how to evaluate the delivery requirement of SOP 97-2.

The staff commented that this type of arrangement seems to be growing in popularity, although it is not all that common at this point. (Priority level 2.)

## .07   Status of Problem 10

In March, 2000, the EITF reached a consensus on EITF 00-3, *Application of AICPA Statement of Position 97-2, "Software Revenue Recognition," to Arrangements That Include the Right to Use Software Stored on Another Entity's*

¶19,013.03

*Hardware.* EITF 00-3 addresses the accounting issues related to software hosting arrangements. In general, it states that if the customer does not have the option to physically take possession of the software, the transaction is not within the scope of SOP 97-2, and revenue should be recognized ratably over the hosting period as a service arrangement.

However, if the customer has the option to take physical delivery of the software and specific pricing information is available for both the software and hosting components of the arrangement, then the software revenue may be recognized when the customer first has access to the software and revenue from the hosting component should be recognized ratably over the hosting period.

Implementation of EITF 00-3 was required for the year ending December 31, 2000.

## .09  Problem 11

An Internet business may provide customers with services that include access to a Web site, maintenance of a Web site, or publication of certain information on a Web site for a period of time. Certain companies have argued that, because the incremental costs of maintaining the Web site and/or providing access to it are minimal (or even zero), this ongoing requirement should not preclude up-front revenue recognition. The staff has historically objected to up-front revenue recognition in these cases, even with an accrual of the related costs.

The SEC staff believes that a staff announcement indicating that fees like this should be recognized over the performance period, which would be the period over which the company has agreed to maintain the Web site or listing, is appropriate. No priority was assigned.

## .11  Status of Problem 11

This problem has not been discussed by the EITF as noted under Issue 00-X3 at the end of this chapter. However, number 10 of the frequently asked questions (FAQ) relating to revenue recognition in SAB 101 appears to answer the questions:

*Question*  In each of the following situations, when should the company receiving the fee recognize the related revenue?

Example 1: A company charges users a fee for nonexclusive access to its Web site that contains proprietary databases. The fee allows access to the Web site for a one-year period. After the customer is provided with an identification number and trained in the use of the database, there are no incremental costs that will be incurred in serving this customer.

¶19,013.11

Example 2: An Internet company charges a fee to users for advertising a product for sale or auction on certain pages of its Web site. The company agrees to maintain the listing for a period of time. The cost of maintaining the advertisement on the Web site for the stated period is minimal.

Example 3: A company charges a fee for hosting another company's Web site for one year. The arrangement does not involve exclusive use of any of the hosting company's servers or other equipment. Almost all of the projected costs to be incurred will be incurred in the initial loading of information on the host company's Internet server and setting up appropriate links and network connections.

*Answer*    Some propose that revenue should be recognized when the initial setup is completed in these cases because the ongoing obligation involves minimal or no cost or effort and should be considered perfunctory or inconsequential. However, the staff believes that the substance of each of these transactions indicates that the purchaser is paying for a service that is delivered over time. Therefore, revenue recognition should occur over time, reflecting the provision of service. In certain cases, the arrangement with the customer may be a multiple-element arrangement, with separate revenue recognition for those initial services.

Question 4 of this document (FAQ) discusses multiple-element arrangements:

*Question*    Although SAB 101 does not establish a framework for accounting for multiple-element arrangements, what factors would the staff consider in assessing whether an arrangement is accounted for as a multiple- element arrangement?

*Answer*    SAB 101 does not modify existing practice in accounting for multiple-element arrangements. Recognizing the diversity in practice in the accounting for multiple-element arrangements, and the complexity of these arrangements, the staff asked the Emerging Issues Task Force (EITF) and the Auditing Standards Board (ASB) to provide additional accounting and auditing guidance on those transactions. The EITF has added Issue 00-21, *Accounting for Multiple-Element Revenue Arrangements*, to its agenda to address the accounting issues. Pending additional guidance, registrants should use a reasoned method of accounting for multiple-element arrangements that is applied consistently and disclosed appropriately. In response to questions, the SEC staff has stated that it will not object to a method that includes the following conditions:

1. To be considered a separate element, the product or service in question represents a separate earnings process. The staff notes that determining whether an obligation represents a separate element requires significant judgment. The staff also notes that the best indicator that a separate element exists is that a vendor sells or could readily sell that element unaccompanied by other elements.

**¶19,013.11**

2. Revenue is allocated among the elements based on the fair value of the elements. The fair values used for the allocations should be reliable, verifiable, and objectively determinable. The staff does not believe that allocating revenue among the elements based solely on cost plus a profit margin that is not specific to the particular product or service is acceptable because, in the absence of other evidence of fair value, there is no objective means to verify what a profit margin should be for the particular element(s).

Additional guidance on allocating among elements may be found in SOP 81-1, paragraphs 35 through 42; SOP 97-2, paragraphs 9 through 14; and SOP 98-9, *Modification of SOP 97-2, Software Revenue Recognition, with Respect to Certain Transactions*. All of the methods of allocating revenue in those SOPs, including the residual method discussed in SOP 98-9, are acceptable. If sufficient evidence of the fair values of the individual elements does not exist, revenue would not be allocated among them until that evidence exists. Instead, the revenue would be recognized as earned, using revenue recognition principles applicable to the entire arrangement as if it were a single-element arrangement. Prices listed in a multiple-element arrangement with a customer may not be representative of fair value of those elements because the prices of the different components of the arrangement can be altered in negotiations and still result in the same aggregate consideration.

## .13  Updated Status of Problem 11

That this issue is not cut, dried, and put on the shelf is obvious from the fact that it was discussed by the Task Force over a two-day period in late June, 2002, then again in November 2002, in January 2003, and in March 2003. At various of these meetings, the Task Force has attempted to make certain revisions to paragraph 4(a) of the November minutes of this Issue to clarify that the provisions do not override higher-level GAAP. At one point, the SEC Observer expressed the view that Issue 00-21 and perhaps the Task Force should reinstate Issue 00-22. The Task Force agreed and the FASB followed up by agreeing to consider adding to the Board's agenda a narrow project that would address Issues 00-21 and 00-22. Consistent with previous requests by the Task Force, the Board is taking into consideration whether the due process afforded a Board project would represent a better forum in which to deal, in greater depth, with the issues and views of constituents on certain matters.

To review: Issue 00-21, *Accounting for Revenue Arrangements with Multiple Deliverables*. Many companies offer complete solutions to their customers' needs. Those solutions may involve:

- The delivery or performance of multiple products.
- Services to be performed.

- Rights to use assets.
- Performance may occur at different points in time or over different periods of time.

The arrangements are often accompanied by initial installation, initiation, or activation services, and generally involve either a fixed fee or a fixed fee coupled with a continuing payment stream. The continuing payment stream generally corresponds to the continuing performance and may be:

- A fixed payment.
- Variable payment based on future performance.
- Composed of a combination of fixed and variable payments.

The issue is how to account for those arrangements.

On the other hand, many software transactions do *not* involve "complete solutions." Therefore, identification of separate components and elements of software transactions and their fair value are necessary to take into consideration for determining the timing of revenue recognition. So, how should "separate components/elements" and "separate deliverables" be defined? The task force considered that tentative conclusions of EITF 00-21 provided some insight into a potential resolution. It states that a deliverable should be segmented and accounted for separately if:

1. There is objective and reliable evidence of fair value to allocate the consideration to the separate deliverables.
2. The deliverable meets at least one of the following criteria at the inception of the arrangement:
   a. It does not affect the quality of use or value to the customer of other deliverables in the arrangement.
   b. It can be purchased from an unrelated vendor without affecting the quality of use or value to the customer of the remaining deliverables in the arrangement.

Software companies may consistently include or exclude all deliverables in an arrangement from revenue (and recognize a liability) for the arrangement if all of the following conditions are met:

1. The deliverable does not affect the quality of use or value of other deliverables or could be purchased from another vendor without loss of the quality of use or value of other deliverables.
2. Any vendor obligation relating to nonperformance would not result in a refund, revenue reversal, or concession.
3. The deliverable is inconsequential or perfunctory.

**¶19,013.13**

No allocation is permitted in the absence of verifiable fair value. Third-party evidence may not be a reliable indicator of vendor specific objective evidence (VSOE) if the product or service is unique to the vendor. When objective and verifiable evidence of fair value is available for the undelivered item(s) but not for one or more delivered items in the arrangement, the residual method (SOP 98-9) can be used to allocate revenue when:

- The undelivered item meets all other applicable criteria for separate accounting.
- The fair value of all the undelivered items is less than the total arrangement fee.

It is important to keep in mind that the residual method cannot be used to *establish* the fair value of an undelivered item. The treatment of the discount is as follows.

> Theresidual method, established in SOP 98-9, allocates the entire discount to the delivered elements. The relative fair value allocation method established in SOP 97-2 allocates a proportionate amount of the entire discount to each unit of accounting in the arrangement based on the fair value of each unit without regard to the discount.

## .15  Revenue Recognition for Multiple Element Arrangements

For more than a year, the Emerging Issues Task Force, its working group and the staff of the FASB had worked on providing this tentative guidance on accounting for multiple element arrangements in relation to revenue recognition.

In July 2001, the chief account of the SEC stepped into the picture. The SEC commended the EITF, its working group and the FASB staff for their hard work. However, the Commission felt that the process that led to the tentative conclusion and comments about the model had made it clear that significant effort must be made to reach an *operational solution* that is consistent with the *fundamentals* of existing GAAP and that provides adequate transparency and protection for investors. In addition, the SEC felt that the tentative conclusions in EITF 00-21 made it clear that developing guidance for revenue recognition related to *multiple element arrangements* is a broad project with many implications that has "outgrown" the size and nature of a project contemplated by the mission of the EITF.

This view had been reflected in comments by some of those task force members, who had stated that the issue requires more *due process and public comments* than can be provided by the EITF's process. The SEC pointed out

¶19,013.15

that several FASB constituents had expressed similar views at the Financial Accounting Standards Advisory Council and in letters to the SEC staff. The SEC concurs with that viewpoint.

Issue No. 00-21, *Revenue Arrangements with Multiple Deliverables*. Many companies offer complete solutions to their customers' needs. Those solutions may involve the delivery or performance of multiple products, services, and rights to use assets, and performance may occur at different points in time or over different periods of time. The arrangements are often accompanied by initial installation, initiation, or activation services and generally involve either a fixed fee or a fixed fee coupled with a continuing payment stream. The continuing payment stream generally corresponds to the continuing performance and may be fixed, variable based on future performance, or composed of a combination of fixed and variable payments. Obviously, this is not a cut and dried procedure. It would appear that there might be as many variations as there are individual companies with individual customers. The issue is, then, how to account for those varied arrangements.

**Status**: At the November 21, 2002, EITF meeting, the Task Force ratified as a consensus the tentative conclusions it reached at the October 25, 2002, EITF meeting, with minor modifications. In addition, the Task Force indicated that the guidance in the consensus was effective for revenue arrangements entered into in fiscal periods beginning after June 15, 2003. At the January 23, 2003, and March 20, 2003, EITF meetings, the Task Force attempted to make certain revisions to paragraph 4(a) of the November minutes of this Issue to clarify that the provisions of this Issue do not override higher-level authoritative literature.

The November 2002 ratification was of a consensus on a model to be used, in the context of a multiple-deliverable revenue arrangement, in determining:

- How the arrangement consideration should be measured,
- Whether the arrangement should be divided into separate units of accounting, and, if so
- How the arrangement consideration should be allocated to the separate units of accounting.

The consensus was reached with the proviso that certain clarifications be made with respect to the scope provisions in paragraph 4(a) of that Issue. At the May 15, 2003, EITF meeting, the Task Force did finalized the scope provisions of Issue 00-21. The guidance is effective for revenue arrangements entered into in annual or interim reporting periods beginning after June 15, 2003.

Alternatively, entities are given the option to report the change in accounting as a cumulative-effect adjustment in accordance with APB Opinion No. 20, *Accounting Changes,* and FASB Statement No. 3, *Reporting Accounting Changes in Interim Financial Statements*. If this is the choice, disclosure should be made in periods subsequent to the date of initial application of the consensus of the amount of recognized revenue that was previously included in the cumulative effect adjustment.

## .17  Scope Language Revisions

At the May 2003 EITF meeting, the Task Force discussed and finalized certain revisions to the scope language in paragraph 4(a) of Issue 00-21. The purpose of those revisions is to clarify the application of Issue 00-21 to a multiple-deliverable arrangement (or a deliverable(s) in multiple-deliverable arrangement) that may already be covered by higher-level generally approved accounting procedures.

The revisions clarify that the higher-level literature, to which one or more of the deliverables in an arrangement are subject, falls into one of the following three categories:

1.  Higher-level GAAP that provides guidance regarding separation of the deliverables and the allocation of arrangement considerations.
2.  Higher-level literature that requires separation of the deliverables that are within its scope from those that are not but provides no guidance regarding allocation of the arrangement consideration to the deliverables that:
    a.  Are covered by higher-level GAAP.
    b.  Are not within the scope of higher-level literature.
3.  Higher-level literature that provides no guidance regarding the separation of deliverables that are within its scope from those that are not or regarding the allocation of arrangement consideration to the deliverables that are within its scope and to those that are not.

The Task Force believes that the following revised scope language adequately covers the application of Issue 00-21 under each of these three circumstances. Accordingly, Task Force members agreed to modify the existing language in the paragraph to indicate that the situations may already be covered by higher-level GAAP. That literature includes, but is not limited to:

*   FASB 13, *Accounting for Leases*
*   FASB 45, *Accounting for Franchise Fee Revenue*
*   FASB 66, *Accounting for Sales of Real Estate*
*   FASB Interpretation 45, *Guarantor's Accounting and Disclosure Requirements for Guarantees, Including Indirect Guarantees of Indebtedness of Others*
*   FASB Technical Bulletin 90-1, *Accounting for Separately Priced Extended Warranty and Product Maintenance Contracts*

- AICPA SOP 81-1, *Accounting for Performance of Construction-Type and Certain Production-Type Contracts*
- AICPA SOP 97-2, *Software Revenue Recognition*
- AICPA SOP 00-2, *Accounting by Producers or Distributors of Film*

This A- and B-level GAAP material may provide guidance with respect to whether and how to allocate consideration of a multiple-deliverable arrangement. The following list describes the three categories into which the higher-level GAAP falls. It also takes into consideration how to decide whether EITF Issue 00-21 or the higher-level GAAP should be selected to determine separate units of accounting and allocating arrangement consideration:

1. If higher-level GAAP provides guidance regarding the determination of separate units of accounting and how to allocate arrangement consideration to those separate units of accounting, the arrangement or the deliverable(s) in the arrangement that is within the scope of that higher-level literature should be accounted for in line with it rather than the guidance in EITF Issue 00-21.

2. If higher-level procedure provides guidance requiring separation of deliverables within its scope from deliverables not within its scope, but does not specify how to allocate arrangement consideration to each separate unit of accounting, the allocation should be performed on a relative fair value basis using the entity's best estimate of the fair value of the deliverables within its scope and those not within its scope. Subsequent accounting (identification of separate units of accounting and allocation of value thereto) for the value allocated to the deliverables not subject to higher-level literature should be governed by the provisions of Issue 00-21.

3. If higher-level GAAP provides guidance regarding neither the separation of the deliverables within its scope from those not within its scope nor the allocation of arrangement consideration to deliverables within its scope and outside of it, then the guidance in EITF 00-21 should be followed for purposes of separation and allocation. If this occurs, it is quite possible that a deliverable subject to the guidance of higher-level GAAP does not meet the criteria in EITF 00-21 to be considered a separate unit of accounting. Consequently, the arrangement consideration that would be allocated to that deliverable should be combined with the amount allocable to other applicable undelivered items within that arrangement. Then, the appropriate revenue recognition should be determined for those combined deliverables as a single unit of accounting.

After considering all of these eventualities, it becomes fairly obvious that each individual "arrangement" requires very individual accounting and allocation treatment.

**¶19,013.17**

Issue 03-5, *Applicability of AICPA Statement of Position 97-2, Software Revenue Recognition, to Non-Software Deliverables in an Arrangement Containing More-Than-Incidental Software.* Task Force consideration of the interaction between EITF Issue 00-21, *Revenue Arrangements with Multiple Deliverables,* and higher-level literature resulted in concern about apparent diversity in practice with respect to the application of the provisions of AICPA SOP 97-2, *Software Revenue Recognition,* to arrangements containing software deliverables and non-software deliverables (for example, computer hardware). A similar Issue had been removed from the EITF agenda in November of 2002 (along with eight other revenue recognition issues) in light of the Board's project on revenue recognition. This Issue takes into consider the narrower issue of whether the provisions of SOP 97-2, particularly the vendor-specific objective evidence (VSOE) requirements, apply to all deliverables in an arrangement containing more-than-incidental software or only software elements (as defined in SOP 97-2).

The Issue is whether nonsoftware deliverables included in an arrangement that contains software that is more than incidental to the products or services as a whole are meant to be included within the scope of SOP 97-2.

**Status**: A consensus was reached after discussion at the EITF's May 15, 2003, meeting. However, the FASB was not asked to ratify that consensus at its May 28, 2003, meeting. It was concluded that the minutes did not accurately reflect the Task Force's consensus.

Therefore, the Task Force considered alternative wording based on Task Force Members' comments, and at the July 31, 2003, EITF meeting a consensus was reached.

The Task Force agreed that in an arrangement that contains more than incidental software to the product or a service as a whole, only software and software-related elements are included within the scope of SOP 97-2. However, software-related elements include software-related products and services, such as those listed in paragraph 9 (i.e., upgrades/enhancements, postcontract customer support, or services) as well as other software-related products for which the software is essential to the functionality of the nonsoftware deliverable. One aspect of reaching the consensus revolved around the Task Force directing the FASB staff to refine the consensus by utilizing the separation criteria of EITF Issue 00-21 multiple deliverables to define "essential to the functionality."

The last step was the Board's ratification of the consensus at its August 13, 2003, meeting. (To become GAAP level C, a consensus of the Task Force must now be ratified by the FASB.)

## .19   The SEC Requests the IASB to Consider the Revenue Recognition Project

At that time, the SEC asked the International Accounting Standards Board (IASB) to undertake a project in partnership with national standard setters, including the FASB, to develop a comprehensive accounting standard for revenue recognition. (This action may well have been the impetus behind the FASB's putting the project on revenue recognition on their agenda.)

The SEC staff would have objected to an EITF consensus on the issue pending completion of a comprehensive revenue recognition standard subject to full due process. Until further standards are developed, they felt that registrants should disclose their accounting policy for revenue recognition. In addition, the staff would not object to a registrant's accounting provided it complied with the broad principles in SAB 101 and the related Frequently Asked Questions document on SAB 101.

The EITF 00-21 working group has met numerous times to address the issue of revenue recognition for multiple element arrangements, including gathering information from various affected industries. Largely because of those working group efforts, it has become clear that this is, indeed, a broad project. Some of the specific observations the SEC staff has noted include:

1. Many of the issues are fundamental revenue recognition questions with ramifications well beyond accounting for multiple element arrangements. As examples, the issues include providing answers to the following questions:

   a. What is a revenue element?

   b. What is a separate earnings process?

   c. What constitutes delivery?

   d. How is fair value of the separable elements in the arrangement determined?

2. As pointed out above, the SEC emphasized that other models for multiple element accounting already exist in GAAP, including SOP 81-1, *Accounting for Performance of Construction-Type and Certain Production-Type Contracts*, and SOP 97-2, *Software Revenue Recognition*. The tentative conclusion would be another model added to the mix, not a comprehensive solution.

3. The question of vendor performance (or lack thereof) is an issue involved in many types of revenue transactions including multiple elements. This issue should be discussed in a broader context.

4. The staff is concerned that, as broad as this issue is, and the resulting implications for all companies that commonly enter into such transactions today, greater due process is necessary to ensure all significant issues have been identified, and there has been adequate input received to afford a transparent standard for investors.

5. Additional time for due process would allow standard setters to study actual practice given the enhanced disclosures now being made as a result of SAB 101.

**¶19,013.19**

6. Revenue is often the single largest item in the financial statements, while *revenue recognition is the single largest issue involved in restatements of financial statements causing the greatest losses for investors*. The development of a high-quality standard for revenue recognition needs to be based on research of these issues and provide adequate investor protection.

The SEC recommended that the IASB work in close partnership with national standard setters on this project. They believe the FASB should play an active leading role on this project. They are of the opinion that such a project provides a significant opportunity for convergence of international accounting standards (including U.S. Standards) toward a single high-quality standard, which would level the playing field for companies worldwide. Convergence should result in "best of breed" accounting standards by drawing on the knowledge of both international and national standards setters.

No final decision had been reached when Issue 00-21 was discussed in June 2002, although there had been numerous meetings and discussions, and several models had been prepared.

## .21   Problem 12

Many Internet companies enter into various types of advertising arrangements (sometimes with other Internet companies) to provide advertising services over a period of time. These arrangements often include guarantees on "hits," "viewings," or "click-throughs."

It is not clear how the provider of the advertising takes progress toward these minimums into account in assessing revenue recognition. This issue could show up in various other industries as well (sales reps who guarantee they will reach a certain level of sales, advertising in other kinds of media, etc.).

The SEC staff mentioned that the terms of these arrangements vary somewhat from contract to contract. The issues that arise in some, but not all, of these contracts may be addressed in SAB 101, *Revenue Recognition in Financial Statements*. (Priority level 3.)

## .23   Status of Problem 12

It would be a good idea for the accountant to pay close attention to the disclosure requirements of SAB 101 until or if the Task Force considers taking a look at this problem. (See Issue 00-X4 at the end of this chapter.)

## .25   Problem 13

There are a growing number of "point" and other loyalty programs being developed in Internet businesses (similar to the airline and hotel industry programs). There are several well-known companies whose business model involves building a membership list through this kind of program. In some cases, the program operator may sell points to its business partners, who then issue them to their customers based on purchases or other actions. In other cases, the program operator awards the points in order to encourage its members to take actions that will generate payments from business partners to the programoperator.

Several issues related to these programs have arisen. The program operators believe that their customers are the companies for whom they provide advertising and marketing services. They view the redemption of the points or other reward as the "cost of sales," not as a revenue-generating activity. Therefore, they do not believe the fact that delivery under the reward occurs later should require revenue deferral. The SEC staff has accepted this argument only when the contracts with the business partners do not require the issuance or offer of any award, and speak merely to performing the advertising, marketing, or customer acquisition activities.

In other cases, the staff has required that some amount of revenue be deferred until the points are redeemed, to reflect that the substance of the arrangement involves multiple elements, one of which has not yet occurred. The same issue could also exist in customer acquisition programs. For example, offers exist whereby an ISP offers six months of free service to people who open accounts at certain online brokerages.

When revenue is recognized up front with an accrual of the redemption costs, a question arises as to whether companies should estimate "breakage" (the amount of rewards that will expire unused). Many Web-based businesses have loyalty programs that would also face this issue. For example, many sites issue rewards that can be used towards future purchases at the site. In recording the liability for those rewards, some argue that the gross amount of the rewards issued should be recorded, while others believe that the recorded amount should be reduced for an estimate of the rewards that will not be used, if this "breakage" can be reliably estimated. (Priority level 2.)

## .27   Status of Problem 13

There has been a great deal of discussion on this problem. The issues and discussion are in EITF 00-22, *Accounting for Points and Certain Other Time-Based or Volume-Based Sales Incentive Offers, and Offers for Free Products or Services to Be Delivered in the Future.* The Task Force has reached no final decisions and there is no additional guidance, but they have identified the issues and reached some tentative conclusions.

The issues are:

*Issue 1.*   How a vendor should account for an offer to a customer, in connection with a current revenue transaction, for free or discounted products or services delivered by the vendor that is redeemable only if the customer completes a specified cumulative level of revenue transactions or remains a customer for a specified time period.

*Issue 2.* How a vendor should account for an offer to a customer, in connection with a current revenue transaction, for free or discounted products or services from the vendor that is redeemable by the customer at a future date without a further exchange transaction with the vendor.

*Issue 3.* How a vendor should account for an offer to a customer to rebate or refund a specified amount of cash that is redeemable only if the customer completes a specified cumulative level of revenue transactions or remains a customer for a specified time period.

*Issue 4.* How a vendor should account for an offer to a customer, in connection with a current revenue transaction, for free or discounted products or services delivered by an unrelated entity (program operator) under an arrangement between the program operator and the vendor that is redeemable only if the customer completes a specified cumulative level of revenue transactions or remains a customer for a specified time period.

*Issue 5.* How a program operator should account for award credits sold (directly or indirectly) to other vendors and consumers.

At the January 2001 meeting, the Task Force reached consensus on Issue 3—that a vendor should recognize a rebate or refund obligation as a reduction of revenue.

Measurement of the obligation should be based on the estimated number of customers that will ultimately qualify for a "prize." However, if the amount of future rebates or refunds cannot be reasonably estimated, a liability (or "deferred revenue") should be recognized for the maximum potential amount of the refund or rebate (that is, no reduction for "breakage" should be made). The Task Force reached a consensus that the following factors may impair a vendor's ability to make a reasonable estimate of the amount of future rebates or refunds:

- Relatively long periods in which a particular rebate or refund may be claimed.
- The absence of historical experience with similar types of sales incentive programs with similar products, or the inability to apply such experience because of changing circumstances.
- The absence of a large volume of relatively homogeneous transactions.

The Task Force also reached consensus that changes in the estimated amount of rebates or refunds, and retroactive changes by a vendor (that is, an increase or a decrease in the rebate amount that is applied retroactively) to a

¶19,013.27

previous offer, should be recognized using a cumulative catch-up adjustment. The vendor should adjust the balance of its rebate obligation to the revised estimate immediately. The vendor should then reduce revenue on future sales based on the revised refund obligation rate as computed.

Entities should have applied the consensus on Issue 3 for the fiscal quarter ending after February 15, 2001. Amounts in prior years presented should be reclassified as a reduction of revenue.

## ¶19,015   Updated Status of EITF 00-22 Relating to Various Incentives

After reaching consensus on Issue 3, the Task Force requested that the FASB staff, together with the Working Group established to address EITF 00-21, on multiple deliverables, make additional progress on the Issue 00-21 model before further developing a revenue recognition approach for EITF 00-22. The Board may add to its agenda a narrow project that would address Issues 00-21 and 00-22. Consistent with previous requests by the Task Force, the Board is considering whether the due process afforded a Board project would represent a better forum in which to comprehensively consider the issues and the views of constituents. (Also see EITF 01-9, above.)

EITF 00-22 basically covers all industries that use point or other loyalty programs to draw and retain customers, including the airline and hospitality industries. Thus, this falls into the category of both old and new economy accounting situations.

The EITF has not yet reached a consensus on the Issue as a whole. In the final analysis, specific industries would be excluded from the scope of the study and discussions inasmuch as many industries are already addressed by higher-level GAAP and rulings; however, there are definite holes in existing guidance. One source points out that the AICPA Industry Audit Guide *Audits of Airlines* does not even mention accounting for frequent-flyer programs (and these are certainly not new or "new economy" means or methods of building a customer base).

## ¶19,017   Prepaid/Intangible Assets Versus Period Costs

Internet businesses often make payments to obtain members or customers or to obtain advertising space, distribution rights, supply agreements, and so on. In some cases, the questions of whether to capitalize or expense such costs and of assessing impairment of the rights obtained are not straightforward. Although similar payments are made by companies that do not have

Internet operations, the frequency with which this issue arises is higher in Internet companies.

## .01   Problem 14

Businesses often make payments for long-term contractual rights (e.g., Internet distribution rights) that are intended to be exploited only through Internet operations. The contractual rights meet the definition of an asset, but the measurement of the probable economic benefits is difficult. Some companies have asserted that these rights are immediately impaired, as their best estimate of the expected cash flows would indicate the asset is not recoverable.

The SEC staff has objected in these situations, and believes impairment should not be recorded unless it can be shown that conditions have changed since the execution of the contract. The evaluation of impairment of these kinds of assets is complicated because, as discussed earlier, the contractual rights purchased may be covered by different accounting standards, depending on the subject of the rights.

The staff pointed out EITF Issue 99-14 discusses *whether* impairment of such contracts should be assessed, but not *how*. They believe that guidance on how to assess impairment is *critical*, and should be provided either as implementation guidance to Issue 99-14 or in a separate issue. Therefore, the staff assigned it priority level 1.

## .03   Status of Problem 14

As mentioned above, the staff considers it of primary importance either to "finish" EITF 99-14 or to consider the "how" as a separate item. However, at this point the issue is not being discussed.

## .05   Problem 15

Many Internet companies enter into various types of advertising arrangements (sometimes with other Internet companies) in which one entity pays the other an up-front fee (or guarantees certain minimum payments over the course of the contract) in exchange for certain advertising services over a period of time. The payers in these arrangements have at times recognized an immediate loss on signing the contract, arguing that the expected benefits are less than the up-front or guaranteed payments.

The staff has indicated that it views these payments as being similar to payments made for physical advertising space, and that any up-front payment should be treated as prepaid advertising costs.

## .07    Status of Problem 15

No priority level was assigned to this problem, but the staff suggested that guidance on these arrangements can be provided along with guidance on Problem 14. Inasmuch as Problem 14 was assigned a level 1 priority, it would follow that this problem also needs expeditious attention. However, at present it is not being discussed.

## .09    Problem 16

Internet businesses often make large investments in building a customer or membership base. Several examples of this are:

- Sites that give users rewards (points, products, discounts, services) in exchange for setting up an account with the site.
- Sites that make payments to business partners for referring new customers or members.
- Businesses that give users PCs and Internet service for free if they are willing to spend a certain minimum amount of time on the Internet each month and are willing to have advertisements reside permanently on their computers.

In each of these cases, a question may arise as to whether the costs represent customer acquisition costs or costs of building a membership listing that qualify for capitalization, for example, by analogy to FASB 91, *Accounting for Nonrefundable Fees and Costs Associated with Originating or Acquiring Loans and Initial Direct Costs of Leases.* (Priority level 3.)

## .11    Status of Problem 16

As evidenced by the priority level 3 assigned by the staff, this is not a pressing problem. They point out that most companies appear to be expensing such costs as incurred; therefore, there is little diversity in practice to make it urgent that this issue be addressed. If and when the issue is addressed, the model should apply broadly to costs of building customer and membership lists.

At present, the Accounting Standards Committee (AcSec) of the AICPA is considering the matter.

## ¶19,019    MISCELLANEOUS ISSUES

## .01    Problem 17

Issued equity instruments often have conversion or exercisability terms that are variable based upon future events, such as the attainment of certain sales levels or a successful initial public offering (IPO). The issuer's accounting does not appear to raise new issues as it is covered in EITF Issues 96-18, *Accounting for Equity Instruments That Are Issued to Other Than Employees for Acquiring, or in Conjunction with Selling, Goods or Services*, and 98-5, *Accounting for Convertible Securities with Beneficial Conversion Features or Contingently Adjustable Conversion Ratios*.

For the holders, the instruments may be within the scope of FASB 133, *Accounting for Derivative Instruments and Hedging Activities*. However, because one or more of the underlyings are often based on the holder's or issuer's performance, FASB 133 will not always apply. In addition, it is not clear that the change in fair value of the instrument should be entirely recognized as a derivative holding gain or loss, versus an increase or decrease in revenues or operating expenses.

The SEC staff believes this issue seems to fit well with other issues being considered by the Derivatives Implementation Group (DIG). (Priority level 2.)

## .03   Status of Problem 17

In March 2000, the EITF reached consensus on EITF 00-8, *Accounting by a Grantee for an Equity Instrument to Be Received in Conjunction with Providing Goods or Services*. This Issue addresses 1) the date a grantee should use to measure the fair value of the equity instruments received, and 2) how the grantee should account for an increase in fair value as a result of reaching designated performance milestones. On the first issue, the Task Force reached consensus that the grantee should measure the fair value of the equity instruments using the stock price and other measurement assumptions as of the earlier of either of the following dates:

- The date the parties come to a mutual understanding of the terms of the equity-based compensation arrangement and a commitment is made for performance by the grantee to earn the equity instruments (a "performance commitment" in the context of the definition in Issue 96-18).
- The Task Force reached consensus on the second issue that:
  - If on the measurement date the quantity or any of the terms of the equity instrument are dependent on the achievement of a market condition, then the grantee should measure revenue based on the fair value of the equity instruments inclusive of the adjustment provisions.
  - That fair value would be calculated as the fair value of the equity instruments without regard to the market condition plus the fair value of the commitment to change the quantity or terms of the equity instruments if the market condition is met.

— If on the measurement date the quantity or any of the terms of the equity instruments are dependent on the achievement of grantee performance conditions, changes in fair value of the equity instrument that result from an adjustment to the instrument upon the achievement of a performance condition should be measured as additional revenue from the transaction.

— Changes in fair value of the equity instruments after the measurement date unrelated to the achievement of performance conditions should be accounted for in accordance with any relevant literature on the accounting and reporting for investments in equity instruments, such as Opinion 18, FASB 115, and FASB 133.

## .05  Problem 18

FASB 131, *Disclosures about Segments of an Enterprise and Related Information*, defines segments based on the information reviewed by top management in making decisions. Therefore, if top management reviews information about the Internet portion of a company's business separately from other operations, the Internet operations should be considered a separate operating segment.

## .07  Status of Problem 18

Because this is what they do, ensuring that FASB 131 is properly applied in this area and others will undoubtedly be a focus of the SEC staff. No priority level was assigned, nor was any further action by an outside group requested. The FASB staff implementation guide, "Segment Information: Guidance on applying Statement 131," is also pertinent.

## .09  Problem 19

The staff has noted that classification of expenses between various categories (costs of sales, marketing, sales, R&D) sometimes varies significantly among Internet companies for costs that appear similar. Examples include Web site development costs and expenses related to the various contractual rights discussed above.

The staff agreed that it is difficult to identify common elements between the classification issues that have arisen, making the preparation of general guidance difficult. (Priority level 3.)

## .11  Status of Problem 19

Since this is not really a new issue, the staff is keeping a close watch, but no discussion is being carried on at present.

¶19,019.05

## .13   Problem 20

When a company prints a coupon in the newspaper, it is common practice to record a liability and marketing expense for the estimated number of coupons that will be redeemed. The Internet provides several new methods of distributing coupons that may raise questions within the existing accounting models. For example:

- Product or service providers post coupons online, often for long periods of time.
- Internet retailers or service providers send e-mails inviting the receiver to get a discount on a purchase.

The staff commented that the area of accounting for coupons, rebates, and discounts is growing more significant, but it is not limited to Internet businesses. Developing a robust model to account for these arrangements would be helpful. (Priority level 2.)

## .15   Status of Problem 20

In accordance with the Emerging Issues Task Force Issue 00-14, *Accounting for Certain Sales Incentives* (EITF 00-14), expenses related to coupon redemptions, formerly classified as marketing and sales expense, are now recorded as a reduction of sales. EITF 00-14 required the implementation of this change effective within all reporting periods beginning in the first fiscal quarter beginning after May 18, 2000, and also requires all prior periods to be reclassified to reflect this modification. The accounting guidance for such programs provided by the EITF consensus No. 00-14 indicates that the Task Force reached a consensus on the issue relating to a sales incentive. This will not result in a loss on the sale of a product or service; therefore, a vendor should recognize the "cost" of the sales incentive at the latter of the following:

- The date at which the related revenue is recorded by the vendor.
- The date at which the sales incentive is offered (which would be the case when the sales incentive offer is made after the vendor has recognized revenue; for example, when a manufacturer issues coupons offering discounts on a product that it already has sold to retailers).

EITF 00-25, *Vendor Income Statement Characterization of Consideration from a Vendor to a Retailer*, picks up where EITF 00-14 left off.

However, when all is said and done, what results is that for coupons, rebates, and discounts offered voluntarily by vendors to customers:

- Cash sales incentives used at the time of sale should be recognized as a revenue reduction at the time of sale.

- Cash incentives that give the customer the right to receive a refund or rebate should be recognized as a reduction of revenue at the sale date based upon an estimate of the amount of incentives claimed by the ultimate customer.
- A free product or service incentives delivered at the time of sale should be recorded at cost as an expense at the time of sale.

The consensus was applicable to the first fiscal quarter starting after May 18, 2000.

(Additional discussions of EITF 00-14 and 00-25 are found at the beginning of this chapter and in Status of Problems 5 and 3, respectively.)

## ¶19,021 CATCH-ALL ISSUE FOR PROBLEMS NOT YET CONSIDERED

That the Emerging Issues Task Force of the FASB took the SEC letter from the SEC chief accountant seriously, and at least worked at considering and discussing all of the concerns raised by the SEC, is supported by the following.

Issue 99-V, "Remaining Issues from the SEC's October 18, 1999 Letter to the EITF." At the November 17-18, 1999 EITF meeting, Task Force members agreed that the issues identified in the SEC's October 18, 1999 letter to the Task Force should be addressed by the Task Force. This Issue is a placeholder for those issues that have not specifically been given an EITF Issue number.

**Status:** Issues identified under this Issue, either have been added to the EITF agenda as EITF Issues (both separately and in combination) (see Issues below) or have been removed from EITF consideration.

**Status:** The Issues identified under this Issue have been removed from the EITF agenda for a variety of reasons, particularly in relation to several of the FASB's projects.

Issue No. 00-x1, *Accounting for the Costs of Computer Files That Are Essentially Films, Music, or Other Content.* A description for this Issue is unavailable at this time.

**Status:** At the November 21, 2002, meeting, the Task Force agreed to remove this Issue from its agenda because it involves a fundamental question regarding the definition of an asset and, therefore, would more appropriately be addressed by the Board.

Issue No. 00-x2, *Accounting for Front-End and Back-End Fees.* A description for this Issue is unavailable at this time.

**Status:** At the November 21, 2002, meeting, the Task Force agreed to remove this Issue as well eight other Issues that are related to revenue recognition from its agenda because the FASB agreed to add to its agenda a major project on recognition of revenues and liabilities in financial statements.

Issue No. 00-x3, *Accounting for Access, Maintenance, and Publication Fees*. A description for this Issue is unavailable at this time.

**Status:** At the November 21, 2002, meeting, the Task Force agreed to remove this Issue as well eight other Issues that are related to revenue recognition from its agenda because the FASB agreed to add to its agenda a major project on recognition of revenues and liabilities in financial statements.

Issue No. 00-x4, *Accounting for Advertising or Other Arrangements Where the Service Provider Guarantees a Specified Amount of Activity*. A description for this Issue is unavailable at this time.

**Status:** At the November 21, 2002, meeting, the Task Force agreed to remove this Issue as well eight other Issues that are related to revenue recognition from its agenda because the FASB agreed to add to its agenda a major project on recognition of revenues and liabilities in financial statements.

## .01   Other "Retired" Issues

*Database and Other Collections of Information.* Issue No. 00-20, *Accounting for Costs Incurred to Acquire or Originate Information for Database Content and Other Collections of Information.* Some companies derive revenues from making databases and other collections of information available to users—electronically or otherwise. The Issue is how the costs of developing or acquiring those collections of information should be accounted for (that is, capitalized and amortized or charged to expense as incurred).

**Status:** At the November 21, 2002, meeting, the Task Force agreed to remove this Issue from its agenda because it involves a fundamental question regarding the definition of an asset and, therefore, would more appropriately be addressed by the Board. It had last been discussed at the September 20-21, 2000, meeting.

*Intellectual Property.* Issue No. 02-G, *Recognition of Revenue from Licensing Arrangements on Intellectual Property.* Licensing arrangements can take many forms, such as arrangements with a specific term or those with an unlimited term. The accounting for licensing arrangements varies in practice. Some may view the licensing of intellectual property as indistinguishable from a lease of a physical asset in which the total arrangement fee should be recognized over the contract term, whereas others may view such licensing arrangements as indistinguishable from the licensing of software or motion picture rights in which revenue is recognized once the license has been conveyed and the seller has no further obligations. The latter group believes their approach is fully consistent with the guidance in AICPA Statements of Position 97-2, *Software Revenue Recognition*, and 00-2, *Accounting by Producers or Distributors of Films*. The issue is when to recognize revenue from licensing arrangements on intellectual property.

¶19,021.01

**Status:** At the November 21, 2002, meeting, the Task Force agreed to remove this Issue as well eight other Issues that are related to revenue recognition from its agenda because the FASB agreed to add to its agenda a major project on recognition of revenues and liabilities in financial statements.

*Accounting for "Points" and other Incentive Offers.* Issue No. 00-22, *Accounting for "Points" and Certain Other Time-Based or Volume-Based Sales Incentive Offers, and Offers for Free Products or Services to Be Delivered in the Future.* An increasing number of point and other loyalty programs are being developed in Internet businesses, in addition to similar programs in the airline and hotel industries. There are companies whose business models involve building a membership list through this kind of program. In some cases, the program operator may sell points to its business partners, who then issue those points to their customers based on purchases or other actions. In other cases, the program operator awards the points in order to encourage its members to take actions that will generate payments from business partners to the program operator. The Issue is how to account for point and other loyalty programs and is scoped broadly to include all industries that utilize point or other loyalty programs, including the airline and hospitality industries.

**Status:** A consensus was reached on Issue 3. The Task Force requested that the FASB staff, together with the Working Group established to address EITF Issue No. 00-21, *Revenue Arrangements with Multiple Deliverables*, make additional progress on the Issue 00-21 model before further developing a revenue recognition approach for this Issue. In the near future, the FASB will be considering adding to its agenda a narrow project that would address Issues 00-21 and 00-22. Consistent with previous requests by the Task Force, the Board is considering whether the due process afforded a Board project would represent a better forum for comprehensive consideration of the issues and the views of constituents. At the November 21, 2002, meeting, the Task Force agreed to remove this Issue, as well as eight other Issues that are related to revenue recognition, from its agenda. The Board agreed to add to its agenda a major project on recognition of revenues and liabilities in financial statements.

## ¶19,023   IF ALL ELSE FAILS

The Office of Internet Enforcement (OIE), formed in July, 1998, administers the Enforcement Division's Internet program. The Internet has brought significant benefits to investors; most notably, enhanced access to information (both in speed and quantity) and lower costs to execute trades. At the same time, unfortunately, the Internet has opened new avenues for fraud artists to attempt to swindle the investing public. To combat this online fraud, the OIE:

1.  Identifies areas of surveillance.
2.  Formulates investigative procedures.

3. Provides strategic and legal guidance to Enforcement staff nationwide.
4. Conducts Internet investigations and prosecutions (a task it shares with the entire Enforcement staff).
5. Performs training for Commission staff and outside agencies.
6. Serves as a resource on Internet matters for the entire Commission.

The OIE coordinates the activities of the "CyberForce," a group of more than 200 Commission attorneys, accountants, and investigators nationwide. In addition to their regular responsibilities, they conduct certain "surf days," which are specific, targeted surveillance efforts to further enhance the Enforcement Division's surveillance activities. These "Enforcement Sweeps" target similar types of Internet misconduct for investigation and, where appropriate, prosecution. This allows for the coordinated filing of Enforcement actions and allows the Commission to deliver its message more forcefully and effectively. The OIE also serves as a liaison on Internet matters with other regulatory agencies and both national and international law enforcement agencies.

The OIE, together with the SEC's Office of Investor Education and Assistance, manages the SEC Complaint Center, which receives more than 1,000 complaints per day concerning Internet-related potential securities violations. These violations involve such scams as phony offerings, market manipulations, affinity frauds (targeting a particular ethnic group), and pyramid and Ponzi schemes.

## ¶19,025  AICPA Top 10 Technologies List

At the November 21, 2002, meeting, the Task Force agreed to remove this Issue from its agenda because it involves a fundamental question regarding the definition of an asset and, therefore, would more appropriately be addressed by the Board. It had last been discussed at the September 20-21, 2000, meeting.

For the fourth consecutive year, professionals in the fields of information technology and accounting have selected Information Security as the number one technology to watch in 2006, according to the results of the 17th annual Top Ten Technologies survey of the AICPA. Four new technologies join six hold-overs on the 2006 list: Assurance and Compliance, IT Governance, Privacy Management, and Spyware Detection and Removal.

The following are the 2006 Top 10 Technologies. Those new to the list are noted.

1. **Information Security**. The hardware, software, processes, and procedures in place to protect information systems from internal and external threats.
2. *NEW* **Assurance and Compliance Applications (e.g. SOX 404, ERM).** Collaboration and compliance tools that enable various stakeholders to monitor, document, assess, test and report on compliance with specified controls.

3. **Disaster and Business Continuity Planning**. The development, monitoring, and updating of the process by which organizations plan for continuity of their business in the event of a loss of business information resources due to impairments such as theft, virus infestation, weather damage, accidents, or other malicious destruction.

4. *NEW* **IT Governance**. IT governance is a structure of relationships and processes to direct and control the enterprise in order to achieve the enterprise's goals by adding value, while still balancing risk versus return over IT and its processes.

5. *NEW* **Privacy Management**. Privacy encompasses the rights and obligations of individuals and organizations with respect to the collection, use, disclosure, and retention of personal information.

6. **Digital Identity and Authentication Technologies**. A way to ensure users are who they say they are—that the user who attempts to perform functions in a system is in fact the user who is authorized to do so.

7. **Wireless Technologies**. Connectivity and transfer of data between devices via the airwaves, i.e. without physical connectivity.

8. **Application and Data Integration**. Using current and emerging technologies, including .NET, web-services, Java, XML (the foundation for XBRL) & Ajax, to facilitate integration of data between heterogeneous applications. In its most basic format, XBRL focuses on the agreement to improve gathering, analyzing and sharing business reporting data.

9. **Paperless Digital Technologies**. Document and content management includes the process of capturing, indexing, storing, retrieving, searching, and managing documents electronically including database management (PDF and other format.

10. *NEW* **Spyware Detection and Removal**. Technology that detects and removes programs attempting to covertly gather and transmit confidential user information without his or her knowledge or permission.

**Honorable Mention**

In addition to the Top Ten Technologies list, this year the AICPA is also including a section for Honorable Mention, the technologies that placed #11–#15 in the final tabulation.

11. **E-mail Filtering including Spam and Malware scanning**. Solutions (software, hardware appliances and/or managed services) that help reduce/eliminate unwanted, nuisance and malicious e-mail delivered to end-user inboxes by employing a number of strategies including white list, black list, content filtering, domain name authentication and real-time SMTP connection monitoring and blocking.

¶19,025

12. **Outsourcing**. Hiring an outside resource to perform all, or portions, of an organization's internal IT support, transaction processing, application support or special projects.

13. **Storage & Backup Technologies**. Technologies that allow additional storage capacity, either locally or over the Web, to be added to a device or network that can then be used for additional space or data backup.

14. **Patch & Network Management Tools**. Tools and strategies to centrally patch, manage, upgrade and maintain applications and operating systems across an enterprise, eg. MS MOM (Microsoft Operation Manager), MS WSUS (Microsoft Windows Server Update Service), Shavlik, Dell Open Manage, ZenWorks, Unicenter TNG, etc.

15. **Technology Competency & Effective Utilization**. The methodology and curriculum by which personnel learn to understand and utilize technology. This includes learning competency and learning plans to increase the knowledge of individuals.

# Chapter 20

# E-Commerce and E-Communication

## CONTENTS

## ¶20,000 OVERVIEW

Forecasts of Internet business—variously called e-commerce, e-business, EC, e-tail, cyber-business or virtual markets—were so astronomical that they strained credibility. Internet commerce was growing in exponential leaps and bounds.

And, yes, the forecasts were overblown. Such growth could not be sustained, but e-commerce is decidedly an important facet of personal and business activities today. Considering the impressive growth in retail sales in 2006 over 2005, as shown by the retail e-commerce figures below, it is fairly obvious that many are finding that buying online is the way to go.

The term "e-commerce" has already been superseded by the term "e-business." E-commerce can be described as obtaining and distributing goods and services over the Internet using digital technology. Even though many use the terms interchangeably, the more encompassing term "e-business" can be defined as including all activities conducted by a business over the Internet. This definition for e-business extends beyond the definition of e-commerce by covering a digital approach to the whole enterprise, including other parts of the IT system and other non-transactional activities, such as recruiting employees through the Internet.

## ¶20,001 ECONOMIC EFFECT OF E-COMMERCE SALES

E-commerce sales are sales of goods and services in which an order is placed by the buyer or price and terms of sale are negotiated over an Internet, extranet, Electronic Data Interchange (EDI) network, electronic mail, or other online system. Payment may or may not be made online.

The Census Bureau of the Department of Commerce announced in August that the estimate of U.S. retail e-commerce sales for the second quarter of 2006, adjusted for seasonal variation and holiday and trading-day differences, but not for price changes, was $26.3 billion, an increase of 4.6 percent (±1.7%) from the first quarter of 2006.

Total retail sales for the second quarter of 2006 were estimated at $984.9 billion, an increase of 0.9 percent (±0.3%) from the first quarter of 2006. The second quarter 2006 e-commerce estimate increased 23.0 percent (±5.4%) from the second quarter of 2005 while total retail sales increased 6.6 percent (±0.5%) in the same period. E-commerce sales in the second quarter of 2006 accounted for 2.7 percent of total sales.

On a not adjusted basis, the estimate of U.S. retail e-commerce sales for the second quarter of 2006 totaled $24.8 billion, an increase of 1.0 percent (±1.7%)* from the first quarter of 2006. The second quarter 2006 e-commerce estimate increased 22.9 percent (±5.4%) from the second quarter of 2005 while total retail sales increased 6.9 percent (±0.5%) in the same period. E-commerce sales in the second quarter of 2006 accounted for 2.5 percent of total sales.

## .01   Estimation Method Used in Sales Estimates

Retail e-commerce sales are estimated from the same sample used for the Monthly Retail Trade Survey (MRTS) to estimate preliminary and final U.S. retail sales. Advance U.S. retail sales are estimated from a subsample of the MRTS sample that is not of adequate size to measure changes in retail e-commerce sales.

A stratified simple random sampling method is used to select approximately 11,000 retail firms whose sales are then weighted and benchmarked to represent the complete universe of more than 2 million retail firms. The MRTS sample is probability based and represents all employer firms engaged in retail activities as defined by the North American Industry Classification System (NAICS). Coverage includes all retailers regardless of whether they are engaged in e-commerce. Online travel services, financial brokers and dealers, and ticket sales agencies are not classified as retail and are not included in either the total retail or retail e-commerce sales estimates. Nonemployers are represented in the estimates through benchmarking to prior annual survey estimates that include nonemployer sales based on administrative records. E-commerce sales are included in the total monthly sales estimates.

## .03   Sampling Updated to Add New Retail Businesses

The MRTS sample is updated on an ongoing basis to account for new retail employer businesses (including those selling via the Internet), business deaths, and other changes to the retail business universe. Because many retail firms are adding e-commerce sales to their traditional sales, they are asked each month to report e-commerce sales separately. For each month of the quarter, data for nonresponding sampling units are imputed from responding sampling units falling within the same kind of business and sales size category. Responding firms account for approximately 85 percent of the e-commerce sales estimate and about 80 percent of the estimate of U.S. retail sales for any quarter.

For each month of the quarter, estimates are obtained by summing weighted sales (either reported or imputed). The monthly estimates are benchmarked to prior annual survey estimates. Estimates for the quarter are obtained by summing the monthly benchmarked estimates. The estimate for the most recent quarter is a preliminary estimate. Therefore, the estimate is subject to revision.

## ¶20,003   ACCOUNTING ISSUES

A study called "Electronic Commerce Trends, Technology and the Security, Control and Audit Implications" was prepared for the Institute of Internal Auditors (IIA) with partial funding from the International Federation of Accountants (IFAC). That report emphasized the need for accountants and auditors of an organization to work closely with management in setting up and developing their e-business and e-communication systems. The study identifies many accounting issues that must be considered.

## ¶20,005 TOPICS FOR CONSIDERATION

The following is a discussion of some of these accounting problems and considerations relating to them.

### .01 Software

The considerable software infrastructure needed to implement an e-commerce strategy will be obtained from software vendors or developed internally. Existing U.S. software related accounting rules governing these transactions are expected to remain unchanged.

***Vendor Software.*** AICPA Statement of Position (SOP) 97-2, *Software Revenue Recognition*, requires that revenue should be recognized on software or software systems arrangements that do not require significant production, modification, or customization of software when delivery has occurred and all of the following tests are met:

1. Persuasive evidence that a sale or lease arrangement exists.
2. Delivery of the product or service has occurred.
3. The seller must not retain any specific performance obligation.
4. The vendor's fee is fixed or determinable.
5. Appropriate recognition is given to the likelihood of returns.
6. Collectibility is probable.

Revenue from software or software system arrangements that require significant production, modification, or customization of software should be accounted for using long-term construction-type contract accounting.

The vendor fee in software arrangements that consist of multiple elements, such as upgrades, must be allocated to the various elements. The portion of a fee allocated to an element should be recognized when the revenue is earned and realized.

***Internally Developed Software.*** *Accounting for the Cost of Computer Software Developed for Internal Uses* (SOP 98-1) requires the costs associated with the acquisition and development of software for internal use to be *capitalized* when both of the following occur:

1. Management authorizes and commits to funding a computer software project and believes that it is probable that the project will be completed and the software will be used to perform the function intended.

2. Conceptual formulation, design, and testing of possible software project alternatives have been completed.

Capitalization of costs should cease when the computer software development project is substantially completed and ready for its intended use. This point occurs when substantially all testing is complete.

Thus, companies developing their e-commerce software internally will find it necessary to:

1. Capitalize the direct costs of the development.
2. Amortize the capitalized cost over the software's useful life.

A high level of uncertainty typically accompanies the introduction of new software applications, such as e-commerce. How reliable are the decisions to commence capitalization of e-commerce development costs and the choice of their related amortization periods?

If there is a question of application for U.S. companies, the issue is of even more concern when dealing with non-U.S. companies. Many of them rely heavily on local accounting standards which may or may not make provision for accounting for software.

## .03   Acquisitions and Mergers

Growth through mergers and acquisitions has become a popular e-commerce strategy. E-commerce companies are seeking to benefit from economies of scale by rapidly expanding their share of existing markets and entering new markets. In nearly all of these business combinations, the accounting for in-process research and development and goodwill could be major issues because of the large amount of money involved and the level of uncertainty associated with potential benefits. An acquired company could present a sizable goodwill factor involving market share, software, and people not on the balance sheet.

Accounting rules in FASB 141 and FASB 142, which are discussed in the Chapter, "Actions of the Financial Accounting Standards Board," apply to these specific topics.

## .05   Contingency Losses

There is a high level of uncertainties associated with e-commerce related contingency losses. Transactions often involve purchases of products and services where the purchaser does not physically inspect the product purchased or interview the service provider directly.

This is not a new phenomenon. Catalog sales companies have operated in this way for many years. The change that the expansion of e-commerce brings is that many companies without any experience in this type of transaction are now engaged in it.

The e-commerce accounting issue that this development raises for these inexperienced companies is:

How do you estimate reliably such contingency losses as returns, volume discounts, and other sales allowances when you do not have an historical record on which to base your estimates of future losses and adjustments?

This uncertainty issue is more important to companies in the U.S. and those other countries, such as the UK, that have contingency losses recognition rules that require reasonable estimates of contingency losses and strictly prohibit the establishment of general reserves.

## .07   Start-Up Activities

E-commerce is not a single technology, but rather a sophisticated combination of technologies and consumer-based services integrated to form a new way of conducting business. This new form, however, is still itself in a start-up mode. The future of e-commerce is bright and viable; the application, however, has not been fully integrated into the business mainstream. For many companies, the introduction of e-commerce sales activities could be considered a start-up activity.

Start-up activities are defined broadly as those onetime activities related to opening a new facility, introducing a new product or service, conducting business in a new territory, conducting business with a new class of customer or beneficiary, initiating a new process in an existing facility, or commencing some new operation. Start-up activities include activities related to organizing a new entity.

According to generally accepted accounting practices (GAAP), start-up activity costs must be expensed as incurred. For U.S. companies that add e-commerce sales activities to their traditional business practices, the question will be: Is this a start-up activity?

If it is not, the costs may be capitalized. Again, this raises the issue of the level of uncertainty associated with the amortization period selected. Outside of the U.S., entities and their investors are confronted with a variety of different accounting treatments of e-commerce start-up sales activities.

Since these e-commerce start-up costs can be very material, management, their shareholders and potential investors need to be aware of the costs and the accounting for them.

## .09   Nondisclosure

In many companies, e-commerce activities are not carried out by a specific organizational unit. Often these activities will spread throughout the operating activities of many organizational units.

Under U.S. operating segment disclosure rules, as well as those of many other countries, only the organizational unit's operating results need be disclosed. If a company chooses to stick by the rules, investors may not be given the company's e-commerce-related operating results. Since, as noted above, e-commerce start-up activities are often unprofitable, nondisclosure may be detrimental to the interests of investors at least in the short run.

## .11  Credit Losses

Electronic payment systems are often an integral part of e-commerce activities. From the accounting point of view, this can be good news and bad news.

From the vendor's point of view, it can be good news since often the buyer's payment is guaranteed by a third party, such as a credit card issuer, that absorbs the bad debt risk. This reduces the uncertainty associated with establishing bad debt reserves.

On the other hand, it can be bad news for the party absorbing the credit risk. With the expansion of e-commerce, many products, customers, sellers, and services outside of the prior experience of the credit grantor will be paid for electronically. Again, the lack of a historical record raises the level of uncertainty associated with making estimates about future events, which in this case is the appropriate level of the bad debt reserve.

## .13  Asset Impairments

Radical changes in the way business is conducted have always led to asset impairments. Therefore, it should be expected that the growth of e-commerce may lead to the impairment of some asset groups. In some cases, asset groups used in traditional business activities may be made obsolete by the introduction of e-commerce. In fact, the rapid evolution of e-commerce and its associated technologies will define technical obsolescence in terms of months, not years. The "new" assets may be impaired very quickly. In other circumstances, some asset groups devoted to e-commerce may become impaired as a result of the inability of the company to implement its e-commerce strategy successfully.

Historically, management has been slow to recognize asset impairment losses. This attitude will probably not change; therefore, balance sheets of companies engaging in e-commerce could very possibly include overvalued assets.

## .15  Customer Solicitation Costs

Many of the companies engaged in e-commerce will have to spend considerable sums of money to build their e-commerce customer base. Some may capitalize part of these customer solicitation costs.

U.S. accounting standards generally require these customer solicitation costs to be expensed as incurred. The only exception is the cost of direct mail advertising. It can be capitalized only if the company can base the amortization period choice on a reasonable estimate of the direct mailings' response rate. Since for many companies, e-commerce will be a new business activity, they will not have a historical record of response rates upon which to base their estimate of future response rates.

Outside of the U.S., advertising costs are generally accounted for under the local intangible assets rules, which may permit capitalization of advertising costs. Companies with limited e-commerce experience that capitalize direct mail advertising costs must be very cautious since their historical response-rate record may be inadequate.

## .17  Materiality

Under generous interpretations of what is *material*, the sales, costs, assets, and liabilities of a company's e-commerce start-up activities may be regarded as *immaterial*. This could be a problem. In recent years, some managers have adopted the point of view that since U.S. GAAP does not apply to immaterial items, they can account for immaterial items in any way they choose.

As shown in the Chapter, "Materiality", the SEC has changed all of this. A cavalier attitude toward materiality is unacceptable practice. The new definition of materiality in essence says, "if it's material to investors, it's material." Under this test, relatively small amounts can be material in a high price-earnings ratio-valued stock situation.

## .19  Uncertainty

E-commerce is a new form of business and, like many new business forms, there can often be a high level of uncertainty associated with the future prospects of many of those engaging in it. Since accounting involves many estimates of future events, this uncertainty can create major accounting problems involving contingency loss estimates, recognition of intangibles, asset impairment loss recognition, and amortization period choices. Consequently, the reliability of management estimates will be crucial to the welfare of the entity.

## ¶20,007   E-BUSINESS ACCOUNTING PRINCIPLES AND CRITERIA

Management is responsible for the attainment of the enterprise's objectives *in accordance with the business strategy it has defined.* If an e-business system is used for this purpose, it is important that those in management make appropriate arrangements to manage the ensuing risks. An enterprise's e-business strategy, as an integral part of the information technology (IT) strategy, ordinarily includes consideration of *all aspects of business risks, including IT risks.* Consequently:

1. Management assesses IT risks with respect to information reliability.
2. Information reliability, in turn, depends on IT system reliability.
3. IT system reliability depends on IT controls.

It is important that management implements IT controls that operate effectively to help ensure that an IT system performs reliably. Information generated by an IT system will be reliable where that system is capable of operating without material error, fault, or failure during a specified period. This also applies to accounting information. The following *principles* may be used to evaluate whether processed accounting information is reliable:

1. Principles for accounting information security.
2. Principles for appropriate accounting information processing.

The reliability of accounting information relating to the entire e-business process is increased if the accounting system satisfies both accounting information security principles and the principles for appropriate accounting information processing.

The principles for appropriate accounting information processing are fulfilled where the e-business system and the entire IT system safeguards comply with the following general criteria for the input, processing, output and storage of information and data about e-business transactions:

1. Completeness.
2. Accuracy.
3. Timeliness.
4. Assessability.
5. Order.
6. Inalterability (logging of alterations).

The *completeness* criterion refers to the extent and scope of processed e-business transactions—that is, the recipient of transactions determines that all transactions are input completely into the e-business system. Each transaction should be individually identifiable and recorded separately. The completeness of the recorded entries should be demonstrably preserved throughout processing and for the duration of the retention period.

In accordance with the *accuracy* criterion, processed information should accurately reflect e-business transactions—that is, recorded transactions should reflect the actual events and circumstances in conformity with the applicable financial reporting framework.

Under the *timeliness* criterion, e-business transactions should be recorded on a timely basis—that is, as soon as possible after the transaction has occurred. When time elapses between the occurrence of a transaction and its recording, further appropriate action may become necessary to determine completeness and accuracy of the entry recorded.

Under the criterion of *assessability*, each item and disclosure in the financial statements should be verifiable in that it can be traced back to individual entries in the books and records and to the original source documents that support that entry. Furthermore, the criterion of assessability implies that an expert third party should be able to gain an insight into the transactions and position of the enterprise within a reasonable period of time.

To meet the *order* criteria, accounting entries in an accounting system should be organized in both chronological order (a journal function) and by nature (by type of asset, liability, revenue or expense—a ledger function). Transactions and their recording should be identifiable and capable of conversion into human-readable format in a reasonable period of time.

In accordance with the criterion of *inalterability*, no entry or record may be changed after the posting date so that its original content can no longer be identified, unless the change to the original content can be identified by means of a log of such alterations. Therefore, alterations of entries or records should be made in a way that both the original content and the fact that changes have been made are evident or can be made evident. For program-generated or program-controlled entries (automated or recurring vouchers), changes to the underlying data used to generate and control accounting entries would also be recorded. This applies, in particular, to the logging of modifications of settings relevant to accounting or the parameterization of software and the recording of changes to master data.

Before accepting a transaction for processing, it would be useful to verify the following:

1. That all transaction details have been entered by the customer.
2. The authenticity of the customer.
3. The availability of the products or services to be supplied.
4. The reasonableness of the order, for example, to identify an unusually large quantity resulting from an input error, or to identify erroneous duplicate orders.
5. The pricing structure applied, including delivery costs, where appropriate.
6. The method of payment or credit worthiness of the customer.
7. The non-repudiability of the transaction in that its author cannot later deny having entered into it.

In an e-business process, it is often not possible to provide evidence of transactions by way of conventional vouchers. Despite this fact, transactions

¶20,007

should continue to be supported by appropriate documentary evidence (i.e., the source document entry function).

## ¶20,009  TAXING PROBLEMS

What of the tax accountant? The accounting for e-commerce will require organizations to review current policies and procedures. Accounting concerns such as recording multiple tax payments, which might not be an issue in a paper-based trading environment, could quickly become a major concern. Very possibly, other tax concerns will develop with many more questions than answers:

1. How soon will the federal government decide that it really should get its share from all of these Web sites?
2. Will there be a flat electronic tax applied to every e-business transaction?
3. How will an organization account for and respond to different tax regulations governing commerce as they vary by country, by state, by county, by city?
4. Will there be some form of interstate or intercountry tax?
5. How would these taxes (if forthcoming) affect the cost of doing e-business?
6. Who will collect the appropriate taxes, and how will the taxes be submitted to the proper taxing authority?
7. Will electronic transactions be taxed in their city/state/country of origin or at some other destination (or all of the above)?
8. What new procedures will be designed to account for varying tax revenue, which will be transferred to organizations in distant countries and various states?

These and many additional questions, which affect tax accounting for Web-based commerce, will need to be addressed on an international level. In the meantime, they are being considered here on a national level.

## .01  Commission on Electronic Commerce

Even discounting the global aspects of Internet taxation, there are more than enough questions relating to domestic taxes. "The Internet Tax Freedom Act," enacted by Congress in October 1998 established a three-year moratorium on "new Internet tax" and set up the Advisory Commission on Electronic Commerce. It is made up of 19 members—13 representatives from governmental and nonprofit entities and 6 from private-sector industry.

They are assigned the task of conducting a thorough study of "Federal, state and local and international taxation and tariff treatment of transactions using the Internet and Internet access and other comparable intrastate, interstate or international sales activities."

Consensus appears to be growing to extend the ban on levying "new" taxes on the Internet for as much as three-to-five years beyond the present cutoff date of October 22, 2001. Congress has extended the original moratorium twice. The most recent extension, titled the Internet Tax Nondiscrimination Act is currently scheduled to expire in November 2007.

But what of the "old" taxes? Yes, there are some and there could be more, regardless of a moratorium.

1. Consumers in some areas are supposed to pay use taxes on those purchases on the Internet for which no sales tax was paid. (In fact, some states include the appropriate tax form in their income tax package as a reminder.)

2. Sales tax must be paid if the buyer lives in a state in which the e-business has a facility such as a retail store, warehouse, or factory in that state. (Therefore, many e-retailers that actually do have a physical site of any variety have located them in the states that have no retail sales tax.)

3. Then there is the distinction between "new" and "old." If the state and local governments begin losing too much tax revenue from e-commerce, they might decide that sales tax is an "old" tax and just extend it to e-commerce.

## .03  Taxation of International E-Commerce Sales

An online merchant selling to international customers must pay careful attention to the tax implications of those sales. In general, once a company crosses a certain threshold of activity in a foreign country, the company becomes subject to income tax in that foreign country. In many cases, a company must have a "permanent establishment" in the foreign country before that country will subject the company to income tax on the company's business profits from that country. Thus, for example, an American online vendor of digitally or physically delivered products that does not have equipment or personnel located in Japan generally would not be subject to Japanese income tax on its sales. However, there are important exceptions to this general rule. Some payments from customers in a foreign country may be subject to withholding tax by the foreign country (e.g., if the foreign country determines that the payments are "royalties" or other payments subject to withholding).

Electronically delivered goods should be treated like any other sale to a foreign customer. It generally is the responsibility of customer/importers to declare their purchase and pay any taxes. Tax and tariff information on a country-by-country basis is available, or a Commercial Specialist in the targeted country offers more information.

In addition, a foreign country may impose other types of taxes, such as value-added tax (VAT), on sales into its jurisdiction. For example, as of

July 1, 2003, the EU member states began taxing sales of electronically supplied products and services by non-EU firms to nonbusiness customers located in the EU. Non-EU providers of electronically supplied products and services are now required to register with a tax authority in a member state and collect and remit VAT based on the VAT rate of the member state in which their customer is located. More information on online taxation can be obtained from the Department of Commerce.

## ¶20,011   CAUTIONS FOR E-COMMUNICATION WEB SITE USE

With the Internet now playing an increasingly important role in investing and financial reporting, the Securities and Exchange Commission Private Securities Litigation Reform Act of 1995 may be cited frequently. It is important that companies be aware of pitfalls that could lead to a new wave of litigation.

Following are several cautions that could reduce the legal risks from electronic disclosures, particularly those associated with company Web sites:

1.  Meaningful, obvious, clearly worded cautionary disclaimers must accompany any and all "forward-looking" statements.
2.  Some of these forward-looking statements may appear in varied guises: transcripts of speeches, press conferences, and quotes should be treated as written disclosures and must include an appropriate written disclaimer situated as closely as possible to the statement.
3.  A full set of financial statements and notes should always be included. "Selected" portions, summations, "fractured"financial statements, even a complete set without the footnotes, could be an invitation for litigation.
4.  A company should not commit to update disclosures and should include on its Web site disclaimers regarding the absence of any obligation to do so. However, the site should be monitored very closely for any information that is outdated or misleading.
5.  Management should be wary of any "selectivity" relating to analysts. Do not frame, inline, or link to analysts' sites or include analysts' comments on the company's site. If a list of analysts covering the company is provided, the names of *all* analysts must be included, not just those with favorable comments.
6.  Probably the most cogent advice relating to "chat rooms" (for the company as well as the investor) has come from the chairman of the SEC in a much publicized speech:
    "Chat rooms, which increasingly have become a source of information and misinformation for many investors, have been compared to a high-tech version of morning gossip or advice at the company water

cooler. But, at least you knew your co-workers at the water cooler. For the future sake of this medium, I encourage investors to take what they see over chat rooms—not with a grain of salt—but with a rock of salt."

Obviously, it is in the best interest of the company to establish well-defined policies for employee participation in chat room discussions about their jobs and their organization.

7. Keeping in mind the seemingly never-ending abilities of the "hackers" to access a mainframe and compromise a Web site, it is paramount that there should be continuing reevaluation of a system's security measures.

## ¶20,013  INTERNATIONAL GUIDANCE HELPS AUDITORS ADDRESS E-COMMERCE RISKS

Increasing use of the Internet for e-business related to various modes of business relationships is introducing new elements of risk that need to be considered by accountants when planning and performing the audit of financial statements. These business relationships include:

- Business to consumer.
- Business to business.
- Business to government.
- Business to employee.

To assist auditors in identifying and assessing these risks, IFAC's International Auditing Practices Committee (now the International Auditing and Assurance Standards Board, or IAASB) issued a new practice statement, *Electronic Commerce—Effect on the Audit of Financial Statements*, in May, 2002. (The IAASB is an IFAC committee that works to improve the uniformity of auditing practices and related services throughout the world by issuing pronouncements on a variety of audit and assurance functions and by promoting their acceptance worldwide.)

Such usage is introducing new elements of risk that need to be considered by accountants when planning and performing the audit of financial statements.

Impetus for the study was the realization that growth of Internet activity without close attention *by the entity* to those risks could affect the auditor's assessments of the risks. It was pointed out that an entity's e-commerce strategy could affect the security of the financial records and the completeness and reliability of the financial information produced. Even with "due diligence" by the most sophisticated IT technician, hackers appear to be able to access almost any computer. But that doesn't mean that every effort should not be made to enhance security.

## .01  Focus of Attention

To assist auditors in identifying and assessing the risks, this new International Auditing Practice Statement (IAPS) helps auditors address e-commerce issues by focusing on the following:

1. The level of skills and knowledge required to understand the effect of e-commerce on the audit.
2. The extent of knowledge the auditor should have about the entity's business environment, activities and industries.
3. Business, legal, regulatory, and other risks faced by entities engaged in e-commerce activities.
4. Internal control considerations, such as an entity's security infrastructure and transaction integrity.
5. The effect of electronic records on audit evidence.

The guidance in this statement is particularly relevant to the application of three International Standards on Auditing (ISAs): ISA 300, *Planning;* ISA 310, *Knowledge of the Business;* and ISA 400, *Risk Assessments and Internal Controls*.

The statement was written for situations in which an organization engages in commercial activity over a public network, such as the Internet. However, much of the guidance it contains can also be applied when the entity uses a private network.

While much of the guidance will be helpful to accountants engaged in auditing entities organized primarily for e-commerce activities, or "dot.coms," it is not intended to deal with all audit issues that could be addressed in the audit of such entities. Furthermore, additional accounting information related to e-commerce is provided in a paper described below.

## .03  IFAC Issues New Paper on E-Business

"E-Business and the Accountant: Risk Management for Accounting Systems in an E-Business Environment" issued by IFAC presents certain risk management aspects of e-business relevant to accounting and financial reporting from a managerial perspective.

Directed to the management of organizations, including accountants, "E-Business and the Accountant" points out how e-business changes the way business is conducted and that e-business consequently introduces new risks that enterprises may need to address by implementing a technology infrastructure and controls to mitigate those risks. The paper points out that e-business and its technological environment will have a significant impact on accounting systems and the evidence available to support business transactions, which in turn will lead to changes in the accounting records maintained and accounting procedures followed.

The document notes that accountants and auditors may be faced with new challenges and regulations and may need to:

1.  Apply new techniques in an e-business environment.
2.  Develop accounting systems based on the business processes employed.
3.  Ensure that transactions are appropriately recorded.
4.  See that transactions are in compliance with local and international legislation and regulations.
5.  Abide by current and evolving accounting standards and guidance.

To help minimize risks in relation to these issues, the paper provides a useful framework of concepts with which accountants and others can analyze e-business from an accounting point of view. It includes best practice guidelines on e-business accounting principles and criteria, such as accounting information security and accounting information processing. It also outlines criteria for a functioning accounting system.

## ¶20,015  THE IASC STUDY: *BUSINESS REPORTING ON THE INTERNET*

The International Accounting Standards Committee published a study of business and financial reporting on the Internet in November, 1999, as the first step in a possible project to develop accounting standards in that area.

The study examines:

1.  The current technologies available for electronic business reporting.
2.  What companies around the world are actually doing (this involved a detailed analysis of the Web sites of the 30 largest companies in each of 22 countries, 660 companies in all).
3.  The sort of standards for electronic business reporting that are needed now, within the constraint of today's technologies.
4.  The shortcomings of financial reporting on the Internet within current technologies.
5.  The technological changes that are on the horizon and how they can improve electronic reporting.

### .01  Changes in Paper Financial Reports

Technology has altered irreversibly not only the physical medium of corporate financial reporting, but also its traditional boundaries. The Committee realized that paper reports are being supplemented—and, for many users, replaced—by electronic business reporting, primarily via the Internet. They became aware that investors and lenders had moved far beyond traditional financial statements and related note disclosures.

Four experts from the academic world authored the IASC study, *Business Reporting on the Internet*. It illustrates to accounting policy makers the nature of changes occurring in business reporting and explains how those changes are affecting the dissemination of accounting and financial information.

The study also identifies the effects those changes may have on accounting standard-setting in the future. The report charts a course of IASC—and, in fact, the rest of the accounting world—to follow in helping to ensure that high-quality electronic data is available for the users of business and financial information.

## .03   A Code of Conduct for Web-Based Business Reporting

Among other recommendations, the study urges IASC to adopt a Code of Conduct for Web-based business reporting. The report is designed to enhance the quality of business reporting information provided on the Web by corporations. The authors of the suggested Code are quick to point out that it is not intended to be a permanent solution to resolving the issues related to business reporting online since technology will continue to change and develop, and user expectations and demands will change. A complete draft of a proposed Code is included in the report.

## .05   E-Business Reporting Language

The study recommends that a global electronic business reporting language (BRL) be developed to meet the needs of those who look to the Internet for financial and operating information.

Those represented in the consortium should include:

1. The IASC.
2. Global information distributors.
3. Software developers.
4. Securities regulators.
5. National accounting standard setters.
6. International accounting firms.
7. Others. (Presumably "others" will become evident as e-business and e-communication become better defined!)

## ¶20,017   FASB's Business Reporting Research Project

Many organizations are interested in this new information technology and do in-depth studies to discover the advantages as well as the pitfalls of its use. The FASB is one of the most recent to publish a very comprehensive study.

### .01   The Three-Part Study

The report, *Electronic Distribution of Business Reporting Information*, published in January 2000, is the first section of a broader study—the Business Reporting Research Project. The objective of the FASB is to determine the kind of business information corporations are reporting outside of financial statements.

The first portion describes the electronic distribution of business information and investigates the possibilities and problems of the Internet on the reporting process.

The second will deal with the redundancies between SEC and FASB reporting requirements, thus helping to eliminate overlapping and duplication.

A third portion will discuss the results of 10 selected industries' business reporting practices.

### .03   Objectives of the First Study

Growth of the Internet as a medium for delivering business reporting information has altered the way that information flows from companies to investors and creditors. The structure will continue to change as companies bring new technologies to the process and as information users find new ways to access and analyze information.

The stated objectives of the first FASB study were to:

1. Survey the state of reporting information over the Internet.
2. Identify notable practices.

### .05   Financial Information Online

More and more companies are using the Internet to disseminate information about themselves. This includes stock quotes and the latest annual report, as well as forward-looking information, detailed plans about new products and services, and other material from outside the financial statements.

The Internet offers vast amounts of fiinancial information available to the nonspecialist investor and allows delivery of that information instantaneously and at very low cost. Any investor with a computer and a modem can obtain information that was previously available, as a practical matter, only to a limited range of company officials, professional investment analysts, and the financial press.

Some of the present practices observed in the report include:

1. Transcripts of management presentations.
2. Analyst's reports on the company.
3. Traditional financial information.
4. Live and archived audio-visual versions of meetings that were previously open only to selected analysts.

The FASB report discusses legal and other issues that are of interest to companies using or thinking about using the Internet for distributing business information.

## ¶20,019   THE SEC ON REPORTING IN THE NEW ECONOMY

As the Securities and Exchange Commission makes quite evident, they are not about to let e-communication and e-trading progress too far without adequate protection for the investor. New industries, spurred by new services and new technologies, are creating new questions and challenges that must be addressed.

Rules for valuation of manufacturing inventory or assessing what a factory is worth are well established. But what of the value of R&D invested in a software program, or the value of a user base on an Internet shopping site? As intangible assets continue to grow in size and scope, more and more people are questioning whether the true value — and the drivers of that value — is being reflected in a timely manner in publicly available disclosure.

To look into these questions, a group of leaders from the business community, academia, the accounting profession, standard-setting bodies, and corporate America is being formed to examine whether the current business reporting framework can more effectively handle these changes in our economy.

As always, the SEC embraces free market principles to foster greater competition, while ensuring effective regulatory oversight to protect investor interest. To that effect, they are simultaneously taking a very close look at the many complaints about online trading.

## ¶20,021   ELECTRONIC DATA INTERCHANGE (EDI)

Electronic commerce involves individuals as well as organizations engaging in a variety of electronic business transactions (without paper documents) using computer and telecommunication networks. These networks can be either private or public, or a combination of the two. Actually the big leap in e-business has been in conducting business over the Internet (specifically the Web).

This is due to the Web's surge in popularity and the acceptance of the Internet as a viable transport mechanism for business information. The use of a public network-based infrastructure like the Internet can reduce costs and make it feasible for small as well as large companies to extend their services and products to a broad customer base.

Electronic commerce has been defined as a means of conducting business electronically via online transactions *between merchants and consumers;* traditionally, the definition of electronic commerce had focused on EDI as the primary means of conducting business electronically *between entities having a preestablished contractual relationship.*

EDI involves computer application-to-computer application transmission of business documents in a predetermined, standard format. While e-commerce is targeted for global trading and is suited to anyone interested in online commerce, EDI is best suited for a selected group of trading partners.

EDI improves business operations dealing with high volumes of transactions by providing electronic information exchange between those trading partners. Such an established electronic connection reduces data entry errors by eliminating repetitive tasks and lowers administrative overhead costs associated with paper-based processing methods.

E-commerce and EDI, whatever its nature, will require accounting professionals of those organizations using the new technology to reexamine the nature of the entity's business practices and the manner in which transactions are recorded. This might be especially true for organizations which, up until their entrance into e-commerce, had only domestic trading partners and never sold directly to the consumer. E-commerce is changing the conduct of business, as most organizations have known it.

## ¶20,023   Glossary of Terms

This glossary provides common definitions of some of the terms in contacts with clients or e-business vendors. Some of the definitions have been simplified for conciseness and ease of understanding. We are all familiar with many of the terms, although we would be hard-pressed actually to define them, thus:

**Affiliate Programs.** Cooperative arrangements that involve providing a link to another Web site in exchange for a commission on purchases made by users following that link to the other Web site.

**Access Provider.** An intermediary remote computer system through which a user may then connect to the Internet.

**Acrobat Reader.** A software application from Adobe that provides the formatted display of documents in portable document format (see PDF).

**Applet.** A JAVA program designed to perform a specific task within a larger program. Applets may be embedded and run from within another application such as a Web page.

**Applications Programming Interface.** A program or data mapping mechanism that allows separate applications to work together by mapping data in one application to the format required in another application.

**Application Service Provider (ASP).** An organization that provides software applications over the Internet. A common example is an Internet Service provider (ISP).

**ADSL.** See Asymmetric Digital Subscriber Line.

**ASP.** See Application Service Provider

**Asymmetric Digital Subscriber (ADSL).** A dedicated connection to the Internet that is suitable for individual and small business use. It is quicker for downloads than for uploads.

**Authentication (authorization).** The process a computer used to "verify" a user attempting to access the computer. Authentication may include user names, passwords, encryption, digital security certificates and signatures and other forms of security checking prior to allowing access to a computer, Web site, systems, files or data.

**Auto-Responder.** A feature of some e-mail programs that can be set to provide an automatic response to incoming messages. It is frequently used by business to acknowledge the receipt of a customer's messages and to provide a timeframe for the response. It is also used by individual employees to send a response to messages when they are out of the office.

**Backbone.** A top-level, high-speed connection to the Internet that serves as a major access point for ISPs and major users of the Internet (e.g., large business).

**Bandwidth.** The amount of information that can be carried through a communication system in a set time.

**Banner.** A graphical display, usually an ad, that is displayed on a Web page.

**Bit.** A single binary value, either 0 or 1, used to store data or provide instructions to a computer. Bits are collected in multiples, called bytes.

**Bookmarks/Favorites.** A list of Web pages visited and to which one will likely return that are created by Internet browsers, such as Netscape and Internet Explorer. These bookmarks are direct links to the Web page.

**Browser.** A user interface program that allows access to the Internet. The most well-known browsers are Internet Explorer and Netscape Navigator.

**Business Intelligence (BI).** Organizing, searching, analyzing and reporting trends or business specific information from data contained in Web sites, business applications and/or databases.

**Business Process Reengineering (BPR).** Analysis and reengineering of specific business processes and management systems to eliminate redundancy and non-value-added steps and to improve efficiency and performance.

**Certificates.** A security mechanism used in Internet communications to ensure that the Web site and data or communications conducted with it are trusted and secure.

**C-Commerce (Collaborative Commerce).** Technology-enabled business interactions among anyone involved in a business process, including internal employees, suppliers, business partners and customers.

**Contact Center.** A component of customer relationship management (CRM), that is a centralized support center for all customer contact channels, including phone, e-mail, Internet, fax, mail or other forms of communication between customers and their providers of goods or services.

**Cookie.** A small text file that is put on users' hard drives when they visit a Web page so that other Web pages can remember certain information about the user.

**Customer Relationship Management (CRM).** An organizational strategy to maximize revenue, profitability and brand loyalty by focusing business processes and information analysis around customer intelligence. Key investment in technologies that connect internal business systems with external customer-facing systems to improve response to customer demands and related product, revenue and profitability mixes.

**Database Management System (DBMS).** Software that enables systematic data storage and retrieval in a repeatable mechanism to create, update and report on large amounts of data.

**Data Mining.** Sorting and analyzing trends or meaningful patterns across large amounts of data.

**Digital Signature.** A code that can be attached to a transmission (e.g., e-mail message, order request) that authenticates the sender.

**Domain Name.** A name designated to represent a location on the Internet, such as the address for a Web site.

**Domain Name Server (DNS).** A server that associates a number (an Internet Protocol, or IP address) with a text-based domain name.

**DNS.** See Domain Name System.

**E-Business.** All activities conducted by a business over the Internet.

**E-Commerce.** The procurement and distribution of goods and services over the Internet using digital technology.

**E-Marketplace.** An online marketplace where buyers and sellers can exchange goods and services. Normally relates to business-to-business transactions.

**Encryption.** The encoding of a message or electronic transmission to prevent unauthorized access.

**Enterprise Resource Planning (ERP).** Large-scale business software applications that support key management functions of the enterprise, such as financial, manufacturing, human resources, procurement, customer relationship management and other key business processes.

**Favorites.** See Bookmarks.

**FAQ.** See Frequently Asked Questions.

**Firewall.** Hardware and software used to prevent unauthorized access to a computer or network.

**Frequently Asked Questions (FAQs).** A list of answers to commonly asked questions, especially on a Web site.

**GIF.** See Graphics Interchange Format.

**Graphical User Interface (GUI).** A graphical tool that allows users to access the features and functionalities of a software application. On the Web, it refers to the parts of the Web site the users actually see, and would not include the back end software such as the database and programs that power the site.

**Graphics Interchange Format (GIF).** One of the two most common formats for graphics on the Web (the other being JPEG).

**Hyperlink.** A highlighted link or graphic within a hypertext document or Web page that will take the user to another place within the same Web page or to another Web site or page.

**Intranet.** A secure network within a company accessible only by internal users of the company network. Intranets are protected by firewalls and other security mechanisms that prevent unsecure parties from accessing internal data.

**Java.** A programming language developed by SUN Microsystems that has been widely adopted for developing Internet applications.

**JPEG.** A compression format used for Internet graphics or images.

**Knowledge Management (KM).** An organizational strategy to use technology to capture, organize, access and manage the "knowledge" assets of a business. The deployment of "content management" systems to provide storage, search, retrieval and use of information assets across collaborative groups of people within an organization.

**LAN (Local Area Network).** A computer network established within a specific area, such as a university or business headquarters. LANs were developed to facilitate the exchange and sharing of data, software, printers, and storage within an organization.

**Middleware.** Software applications that support integration of different data, programs, databases, and Web sites across or between multiple computer systems.

**PDF (Portable Document Format).** A file format created by Adobe that delivers and displays an entire document with text and complex graphics in a single readable file.

**PDA (Personal Digital Assistant).** Any small, mobile, handheld device that creates, stores and retrieves data. Many PDAs may also connect to the Internet through wireless technology for sending and retrieving data such as e-mail.

**Permission Marketing.** Involves persuading customers to physically request that marketing information be sent to them (sometimes called opt-in marketing).

**Personalization.** Individual user's ability to configure their own preferences for information selection and display on their access pages to a Web site or application.

**POP (Post Office Protocol or Point Of Presence).** Refers to one common way that e-mail software gets mail from a mail server. Point of presence usually refers to the locations where a dial-up connection to a mail server is available.

**Portal.** A Web site used as a primary starting point to get to other Web sites. It often refers to search directories such as Yahoo and Search engines such as Google.

**Search Directory.** A human-compiled directory of information on the Web sorted under meaningful categories (e.g., Yahoo, About, open directory).

**Search Engine.** A computer program that automatically seeks out Web sites, creates an index of these sites and then allows you to search the index (e.g., Altavista, Alltheweb, Hotbot).

**Secure Sockets Layer (SSL).** A communication protocol developed to securely transmit data on the Internet. Data is encrypted prior to being transferred over SSL to its destination. Many Web sites support SSL to confidentially process user information, such as credit card payments.

**Service-Level Agreement (SLA).** An agreement between an ASP and a user that describes the level of service expected throughout the duration of the contract.

**SLA.** See Service-Level Agreement.

**SPAM.** A term used to describe unsolicited and unwanted messages sent to an e-mail address or to an online discussion group.

**Splash Page.** An initial web page that is used to capture the user's attention and is usually a lead-in to the home page.

**Structured Query Language (SQL).** A standard programming language use for updating and retrieving data from a database.

**SSL.** See Secure Sockets Layer.

**Stickiness.** A term used to describe the ability of a Web site to keep users on the site. Usually measured by the average length of time visitors spend on a Web site.

**Supply Chain Management (SCM).** Business processes and technology-based applications that support the process of planning, producing, ordering, stocking, delivering and supporting goods, services and information from a supplier to a customer.

**T1 (also T3).** High-speed, high-bandwidth, dedicated connections to the internet. T1 offers 20 times the bandwidth of a 56K modem. A T3 connection is made up of 28 T1 lines.

**24/7.** Refers to services offered 24 hours a day, 7 days a week.

**Telephony.** A general term applied to any type of voice communication as opposed to data communication.

**Traffic.** Refers to the amount of visitors that a Web site receives.

**Transition Logs.** Reports designed to create an audit trail for each online transaction and its terminal of origin, time, user, and details.

**URL.** See Uniform Resource Locator.

**Uniform Resource Locator (URL).** Another way of describing a Web page address. When a URL is entered into a Web browser, it will be bring the user to that site.

¶20,023

**Viral Marketing.** Involves using the customer as a sales person to encourage others to use a product/service.

**WAN (Wide Area Network).** A computer network established across an expanded area, such as between hospital sites, city utilities sites, or multiple corporate subsidiaries. Several local area networks (LANs) can be interconnected into a WAN.

**Web Site.** Generally a set of Web pages all located within the same URL.

**World Wide Web (or WWW or the Web).** A series of hypertext markup language (HTML) documents all connected using the Internet.

**www.** See World Wide Web.

**Workflow Management.** Supports the ability to define specific business rules or data events that are automatically routed to users and managers for review or action.

## ¶20,025   AN E-BUSINESS CHECKLIST

Keys to the success of any project include executive support and constant communication. Usually a steering committee of executives is established to report regularly on a project. This allows project decisions to be made quickly. Any business policy or business process change requires this. "Quickly" is often important because usually any decision that delays a project adds costs to the project.

Using this checklist could assist in developing successful project policies.

1. Is there an executive who can serve as a project liaison with senior management?
   ☐ yes   ☐ no

2. Is there a cross-departmental team of both business and Information Technology users assigned to the implementation of the project?
   ☐ yes   ☐ no

3. Are the business objectives of both the organization and the project clearly identified and agreed upon?
   ☐ yes   ☐ no

4. Are business and information managers fully aware of the plans and strategies of the organization?
   ☐ yes   ☐ no

5. What benefits and improvements can be expected from this project, and how will they be measured?

   _____

   _____

   _____

6. Which business processes will be improved, and how will customers benefit?

_____

_____

_____

7. Are the people involved in the project development and implementation capable and reliable?
   ❏ yes  ❏ no

8. Are there sufficient resources to implement the new project while adequately supporting the old system?
   ❏ yes  ❏ no

9. Has the total cost of the project been identified and estimated, including staffing, training, and any external consulting that may be required?
   ❏ yes  ❏ no

10. Has a detailed business case, supported by resource and technical plans, been prepared along with a proper project proposal?
    ❏ yes  ❏ no

11. Can the implementation of the project be "phased" in stages to deliver incremental early successes as opposed to the "big bang" approach in which success is not identified until the entire project is complete?
    ❏ yes  ❏ no

12. Is there an experienced project leader dedicated full time to the management of the teams, tasks, and external consultants on a daily basis?
    ❏ yes  ❏ no

13. Have effective means of communicating developments and progress to all staff members been put in place?
    ❏ yes  ❏ no

14. Have the role, responsibilities and time commitment of the people involved been clearly set out and accepted by them?
    ❏ yes  ❏ no

15. Are information and communication strategies and systems reviewed frequently?
    ❏ yes  ❏ no

16. Is it possible to benchmark the business and information systems against those of the company's peers and competitors?
    ❏ yes  ❏ no

17. Does the project help achieve the strategic objectives of the business?
    ❏ yes  ❏ no

# Chapter 21

# Insurance Accounting

## CONTENTS

## ¶21,000 OVERVIEW

There is nothing like front-page accounting scandals to focus the attention of regulators, standard setters, trade associations, Congress, investors and assorted bystanders to focus upon a particular industry. So it is with the insurance industry and the revelations about the accounting machinations of AIG, General Re, PricewaterhouseCooper, and/or their officials.

The Securities and Exchange Commission pointed out that the problem was not about a violation of "technical accounting rules." Rather, it involved the deliberate or extremely reckless efforts by senior corporate officers of a facilitator company (General Re) to aid and abet senior management of an issuer (AIG) to structure transactions having no economic substance. The intent was to fashion transactions expressly for the purpose of providing a specific false accounting effect in the issuer s financial statement.

As noted last year, the National Association of Insurance Commissioners was the first to respond, and has been busy ever since considering ways and means of preventing future abuses, as discussed later in this chapter. The Financial Accounting Standards Board could but step into the fray, and the House and Senate both felt compelled to sponsor hearings on the direction of the industry.

## ¶21,001 FASB SEEKS WAYS TO IMPROVE FINANCIAL REPORTING FOR INSURANCE

As part of a broader initiative to improve financial reporting for insurance accounting, the FASB is considering constituent views and perspective on the potential bifurcation of insurance and reinsurance contracts into insurance components and finance components. In May 2006, the FASB issued an Invitation to Comment (ITC). Feedback from this ITC will be evaluated by the Board to determine whether or not to issue an Exposure Draft on the subject.

This action is indicative of the Board s concern about a possible lack of transparency in the financial statements of both policyholders and (re)insurance companies relating to the depiction of insurance risk associated with contracts that include terms or features that significantly limit the actual amount of risk transferred. Statement No. 5, *Accounting for Contingencies*, paragraph 44, requires that all insurance and reinsurance contracts indemnify the insured against loss or liability. FASB Statement No. 113, *Accounting and Reporting for Reinsurance of Short-Duration and Long-Duration Contracts*, provides further guidance for determining the transfer of significant insurance risk for reinsurance arrangements. Those contracts that do not transfer significant insurance risk are accounted for as deposits (similar to a financing or loan, with loan repayments taking the form of periodic insurance premium payments). Such contracts are frequently referred to as finite risk contracts, although this ITC is not limited to finite risk contracts.

The guidance in current Standards for insurance accounting is primarily directed toward financial reporting by the insurance and reinsurance companies. However, these Standards provide only limited guidance on how to account for insurance contracts by policyholders. Moreover, insurance and reinsurance contracts often have both insurance components and financing components, which are combined and accounted for simply as "insurance contracts," when, in actuality, they may more specifically be financing measures. This, along with other factors, has led to some of the accounting irregularities. As a result, the Board is gathering information about whether bifurcation would improve financial reporting by providing users of financial statements with better information about the economic substance of insurance arrangements.

## .01 Possible Separation of Insurance and Financing Components

Bifurcation would divide some or all of such contracts into two main components for financial reporting purposes:

1. Components of such contracts that transfer significant insurance risk would be accounted for under existing insurance accounting guidance and generally provide an income statement benefit (recovery) in the period of an insured loss.
2. Financing components that are accounted for as deposits would be recorded as an asset by the policyholder. Any recovery from an insured event would reduce the deposit and not have a significant income statement benefit.

The Invitation to Comment requests specific information from buyers and sellers of insurance and reinsurance contracts and the users of their financial statements.

(Earlier discussions of the Board leading up to the decision to issue this ITC are touch on in the section dealing with the distinction between insurance and financing later in this chapter.)

## .03 Broad Sampling of Potential Users Needed

The FASB is encouraging the active participation of all constituents in this process; however, they are particularly interested in hearing from noninsurance company policyholders—including small organizations and private companies. The Board believes that bifurcation could have a significant impact on the way some insurance contracts are accounted for. They are also attempting to ensure that all parties have an opportunity to consider the issues carefully and to express their points of view.

This preliminary process is important because, as mentioned above, the Board's plan is to study and analyze the input from the ITC thoroughly and carefully before deciding whether a bifurcation proposal should be developed for inclusion in an Exposure Draft on risk transfer. It stands to reason that a broad sampling of opinion from potential users of the information is important.

## ¶21,003   OTHER FORMS OF INSURANCE RECEIVE ATTENTION

As mentioned above, a scandal brings attention to an industry. In the case of the insurance industry, the spotlight appears to have opened up many avenues of concern. In addition to the more "public" problems facing the insurance industry, the FASB has been made aware of other problems that call for their attention. Not only are finite insurance and reinsurance drawing regulatory attention, but now financial guarantee insurance contracts are also being scrutinized. That, in turn, opened the way for consideration of other insurance products with similar characteristics, such as mortgage guarantee contracts and credit insurance.

When questions arose about the differences relative to the timing of the recognition of claim liabilities for financial guarantee contracts issued by insurance companies, there seemed to be no easy answer for the proper treatment. FASB Statement No. 60, *Accounting and Reporting by Insurance Enterprises,* provides the primary source of accounting and reporting guidance for all insurance enterprises, but it was adopted *before* the financial guarantee industry came into prominent existence and does not adequately cover the unique characteristics of financial guarantee insurance. FASB 60 provides different revenue and expense recognition guidance depending upon whether a contract fits within the Statement 60 definition of a short- or long-duration contract. Financial guarantee contracts have attributes of both, and therein, lies much of the problem. Diversity in practice has resulted because the statement does not provide sufficient guidance—in part, from the variety of accounting models that exist for similar contracts.

It was at the June 8, 2005 meeting that the Board decided to add a project to consider the accounting by insurers for financial guarantee insurance. The scope was limited to contracts issued by insurance companies that indemnify the holder against losses from payment default on a financial obligation that are *not* considered derivative contracts due to meeting the exception in paragraph 10(d) of Statement 133. Plans for the project were confined to contracts written by insurance companies currently within the scope of FASB Statement No. 60, *Accounting and Reporting by Insurance Enterprises.* However, consideration of the accounting model was not limited to the short- and long-duration models described in Statement 60.

By the end of October 2006, the Board had decided to have the staff draft an Exposure Document for the Board s consideration, and planned to issue an Interpretation before the end of the year. Until such time as the Board issues at least one of these documents, the current rules are in effect. The information about the discussions is provided for the convenience of constituents who want to follow the Board s deliberations so that they can gauge the direction of the members' thinking. All of the conclusions reported are tentative and may be changed at future Board meetings. Measures are final only after a formal written ballot is cast to issue a final Statement, Interpretation, or FSP.

## .01    Planned Guidance

In the meantime, the Board is considering the appropriate accounting model for financial guarantee contracts. They have decided not to put too many restraints on this project, but to provide guidance relative to:

* The timing of claim liability recognition.
* Premium recognition.
* The related amortization of deferred policy acquisition costs.

This is specifically for financial guarantee contracts issued by insurance companies that are *not* accounted for as derivative contracts under FASB Statement 133.

A financial guarantee contract guarantees the holder of a financial obligation the full and timely payment of principal and interest when due and is typically issued in conjunction with municipal bond offerings and certain structured finance transactions. The goal is to reduce diversity in accounting by financial guarantee insurers so that the users are able to understand the insurers' financial statements better and to compare those statements more readily. In their process of deciding upon the appropriate accounting model for financial guarantee contracts, the Board also will examine the appropriate accounting model for other insurance products with similar characteristics, such as the mortgage guarantee contracts and trade credit insurance.

## ¶21,005    FASB CONSIDERS DISTINCTION BETWEEN INSURANCE AND FINANCINGS

To no one's surprise, at its April 2005 meeting, the FASB Board decided to add a project to consider risk transfer in insurance and reinsurance contracts. The project will include developing a definition of insurance contracts and exploring simplified approaches to bifurcating insurance contracts. At the June 2005 educational session, the Board directed the staff to draft for Board consideration definitions of insurance contract, insurance risk, and related terms based on the definitions and related descriptive material in IASB's IFRS 4, *Insurance Contracts*.

Because of the recent insurance scandal, questions have arisen concerning the determination of whether an insurance or reinsurance contract transfers significant insurance (reinsurance) risk. The determination of significant risk transfer is necessary to determine whether the contract is accounted for as an insurance or reinsurance arrangement or whether it is accounted for as a financing arrangement (similar to a loan). Also, certain finite-risk or financial insurance and reinsurance contracts contain risk-limiting features that can make the risk transfer analysis difficult.

Statement 5, paragraph 44, requires that all insurance and reinsurance contracts indemnify the insured against loss or liability. FASB Statement No. 113, *Accounting and Reporting for Reinsurance of Short-Duration and Long-Duration Contracts,* provides further guidance for determining the transfer of significant insurance risk for reinsurance arrangements. Those contracts that do not transfer significant insurance risk are accounted for as deposits (similar to a financing or loan, with loan repayments taking the form of periodic insurance premium payments).

Regardless of whether a policyholder is a noninsurance or insurance enterprise, only to the extent that an insurance (or reinsurance) contract indemnifies or transfers significant insurance risk from the policyholder to the insurer does it qualify for insurance accounting. This project's objective is to define an insurance contract and provide further assistance in identifying those contracts that transfer significant insurance risk. In addition, the project will explore the notion of bifurcation of insurance contracts into risk transfer and financing segments for purposes of establishing the appropriate accounting for those contract segments.

The objective of the project is to clarify what constitutes transfer of significant insurance risk in insurance and reinsurance contracts first by defining insurance contracts and related terms. Simple approaches to bifurcation of insurance contracts that include both insurance and financing elements also will be explored. The project is intended to improve the representational faithfulness of accounting for insurance and reinsurance contracts by more clearly defining which contracts or portions thereof should be accounted for as insurance and which should be accounted for as deposits (financings). The resulting increased transparency in accounting and reporting by insureds should help users of financial statements better understand the economic impact of those contracts.

As always, Board decisions are *tentative* and do not change current accounting. Until such time as official positions of the FASB are adopted, the FASB Statements discussed at the end of this chapter are the official U.S. GAAP.

## ¶21,007 NAIC APPROVES FINITE REINSURANCE DISCLOSURE REQUIREMENTS

After being early responders to the accounting scandals in the insurance business resulting from misuse of finite insurance by some high-profile insurers, the National Association of Insurance Commissions (NAIC) did not just sit back to let the air clear. During several months of work, State insurance regulators, working in a coordinated manner through the NAIC, evaluated existing relevant statutory financial reporting to develop improved disclosure requirements.

In October 2005, the NAIC Executive and Plenary Committees and the full body of the NAIC approved enhanced disclosure requirements for insurers that utilize reinsurance with limited risk transfer features (finite reinsurance).

The disclosures adopted for the 2005 annual statement required a property and casualty insurer to report to state insurance regulators the contract terms and management objectives of any finite reinsurance agreement that has the effect of altering policyholders' surplus by more than three percent, or representing more than three percent of ceded premium or losses. The adopted proposal also requires the insurer s CEO and CFO to sign an attestation that there are no side agreements and that risk transfer has occurred.

The belief is that the adoption of this proposal provides financial regulators greater transparency needed to assess the impact of finite reinsurance on the industry and on individual insurers.

## ¶21,009  MODEL AUDIT RULE

In June 2006, the NAIC amended its Model Regulation Requiring Annual Audited Financial Reports in such a manner that it was obviously influenced by the Sarbanes-Oxley Act.

The amendments relate to:

- Auditor independence.
- Corporate governance.
- Internal control over financial reporting.

These revisions provide that insurance companies should have an audit committee and indicate that some audit committee members may need to be independent from management. The adopted revisions also provide that insurance companies with $500 million or more in direct and assumed premium should file a report with the state insurance department regarding its assessment of internal control over financial reporting. The effective date for many of the provisions is January 1, 2010, but an effective date of December 31, 2010, has been set for the provision related to the internal control report.

The adopted amendments resulted from a vetting process by the Financial Condition Committee, which began consideration of the Model Audit Rule in March 2006 after a process begun in 2003 by the NAIC/AICPA Working Group. An Implementation Guide to assist in the application of and compliance with the new requirements has been drafted and was adopted by the Financial Condition (E) Committee in September 2006. It is anticipated that the full NAIC Membership will adopt this guide in December 2006.

## .01  Influence of Sarbox on Private Insurance Companies

The changes resulting from Sarbox requirements have had a profound effect upon public companies and their auditors, but privately held insurance companies in the U.S. have been relatively slow in reacting. However, discussion at the National Association of Insurance Commissioners has prompted regulators and working groups to review the current Model Regulation requiring annual audited financial reports to consider appropriate components of the Act in their deliberations.

The NAIC and AICPA cite the advantage they had in being able to consider the criticism leveled at SOX during their work on the Model Audit Rule. They could utilize the lessons learned to formulate a measured and cost-effective approach to help strengthen auditor independence, corporate governance and internal control over financial reporting of insurance companies. The two organizations, working together, established three subgroups to review Sarbox and the reaction to its provisions in recommending application of some of its rulings to the nonpublic insurance world.

*Title II Addresses External Auditor Independence.* The Title II Subgroup has recommended adopting auditor independence requirements prohibiting audit firms from providing audit clients such *nonaudit* services as:

- Bookkeeping.
- Financial information systems design and implementation.
- Actuarial services.
- Internal audit outsourcing services.
- Management or human resource services.
- Expert services unrelated to the audit.

The requirements also require the engagement partner to rotate off the audit client every five years and to wait five years before returning to that client.

*Title III Deals with Corporate Responsibility and Governance.* The Title III Subgroup proposed that each company that meets certain premium volumes must form and maintain an audit committee. Key provisions include:

- The audit committee would be solely responsible for the appointment, compensation and oversight of the external auditors.
- Each member of the audit committee would be required to be a member of the company's board of directors. Depending upon the size of the company, some audit and board members would need to be independent. Independence, in this context, is defined as "a person who does not accept any consulting, advisory or other compensatory fee from the company or its affiliates." An exception to this would be given in those states that have conflicting laws.

- For insurers with a holding company ownership structure, a separate audit committee is not required for each legal entity, but only at the "ultimate controlling person" level.

***Title IV Addresses Section 404 of the Act.***   The Title IV Subgroup revisions require management to file a report with the state insurance department regarding its assessment of internal controls over financial reporting. The report must include the following information:

1. A statement by management that it is responsible for establishing and maintaining adequate internal controls over financial reporting.
2. A statement that management has established such controls and an assertion that these controls are effective to provide reasonable assurance regarding the reliability of the statutory financial statements
3. A statement regarding the process or approach utilized by management in this evaluation
4. Disclosure of any unremediated material weaknesses in internal controls over financial reporting

The independent auditors will consider this report during the planning and performance of the annual audit. However, the independent auditors are not required to issue an auditor s opinion on the effectiveness of a company's internal controls over financial reporting. In addition, the proposed revisions require the insurer to file the independent auditor's communication regarding any unremediated material weaknesses noted during the course of an audit with the state insurance department.

Title IV of the internal control requirements recommended above will not apply to companies writing less than $500 million in annual gross (direct and assumed) premium. Given the work that companies will need to do to comply with these requirements, an extensive implementation time frame has been granted.

# ¶21,011   INSURANCE REGULATION BILLS INTRODUCED IN CONGRESS

In the summer of 2006, the NAIC commended the National Governors Association (NGA) and the National Conference of State Legislatures (NCSL) for emphasizing the importance of state-based insurance regulation. The statement indicated that the organizations' stand that States are in a better position than the federal government to consider *both* the interests of U.S. insurance consumers and competing insurance companies.

The NGA and NCSL had announced opposition to the National Insurance Act of 2006 (S.2509), which seeks to restructure the existing system of state insurance regulation by establishing a federal insurance regulatory authority. The NAIC believes that support from the NGA and NCSL emphasizes their belief in the importance of current proven regulatory expertise and the existing framework to provide consumer protection.

Actually almost identical bills were referred to Congressional committees during 2006—the one mentioned above was referred to the Senate Banking, Housing, and Urban Affairs Committee, the companion bill, the National Insurance Act of 2006 (H.R.6225), to the House Financial Services Committee.

The House version would create a federal regulatory agency within the Treasury Department. However, according to the sponsor, it would leave the current state regulatory system in place because an insurance provider could choose to be regulated by the 50 states or by an Office of National Insurance. It has been pointed out that the concept is not new inasmuch as the banking system operates within a similar framework.

The U.S. Treasury, academic experts, and market participants recently testified that the state-based system of regulation needs modernization. Their contention is that uniformity of regulation, which is lacking at state level, would be achieved with federal oversight. Their position is that one set of rules would enable insurance providers to reduce compliance costs and reduce barriers to market entry.

After the exposure of irregularities in the insurance industry, it us not surprising that Congress should consider regulatory provisions relating to the industry; however, as has been suggested, the current regulatory system has evolved over a period of 135 years. It is not probable that any sweeping change to this system will occur in the near future.

On the other hand, it is quite possible that some Federal legislation may help in unifying State insurance commissions and the NAIC in dealing with industry regulation. An example of this type of legislation is H.R. 5637: *Nonadmitted and Reinsurance Reform Act of 2006*, a bill to streamline the regulation of nonadmitted insurance and reinsurance, and other purposes.

This bill passed in the House by unanimous roll call vote, and was sent to the Senate in September 2006. If it becomes law, it would streamline tax collection and supervision for surplus lines and reinsurance policies. It is seen by many as an alternative, federal standards approach to the creation of a new federal insurance regulator. Additional federal standards bills are expected to follow.

## ¶21,013   IASB Standards on Insurance

The International Accounting Standards Board (IASB) issued International Financial Reporting Standard 4, *Insurance Contracts* (IFRS 4) in March 2004. The publication of this IFRS provided, for the first time, guidance on accounting for insurance contracts, and marked the first step in the IASB's project to achieve the convergence of widely varying insurance industry accounting practices around the world.

In developing IFRS 4, the IASB balanced the urgent need for an international standard on accounting for insurance contracts with the recognition that developing a global consensus on a rigorous and comprehensive approach would require extensive consultation beyond the timeframe available. In particular, consultation on a completely new international approach could not be completed in time to meet the starting date of 2005 set by the European Union and other jurisdictions. In that light, IFRS 4 completes only the first phase of the IASB's insurance project. It is aimed at introducing improved disclosures for insurance contracts, and modest improvements to recognition and measurement practices, without requiring extensive changes that might need to be reversed when the IASB completes the second phase of this project.

The IFRS applies to all insurance contracts (including reinsurance contracts) that an entity issues and to reinsurance contracts that it holds, except for specified exemptions.

Although this is the beginning of the International Accounting Standard Board's Summary of IFRS 4, it is probable that the IASB will also attempt to further explain reinsurance, finite insurance, financings, and their distinctions in the second phase because of the accounting abuse and misuse of those insurance vehicles. Plans had already been made to address broader conceptual and practical issues related to insurance accounting in the second phase. These will be the subject of IASB deliberations and consultations with interested parties that resumed in the second quarter of 2004. A working party composed of experts active in the insurance industry and the accounting profession, representatives of the appropriate regulatory and supervisory authorities, and investment analysts are involved in this phase of the work. Although the completion of any long-term solution for insurance contracts may take several years to complete, the IASB is willing to revise IFRS 4 in the short term in the light of any immediate solutions arising from the working party's discussions.

(A discussion of IFRS 4 appears in the Chapter "International Standards: Accounting.")

## .01  IASB's Phase II Insurance Project

Since the IASB, like the FASB, has an active project on accounting for insurance contracts on their agenda, the two organizations are now approaching the project using a modified joint approach. Under this approach, the IASB intends to issue a Discussion Paper containing its tentative decisions on the accounting for insurance contracts for public comment.

The FASB will then issue an Invitation to Comment containing the IASB Discussion Paper to obtain input from its constituents on the IASB s preliminary views. The feedback received on that Invitation to Comment will be used by the Board in deciding whether to add a joint project with the IASB to develop a comprehensive standard on accounting for insurance contracts to its agenda.

The IASB expects to issue its Discussion Paper in the first quarter of 2007. The FASB expects to issue that ITC shortly thereafter, also during the first quarter 2007.

After completing IFRS 4, the IASB project is now in phase II with the Board currently exploring approaches that use the following three building blocks to measure insurance liabilities:

- Explicit current estimates of the expected (i.e. probability-weighted) future cash flows from existing insurance contracts.
- Discounting those cash flows to reflect the time value of money.
- Explicit risk margins.

The Board is working towards a Discussion Paper, as mentioned above. To get to an Exposure Draft would probably take at least 18 months after publication of a paper, and a final standard would require at least another 12 months.

## ¶21,015 IRS Updating Reporting Requirements of Insurance Companies

The Internal Revenue Service released updated draft instructions for Schedules M-3 for the 2006 tax year and an updated draft of the new Form 8916 that will be filed by certain insurance-related corporations to reconcile taxable income.

The draft instructions, dated April 25, 2006, are for Schedules M-3 that are filed with Forms 1120, 1120-L, 1120-PC, 1120S and 1065, and Form 8916.

Large and Mid-Size Business stakeholders provided the IRS with constructive suggestions to make Schedule M-3 a more effective tool for taxpayer reconciliation of book to tax income, according to the IRS Large and Mid-Size Division. They point out that Schedule M-3 improves transparency and disclosure, enabling the IRS to target and address areas of high risk and noncompliance.

One important instruction focuses on the Form 1065 Schedule M-3 requirement to disclose "reportable entity partners." Accordingly, partnerships must identify on the Schedule M-3 those partners that have themselves filed a Schedule M-3 that own or are deemed to own, directly or indirectly, a 50% or greater interest in the income, loss or capital of the partnership on any day of the partnership tax year on or after June 30, 2006.

This reporting requirement is also imposed on the partners and is detailed in the Schedule M-3 instructions for Form 1065, 1120, 1120-L, 1120-PC and 1120S.

**¶21,015**

A change relating to cost of goods sold is reflected in the draft instructions for Schedule M-3 for Forms 1065, 1120 and 1120S. At the suggestion of stakeholders, a new required attachment will be used for cost of goods sold. The updated draft of new Form 8916 expands the initial draft released on April 4, 2006, to provide clearer reconciliation by certain corporate groups that include an insurance company.

## ¶21,017 FINANCIAL ACCOUNTING STANDARDS BOARD STATEMENTS THAT COVER ACCOUNTING AND REPORTING BY INSURANCE ENTERPRISES

Four statements apply to insurance entities. The basic document is FASB 60, *Accounting and Reporting by Insurance Enterprises.* It has been amended and amplified by the three other statements in the following discussions.

### .01 FASB 60, *Accounting and Reporting by Insurance Enterprises*

In June 1982, the Financial Accounting Standards Board extracted the specialized principles and practices from the AICPA insurance industry related Guides and Statements of Position to produce Standard No. 60, *Accounting and Reporting by Insurance Enterprises.* It established financial accounting and reporting standards for insurance enterprises other than mutual life insurance enterprises, assessment enterprises, and fraternal benefit societies.

The Statement classified insurance contracts as short-duration or long-duration contracts. Long-duration contracts include contracts, such as:

- Whole-life.
- Guaranteed renewable term life.
- Endowment.
- Annuity.
- Title insurance contracts that are expected to remain in force for an extended period.

All other insurance contracts are considered short-duration contracts and include most property and liability insurance contracts.

Premiums from short-duration contracts ordinarily are recognized as revenue during the period of the contract in proportion to the amount of insurance protection provided. Claim costs, including estimates of costs for claims relating to insured events that have occurred but have not been reported to the insurer, are recognized when insured events occur.

Premiums from long-duration contracts are recognized as revenue when due from policyholders. The present value of estimated future policy benefits to

¶21,017.01

be paid to or on behalf of policyholders less the present value of estimated future net premiums to be collected from policyholders are accrued when premium revenue is recognized. Those estimates are based on assumptions applicable at the time the insurance contracts are made, including:

- Estimates of expected investment yields.
- Mortality.
- Morbidity.
- Terminations.
- Expenses.

Claim costs are recognized when insured events occur.

Costs that vary with and are primarily related to the acquisition of insurance contracts (acquisition costs) are capitalized and charged to expense in proportion to premium revenue recognized.

Investments are reported as follows:

- Common and nonredeemable preferred stocks at market.
- Bonds and redeemable preferred stocks at amortized cost.
- Mortgage loans at outstanding principal or amortized cost.
- Real estate at depreciated cost.

Realized investment gains and losses are reported in the income statement below operating income and net of applicable income taxes. Unrealized investment gains and losses, net of applicable income taxes, are included in stockholders' (policyholders') equity.

### .03    FASB 97, *Accounting and Reporting by Insurance Enterprises for Certain Long–Duration Contracts and for Realized Gains and Losses from the Sale of Investments*

FASB Statement 97 amends Statement 60 by concluding that the accounting methods required by Statement 60 are not appropriate for insurance contracts in which the insurer can vary amounts charged or credited to the policyholder's account or the policyholder can vary the amount of premium paid.

The Statement outlines the accounting methods for three different classifications of long-duration life and annuity products. These classifications are:

1. Universal life-type policies.
2. Limited payment policies.
3. Policies not covering significant mortality or morbidity risks.

*Universal Life-Type Policies.*   Universal life-type policies must utilize a retrospective deposit method. The liability for this type of policy will be equal to the gross account balances before deduction of surrender charges. Revenues reported will be made up of charges assessed against the policy for mortality, expenses, and surrenders. These charges are presumed to be earned in the period during which they were assessed; however, charges, such as front-end fees, for example, assessed a limited number of times are deferred as unearned revenue.

For universal life-type policies, acquisition costs will be deferred and amortized in relation to present value of estimated future gross profits. Interest accrues to the unamortized balance of the deferred acquisition costs. The estimated gross profits are computed from estimated future mortality charges minus the estimated benefit claims exceeding:

1. The related account balances.
2. Expense charges minus the policy's estimated administration costs.
3. Estimated surrender charges.
4. Estimated future earnings based on investment yields of the policyholder's account balances, minus the estimated interest to be credited to account balances.

When the estimates of future gross profits are reevaluated, the amortization of deferred acquisition costs accrued to date must be adjusted and recognized in current operations. Any deferred revenues, including deferred front-end fees, are recognized as income on the same basis as the amortization of deferred acquisition costs.

*Limited-Payment Policies.*   Limited-payment policies consist of life insurance and annuity policies with fixed and guaranteed terms having premiums that are payable over a period shorter than the period during which benefits are paid. The premiums for this type of policy are reported as revenues (reserves are computed in accordance with rulings set forth in Statement 60). However, the accumulated profit, formerly shown as a percentage of premiums, is deferred. The amount of coverage must be related to life insurance in force or expected future annuity benefit payments.

*Policies Not Covering Significant Mortality or Morbidity Risk.*   Policies not covering significant mortality or morbidity risks, such as *guaranteed investment contracts* (GICs) and some types of annuities, are shown as interest-bearing or other financial instruments, rather than as insurance contracts. Therefore, the accounting for these policies would show the account balance as a liability, and premiums as deposits rather than as revenues. Deferred acquisition costs would primarily be amortized in relation to future interest margins.

¶21,017.03

Policies including accident and health insurance not falling under one of these three classifications remain within the requirements of Statement 60.

Statement 97 also requires that property/casualty and stock life insurance companies must provide one-step income statements for realized investment gains or losses instead of the currently required two-step statement. The latter shows operating income after taxes but before net realized investment gains or losses. The one-step income statement presents realized investment gains or losses on a pretax basis with revenues, investment income, and expenses to show income before taxes.

## .05 FASB 113, *Accounting and Reporting for Reinsurance of Short–Duration and Long–Duration Contracts*

**Definitions.**   The following definitions of terms relate to this Statement. They will be helpful in understanding their exact meaning in this Statement.

*Amortization*—The act or process of extinguishing a debt, usually by equal payments over a specific period of time. The liquidation of a financial obligation on an installment basis.

*Assuming Enterprise*—The receiving company in a reinsurance contract. The assuming enterprise (or reinsurer) receives a reinsurance premium and, in turn, accepts an obligation to reimburse a ceding enterprise under specified terms; reinsures on a risk or exposure.

*Ceding Enterprise*—The company seeking a reinsurance contract. The ceding enterprise exchanges a reinsurance premium for the right to reimbursement from the assuming enterprise under specified terms. The insurer that cedes all or part of the insurance or reinsurance it has written to another insurer. Also known as the *direct writer.*

*Contract Period*—The length of time over which the specified terms are covered by the reinsured contracts.

*Covered Period*—Same as contract period (above).

*Fronting Arrangements*—Reinsurance provisions in which the ceding enterprise issues a policy to the assuming enterprise to reinsure all or substantially all of the insurance risk.

*Incurred But Not Reported (IBNR)*—Refers to losses that have occurred but have not been reported to the insurer or reinsurer.

*Indemnification*—Action of compensating for the actual loss or damage sustained; the fact of being compensated; the payment made for loss or damage.

*Insurance Risk*—The risk caused by the uncertain nature of the underwriting risk relating to the amount of net cash flows from premiums, commissions, claims, and claim settlement expenses paid as a result of contract specifications and the equally uncertain nature of the timing risk, which involves the timing of the receipt and payment of those cash flows. Actual or imputed investment returns are not an element of insurance risk. An insurance risk encompasses the possibility of adverse events occurring outside the control of the insured.

*Long-Duration Contract*—A contract expected to cover a prolonged period of time; in contrast to a short-duration contract (*see* Short-Duration Contract). While the time element is obvious from the long/short descriptive terms applied, the nature of the services rendered and the degree of control by the insurance company also differ. Along with insurance coverage, the long-duration carrier provides additional services and functions for the policyholder, including loans secured by the insurance policy, various options for payment of benefits, etc. The contract is usually not unilaterally controlled as is the short-duration type. It is customarily noncancellable, guaranteed renewable, and has fixed contract terms.

Most life and title insurance policies are considered long-duration contracts, while accident and health insurance policies depend on the expected term of coverage for the determination of long- or short-duration.

*Offsetting*—Showing a recognized asset and a recognized liability as a net amount on a financial statement. As a result of offsetting the assets and liabilities in reinsurance contracts, pertinent information could be lost and financial statement relationships altered.

*Prospective Reinsurance*—Reinsurance in which an assuming enterprise agrees to reimburse a ceding enterprise for losses that may be incurred as a result of future insurable events covered under contracts subject to the reinsurance. A reinsurance contract may include both prospective and retroactive reinsurance provisions.

*Reinsurance*—A device whereby an insurance company lessens the catastrophic hazard in the operation of the insurance mechanism; insurance for the insurer.

*Reinsurance Receivables*—All amounts recoverable from reinsurers for past and unpaid claims and claim settlement expenses, including estimated amounts receivable for unsettled claims, claims incurred but not reported, or policy benefits.

*Reinsurer*—*See* Assuming Enterprise.

*Retroactive Reinsurance*—Reinsurance in which an assuming enterprise agrees to reimburse a ceding enterprise for liabilities incurred as a result of past insurable events covered under contracts subject to reinsurance. A reinsurance contract may include both prospective and retroactive reinsurance provisions.

*Retrocession*—The process by which the reinsurer, or assuming enterprise, in turn, becomes a party in a reinsurance contract with still other reinsurers.

*Settlement Period*—The estimated period over which a ceding enterprise expects to recover substantially all amounts due from the reinsurer under the specified terms of the reinsurance contract.

*Short-Duration Contract*—An insurance policy not expected to cover an extended period of time. A carrier primarily provides insurance for a short, fixed period. The insurance carrier has more one-way control than in the long- duration contract (*see* Long-Duration Contract). The various specified terms of the contract, including amount of premiums and coverage, may be altered or canceled at the end of any contract period by the insurance company. Short- duration contracts include most property and liability policies and, to a lesser extent, some short-term life policies.

*Statutory Accounting*—The accounting system followed by insurance companies as required by the statutes of the various states. These procedures are geared to the National Association of Insurance Commissioners' (NAIC's) standardized reporting format. Differs in some instances from GAAP, but because the principal emphasis is on reflecting the ability of the insurer to meet its contract commitments, tends to be conservative.

***General Provisions of the Statement.***    FASB Statement 113, *Accounting and Reporting for Reinsurance of Short-Duration and Long-Duration Contracts* amends FASB Statement 60, *Accounting and Reporting by Insurance Companies,* and was effective for fiscal years starting after December 15, 1992. This rule eliminated the former practice of reporting assets and liabilities related to insurance contracts net of the effects of reinsurance. Statement 60, which is the basic document dealing with specialized insurance accounting and reporting practices, had continued the statutory accounting practice of offsetting reinsurance assets and liabilities. However, this procedure is now considered inconsistent with the generally accepted criteria for offsetting. Under this rule, the practice is eliminated for general-purpose financial statements.

Beginning in 1993, reinsurance receivables and prepaid reinsurance premiums are reported as assets. Reinsurance receivables include amounts related to (a) claims incurred but not reported and (b) liabilities for future policy benefits. Estimated reinsurance receivables are recognized in a manner consistent with the related liabilities.

Statement 113 set up a method of determining whether a specific contract qualified for reinsurance accounting. The accounting standard revolves around determination of whether the reinsurance is long-duration or short-duration, and, if short-duration, whether it is prospective or retroactive insurance. A contract must result in a reasonable possibility that the reinsurer may realize a significant loss from assuming insurance risk, or the contract does not qualify for reinsurance accounting, but must be accounted for as a deposit. All reinsurance contracts prohibit the reinsurance from recognizing immediately a gain if there remains a chance of liability to the policyholder by the ceding enterprise.

To further clarify the financial picture, the reinsurer is required to provide footnote disclosures explaining all facets of the terms, nature, purpose, and effect of ceded reinsurance transactions. In addition, disclosures of concentrations of credit risk associated with reinsurance receivables and prepaid premiums are also required under the provisions of FASB 105, *Disclosures of*

*Information About Financial Instruments with Off-Balance-Sheet Risk and Financial Instruments with Concentrations of Credit Risk.*

*Cause for Concern.* A portion of the impetus for consideration, or reconsideration, of the accounting and reporting for reinsurance has evolved from the general concern about the highly visible failure of some insurance companies. Risk relating to reinsurance has been considered germane to some of the failed enterprises.

Among the concerns voiced in regard to reinsurance have been:

1. The effect of reinsurance accounting relating to contracts that did not provide indemnification for the ceding party against loss or liability.
2. The fact that FASB Statement 60 did not provide sufficient guidance relating to reinsurance accounting. Among other weaknesses, this led to acceleration of the recognition of income relating to reinsurance contracts.
3. The absence of requirements for disclosure of reinsurance transactions. The policyholder was seldom aware of any reinsurance arrangement.
4. The inconsistency between the widespread use of *net* accounting for reinsurance-related assets and liabilities in spite of not meeting the established criteria for offsetting.

Therefore, the thrust of the Statement is: (a) as already noted, to address these perceived problems; (b) to provide guidance in the determination of whether specific reinsurance contracts actually make provision for indemnification of the ceding enterprise to qualify for reinsurance accounting; and (c) to establish the necessary accounting methods.

Statement 113 did *not* change practice in accounting for reinsurance *assumed* other than to require certain disclosures relating to reinsurance by all insurance companies.

For short-duration contracts to qualify for reinsurance accounting, there should be a positive answer to the following questions:

1. Does the reinsurer assume significant insurance risk under the reinsurance provisions of the underlying insurance contracts?
2. Is there a reasonable possibility that the assuming enterprise may be faced with a significant loss as a result of this contract?
3. Is there a possibility of a significant variation in the amount or timing of payments by the reinsurer?

A ceding company's evaluation of whether it is reasonably possible for a reinsurer to realize a significant loss should be based on a present value analysis of cash flows between the ceding and assuming enterprises under reasonably possible outcomes. When the ceding company reaches the conclusion that the reinsurer is not exposed to the possibility of significant loss, the ceding company can decide that it is indemnified against loss or liability related to insurance risk only if *substantially all* of the insurance risk relating to the reinsured portion of the specific underlying insurance policy has been assumed by the reinsurer. Thus, any insurance risk remaining with the ceding company must be of little or no importance or of a trivial nature if the ceding company decides to consider itself indemnified against loss or liability.

For a long-duration contract to qualify for reinsurance accounting, there must be a reasonable probability that the reinsurer may realize significant loss from assuming the insurance risk. FASB Statement 97, *Accounting and Reporting by Insurance Enterprises for Certain Long-Duration Contracts and for Realized Gains and Losses from the Sale of Investments*, defines long-duration contracts that do not subject the insurer to mortality or morbidity risks as investment contracts. Consistent with that definition, if a contract does not subject the reinsurer to the reasonable possibility of significant loss from the events insured by the underlying insurance contracts, it does not indemnify the ceding enterprise against insurance risk.

FASB 113 mandates that reinsurance contracts can lead to recognition of immediate gains only if the reinsurance contract is a legal replacement of one insurer by another and the ceding company's liability to the policyholder is extinguished.

Amounts paid for prospective reinsurance of short-duration insurance contracts must be accounted for as prepaid reinsurance premiums. They are to be amortized over the remaining contract period in proportion to the amount of insurance protection provided.

Amounts paid for retroactive reinsurance of short-duration insurance contracts must be reported as insurance receivables to the extent those amounts do not exceed the recorded liabilities relating to the reinsured contracts. If the recorded liabilities exceed the amount paid, reinsurance receivables should be increased to reflect the difference and the resulting gain should be deferred. The deferred gain is to be amortized over the estimated remaining settlement period. If the amount paid for retroactive reinsurance exceeds the recorded related liabilities, the ceding company must increase the related liabilities or reduce the reinsurance receivable, or both, at the time the reinsurance contract is entered into. The excess is charged to earnings.

If, when both prospective and retroactive provisions are included in a single short-duration reinsurance transaction and it is deemed impracticable to account for every provision separately, retroactive short-duration reinsurance contract accounting must be used. Amortization of the estimated costs of insuring long-duration insurance contracts depends on whether the reinsurance contract is long- or short-duration. These costs should be amortized over the remaining life of the underlying insured contracts if the contract is long-duration, or over the reinsurance contract period if the reinsurance contract is short-duration. Determining whether a contract that reinsures a long-duration insurance contract is long- or short-duration is a matter of judgment.

*Disclosure Requirments.*   The financial statements of all insurance companies must now disclose the following information:

1. The nature, purpose, and effect of ceding and reinsurance transactions on the insurance company's operations.
2. The ceding company must disclose the amount of earned premiums ceded and recoveries recognized under reinsurance contracts in footnotes to the financial statement, unless these are reported separately in the statement of earnings.
3. Premiums from direct business, reinsurance assumed, and reinsurance ceded, on both a written and earned basis, must be disclosed for short-duration contracts.
4. For long-duration contracts, premiums and amounts assessed against policyholders from direct business, reinsurance assumed and ceded, and premiums and amounts earned must be disclosed.
5. Companies must detail the methods used for income recognition on their reinsurance contracts.

### .07   FASB 120, *Accounting and Reporting by Mutual Life Insurance Enterprises and by Insurance Enterprises for Certain Long–Duration Participating Contracts*

FASB 120 is the result of considerable cooperation between the Financial Accounting Standards Board and the American Institute of CPAs to provide guidance in accounting, reporting, and disclosure procedures to mutual life insurance companies. Prior to the enactment of this standard and those rulings cited below, these companies reported financial information to their creditors and policyholders primarily following the statutory provisions of various state insurance regulatory bodies. The companies are now to report insurance and reinsurance activities according to GAAP.

The thrust of this Statement is to apply the provisions of FASB 60, *Accounting and Reporting by Insurance Enterprises;* FASB 97, *Accounting and Reporting by Insurance Enterprises for Certain Long-Duration Contracts and for Realized Gains and Losses from the Sale of Investments,* and FASB 113, *Accounting and Reporting for Reinsurance of Short-Duration and Long-Duration Contracts,* to mutual life insurance enterprises, assessment enterprises and to fraternal benefit societies. Certain participating life insurance contracts of those same enterprises have also been addressed in the AICPA's Statement of

Position 95-1, *Accounting for Certain Activities of Mutual Life Insurance Enterprises.* Both become effective for financial statements for fiscal years beginning after December 15, 1995.

The three earlier FASB Statements had specifically exempted mutual life insurance enterprises from their requirements. FASB Interpretation 40, *Applicability of Generally Accepted Accounting Principles to Mutual Life Insurance and Other Enterprises,* did not address or change the exemption of mutual life insurance companies from these Statements. Interpretation 40 had been scheduled to become effective earlier but the date was changed to permit simultaneous application with FASB 120 and SOP 95-1.

It was because there seemed to be little authoritative accounting guidance relative to the insurance and reinsurance activities of mutual life insurance enterprises that the FASB, along with the AICPA, decided to extend the requirements of the above mentioned standards to them. The AICPA's Statement of Position 95-1 sets guidelines for participating insurance contracts of mutual life insurance companies when:

1.  They are long-duration participating contracts that are expected to pay dividends to policyholders based on the actual experience of the insurer.
2.  The annual policyholder dividends are paid in a way that identifies divisible surplus, then distributes that surplus in approximately the same proportion that the contracts are estimated to have contributed to that surplus. Otherwise, accounting and reporting for these contracts are covered by the four basic FASB insurance enterprise standards listed above.

The effect of initially applying FASB 120 was reported retroactively through restatement of all previously issued annual financial statements presented for comparative purposes for fiscal years beginning after December 15, 1992.

# Chapter 22
## Expert Witness

## CONTENTS

## ¶22,000 OVERVIEW

With the plethora of high profile legal cases which have inundated the news in the last few years, we've all become trial experts. After being briefed on a variety of cases, we're aware of all the legal terms—and ramifications.

But of a less spectacular nature has been the steady increase of experts in more dignified, straightforward, less publicized cases; in fact, to the lay person, these are often downright boring. However, to the accountant who has found his niche as an "expert witness," they are not only fascinating, but can be quite remunerative. (After all, it was accounting that finally put Al Capone behind bars.) Many accountants are discovering they can increase business, gain public awareness, and enjoy using their special knowledge and experience as expert witnesses. Their financial knowledge and ability to follow a paper trail of figures gives them importance as investigators as well as witnesses in complicated court cases involving financial dealings. There can also be pitfalls along the way.

The need for the accountant as an "expert witness" has increased proportionately with the growing complexity of business affairs. For a number of years, the courts had permitted a rather liberal use of experts in trials; however, the days of relative immunity from prosecution of the expert witness seem to have ended as litigation threatened to become a national pastime. Obviously, the more lawsuits, the more losers. And the loser has to take it out on someone. (That loser may be the opposing party—or it could be the accountant's client.) Why not go after that expert who caused all the trouble? And his firm, too!

## ¶22,001  ENGAGEMENT LETTER

Therein lies the raison d'être of a well thought-out, carefully constructed engagement agreement containing buffers against both parties. This agreement needs, at the minimum, to spell out carefully:

1. What the accountant has agreed to do.
2. What information the client *must* make available to the expert witness to enable him or her to investigate the evidence and reach an opinion.
3. Lines of effective communication with both the client(s) and the attorney(s).
4. What the client can expect if the accountant is *required* to reveal on the stand any and all information on which his opinion is based.
5. That the attorney *must* keep the accountant informed in a timely fashion of any and all legal requirements such as filing times, submission of written documents, when any graphic presentations are due, and the like.

The corollary of this is, of course, that the accountant needs to guarantee to do or not do several things of concern to the client and/or attorney. If the accountant feels that he may not "fit the bill" as an expert witness in a case, he must not accept the engagement. The accountant must:

1. Possess the necessary qualifications and background.
2. Be cognizant of the accounting profession's technical and ethical standards applicable to litigation services, specifically those applying to expert witnesses.

3. Schedule adequate time and opportunity to investigate the case thoroughly.

4. Be prepared to furnish testimony in a forceful, confident manner.

5. Be prepared to defend a position "properly taken" in a polite, matter-of-fact manner in cross-examination.

6. Keep foremost in mind that the objective is to aid the client and attorney in winning the case, but *not* at the cost of the accountant's integrity.

7. Remember that the expert witness is *not* a client advocate, but an advocate of the accountant's own opinion and point of view.

8. Be positive that there can be no taint of conflict of interest that could be detrimental to the case.

9. Steer away from any engagement where there could be a possibility of divulging privileged information.

10. Withdraw as expeditiously as possible if there are any doubts about the litigation in question.

11. Adhere to the strategy of the lawyer, but here again, *not* at the expense of the accountant's integrity.

## ¶22,003  Prep Time

Preparing for the first trial may be the most difficult part of joining the growing number of accountants entering the expert witness niche. This is the time when the accountant, if he's been lucky or hasn't served on a jury, really becomes familiar with the down-to-earth aspects of the judicial system.

There's nothing like familiarity in developing confidence and ease of presentation; therefore, preparation should include:

1. Becoming familiar with the general rules governing real-life courtroom procedure in the locale where the testimony will be given.

2. A visit to a court, preferably one where there is a trial being held involving an accountant expert witness. In metropolitan areas, this should be relatively easy.

3. When apprised of the specific court assignment of the case, the accountant should visit the particular judge's courtroom to observe his attitude and demeanor.

4. Role playing. This activity is recommended for all sorts of therapy, where it may or may not work, but it definitely works in a situation like this. (The attorneys had to play out their role for moot court in law school. Why not the accountant turning expert witness?) Partners, staff and/or family members make great critics — as well as actors in this courtroom drama. Even a full-length mirror can ask questions and talk back.

## ¶22,005  DEFINITION OF AN EXPERT WITNESS

The courts uniformly agree that the accountant possesses the qualifications of an expert witness on any subject matter falling within the scope of his experience, training, and education.

There are perhaps as many definitions of an "expert witness" as there are statutes, judges, and writers concerned with testimony. The following definition of an expert witness is designed to cover all aspect of "expert" definitions (without any whereases or wherefores): *A witness is an expert witness and is qualified to give expert testimony if the judge finds that to perceive, know, or understand the matter concerning which the witness is to testify requires special knowledge, skill, experience, training, and/or education, and that the witness has the requisite special knowledge, skill, experience, training, and/or education deemed necessary and appropriate.*

If the opposing party offers any objection to the use of an expert's testimony, the accountant's special knowledge, skill, experience, training, or education must be shown before the witness may testify as an expert. Regardless, this information should be made known to the court. A witness's special knowledge, skill, training, or education may be shown by his own testimony, but it will probably "set" better with the jury if the lawyer elicits the pertinent information from the witness relating to his or her education, experience, and specialized knowledge.

Since the basic requirement of an expert witness is that the witness possess the ability to interpret, analyze, and evaluate the significant facts on a question concerning which just a judge or a judge and jury need assistance to resolve, it is imperative that they be aware of the accountant's background. This expertise must be demonstrated in a positive but unassuming manner to be effective. No one likes a braggart.

The courts have uniformly accepted the accountant as an expert. In the majority of cases, the primary and most significant criteria in guidance of a trial court's determination of qualifications of an expert witness are based on occupational experience. Equally significant is the judicial recognition of the special knowledge acquired by an accountant relating to a particular industry, trade, occupation, or profession to qualify her as an expert on particular business and trade practices and on other factors relating to costs and gross profit margins.

In actual practice, it is rare that the trial court will refuse to permit the witness to testify as an expert because he is insufficiently qualified. Rather, any weakness or deficiency will show up in the quality and impact of the testimony rather than its admissibility.

Therefore, it is imperative that an accountant be very cautious about accepting an assignment that may be beyond his or her area of expertise.

# ¶22,007  FUNCTION OF THE EXPERT WITNESS

The function of the expert witness is to form an opinion or inference on matters when individuals in the normal course of affairs would probably not be able to do so. Therefore, an expert witness is needed in any case where by reason of his special knowledge, the expert is able to form a valid opinion on the facts while the man on the street would—or should—not.

Courts vary in their conception of when the expert is needed. Some courts maintain that expert testimony is admissible only when the subject matter is beyond the common experience of the ordinary juror who would then be unable to reach an informed opinion or draw a valid inference from the facts. In effect, they apply a "strict" test of necessity. More often, the determination is made on the basis of whether this testimony would be of "assistance" to the judge or jury.

# ¶22,009  BASIS OF INVESTIGATION

In his investigation preparatory to giving testimony, an expert may rely upon various sources. He may:

1. Rely on known facts if such facts are material to the inquiry.
2. Obtain information gained from a demonstrably reliable source.

   This could include previous audit reports, certified financial statements, books and records of the business—even though they were not kept by the expert witness—or demonstrable customs and practices within the business or industry of the client for whom the expert is testifying.
3. If the expert has firsthand knowledge of the situation, inferences or opinions may be stated directly. However, care should be taken to be absolutely sure that the practitioner states fully the facts relied upon, the reliable source, and the permissibility of the basis upon which an opinion was founded. Otherwise, the testimony will do more harm than good. If a judge and/or jury become aware of even one instance in which the accountant has slipped up, his expertise will henceforth be open to question.

In addition, the expert witness must have a thorough knowledge of the substantive issue in the case. The investigation and subsequent conclusion may be incomplete and unrelated to the issue if he either has not been informed properly of the particulars in a case, or has not done his homework thoroughly. It is also necessary that he know the issues of the case so that he can anticipate and respond promptly and forcefully to cross-examination and avoid answers that are incomplete, confusing, and irrelevant. In other words, the expert must be made privy to all relevant facts in the case as well as to the direction of the lawyer's attack or counterattack.

The "need to know" policy should not be carried so far that the accountant appears "in the dark" or at best ill-informed. Therefore, it is important for the accountant to ascertain whether the attorney is willing to work closely with the "expert witness." If the accountant finds it impossible to work in good faith with a particular attorney or law firm, he should withdraw from the case, if possible, or at least refuse to work with that individual or firm in the future. Failure to be aware of or to consider all of the facts not only diminishes the value of the expert's testimony to the case but quite often leaves the expert vulnerable to attack on cross-examination. Not only can the accountant become surprised and confused by the additional facts, but the image as an expert will be damaged in the minds of the judge and jury. The individual's credibility and reputation could be severely damaged.

## ¶22,011   EXHIBITS

It is almost mandatory that the expert witness prepare, or have prepared, some type of exhibit for several obvious reasons, not the least of which is the fact that very few individuals can make any sense of numbers from just *hearing* them. Oversize charts, graphs, schedules, diagrams—whatever aids the court in visualizing the accountant's findings—can be useful in focusing their attention. Visual aids not only help the expert witness explain his conclusions but they can have a greater impact on the judge and jury. *If* these graphics can be presented in an interesting, imaginative way, they might also tend to lessen the tedium of often very dry facts and figures.

This "demonstrative evidence" (in the parlance of the court) must not appear to be a way of "lecturing" to the judge and jury. At the same time, these are not people preparing for the CPA exam. The visual materials must present readily understood, clearly identifiable steps the accountant took in arriving at opinions and conclusions—not just a jumble of numbers.

It may be appropriate to provide copies of the material to the judge and the members of the jury so that they can use both eyes and ears to follow the testimony of the expert. Even then, it is probably better to have too little information on a graph or schedule than too much.

## ¶22,013   UNDERSTANDABLE TESTIMONY

Expert testimony is valuable only when it is understood by the judge and jury. The expert must be able to explain and defend her opinion in language reasonably understood by the layman. Everyone complains about "legalese."

What about "accountantese"? It should always be kept in mind that the very reason the expert is testifying is that the subject matter is beyond the common knowledge and experience of the average juror.

A common error committed by the accounting expert is to use technical language in testimony without offering an explanation of its meaning.

Terms like *earnings per share, stockholder's equity,* and *retained earnings* may have a nice ring to them. However, if the testimony must necessarily involve technical accounting terms and concepts of this caliber, they must be defined and explained in a clear and simple manner.

## ¶22,015   CROSS-EXAMINATION

An accountant testifying as an expert may be cross-examined to the same extent as any other witness.

Therefore, the expert should assume that his opinion will be rigorously challenged on cross-examination. The fact that the subject matter is being litigated indicates conflicting theories or facts upon which an opinion may be based. In order to preserve the value and effectiveness of testimony given as an expert, the witness should anticipate what may be brought up in cross-examination. Thorough preparation, awareness of other aspects of a case, anticipation of where the "attack" may come will all aid in the individual's holding up well in this phase of a court appearance. Now is the time when the opposing counsel will attempt to discredit the expert witness concerning qualifications, knowledge of the subject matter, the validity of the source of relevant information, and the basis for arriving at the stated opinion and conclusions.

It is important for the accountant to remember that this is the lawyer's job. Since the purpose of cross-examination is to diminish or destroy the expert's conclusions, the lawyer may be argumentative, supercilious, and aggressive in an attempt to catch the witness off balance—to make the expert react too quickly and speak before thinking. Instead, this is the time when remaining courteous, unemotional, and firmly convinced of the correctness of previous statements pays off.

One of the techniques used in cross-examination is to show a contradiction or omission of facts upon which the expert founded an opinion. For this reason, it is essential that the expert make a thorough investigation, have knowledge of all relevant theories and material facts, and be prepared to support that opinion rationally on cross-examination. If the expert has adequately prepared, she can reasonably anticipate any weak or questionable aspects of the testimony and be ready to cope with them quickly and spontaneously on cross-examination.

## ¶22,017  REBUTTAL

Rebuttal testimony provides the opposing party with an opportunity to introduce evidence that refutes the prior evidence of the other side in the case. The opposing side may decide to offer in rebuttal its own expert to directly refute the testimony of the original expert. Rebuttal testimony may not go beyond the scope of the original evidence. In other words, a party may not introduce new evidence but is limited to a direct rebuttal of prior evidence. However, there is still plenty of opportunity for accounting expert witness No. 2 to question the validity of the original expert's assumptions, opinions, and conclusions concerning alternative ways of looking at a situation.

If the original expert has considered and discussed the cause for litigation from every possible angle, the impact of a rebuttal expert witness who attempts to base opinion on opposing theories and facts has basically been forestalled, because that ground has already been covered, and discarded.

## ¶22,019  LEGAL MATTERS

What are these weighty matters which the expert witness is going to investigate, form opinions concerning, testify to, be cross-examined about or offer rebuttal to? As might be expected, there may even be a "mini-niche" within this niche where the accountant could decide to specialize. Among the more likely spots are:

1.  Tax cases-civil, criminal, fraud—both state and federal. It is difficult to imagine a tax case that does not involve accounting problems. Attorneys for both the government and the taxpayer can be expected to have a general knowledge of accounting principles, but they have other responsibilities in the case. Enter the practitioner investigator and witness to refute the charge of "willful attempt to evade taxes," or just an assertion of deficiency in tax payments.

2.  Divorce cases. In states with community property laws, this can become extremely involved in tracing and determining which funds are community property, separate property, proceeds from separate property, commingled funds, and separate funds of various descriptions.

3.  Probate proceedings. Wills, state inheritance taxes, and federal estate taxes in states with community property laws also often need testimony from investigative accountants. In fact, the distinction between separate and community property is often crucial in figuring the amount of state inheritance and federal estate taxes owed.

4.  Partnership dissolution and/or valuation of partnership interest. The accountant is frequently employed as an expert to prepare a partnership

accounting of a dissolved partnership. Following is a sampling of the items that will come to the attention of the accountant in preparing her report for submission to the court:

a. Contractual agreements among the partners expressly providing for a partnership accounting for capital or profits.

b. Capital contributions reflected in the partnership agreement, additional loans, and restrictions or limitations on the right of a partner to withdraw the profits or capital.

c. Present fair market value (FMV) of property previously contributed by a partner.

d. Allocation of profits and losses for the current year in accordance with the partnership agreement.

5. Corporate suits brought by shareholders; corporate fraud cases. These involve not only large corporations, but also very small ones that have been inundated in the flood of litigation in the U.S.

The accountant must, obviously, have an understanding of the pertinent substantive law before being competent to undertake an investigation of the facts and testify as an expert witness—giving an opinion and conclusions concerning a legal as well as a financial matter.

It becomes fairly obvious that the neophyte expert witness needs to do some investigating to determine just what laws apply to the niche he has chosen to delve into. The particular state laws are undoubtedly the place to begin the investigation since each will be somewhat different—some more than others.

# Chapter 23

## Keep It Honest and Profitable

## CONTENTS

## ¶23,000  OVERVIEW

Any business organization that does not have an established system of fraud control and other internal controls in place should have one; any organization that does have such a policy should review and update it periodically. If the system has developed haphazardly—reactively rather than proactively—it probably needs a thorough overhaul.

Enron is not the only cataclysmic event that has spurred change, reform, legislation and a closer look at business practices in general and accounting and auditing practices in particular. Other occurrences have also resulted in an attempt to bring honesty and increased productivity to the business world.

Action was taken in response to the series of savings and loan failures and spectacular frauds during and after the Watergate era. Increased emphasis was placed on improving the quality of financial reporting through *business ethics*, effective *internal controls*, and *corporate governance*. Concentrated effort was made to correct the existing situation and to prevent future fiascoes. In the latter attempt, the effort appears to have failed spectacularly.

More recently, Section 404 of the Sarbanes-Oxley Act of 2002 requires public companies (those required to register with the SEC) to include with their annual report to the Securities and Exchange Commission a seperate assessment report, indicating the effectiveness of the company's internal controls. The report to the SEC is further required to be attested to and seperately reported on by the external auditors for the company. As noted in Chapter 26, "The Sarbanes-Oxley Act of 2002," each annual report must contain a report stating the reponsibility of management for establishing and maintaining an adequate internal control structure and procedures for financial reporting.

The report by management on its internal control is required to disclose the criteria against which its internal control effectiveness has been measured. The general industry standard used as a measurement criterion is the Committee on Sponsoring Organizations (COSO) framework discussed below. The assessment of internal control effectiveness is to be made as of the end of the fiscal year being reported on and any changes in internal control that have occurred during the year should also be indicated

On June 17, 2004, the PCAOB adopted *Auditing Standard No. 2, An Audit of Internal Control Over Financial Reporting Performed in Conjunction with An Audit of Financial Statements*. This document supplies the specifics necessary for management to provide an assessment of its internal controls as well as for outside auditors to perform their audit of management's report. Especially helpful is a section on definitions used in dealing with internal controls. For example, an internal *control deficiency* exists, according to the standard, "when the design or operation of a control does not allow management or employees, in the normal course of performing their assigned functions, to prevent or detect misstatements on a timely basis." The standard further indicates that its performance and reporting directions are based on the COSO framework.

## ¶23,001    THE COMMITTEE OF SPONSORING ORGANIZATIONS (COSO)

One of the reactions to that upheaval was the Committee of Sponsoring Organizations, formed in 1985 to establish and support the National Commission on Fraudulent Financial Reporting. The National Commission was organized as an independent private-sector initiative to study the causal factors that can lead to fraudulent financial reporting. It developed recommendations for public companies and their independent auditors, for the Securities and Exchange Commission (SEC) and other regulators and for educational institutions.

The National Commission (otherwise referred to as the "Treadway Commission," in honor of its first chairman, a former Commissioner of the SEC) was jointly sponsored by the five major U.S. financial professional associations:

1. The American Institute of Certified Public Accountants (AICPA).
2. The American Accounting Association (AAA).
3. The Institute of Internal Auditors (IIA).
4. The Institute of Management Accountants (IMA).
5. The Financial Executives Institute (FEI).

However, it was wholly independent of each of the sponsoring organizations and contained representatives from industry, public accounting, investment firms and the New York Stock Exchange.

## .01    The COSO Framework for Internal Control

The COSO sponsored the development and publication of *Internal Control—Integrated Framework*, which provides the COSO model. The model outlines a sound basis for establishing internal control systems and for determining their effectiveness in practice. It does not attempt to reinvent internal controls but to define them in broader terms and to provide a framework for describing and evaluating the effectiveness of internal controls within a control environment.

The COSO basis for internal controls is widely accepted:

1. It has been incorporated into generally accepted accounting principals (GAAP) with the adoption of *Statement on Auditing Standards No. 78* by the AICPA.
2. The COSO framework has also been adopted by the financial services industry in response to the Federal Deposit Insurance Improvement Act requirements for assessing internal controls.
3. The Office of Management and Budget (OMB) Circular A-123, "Management Accountability and Control," of June 21, 1995, provides the requirements for assessing controls under COSO. OMB Circular A-123 uses the term "management control" to cover all aspects of internal control over an agency's operations (operational, financial and compliance).
4. The General Accounting Office (GAO) standards provide the measure of quality against which controls in operation are assessed, and the COSO model is the model accepted by GAO.
5. Many large and small companies use the framework as the basis for their internal control procedure, as does the Small Business Administration.

## .03   Components of Internal Control

The COSO determined that a comprehensive assessment of risk and improved internal controls were necessary to manage business risk effectively. The standards and guidance developed by the committee are referred to as the COSO Internal Control Framework. According to COSO, internal control consists of five interrelated components:

1. *The control environment.* The control environment, as established by the head of the organization and senior managers, sets the tone and influences the control consciousness of employees. Control environment factors include integrity and ethical values, employee competence, leadership philosophy and style, and assignment of authority and responsibility.
2. *Risk assessment.* Risk assessment is the identification and analysis of relevant risks to the achievement of the organization's objectives. It forms the basis for determining how risks should be managed.
3. *Control activities.* Control activities are the policies and procedures that help to ensure that management directives are carried out. They also help to ensure that necessary actions are taken to address any risks to the achievement of the organization's objectives.
4. *Information and communication.* Information and communication systems enable the organization's managers and employees to capture

and exchange the information needed to conduct, manage and control its operations.

5.  *Monitoring.* The entire process must be monitored to assess the quality of the internal control system's performance over time. Ongoing monitoring occurs in the course of operations:

    a.  As part of regular management and supervisory activities.

    b.  For employee performance of their duties.

Separate periodic evaluations assess the effectiveness of the internal control process and the ongoing monitoring procedures.

## .05  The COSO Definition of Internal Control

Internal control is a process, effected by an entity's board of directors, management and other personnel, designed to provide reasonable assurance regarding:

1.  Effectiveness and efficiency of operations.
2.  Reliability of financial reporting.
3.  Compliance with applicable laws and regulations.

## .07  Key Concepts Considered by COSO

Following are those key concepts assumed by COSO's model and framework:

1.  Internal control is a *process.* It is a means to an end, not an end in itself.
2.  Internal control is effected by *people*—it is not merely policy manuals and forms, but people at every level of an organization.
3.  Internal control can be expected to provide only *reasonable assurance*, not absolute assurance, to an entity's management and board.
4.  Internal control is geared to the achievement of *objectives* in one or more separate but over-lapping categories.

(Note: Checklists at the end of the chapter should give a good idea of whether internal control is adequate for a particular organization.)

## ¶23,003  The Foreign Corrupt Practices Act (FCPA)

Investigations by the Securities and Exchange Commission in the mid-1970s showed that more than 400 U.S. companies admitted making questionable or outright illegal payments in excess of $300 million to foreign government officials, politicians and political parties.

When the Foreign Corrupt Practices Act (FCPA) was enacted by Congress in 1977, the act was characterized by the American Bar Association as the most extensive application of federal law to the regulation of business since the passage of the 1933 and 1934 Securities Acts. As a matter of fact, the FCPA is an amendment to the 1934 Securities Exchange Act and is generally administered by the SEC.

One reason for the significance of this statutory requirement is that it represents the first time, historically, that the U.S. Congress legislated an accounting rule. GAAP, of course, have always been developed and promulgated by private-sector authorities—the AICPA, the Financial Accounting Standards Board (FASB), the AAA and other authoritative sources. However, indications at present are that this may not hold true in the future.

## .01   Importance of the Act to the Accounting Profession

Primarily as a result of the enactment of the FCPA, internal accounting controls have become a significant point of concern for corporate management, the public accounting profession and the Securities and Exchange Commission.

Section 102 of the FCPA titled "Accounting Standards" specifies that all corporations required to file with the SEC must "Make and keep books, records, and accounts, which, in reasonable detail, accurately and fairly reflect the transactions and dispositions of the assets of the issuer."

## .03   The Accountant's Responsibility

Again, the significance of the act is the explicit statutory recognition by the federal government given to accounting controls and control systems. The accountant's responsibility is to plan a system that constantly monitors for errors, irregularities, malfeasance, embezzlement and fraudulent manipulation of the accounts. The accountant is, in fact, the monitor who must continually evaluate the effectiveness of the system and monitor compliance with the requirements of the statute. This, of course, also includes compliance with GAAP, because the statute explicitly includes GAAP in the wording of the act.

That the statutory requirement applies to publicly held corporations led, initially, to the misunderstanding that it is of no concern to public accountants who are not involved in auditing public corporations. But auditors must be mindful of the Statement on Auditing Procedure No. 1, which applies to the scope of the examination of *all companies*, whether public or private corporations, partnerships or other forms of business organizations. This Statement specifically references creditors, for example, who are a primary user of financial statements and to whom an auditor has a potential liability for materially misleading financial statements accompanying applications for credit to financial institutions, regardless of honest error or fraudulent intent.

## .05 Compliance Problems

What can an accountant do to ascertain compliance with the 1977 act? Because neither the act nor the professional literature actually specifies criteria for evaluating a system's adequacy or materiality levels, compliance can be demonstrated by an intent to comply. This makes it difficult for management, directors, independent auditors, and legal counsel to be sure of compliance with the act as far as the government is concerned.

The following suggestions may be helpful both to the accountant and to management for establishing intent to comply. There should be:

1. Records of memos and minutes of meetings held by management, the board of directors and the audit committee (if there is no audit committee, one should be instituted) concerning internal accounting control concepts. The discussions should include legal counsel, internal auditors and independent auditors.

2. Statements for the record of intention to comply.

3. A record of all company meetings with the accounting personnel and internal audit staff held to ensure that they understand the importance of compliance and are capable of monitoring compliance.

4. A written program for continuing review and evaluation of the accounting controls system.

5. Letters from the independent auditors stating that no material weaknesses in internal accounting controls were discovered during the audit or that suggested needed improvements have in fact been made. If necessary, the independent auditors' comments should also include other deficiencies discovered during the audit. Management's written plans to correct these deficiencies should be included.

6. A record of periodic review and approval of the evaluation of the system by senior management, the audit committee and the board of directors.

7. Instructional manuals for the development of methods and techniques for describing, testing and evaluating internal controls.

8. Training programs conducted for internal auditors and other company personnel responsible for internal controls.

9. Changes in internal controls to overcome identified deficiencies that are initiated and documented.

10. A formal written code of conduct appropriately communicated and monitored. (Note: the SEC regards a corporate written code of conduct as imperative. At the same time, a non-listed corporation might find that

such a written code is even more important as a protection in case of litigation.)

11. Documentation that compliance testing was done by direct visual observations during the period being audited.

## .07   1988 Amendment to the FCPA

The basic act was amended in 1988 to spell out and clarify certain provisions of the act. As more and more small businesses became involved in world trade, it became essential for persons doing business overseas to understand fully the FCPA and its implications. It is an extremely important law that can result in grave consequences for those who disregard it. This law criminalizes certain conduct by or on behalf of U.S. entities doing business abroad. There are two basic parts of this law:

1. *Anti-bribery provisions,* which prohibit the payment of bribes to foreign officials to obtain business. This measure applies to *all* entities, *not* just listed companies. (See below.)

2. *Accounting provisions,* which require *public* companies to maintain accurate books and records, and an *adequate internal accounting control system.* The accounting rules apply only to companies that are required to report financial information under the Securities laws. These accounting and recordkeeping rules are broad and should be thoroughly understood.

## .09   Anti-Bribery Provisions of the FCPA

Under the FCPA, a "U.S. person" is precluded from providing certain things to a "foreign official" to get that foreign official to behave contrary to the obligations of his or her position. Specifically, the FCPA prohibits any U.S. person from corruptly proposing or giving money or other things of value to a foreign official, an official of a foreign political party, a candidate for foreign political office, or a foreign political party for the purposes of:

1. Influencing any act or decision of such foreign official in his official capacity.

2. Inducing such foreign official "to do or omit to do" any act in violation of a lawful duty of such official.

3. Inducing such official to use his or her influence with a foreign government or instrumentality thereof to affect or influence any governmental act or decision.

4. Securing any improper advantage.

## .11  Accounting Provisions: Financial Policies and Internal Control

The FCPA states that corporations filing with the SEC are required to keep an accurate accounting of all financial transactions, including payment of commissions, consulting fees, service fees, facilitating payments and gratuities. All financial transactions must be characterized accurately in company financial records. Mislabeled or hidden transactions can result in liability for the company under the accounting provisions of the FCPA.

A company's *finance policies* and *internal controls* must ensure that all such transactions are properly and fully recorded. Therefore, it is mandatory that appropriate contracts govern international relationships and that all terms and conditions regarding payment under those contracts are clearly spelled out.

The statute requires publicly held companies to develop and maintain a system of internal accounting controls sufficient to ensure:

1. That transactions are executed in accordance with management's general or specific authorization.
2. That transactions are recorded as necessary to permit preparation of financial statements in conformity with GAAP or any other criteria applicable to such statements.
3. That the system maintains accountability for assets.
4. That access to assets is permitted only in accordance with management's general or specific authorization.
5. That the recorded accountability for assets is compared with existing assets at reasonable intervals, with appropriate action taken with respect to any difference.

*The Role of the Auditor.*  The significance of the act, insofar as auditors are concerned, is the explicit statutory recognition given to accounting controls. The auditor's objective is to plan the examination to search for errors or irregularities that would have a material effect on the financial statements and to use skill and care in the examination of the client's internal control system. Although the independent auditor is not part of a company's internal accounting control system, the auditor must evaluate the effectiveness and monitor compliance of internal accounting control systems.

## .13  Further Discussion of the Anti-Bribery Provisions

Because the scope of the FCPA is very broad, additional discussion of the anti-bribery provisions seems appropriate. It is important to keep in mind that the act covers not only large public companies but essentially any person residing in the United States as well as businesses incorporated in the United States or those that have their principal place of business in the United States. While the original intent of the law was to cut off large bribery-type payments to foreign officials, *any business, large or small*, that exports a product outside of the United States should be aware of the law.

According to the FCPA, covered companies, their employees and agents are prohibited from making, authorizing or promising payments or gifts of money or anything of value corruptly. In other words, no person may make a payment or gift to influence the recipient in any official act, such as failing to perform an official duty. Nor can any person give a gift to induce an individual to use his or her influence with his or her government or business for the entity's business benefit. (The prohibitions apply when the recipient is a foreign official, a foreign political party, a party official, a candidate for a foreign political office or any individual who will transmit some or all of the payment or gift to an illegal recipient.) Payments for seemingly *routine* matters—for example, expediting a shipment or speed up issuance of a permit—*may* violate the FCPA.

The Department of Justice has established a Foreign Corrupt Practices Act Opinion Procedure from which any U.S. company or national may request a statement from the Department's present enforcement policy in relation to anti-bribery provisions of the FCPA regarding a proposed business arrangement or action.

Although the Department of Commerce has no enforcement role regarding the FCPA, it supplies general guidance to U.S. exporters who have questions about the FCPA and about international developments concerning the FCPA.

## .15 Relevant Definitions

A *U.S. person* is defined as:

1. Domestic concerns (i.e., U.S. citizens, residents, business entities organized under the laws of any U.S. state or territory, and business entities with their principal place of business in the United States).
2. Issuers of stock traded on a stock exchange.
3. Officers, directors, employees, agents, and stockholders of domestic concerns.

A *foreign official* is considered to be:

1. Any officer or employee of a foreign government or instrumentality thereof or any person acting in an official capacity for or on behalf of any such government or instrumentality.
2. Officers and employees of state-owned enterprises.
3. Political parties and candidates.

4. Officers or employees of public international organizations such as the United Nations.

## .17 Sanctions for Violating the FCPA

The consequences for a violation of the FCPA are severe, both for a company and for individuals.

Fines and penalties for violations of the *anti-bribery provisions* are as follows:

1. Maximum criminal fine for a business entity is $2 million.
2. Maximum criminal fine for individuals is $100,000. Maximum imprisonment term is 5 years.
3. Civil penalty of $10,000 may also be imposed.

A fine imposed on a corporate employee or representative may not be paid directly or indirectly by the corporation.

For violations of the *accounting provisions*, there is no criminal liability, except the FCPA specifically criminalizes conduct by persons who knowingly circumvent a system of internal accounting controls or who knowingly falsify books and records. Fines and penalties are as follows:

1. Fines for individuals up to $1 million; imprisonment for up to 10 years or both.
2. Fines for corporations may be up to $2.5 million.

## .19 FCPA Red Flags

The following types of activities may involve FCPA violations:

1. Money or property passed through a consultant or representative to a public official to obtain certain government actions.
2. Use of consultants or representatives who are closely connected intermediaries with the government or a political party of the country in which the corporation is doing business.
3. Gifts or gratuities to government officials or political party officials, candidates for public office, or their families.
4. Extravagant entertaining of government officials or party leaders or their families.
5. Indirect payments to government officials or their families.
6. Use of company facilities by such government officials.

¶23,003.19

7. Negative information (flawed background) is discovered as part of due diligence.
8. A representative refuses to make FCPA-related certification.
9. A request for unusually large commissions, retainers, or other fees.
10. An unusual method of payment or payment in a third country proposed by representative.
11. Retention of a contingent fee representative when procurement decision is imminent.

## .21  1998 Amendment to the FCPA

In 1998, the International Anti-Bribery and Fair Competition Act of 1998 amended the FCPA to implement the Organization for Economic Cooperation and Development (OECD) Convention on Combating Bribery of Foreign Public Officials in International Business Transactions. The 1998 amendments:

1. Clarify that the act applies to payments to obtain any "improper advantage."
2. Assert nationality jurisdiction over U.S. companies and nationals that take any act in furtherance of a bribe, even in the absence of an interstate commerce nexus.
3. Expand the definition of foreign officials to include officials of *international public organizations.*
4. Provide for criminal liability over *foreign companies and nationals* that take any act in furtherance of a bribe *within the territory of the United States.*
5. Eliminate a *disparity in penalties* between U.S. nationals and non-U.S. nationals employed by or acting as agents of U.S. companies.

## .23  Preventing Non-Compliance

Any entity exporting products or services or preparing to export, must make sure that all employees and agents understand the requirements of the FCPA. To emphasize the importance of abiding by the provisions of the FCPA, a business should establish written policy statements concerning proper conduct. It would be appropriate for those policy statements to address not only bribery of foreign officials but also officials in the U.S.

Individuals responsible for the actual exporting activities, especially those that may come in direct contact with foreign officials or appoint local representatives who will do so, should be especially aware of the FCPA rules. The policy should also stipulate that employees should not accept any gifts or payments that could be interpreted as intent to persuade the company to act in a certain way.

## .25    Annual Report to Congress on the OECD Convention

The third annual report to the U.S. Congress on the implementation of the Organization for Economic Cooperation and Development Anti-Bribery Convention was given by the Commerce Department on June 29, 2001.

Among other disturbing findings, the report noted that the U.S. government has received reports indicating that the bribery of foreign public officials influenced the awarding of billions of dollars in contracts around the world. For example, in the period from May 1, 2000, to April 30, 2001, the competition for 61 contracts worth $37 billion may have been affected by bribery of foreign officials. Of those contracts, U.S. firms are believed to have lost at least nine, worth approximately $4 billion. Firms from Convention signatory countries continue to account for about 70 percent of these allegations.

The government's original aim was to stop the flagrant bribery of foreign officials and to restore public confidence in the integrity of the American business system. When it became obvious that American businesses where at a disadvantage because of bribery by foreign firms, the government joined other signatories in the Convention in the hopes that this vehicle could foster fair dealings globally.

The expanded FCPA conforms with the Convention on Combating Bribery of Foreign Officials in International Business Transactions, which has been adopted by 33 countries worldwide.

## ¶23,005    EXACTLY WHAT IS THE INTERNAL CONTROL SYSTEM (ICS)?

When considering a topic of this magnitude—the importance and complexity of internal control systems—it is important to understand what they are and why they are used before getting into the nitty-gritty technical aspects. Internal control serves at least two very important functions—effective use of assets (including personnel) and prevention of fraud.

A system can be thought of as a way of thinking. That is, it involves the evaluation of both the methods and the application of those methods to an entity's controls system. Evaluation techniques require:

1. Thoughtful consideration.
2. Rigorous study and research.
3. Objective analysis.

These three attributes are ways of thinking that in turn provide an orderly approach for reviewing an organization's techniques and procedures in order to appraise the adequacy of its ICS. And, if it appears not to be working, this is the time for trying to figure out why—and to fix it.

## .01 Internal Accounting and Administrative Control

Internal control, according to the Professional Auditing Standards, is subdivided into accounting control and administrative control. Two levels of objectives are implicit in the Standard. The ultimate goals are the *safeguarding* of assets and the *reliability* of financial records.

*Accounting Control.* The plan of organization and all methods, procedures and records that are concerned with, and relate directly to, safeguarding assets and the reliability of financial records are considered to be accounting controls. Consequently, they are designed to provide reasonable assurance that:

1. Transactions are executed in accordance with management's general or specific authorization.
2. Transactions are recorded as necessary:
   a. To permit preparation of financial statements in conformity with GAAP or any other criteria applicable to such statements.
   b. To maintain accountability for assets.
3. Access to assets is permitted only in accordance with management's authorization.
4. The recorded accountability for assets is compared with the existing assets at reasonable intervals and appropriate action taken with respect to any differences.

*Administrative Control.* The plan of organization and all methods and procedures that are concerned mainly with operational efficiency and adherence to managerial policies, such as sales policies, employee training, and production quality control, are elements of administrative control. This is usually only indirectly related to the financial records.

Administrative control includes, but is not limited to, the plan of organization and the procedures and records that are concerned with the decision processes leading to management's authorization of transactions. Such authorization is a management function directly associated with the responsibility for achieving the objectives of the organization and is the starting point for establishing account control of transactions.

## ¶23,007    FUNDAMENTALS OF A SYSTEM OF INTERNAL ACCOUNTING CONTROL

There is, necessarily, a relationship between the size of an organization and the development of its internal control system. Although complete separation of functions and the internal auditing department may well be impossible in smaller companies, effort should be made, as much as possible, to set in place the procedures, policies, and controls that support the following guidelines:

1. *Responsibility.* There should be a plan or an organizational chart that places the responsibility for specified functions on specific individuals in the organization. The responsibility for establishing and maintaining a system of internal accounting control rests with management. The system should be continuously supervised, tested, and modified as necessary to provide reasonable (but not absolute) assurance that objectives are being accomplished, all *at costs not exceeding benefits.*

2. *Division of duties.* The idea here is to remove the handling and recording of any one transaction from beginning to end from the control of any one employee. Making different employees responsible for different functions of a transaction actually serves as a cross-check, which facilitates the detection of errors—accidental or deliberate.

3. *Use of appropriate forms and documents.* Efficient design of forms and documents aids in the administration of the internal control system. Mechanical and electronic equipment can also be used to expedite the process of checking. Both of these methods provide control over accounting data.

4. *Internal auditors.* Periodic review of all of the preceding elements of the internal control system should be carried out by an internal audit staff. The function of this staff is to check the effectiveness of the policies, procedures, and controls mentioned.

## .01    Basic Elements of a System of Internal Accounting Control

The elements of a satisfactory system of internal control include:

1. A plan of organization that provides appropriate segregation of functional responsibilities.
2. A system of authorization and record procedures adequate to provide reasonable accounting control of assets, liabilities, revenues and expenses.
3. Sound practices to follow in the performance of duties and functions of each of the organizational departments.
4. Personnel of a quality commensurate with responsibilities.

One important element in the system of internal control is the independence of the operating, custodial, accounting and internal auditing functions.

There should be a separation of duties so that *records exist outside each department to serve as controls over the activities within that department.* Responsibilities for various functions and delegation of authority should be clearly defined and spelled out in organizational charts and manuals.

Conflicting and dual responsibility must be avoided. The initiation and authorization of an activity should be separate from the accounting for it. Custody of assets should be separated from the accounting for them.

## .03 Relationship of an Internal Control System to Outside Accountants

The efficiency of an internal control system becomes important to a company's outside, independent auditors. Before determining how thorough an audit should be made, the internal control system must be reviewed. An efficient system may do away with certain audit procedures that might otherwise be necessary. Conversely, a poor internal control system may necessitate a far more costly review on the part of the auditor.

## ¶23,009 INTERNAL CONTROL FOR INVENTORIES

It is obvious that merchandising and manufacturing companies in particular need to keep a complete, secure inventory of goods held for sale. Management is responsible for determining and maintaining the proper level of goods in inventory because:

1. If inventory is too low, sales opportunities may be missed.
2. If inventory is too large, the business pays unnecessarily high costs for storing, insuring and providing security. As a result, the company's cash flow becomes one sided—cash drains out to purchase inventory, but cash does not flow in from sales.

Merchandising companies classify all goods available for sale in one inventory category. Manufacturing companies generally use three inventory categories: finished goods, work-in-process and raw materials and supplies. This chapter emphasizes inventory for manufacturing companies, but many of the principles and practices also apply to merchandising companies.

Following is a discussion of internal control procedures that can be used in conjunction with different types of inventories: goods for resale, finished goods, materials and work in process.

## .01  Inventories of Merchandise Purchased for Resale and Supplies

The departments involved in internal control in merchandise and supplies inventories are purchasing, sales, receiving, accounts receivable, and accounts payable. The following controls should be implemented:

1. The purchasing department approves the purchase orders for merchandise to be bought. In a small company, the owner or manager may be the one to approve these purchase orders, which should be sequentially numbered and traced to final destination.

2. After okays from the purchasing manager have been received, requests for price quotations are usually sent out. These requests should go to various sources, and the company quoting the lowest price will be the one from which the purchases are made, unless there is some overriding consideration.

3. In the selling department, an updated individual quantity record for each type of unit is kept on perpetual inventory stock cards. It is usually the responsibility of inventory clerks to keep these cards up to date:

   a. The number of units of merchandise ordered is entered on the inventory stock cards by one clerk.

   b. The number actually received is entered from the receiving list by a different clerk.

   c. The number sold or used is recorded by still another clerk from sales lists or salesperson's orders.

   These stock cards indicate the need for reorders. They should be checked against a purchase requisition by the manager of the selling department or other person in control of the merchandise stock. In a business too small to have a separate selling department, the owner or manager should perform these functions.

   After the number of units ordered, received and issued have been recorded on the inventory cards, the balance represents the number of units actually on hand. A well-rounded perpetual card system usually includes detailed unit costs for ready computation under the LIFO, FIFO or average method.

4. In the receiving department, the receiving clerk should not be allowed to see purchase order records or purchase requisitions. Receiving reports are checked against the perpetual inventory stock records and a notation is made on these stock record cards indicating the date, order number, and quantity received.

   Even where a business is too small to have a perpetual inventory, a receiving report should be made. It should then be checked against the purchase orders and a notation as to the day and quantity received made on those purchase orders.

¶23,009.01

5.  In the accounts payable department, the receiving report is checked against the merchandise stock record, then sent to the accounts payable department, where it is verified against the seller's invoice. The purchasing agent should have approved the price on the seller's invoice before that invoice was sent to the accounts payable department.

    A clerk in the accounts payable department should verify all extension totals on the invoice. If the vendor's invoice and receiving report are in agreement, the invoice is then entered into a purchase journal or voucher register for future payment. Any discrepancy between quantity received and quantity on the seller's invoice will necessitate holding up payment until an adjustment is made by the seller.

## .03   Finished Goods Inventories

The departments involved in internal control of finished goods inventories are manufacturing, cost accounting, accounts receivable and sales. The following controls should be implemented:

1.  It is necessary to ascertain the quantity of units completed from the production record and transferred to the shipping department or warehouse. The daily report of finished goods units transferred to the shipping department or warehouse indicates the number of finished units available to the sales department.
2.  The unit cost of finished goods delivered to the sales department must be computed. This information is obtained from the unit cost sheet (for a process cost accounting system) or from the job-order cost card (in a job-order cost accounting system). (For more information see Chapter 15 on cost accounting.)
3.  Finished goods inventory cards should be set up. For each item, the following should be recorded:
    a.  The quantity received at the warehouse.
    b.  The quantity shipped on orders.
    c.  The balance remaining at specified unit costs.
        The number of finished goods units in the warehouse or stockroom should tie in with this finished goods inventory file.
4.  Periodically, a physical count of the finished goods inventory is required. It should tie in with the finished goods inventory file.

## .05   Raw Materials and Supplies Inventories

The departments involved in internal control for raw materials and supplies inventory are stores, purchasing, accounts payable, and manufacturing.

The following controls should be implemented:

1. In the stores department, the storekeeper must safeguard the raw materials and supplies inventories—both physically and by accounting control. No raw materials or supplies can leave without a stores requisition. Quantity control at minimum levels is also the responsibility of the storekeeper. The storekeeper should maintain a stores record for each item, listing:

   a. The maximum and minimum quantities.

   b. Quantity ordered and number.

   c. Quantity received.

   d. Quantity issued.

   e. Balance on hand.

   When stores cards show minimum quantities, a stores ledger clerk pulls those cards from the file to make sure that materials or supplies are ordered to cover minimum needs. Quantities shown on the stores record should be verified by making an actual count of the stores items that are to be ordered. A purchase requisition is then filled out from the stores records. The quantity of each item ordered is approved by the storekeeper who knows the average monthly consumption of each item.

   The ordering of special equipment by department heads also goes through the storeroom after having the necessary executive approval. The purchase requisition is then forwarded to the purchasing agent.

   In the stores department, a receiving report is prepared in triplicate by the receiving clerk:

   a. One copy goes to the stores ledger clerk.

   b. The second is sent to the accounts payable department.

   c. The third is kept by the receiving clerk.

   The receiving clerk puts the stores items in proper places within the storeroom after preparing the receiving report. Ideally, location numbers are used to facilitate ready accessing.

   The stores ledger clerk gets a copy of the receiving report and makes a record of the quantity and the order number on the stores ledger card affected by the items received.

2. In the purchasing department, the purchase agent places the order for the quantity needed on the quantity requisition. If the agent feels the quantity ordered is excessive, he or she may look into the storekeeper's purchase requisition. The next step is to request price quotations from various supply companies. The order should normally be placed with the lowest bidder. The purchase agent also verifies the prices on the seller's invoices by comparing them to the price quotations.

3. In the accounts payable department, no bill should be approved for payment until:

   a. Materials ordered have actually been received.

   b. Materials have been inspected and are in good condition.

   c. The prices of the seller's invoice match the quotations.

4. In the manufacturing department, different individuals have authority to sign stores requisitions to withdraw materials from the storeroom. Usually, a foreman prepares a stores requisition when raw materials or supplies are needed in any of the manufacturing departments.
   This requisition contains:

   a. The account name and number.

   b. The department name and number.

   c. The job order number.

   d. The quantity of material issued.

   e. The stores item name and classification symbol.

   f. The name of the person to withdraw materials from the storeroom.

   g. The unit price of the item and the total cost of items withdrawn from the storeroom.

## .07   Work-in-Process Inventory

The departments involved in internal control of work-in-process inventories are manufacturing and cost accounting. The following controls should be implemented:

1. In the manufacturing department, stores requisitions are prepared by shop foremen for materials that are to be charged to the work-in-process inventory account. Quantities of materials are obtained from engineering or administrative departments. Specifications for raw materials are usually shown on a bill of materials (a list of different items required to complete an order). The stores requisition will specify:

   a. Quantity.

   b. Price.

   c. Cost of each item of raw material requisitioned.

   d. Job order number.

   Time tickets are prepared by the workers and approved by a foreman in the department in which work is performed before it is charged to the work-in-process inventory account. Each labor operation may have a standard time for performing a certain operation, as predetermined by the engineering department. There may also be a predetermined standard wage rate, determined by the head of the manufacturing department and known by the payroll department.

The cost accounting department is responsible for the amount of manufacturing expense charged to the work-in-process inventory account.

2.  In the cost department:

    a.  Raw material cost is computed from sales requisitions.

    b.  Direct labor costs are obtained from time tickets.

    c.  Manufacturing expense is estimated from prevailing overhead rates.

    Internal control methods for the work-in-process inventory account depend on whether the firm has a process cost accounting or job-order cost accounting system.

    The chief point of internal control for work-in-process inventories is computing costs. Product costs are analyzed by operations, departments and cost elements. This permits measurement of the cost of products at different stages of completion. The number of partly finished units when multiplied by a cost at a particular stage should come close to the value in the work-in-process inventory account.

## .09  Taking Count—The Physical Inventory

The two most significant factors of inventory control are knowing what should be on hand based on paper controls and then verifying what actually is on hand from a physical count.

***The Perpetual System—Knowing What Should Be on Hand.***    In many firms, not enough effort and emphasis are put into the timely keeping of detailed perpetual inventory stock records, the most basic control available. The nature and extent of the records to maintain vary from company to company, but at the least, there should be a constantly updated record of the units handled. The "ins" and "outs" are posted, showing the new morning's balance on hand, or rather, the balance that *should* be on hand. If expanded to the fullest, the system would also include:

1.  Unit costs of acquisitions (in manufacturing, detailed material, labor and overhead costs assigned).

2.  Unit sales deleted at cost (based on the company's flow-of-cost assumption of LIFO, FIFO or average costs).

3.  Balance on hand extended at cost.

4.  Back-order positions, write-downs, destructions and, most important, locations in the storage area (by location number or description) are shown on the individual record.

5.  The total sales income for that particular unit shown on the individual record and displaying unit gross profits.

¶23,009.09

Retail stores using the gross profit method of valuing inventories usually maintain controls over entire departments, or sections of departments rather than by individual units. Extended values are at retail, showing markups and markdowns as well as bulk cost figures.

The general-ledger summary inventory asset account should (where the system provides cost-flowing movement) always tie in to the total of the subsidiary perpetual system (at least monthly). They should be matched as often as possible and all differences traced to eliminate any weaknesses in the system. The point is—know what should be on hand!

*The Physical Count—Verifying What Is Actually on Hand.*   At least once a year, a physical count of the entire inventory should be taken, usually as of the balance sheet date. Management, not the auditor, is responsible for taking this physical inventory. The auditor is only an observer of methods, count and valuation. Personnel may help establish the system of counting, the tags to use, the methods of ensuring a full count, the cut-off procedures and the pricing. The auditor should observe the process to be satisfied about the reasonability of the total value acceptable for attestation.

The method of tagging, counting, weighing or measuring, locating and recounting—the assignment of personnel—all the procedures should be set in advance and followed (unless properly authorized changes develop).

As to the nitty-gritty of an actual inventory count, considerations include:

1.   Particular items should be counted by employees who do not have custody of the items.

2.   Supervisors should be responsible for assigning each employee to a specific set of inventory tasks.

3.   Employees who help take inventory are responsible for verifying the contents of any and all containers and storage places, including boxes, barrels, tubs and closets.

4.   Prenumbered tally sheets are provided to all employees involved in actually taking the inventory.

5.   The tally sheets provide evidence to support reported inventory levels and show exactly who is responsible for the information they include.

6.   Access to inventory should be limited until the physical inventory is completed.

7.   If any items are scheduled for shipping during a physical inventory, they should be segregated and not included in the count.

8.   If shipments are received during a physical inventory, they also should be segregated and counted separately.

9.   After the regular counting, a supervisor should verify that all items have been counted and that none has been counted twice.

¶23,009.09

The auditor should become familiar with the nature of the products handled, the terminology, the packaging, the principles of measurement and all of the precautions have been taken before the actual process is scheduled. Such education in the client's processes should not be obtained at the sacrifice of counting-time.

The auditor is concerned with the final evaluation of that physical inventory. The perpetual records, as such, and errors therein are not a necessary part of the audit process, though weaknesses should be commented upon in the management letter.

However, a history of *accurate* internal control of inventory can substantially reduce the extent of testing by the auditor. When it can be expected that variations from perpetual inventories will be small and within tolerable limits, the auditor may choose to use statistical random sampling in testing either an immediately prior physical count or in counting only those items *drawn by the auditor* (without advance notice) for random selection.

If the sample then indicates an unacceptable rate of error, the auditor may request another (or full) physical count, or may, with management's consent, adjust the overall value of the inventory to an amount indicated by the sample, with management required to investigate the error in the ensuing fiscal year. When an effective perpetual inventory control is in use, management usually cycle-counts the inventory. This may occur once or several times during the year. Unscheduled testing of bits and pieces throughout the year will keep everyone aware of attention given to the inventory; however, it must be covered entirely at least annually.

There are often *portions* of an inventory that would require more time and effort for the physical count than the relative merit of those portions warrants. Such items may be reasonably estimated (with joint approval of management and auditor), based on such elements as:

a. Last year's value.
b. Movement during the year.
c. Space occupied.
d. Weight.
e. Sales and purchases, using an estimated gross profit method.

The accuracy of a physical inventory even with the most sophisticated computerized system, may always be in doubt if there is no perpetual record for comparison. *A perpetual inventory is meaningless unless tested periodically to a physical count.* A history of accurate perpetual records can be justification for an auditor's using statistical sampling for year-end evaluation. Moreover, management itself can use statistical sampling techniques for cycle-counting. Tie-in to the general-ledger asset account should be made regularly by management. The financial statement value of the inventory must be at *cost* or *market*, whichever is lower. Standards are unacceptable, unless approximating cost.

¶23,009.09

## ¶23,011   INTERNAL CONTROL FOR EXPENSES

Each of the various types of expenses requires special internal control procedures. These procedures are covered in the following paragraphs.

### .01  Manufacturing Expenses

The departments involved in internal control of manufacturing expenses are factory production, factory service and accounts payable. The following controls should be implemented:

1.  In the manufacturing service and producing department, small tools that are not constantly being used should be kept in the tool room. Each worker requiring such tools can be given metal checks, each stamped with a personal number. The tool room attendant will release a tool to a worker in exchange for a metal check bearing the worker's number. The check is retained in the tool room until the tool is returned, at which time the check is returned.

    The department supervisor has the responsibility of approving a requisition for a new tool when one wears out.

2.  Charges for freight and shipping on incoming supplies should be charged to the account to which the supplies are charged. Copies of the freight or shipping bills should be attached to supply invoices. Supplies inventory is, therefore, charged for these freight and shipping charges instead of an expense account.

3.  Numerous types of shop supplies, such as brooms, oil, waste, solder, wire, are part of the raw materials and supplies inventory. They should be kept in the storeroom and issued only by a stores requisition, signed by an authorized individual. The individual who indicates the need for such supplies (usually a supervisor) should indicate the job order number or departmental expense account number to which the material is to be charged on the stores requisition.

4.  Workers categorized as indirect laborers should have an identification number when they work in a specific department. A time clock card should be kept and verified by a supervisor or timekeeper.

### .03  Selling Expenses

The departments involved for internal control of selling expenses are sales and accounts payable. The following controls should be implemented:

1.  Salespersons' salaries should be okayed by the sales department manager before a summary is sent to the payroll department. The basis for the summary is the salesperson's daily report. Commissions earned are verified

from duplicate sales invoices mailed to the customer. These are computed in the sales department and approved by the sales department manager.

2. To prevent padding of travel expenses, many companies allow flat rates or maximum amounts for each day of the week. Unusual amounts should require an explanation from the salesperson.

3. The office manager retains control over outgoing mail and postage. A mail clerk usually affixes the postage. Control of postage expenses involves limiting the number of office workers who have access to stamps or a postage meter.

4. Telephone expenses can be controlled by maintaining a record of all outgoing calls. Long distance calls should be reported indicating the party making the call and where the call is going. From the long distance call record, telephone expenses are distributed by departments.

5. Subscriptions to publications and dues of various organizations and professional societies should be approved by the sales manager before a voucher is prepared.

6. All bills approved by the sales manager are sent to the accounting department for payment.

## .05  Administrative Expenses

The departments involved in internal control of administrative expenses are administrative and accounts payable. Internal control for administrative expenses is very similar to that for the sales department. Bills for administrative expense items should be approved by an administrative department executive before they are sent to the accounts payable department for payment.

## .07  Financial and Other Expenses

In corporations that have special departments to control financial problems in the company, a treasury department or similar department will handle expenses in the nature of interest and discount and dividends and may even supervise handling of cash. The financial department may also have the responsibility for authorizing credit extended to customers.

The departments involved in internal control for factory payrolls are timekeeping, payroll, accounts payable and the particular manufacturing division. The following controls should be implemented:

1. A credit manager in the financial department should have the responsibility for approving sales orders above a specific amount. The manager should be in constant touch with the accounts receivable department to determine whether or not a customer has been regular in payments.

The treasurer has the responsibility for authorizing bad debt write-offs. The write-off itself should be made by someone in the accounts receivable department on the authority of the financial department executive—not the sales manager.

2. The financial department executive or office manager approves expenditures such as interest and bank discounts, office expenses and supplies. After approval of these items, invoices are sent to the accounts payable department.

## .09  Salaries and Wages

The departments involved in internal control for factory payrolls are timekeeping, payroll, accounts payable, and the particular manufacturing division. The following controls should be implemented:

1. In the timekeeping department, each worker is given an identifying number that will serve to identify his or her department. A badge with this number serves as identification when presence within the factory is checked each day.

2. It is the duty of a time clerk to check the presence of each worker once or twice a day, every day. This is to eliminate the possibility of one person punching the time clock for another who is absent. Absences are noted in a time book. These are then checked against the employee's time ticket, time clock card, or payroll sheet at the end of each specific pay period.

3. Care should be taken to prevent one worker punching another worker's time clock card. The time clock card indicates the number of hours the worker is present each day in the plant and can be used to verify either daily or weekly the hours shown on daily time tickets.

4. In the manufacturing department, a time ticket that lists the worker's name, number of hours worked on different jobs and labor operations, and total hours worked is prepared. It must be approved by the foreman of the department in which the work is performed.

5. In the payroll department, time tickets are verified against the time clock cards and the timekeeper's time clock book. The time ticket is then given to a clerk who inserts the hourly or piecework rate of each worker. Another clerk computes the earnings. The time tickets are then used for working up the payroll sheet. The time tickets are sent to the cost accounting department to prepare a payroll distribution sheet. The payroll sheet becomes the record by which the worker is paid. After the payroll sheet has been completely okayed, it is sent to the accounts payable department for payment. Payment to each worker, either by check or cash, should be receipted.

¶23,011.09

In the accounts payable department, the payroll sheet serves as the basis for payment.

## .11  Office Payroll

The following controls should be implemented for the office payroll:

1.  In the sales department, the sales manager approves the daily sales reports. From these reports, a record of the salesperson's days is prepared. The record is sent to the payroll department after approval by the sales manager. The manager in the sales department also approves the records of work performed by the sales office force before sending it to the payroll department.
2.  In the administrative department, the office manager approves time worked by the office force and then sends it to the payroll department. Salaries of top executives are often placed on a special payroll. Their salaries are usually known by the paymaster who prepares their checks and sends them directly to the executives' offices.
3.  The treasurer or financial department office manager similarly approves the work performed by the clerical personnel in his or her department.
4.  Upon receiving these authorized reports from the various departments, the paymaster sets them up on a payroll sheet and after computing the applicable salary for each office worker, takes all applicable deductions and indicates a net salary for each employee.
5.  In the accounts payable department, payment for these office workers' salaries is prepared from the payroll sheets.

## ¶23,013  Internal Control for Cash

Where currency is available, internal control is most necessary. Incoming checks may be used in manipulating accounts receivable and must be controlled. Accounts receivable control becomes part of cash control, and vice versa. Cash disbursements and petty cash also need special internal controls. Details follow.

## .01  Cash Receipts

The departments involved in internal control of cash receipts are selling, treasury or cashier's and accounts receivable. The following controls should be implemented:

1.  In the selling department, cash sales should be recorded in a register. A numbered sales slip should be made up for each sale. These slips should be used in numerical order.

2. In the cashier's department, an employee should count the cash at the end of the day. Except for a small amount left to make change, all cash should be removed. The total daily cash receipts should be recorded on slips and placed in the same pouch as the cash itself. The pouch should then be turned over to a clerk (a different employee from the one who counted the cash in the register) who will make out a bank deposit slip. Still another clerk in the cashier's department should read the cash register totals of the day or remove the cash sales slips.

   The cash removed from the register must agree with the tape and the total of cash slips, which are numbered sequentially (all numbers must have been accounted for). The sales readings are then compared with the amount of cash removed from the registers by the cashier. Small discrepancies are charged to a cash short or over account. Larger discrepancies call for an explanation.

3. In the accounts receivable department, incoming mail should be opened by a bonded clerk. All checks, currency, and money orders are listed by this clerk on a cash-received record. The cash-received record lists date of receipt, name of sender and amount. The record and totals are then sent to the accounts receivable department to be properly applied to the customers' accounts. The cash is sent to the cashier's office and subsequently given to the deposit clerk.

4. In the accounts receivable department, the record of cash received is used to credit customers' accounts. This record then goes to the general accounting department where it is compared with daily deposit slips of cash received from customers before it is entered on the books.

## .03   Cash Disbursements

The departments involved in the internal control of cash disbursements are accounts payable and voucher.

In the accounts payable department, purchase of any item must have prior approval from the authorized person in charge of the department in which the expenditure originates before it comes to the accounts payable department. Where a voucher system is in operation, vouchers are prepared for each expenditure. Information on the voucher matches that shown on the seller's invoice. Vouchers are entered in the voucher register after having been approved by the head of the voucher department and then placed in a pending file for future payments.

## .05   Petty Cash

The departments involved in the internal control of petty cash are selling, administrative or others in which there is a need for such petty cash funds, and accounts payable.

¶23,013.03

In any department where it is necessary to have a petty cash fund, at least two individuals should have the responsibility for handling petty cash. One individual inspects and approves the item for payment. The other has charge of the petty cash fund and pays the vouchers as they are presented. Each petty cash voucher should list the date, amount paid and name of the account to be charged. A bill or other receipt, if there is one, should be attached to the voucher. The employee who controls the petty cash fund should compare the receipts attached to the petty cash vouchers with the vouchers.

When the petty cash fund needs reimbursement, the person controlling the fund totals those petty cash vouchers which have been paid out and presents them to the accounts payable department. This department then arranges for the necessary reimbursement.

## .07  Accounts Receivable

The departments responsible for internal control of accounts receivable are accounts receivable and sales.

Copies of sales slips from the sales department are used to charge customers' accounts. Copies of any credits due customers come from the sales department. These records are sent to the accounts receivable department, where, if possible, one clerk should have the responsibility for entering only debits to customers' accounts and another for posting credits, such as for returned merchandise or receipt of a note. Still a third employee should enter the credit in the customer's account for cash received.

Sending statements at the end of each month is a good way to check the accuracy of the customer's accounts.

## .09  Notes Receivable

The departments responsible for internal control of notes receivable are treasury and accounts receivable.

In the treasury department, a record of notes held from customers is maintained. A record is then sent to the accounts receivable division where a clerk makes the proper credits. A copy is sent to the general accounting department to reflect the charge to the control account—notes receivable. The treasurer keeps the notes until maturity date or until discounted with the bank. A subsidiary note register should be kept if the company receives a large number of such notes.

## .11  Cash and Bank Reconciliations

Cash is the lifeblood of the company. It is the center upon which the whole circle of business activity pivots. Here is the reservoir through which all flows— in and out. Preferably more of the former.

¶23,013.11

It is surprising to find that tests of cash receipts and cash disbursements are usually limited by management (through intermediaries) to monthly bank reconciliations. Nothing is more effective than unannounced, non-routine, spot tests of the cash-handling procedures (for that matter, *any* business procedure) by the highest authority within the company. Think of the impact made on an employee who *knows* there may be an impromptu test by the president of the company—at any time! Imagine the psychological impact if this is done periodically, but irregularly. Such tests of the application of payments on account—receivables and payables—encourage peak, honest, performance.

Bank reconciliations by and of themselves cannot stand alone as proof of cash authenticity. They prove only the activity within that one period and serve to lend to prior reconciliations substantiation of then-listed outstanding checks. The current reconciliation is technically unproved until the outstanding checks and uncredited deposits in transit appear.

Reconciliations should be tested by someone other than the original preparer.

Block-proofs of cash should also be used occasionally to test an entire year's transactions. Here, all deposits are matched to all receipts recorded (in total); and all recorded disbursements are matched to total bank charges for cleared checks and minor items, with consideration given to opening and closing transit items.

The theory behind the mechanics of the bank reconciliation is to update the bank figures (on a worksheet) to reflect all transit items that have not yet cleared the bank, as follows:

| | |
|---|---|
| Bank shows a balance of | $ 10,500 |
| Add deposits in transit | 2,000 |
| | 12,500 |
| Less checks outstanding (itemized) | 600 |
| Adjusted bank balance | $ 11,900 |
| Balance per books shows | $ 11,909 |
| Difference | $      9 (more on books) |

Having taken the preliminary steps of determining the deposits in transit (by checking the bank credits against recorded receipts) and the outstanding checks (by checking off all returned canceled checks against the listing of those issued or carried over), a remaining difference of $9 is noted.

In the following order, the most expedient ways to find this difference are to:

1. Look at the bank statement for any bank charge not yet recorded in the general ledger.

¶23,013.11

2. Look at the books for any $9 debit (or combination) on the books and not on the statement.

3. Match the bank's opening pickup balance to the closing one on the last statement to determine whether the $9 is indicative of a transposition. Specifically,

   a. Match deposits to receipts recorded.

   b. Check general-ledger footings and subtraction.

   c. Check summary postings into the general ledger from the original source.

   d. Check footings in the books of original entry (receipts, disbursements and general journal).

4. Having exhausted the above possibilities and still not having found the difference, check the face amount of each check to the amount charged by the bank (each check is canceled with a clearance date).

5. Now match the listing of the check to the actual check. (Steps 4 and 5 are interchangeable).

6. Not yet? Prove the bank's additions.

7. If still elusive, it probably has been missed above or a transposition error has been made in listing transit checks or deposits; or, it may be an error made last month that was missed.

## ¶23,015  FILE MAINTENANCE

How costly is the time wasted in frustrating searches for misfiled data, when initial precautions and firm rules might have assured quick access to, and retrieval of, needed documents by competent, authorized personnel. One of the most important, yet least emphasized, facets of the business enterprise is the establishment and proper maintenance of an effective, accurate filing system. Following are some suggestions for doing just that:

1. Establish firm rules for filing.

2. Provide adequate accessible filing space for current files.

3. Pinpoint responsibilities for filing and accessing files.

4. Follow legal requirements for record retention.

5. Establish an annual policy of removing outdated files.

6. Utilize flow charts when appropriate.

7. Have sufficient copies of documents (e.g., purchase orders, sales shipping papers, and all papers) ultimately tied to a sales or vendor's invoice, to allow for a complete numerical file of each document.

¶23,015

*A List of File Categories.* File maintenance embraces all of the following:

1. Sales invoices to customers—both alphabetic and numeric files.
2. Vendor invoices—alphabetic, sometimes with copy of paid voucher check or numbered voucher. Some firms keep invoices segregated in an unpaid file until paid.
3. Canceled checks—kept by month in reconciled batches. Do not intermingle different batches.
4. Correspondence files—for customers, vendors, others.
5. Permanent files—organizational information, legal documents, leases, minutes and deeds. These are usually kept in fireproof areas and accessibility is limited.
6. Other:
    a. Tax files.
    b. Payroll and personnel files.
    c. Backup for journal entries.
    d. Investment files—security transactions.
    e. Petty cash voucher files.
    f. Purchasing department files—such as supplies and bids (costs).
    g. Credit department files.
    h. Prior years' books of entry.
    i. Data from subsidiary companies owned.
    j. Advertising programs, literature.

*Computer Files—Considerations.* Computer files present some unique problems that should be given special consideration. At a minimum, it is important to:

1. Have security protection—access, codes, permanent tapes or disks of programs and updated balance files for accounts receivables, payables, general ledger, payrolls. Keep enough of these changing files for reruns or accumulation runs, as needed for emergencies.
2. Keep hard copy until sure replacement hard copy is accurate, or as necessary for continuous file.
3. Be prepared for manual emergency work, if the computer goes down suddenly.
4. Pinpoint responsibility for keeping logs right through storage, updating software, and general housekeeping functions.

¶23,015

## ¶23,017  INTERNAL CONTROLS FOR A SMALL BUSINESS ENTERPRISE

There are many definitions of a small business. The most commonly accepted one is the U.S. Department of Commerce classification of an enterprise of fewer than 500 employees as a small business concern. Using this definition, there are millions of non-agricultural small business establishments in the United States.

In a small business organization of only a few people, little reliance can be placed on internal controls involving a segregation of duties, as it is among several persons in a large organization. However, that is no excuse for ignoring the importance of some degree of internal controls. Limited personnel who perform more than one related function and are associated with the handling of a company's money should trigger an assessment of the need for the establishment of at least a modified control system.

A plan of organization that provides at least a limited segregation of functional responsibilities within the constraint of a small staff should be developed. In a small business, the segregation is not so much between employees as between the owner and employees. An alert and able owner can provide about as much control as the segregation of duties does in a large organization.

The owner of a small business usually is the key person in its management. Unlike in a large organization, in the small business, the owner represents one of the effective components of a control system—that of personal observation. Principally, the owner can personally focus attention on selective areas of the business, such as reconciling the bank statement—one of the prime areas of control for a manager with limited time and staff.

The selection of a few areas for control is an important step. A tendency to over-control must be avoided in order to prevent a negative cost benefit allocation of time and expense. There is no need to control pencils and paper clips; the effort should be directed toward areas where the risk of error and material loss are greatest. Careful evaluation can uncover areas over which no control is exercised, but that are significant enough for procedures to be established for their control.

The checklists that follow have been developed as an economic and simplified guide for the responsible person in a small business to conduct periodic internal audits for the implementation and continuous review of the activities in the various areas of the business.

Too many companies give little if any thought to fraud prevention until after the fact. Then, any plan is a reaction to a specific situation rather than well-thought-out proactive steps and procedures to prevent misappropriation in any form from taking place in the future. Here, if not earlier, the accountant can come to the rescue with a skeleton plan that can be fleshed out with input from the owner and managers. Even this plan should be reconsidered periodically.

¶23,017

From these checklists, which include the significant areas of any business, can be selected those areas most important to the individual user. While a small business does not need accounting controls as sophisticated and expensive as those of a large company, neither can a small business be lax and informal with respect to procedures that can prevent possible mismanagement of assets or even embezzlement or fraud. The checklists indicate procedures that can lead to a suitable system.

## .01    Internal Controls Checklists for Small Business Entities

The following checklists provided in Forms 23-1 through 23-9 should help management keep tabs on what is and is not being done to prevent fraud and to foster efficiency. (After selecting the areas that are considered to be necessary for some degree of control, the user can refer back to sections in this chapter for additional detail about each checklist deemed appropriate for the particular enterprise.)

| Form 23-1 General Internal Control Checklist | | | | |
|---|---|---|---|---|
| | N/A | Yes | No | Action or Remarks |
| 1. Are accounting records kept up to date and balanced monthly? | | | | |
| 2. Is a standard chart of accounts with descriptive titles in use? | | | | |
| 3. Are adequate and timely reports prepared to ensure control of operations? a. Daily reports? b. Monthly financial statements? c. Ratio analysis, such as cost of goods sold or gross profit? d. Comparison of actual results with budget? e. Cash and other projections? | | | | |
| 4. Do the owner/directors take an active interest in the financial affairs and reports available? | | | | |
| 5. Are personal expenses kept separate from business expenses? | | | | |
| 6. Are employees who are in a position of trust bonded? | | | | |
| 7. Are the director and employees required to take annual vacations, and are their duties covered by another? | | | | |
| 8. Are monthly bank reconciliations reviewed by the owner and director? | | | | |
| 9. Do employees appear to be adequately trained and technically competent? | | | | |
| 10. Are job descriptions prepared and updated regularly to reflect current thinking? | | | | |

| | | | | |
|---|---|---|---|---|
| 11. Are volunteers properly trained and supervised? | | | | |
| 12. Is there appropriate separation of duties? | | | | |
| 13. Are minutes up to date and complete? | | | | |
| 14. Are authorized signatories for bank accounts designated with due diligence? | | | | |
| 15. Are account reconciliations performed regularly by personnel independent of the bank account? | | | | |
| 16. Are bank statements received directly by the person doing the bank reconciliation? | | | | |
| 17. Are the reconciliations reviewed by a qualified appropriate independent person? | | | | |
| 18. Is there a built-in system of checks and balances? | | | | |
| 19. Are governmental reporting requirements being complied with in a timely manner? | | | | |

¶23,017.01

| Form 23-2 Accounts Receivable and Sales Checklist | | | | |
|---|---|---|---|---|
| | N/A | Yes | No | Action or Remarks |
| 1. Are work orders, sales orders, shipping documents and invoices prenumbered and controlled? | | | | |
| 2. Would the existing system disclose any shipments being made without recording a sale (such as for sales on consignment and samples)? | | | | |
| 3. Is a credit check approved by owner? | | | | |
| 4. Are sales invoices reviewed for accuracy of price, terms, extensions and footings? | | | | |
| 5. Is an aged trial balance prepared monthly, reconciled to the general ledger and reviewed by the owner? | | | | |
| 6. Are monthly statements:<br>a. Reviewed by owner?<br>b. Mailed to all accounts? Does each account have a permanently assigned "account number"?<br>c. Are zero and credit balance statements mailed? | | | | |
| 7. Are write-offs, credit memos and special terms approved by the owner and directors? | | | | |
| 8. Is there sufficient separation of the receipts function and the application of payments to the accounts receivable? | | | | |
| 9. Are notes and other receivables under separate control? | | | | |
| 10. If there are any pledges receivable:<br>a. Are they properly recorded?<br>b. Is there collection follow-up? | | | | |
| 11. Is there a collections method in place either in-house or by a reputable agency? | | | | |
| 12. Is a schedule of late charge fees in place? | | | | |
| 13. Is there a schedule of charges for bounced checks? | | | | |

¶23,017.01

| | N/A | Yes | No | Action or Remarks |
|---|---|---|---|---|
| **Form 23-3**<br>**Cash Receipts Checklist** | | | | |
| 1. Does the accounting system provide means to identify, classify, record and report cash transactions? | | | | |
| 2. Is mail opened by director or owner or someone other than the bookkeeper? | | | | |
| 3. Are receipts copied with payment and listed prior to turning them over to the bookkeeper? | | | | |
| 4. Are they subsequently traced to the cash receipts journal? | | | | |
| 5. Does the client have adequate documentation of cash receipts? | | | | |
| 6. Are checks immediately endorsed "for deposit only" and deposited promptly and intact? | | | | |
| 7. Are over-the-counter receipts controlled, as by cash register and prenumbered receipts? | | | | |
| 8. Are these reviewed by owner or director? | | | | |
| 9. Is there a follow-up policy established to collect on bounced checks? | | | | |
| 10. Are over-the-counter cash receipts compared against register tapes and a count of sales tickets? | | | | |
| 11. Does the bank confirm deposits directly to someone independent of the cash deposit function? | | | | |
| 12. Does the bank alert the cash manager to incoming wires? Are they recorded properly? | | | | |
| 13. Are cash receipts managed according to policy? | | | | |

| Form 23-4 Inventories Checklist | N/A | Yes | No | Action or Remarks |
|---|---|---|---|---|
| 1. Are perpetual inventories maintained? | | | | |
| 2. Are they verified periodically by someone not normally in charge of inventories? | | | | |
| 3. Where perpetual records are not in use: a. Are periodic physical counts taken by responsible employees? b. Is owner exercising control by review of gross profit margins? | | | | |
| 4. Are physical facilities organized to discourage pilferage by employees and others? | | | | |
| 5. Are policies established to ensure all employee purchases are approved by a manager? And properly logged? | | | | |
| 6. Are off-premises inventories controlled? | | | | |
| 7. Is customer's merchandise on the premises physically segregated and under accounting control? | | | | |
| 8. Are inventories reviewed periodically for old, obsolete, or overstocked items? | | | | |

| | | | | |
|---|---|---|---|---|
| **Form 23-5** **Accounts Payable, Purchases and Disbursements Checklist** | | | | |
| | **N/A** | **Yes** | **No** | **Action or Remarks** |
| 1. Are prenumbered purchase orders used and are these approved by the owner or director? | | | | |
| 2. Are competitive bids required above prescribed limits? | | | | |
| 3. Are payments made from original invoices? | | | | |
| 4. Are supplier statements compared with recorded liabilities? | | | | |
| 5. Are all disbursements made by prenumbered checks and accounted for by someone independent of the disbursement function? | | | | |
| 6. Is the owner's or director's signature required on all checks? <br> a. Does owner or director sign checks only when they are accompanied by original supporting documentation? <br> b. Is the documentation adequately canceled to prevent reuse? <br> c. Do the persons responsible for the expenditure sign "ok to pay"? <br> d. Is the computer set to note the date and amount of the last payment on scheduled payments (e.g., phone and utilities bills) so that variations in billing are apparent? | | | | |

| | | | | |
|---|---|---|---|---|
| 7. Is there evidence that the following items have been checked before invoices are paid?<br>a. Prices, trade discounts and sales tax?<br>b. Receipt of goods or services? | | | | |
| 8. Are voided checks properly redeposited and stored? | | | | |
| 9. Is the disbursement officer independent of the accounting function? | | | | |
| 10. Is there a petty cash fund with one person responsible for its security and disbursement? | | | | |
| 11. Are vouchers used for petty cash disbursement? | | | | |
| 12. Are periodic reconciliations of the petty cash fund conducted by someone independent of the function? | | | | |
| 13. Is the size of the petty cash fund appropriate for its anticipated use? | | | | |

| Form 23-6 Investments Checklist | | | | |
|---|---|---|---|---|
| | N/A | Yes | No | Action or Remarks |
| 1. Is access to certificates, notes and other investment documents carefully spelled out and appropriately monitored? | | | | |
| 2. Is the physical possession of investment securities appropriately safeguarded? | | | | |
| 3. Is there a formalized investment policy? | | | | |
| 4. Is income from investments accounted for monthly? | | | | |
| 5. Is there effective utilization of temporary excess funds? | | | | |
| 6. Are investment securities of the type specified by management policy? | | | | |
| 7. Do the investment maturities fit the current cash flow plan? | | | | |
| 8. Do the returns of the portfolio warrant the risks? | | | | |
| 9. Are brokers' statements reconciled to the general ledger and the investments ledger by someone independent of the function? | | | | |
| 10. Are brokerage confirmations sent directly to someone independent of the investment function? | | | | |
| 11. Are periodic inventory counts made of the securities portfolio? | | | | |
| 12. In case of not-for-profit organizations:<br>a. Is dual control exercised over certificates?<br>b. Is there a written investment policy?<br>c. Does the board approve sales and purchases?<br>d. Is the return on investment checked periodically by the board? | | | | |

**¶23,017.01**

| Form 23-7<br>Property, Plant and Equipment Checklist | | | | |
|---|---|---|---|---|
| | N/A | Yes | No | Action or Remarks |
| 1. Are there detailed and updated records to support general-ledger totals for assets and accumulated depreciation? | | | | |
| 2. Are the owner or directors acquainted with assets owned? | | | | |
| 3. Is approval required for sale or acquisition of assets? | | | | |
| 4. Are there physical safeguards against theft or loss of small tools and other highly portable equipment? | | | | |
| 5. Is there a policy distinguishing capital and expense items? | | | | |
| 6. Is there a policy regarding security of building and well-being of employees? | | | | |

| Form 23-8<br>Insurance Checklist | | | | |
|---|---|---|---|---|
| | N/A | Yes | No | Action or Remarks |
| 1. Is insurance maintained in all major cases and is this coverage reviewed periodically by a qualified individual? | | | | |
| 2. Is insurance coverage adapted to needs of the specific type of organization? | | | | |
| 3. Are insurance claims checked carefully? | | | | |
| 4. Fidelity bonding helps to limit the loss on fraud; however, is there an understanding of just what the insurance covers and when to file claims? | | | | |

¶23,017.01

| | N/A | Yes | No | Action or Remarks |
|---|---|---|---|---|
| **Form 23-9** **Payroll Checklist** | | | | |
| 1. Is owner or director acquainted with all employees and does he or she approve all new hires and changes of pay rates? | | | | |
| 2. Is there a folder for each employee containing full documentation, including an employment application, W4, authorizations for deductions and signed employee handbook. | | | | |
| 3. Are there controls to prevent the payroll from being inflated without the knowledge of owner or director by fictitious employees, padded hours or inappropriate overtime? | | | | |
| 4. Does the owner or director sign all payroll checks and approve all state taxes and IRS deposits? | | | | |
| 5. If payroll is prepared by a bank or service bureau, does the owner or director of the company periodically review each check and related journals prior to distribution to employees? | | | | |
| 6. Are voided checks properly redeposited and stored? | | | | |
| 7. Is the payroll bank reconciliation balanced by someone other than the preparer? | | | | |
| 8. Is the payroll paid from a separate bank account? | | | | |
| 9. Is someone responsible for keeping current on change in payroll tax code laws? | | | | |
| 10. Is someone in charge of "scheduling" eligibility for and payment of simplified employee pensions (SEPs)? | | | | |

¶23,017.01

## ¶23,019  EMBEZZLEMENT

Embezzlement is the fraudulent appropriation of property by a person whom management has trusted. *Trusted* is the key word. A company can be losing money before suspecting that an embezzlement might be taking place, because this crime is usually committed by someone in a position of trust. Losses can be small amounts taken from a cash register or large sums of money stolen through manipulating the books. A set of simple controls built into the accounting system can prevent an embezzling operation. At the least, proper controls can document incriminating evidence in the absence of which it would be difficult to estimate a loss for insurance purposes or to prove in the courts that the losses resulted from a crime.

Companies with fewer than 100 employees tend to be more vulnerable to internal thefts because the smaller company is generally more lax about internal controls than a larger establishment would be. If employees feel that they are not getting a fair deal and are not being treated with respect, they may feel justified in getting what they feel they deserve, which may be anything from products or equipment and supplies to increasingly larger sums of cash. Therefore, just as in health care for the individual, *prevention* of disease within an organization must be the watchword.

## .01  Detecting and Preventing Embezzlement

This discussion reviews procedures for the detection and prevention of dishonest practices. It can be helpful first to understand a few of the usual methods of embezzlers in diverting company funds to their own pockets. Such an understanding can be a framework for developing the record keeping and control procedures to safeguard the company's money and other property vulnerable to misappropriation by an employee. (In general, however, an embezzler's methods are limited only by his or her creativity.)

*Authority in Important Areas.*    As mentioned previously, by definition an embezzler is usually a trusted employee enjoying the complete confidence of his or her employer. Usually, the embezzler has authority in such important areas as managing the checkbook. The easiest opportunity is sales for cash with no recording of the transaction in the books and no relevant paperwork. Prenumbered invoices or simply cash register receipts can be used for all sales with appropriate monitoring procedures to ensure that cash sales are being recorded. In addition, when employees know written records are maintained, the temptation to embezzle is lessened.

*Lapping.*    A complicated method of embezzlement is termed *lapping*. Lapping involves temporarily withholding receipts, such as payments by a customer on accounts receivable, and is a continuing process that usually starts with a small amount and runs into thousands of dollars before it is detected.

**Example:** An employee opens mail or receives cash and checks as payment on open accounts. The employee pockets a $100 cash payment by a customer named Paul. To avoid Paul's complaining at a later time about failure for his account to be credited, $100 is next taken from a $200 subsequent payment by a customer named Peter and credited to Paul's account. The embezzler pockets the $100 difference. (Note that the amount pyramids; it has to in order for the embezzler to continue to profit.) The lapping procedure continues with the employee absconding with increasingly larger amounts of money involving a steadily increasing number of customer accounts.

Prevention requires detailed recordkeeping procedures of invoices and other supporting working papers and periodic unscheduled audits of the accounts, along with confirmation of accounts receivables. Without adequate internal control procedures, detection of lapping is difficult and can continue for years. One red flag, however, is the discovery that an employee is keeping personal records of transactions outside of the established accounting system. Another is not taking vacations For this reason, many companies and organizations such as banks and brokerage firms require employees responsible for funds management to take regular vacations; it has happened that the substitute employee discovers irregularities. Beware of brown baggers who make a habit of not leaving the premises for lunch—it may not be just an economy measure.

*Check-Kiting.*   Check-kiting is one of the most popular operations in small and large companies alike. For a successful check-kiting operation, the employee must be in the position both to write checks and to make deposits in two or more bank accounts. One account is the embezzler's personal account and the other is the business checking account.

The check-kiter plays the float (e.g., the number of days between the deposit of a check and collection of funds). There may be several days between the date when a check drawn on Bank A is deposited in Bank B and the date the check clears Bank A for payment. An easy kite is accomplished simply by cashing a check at Bank B and then covering the amount on the morning of the day the check is expected to reach Bank A.

As the process is repeated the kited checks become increasingly large. More cash is withdrawn from Bank B and the kiting continues as long as the shortage is covered on time in Bank A. Finally, the kite breaks; this occurs when Bank A refuses to honor a check because the funds on deposit are insufficient to cover the kited check, or because the check reached Bank A a day earlier than usual.

A temporary kite can be used by a dishonest employee who has stolen cash in a separate operation. The cash shortage can be concealed at the end of an accounting period by depositing a kited check into the company account. This deposit brings the bank balance into reconciliation with the book balance on the statement date.

**¶23,019.01**

The best preventive measure against kiting (or to detect suspected kiting) is for the owner of the business to request cut-off statements from the bank at periodic intervals which, in turn, should be irregular intervals.

*Payroll Fraud.*   Payroll frauds are a frequent source of loss (and one of the more lucrative for the embezzler). The usual practice is to add the names of relatives or fictitious individuals to the company payroll, enabling the embezzler to draw several weekly paychecks instead of one. The best preventive measure is a policy that no person is added to the payroll without the personal authorization of the owner, or a responsible personnel manager in the organization. Also, frequent and regular payroll audits can reveal more paychecks being drawn than the company has employees.

*Dummy Suppliers.*   A typical embezzling procedure is for the dishonest employee to open an account on the books for a dummy supplier and issue checks to the nonexistent supplier for fictitious purchases. Established purchase procedures and a tight inventory controls system can discourage an employee from using false vouchers to process purchases of nonexistent merchandise.

## ¶23,021   WAYS TO DETER FRAUDULENT FINANCIAL REPORTING

In a survey conducted by the Association of Certified Fraud Examiners (ACFE) people were asked to respond to a question relating to the prevention of fraud in financial reporting. The organization noted that in the wake of Enron, there are calls for reform in the way CPAs conduct their audits. The question is, how to go about it. After compiling a list of possible solutions, the ACFE asked, "Which one of these measures do you think would likely have the greatest impact on deterring fraudulent financial reporting?" The measures and percentages of respondents who chose them follow:

- 28% Encouraging whistleblowers.
- 25% Surprise audits.
- 24% Assigning at least one certified fraud examiner to every public audit.
- 13% Requiring that auditors diligently inquire about fraud during the audit.
- 9% Requiring personal financial disclosures from insiders.

### .01   Clues for the Alert Fraudbuster

A number of clues can alert the owner or manager of a business to suspect dishonest practices:

1. An unusual increase in sales returns can conceal accounts receivable payments.

2. Unusual bad-debt write-offs can cover a fraudulent practice.
3. A decline in credit sales that is unusual can indicate possible unrecorded sales.
4. An unexpected large drop in profits or increase in expenses can be a red flag.
5. An increasing rate of slow collections of receivables can conceal an embezzlement.

In addition to an accounting system that incorporates a system of internal controls, there are precautions an owner can take to reduce the possibility of fraudulent losses:

1. A careful check of prospective employees' backgrounds.
2. Knowing the employees' personal lifestyles, insofar as possible.
3. Having company mail addressed to a post office box to which only the owner has access.
4. Having only the owner or a key person collect and open company mail.
5. Allowing only the owner to manage the funds, write checks, and make deposits.
6. Conducting periodic examination of all canceled checks, especially the endorsements on them.
7. Requiring that unusual discounts and bad-debt write-offs be approved by the owner, or manager.
8. Making sure that all employees responsible for company funds are bonded.
9. Making sure, if possible, that the preparation of the payroll and payment of employees are done by different persons, especially if cash is disbursed on payday.
10. Never signing blank checks!

# PART V

---

## SEC ACCOUNTING AND OVERSIGHT

# Chapter 24

# The Securities and Exchange Commission—Organization and the Acts

# ¶24,000  OVERVIEW

In a confusing and contentious regulatory environment, it is more important than ever before to understand the role, rules, and regulations of our regulatory bodies. The Securities and Exchange Commission has been in the news constantly and is a source of great curiosity to the public at large. Both tax professionals and their clients can enhance their understanding of current affairs by knowing what the SEC can—and cannot—do.

In the late 1920s there was widespread speculation in the stock market. When the market crashed in 1929, the public demanded protective action by their legislators. Congressional committees held hearings into all phases of the securities industry, investment banking, and commercial banking activities prior to the market crash. As a result of these hearings, eight Federal statutes were enacted between 1933 and 1940 (with a ninth in 1970), bringing the securities markets and the securities business under federal jurisdiction. These laws are referenced as the "truth in securities" statutes. They include the Securities Act of 1933, the Securities Exchange Act of 1934, the Public Utility Holding Company Act of 1935, the Maloney Amendment to the Securities Exchange Act of 1934, and the Federal Bankruptcy Code. Also included are the Trustee Indenture Act of 1939, the Investment Company Act of 1940, the Investment Advisers Act of 1940, the Securities Investor Protection Act (SPIC) of 1970, and the Securities Act Amendments of 1975.

**SEC REGIONAL AND DISTRICT OFFICES**

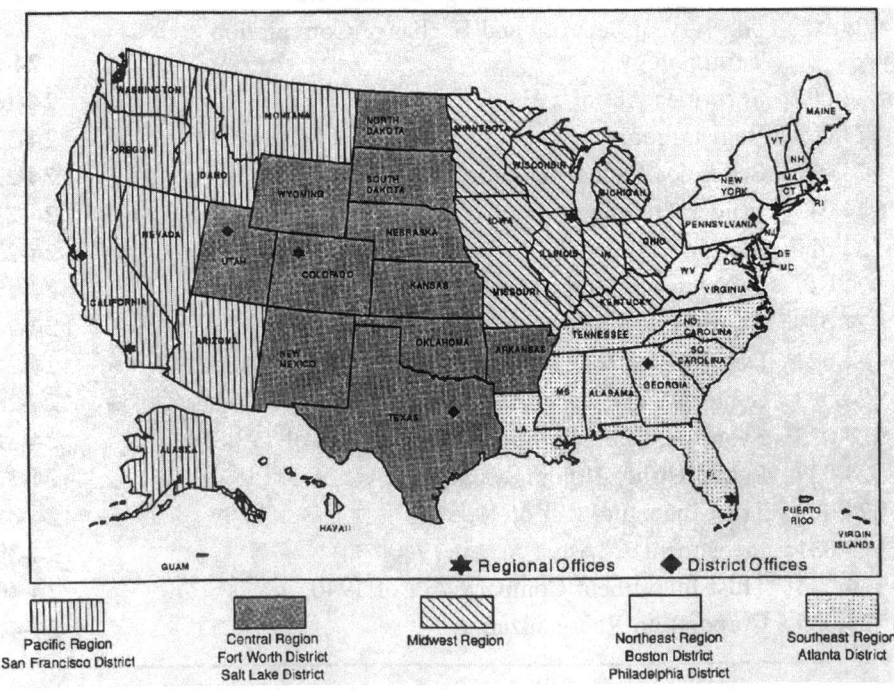

# ¶24,001    SEC ADDRESSES: HEADQUARTERS AND REGIONAL AND DISTRICT OFFICES

## *SEC HEADQUARTERS*

450 Fifth Street, NW
Washington, DC 20549
Office of Investor Education and
  Assistance
(202) 942-7040
e-mail: help@sec.gov

## *PACIFIC REGION*

*San Francisco District*
Alaska, Arizona, California, Guam,
Hawaii, Idaho, Montana, Nevada,
Oregon, Washington
  Pacific Regional Office
  5670 Wilshire Boulevard
  11th Floor
  Los Angeles, CA 90036-3648
  (323) 965-3998
  e-mail: losangeles@sec.gov

San Francisco District Office
44 Montgomery Street
Suite 1100
San Francisco, CA 94104
(415) 705-2500
e-mail: sanfrancisco@sec.gov

## *CENTRAL REGION*

*Fort Worth District, Salt Lake District*
Arkansas, Colorado, Kansas,
Nebraska, New Mexico, North
Dakota, Oklahoma, South Dakota,
Texas, Utah, Wyoming

Central Regional Office
1801 California Street
Suite 4800
Denver, CO 80202-2648
(303) 844-1000
e-mail: denver@sec.gov

Fort Worth District Office
801 Cherry Street
19th Floor
Fort Worth, TX 76102
(817) 978-3821
e-mail: dfw@sec.gov

Salt Lake District Office
500 Key Bank Tower
Suite 500
50 South Main Street
Salt Lake City, UT 84144-0402
(801) 524-5796
e-mail: saltlake@sec.gov

## *MIDWEST REGION*

Kentucky, Illinois, Indiana, Iowa,
Michigan, Minnesota, Missouri, Ohio,
Wisconsin

  Midwest Regional Office
  175 W. Jackson Boulevard
  Suite 900
  Chicago, IL 60604
  (312) 353-7390
  e-mail: chicago@sec.gov

## *NORTHEAST REGION*

*Boston District, Philadelphia District*
Connecticut, Delaware, District of
Columbia, Maine, Maryland,

¶24,001

Massachusetts, New Hampshire,
New Jersey, New York,
Pennsylvania, Rhode Island,
Vermont, Virginia, West Virginia

Northeast Regional Office
233 Broadway
New York, NY 10279
(646) 428-1500
e-mail: newyork@sec.gov

Boston District Office
73 Tremont Street
Suite 600
Boston, MA 02108-3912
(617) 424-5900
e-mail: boston@sec.gov

Philadelphia District Office
The Curtis Center
Suite 1120E
601 Walnut Street
Philadelphia, PA 19106-3322
(215) 597-3100
e-mail: philadelphia@sec.gov

### SOUTHEAST REGION

*Atlanta District*
Alabama, Florida, Georgia,
Louisiana, Mississippi, North
Carolina, Puerto Rico, South
Carolina, Tennessee, Virgin
Islands

Southeast Regional Office
1401 Brickell Avenue
Suite 200
Miami, FL 33131
(305) 536-4700
e-mail: miami@sec.gov

Atlanta District Office
3475 Lenox Road, N.E.
Suite 1000
Atlanta, GA 30326-1232
(404) 842-7600
e-mail: atlanta@sec.gov

## ¶24,003  THE SECURITIES AND EXCHANGE COMMISSION

The Commission is composed of five members: a Chairman and four Commissioners. Commission members are appointed by the President, with the advice and consent of the Senate, for five-year terms. The Chairman is designated by the President. Terms are staggered; one expires on June 5th of every year. Not more than three members can be of the same political party.

Under the direction of the Chairman and Commissioners, the SEC staff ensures that publicly held entities, broker-dealers in securities, investment companies and advisers, and other participants in the securities markets comply with federal securities laws. These laws are designed to facilitate informed investment analyses and decisions by the investment public, primarily by ensuring adequate disclosure of material significant information. Conformance with federal securities laws and regulations does not imply merit of securities. If information essential to informed investment analysis is properly disclosed, the Commission cannot bar the sale of securities which analysis may show to be of questionable value. Investors, not the Commission, must make the ultimate judgment of the worth of securities offered for sale.

The Commission's staff is composed of lawyers, accountants, financial analysts and examiners, engineers, investigators, economists, and other professionals. The staff is divided into divisions and offices, including eleven regional and district offices, each directed by officials appointed by the Chairman.

## ¶24,005 GLOSSARY OF SECURITY AND EXCHANGE COMMISSION TERMINOLOGY

The Securities and Exchange Commission in Article 1, Rule 1-02, Title 17, Code of Federal Regulations (which is Accounting Regulation S-X), defines the meaning of terms used by the SEC in its Accounting Rules and Regulations. Also, many of the terms are defined as they appear in the Securities Act of 1933, the Securities Exchange Act of 1934, in Regulations S-K and D, and in the various Forms which publicly held corporations must file periodically with the SEC.

Occasionally, the Commission will use a term in a rule which in context will have a meaning somewhat different from its commonly understood meaning. Many of the definitions as they are written in the statutes and accounting regulations are lengthy and legalistic in style. The objective here is to "delegalize" the "legalese" in the interests both of clarity and brevity. The definitions are not, therefore, verbatim as developed by the Commission.

**Accountant's Report.** In regard to financial statements, a document in which an independent public accountant or certified public accountant indicates the scope of the audit (or examination) which has been made and sets forth an opinion regarding the financial statements taken as a whole, or an assertion to the effect that an overall opinion cannot be expressed. When an overall opinion cannot be expressed, the reasons therefore should be stated.

**Accounting Principle, Change In.** Results from changing one acceptable principle to another principle. A change in practice, or in the method of applying an accounting principle, or practice, is also considered a change in accounting principle.

**Affiliate.** One that directly or indirectly, through one or more intermediaries, controls or is controlled by, or is under common control with, the person specified (see **Person** below).

**Amicus Curiae** ("Friend of the Court"). An SEC advisory upon request of a court which assists a court in the interpretation of some matter concerning a securities law or accounting regulation.

**Amount.** When used to reference securities means:

a. The principal amount of a debt obligation if "amount" relates to evidence of indebtedness.

b. The number of shares if "amount" relates to shares.

c. The number of units if "amount" relates to any other type of securities.

**Application for Listing.** A detailed questionnaire filed with a national securities exchange providing information concerning the corporation's history and current status.

**Assets Subject to Lien.** Assets mortgaged, pledged, or otherwise subject to lien, and the approximate amounts of each.

**Associate.** When used to indicate a relationship with any person (see **Person** below), any corporation or organization, any trust or other estate, and any relative or spouse of such person, or any relative of such spouse.

**Audit** (or **examination**). When used in regard to financial statements, an examination of the statements by an accountant in accordance with generally accepted auditing standards for the purpose of expressing an opinion.

**Audit Committee.** A special committee of the board composed of directors who are *not* (if possible) officers of the company. The SEC wants the Audit Committee to assume the responsibility for arranging the details of the audit. In addition, an audit committee's major responsibilities include dealing with the company's financial reports, its external audit, and the company's system of internal accounting control and internal audit. The duties and responsibilities of audit committee members should be reasonably specific, but broad enough to allow the committee to pursue matters believed to have important accounting, reporting and auditing consequences.

**Balance Sheet.** Includes statements of assets and liabilities as well as statements of net assets unless the context clearly indicates the contrary.

**Bank Holding Company.** A person who is engaged, either directly or indirectly, primarily in the business of owning securities of one or more banks for the purpose, and with the effect of exercising control.

**Blue Sky Laws.** Terminology for State securities laws.

**Broker.** A person in the business of buying and selling securities, for a commission, on behalf of other parties.

**Call.** (See **Option** below.)

**Censure.** A formal reprimand by the SEC for improper profesional behavior by a party to a filing.

**Certificate.** A document of an independent public accountant, or independent certified public accountant, that is dated, reasonably comprehensive as to the scope of the audit made, and states clearly the opinion of the accountant in respect to the financial statements and the accounting principles and procedures followed by the registrant (see **Registrant** below).

**Certification.** It is the accountant's responsibility to make a reasonably unqualified certification of the financial statements. It is important for the auditor to incorporate in the certificate an adequate explanation of the scope (see **Scope** below) of the audit.

**Certified.** When used in regard to financial statements, examined and reported upon with an opinion expressed by an independent public or certified public accountant.

**Certiorari, Writ of.** An order issued by a superior court directing an inferior court to deliver its record for review.

**Chapter X Bankruptcy.** Voluntary or involuntary reorganization of a corporation with publicly held securities.

**Chapter XI Bankruptcy.** Deals with individuals, partnerships and with corporations whose securities are not publicly held. Affects only voluntary arrangements of unsecured debts.

**Charter.** Includes articles of incorporation, declarations of trust, articles of association or partnership, or any similar instrument, as amended, affecting the organization of an incorporated or unincorporated person.

**Civil Actions.** Involves the private rights and remedies of the parties to a suit; actions arising out of a contract.

**Class of Securities.** A group of similar securities that give shareholders similar rights.

**Closed-End Investment Company.** A corporation in the business of investing its funds in securities of other corporations for income and profit. Investors wishing to "cash out" of the investment company do so by selling their shares on the open market, as with any other stock.

**Closing Date.** Effective date (see **Effective Date** below) of a registration statement.

**Comment Letters.** (See **Deficiency Letter** below.)

**Common Equity.** Any class of common stock or an equivalent interest, including but not limited to a unit of beneficial interest in a trust or a limited partnership interest.

**Compensating Balance.** Restricted deposits of a borrower required by banks to be maintained against short-term loans. A portion of any demand, time, or certificate of deposit, maintained by a corporation, or by any person on behalf of the corporation, which constitutes support for existing borrowing arrangements of the corporation, or any other person, with a lending institution. Such arrangements include both outstanding borrowings and the assurance of future credit availability.

**Consent Action.** Issued when a person agrees to the terms of an SEC disciplinary action without admitting to the allegations in the complaint.

**Consolidated Statements.** Include the operating results of a corporation's subsidiary(ies) with inter-company transactions eliminated.

**Control** (including the terms "controlling," "controlled by," "under common control with"). The possession, direct or indirect, of the power to direct or cause the direction of the management and policies of a person, whether through the ownership of voting shares, by contract, or otherwise.

**Cooling-Off Period.** The period between the filing and effective date (see **Effective Date** below) of a registration statement.

**Criminal Action.** Suits initiated for the alleged violation of a public law.

**Dealer.** A person in the business of buying and selling securities for his or her own account.

**Deficiency Letter.** A letter from the SEC to the registrant setting forth the needed corrections and amendments to the issuing corporations' registration statement.

**Delisting.** Permanent removal of a listed security from a national securities exchange.

**Depositary Share.** A security evidenced by an American Depositary Receipt that represents a foreign security or a multiple of or fraction thereof deposited with a depositary.

**Development Stage Company.** A company is considered to be in the development stage if it is devoting substantially all of its efforts to establishing a new business and either of the following conditions exists.

1. Planned principal operations have not commenced.

2. Planned principal operations have commenced, but there has been no significant revenue therefrom.

**Disbarment.** Permanent removal of a professional's privilege to represent clients before the SEC.

**Disclosure.** The identification of accounting policies and principles that materially affect the determination of financial position, changes in financial position, and results of operations.

**Domiciled Corporation.** A corporation doing business in the state in which its corporate charter was guaranteed.

**Due Diligence Meeting.** A meeting of all parties in the preparation of a registration statement to assure that a high degree of care in investigation and independent verification of the company's representations has been made.

**Effective Date.** The twentieth (20th) day after the filing date of a registration statement or amendment unless the Commission shortens or extends that time period.

**Employee.** Any employee, general partner, or consultant or advisor, insurance agents who are exclusive agents of the registrant, its subsidiaries or parents. It also includes former employees as well as executors, administrators or beneficiaries of the estates of deceased employees, guardians or members of a committee for incompetent former employees, or similar persons duly authorized by law to administer the estate or assets of former employees.

**Equity Security.** Any stock or similar security; or any security convertible, with or without consideration, into such a security, or carrying any warrant or right to subscribe to or purchase such a security, or any such warrant or right.

**Examination.** (See **Audit** above.)

**Exchange.** An organized association providing a market place for bringing together buyers and sellers of securities through brokers.

**Exempt Security.** One that is not required to be registered with the SEC.

**Exempt Transaction.** A transaction in securities that does not require registration with the SEC.

**Expert.** Any specialist, accountant, attorney, engineer, appraiser, etc., who participates in the preparation of a registration statement. Broadly, any signatory to the registration statement is assumed to be an expert.

**Fifty-Percent-Owned-Person.** A person whose outstanding voting shares are approximately 50 percent owned by another specified person directly, or indirectly, through one or more intermediaries.

**Filing.** The process of completing and submitting a registration statement to the SEC.

**Filing Date.** The date a registration statement is received by the SEC.

**Financial Statement.** Includes all notes to the statements and all related schedules.

**Fiscal Year.** The annual accounting period or, if no closing date has been adopted, the calendar year ending on December 31.

**Float.** The difference on a bank's ledger and a depositor's books caused by presentation of checks and deposits in transit.

**Footnote.** Appended to financial statements as supplemental information for specific items in a statement.

**Foreign Currency.** Any currency other than the currency used by the enterprise in its financial statements.

**Forms.** Statements of standards with which registration statements and other filings must comply. Essentially, SEC forms are a set of instructions to guide the registrant in the preparation of the SEC reports to be filed; the forms are not required to be precisely copied.

**Form S-1.** A registration statement (see **Registration Statement** below) is filed on Form S-1 for companies issuing securities to the public. This form incorporates specified standards for financial statements and auditor's report.

**Form 8-K.** A report which is filed only when a reportable event occurs which may have a significant effect on the future of a company and on the value of its securities. Form 8-K must befiled not later than 15 days after the date on which the specified event occurs.

**Form 10-K.** The annual report to the SEC which covers substantially all of the information required in Form S-1. Form 10-K is due 90 days after a company's December 31 fiscal year, or by March 31 of each year.

**Form 10-Q.** A quarterly report containing *unaudited* financial statements. If certain types of events occur during the period, they must be reported on the Form. The 10-Q is due 45 days after the end of the first three fiscal quarters.

**Going Private.** The term commonly used to describe those transactions having as their objective the complete termination or substantial reduction of public ownership of an equity's securities.

**Going Public.** Registering a new issue of securities with the SEC. *Going public* is closely related to the process of applying for listed status on one or more of the exchanges, or registering for trading in the over-the-counter market.

**Indemnification Provision.** An agreement protecting one party from liability arising from the occurrence of an unforeseeable event.

**Independent Accountants** *(CPA).* Accountants who certify financial statements filed with the SEC. Accountants must maintain strict independence of attitude and judgment in planning and conducting and audit and in expressing an opinion on financial statements. The SEC will not recognize any public accountant or certified public accountant that is not independent.

**Information Statement.** A statement on any pending corporate matters furnished by the registrant to every shareholder who is entitled to vote when a proxy is not solicited.

**Initial Margin Percentage.** The percentage of the purchase price (or the percentage of a short sale; see **Short Selling** below), that an investor must deposit with his/her broker in compliance with Federal Reserve Board margin requirements.

**Injunction.** A court order directing a person to stop alleged violations of a securities law or regulation.

**Insurance Holding Company.** A person who is engaged, either directly or indirectly, primarily in the business of owning securities of one or more insurance companies for the purpose, and with the effect, of exercising control.

**Integrated Disclosure System (IDS).** An extensive revision of the mandatory business and financial disclosure requirements applicable to publicly-held companies. It establishes a uniform and integrated disclosure system under the securities laws. The IDS adopted major changes in its disclosure systems under the Securities Act of 1933, and the Securities Exchange Act of 1934. The changes include amendments to Form 10-K and 10-Q, amendments to the proxy rules, amendments to Regulation S-K which governs the non-financial statement disclosure rules (see **Regulation S-K** below), uniform financial statement instructions, a general revision of Regulation S-X which governs the form, content, and requirements of financial statements (see **Regulation S-X** below), and a new simplified form for the registration of securities issued in business combinations.

**Issuer.** Any corporation that sells a security in a public offering.

**Letter-of-Consent.** Written permission from participating experts to include their names and signatures in a registration statement.

**Line-of-Business Reporting.** Registrants must report financial information regarding segments of their operations. The SEC does not define the term "line-of-business." Rather, the responsibility of determining meaningful segments that reflect the particular company's operations and organizational concepts is the responsibility of management. No more than ten classes of business are required to be reported.

¶24,005

**Listed Status.** Condition under which a security has been accepted by an exchange for full trading privileges. As long as a corporation remains listed on an exchange, it must file periodic reports to its stockholders.

**Listing.** A corporation applying to list its securities on an exchange must file a registration statement and a copy of the application for listing with the SEC.

**Majority-Owned Subsidiary.** A subsidiary more than 50 percent of whose outstanding voting shares is owned by its parent and/or the parent's other majority-owned subsidiaries.

**Managing Underwriter.** Underwriter(s) who, by contract or otherwise, deals with the registrant; organizes the selling effort; receives some benefit directly or indirectly in which all other underwriters similarly situated do not share in proportion to their respective interests in the underwriting; or represents any other underwriters in such matters as maintaining the records of the distribution, arranging the allotments of securities offered or arranging for appropriate stabilization activities, if any.

**Margin Call.** The demand by a broker that an investor deposit additional cash (or acceptable collateral) for securities purchased on credit when the price of the securities declines to a value below the minimum shareholder's equity required by the stock exchange.

**Material.** Information regarding any subject that limits the information required to those matters about which an average prudent investor ought reasonably to be informed.

**Mutual Fund.** Not legal terminology. It is a financial term commonly used in street jargon to mean an open-end investment company (see **Open-End Investment Company** below) as defined in the Investment Company Act of 1940.

**National Association of Securities Dealers, Inc. (NASD).** An association of brokers/dealers who are in the business of trading over-the-counter securities.

**Net Sales.** Income or loss from continuing operations before extraordinary items and cumulative effect of a change in accounting principle.

**New York Stock Exchange** (and **Regional Exchanges**). An association organized to provide physical, mechanical, and logistical facilities for the purchase and sale of securities by investors through brokers and dealers.

**No-Action Letter.** The SEC's written reply to a corporate issuer of securities stating its position regarding a specific filing matter.

**Notification.** Filing with the SEC the terms of an offering of securities that are exempt from registration.

**Offering Date.** The date a new security can be offered to the public.

**Open-End Investment Company.** A corporation in the business of investing its funds in securities of other corporations for income and profit. An open-end company continuously offers new shares for sales and redeems shares previously issued to investors who want to cash out.

**¶24,005**

**Opinion.** A required statement in the certification that the auditor believes the audit correctly reflects the organization's financial condition and results of operation.

**Option.** The contractual privilege of purchasing a security (Call) for a specified price, or delivering a security (Put) at a specified price.

**Over-the-Counter Securities.** Corporate and government securities that are not listed for trading on a national stock exchange.

**Parent.** A "parent" of a specified person(s) is an affiliate controlling such person(s) directly or indirectly through one or more intermediaries.

**Pension Plan.** An arrangement whereby a company undertakes to provide its retired employees with benefits that can be determined or estimated in advance.

**Person.** An individual, corporation, partnership, association, joint-stock company, business trust, or unincorporated organization.

**Predecessor.** A person from whom another person acquired the major portion of the business and assets in a single succession or in a series of related successions. In each succession the acquiring person acquired the major portion of the business and assets of the acquired person.

**Prefiling Conference.** A meeting of corporate officers and experts outlining the SEC requirements for the filing of a registration statement. Occasionally an SEC staff member will attend.

**Previously Filed or Reported.** Previously filed with, or reported in a definitive proxy statement or information statement, or a registration statement. Information contained in any such document will be assumed to have been previously filed with the exchange.

**Principal Holder of Equity Securities.** Used in respect of a registrant or other person named in a particular statement or report, a holder of record or a known beneficial owner of more than 10 percent of any class of securities of the registrant or other person, respectively, and of the date of the related balance sheet filed.

**Promoter.** Any person who, acting alone or in conjunction with one or more other persons, directly or indirectly takes initiative in founding and organizing the business or enterprise of an issuer. Any person is a promoter who, in connection with the founding and organizing of the business or enterprise of an issuer, directly or indirectly receives in consideration of services or property, or both services and property, 10 percent or more of any class of securities of the issuer or 10 percent or more of the proceeds from the sale of any class of securities. However, a person who receives such securities or proceeds either solely as underwriting commissions or solely in consideration of property shall not be deemed a promoter within the meaning of this paragraph if such person does not otherwise take part in founding and organizing the enterprise.

**Prospectus.** Document consisting of Part 1 of the registration statement filed with the SEC by the issuing corporation that must be delivered to all purchasers of newly issued securities.

**Proxy.** A power of attorney whereby a stockholder authorizes another person, or group of persons, to act (vote) for that stockholder at a shareholders' meeting.

**Proxy Statement.** Information furnished in conjunction with a formal solicitation in the proxy for the power to vote a stockholder's shares.

**Put.** (See **Option** above.)

**Red-Herring Prospectus.** Preliminary prospectus with a statement (in red ink) on each page indicating that the security described has not become effective, that the information is subject to correction and change without notice, and is not an offer to buy or sell that security.

**Refusal.** SEC action prohibiting a filing (see **Filing** above) from becoming effective.

**Regional Exchanges.** (See **New York Stock Exchange** above.)

**Registrant.** An issuer of securities for which an application, a report, or a registration statement has been filed.

**Registration.** Act of filing with the SEC the required information concerning the issuing corporation and the security to be issued.

**Registration Statement.** The document filed with the SEC containing legal, commercial, technical, and financial information concerning a new security issue.

**Regulation S-K.** An authoritative statement of disclosure standards under all securities acts. Regulation S-K establishes the standards of disclosure for non-financial information not included in financial statements, footnotes or schedules.

**Regulation S-X.** The principal document reporting for financial statements, footnotes and schedules' standards under all securities acts. No filing can be made without reference to Regulation S-X. It integrates all accounting requirements prior to February 21, 1940, into a single regulation.

**Related Party.** One that can exercise control or significant influence over the management and/or operating policies of another party, to the extent that one of the parties may be prevented from fully pursuing its own separate interests. Related parties consist of all affiliates of an enterprise, including its management and their immediate families, its principal owners and their immediate families, its investments accounted for by the equity method, beneficial employee trusts that are managed by the management of the enterprise, and any party that may, or does, deal with the enterprise and has ownership of, control over, or can significantly influence the management or operating policies of another party to the extent that an arms-length transaction may not be achieved. Transactions between related parties are generally accounted for on the same basis as if the parties were not related, unless the substance of the transaction is not arm's length. Substance over form is an important consideration when accounting for transactions involving related parties.

**Replacement Cost.** The lowest amount that would have to be paid in the normal course of business to obtain a new asset of equivalent operating or productive capability.

**Restricted Security.** Private offering of an issue that cannot be resold to the public without prior registration. Also called "investment letter" securities for the letter that the purchaser of such securities must submit to the SEC stating that the securities are being acquired for investment purposes, not for immediate resale.

**Right.** Provides current security holders the privilege of participating on a pro rata basis in a new offering of securities.

**Roll-Up Transaction.** Any transaction or series of transactions that, directly or indirectly through acquisition or otherwise, involves the combination or reorganization of one or more partnerships. The term includes the offer or sale of securities by a successor entity, whether newly formed or previously existing, to one or more limited partners of the partnership to be combined or reorganized, or the acquisition of the successor entity's securities by the partnerships being combined or reorganized.

**Rules of Practice.** Establishes standards of conduct for professionals practicing before the SEC.

**Sale.** Every contract of sale, disposition, or offer of a security for value (see **Security** below).

**Schedule.** Detailed financial information presented in a form prescribed by the SEC in Regulation S-X.

**Scienter.** Intent to deceive, manipulate, or defraud. Requires proof that defendant knew of material mistatements or omissions; that defendant acted willfully and knowingly.

**Scope** (of an Audit). A complete, detailed audit. The auditor includes in the certificate an adequate explanation of the extent of the audit.

**Securities Act of 1933.** Requires the disclosure of financial data for issues not exempted from registration and prohibits fraudulent acts and misrepresentations and omission of material (see **Material** above) facts in the issue of securities.

**Securities Exchange Act of 1934** (The **Exchange Act**). Covers the regulation of stock market activities and the public trading of securities. The regulations covered are the disclosure of significant financial data, the regulation of securities market practices and operation, and control of credit (margin requirements) extended for the purchase and short sales of securities.

**Security.** Any instrument representing a debt obligation, an equity interest in a corporation, or any instrument commonly known as a security. In the Securities Act, security is defined to include by name or description many documents in which there is common trading for investment or speculation.

¶24,005

Some, such as notes, bonds and stocks, are standardized and the name alone carries well settled meaning. Others are of a more variable character and were necessarily designated by more descriptive terms, such as transferable share, investment contract, and in general any interest or instrument commonly known as a security.

**Selling Group.** Several broker/dealers who distribute a new issue of securities at retail.

**Share.** A share of stock in a corporation or unit of interest in an unincorporated person.

**Short-Selling.** Selling a security that is not owned with the expectation of buying that specific security later at a lower market price.

**Significant Subsidiary.** A subsidiary (including its subsidiaries) in which the registrant's (and its other subsidiaries') investments in and advances to exceed 10 percent of the total assets of the registrant and its subsidiaries consolidated as of the end of the most recently completed fiscal year. For a proposed business combination to be accounted for as a pooling of interests, this requirement is also met when the number of common shares exchanged by the registrant exceeds 10 percent of its total common shares outstanding at the date the combination is initiated, or the registrant's (and its other subsidiaries') proportionate share of the total assets, after intercompany eliminations, of the subsidiary exceeds 10 percent of the total assets of the registrant and its subsidiaries consolidated as of the end of the most recently completed fiscal year.

**Small Business Issuer.** An entity that (a) has revenues of less than $25,000,000; (b) is a U.S. or Canadian issuer; (c) is not an investment company; (d) if a majority-owned subsidiary, the parent corporation is also a small business issuer.

**Solicitation.** Any request for a proxy or other similar communication to security holders.

**Sponsor.** The person proposing the roll-up transaction. (See **Roll-Up Transaction** above.)

**Spread.** The difference between the price paid for a security by the underwriter and the selling price of that security.

**Stockholders' Meeting, Regular.** The annual meeting of stockholders for the election of directors and for action on other corporate matters.

**Stockholders' Meeting, Special.** A meeting in which only specified items can be considered.

**Stop Order.** An SEC order stopping the issue or listing of a security on a stock exchange.

**Subsidiary.** An affiliate controlled by a specified person directly, or indirectly, through one or more intermediaries.

**Substantial Authoritative Support.** FASB principles, standards and practices published in Statements and Interpretations, AICPA Accounting Research Bulletins, and AICPA Opinions, except to the extent altered, amended, supplemented, revoked or superseded by an FASB Statement.

¶24,005

**Succession.** The direct acquisition of the assets comprising a going business, whether by merger, consolidation, or other direct transfer. This term does not include the acquisition of control of a business unless followed by the direct acquisition of its assets.

**Successor.** The surviving entity after completion of the roll-up transaction, or the entity whose securities are being offered or sold to, or acquired by, limited partners of the partnerships or the limited partnerships to be combined or reorganized.

**Summary Prospectus.** A prospectus containing specific items of information which subsequently will be included in the registration statement.

**Suspension.** An SEC order temporarily prohibiting the trading of a security on the stock exchange, usually invoked by the SEC when a news release is pending which may cause a disorderly market in that security. Trading is usually resumed shortly after the information has been publicly disseminated.

**Totally Held Subsidiary.** A subsidiary substantially all of whose outstanding securities are owned by its parent and/or the parent's other totally held subsidiaries. The subsidiary is not indebted to any person other than its parent and/or the parent's other totally held subsidiaries in an amount which is material in relation to the particular subsidiary, excepting indebtedness incurred in the ordinary course of business which is not overdue and which matures within one year from the date of its creation, whether evidenced by securities or not.

**Underwriter.** (See **Managing Underwriter** above.)

**Unlisted Trading Privileges.** A security issue authorized by the SEC for trading on an exchange without requiring the corporation to complete a formal listing application.

**Voting Securities.** Securities whose holders are presently entitled to vote for the election of directors.

**Warrant.** A security that grants the holder the right to purchase a specific number of shares of the security to which the warrant is attached at a specified price and usually within a stated period of time.

**Wholly-Owned Subsidiary.** A subsidiary substantially all of whose outstanding voting securities are owned by its parent and/or the parent's other wholly-owned subsidiaries.

# ¶24,007    SECURITIES ACT OF 1933

The *truth in securities* law has two main objectives:

1. To require that investors are provided with material information concerning securities offered for sale to the public.
2. To prevent misrepresentation, deceit, and other fault in the sale of securities.

The primary means of accomplishing these objectives is by requiring full disclosure of financial information by registering offerings and sales of securities. Securities transactions subject to registration are mostly offerings of debt and equity securities issued by corporations, limited partnerships, trusts and other issuers. Federal and certain other government debt securities are not. Certain securities and transactions qualify for exemptions from registration provisions. They are included in the discussion that follows.

## ¶24,009   REGISTRATION

Registration is intended to provide adequate and accurate disclosure of material facts concerning the company and the securities it proposes to sell. This enables investors to make a thorough appraisal of the merits of the securities and exercise informed judgment in determining whether or not to purchase them.

Registration requires, but does not guarantee, the accuracy of the facts represented in the registration statement and prospectus. However, the law does prohibit false and misleading statements under penalty of fine, imprisonment, or both. Investors who purchases securities and suffer losses have important recovery rights under the law if they can prove that there was incomplete or inaccurate disclosure of material facts in the registration statement or prospectus. If such misstatements are proven, the following could be liable for investor losses sustained in the securities purchase:

1.  The issuing company.
2.  Its responsible directors and officers.
3.  The underwriters.
4.  The controlling interests.
5.  The sellers of the securities.
6.  Others that are affiliated with the securities of the issuer.

Registration of securities does not preclude the sale of stock in risky, poorly managed, or unprofitable companies. Nor does the Commission *approve or disapprove* securities on their merits; and it is unlawful to represent otherwise in the sale of securities. The only standard which must be met when registering securities is adequate and accurate *disclosure* of required material facts concerning the company and the securities it proposes to sell. The fairness of the terms, the issuing company's prospects for successful operation, and other factors affecting the merits of investing in the securities have no bearing on the question of whether or not securities can be qualified for registration.

## .01  The Registration Process

To facilitate registration by different types of enterprises, the Commission has special forms that vary in their disclosure requirements, but generally provide essential facts while minimizing the burden and expense of complying with the law. In general, registration forms call for disclosure of information such as:

1. Description of the registrant's properties and business.
2. Description of the significant provisions of the security to be offered for sale and its relationship to the registrant's other capital securities.
3. Information about the management of the registrant.
4. Financial statements certified by independent public accountants.

Registration statements become public immediately upon filing with the SEC. After the registration statement is filed, securities can be *offered* orally or by summaries of the information in the registration statement, but it is unlawful to *sell* the securities until the *effective date* which is on the 20th day after filing the registration statement, or on the 20th day after filing the last amendment, if any. The SEC can issue a *stop order* to refuse or suspend the effectiveness of the statement if the Commission concludes that material deficiencies in a registration statement appear to result from a deliberate attempt to conceal or mislead. A stop order is not a permanent prohibition to the effectiveness of the registration statement, or to the sale of the securities, and can be lifted and the statement declared effective when amendments are filed correcting the statement in accordance with the requirements in the stop order decision.

There are exemptions to the registration requirements:

1. Private offerings to a limited number of persons or institutions who have access to the kind of information that registration would disclose and who do not propose to redistribute the securities.
2. Offerings restricted to residents of the state in which the issuing company is organized and doing business.
3. Securities of municipal, state, federal and other governmental instrumentalities, such as charitable institutions and banks.
4. Offerings not exceeding certain specified amounts made in compliance with regulations of the Commission.
5. Offerings of small business investment companies made in accordance with the rules and regulations of the Commission.

Regardless of whether or not the securities are exempt from registration, anti-fraud provisions apply to all sales of securities involving interstate commerce or the mails.

The small business exemption from registration provides that offerings of securities under $5 million can be exempt from full registration, subject to conditions the SEC prescribes to protect investors. Certain Canadian and domestic companies are permitted to make exempt offerings.

---

**UNITED STATES**
**SECURITIES AND EXCHANGE COMMISSION**
**Washington, D.C. 20549**

**FORM 10**

**GENERAL FORM FOR REGISTRATION OF SECURITIES**
**Pursuant to Section 12(b) or (g) of The Securities Exchange Act of 1934**

---

(Exact name of registrant as specified in its charter)

---

(State or other jurisdiction of incorporation or organization)          (I.R.S. Employer Identification No.)

---

(Address of principal executive offices)          (Zip Code)

Registrant's telephone number, including area code —————————————

Securities to be registered pursuant to Section 12(b) of the Act:

| Title of each class to be so registered | Name of each exchange on which each class is to be registered |
|---|---|
| | |
| | |

Securities to be registered pursuant to Section 12(g) of the Act:

---

(Title of class)

---

(Title of class)

---

**INFORMATION REQUIRED IN REGISTRATION STATEMENT**

**Item 1. Business.**

Furnish the information required by Item 101 of Regulation S-K (§ 229.101 of this chapter).

¶24,009.01

**Item 2. Financial Information.**
Furnish the information required by Items 301 and 303 of Regulation S-K (§§ 229.301 and 229.303 of this chapter).

**Item 3. Properties.**
Furnish the information required by Item 102 of Regulation S-K (§ 229.102 of this chapter).

**Item 4. Security Ownership of Certain Beneficial Owners and Management.**
Furnish the information required by Item 403 of Regulation S-K (§ 229.403 of this chapter).

**Item 5. Directors and Executive Officers.**
Furnish the information required by Item 401 of Regulation S-K (§ 229.401 of this chapter).

**Item 6. Executive Compensation.**
Furnish the information required by Item 402 of Regulation S-K (§ 229.402 of this chapter).

**Item 7. Certain Relationships and Related Transactions.**
Furnish the information required by Item 404 of Regulation S-K (§ 229.404 of this chapter).

**Item 8. Legal Proceedings.**
Furnish the information required by Item 103 of Regulation S-K (§ 229.103 of this chapter).

**Item 9. Market Price of and Dividends on the Registrant's Common Equity and Related Stockholder Matters.**
Furnish the information required by Item 201 of Regulation S-K (§ 229.201 of this chapter).

**Item 10. Recent Sales of Unregistered Securities.**
Furnish the information required by Item 701 of Regulation S-K (§ 229.701 of this chapter).

**Item 11. Description of Registrant's Securities to be Registered.**
Furnish the information required by Item 202 of Regulation S-K (§ 229.202 of this chapter).

**Item 12. Indemnification of Directors and Officers.**
Furnish the information required by Item 702 of Regulation S-K (§ 229.702 of this chapter).

**Item 13. Financial Statements and Supplementary Data.**
Furnish all financial statements required by Regulation S-X and the supplementary financial information required by Item 302 of Regulation S-K (§ 229.302 of this chapter).

**Item 14. Changes in and Disagreements with Accountants on Accounting and Financial Disclosure.**
Furnish the information required by Item 304 of Regulation S-K (§ 229.304 of this chapter).

¶24,009.01

## Item 15. Financial Statements and Exhibits.

(a) List separately all financial statements filed as part of the registration statement.

(b) Furnish the exhibits required by Item 601 of Regulation S-K (§ 229.601 of this chapter).

## SIGNATURES

Pursuant to the requirements of Section 12 of the Securities Exchange Act of 1934, the registrant has duly caused this registration statement to be signed on its behalf by the undersigned, thereunto duly authorized.

_____
(Registrant)

Date _____      By _____
(Signature)*

_____
*Print name and title of the signing officer under his signature.

## GENERAL INSTRUCTIONS

### A. Rule as to Use of Form 10.

Form 10 shall be used for registration pursuant to Section 12(b) or (g) of the Securities Exchange Act of 1934 of classes of securities of issuers for which no other form is prescribed.

### B. Application of General Rules and Regulations.

(a) The General Rules and Regulations under the Act contain certain general requirements which are applicable to registration on any form. These general requirements should be carefully read and observed in the preparation and filing of registration statements on this form.

(b) Particular attention is directed to Regulation 12B [17 CFR 240.12b-1-240.12b-36] which contains general requirements regarding matters such as the kind and size of paper to be used, the legibility of the registration statement, the information to be given whenever the title of securities is required to be stated, and the filing of the registration statement. The definitions contained in Rule 12b-2 [17 CFR 240.12b-2] should be especially noted.

### C. Preparation of Registration Statement.

(a) This form is not to be used as a blank form to be filled in, but only as a guide in the preparation of the registration statement on paper meeting the requirements of Rule 12b-12 [17 CFR 240.12b-12]. The registration statement shall contain the item numbers and captions, but the text of the items may be omitted. The answers to the items shall be prepared in the manner specified in Rule 12b-13 [17 CFR 240.12b-13].

(b) Unless otherwise stated, the information required shall be given as of a date reasonably close to the date of filing the registration statement.

(c) Attention is directed to Rule 12b-20 [17 CFR 240.12b-20] which states: "In addition to the information expressly required to be included in a statement or

¶24,009.01

report, there shall be added such further material information, if any, as may be necessary to make the required statements, in light of the circumstances under which they are made, not misleading."

### D. Signature and Filing of Registration Statement.

Three complete copies of the registration statement, including financial statements, exhibits and all other papers and documents filed as a part thereof, and five additional copies which need not include exhibits, shall be filed with the Commission. At least one complete copy of the registration statement, including financial statements, exhibits and all other papers and documents filed as a part thereof, shall be filed with each exchange on which any class of securities is to be registered. At least one complete copy of the registration statement filed with the Commission and one such copy filed with each exchange shall be manually signed. Copies not manually signed shall bear typed or printed signatures.

### E. Omission of information Regarding Foreign Subsidiaries.

Information required by any item or other requirement of this form with respect to any foreign subsidiary may be omitted to the extent that the required disclosure would be detrimental to the registrant. However, financial statements, otherwise required, shall not be omitted pursuant to this instruction. Where information is omitted pursuant to this instruction, a statement shall be made that such information has been omitted and the names of the subsidiaries involved shall be separately furnished to the Commission. The Commission may, in its discretion, call for justification that the required disclosure would be detrimental.

### F. Incorporation by Reference.

Attention is directed to Rule 12b-23 [17 CFR 240.12b-23] which provides for the incorporation by reference of information contained in certain documents in answer or partial answer to any item of a registration statement.

---

## ¶24,011  SECURITIES EXCHANGE ACT OF 1934

The 1934 Act extends the disclosure doctrine of investor protection to securities that are listed and registered for public trading on U.S. national securities exchanges. In 1964 the SEC was authorized by Congress to include disclosure and reporting requirements to equity securities in the over-the-counter market. The object of the 1934 Act is to ensure *fair and orderly securities markets* by prohibiting certain types of activities and by setting forth rules regarding the operation of the markets and the participants.

Companies wanting to have their securities registered and listed or publicly traded on an exchange must file a registration application with the exchange and the SEC. Companies whose equity securities are traded over-the-counter must file a similar registration form. SEC rules prescribe the content of registration statements and require certified financial statements. After a company's securities have become registered, annual and other periodic reports to update information contained in the original registration statement must be filed.

The 1934 Act governs the solicitation of proxies (votes) from holders of registered securities, both listed and over-the-counter, for the election of directors and for approval of other corporate action. All material facts concerning matters on which shareholders are asked to vote must be disclosed. In 1970 Congress amended the Exchange Act to extend its reporting and disclosure provisions to situations where control of a company is sought through a tender offer to other planned stock acquisitions of over five percent of a company's equity securities by direct purchase or by a tender offer. Disclosure provisions are supplemented by other provisions to help ensure investor protection in tender offers.

## ¶24,013  INSIDER TRADING

Insider trader prohibitions are designed to curb misuse of material confidential information not available to the general public. Examples of such misuse are buying or selling securities to make profits or avoid losses based on material nonpublic information, or by telling others of the information before such information is generally available to all shareholders. The *Insider Trading Sanctions Act of 1984* allows imposing fines up to three times to profit gained or losses avoided by use of material nonpublic information. All officers and directors of a company and beneficial owners of more than ten percent of its registered equity securities must file an initial report with the SEC and with the exchange on which the stock is listed, showing their holdings of each of the company's equity securities. Thereafter, they must file reports for any month during which there was any change in those holdings, and any profits obtained by them from purchases and sales, or sales and purchases, of such equity securities within any six-month period can be recovered by the company or by any security holder on its behalf. Insiders are also prohibited from making short sales of their company's equity securities.

## ¶24,015  MARGIN TRADING

The 1934 Act authorizes the Board of Governors of the Federal Reserve System to set limits on the amount of credit which can be extended for the purpose of purchasing or carrying securities. The objective is to restrict excessive use of credit in the securities markets. While the credit restrictions are set by the Board of Governors, investigation and enforcement is the responsibility of the SEC.

## ¶24,017    DIVISION OF CORPORATION FINANCE

Corporation Finance has the overall responsibility of ensuring that disclosure requirements are met by publicly held companies registered with the SEC. Its work includes: reviewing registration statements for new securities; proxy material and annual reports the Commission requires from publicly held companies; documents concerning tender offers, and mergers and acquisitions in general.

This Division renders administrative interpretations to the public of the Securities Act and the Securities Exchange Act, and to prospective registrants, and others. It is also responsible for certain statutes and regulations pertaining to small businesses and for the Trust Indenture Act of 1939. Applications for qualification of trust indentures are examined for compliance with the applicable requirements of the law and the Commission's rules. Corporation Finance works closely with the Office of the Chief Accountant in drafting rules and regulations which prescribe requirements for financial statements.

## ¶24,019    TRUTH IN SECURITIES LAWS

The objectives of the laws are twofold. First is the protection of investors and the public against fraudulent acts and practices in the purchase and sale of securities. The second objective is to regulate trading in the national securities markets. For example:

1. "To provide full and fair disclosure of the character of securities sold in interstate and foreign commerce and through the mails, and to prevent fraud in the sale thereof, and for other purposes." (Securities Act of 1933.)
2. "To provide for the regulation of securities exchanges and the over-the-counter markets operating in interstate and foreign commerce and through the mails, to prevent inequitable and unfair practices on such exchanges and markets, and for other purposes." (Securities Exchange Act of 1934.)
3. "To provide for the registration and regulation of investment companies and investment advisers, and for other purposes." (Investment Company Act of 1940 and the Investment Advisers Act of 1940.)

## ¶24,021    DEVELOPMENT OF DISCLOSURE: 1933 AND 1934 ACTS

Two separate disclosure systems developed under the two principal securities laws. Generally, the Securities Act of 1933 regulates the *initial* public distribution of securities. The disclosure system developed under the 1933 Act emphasizes the comprehensive information about the issuer, because it was developed primarily for companies going public for the *first time* and about which the public had very little information.

The Securities Exchange Act of 1934 regulates the trading of securities in *publicly held companies* which are traded both on the exchanges and in the over-the-counter markets. The dual disclosure system developed under the 1933 and 1934 Acts deals primarily with the form and content of financial and business data in the annual reports to the SEC and to shareholders, and concerns proxy statements as well as the dissemination of interim data. The emphasis of this disclosure system is on periodic information concerning issuers already known to security holders, and the purpose is to keep the data up-to-date.

The dual system generated a large number of registration and periodic reporting forms, each with its own set of instructions. Many publicly-held companies filed numerous registration statements and distributed related reports to the public containing the same information produced several times in slightly different forms, repeating much information that was already available within the financial community.

In addition, the audited primary financial statements prepared in conformity with GAAP that were included in the annual reports to shareholders, were not explicitly covered by the very detailed disclosure requirements in S-X. These mandated the form and content of the audited primary financial statements that were included in documents filed with the SEC and in prospectuses. However, since the financial statements had to be in conformity with GAAP there were no essential differences between the two.

Financial statements that conformed to S-X included numerous additional technical disclosures to satisfy the needs of professional financial analysts and the SEC staff. Uniform financial disclosure requirements for virtually all documents covered by either the 1933 or the 1934 Acts as well as for nonfinancial disclosures under the 1934 Act and for a major portion of those required under the 1933 Act have been formulated. To reach the objective, where identical disclosures are included both in documents filed with the Commission and distributed to security holders in prospectuses, proxy statements and annual reports, the Commission has two basic regulations. These are Regulation S-X (see Chapter 16) which covers the requirements for audited primary financial statements, and Regulation S-K which covers most of the other business, analytical, and unaudited financial disclosures.

Regulation S-K covers analytical and unaudited supplementary financial disclosures under the 1934 Act and most disclosures under the 1933 Act. One of the key requirements in Regulation S-K is the *Management's Discussion and Analysis of Financial Condition and Results of Operations*. The discussion must cover the three years presented in the audited financials and treat not only results of operations, but also financial condition and changes in financial condition. Although the requirement is for three years, the SEC suggests that when trends are being discussed, references to five years of selected financial data are appropriate.

¶24,021

The discussion and analysis is filed under the Securities Acts, as well as included in all annual reports and prospectuses. Accordingly, companies should document the adequacy of their systems and procedures for analyzing past results to be sure that there is an adequate and reliable information base for the management discussion and analysis, including decisions as to scope and content. Since future plans and expectations, such as capital expenditure commitments, are important in formulating management's discussion and analysis, it may be prudent to reappraise internal financial forecasting procedures periodically.

Although forward-looking information is not mandated, the specifically required information is such that financial analysts will be able to work out a forecast of future operating results. As practice develops, managements may find it preferable simply to include formal financial forecasts and comply with the safe harbor rules, rather than rely solely on the forecasts analysts will make based on data presumed to be reliable.

*Form S-15*. When a company acquires a business that is relatively minor when compared to the acquiring company, a process that was difficult because of the complexity and cost of registration requirements is greatly simplified by the use of Form S-15 for the registration requirements. Form S-15 enables an issuer to provide an abbreviated prospectus accompanied by the issuer's latest annual report to shareholders instead of larger documents. This procedure is limited to cases where the acquiring company's key financial indices as specified in the regulations are not affected by more than 10% by the acquired company, and where State law applicable to the merger does not require a vote by the security holders of the company being acquired. There are other restrictions, however, and it is likely this simplified procedure will be most usable for mergers where the company to be acquired is closely-held and will not become a significant part of the combined company.

Three copies of Form S-15 must be filed with the SEC. One copy must be signed manually by an officer of the registrant, or by counsel, or by any other authorized person. The name and title of the person signing Form S-15 should be typed or printed under that person's signature.

## ¶24,023  Synopsis: The Securities Act of 1933

In 1933, the first Federal legislative act designed to regulate the securities business on an interstate basis was passed. Its expressed purpose was:

"To provide full and fair disclosure of the character of securities . . . and to prevent frauds in the sale thereof, and for other purposes." There are four things to note:

1.  It related to newly-issued securities, not to those already in the hands of the public.

¶24,023

2. It called for full and fair disclosure of all the facts necessary for an intelligent appraisal of the value of a security.
3. It was designed to prevent fraud in the sale of securities.
4. This legislation led to the Securities Exchange Act of 1934 establishing the Securities and Exchange Commission which would administer both acts.

There are 26 sections to the Act:

**Section 1.** "This title may be cited as the Securities Act of 1933." Various court decisions have very liberally interpreted the meaning of "securities" as covered by the Act. One decision contains the following: ". . . that this statute was not a penal statute but was a remedial enactment . . . A remedial enactment is one that seeks to give a remedy for an ill. It is to be liberally construed so that its purpose may be realized." (SEC v Starmont, (1940) 31 F. Supp. 264.)

**Section 2.** Definitions. This section defines many of the terms used throughout the other sections of the Act. Importantly, it contains definitions of "security," "person," "sale," "offer to sell," and "prospectus," among many others. Several important Rules of the SEC are directly derived from this section, including Rule 134 (discussed in Section 5).

**Section 3.** Exempted Securities. Some securities, such as those issued or guaranteed by the United States, are exempted from the provisions of the Act.

**Section 4.** Exempted Transactions. Describes the transactions for which Section 5 does not apply.

**Section 5.** Prohibitions Relating to Intrastate Commerce and the Mails. It is unlawful to offer any security for sale "by any means or instruments of transportation or communication in interstate commerce or of the mails," unless a registration statement is in effect as to that security. It also prohibits the transportation by any means of interstate commerce or the mails of such a security for the purpose of sale or delivery after sale.

This Section further requires that any security that is registered cannot be sold without prior or concurrent delivery of an effective prospectus that meets the requirements of Section 10(a) of the Act.

There have been two important Rules promulgated by the SEC under this Section. The first, Rule 134, defines the types of advertising and of letters or other communications that can be used without prior or concurrent delivery of a prospectus. This Rule is frequently violated in letter form and also in telephone conversations. SEC Release 3844 of October 8, 1957, shows the importance of delivering a prospectus either before or at the same time that an attempt to sell is made. This Release states that a prospectus is defined to include any notice, circular, advertisement, letter, or communication, written or by radio or by television, which offers any security for sale except that any communication sent or given after the effective date of a registration statement shall not be deemed a prospectus if, prior to or at the same time with such a communication, a written prospectus meeting the requirements of Section 10 of the Act was sent or given.

Thus, any letter that gives more information than that allowed by Rule 134 becomes itself a prospectus, unless it is preceded or accompanied by the actual prospectus. A letter prospectus is in violation of Section 5 since it could not possibly comply with the requirements of Section 10.

The second, Rule 433, deals with the so-called "red-herring" prospectus which cannot be used as an offer to sell, but merely to disseminate information prior to the delivery of a regular prospectus which does offer the security for sale.

**Section 6.** Registration of Securities and Signing of Registration Statement. This Section details what securities may be registered and how such registration is to be done.

**Section 7.** Information Required on Registration Statement. This Section gives the SEC broad powers in regulating what must appear in a registration statement. In part, the section reads:

"Any such registration statement shall contain such other information, and be accompanied by such other documents, as the Commission may by rules or regulations require as being necessary or appropriate in the public interest or for the protection of investors."

**Section 8.** Taking Effect of Registration Statements and Amendments Thereto. Registration statements normally become effective on the twentieth day after filing, under this section. However, the SEC is empowered to determine whether or not the statement complies with the Act as to completeness and may refuse to allow the statement to become effective unless amended. If it appears to the SEC that untrue statements have been included, the Commission may issue a stop order.

**Section 9.** Court Review of Orders. As with any other act of Congress, provision is made so that any person who is aggrieved by an order of the administrative body (in this case the SEC) may obtain a review of the order in the Federal courts.

**Section 10.** Information Required in Prospectus. A prospectus must contain the same information as that contained in the registration statement. In addition, the SEC is given the authority to define the requirements for any additional material which that body considers necessary in the public interest. "Red herring" requirements and the manner of use of this type of preliminary prospectus are also detailed in this Section.

Note the application of Rule 134, discussed under Section 5, with respect to an "incomplete" prospectus.

One part of the Section, 10(3), relates to the length of time a prospectus may be used (that is, be considered an effective prospectus).

Under this Section of the Act, the SEC issued Rule 425, which requires the statement at the bottom of the first page of all prospectuses "These securities have not been approved or disapproved by the Securities and Exchange

Commission nor has the commission passed upon the accuracy or adequacy of this prospectus. Any representation to the contrary is a criminal offense.''

**Section 11.** Civil Liabilities on Account of False Registration Statement. Anyone directly connected with a company or signing the registration statement is subject to suit at law or in equity should the registration statement contain an untrue statement or fail to include a material fact necessary to make the statement not misleading.

**Section 12.** Civil Liabilities. If any person offers to sell or does sell a security in violation of Section 5, or uses any fraudulent means to sell a security, he or she is liable to civil suit for damages. This liability is in addition to any criminal liability arising under the Act.

**Section 13.** Limitation of Actions. Specified are the time limits within which civil suits may be instituted under Sections 11 and 12.

**Section 14.** Contrary Stipulations Void. Any provision in the sale of a security that binds the purchaser to waive the provisions of this Act or of the rules and regulations of the SEC is void. In other words, no one buying a security can relieve the seller from complying with the Act and with the rules issued under the Act.

**Section 15.** Liability of Controlling Persons. A dealer or broker is liable under Section 11 or 12.

**Section 16.** Additional Remedies. "The rights and remedies provided by this title (the Act) shall be in addition to any and all other rights and remedies that may exist at law or in equity."

**Section 17.** Fraudulent Interstate Transactions. As interpreted by the SEC, this section might be referred to as a "catch-all" section.

(a) "It shall be unlawful for any person in the offer or sale of any securities by the use of any means or instruments of transportation or communication in interstate commerce or by the use of the mails, directly or indirectly.

1. to employ any device, scheme or artifice to defraud, or
2. to obtain money or property by means of any untrue statement of a material fact or any omission to state a material fact necessary in order to make the statements made, in the light of the circumstances under which they were made, not misleading, or
3. to engage in any transaction, practice or course of business that operates or would operate as a fraud or deceit upon the purchaser."

Both TV and radio have been included by the SEC as "communication in interstate commerce" because it is impossible to control their area of reception.

While Section 17(a) refers only to the criminal courts in the term "unlawful," a court decision makes it clear that civil liability, in addition to criminal liability is incurred by violation of the section.

Court decisions also implement and amplify the language of the Act itself, with respect to the phrase "or by use of the mails." It would appear that Section

¶24,023

17 only applies to interstate mailings. However, the courts have ruled that if one used the mails *within one State* on an *intrastate* offering, and violated any provision in Section 17(a), that person is as guilty as if he or she had mailed across a state line.

Subparagraph (b) of Section 17 makes it illegal for anyone to publish descriptions of securities when the publisher is paid for such publicity, without also publishing the fact that compensation has been, or will be, received.

Section 17(c) makes the Section applicable to those securities exempted under Section 3. In other words, fraud is fraud whether in connection with exempt or other securities.

**Section 18.** State Control of Securities. "Nothing in this title (the Act) shall affect the jurisdiction of the Securities Commission . . . of any State . . . ." In other words, all the provisions of the Federal act *and* all the laws of the State in which business is being conducted must be complied with.

**Section 19.** Special Powers of Commission. The Commission has the authority to make, amend, and rescind such rules and regulations as may be necessary to carry out the provisions of the Act. Commissioners or their representatives are also empowered to subpoena witnesses and to administer oaths.

**Section 20.** Injunctions and Prosecution of Offenses. The SEC is empowered to make investigations and to bring criminal actions at law against persons deemed to have violated the Act. The wording of the section is interesting in that it gives the Commission power to act "whenever it shall appear . . . that the provisions of this title (the Act) . . . have been *or are about to be* violated . . . ."

**Section 21.** Hearings by Commission. "All hearings shall be public and may be held before the Commission or an officer or officers of the Commission designated by it, and appropriate records shall be kept."

**Section 22.** Jurisdiction of Offenses and Suits. Jurisdiction of offenses and violations and certain rules in connection with them, are defined in this section. Jurisdiction is given to the District Courts of the United States, the U.S. Court of any Territory, and the U.S. District Court of the District of Columbia.

**Section 23.** Unlawful Representations. The fact that the registration statement for a security has been filed or is in effect does not mean that the statement is true and accurate, or that the Commission has in any way passed upon the merits of the security. It is unlawful to make any representations to the contrary.

In short, the words in the registration statement (*and* the prospectus) have been made under the penalties of fraud. The registrants are liable, even though the Commission has not certified the truth and accuracy of the statements or of the worth of the security.

**Section 24.** Penalties. "Any person who willfully violates any of the provisions of this title (the Act), or the rules and regulations promulgated by the Commission under authority thereof . . . shall upon conviction be fined not more than $10,000.00 or imprisoned not more than five years, or both."

**Section 25.** Jurisdiction of Other Government Agencies Over Securities. Nothing in the Act shall relieve any person from submitting to other U.S. Government supervisory units information required by any provision of law.

**Section 26.** Separability of Provisions. If any one section of the Act is invalidated, such findings will not affect other sections.

**Schedule A.** Sets forth the requirements for the registration of securities.

**Schedule B.** Sets for the registration requirements for securities issued by a foreign government or political subdivision thereof.

# ¶24,025  SYNOPSIS: THE SECURITIES EXCHANGE ACT OF 1934

The Securities Act of 1933 protects investors in the purchase of newly-issued securities. The Securities Exchange Act of 1934 concerns the regulation of trading in already issued securities.

The stated purpose of the 1934 Act is "to provide for the regulation of securities exchanges and of over-the-counter markets operating in interstate and foreign commerce and through the mails, to prevent inequitable and unfair practices on such exchanges and markets, and for other purposes."

The Act has been of importance in prohibiting abuses and manipulations through its creation of the SEC and later of the self-regulatory National Association of Securities Dealers, Inc.

The Act has 34 sections:

**Section 1.** Short Title. "This Act may be cited as the Securities Exchange Act of 1934."

**Section 2.** Necessity of Regulation. Citing that transactions in securities are affected with a national public interest, this section states that it is necessary to regulate and control such transactions and other matters in order to protect interstate commerce, the national credit, the Federal taxing power, to protect and make more effective the national banking system and Federal Reserve System, and to insure the maintenance of fair and honest markets in such transactions.

Parts of Sections 2(3) and 2(4) explain the effects of "rigged" markets and manipulative practices:

**Section 2(3).** Frequently, the prices of securities on such exchanges and markets are susceptible to manipulation and control, and the dissemination of such prices gives rise to excessive speculation, resulting in sudden and unreasonable fluctuations in the prices of securities which (a) cause alternately unreasonable expansion and unreasonable contraction of the volume of credit available for trade, transportation, and industry in interstate commerce . . . (c) prevent the fair valuation of collateral for bank loans and/or obstruct the effective operation of the national banking system and Federal Reserve System.

**Section 2(4).** "National emergencies, which produce widespread unemployment and the dislocation of trade, transportation, and industry, and which burden interstate commerce and adversely affect the general welfare,

are precipitated, intensified, and prolonged by manipulation and sudden and unreasonable fluctuations of security prices and by excessive speculation on such exchanges and markets, and to meet such emergencies the Federal Government is put to such great expense as to burden the national credit."

**Section 3.** Definitions. In addition to defining 38 technical terms used in the Act, this Section gave the Securities Exchange Commission and the Federal Reserve System the authority to define technical, trade, and accounting terms so long as such definitions are not inconsistent with the provisions of the Act itself.

**Section 4.** This Section established the Securities and Exchange Commission. Prior to the Commissioners' taking office, the Securities Act of 1933 was administered by the Federal Trade Commission.

**Section 5.** Transactions on Unregistered Exchanges. Under this Section, it became illegal for transactions to be effected by brokers, dealers, or exchanges on an exchange unless the exchange was registered under Section 6 of the Act.

**Section 6.** Registration of Exchanges. Combined with Section 5, this Section sets forth the requirements for exchanges to be registered and the method of registration. Exchanges file their rules and regulations with the SEC and must agree to take disciplinary action against any member who violates the Act or violates any of the rules and regulations issued by the SEC under the Act.

**Section 7.** Margin Requirements. The Board of Governors of the Federal Reserve System is given the power to set margin requirements for any securities, which requirements may be changed from time to time at the discretion of the Board. Under this authority, the Board issued Regulation T and Regulation U. Regulation T governs the extension and maintenance of credit by brokers, dealers, and members of national securities exchanges. Regulation U governs loans by banks for the purpose of purchasing or carrying stocks registered on a national securities exchange.

**Section 8.** Restrictions on Borrowing. In four parts, this Section (a) details from whom brokers or dealers may borrow money on listed securities, (b) lays the foundation for the SEC's "net capital rule," (c) deals with pledging and co-mingling of customers' securities, and (d) states no broker or dealer may lend or arrange for the lending of any securities carried for the account of a customer without the written consent of the customer.

**Section 9.** Prohibition Against Manipulation. Both this Section and Section 10 deal with manipulative practices that are intended to make money for those in the Securities business at the expense of the general public.

Section 9 makes it unlawful to do certain things that constitute manipulation, such as: (a) creating a false or misleading appearance of active trading in a security, (b) giving of information to potential investors as to the likelihood of a rise or fall in price solely for the purpose of causing the market price to react to purchases or sales by such potential investors, (c) making false or misleading statements about a security, (d) "pegging" or "fixing" prices, (e) improper use of puts, calls, straddles, or other options to buy or sell. Transactions in which there is no real change in ownership are also specifically prohibited.

¶24,025

**Section 10.** Regulation of Manipulative and Deceptive Devices. Section 10 first forbids the use of short sales or stop-loss orders that violate any rules or regulations the Commission may set to protect investors. Its wording, then, becomes much more inclusive than Section 9 or the first part of Section 10, since it forbids in general "any manipulative or deceptive device or contrivance . . . ."

**Section 11.** Trading by Members of Exchanges, Brokers, and Dealers. Authority is given to the Commission to set rules and regulations as to floor trading by members, brokers, or dealers for their own accounts and to prevent excessive trading off the floor of the exchanges. A part of this Section deals with the roles of the odd-lot dealers and the specialist on the floor of the exchange. Further, the Section places a limitation on certain customer credit extension in connection with underwritings.

**Section 11A.** National Market System for Securities; Securities Information Processors. Concerns the planning, developing, operating, or regulating of a national market system.

**Section 12.** Registration Requirements for Securities. It is unlawful for any broker or dealer to effect transactions in a security or a national securities exchange unless a registration statement is effective for that security. Information stating how such registration is to be accomplished is given here. The SEC is given authority to allow trading on one exchange in securities that are listed on another exchange (such securities are said to have "unlisted trading privileges").

**Section 13.** Reports. All companies whose securities are listed on a national securities exchange must file reports at such intervals and in such form as the SEC may require. The purpose of requiring such reports was to ensure that enough information was available on any company to enable an investor to make an intelligent decision concerning the worth of its securities.

**Section 14.** Proxies. Paragraph (a) of this Section gives the SEC the authority to make rules and regulations as to the solicitation of proxies and makes it illegal to solicit proxies other than in accord with such rules and regulations. Several rules have been issued under this Section which detail the manner in which proxies may be solicited and the information that must be given to shareholders whose proxies are being solicited. All of these rules are designated to ensure that the recipient of a proxy solicitation will understand what it is that he or she is being asked to sign and to give enough background on the matter in question so that the shareholder can make an intelligent decision about how to vote.

Paragraph (b) relates to the giving of proxies by broker or dealers in connection with securities held for the accounts of customers. It is standard practice for broker/dealers to vote proxies for shares held in their names for customers directly in accord with the wishes of the customers themselves.

**Section 15.** Over-The-Counter Markets. It is mandatory that all brokers and dealers who deal in the over-the-counter market (on other than an intrastate basis) be registered with the SEC. Further, the Section states that registration will be in accord with rules and regulations issued by the Commission. "Intrastate" means that the broker or dealer deals in intrastate securities as well as doing business only within his state. Here, as elsewhere in the Act, the "use of mails," even if within one State, places the user under the Act.

Section 15 also defines the grounds for denial of registration, for suspension, or for revocation of registration. Basically, these grounds are:

1. Making false or misleading statements in the application for registration.
2. Having been convicted within the last ten years of a felony or misdemeanor involving the purchase or sale of any security or arising out of the business of a broker or dealer.
3. Being enjoined by a court from engaging in the securities business.
4. Having willfully violated any of the provisions of the 1933 Act or of the 1934 Act. (After passage of the Investment Advisers Act of 1940 and the Investment Company Act of 1940, violation of those Acts also became grounds for suspension or revocation.)

Sections 9 and 10 dealt with manipulation with respect to securities listed on a national exchange. Section 15 adds a prohibition against over-the-counter manipulation as defined by the Commission. Some of the practices that have been so defined are:

1. Excessive prices that are not fairly related to the market.
2. False representations to customers.
3. Taking of secret profits.
4. Failure to disclose control of a market.
5. Creating false impression of activity by dummy sales.
6. "Churning," or unnecessary purchases and sales in a customer's account.

Another important rule of the SEC under Section 15 seeks to protect investors by forbidding certain practices in connection with pledging or comingling of securities held for the accounts of customers. This rule specifically applies to over-the-counter broker/dealers; a similar rule, under Section 8, applies to broker/dealers who are members of or do business through members of a national exchange.

**Section 15A.** Registration of National Securities Associations. Aided by the Maloney Act of 1938, which amended the original Act by adding this Section, the formation of associations, such as the National Association of Securities Dealers, was authorized.

**Section 15B.** Concerns municipal securities dealers and transactions in municipal securities.

Section 15(c)(3) requires financial responsibility on the part of broker/dealers.

Sections 12 and 13 deal with registration and report requirements for listed securities. Section 15(d) is a corresponding list of requirements with respect to unlisted securities.

**Section 16.** Directors, Officers, and Principal Stockholders. Requires statements of ownership of stocks by "insiders" and other related information.

**Section 17.** Accounts and Records. Not only does this Section require that all brokers and dealers maintain records in accord with such rules and regulations as the SEC may set forth, but it also authorizes the SEC to make examinations of any broker's or dealer's accounts, correspondence, memoranda, papers, books, and other records whenever the Commission deems it in the public interest. Rules and regulations issued by the SEC under this Section state the types of records that must be kept. In practice, an SEC examiner may walk into a broker/dealer's office and ask that all files and books be opened for inspection. Under the law, no broker/dealer may refuse the examiner access to any and all correspondence and records. A broker/dealer can have his or her registration suspended or revoked by failure to keep copies of all correspondence or to keep books and records as required by the SEC.

**Section 17A.** Settlement of Securities Transactions. Concerns the clearance and settlement of securities transactions, transfer of ownership, and safeguarding of securities and funds. Congress directed the SEC to facilitate the establishment of a national system for securities clearings.

**Section 18.** Liability for Misleading Statements. In a rather unusual statement of law, this Section makes a person both criminally and civilly liable for any misleading statements made in connection with the requirements of Section 15 of this Act.

**Section 19.** Registration, Responsibilities, and Oversight of Self-Regulatory Organizations. The SEC has the power to suspend for 12 months or revoke the registration of any national securities exchange or of any security, if the Commission is of the opinion that such action is necessary or appropriate for the protection of investors. Further, authority is granted the SEC to suspend or expel from an exchange any member or officer who has violated any of the provisions of this Act.

Other provisions of this Section give the SEC broad powers in supervising the rules of national securities exchanges, which the Commission may require to be changed or amended. In other words, the SEC supervises the members of an exchange through the exchange itself as well as on an individual basis.

**Section 20.** Liabilities of Controlling Persons. In effect, this Section states that if A commits an illegal act under the direction of B, who controls A, then both A and B are equally liable under the law. Section 20 also makes it illegal for any "controlling person" to "hinder, delay, or obstruct" the filing of any information required by the SEC under this Act.

**Section 21.** Investigations; Injunctions and Prosecution. In the Securities Act of 1933, Sections 19 and 20 gave the SEC special powers in the areas of investigation, subpoenaing of witnesses, prosecutions of offenses and the like. Section 21 of this Act is similar in its provisions.

**Section 22.** Hearings. It is interesting to note the difference in wording with respect to hearings in the 1933 Act and in this Act. Section 21 of the 1933 Act states that "All hearings *shall* be public . . . ." Section 22 of the 1934 Act states "Hearings *may* be public . . . ."

**Section 23.** Rules and Regulations. Power to make rules and regulations under this Act is specifically given the SEC and the Board of Governors of the Federal Reserve System by this Section. Both bodies are required to make annual reports to Congress.

**Section 24.** Public Availability of Information. To protect those required to file under this Act, this Section makes it possible for certain information, such as trade secrets, to be made confidential and not a matter of public record. This Section also forbids any member or employee of the Commission to use information that is not public for personal benefit.

**Section 25.** Court Review of Orders and Rules. Like Section 9 of the 1933 Act, this Section reserves final judgment on any issue to the courts, rather than to the Commission itself.

**Section 26.** Unlawful Representations. It is unlawful to make any representation to the effect that the SEC or the Federal Reserve Board has passed on the merits of any issue. Also, the failure of either body to take action against any person cannot be construed to mean that that person is not in violation of the law.

**Section 27.** Jurisdiction of Offenses and Suits. Jurisdiction of violations of this Act is given to the district courts of the United States.

**Section 28.** Effect on Existing Law. "The rights and remedies provided by this title (the Act) shall be in addition to any and all other rights and remedies that may exist in law or at equity . . . ." The Section also leaves jurisdiction of offenses against a State law with the State.

**Section 29.** Validity of Contracts. No one can avoid compliance with the provisions of this Act by getting someone else to waive the requirements in any contract. Any contract that seeks to avoid the provisions of this Act are automatically void.

**Section 30.** Foreign Securities Exchange. It is unlawful to deal in securities whose issuers are within the jurisdiction of the United States on a foreign exchange in any manner other than that in which dealing in such securities would have to be handled in this country. In other words, the laws of the U.S. exchanges cannot be circumvented by placing business through a foreign exchange.

**Section 31.** Transaction Fees. Each national securities exchange is required to pay an annual fee to the Commission.

**Section 32.** Penalties. Individuals may be fined a maximum of $1,000,000 or sentenced to a maximum term of imprisonment of 10 years, or both, for violations of the Act.

¶24,025

**Section 33.** Separability of Provisions. An escape section that states that if any one section of the Act is found to be invalid, such findings shall have no effect on the other sections.

**Section 34.** Effective Date, July 1, 1934.

# ¶24,027  PUBLIC UTILITY HOLDING COMPANY ACT OF 1935

Interstate holding companies engaged through subsidiaries in the electric utility business or in the retail distribution of natural or manufactured gas are subject to regulation under the Act. These systems must register with the SEC and file initial and periodic reports. Detailed information concerning the organization, financial structure, and operations of the holding company and its subsidiaries is contained in these reports. If a holding company or its subsidiary meets certain specifications, the Commission can exempt it from part or all of the duties and obligations otherwise imposed by statute. Holding companies are subject to SEC regulations on matters such as structure of the system, acquisitions, combinations, and issues and sales of securities.

The most important provisions of the Act are the requirements for physical integration and corporation simplification of holding company systems. Integration standards restrict a holding company's operations to an *integrated utility system*. An integrated system is defined as one:

1. Capable of economical operation as a single coordinated system.
2. Confined to a single area or region in one or more states.
3. Not so large that it negates the advantages of localized management, efficient operation, and effective regulation.

The original structure and continued existence of any company in a holding company system must not necessarily complicate the corporate structure of the system or result in the distribution of voting power inequitably among security holders of the system.

The SEC can determine what action, if any, must be taken by registered holding companies and their subsidiaries to comply with Act requirements. The SEC can apply to federal courts for orders compelling compliance with Commission directives.

## .01  Acquisitions

To be authorized by the SEC, the acquisition of securities and utility assets by holding companies and their subsidiaries must meet the following standards:

1. The acquisition must not tend toward interlocking relations or concentrating control to an extent detrimental to investors or the public interest.

**¶24,027.01**

2. Any consideration paid for the acquisition, including fees, commissions, and remuneration, must not be unreasonable.

3. The acquisition must not complicate the capital structure of the holding company systems or have a detrimental effect on system functions.

4. The acquisition must tend toward economical and efficient development of an integrated public utility system.

## .03 Issuance and Sale of Securities

Proposed security issues by any holding company must be analyzed and evaluated by the SEC staff and approved by the Commission to ensure that the issues meet the following tests under prescribed standards of the law:

1. The security must be reasonably adapted to the security structure of the issuer, and of other companies in the same holding company system.

2. The security must be reasonably adapted to the earning power of the company.

3. The proposed issue must be necessary and appropriate to the economical and efficient operation of the company's business.

4. The fees, commissions, and other remuneration paid in connection with the issue must not be unreasonable.

5. The terms and conditions of the issue or sale of the security must not be detrimental to the public or investor interest.

Other provisions of the Act concern regulating dividend payments, intercompany loans, solicitations of proxies, consents and other authorizations, and insider trading.

## ¶24,029 TRUST INDENTURE ACT OF 1939

This Act applies to bonds, debentures, notes, and similar debt securities offered for public sale and issued under trust indentures with more than $7.5 million of securities outstanding at any one time. Even though such securities are registered under the Securities Act, they cannot be offered for sale to the public unless the trust indenture conforms to statutory standards of this Act. Designed to safeguard the rights and interests of the investors, the Act also:

1. Prohibits the indenture trustee from conflicting interests which might interfere with exercising its duties on behalf of the securities purchasers.

2. Requires the trustee to be a corporation with minimum combined capital and surplus.

3. Imposes high standards of conduct and responsibility on the trustee.

4. Precludes, in the event of default, preferential collection of certain claims owing to the trustee by the issuer.

5. Provides that the issuer supply to the trustee evidence of compliance with indenture terms and conditions.

6. Requires the trustee to provide reports and notices to security holders.

Other provisions of the Act prohibit impairing the security holders' right to sue individually for principal and interest, except under certain circumstances. It also requires maintaining a list of security holders for their use in communicating with each other regarding their rights as security holders.

In 1987 the Commission sent a legislative proposal to Congress which would modernize procedures under the Act to meet the public's need in view of novel debt instruments and modern financing techniques. This legislative proposal was adopted and enacted into law in 1990.

## ¶24,031  INVESTMENT ADVISERS ACT OF 1940

This law establishes a pattern of regulating investment advisers. In some respects, it has provisions similar to the Securities Exchange Act provisions governing the conduct of brokers and dealers. This Act requires that persons or firms compensated for advising others about securities investment must register with the SEC and conform to the statutory standards designed to protect investors.

The Commission can deny, suspend, or revoke investment adviser registrations if, after notice and hearings, it finds that grounds for a statutory disqualification exist and that the action is in the public interest. Grounds for disqualification include conviction for certain financial crimes or securities law violations, injunctions based on such activities, conviction for violating the mail fraud statute, willfully filing false reports with the SEC, and willfully violating the Advisers Act, the Securities Act, the Securities Exchange Act, the Investment Company Act, or the rules of the Municipal Securities Rulemaking Board. The SEC can recommend criminal prosecution by the Department of Justice for violations of the laws, fraudulent misconduct or willful violation of Commission rules.

The law contains antifraud provisions and empowers the Commission to adopt rules defining fraudulent, deceptive, or manipulative acts and practices. It requires that investment advisers:

1. Disclose the nature of their interest in transactions executed for their clients.

2. Maintain books and records according to SEC rules.

3. Make books and records available to the SEC for inspections.

## ¶24,033   TRUST INVESTMENT COMPANY ACT OF 1940

Activities of companies engaged primarily in investing, reinvesting, and trading in securities, and whose own securities are offered to the public, are subject to statutory prohibitions and to SEC regulations under this Act. Public offerings of investment company securities must be registered under the Securities Act of 1933. It is important that investors understand that the SEC does not supervise the investment activities of these companies and that regulation by the Commission does not imply safety of investment in them.

In addition to the registration requirement for investment companies, the law requires that they disclose their financial condition and investment policies to provide investors complete information about their activities. This Act also:

1.  Prohibits investment companies from substantially changing the nature of their business or investment policies without stockholder approval.
2.  Prohibits persons guilty of securities fraud from serving as officers and directors.
3.  Prevents underwriters, investment bankers, or brokers from constituting more than a minority of the directors of the companies.
4.  Requires that management contracts and material changes be submitted to security holders for their approval.
5.  Prohibits transactions between companies and their directors, officers, or affiliated companies or persons, except when approved by the SEC.
6.  Forbids investment companies to issue senior securities except under specific conditions and upon specified terms.
7.  Prohibits pyramiding of such companies and cross-ownership of their securities.

Other provisions of the Act involve advisory fees, nonconformance of an adviser's fiduciary duty, sales and repurchases of securities issued by investment companies, exchange offers, and other activities of investment companies, including special provisions for periodic payment plans and face-amount certificate companies.

Investment companies must register securities under the Securities Act, and also must file periodic reports and are subject to the SEC proxy and insider trading rules.

## ¶24,035   CORPORATION REORGANIZATION

Reorganization proceedings in the U.S. Courts under Chapter 11 of the Bankruptcy Code are begun by a debtor voluntarily, or by its creditors. Federal bankruptcy law allows a debtor in reorganization to continue operating under the court's protection while the debtor attempts to rehabilitate its business and work out a plan to pay its debts. If a debtor corporation has publicly issued securities outstanding, the reorganization process may raise many issues that materially affect the rights of public investors.

Chapter 11 authorizes the SEC to appear in any reorganization case and to present its views on any issue. Although Chapter 11 applies to all types of business reorganizations, the SEC generally limits its participation to proceedings involving significant public investor interest, i.e., protecting public investors holding the debtor's securities, and participating in legal and policy issues of concern to public investors. The SEC also continues to address matters of traditional Commission expertise and interest relating to securities. When appropriate, the SEC comments on the adequacy of reorganization plan disclosure statements and participates where there is a Commission law enforcement interest.

Under Chapter 11, the debtor, official committees, and institutional creditors negotiate the terms of a reorganization plan. The court can confirm a reorganization plan if it is accepted by creditors for:

1. At least two-thirds of the amounts of allowed claims.
2. More than one-half the number of allowed claims.
3. At least two-thirds in amount of the allowed shareholder interest.

The principal safeguard for public investors is the requirement that a disclosure statement containing adequate information be transmitted by the debtor or plan proponent in connection with soliciting votes on the plan. In addition, reorganization plans involving publicly-held debt usually provide for issuing new securities to creditors and shareholders which are exempt from registration under Section 5 of the Securities Act of 1933.

# Chapter 25

# The Securities and Exchange Commission—Materiality

## CONTENTS

# ¶25,000   OVERVIEW

The Securities and Exchange Commission staff is thinking about materiality again. One of the concerns being mentioned is the iron curtain versus rollover issue. Not all materiality problems were considered or solved by the SEC's Staff Accounting Bulletin No. 99. The SEC staff believes that more guidance may be needed in this particular area as well as others. The Commission has given a considerable amount of thought to the issue over the last year or so. The Commission has not completed the analysis, but is planning to do so in the near future. As with any undertaking dealing with amorphous concepts like materiality there will be some difficult issues to consider.

# ¶25,001   SEC CONSIDERING PROBLEMS RELATING TO MATERIALITY

The SEC's Staff Accounting Bulletin No. 99 includes significant discussion of how materiality should be evaluated and provides detailed guidance in some areas, but it has not resolved all of the issues regarding materiality evaluations. Members of the staff believe that, to some extent, it has had the effect of causing confusion about how quantitative and qualitative considerations on materiality should be analyzed. It has been pointed out that some of the most difficult discussions are those having to do with the evaluation of materiality of errors. The staff has given careful consideration to that and other problems, including the following.

## .01   Areas to Consider in Evaluation of Materiality of Errors

It is important to remember that accounting for something in a way that is not consistent with GAAP is still an error, regardless of whether the item is material. That is, just because an item is small does not mean that no accounting standards apply to it. It just means that accounting for it incorrectly does not materially misstate the financial statements.

Before a registrant decides not to apply specific requirements of GAAP because of materiality, the registrant and its auditors have an obligation to appropriately evaluate whether the impact of not applying that required guidance is material, as discussed in SAB Topic 1.M. That evaluation should be documented and completed for each reported financial period. The registrant's methodology for determining the quantitative impact of not applying the required guidance must allow the registrant and its auditor to reliably measure the difference for each reported financial period. If the pool of transactions to which the relevant accounting guidance has not been applied is not homogenous or varies from period to period, a sampling technique will most likely not allow the registrant and its auditor to reliably measure the impact of not applying GAAP.

Registrants need to keep in mind that, just like every other area of financial reporting, the initial conclusion about whether an error is material is the company's to make. Management should not merely ask its auditors whether an error must be corrected. Instead, an analysis should be done, considering all relevant qualitative and quantitative factors, to support a conclusion about whether the error represents a material misstatement, alone or in combination with other errors. Only after the registrant has reached a conclusion as to the materiality of an item should an auditor do so.

The SEC staff has asked that management not outsource the decision to the Commission. Too often SEC staff gets submissions from registrants seeking concurrence with not restating for an error based on materiality before they attempt to analysis why the error should not be considered material. In some cases, the submission has indicated that neither the registrant nor the auditors had yet reached a conclusion. The SEC explains that the Commission is not in a position to do the analysis. Commission personnel do not know as much about the entity's situation as management and the auditors do. However, the SEC will provide opinions on materiality considerations after the company and its auditors have completed their analyses.

The staff is considering an aspect of materiality analyses that is rarely talked about: the so-called income statement versus balance sheet approach question.

1. The *income statement method* of evaluating materiality, which is also called the *current-period or rollover method,* considers as an error the amounts recorded in the current period income statement that should not have been.

2. The *balance sheet method,* which is also called the *cumulative or iron curtain method,* considers as an error the total effect of all amounts that have been recorded in the company's books during the current or prior periods.

## .03  Difference Between Iron Curtain and Rollover Methods

A simple example demonstrates the difference between these two methods: if a company increases a reserve $10 more than necessary each year for three years, the rollover method treats the error as being $10 in each year, whereas the iron curtain method treats the error as $10 in the first year, $20 in the second, and $30 in the third.

Assume that $10 would be immaterial to all periods, but $30 would be material. Under the rollover method, there is never a material error, unless the company wants to reverse the accrual in the fourth year, because doing so would put $30 out of period. So, under the rollover method, eliminating the overaccrual becomes a material error. Under the iron curtain method, the error would need to be corrected in year three, as it became material that year.

Auditing standards briefly mention this debate in a footnote, noting only that "The measurement of the effect, if any, on the current period's financial statements of misstatements uncorrected in prior periods involves accounting considerations and is therefore not addressed in this section." Because the debate is an accounting one, not an auditing one, a problem arises. Unfortunately, accounting literature does not deal with this at all.

The SEC believes that auditors generally believe the iron curtain method is the preferable method in most situations. For various reasons, both methods are used in practice and have been accepted by auditors and regulators. This is often considered to be a policy election, and the fact that the accounting literature does not specify which method to use appears to support acceptability of both methods. However, a company seldom, if ever discloses—in its summary of accounting policies or elsewhere—which method it uses to evaluate errors and why.

## ¶25,003  POSSIBLE DIRECTION OF NEW GUIDANCE

Previous initiatives to provide guidance on which method should be selected for particular situations have been made, with no substantive progress. Recent events have the SEC thinking that the time has come to provide more guidance in this area. Although there are no plans ready to provide that guidance immediately, representatives of the Agency have been bringing up the topic of materiality in speeches and round tables, and specifically discussing the iron curtain and rollover methods. The indications are that the SEC is likely to be asking for more input and information in this area in the near future, with a view toward providing guidance to resolve the question that has troubled accountants and auditors for some time.

Indications are that the SEC plans to tell companies that small, annually recurring items that normally would not be disclosed and that have a bigger impact on the balance sheet than on the income statement cannot be deemed immaterial simply because they have only a small impact on the income statement. It is not too imaginative to believe that accountants and auditors might be wise to consider carefully just what is and is not material in the light of the SEC's renewed interest in the topic. At the same time, SAB 99 still provides the accepted guidance.

## ¶25,005  SEC STAFF ACCOUNTING BULLETIN 99

The Securities and Exchange Staff Accounting Bulletin (SAB) 99, *Materiality*, issued in August, 1999 delineates the staff's views concerning reliance on certain quantitative benchmarks to assess materiality in preparing financial statements and performing audits of those financial statements. The SEC has decided that the practice of adopting an arbitrary margin of error is inappropriate. SAB 99 concludes that misstatements are not immaterial simply because they fall beneath a numerical threshold.

The SEC is quick to point out that statements in the staff accounting bulletins are not rules or interpretations of the Commission, nor are they published as bearing the Commission's official approval. However, they do represent interpretations and practices followed by the Division of Corporation Finance and the Office of the Chief Accountant in *administering the disclosure requirements of the federal securities laws.* To put it bluntly, anyone ignoring this SAB, is putting himself, herself and/or their company at risk: this new materiality test is the standard the SEC will use for enforcement purposes.

It should be emphasized that SAB 99 does not constitute a new approach to the consideration of "materiality," but is an attempt to "shore up" the definition of the concept and in so doing reemphasize the Commission's foremost goal—the protection of the investor. Therefore, it provides guidance in applying materiality thresholds to the *preparation of financial statements filed with the Commission and the performance of audits of those financial statements.*

## .01   Misusing the "Rule of Thumb"

The SEC staff has been cognizant of the fact that many registrants gradually adopted as "rules of thumb" a 5% quantitative margin of error in preparing their financial statements, and that auditors also have used these thresholds in their evaluation of whether items might be considered material to users of a registrant's financial statements. One rule of thumb in particular suggests that the *misstatement* or *omission* of an item that falls under a 5% threshold is not material in the absence of particularly "egregious circumstances, such as self-dealing or misappropriation by senior management." (In this SAB, "misstatement" or "omission" refers to a financial statement assertion that would not be in conformity with GAAP.)

The staff reminds registrants and the auditors of their financial statements that exclusive reliance on this or any percentage or numerical threshold has no basis in the *accounting literature* or the *law.*

The use of a percentage as a numerical threshold, such as 5%, may provide the basis for a *preliminary* assumption that, without considering all relevant circumstances, a deviation of less than the specified percentage with respect to a particular item on the registrant's financial statements is unlikely to be material. The staff has no objection to such a "rule of thumb" as an *initial* step in assessing materiality. But the bulletin cautions that quantifying the magnitude of a misstatement in percentage terms can be only the beginning of an analysis of materiality; it cannot be used as a substitute for a *full analysis* of all relevant considerations.

## ¶25,007  DEFINING MATERIALITY

Materiality concerns the significance of an item to users of a registrant's financial statements. A matter is "material" if there is a substantial likelihood that a reasonable person would consider it important. Early in its existence, the Financial Accounting Standards Board made this clear. In its Statement of Financial Accounting Concepts 2, the FASB stated the essence of the concept of materiality as follows: *The omission or misstatement of an item in a financial report is material if, in the light of surrounding circumstances, the magnitude of the item is such that it is probable that the judgment of a reasonable person relying upon the report would have been changed or influenced by the inclusion or correction of the item.*

This Statement is almost identical to that expressed by the courts in interpreting the federal securities laws. In 1976, the Supreme Court held that a fact is material if there is "a substantial likelihood that the fact would have been viewed by the reasonable investor as having significantly altered the 'total mix' of information made available."

Thus, we see that an assessment of materiality requires that the facts be considered in the context of the "surrounding circumstances," according to accounting literature, or the "total mix" of information, in the opinion of the Supreme Court.

## ¶25,009  QUALITATIVE AND QUANTITATIVE FACTORS ARE IMPORTANT

In the context of a misstatement of a financial statement item, while the "total mix" includes the *size* in numerical or percentage terms of the misstatement, it also includes the *factual context* in which the user of financial statements appraises the financial statement item. Therefore, financial management and the auditor must consider both "quantitative" and "qualitative" factors in assessing an item's materiality. Court decisions, Commission rules and enforcement actions, and accounting and auditing literature have all considered "qualitative" factors in various contexts.

The FASB has repeatedly emphasized that materiality cannot be reduced to a numerical formula. In FASB Statement 2, the FASB noted that some commenters had urged it to promulgate quantitative materiality guides for use in various situations. The FASB decided against a blanket approach as representing only a "minority view" and went on to explain, "The predominant view is that materiality judgments can properly be made only by those who have all the facts."

According to FASB 2, an additional factor in making materiality judgments revolves around the *degree of precision* that can be attained in *estimating* the judgment item. The amount of deviation that is considered immaterial may increase as the attainable degree of precision decreases. As an example, the SAB points out that *accounts payable* usually can be estimated more accurately than can *contingent liabilities* arising from litigation or threats of it. Therefore, a deviation considered to be material in figuring accounts payable may be quite trivial when considering contingent liabilities.

## ¶25,011  FASB CONSIDERATIONS AND OPINION

The FASB's present position is that no general standards of materiality can be formulated to take into account all the considerations that enter into an experienced human judgment. The Board noted that, in certain limited circumstances, the SEC and other authoritative bodies have issued quantitative materiality guidance, citing as examples guidelines ranging from 1 to 10% with respect to a variety of disclosures. They looked at contradictory studies: one showing a lack of uniformity among auditors on materiality judgments; another suggesting widespread use of a "rule of thumb" of 5 to 10% of net income. They also considered whether an evaluation of materiality could be based solely on anticipating the market's reaction to accounting information.

In the end, the FASB rejected any simplified approach to discharging "the onerous duty of making materiality decisions" in favor of an approach that takes into account *all relevant considerations.* In so doing, it made clear that, "Magnitude by itself, without regard to the nature of the item and the circumstances in which the judgment has to be made, will not generally be a sufficient basis for a materiality judgment."

## ¶25,013  SMALL FIGURES MAY CAUSE BIG MISSTATEMENTS

Evaluation of materiality requires a registrant and its auditor to consider all the relevant circumstances, and the staff believes that there are numerous circumstances in which misstatements below 5% could well be material. As does the SEC Chairman who pointed out that given the attitude of investors in the stock market today, *everything* matters when "...missing an earnings projection by a penny can result in a loss of millions of dollars in market capitalization."

SAB 99 takes into consideration this concern that *qualitative factors* may cause misstatements of quantitatively extremely small amounts to be material. Thus, the bulletin, in effect, cautions the auditor that as a result of the interaction of quantitative and qualitative considerations in materiality judgments, misstatements of relatively small amounts that come to the auditor's attention *could* have a material effect upon the financial statements. Among those considerations that may well render material a quantitatively small misstatement of a financial statement item are whether the misstatement:

1. Results from an item capable of precise measurement or from an estimate and, if so, the degree of imprecision inherent in the estimate.
2. Masks a change in earnings or other trends.

3. Hides a failure to meet analysts' consensus expectations for the enterprise.
4. Actually changes a loss into income or vice versa.
5. Concerns a *segment* or other portion of the registrant's business that has been identified as playing a *significant role* in the registrant's operations or profitability.
6. Affects the registrant's compliance with regulatory requirements.
7. Affects the registrant's compliance with loan covenants or other contractual requirements.
8. Has the effect of increasing management's compensation, for example, by satisfying requirements for the award of bonuses or other forms of incentive compensation.
9. Involves concealment of an unlawful transaction.
10. Aims toward smoothing earnings artificially to give a false impression of stability.

The bulletin does not claim this to be an exhaustive list of the circumstances that may affect the materiality of a quantitatively small misstatement, but it certainly makes the decision process a little more exhausting than merely adhering to some predetermined "percentage."

## ¶25,015 OTHER CONSIDERATIONS

Other factors and situations may bring to question the materiality of a quantitatively small misstatement of a financial statement item:

1. The demonstrated volatility of the price of a registrant's securities in response to certain types of disclosures may provide guidance as to whether *investors* regard quantitatively small misstatements as material.
2. Consideration of potential market reaction to disclosure of a misstatement is by itself "too blunt an instrument to be depended on" in considering whether a fact is material. However, when management or the independent auditor expects (based, for example, on a pattern of market performance) that a known misstatement *may* result in a significant positive or negative market reaction, that expected reaction should be taken into account when considering whether a misstatement is material.

Even if management does not expect a significant market reaction, a misstatement still may be material and should be evaluated under the criteria discussed in this SAB.

## ¶25,017  "MANAGED" EARNINGS—HERE, THERE, AND EVERYWHERE

For the reasons noted above, the staff believes that a registrant and the auditors of its financial statements should *not* assume that even small intentional misstatements in financial statements—for example those pursuant to actions to "manage" earnings—are immaterial. (Intentional management of earnings and intentional misstatements, as used in SAB 99, do not include insignificant errors and omissions that may occur in systems and recurring processes in the normal course of business.)

While the *intent* of management does not render a misstatement material, it may provide significant evidence of materiality. The evidence may be particularly revealing when management has intentionally misstated items in the financial statements to "manage" reported earnings.

In such an instance, management has presumably done so believing that the resulting amounts and trends *would be significant* to users of the registrant's financial statements. Or have the earnings been "managed" just enough to meet or marginally exceed the expectations of securities analysts who appear to be very significant players in today's volatile markets?

SAB 99 mentions that assessment of materiality should occur not only in annual financial reports, but also during the preparation of each quarterly or interim financial statement. After all, savvy investors and even less well informed ones are known to research these statements.

## .01  Consider the Investor

The staff believes that investors generally would regard as significant a management practice to overstate or understate earnings up to an amount just short of a percentage threshold in order to "manage" earnings. Investors presumably also would regard with a jaundiced eye an accounting practice that, in essence, rendered all earnings figures subject to a management-directed margin of misstatement.

The materiality of a misstatement may be judged based upon where it appears in the financial statements. For example, if a misstatement involves a segment of the registrant's operations, in assessing materiality of a misstatement to the financial statements taken as a whole, registrants and their auditors should consider:

1. The *size* of the misstatement.
2. The *significance* of that particular segment information to the financial statements as a whole.

A misstatement of the revenue and operating profit of a relatively small segment which management indicates is important to the future profitability of the entity is more likely to be material to investors than a misstatement in a segment that management has not identified as especially important. In assessing the materiality of misstatements in segment information, as with materiality generally, situations may arise in practice where the auditor will conclude that a matter relating to segment information is *qualitatively material* even though, in his or her judgment, it is *quantitatively immaterial* to the financial statements as a whole.

## ¶25,019  AGGREGATING AND NETTING MISSTATEMENTS

In determining whether multiple misstatements cause the financial statements to be materially misstated, registrants and the auditors of their financial statements should consider the effect of each misstatement separately, and in the aggregate.

Obviously, the concept of materiality takes into consideration that some information, whether viewed individually or as a part of the whole report, may be required for fair presentation of financial statements in conformity with GAAP in one context or the other. Furthermore, it is necessary to evaluate misstatements in light of quantitative and qualitative factors. It is also necessary to consider whether the following can materially misstate the financial statements taken as a whole:

1. Individual line item amounts
2. Subtotals
3. Totals

This requires consideration of:

1. The significance of an item to a particular type of business enterprise; for example, inventories to a manufacturing company. (An adjustment to inventory seen as immaterial to pretax or net income could be material to the financial statements because it could affect a working capital ratio or cause the registrant to be in default of a loan covenant.)
2. The pervasiveness of the misstatement—whether it affects the presentation of numerous financial statement items.
3. The effect of the misstatement on the financial statements taken as a whole.

Accountants and auditors should consider whether each misstatement is material, regardless of its effect when combined with other misstatements. The literature notes that the analysis should consider whether the misstatement of "individual amounts" causes a material misstatement of the financial statements taken as a whole. As with materiality generally, this analysis requires consideration of both quantitative and qualitative factors.

¶25,019

If the misstatement of an individual amount causes the financial statements as a whole to be materially misstated, that effect cannot be eliminated by other misstatements whose effect may be to diminish the impact of the misstatement on other financial statement items.

Quantitative materiality assessments often are made by comparing adjustments to revenues, gross profit, pretax and net income, total assets, stockholders' equity, or individual line items in the financial statements. The particular items in the financial statements to be considered as a basis for the materiality determination depend on the proposed adjustment to be made and other factors, such as those identified in this SAB. For example, an adjustment to inventory that is immaterial to pretax income or net income may be material to the financial statements because it may affect a working capital ratio or cause the registrant to be in default of loan covenants.

## .01  Aggregation May Lead to Aggravation

If a registrant's revenues are a material financial statement item and if they are materially overstated, the financial statements taken as a whole will be materially misleading even if the effect on earnings is completely offset by an equivalent overstatement of expenses. Even though *one misstatement* of an individual amount may not cause the financial statements taken as a whole to be materially misstated, it may nonetheless, when *aggregated with other misstatements*, render the financial statements taken as a whole to be materially misleading.

Registrants and the auditors of their financial statements should consider the effect of the misstatement on *subtotals* or *totals*. The auditor should aggregate all misstatements that affect each subtotal or total and consider whether the misstatements in the aggregate affect the subtotal or total in a way that causes the registrant's financial statements taken as a whole to be materially misleading.

The staff believes that, in considering the aggregate effect of multiple misstatements on a subtotal or total, accountants and auditors should exercise particular care when considering misstatement of an estimated amount with a misstatement of an item capable of precise measurement. As noted above, *assessments of materiality should never be purely mechanical;* given the imprecision inherent in estimates, there is by definition a corresponding imprecision in the aggregation of misstatements involving estimates with those that do not involve an estimate.

Registrants and auditors also should consider the effect of misstatements from prior periods on the current financial statements. For example, the auditing literature states that matters underlying adjustments proposed by the auditor but not recorded by the entity could potentially cause future financial statements to be materially misstated, even though the auditor has concluded that the adjustments are not material to the current financial statements. This may particularly be the case where immaterial misstatements recur in several years and the cumulative effect becomes material in the current year.

## ¶25,021 Intentional Immaterial Misstatements

The SEC reemphasizes their caution that a registrant may *not* make intentional immaterial misstatements in its financial statements. A registrant's management may never intentionally make adjustments to various financial statement items in a manner inconsistent with GAAP.

In any accounting period in which such actions might be taken, it could be that none of the individual adjustments would be considered material, nor would the aggregate effect on the financial statements taken as a whole be material *for the period.*

The adjustments could even be considered irrelevant; however at the same time, they could actually be unlawful. In the books and records provisions under the Exchange Act, even if misstatements are immaterial, registrants must comply with the law. Under these provisions, each registrant with securities registered pursuant to the Act, or required to file reports pursuant to it, must:

1. Make and keep books, records, and accounts, which, in *reasonable detail*, accurately, and fairly reflect the transactions and dispositions of assets of the registrant.
2. Maintain internal accounting controls that are sufficient to provide *reasonable assurances* that, among other things, transactions are recorded as necessary to permit the preparation of financial statements in conformity with GAAP.

FASB Statements of Financial Accounting Standards generally include the statement: "The provisions of this Statement need not be applied to immaterial items." This SAB does not countermand that provision of the Statements. However, it does vanquish the 5% of net income quantitative test often applied in the past. The SEC admits that, in theory, this language in the FASBs is subject to interpretation that a registrant may intentionally record immaterial items in a manner that would unquestionably be contrary to GAAP if the misstatement were considered material. It should be carefully noted, however, that the staff believes the FASB did not intend such a conclusion. Regardless, some companies have in the past apparently interpreted the sentence in just that fashion. They evidently felt they could ignore certain immaterial transactions and misapply GAAP to so-called immaterial transactions with impunity. No more!

Both the U.S. Code and the Securities Exchange Act indicate that criminal liability may be imposed if a person knowingly circumvents or knowingly fails to implement a system of internal accounting controls or knowingly falsifies books, records, or accounts. This should make it perfectly clear that any degree of "cooking the books," setting up "cookie jar reserves," "managing," or otherwise obfuscating may result in violations of the securities laws.

## ¶25,023   THE PRUDENT MAN CONCEPT

In this context, determinations of what constitutes "reasonable assurance" and "reasonable detail" are based not on a "materiality" analysis but on the level of detail and degree of assurance that would satisfy *prudent* officials in the conduct of their own affairs. The books and records provisions of the Exchange Act, in which this is developed, originally were passed as part of the Foreign Corrupt Practices Act (FCPA). In the conference committee report regarding the 1988 amendments to the FCPA, the report stated, "The conference committee adopted the prudent man qualification in order to clarify that the current standard does not connote an unrealistic degree of exactitude or precision. The concept of reasonableness contemplates the weighing of a number of relevant factors, including the costs of compliance."

## ¶25,025   "REASONABLENESS" SHOULD NOT BE UNREASONABLE

The SEC staff is well aware of the fact that there is little authoritative guidance regarding the "reasonableness" standard in the Exchange Act. A principal statement of the Commission's policy in this area was set forth in a 1981 address by the SEC Chairman who noted that, like materiality, "reasonableness" is not an "absolute standard of exactitude for corporate records."

Unlike materiality, however, "reasonableness" is not solely a measure of the significance of a financial statement item to investors. "Reasonableness," here reflects a judgment as to whether an issuer's failure to correct a known misstatement brings into question the purposes underlying the accounting provisions of the Exchange Act. In assessing whether a misstatement results in a violation of a registrant's obligation to keep books and records that are accurate "in reasonable detail," registrants and their auditors should consider, in addition to the factors discussed above concerning an evaluation of a misstatement's potential materiality, the following factors.

1. *The significance of the misstatement.* Though the staff does not believe that registrants need to make in-depth determination of significance regarding all immaterial items, it is "reasonable" to treat misstatements whose effects are clearly inconsequential differently from possibly more significant ones.

2. *How the misstatement arose.* It is undoubtedly never "reasonable" for registrants to record misstatements or not to correct known misstatements, even immaterial ones, as part of an ongoing effort directed by or known to

senior management for the purposes of "managing" earnings. On the other hand, insignificant misstatements that arise from the operation of systems or recurring processes in the normal course of business generally will not cause a registrant's books to be inaccurate "in reasonable detail."

To carry it a step further, the SEC appears to be emphasizing the caution that criminal penalties *will be imposed* where acts of commission or omission in keeping books or records or administering accounting controls *are deliberately aimed at* falsification, or circumvention of the accounting controls set forth in the Exchange Act. (This would also include the deliberate falsification of books and records and other conduct calculated to evade the *internal accounting controls requirement* which is about to come under close scrutiny by the Commission. See below.)

3. *The cost of correcting the misstatement.* The books and records provisions of the Exchange Act do not require registrants to make major expenditures to correct small misstatements. (To put it succinctly, thousands of dollars should ordinarily not be spent conserving hundreds.) Conversely, where there is little cost or delay involved in correcting a misstatement, failure to do so is unlikely to be "reasonable."

4. *The clarity of authoritative accounting guidance with respect to the misstatement.* In instances where reasonable individuals could differ about the appropriate accounting treatment of a financial statement item, a failure to correct it may not render the registrant's financial statements inaccurate "in reasonable detail." On the other hand, when there is little basis for reasonable disagreement, the case for leaving a misstatement uncorrected is decidedly weaker.

The SEC acknowledges that there may be additional indicators of "reasonableness" that registrants, their accountants and auditors may take into consideration. Because the judgment is seldom unanimous, the staff will be inclined to continue to defer to judgments that "allow a business, acting in good faith, to comply with the Act's accounting provisions in an innovative and cost-effective way."

## ¶25,027    THE AUDITOR'S RESPONSE TO INTENTIONAL MISSTATEMENTS

The Exchange Act requires auditors to consider several courses of action when discovering an illegal act which is defined as "...an act or omission that violates any law, or any rule or regulation having the force of law."

The statute specifies among other things that:

1. These obligations are triggered regardless of whether or not the illegal acts are considered to have a material effect upon the financial statements of the issuer.

2. The auditor is required to inform the appropriate level of management of an illegal act unless it is clearly "inconsequential."

3. When an auditor discovers an intentional misstatement of immaterial items in a registrant's financial statements which violates the Exchange Act and thus is an illegal act, the auditor must take steps to see that the registrant's audit committee is "adequately informed" about the illegal act. (Since the provisions of the Act are triggered regardless of whether an illegal act has a material effect on the registrant's financial statements, when the illegal act is a misstatement in the registrant's financial statements, the auditor is required to report that illegal act to the audit committee irrespective of any "netting" of the misstatements with other financial statement items.)

Auditors who become aware of intentional misstatements may also be required to:

1. Reevaluate the degree of audit risk involved in the audit engagement.
2. Determine whether to revise the nature, timing, and extent of audit procedures accordingly.
3. Consider whether to resign.

Cases of intentional misstatements may serve as a signal of the existence of reportable conditions or material weaknesses in the registrant's system of internal accounting control that should have been designed to detect and deter improper accounting and financial reporting.

## .01  Management's Role

As stated by the National Commission on Fraudulent Financial Reporting (also known as the Treadway Commission) in its 1987 report, the *tone* set by top management, the corporate environment, or the culture within which financial reporting occurs is the most important factor contributing to the integrity of the financial reporting process. Even if there is an in-depth set of written rules and procedures, if this tone is lax or permissive, fraudulent financial reporting is more likely to occur.

Here again, it is up to the auditor to report to a registrant's audit committee any *reportable conditions or material weaknesses* in a registrant's system of internal accounting control that he or she uncovers in the course of the examination of the registrant's financial statements.

## ¶25,029  GAAP Takes Precedence Over Industry Practice

It has been argued that registrants should be permitted to continue to follow an *industry* accounting practice even though that practice is—or has become—inconsistent with authoritative accounting literature. Such a situation might occur:

1. If a practice is developed when there are few transactions.
2. The accounting results are clearly inconsequential.
3. That particular industry practice never changed despite a subsequent growth in the number or materiality of such transactions.

Regardless of how or why the practice had developed, this may *not* be considered a valid argument for its continued use. Authoritative literature *always* takes precedence over industry practice that is contrary to GAAP.

## .01   Determining Appropriate Accounting Treatment

As pointed out above, SAB 99 is not intended to change current law or guidance in the accounting or auditing literature. This SAB and the authoritative accounting literature cannot specifically address all of the novel and complex business transactions and events that may occur. Accordingly, registrants may at times account for, and make disclosures about these transactions and events based on analogies to similar situations or other factors.

The SEC staff may not, however, always be convinced that a registrant's determination is the most appropriate under the circumstances. When disagreements occur after a transaction or an event has been reported, the consequences may be severe for registrants, auditors, and, most important, for the *users of financial statements* who have a right to expect consistent accounting and reporting for, and disclosure of, similar transactions and events.

The SEC, therefore, encourages registrants, their accountants and auditors to discuss on a timely basis with the staff proposed accounting treatments for, and disclosures about, transactions or events not specifically covered by the existing accounting literature. This caution should also apply in instances where there is any question in the mind of any of the entity's "team" concerning the appropriateness of a particular procedure. In more forceful terms, "Don't let creative accounting get you or your firm into trouble."

# Chapter 26

# The Sarbanes-Oxley Act of 2002

## CONTENTS

# ¶26,000  OVERVIEW

In October and November, 2006, the Securities and Exchange Commission, the Public Company Accounting Oversight Board, various global-wide standard-setters were all expressing concern over the provisions of Sarbanes-Oxley

The SEC and the PCAOB were planning to revise the Sarbanes-Oxley corporate governance law, possibly by December, to lower compliance costs for public companies based on their market values. The aim was to make significant changes to implementation of Section 404 of Sarbanes-Oxley to make the process less costly and more effective.

The average public company pays $3.8 million a year to comply with Sarbanes-Oxley, according to Financial Executives International, an association of 15,000 chief financial officers and other corporate officials.

Business groups had complained to the SEC and the PCAOB that 404 is burdening smaller companies. The claim is that higher auditing and legal fees are driving initial public offerings overseas. On the other hand, many investors' groups and firms believe that this measure's reaction to the accounting fraud perpetrated by Enron and WorldCom, for example, is worth the cost and effort to make it work. After all, lack of oversight and internal control cost investors in these companies about $65 billion, according to government figures and shareholder lawsuits.

The staffs of the SEC and the PCAOB issued a joint statement in November that considerable progress had been made in the attempt to improve guidance on SOX. The agencies are coordinating their efforts to assure that implementation of section 404 of Sarbanes-Oxley continues to strengthen investor protections while reducing unnecessary or disproportionately high costs.

PCAOB planned to amend AS2 in December 2006 to define how Sarbanes-Oxley audits should be conducted. The revision is expected to advise companies and auditors to focus on "what really matters, what's material to the preparation of the financial statements, and to ignore what isn't essential."

At about the same time, the SEC has stated that they will propose guidelines to help companies interpret Sarbanes-Oxley in a way that saves both time and money. The revisions should make audits "top-down, risk-based" and "permit reliance on the work of others,"

# ¶26,001  PEERING INTO THE FUTURE

Under pressure from accounting scandals at Enron, Congress reached an agreement with lightning speed on legislation to overhaul the rules governing the accounting profession. With the time constraint of the August congressional recess forcing their hand, House and Senate members hammered out a compromise on reform legislation in less than a week and reached an accord on July 24, 2002. The compromise called for the creation of an independent Accounting Oversight Board governed by the Securities and Exchange Commission (SEC).

Despite pressure to tone down the language and requirements of the Sarbanes-sponsored Senate bill, which placed stringent limits on the consulting services that audit firms can provide to public company audit clients, the strictures prevailed. Moreover, the act included House measures on stiffer criminal penalties for corporate crimes.

Adoption of the legislation marked a drastic shift for the accounting profession, which has, thus far, been self-regulated. The legislation makes control of the accounting profession similar to that of the brokerage industry's regulation under the NASD.

The bill places a federal government bureaucracy at the helm of accounting regulation. It is hoped that this new oversight structure will renew the faith the public had in auditors and the financial statements that they helped prepare. On the other hand, it will take a little while to see how closely the SEC and the Oversight Board itself follow the dictates of the law.

The American Institute of Certified Public Accountants (AICPA) noted that the changes demanded by the legislation would be dramatic and challenging for the accounting profession. The AICPA has pledged to work cooperatively with firms engaged in conducting public company audits in adapting to changes mandated by the new legislation. One immediate problem facing the AICPA is the appropriate role of its SEC Practice Section, within the framework of the new oversight board. At this juncture, it is a little difficult to foresee fully just what the role of the AICPA, Financial Accounting Standards Board (FASB), and other professional and standard-setting organizations may be.

An official of the SEC, speaking before a group of accountants at the end of January 2003, remarked that the past two weeks had been ". . . the busiest two weeks of rulemaking in the history of the Commission." He stated his belief that to restore the honor and credibility of the accounting profession, all participants must focus on one thing—doing what is best for investors.

These are still busy rulemaking activities going on with little indication that they will stop soon. Many feel that the rulemaking has gone too far, too fast. On the other hand, many supporters of SOX and the PCAOB applaud the progress that has been made in placing some limits and controls upon corporations and management for the benefit of the investor.

## ¶26,003  FOCUSING ON INVESTORS

Several of the initiatives under way at the SEC addressed the issue of focusing on investors. Much of this activity was generated by the passage of the Sarbanes-Oxley Act. In that time, the Commission adopted nine final rules implementing both the legislative mandates of the Act and, in some cases, additional reforms that the Commission and Commission staff deemed necessary to advance the interests of investors. Those rules relate to:

1. CEO and CFO certifications.
2. Pro forma financial information.
3. Codes of ethics for senior executives.
4. Financial experts on audit committees.
5. Trading during pension fund blackout periods.
6. Disclosure of material off-balance-sheet transactions.
7. Retention of audit records.
8. Independence standards for public company auditors.
9. Standards of conduct for attorneys.

## .01  Importance to the Accounting Profession

Three of these initiatives undertaken by the SEC that are believed to have the potential for having the most significant effect upon the accounting profession are:

1. The establishment of the Public Company Accounting Oversight Board.
2. The adoption of new independence standards for public company auditors.
3. The efforts under way to improve the accounting standard-setting process and bring about international convergence of accounting standards.

The list of rules noted above indicates that the Act requires significant reform in all aspects of financial reporting and the disclosure system. The status of both registrants and auditors has been changed drastically. Other members of the capital market system, including investment bankers, analysts, and attorneys will now also operate under new and more stringent regulation.

## .03  Sarbanes-Oxley More Than a List of Specifics

Details of the Act follow, but the Commission considers that the underlying themes are relatively simple, straightforward, and intended to restore market credibility. They include some old-fashioned truths about life in general as well as warnings for avoiding trouble in the corporate world:

- Each person must accept responsibility for his or her own behavior.
- Being an accomplice to, or ignoring, a bad deed may be the same as doing the bad deed.

- Those who carry out bad deeds shall be punished.
- Appearance counts.

## ¶26,005  TYPES OF SERVICES CONSIDERED UNLAWFUL

The big accomplishment was to bring to fruition what the SEC and FASB had been trying to accomplish (with little success) before all the scandals came to light. Accounting firms are now barred from providing:

1. Bookkeeping or other services related to the accounting records or financial statements of public company audit clients.
2. Financial information systems design and implementation services.
3. Appraisal or valuation services, fairness opinions, or contribution-in-kind reports.
4. Actuarial services.
5. Internal audit outsourcing services.
6. Management functions or human resources.
7. Broker or dealer, investment advisor, or investment banking services.
8. Legal services and expert services unrelated to the audit.
9. Any other service that the Board determines, by regulation, is impermissible.

However, the Board does have the power to grant exceptions. Under certain conditions, some services may be performed if prior approval has been sought and granted. A similar measure in the House bill would have barred only consulting on system implementation and internal audits for audit clients. There are those who feel that Congress did not need to set hard and fast rules regarding independence and non-audit services. Some knowledgeable commenters consider those are matters better attended to by an expert regulatory body. On the other hand, if such matters are actually spelled out, obfuscation might not prevail.

The final legislation took the tougher measures proposed by the House on penalties for corporate crimes. A new securities fraud section was established to handle white-collar crime. Conviction carries a maximum penalty of a 25-year prison term, and penalties for mail and wire fraud are increased to 20 years.

## ¶26,007  THE PUBLIC COMPANY ACCOUNTING OVERSIGHT BOARD

The Oversight Board has the power to:

1. Establish auditing.
2. Set up quality control.

3. Draft ethics and independence standards for public company auditors.
4. Investigate and discipline accountants.
5. Apply oversight of foreign firms that audit the financial statements of companies under U.S. securities laws.

Because the measure was passed so quickly and powered by such emotional fervor, there may be even more need for "technical corrections" than the many that are necessary for even the most routine legislation. The first of these corrections, Public Law 108-44, the *Accountant, Compliance, and Enforcement Staffing Act of 2003* was enacted and signed into law July 3, 2003. The purpose of this change is to "provide for the protection of investors, increase confidence in the capital markets system, and fully implement the Sarbanes-Oxley Act of 2002 by streamlining the hiring process for certain employment positions in the Securities and Exchange Commission." Board membership qualifications and constraints include the following:

1. The Board is made up of five financially literate members who are appointed for five-year terms.
2. Two of the members must be or have been CPAs.
3. The remaining three *must not be and cannot have been* CPAs.
4. The Chair may be held by one of the CPA members, provided that he or she has not been engaged as a practicing CPA for five years.
5. The Board's members are to serve on a full-time basis.
6. No member may, concurrent with service on the Board, share in any of the profits of, or receive payments from, a public accounting firm, other than "fixed continuing payments," such as retirement payments.
7. Members of the Board are appointed by the SEC after consultation with the Chairman of the Federal Reserve Board and the Secretary of the Treasury.
8. Members may be removed by the SEC "for good cause."

## .01  Responsibilities of the Board Related to Auditing Standards

The Oversight Board is expected to:

1. Cooperate on an ongoing basis with designated professional groups of accountants and any advisory groups convened in connection with setting auditing standards. Although the Board can, to the extent that it deems appropriate, adopt standards proposed by those groups, the *Board will have authority to amend, modify, repeal, and reject any standards suggested by the groups*. The Board is to report on these standard-setting activities to the Commission annually.

2. Require registered public accounting firms to "prepare, and maintain for a period of not less than seven years, audit work papers, and other information related to any audit report, in sufficient detail to support the conclusions reached in such report."

3. Require a second partner in public accounting firms to review and approve audit reports that registered accounting firms must adopt related to quality control standards.

4. Adopt an audit standard to implement the internal control review required by the act. This standard must require that the auditor evaluate whether the internal control structure and procedures include records that:

    a. Accurately and fairly reflect the transactions of the issuer.

    b. Provide reasonable assurance that the transactions are recorded in a manner that will permit the preparation of financial statements in accordance with GAAP.

    c. Include a description of any material weaknesses in the internal controls of the particular firm.

## .03 Mandatory Registration and Other Oversight Functions

The Board will be responsible for:

1. Registering public accounting firms. In order to audit a public company, a public accounting firm must register with the Board. The Board is empowered to collect a registration fee and an annual fee from each registered public accounting firm in amounts that are "sufficient" to recover the costs of processing and reviewing applications and annual reports.

    The Board is required to establish a reasonable annual accounting support fee in an amount necessary or appropriate to maintain the Board. This fee will be assessed on issuers only.

    The registration requirement also applies to foreign accounting firms that audit a U.S. company. This would include foreign firms that perform some audit work, such as in a foreign subsidiary of a U.S. company that is relied on by the primary auditor.

2. Establishing (or adopting, by rule) auditing, quality control, ethics, independence, and other *standards* relating to the preparation of audit reports for issuers.

3. Conducting inspections of accounting firms. Annual quality reviews (inspections) must be conducted for firms that audit more than 100 issues; all other inspections must be conducted every three years. The SEC or the Board may order a special inspection of any firm at any time.

4. Conducting investigations and disciplinary proceedings and imposing appropriate sanctions. All documents and information prepared or received by the Board are treated as confidential and privileged as an evidentiary matter in any proceeding in any federal or state court or administrative agency, unless they are presented in connection with a public proceeding or released in connection with a disciplinary action. However, all such documents and information can be made available to the SEC, the U.S. Attorney General, and other federal and appropriate state agencies. Disciplinary hearings will be closed unless the Board orders that they be public, for good cause, and with the consent of the parties. Sanctions can be imposed by the Board upon a firm if it fails to supervise, within reason, any associated person with regard to auditing or quality control standards, or otherwise. No sanctions report will be made available to the public unless and until stays pending appeal have been lifted.

5. Performing such other duties or functions as necessary or appropriate.

6. Enforcing compliance with the act, the rules of the Board, professional standards, and the securities laws relating to the preparation and issuance of audit reports and the obligations and liabilities of accountants with respect to them.

7. Setting the budget and managing the operations of the Board and the staff of the Board.

## ¶26,009    SEC OVERSIGHT OF THE OVERSIGHT BOARD

The Securities and Exchange Commission:

1. Has oversight and enforcement authority over the Board.

2. Can give the Board additional responsibilities, other than those specified in the Act.

3. May require the Board to keep certain records.

4. Has the power to inspect the Board itself, in the same manner as it can with regard to self-regulatory organizations, such as the NASD.

5. Is to treat the Board as if it were a registered securities association; that is, a self-regulatory organization.

6. Requires that the Board file proposed rules and rule changes with the SEC and may approve, reject, or amend such rules.

7. Requires that the Board notify the SEC of pending investigations involving potential violations of the securities laws and coordinate its investigation with the SEC Division of Enforcement, as necessary, to protect an ongoing SEC investigation.

8. May, by order, censure or impose limitations on the activities, functions, and operations of the Board if it finds that the Board has violated the act or the securities laws. The same applies if the Board has failed to ensure the

compliance of accounting firms, with applicable rules, without reasonable justification.

9. Requires that the Board must notify the SEC when it imposes any "final sanction" on any accounting firm or associated person. The Board's findings and sanctions are subject to review by the SEC. The SEC may enhance, modify, cancel, reduce, or require remission of such sanction.

## .01 SEC Announces Committee to Advise Small Public Companies

In its role as overseer, the Securities and Exchange Commission in December 2004 announced the establishment of an advisory committee to assist in examining the impact of the Sarbanes-Oxley Act, as well as other aspects of the federal securities laws affecting smaller public companies.

Two cochairs were appointed to head the committee, which will be known as the Securities and Exchange Commission Advisory Committee on Smaller Public Companies. Its areas of inquiry are:

- Frameworks for internal control over financial reporting applicable to smaller public companies, methods for management's assessment of such internal control, and standards for auditing such internal control.
- Corporate disclosure and reporting requirements and federally imposed corporate governance requirements for smaller public companies, including differing regulatory requirements based on market capitalization, or other measurements of size or market characteristics.
- Accounting standards and financial reporting requirements applicable to smaller public companies.
- The process, requirements, and exemptions relating to offerings of securities by smaller companies, particularly public offerings.

The Advisory Committee is charged with considering the impact of the Sarbanes-Oxley Act of 2002 in each of these areas. The SEC will direct the committee to conduct its work with a view of protecting investors, considering whether the costs imposed by the current securities regulatory system for smaller public companies are proportionate to the benefits, identifying methods of minimizing costs and maximizing benefits, and facilitating capital formation by smaller companies. The Chairman also stated the Commission expects the committee to provide recommendations about where and how the Commission should draw lines to scale regulatory treatment for companies based on size.

***SEC Appoints Members of Advisory Committee.*** In March 2005, the SEC Chairman appointed the 19 additional members of the Commission's Advisory Committee on Smaller Public Companies to bring the total number of members of the Advisory Committee to 21. At that time, the Chairman also announced that representatives of three groups, the Public Company Accounting Oversight Board, the Financial Accounting Standards Board, and the North American Securities Administrators Association, had accepted invitations to become official observers of the committee.

The SEC established the advisory committee to examine the impact of the Sarbanes-Oxley Act and other aspects of the federal securities laws on smaller companies. The Commission stated that that Sarbanes-Oxley Act had already benefited America's investors enormously and would spur further improvements in the securities markets.

The role of the advisory committee is to advise the SEC on how best to ensure that the costs of regulation for smaller companies under the Act and other securities laws are commensurate with the benefits. The appointments to the Advisory Committee are intended to ensure that the Commission receives input on these issues from a broad range of market participants, including individuals from diverse industries, geographical areas, professions, and categories of smaller companies and investors. Selection of members took into consideration the varied interests to be represented and a fair balance of points of view.

## ¶26,011  ACCOUNTING STANDARDS

The SEC is authorized to recognize, as generally accepted, any accounting principles established by a standard-setting body that meets the bill's criteria, which include requirements that the body:

1. Be a private entity.
2. Be governed by a board of trustees (or equivalent body), the majority of whom are not, nor have been, associated with a public accounting firm for the past two years.
3. Be funded in a manner similar to the Board.
4. Have adopted procedures to ensure prompt consideration of changes to accounting principles by a majority vote.
5. Consider, when adopting standards, the need to keep them current and the extent to which international convergence of standards is necessary or appropriate.

## ¶26,013  PUBLIC COMPANY AUDIT COMMITTEES

The audit committee of the issuers plays an important part in overseeing many of the provisions of the Sarbanes-Oxley Act.

## .01  Qualifications and Responsibilities

Each member of the audit committee must be a member of the board of directors of the issuer and otherwise be independent. "Independent" is defined as not receiving (other than for service on the board) any consulting, advisory, or other compensatory fee from the issuer. In addition, no member may be an "affiliated" person of the issuer or of any of his or her subsidiaries. However, the SEC may make exemptions for certain individuals *on a case-by-case basis*. The SEC is expected to announce rules to require issuers to disclose whether at least one member of its audit committee is a "financial expert."

Each issuer must provide appropriate funding to the audit committee to allow the committee to carry out its responsibilities. The audit committee of an issuer, in turn, is directly responsible for the appointment, compensation, and oversight of the work of any registered public accounting firm employed by that issuer. The audit committee must also establish procedures for receiving, retaining, and handling complaints received by the issuer regarding accounting, internal controls, and auditing. In addition, the committee must engage independent counsel or other advisors that it determines necessary to carry out its duties.

## .03  Auditor Reports to Audit Committees

The accounting firm must report to the audit committee all critical accounting policies and practices to be used and any alternative disclosures and treatments of financial information within GAAP that have been discussed with management, along with the ramifications of their use and the treatment preferred by the firm. Other nonaudit services, including tax services, require preapproval by the audit committee on a case-by-case basis and must be disclosed to investors in periodic reports.

## ¶26,015  MANAGEMENT ASSESSMENT OF INTERNAL CONTROLS

The Sarbanes-Oxley Act requires that each annual report of an issuer contain an internal control report, which is to state the responsibility of management for establishing and maintaining an adequate internal control structure and procedures for financial reporting. It also must contain an assessment, as of the end of the issuer's fiscal year, of the effectiveness of the internal control structure and procedures of the issuer for financial reporting. Each issuer's auditor must attest to, and report on, the assessment made by the management of the issuer. An attestation made under this section must be in accordance with standards for attestation engagements issued or adopted by the Board. An attestation engagement may not be the subject of a separate engagement.

The legislation directs the SEC to require each issuer to disclose whether it has adopted a code of ethics for its senior financial officers and the contents of that code. It directs the SEC to revise its regulations concerning prompt disclosure on Form 8-K to require immediate disclosure "of any change in, or waiver of," an issuer's code of ethics.

## ¶26,017 FINANCIAL REPORT REQUIREMENTS IN THE ACT

Nothing is more important to a business entity, large or small, its creditors, investors, even its employees and rank-and-file officers and directors than a true and honest financial report. When ranking officers do not play by the rules (however flawed the rules) and skew that report to their own advantage, all and sundry suffer in the final analysis.

Much of the Sarbanes-Oxley Act is drafted to attempt to improve the quality and reliability of these reports.

Each financial report must be prepared in accordance with GAAP and must "reflect all material correcting adjustments . . . that have been identified by a registered accounting firm. . . ." In addition, each annual and quarterly financial report is required to disclose all material off-balance-sheet transactions and any other relationships with unconsolidated entities that may have a material current or future effect on the financial condition of the issuer.

The SEC is expected to issue rules providing that pro forma financial information must be presented in such a manner that it does not contain an untrue statement or omit a material fact that, by its omission, would make the pro forma financial information misleading.

*Officer and Director Penalties.*    If an issuer is required to prepare a restatement owing to *material noncompliance* with financial reporting requirements, the chief executive officer and the chief financial officer are required to reimburse the issuer for any bonus or other incentive- or equity-based compensation received during the 12 months following the issuance or filing of the non- compliant document. They must also reimburse the issuer for any profits realized from the sale of securities of the issuer during that period.

In any action brought by the SEC for violation of the securities laws, federal courts are authorized to "grant any equitable relief that may be appropriate or necessary *for the benefit of investors.*"

*Improper Influence on Conduct of Audits.*    It shall be unlawful for any officer or director of an issuer to take any action to fraudulently influence, coerce, manipulate, or mislead any auditor engaged in the performance of an audit for the purpose of rendering the financial statements materially misleading.

*Corporate Responsibility for Financial Reports.*    The CEO and CFO of each issuer are ordered to prepare a statement to accompany the audit report to certify the "appropriateness of the financial statements and disclosures contained in the periodic report, and that those financial statements and disclosures fairly present, in all material respects, the operations and financial condition of the issuer." In particular, section 301 of the Act (*Corporate Responsibility for Financial Reports*) requires each annual or quarterly report filed to contain a statement that:

1. The signing officer has reviewed the report;
2. Based on the officer's knowledge, the report does not contain any untrue statement of a material fact or omit to state a material fact necessary in order to make the statements made, in light of the circumstances under which such statements were made, not misleading;
3. Based on such officer's knowledge, the financial statements and other financial information included in the report fairly present in all material respects the financial condition and results of operation of the issuer as of, and for, the periods presented in the report;
4. The signing officers:
   (a) Are responsible for establishing and maintaining internal controls;
   (b) Have designed such internal controls to ensure that material information relating to the issuer and its consolidated subsidiaries is made known to such officer by others within those entities, particularly during the period in which the periodic reports are being prepared;
   (c) Have evaluated the effectiveness of the issuer's internal controls as of a date within 90 days prior to the report;
   (d) Have presented in the report their conclusions about the effectiveness of their internal controls based on their evaluations as of that date;
   (e) Have disclosed to the issuer's auditors and the audit committee of the board of directors (or persons fulfilling the equivalent function):
      (i) All significant deficiencies in the design or operation of internal controls that could adversely affect the issuer's ability to record, process, summarize, and report financial data and have identified for the issuer's auditors any material weaknesses in internal controls; and
      (ii) Any fraud, whether or not material, that involves management or other employees who had a significant role in the issuer's internal controls; and
   (f) Have indicated in the report whether or not there were significant changes in internal control or in other factors that could significantly affect internal controls subsequent to the date of their evaluation, including any corrective actions with regard to significant deficiencies and material weaknesses.

¶26,017

In response to questions about the actual implementation of the requirements of the corporate responsibility statements, the SEC has issued, in question and answer format, a number of clarifications. Many relate to highly technical issues while the following have general import.

**Question 12:** If the same individual is both the principal executive officer and principal financial officer, must he or she sign two certifications?

**Answer:** The individual may provide one certification and provide both titles underneath the signature.

**Question 13:** A CEO resigned after the end of the quarter but before the filing of the upcoming Form 10-Q. The company appointed a new CEO prior to the filing. Who signs the certification?

**Answer:** The new CEO, because he or she is the principal executive officer at the time of filing.

**Question 15:** An issuer currently does not have a CEO/CFO. Who must execute the certifications required by Rules 13a-14 and 15d-14?

**Answer:** as set forth in paragraph (a) of Rules 13a-14, where an issuer does not have a CEO/CFO, the person or persons performing similar functions must execute the required certification.

A violation of this section must be knowing and intentional to give rise to liability.

## ¶26,019 SEC Involvement in the Act

Not only is a new Board created by the Sarbanes-Oxley Act, but the Securities and Exchange Commission is given control of it, additional oversight assignments, study problems, and added funds and laborpower to accomplish the job. Throughout this chapter, the SEC figures prominently in new and revised rules and regulations. Following are some additional areas of the Commission's role in the new legislation. Among the provisions is a section that empowers the SEC to prohibit a person from serving as an officer or director of a public company if the person has committed securities fraud. This, and many of the other measures, would seem to be iteration of provisions that have been in place, but they need to be emphasized.

### .01 Study and Report on Special-Purpose Entities

The Commission is to study off-balance-sheet disclosures to determine (1) the extent of such transactions (including assets, liabilities, leases, losses and the use of special purpose entities) and (2) whether generally accepted accounting rules result in financial statements of issuers reflecting the economics of such off-balance-sheet transactions to investors in a transparent fashion. The Commission is to make a report containing its recommendations to Congress.

## .03 Miscellaneous Assignments

Various sections of the legislation include the requirements placed on firms and their officers and the specifically assigned oversight tasks to the Commission. Among them are:

1. A direction that the SEC require each issuer to disclose whether it has adopted a code of ethics for its senior financial officers and the contents of that code. The SEC is also directed to revise its regulations concerning prompt disclosure on Form 8-K that requires immediate disclosure of any change in, or waiver of, an issuer's code of ethics.
2. The expectation that the SEC will issue rules providing that pro forma financial information must be presented in such a manner that it does not contain an untrue statement or omit to state a *material fact* that, by its omission, would make the pro forma financial information misleading. (Many firms that have rather straightforward financial reports have managed to produce questionable pro forma information and have defined materiality rather loosely.)

## .05 Officer and Director Penalties

The SEC is empowered to issue an order to prohibit, conditionally or unconditionally, permanently or temporarily, any person who has violated section 10(b) of the 1934 Act from acting as an officer or director of an issuer if the SEC has found that such person's conduct demonstrates unfitness to serve as an officer or director of any such issuer:

(Section 10: It shall be unlawful for any person, directly or indirectly, by the use of any means or instrumentality of interstate commerce or of the mails, or of any facility of any national securities exchange—[b] To use or employ, in connection with the purchase or sale of any security registered on a national securities exchange or any security not so registered, or any securities-based swap agreement (as defined in section in the Gramm-Leach-Bliley Act), any manipulative or deceptive device or contrivance in contravention of such rules and regulations as the Commission may prescribe as necessary or appropriate in the public interest or for the protection of investors.)

## .07  Appearance and Practice Before the Commission

The SEC may censure any person or temporarily bar or deny any person the right to appear or practice before the SEC if the person does not possess the requisite qualifications to represent others, lacks character or integrity, or has willfully violated federal securities laws.

## .09  Rules of Professional Responsibility for Attorneys

The SEC is required to establish rules setting minimum standards for professional conduct for attorneys practicing before it.

## .11  Study and Report

The SEC is ordered to conduct a study of "securities professionals" (public accountants, public accounting firms, investment bankers, investment advisors, brokers, dealers, and attorneys) who have been found to have aided and abetted a violation of federal securities laws.

## .13  Temporary Freeze Authority

The SEC is authorized to freeze an extraordinary payment to any director, officer, partner, controlling person, agent, or employee of a company during an investigation of possible violations of securities laws.

## ¶26,021  MEASURES RELATING TO CORPORATE OFFICERS

Because many of the problems facing corporations and the stock market at present result from actions by ranking corporate officers, a number of provisions in this legislation deal directly with corporate governance and related matters:

1.  *Prohibition of insider trades during pension fund black-out periods.* The Act prohibits the purchase or sale of stock by officers and directors and other insiders during black-out periods. Any profits resulting from sales in violation of this section "shall inure to and be recoverable by the issuer." If the issuer fails to bring suit or prosecute diligently, a suit to recover such profit may be instituted by "the owner of any security of the issuer."

2.  *Prohibition of personal loans to executives.* Generally, it will be unlawful for an issuer to extend credit to any director or executive officer. Consumer credit companies may make home improvement and consumer credit loans and issue credit cards to its directors and executive officers, if it is done in

the *ordinary course of business* on the same terms and conditions made to the general public.

3. *Timely disclosures.* Issuers must disclose information on material changes in the financial condition or operations of the issuer on a rapid and current basis. Directors, officers, and 10 percent owners must report designated transactions by the end of the second business day following the day on which the transaction was executed.

4. *Conflicts of interest.* The CEO, Controller, CFO, Chief Accounting Officer, or person in an equivalent position cannot have been employed by the company's audit firm during the one-year period proceeding the audit.

5. *Audit partner rotation.* The lead audit or coordinating partner and the reviewing partner must rotate off of the audit every 5 years.

6. *Tampering with an official proceeding.* The Act makes it a crime for any person to corruptly alter, destroy, mutilate, or conceal any document with the intent to impair the object's integrity or availability for use in an official proceeding or to otherwise obstruct, influence or impede any official proceeding. Perpetrators are liable for up to 20 years in prison and a fine.

7. *Sense of congress regarding corporate tax returns.* It is the sense of Congress that the federal income tax return of a corporation should be signed by the chief executive officer of such corporation.

## ¶26,023   TREATMENT OF SECURITIES ANALYSTS BY REGISTERED SECURITIES ASSOCIATIONS

National Securities Exchanges and registered securities associations must adopt conflict-of-interest rules for research analysts who recommend equities in research reports.

## ¶26,025   GAO STUDIES

The Government Accountability Office (GAO) has also been assigned a part in the new legislations. Its task is to conduct two studies.

### .01   The Effect of Consolidation of Public Accounting Firms

The first is a study regarding the consolidation of public accounting firms since 1989, including the present and future impact of the consolidation and the solutions to any problems discovered. According to the GAO report, issued in July 2003, the Sarbanes-Oxley Act called for the study because "the audit market for large public companies is an oligopoly, with the largest firms auditing the vast majority of public companies and smaller firms facing significant barriers to entry into the market. Mergers among the largest firms in the 1980s and 1990s and the dissolution of Arthur Andersen in 2002 significantly increased concentration among the largest firms, known as the "Big 4." These four firms currently audit over 78 percent of all U.S. public companies and 99 percent of all public company sales."

The study found no evidence of impaired competition to date due to the consolidation. Other findings of the report include:

- A lack of correlation between the consolidation of accounting firms and accounting fees.
- A lack of correlation between audit quality and auditor independence.
- A lack of correlation between accounting firm consolidation and capital formation—with the exception of smaller companies seeking to raise capital.

A limitation of the study noted by the GAO is that it covers the past, which may not be indicative of future changes in the above categories. The GAO also found that smaller accounting firms faced significant barriers to entry—including lack of staff, industry and technical expertise, capital formation, global reach, and reputation—into the large public company audit market.

## .03    Effect of Mandatory Rotation

The second is a study of the potential effects of requiring mandatory rotation of audit firms for publicly traded corporations. This study, issued in November of 2003, determined that "mandatory audit firm rotation may not be the most efficient way to strengthen auditor independence and improve audit quality considering the additional financial costs and the loss of institutional knowledge of the public company's previous auditor of record." The report was based in part on surveys conducted by the GAO of the largest audit firms and Fortune 1000 publicly traded companies. These stakeholders believe the costs of mandatory auditor rotation will exceed the benefits. Most also believe that the current requirements for audit partner rotation, auditor independence, and other reforms, when fully implemented, will sufficiently achieve the intended benefits of mandatory audit firm rotation.

The arguments for and against mandatory audit firm rotation concern whether the independence of a public accounting firm auditing a company's financial statements is adversely affected by a firm's long-term relationship with the client and the desire to retain the client.

**¶26,025.03**

## ¶26,027   AMENDMENTS TO THE SARBANES SENATE BILL

Rather than rely on other laws to punish those who dispose of evidence, shred documents, and otherwise attempt to impede investigations, Congress has spelled out the crime and punishment in amendments to the Sarbanes-Oxley Act.

### .01   The Corporate and Criminal Fraud Accountability Act of 2002

It is a felony to knowingly destroy or create documents to "impede, obstruct or influence" any existing or contemplated federal investigation. Auditors are required to maintain all audit or review work papers for five years.

The statute of limitations on securities fraud claims is extended to the earlier of five years from the fraud or two years after the fraud was discovered, from three years and one year, respectively.

Employees of issuers and accounting firms are extended whistle-blower protection that would prohibit the employer from taking certain actions against employees who lawfully disclose private employer information to, among others, parties in a judicial proceeding involving a fraud claim. Whistle-blowers are also granted a remedy of special damages and attorney's fees.

A new crime for securities fraud has penalties of fines and up to 10 years of imprisonment.

### .03   White-Collar Crime Penalty Enhancement Act of 2002

The provisions include a long list of penalties that have increased the time of imprisonment and amount of fines for specified crimes as follows:

1.  The maximum penalty for mail and wire fraud is increased from 5 to 10 years.
2.  Tampering with a record or otherwise impeding any official proceeding is classified as a crime.
3.  The SEC is given authority to seek a court freeze of extraordinary payments to directors, officers, partners, controlling persons, and agents of employees.
4.  The U.S. Sentencing Commission is to review sentencing guidelines for securities and accounting fraud.
5.  The SEC may prohibit anyone convicted of securities fraud from being an officer or director of any publicly traded company.

6. Financial Statements filed with the SEC must be certified by the CEO and CFO.

7. The certification must state that the financial statements and disclosures fully comply with provisions of the Securities Exchange Act and that they fairly present, in all material respects, the operations and financial condition of the issuer.

8. Maximum penalties for willful and knowing violations of this section are a fine of not more than $500,000 and/or imprisonment of up to five years.

## ¶26,029  ALL ACCOUNTANTS NEED TO BE AWARE OF PROVISIONS

Nonpublic companies' CPAs also need to study the implications of the act. Many of the reforms should probably be considered best practices that will result in new regulations by federal and state agencies.

Unquestionably, this act dramatically affects the entire accounting profession. It impacts not just the largest accounting firms, but also any CPA actively working as an auditor of, or for, a publicly traded company or any CPA working in the financial management area of a public company. In fact, the trickle-down or cascade effect will certainly mean that every accountant should be familiar with the new requirements in the field.

## ¶26,031  ACTIONS RESULTING FROM SARBANES-OXLEY

The SEC released a policy statement in April 2003 reaffirming the Financial Accounting Standards Board as a Designated Private-Sector Standard Setter. The Commission determined that the FASB and its parent organization, the Financial Accounting Foundation (FAF), satisfy the criteria in section 108 of The Sarbanes-Oxley Act of 2002 and, accordingly, FASB's financial accounting and reporting standards are recognized as "generally accepted" for purposes of the federal securities laws. As a result, registrants are required to continue to comply with those standards in preparing financial statements filed with the Commission, unless the Commission directs otherwise. The determination is premised on an expectation that the FASB, and any organization affiliated with it, will address the issues set forth in this statement and any future amendments to this statement, and will continue to serve investors and protect the public interest.

This policy statement updates the SEC's Accounting Series Release 150, issued on December 20, 1973, which expressed the Commission's intent to continue to look to the private sector for leadership in establishing and improving accounting principles and standards through the FASB with the expectation that the body's conclusions will promote the interests of investors.

## ¶26,033    SEC's Relationship with the FASB

The federal securities laws set forth the Commission's broad authority and responsibility to prescribe the methods to be followed in the preparation of accounts and the form and content of financial statements to be filed under those laws, as well as its responsibility to ensure that investors are furnished with other information necessary for investment decisions. To assist it in meeting this responsibility, the Commission historically has looked to private sector standard-setting bodies designated by the accounting profession to develop accounting principles and standards. At the time of the FASB's formation in 1973, the Commission reexamined its policy and formally recognized pronouncements of the FASB that establish and amend accounting principles and standards as "authoritative" in the absence of any contrary determination by the Commission. The SEC concluded at that time that the expertise and resources the private sector could offer to the process of setting accounting standards would be beneficial to investors.

The Sarbanes-Oxley Act amends section 19 of the Securities Act of 1933 to establish criteria that must be met in order for the work product of an accounting standard-setting body to be recognized as "generally accepted." A new subsection indicates that, in carrying out its authority under the Securities Exchange Act of 1934, the Commission may recognize as "generally accepted" for purposes of the federal securities laws any accounting principles established by a standard-setting body that:

- Is organized as a private entity.
- Has, for administrative and operational purposes, a board of trustees serving in the public interest, the majority of whom are not, concurrent with their service on such board, and have not been during the two-year period preceding such service, associated persons of any registered public accounting firm.
- Is funded as provided by the Sarbanes-Oxley Act.
- Has adopted procedures to ensure prompt consideration, by majority vote of its members, of changes to accounting principles necessary to reflect emerging accounting issues and changing business practices.
- Considers, in adopting accounting principles, the need to keep standards current in order to reflect changes in the business environment, the extent to which international convergence on high-quality accounting standards is necessary or appropriate in the public interest and for the protection of investors.

Representatives of the FASB and FAF requested that "[t]he FASB . . . continue to be the designated organization in the private sector for establishing standards of financial accounting and reporting." In reaffirming the FASB's position, the SEC pointed out that the Act does not restrict the Commission's ability to develop accounting principles on its own, nor does it limit the number of private-sector bodies the Commission may recognize.

## .01 Qualification and Recognition of the FASB

In assessing compliance with the provisions of section 108, the SEC evaluated the organizational structure, operations, and procedures of both the FAF and the FASB.

The FAF is composed of independent trustees and is responsible for overseeing, funding, and appointing members of the Board, as well as selecting members of an advisory body. The Commission was informed that the majority of the FAF trustees is not, and has not been during the two-year period preceding their service on the FAF, associated with a public accounting firm. Based on their past relationship with the FAF, the SEC believes that the FAF serves the public interest. Accordingly, the FAF meets the applicable criteria in section 108 of the Sarbanes-Oxley Act for the board of trustees of a recognized private sector accounting standard setter.

The Board is responsible for promulgating financial accounting and reporting standards. It currently has seven members who have expertise in accounting and financial reporting. Members generally are appointed for five- year terms and can be reappointed to one additional term. Board members are full-time employees of the FAF.

## .03 Commission Oversight of FASB Activities

Whereas the SEC consistently has looked to the private sector to set accounting standards, the securities laws, including the Sarbanes-Oxley Act, clearly provide the SEC with authority to set accounting standards for public companies and other entities that file financial statements with the Commission. In addition, recognition of standards set by a private sector standard-setting body as "generally accepted" is only appropriate under section 108 of the Sarbanes-Oxley Act if, among other things, the Commission determines that the private-sector body "has the capacity to assist the Commission in fulfilling the requirements of . . . the Securities Exchange Act . . . because, at a minimum, the standard setting body is capable of improving the accuracy and effectiveness of financial reporting and the protection of investors under the securities laws." As previously noted, section 108 also emphasizes the Commission's responsibility to determine that the standard-setting body:

- Has "procedures to ensure prompt consideration . . . of changes to accounting principles necessary to reflect emerging accounting issues and changing business practices."
- Considers the need to amend standards "to reflect changes in the business environment."
- Considers, to the extent necessary or appropriate, international convergence of accounting standards.

Given the Commission's responsibilities under the securities laws and specific responsibilities under the Sarbanes-Oxley Act to make findings regarding the procedures, capabilities, activities, and results of any designated accounting standards-setting body, the SEC believes that:

- The FAF and FASB should give the SEC timely notice of, and discuss with it, the FAF's intention to appoint a new member of the FAF or FASB. The FAF makes the final determinations regarding the selection of FASB and FAF members. However, to fulfill its statutory responsibilities, the SEC provides the FAF with its views, and expects that they will continue to be taken into consideration in making the final selection. The SEC, FAF, and FASB share the belief that the qualifications and appropriateness of each member of the FAF and the FASB are critical if the FASB is to continue to be a premier private sector standards-setting body.
- The FASB, in its role of "assist[ing] the Commission in fulfilling the requirements of the Securities Exchange Act," should provide timely guidance to public companies, accounting firms, regulators, and others on accounting issues that the Commission considers to be of immediate significance to investors. The Commission and its staff, however, do not prohibit the FASB from also addressing other topics and do not dictate the direction or outcome of specific FASB projects so long as the conclusions reached by the FASB are *in the interest of investor protection.*

  The SEC staff will continue to refer issues to the FASB or one of its affiliated organizations when those issues may call for new, amendments to, or formal interpretations of, accounting standards. The FASB is expected to address such issues in a timely manner. On occasions when the FASB determines that consideration of the issue is inadvisable or that the issue cannot be resolved within the time frame acceptable to the SEC, it is expected that the Board will notify the Commission or its staff promptly, provide its views regarding an appropriate resolution of the issue, and work with the Commission to ensure the protection of investors from misleading or inadequate accounting or disclosures.

  One such affiliated organization is the Emerging Issues Task Force (EITF), which comprises approximately 13 members who serve, generally without compensation, on a part-time basis. EITF members are partners in

¶26,033.03

large, medium-sized, and small accounting firms; business executives; financial analysts and other users of financial statements; and academics. Upon ratification of an EITF consensus by the FASB, the consensus is published as part of the EITF's minutes and may be relied upon by SEC registrants and others in the preparation of financial statements that purport to conform to generally accepted accounting principles.

- Because the SEC and FASB share the common goal of providing investors with the disclosure of meaningful financial information, the Commission anticipates continuation of the collegial working relationship with the FASB. It expects that, when requested to do so, the FASB will make information and staff reasonably available to facilitate the understanding and implementation of a particular FASB standard.

The SEC and its staff intend to work with the FAF and the FASB to ensure that proper oversight procedures and policies are in place to allow the SEC to assess whether the FASB continues to meet the characteristics of an accounting standard setter that are discussed in the Sarbanes-Oxley Act.

## .05  Key FASB Initiatives

As noted earlier, the SEC has treated FASB accounting standards as authoritative since 1973. In order for U.S. accounting standards to remain relevant and to continue to improve, however, the Commission expects the FASB to:

- Consider, in adopting accounting principles, the extent to which international convergence on high-quality accounting standards is necessary or appropriate in the public interest and for the protection of investors, including consideration of moving toward greater reliance on principles-based accounting standards (rather than specifics) whenever it is reasonable to do so. The SEC expects that, during its deliberations of any accounting issue, the FASB will carefully consider international accounting and financial reporting standards that cover that same issue. This has been done in the past and increasingly so in recent years as it becomes clear that it is, indeed, a global economy.
- Take reasonable steps to continue to improve the timeliness with which it completes its projects while satisfying appropriate public notice and comment requirements.
- Continue to be objective in its decision making and to weigh carefully the views of its constituents and the expected benefits and perceived costs of each standard.

## .07 FASB's Independence

Although effective oversight of the FASB's activities is necessary in order for the Commission to carry out its responsibilities under the securities laws, the SEC continues to recognize the importance of the FASB's independence. Therefore, the Commission's determination is that the FASB should continue its role as the preeminent accounting standard setter in the private sector. In performing this role, the SEC feels that the Board must use independent judgment in setting standards and should not be constrained in its exploration and discussion of issues. This is necessary to ensure that the standards developed are free from bias and have the maximum credibility in the business and investing communities.

## .09 Conclusion of the Commission

Based on available information, the SEC has reached several conclusions. The organizational structure, operating activities, and procedures of the FAF and FASB were deemed to meet the criteria in section 108 of the Sarbanes-Oxley Act. As mentioned, one of the statutory criteria is that the recognized accounting body be funded as provided in section 109 of the Act. These funding provisions replace the FAF's funding responsibilities; the FAF will continue to be responsible for the fee requests, including establishing the FASB's budget for review by the Commission each year. The SEC stated that it is providing the endorsement of the FASB so that it can begin to work with the Public Company Accounting Oversight Board to implement these funding mechanisms. The recognition of the FASB by the SEC is in anticipation of, and with the expectation that, this funding will be forthcoming in the near term. There has been a great deal of discussion concerning the source of this funding.

The FASB has the capacity to assist the Commission in fulfilling the requirements of the Securities Act of 1933 and of the Securities Exchange Act of 1934 and is capable of improving both the accuracy and effectiveness of financial reporting and the protection of investors under the securities laws. The FASB does not act alone, but receives input relating to standard setting and interpretation from, among other sources, a standing advisory body, the Financial Accounting Standards Advisory Council (FASAC), which is composed of members from the accounting and business communities, academia, and professional organizations. All share an interest in fostering quality financial reporting and disclosure. FASAC's primary mission is to advise the FASB on its projects and agenda. In addition, the FASB has established a User Advisory Council (UAC) to assist the FASB in raising awareness of how investors and investment professionals, equity and credit analysts, and rating agencies use financial information. The FASB has recruited more than 40 professionals, representing a variety of investment and analytical disciplines, to participate on the UAC. Council meetings will concentrate on major Board projects that could significantly change financial information currently available to users. Early meetings have covered a range of issues including accounting for financial instruments, revenue recognition, and pension accounting.

The standards set by the FASB should be recognized as "generally accepted" under section 108 of the Sarbanes-Oxley Act. (At the same time, the Sarbanes-Oxley Act states, "Nothing in this Act, . . . shall be construed to impair or limit the authority of the Commission to establish accounting principles or standards for purposes of enforcement of the securities laws.")

As required under the securities laws, including the Sarbanes-Oxley Act, the Commission will monitor the FASB's procedures, qualifications, capabilities, activities, and results, as well as the FAF's and FASB's ongoing compliance with the expectations and views expressed in this policy statement.

The SEC will issue an appropriate revision of this policy statement if it determines that the FAF or FASB no longer meets the statutory criteria or expectations discussed in the policy statement, or if it is otherwise necessary or appropriate to do so. The occasions when the Commission has not accepted a particular FASB standard have been extremely rare because of its past and continuing recognition and support of the Board's independence. The Commission and its staff do not prohibit the FASB from addressing a particular topic and do not dictate the direction or outcome of specific FASB projects provided that the conclusions reached by the FASB are in the interest of investor protection.

## ¶26,035    SEC ADOPTS ATTORNEY CONDUCT RULE UNDER SARBANES-OXLEY ACT

In January 2003, the SEC adopted final rules to implement section 307 of the Sarbanes-Oxley Act by setting "standards of professional conduct for attorneys appearing and practicing before the Commission in any way in the representation of issuers."

In addition, the Commission approved an extension of the comment period on the "noisy withdrawal" provisions of the original proposed rule and publication for comment of an alternative proposal to it. There was much concern expressed regarding the effects of the original "noisy withdrawal" proposal. The American Bar Association was particularly concerned about several issues, including the client confidentiality aspects of the provisions.

On November 6, 2002, the Commission voted to propose the new standards of professional conduct. That proposal more specifically defined the role and activities of a lawyer who is *appearing and practicing before the Commission* in the representation of an issuer. Attorneys were required to report evidence of a material violation "up the ladder" within an issuer. In addition, under certain circumstances, these provisions permitted or required attorneys to effect a so-called "noisy withdrawal" — that is, to withdraw from representing an issuer and notify the Commission that they have withdrawn for professional reasons.

## .01 Provisions of the Rule

The rules adopted by the Commission:

- Require an attorney to report evidence of a material violation, determined according to an objective standard, "up the ladder" within the issuer to the chief legal counsel or the chief executive officer of the company or the equivalent.
- Require an attorney, if the chief legal counsel or the chief executive officer of the company does not respond appropriately to the evidence, to report the evidence to the audit committee, another committee of independent directors, or the full board of directors.
- Clarify that the rules cover attorneys who are providing legal services to an issuer, who have an attorney-client relationship with the issuer, and who are aware that documents they are preparing or assisting in preparing will be filed with or submitted to the Commission.
- Provide that foreign attorneys who are not admitted in the United States and who do not advise clients regarding U.S. law would *not* be covered by the rule, whereas foreign attorneys who provide legal advice regarding U.S. law would be covered to the extent they are appearing and practicing before the Commission unless they provide that advice in conjunction with U.S. counsel.
- Allow an issuer to establish a "qualified legal compliance committee" (QLCC) as an alternative procedure for reporting evidence of a material violation. Such a QLCC would consist of at least one member of the issuer's audit committee (or an equivalent committee of independent directors) and two or more independent board members, and would have the responsibility, among other things, to recommend that an issuer implement an appropriate response to evidence of a material violation. One way in which an attorney could satisfy the rule's reporting obligation is by reporting evidence of a material violation to the issuer's QLCC.
- Allow an attorney, without the consent of an issuer client, to reveal confidential information related to his or her representation to the extent the attorney reasonably believes it is necessary in order to:

—Prevent the issuer from committing a material violation likely to cause substantial financial injury to the financial interests or property of the issuer or investors.

—Prevent the issuer from committing an illegal act.

—Rectify the consequences of a material violation or illegal act in which the attorney's services have been used.

- State that these Commission rules govern in the event the rules conflict with state law, but will not preempt the ability of a state to impose *more rigorous* obligations on attorneys that are not counter to the SEC rules.

- Affirmatively state that the rules do not create a private cause of action and that authority to enforce compliance with the rules is vested exclusively with the Commission.

## .03   Definition Modified

Further, the final rules modify the definition of the term "evidence of a material violation," which defines the trigger for an attorney's obligation to report up the ladder within an issuer's ranks. The revised definition confirms that the SEC intends an *objective* triggering standard, rather than a *subjective* one.

This "trigger" must involve credible evidence, based on which it would be unreasonable, under the circumstances, for a prudent and competent attorney not to conclude that it is reasonably likely that a material violation *has occurred, is ongoing, or is about to occur.*

# Chapter 27

# Public Company Accounting Oversight Board

## CONTENTS

# ¶27,000  OVERVIEW

The Securities and Exchange Commission had taken another step toward improving the implementation of the Sarbanes-Oxley investor protection law in July 2006. At that point, it published a Concept Release as a prelude to its forthcoming guidance for management in assessing a company's internal controls for financial reporting.

Following its May 10, 2006, Roundtable devoted to Sarbanes-Oxley Section 404 implementation concerns, the Commission had issued a roadmap setting out a plan for improving guidance. The Concept Release, issued July 11, 2006, discussed below, is one of the milestones on that roadmap. It brought the SEC one step closer to issuing guidance for management that has been lacking since the law was enacted in 2002.

In early October 2006, the SEC announced that they were planning to consider, at an open meeting of the Commission to be held on Dec. 13, 2006, recommendations regarding Section 404 of the Sarbanes-Oxley Act of 2002. The SEC explained that the proposed guidance to management is an important next step in making Section 404 of the Sarbanes-Oxley Act cost-effective and risk-based. At that time the Commission felt that this initiative, as well as foreign private issuer deregistration, would be addressed before year-end.

# ¶27,001  RELIEF FROM SECTION 404 COMPLIANCE FOR SMALLER PUBLIC COMPANIES, FOREIGN PRIVATE ISSUERS

The Securities and Exchange Commission issued two releases in August 2006 to grant smaller public companies and many foreign private issuers further relief from compliance with Section 404 of the Sarbanes-Oxley Act of 2002. The relief is in furtherance of the steps for Sarbanes-Oxley implementation announced on May 17, 2006, and includes some new initiatives not previously announced.

The July 11, 2006, publication of a Concept Release solicited public comment on guidance for management the SEC planned to issue to assist companies in assessing their internal controls over financial reporting. The Commission has exerted continuing effort to be sensitive and responsive to the particular needs of smaller public companies and foreign private issuers to minimize the burdens that Section 404 might cause/ have caused them from the very beginning.

By offering further relief for smaller companies and most foreign issuers, these actions allow time for the Commission and the PCAOB to redesign Section 404 implementation in a way that is efficient and cost effective for investors, according to the SEC.

A summary of the subjects of the two releases appears below:

## .01  Relief from Section 404 Compliance Dates for Smaller Companies (Non-Accelerated Filers)

The Commission is proposing to grant relief to smaller public companies by extending the date by which non-accelerated filers must begin providing a report by management assessing the effectiveness of the company's internal control over financial reporting. The initial compliance date for these companies would be moved from fiscal years ending on or after July 15, 2007, until fiscal years ending on or after Dec. 15, 2007. The Commission also proposes to extend the date by which non-accelerated filers must begin to comply with the Section 404(b) requirement to provide an auditor's attestation report on internal control over financial reporting in their annual reports.

This deadline would be moved to the first annual report for a fiscal year ending on or after Dec. 15, 2008. This proposed extension would result in all non-accelerated filers being required to complete only the management's portion of the internal control requirements in their first year of compliance with the requirements. This proposal is intended to provide cost savings and efficiency opportunities to smaller public companies and to assist them as they prepare to comply fully with Section 404's reporting requirements. This proposed extension will provide these issuers and their auditors an additional year to consider, and adapt to, the changes in Auditing Standard No. 2 that the Commission and the Public Company Accounting Oversight Board intend to make, as well as the guidance for management the SEC intends to issue, to improve the efficiency of the Section 404(b) auditor attestation report process.

Approximately 44% of the domestic companies and 38% of the foreign private issuers that file periodic reports with the Commission are non-accelerated filers.

## .03  Relief from Section 404(b) Compliance Date for Certain Foreign Private Issuers

The Commission is granting relief from Section 404(b) compliance for foreign private issuers that are accelerated filers (but not large accelerated filers), that file their annual reports on Form 20-F or 40-F. These companies will have their compliance deadline extended for an additional year, so that they will not begin complying with the Section 404(b) requirement to provide an auditor's attestation report on internal control over financial reporting in their annual reports until fiscal years ending on or after July 15, 2007.

This group of issuers will be required to comply only with the Section 404 requirement to include management's report in the Form 20-F or 40-F annual report filed for their first fiscal year ending on or after July 15, 2006. They will not need to comply with the requirement to provide the registered public accounting firm's attestation report until they file a Form 20-F or 40-F annual report for a fiscal year ending on or after July 15, 2007.

The Commission's data indicate that about 23% of the approximately 1,200 foreign private issuers that are subject to the Exchange Act reporting requirements are accelerated filers that will receive the one-year extension of the compliance dates for the Section 404(b) auditor attestation requirement. Because approximately 38% of foreign private issuers are non-accelerated filers that will benefit from the steps outlined in Item 1 above, over 60% of the community of foreign private issuers will receive a measure of relief as a result of the actions we're announcing today. The Commission's actions today do not change the date by which a foreign private issuer that is a large accelerated filer must comply with both the Section 404(a) and (b) requirements. These filers are required to include both a report by management and an attestation report by the issuer's registered accounting firm on internal control over financial reporting in their Form 20-F or 40-F filed for a fiscal year ending on or after July 15, 2006.

## .05 Proposed Transition Relief for Newly Public Companies

In the same release in which it proposes an extension of the Section 404 compliance dates for non-accelerated filers, the Commission also proposes a transition period for newly public companies. This transition relief would apply to any company that has become public through an IPO or a registered exchange offer, or that otherwise becomes subject to the Exchange Act reporting requirements. It would include a foreign private issuer that is listing on a U.S. exchange for the first time. To provide meaningful relief to companies that are new to the U.S. markets and our reporting requirements, the Commission is proposing to amend its rules so that a company would not be required to provide either a management assessment or an auditor attestation report until it has previously filed one annual report with the Commission.

This relief is being proposed in recognition of the fact that preparation of a newly public company's first annual report can be a time and resource intensive process that may quickly follow an IPO or initial listing. By not requiring the Section 404 reports until a newly public company files its second annual report with the SEC, the Commission hopes to increase the efficiency and effectiveness with which those companies ultimately meet their Section 404 compliance obligations.

The SEC was well aware of the fact that the Section 404 reporting requirements impose a special burden on foreign private issuers, smaller companies and newly public companies. Because these companies play an important role in U.S. capital markets, the Commission believes these releases illustrate their commitment to improving the efficiency and effectiveness of Section 404 implementation for them.

They believe the proposed transition relief for newly public companies should enhance the attractiveness and cost-effectiveness of participating in the markets both for companies contemplating IPO's and for foreign companies considering listing in the U.S. for the first time, without sacrificing important investor protections.

## ¶27,003  SARBANES-OXLEY 404 IMPROVEMENTS LAID OUT AT MAY 2006 ROUNDTABLE

At the May Roundtable, it came as no surprise that participants feel that while Section 404 had produced benefits, its implementation had been unduly costly. The Commission also received specific feedback about issues that remain to be addressed, and actions that the SEC and the Public Company Accounting Oversight Board could take to make the internal control assessment and auditing more efficient and more effective.

The Advisory Committee on Smaller Public Companies reported, following a year-long study, that companies, which have not yet undertaken the process, have special concerns about both costs and procedures. The guidance for management, which is the subject of the Concept Release, is intended to assist in dealing with all of these issues and concerns.

The SEC announced that their goal is to develop practical guidance for companies to help improve the reliability of financial reporting and to make Section 404 implementation more efficient and cost effective for investors. The public comment received in response to the Concept Release is expected to help the SEC write meaningful guidance for all public companiesy — large, small, foreign, and domestic — for the benefit of all of their shareholders.

The Commission anticipates that the forthcoming guidance for management will cover at least these areas:

- Identification of risks to financial statement account and disclosure accuracy and the related internal controls that address the risks, including how management might use company-level controls to address the risk.
- Objectives of the evaluation procedures and methods or approaches available to management to gather evidence to support its assessment.
- Factors management should consider in determining the nature, timing, and extent of its evaluation procedures.
- Documentation requirements, including overall objectives of the documentation and factors that might influence documentation requirements.

The Concept Release seeks feedback on each of these topics and on whether guidance should be provided in other areas as well.

According to the Commission, quality financial reporting is a critical cornerstone to our capital markets, and investors are entitled to rely upon it. Section 404 has a key role to play in enhancing the reliability of public companies' financial statements. It is expected that the issuance of the Concept Release will garner useful and broad-based public comment that can help to improve the implementation of Section 404 for both issuers and investors.

The resulting guidance is expected to help companies further improve and streamline their processes for assessing the effectiveness of internal controls. The intent is for the guidance to be flexible and scalable, so that it will assist companies of all sizes.

The Commission continues to move forward on the other steps it announced in May, and will be sensitive and responsive to the particular needs of smaller issuers, both domestic and foreign, while seeking to reduce costs and facilitate a more efficient and effective process to minimize the burdens that Section 404 may impose. The Commission and its staff will also continue to work with the Public Company Accounting Oversight Board on revisions to Auditing Standard No. 2, which implements Section 404 for auditors, so that it will more efficiently and workably protect investors in companies of all sizes.

## ¶27,007  OVERSIGHT BOARD CHARGED WITH RESTORATION OF INVESTORS' FAITH

Under the Sarbanes-Oxley Act, the Public Company Accounting Oversight Board (PCAOB) was charged with the responsibility for all aspects of supervision of auditors who serve public clients, subject to the Securities and Exchange Commission's (SEC's) oversight. With the auditing profession's image in tatters and investors' confidence almost nonexistent, the goal of the Board is to improve the quality of the independent audit in an attempt to restore the investors' faith in the system.

For whatever reasons, the self-regulatory system did not work; therefore, there will, henceforth, be close supervision and regulation from without. The Oversight Board's statutory responsibilities include:

- Registering CPAs and public accounting firms that prepare audit reports for public companies. This was required to be within 180 days of the Commission's determination that the Oversight Board was operational (April 25, 2003).
- Establishing auditing, quality control, ethics, and independence standards for auditors and audit firms.
- Conducting inspections, investigations, and disciplinary proceedings of public accounting firms and their associated persons that work on public companies.

- Enforcing compliance with the rules of the Oversight Board and professional standards.

## ¶27,009   VARIED RESPONSIBILITIES ASSIGNED TO THE PCAOB

The Sarbanes-Oxley Act established the Public Company Accounting Oversight Board, to be organized as a nonprofit corporation, with SEC administration and oversight. The PCAOB's mission is to oversee the audits of public companies and related matters. Its more specific tasks as described in the Act include:

- *Auditor registration.* All auditors of public companies must register with the PCAOB, identify public audit clients, identify all accountants associated with those clients, list fees earned for audit and nonaudit services, explain their audit quality control procedures, and identify all criminal, civil, administrative, and disciplinary proceedings against the firm or any of its associated persons in connection with an audit.
- *Inspection of CPA firms.* The PCAOB must inspect all CPA firms that audit public companies to assess compliance with the law, SEC regulations, rules established by the PCAOB, and professional standards. Firms that audit more than 100 public companies will be inspected annually. Firms that audit 100 or fewer public companies must be inspected at least once every three years. If violations are found, the PCAOB must take disciplinary action.
- *Audit, quality control, ethics, and independence standards.* The PCAOB must adopt audit, quality control, ethics, and independence standards. In doing so, the PCAOB may look to standards established by recognized professional organizations such as the AICPA.
- *Quality control.* The PCAOB's quality control standards must require that registered firms properly supervise all work, monitor compliance with ethics and independence rules, and establish internal systems for consultation, professional development, and client acceptance and retention.
- *Restrictions on services to audit clients.* The Act restricts consulting work that auditors can do for their audit clients. The PCAOB may enumerate additional prohibited services to those covered in the Act.

## ¶27,011   FINAL RULES FOR INSPECTIONS

Following through with the responsibility for the inspection of CPA firms, the PCAOB adopted final rules relating to inspections of registered public accounting firms in October 2003. These rules will not take effect unless approved by the Securities and Exchange Commission.

¶27,011

Section 104(a) of the Sarbanes-Oxley Act directs the Board to conduct a continuing program of inspections to assess the degree to which each registered public accounting firm and its associated persons are complying with the Act, the Board's and the Commission's rules, and professional standards in connection with audits, audit reports, and related matters involving U.S. public companies.

Consistent with the Act, the Board's rules subject registered public accounting firms to such regular and special inspections as the Board may from time to time conduct. The rules establish a schedule for regular inspections that is consistent with Section 104(b)(1) of the Act, including annual inspections for firms that do the largest volume of audit work and at least triennial inspections for other firms that do some volume of audit work. Special inspections are not subject to a schedule and would be conducted as necessary or appropriate to address issues that come to the Board's attention.

## .01 Some Early Questions Being Answered

Some of these questions were answered, pending SEC approval, when the final inspection rules, *Inspections of Registered Public Accounting Firms*, were announced in October 2003. These rules establish a procedural framework for the PCAOB's inspection program as directed under Section 104(a) of the Sarbanes-Oxley Act. The rules provide for:

- Annual inspections for firms issuing audit reports for more than 100 issuers during the prior calendar year.
- Triennial inspections for firms that issued or played a substantial role in the preparation of audit reports for 1 to 100 issuers during any of the three prior calendar years.
- Special inspections to be conducted as necessary.
- Reporting information of possible violations of law or professional standards to the SEC, state regulatory authorities, and other regulators and law enforcement authorities.
- A process by which a firm may submit written comments on a draft inspection report prior to issuance of a final inspection report.
- A portion of the final inspection report related to criticisms or potential defects of a firm's quality control system to be made public if not resolved with the PCAOB within 12 months of the report's issuance.
- Issuance of general reports discussing criticisms or potential defects of a firm's quality control system that do not identify the firm unless the information was previously made public.

## ¶27,012  LOOKING BACK AT RESULTS OF FIRST YEAR OF OPERATION UNDER SARBANES-OXLEY

Two messages came through clearly: one that the Commission had anticipated and applauded, the other that it appears to discount to a great extent. Much of the discussion revolved around two points:

- The Commission has been gratified by the fact that many, even most, of those involved realize that compliance with Section 404 is producing benefits that include a heightened focus on internal controls at the top levels of public companies. The Commission's hope is that this focus will produce better financial reporting. The purpose of the legislation was to provide a more honest, transparent in-depth picture of an entity's financial condition, and to reassure investors wary of financial reports after the Enron debacle.

- To no one's surprise, much of the discussion was about the significant expenditures required for implementation in the first year. The Commission believes that although a portion of the costs probably reflects start-up expenses from the new requirement, it also appears that some nontrivial costs may have been unnecessary, as a result of excessive, duplicative, or misfocused efforts.

In response to the concerns raised about the costs, the SEC staff was asked at the end of the roundtable attended by issuers, accountants, auditors, and investors, to consider whether additional guidance and clarification of certain issues was appropriate. The staff responded in May 2005 with a "Staff Statement on Management's Report on Internal Control Over Financial Reporting" to provide such guidance. The Commission believes that the most important point made by the guidance is that it is management's responsibility to determine the *form and level* of controls appropriate for each company and to tailor their assessment and the testing accordingly.

### .01  Various Forms of Guidance and Advice Available

The SEC also feels that registered public accounting firms should recognize that there is a *zone of reasonable conduct* by companies that should be recognized as acceptable in the implementation of Section 404. The SEC staff guidance complements the guidance that the PCAOB attempted to provide with respect to the application of its Auditing Standard No. 2, *An Audit of Internal Control over Financial Reporting Performed in Conjunction with an Audit of the Financial Statements.*

## .03  Commission Offers Suggestions for Easing Implementation

In addition, because of the importance the SEC places on effective and efficient implementation of Section 404, the following points were itemized:

1. Almost all of the significant complaints related not to the Act or the rules and auditing standards implementing Section 404, but to a mechanical, and even overly cautious, way in which those rules and standards had been applied in many cases. Both management and external auditors must bring *reasoned judgment* and a top-down, risk-based approach to the 404 compliance process. A one-size-fits-all, bottom-up, check-the-box approach that treats all controls equally is less likely to improve internal controls and financial reporting than reasoned, professional judgment focused on reasonable-as opposed to absolute—assurance.

2. In the future, the SEC expects the internal control audit to be better integrated with the audit of a company's financial statements. If management and auditors integrate the two audits, both internal and external costs of Section 404 compliance should fall for most companies.

3. Internal controls over financial reporting should reflect the nature and size of the company to which they relate. Particular attention should be paid to making sure that implementation of Section 404 is appropriately tailored to the operations of smaller companies. Auditors should not use standardized "checklists" that may not reflect an allocation of audit work weighted toward high-risk areas (and weighted against unnecessary audit focus in low-risk areas).

4. The SEC believes in the use of a top-down approach that begins with company-level controls, to identify for further testing only those accounts and processes that are, in fact, relevant to internal control over financial reporting, and use the risk assessment required by the standard to eliminate from further consideration those accounts that have only a remote likelihood of containing a material misstatement.

5. The Commission believes that frequent, frank dialogue among management, auditors, and audit committees with the goal of improving internal controls and the financial reports upon which investors rely will not constitutes a violation of the independence rules.

## .05  SEC Urges Continued Focus on "Getting It Right"

The SEC believes that the entire financial reporting community, including investors, auditors, management, and regulators, shares the common goal of improving the reliability of financial reporting and the information available to the market. With the experience of the first round of Section 404 implementation, the Commission urges continued focus on the lessons learned and ways to improve the process. The belief is that Section 404 is too important not to get right, but getting it right requires both effective and efficient implementation.

## ¶27,013  STEPS FOR SARBANES-OXLEY IMPLEMENTATION

In May 2006 the Securities and Exchange Commission announced a series of actions it intended to take to improve the implementation of the Section 404 internal control requirements of the Sarbanes-Oxley Act of 2002. These actions included issuing SEC guidance for companies and working with the Public Company Accounting Oversight Board (PCAOB) on revisions of its internal control auditing standard. Their actions are based on extensive analysis and commentary in recent months from investors, companies, auditors, and others.

The expected actions included SEC inspections of PCAOB efforts to improve Section 404 oversight and another, brief postponement of the Section 404 requirements for the smallest company filers. However, the SEC emphasized that ultimately all public companies will be required to comply with the internal control reporting requirements of Section 404.

The steps announced in May were designed to further improve the reliability of financial statements and to protect investors better while making the Section 404 process more efficient and cost effective. It was also of importance to ascertain whether PCAOB inspection process is succeeding in increasing the efficiency and cost-effectiveness of the audit process.

At that time, the Commission listed a variety of sources from which they had obtained information concerning the operation and effects, both good and not-so-good, of Section 404, including:

- The May 10, 2006, SEC Roundtable on Second-Year Experiences with Internal Control Reporting and Auditing Provisions.
- Written comments received in connection with the Roundtable.
- The April 23, 2006, Report of the SEC Advisory Committee on Smaller Public Companies.
- The April 2006 Report from the U.S. Government Accountability Office (GAO) entitled *Sarbanes-Oxley Act, Consideration of Key Principles Needed in Addressing Implementation for Smaller Public Companies.*
- Feedback from issuers, auditors, investors, and others since the Sarbanes-Oxley internal control reporting requirements went into effect.

The actions the Commission announced in May represent key steps toward addressing issues raised by participants involved in the critical process of reporting to investors on the effectiveness of companies' internal control over financial reporting, according to the SEC.

## .01   Actions the Commission Expects to Take

The Commission has received many requests for additional guidance for management on how to complete its assessment of internal control over financial reporting, as required by Section 404(a) of the Sarbanes-Oxley Act. To prepare for the issuance of management guidance, the Commission intends to take the following steps:

- *Concept Release and Opportunity for Public Comment.* The Commission expects to issue a Concept Release covering a variety of issues that might be the subject of Commission guidance for management. With the Concept Release, the Commission solicited  views on the management assessment process to ensure that the guidance the Commission ultimately proposes addresses the needs and concerns of all public companies. The Commission is also  seeking input on the appropriate role of outside auditors in connection with the management assessment required by Section 404(a) of Sarbanes-Oxley, and on the manner in which outside auditors provide the attestation  required by Section 404(b), to assist in the consideration of possible alternatives to the current approach.

- *Consideration of Additional Guidance from COSO.* The Commission has long been supportive of the Committee of Sponsoring Organizations of the Treadway Commission (COSO) as it works to provide guidance on COSO's 1992 Internal Control - Integrated Framework to address the needs of smaller companies. The Commission anticipates that this forthcoming guidance will help organizations of all sizes to understand and apply the control framework better as it relates to internal control over financial reporting. As the SEC develops guidance for management on how to assess its internal control over financial reporting, they will consider  the extent to which the additional guidance that COSO provides is useful to smaller public companies in completing their Section 404(a) assements.

- *Issuance of Guidance.* Commentary submitted to the Commission has suggested that management assessments under Section 404 have not fully reflected the top-down, risk-based approach the Commission intended. Building from the information gathered in response to the Concept Release, and from the anticipated COSO guidance, the Commission currently anticipates that it will issue guidance to management to assist in its performance of a top-down, risk-based assessment of internal control over financial reporting. To ensure that this guidance is of help to non-accelerated filers and smaller public companies, the Commission intends that this future guidance will be scalable and responsive to their individual circumstances. The guidance will also be sensitive to the fact that many companies have already invested substantial resources to establish and document programs and procedures to perform their assessments over the last few years. The form of the guidance has yet to be determined.

## .02  Revisions to Auditing Standard No. 2.

The PCAOB announced in May 2006 that it intends to propose revisions to its Auditing Standard No. 2, An Audit of Internal Control Over Financial Reporting Performed in Conjunction with an Audit of Financial Statements. Any final revision of AS No. 2 would be subject to SEC approval. For the provisions proposed, see the section, "Audit Standard Setting" below.

## .03  SEC Oversight of PCAOB Inspection Program

The PCAOB announced on May 1, 2006, that it would focus its 2006 inspections on whether auditors have achieved cost-saving efficiencies in the audits they have performed under AS No. 2, and on whether auditors have followed the guidance that the PCAOB issued in May and November 2005 urging them to do so. As part of the Commission's oversight of the PCAOB, the Commission staff inspects aspects of the PCAOB's operations, including its inspection program. Among other things, upon completion of the PCAOB's 2006 inspections, the staff will examine whether the PCAOB inspections of audit firms have been effective in encouraging implementation of the principles outlined in the PCAOB's May 1, 2006, statement.

## ¶27,015  AUDIT STANDARD SETTING

With regard to standard setting, the first question was whether the Board would set its own standards or adopt standards recommended by an advisory group. Regardless of that decision, any new rules would require SEC approval. Effectively ending the era of self-regulation for the public accounting and auditing industry, the PCAOB unanimously voted to review the existing auditing standards and to write new ones. This, in effect, replaces the Auditing Standards Board (ASB) of the American Institute of Certified Public Accountants (AICPA) as the highest authority for standard-setting guidance of public companies. The Sarbanes-Oxley Act had allowed the PCAOB the option of delegating that authority to an industry group such as the ASB, but the PCAOB decided to accept the responsibility of developing its own guidance. Accounting, investment, and financial experts were asked to assist in developing the new auditing standards.

In the interim—or transition period—the SEC issued an order that the adoption of interim professional standards be consistent with the requirements of the Act and the federal securities laws. These interim professional standards were considered necessary for use in connection with the audits of public companies and for the protection of investors.

Under the Sarbanes-Oxley Act, the PCAOB's duties include the establishment of auditing, quality control, ethics, independence, and other standards relating to public company audits. In connection with this standard-setting responsibility, section 103 of the Act provides that the PCAOB may adopt any portion of any statement of auditing standards or other professional standards that the PCAOB determines satisfy the requirements of the Act and that were proposed by one or more professional groups of accountants as initial or transitional standards, to the extent the PCAOB determines necessary. This section of the Act also provides that any such initial or transitional standards must be separately approved by the Commission at the time it makes the determination required by the Act, without regard to the procedures that otherwise would apply to Commission approval of PCAOB rules.

On April 16, 2003, the Board adopted some pre-existing standards as interim standards to be used on an initial, transitional basis. PCAOB Rules 3200T, 3300T, 3400T, 3500T, and 3600T describe the standards that the Board adopted and required registered public accounting firms and their associated persons to comply with as the interim standards to the extent *not superseded or amended by the Board.* Ifany one of the new Standards addresses a subject matter that also is addressed in the interim standards, the affected portion of the interim standard should be considered superseded or effectively amended.

The Board also has made certain conforming amendments to the interim standards to reflect the effect of the adoption of PCAOB standards. The present electronic version of the interim standards reflects those amendments. If and when the interim standards are used, it is the responsibility of the CPA firm and its associated persons (and anyone else using the interim standards) to determine whether a particular interim standard has been superseded or amended.

The Board cautions that the electronic version of the interim standards may be updated from time to time to correct typographical or other technical errors. Within a year and one-half, five final standards were issued that take precedence over at least some provisions of these interim standards:

- Auditing Standard No. 1 modifies the auditor's report.
- Auditing Standard No. 2 deals with internal controls reporting.
- Auditing Standard No. 3 sets forth the rules for audit documentation.
- Rule 3100 dictates auditor compliance with PCAOB Professional Practice Standards.
- Rule 3101 deals with certain terms used in the Auditing and Professional Practice Standards.

The three PCAOB Auditing Standards supersede the applicable sections of temporary rules and the two Rules relate to them. Another measure, Auditing Standard No. 4. was added in 2006.

¶27,015

## .01  Auditing Standard No. 1

Effective February 5, 2004, PCAOB Auditing Standard No. 1, *References in Auditors' Reports to Standards of the Public Company Accounting Oversight Board*, required that auditors' reports on audits and other engagements relating to public companies include a reference stating that the engagement was performed *in accordance with the standards of the PCAOB*. This replaces previous reference to generally accepted auditing standards (GAAS). Therefore, auditors are to *cease referring to GAAS in audit reports* relating to financial statements of issuers of public companies and instead refer to "standards of the Public Company Accounting Oversight Board (United States)." However, it should be noted that the Standard is applicable *only* to auditors' engagements that are governed by PCAOB rules.

PCAOB Rule 3100 requires registered public accounting firms and their associated persons to comply with the applicable auditing and related professional practice standard established or adopted by the PCAOB. Because of this, according to the Securities and Exchange Commission, and because the PCAOB has adopted interim standards incorporating generally accepted auditing standards, references to GAAS *and* standards established by the AICPA are now *superseded*.

As noted, Standard No. 1 requires that an auditor's report issued in connection with any engagement performed in accordance with the auditing and related professional practice standards of the PCAOB state that it was performed in accordance with "the standards of the Public Company Accounting Oversight Board (United States)." According to the SEC, given the possible confusion between Commission rules and staff guidance references in the federal securities laws, on the one hand, and the PCAOB's rules, on the other, the Commission decided some guidance was necessary. Therefore, they published interpretive guidance based upon comments and queries received prior to their approval of the Standard. With that approval, references in SEC rules and staff guidance and in the federal securities laws to GAAS or to specific standards under GAAS, as they relate to issuers, should be understood to mean the standards of the PCAOB plus any applicable rules of the Commission.

Although the PCAOB has indicated that Auditing Standard No. 1 supersedes references to GAAS, GAAP, "auditing standards generally accepted in the United States of America," and "standards established by the AICPA," this Standard *does not* supersede other SEC rules or regulations.

- **Rule 3200T, Interim Auditing Standards.** In connection with the preparation or issuance of any audit report, a registered public accounting firm and its associated persons must comply with generally accepted auditing standards, as described in the AICPA Auditing Standards Board's (ASB's) Statement of Auditing Standards (SAS) 95 (AU 150) and as in existence on April 16, 2003.

Public accounting firms were not required to be registered with the Board until October 23, 2003. The Board intended that the Interim Auditing Standards apply to public accounting firms that would be required to be registered after the mandatory registration date and to associated persons of those firms, as if those firms had already registered.

- **Rule 3300T, Interim Attestation Standards.** In connection with an engagement described in the ASB's Statements on Standards for Attestation Engagements (SSAE), and related to the preparation or issuance of audit reports for issuers, a registered public accounting firm and its associated persons must comply with these standards and related interpretations and Statements of Position in existence on April 16, 2003.

- **Rule 3400T, Interim Quality Control Standards.** A registered public accounting firm and its associated persons should comply with quality control standards as described in the ASB's Statements on Quality Control Standards (SQCSs) and in existence on April 16, 2003, and with the AICPA SEC Practice Section's Requirements of Membership in existence on April 16, 2003.

- **Rule 3500T, Interim Ethics Standards.** In connection with the preparation or issuance of any audit report, a registered public accounting firm and its associated persons are to comply with ethics standards as described in the AICPA's Code of Professional Conduct Rule 102 and interpretations and rulings in existence on April 16, 2003.

- **Rule 3600T, Interim Independence Standards.** In connection with the preparation or issuance of any audit report, a registered public accounting firm and its associated persons are required to comply with independence standards as described in the AICPA's Code of Professional Conduct Rule 101 and interpretations and rulings in existence on April 16, 2003, as well as with Standards 1, 2, and 3 and Interpretations 99-1, 00-1, and 00-2 of the Independence Standards Board. (The Board's Interim Independence Standards do not supersede the Commission's auditor independence rules. Therefore, to the extent that a provision of the Commission's rule is more restrictive or less restrictive than the Board's Interim Independence Standards, a registered public accounting firm must comply with the more restrictive rule.)

Each of the interim standards described would remain in effect until modified or superseded either by PCAOB action approved by the Commission as provided in the Act or by Commission action pursuant to its independent authority under the federal securities laws and those rules and regulations.

## .03 Auditing Standard No. 2

Auditing Standard No. 2, *An Audit of Internal Control Over Financial Reporting Performed in Conjunction with an Audit of Financial Statements,* was approved by the PCAOB on March 9, 2004, and approved and adopted by the SEC on June 17, 2004. Auditing Standard No. 2 focuses on the elements of the audit process that should be of particular importance to management and audit committee members, so as to give such persons an overview of the process and an of idea of what will be expected of management during the process. It also highlights the PCAOB's (and indirectly the SEC's) views with respect to:

- The oversight responsibilities of the audit committee and the implications of ineffective oversight.
- The advantages to establishing an effective, competent, and objective internal control function.
- The implications of disagreements about whether management has made appropriate public disclosure of changes in internal control over financial reporting.
- The disclosure implications of a finding of a material weakness.

Alternatives are available to management to provide additional disclosure (over and above that required in its report) concerning internal control over financial reporting.

***Background of Standard No. 2.***    Section 404(a) of the Act and related rules adopted by the SEC require each reporting company (other than a registered investment company) to include a report of management on the company's internal control over financial reporting in its annual report. This measure is a direct attack upon the plea of ignorance put forth by many of the upper echelon of management in the recent scandals. This report is to cover the following:

1. It must state management's responsibility for establishing and maintaining an adequate internal control structure and procedures for financial reporting.
2. It must also contain an assessment, as of the end of the company's most recent fiscal year, of the *effectiveness* of the company's internal control over financial reporting and procedures for financial reporting.
3. Each reporting company's independent auditor must attest to management's assessment of the company's internal control over financial reporting.
4. Each reporting company is to file the independent auditor's attestation report as part of the company's annual report.
5. Management is required to evaluate any change in the company's internal control over financial reporting that occurred during the relevant fiscal period that has materially affected or is reasonably likely to materially affect, the company's internal control over financial reporting.

The attestation and report required by Section 404(b) must be made in accordance with standards for attestation engagements "issued or adopted" by the PCAOB. Auditing Standard No. 2 is the PCAOB's standard for this purpose.

## .05 Auditing Standard No. 3

In August 2004 the SEC approved PCAOB Auditing Standard No. 3, *Audit Documentation*, which requires registered public accounting firms to prepare and maintain, for at least seven years, audit documentation in sufficient detail to support the conclusions reached in the auditor's report. The Standard also imposes unconditional responsibility on the principal auditor to obtain certain audit documentation from another auditor (who, although not named in the audit report, has performed part of the audit work used by the principal auditor) prior to the audit report release date. The Standard was effective for fiscal years ending on or after November 15, 2004, for all engagements conducted in accordance with PCAOB standards (audits of financial statements, audits of internal control over financial reporting and reviews of interim financial information).

At the same time that it approved the proposed Auditing Standard No. 3, the SEC also approved an Amendment to Interim Auditing Standards—AU sec. 543, *Part of Audit Performed by Other Independent Auditors.* (This measure is discussed below.)

Auditing Standard No. 3 establishes general requirements for documentation the auditor should prepare and retain in connection with engagements conducted pursuant to the standards of the PCAOB. Such engagements include:

- An audit of financial statements.
- An audit of internal control over financial reporting.
- A review of interim financial information.

This standard does not replace specific documentation requirements of other standards of the PCAOB.

***Documentation Requirement.*** The auditor must prepare audit documentation in connection with each engagement conducted pursuant to the standards of the PCAOB. Audit documentation should be prepared in sufficient detail to provide a clear understanding of its purpose, source, and the conclusions reached. Also, the documentation should be appropriately organized to provide a clear link to the significant findings or issues. Examples of audit documentation include memoranda, confirmations, correspondence, schedules, audit programs, and letters of representation. Audit documentation may be in the form of paper, electronic files, or other media.

Because audit documentation is the written record that provides support for the representations in the auditor's report, it should:

1. Demonstrate that the engagement complied with the standards of the PCAOB.
2. Support the basis for the auditor's conclusions concerning every relevant financial statement assertion.
3. Demonstrate that the underlying accounting records agreed or reconciled with the financial statements.

*Steps to be Followed in Documentation.* The auditor must document the procedures performed, evidence obtained, and conclusions reached with respect to relevant financial statement assertions. Audit documentation must clearly demonstrate that the work was in fact performed. This documentation requirement applies to the work of all those who participate in the engagement as well as to the work of specialists the auditor uses as evidential matter in evaluating relevant financial statement assertions. Audit documentation must contain sufficient information to enable an experienced auditor, having no previous connection with the engagement to:

1. Understand the nature, timing, extent, and results of the procedures performed, evidence obtained, and conclusions reached.
2. Determine who performed the work and the date such work was completed as well as the person who reviewed the work and the date of such review.

## .07 Amendment to Interim Auditing Standard

The interim auditing standard, AU sec. 543.12, adopted by the PCAOB in April 2003, is amended as follows.

When the principal auditor decides not to make reference to the audit of the other auditor, in addition to satisfying him- or herself as to the matters described in AU sec. 543.10, the principal auditor must obtain, and review and retain, the following information from the other auditor:

1. An engagement completion document consistent with paragraphs 12 and 13 of PCAOB Auditing Standard No. 3.
2. This engagement completion document should include all cross-referenced, supporting audit documentation.
3. A list of significant fraud risk factors, the auditor's response, and the results of the auditor's related procedures.

4. Sufficient information relating to significant findings or issues that are inconsistent with or contradict the auditor's final conclusions, as described in paragraph 8 of PCAOB Auditing Standard No. 3.

5. Any findings affecting the consolidating or combining of accounts in the consolidated financial statements.

6. Sufficient information to enable the office issuing the auditor's report to agree or reconcile the financial statement amounts audited by the other firm to the information underlying the consolidated financial statements.

7. A schedule of audit adjustments, including a description of the nature and cause of each misstatement.

8. All significant deficiencies and material weaknesses in internal control over financial reporting, including a clear distinction between those two categories.

9. Letters of representations from management.

10. All matters to be communicated to the audit committee.

The principal auditor must obtain, and review and retain, such documents prior to the report release date.

In addition, the principal auditor should consider performing one or more of the following procedures:

1. Visit the other auditor and discuss the audit procedures followed and results thereof.

2. Review the audit programs of the other auditor. In some cases, it may be appropriate to issue instructions to the other auditor as to the scope of the audit work.

3. Review additional audit documentation of the other auditor relating to significant findings or issues in the engagement completion document.

## .09   Auditing Standard No. 4

In February 2006, Auditing Standard No. 4, *Reporting on Whether a Previously Reported Material Weakness Continues to Exist*, was approved by the Securities and exchange Commission. This Standard establishes requirements that apply when an auditor is engaged to report on whether a material weakness in internal control over financial reporting has been eliminated. AS 4 institutes a stand-alone engagement that is entirely voluntary, performed only at the company's request after the company, has disclosed a material weakness.

Like other attestation service, an auditor's report under this Standard is based on an evaluation of management's statement that the material weakness has been eliminated. Management is required to present a written report that will accompany the auditor's report that contains specified elements. Unlike an auditor's report on internal control over financial reporting, in which the assessment is required to be as of the date of the annual financial statements, an auditor's report on whether a material weakness continues to exist may be as of any date set by management.

That date represents management's belief that that is the day the material weakness no longer exists. They also believe that the company has adequately assessed the effectiveness of the specified controls that address the material weakness. The auditor's opinion relates to the existence of a specifically identified material weakness as of a specified date.

To establish the narrow focus of this engagement clearly, AS 4:

- Requires the auditor's report to describe the material weakness.
- Identify all of the specified controls that management asserts address the material weakness.
- Identify the stated control objective achieved by these controls.
- Include language to emphasize that the auditor has not performed procedures sufficient to reach conclusions about the effectiveness of any other controls or provided an opinion regarding the effectiveness of internal control over financial reporting overall.

Because of the narrow focus of this engagement, qualified opinions are not permitted - the auditor's opinion as to whether a previously reported material weakness continues to exist may be expressed as either "the material weakness exists" or "the material weakness no longer exists."

## .11  Revisions to Auditing Standard No. 2.

The PCAOB announced in May 2006 that it intends to propose revisions to its Auditing Standard No. 2, *An Audit of Internal Control Over Financial Reporting Performed in Conjunction with an Audit of Financial Statements*. Any final revision of AS No. 2 would be subject to SEC approval. The proposed revisions would:

- Seek to ensure that auditors focus during integrated audits on areas that pose higher risk of fraud or material error.
- Incorporate key concepts contained in the guidance issued by the PCAOB on May 16, 2005.
- Revisit and clarify what, if any, role the auditor should play in evaluating the company's process of assessing internal control effectiveness.

The Commission will work closely with the PCAOB to ensure that the proposed revisions to AS No. 2 are in the public interest and consistent with the protection of investors.

¶27,015.11

## ¶27,017    PCAOB Proposes Rules to Collect Fees to Fund Budget

The Sarbanes-Oxley Act established the Board as a nonprofit corporation. The Board was formed to oversee the audits of public companies that are subject to the securities laws, and related matters, in order to protect the interests of investors and further the public interest in the preparation of informative, accurate, and independent audit reports for companies whose securities are sold to, and held by and for, public investors. As such, the Board is subject to, and has all the powers conferred upon a nonprofit corporation by, the District of Columbia Nonprofit Corporation Act.

Section 109 of the Sarbanes-Oxley Act provides that funds to cover the Board's annual budget (less registration and annual fees paid by public accounting firms) are to be collected from public companies (i.e., "issuers," as defined in the Act). The amount due from such companies is referred to in the Act as the Board's "accounting support fee." (The Big Four and other major firms will also pay hefty fees—those referred to above as "registration and annual fees"—to be regulated by the PCAOB.)

The Board decided to apply a similar sliding-scale fee structure to corporations registered with the SEC. The schedule discussed below could require some large-capitalization companies to pay as much as $1 million in annual fees.

The 2003 operating budget approved by the Board projected $68 million in revenues for the year to come from the "accounting support fees" paid by corporations. The Oversight Board's budget expects that 97 percent of SEC registrants will pay these bills.

The initial registration fees collected from audit firms was not included in the Board's 2003 budget, because the exact fee structure had not yet been determined. Those fees go toward reducing the accounting support fee for 2004 budget expenses.

The government supplied more than 15 million to the PCAOB to cover the Board's startup costs. According to Board members, they intended to repay the advances in full during their first year of operation.

The biggest line item in the PCAOB's 2003 budget was payroll, with $28.9 million slotted for salaries, benefits, and payroll taxes. This reflected the Board's hiring plans, which called for the agency to grow from initial personnel of eight in January 2003 to 216 by the end of the year.

The staff and salary allocation for 2006 presented quite a contrast to the beginning year of PCAOB operation. The Board expected to begin 2006 with approximately 427 employees and to increase that number to 537 by the end of the year. A majority of the new employees were expected to be experienced auditors. They would conduct the Board's program of inspections to assess the degree of compliance by registered public accounting firms with the Act, the rules of the Board, the rules of the Commission, and auditing and related professional practicestandards, in connection with those firms audits of the financial statements of public companies. The 2006 budget for salaries, includes salaries and related expenses for merit and other salary adjustments and awards—$78,622,000. Employee benefits and payroll taxes added another $8,214,000 and $4,098,000, respectively, to the salary total.

The Board has adopted five proposed rules relating to public company funding of the Board's operations, plus certain definitions to implement section 109 of the Sarbanes-Oxley Act.

## .01   Details of the Schedule of Fees for Accounting Support

The Board's proposed rules provide for the equitable allocation, assessment, and collection of the fees from public companies. The fee is payable by two classes of issuers:

1. Publicly traded companies with average, monthly U.S. equity market capitalization during the preceding year, based on all classes of common stock, of greater than $25 million. (This is the threshold figure for small business issuers.)

2. Investment companies with average, monthly U.S. equity market capitalizations (or net asset values) of greater than $250 million. In recognition of the structure of investment companies and the relatively less complex nature of investment company audits (as compared to operating company audits), investment companies would be assessed at a lower rate.

All other issuers, including the following, would be allocated shares of zero:

- Those not required to file audited financial statements with the Commission.
- Employee stock purchase, savings, and similar plans.
- Bankrupt issuers that file modified reports.

## .03   Computation of Accounting Support Fee and Allocation

Once each year, the Board will compute the accounting support fee. This fee will equal the sum that the Board has arrived at to cover the proposed budget for that year, as approved by the Commission, less the amount of registration and annual fees received during the prior year from public accounting firms.

In establishing rules for the allocation of the accounting support fee, the Board was guided by two major principles required by section 109 of the Act. Generally, the accounting support fee must be allocated in a manner that reflects the proportionate size of issuers, and within that framework, the accounting support fee must be allocated in an equitable manner. These two principles are related in that, at least as a general matter, the size of issuer serves as an indication of the complexity of an audit, which could be an equitable measure on which to base allocation of the accounting support fee.

With respect to the measurability of issuers' proportionate size, the Board faces certain limitations. To explain, first, although section 109 provides a formula based on equity market capitalization by which to measure the proportionate size of issuers, market data may not be reliable or even regularly available with respect to some issuers, including:

- Issuers whose securities are not traded on an exchange or quoted on NASDAQ.
- Issuers whose securities are otherwise illiquid.
- Certain investment companies, such as unit investment trusts and insurance company separate accounts.
- Issuers whose only publicly traded securities are debt securities do not have equity market capitalization.

Second, to the extent that there are issuers, as that term is defined in the Act, that are not required to file audited financial statements, it may not be equitable to allocate any share of the accounting support fee to them. Further, although most investment companies file annual audited financial statements, the assets of many of those companies consist of investments in issuers who will have themselves been allocated shares of the accounting support fee.

In order to allocate the accounting support fee among issuers in a manner that reflects the overarching principles and the inherent limitations of available data, the Board's proposed rules divide issuers into four classes:

1. All issuers whose average, monthly U.S. equity market capitalization during the preceding calendar year, based on all classes of common stock, is greater than $25 million and whose share price on a monthly, or more frequent, basis is publicly available. (*Equity Issuers class*)
2. Registered investment companies and issuers who have elected to be regulated as business development companies whose average, monthly market capitalization (or net asset value), during the preceding calendar year, is greater than $250 million and whose share price (or net asset value) on a monthly, or more frequent, basis is publicly available. (*Investment Company Issuers class*)

    As discussed below, the allocation formula scales down market capitalization (or, in the case of investment companies whose securities are not traded on an exchange or quoted on NASDAQ, net asset value) of investment companies by 90 percent, such that a $250 million investment company would be allocated a share equal to that of a $25 million operating company.

3. All issuers who, as of the date the accounting support fee is calculated under SEC Rule 7100,:

   a. Have a basis, under a Commission rule or pursuant to other action of the Commission or its staff, not to file audited financial statements,

   b. Are employee stock purchase, savings, and similar plans—interests that constitute securities registered under the Securities Act of 1933—as amended, or

   c. Are subject to the jurisdiction of a bankruptcy court and satisfy the modified reporting requirements of Commission Staff Legal Bulletin 2. (*Issuers Permitted Not to File Audited Financial Statements and Bankrupt Issuers That File Modified Reports class*)

4. All other issuers (i.e., issuers who do not fall into classes 1, 2, or 3 (*All Other Issuers class*)

A company's status as an issuer (or as an investment company, business development company, issuer excused from filing audited financial statements, or bankrupt issuer) will be determined as of the date on which the amount of the annual accounting support fee is set. Companies that are not issuers on that date will not be required to pay any fee during that year.

The accounting support fee will be allocated among the issuers in the four classes in the following manner. Each company in the Equity Issuer and Investment Company Issuer classes will be allocated an amount equal to the accounting support fee, multiplied by a fraction. The numerator of the fraction will be the issuer's average, monthly market capitalization during the preceding calendar year. The denominator will be the sum of the average, monthly market capitalizations of all Equity and Investment Company Issuers. For purposes of this allocation, however, the market capitalization of an investment company issuer will be 10 percent of the investment company's market capitalization or net asset value. All issuers in the other two classes—issuers permitted not to file and all other issuers—will be allocated a share of zero. Issuers will be required to pay their allocated shares of the accounting support fee, rounded to the nearest hundred. Accordingly, issuers whose shares of the accounting support fee are less than $50 will have their shares rounded to zero and will not be assessed a fee.

## ¶27,019 REGISTRATION REQUIRED OF ALL PUBLIC FIRMS

The PCAOB has adopted a registration system for public accounting firms, including non-U.S. firms. The Sarbanes-Oxley Act of 2002 made it unlawful to play a substantial role in preparing or issuing an audit report on a public company without being registered with the PCAOB. Foreign auditors have been given an additional six months to comply with the new guidelines.

The Board fixed upon an all-electronic Web-based registration system. Domestic firms that audit U.S. companies were given until approximately October 24, 2003, to complete the registration process; foreign firms, until April 26, 2004.

This additional time should give the non-U.S. auditors an opportunity to determine how any of these rules might affect their home-country and international rules as well as allowing U.S. regulators to resolve compliance concerns raised by the auditors and government officials. PCAOB members view this as one of the most controversial matters facing the Board. They agree that they must be prepared to work with their foreign counterparts to find ways to accomplish the oversight goals and protect investors' interests without subjecting foreign firms to unnecessary burdens or conflicting requirements. They believe the 180-day deferral of foreign firm registration affords an opportunity to explore ways of accomplishing that goal with non-U.S. accounting oversight bodies. Regardless, the Sarbanes-Oxley accounting reform law left the PCAOB with no justification for exempting non-U.S. firms.

The Board agrees for the need to avoid unnecessary administrative burdens on public accounting firms arising from the oversight of multiple jurisdictions, but it also believes that, regardless of where they are located, all auditors who participate in the preparation or issuance of audit reports for U.S. issuers should be governed by the same rules and oversight requirements. Early objections, which threatened to become rancorous, rapidly dissipated in the light of yet another prominent non-U.S. firm and its top officials being exposed as equally capable as their U.S. counterparts of malfeasance and corporate skullduggery.

## .01   Some Specifics

The Board did make a concession for foreign audit firms that find themselves subject to home-country legal restrictions that prohibit them from disclosing information sought by the PCAOB. In response to concerns raised by non-U.S. accountants during a meeting with PCAOB members early in the formation process, the Board agreed to allow accountants to withhold information if they could document that disclosure would violate non-U.S. laws.

The Board's new registration rules—which are still subject to approval by the Securities and Exchange Commission—also include provisions that:

- Entitle accounting firms to a hearing before the PCAOB if the Board determines that the registration application is inaccurate or incomplete.
- Confirm that the information in these registration applications will be made publicly available as soon as practicable after the Board approves or rejects them.

¶27,019.01

- Allow both foreign and domestic firms to request confidential treatment of any portion of an application that contains nonpublic personal or proprietary information.
- Eliminate a controversial requirement in the proposed version of the rule that would have required accounting firms to provide additional financial information about their revenue source.
- Narrow the types of criminal, civil, and administrative proceedings that accounting firms must disclose in their registration applications.

## .03    Concerns over Foreign Company Registration

As late as mid-October 2003, European representatives were trying to reach a compromise relating to the mutual supervision of accountants. Although they were given a later date to comply with the U.S. rules, foreign accounting firms that audit U.S. companies must comply with the new accounting oversight board's registration process. The European Union still does not like the idea, but a compromise that will placate both sides may be possible. On the other hand, any firm that affects the financial status of U.S. companies must be overseen by the PCAOB, or the Board will be defeated almost before it is up and operating.

As noted above, the PCAOB mandates that European firms that audit U.S. public companies be registered. One European representative agreed that European firms could register with the U.S. accounting oversight board if the two sides reach an agreement on enforcement.

In late October, the PCAOB released a briefing paper that describes the broad parameters of the Board's approach to the oversight of non-U.S. accounting firms. In the briefing paper are the Board's plans for oversight of non-U.S. registered public accounting firms, based on cooperation with appropriate non-U.S. auditor oversight authorities. This cooperative approach would allow the Board to fulfill its responsibilities to protect the interests of investors and to further the public interest, in keeping with the statutory authority granted to the Board. Plans outlined in the briefing paper include:

- A framework to permit varying degrees of reliance on a firm's home country system of inspections, based on a sliding scale depending upon the strength of the particular country's system.
- Modification of the registration form to permit, where applicable, the inclusion of certain information about a non-U.S. firm's home country oversight system to facilitate coordination between the two systems.
- A 90-day extension of the Board's deadline for non-U.S. firm registration in order to allow sufficient time for the Board to have final rules in place, as well as to permit non-U.S. firms additional time to understand and prepare for registration.

## ¶27,021   BOARD SETS CRITERIA FOR ADVISORY GROUP

The PCAOB has adopted a rule relating to the formation of advisory groups under section 103 of the Sarbanes-Oxley Act. The rules were submitted to the Securities and Exchange Commission for approval. Pursuant to section 107 of the Act, Board rules do not take effect unless approved by the Commission.

In order to obtain the advice of a broad range of experts, the Board will form a Standing Advisory Group (SAG), which may be divided into subgroups by the Board if needed for specialized advice. The Board may also establish one or more ad hoc task forces to assist the staff with various specialized responsibilities—the drafting of technical language, among other things.

### .01   First Advisory Group Formed

In line with the rule that provides that the Board may form such advisory groups to assist in carrying out its responsibilities, the Board adopted Rule 3700 on the formation of its first advisory group.

Advisory groups must be composed of individuals with expertise in a variety of fields, including accounting, auditing, corporate finance and corporate governance, investing in public companies, and other areas that the Board deems relevant to one or more of the auditing or professional practice standards.

The rule also provides that members of any advisory group are selected by the Board based upon nominations, including self-nominations, received from any person or organization. Membership in an advisory group is personal to the member, and the duties and responsibilities of the member cannot be delegated to others. Further, the rule provides for members to be subject to the provisions of the Board's Ethics Code.

### .03   Ground Rules for the Standing Advisory Group

The Board voted to issue a Release discussing nominations and qualifications of members, terms and conditions of membership, the conduct of meetings, and other matters related to its use of a Standing Advisory Group. The Board contemplates that the SAG will initially have approximately 25 members. The SAG will be composed of individuals with a variety of backgrounds, including practicing auditors, preparers of financial statements, investors (both individual and institutional), and others (e.g., from academia and state accounting regulators). In order to achieve this diversity, the Board expects that no one field of expertise will predominate among the SAG membership. Although SAG members may be employed or otherwise affiliated with particular organizations, the Board expects SAG members to serve in their individual capacities and not to serve as representatives of particular interests, groups, or employers.

In determining appointments to the SAG, the Board intends to solicit nominations, including self-nominations. In evaluating nominations for the SAG, the Board will seek individuals with an interest in the quality of the audits of public companies.

Unless the appointment is revoked for cause, as determined by the Board, or unless the SAG member voluntarily resigns, SAG membership will be for a term of two years; provided, however, that approximately 50 percent of the initial members will be appointed for a three-year term to ensure continuity. Members will not be limited in the number of terms they may serve.

In addition to requiring compliance with certain provisions of the Board's Ethics Code, the Board requires as conditions of membership that SAG members:

- Act in the public interest in their individual capacities.
- Withdraw or recuse themselves from certain matters that pose potential conflicts.
- Attend meetings and dedicate 50 to 100 hours per year (and more if needed) to SAG service on a voluntary basis.

The SAG will hold at least two open meetings a year (and may have more). Any final decisions on recommendations to the Board are made at open meetings. Presentation of SAG recommendations are made to the Board at open meetings of the Board.

## .05 Role of the SAG

The role of the SAG will be to assist the Board in reviewing existing Standards, in evaluating proposed Standards recommended by Board staff, Board-formed technical task forces, or others, and recommending to the Board new or amended Standards. The role of the SAG will not ordinarily include technical drafting (which will be performed by the Board's staff, with the assistance of ad hoc task forces, when necessary). Instead, the Board will look to the SAG to provide advice and insight concerning:

- The need to formulate new Standards.
- The advisability of changing or amending existing Standards.
- The possible impact of proposed new or changed Standards.
- Participation in the standards-setting process.

## .07 Meetings and Board Relations

The Board decided that the first Chair of the SAG, also acting as general liaison to the Board, will be the Board's Chief Auditor and Director of Professional

Standards. He or she will be a nonvoting member of the Group. The Board will approve the agenda for all annual, semiannual, or quarterly SAG meetings. Agenda items may also be added when the Board determines that the assistance of the SAG is required in response to emerging issues or problems.

The SAG will meet in person at least three times each year. These meetings will be open to the public. Meetings of the SAG may also be held, at the direction of the Board or the Chair, during the intervening quarters. At the direction of the Chair, monthly meetings of the SAG may be held by video or teleconference.

The Board's Standing Advisory Group acts to advise the Board on the establishment of auditing and related professional practice standards. It is to be composed of 31 highly qualified persons representing the auditing profession, public companies, investors, and others. The Board also has granted six organizations observer status with speaking rights at all SAG meetings. Those six organizations are the Financial Accounting Standards Board, the Government Accountability Office, the International Auditing and Assurance Standards Board, the Securities and Exchange Commission, the Department of Labor, and the Auditing Standards Board of the American Institute of Certified Public Accountants.

Final decisions on recommendations to the Board and related activities will be conducted at the annual, semiannual, or other open meetings of the SAG. The meetings held in the quarters between the annual and semiannual meeting, if any, and monthly meetings will not generally be open to the public.

If so directed by the Chair of the SAG, the Group may convene hearings, roundtable discussions, or other fact-finding activities designed to assist them in the development of recommendations to the Board. Because the Board expects the SAG to make decisions in an efficient manner, the Group need not defer decisions on recommendations for the annual or semiannual open meetings. They may make decisions on recommendations at any meeting, so long as it is open to the public in some manner, including, at the direction of the Chair, telephonically.

# PART VI

---

## INVESTMENTS

# Chapter 28

## The CPA as Financial Planner

## CONTENTS

## FORMS

## ¶28,000 OVERVIEW

"Faced with a turbulent stock market, rising energy prices and other signs of an economy in flux, Americans are increasingly worried about their finances. And though individual investors admit to financial planners' expertise, few consult one." This is according to a survey commissioned by the American Institute of Certified Public Accountants' (AICPA's) personal financial specialist examination committee. The survey polled 636 Americans ages 18 to over 55 with annual income of more than $75,000.

Almost all respondents (91 percent) said they manage their finances themselves, doing their own research and obtaining advice from family, friends, the Internet, or a broker. The AICPA suggested that CPA/PFS practitioners may see potential market opportunities in this and the survey's other findings.

The CPA who is not a PFS might be interested in seeing that this is not an overcrowded niche. At present, of the 330,000 AICPA members, there are approximately 3,000 who hold the designation. For CPAs interested in obtaining the Personal Financial Specialist (PFS) designation, the requirements are given at the end of this chapter.

This designation becomes more and more important as highly publicized scandals continue to develop within the financial services industry. Honest professionals can take advantage of an opportunity to expand their business in both size and scope. By now, everyone in the profession is aware of the problems with KPMG and their government settlement. Although KPMG has fully cooperated with the government probe, covering 1996–2002, of their tax shelters, the fact remains that many people have lost gigantic amounts of money with these investments. The KPMG fines at present total at least $456 million—and the government has missed as much as $1.4 billion in revenue. What this means to the CPA/PFS is that both from enlightened self-interest and self-defense, a thorough familiarity with the types of investments within the sphere of their practice is an absolute.

## ¶28,001 SETTING FEES FOR FINANCIAL PLANNING

The idea of financial planning is popular. There are many plan types available, with costs from zero to thousands of dollars. Fees are usually based on a double matrix of how much money a client has and how complicated and complete the plan needs to be. Only the financial specialist can determine how much time and paperwork should be generated by a specific client's plan. Clearly, financial considerations are always a concern with a fee-related product. A survey of local fellow professionals about planner fees should help an individual entering the financial planning niche to price his or her services to scale.

## ¶28,003  INFLATION AND FINANCIAL PLANNING

A major obstacle to anyone's financial future is inflation. For example, a million dollars is not what it once was. As a matter of fact, it's about $150,000 in 1950 dollars. However, that $150,000, indexed in the Dow Jones Industrials, would be $3,000,000 now. Appropriately invested, the client's money reaps the benefits of:

1.  Asset growth.
2.  Income enhancement.
3.  Inflation hedge.

Inflation is a major issue, but if the CPA/PFS prepares a good financial plan, with appropriately allocated investments, that plan becomes a buffer, equalizer and fighter against inflation and other risks. A millionaire today must not be cavalier with money, or he or she will not be a millionaire for very long. The planner must address these serious and ongoing client needs. Just to keep pace, the individual must have a plan that reaps at least a modest return on investment.

## ¶28,005  WHO NEEDS A FINANCIAL PLAN?

The CPA/PFS should begin with a financial plan for each client. It is a blueprint for that client's future — tailored to that individual's financial needs. In a survey of clients, friends, and professional associates, the chances are each of them supports the principles of financial planning.

*Everyone* needs a financial plan. As the AICPA survey confirmed, the chances are very good that few of these individuals have completed comprehensive financial plans. It is *planning* and *action* on those plans that lead to financial success.

Financial success is usually described as *the ability to meet current expenses, fund college educations and enjoy a prosperous retirement*. Weighing, evaluating, and accomplishing such goals is the responsibility of the planning specialist who can help address economic problems. The tools in the form of financial planning are available for anyone.

## ¶28,007  PLANNING A CONSTRUCTIVE DIALOGUE WITH THE CLIENT

The clients come to the office and have a meeting centered around a basic financial plan prepared for that meeting. The plan is in a format suited to the needs of the client. It concretely addresses the college saving needs, an asset allocation for the savings account, and a look at the investments in the retirement plan. The goal is to create happy and financially secure clients.

You have heard repeatedly that the clients have considered all of these financial concerns, but they have not been formalized. You as a financial planner can do much to make the session a success for the clients, with benefits that can create a lifetime pattern of planning and investments:

1. Ask the clients why they are seeking advice.
2. Determine as clearly as possible what the client perceives the family's needs to be. (It is important to establish the clients in the planning loop from the very beginning, even if they have only vague ideas of their needs.)
3. Explain in detail the planning points. The primary concern is to assess the financial security of the client.
4. Lead a frank discussion of successes and concerns with the clients.
5. Help them evaluate how closely the planning suggestions are to how they visualize their situation, and ask what they will do to implement the action points.
6. Help the clients weigh and prioritize, based on educated judgment, what is best for them. (Of course, the client ultimately has the personal responsibility for acting or not acting on advice.)

### .01  Need Based Planning

Aspects of the financial planning process include:

1. Current needs.
2. College funds.
3. Retirement.
4. Trusts and wills.
5. Insurance.
6. Mortgages.
7. Gifts and charities.
8. Asset allocation.

But clients all have different needs. The task is to determine these needs and to evaluate the level of sophistication and the amount of detail each case requires. Some clients need only a basic, boilerplate plan; others require extensive, tailored plans.

**¶28,007**

For example, a young couple several years into their working lives requires a basic plan with fundamental goals to see them along the proper path to a good financial future. On the other hand, the owner of a private company with 200 employees and a 30-year record of sales has vastly more elaborate requirements as he or she zeros in on retirement and succession planning.

The financial planner may start the client with basics, but learn that a more elaborate plan is required. CPAs are uniquely placed to gauge the extent of each client's needs because of their familiarity with every aspect of the clients' financial situation.

As the clients' assets grow and their lives become more complex, their plan will require revision and reworking. Planning is a dynamic process that involves everything from mundane number-crunching to the most trendy visualization. In other words, it is an ongoing process subject to change. The clients should understand that having a plan is a major step forward but that the plan will evolve and change in light of the unexpected events and changes that everyone experiences.

## ¶28,009 ACCELERATING THE CLIENT PLANNING PROCESS

An endless array of self-help books, computer software, and online applications can be tailored to a personalized product. The CPA is concerned primarily with getting a plan in place and implementing it; form means very little exclusive of function. A consistent review process dramatically improves the product and moves the plan toward accomplishment. The client's life changes and, as a consequence, so does the financial plan.

Fine tuning the process of financial planning is true value added from a professional standpoint in the CPA/client relationship. Together, they can determine whether the goals are being met, surpassed or not achieved. The plan should be updated and revised periodically to incorporate changes in the client's financial picture. Information useful in a plan update would be:

1. Performance on an annual basis of all securities accounts.
2. Salary changes that can affect a plan immediately.
3. Sizable gifts of financial or other assets that change the client's net worth.
4. Inheritances or bequests that have a material effect on the client's financial picture.
5. Changes in rates of saving or spending that alter the course of the plan.
6. Tax or contribution changes affecting the retirement plan.

## ¶28,011 SEVEN KEY AREAS OF FINANCIAL PLANNING

Some subjects appear in any financial plan. The client picture evolves from a format that follows this order or something similar. However, the contents are tailored for each client, either directly by the accountant or with the help of other financial service industry professionals. These subjects are:

1. *Net worth*—Establish with total clarity the client's current financial picture. Otherwise, there is no basis upon which to complete a plan. Many clients do not understand and therefore are unaware of their own financial profile. Clients are amazed to learn the simple fact that net worth is simply all assets minus all liabilities.

   Net worth is the total of the client's equity in a home, all securities in and out of retirement plans, value of business and other real estate holdings, cash value of insurance, collectibles and personal property minus all bills, taxes and loans owed. A simple net worth statement is created, but it can be broken down to more specific classifications, if needed. (See Form 28-1.) For example:

   a. *Liquid versus illiquid assets.* Most clients do not understand liquidity. Money market funds, most stocks and bonds and mutual funds are totally liquid. If the need is there, they can be liquidated in minutes. Many other investments are relatively illiquid—limited partnerships, private placements, most real estate and some insurance products—because they take a while to sell or liquidate.

   b. *Investment versus personal assets.* Brokerage accounts are definitely investment assets. Most collectibles, such as antiques and art works, however dearly the client may prize them, are in the final analysis personal assets.

   c. *Active versus passive investments.* Active investments are those over which the CPA and the client have management control. Passive investments are investments whose performance cannot be directly influenced. An IRA account, for example, is an active investment because it is self- directed. Social Security, on the other hand, is passive because the individual cannot impact what the managers do with the contributions. (This is true at the present time, but that could change.)

2. *Social security*—The client's Social Security statement should be checked to confirm and establish benefits. Are all contributions accounted for, and are projected benefits calculated correctly? This may be done for all members of the client's family.

3. *Retirement planning*—Most financial planning somehow relates to retirement planning. Clients may have little notion of how well or poorly they are prepared for retirement. Several planning steps help to clarify this picture.

   a. Clients should be required to calculate, as closely as possible, their financial needs in retirement. The financial planner should remind the clients that many current needs during the earning years are unrelated to retirement needs—commuter expenses, business attire, lunch and entertainment expenses, business usage books and journals; the list is long.

b. It is important to determine whether any corporate or government retirement plans have Cost of Living Adjustments (COLAs) attached to them.

## Form 28-1
## Figuring the Client's Net Worth

| 1. Personal Assets | Dollar Value | | |
|---|---|---|---|
| Primary Residence Market Value | $ | | |
| Secondary Residence Market Value | $ | | |
| *Personal Property:* | | | |
| Furnishings | $ | | |
| Vehicles | $ | | |
| Jewelry | $ | | |
| 2. Investment Assets | | | |
| Market Value of Securities Accounts | $ | | |
| Market Value of Retirement Accounts | $ | | |
| Market Value of Collectibles | $ | | |
| Market Value of Bank Accounts | $ | | |
| Cash Value of Life Insurance Policies | $ | | |
| Cash Value of Debts Owed to Client | $ | | |
| Cash Value of Business Owned by Client | $ | | |
| Market Value of Investment Real Estate | $ | | |
| **TOTAL ASSETS** | $ | | |
| 3. Liabilities | | | |
| *Outstanding Loan Balances:* | | Dollar Cost | |
| Real Estate | | $ | |
| Business | | $ | |
| Vehicles | | $ | |
| Consumer | | $ | |
| All Others | | $ | |
| *Taxes Payable:* | | | |
| Real Estate | | $ | |
| Income Tax | | $ | |
| **TOTAL LIABILITIES** | | $ | |
| 4. Net Worth Calculation | | | Net Worth |
| Assets | | | $ |
| –Liabilities | | | $ |
| =Net Worth | | | $ |

## Form 28-2
## Retirement Planning Questionnaire

1. Where are you planning to live when you retire?

    City _____    State _____

2. Can you pay off all your debts before or at retirement?           Yes ☐          No ☐

3. Are your securities (personal wealth) and self-directed           Yes ☐          No ☐
   retirement (pension income) accounts allocated in a manner
   reflecting your future wants/needs as determined with the CPA?

4. Have you and your CPA addressed current and future federal and    Yes ☐          No ☐
   state income tax considerations and consequences?

5. Have you and your CPA thoroughly and accurately mapped out        Yes ☐          No ☐
   your retirement expenses/income by projecting a current and future
   budget?

6. Will you continue to work for fulfillment and/or supplemental     Yes ☐          No ☐
   income?

---

    a. Clients must keep current concerning the deductibility of any of the various voluntary contribution plans they may be eligible for; they should not ignore a deductible or pre-tax contribution at the expense of a post-tax plan.

    b. Both the CPA and the client should keep current with all retirement legislation. (See Form 28-2.)

4. *College planning*—Any client who has the responsibility for educating a child should address that obligation as soon as possible. The importance and magnitude of the event is an opportunity for the financial planner to make a genuinely valuable contribution to a client's life.

    College planning is not an area for procrastination. College costs have grossly outpaced the rate of inflation in this country. The notion of a child's somehow earning his or her way through college, as earlier generations did, is now completely out of the realm of possibility. Any child who can earn the costs of a median priced private school should probably be setting up his or her own business.

    Taking into consideration the age of the child/children, the accountant and the clients should, among other considerations, discuss when and if the student(s) should become part of the financial planning process, and whether to discuss with them the extent of the financial help they can expect.

    Form 28-3 is designed as a questionnaire to aid the accountant in determining what the clients' planning needs may be. The CPA may then rephrase the questions to submit to clients for their input. (See Form 28-3.)

**Form 28-3**
**College Planning Questionnaire**

1. How many children will the client help through college?

2. How much will the college of choice cost?

3. What is the current age of the children?

4. How will the client get started to meet the obligations?

5. How will you, the CPA, help determine the investment choices?

6. What investment selections will you help the client use for a small child, a high school student, or a young adult?

7. What level of risk is the client prepared to assume with the college investments?

8. What investment strategies are appropriate for each student's goals?

9. Where do you, the CPA, go if you need help?

10. How do you assist the client in learning about scholarships and other financial aid?

11. How do you help the client and student reduce college costs without impairing the educational experience?

¶28,011

5. *Insurance and employee benefits*—All insurance and benefit information should be identified and evaluated with two distinct goals in mind:

   a. From a practical standpoint, does the client have enough, too much or just the right amount of coverage for perceived needs? From a financial planning standpoint, needs must be addressed relative to all forms of insurance—life, fire and casualty, homeowners or renters, automobile, umbrella liability, medical, dental, long-term health care, personal property and disability.

   b. Insurance planning must also be addressed from a financial feasibility standpoint. Insurance represents a very significant financial investment. The CPA can address every opportunity to obtain the best for the least for the client.

      —The client must become aware of the fact that to have inexpensive automobile insurance with a company that is rated low for paying claims is no bargain.

      —On the other hand, to buy an umbrella liability policy (which is permitted for bundling two or three of the primary types of insurance—life, property, and automotive—with one company) is great financial planning and money management.

      —Worksheets can help in determining how much of each type of insurance the client needs and can afford.

      —For variable life and annuity products, the mutual fund selection can be determined using an asset allocation matrix that isolates the client's risk parameters. (See Form 28-4.)

6. *Estate planning (wills, trusts, and estate documents)*—Determination should be made of needs from an estate planning standpoint, then an attorney should be selected to put together the final product. The resulting documents should be reviewed each time the financial plan is reviewed.

   Clients should always be cognizant of the fact that *estate planning is as dynamic as financial planning*. The list of life changes they go through from an estate planning standpoint are seemingly endless. For example, they may change their minds about who:

   a. Gets what.

   b. Administers their estate.

   c. Is the successor trustee.

   d. Rears the children if the parents die.

7. *Taxes*—The CPA can do more than any other financial planner to accomplish tax-related goals for clients. He or she can help minimize taxes, invest for a tax exempt or tax deferral goal, determine exemptions, prepare forms, anticipate problems and resolve all tax issues. (See Form 28-5.)

**¶28,011**

**Form 28-4**
**Insurance and Employee Benefits Checklist**

| | |
|---|---|
| **1. Life Insurance Coverage** | |
| Face Amount | $ |
| Cash Value | $ |
| Annual Premium | $ |
| Carrier | |
| Type of Policy | |
| **2. Disability Income Coverage** | |
| Amount of Benefit | $ |
| Annual Premium | $ |
| Carrier | |
| Type of Policy | |
| **3. Employee Benefits** | |
| Pension Income | $ |
| Cost of Living Adjustment Provision (If Provided) | % |
| Survivor Benefit | %/$ |
| Social Security Income | $ |
| Survivor Benefits | %/$ |
| Other Employee Benefits | $ |
| Other Retirement Benefits | $ |
| **4. Health Insurance Coverage** | |
| Amount of Benefits | $ |
| Annual Premium | $ |
| Carrier | |
| Type and Scope of Coverage | |
| **5. Dental Insurance Coverage** | |
| Amount of Benefits | $ |
| Annual Premium | $ |
| Carrier | |
| Type and Scope of Coverage | |
| **6. Long-Term Medical Coverage** | |
| Amount of Benefits | $ |
| Annual Premium | $ |
| Carrier | |
| Type and Scope of Coverage | |

¶28,011

**Form 28-5**
**Client Tax Pointer Menu and Checklist**

_____ 1. Income Planning

_____ 2. Retirement Planning

_____ 3. Investment Planning

_____ 4. Estate Planning

_____ 5. Education/Child Planning

What the Client Can Do to Facilitate the Process:

_____ 1. Keep clean expense records.

_____ 2. Save all financial statements.

_____ 3. Report any significant financial changes.

_____ 4. Address securities gain or loss before year end.

_____ 5. Schedule a mid-year planning review.

_____ 6. Practice responsible document control.

_____ 7. Collect and retain all records and organize them.

_____ 8. Leave nothing to the last minute.

---

# ¶28,013   Sample Questions for the Planning Process

Form 28-6 provides an assortment of financial planning questions only the clients can answer because the questions are case specific. They should consider all of these questions regarding their financial status carefully because the answers are germane to their financial plan.

Answers to each of these questions may be written prior to their first financial planning meeting if the CPA has worked with them previously or after an introductory financial planning session (if they are relatively new clients).

Of course, the individual CPA/PFS will be in a position to determine whether any, all or a portion of these forms and questions are appropriate for individual clients. For that reason, they are on the CD-ROM (see Form 28-6).

## Form 28-6
## Financial Planning Checklist

1. Where do you work? _____

2. Your title _____ Length of service _____

3. How much is your annual income? _____
   Where does it come from? _____

4. If you are responsible for paying for educational expenses, for whom?
   _____

5. When do you plan to retire? _____

6. How much in post-tax dollars is required? _____

7. What pensions do you have? _____
   _____

8. What is the estimated pension income? _____

9. Is there a survivor benefit? _____

10. What self-directed plans do you have? _____

11. How much are they worth? _____

12. What are the current investments? _____

13. Do you believe these investments are appropriately allocated at present?
    _____

14. What long-term disability income coverage and life insurance do you
    carry? _____

15. Do you have a will and, if appropriate, a living trust with unified credit
    provisions? _____

16. What are your personal assets? _____

17. How much are they worth? _____

18. How much money do you save each year? _____
    Where does it go? _____

19. Do you consider your risk profile conservative, moderate, or aggressive?
    _____

20. Do you consider this allocation suitable for your risk profile? _____
    _____

## ¶28,015   RAMIFICATIONS OF ADVISING CLIENTS ON INVESTMENTS

The Investment Advisers Act of 1940 requires investment advisers to register with the Securities and Exchange Commission (SEC) and comply with certain requirements, unless exempted from registering or excepted from the definition of investment adviser.

The act defines "investment adviser" as a person who provides advice about securities for compensation, as part of a business. The definition specifically excludes the activities of an accountant that are *solely incidental* to the individual's practice of accounting. However, the SEC and the staff have traditionally interpreted the exclusion narrowly.

As more CPAs are providing comprehensive financial planning to clients (which almost necessarily requires providing advice about securities), they are increasingly registering as investment advisers. Much of the remainder of this chapter deals with information that should help the financial adviser be aware of what is entailed in becoming an investment adviser.

In 1996, changes to the act created a threshold for registering as an investment adviser with the SEC. Advisers who provide investment advice and manage more than $25 million in assets must register with the SEC. Those who manage less than $25 million are regulated by the individual states. The AICPA points out that the decision to register and the ensuing requirements involve complex legal issues. With this in mind, it is advisable to consult an attorney regarding the attendant legal issues.

As outlined at the end of the chapter, the AICPA also allows some credit toward its PFS designation for passing the examination for the following: Certified Financial Planner, Chartered Financial Consultant, Chartered Financial Analyst, National Association of Securities Dealers (NASD) Series 65, NASD Series 66 and NASD Series 7.

## ¶28,017   INVESTMENT KNOWLEDGE

The client often feels that investing has a language unto its own and that that language is as elusive as Sanskrit. In a survey to determine investment literacy and behavior, a study by the New York Stock Exchange concluded that few Americans know the basics of investing, and fewer still know how to put them to work. The CPA has a greater background familiarity with these basics because of the tax consequences of investing, but most of the experience with the investment process is passive—responding to the tax forms of clients.

The CPA can help the client along by focusing on three big concerns:

1.  Determine the client's life goals.

2. Formulate an investment plan and put it into place.
3. Determine which investments will help reach those goals.

The clients should fill in their knowledge gap with a plan that teaches them how to make sound, informed financial decisions necessary to achieve their goals. This is key for retirement planning because:

1. Many employers are abandoning corporate managed pension plans.
2. Social Security faces a problematic future at best.
3. Companies are increasingly implementing retirement plans that place the burden of investment decisions on the plan participants.

Developing a sound financial plan is a value-added service for the client because it facilitates making the right investment decisions for the client's future. Because participants' feelings about this newly acquired responsibility run the gamut from exciting to horrific, the financial planner plays a key role in helping them determine the appropriate investment choices.

An endless array of investment information is readily available. Knowledgeable use of that information is the goal. There are right and wrong ways to advise the client to invest money. Investing is not as subjective as one might suppose, especially as perceived by the regulatory agencies.

Knowledgeable investing is informed investing. Informed investing is more than simply reading weekly business magazines. Planning specialists must establish a regular and systematic investigative process regarding the workings of all the investments selected for client portfolios.

Well-chosen professional investment publications, especially from SEC-regulated sources of information such as brokerage firms and mutual fund companies, are an excellent source of information for risk evaluation and other expertise. Professional financial planners provide added value for the client because they are able to sift through the myriad sources of information. They can then make an educated judgment regarding which sources to rely upon and which sources to ignore. Clients are rarely competent at performing a task like this because they do not have the resources or the background to do so.

## ¶28,019  RISK TOLERANCE

Determining risk tolerance is a nearly impossible task for most individuals because few are aware of the factors that should be taken into consideration. Objectivity is essential when selecting investments to fund an individual or family's future. Risk control at either extreme—conservative or high risk—demands the most objective analysis.

The value added by professional financial planning cannot be exaggerated. In the prevailing self-service approach to personal finance, millions of investors become sitting ducks for investment fraud and abuse. Much of this is a direct result of not understanding risk. An accountant offers all of his or her clients, at minimum:

1. A sounding board for each investment selection.
2. A leg up on specific areas of financial planning.
3. Knowledgeable product information.
4. Expertise about the investment industry.

## .01 Establishing the Client's Tolerance for Risk

The investor must be required to take a close look at risk. What is meant by risk? Some basic factors must be taken into consideration to establish risk in a client's financial plan, specifically, the client's:

1. Age.
2. Income and net worth.
3. Knowledge of securities.
4. "Pain tolerance."

While the first three factors are easy to measure, the fourth is a factor very difficult to determine. The client may have a conservative, moderate, speculative or high risk profile. Estimating his or her reaction to financial pressure is very important. If the client invests within a comfort level, then he or she will successfully endure the relative highs and lows of investing and the sometimes erratic behavior of the financial markets.

## .03 Crystalizing the Client Investment Profile

To acquire a clear picture of a client's investment profile, the CPA can do the following:

1. Require the client to consider the questions in Form 28-6.
2. Have the client prepare written responses to the questions in Form 28-7A.
3. Consider the factors pinpointed in Form 28-7B.
4. Meet with the client to interpret these answers.
5. Formulate an action plan.

**Form 28-7A**
**Investment Profile: Client Questionnaire**

1. How secure do you consider your income and its potential for growth?
   _____

2. Do you think your present investments are right for you? Give each of them a report card grade ranging from A to F.
   _____
   _____
   _____

3. Total your fixed (financial obligations that do not change) and variable (financial obligations that do change) expenses.
   _____
   _____

4. How old are you? _____

5. How many dependents do you have? _____

6. At what age would you like to retire? (See Form 28-2.) _____

7. Estimate your required retirement income.
   _____
   _____
   _____

8. Calculate your net worth exclusive of home equity. (See Form 28-1.)
   _____
   _____
   _____

9. Do you need help to reduce the level of debt and put a savings plan into effect?
   _____
   _____

10. How do you feel about the ups and downs of the stock market?
    _____
    _____
    _____

11. How do you feel about the risk of losing money in the stock market?
    _____
    _____

12. Do you prefer low risk/low return investments to more volatile, high risk/high return ones?
    _____
    _____

13. Do you think you have the patience to see a financial plan through from beginning to end?
    _____
    _____

**¶28,019.03**

**Form 28-7B**
**Investment Profile: Client Assessment**

1. Assess the security of the client's income and its potential for growth.
   _____
   _____
   _____

2. Examine the client's past investment profile and prepare a report card on these investments.
   _____
   _____
   _____

3. Determine the client's fixed and variable expenses.
   _____
   _____
   _____

4. How old is the client? _____
5. How many dependents does the client have? _____
6. At what age would the client like to retire? _____
7. Estimate the client's required retirement income and project upward for inflation. _____
   _____

8. Calculate the net worth of the client exclusive of home equity.
   _____
   _____

9. Does the client need help to reduce the level of debt and put a savings plan into effect?_____
   _____

10. What is the client's response to market volatility and how does the client perceive it as a factor in determining risk? _____
    _____

11. What is the client's response to losing money?
    _____

12. Does the client prefer low risk/low return investments? _____

13. Does the client exaggerate or understate his or her personal profile?
    _____
    _____

14. Does the client have the patience to see a financial plan through from beginning to end? _____
    _____

**¶28,019.03**

## ¶28,021  MARKET RISK

Risk in the securities industry is an attempt to assess the possibility of loss on investments. Many risks are quantifiable and not nearly as vague as many other forms of uncertainty. There are elaborate measurements of risk that the CPA and the client are not called upon to learn or understand. However, there are some forms of risk that financial planners would be advised to familiarize themselves with, because these forms of risk provide information about the investments themselves.

### .01  Taking a Closer Look at Risks

Because there are many kinds of risk, the financial planner must be aware of them as they relate to securities. Most risks in securities are measurable: they address the possible loss of the money the client has put into an investment. Common risks that affect a client investment profile are:

1.  *Inflation risk*—the risk that the purchasing power of the client's funds will decrease over time. With increasing life expectancy, inflation plays a part in long-term concerns. For retired people, the concern of spiraling costs is significant, particularly if they have fixed pension income and fixed income securities.
2.  *Interest rate risk*—the risk that the client will lock in a rate of return on a fixed income security that is no longer competitive with other securities. People always expect the most for each dollar. In the current environment of low interest rates on fixed income vehicles, the client needs the highest rates attainable commensurate with the level of risk. This concern is especially true with the longer duration notes and bonds because the investor is often locked in by these vehicles.
3.  *Liquidity risk*—the risk that the clients will be unable to sell their investment when they need cash. The most prominent historical examples of this type of risk are private placements and limited partnerships. Many are without an orderly market, and sales are rarely accomplished quickly.
4.  *Exchange risk*—the risk that an investment loses money because of currency fluctuations. Many investors realize significant cash flows in non-dollar-denominated foreign investments. Often, as these investments are exchanged for dollars, the clients net less money than they expected. Because the dollar has been such a strong currency, the foreign currency is exchanged for far fewer dollars than previously.
5.  *Credit risk*—the risk that a rating sensitive investment goes down in value owing to a lowering of investment opinion. When Orange County, California, bonds went into default several years ago, many of the bonds went from AAA (the very highest rating) to "in reorganization" (the lowest

rating) in one day. The bondholders experienced immediate significant capital, cash flow and liquidity loss because of the credit collapse brought on by the county's default.

6. *Event risk*—the risk that something catastrophic will happen that affects the price of an investment. The most serious examples include:

   a. The loss of major executives in travel accidents.

   b. The nationalization of a foreign company.

   c. The discovery that a product causes terminal illness.

   d. Announcement of a major safety issue for employees and surrounding neighbors.

   Electric utilities provide classic examples of event risk that are all too familiar. Every nuclear episode in American history resulted in tremendous loss of capital and default on debt. After the event, investors could do nothing but commence endless litigation. Many of these companies have taken years to recover from such episodes.

7. *Principal risk*—the risk that the value of the investment will drop. This is most common with aggressive stock, options and futures investments. The principal value of these investments can gyrate wildly over time because they can appear to the novice investor to have "minds of their own." While physicists noted that "matter can neither be created nor destroyed," it should be obvious to the CPA that those scientists had had no experience with money management. *Principal can be created and destroyed* very quickly, indeed!

8. *Regulatory risk*—the risk that a legislative or political act will cause an investment to decline. In an environment where government regulation determines an increasingly large part of domestic corporate policy, it appears that even profit margins could be dictated by regulatory agencies.

## ¶28,023  ASSET ALLOCATION AND THE SPREAD OF RISK

In financial planning, investments and asset allocation, the key to success is diversity. This goal can be accomplished through a variety of investments in the securities industry. The determination of *how to diversify* is what asset allocation is all about. The CPA/PFS should work out with the client an appropriate blend of stocks, bonds and cash. Clients should diversify investments through asset allocation to protect the total portfolio from major downside moves without too stringently limiting upside potential. Stocks can go up, bonds can go down, balanced mutual funds can go sideways. The variations are endless, and they can all move simultaneously. By selecting a variety of investments, clients give their portfolios a better chance of remaining stable in a negative environment (for any of the asset classes) and thus of realizing maximum returns over the long term.

Asset allocation is more than a buzzword; it is a concept as old as money itself. What makes the term fresh is its usefulness for the contemporary client. The CPA/PFS can assist clients in building an investment portfolio and in achieving their financial goals using asset allocation as a tool. In today's environment, it is both profitable and smart to stick with successful applications of asset allocation because the markets are so volatile.

To summarize, the CPA/PFS takes three types of investment—stocks, bonds and cash—and stirs. Much of asset allocation is simple; but, in the real-world application, financial concepts can become complex. The specialist should be the client's interpreter for complex terms, issues and scenarios surrounding investment and asset allocation. However, there is no need to make them more difficult than they already are. Any areas that clients might find particularly interesting can be explored in depth with the CPA/PFS as mentor.

All three classes of investment—stocks, bonds and cash—perform well, poorly, neutrally, in tandem, out of sync and randomly over extended periods of time. To determine the percentage to allocate to each of these classes requires a financial plan based not on what the CPA/PFS and client think *might* happen, but on *what has happened* before and *what is currently happening* in the financial markets.

CPAs/PFSs cannot formulate a plan without a clear understanding of these securities. They must plan to consider the securities their client base will be most apt to deal with, and exclude all the techniques and vehicles that do not apply to their particular clients. Many stock and bond trading activities generate a great deal of press interest and coverage that is meaningless in the normal course of investing. CPAs/PFSs should look at stocks, bonds, and mutual funds (which are overwhelmingly made up of only stocks or bonds) for their clients, learn what they are, which kinds are available, and which are appropriate for each type of client's account.

Today, the CPAs/PFSs face a more difficult task than they did even 10 years ago. Paradoxically, while the world has shrunk because of communications and information technology, the investment universe has expanded as a consequence of communications technology. As markets fluctuate through wider and wider volatility bands, the advisor must understand and accommodate this volatility.

No CPA/PFS advises or expects a client to split savings 50/50 between the S&P 500 index and the 10-year U.S. Treasury note, then sit back and await retirement. While sometimes this might be an adequate strategy, it is no guarantee of superior returns. Personal financial needs, investment diversification, and personal risk profiles complicate such a simplistic approach. What kind of money the client needs, for what, and for how long, changes radically over a life span. A lack of diversification may expose the client to unnecessary investment risk and could result in poor long-term investment performance. The client's individual risk profile properly determined can prevent more losses than all other investment strategies combined.

¶28,023

## .01   Asset Allocation: How to Put It All in Place

What has been accomplished thus far is to recognize the need for a financial planning approach to investments. It then becomes necessary to:

1.  Determine the client's goals (particularly as they relate to retirement and college savings).
2.  Help the client implement the plan.
3.  Aid the client in selecting the investments once the individual risk profile has been established.
4.  Review, update, and refine the plan and strategy to confirm that the client is on course to reach those goals.
5.  Check periodically to ascertain whether that course reflects the client's current thinking.

The CPA/PFS can be of great help in implementing these steps, but the plan and strategies are the clients' concern and are central to their own needs. The CPA/PFS and client should know by now the investment options in stocks, bonds and mutual funds. Now they must determine what to do to put this knowledge to work.

To allocate assets, the client is directed in the current era *toward total* return. While as time passes, this approach may change, it is currently the orientation of most securities investment. Most clients want to outpace inflation and maximize returns with a bias toward asset growth. However, they cannot ignore the attractions of cash flow from both bond interest and stock dividends.

As a secondary concern, behind the primary goal of realizing dreams, asset allocation allows the client to dream comfortably. The CPA/PFS needs to create a balance of risk to return with as little portfolio volatility as possible. Stocks and bonds often behave differently from one another. They do not move together as a single force.

## .03   Portfolio Management

While there is no need to start courses in modern portfolio theory, understanding some portfolio management basics helps in creating a diversified portfolio. For the client to achieve this, with the help of the CPA/PFS, is the most valuable aspect of investing. Asset allocation is the engine that drives the investment car. Determining this allocation is not easy, nor is portfolio management. There is much to learn before setting out to select securities for a portfolio. All the planning in the world is of no use unless it is successfully implemented by investment in a portfolio of stocks, bonds and cash. Portfolio management aims to accomplish this with:

1. Above-average returns.
2. Appropriate risk levels.
3. Diversity.
4. The long-term view.

## .05  Putting Asset Allocation to Work

The assumption of responsibility for portfolio management is the direction of asset allocation. It is the action steps of the asset allocation program. After establishing how to allocate assets from the client's financial plan, the CPA/PFS should use that plan to determine how to invest by:

1. Researching what stocks, bonds and cash to invest in. The CPA/PFS should obtain information from other financial advisors, investment publications, newspapers, books, magazines, radio, TV, investor seminars, and personal ideas.
2. Determining how to weigh a portfolio. This involves finalizing the mix of stocks, bonds and cash and evaluating choices based on suitability, risk, value, industry particulars and any other factors of interest to the CPA/PFS or client before investing.
3. Taking steps that portfolio management demands, including regular securities quote examination and regular reading about investment theory.
4. Establishing when the client should contact the CPA/PFS, such as in cases of undue volatility, especially good or poor investment performance, or when anything crops up that the client simply does not understand.
5. Instructing clients who manage their own portfolios to call for help in the event of red flags—episodes of significance to an investment that are negative in their effect.

## .07  Further Concerns

The goal is to accomplish positive things, but a similar goal is to avoid negative results. The financial specialist must watch for illogical investments—those that are unsuitable, perform all the same or are current fads:

1. *Unsuitable investments*—These are investments not suited to the clients' goals. The typical poor choices for clients are investments that exceed their risk parameters. Most familiar are investments such as hot stock funds, heavily leveraged funds, or highly specialized or concentrated sec-

tor funds. A less obvious poor choice would be a large dividend paying stable stock in a growth portfolio.

2. *Perform all the same* — These investments are so similar that the client cannot be said to have diversified at all. For example, selecting three different domestic small capitalization mutual funds is not investment diversity — it is investment redundancy; all are much the same and tend over time to perform the same as one another. To own six power utilities, three phone companies, and two natural gas distribution stocks sounds diversified, but, really, the client simply owns eleven utility stocks. A better allocation would be several utility stocks plus an assortment of consumer growth stocks and an insurance or bank stock.

3. *Current fads* — The last few years have seen so many retail investment products come and go in popularity that one is hard put to select a few for examples:

   a. The limited partnership vehicle, where the client participated in partnership activities but could not lose more than his or her original investment, seems to have departed forever.

   b. The ubiquitous short-term, multimarket income funds have been rolled into other income funds, never to resurface.

   c. Current investment fads have included new issues and Internet stocks — some have tomorrows, most do not.

In summary, the CPA/PFS should assess client needs, set up an asset allocation plan that complements the financial plan and risk profile and then create a set of portfolio rules related to periodic reviews, buy/sell strategies and an overall plan that is customized to the client's needs.

## .09   What Asset Allocation Looks Like

Asset allocation relates to all this by answering the question, "What should the client invest in?" While more specific asset allocation comes in some detail later, for current uses, what the client invests in is a mixture of stocks, bonds and cash. Each asset class has volatility factors, with cash being least volatile, stocks being most volatile, and bonds somewhere in between.

*Stocks.*   Regarding stocks, it is important to determine whether the client should consider growth, value, domestic or foreign stocks:

1. Growth stocks increase in price and trading volume, usually from increasing earnings momentum.

2. Value stocks sell at what are perceived to be low prices relative to their liquidation and market worth.

3. Domestic stocks are in companies whose headquarters are located in the United States.

4. Foreign stocks are in companies whose headquarters are located in foreign countries.

**Bonds.**   With bonds, the CPA/PFS simply suggests a class of bonds suitable for the client and then creates a portfolio fit to that suitability — or invests in a strategic income mutual fund and lets a manager take care of all this for the client. Classes of bonds are:

1. Short Term: one year or less.
2. Intermediate Term: one to five years.
3. Long Term: six years or more.
4. Investment Grade: rated BBB or above.
5. Junk: rated BB or below.

As a precaution, the CPA/PFS should orient the client toward being as aggressive as the clients' risk profile and temperament allow. Investors can become so preoccupied with avoiding loss that they fail to generate suitable gains. This error results in a serious overweighing of income and neglect of growth, especially in a low interest/low inflation environment.

## .11   The Need to Diversify

To achieve their goal of financial independence in retirement and adequate savings for educational expenses, most clients fall into these broad areas of investment:

1. Capital preservation.
2. Current income.
3. Total return.
4. Long-term growth.
5. Aggressive growth.

These five sample programs should not be routinely changed. They are definitely not cursory guides to be abandoned at a whim but are commonly accepted and long-established guidelines used throughout the financial services industry. There are some compelling reasons to follow these allocations for the investors they describe. Of course, all are subject to revision and should certainly be reviewed in relation to client holdings quarterly, semiannually or at least annually. This is to make certain that the client weighting is appropriate and, if so, that the assets are still allocated as the weighting requires. If one asset class outperforms the other two by a wide margin, there could be some reallocation of assets to get the percentages back in line. Also, the exact percentages are a guideline, not hard-and-fast rules.

A description of each of these and the mix that should make up the portfolio is discussed below.

*Capital Preservation.* Capital preservation, the most conservative class, is made up of 25 percent cash, 55 percent bonds, and 20 percent stock. The 25 percent cash is for client-perceived immediate or near immediate cash needs and has no volatility. The 55 percent bonds are to generate current spending income. The 20 percent equity allocation functions primarily as an inflation and asset hedge, but secondarily to generate increased net worth and capital gains over the long-term. As the most conservative strategy, the return can be only modestly rewarding because of the near absence of growth and the large percentage of money fund assets. However, the CPA assumes here the genuine need for liquidity and capital preservation at the expense of any other strategy.

With the actual potential for negative real returns (realized returns adjusted for rate of inflation), this risk parameter and asset allocation is for a very small portion of the client population. This client might be someone who is fully retired, with adequate assets for future needs. The only financial concern would be a sudden significant capital loss.

Capital preservation might be a suitable entry-level investment and asset allocation stance for a client attempting to invest for the first time. However, if that client has a very long-term outlook, the CPA/PFS could work toward a more aggressive stance over a period of time as the client became more comfortable with the process.

*Current Income.* The current income class, the next asset allocation level in terms of risk tolerance, the CPA allocates 30 percent to stocks, 60 percent to bonds, and 10 percent to cash. The stocks should be total return stocks with dividends consistent with the S&P 500 dividend; the bonds should be of whatever duration the client is comfortable with; the cash is for unexpected needs. A current income allocation can be adjusted to be as conservative or moderate as the client wants to make it:

1. If conservative, the client is looking at small real returns and, it is hoped, no losses.
2. If moderate, the client can make a very good return with total return stocks, especially large capitalization ones. A more aggressive duration stance with the bonds would be in order.

The current income client is one for whom declining purchasing power, inflation, rising prices and other future dollar concerns may be a problem. However, the problem is not a severe one because this client should have a comfortable amount of money. Similar to the prototypical capital preservation client, losses are a very significant source of unrest for the client.

*Total Return.* The total return portfolio is a mixture of income and growth. It should be 40 percent stocks, 50 percent bonds, and 10 percent cash. The client can "barbell" risk (have one end speculative and the other end conservative) and have aggressive growth and moderately long-term, highest-grade bonds. Or the client can look for the middle ground with total return stocks and capital-appreciation-oriented bonds. The cash, once again, is for sudden expenses. Total return is the middle-of-the-road category that fits the middle of the bell curve for the middle client. It represents Everyman. This client is an employed individual who is trying to increase his or her net worth through securities investment and simply wants a good return without great downside risk. This client is more than happy to give up the investment grand slam home run and settle for singles, doubles, and the occasional triple or homer. Most clients are comfortable with this mix or long-term growth because these allocations approximate the financial commitment for which most clients qualify. Most clients would like to have growth and income and would be hard put to delineate a preference for either. The risk/reward tends here toward a double-digit return, without great unease in most times of market upheaval.

*Long-Term Growth.* Long-term growth is set up with 70 percent stocks, 20 percent bonds, and 10 percent cash. The stock component makes investments in all areas of growth and value, capitalization and domestic and foreign. The bonds generate income to reinvest (some appreciation, ideally) and function as a hedge in down stock markets. The cash is for emergencies or special investment opportunities. Long-term growth is for the somewhat aggressive growth client who has no more than modest current income needs, but recognizes the virtues of a bond cash flow and its stabilizing influence. This client may be younger, higher income, or more aggressive than the total return client, hence the stronger predisposition toward growth. As with total return, however, the growth allocation can be very aggressive, if weighted in speculative or high-risk areas of equities. The growth component is then accentuated at the expense of the income side of the equation, but it requires significant portfolio management to accomplish significant returns. For example, for the client to realize the full benefit of such a program, considerable research would go into determining which individual equities to invest in and in what industry groups. Even if mutual funds are utilized, considerable research should go into determining which funds, from what fund family, in what types, because the goal of such a program is to hit home runs. A normal growth component with a normal rate of return would not be an adequate goal.

*Aggressive Growth.*     Aggressive growth, which suits people with no income needs whatsoever and few liquidity needs, is 80 percent stocks, 10 percent bonds, and 10 percent cash. The stocks are all classes, mostly pure growth with no income component; the bonds are zero coupon bonds maturing in the distant future to generate maximum capital gains potential; the cash is for special investment opportunities. Aggressive growth requires far more hands-on portfolio management than capital preservation—the opposite end of the investment spectrum—because the CPA/PFS and client need to be concerned about more aspects of the market. The aggressive growth client must spend a great deal of time trading the account and investing or, if not, he or she, must plan to hire a money manager who can handle everything. This would include discretionary trading with confirms, monthly statements, and performance reviews on a systematic basis with the CPA/PFS. The likelihood of significant losses and gains is much greater because the volatility of the account and its constituent parts is much greater. More aggressive means more risk and thus more responsibility, attention, review, activity, trading positions . . . and problems.

*Warning:* These are active accounts that often turn sour as short-term trading accounts using options and futures and other high-risk tools to achieve perceived maximum performance.

## .13   How to Select an Asset Allocation Option

If the client were to conclude that direct investment in stocks, bonds and cash under any of these five programs for asset allocation is beyond them, the mutual fund industry is only too happy to come to their rescue. This group of clients can create their own portfolio made up of different mutual funds. They can:

1. Select sector, index, or style funds for the equity allocation.
2. Invest in sector or strategic income funds to meet the bond allocation.
3. Have any type of money market fund that suits them for the cash.

If even this level of involvement in the selection process taxes the client's time or inclination, there are global asset allocation funds that contain domestic and foreign equities, debt and cash. Within this group is an answer to almost any investment need, because the group contains as widely variant a group of funds as any in the industry. Some are extraordinarily well diversified with hundreds of positions in numerous countries, markets and securities adding up to billions of dollars.

The best of them have betas (measure of volatility relative to the stock market) under that of the S&P 500 Index. However, some of these same funds have among the worst returns of any mutual funds in existence, either equity or debt. The class enjoys almost total flexibility because they have no real investment guidelines. This, of course, can be unnerving to many clients. But at their very best, they approach the concept of one-stop shopping investment. The task is to find a fund with an investment philosophy consistent with the risk parameters and asset allocation of the particular client—and send in the money.

Caveat emptor is still the order of the day, with required reviews and all other portfolio procedures, but most of the job is done by the fund managers.

## .15   Conclusion

A number of financial issues face client and advisor today. Among these issues are:

1.  The end of "Big Brother" corporate pension plans.
2.  The rocky future of Social Security.
3.  The end or drastic curtailment of many government social service and entitlement programs.
4.  The propensity toward increased life expectancy.
5.  Skyrocketing health care costs.

The way to address these issues for the CPA/PFS and their clients is through life savings, self-directed retirement plans, college savings and other financial vehicles that in a knowledgeable and deliberate fashion solve the clients' financial problems for themselves. The CPA/PFS and client must be their own best caretakers. Financial planning, risk profile and asset allocation investment are the tools of the CPA/PFS and client relationship, they will help the CPA/PFS take better care of their clients. The sooner the individual's goals are quantified and set, the more apt the client is to achieve them.

The CPA/PFS and the client need to assess the investments using accurate performance techniques and strategies that allow the advisor to fill out an objective report card on the client's investments. After they have selected the investment, they must regularly track their performance. The CPA/PFS and client learn enough about investment appraisal and performance information sources to judge success and failure. They know to quantify everything and use quantitative analysis rather than the subjective language of adjectives such as "good" and "bad" or "safe" and "risky."

Asset allocation has characteristically appealed to, and been practiced by, large institutions and individuals with high net worth. The CPA/PFS and their clients should learn that the benefits of asset allocation apply to everyone. The primary explanation for the success of asset allocation is that diversification properly practiced actually works. The clients can index, create their own portfolio of individual securities, or select an asset allocation mutual fund. The choice is up to the CPA/PFS and his or her clients. Market timing, rampant speculation, in-and-out trading or unsuitable investments of any kind do not work for anyone.

Who wins and who loses in the investment arena is easily determined: long-term, high-quality, patient investors win more often than not. There is no perfect plan or set-in-stone portfolio for everyone. Each client is different. The challenge for the CPA/PFS is to determine what is best for each and every one of them.

## ¶28,025  COMMON INVESTMENT MISTAKES

Avoiding common investment mistakes may seem to the client to be a function of logic, but in the excitement and confusion of the moment, mistakes occur. Although the risks previously addressed are beyond anyone's control, the next series of mistakes are not. The financial specialist is largely in control of the client's financial destiny. One really bad investment can ruin an entire portfolio. While it is impossible to generate record profits and performance year after year, it is relatively easy to avoid disastrous returns if the client listens to advice and avoids that "big loss."

The following disasters can be avoided by using common sense and a generous application of self-discipline. The astute CPA/PFS will not:

1.  *Put all the client's eggs in one basket*.   The securities industry calls disproportionately large securities positions "concentrated positions." The brokerage firms will not lend the normal percentages of money on concentrated positions. They consider the risks of doing so inherently excessive. They prefer that a client have a diversified portfolio—as should the planner. Enron employees who had all of their 401(k)s in company stock are an extreme example of the peril of holding a concentrated position.

2.  *Have misplaced faith in a particular stock*.   To believe in XYZ Company wholeheartedly could be likened to falling under a spell. When something goes wrong with a company, something has gone wrong, period. Stock prices per se and securities prices in general tell a story by their movements. A continually declining security often unfolds as a sad story.

3.  *Leave the client's statements and confirmations in their envelopes unopened*.   The disclosure laws exist for the investor's well-being and protection. Open all mail and act/react in a timely manner.

4.  *"Churn" the client*.   The CPA/PFS should also never let them be churned by someone else or allow them to churn themselves. Clients never traded themselves out of difficult spots by excessive trading activity. Checkmate in securities is always checkmate—and the game is over. The costs of excessive trading, which you can easily calculate, eliminate all but the most extraordinary profits. (Many former online traders learned this the hard way.)

5.  *Try to out-think the market*.   The market is smarter than any individual, even a professional analyst, and functions at speeds no human can match; it is impossible to fight against the direction of the market.

6. *Follow a guru*.   If the CPA were to make a list of gurus going back to the gold boom of the late 1970s, how many of them would have passed the test of time?

7. *Ignore gut reactions*.   This includes hunches, intuition and natural inclinations. The accountant's and client's first impulses, with intelligence guided by experience, are more often than not correct.

8. *Look backward*.   The missed opportunities are in the past. Learn from experience and look ahead.

9. *Aim too high*.   No one makes spectacular securities profits out of nowhere with no risk.

10. *Stagnate*.   When things are not going well and have not gone well for a long time, even standing pat can be interpreted as stagnating. When this happens, it is time to decide upon a course of action.

# ¶28,027   Good Advice

Many clients are content to rely upon their life experience as their sole frame of reference for evaluating potential investments. If the clients believe the planner will achieve their goals expeditiously and cost-effectively, the CPA (from enlightened self-interest) should inject some third party into the picture. For the protection of both the adviser and the client, it is wise to enlist the aid of a qualified investment professional to increase securities knowledge. Investing has become increasingly complicated and has taken on a life of its own; no one should try to go it alone.

Whether the CPA elects to be self-reliant, seek occasional or ongoing professional advice and information, the following suggestions are sound advice. These are tried-and-true axioms that make sense and are of genuine benefit:

1. *Cut losses*.   A client can forget a 15 percent loss in no time and it means little in the overall picture. A 50 percent loss is remembered forever.

2. *Know what the client owns and why*.   Intermediate notes are selected for a decent cash flow and stable asset price. They cannot somehow be expected to turn into a growth stock—in any market environment.

3. *Let profits ride*.   Sell losers, not winners. If the clients sell their winners to make up for losers, they end up with all losers.

4. *Read quarterly and annual reports*.   Their existence is required for a reason—disclosure, disclosure, disclosure. . . .

5. *Deal only in quality investments*.   In time, quality always wins out. It must be remembered that everyone makes mistakes. The goal is to minimize mistakes by discarding a bad investment before the investment turns completely

sour. While too much risk is a recipe for failure, without some degree of risk, there will not be adequate returns.

6. *Plan for failure*.   Clients always want big returns. But it is best to have an exit strategy with any investment, should things go wrong. If XYZ Company stock is down and the clients have a red flag price to cut losses, they must abide by the initial decision regarding the investment and cut losses. To maintain control of each portfolio, the client needs a plan of action for failure as well as one for success for each investment.

## .01   Minimizing Risk

A successful strategy to minimize risk is to keep careful records of all trades and pay close attention to investment statements. With a record of investment performance, the accountant can do an adequate job of performance appraisal. No one can intelligently appraise how investments are performing without good records. Securities awareness must expand as clients become owners of more and more different investments.

## ¶28,029   ACCREDITATION REQUIREMENTS FOR THE PFS DESIGNATION

In December 2000, the AICPA announced a new set of guidelines to satisfy requirements for the Personal Financial Specialist credential. Candidates are now to be evaluated on a point system. A minimum of 100 points is required for the designation. These points are based in three specific areas: business experience, life-long learning, and examination.

To qualify for the PFS designation, an individual must:

1. Be a member in good standing of the AICPA.
2. Hold a valid and unrevoked CPA certificate issued by a legally constituted state authority.
3. Pass the PFS examination. (The requisite experience may be obtained before or after taking the PFS exam.)
4. Agree to comply with all the requirements for reaccreditation.
5. Have at least 250 hours of relevant business experience per year in personal financial planning activities for the three years immediately preceding the PFS application. This experience is drawn from six financial planning disciplines:
   a. The personal financial planning process (setting goals).
   b. Personal income-tax planning.
   c. Risk-management planning.
   d. Investment planning.

  e. Retirement planning.

  f. Estate planning.

6. Upon successful completion of the PFS exam, the applicant will be asked to submit six references to substantiate working experience in personal financial planning.

The first two requirements must be met at the time of registration in order to sit for the examination. References are required only after the applicant has been notified of successful completion of the examination. He or she then has three years in which to submit the work references. If that time has elapsed, the examination score will be invalidated. The individual will then be required to retake and pass the examination to become accredited.

## .01 Additional Information Relating to the Point System

In addition to the areas covered above in item 5, business experience also includes teaching college-level personal financial planning courses.

Life-long learning points may be earned through continuing professional education (CPE) courses, self-directed reading and research programs, conference presentations and professional writing. Advanced degrees, such as a juris doctor and master of business administration, are considered. Participants on the committees of nationally renowned personal financial planning associations also receive life-long learning credit.

As stated, all PFS candidates are required to pass an examination, the Comprehensive PFS Examination. In addition, several other certification exams are eligible for points toward accreditation: Certified Financial Planner, Chartered Financial Consultant, Chartered Financial Analyst, National Association of Securities Dealers (NASD) Series 65, NASD Series 66 and NASD Series 7. The AICPA cautions that some of these additional exams will require the applicant to obtain a greater number of points in business experience and life-long learning.

## .03 Reaccreditation Requirements

To maintain the PFS accreditation, the accountant must pay an annual reaccreditation fee and recertify his or her accreditation every three years. To do so, the requirements are:

1. Be a member in good standing of the AICPA.
2. Have a valid and unrevoked CPA certificate issued by a legally constituted state authority.

3. Have at least 750 hours of experience in personal financial planning over the preceding three years. Experience must be in each of the six financial planning disciplines listed above.

4. Take at least seventy-two hours of financial planning courses in prescribed disciplines every three years.

5. Submit a written statement of intent to continue to comply with all the requirements for reaccreditation.

6. Submit a completed internal practice review questionnaire (IPRQ), as amended from time to time. The questionnaire asks the CPA/PFS to provide information to determine whether he or she has met the reaccreditation requirements. The CPA/PFS agrees to submit supporting data, including work papers, for external review of personal financial planning activities upon request.

Every three years, all CPAs/PFSs must be reaccredited to maintain the designation. If reaccreditation requirements are not met, the accreditation ceases and all initial requirements, including examination, must be repeated to regain accreditation. A waiver may be requested and will be granted if, in the sole judgment of the AICPA, there is justification.

## .05   The Personal Financial Planning Experience Requirement

As mentioned previously, PFS candidates must have at least 250 hours of experience in personal financial planning activities in each of the three years preceding the initial accreditation application. Candidates for reaccreditation must have at least 750 hours of personal financial planning experience over the three years preceding their reaccreditation.

Although the CPA must have some experience in each of the planning areas, there is no specific or minimum amount of time required for any one area. The following summary highlights some of the services provided by CPA financial planners and provides examples of activities that may qualify as personal financial planning experience.

*The Personal Financial Planning Process.*   In addition to all the activities involved in setting up and augmenting a basic financial plan, as described earlier, the AICPA goes even further and suggests other services that may qualify for experience. Among these are reviewing spending patterns, developing cash flow management, budgeting recommendations and performing time-value-of-money calculations.

*Personal Income Tax Planning.*   As stated earlier, this is the area in which the CPA is already the most conversant with the clients' situation. If these are not new clients, the accountant is unquestionably already doing much of what the AICPA considers to be qualifying experience toward the

PFS designation: "Advising clients regarding the federal and state income tax consequences of their financial decisions, including matters such as timing income and deductions; making charitable contributions; utilizing net operating losses, capital losses, or passive activity losses; establishing and maintaining employee fringe benefit plans; taking retirement plan distributions; and bankruptcy. Helping clients split income among family members through the use of family partnerships, employment arrangements, gifts and trusts, installment sales, etc. Advising clients on the issues related to personal decisions such as marriage or divorce (property settlements, retirement plan asset division, alimony and child support)."

*Risk Management Planning.*     In this chapter, risk is considered from two very distinct aspects: that relating to the types of risk that can be ameliorated or completely covered by insurance and the types of risk encountered in investing.

The AICPA emphasizes insurance as an important aspect of managing risk. That aspect has been rather fully covered in this chapter. Certainly, it is important to analyze clients' exposure to risk and review with them methods for managing risk and to help them minimize financial risks from disability, illness, property damage, and personal and professional liability. As a part of their tax planning, the planner will automatically review with clients the income and estate tax aspects of their insurance coverage.

*Investment Planning.*     This is the area in which the CPA/PFS must exercise the most caution. Being a tax adviser and an investment adviser are two distinct roles. That is the reason much of this chapter is devoted to the discussion of the investment activities the AICPA includes as credit toward the PFS designation. Among their list, they include: ". . . recommending investments or helping clients build portfolios (consider registration requirements); managing client assets." A veiled caution, but a caution nonetheless.

*Retirement Planning.*     Added to material considered above are ". . . reviewing with clients the limits on and tax consequences of contributions to or distributions from retirement plans; planning for the post-retirement succession of a closely held business."

*Estate Planning.*     If the speculation about the effects of the new tax law on estate planning hold true, many CPAs may be very actively involved in this area of planning. Regardless of new legislation, the steps mentioned and the AICPA suggestions will remain: ". . . reviewing with clients the tax and probate considerations of various forms of property ownership and making recommendations on the titling of assets; recommending or reviewing various instruments (wills, powers of attorney, trusts) for use in achieving goals; planning for the post-mortem succession of a closely held business (buy-sell agreements, estate freeze techniques, valuation issues, etc.)."

¶28,029.05

# Chapter 29

# Equity Strategies

## CONTENTS

## ¶29,000 OVERVIEW

Because of the widespread nature of investment by clients, the CPA/ personal financial specialist (PFS) must learn and know about equities, debt and other investment vehicles. In the 1950s, only wealthy people owned stocks and bonds. Now, most clients have investment portfolios. For the CPA, there is a sea of certification and licensing possibilities that are available on both a state and federal level to address these needs.

Many aspects of the certification process have been made confusing as more and more investment titles have been created. The fate of AICPA special designations has been decided at least for the time being. In October 2003, the group's Governing Council voted to retain the three designations—the Personal Financial Specialist, Certified Information Technology Professional, and the Accredited in Business Valuation—in addition to earmarking $16 million in funding for them. They also approved a resolution by the Board to kill an annual review of the credentials, but agreed that the designations become self-supporting by specific dates, and attract a minimum number of credential holders.

The PFS must hit the break-even target on July 31, 2006, while the CITP and the ABV must reach that goal by July 31, 2008. At their break-even dates the PFS must have 3,600 holders, while the ABV and CITP must have 2,700 and 1,700, respectively. Currently there are 3,188 PFS holders, while the ABV and CITP have 1,536 and 527, respectively.

In its resolution, the Board offered funding recommendations for Personal Financial Planning ($4.6 million in excess of revenues through 2006), Information Technology ($5.6 million in excess of revenues through 2008), and Business Valuation/Forensic & Litigations Services ($5.75 million in excess of revenues through 2008). The Council adopted these recommendations.

Council also agreed with the Board's determination that retention strategies should not include a national branding campaign because of the cost and effort necessary to achieve that level of recognition. Rather, the AICPA has agreed to develop marketing tools to aid the credential holders in promoting the designations in their local markets.

The National Accreditation Commission (NAC), which oversees the credential programs, has decided that credential holders will receive annual statements on each designation as a quasi-progress report and that the commission would coordinate with the executive committee for each designation to map out implementation and marketing strategies.

The AICPA will develop a variety of resources to help credential-holding practitioners provide services to their clients and employers. The NAC will coordinate its activities with the executive committees of each underlying discipline to achieve an integrated approach to help members succeed in their specialty areas.

The National Association of Securities Dealers (NASD) administers all licenses for the Securities and Exchange Commission (SEC). However, even if the CPA elects not to pursue a PFS designation or any of the various financial services licenses, he or she had best be familiar with stocks, bonds, and their corresponding mutual funds—if only from the standpoint of self-defense!

**¶29,000**

## ¶29,001    WHAT THE DIFFERENT TYPES OF STOCK INVESTMENTS OFFER

When the CPA/PFS discusses the types of stock investments that are available to the client, he or she must first look at what can be done for the client—the professional must define the parameters for measuring results. Results in the stock arena are measured in three ways: growth, income, and total return. These measures in turn must be assessed in the context of relative volatility or risk.

To make the best choice for the client, the CPA/PFS must know what these three goals mean and what they have to offer the client as an investor. Each offers something different:

- Growth increases net worth.
- Income is cash flow to the shareholder.
- Total return is a combination of both growth and income.

Examining each type of investor and providing an example of each may help matching a particular investor with the appropriate stocks.

### .01    The Growth Investor

Growth investors typically are those with an ongoing need to increase their net worth and are willing to accept some risk and volatility to accomplish this goal. A growth-oriented investor tends to be either middle class or wealthy. If the investor is wealthy, watching growth stocks is an enjoyable experience. If an investor is of moderate means, seeing a measurable increase year after year in net worth is exhilarating. However, the median investor must be more circumspect in choosing stock, because money is often illiquid and cannot be easily replaced. These investors should look back to when they had very little and should continue looking forward to when they will need a lot. The CPA/PFS needs to help median investors keep their feet firmly on the ground. They have little margin for error, especially when their time considerations are factored into the equation.

Growth stocks are what equity investments are all about. When they perform well, the world is seen through the snappiest rose-tinted glasses. For example, Mary Sue is an administrative manager working at a large computer sales company and makes $35,000 per year. She receives $10,000 per year from her widowed mother to put away for her children's education and often is able to supplement that with a portion of her annual bonus of $5,000 to $15,000. What kind of stocks should she buy for her children? Growth stocks. They have no need for current income, as they are students in school, but their needs for college are almost limitless. Mary Sue's plan of action should be to research and select industries she feels will provide real growth during her children's school years and start a portfolio of the industry leaders in her chosen groups. She can consider as many industry groups as she wants, define her parameters, and start narrowing down her choices. With several good candidates, she then chooses stocks and proceeds to invest her money. She does not have to make perfect choices, but she should look for some research consensus about her selections.

## .03   The Income Investor

An income stock is not as glamorous as a growth stock, but it performs a noble function. It is very kind to one's standard of living because it generates a usable cash flow, cushions downturns in growth stocks, and provides a supplement to fixed income investments that neither increase dividends as earnings increase nor have the potential for even modest growth while tracking inflation.

Aunt Sally is a representative income stock investor. During the Carter era, she was happy to roll over short- and intermediate-term fixed income instruments, such as Certificates of Deposit and Treasury Bills, but now the yield advantage of those investments is ancient history. Sally must turn to stocks because the inflation of the ensuing years has eroded the purchasing power of her remaining fixed income investments and she simply has to have more cash flow. For a number of reasons, stocks with big dividends are the answer. She is not happy about buying stock, but the advantages from an income standpoint far outweigh the risks.

The following are reasons for moving to a stock income portfolio:

- Income stocks pay higher yields than comparable fixed income investments because stock investments are more risky than bond investments—the yields are higher because there is no set rate or income for a set rate of time.
- Historically, successful income stocks tend to increase their dividends—a real plus for the income investor. As time and inflation marches on, the investor receives more and more dividends, which hopefully keep pace with her need for more income.
- The growth component inherent in stock investing cannot be ignored—if the value of the stocks appreciate, and should the need arise, some of the stock can be liquidated to generate cash for Sally. Her profits can then be used to pay her obligations.

## .05   The Total Return Investor

Total return stocks are the best of both worlds—growth increases net worth and income generates cash flow to supplement other income. It is prototypical money management because the growth and income stocks complement each other and are a balancing factor that is required by many investors. Most people have both net worth and income-sensitive concerns.

Phil is looking forward to retirement in several years. He has almost enough to live on happily in retirement, but he is worried about having to dip into his principle later in life. He is more than a little concerned about the future of Social Security, and whether his pension plan, which does not have cost-of-living adjustments, will be sufficient for future living expenses. Phil needs everything stock investment has to offer—growth and income.

Phil can afford to be moderately aggressive because he is well established for life. But he has to watch his balance. If he generates some decent dividend income before he needs it, he can use his cash flow to address his upcoming requirements later in life. He needs help in seeking out the highest-quality total return stocks the industry provides and starting to build positions in them now.

## ¶29,003  DETERMINING AN INVESTMENT PROFILE HELPS INVESTORS MAKE THE RIGHT CHOICES

Different personalities and incomes have different profiles. The extent to which clients are comfortable with risk cannot be overstated. The more clients and their CPA/PFSs learn about stocks, the more comfortable they can be with volatility when facing the long-term horizon. The more concerned a person is with risk, the more cautiously a person should ease into stock investment. Starting out, investments should be the most conservative, household name, investment grade stocks. As stock investors learn more about the market and are more comfortable with its volatility, they can expand their horizons. They can naturally progress to more risk-oriented investments, so they can realize a suitable return on their investments.

For the more savvy investors who know their own profile and their own needs well, the learning process has not ceased. They just simply have to look for more sophisticated strategies and techniques to accomplish their goals. Warren Buffet is the premier stock investor in history. Who thinks he is done learning? Not a chance—there are always ways to grow in this field.

## ¶29,005  FITTING STOCKS INTO AN INVESTMENT PLAN

The clients are all in different places with different goals for their financial plan, but the roads to success for everyone are actually very similar. Stocks fit all but the most conservative, short-term, risk-adverse investment profiles. For some, stocks are not an option until certain criteria related to debt and other financial obligations are met. But, once they are met, stocks are the best and sometimes the only way to reach their goals.

How does the CPA/PFS fit stock into an investment plan? Simply put, he or she calculates how much discretionary cash the clients have—what do they have, what do they owe, how much can they invest? It is always best to pay off all consumer debt first and then figure how much and for what purpose the clients wish to invest. This will require some financial planning on their part. Some generalizations about stock investing are true:

- The youthful investor has a strong growth bias. It is often easy to be too conservative with college savings plans or retirement plans like 401(k)s and allow the seriousness of the task to inhibit the aggressiveness necessary to achieve the goal of making enough money.

- The middle-aged investor is often total return oriented. This is not only because of a more conservative bias toward some income, but also because the type of stocks middle-aged investors conventionally need and select are often total return stocks. Why? Cash must be generated, but a growing portfolio for the future is needed, too.

- The mature investor overwhelming gravitates toward income stocks. The retired investor rarely reflects an aggressive growth profile because most wealth accumulation was accomplished during peak earnings years. This investor is more concerned with safety of principle and earning a decent, rather than spectacular, return on investments. Volatility is often very unsettling to mature investors, as it is reminiscent of the stock market crash of 1929 and the Great Depression.

## .01 Direct Investment Puts the Investor in Charge

Many people want to be the masters of their own fates. Direct investment allows people to rely upon everything they know about themselves and their world. Hunches, research, tips—are all figured in here.

For example, a mother actively involved with her four children's spending begins to notice a pattern in their consumer trends. She starts buying stocks in the various companies that provide the consumer goods that her children and their friends have shown the most loyalty to over their childhood years. She determines for herself the industry groups, companies, and weightings for each stock in the family portfolio.

## .03 Managed Accounts Let Investors Tap Experienced Advisors

Managed accounts help the investor stay in the driver's seat, but they will have—and need—an expert traveler to help on the trip. The CPA/PFS and the client can control the overall strategy, the investment parameters, the buying and selling level, and the asset allocation through the guidelines established for the manager. The professional and client tell the managers what they want and the manager will do it for them. Managed accounts are for people who have neither the time nor drive to acquire the knowledge needed to make a portfolio, but who can afford an advisor who will accomplish all this for them. Together, the CPA/PFS, client, and money manager can make a great team.

## .05    Mutual Funds Provide Diversity and Simplicity

Diversity is achieved through investing in many types of stock funds with many types of stocks in them. Simplicity is achieved with ease of investment and ease of understanding. Mutual funds take much of the work out of investing in stocks. The investors have one end of the stock spectrum to the other end of the stock spectrum all growing and playing in a system of checks and balances as the fund families compete for the investment dollar. They attempt to keep pace with whatever index their fund is pegged to—all the CPA/PFS has to do is select a fund, have the client provide a lump sum of money to start the position, continue to contribute money to this fund, if successful, and watch it grow. A merry-go-round to some, but to others, it is the only way to go. Managed money and mutual funds are the vehicle of choice if the client choses not to own individual stocks.

Integral to the evaluation and analysis of mutual funds is consideration of the manager or management team, sales charges or other fees as well as the investment objectives of the fund.

## .07    Index Funds Offer Proven Results

The CPA/PFS and client may know the indexes of stocks better than the stocks themselves. Furthermore, they may better know the indexes than the various mutual funds and their families. Everyone knows them as the Dow Jones Industrials, the S&P 500, the Value Line Index, and a host of other proprietary performance measurements. Almost any index (domestic and foreign) that anyone can name has a corresponding index fund available for retail investment. The past few years have seen the addition of a growing number of exchange traded funds (ETFs) as well—broadening and deepening the investor's choices. These index funds track specific sectors or industries such as financial services or energy. The returns on these funds are the returns on the indexes because the funds perfectly (less management fees) mirror the performance of the indexes they duplicate. Like conventional managed mutual funds, but even more so, the index funds take pressure off the investor because they not only remove stock picking from the investor area of responsibility but also the task of fund picking. All the investor does is pick an index and commit money—it is as simple as that. Indexes are good choices for both novice and experienced investors because their benefits for the investor are clear:

- They are "no brainer" investments.
- They have immense diversification.
- The costs of most index products are minimal.
- For some, index funds comprise the investor's plan of action for asset allocation—and asset allocation can be the key to an investor's success.

## ¶29,007 CHOOSING STOCK INVESTMENT STRATEGIES THAT WORK FOR THE CLIENT

There are many ways to invest in the stock market. What will be significant is the strategy that works for the client's personality and needs of the time. Fortunately, stock investment strategies that work well are plentiful. Clients will undoubtedly change their strategy as time changes their investment outlook. Knowing investment options and using these strategic tools will make investing more interesting and financially rewarding for the client.

### .01 Investing for Appreciation: Building a Nest Egg

The first and most common strategy is growth investing. It offers the glistening opportunity of building a nest egg. Growth moves in mysterious ways. Even in the best of times and strongest of markets, many excellent stock fund managers underperform the benchmark stock indexes they are measured against. In contrast, it is much easier for bond fund managers to perform in the vicinity of their benchmarks. Bonds are much easier to successfully manage because there are fewer variables in the debt universe than there are in the equity universe. Equity managers are stock pickers by choice, and it is hoped the CPA/PFS and their clients are doing it by choice, too.

Imagine that a client just read in the paper about a new company that created a running shoe sole that will last for years. The client is a runner and knows that no running shoe lasts longer than 300 miles, so the prospect of buying some of these shoes is very exciting. As a CPA/PFS, the immediate thought is that the client might be able to get in early on what might have enormous implications not only for running shoes, but for footwear per se. The first thing is to determine whether the shoe manufacturer is a publicly held company. Once the professional has done that, and discovered that the public can actually own the stock, the research process starts preparatory to investing in the company:

1. The CPA/PFS finds out what brokerage firms, if any, cover the stock.
2. The CPA/PFS goes on-line or calls the brokerage firm and asks for copies of any available research reports.

3. The CPA/PFS reads the reports and, if they are positive, calls the share-holder relations area of the company and requests public data available on the company—quarterly and annual reports, balance sheets, financial statements, and publicity releases.

Once the CPA/PFS has digested all of this, and it appears to be a positive step, it is time to determine how much money the client is comfortable committing to the stock and then purchasing it.

Growth starts with ownership in a business that succeeds. What helps a business succeed? Following are some universal concepts of startups that become successful businesses and therefore growth stocks:

- There is a market for the product that the company sells. The existence of a product does not necessarily mean there is a market for that product.
- The product truthfully and successfully meets the needs of a ready market. The existence of a market does not necessarily mean there is a product for that market.
- The product is produced by a well-managed company, and the company provides an environment and opportunity for success for its employees and its product. The performance of the technical tasks necessary to the development of a product is totally different from the performance necessary for running a successful company. Managers are managers; inventors are inventors; salespeople are salespeople. It is necessary to determine whether the stock choice has strong divisions of power to support the overall excellence of the product.
- The company must be capable of functioning in the 21st century: management is not only personnel oriented but also now systems and processor oriented.
- The business historically generates significant operating cash flows.

What does all this mean to the CPA/PFS as an advisor and the client as a stock investor? It means each can devote common sense to stock choices and become capable fundamental analysts. Fundamental analysts study, assess, and judge the overall strength of a company from every informational point of view imaginable. Although few in the public may ever be able to analyze figures that well, many can use instinctive judgments based on experience, learning, and observation.

A client comes to the CPA/PFS with a hot stock tip. What should the CPA/PFS do?

1. Check the performance of the stock—its past, its perceived future.
2. Check the company for strength and stability in today's market.

¶29,007.01

3. Check plans for the future. Does this stock have a plan and a place in tomorrow's market?
4. Determine need. A strong need is the fuel for success.
5. Determine competition—is something else out there to compare it to?

The growth goal is to hit home runs. The growth stock investor wants to increase money as quickly as possible. Although people often say they would be content with "a sustained period of growth with inflation-adjusted returns somewhat above Treasury rates," they are really often impatient. The CPA/PFS must never lose sight of the client's true goals.

## .03 Aggressive Investing: More Risk, More Potential

By looking at the most aggressive form of equity investment, venture capital (which is oriented toward seed money in various stages of an uncreated company's development), the CPA/PFS can gain a picture of what to look for in any type of stock. Stocks are often classed as investment grade, good quality, speculative, or high risk. Venture capital is in the high-risk category. The client initially may never think of plunking down hard-earned capital for a venture capital investment, but as the portfolio expands and securities knowledge grows, it is not uncommon for a client to discover the benefits of aggressive growth.

Angel investing is business startup financing. There are investment services throughout the United States that help match companies and investors in various equity projects in various stages of development. For example, Uncle Ed Jones has just invented a substance that will keep guns in storage clean and rust-free for years in any climate or environment. Hunters and target shooters throughout the county buy his goop and his family quickly realizes he has a niche product that is a telemarketing dream—cheap, easy to make, and appeals to lots of people. What to do now? None of them has either the capital or the expertise necessary to market Gun Goop. Where do they go and what do they do to set the wheels in motion? There are venture capital placement and financing services in every major city in the United States. Uncle Ed and the family find a silent partner and are on their way to becoming the gun collector's answer to rust and storage problems. If the company continues to succeed because of excellent management, marketing, and sales, a public offering may materialize.

Everyone would like to be part of an investment early in its growth cycle. However, startups are by definition the birth of a company; they are also long-term commitments that might go nowhere. Ideally, an equity investor selects companies that are building for a successful future, with a goal of having a good profit run for years.

**¶29,007.03**

What is there in these private capital activities that helps the CPA/PFS learn more about stock picking tasks? As the most selective investors in the world, venture capitalists look for the following qualities in a company, and so should CPAs/PFSs and their clients:

- The company's products have a broad, general appeal or alternatively, a specialized niche with favorable gross-profit margins.
- The management teams are experienced in their company's product area. Regardless of the quality of the product, if the company fails, so will the stock.
- Today's technology is capable of handling the company's current needs and those of the intermediate future. Inventory and distribution are essential elements of business.
- There are excellent reasons for the consumer to buy the company's products. The cost is reasonable and the product is reliable.
- The company's revenues exceed expenses, and expenses are production generated. Value, not creative management, sells the product; it has been approved by the appropriate government agencies, and it can stand on its own as a successful product.
- The product is what started the company and the product remains the powerful source of revenue for the company, as opposed to creative number crunching.
- Cash flow from operations is reinvested in the growth of the company.

Is it risky? Yes, of course. However, if the CPA/PFS is research oriented with an knowledge of marketing trends and opportunities, companies and economics, this may dramatically increase net worth for the clients.

## .05    Stock Investing for Income: Returns Investors Can Use Today

For the investor facing a conventional retirement dependent upon a combination of corporate or government pensions, Social Security, IRAs and 401(k)s, and personal savings, investing for income becomes increasingly significant as time passes.

From an asset allocation standpoint, the closer a person is to retirement, the larger cash flow needs may become. Cash flow, as previously stated, mitigates many of the unappealing aspects of stock investment.

Before discussing income stock investments, it is important to point out that some income-oriented stock investments can be less risky and safer investments than corporate bonds. Not only may the underlying credit rating services' opinions be higher, but with the potential of rising income from increased stock dividends, they pay better.

¶29,007.05

Investors often fail to understand that an income flow changes the longer-term appreciation pattern of stock investing into one of immediate rewards and gratification. Stocks that pay dividends pay them every quarter. Stocks, of course, lack a maturity, and the dividend can be reduced, so they do not have a stated fixed interest payment, as with bills, notes, or bonds. This is not necessarily a detriment. Investors often take smaller than expected fixed income interest payments because they are afraid to assume holding periods with maturities dictated by longer-term debt securities. However, that is a mistake — bills, notes, and bonds are fully as liquid as stocks and can be very volatile, especially in the longer maturities. Investors have a mind-set about fixed income investments that is totally foreign to the stock arena. The benefit to investors is that they can create a regular income stream that has the distinct possibility of increasing significantly in value as the years go by.

Dividend income flows are usually measured in two ways: they are (1) stated as a function of cash flow (the amount of dollars and cents of income that goes directly into the hands of the shareholder), or (2) as a dividend yield, which is a percentage expression of the current amount of the dividend in cash divided by the current value of the underlying stock that pays the dividend.

For example, the shareholder can earn a 4 percent yield at the time of investment in XYZ. He or she can expect this to continue indefinitely, with a reasonable expectation of having that dividend increased if the company prospers and the board of directors continue to care about satisfying its existing income-oriented shareholders and trying to attract new investors.

The board of directors of XYZ determines the whether, how much, and when of dividend payments. Particularly in the blue chip arena, dividend issues can be a major source of board and shareholder focus. To the board, dividend payments are often reflective of the board's ability to generate earnings and willingness to distribute some of these earnings to the shareholders. To the shareholders, dividends represent a tangible manifestation of their ownership of the stock of XYZ. If the stock increases in value, they are of course pleased; but their ability to do much with this increase in value is very limited unless they sell XYZ. This is certainly a poor way to reward XYZ and its board for going up in value.

Cash dividends are a continuing inducement every 13 weeks to continue to own XYZ — the clearest validation to stockholders of their investment ownership in the company.

A less tangible, but certainly important, benefit of dividend cash flow is that it tends to stabilize the price of a stock in a down market. Many times, a stock declining in value bottoms out, not because investors are no longer selling it, but because new investors are buying it for the cash flow. This is particularly the case with very large capitalization stocks that have a historically secure dividend with a regular record of increasing (or, at least, not reducing) these dividends. Knowledgeable investors are very aware of the bargains created when stocks decline in value that have not missed or reduced their dividends

**¶29,007.05**

in decades or have increased their dividend payouts regularly for decades. These stocks generally bounce off 52-week lows or sharp market-related declines very quickly.

What this all means to an investor is that it is important to understand income stock investing. Income stock investing exemplifies cash flow management, the answer to almost every financial issue. The benefits to the investors are as many as they have uses for cash flow. Whether used to buy bread, reinvest in more securities, or give to a favorite charity, stock dividends are an immediate benefit of investing that anyone can appreciate.

An incentive for long-term investing provided by U.S. fiscal policy is the favorable long-term capital gains income tax rate. Clients should be educated on the benefits generated by holding stocks for longer than a year and the resulting 15% income tax rate applicable on gains generated.

## .07  Speculative Investments: Taking a Chance with Excess Funds

These stocks pay no dividends, often earn very little money, and can be depended upon to seesaw in price with mind-numbing regularity. However, as they trade through ranges of higher highs and, as is hoped, higher lows, the investor can benefit from rapidly accelerating price appreciation that could never be realized in more staid, blue chip growth, income, or total return stocks. Speculation often has a negative connotation, but the fact remains that a great deal of wealth in this country was created by investing in speculative growth companies. The U.S. government and Internal Revenue Service are fully cognizant of the value of this type of investing. They encourage it by the favorable tax treatment of stock gains.

At the other end of the spectrum are speculative recovery situations in blue chip fallen angels. The domestic automotive industry, domestic computer hardware industry, and international money center bank stocks are examples of industry groups that have seen primary constituents collapse over the years. However, phoenix-like, they have sprung from their own ashes to achieve extraordinary levels of return for their steely nerved value investors.

The most popular speculative stocks are the lower-priced, over-the-counter "story" stocks. They are often perceived by their investors as undiscovered gems that will become the blue chip index stocks of the future. They usually have no solid track record of earnings, products, or performance, but they are as long on expectations as they are short on results. They usually have a need to generate cash flow and have no idea from whence it will appear. Nevertheless, sometimes, they develop a product that changes the world.

Many types of aggressively traded speculative and high-risk vehicles are usually unprofitable. Whereas for some, penny stock, option, futures, and hard asset trading may be genuinely appealing, unless these investments are traded under expertly managed conditions, it is likely the retail speculator will lose

¶29,007.07

every cent invested. As a confirmation of this cautionary statement, it is difficult for the conventional retail client to gain approval from a wire house, discount, or bank brokerage firm to trade these vehicles. However, the primary benefit to the investor is that these securities and others contained in high-risk managed money portfolios do sometimes generate enormous trading profits. The road can be extraordinarily bumpy, but there are widely available, fully audited, remarkably profitable portfolios for the CPA/PFS to investigate should these techniques and strategies have appeal to a client. For the investor who is predisposed toward extreme risk and volatility, the return that can be earned on these investments may dramatically enhance the cumulative return of the total portfolio.

To conclude, when analyzing high-risk investments, the distinction between speculation and gambling may seem nonexistent. However, there is a genuine difference between the two. Speculation involves a measurement of risk and reward parameters, whereas gambling is often a chance, random event based on luck. Speculation is attractive to investors because some of the largest capitalization stocks in existence were recently speculative stocks with names familiar to basically no one.

The investor is trying to become someone who puts money into investments that will earn a reasonable and regular return consistent with that investment. Over the long term, investors look to both appreciation and income to resolve financial issues. The mind-set a speculator must cultivate with speculative investments is a totally short-term view that revolves around actively trading securities. The benefits to the securities investor are abundantly clear—quick profits. Although the risks are more immediate and apparent than with long-term investments, the truth is that the potential rewards are enough to overcome any objections for some people.

## ¶29,009 Successfully Coping with Market Fluctuations

Risk concerns become most stressful when the client addresses the area of market timing. Ideally, investors want to invest money in the stock market and receive an excellent return on their investment commensurate with their risk-to-reward profiles. Market timing is the notion that an investor buys at the trough of a down cycle in price. This way, the investor earns more than by simply buying when there is money to invest. The equity investor of today attempts to identify when the market is at its peak, but no one can truly do this. A successful investor is aware of various techniques and patterns that provoke a course of action when markets fluctuate excessively and threaten to undermine the most determined investor's confidence.

Study after study shows that market timing works only in hindsight; the long-term investor usually makes money, regardless of timing. From an asset allocation standpoint, what is important is that the investor is invested. The key is to own stock, but, how does one cope with market fluctuations?

Historically, bear markets have been brief. Corrections generally have been sharp and of a relatively brief duration. The worst nightmare is to invest at a peak, have a sudden correction in the market and prices drop, and have another three-year bear market begin. There is no corrective action the investor can take, but doing nothing is actually doing something. When invested in good-quality growth companies, the client has bought in for the long term. To be proactive in a bear market, the client must continue to invest, as money becomes available or even systematically. This is known as dollar-cost averaging. The virtue of repeated investing at regular intervals is that, if there is a long-term upward trend, in time the investor makes money. If clients are not out for a quick killing in the market, or they have not borrowed on margin to invest, or their immediate livelihood is not predicated on the performance of this investment, time is a friend.

For example, dollar-cost averaging results in buying more shares in down markets and fewer shares in up markets. Volatility is advantageous, because the client would never buy at the lowest lows if securities never changed in value. Indeed, a narrow trading band does not benefit dollar-cost averaging, because the security is trading near its median price.

To illustrate, David buys XYZ stock regardless of its price every month. If he buys $1,000 per month and his stock is $100 per share at the start of the year, goes up to $120 per share, down to $60 per share, and finishes out the year back at $100 per share, what does David accomplish? David can end up with about 10 percent more shares than if the stock traded only up or down $10, because he never would have bought his inexpensive shares. In the long run, David ends up owning many more shares of XYZ.

## ¶29,011  VALUE AND GROWTH STOCK INVESTING

Both value and growth have strengths and weaknesses. There are no perfect solutions for investment, or there would be only a few investments from which to choose. Fortunately, there are plenty of investments available to earn the client's money. Three basic characteristics of value and growth help summarize their styles:

1. Value focuses on past performance to determine what is undervalued; growth is very forward looking to project anticipated earnings momentum.
2. Value opportunities are created by the predictably bad behavior of investors; growth opportunities depend on corporate management to make the right decisions to fulfill expectations.

3. Value focuses on out-of-favor basic industries that are staples of society; growth looks at glamour industries for explosive returns.

4. Value is often generated by the short-sightedness of investors. Studies have shown that markets frequently overreact to recent bad news resulting in over-selling stocks beyond otherwise supportable values. Such stocks, if the source of the bad news was overblown, tend to out perform the market in subsequent years.

The CPA/PFS can work through stocks' realistic possibility of increase based on these parameters. This exercise will narrow the field and offer direction toward attainable goals as clients choose to buy stock.

## .01  Value Stock Investing

A traditional solution for a bear market is for the CPA/PFS to look for relative value every time the investor makes a securities purchase. The difficulty lies in defining "value." The answer is to buy a quality stock that has rising earnings prospects; that is, it is selling at a discount to itself, its industry group, or the market. This applies to individual stocks, groups, or even markets.

Several examples of value investing follow:

- A stock has had bad earnings because of a one-time charge against earnings for a write-off. Ignoring long-term excellent prospects, institutional investors sell the stock and in one week the stock is off 20 percent. The stock is an A rated equity by Standard & Poor's, analysts still like its long-term appreciation potential, and the stock's 2 percent dividend is perceived as secure. For value and fundamental analytical reasons, the CPA/PFS selects it and the client buys it.

- A group of software stocks has lagged the market. Every time the group starts to rally, one of the companies announces bad earnings, has some negative event, or runs afoul of regulatory agencies. Because the CPA/PFS decides the product the group provides is essential to the United States, he or she picks several of the best stocks in the group, and clients buy them.

- A country has settled its differences with its neighbors and a new government has taken power thanks to supervised elections. The new leaders embrace capitalism wholeheartedly and immediately move to privatize (sell to the public through a stock offering) the telephone company of this emerging nation. Clients buy the stock on the offering. They consider the telephone company a proxy for the whole country, whose prospects the CPA/PFS analyzes and likes. The CPA/PFS considers this an index for the country's fledgling market and concludes that it will take off during this period of enlightened rule.

Much can go wrong, which is why there are always contrary convictions. Because there is a case for three hypothetical investments, playing devil's advocate helps explain when not to make these investments. These are the cases for not investing in any of the preceding three choices:

1. The client decides not to buy the stock. The CPA/PFS decides not to endorse the stock because of its 20 percent drop in one week. They are not totally confident of the company's long-term prospects, because no analyst expected this write-off. What bad news will the next announcement bring?

2. The client decides against investing in stocks in this underperforming software group. A chain is only as strong as its weakest link. The CPA/PFS cannot decide whether it is profit margins, management, or the cost of financing, but there is something wrong.

3. The client decides to look at another country for foreign investment. The new government seems open to U.S. involvement, but what if they receive all this cash and nationalizes its telephone company again? Even if the government is stable, emerging markets regularly collaspe and close for months on end.

Investors must constantly evaluate the risk-to-reward parameters of value stocks. If they are engaged in direct investment, they must continually draw conclusions on examples like these. If the clients have managed money or mutual funds, the portfolio manager is responsible for making these decisions.

## .03   Growth Stock Investing

If value investing and all it entails seems too demanding, perhaps the investor is better suited to investing for growth. Growth stocks show great earnings momentum. They are concentrated in the glamour stocks that are all household names, rather than in the fallen angels of esoteric industries that are impossible to understand.

Following are some pithy investment ideas for growth stocks:

- Buy USA! In a risk-averse world, the only safe place to invest money is in the United States. Here is where the earnings are. Every other country is subject to high risk, and why assume more risk than the minimum needed to take the investors where they want to go?

- Buy technology! In a post-industrial society, all that matters is information services. Brains are more important than brawn and technology is where the brains are. Who cares about the last three years—it will all work out over time.

¶29,011.03

Once again, as with value investing, what can go wrong? The answer is plenty. Look at the other side of the coin:

- Buy foreign! Many foreign markets have outperformed the U.S. markets. They will continue to do so as long as they continue to develop at the extraordinary rate of growth they have demonstrated for the past decade.
- Forget about technology! The margins in the high-tech industries have shrunk to such an extent that it is impossible to accurately forecast earnings for any of these companies. The technology area soon will be left with only nine or ten companies. The rest will vanish.

## ¶29,013  HIGH-QUALITY VERSUS LOW-QUALITY STOCKS

If the investor would rather not juggle value versus growth, another stock strategy is selecting high-quality versus low-quality stocks. Low-quality stocks in theory provide significantly greater returns over time because the investor assumes more risk. Unfortunately, this approach can be disappointing. Sometimes, low-quality stocks, when price/earnings ratios are compared, trade at a premium to quality. Therefore, investors have a good chance of losing significantly more money than they can make because they have paid for the privilege of assuming more risk. That is a lose-lose proposition if ever there was one. If the investors have bought low-quality stock, when the high-and low-quality stocks start to trade in line again, the investors may lose in another way. Their low-quality stocks come back to the mean, in addition to underperforming the good-quality stocks. From a commonsense standpoint, most people cannot address such issues because most people simply do not have several dozen (let alone hundreds) of stock positions. The primary benefit of understanding high-quality versus low-quality stock is to gain an understanding of which types of mutual funds to invest in either inside of or outside of a self-directed retirement plan. Although value and growth questions are not too much of an issue with fund choices, most conservative stock funds are of high quality, and most speculative stock funds are of low quality. When it is time for the CPA/PFS to vote with the client's money, the CPA/PFS and clients must choose the quality with which they feel most comfortable.

Fortunately, over longer periods of time, growth stocks and value stocks alternate leadership positions in the market, lending to the wisdom of diversifying across both categories of investments.

## ¶29,015  SMALL, MIDDLE, AND LARGE CAPITALIZATION STOCKS

The CPA/PFS could take a totally different tack and decide to concentrate on selecting weightings between small, mid, and large capitalization stocks.

Such stocks define the size of a company. Small capitalization stocks are stocks of up to $10 billion in market capitalization (number of outstanding shares of common stock multiplies by market price), mid caps are up to $100 billion, and large caps can be as much as $500 billion in value of outstanding shares. The larger the capitalization, the larger the trading volume and the better the liquidity. Larger capitalization stocks have more research and media coverage than do small caps. However, small and mid cap stocks traditionally have greater gain potential. It is possible to make a modest investment and have a sizable windfall profit within a few years' time in these less-well-known stocks.

Small cap stocks have historically outperformed large cap stocks, but during certain periods, large cap stocks have survived better than small cap stocks. Some calculate that the earnings streams of small cap are more dependable than large cap because their revenues are not dependent on foreign countries for income. In some corrections, the entire episode seemed to be generated by foreign markets. However, the thought of concentrating on small cap stocks can be dangerous. The professional knows that most small and mid cap stocks are over-the-counter stocks. The NASDAQ, where these stocks are traded, suffered drastic losses during the early years of this century.

## ¶29,017 SOLUTIONS

Solutions are not simple. After examining value and growth, high-quality versus low-quality, and small, medium, and large capitalization stocks, the CPA/PFSs and their clients may feel overwhelmed. There are pitfalls, but stock investing can be financial rewarding for the clients and their families. Historically, large-company stocks return about 10 percent per year (this is sometimes also expressed as 7 percent plus inflation) and small company stocks return 12 percent per year. Treasury bills return about 3 percent, long-term bonds about 6 percent. What matters ultimately is that an investor own stock. The CPA/PFS must determine with the client a comfort level with risk and reward parameters and then create a stock investment plan that is consistent with this risk profile. With the help of the CPA/PFS, clients must invest money and leave it invested, periodically add to their portfolio, and consider the long term. All these equity investment approaches work over time to a greater or lesser degree—that is why they exist. The benefits of stock investing ultimately outweigh the risks over an extended time period.

## ¶29,019 CONTROLLING RISK THROUGH DIVERSIFICATION

What do the institutional money managers responsible for managing multibillion dollar portfolios and funds do with money? The best lessons in the investment world come from success stories. Modern money management, despite many well-publicized fiascoes, is doing a better job of generating profits and managing risk for clients. Investors can learn a lot from what is applicable to the retail stock portfolio. In the past few years, money managers have attempted to "style invest," which is rotating between value and growth. However, the attempt to correctly time switching between value and growth is only marginally less frustrating than trying to define the styles themselves. Understanding what they are trying to do has clear benefits to stock investors because money management issues are a macrocosm of everything individual investors are trying to accomplish.

Style switchers try to invest in the up cycle of whichever style—value or growth—is outperforming the other. For example, if there is a perception that blue chip basic industry stocks have hit their peak, managers switch over to explosive growth, small capitalization, over-the-counter stocks. When value outperforms, growth underperforms—there is a cycle to that performance. There is a reversal and growth outperforms value. The managers then reverse direction and sell their small caps and go back to the large caps. Market timing is anything but neutral—it is totally subjective, because investors are completely dependent on the manager's insights to switch styles. This method is not foolproof. Sometimes the waxing and waning of value and growth only reveals itself in hindsight.

## ¶29,021 Constructing a Stock Portfolio That Makes Sense

The CPA/PFS is looking for the accurate equity portion of the client's asset allocation. This is not as difficult as it sounds, because there are standard measurements available. From a securities standpoint, the number of different types of investors is by no means infinite. The investor should look for interlocking relationships between a number of different, conventional financial planning characteristics. The financial planning process can address the issues of stock selection.

The CPA/PFS must initially address age, net worth, income, retirement, and educational needs. The benefit of considering these characteristics for investors is that these considerations force them to quantify their seemingly subjective financial profile into totally objective numbers. Then the CPA/PFS and the clients determine what needs to be done. "What needs to be done" determines the type of stock portfolio the client constructs and the selection of the investments that go into that portfolio.

Furthermore, job stability and tenure, expected inheritances, and counterbalancing of financial needs and desires all affect stock blend. Although there is no need to assume more risk than needed to reach goals, the situation may dictate that the way to achieve these ends is to assume a more aggressive stance than the client might otherwise deem acceptable.

# ¶29,023  The CPA/PFS as a Star Stock Picker

The keys to success in stock investing are as follows:

1. *Invest for the long haul.* The client as an investor becomes a long-term position builder. Not everyone has the money or the inclination to become involved in a systematic investment plan. But, the CPA/PFS must approximate that system, as it is what works best and makes the most money for the client.

2. *Invest in quality earnings streams.* The CPA/PFS must make the right selection to start building the client's positions. The way to create wealth is to determine the right choices, either of stocks, money managers, or funds, and hold them as long as they show appropriate growth. Stock performance is a direct reflection of earnings growth expectations.

3. *Stay invested.* Clients will see downswings. Given the extreme cyclical nature of investing, they will also have the opportunity to revel in upswings.

4. *Once a decision has been made, run with it.* Stock prices often are a reflection of variables neither the CPA/PFS nor their clients can control. Clients must remember why they bought their shares but be alert to any changes within the company other than the price of the stock.

## .01  Investment Rationale

There is a longstanding belief that markets are somehow removed from the economies in which they are located. The adherents to this theory believe that markets behave in a random pattern and are reflective of nothing. This could not be further from the truth. Markets are efficient processors of information and respond to all the information an economy provides them. Critics have complained many times that governments become slaves to their financial markets, but markets clearly reflect investors' opinions of the effectiveness of governments.

Therefore, as an investment professional, CPA/PFSs must accommodate these vagaries into their clients' investment and asset allocation plans. The CPA/PFS cannot respond to upswings and downturns. He or she must remain optimistic that the client's money is where it belongs and have faith in the system that accommodates these markets. The key to success in equity investment is the continued accumulation of quality holdings that become larger and larger positions with a lower and lower cost basis.

## .03  How the CPA/PFS and Clients Put It All Together

Regardless of whether clients use a simple or complex plan, professionals must cultivate discipline and responsibility. Professional behavior is far more important than style because it has a far greater impact on the clients' long-term performance results. The ways to establish behavior characterized by discipline and responsibility are the following:

1. Complete a financial plan.
2. Establish a clear risk profile.
3. Know the client.
4. Pick a strategy that is suitable for the client.
5. Find research to explain, support, and expand the strategy.
6. Invest the client's money in a few well-chosen stocks.
7. Continue to search for and identify new candidates.
8. Listen to and talk with other professionals, shareholders, and investors, but use them as guides, not leaders.
9. Keep the long-term view in mind.
10. Look for consumer trends that support or refute stock picks.

To maintain professional standing, CPAs/PFSs should be aware that:

- Traders pay a lot of unnecessary brokerage fees, which affects performance negatively.
- Sellers generate capital gains tax liabilities.
- Hot trend followers tend to escalate their risk parameters with each failure and ultimately lose money.
- Strategies that require a lot of time, reading, and computer work are by definition too elaborate for most investors.
- Excessive diversification usually is for giant mutual funds that are regulated by the SEC.

It is impossible to know whether any long-term strategy will continue to be successful, but the strategies examined above have enjoyed historic and present successes. With reasonable diversification, disciplined investment, and a responsible approach to methodology, investors should earn excellent long-term results and achieve all of their long-term goals.

# Chapter 30

# Advanced Equity Strategies

## CONTENTS

## ¶30,000 OVERVIEW

Although initial public offerings (IPOs) decreased rapidly in number in the wake of the turmoil over the accounting scandals at the turn of the century and frequently fell below the initial selling price, indications are that this is changing. Analysts and financial professionals are predicting that IPOs worth considering will be appearing in the near future. In fact, 2004-2006 have been good years for new issue equity securities. It is absolutely necessary that the responsible CPA/ personal financial specialist (PFS) be aware of this activity and other aggressive equity strategies. The lively interest in stock concepts will continue as long as the equity arena continues to attract money from almost every class of active securities investor.

## ¶30,001   INITIAL PUBLIC OFFERINGS

It is difficult for the individual investor to be the early bird on an IPO. However, although the majority of shares usually go to mutual funds and other institutions, that does not mean they all do. Therefore, if the client wants to give it a try, there are right and wrong ways to go about it. The CPA/PFS must understand the IPO process. An IPO is the first time a company raises money from the public by issuing its stock. In order to do so, the company goes to an investment banking firm to discuss, establish, and complete the process of selling its stock. The investment bank appraises the value of the company, figures out how many shares to sell and at what price, and then buys the stock from the company and sells it. After the company receives money from the investment bank, it is out of the loop.

The stock is then sold through a selling syndicate. The company receives X amount of money, the investment banking firm sells it at X plus its markup, and the selling syndicate marks it up still more for sale to the public. Although the investor pays no direct stock commissions to buy IPOs, there is plenty of "selling concession" built into the price of any offering. The benefit for the investor is the opportunity to invest in new companies that they hope will become the Microsofts and Intels of the future. The results can be somewhat different and much more complicated, but finding tomorrow's hot stock is what IPOs are all about.

## .01   Entering the IPO Fray

As mentioned, there is a right way and a wrong way to approach the IPO market. For the client to profit, the CPA/PFS must follow the "rules of engagement":

1. *Learn the IPO game.* The company must need money or it would not be going public. This is not necessarily bad, however, the client does not want to invest money in some executive branch's estate planning exercise, in a company whose board thinks earnings have peaked, or in a company that is desperate to expand or buy new property simply to maintain market share. The CPA/PFS should perform the necessary research to identify the company's reasons for going public.
2. *Select the right broker.* New issue trading is a specialty and clients benefit from hiring an expert for this activity. A broker should be able to show the CPA/PFS which IPOs have been allocated stock, in what volume, where the stock has gone, and how the various underwritings did.
3. *Open the account at a large wirehouse brokerage office.* Big wirehouse deals have tended to outperform their smaller counterparts' performances in this area. Discount brokerages rarely participate in any worthwhile deals.

4. *Spread around the accounts.* If clients have enough assets, deposit them at all the big wirehouses and do some business with all of them. The more professional relationships the CPA/PFS has, the more apt the clients are to be in the right place at the right time to purchase IPO stock.

5. *Remember, the best clients have the opportunity to buy the most stock.* IPO participation often takes on highly political sales-driven overtones. Brokerage clients are repaid for previous business with their firm's IPO allocations.

6. *Collect prospectuses and research choices.* Earnings of new issues average falling 20 percent to 30 percent in the year following a stock offering.

7. *Put in an indication of interest (IOI) as fast as possible.* If clients think they want a stock, ask immediately—too soon is better than too late. The client can always pull an order before the deal is released. Prospectuses are often impossible to understand, especially because so many new issues are either high-tech or biotech stocks. In whatever order the CPA/PFS prefers, he or she will often have to rely on either gut instinct or the investment professional.

8. *Avoid pressure sales.* Securities are sold rather than bought: rather than actively buy securities for themselves, conventional retail brokerage clients are shown products by their brokers and choose their investments from what they are shown. If someone is trying hard to persuade the client to buy something, the client probably does not want it.

9. *Stick to the plan.* The CPA/PFS should be careful to invest in what the client wants and be very cautious about investing in anything else.

10. *Flip new issues.* "Flipping" new issues is the technique of buying an IPO and immediately selling it into the market. The client realizes an immediate gain or loss and goes onto the next deal immediately. This is what many institutions do with new issues and perhaps so should the clients. Most new issues tend to track down in price and volume over a period of time as their fundamentals deteriorate. See point 1 above.

If the CPA/PFS and client really like a stock and yet cannot buy the stock on the IPO, he or she should buy it later in the open market. IPOs that do well usually continue to do well for some time, so subsequent investors tend to do well, too. Half the new deals close down from their opening price at the end of their first trading day. Often, the stocks are cyclical (rise fast in good times; decline fast in bad) and, as previously discussed, are at or near a peak in their cycle.

Good clients of large wirehouses rarely get burned by IPOs. It pays to be a good client (an active fee-generating market participant) in the new issue arena. Many IPOs never receive research coverage from the large wirehouses, the stocks drift off in price and volume, and the companies' images are permanently damaged. Brokers are very careful to avoid such deals, but the CPA/PFS would be hard put to determine this alone. Salespeople tend to know quickly which issues are hot and which issues are bad investments.

¶**30,001.01**

## .03 Investment Banking Today: The IPO Scene

At this point, any resemblance between investment banking relationships today and the banking relationships of yesteryear is virtually coincidental. There is an industry-wide problem of too many bankers courting too few clients. In an era of corporate consolidations, as opposed to expansions, this problem can only worsen. The unhappy byproduct of all this is a lowering of banking standards and parameters when faced with the necessity to "do deals." Particularly as investment banking relates to smaller companies, this courtship ritual can easily prove fatal. The successful, new, publicly owned company has employees whose expertise in their specialty is unquestioned, but their knowledge of business is nonexistent. These companies may have complete contempt for "bean counters," except as the bean counters relate to their own personal beans. The owners succumb completely to the untoward advances of the various investment bankers that come calling. They select the banker who makes them feel the best about themselves and start down the road to what often becomes a disastrous union.

Although this all sounds pretty pessimistic, there are some distinct benefits to the investor who understands this process. Everyone hears about and remembers the highly successful IPOs; everyone hears about and ignores the failures. The nature of the American investor is to be optimistic. Given the past few years of stock market performance, American investors are not as optimistic as they were, but hope springs eternal. Therefore, the investor should be aware that sometimes things could go very wrong with an investment. The CPA/PFS who studies and learns from these negative episodes may be in a better position to avoid such failures.

Although in hindsight it is almost impossible to decide who is to blame for the thousands of IPOs that have failed over the years, it is a somewhat easier task to discover what went wrong. The investor can be "on guard" and watch for the telltale signs of problems. Armed with knowledge about stock liquidity, research coverage, and trading volume, the CPA/PFS can help clients either avoid or escape such offerings with minimal damage.

It is safe to say that almost no company going public really understands the machinations of Wall Street, but certainly may understand these machinations once the deal is complete. Because of the company's justified enthusiasm, it is often caught up in a process that has no relationship with the quality of what has come before it. The employee's abilities, the company's products, and its future—all are swept aside by the normal desire to quantify the business it has created. The business sections of local papers are riddled with stories about the founders and board members of "fallen angels" and "orphans" that still have excellent products, good management, and fine futures. However, all this is tainted by the fact that the stock has become a "single-digit midget" since its much-ballyhooed regional offering.

What happened? The companies experienced too much, too soon from a securities standpoint and simply fell apart. Whether an earnings issue, a product issue, or an accounting issue, it does not matter. What does matter, however, is that, in the stock market, "down" is usually "out" for small capitalization companies.

From the point of view of the retail investor, it is most important for the CPA/ PFS to watch for the slightest suggestion that IPO earnings may disappoint. There are numerous small deals that have immediate liquidity problems because they never earn research coverage from national, regional, or even local brokerage firms. For example, XYZ Technology comes to market; the deal is a success, trading up to $15 from its IPO price of $12. Everyone is happy . . . for the moment. No brokerage firm picks up research coverage of XYZ Technology. Although assured by its bankers that its stock would be a popular issue with analysts, the opposite proves to be the case. The issue receives several months of unnecessary price support—unnecessary because it is trading above its offering price—but even the tout services do not pick up the stock. Worse yet, XYZ Technology is about to end its softest sales quarter and realizes it will have to announce a decline in revenues and earnings for the quarter. When XYZ was still a private company, this issue did not matter because everyone inside the company knew this happened every year or so. The public shareholders, however, are not so understanding, nor are they as sanguine about XYZ Technology's future. The stock, in a week, goes from $14 to $5, perhaps on its way to zero.

When the public sees the largest capitalization, most well-known companies announce the probability of lower earnings (usually, after the market close), the market responds immediately on the next day's opening, and the response is harsh.

Factor in the response of such negative news with high tech and biotech stocks, remembering that most IPOs are small to mid cap high tech and biotech companies, and the offerings have the makings of some real disasters.

## .05  Conclusion on IPOs

To conclude the discussion of IPOs, 5 percent to 10 percent of the price of an IPO pays for fees. If the CPA/PFS is of the opinion that the deal has run its course at the current price, he or she should sell. There is too much excess built into the price of any deal to wait. The CPA/PFS must keep careful track of all public discussions of the deals before, during, and after their release. The Internet can be invaluable here. If there is a lot of negative publicity from legitimate sources, or if there is a suggestion that a price may be lowered to improve its appeal, the client's IOI should be pulled immediately, as this indicates an impending disaster. Conversely, if the broker calls and says the price range on a deal has been raised, the CPA/PFS should thank him or her and anticipate a nice lunch together—on the client, as the stock is probably a winner. If the CPA/PFS notices an investment banker consistently in litigation over deals, particularly with former banking clients, he or she should not participate in the banker's deals—in investment banking, where there is smoke, there is often fire.

## ¶30,003  FOREIGN STOCKS

Conventional wisdom, a term that often proves to be an oxymoron, says that some foreign exposure in equities is necessary in all accounts because of an eventual return of inflation and the high performance of some overseas equity markets. Factually, 60 percent of the world's equity assets are nondomestic, but only 15 percent of domestic investment is foreign. For example, John Doe participates in only 15-percent ownership in foreign stocks here, although 60 percent of the world's equity is in foreign investment and available for John Doe to buy. By equity size alone, some foreign stock exposure should have the effect of hedging a domestic stock portfolio, because often what makes U.S. markets go down has the opposite effect abroad. Although this is not uniformly the case, there is some valid historic precedent for such belief. As seen time and again, moderation is often the key to success, in any areas of investment.

Also, there is a belief that foreign exposure can enhance the overall return of a stock portfolio while insuring against domestic market volatility. Foreign stocks are attractive from a diversification standpoint. There is more out there left untouched by many investors because they either do not want what they do not know or they cautiously want what is familiar to them.

The primary risk of investment in foreign equity markets is currency exposure. Foreign exchange rates come into play as investors buy foreign-currency-denominated securities with U.S. dollars and reconvert back to U.S. dollars from foreign currency dividends or sale proceeds. If the dollar weakens in relation to a foreign stock's currency, the investors make money; if the dollar strengthens in relation to a foreign stock's currency, the investors lose. For example, investors buy XYZ foreign stock here; the stock continues to rise in its home country, but here the dollar becomes stronger and stronger. The stock simply does not go up in price. In the opposite case, a stock remains flat in its home country, but its currency strengthens in relationship to the dollar—the domestic shareholder sees his or her investment go up in price.

Another foreign investment concern is the actual costs of buying and selling foreign securities in their markets. Some foreign markets have huge buy/sell costs. Of course, time zone constraints, money settlement problems, and the always present issue of liquidity can all cause problems.

Most retail investors make foreign securities purchases in the form of mutual fund choices. The costs of foreign investment are still there, although greatly reduced by volume fund purchases. There are so many foreign funds, both closed and open ended, that there is not a single market, vehicle, or strategy that a person cannot invest in through mutual funds. In the mutual fund arena it is important to distinguish between foreign funds and international funds. Foreign funds invest in other-than-U.S. stocks while international funds may own U.S. stocks as well as foreign equities. Also, as will be explained more fully, funds owning international corporations tend to blunt the distinction between domestic and foreign investing.

Mutual funds will always mirror the best and worst of any investment plan. They facilitate diversification for an investor—but that is the very nature of mutual funds, not just foreign stock ones. Investors can probably have a higher than usual return and lower than usual risk (volatility) portfolio with some foreign exposure. However, in times of extreme and dramatic domestic downside stress, the foreign markets react accordingly to the downside, often even to a degree in excess of domestic corrections. In addition, these markets tend to stabilize more slowly.

## ¶30,005  EMERGING MARKETS

Emerging markets, quite simply, are markets in countries whose output of goods and services falls below the average per capita output of goods and services for the world. Above average countries are considered developed. If a country does not exceed the average production of the world, it is an emerging nation economically, regardless of its age or history. Emerging markets are the most aggressive growth and value areas in the equity universe. The greatest opportunities and the greatest risk are in the global emerging markets. Geographically, investment is spread through Latin America, emerging Asia, emerging Europe, and South Africa. As with generic foreign investment, if domestic markets continue to do better, a very selective posture should be assumed with emerging markets investment.

The historic tendency is for emerging markets to underperform U.S. markets when the U.S. is outperforming other markets. However, emerging markets tend to outperform the established, mature foreign markets when U.S. markets are under performing globally. Therefore, when U.S. markets are doing well, they tend to outperform all foreign investment, but when foreign markets are doing well relative to U.S., the emerging markets tend to do the best of all.

When considering the matter of investing in foreign markets, significant issues of risk must be addressed by the individual investor:

- Is the market liquid? Some countries have constant liquidity problems that should dissuade all but the most determined investors. However, there are some countries absolutely determined to present the maximum liquidity they can generate in hopes of attracting "serious money" investment from well-developed countries and their investors.
- Does the country present an investor-friendly profile to the world? This issue is linked to the question of liquidity and hinges on whether the country is open-minded about and willing to encourage international investment. If a country is hostile to capitalism, there is no reason to invest there. Conversely, if a country has laws friendly to investment and securities regulations supporting the privatizing of its industrial and utility companies, why not take a look?
- Does a country have the capability of harnessing its aspirations? All the material and natural resources in the world are worthless if no one can mine, drill, or harvest them and there is nobody there who can develop a local use for them.

- Will opening up a country to investment benefit or brutalize its nascent markets? Anyone can make a strong case for either view in any country— it is the job of investors to sort out each country's potential prior to investment.

As time goes by and these markets mature, their dependency upon U.S. market performance should diminish. "Decoupling" will be accomplished as managers take a bottom-up approach to looking at individual companies. More and more of these companies will then find themselves in the country and regional fund trading here in the U.S. They will have increased liquidity as they become more familiar to domestic investors, both retail and institutional. However, investors cannot forget that, uniformly, these countries are characterized by nonstandard methods of accounting and reporting, a lack of market regulation, and currency risks. Any of these factors can quickly eliminate any profits or diversification benefits that might be gained from the stocks.

For the domestic retail investor who is determined to invest in emerging markets, there are two reasonable ways to participate in these markets:

1. Invest in America–Buy domestic stocks that earn a large percentage of their profits in countries or regions that captivate the investor. The client can own direct participation in the economies of these countries and regions without direct involvement with their markets.
2. Buy the mutual funds of the countries or regions that the CPA/PFS and client select. In particular, the close-ended funds are often covered by the big wirehouses and, therefore, are managed with care. Although the specialty funds often generate enormous losses, the expertise of a manager can generate more success than clients might on their own.

## ¶30,007  CONVERTIBLE BONDS

For investors who are concerned about the stock market, convertible bonds and convertible preferred stock can be the perfect hybrid investment. They can be perfect for modest or indirect stock or bond exposure, because convertibles are a true hybrid fixed income and equity product.

Like everything in securities, there are two sides to every story. Convertible securities are generally issued as debt securities, but when certain price conditions are met, they can be converted into equity securities. Proponents of convertibles like the bonds because, if a stock rises, the bonds can be converted into that stock. In addition, convertibles typically generate much higher income than do comparable stocks. Naysayers on convertibles consider them the worst of both debt and equity investments—the yields never approach straight debt yields and the appreciation never approaches straight equity appreciation.

Converts are true "total return" vehicles, with the strengths and weaknesses inherent in total return investments per se. The individual receives the yield that the bond or preferred stock pays, plus the predetermined amount of appreciation built into the bond if it is achieved by the issuer's common stock. Because the convertible instruments are issued at a convertible price 20 percent or 25 percent or so above the then current price of the stock, they do not participate dollar for dollar as the stock appreciates. However, they can gain 60 percent to 70 percent of upside, yet appear to have only 30 percent to 40 percent of downside stock market risk. They tend to trade like bonds in bad stock market periods and like stock during good stock market times. This seeming irrationality makes perfect sense when one considers that converts are hybrid products of debt and equity.

## .01    Picking Convertible Securities

The traditional issuer of convertibles is usually a small- or mid-capitalization company with extraordinary growth and the presumed capability of sustaining this growth. These bonds are rarely particularly seasoned. Best estimates suggest that convertibles of rising market stars last three to five years before they are converted en masse to equities and cease to exist.

Most investors are best off selecting an appropriate mutual fund or money manager for investment in convertible securities. The primary benefits of mutual fund investment and money management for the investor are the usual ones inherent to mutual fund investment and money managers per se—professional management, diversification, and relief from responsibility. Furthermore, there are elements of significance attached to convertible investment that make the alternative, individual issue selection difficult for the retail investor:

1. *Rating issues.* The usual convertible issuer is rated below investment grade (BBB). Not only are retail investors incapable of learning about or understanding the nuances of lower-quality debt, but often they cannot buy junk debt directly. Junk debt is a small segment of the domestic bond market and convertible debt is a small segment of junk debt. Therefore, there are genuine inventory problems that are too great a hurdle for even the most determined investor to overcome.

2. *Timeliness of portfolio management.* Because of the volatility of the underlying stocks of most convertible issues, the buy-and-hold investor takes a decided back seat in this area of investment. The convertible issues are constantly changing their natures in the face of complex issues related to their highly specialized market. For example, because of the comparatively small size of this market, there is a strong tendency (particularly to the downside) to overreact temporarily to news that immediately relates to major issues or issuers (especially technology or biotech).

¶30,007.01

3. *New issue securities.* Because most new issue convertible debt is priced at or near par, they do not have the peculiar premiums and discounts with which many seasoned issues trade. These premiums and discounts are reflections of the trading price of the convertible securities underlying equity prices—successful stocks have premium convertibles, unsuccessful stocks have discount convertibles. The retail client cannot normally expect to participate in the new issue convertibles, because they often carry sizable bond investment minimums.

4. *Portfolio turnover.* For many reasons (e.g., calls, rating changes, equity behavior, and mergers and acquisitions), convertible portfolios' turnover of securities tends to be both rapid and significant. This extreme activity makes the services of a mutual fund or money manager much more desirable for the more practical retail investor who cannot make the necessary time commitment to keep pace with the price and market activity.

5. *Convertible preferred stock.* Convertible preferred stock is a hybrid investment of a hybrid investment. These are hard for anyone to understand— and there are many kinds, with varying levels of liquidity. They are a retail "made for packaging" product.

## ¶30,009   MICRO-CAPITALIZATION STOCKS

"Micro-capitalization stocks" are often fancy words for "penny stocks." Many small-cap specialists have had to ratchet up their limits of what constitutes "small" as the market has moved upward. Formerly, $250 million was the upper limit—it may now be $1 billion.

As mutual fund managers who specialize in micro-caps are forced to step up to the plate with larger capitalization limits, the issue of concern is the extent to which these portfolios still mirror the principles with which they were created. Even though the managers may actually remain consistent in their investment philosophies, the makeup of their fund portfolios may change dramatically. This would happen as the securities within the fund grow or reflect higher capitalization limits, thus putting managers in the awkward position of drifting away from their stated style.

All concerns notwithstanding, the micro-cap stock, perhaps as a function of terminology and "language inflation," has taken on a life of its own and an identity of the old small cap stock. These stocks are currently perceived as corporations of $250 million capitalization and less, sometimes $500 million, sometimes and $100 million. They account for 5,000 or so companies, which constitute 70 percent to 80 percent of the publicly traded stocks in the U.S.

Every investor who owns stocks is interested in micro-cap stocks, because they are the penny stocks that can increase in value a hundred- or even a thousandfold.

However, the stocks are invariably thinly traded, the markets and the market makers are often nonprofessionals, and the cost of "doing business" is very high. Nevertheless, long-term, micro-capitalization stocks have outperformed large capitalization stocks. Research sources are available from the mutual fund rating services. For the direct investment oriented, the investor can often talk directly to the highest level of management in a micro-cap company.

There are about 50 mutual funds that invest in micro-caps, and their results are often astonishing. Up and down years of 50 percent are not uncommon. If ever there is an area where the fund manager provides added value, it is in the area of micro-cap portfolio management. Even with all the research available, most investors would benefit from the mutual fund vehicle for this type of security. Happily, there are a number of micro-cap funds that enjoy the highest mutual fund ratings available from the various rating services.

# Chapter 31

## Debt Securities

## CONTENTS

## ¶31,000 OVERVIEW

Professional responsibility for filling out income tax returns dictates that personal financial planning be addressed with clients. Personal income

¶31,000

tax planning is the most obvious issue for the CPA/PFS, but risk management planning, after the bond crises of 1994 and 1999 and the continuing stock problems generated since 2000, is very significant. Therefore, investment planning for retirement and college savings (all with an eye toward eventual estate planning) is utmost in the mind of the CPA/PFS. Conscientious asset allocation leads to effective risk management.

Many investors during the recent past have thought of bonds as dull, boring, and lacking the historic return of stocks. However, bonds are, without any possible argument, a necessary component of every investor's securities portfolio. Bonds are simply IOUs from their issuer (borrower). The issuer is whoever creates bonds to borrow money—the U.S. government, foreign countries, companies big and small, cities, states, hospitals, and schools. The list is endless. The investor is given a date when the money he or she has loaned to the issuer will be paid back and in the interim the investor is paid interest on the bond. The issuer sells these instruments to investors as debtor to creditor. The bondholder has no equity in the borrower's company. There is no sharing of earnings like the privileges bestowed on shareholders who buy stock. Bonds are loans that are packaged as securities.

## ¶31,001  WHY BONDS DO NOT WIN POPULARITY CONTESTS

The last few years have conditioned an exhausted public to the notion that equities are worth the patience, whereas cash and bonds are not. There were some good reasons to believe that bond investments were a waste of capital in the former environment. Bond yields (income from debt instruments) had been low compared to stock returns, and bonds' total returns (income plus appreciation) had been poor. Celebrated bond debacles in junk, municipal, and foreign debt securities had shaken investor confidence. The majority of investors had no need for income, anyway—they were trying to shelter, defer, and postpone the tax consequence of current income, with the help of their CPA. If investors were avoiding as much taxable income as possible, it is easy to understand why investors lacked curiosity about how to generate still more current income from passive bond investment. Hold and grow; wait and pay (taxes, that is)—the mind-set for most investors.

The CPA/PFS can make a case for some debt exposure in a portfolio. The debt allocation can be invested in some lively bond sectors that will more than hold one's attention as the years pass by. If the client wants to invest in a conservative fashion, he or she can invest in Treasury securities of short- and intermediate-term maturity. Short- to intermediate-term maturity would be from overnight to five years' duration. This strategy will keep the portfolio of bonds very safe, which is a boon in these trying times. If the client wants to brighten things up a bit, there are plenty of lively bond investments—all over the world (i.e., all kinds of junk bonds, emerging nation debt, British bank debt, non-dollar denominated bonds, and zero coupon bonds).

## ¶31,003   THE ROLE BONDS PLAY IN ASSET ALLOCATION

There are several reasons to accept the notion of diversification among stocks, bonds, and cash. Historically, bonds are prone to less risk and less return than stocks. Recent years have occasionally seen bonds outperform stocks; but, historically, this is the exception. From a diversification and asset allocation viewpoint, what makes investing in both classes of securities so useful is that, when one goes down, the other often goes up. Therefore, in a volatile or bearish market, either in equity or debt, the most dramatic swings in portfolio value can be mitigated by diversification. The reason most people own bonds in a balanced portfolio is to provide solace when the stock market goes down.

The fact that corrections until the past few years have been sharp, brief, and followed by rapid recovery does not refute the theory of diversification. It means that diversification, in hindsight, has not been necessary—lately. However, as the public has experienced in a recent, extended bear market (which the boomer generation and younger investors had never experienced before), bonds regained their prestige and luster by virtue of their income and relative stability. Because their virtues are somewhat subtle, investors easily missed their importance.

Two general categories of risk are systematic and unsystematic risk. The first type includes risks such as the general fluctuation of interest rates that cannot be reduced by diversifying a portfolio—since the entire portfolio is affected. Other types of risk considered systematic include reinvestment rate risk, purchasing power risk, market risk, exchange rate risk, and political risk. Unsystematic risk, also called diversifiable risk, includes risks specific to individual businesses or industries. These risks may be controlled by diversifying the investments in an investor's portfolio. This category includes business risk, financial risk, default risk, credit risk, liquidity risk, call risk, event risk, and prepayment risk.

## ¶31,005   BOND RISKS

Risks associated with bonds may be divided into two groups. The first are those facing the market as a whole and therefore not curable by diversifying among bonds. These risks, called systematic risks, cause bonds as a whole, as opposed to individual bonds, to move in tandem—the market moves in response to them. Some of the more basic systematic bond risks follow:

- *Interest rate risk*—the possibility of lost potential income caused by rates rising during the holding period of a lesser paying instrument. The bondholder owns bonds at 6 percent and as rates rise, bonds of a similar type pay 8 percent.
- *Inflation risk*—the lost value of money due to inflation. The bondholder owns a fixed income portfolio that pays $30,000 per year income, but the

purchasing power continues to drop as inflation continues to erode purchasing power.

- *Currency risk*—the money lost because foreign-currency-denominated bonds and their income payout drops as the dollar becomes stronger. A foreign bond pays 10 percent in its own currency, but its currency is so weak versus the dollar that the bondholder realizes a yield of only 3 percent after currency exchange.

- *Political or geo-political risk*—the possibility of an international incident, for example, having an overall positive or negative effect on the bond market.

- *Legislative risk*—the possibility that the bondholder will lose money because regulatory, tax, or other legislation will negatively effect the holdings. The government declares private purpose municipal debt no longer tax exempt—a 3-percent tax-exempt bond is now generating fully taxable income in a taxable environment that pays twice as much.

In addition there are other risks unique to a specific bond issue. These risks, called unsystematic risk, are partially overcome by diversifying among bonds.

- *Due diligence risk*—the possibility that an issue is rated improperly and will default with no warning. A county historically issuing AA and AAA debt defaults after declaring bankruptcy. The holdings in that county are of little value, less liquidity, and no longer pay interest payments.

- *Default risk*—the possibility that the issuer will not pay back. A corporation goes out of business and the bondholders are left with worthless bonds and consequently no interest payments forthcoming.

- *Event risk*—lost money because of a catastrophic event attached to the bond issuer. The bondholder owns hospital bonds and the hospital closes indefinitely after earthquake damage.

- *Call risk*—the possibility that a bond will be redeemed or called-in before its stated due date.

## ¶31,007 How to Select Bonds

All investors attempt to outsmart compelling obstacles to make correct investment choices. To avoid the risks mentioned and to take bond selection into the realm of logic and reason in order to offset those risks, the CPA/PFS should assess the extent to which the bond investments are exposed to these risks. This involves studying analysts' comments about the bonds and subscribing to the monthly Standard & Poor's or Moody's or other corporate bond guides. Bond ratings are attempts to determine default risk. A typical bond rating comment is full of various balance sheet and financial statement numbers translated into a series of ratios that are explained and interpreted by the analyst preparatory to articulating an opinion. The CPA/PFS then uses this information to determine the risks and judge portfolio appropriateness.

## ¶31,009   FIXED INCOME ANALYSTS AND FIXED INCOME MARKETS

The fixed income analyst is an individual who rates bonds and suggests investment strategies. Investors want increasingly more sophisticated products that perform at high rates of return. The financial officers of the issuers and the banking firms want the analysts to help with origination, trading, sales, and investment decisions. The issues themselves are difficult to understand and evaluate. The generalists of yesterday are gone, replaced by gifted specialists trained in sophisticated quantitative research. If investors are unclear about which bonds to select for their investment portfolio, an income analyst can help tremendously—bonds have their own language and the CPA/PFS and his or her clients are advised to ask for help. As of now, credit rating services are the best place for the CPA/PFS to find facts on bonds; these facts on bonds will help the CPA/PFS decide whether the client should invest in them. The CPA/PFS looks at the various publications of the major bond rating services to determine the level of rating considered an acceptable minimum and then buys bonds at or above that rating.

## ¶31,011   CREDIT RATING SERVICES

Credit-rating services are all private firms. They are not government agencies with legislative power behind them, yet (and this is the source of some problems) their opinions are legislated into the operating rules of many public entities, both here and abroad. For example, rating service opinions determine how many public funds are invested. The rating services exert tremendous pressure and wield tremendous power through their examinations. The problem is this: credit rating services comment upon issuer default risk, and, like personal credit reports, these comments assume a life far beyond their actual area of expertise. Credit rating services have repeatedly cautioned that no one should rely on their opinions for anymore than what they are—credit ratings.

## ¶31,013   DIFFERENT TYPES OF BONDS

From an asset allocation standpoint, the CPA/PFS should focus on the same diversity mode that is used for stocks.

## .01   U.S. Treasury Securities

The safest debt investments for someone who cannot afford to lose money are U.S. Treasury securities, which are backed by the full faith and credit of the U.S. government. The most popular vehicles for investment are 3-, 6-, 9-, and 12-month Treasury bills issued at a discount in $1,000 denominations. The accretion from the discounted purchase price to the face value is interest income. Those who have a longer time horizon often invest in 2-, 3-, or 5-year Treasury notes. There are also 10- and 30-year notes and bonds, but neither is primarily a retail investment vehicle. The investor pays no state or local taxes on any Treasury issue.

## .03   Certificates of Deposit

Insured Certificates of Deposit (CDs) are similar to U.S. Treasury securities in that the Federal Deposit Insurance Corporation (FDIC) has the full faith and credit of the U.S. government. CDs of two years' maturity or less have been popular with investors for years. CDs often have lower rates than Treasuries of comparable maturity, though, and the taxpayer pays state and local taxes on them. Because the banks do not necessarily want money from investors (remember, to them, CDs are a liability), they are not often promoted as an attractive product. Although they are insured up to $100,000, most short-term income vehicles are very safe, so the investor may have no need for FDIC insurance. The highest CD rates are usually available through brokered CDs, so it is worth talking to a broker about CDs and other short- and intermediate-term income investments. For example, the brokerages also sell retail deposit notes (RTNs) and medium-term notes (MTNs), many of which pay monthly. The RTNs also have FDIC insurance. Certificates of deposit are subject to the income reporting requirements of original issue discount bonds (see below). That is, if the duration of the CD is more than one year, a cash basis owner is still required to report interest income although no cash payments have been received.

## .05   Money Market Funds

From a practical standpoint, most people's short- or intermediate-term cash investment needs are best served by money market funds. There is minimal risk attached to these funds. Investors who are risk adverse can invest in money market funds available in Treasury, government, insured, and/or tax-free formats. In addition, for somewhat longer maturities, in the area of a year or so, there are an assortment of both open-ended and closed-ended money fund and intermediate-term mutual fund clones and spin-offs. However, they are definitely not actual money market funds because their net asset value can vary—occasionally widely.

## .07   Zero Coupon Bonds

Wild and woolly bond products can generate stock-like gains, or losses, because of their volatility. The most widely used and least understood bond vehicle is the zero coupon bond. Many college savings accounts, which are very serious money, are full of them, because these accounts generally have a longer time horizon and because the accrued but unpaid interest income is sheltered in these accounts as it is in IRAs and profit sharing plans. Among the characteristics of these bonds are the following:

- The long maturities are volatile.
- They have standard deviation that cannot be identified with conservative investment.
- There is not a penny of cash flow between origination and maturity.
- The deep discount they are issued at is de facto leverage.
- When things go wrong with the bond market, they go unbelievably wrong with zero coupon bonds.
- They produce taxable income without corresponding cash payments.

With no cash flow and the pseudo-leverage, zeros in a bear market works against the holder to an extent far greater than coupon issues, precisely because there is no cash flow to mitigate declining value. Of course, this reverses itself in a bull market, because there is no cash flow coming out of zeros for which to find a home. Therefore, because the investor has no reinvestment responsibilities in a low interest environment, the zero coupon investments go up further and faster than any other debt type. Investors want cash flow in a bear market because they invest at a high rate. They do not want cash flow in a bull market because they are investing at low rates. Interest rate risk is extremely high on zeros—a long-term zero can lose 20 percent to 30 percent of its value with a 1-percent rise in rates, depending on its maturity, issuer, and the prevailing rate. They are, for the adventurous, one of the great, pure interest-rate trading plays, in the form of the U.S. Treasury strips. There is absolutely no risk other than interest rate sensitivity risk, because none of the other types of risk apply to a direct obligation of the government. Many packaged zero coupon products can have standard deviations of 30, 40, even 50 percent.

Zero coupon bonds purchased from the original issuer generate a form of income called original issue discount (OID). If the bonds are held by an individual outside a tax sheltering vehicle (such as an IRA or college savings account) the bond will generate annual taxable interest income, OID, without any corresponding cash interest payments. Inside an IRA or other tax sheltering investment vehicle the cashless income is still reported but its effects are mitigated. The owner of a zero coupon bond needs to add the OID income reported each year to the basis of the obligation so that upon redemption there is no gain or loss.

¶**31,013.07**

## .09  Foreign Debt

Another often used but rarely understood investment item is foreign debt. Most carry some varying level of currency risk, unless they are dollar denominated, in which case, their income stream is paid in dollars. Many carry political risk, although plenty of countries' stability is not an issue. There is a reasonable concern of political unrest in a lot of countries, but the chances of currency problems are far greater. With the dollar in a steady downtrend the past few years, many foreign bond bets dependent upon dollar weakness have made vast sums of money.

A continued weak dollar could make quality foreign bond investing attractive for the domestic investor, retail or institutional. As international bond yields go up and divorce in interest rate parity with U.S. rates, there is very great impetus to pay a premium to acquire more risk. If the risk is hedged, the expense of hedging the risk is so modest that the investor can end up with much more money than would be received from relatively passive domestic investment. This investment can be inexpensive and have modest risk to gain higher returns when compared to less adventurous domestic investments.

When international debt return advantage is uncertain relative to domestic debt, investors are almost forced out of high-quality foreign debt. Then, if trying to significantly outperform a domestic debt index, they are led into the more problematic distressed debt. From an asset allocation standpoint, purely as a strategic activity, many institutions insist on foreign debt. However, as a retail investor, unless the investor has a huge portfolio, one can basically forget about direct investment. An average investor cannot invest directly in international bonds as cheaply or as easily as he or she can in stocks. There are dozens of stock exchange listed foreign companies, but no debt. The bond buying costs are significant and the liquidity is always an issue.

It is hard to make much of a case for direct investment in sovereign foreign debt, Brady bonds, or overseas junk bonds because there is never a level playing field for retail investors. There are so many risks and they are of such significant magnitude that it is hard to make much of a case for funds, either. Some of the biggest fund problems immediately relate to foreign income funds. A straight international debt sector fund has too much standard deviation for too little potential return and the managers are tightly restricted by the legislated style of the fund.

## .11  Junk Bonds

What about homebred junk? It is very easy to make a good case for almost any investor owning some "high yield domestic debt," as junk is more properly termed. Junk bonds are those rated BB or lower by a recognized rating service. In well-managed, highly diversified funds, they are powerful investment vehicles almost anyone can own. Although the area has been tainted by notoriety, it deserves a fresh look from a new perspective.

Junk bonds are a tremendous enhancement for income-oriented portfolios in a low-interest environment. They usually pay significantly more than Treasuries or high-quality corporate debt. Furthermore, junk bonds are a good diversification tool. They generate income as a debt instrument (of course, because they are junk, they have the biggest coupons). When the bond market declines, junk bonds tend to behave more like stocks (they are allied with the equity of their companies rather than with conventional debt products). Not only do they not decline as much as high quality debt, they are sometimes less volatile than Treasuries of comparable maturity.

Performance in high yield is a function of security selection, diversification, and risk management. The ability to predict credit upgrades is the focus of a lot of this expertise—one needs to know a lot about credits or a lot about math to do well in this area. With these standards in mind, a well-regarded junk bond mutual fund is the best vehicle for this investment for the retail investor. The diversification includes different issuers, issues, maturities, credits, and industries. They can also buy the private placements of junk debts. They can drastically reduce costs (bonds cost a lot more than stocks), demand "equity kickers" (i.e., stock inducements to buy bonds) from issuers, enhance returns with leverage, and quickly respond to market and credit analysis issues.

Only 20 percent of the deals are rated B or lower, as compared to 65 percent 15 years ago. Liquidity is more adequate, as many issues have decent balance sheets, good cash flow, and viable and successful franchises. So why not buy the debt? Most of the current era problems relate to accounting event risks that nobody can predict but that are certainly going to crop up occasionally—this is still junk debt, after all. But now a one-time "notable event" is the norm for an issuer, rather than terminal default, and once the problem is solved, the risk is gone, and the debt begins to trade toward par with other issues in its sector of the market.

Fund managers can evaluate and process information of this type best, so the client essentially hires a fund manager when the CPA/PFS selects a fund for the expertise of the fund manager. A case can be made for timeliness in junk debt management, which eliminates the conventional investor from the picture. An average investor simply has no time to devote to active securities management. Good fund managers have access to far more information (company, research, and rating) than the average investor ever would. In fact, they can go straight to the "horse's mouth," if the need arises. Whereas most income funds are for people who have time or cash restraints, in the area of junk, a manager can provide genuine value added for the investor, large or small. Many institutional investors buy funds that normally shun the fund industry as a matter of principle. In addition, the diversification necessary in a portfolio of this nature is beyond almost any investor (not to mention that some junk debt comes in minimum orders of $5 million). A junk bond fund manager has something to do that cannot realistically be done by the client, so these services are quite beneficial for those who want junk.

¶31,013.11

*Distressed Junk Bonds.*    Special situations with distressed bonds are the province of the professional money manager. Distressed bonds cause major valuation and transaction cost problems because, although an investor pays perceived bargain prices for bad deals, the investor can still end up losing all the money. No one ever lost all their money paying too much for high-quality deals, but they have often lost everything buying bad deals cheaply. As stated, transaction costs are always significant in bonds because they cost so much more than stocks. By definition, distressed junk bonds require tricky evaluation above and beyond normal debt issues. Distressed junk is not a popular investment vehicle, so information is usually difficult to obtain, pricing is inefficient, and risk evaluation is extraordinarily difficult. The same logic regarding junk bond funds applies in spades to distressed junk bonds.

Looking for a junk fund is a difficult task. What a professional can do is rely upon the mutual fund rating services to reveal certain important facts about returns, risk, and consistency. The ideal junk bond fund is very similar to a balanced fund or total return fund—income and growth are both components of the return. These funds have averaged about 8 percent to 10 percent per year for the last decade or so, and the investor should expect the same return from a junk fund.

More of the return will be from income and less of it will be gain than that of a balanced or total return fund. At times, as discussed, the junk market acts like an equity market, so gains have to show in fund performance distributions, or the manager is not doing the job. In addition, for the increased risk, there should be demonstrably more cash flow than in a comparable high-quality corporate or government mutual fund. If not, why bother with the extra risk? That is, unless there are big capital gains distributions. A moderate cash flow may indicate a rise in credit quality in the fund or large investments in distressed securities. Both conditions and suitability are important for the CPA/PFS to assess. The evaluator may want junk to be junky or may want nothing to do with distressed debt. Do not prejudge a situation like relatively modest cash flow without finding out why it exists and what is at the root of the condition. Parenthetically, the CPA/PFS cannot assume that the highest yielding junk fund is the best one, because, until the he or she finds out where the money is coming from, there is no clue as to what the fund is doing. The fund may be passing back a lot of principal, it may generate huge gains on concentrated speculative positions—the professional has to find out for him- or herself, with or without the help of an investment or securities professional.

The CPA/PFS should find funds that are at or slightly above their index, especially in regard to income (cash flow from interest and dividends). It is important to see a stable return with stable net asset value. In addition, extreme volatility in high-yield bond funds would suggest really low-rated and distressed debt, which is fine for some of the fund assets. Currently, about two-thirds of junk is rated BB, the remaining third is B. Many funds are two-thirds B and one-third BB, so investors have to pay close attention to portfolio weight before selecting a fund. Although it is true that no one can control what returns are, an investor certainly can control what risk is assumed. There is no reason to accept anymore risk than predetermined return expectations require.

**Risk in Junk Bonds.**   There are three types of risk in junk:

1. *Interest rate risk.* This is the risk that market rates will go up and the investor will have less income than prevailing bonds, and then the value of the bonds will go down accordingly to meet the income levels of the new debt.
2. *Stock risk.* The stock market is subject to tremendous volatility in the speculative and high-risk stock areas. It is the speculative and high-risk areas, which represent the issuers of junk debt.
3. *High-yield debt risk.* High-yield debt comes in and goes out of fashion and prominence independent of what goes on in other markets. The risk is owning junk bonds or junk bond funds as they go out of fashion and their liquidity dries up. A lot of the go-go junk bond mutual funds of the 1970s and 1980s had to be absorbed into other funds because net asset values disappeared—often at great loss of income and principal to shareholders.

Interest rate risk is completely normal to all debt. The stock risk is because junk trades with equities and is open to the same risks as the stock market. Finally, there are some aspects of junk, which are idiosyncratic to junk, and they impose their own risks on the market.

## .13   Strategic Income Fund

The best way to answer the question of what strategic income funds are is to make the statement, "All of the above." They are the "open season on anything" funds of the debt world. Obviously, there are some position limits, but these funds are nowhere near as constrained as conventional income funds. Strategic income funds are similar to both the balanced/total return funds and the junk bond funds. They often have double-digit returns from a combination of income and gain. Because they participate in a variety of debt and equity markets, both domestically and internationally, they fit perfectly into a passive asset allocation framework dedicated to income.

The diversity of the fund format incurs a very high level of operating costs, so high expense ratios should be no surprise. If the CPAs/PFSs can understand plain vanilla debt or debt funds, they can understand the mutual fund rating service reports on these funds. It is important to find which fund has an investment philosophy similar to that of the CPAs/PFSs and their clients by reviewing a fund's:

1. *Research stance.* Which securities does it like and which securities do they not like?

2. *Asset allocation.* What mix of debt, equity, and cash does it normally employ?
3. *Market weightings.* Where does it put money?
4. *Economic, social, and political focus.* Does it have an ax to grind? What does it believe in and is it compatible with the view of the universe held by the CPAs/PFSs and their clients?

The goal of most of these funds is to provide maximum income with minimum volatility. They generate maximum income by having unlimited access to any income vehicles; they generate minimal volatility because of their ability to diversify across all income investments. The primary areas of investment are U.S. government debt, foreign debt of all classes, and domestic junk bonds. The managers also look at the emerging markets, domestic and foreign stocks with high dividends, domestic and foreign preferred stock, and all grades of domestic debt. All of the funds tend to be "custom blends," thus apple-to-apple comparisons between funds are impossible. Once again, this means the professional has to look at philosophy rather than numbers when doing homework. Low-risk strategic income funds generate less income than high-risk funds, so the CPA/PFS cannot simply pick the highest yielding fund and think the job is done. The indexes used for strategic funds are so hypothetical that they apply to no funds in the strategic fund universe other than by coincidence.

## .15 Tax-Free Municipal Bonds

There are some specific matters related to bonds with which every experienced investor should be familiar. Municipal bonds are bonds that carry no federal tax liability for interest payments. They are usually free of taxes in the states from which they are issued. Some states do not tax municipal interest if it is from another state and accept any municipal interest of any state as free from their taxes. Furthermore, some cities that have income taxes exempt the interest payments from their municipal debt from tax liability. Finally, Puerto Rico and a few other territories issue bonds whose interest payments are exempt from tax liability in all states.

The rate of return is adjusted for the fact that there are no tax consequences. The CPA/PFS must calculate whether tax-free or fully taxable debt is best for the client. (As a happy medium, there is never any state or local tax on Treasury obligations.)

There are investment rules that are peculiar to tax-free debt. In addition, some rules that are generic to all bond investment apply more specifically in some cases or somewhat differently in other cases to tax-free debt. Generally, anything that happens to an issuer of a financial nature is of interest to investors. Issuers are state, county, municipal, or other taxing authorities.

CPAs/PFSs should learn about municipal bonds before clients buy any. Furthermore, the CPA/PFS should learn about all the bonds their clients are buying. If the client decides to invest in municipal bonds for tax-free income, the professional must decide whether to invest in individual bonds or mutual funds and address price and default risk. Price risk is usually a function of the maturity of the bonds. The longer the maturity, as already seen, the more apt the bonds are to be volatile in a lively interest rate scenario. Default risk for municipal debt is an extensive list, but not as common an event.

*Minimizing Common Default Risks.*    Some of the common default risks are:

- *Natural disasters.* Earthquakes, fires, floods, hurricanes, and tornadoes.
- *Fiscal mismanagement.* Profligate spending or poor money management.
- *Taxing authority regulations.* Changes that effect issuers or investors.
- *Revenue declines.* Inability to pay income or principal when due.
- *Infrastructure problems.* Problems with everything from sewers to the mayor's mansion.
- *Specific project failures.* Failure to meet deadlines, failure to complete projects, failure of project as a revenue source.

To minimize common default risks and other non-market-related risks, the investor can simply select insured bonds. Bond insurance and how it works will be discussed in more, but for current purposes, suffice it to say that the insurance is a valuable retail investor feature that mitigates the covered risks. The costs to the issuer and thus to the investor are minimal. Municipal debt insurance works—for issuer and investor.

The retail investor must be careful not to become entranced by the tax-free nature of municipal debt. The CPA/PFS who prepares taxes can calculate whether taxable or tax-free debt yields the most to the client. The tax issue is not significant intrinsically—what matters is what income is brought to the bottom line. As a rule of thumb, if the client is in a high tax bracket, more is earned from municipal debt. If the client is in a low or medium tax bracket, even after the CPA/PFS allows for a tax liability, more may be earned from taxable corporate or government bonds. Most everything depends upon the interest rate spread between taxable and tax exempt income. Currently, tax-free bonds are appropriate relative to Treasuries for taxpayers in all but the lowest brackets. The reason for this is that some municipals yield more than Treasury securities do.

## .17  Income Tax Aspects of Municipal Bonds

Although municipal bonds are generally tax free, this refers to the income tax effect of their interest payments. The sale of a municipal bond still results in a taxable capital gain or loss and municipal bonds held in an estate are still subject to estate tax or if given, subject to gift tax.

A municipal bond purchased on a secondary market (as opposed to the original issuer) after April 30, 1993, may have a market discount. A market discount arises when the value of a bond decreases after its issue date, generally because of an increase in interest rates. Market discount is the amount of the stated redemption price of a bond at its maturity that is more than your basis in the bond immediately after its acquisition. In such a situation, if the bond is held to maturity, it will pay the bondholder back its face amount. In so doing the bondholder receives back not only his or her original investment but the difference between the discounted price paid and the face amount. What is the taxable character of this difference? It is *not* additional tax-free income. When you buy a market discount bond, you can choose to accrue (on a daily basis) the market discount over the period you own the bond and include it in your income currently as taxable interest income. As you accrue the discount and record the amount in taxable income, you are simultaneously increasing your basis in the bond. If the bond is subsequently redeemed for is face value you will have no gain or loss. If this is not done then any gain resulting when the bond is disposed of (up to the amount of the market discount) is treated as ordinary income (not capital gain). These market discount rules apply to taxable bonds as well but the effect there is less dramatic because the bondholder is not assuming all income from the bond is tax-exempt. There the difference is one of converting the accretion from the discounted basis to the face amount as ordinary income (whether done ratably or at the time of sale or redemption) rather than treating as capital gain.

Certain municipal bonds may produce income subject to alternative minimum tax. These bonds, referred to as private activity bonds, are debt instruments where more than 10 percent of the proceeds of the issue was used for a private business or 10% of the principle or interest is secured by private business property. Interest received on privative activity bonds issued after August 7, 1986 is generally a "tax preference item" for calculation of alternative minimum tax although the interest is otherwise tax-exempt like other municipal bonds.

The original issue discount (OID) on tax-exempt state or local municipal bonds is also tax-exempt. Interest on federally guaranteed state or local tax-exempt bonds issued after 1983 is generally taxable.

## .19 Municipal Bond Mutual Funds

Many investors avoid the issue of individual bond selection by investing in a municipal bond mutual fund. There are four basic types of municipal funds:

1. *State and federal tax-free bond funds.* These single-state funds are the most common type of fund. They have the name of a state somewhere

in their title, thus delineating the contents of and stated potential investors for that fund.

2. *State and federal tax-free high-yield bond funds.* High yield comes to the municipal arena. These funds invariably have mostly investment-grade paper, but lower and not-rated paper exceeds the limits imposed on conventional funds. Although there are certainly more risks associated with these funds, they are usually the stellar performers of their respective fund group and generally enjoy astronomically high ratings and regard by fund rating services.

3. *State and federal tax-free insured bond fund.* Funds that are almost exclusively insured paper. They are at the opposite end of the spectrum from the high-yield funds and all but the most reactionary would consider them very safe. They generally have comparatively low yields and are regularly criticized by the rating services as unnecessary from a safety standpoint and an overprotection from risk.

4. *State and federal tax-free money market and intermediate bond funds.* Short- and intermediate-term paper makes up these funds. These funds can have anything from one month's to several years' duration. They earn high marks for safety of principal and stability of net asset value.

5. *Federal tax-free funds, called "national" or "general" tax-free funds.* If they are owned in a state where there is a state income tax, they are often fully taxable interest-bearing vehicles for that state (but still not federally). Except for the amount of the total income generated by that state, which is still tax-free, the fund income is subject to state income tax. These funds can have all 50 states and the various territories represented in their portfolio.

The state and federal funds are usually concentrated in the long-term debt of their issuer, characteristically 10 to 30 years. The insured funds have the same timeframe, as do the high-yield funds. High-yield tax-free funds are very similar to their taxable corporate counterparts. The "high-yield" component relates to:

- *Lower ratings.* Under BBB paper makes up a large percentage of the fund's assets. BBB and above are investment grade, "bank-quality" paper; all other ratings are junk.
- *Less favorable call and refunding provisions.* This is call risk and refunding provision risk exposure that limits dependability of income.
- *Secondary or junior debt.* This is debt subordinate to senior debt of issuers that are perceived as unstable.
- *Special situations.* This is debt issued to cover the more problematic aspects of municipal issuance.
- *Non-rated debt.* Debt sold directly to the fund without rating.

¶31,013.19

Municipal debt is so credit sensitive that, as a total return item, high-yield muni funds often do not outperform conventional funds. Insured funds, however, almost always under perform their uninsured counterparts. Should investors want insured municipals, their interests are best served by directly investing in those bonds.

Like most insurers, muni insurers do not insure any entity that needs insurance. They have no time for higher-risk issuers—they are poor credit risks. The representative issuer who gets insurance is an issuer of A or AA credit quality. The insured debt is automatically upgraded to AAA—because it is insured. The issue is generally sold at one-tenth or two-tenths of a percent lower yield than comparable uninsured issues of the same maturity. It is a very cheap price for the retail investor to pay for this feature. Some financial advisors stopped recommending to their individual clients anything but insured debt all the way back in the early 1980s. The retail muni investor is most impressed with safety, liquidity, and stability, all of which are immeasurably enhanced by municipal insurance.

## ¶31,015   DEBT MATURITIES

The issue that every investor talks about the most is maturity. There are several levels of maturity: short term is up to one year, intermediate term is one to five years, and long term is six or more years.

An endless debate concentrates on short-term versus long-term risk. Long-term risk relates to price risk; income risk applies to short-term issues. Normally, short-term debt pays less than long-term debt. When interest rates are low, most investors are best served by investing in intermediate- and long-term debt. However, there is not a single uncertainty related to debt maturities that diversification cannot help. From an asset allocation standpoint, whether debt maturity is short, intermediate, or long term, all deserve a place in the investor's portfolio and are beneficial for the achievement of fixed income goals. They will play off against each other as time goes by and soften the blow of the errors—errors that everyone makes, no matter how well laid their plans. Specific asset allocation between short, intermediate, and long term are up to the CPAs/PFSs and their clients. There is a place for short-, intermediate-, and long-term debt, but it is all determined by the needs of the individual investor. Factors related to risk, age, income needs, credits, and comfort level are part of the equation.

Extending maturities often does not result in generating more income for the fixed income investor. Therefore, benefits to the investor may be marginal. However, extending maturity does address several negative issues for the fixed income investor. First, if short-term rates decline and they have nothing but cash, the chances are very good that intermediate and long-term rates will also decline.

If the investor prefers capital preservation and liquidity, which basically describes a short-term income vehicle investor, an asset allocation shift of money to longer maturities may be unsatisfactory both because of time of maturity and size of dollar commitment. However, many investors falsely exaggerate their need for capital preservation and liquidity. Although it may be true that investors are intimidated by long-term bonds or mutual funds, it is equally true that, from an income orientation, they only hurt themselves by not investing in long-term bonds or mutual funds. Somehow, some way, these investors must truthfully assess their need for liquidity and inability to accept principal fluctuation or they will be unable to realize the benefits available to them from a traditional fixed income investment.

Current income investors are much more pragmatic about maturities, although they can error through aggressive investments. Some income investors chase yield and own only the most long-term debt available. These investors can be carried away with income stream and disregard the multitude of risks they assume grasping for all that income. Owning too many large positions in long-term debt is not really a problem in an era where all municipal and corporate debt is skewed in favor of the issuer (not in favor of the investor) from a call "protection" standpoint. All municipal and corporate debt seems to be called away well before its time. However, large positions of low-rated debt and equity certainly can be a problem. The reason for this is risk and its relationship to the individual investor's risk profile. Across asset classes, assuming great credit risk in both junk debt and high-dividend payout, low-quality stocks is inappropriate financial planning, money management, and asset allocation. The most beneficial risk level to the investor is one that has been created by a balanced portfolio. The CPA/PFS must look for a balance.

Capital appreciation investors are similar to total return investors, but in the bond arena. They seek to manage capital gains, but they want coupon income, too. The exception is traders who assume positions in zero coupon bonds. Since there is no cash flow (but interest continues to accrete passively onto the bond), these investors are actively seeking only capital gains. The conventional capital appreciation investor is trying to capitalize on perceived future changes in interest rates, asset value variances, and yield curve differences.

## ¶31,017   PAR, PREMIUM, OR DISCOUNT BONDS

Another issue is whether to invest in par ($1,000 per bond), premium (priced above par), or discount (priced below par) bonds. In the recent past, investors who bought premium debt have locked in attractive yields compared to discount and par bonds with similar maturities. With premium bonds, the cash flow from having a larger coupon causes the price to be higher, to compensate for the bigger coupon cash flow. All bonds pay off at par, unless they are called or refunded at a premium, so all that premium normally disappears. However, increased income more than makes up for the lost premium. Premium bonds are relatively defensive in nature, because in a bull market they tend to lag the performance of lower coupon issues because of "reinvestment" risk. The bond-holders have more income to find a home for if they own large coupon, premium issues. However, in a bear market, when interest rates rise and bond values decline, the large coupon buoys the premium bond relative to par and discount issues. Whether rates go up, down, or sideways, from a capital preservation standpoint, premium bonds are less volatile than par or discount issues. Simply put:

- Premium bonds are for maximum cash flow, cost the most money, and go down less in a bad market.
- Discount bonds have the least cash flow, cost the least money, but go up the most in a good market.
- Par bonds are the happy medium. They cost $1,000 per bond, which is their face value and value at maturity, generate income exactly at the rate of the current environment, and behave as the market behaves because they represent the market at the time of their issuance, because their coupon is "current."

Note that in the case of premium bonds, producing greater cash flow is the result of paying a higher price for the bond. The overall economic effect may thus only be receiving more cash because of parting with more cash.

If you buy a bond at a discount when interest has been defaulted or when the interest has accrued but has not been paid, the transaction is described as trading the bond "flat." When you receive the defaulted or unpaid interest it is not taxable income to you as it was accounted for in the purchase price. When you receive the payment of the unpaid or defaulted interest it is a return of capital and it reduces your basis in the bond. Interest that accrues after the date of purchase is taxable to the purchaser.

## ¶31,019    Bond Calls

Calls in the past few years of gradually declining interest rates have become a major bond investment. Calls are provisions in bond covenants, which allows the issuer to retire a bond and pay back the investor before the bond matures. Investors, however, earn a higher yield on callable bonds as compared to noncallable bonds. They pay more as a payment for uncertainty about the life of the bond. A noncallable bond has a set maturity date that cannot be altered by calls or refunding.

Bonds are called for several reasons:

- To reduce financing costs and retire or reissue at a lower rate of interest. An issuer is flush and pays off its debt or, at least, refinances it at a lower rate of interest.
- To change cash flow. An issuer receives a better return on its money by paying off debt rather than investing it.
- To replace with different investment vehicle, turning bonds into preferred stock, private placements, or some other loan vehicle.
- To change duration—exchange long-term debt for shorter-term debt.

## ¶31,021  BOND LADDERS

Probably the most misunderstood and least utilized damage control strategy for calls and other problems is bond laddering. Bond ladders extend through various maturities as a diversification tool. The investor starts with an equally or near equally weighted series of maturities. Some examples would be:

- 1, 2, 3, 4, and 5 years.
- 1, 3, and 5 years.
- 1, 3, 5, and 10 years.

As each issue matures, the CPA/PFS and client reinvest at the longest maturity in the series and continue to "roll out" (extend to the longest maturity) at the same or similar maturity. Ladders are useful for various reasons. Ladders are more flexible than single-maturity portfolios. If liquidity needs surface, there is always a part of the portfolio near maturity and therefore trading near par, so price risk concerns are minimal. If the client needs money and owns a note maturing in seven months, he or she can sell it very near par with no loss of principal, unless there is a major problem. In addition, because of continued income stream and regular principal distributions, the ladder strategy amounts to dollar cost averaging. The investor gets the level of income associated with all the levels of maturity the CPA/PFS and client select. The client's income is somewhere near the median maturity of the portfolio weighting. Interest rate fluctuations have minimal significance. There is no rate chasing with the fixed ladder format. There is no need to predict rates or second-guess economic developments. The CPA/PFS has covered all the bases. Ladders can structure income and principal needs precisely. An investor can set up a five-year college savings plan, for example, with a ladder lasting five years and then scale in maturities to correspond with each September financing. Zero coupon bond ladders are used constantly for this purpose.

Practically, what the investor accomplishes with a ladder is a hedge strategy. The investor combines short-term liquidity with long-term returns and avoids the worst extremes of each. There is always something that can go wrong with any investment, but there is not much that can go wrong with a bond ladder. The investor can miss out on gains in a bull market, but the strategy is supposed to be used to avoid market issues — down and up. If the CPA/PFS is inattentive to the ratings or calls of the portfolio, a mistake here and there leading to premature return of principal or loss of it or income through default can certainly spoil the ladder. Nonetheless, it does not make sense to ladder bonds laden with call provisions and poor rating. If that is what the client wants, he or she should simply select a strategic income fund that corresponds with investment needs.

## ¶31,023 BOND MUTUAL FUND LADDERS

Regarding funds, funds can be used to create a passive ladder by asset allocation between money market, intermediate-term, and long-term income funds. Because many laddered funds are available, the CPA/PFS need only carefully examine the information reports from the mutual fund rating service to select the one that best suits the client. What is interesting with funds, whether laddered by using several funds or one internally laddered by its manager, is an income comparison with directly owned bonds. Bonds are much more expensive than stocks to buy. So, if the professional can isolate funds with low expense ratios and 12b-1 fees, the client might come out well ahead of buying own bonds alone. However, there is no such thing as a set dividend from a mutual fund. The dividends can be changed at the whim of the fund family's board of directors — even the fund managers and traders are often not consulted. Funds will eventually reflect the interest rate environment of the client's portfolio. In the interim, the strategy works very well because the manager addresses call and credit risks with far more expertise than the nonprofessional. Even given compensating fund expenses, fund managers can also buy bonds at far cheaper prices than retail investors.

## ¶31,025 DURATION

Duration is an attempt to quantify various aspects of current bond performance to predict future performance. It addresses such issues as why long-term debt is more volatile than short-term debt and why low-coupon issues are more volatile to the downside than high-coupon issues. It is similar to stock beta in that it measures volatility, but it is more oriented toward future performance than past.

Duration determines the investor's breakeven point on a bond. It takes into consideration maturity, coupon, yield, and call. It is a technique utilized by investors to compare sensitivity to the interest rate environment of various bonds. The hope is that CPAs/PFSs will use duration to make bond investing more simple, safe, and profitable for their clients.

Duration is a number that tells how long it will take the income and principal payments of a bond to pay back the original investment on that bond. For example, the investor buys a 30-year Treasury bond for $1,000. The bond has a 5-percent coupon, so the client receives $50 per year ($25 per semiannual payment) in interest payments for 30 years. At the end of 40 payments (20 years), the investor has broken even. The duration, then, is 20 years. The larger the interest payment, the shorter the duration. If an investor selects a 15-percent coupon nonrated junk bond with a 20-year maturity, he or she would receive $75 per 6-month payment, $150 per year, and have a break even of 14 payments or seven years. Therefore, the 20-year junk bond (assuming it does not default) duration is seven years.

The CPA/PFS can use duration to evaluate both bonds and mutual funds. Duration is multiplied times interest rate fluctuation to find the expected volatility response to a change in rates. For example, if rates drop 1 percent, then the 30-year Treasury example above will go up about 20 percent in value. On the other hand, if rates go up one-half percent, because values react inversely to rate fluctuations, the 30-year Treasury will drop approximately 10 percent in value.

The CPA/PFS can do the same calculation for mutual funds, too. The information sheets from the mutual fund rating service give duration figures for funds, although it is more accurate to contact fund families with all choices to learn the current duration of the portfolio if the CPA/PFS and client are making a new investment. As an example, a mutual fund with a duration of 10 years would fall 5 percent in value if there were a half-point drop in rates, exactly like with an individual bond.

As anyone can gather, nothing has longer duration than a zero coupon bond, because there is no cash flow until it pays off at maturity. A 30-year Treasury strip will rise 30 percent in value if interest rates drop 1 percent, which is why these securities are a rate speculator's dream product. No coupon issue would ever perform even close to that. Alas, if rates rise 1 percent, a 30-year Treasury strip's value can drop 30 percent, too.

How can the CPA/PFS use duration as a technique for successful retail debt investment? If the CPA/PFS and client believe in declining interest rates long term, the client should invest in long-duration debt. If the CPA/PFS and client believe the trend is the opposite direction, the client should invest in short- duration debt. Essentially, duration is a tool that forces the investor to take a stand on rates and inflation. Although speculators love to take stands, nobody likens that behavior to plain vanilla debt investment. Plain vanilla investors like market-neutral stances. Much of the appeal of ladders is to avoid the pitfalls of duration. The examples are intentionally somewhat extreme to accentuate the vivid reality of duration.

¶31,025

There are many ways to calculate duration and many variables, such as call provisions and future value dollar calculations, to muddy the duration formulas. The CPA/PFS must always remember that:

- Duration changes with calls or prerefunding.
- A larger coupon means shorter duration and less volatility.
- Duration does not consider credit quality or other unrelated risk issues.

The CPA/PFS now knows that bonds range from ownership of simple debt instruments to extraordinarily complex products. Like many concepts and ideas that seem to flourish only in ivory towers, the climb to learn what makes bonds important investments reveals something both simple and profound. Bonds are loaded with depths of usefulness for every investor. There are plenty of reasons the debt markets continue to dwarf the stock markets in size. The CPA/PFS asset allocation plan has surged with their strength the last few years.

# Chapter 32
## Demystifying Funds

## CONTENTS

## ¶32,000  OVERVIEW

Everybody loves mutual funds. The average mutual fund investor is a Baby Boomer 44 years old, married, employed, with investments in three different funds in two different mutual fund families. The household income is $60,000 per year, and the family has $50,000 in assets. In addition, the average fund owner knows absolutely nothing about what he or she owns.

The basic cause of confusion regarding mutual funds is the rapid growth and expansion of this nation's, and the entire investment world's, reliance upon this vehicle. The mutual fund vehicle is asked to be both the savior and the scapegoat for the investing public.

Approximately 90,000,000 people, representing over 50,000,000 U.S. households, own funds. The primary source of this meteoric rise in numbers is retirement plan assets. The shift from corporate-managed pension plans to self-directed retirement vehicles opened an ever-widening gate for the novice investor. Today, it is rarely the company's responsibility for planning successful employee pensions; usually, it is financially naive employees responsible for selecting successful investments for themselves. This has given new meaning to the term "dartboard investing."

Currently, almost 50 percent of all mutual fund assets are invested in stocks, with about 25 percent in bonds, and the remainder in money market funds. This is a compromised breakdown because there is a wide variety of fund types, many of which defy conventional asset labels and commingle asset types. Not every formula is the same.

## ¶32,001  THE MUTUAL FUND INDUSTRY

Wall Street is as fond of mutual funds as are investors. From a traditional investment banking standpoint, issuer products have been largely stocks or bonds. Furthermore, most of the attention was concentrated on the institutional investors, who would buy most of the stocks or bonds in a banking issue for their own use — investment, pension plans, cash flow needs, or whatever. In recent years, however, mutual funds (overwhelmingly directed toward the retail investor) have assumed a larger and larger slice of the investment banker pie. Not surprisingly, Wall Street pays attention.

Both open-ended and closed-ended mutual funds have generated enormous banking fees and enjoyed enthusiastic acceptance with investors. "Enthusiastic acceptance" describes a huge asset shift — and assets mean a lot to Wall Street. Of late, the most institutionally driven of investment banking firms have signed mutual fund distribution contracts with the large retail wire houses and discount brokerage firms. This is a revenue expanding and gathering activity for both.

Today, the retail investor directly owns half of all U.S. financial assets and will acquire more as savings and retirement investment expands and grows.

Much of this money resides in mutual fund investments. The scramble is still unfolding regarding how this class will grow and best be harnessed by both institutions and investors.

Another measure of the fund industry's success is its seemingly daily consolidation. Mutual fund families are on a merger course that rivals the consolidation mania of the rest of the financial services industry itself. As the families consolidate, so do the funds. Happily, all this appears beneficial for the investor, too, because the investor has more funds to choose from within the expanded family groups.

To summarize, mutual fund management is a primary source of income to the financial services industry. That income is largely impervious to market fluctuations because funds need management in bad years as well as good years. Long-term investing is simply that: there will be both up and down cycles. It is the overall, long-term, extended holding period (5–10-year) return that is important to the investor because the long time frame is where the benefits lie—not short term. The investor, once again, pays fees no matter what goes on with the markets.

## ¶32,003  WHAT YOU BUY IS WHAT YOU GET

On the other hand, investors can get quite a bit for what they pay. The average mutual fund investor owns $25,000 worth of funds. Almost 80 percent of those funds are selected with the help of an investment professional. There are three basic types of funds: stock, bonds and money market funds. Three-quarters of all fund owners own stock funds, half own bond funds, and half own money market funds. Almost all owners own two or three of the three types of funds. Half are comfortable with risk, a quarter are somewhat speculatively inclined, and almost 10 percent are either totally risk adverse or totally high risk oriented, putting them at either extreme of the investor bell curve. Each investor's fee facilitates finding each investor the correct fit.

How do the mutual fund investors get what they pay for? Probably only a small percentage of fund investors understand diversification and asset alloca-tion. Consequently, most investors in mutual funds don't know what they own. Only a fraction of investors could ever hope to duplicate their fund performance on their own. Quite simply this is what they pay for—high returns from invest-ments they may know nothing about and have no input in selecting. This rep-resents an enormous opportunity for the CPA/PFS to add value.

## ¶32,005  WHAT ARE MUTUAL FUNDS?

What are these behemoths we call mutual funds? They're everyone who wants to commingle their money to work more aggressively to increase their wealth. They prefer to do it with a collectively huge sum of money rather than individually with a small amount of money. The benefit to the investor is that a small amount of money makes an investor part-owner in fabulous wealth that is invested for them according to a prospectus plan.

For the most part, they are pooled assets historically created for two types of investors. These investors were people with little time or with moderate amounts of money—as little as $100. Like most antiquated investment rules, these investor profiles have expanded with time, but the rules still apply to the most representative types of mutual fund shareholders, those with little time and moderate amounts of money. These pooled assets make investing easier because, once the investor designates a fund type, the mutual fund management company assumes responsibility for everything else. The selection, diversification, buying and selling—all are the direct responsibility of the manager.

If the manager has selected correctly, funds can perform extremely efficiently. Consequently, people with a lot of money invest in funds for the extraordinary level of performance they can enjoy. Many of the investment banking firm mutual funds were created for this group. A mutual fund can own hundreds or even thousands of individual issues. This makes the whole process cost-effective. Purchases in bigger blocks generate fewer fees. In addition, some investors who enjoy spending time studying investments spend it examining and rating different funds. They do this because mutual fund investment can be a cost-efficient way to diversify assets. Most funds have diversification above and beyond almost any investor's dreams.

There is a major disadvantage to all of this. By delegating responsibility to a manager, the investor loses control over the investment and, thus, his or her money. The investor's choice is confined to buying and selling the fund. Many investors view security selection as a sport. It is important for the CPA to rein in this activity.

Direct stock and bond investment costs end as soon as the client buys the security; mutual fund fees are ongoing. Fund fees only rarely are tied to returns. In other words, fees are rarely dictated by performance. Usually, they are fixed, regardless of how the market or how the funds behave. With high turnover (of assets in the fund) and increasingly modest disclosure requirements (of activity generated within the mutual fund), interested investors often have no idea (other than asset class) what they own or what they have earned.

To top it off, the primary fund support document, the prospectus, may be difficult to understand. However, recent prospectus requirements were cut and edited to modest-sized disclosure documents by the Securities and Exchange Commission's Rule on the "Profile" disclosure option. Another SEC Rule mandates the use of "Plain English" for disclosure documents. (Both SEC Rules are explained in other chapters.)

Not all funds have these various disadvantages. Furthermore, many have them to a lesser extent than their more confusing or complicated mutual fund rivals. It is true that some mutual funds' portfolio guidelines are almost impossible to understand. Incredibly enough, however, mutual fund companies are regularly rated, based on the reporting documents to shareholders and their shareholder relations departments. But their portfolio guidelines never win awards for clarity.

## ¶32,007  OPEN-ENDED AND CLOSED-ENDED MUTUAL FUNDS

There are two types of mutual funds: open ended and closed ended. By far the most common, popular and largest are open ended, so-called because they can continue to take in new money every trading day, thus creating new shares that represent a pro rata portion (the investor's share of the pot) of the fund's assets. Open-ended funds are listed in the mutual fund section of the business section of the newspaper, fund family by fund family. They are priced by their net asset value (total net value of the fund divided by the number of shares in the fund) at the close of the trading day. There are no fluctuating quotes during the course of the market day.

Closed-ended funds, on the other hand, trade throughout the day on an exchange the same way stocks do—their prices fluctuate during the course of the day and are listed and quoted daily under their proper exchange listing. Closed-ended funds are always listed under the exchange quotes (in alphabetical order) of the exchange on which they are listed (usually the New York Stock Exchange and American Stock Exchange). They are not priced by their net asset value the way open-ended funds are. The two can vary widely—market (price) value and underlying asset value. Most closed-ended funds sell at either a premium (above) or a discount (below) to their underlying net asset value. Net asset value is total fund assets remaining after total fund liabilities, such as trading fees and margin interest, have been subtracted. XYZ Fund owns $125,000,000 of stock (after all liabilities are subtracted from fund assets) and there are 10,000,000 shares outstanding. Therefore, the net asset value is $12.50 ($125,000,000 divided by 10,000,000 shares=$12.50).

Closed-ended funds tend to be a bit more esoteric as investment items than open-ended funds because little about them is as cut-and-dried as open-ended funds. Discounts to (prices below) their net asset value are much more common than premiums (prices above), so people tend to assume there is something wrong with closed-ended funds per se. Many of the funds are made up of foreign, illiquid, or small capitalization securities; therefore, many investors are wary of investing in something they are unfamiliar with and do not understand. Closed-ended funds often employ leveraging (borrowing) to enhance cash flow, gains or total return—many clients want nothing to do with leveraged securities purchases in any form and should avoid closed-end funds altogether.

## ¶32,009  MUTUAL FUND SALES COSTS

Far more popular than worrying about closed-ended funds and their investment practices is the issue of mutual fund costs. A large library could be filled with the book, magazine, newspaper, TV and radio coverage of mutual fund costs. They all so thoroughly contradict one another and come to such contrary conclusions that, other than as a cure for insomnia, they may be collectively without value. As an introduction to mutual fund costs, the CPA/PFS must remember there are no free lunches in the mutual fund industry. Mutual fund companies are not philanthropic entities. They are in the business of making money for themselves and their clients. If they don't, they don't survive.

## .01 Definitions of Sales Fees of Mutual Funds

The issue of cost arises because there is a multiplicity of pricing matrixes for the same or very similar products. The sales fees of mutual funds are called "loads." There are front-ended loads, no-loads, back-ended (trailing) loads, and level-load funds. In addition, there are internal charges, called 12(b)-1 fees and management fees, which serve to further muddy the waters. Enumerated, stated and defined are all the loads:

1. *Load*—the different types of sales charges associated with open-ended mutual fund purchases.
2. *Front-ended load*—up-front pay for the purchase.
3. *No-load*—no direct purchase or sell costs are associated with investment. However, there are internal fees (to make up for no direct sales charges), which can be considerable.
4. *Back-ended (trailing) load*—a fee is attached if the fund is liquidated within a stated time period that declines at stated intervals, usually yearly, as ownership continues.
5. *Level-load*—a combination of front-ended and back-ended (trailing) load in which a reduced front-ended charge is paid upon purchase and a reduced back-ended (trailing) load is paid if the investment is liquidated early in holding period.
6. *Internal charges*—fees paid within the fund itself for the ongoing expenses of the fund.
7. *12(b)-1 fees*—fees charged to fund assets for mutual fund advertising and sales.
8. *Management fees*—administrative and trading costs charged to the fund assets.

## .03 The Significance of Fund Costs

To an investor, these charges are at best inconsequential and at worst blinding. At one end of the spectrum, there are investors who ignore the costs of a product and simply invest passively, regardless of the price. At the other end, are investors who ignore every characteristic of a fund except its costs. The realistic approach lies somewhere between the two extremes. The consequence of mutual fund costs is significant because of the nature of mutual fund investing itself. A single year of sales and related fees may not seem like much, but mutual fund investment is perceived as a long-term commitment. With time (as these fees never go away), the costs of a fund are clearly significant, because they affect fund performance. The more sophisticated a fund's investment mission, the more sizable are their fees. There are no superexpensive plain-vanilla index funds; there are no bargain-basement leveraged, international, multi-sector commodities pools. Often, then, but not always, the investors pay for what they get. However, it is a mistake to assume that the highest fees necessarily guarantee the investor the best manager or performance. The highest fees simply provide the investor with the most costly securities—much of the time.

High costs generate virulent controversy because investors do not like to pay them and, as already stated, the costs do not go away. It is incorrect to assume that someone who attacks mutual fund fees is simply a crank unwilling to pay fair value for services rendered. Studies suggest that, when mutual funds perform above the average of income funds, their success is directly related to modest costs. Conversely, these studies suggest that, when funds perform below the average, they lose too much return to the cost of the fees. Internal fees rarely scale down as funds grow in size; some studies suggest that fees tend to go up as funds do better! So, one is at a loss to determine exactly what is fair. "Fair" pricing structure in mutual funds may be impossible to define, but everyone is well advised to pay attention to all of these costs.

## .05 How Mutual Fund Costs Affect Performance

Less subjectively, it can be said that a lot of effort has been expended trying to answer questions about mutual fund costs and almost all of that effort focuses on performance. How do costs affect performance? Respected research offers conflicting data. One company that researches, evaluates, and comments on mutual funds, has concluded that, over the long run (10 years), fund returns are not influenced by the type of sales charges a fund family uses. This company perceives the real issue to be whether investors receive fair value for whatever expense they generate determining their mutual fund selections. The company addresses investor need by looking at:

1. What the investor can expect from a fund.
2. Products offered by the different fund families—by segregating all the various types of funds and defining them in plain English.
3. Value added by the fund family—by determining the role played in various fund classes and types by managers, trading costs and management fees.

Of mutual fund sales, 25 to 30 percent are no-load. Much of the no-load sales are in defined contribution retirement plans, an area that load-fund families are aggressively targeting. More and more investors feel the need to consult professional advice and are unwilling to go the investment route solo with direct-marketed (not broker-sold) mutual funds. Supporting the point, more and more direct-marketed fund families have sprouted broker-marketed fund subsidiaries, often with different names. Broker-sold funds, through the CPA/ personal financial specialist (PSF) may be less risky than direct-marketed funds for the novice investor. The financial advisor can help select the clients' fund choices and provide them with research and documentation. Most investors cannot confidently or wisely select mutual funds on their own.

Even more confusing, a financial journal has concluded that no-load mutual fund investors made more money than load investors, but that their superior results came from more aggressive investment. The problem with this conclusion is that it does not:

1. Address the suitability of the specific mutual fund for the investor.
2. Take into consideration the goals set by the individual investor.
3. Consider how asset allocation was able to offset market upsets to the good or detriment of the fund.

It is difficult to congratulate an investor group on performance achieved as a happy by-product of ignorance of their own investment profile. On the other hand, if professional advisors tend to defer to a conservative investment posture to police clients "for their own good," the clients must wonder what is going on. Until the mid-1990s, pension plan investment tended to be biased toward capital preservation and low volatility.

Hindsight demonstrates in this instance that professional advice that is too conservative is fully as undesirable as the opposite stance. It can be very difficult for the CPA to ascertain a clear picture of how a mutual fund is doing in relation to individual client's needs.

## .07  Conclusions About Mutual Fund Costs

It should be clear that cost problems in the mutual fund industry are not going away. Perhaps most inequitable is the fact that all of the costs in all of the sale configurations are borne by the investors. The investor pays for everything. Almost no fund fees are tied to the performance of the mutual fund. Consequently, the investor reads all about the gains of mutual funds but has no familiarity with the costs incurred by the fund itself. Many assumptions are made about mutual funds because the investor believes that they all behave the same as the other funds of their class and variety. They do not.

¶32,009.07

For a moment, the CPA should look at the conventional buying and selling of securities. One of the most incorrect statements made about the financial services entities that sell securities is that the industry does not care whether the market goes up or down. The conventional belief is that, buying or selling, the client has to pay a commission, so the broker makes out no matter what. Well, that's just plain silly. What is true is that the money managers who manage mutual funds often do not share the responsibility for good or bad results with mutual fund shareholders the way they do with other financial commitments. To say managers are neither rewarded for good performance nor penalized for bad is incorrect and an exaggeration. They receive better bonuses if all goes well; they are fired if things do not. However, the fund companies themselves receive the same fees regardless of the results. While it is true clients exit poor performing funds, their money tends to remain with the same mutual fund family—they simply switch to a better-performing fund within that family. The fund company still gets their fees.

Direct-sales clients can come and go as they please because they pay no direct sales fees to inhibit their departure; however, broker-sold fund families have better retention because sales regulatory principles that govern broker practices discourage switching between fund families. One would be hard put to determine which is the better practice.

## .09   So ... What's the Answer?

The SEC requires mutual fund families to share in gains and assume responsibilities in losses if a performance-based fee program is implemented. Over an extended holding period, the fees might be the same with or without a performance-based fee program. To determine that would require still another industry study. One would suspect that the gigantic fund families (as they continue to consolidate) would not really care much. However, smaller companies with specialized funds would experience significant revenue volatility. Particularly acute would be problems that a prolonged downturn in their markets would create because these companies would lose assets. For example, any specialty fund loses money under management when its area of specialization falls out of favor.

## .11   The Answer Is ....

Like so many seemingly simple investment questions, there are sadly no simple answers. The global investment public continues to rely on the mutual fund industry to manage assets; therefore, the way that industry is compensated will be scrutinized. Who knows what will come of it?

Costs are more relevant an issue to the investor than ever before with their shift toward allocating capital to equity funds. The reason for this is that the cost of equity funds so grossly exceeds that of debt funds. All debt funds charge about the same amount of money to do the same thing, which is why they all tend to have about the same yield. This is anything but the case with equity funds. In a bull market, the return on successful equity funds is so high that most clients cannot see the costs that they are paying to own the funds. This is not a good situation, because it creates opportunities for shareholder abuse. However, in a bear market, every client is aware of where every penny (that they do not receive) goes. Hence, fund fees and sales charge abuses are less apt to be a problem. The issue of costs with income funds (which generate a cash flow to the client as opposed to growth, as with an equity fund) is largely self-policed in a low interest rate environment. Excessive costs eliminate yield, which is the reason most investors buy debt funds. Thus, costs tend to remain low or investors do not invest in the fund. If costs are high, they eat up the yield and investors select a different fund for their income.

## ¶32,011 STOCK MUTUAL FUNDS

Again, in an equity bull market, performance can conceal a multitude of sins, let alone bury internal costs. Until 1994, a terrible year for both equity and debt securities, stock and bond fund cash flows were about equal. By 2000, the net inflow to bond funds became essentially zero. Equities account for nearly 40 percent of all household financial assets, much of them contained in mutual funds concentrating in equities. The retail investor has, for several years, been a net seller of directly owned equities.

Interestingly, from a performance standpoint, most equity mutual funds, if compared to the Standard & Poor's 500 Index, do not do well. The S&P 500 is the accepted measurement and usual index for equity performance measurement. Large equity funds have a difficult time beating their index (once again, usually, but by no means always, the S&P 500). Some of the index funds have a hard time duplicating the performance of their index.

### .01 What's an Investor to Do?

A head-banging exercise in equity fund investment futility is to try to pick funds with the aid of mass media periodical rankings. None of these publications agrees on much of anything and their choices are often atrocious performers, even if their selection is not entirely capricious. They do seem to try, and yet routinely fail. So, the CPA/PFS and client can go ahead and read periodical rankings, but they must keep in mind the lack of reliability.

### .03 Special and Sector Equity Funds

While nobody can begin to sort out magazine fund rankings, what is true is that if such specialized sectors as real asset funds, emerging economy funds, socially responsible funds, or other esoteric types suit the client's fancy, the CPA should learn a lot about how to evaluate funds. Nothing out there can help very much. Many of these funds are completely uncharacteristic and capricious in their investment styles. They often have abominable performance by any standard of measurement and are despised by the rating services. The financial planner is going to have to take down and tear apart each fund one by one to glean any uniqueness or value for the client. They are often bad investments.

## .05    Equity Funds: Costs and Conclusions

To conclude remarks on equity funds, the CPA and client cannot afford to ignore investment costs. The most common measurement of costs is expense ratios. They are a statement of costs expressed as a percentage of assets. For example, if the net asset value of a fund is $25.00 and the expenses total 50 cents, then 2 percent of the assets go to expenses. The expense ratios vary from less than 1 percent to as much as 10 percent in growth-oriented mutual funds. Once again, there is no correlation, good or bad, between expenses and performance over time. However, a "study of studies" suggests that:

1. Large capitalization fund performance is affected negatively by large fees.
2. Small capitalization stock fund performance is related positively to high expense ratios.
3. There is no correlation between costs and global fund performance. Therefore, it cannot be that the more esoteric the investment, the more money needs to be spent on the funds.

With equity mutual funds, there is really only one way to find a correlation between costs and performance. The solution is to take a long list of stock funds, break down what their expenses are allotted to, and determine whether any particular expense correlates with either positive or negative performance. Nobody wants to be the one to try to do it, though. Can anyone imagine calling a variety of privately owned investment companies to ask them for a list of their expenses, broken down item by item, for each fund? "Go fish!"

## ¶32,013    BOND FUNDS

A bond fund is a mutual fund made up almost entirely, but by no means exclusively, of bonds. There are numerous income-generating securities that can end up in a bond fund—from simple money market instruments to the sophisticated synthetics or derivatives. Their primary purpose is to generate a cash flow the investor can use for immediate spending.

Bond fund costs, happily, are clearer and easier to understand than equity fund costs. Since bond funds tend to be specialized and simple to categorize, they are easier than stock funds to evaluate. Bond funds, in brief, usually under perform their indexes, especially on a risk-adjusted, post-expense basis. In a low-interest-rate environment, the only way a manager can perform at or above his or her index is to increase his risk significantly (on a relative basis to that index and to funds like it).

In addition, the manager can try to enhance the return with strategies that few individual investors would ever consider, let alone try to do or be able to understand, on their own. At the most elementary level, very few individuals use margin to buy bonds on credit, either for income or gain. At its most sophisti-cated, money managers have sizable commitments to synthetically created securities, derivatives of conventional bonds, uncommon option and futures strategies . . . the list is endless.

While the aggressive management of bond funds is not categorically bad (investors do, after all, pay a fund manager to do better than they think they can do on their own), the investment public has seen some mind-boggling bond fund disasters over the last 20 years. Many of these misfortunes arose because a fund manager failed to realize exceptional returns for his or her shareholders. Although it is ludicrous to say fund managers' errors were made in an effort to offset large expenses, this strategy did play a role in these fiascoes. For example, common sense dictates that if a manager of anything—mutual fund or fast food restaurant—has large expenses, the manager tries to do the best he or she can to cover expenses.

## .01 Bond and Other Income Fund Costs

One service has claimed that risks and high expense ratios in income funds go hand in hand, especially large 12(b)-1 fees. Bond fund promotion costs through 12(b)-1 fees are so large that the effects on yield are perceptible. Evi-dently, aside from assuming more credit risk, expensive funds have longer duration (more volatility), use margin (leveraged purchases) and employ options and futures strategies (high risk) more often. Another of the largest managers of income funds was accused for years of buying premium bonds in its income funds only to beef up yields to cover enormous advertising costs. Of course, premiums disappear as bonds approach par value at maturity, so a lot of money just disappears from net asset value—but cash flow stays higher in the meantime.

How much of all this quibbling becomes "chicken and egg" controversy is arguable. The 12(b)-1 fees are so controversial and confusing that one can safely predict an eventual legislated end to their existence. The consumer is confused by the blend of internal sales, management and distribution fees, and logic suggests that these fees in their current form cannot last much longer. Full disclosure of costs would mitigate most of the problems attached to mutual fund fees.

## .03    Junk Bond Funds

Before addressing fund selection, there are a few special types of bond funds the financial planner should understand. Even in an equity-obsessed universe, these income funds generate a large amount of press coverage and should be understood by the financial advisor. The most notorious of all bond vehicles, in or out of a mutual fund, are junk bonds. Junk bonds are lower-rated debt that is not investment or "bank quality" debt—which must be rated BBB or better. Despite the general antipathy generated by the sector, the fact remains that junk (or high-yield bonds, to be less pejorative) generates large cash flow and excellent total return. It took a while, after Michael Milken, but lower-rated debt has returned to the generally high level of performance conventionally associated with this investment before the junk market collapse.

Junk bonds historically have returned about 50 percent more than Treasury bonds. In a time when few companies default, where there is little inflation and the economy usually chugs along quite nicely, the risks of lower-rated debt (particularly diversified in a large mutual fund investment pool) seems well worth the risk to many investors. Of particular note is that, as more companies continue to turn their performance around for the better, credit upgrades resulting from these turnarounds can only enhance the value of junk bond portfolios. An example would be all the debt issued to fund the growth and development of the major high-tech companies. When the companies were created in the 1960s and 1970s, those that were able to issue debt were rated very low. However, as some of these companies became large capitalization companies of immense value, their debt was upgraded accordingly and traded in line with the higher-quality debt to which they became comparable.

## .05    Global Bond Funds

Global bond funds enjoy reputations similar to junk bond funds. Most countries have debt that is rated below investment grade. Many countries enjoy decent ratings simply because their debt is guaranteed or backed by the U.S. government. Thanks to the collapse of short-term multimarket income funds several years ago (when much foreign debt either defaulted or dropped like a stone as the dollar strengthened), many clients respond to the mention of global bond funds with genuine loathing. The reason for this antipathy is that the short-term multimarket income funds fell apart never to recover, and they generated legal proceedings that continue to this day.

Global bond funds are sophisticated investments with multiple risks that are rather difficult to understand. Without an elaborate discussion of bond fund risks, suffice it to say that if global debt is a client's interest rate vehicle of choice, the CPA/PFS must do some homework preparatory to selecting a fund and investing the client's hard-earned money in it.

The CPA must learn about those countries that a "chosen" fund invests in. It would be unwise under any circumstances to invest in countries the client does not like. On the other hand, it would be interesting for the client to invest in countries that he or she does like. The CPA must always remember—debt securities are loans; hence, loans should be made to countries clients want to lend their money to, because that is exactly what they are doing. Then, it is important to examine the nature of the fund's currency exposure—do they own mostly dollar-denominated securities? Or are they all tied up with a lot of soft currency paper? As has been discussed, the CPA should determine whether the fund's expense ratio is consistent with the costs of implementing the investment strategy stated in its prospectus. For example, a plain vanilla fund without leverage or advanced trading strategies should have significantly lower expenses than one with sophisticated futures, options, currency and derivative plays.

## .07    Emerging Markets Bond Funds

Closely aligned to global bond fund investing are emerging markets bond fund investing. While global funds can invest in domestic and foreign debt from highest to lowest quality, emerging market bond funds invest only the debt of developing nations. The debt of emerging nations by definition is often of highest credit risk, illiquid and tied to currencies that are not traded on global markets. The fact that these currencies are often pegged to the dollar helps stabilize them, but the risks attached to these countries can quickly eliminate this advantage. It is safe to say that most emerging nation debt funds trade like high-risk equity funds with an income kicker (in the form of cash flow) attached to them. The emerging debt fund group is a vehicle designed to generate a huge cash flow, but certainly things go wrong. Every kind of risk can apply to a greater or lesser extent to emerging market debt.

## .09    Insured Municipal Bond Funds

The last bond fund the CPA should learn about is the insured municipal bond fund. Many investors become very concerned with municipal bond fund problems—problems they think owning an insured fund will cure. What they want is so many layers of protection that they ignore the fact that they may give up more income than their concern justifies. For example, if a person wants insured debt, he or she should invest in direct ownership of individual issues. Then, the investor will have fixed cash flow and fixed maturity, which do not exist in funds.

Now, to be totally contradictory, if there are high-yield (lower-rated) mutual funds of a state, the CPA should examine these offerings. The default risk of municipal debt is slight. Funds managers have mind-numbing diversity to consider in any single state's municipal funds; there are hundreds of issuers and thousands of issues. A good municipal fund manager might generate very high yields for the client unconstrained by conventional rating.

## .11  Bond Funds and Risk

Bond funds have significant risk. The types of risk associated with income-oriented investment that directly apply to income mutual funds follow:

*Interest Rate Risk.*    There's not a thing anyone can do about interest rates, unless they are on the Federal Reserve Board. If the CPA and the client are afraid of rates rising and eroding the value of a fund position, they should switch into the fund family's money market fund or intermediate term bond fund. Rate issues generate much less significant principal risk in intermediate-term maturities than in long-term ones. Of course, for all practical purposes, principal is not at risk in a money market fund, regardless of rate fluctuations.

*Credit Risk.*    If the CPA and client do not like lower-rated debt because of a fear of default, the client should not own any lower-rated debt, period. The incremental return is not worth the fact that the client will never stop worrying about his or her position.

*Sector Risk.*    Sector risks are very real. Most single state municipal funds are very responsive to their state's financial well-being. However, the municipal markets are comparatively stable, state to state, because they operate in fairly benign isolation and suffer from a chronic supply shortage of bonds. On the other hand, with most high-risk global, junk or emerging market funds, an investor must exercise great restraint, from an asset allocation standpoint. High yield seduces many investors with visions of chunks of cash flow dancing in their heads into overcommitting assets. Concentrated positions in low-rated and high-risk securities makes no sense in income-oriented investments—to place 25 percent of your principal at risk to generate 4 percent more income per year is hardly sound money management. Junk funds are good for income enhancement, but the client cannot overcommit to them. Murphy's Law is fully operative with greedy income investors. They are always punished.

*Style Risk.*    The CPA/PFS must be well-versed in leverage, options and futures strategies, derivatives and foreign exchange risk before employing these strategies to invest the clients' money in funds. Also, the financial advisor must read the prospectuses and quarterly reports of all these funds to determine which employ risk or risk management strategies and to attempt to learn exactly how they affect the performance of the funds.

## ¶32,015   SELECTING A MUTUAL FUND—PROFESSIONAL RATING SERVICES

How do the CPA and client select mutual funds? There is not a single investor out there who does not have an opinion on mutual fund selection. Most professionals rely upon one or more of the professional rating services. They are providers of services that the CPA and client can purchase direct, buy from professional advisors or find at local libraries that have a strong investment information presence.

With the American urge to quantify and rank anything, the CPA and client can even attempt to rate the rating services, but there is no reason to recommend it. They all have more to offer investors than anyone can ever use. It is best to screen funds with as many services as are available. However, all they address is the past; they cannot be held accountable for the future.

Most use some sort of a grading system similar to the way movies are rated. As with movies, they often conceal as much as they reveal. The ratings are no substitute for personal involvement. For example, stars are used to screen types of funds. If a style of fund is made up of 15 to 20 funds and almost all of them are 1- to 2-star funds (on a scale of 1 to 5, 5 being high), the CPA and client must have the courage of their convictions before allocating to that sector. More narrowly, if the CPA and client pick a universe made up of 30 to 40 funds and 3 of them are 5 stars and the remainder are 2, 3, and a few 4 stars, then the CPA and client should certainly look at the three 5-star funds first.

## .01   Grading Mutual Fund Professional Rating Service Analysts

The CPA/PFS must learn to analyze the analysts. For example, few bond funds are 5-star funds, compared with balanced (equity and debt geared toward total return of both growth and income) or equity funds. There is a perception, however misguided, that bond fund managers do little to earn their money and they do little to enhance bond fund performance legitimately. Does that mean the investor should not buy a bond fund? Absolutely not—they are simply unpopular or uninteresting to mutual fund analysts. To summarize, the CPA and client must use ratings and rating services responsibly—as a tool of logic and research. They are of benefit because they perform a task nobody can perform on their own, but the CPA must learn how to read them and what they mean. Do be careful to read between the lines.

## .03   How to Access Professional Rating Service Information on Mutual Funds

The retail public dissemination of mutual fund information has been carried on by the rating services for 20 years now. This information was formerly the province of institutions alone. These services went from statistical disseminators to consumer advocates and industry reformers. As a reader of the editorials in their various guides (whichever the CPA elects to use), the financial advisor or client will learn that they are aggressive people. It is not a stretch to say that every mutual fund investor owes these services a debt of gratitude for all they have done for the investor over the past decade. Their database has been used to destroy myth after myth after myth about mutual funds.

The companies most likely to apply to the CPA and their clients are the purely retail services. For the most part, all do the same thing—provide hard copy and software subscriptions. Investors can benefit from them all; they should inspect everything that is available.

All of the services receive ample criticism. Much of the criticism centers on the services' inability to predict the future (which they do not try to do), the lack of dependability of their star systems (which they readily acknowledge), and their inapplicability for fund-trading strategies (which is a pastime that does not work and they discourage). If the CPA or client wants to be a student of mutual fund investment, these are the textbooks.

## ¶32,017   PERIODICALS: BENEFITS TO THE CPA AND CLIENT

In addition to rating service publications, financial magazines often produce excellent comparative spreadsheets in their mutual fund lists. As with any analytical service in any field, the rankings are to be viewed very carefully—the writer's and editorial staff's likes and the financial planner's and clients' interests might not be the same. The primary benefit to the CPA and client is that the periodicals deal with a huge number of funds and can be used as a starting point to narrow down the focus to the more detailed commentaries available elsewhere.

## ¶32,019   COMPUTER SOFTWARE: BENEFITS TO THE CPA AND CLIENT

Various services provide software loaded with charts and information. The CPA can customize his or her fund searches with databases used by professional fund managers. The personal computer has proven to be a valuable tool, tremendously beneficial for the retail investor willing to make the financial, time and learning commitment necessary to negotiate the minefields of computer securities services.

## ¶32,021   INTERNET SERVICES: BENEFITS TO THE CPA AND CLIENT

Information sifting on the computer may ultimately prove to be the only way to keep timely track of mutual funds. The CPA can find a biography on almost any manager, find the most recent portfolios of many funds and certainly find past performance on any public fund.

## ¶32,023   ADVICE ON MUTUAL FUNDS ADVICE

While the preceding information, well used, can help the CPA and client both to police current holdings and to search for new possibilities, the fact remains that no method of research will ever guarantee success. However, these are some ideas to consider that are perceived as generally helpful:

1.  "Past performance is no indication of future returns" is a sentence printed in bold type on every piece of mutual fund literature legitimately distributed in the U.S. Beware of astronomical performance claims, particularly unaudited ones. There are ways to compute past performance that, while observing the rules, really gild the lily regarding true returns. Buyers beware!

2.  Assess risk to determine whether a fund actually fits the client risk parameter. Many services attempt to assess risk and the CPA and client should be aware that what seems and what is, on the risk front, are often two entirely different matters. For example, most people who buy mutual funds in banks think FDIC insurance covers their fund investments. Not so.

3.  Once again, there are absolutely no free lunches. The CPA and client can determine for themselves how to elect to pay for mutual fund investments. Costs in funds are a given. No one can avoid expenses of significance attached to mutual funds. The financial advisor and client should simply accept this fact if they are going to invest a significant amount of assets in these vehicles.

4.  Shop around. Which funds in the proper style post a history that is compatible with that notion of reality for that type of investment? Then, the CPA should do the same cost studies done with any other major family purchase.

## ¶32,025  GENERAL GUIDELINES ON SELECTING A MUTUAL FUND

To select funds, the CPA should consider this advice:

1. Know why a client should invest in a certain fund and what the client wants from it.
2. Scan research tools for as large a universe of choices as the fund type includes.
3. Narrow the field by negative feedback—anything that doesn't jibe, get rid of immediately.
4. Find all research and marketing material available on the funds that remain in the group and cull this herd.
5. If there are several choices left, go with an instinctive choice and invest the money.

## ¶32,027  STEPS TO AVOID

There are many ways to subvert best efforts and lose potential return. Some thoughts to keep in mind:

1. Most investors evidently do not realize (earn) the return their funds post because they tend to buy high and sell low. They switch around too often, usually chasing last period's best performers. By its very nature, fund investment is supposed to be long term.
2. If the client takes out income and distributions for any reason other than need, he or she is making a big mistake. Posted results of funds always assume reinvestment of all distributions. At any given time, as much as 75 percent of the return of the S&P 500 has been as a consequence of the reinvestment of dividends and those dividends' subsequent appreciation.
3. If clients ignore the tape because they cannot acknowledge mistakes but move so fast it is obvious they do not know what they are doing, fund-switch services and hotlines are perfect for them. Then they can lose money much more quickly and get it over with sooner. The CPA has no time for such clients as "investors."
4. New funds should not be ignored categorically, especially those with a high turnover rate. New funds often outperform their more established rivals, and high-turnover funds in aggressive growth are often found at the top of their class.
5. The CPA can do much to see that the client's long-term goals are being met. Once they have selected the client's funds and invested the money,

they are not done. The responsibilities of an educated financial advisor and investor never end.

6.   Keeping careful track of the client's funds and their price fluctuations is mandatory. The CPA should read the semiannual portfolio summaries to determine the contents of the funds. Could the advisor happily have the client own these items through direct investment? The CPA should assume the responsibility of determining that fund portfolios remain consistent with the client's goals and objectives. This is particularly true from a risk/reward standpoint.

7.   With funds in taxable accounts, the CPA must help determine post-tax rate of return. The rating services data sheets can help, as they calculate post-tax returns at the maximum marginal tax rate. With a post-tax rate of return, the CPA can determine whether (on a risk-adjusted basis), the client is at the bottom of the ladder (least risk for potential return) or appropriately invested. The CPA can be of immeasurable value in this exercise. He or she can see to it that the client gets the numbers right and can use reason (rather than emotion) to evaluate the investments.

## ¶32,029   CONCLUSION

There is a lot to think about here. Mutual funds have gone from one of the least popular investment vehicles on the U.S. investment scene to the most widely disseminated in fewer than 20 years. Funds can become only more and more predominant. In an era of rapidly expanding financial self-determination, it benefits CPAs/PFSs to become as expert as they are capable of becoming as quickly as possible. Mutual fund selection is alternately the most intimidating and most exciting of investment processes. Unfortunately, most people assume it is the simplest and safest. The CPA won't make this mistake.

# Chapter 33
## Mutual Funds

## CONTENTS

# ¶33,000  OVERVIEW

The mutual fund industry, after escaping the financial industry scandals of the past few years, has grabbed almost all of the financial page tabloid headlines in the last year. Although initially slow to react, as the magnitude of the malaise became well known, the industry enacted various reforms or are in the final stages of approval in reaction to the problems.

# ¶33,001  FUNDS REACTION TO WIDESPREAD SCANDAL

By 2006, the chairman of a fund family must be independent of that fund family. In addition, three-fourths of the board of directors must be independent, too, by 2006. The SEC passed the new rules, briefly outlined below, after the congressional legislators had failed to enact any rules. However, Washington may soon pass rules related to after-hours trading.

There are several hundred thousand employees of the mutual fund industry. Obviously, some of them were unconcerned with the trust the investment community had placed in their actions. However, some of the specific concerns are yet to have a clear case made for the propriety or impropriety of their existence. Market timing, for example, has yet to be proven to be an infringement on shareholder value and rights.

The SEC effort, nevertheless, has been quite rapid, determined, and fair in an attempt to restore confidence to a beleaguered investment public. Whereas the level of compliance and self-regulation of the mutual fund industry are open to question, the fact of the matter is that some media representatives may underestimate the level of disclosure of the fund industry and/or the ability of investors to determine their own investment choices accurately.

What certainly does matter is that the mutual fund vehicle is a universal vehicle and the CPA/PFS must be very familiar and current with the fund industry to understand and help realize their clients' interests and goals.

## .01  Disclosure Regarding Approval of Investment Advisory Contracts

In June 2004, the SEC voted to adopt amendments to its rules and forms that are designed to improve the disclosure that mutual funds and other registered management investment companies provide their shareholders concerning the basis for the fund board's approval of an investment advisory contract. The amendments are intended to encourage fund boards to consider investment advisory contracts more carefully and to encourage investors to consider more carefully the *costs and value of the services* rendered by the fund's investment adviser.

**¶33,000**

The amendments will require fund shareholder reports to discuss, in reasonable detail, the material factors and the conclusions with respect to these factors that formed the basis for the board of directors' approval of advisory contracts during the most recent fiscal half-year. Because fund shareholder reports will contain disclosure with respect to *all* advisory contracts approved by the board, the amendments will remove the existing requirement for disclosure in the Statement of Additional Information.

The amendments do not basically change the rules discussed in this Chapter, but will include the following enhancements to the existing disclosure requirements in fund proxy statements that will parallel the disclosure in fund shareholder reports:

1. *Selection of Adviser and Approval of Advisory Fee.* The amendments will clarify that the fund must discuss both the board's selection of the investment adviser and its approval of amounts to be paid under the advisory contract.

2. *Specific Factors.* The fund will be required to include a discussion of:
    (a) The nature, extent, and quality of the services to be provided by the investment adviser;
    (b) The investment performance of the fund and the investment adviser;
    (c) Costs of the services to be provided and profits to be realized by the investment adviser and its affiliates from the relationship with the fund;
    (d) The extent to which economies of scale would be realized as the fund grows; and
    (e) Whether fee levels reflect these economies of scale for the benefit of fund investors.

3. *Comparison of Fees and Services Provided by Adviser.* The fund's discussion will be required to indicate whether the board relied upon comparisons of the services to be rendered and the amounts to be paid under the contract with those under other investment advisory contracts, such as contracts of the same and other investment advisers with other registered investment companies or other types of clients (e.g., pension funds and other institutional investors).

Fund reports to shareholders for periods ending on or after March 31, 2005, and fund proxy statements filed on or after Oct. 31, 2004, will be required to comply with these amendments.

## .03  Investment Company Governance

The Commission also voted to adopt amendments designed to improve the governance of investment companies (funds) and the independence of fund directors. These amendments are the latest in a series of reforms the Commission is adopting to solve problems that have made media headlines relating to the mismanagement of mutual funds.

The SEC pointed out that mutual fund boards of directors play an important role in protecting fund investors. They have overall responsibility for the fund and they oversee the activities of the fund adviser and negotiate the terms of the advisory contract, including the amount of the advisory fees and other fund expenses. Certain exemptive rules under the Investment Company Act require the oversight and approval of the independent directors if the fund engages in transactions with the fund manager and other affiliates, which transactions can involve inherent conflicts of interest between the fund and its managers. The Commission adopted the following amendments to these rules, to further the independence and effectiveness of the fund's independent directors in overseeing or approving these transactions:

- *Independent Composition of the Board.* Independent directors will be required to constitute at least 75 percent of the fund's board. An exception to this 75 percent requirement will allow fund boards with three directors to have all but one director be independent. This requirement is designed to strengthen the presence of independent directors and improve their ability to negotiate lower advisory fees and other important matters on behalf of the fund.

- *Independent Chairman.* The board will be required to appoint a chairman who is an independent director. The board's chairman typically controls the board's agenda and can have a strong influence on the board's deliberations.

- *Annual Self-Assessment.* The board will be required to assess its own effectiveness at least once a year. Its assessment must include consideration of the board's committee structure and the number of funds on whose boards the directors serve.

- *Separate Meetings of Independent Directors.* The *independent* directors will be required to meet in separate sessions at least once a quarter. This requirement could provide independent directors the opportunity for candid discussions about management's performance and could help improve collegiality.

- *Independent Director Staff.* The fund will be required to authorize the independent directors to hire their own staff. This requirement is designed to help independent directors deal with matters on which they need outside assistance.

Compliance with these amendments will be required 18 months after their publication in the *Federal Register.*

¶33,001.03

## ¶33,003    KINDS OF DISTRIBUTIONS

There are several kinds of distributions that a shareholder can receive from a mutual fund. They include:

1. Ordinary dividends.
2. Capital gain distributions.
3. Exempt-interest dividends.
4. Return of capital (nontaxable) distribution.

## .01    Tax-Exempt Mutual Fund

Distributions from a tax-exempt mutual fund—one that invests primarily in tax-exempt securities—can consist of ordinary dividends, capital gains distributions, undistributed capital gains, or return of capital like any other mutual fund. These contributions follow the same rules as a regular mutual fund. Distributions designated as exempt-interest dividends are not taxable.

A mutual fund may pay exempt-interest dividends to its shareholders if it meets certain requirements. These dividends are paid from tax-exempt interest earned by the fund. Since the exempt-interest dividends keep their tax-exempt character, the taxpayer does not have to include them in income, but may need to report them on his or her return. The mutual fund will send the taxpayer a statement within 60 days after the close of its tax year showing the amount of exempt-interest dividends. Although exempt-interest dividends are not taxable, they must be reported on the tax return if one is required to be filed. This is an information reporting requirement and does not convert tax-exempt interest to taxable interest.

## .03    Return of Capital

A distribution that is not out of earnings and profits is a return of the investment, or capital, in the mutual fund. The return of capital distributions are not taxed as ordinary dividends and are sometimes called tax-free dividends or nontaxable distributions that may be fully or partly taxable as capital gains.

A return of capital distribution reduces the basis in the shares. The basis cannot be reduced below zero. If the basis is reduced to zero, the taxpayer must report the return of capital distribution on the tax return as a capital gain. The distribution is taxable if, when added to all returns of capital distribution received in past years, it is more than the basis in the shares. Whether it is a long-term or short-term capital gain depends on how long the shares had been held.

## .05   Reinvestment of Distributions

Most mutual funds permit shareholders to automatically reinvest distributions, including dividends and capital gains, in more shares in the fund. Instead of receiving cash, distributions are used to purchase additional shares. The reinvested amounts must be reported to the IRS in the same way as if the reinvestment were received in cash. Reinvested ordinary dividends and capital gains distributions must be reported as income; reinvested exempt-interest dividends are not reported as income.

## ¶33,005   FOREIGN TAX DEDUCTION OR CREDIT

Some mutual funds invest in foreign securities or other instruments. A mutual fund may choose to allow an investor to claim a deduction or credit for the taxes the fund paid to a foreign country or U.S. possession. The notice to the fund's investors will include their share of the foreign taxes paid to each foreign country or possession, and the part of the dividend derived from sources in each country or possession.

## ¶33,007   BASIS

The basis in shares of a regulated investment company (mutual fund) is generally figured in the same way as the basis of other stock. The cost basis of purchased mutual fund shares often includes a sales fee, also known as a *load charge*. In certain cases, the entire amount of a load charge incurred after October 3, 1989, cannot be added to the cost basis, if the load charge gives the purchaser a reinvestment right.

## .01   Commissions and Load Charges

The fees and charges paid to acquire or redeem shares of a mutual fund are not tax deductible. They are usually added to the cost of the shares and increase the basis. A fee paid to redeem the shares is usually a reduction in the redemption price (sales price) in the case of mutual funds.

## .03   Keeping Track of the Basis

The investor in mutual funds should keep careful track of his or her basis because the basis is needed to figure any gain or loss on the shares when they are sold, exchanged, or redeemed. When mutual fund shares are bought or sold, the confirmation statements should be kept to show the price paid for the shares, and the price received for the shares when sold. If the shares are acquired by gift or inheritance, the investor needs information that is different from that in a confirmation statement for figuring the basis of those shares. The basis of shares of a mutual fund is important to know in figuring a gain or loss, with the basis dependent upon how the shares are acquired.

## .05  Shares Acquired by Inheritance

If mutual funds shares are inherited shares, the basis is the fair market value (FMV) at the date of the decedent's death, or at the alternate valuation date, if chosen for estate tax purposes. In community property states, each spouse is considered to own half the estate. If one spouse dies and at least half of the community interest is includable in the decedent's gross estate, the FMV of the community property at the date of death becomes the basis of both halves of the property.

## .07  Adjusted Basis

After mutual fund shares are acquired, adjustments may need to be made to the basis. The adjusted basis of stock is the original basis, increased or reduced. The basis is increased in a fund by 65 percent of any undistributed capital gain that is included in the taxpayer's income. This has the effect of increasing the basis by the difference between the amount of gain included in income and the credit claimed for the tax considered paid on that income. The mutual fund reports the amount of undistributed capital gain.

## .09  Reduction of the Basis

The basis must be reduced in the fund by any return of capital distributions received from the fund. The basis is not reduced for distributions that are ex-empt-interest dividends.

## ¶33,009  SALES, EXCHANGES AND REDEMPTIONS

When mutual fund shares are sold, exchanged, or redeemed, the investor will usually have a taxable gain or deductible loss. This includes shares in a tax-exempt mutual fund. The amount of the gain or loss is the difference between the adjusted basis in the shares and the amount realized from the sale, exchange, or redemption.

Gains and losses are figured on the disposition of shares by comparing the amount realized with the adjusted basis of the owner's shares. If the amount realized is more than the adjusted basis of the shares, a gain results; if the amount realized is less than the adjusted basis of the shares, a loss results. The amount received from a disposition of mutual fund shares is the money and value of any property received for the shares disposed of, minus expenses of sale such as redemption fees, sales commissions, sales charges, or exit fees.

The exchange of one fund for another fund is a taxable exchange, regardless of whether shares in one fund are exchanged for shares in another fund that has the same distributor or underwriter without paying a sales charge. Any gain or loss on the investment in the original shares as a capital gain or loss must be reported in the year in which the exchange occurs. Service charges or fees paid in connection with an exchange can be added to the cost of the shares acquired. Mutual funds and brokers must report to the IRS the proceeds from sales, exchanges, or redemptions. The broker must give each customer a written statement with the information by January 31 of the year following the calendar year the transaction occurred. The broker must be given a correct taxpayer identification number (TIN); a social security number is acceptable as a TIN.

## .01   Identifying the Shares Sold

When mutual fund shares are disposed of, the investor must determine which shares were sold and the basis of those shares. If the shares were acquired all on the same day and for the same price, figuring their basis is not difficult; however, for shares that are acquired at various times, in various quantities, and at various prices, determining the cost basis can be a difficult process. Two methods can be used to figure the basis, the cost basis, or the average basis.

Under the cost basis one of the following methods can be chosen:

1. Specific share identification.
2. First-in first-out (FIFO).

If the shares sold can be definitely identified, the adjusted basis of those particular shares can be used to figure a gain or loss. The shares can be adequately identified, even if bought in different lots at various prices and times, if:

1. The buyer specifies to the broker or other agent the particular shares to be sold or transferred at the time of the sale or transfer.
2. The buyer receives confirmation of the specification from his or her broker in writing within a reasonable time.

The confirmation by the mutual fund must state that the seller instructed the broker to sell particular shares. The owner of the shares has to be able to prove the basis of the specified shares at the time of sale or transfer.

If the shares were acquired at different times or at different prices, and the seller cannot identify which shares were sold, the basis of the shares acquired initially (first-in, first-out) is used as the basis of the shares sold. Therefore, the oldest shares still available are considered sold first. An adequate record should be kept of each purchase and any dispositions of the shares, until all shares purchased at the same time have been disposed of completely.

## .03  Average Basis

The average basis can be used to figure a gain or loss when all or part of the number of shares in a regulated investment company are sold. This choice can be made only if acquired at various times and prices, and the shares were left on deposit in an account handled by a custodian or agent who acquires or redeems those shares. The investor may be able to find the average basis of the shares from information provided by the fund. Once the average basis is used, it must continue to be used for all accounts in the same fund. However, a different method can be used for the shares in other funds.

To figure average basis, one of the following methods can be used:

1. Single-category method.
2. Double-category method.

*Single-Category Method.*   In the single-category method, the average cost is found of all shares owned at the time of each disposition, regardless of how long the shares were owned. Shares acquired with reinvested dividends or capital gains distributions must be included. Even if only one category is used to compute the basis, it is possible to have short-term or long-term gains or losses. To determine the holding period, the shares disposed of are considered to be those acquired first. The following steps are used to compute the basis of shares sold:

1. The cost of all shares owned is added.
2. The result of Step 1 is divided by the number of shares owned. This gives the *average basis* per share.
3. The result of Step 2 is multiplied by the number of shares sold. This gives the basis of the shares sold.

The basis of the shares determined under average basis is the basis of all the shares in the account at the time of each sale. If no shares were acquired or sold since the last sale, the basis of the remaining shares at the time of the next sale is the same as the basis of the shares sold in the last sale.

*Double-Category Method.*   In the double-category method, all shares in an account at the time of each disposition are divided into two categories: short-term and long-term. The adjusted basis of each share in a category is the total adjusted basis of all shares in that category at the time of disposition, divided by the total shares in the category.

The investor can specify to the custodian or agent handling the account from which category the shares are to be sold or transferred. The custodian or agent must confirm in writing the seller's specification. If the investor does not specify or receive confirmation, the shares sold must first be charged against the long-term category and then any remaining shares sold against the short-term category.

When a share has been held for more than one year, it must be transferred from the short-term category to the long-term category. When the change is made, the basis of a transferred share is its actual cost or adjusted basis; if some of the shares in the short-term category have been disposed of, its basis falls under the average basis method. The average basis of the undisposed shares would be figured at the time of the most recent disposition from this category.

## .05  Holding Period

When mutual fund shares are disposed of, the holding period must be determined. The period starts by using the trade date—the *trade date* is the date on which the holder of the shares bought or sold the mutual fund shares. Most mutual funds will show the trade date on confirmation statements of the purchases and sales.

## ¶33,011  INVESTMENT EXPENSES

The expenses of producing taxable investment income on a *nonpublicly* offered mutual fund during the year are generally deductible expenses; these include counseling and advice, legal and accounting fees, and investment newsletters. These are deductible as miscellaneous itemized deductions to the extent that they exceed 2 percent of adjusted gross income. Interest paid on money to buy or carry investment property is also deductible.

A nonpublicly offered mutual fund is one that:

1. Is not continuously offered pursuant to a public offering.
2. Is not regularly traded on an established securities market.
3. Is not held by at least 500 persons at all times during the tax year.

Generally, mutual funds are *publicly* offered funds. Expenses of publicly offered mutual funds are not treated as miscellaneous itemized deductions because these mutual funds report only the net amount of investment income after the investor's share of the investment expenses has been deducted.

Expenses on the shares of nonpublicly offered mutual funds can be claimed as a miscellaneous itemized deduction subject to the 2 percent limit.

Expenses cannot be deducted for the collection or production of exempt-interest dividends. Expenses must be allocated if they were for both taxable and tax-exempt income. One accepted method for allocating expenses is to divide them in the same proportion that the tax-exempt income from the mutual fund is to the total income from the fund.

The amount that can be deducted as investment interest expense must be limited in two different ways. First, the interest cannot be deducted for the expenses borrowed to buy or carry shares in a mutual fund that distributes only tax-exempt dividends. Second, investment interest is limited by the amount of investment income. Deductions for interest expense are limited to the amount of net investment income. Net investment is figured by subtracting investment expenses other than interest from investment income. Investment income includes gross income derived from property held for investment, such as interest, dividends, annuities, and royalties. It does not include net capital gains derived from disposing of investment property, or capital gains distributions from mutual fund shares. Investment interest that cannot be deducted because of the 2% limit can be carried forward to the next tax year, provided that net investment income exceeds investment interest in the later year.

## ¶33,013  BACKGROUND OF SEC FINAL RULES AND AMENDMENTS ON INDEPENDENT FUND ADVISORS

Mutual funds are organized as corporations, trusts or limited partnerships under state laws and thus are owned by their shareholders, beneficiaries or partners.

Like other types of corporations, trusts or partnerships, a mutual fund must be operated for the benefit of its owners. However, unlike most business organizations, mutual funds are typically organized and operated by an investment adviser who is responsible for the day-to-day operations of the fund. In most cases, the investment adviser is separate and distinct from the fund it advises, with primary responsibility and loyalty to its own shareholders.

Therefore, the "external management" of mutual funds presents inherent conflicts of interest and potential for abuses that the Investment Company Act and the Securities and Exchange Commission (SEC) have addressed in different ways.

One of the ways that the Act addresses conflicts between advisers and funds is by giving mutual fund boards of directors, and in particular the disinterested directors, an important role in fund governance. In relying upon fund boards to represent fund investors and protect their interests, Congress avoided the more detailed regulatory provisions that characterize other regulatory schemes for collective investments.

The SEC has similarly relied extensively on independent directors in rules that exempt funds from provisions of the Investment Company Act.

## .01   SEC Study of Role of Independent Directors

The SEC pointed out that millions of Americans had been investing in mutual funds, which experienced a tremendous growth in popularity over the previous 20 years. In 1999 and 2000, because of that growth and the growing reliance on independent directors to protect fund investors, the SEC felt compelled to study:

1. The governance of investment companies.
2. The role of independent directors.
3. SEC rules that rely on oversight by independent directors.
4. The information that funds are required to provide to shareholders about their independent directors.

They held a roundtable discussion at which independent directors, investor advocates, executives of fund advisers, academics and experienced legal counsel offered a variety of perspectives and suggestions. After evaluating the ideas and suggestions offered by roundtable participants, the SEC proposed a package of rule and form amendments that were designed to:

1. Reaffirm the important role that independent directors play in protecting fund investors.
2. Strengthen their hand in dealing with fund management.
3. Reinforce their independence.
4. Provide investors with better information to assess the independence of directors.

In addition to input from the roundtable, in response to their usual policy of requesting comments to proposed rule changes, amendments and additions, the SEC received 142 comment letters on the proposals, including 86 letters from independent directors.

Commenters generally supported the efforts to enhance the independence and effectiveness of fund directors, although many offered recommendations for improving portions of the proposals. Many of these letters were taken into consideration in formulating the final rules and amendments.

## .03   Early Results of Study

The SEC believes that the efforts to improve the governance of mutual funds on behalf of mutual fund investors began to have effect even before the final adoption. The roundtable discussions and proposed rules provoked a great deal of discussion among directors, advisers, counsel, and investors about governance practices and policies. After the roundtable, an advisory group organized by the Investment Company Institute (ICI) made recommendations regarding fund governance in a "best practices" report.

Many boards adopted the recommendations set forth in the ICI Advisory Group Report. Some groups of independent directors hired independent counsel for the first time. Director nomination and selection procedures have been revised.

During the next year, Commissioners and members of the staff began meeting with independent directors and sharing ideas and concerns regarding the governance of mutual funds. A former SEC chairman established the Mutual Fund Directors Education Council, a broad-based group of persons interested in fund governance and operations. Their main purpose is to foster the development of educational activities designed to promote the efficiency, independence, and accountability of independent fund directors.

The American Bar Association formed a task force to examine the role of counsel to independent directors, and the task force released a report offering guidance to counsel and fund directors regarding standards of independence for counsel, and guidelines for reducing potential conflicts of interest (ABA Task Force Report).

All of these initiatives have focused attention on the important role of independent directors, and their importance in promoting and protecting the interests of fund shareholders.

## ¶33,015 THE SEC ADOPTS FINAL RULES AND AMENDMENTS ON FUND GOVERNANCE

In January 2001, the SEC adopted amendments to certain exemptive rules under the Investment Company Act of 1940 relating to investment company governance based upon changes that were proposed in October 1999. Many of the proposed rule and form amendments were basically those initially proposed. However, the final amendments, summarized below, contain several modifications made as a result of suggestions made during the comment period. In line with the original proposals, the rule and form changes cover three areas:

1. Rule amendments relating to directors.
2. Conditions for reliance on certain exemptive rules.
3. Changes in disclosure requirements.

These amendments are designed to enhance the independence and effectiveness of boards of directors of investment companies and to better enable investors to assess the independence of those directors.

**¶33,017 THE ROLE OF INDEPENDENT DIRECTORS OF INVESTMENT COMPANIES**

The SEC's first order of business was adopting amendments to require (for funds relying on these "certain exemptive rules") that:

1. Independent directors constitute a majority of the fund's board of directors.
2. Independent directors select and nominate other independent directors.
3. Any legal counsel for the fund's independent directors is an independent legal counsel—that is, he or she does not also represent the fund's management or close affiliates.

The three new conditions are generally the same as had been proposed, though some clarifications and modifications were made. Specifics of these items are discussed in some detail below.

## .01 Independent Directors Constitute Majority of Fund's Board

Rather than the 40 percent previously required by the Investment Company Act of 1940, the Commission adopted a simple majority independence requirement. They had originally proposed a two-thirds supermajority requirement, but adopted the simple majority in response to public comments.

According to the adopting release, a majority independence requirement will permit, under state law, the independent directors to have a strong influence on fund management. It should enable them to represent shareholders better by being in a stronger position to elect officers, call meetings and solicit proxies.

To allow funds time to implement this provision, compliance is required after July 1, 2002.

In connection with this new requirement, the Commission also adopted a new rule that suspends the board composition requirement *temporarily* in the event of the death, disqualification or bona fide resignation of a director. The final rule provides that if the remaining directors can fill the vacant board position, the suspension is for 90 days; if a shareholder vote is required, the suspension is for 150 days. This time period begins to run when the fund no longer meets the board composition requirement, even if the fund is not yet aware of its non-compliance. The effective date for this specific rule was February 15, 2001.

## .03 Independent Directors Select, Nominate Other Independent Directors

This rule amendment was adopted substantially as proposed. The adopting release clarifies that a fund's adviser may be involved in the nomination process.

The independent directors must maintain control of the nomination process; however, the adviser may suggest candidates at the independent directors' invitation and provide administrative assistance in the selection and nomination process.

The self-nomination requirement is not intended to supplant or limit the ability of shareholders under state law to nominate directors. At the same time, the involvement of shareholders or the adviser does not excuse the independent directors from their responsibility to canvass, recruit, interview and solicit candidates.

The self-nomination requirement is prospective only. Current independent directors who were selected through a different process may continue to serve as independent directors but—beginning after July 1, 2002—all *new* independent directors must be researched, recruited, considered and formally named by the existing independent directors.

## .05 Legal Counsel for Independent Directors Must Be an "Independent Legal Counsel"

This rule's conditions were modified in response to the large number of comments the SEC received relative to it. The proposal defined "independent legal counsel" in narrow terms. Many commenters felt that this explicit definition of "independent" could have unintended negative results:

1. Discouraging the independent directors from even consider selecting their own counsel.
2. Limiting the pool of eligible counsel unnecessarily.
3. In some instances, possibly forcing independent directors to terminate longstanding relationships with counsel.

In line with the final rule, as well as with the proposal, independent directors are not required to have counsel. However, if they do, that counsel must be an "independent legal counsel," as determined by the independent directors. A "person"—the lawyer, his or her firm and partners and employees—is considered an independent legal counsel if the independent directors:

1. Determine that any representation of the fund's investment adviser, principal underwriter, administrator or their control persons during the past two fiscal years is or was "sufficiently limited" that it is unlikely to adversely affect the professional judgment of the person in providing legal representation.
2. Have obtained sufficient background information from the counsel for them to determine at that time that any relationship is, indeed, "sufficiently limited." The legal counsel must update the independent directors promptly on any relevant information if the counsel begins or materially increases his or her representation of a management organization or control person.

¶33,017.05

Directors may rely on information provided by counsel for these decisions.

The final rule requires that the independent directors determine whether a person is an independent legal counsel at least annually. The basis for the determination must be recorded in the board's meeting minutes. If the board receives information from counsel concerning his or her representation of a management organization or a control person, the fund can continue to rely on the relevant exemptive rules for up to three months. This period should provide sufficient time for the independent directors to make a new determination about the counsel's independence under the circumstances or, on the other hand, to hire a new independent legal counsel.

The SEC states that in making the determination of whether counsel is an independent legal counsel, the judgment of the independent directors must be *reasonable* and should take into consideration all relevant factors in evaluating whether the conflicting representations are sufficiently limited. For example, the independent directors should consider such factors as:

1. Is the representation current and ongoing?
2. Does it involve a minor or substantial matter?
3. Does it involve the fund, the adviser, or an affiliate, and if an affiliate, what is the nature and extent of the affiliation?
4. The duration of the conflicting representation.
5. The importance of the representation to counsel and his firm, including the extent to which counsel relies on that representation economically.
6. Does it involve work related to mutual funds?
7. Whether or not the individual who will serve as legal counsel was or is involved in the representation. (In the opinion of the SEC, this would exclude a lawyer from simultaneously representing the fund's adviser and independent directors in connection with such matters as the negotiation of the advisory contract or distribution plan or other *key areas* of conflict between the fund and its adviser.)

Compliance with the independent legal counsel provision also became effective July 1, 2002.

## ¶33,019  AMENDMENTS TO EXEMPTIVE RULES TO ENHANCE DIRECTOR INDEPENDENCE AND EFFECTIVENESS

In amending the 10 rules to exempt funds and their affiliates from certain prohibitions of the Act, the SEC added conditions to the Exemptive Rules to require that, for funds relying upon those rules, the independence and effectiveness of independent directors must be guaranteed. The efforts in that direction have been discussed above.

The SEC pointed out that some commenters questioned the need to amend the rules, because each rule already requires independent directors to approve separately some of the fund's activities under the rule. In truth, these rules were selected because they require the independent judgment and scrutiny by the independent directors in overseeing activities that are beneficial to funds and investors *but involve inherent conflicts of interest between the funds and theirpgdk/ managers*. The amendments are designed to increase the ability of independent directors to perform their important responsibilities under each of these rules.

## .01 Amendments to Exemptive Rules

The 10 rules exempting funds and their affiliates from certain stipulations of the Investment Company Act make the following actions possible:

1. Permission for funds to purchase securities in a primary offering when an affiliated broker-dealer is a member of the underwriting syndicate.
2. Permission to use fund assets to pay distribution expenses.
3. Permission for fund boards to approve interim advisory contracts without shareholder approval.
4. Permission for securities transactions to take place between a fund and another client of the fund's adviser.
5. Permission for mergers between certain affiliated funds.
6. Permission for funds and their affiliates to purchase joint liability insurance policies.
7. Specific conditions under which funds may pay commissions to affiliated brokers in connection with the sale of securities on an exchange.
8. Permission for funds to maintain joint insured bonds.
9. Permission for funds to issue multiple classes of voting stock.
10. Permission for the operation of interval funds by enabling closed-end funds to repurchase their shares from investors.

## ¶33,021 ADDITIONAL RULE CHANGES

Other rule changes affecting independent directors and their qualification duties and responsibilities have been adopted, including:

### .01 Joint Insurance Policies

A rule of the Investment Company Act has been amended so that funds may now purchase joint "errors and omissions" insurance policies for their officers and directors, but *only* if the policy does not exclude:

1. Bona fide claims brought against any independent director by a co-insured.
2. Claims brought by a co-insured in which the fund is a co-defendant with an independent director.

This provision became effective July 1, 2002.

## .03    Independent Audit Committees

The SEC also adopted a new rule exempting funds from the Act's requirement that shareholders vote on the selection of the fund's independent public accountant if the fund has an audit committee composed *wholly* of independent directors.

The rule will permit continuing oversight of the fund's accounting and auditing processes by an independent audit committee instead of the shareholder vote. Commenters agreed that the shareholder ratification had become largely perfunctory and that an independent audit committee could exercise more meaningful oversight.

Consistent with the proposed rule, the final rule provides that a fund is exempt from having to seek shareholder approval if:

1. The fund establishes an audit committee composed solely of independent directors to oversee the fund's accounting and auditing processes.
2. The fund's board of directors adopts an audit committee charter setting forth the committee's structure, duties, powers, and methods of operation or sets out similar provisions in the fund's charter or bylaws.
3. The fund maintains a copy of such an audit committee charter. Some commenters questioned whether the proposed rule would require the audit committee to supervise a fund's day-to-day management and operations. The rule does not require, nor was it intended, that an audit committee perform daily management or supervision of a fund's operations.

The effective date for this particular rule was February 15, 2001.

## .05    Qualification as an Independent Director

A new rule conditionally exempts individuals from being disqualified from serving as independent directors because they invest in index funds that hold shares of the fund's adviser or underwriter or their controlling persons. The rule as *proposed* would have applied only if the value of securities issued by the adviser or controlling person did not exceed 5 percent of the value of any index tracked by the index fund. The SEC has *modified the final rule* to provide relief if a fund's investment objective is to replicate the performance of one or more "broad-based" indices. The effective date for this rule was February 15, 2001.

In addition, the SEC has rescinded a rule that provides relief from a section of the Investment Company Act defining when a fund director is considered to be independent. The SEC had proposed amending the rule to permit a somewhat higher percentage of a fund's independent directors be affiliated with registered broker-dealers, under certain circumstances. The enactment of the Gramm-Leach-Bliley Act amended the Act to establish new standards for determining independence under the same circumstances, thus making the proposed amendments redundant. The rescission became effective on May 12, 2001.

## .07   Recordkeeping Requirements

The rule was amended to require funds to preserve for at least six years any record of:

1. The initial determination that a director qualifies as an independent director.
2. Each subsequent determination of whether the director continues to qualify as an independent director.
3. The determination that any person who is acting as legal counsel to the independent directors is an independent legal counsel.

These requirements are designed to permit the SEC's staff to monitor a fund's assessment of director independence. Compliance with this requirement was required after July 1, 2002.

## ¶33,023   DISCLOSURE REQUIREMENTS

As is to be expected the SEC has adopted rule and form changes that will require funds to *disclose additional director information* beyond that currently available in a fund's statement of additional information (SAI) and proxy statements. The amendments were adopted with several modifications to tailor them more closely to the goal of providing shareholders with better information without overburdening directors.

All of these new registration statements and post-effective amendments that are annual updates to effective registration statements, proxy statements for the election of directors, and reports to shareholders filed on or after January 31, 2002 must comply with the new disclosure requirements. The new requirements are discussed below.

## .01  Basic Information About Fund Directors

The Commission has adopted, as they had proposed, requirements that basic information about the identity and experience of directors should be outlined in tabular form and included in the fund's annual report to shareholders, the SAI and any proxy statement for the election of directors. Specifically, the table must disclose detailed information about each and every director:

1. Name, address, and age.
2. Current positions held with the fund.
3. Term of office and length of time served.
4. Principal occupations during the past five years.
5. Number of portfolios overseen within the fund complex (as opposed to the current requirement to disclose the number of registered investment companies overseen).
6. Other directorships held outside the fund complex.
7. The relationship, events, or transactions that make each "interested" director an "interested person" of the fund.

The annual report is required also to include a statement that the SAI has additional information about the directors that is available without charge upon request.

## .03  Ownership of Equity Securities in Fund Complex

The proposed requirement to disclose the amount of equity securities of funds in a fund complex owned by each fund director was adopted with certain modifications, as described below.

***Disclosure of Amount Owned.***  The SEC responded to comments that fund disclosure of the dollar amount of directors' fund holdings was not necessary to demonstrate alignment of directors' interests with those of shareholders and would impinge on directors' privacy. The provision adopted requires disclosure of a director's holdings of fund securities using specified dollar ranges rather than an exact dollar amount. Commenters considered the exact amount impinged too greatly upon the director's privacy. The rule incorporates the following dollar ranges: none; 0–$10,000; $10,001–$50,000; $50,001– $100,000; over $100,000.

***Beneficial Ownership.***  The SEC received a number of comments requesting clarification about the types of director holdings that would be disclosed under the proposal. Based on these comments, the Commission reevaluated the proposal to require disclosure of securities owned beneficially and of record by each director.

¶33,023.01

Under the original proposal, beneficial ownership would have been determined in accordance with a rule of the Exchange Act, which focuses on a person's voting and investment power. In view of the objective of providing information about the alignment of directors' and shareholders' interests, they believe that disclosure of record holdings should not be required and that the focus of beneficial ownership should be on whether a director's economic interests are tied to the securities rather than on his or her ability to exert voting power or to dispose of the securities.

As a result, disclosure of director holdings will be required only in those instances where the director's economic interests are tied to the securities and will not be triggered solely by his or her ability to exert voting power or to dispose of the securities.

***Disclosure of Ownership of Funds Within the Same Family of Investment Companies.*** The proposal that directors disclose their aggregate holdings in a fund complex was modified to require disclosure of:

1. Each director's ownership in every fund that he oversees.
2. Each director's aggregate ownership of all funds that he oversees within a fund family.

The ownership in specific funds demonstrates a director's alignment of interests with shareholders. The SEC realized that a director may have legitimate reasons for not having shares of a specific fund in his or her portfolio; however, the adopting release states that the requirement to disclose aggregate ownership should help to negate any inference that otherwise could be made about why a director has chosen not to own shares of a particular fund.

To determine a director's holdings in a fund complex, the SEC agreed with public comments that the proposed definition of fund complex was too broad. Instead, the Commission adopted a more specific definition of "family of investment companies," to include only funds that have the same investment adviser or principal underwriter and actually publicize themselves to investors as related companies for purposes of investment and investor services.

The equity ownership information must be included in the SAI and any proxy statement relating to the election of directors. For the proxy statement, the equity ownership information must be provided as of the most recent practicable date, as proposed, in order to ensure that shareholders receive up-to-date information when they are asked to vote to elect directors.

For the SAI, the SEC modified the proposal to require that the equity ownership information be provided as of the end of the last completed calendar year. They believe that this modified time period requirement facilitates our goal that investors receive equity ownership information to evaluate whether directors' interests are aligned with their own and imposes less of a burden on directors, especially those who serve multiple funds with staggered fiscal years.

¶33,023.03

*Conflicts of Interest.* Consistent with the proposal, fund SAIs and proxy statements will be required to disclose three types of circumstances that, according to the adopting release, could affect the allegiance of fund directors to shareholders. These are the positions, interests and transactions and relationships of directors and their immediate family members with the fund and persons related to the fund. The proposal was modified in several significant respects in response to comments that it was too broad.

*Persons Covered.* The final rule excludes "interested" directors from the conflict of interest disclosure requirements in both the SAI and proxy statement.

In addition, the SEC narrowed the scope of "immediate family members" covered by the disclosure requirements to a director's spouse, children *residing in the director's household,* including step and adoptive children and dependents of the director. The SEC concluded that these are family members from whom directors can reasonably be expected to obtain the required information. Thus, in contrast to the proposal, the final disclosure requirements do not apply to the director's parents, siblings, children not residing with the director or in-laws.

On the other hand, the SEC did not go to the extent of adopting a suggestion made by some commenters to limit disclosure about positions, interests and transactions and relationships of a director's family members to those about which the director has actual knowledge.

The SEC excluded administrators from the persons related to the fund that are covered by the requirements. This exclusion is limited to administrators that are not affiliated with the fund's adviser or principal underwriter. Entities (including administrators) that control, are controlled by or are under common control with the adviser or principal underwriter will be covered by the disclosure requirements.

Despite these modifications narrowing the disclosure requirements, the adopting release strongly suggests examining any circumstances that could *potentially impair* the independence of independent directors, regardless of whether or not such circumstances are actually spelled out in the SEC's disclosure requirements.

*Threshold Amounts.* The SEC adopted a $60,000 threshold for disclosure of interests, transactions and relationships. For this provision, it is necessary for a director's interest to be aggregated with those of his immediate family members.

The adopting release warns funds that the $60,000 threshold should not be equated with materiality. The statement is made that "a transaction between a director and a fund's adviser may constitute a material conflict of interest with the fund or its shareholders that is required to be disclosed, regardless of the amount involved, if the terms and conditions of the transaction are not comparable to those that would have been negotiated at 'arm's length' in similar circumstances.''

*Time Periods.*   The SEC also modified some of the proposed time periods for disclosure of conflicts of interest in the proxy statement and SAI. In the proxy statement, disclosure of positions and interests of directors and their immediate family members is required, as proposed, for a five-year period. Disclosure of material transactions and relationships must be provided from the beginning of the last two completed fiscal years. In the SAI, disclosure of positions and interests of directors and their immediate family members, as well as disclosure of material transactions and relationships is required for the two most recently completed calendar years, rather than fiscal years.

*Routine, Retail Transactions and Relationships.*   The adopting release clarifies that the exception from the disclosure requirements for routine, retail transactions and relationships, such as credit card or bank or brokerage accounts (unless the director is accorded special treatment), extends to residential mort-gages and insurance policies as well as other routine transactions not specifically enumerated.

*The Board's Role in Fund Governance.*   The SEC has adopted, as pro-posed, disclosure requirements in the proxy rules and SAI relating to board committees. Funds must identify each standing committee of the board in both the SAI and any proxy statement for the election of directors. Funds also are required to provide:

1.  A concise statement of the functions of each committee.
2.  Names of the members of the committee.
3.  Information regarding the number of committee meetings held during the last fiscal year.
4.  An indication of whether the nominating committee would consider nomi-nees recommended by fund shareholders; if so, procedures for submitting recommendations should be provided.

*Approval of the Advisory Contract.*   Funds must also disclose in the SAI the board's basis for approving an existing advisory contract. In response to comments that this disclosure would become "boilerplate," the adopting release specifies that boilerplate language is not adequate; funds are required to provide appropriate detail regarding the board's basis for approving an existing advisory contract, including the particular factors forming the basis for this determination.

*Separate Disclosure.*   Funds must present all disclosure for *independent directors* separately from disclosure for *interested directors* in the SAI, proxy statements for the election of directors and annual reports to shareholders. The

SEC felt this would aid shareholders in understanding information about directors and in evaluating the effectiveness of independent directors to oversee fund operations.

*Compliance Date for Disclosure Amendments.* All new registration statements and post-effective amendments that are annual updates to effective registration statements, proxy statements for the election of directors and reports to shareholders filed on or after January 31, 2002, must comply with the disclosure amendments. Based on the comments, the SEC felt that this would provide funds with sufficient time to make the necessary changes to disclosure documents.

# Chapter 34

# Mutual Fund "Profile" Disclosure Option

## CONTENTS

## ¶34,000 OVERVIEW

The Securities and Exchange Commission has adopted a new Rule that permits an open-end management investment company (mutual fund) to offer investors a user-friendly disclosure document called a "profile." This document summarizes key information about the fund, including the fund's investment strategies, risks, performance, and fees, in a concise, standardized format.

A fund that offers a profile will be able to give investors a choice of the amount of information that they wish to consider before making a decision about investing in the fund; investors will have the option of purchasing the fund's shares after reviewing the information in the profile or after requesting and reviewing the fund's prospectus (and other information). An investor deciding to purchase fund shares based on the information in a profile will receive the fund's prospectus with the confirmation of purchase.

The SEC also adopted amendments to Rule 497 under the Securities Act to require a fund to file a profile with the Commission at least 30 days prior to the profile's first use. At the same time, they adopted revisions to the prospectus disclosure requirements in Form N-1A, the registration statement used by funds. The revisions should *minimize* prospectus disclosure about technical, legal, and operational matters that generally are common to all funds and thus *focus prospectus disclosure on essential information* about a particular fund. The reasoning is that the simplified general information should enable the average investor to make better informed decisions about investing in that fund.

## ¶34,001    NEED FOR SIMPLIFIED DISCLOSURE INFORMATION

As more investors turn to funds for professional management of current and retirement savings, funds have introduced new investment options and shareholder services to appeal to investors. While benefiting from these developments, investors also faced an increasingly difficult task in choosing from the many different fund investments. The SEC, fund investors, and others realized it was in everyone's best interest to improve fund disclosure documents to help investors evaluate and compare them.

In the Commission's view, the growth of the fund industry and the diversity of fund investors warranted a new approach to fund disclosure to offer more choices in the format and the amount of information available about these investments. (Particularly, it would seem, since so many relatively "uninitiated" investors were testing the mutual fund market.)

The Profile summarizes key information about a fund, including its investment objectives, strategies, risks, performance, fees, investment adviser and portfolio manager, purchase and redemption procedures, distributions, tax information and the services available to the fund's investors.

It was designed to provide summary information about a fund that could assist an investor in deciding whether to invest in that particular fund immediately, or to request additional information about it before deciding whether or not to buy shares in it.

Rule 498 requires a fund to mail the prospectus and other information to the requesting investor within 3 business days of a request. An investor deciding to purchase fund shares based on the Profile receives the fund's prospectus with the purchase confirmation.

## ¶34,003    PROFILE REQUIREMENTS UNDER RULE 498

1. *Standardized Fund Summaries.* The profile includes concise disclosure of 9 items of key information about a fund in a specific sequence.

2. *Improved Risk Disclosure.* A risk/return summary (also required at the beginning of a fund's *prospectus*) provides information about a fund's investment objectives, principal strategies, risks, performance, and fees.

3. *Graphic Disclosure of Variability of Returns.* The risk/return summary provides a bar chart of a fund's annual returns over a 10-year period that illustrates the variability of those returns and gives investors some idea of the risks of an investment in the fund. To help investors evaluate a fund's risks and returns relative to "the market," a table accompanying the bar chart compares the fund's average annual returns for 1-, 5-, and 10-year periods to that of a broad-based securities market index.

4. *Other Fund Information.* The profile includes information on the fund's investment adviser and portfolio manager, purchase and redemption procedures, tax considerations, and shareholder services.

5. *Plain English Disclosure.* The Commission's plain English disclosure requirements, which are designed to give investors understandable disclosure documents, apply to the profile. The plain English rule requires the use of plain English writing principles, including short sentences, everyday language, active voice, tabular presentation of complex material, no legal or business jargon, and no multiple negatives. (For a discussion of this rule, see Chapter 21.)

## ¶34,005    PROFILES FOR TAX-DEFERRED ARRANGEMENTS

Rule 498 also permits a fund that serves as an investment option for a participant-directed defined contribution plan (or for certain other tax-deferred arrangements) to provide investors with a profile that includes disclosure that is tailored for the plan (or other arrangement).

Profiles tailored for such use can exclude information relating to the purchase and sale of fund shares, fund distributions, tax consequences, and fund services otherwise required in a profile.

## ¶34,007    PILOT PROFILE PROGRAM

The Commission tested various options for improving fund disclosure documents in a pilot program conducted with participation by the Investment

Company Institute (ICI) and several large fund groups, in which the funds used profile-like summaries with their prospectuses. The Pilot Profile summarized important information about specific funds to determine whether investors found these profiles helpful in making investment decisions. Focus groups conducted on the Commission's behalf responded positively to the profile concept, indicating that a disclosure document of this type would assist them in making investment decisions. Fund investors participating in a survey sponsored by the ICI also strongly supported the profile idea.

## ¶34,009    OTHER INVESTMENT COMPANIES EXCLUDED FROM PROFILE OPTION

The Commission has decided that other types of investment companies, such as closed-end investment companies, unit investment trusts, and separate accounts that offer variable annuities do not come within the scope of Rule 498. It is available only to mutual funds.

Although the Agency recognizes that a short, summary disclosure document such as the profile could potentially benefit investors in other types of investment companies, it has concluded that it would be prudent to assess the use of profiles by mutual funds over a period of time before considering a rule to allow other types of investment companies to use similar summary documents. As the Commission gains experience with funds' use of the profile and analyzes the results of other pilot profile programs that are underway, it will undoubtedly consider expanding use of the concept to other types of investment companies if things work out as well as they anticipate.

## ¶34,011    MULTIPLE FUNDS DESCRIBED IN A PROFILE

The SEC decided that a profile that describes more than one fund can be consistent with the goal of a summary disclosure document that assists investors in evaluating and comparing funds. In fact they believe that describing more than one fund or class of a fund in a profile can be a useful means of providing investors with information about related investment alternatives offered by a fund group (e.g., a range of tax-exempt funds or different types of money market funds) or about the classes of a multiple class fund. However, profiles describing multiple funds must be organized in a clear, concise, summary manner in a format designed to communicate the information effectively. Thus, a profile that offers the securities of more than one fund or class does not need to repeat information that is the same for each one described in the document.

# ¶34,013 COVER PAGE

Rule 498 requires the cover page of a fund's profile to include certain basic information about the fund and to disclose that the profile is a *summary disclosure document*. The cover page identifies it as a "profile" without using the term "prospectus." It includes a legend explaining the profile's purpose, and displays the fund's name. A fund also could describe its investment objectives or its type or category (e.g., that the fund is a growth fund or invests its assets in a particular country). The cover page must state the approximate date of the profile's first use.

## .01 Required Legend

The new rule requires the following legend on the cover page, or at the beginning, of a profile:

"This profile summarizes key information about a Fund that is included in the Fund's prospectus. The Fund's prospectus includes additional information about the Fund, including a more detailed description of the risks associated with investing in the Fund that you may want to consider before you invest. You may obtain the prospectus and other information about the Fund at no cost by calling _____."

A toll-free (or collect) telephone number that investors can use to obtain the prospectus and other information must be provided. The fund may also indicate, as applicable, that the prospectus and other information is available on the fund's Internet site or by e-mail request.

When additional information is requested, a 3-business day mailing requirement applies. Since many funds use intermediaries in distributing or servicing their shares, revised Rule 498 also permits the legend to state that additional information in such a case may be obtained from financial intermediaries. The 3-business day rule applies here also.

# ¶34,015 RISK / RETURN SUMMARY

The first 4 items of the profile must contain information that would be substantially identical to the proposed risk/return summary at the beginning of every prospectus. The following discussion summarizes the main features of the risk/ return summary required by Form N-1A and discusses specific disclosure required in the profile.

## .01 Fund Investment Objectives / Goals

To assist investors in identifying funds that meet their general investment needs, the risk/return summary requires a fund to disclose its investment objectives or goals.

## .03    Principal Investment Strategy

The risk/return summary requires a fund to summarize, based on the information provided in its prospectus, how the fund intends to achieve its investment objectives. The purpose of this disclosure is to provide a summary of the fund's principal investment strategies, including the specific types of securities in which the fund invests or will invest principally, and any policy of the fund to concentrate its investments in an industry or group of industries.

In addition, a fund (other than one that has not yet been required to deliver a semi-annual or annual report) must provide the following disclosure:

"Additional information about the Fund's investments is available in the Fund's annual and semi-annual reports to shareholders. In the Fund's annual report you will find a discussion of the market conditions and investment strategies that significantly affected the Fund's performance during the last fiscal year. You may obtain either or both of these reports at no cost by calling _____."

## .05    Principal Risks of Investing in the Fund

***Summary Risk Disclosure.***    The risk summary gives a fund the option to include disclosure in its profile about the types of investors for whom the fund is intended and the types of investment goals that may be consistent with an investment in the fund.

***Special Risk Disclosure Requirements.***    A mutual fund profile is required to provide a special disclosure in the risk summary for money market funds to the effect that, "An investment in the Fund is not insured or guaranteed by the Federal Deposit Insurance Corporation or any other government agency. Although the Fund seeks to preserve the value of your investment at $1.00 per share, it is possible to lose money by investing in the Fund."

A fund advised by or sold through a bank would disclose in the risk summary of its profile: "An investment in the Fund is not a deposit of the bank and is not insured or guaranteed by the Federal Deposit Insurance Corporation or any other government agency."

***Risk/Return Bar Chart and Table.***    The risk/return summary requires a fund's profile to include a bar chart showing the fund's annual returns for each of the last 10 calendar years and a table comparing the fund's average annual returns for the last 1, 5, and 10 fiscal years to those of a broad-based securities market index.

Obviously, this provision requires a fund to have at least one calendar year of returns before including the bar chart. It requires a fund whose profile does not include a bar chart, because the fund does not have annual returns for a full calendar year, to modify the narrative explanation to refer only to information presented in the table. The provision also requires the bar chart of a fund in operation for fewer than 10 years to include annual returns for the life of the fund.

To show a fund's highest and lowest returns (or "range" of returns) for annual or other periods as an alternative, or in addition, to the bar chart, the Profile ruling requires that a fund disclose (in addition to the bar chart) its best and worst returns for a quarter during the 10-year (or other) period reflected in the bar chart. This information is aimed at disclosing the variability of a fund's returns and the risks by pointing out that a fund's shares may very well be subject to short-term price fluctuations.

*Presentation of Return Information.*    To help investors use the information in the bar chart and table, the profile risk/return summary requires a fund to provide a brief narrative explanation of just how the information illustrates the variability of the fund's returns.

*Bar Chart Return Information.*    The risk/return summary requires calendar-year periods for both the bar chart and table. Under Rule 498, the average annual return information in the table in a fund's profile risk/return summary must be as of the most recent calendar quarter and updated quarterly.

*Bar Chart Presentation.*    The bar chart may include return information for more than one fund. However, the presentation of the bar chart is subject to the general requirement that disclosure should be presented in a format designed to communicate information *clearly and effectively.*

The risk/return summary requires a fund offering more than one class of shares in a profile to include annual return information in its bar chart for only one class. The ruling permits a fund to choose the class to be reflected in the bar chart, subject to certain limitations: the chart must reflect the performance of a class that has returns for at least 10 years (e.g., a fund could not present a class in the bar chart with 2 years of returns when another class has returns for at least 10 years). In addition, if two or more classes offered in the profile have returns for less than 10 years, the bar chart must reflect returns for the class that has returns for the longest period.

## .07    Fees and Expenses of the Fund

The risk/return summary requires a bar chart showing the fund's fees and expenses, including any sales loads charged in connection with an investment in the fund. The fee table must be included in both the profile and the prospectus. This emphasis underlines the SEC's belief that fees and expenses of a fund figure high in a typical investor's decision to invest in a fund. The fee table is designed to help them understand the costs of investing in a particular fund and to compare those costs with the costs of other funds.

¶34,015.07

## ¶34,017 OTHER DISCLOSURE REQUIREMENTS

The profile of a fund must include not only the risk/return summary, but also disclosure about other key aspects of investing in the fund—the other items to be disclosed in sequence: Investment Adviser, Sub-Adviser(s) and Portfolio Manager(s) of the Fund.

The profile requirements are very precise in this respect. This section requires:

1. Identification of the fund's investment adviser.
2. Identification of the fund's sub-adviser(s) (if any):
   a. A fund need not identify a sub-adviser(s) whose sole responsibility for the fund is limited to day-to-day management of the fund's holdings of cash and cash equivalent instruments, unless the fund is a money market fund or other fund with a principal investment strategy of regularly holding cash and cash equivalent instruments.
   b. A fund having three or more sub-advisers, each of which manages a portion of the fund's portfolio, need not identify each such sub-adviser, except that the fund must identify any sub-adviser that is (or is reasonably expected to be) responsible for the management of a significant portion of the fund's net assets. For purposes of this paragraph, a significant portion of a fund's net assets generally will be deemed to be 30% or more of the fund's net assets.
   c. State the name and length of service of the person or persons employed by or associated with the fund's investment adviser (or the fund) who are primarily responsible for the day-to-day management of the fund's portfolio and summarize each person's *business experience* for the last five years.

      A fund with three or more such persons, each of whom is (or is reasonably expected to be) responsible for the management of a portion of the Fund's portfolio, need not identify each person, except that a fund must identify and summarize the business experience for the last five years of each person who is (or is reasonably expected to be) responsible for the management of a significant portion of the fund's net assets. For purposes of this paragraph, a significant portion of a fund's net assets generally will be deemed to be 30% or more of the fund's net assets.

### .01 Purchase of Fund Shares

Under Rule 498, a fund must disclose the minimum initial or subsequent investment requirements, the initial sales load (or other loads), and, if applicable, the initial sales load breakpoints or waivers.

¶34,017

## .03   Sale of Fund Shares

Rule 498 also requires a fund to state that its shares are redeemable; to identify the procedures for redeeming shares (e.g., on any business day by written request, telephone, or wire transfer); to identify any charges or sales loads that may be assessed upon redemption (including, if applicable, the existence of waivers of these charges).

## .05   Fund Distributions and Tax Information

Rule 498 requires a mutual fund's profile to describe how frequently the fund intends to make distributions and what reinvestment options for distributions (if any) are available to its investors.

It also requires a fund to disclose whether its distributions to shareholders may be taxed as ordinary income or capital gains and that the rates shareholders pay on capital gains may be taxed at different rates depending upon the length of time that the fund holds its assets.

If a fund expects that its distributions, as a result of its investment objectives or strategies, primarily will consist of ordinary income or capital gains, it must provide disclosure to that effect. Funds subject to this requirement would include, for example, those often described as "tax-managed," "tax-sensitive," or "tax-advantaged," which have investment strategies to maximize long-term capital gains and minimize ordinary income.

If a fund has a *principal* investment objective or strategy to achieve tax-managed results of this type, the fund would be required to provide disclosure to that effect in the discussion of its investment objectives.

For a fund that describes itself as investing in securities generating tax-exempt income, it must provide, as applicable, a general statement to the effect that a portion of the fund's distributions may be subject to federal income tax.

## .07   Other Services Provided by the Fund

A fund profile should provide a brief summary of services available to the fund's shareholders (e.g., any exchange privileges or automated information services), unless this information has already been provided in earlier sections of the profile. A fund should disclose only those services that generally are available to typical investors in the fund.

## ¶34,019   APPLICATION TO PURCHASE SHARES

The profile may include an application that a prospective investor can use to purchase the fund's shares as long as the application explains with equal prominence that an investor has the option of purchasing shares of the fund after reviewing the information in the profile or after requesting and reviewing the fund's prospectus (and other information) before making a decision about investing in the fund.

## ¶34,021 FILING REQUIREMENTS

A profile is to be filed with the Commission at least 30 days before the date that it is first sent or given to a prospective investor. The first profile filing must be accompanied by the submission of a profile in the format in which it will be distributed to investors. Subsequent filings will not require the additional formatted profile. An amended form of any profile must be filed with the Commission within 5 business days after it is used.

## ¶34,023 MODIFIED PROFILES FOR CERTAIN FUNDS

Funds can tailor disclosure for profiles to be used for investments in defined contribution plans qualified under the Internal Revenue Code, and for funds offered through variable insurance contracts. The Commission believes that this revision will help to ensure that profiles contain information that investors will find meaningful and useful.

Rule 498 permits a profile for a fund offered as an investment option for a plan to include, or be accompanied by, an enrollment form for the plan. An application or enrollment form for a variable insurance contract may accompany the profile for the funds that serve as investment options; however, this is only if the form also is accompanied by a full prospectus for the contract.

The Rule also permits funds to modify the legend and other disclosure in profiles intended for use in connection with defined contribution plans, other tax-deferred arrangements described in the Rule, and variable insurance contracts.

# Chapter 35
# Plain English Disclosure Rule

## CONTENTS

## ¶35,000 OVERVIEW

The Securities and Exchange Commission has adopted a Plain English Disclosure rule incorporating changes made as a result of comments received and the lessons learned from participants in the plain English pilot program. The rule requires issuers to write the *cover page, summary*, and *risk factors section* of prospectuses in plain English. The previous requirements for those sections have been changed to the extent they conflicted with the plain English rule. In conjunction with this rule, the SEC also provides issuers more specific guidance on how to make the entire prospectus clear, concise, and understandable.

The Commission believes that using plain English in prospectuses will lead to a better informed securities market in which investors can more easily understand the disclosure required by the federal securities laws. The rule became effective on October 1, 1998, with the compliance date being the same.

## ¶35,001   INVESTOR PROTECTION

Obviously, the intended purpose of financial reporting should be full and fair disclosure. In fact this is one of the cornerstones of investor protection under federal securities laws. The SEC points out that if a prospectus fails to communicate information clearly, investors do not receive the basic protection intended.

Yet prospectuses have often employed complex, legalistic language, confounding all but the most erudite lawyers, accountants or financial experts. The Commission emphasizes that the proliferation of complex transactions and securities (including all manner of derivatives) has only magnified this problem. A major challenge facing the securities industry and its regulators is the assurance that financial and business information reaches investors in a form they can read *and understand*.

The SEC anticipates, and many public comment letters concur, that implementation of the plain English rule will:

1. Allow investors to make better-informed assessments of the risks and rewards of investment opportunities.
2. Reduce the likelihood that investors make investment mistakes because of incomprehensible disclosure documents.
3. Reduce investors' costs of investing by lowering the time required to read and understand information.
4. Increase consumers' interest in investing by giving them greater confidence in their understanding of investments.
5. Reduce the number of costly legal disputes because investors are more likely to understand disclosure documents better.
6. Lower offering costs because investors will ask issuers fewer questions about the offering.

All well and good, but how is all of this expected to happen?

## ¶35,003   PROSPECTUS SIMPLIFICATION

The Commission stated that the new rules will change the face of every prospectus used in registered public offerings of securities. They expect these prospectuses will be simpler, clearer, more useful, and hopefully, more widely read and understood when clarity prevails:

1. The new rules require issuers to write and design the cover page, summary, and risk factors section of their prospectuses in plain English. Issuers will also have to design these sections to make them inviting to the reader. The new rules will *not* require issuers to limit the length of the summary, limit the number of risk factors, or prioritize risk factors.
2. The SEC is also providing guidance to issuers on how to comply with the current rule that requires the entire prospectus to be clear, concise, and understandable. The goal is to dispense with legalese and repetitions that tend to blur the pertinent information (and facts) that investors actually need in making informed decisions.

With that in mind, the Office of Investor Education and Assistance produced a handbook with practical tips on document presentation. A *Plain English Handbook: How to Create Clear SEC Disclosure Documents*, outlining methods and techniques on how to apply plain English principles to the disclosure documents, is the resulting publication.

## ¶35,005 PLAIN ENGLISH PILOT PROGRAM

To test plain English in disclosure documents, the Division of Corporation Finance experimented with a pilot program in 1996 for public companies willing to file plain English documents under either the Securities Act of 1933 or the Securities Exchange Act of 1934. More than 75 companies volunteered to participate in the pilot program. Many participants got into the spirit of the project to the extent that they even prepared disclosure documents that are not subject to the plain English rule: proxy statements, footnotes to financial statements, management's discussion and analysis of financial condition and results of operations.

Assessment of the results of the pilot program affirmed the SEC's belief that preparing documents in plain English increases investors' understanding and helps them make informed investment decisions. Thus, the package of rules adopted, as well as the handbook, should enable issuers to improve dramatically the clarity of their disclosure documents.

## ¶35,007 RULE 421(D), *THE PLAIN ENGLISH RULE*

Basic rules outline how prospectuses must be prepared. This new ruling requires preparation of the front portion of the prospectus in plain English. The plain English principles apply to the organization, language, and design of the front and back cover pages, the summary, and the risk factors section. Also, when drafting the language in these front parts of the prospectus, the preparer must comply substantially with six basic principles:

1. Short sentences.
2. Definite, concrete, everyday language.
3. Active voice.
4. Tabular presentation or bulleted lists for complex material, whenever possible.
5. No legal jargon or highly technical business terms.
6. No multiple negatives.

Does this all sound very reminiscent of your high school English teacher preparing you to write term papers? It should. And it does seem strange that it takes a Final Rule of the Securities and Exchange Commission to remind prospectus preparers of these basic rules for written communication. (Unless obfuscation is their objective.)

A number of comment letters noted that the rule *dictates* how to write the front of the prospectus. The SEC observed marked improvement in the clarity of disclosure when pilot participants used these recognized, basic principles of clear writing. They decided that the benefits to investors supported *mandating* the use of the principles for the front of the prospectus.

In addition, the cover page, summary, and risk factors section must be easy to read. The text and design of the document must highlight important information for investors. The rule permits the issuer to use pictures, charts, graphics, and other design features to make the prospectus easier to understand.

## ¶35,009   RULE 421(B), *CLEAR, CONCISE, UNDERSTANDABLE PROSPECTUSES*

This ruling currently requires that the entire prospectus be clear, concise, and understandable. These stipulations are in addition to the plain English rule, which applies only to the front of the prospectus.

Amendments to Rule 421(b) also provide guidance on how to prepare a prospectus that is actually clear, concise, and understandable. The amendments set out four general writing techniques and list four conventions to *avoid* when drafting the prospectus. In effect, these amendments codify earlier interpretive advice.

Amended Rule 421(b) requires use of the the following techniques when writing the entire prospectus:

1. Presentation of information in clear, concise sections, paragraphs, and sentences. Whenever possible, the use of short explanatory sentences and bullet lists.

2. Use of descriptive headings and subheadings.

3. Avoidance of frequent reliance on glossaries or defined terms as the primary means of explaining information in the prospectus. Definition of terms in a glossary or other section of the document only if the meaning is unclear from the context. Use of a glossary only if it facilitates understanding of the disclosure.

4. Avoidance of legal and highly technical business terminology.

## .01  How to Comply

The new note to Rule 421(b) provides further guidance on how to comply with the rule's general requirements. Because they make the document harder to read, the note lists the following tactics to *avoid:*

1. Legalistic or overly complex presentations that make the substance of the disclosure difficult to understand.

2. Vague boilerplate explanations that are readily subject to differing interpretations.

3. Complex information copied directly from legal documents without any clear and concise explanation or interpretation of the provision(s).

4. Repetitive disclosure that increases the bulk of the document, but fails to further clarify the information.

## .03  Technical Terminology

Several comment letters stated that the SEC should permit public companies to use legal and technical business terminology. The argument was that high tech companies must use technical terms to distinguish their products or services from others in the industry. The Commission agreed that certain business terms may be necessary to describe operations properly, but cautioned against using excessive technical jargon that only competitors or industry specialists could understand.

The focus of the Plain English Rule is that the disclosure in the prospectus is for the benefit of the *investors*. When too many highly technical terms are employed, the investor soon becomes bogged down in a welter of verbiage and little if anything is "disclosed." If technical terms are unavoidable, the preparer must attempt to make their meaning perfectly clear at the onset.

## .05  Legal Documents

Several comment letters noted that some investors, particularly institutional investors, want to read the specific terms of contracts or of the securities offered. For example, the SEC concedes an investor may want to read the specific language of a loan agreement's financial covenants or an indenture's default provisions.

The current rule permits summarizing an exhibit's key provisions in the prospectus. The issuer is also required to file material contracts and any instruments that define the rights of security holders. The SEC believes this approach generally serves the needs of all investors in the market.

If the language from an exhibit in the prospectus cannot be summarized adequately, then the explicit language may be included, but it must be presented clearly and its meaning to the investor explained precisely.

## ¶35,011    REVISIONS TO REGULATIONS S-K AND S-B

The following revisions to Regulation S-K and S-B, covering requirements applicable to nonfinancial portions of the registration statements, annual and interim reports to stockholders, proxy, and other information statements, are addresses to specific sections of the narrative portions of the disclosure documents. Evidently the SEC hopes that prospective customers and stockholders will be given a better opportunity to understand the written portions of a prospectus and other relevant documents whether they really grasp the financial import of the documents or not. (Regulation S-B applies specifically to "small" businesses.)

### .01    Item 501—Forepart of Registration Statement and Outside Front Cover Page of Prospectus

The formal design requirements for the prospectus cover page have been eliminated but the issuer is required to limit the front cover of the prospectus to one page. It is expected that the revisions will result in a cover page written and designed to focus investors on *key information* about the offering and encourage them to read the important information in the prospectus. The SEC also expects the amendments to give the flexibility needed to design a cover page tailored to the specific company and the offering.

Under the revised disclosure item, the issuer is free to use pictures, graphs, charts, and other designs that accurately depict the company, business products, and financial condition; however, design features and font types that make the disclosure difficult to read or understand are taboo.

The formalized requirements on how to present the mandatory legends on the cover page have been amended. The only restrictions on presentation of these legends are:

1. The legends must be prominent.
2. The print type must be easy to read.

**¶35,011**

The Commission has amended Item 501 to provide two plain English examples of the legend that state the Commission has not approved the offering. The item also provides a plain English example of the legend that states the prospectus is not yet complete. It is commonly printed in red ink and referred to as the "red herring" legend.

The Commission has amended the requirements detailing information that must always be included on the prospectus cover page. The goal is to have the cover page focus only on *key information* about the offering. The issuing company is cautioned to avoid moving unnecessary information to this page.

Original plans were to eliminate the requirement to refer to the risk factors on the cover page; however, comment letters suggested the mandate be retained. Therefore, the cover page must now not only reference the risk factors section but must also cite the page number on which the risk factors begin.

## .03   Cover Page Format

*Retained* on the cover page from previous requirements are:

1. Company name.
2. Title, amount, and description of securities offered.
3. Selling securities holder's offering.
4. Bona fide estimate of range of maximum offering price, and numbers of securities.
5. If price not set, indication of how price will be determined.
6. State-required legends.
7. Date of prospectus.

Adopted changes to Regulation S-K—Item 501 to the prospectus cover page include:

1. Cross reference to risk factors *must include page number.*
2. Bullet list or other design that highlights the information showing *price, underwriting commission, and proceeds of the offering* replaces formatted distribution table.
3. Bullet list or other design that highlights the *best efforts disclosure* replaces the formatted distribution table.
4. Commission legend retained in plain English. Reference to *state securities commissions* to be included.
5. Information concerning *underwriters' over-allotment option and the number of shares* retained on the cover page. Expenses of the offering, the number of shares, commissions paid by others, and other non-cash consideration and finder's fees *moved* to the plan of distribution section.

¶35,011.03

6. Identification of market for securities, trading symbol, underwriters, and type of underwriting arrangements.
7. Prospectus "Subject to Completion" legend retained in plain English.
8. Cover limited to one page.

## .05  Limited Partnership Offerings Risk

Several comment letters suggested that the plain English rule and the revised disclosure requirements should replace earlier interpretive advice on cover page disclosure for *limited partnership* offerings.

The SEC acknowledges that under existing advice, the cover page must list the offering's key risks, resulting in repetitious disclosure of those risks. However, they feel that the unique nature of limited partnership offerings and the risks they present to investors warrant requiring the issuer to highlight these risks on the cover page. Of course, the cover page, summary, and risk factors section must otherwise comply with the plain English rule and the revised disclosure requirements being adopted.

## .07  Item 502—Inside Front and Outside Back Cover Pages

Item 502's amended requirements for the inside front cover page and outside back cover page of the prospectus now significantly limit the information required on these pages. The hope is that this will give further freedom to the issuer to arrange the information in the prospectus from the *investor's viewpoint*.

The Commission prefers that the required table of contents immediately follow the cover page, but the ruling permits the preparer to have the flexibility to include it on either the inside front or outside back cover page of the prospectus. However, if a prospectus is delivered to investors electronically, the table of contents must come immediately after the cover page so that investors need not scroll to the end of the prospectus to see how it is organized.

Although some comment letters recommended elimination of the requirement to disclose the dealer's prospectus delivery obligations, the SEC decided to retain this disclosure on the outside back cover page. They suggest this disclosure is helpful to dealers in reminding them of their legal obligation to deliver the prospectus.

Following are disclosures *previously required* on the inside front or outside back cover pages and their *new location* adopted under Regulation S-K—Item 502:

1. Availability of Exchange Act reports generally—moved to description of business section or, for short-form registration statements, to the incorporation by reference disclosure.

¶35,011.05

2. Identification of market for securities—moved to cover page.

3. Availability of annual reports to shareholders with financial statements for foreign issuers and others not subject to proxy rules—moved to description of business section.

4. Availability of Exchange Act reports incorporated by reference in short-form registration statements—moved to incorporation by reference disclosure.

5. Stabilization legend—moved to plan of distribution section.

6. Passive market-making activities legend—deleted. Disclosure retained in plan of distribution section.

7. Dealer prospectus delivery page—retained on outside back cover as noted above.

8. Enforceability of civil liability provisions of federal securities laws against foreign persons—moved to description of business section.

9. As mentioned above, the table of contents may still be located on either the inside front cover or the outside back cover unless it is sent electronically. Then it must be on the inside front cover.

In line with other changes, Forms S-2, S-3, S-4, F-2, F-3, and F-4 are also being amended.

Along with the list of reports incorporated by reference, the issuer must include information on:

1. How investors may obtain a copy of these reports.

2. How investors may obtain copies of the other reports filed with the SEC.

## .09 Item 503—Summary Information, Risk Factors, and Ratio of Earnings to Fixed Charges

*Summary Information.*    If a summary is included, it must be brief and in plain English. Further, if a summary description of the company's business operations or financial condition is included, the information must be written in plain English even if not identified as a "summary."

Length of the summary is not mandated, but the SEC emphasizes that this section should *highlight the most important features* of the offering. It *should not* include a lengthy description of the company's business and business strategy. They suggest this detailed information is better included in the disclosure in the body of the prospectus.

Although there is no list of items that must be in a summary (if there is one), since the financial statements are an important part of the disclosures made by public companies, the SEC believes the issuer should continue to *highlight financial information* in the summary in a manner readily understood by the user.

*Risk Factors.* When a risk factors section is included in the prospectus, the risk factors must be detailed in plain English avoiding trite "boilerplate" risk factors. Any risk factors must be explained in context so investors can understand the specific risk applicable to that particular company and its operations.

*Ratio of Earnings to Fixed Charges.* Where a summary or similar section is included in the prospectus, amended Item 503 requires showing the ratio of earnings to fixed charges as part of the summarized financial data.

Issuers offering debt securities must show a *ratio of earnings to fixed charges*. Those registering preference equity securities must show the *ratio of combined fixed charges and preference dividends to earnings*. The issuer must present the ratio for each of the last five fiscal years and the latest interim period for which financial statements are presented in the document.

If the proceeds from the sale of debt or preference securities are used to repay any outstanding debt or to retire other securities, and the change in the ratio would be ten percent or greater, a ratio showing the application of the proceeds, the *pro forma ratio*, must be used. If a ratio indicates less than one-to-one coverage, the dollar amount of the deficiency is to be disclosed. The pro forma ratio may be shown only for the most recent fiscal year and the latest interim period. The net change in interest or dividends from the refinancing should be used to calculate the pro forma ratio.

# ¶35,013   COMMENTS ON THE PLAIN ENGLISH REQUIREMENTS

Forty-five comment letters on the plain English proposals generally favored requiring plain English for the front of prospectuses—the cover page, summary, and risk factors section—to ensure that investors receive clear information. They believe that requiring plain English will focus all parties involved in the offering process—issuers, underwriters, trustees, and counsel—on clear and readable disclosure.

Other comment letters raised the following general concerns about the rule:

1. Will the plain English rule increase a registrant's liability?
2. How will the staff review and comment on plain English filings?
3. Will the Commission deny acceleration of a filing if it does not comply with the plain English rule?

After studying these questions, the SEC has concluded that issuers really have little, if any cause, for concern: *following the new rulings* should not alter established procedures and practices for handling relevant matters.

# ¶35,015  COST FACTORS

While project participants who responded to benefit-cost questions had incurred some additional document preparation costs, the majority estimated them to be low and predicted that they would fall over time. The participants anticipated little added, and perhaps even lower, overall cost. Some even predicted they might save money on printing and distribution costs and on the amount of time spent on answering investors' questions. Based on the experiences of pilot program participants, the SEC believes that the substantial benefits to investors of plain English — and the probable ongoing cost savings to issuers — justify the short-term cost to public companies of learning to prepare documents in plain English.

# ¶35,017  UPDATED STAFF LEGAL BULLETIN 7

In June, 1999, the SEC updated Staff Legal Bulletin 7 relating to the Plain English requirements for registration statements filed on or after October 1, 1998, with the Division of Corporation Finance. This bulletin is not a rule, regulation, or statement of the Securities and Exchange Commission, nor have its contents been approved or disapproved by the agency.

## .01  Risk Factor Guidance

According to the staff members responsible for reviewing the filings, the most vexing problem for most issuers involved risk factor disclosures. Amended Item 503(c) of Regulation S-K specifies that issuers should not present risks that could apply to any issuer or any offering. Further, the subheadings must adequately describe the risk that follows.

Item 503(c) seems to be the least understood of the plain English requirements. For this reason, the SEC has provided additional information as well as sample risk factor disclosures and subheadings to help preparers comply with Rule 421(d) of Regulation C and Item 503(c) of Regulation S-K.

## .03  Types of Risk

Risk factors loosely fall into three broad categories:

1. *Industry Risk* — risks companies face by virtue of the industry they're in. For example, many REITs run the risk that, despite due diligence, they will acquire properties with significant environmental issues.
2. *Company Risk* — risks that are specific to the company. For example, a REIT owns four properties with significant environmental issues and cleaning up these properties will be a serious financial drain.

¶35,017.03

3. *Investment Risk*—risks that are specifically tied to a security. For example, in a debt offering, the debt being offered is the most junior subordinated debt of the company.

When drafting risk factors, the issuer should specifically link each risk to the specific industry, company, or investment, as applicable.

## .05 Cautions and Suggestions Relating to Risk Disclosure

After the staff had gained several months' experience issuing plain English comments under the new rule and amendments, they thought it would be helpful to list some of the comments that had been recorded most frequently. By alerting filers to these comments before they file subsequent registration statements, the SEC hopes filers will be able to avoid making these types of mistakes in the future.

Of course, the following selected, abridged comments do not encompass all of the varied plain English comments that were issued. Each prospectus is different and many of the comments issued are unique to the organization of and disclosure in individual prospectuses.

Following are several of the types of cautions made relative to risk disclosure:

1. More than one risk factor should not be "bundled" under one subheading. In order to give the proper prominence and weight to each risk presented, it should be given its own descriptive subheading.

2. Risks should be presented in concrete terms. For example, a reference to "risks due to the 'costs' associated with the benefit plans" is too vague. A better understanding of the risks would be gained by a statement that the "costs" are not expenses of running the plans, but result from the added compensation expense that stems from the shares purchased by or granted to employees and executives under those plans.

3. In each risk factor, the risk should be clearly and succinctly stated as quickly as possible without undue introductory background material and extensive detailed discussion.

4. The issuer should provide the information investors need to assess the magnitude of the risk. For example, a statement that "increases in short-term interest rates could have a material adverse effect" on XYZ Bank's profitability raises more questions than it provides information.

   Why? Are a substantial percentage of XYZ's interest-earning assets in long-term investments that pay fixed rates while the interest paid to depositors fluctuates? If so, what percentage of interest-earning assets are in long-term investments? Explain.

5. Item 503(c) of Regulation S-K states that issuers should not "present risk factors that could apply to any issuer or to any offering."

   For example, a risk disclosed under "Dependence on Key Personnel" could apply to nearly any issuer in an industry or in almost any industry. If general risk factors are retained in a prospectus, they must be clearly explained. How do they apply to a particular industry, company, or offering? Why is there a concern about losing key personnel? Are they about to retire? Are they not bound by employment contracts?

6. If the subheadings in the risk factors section are too vague and generic they will not adequately describe the risk that follows as is required in Item 503(c) of Regulation S-K.

   For example, the subheading "Competition" is certainly not descriptive because all companies operating in a free market economy are subject to competition.

7. To the extent possible, generic conclusions about the risk should be avoided. Statements like "... would have a material adverse effect on ..." operations, financial condition, or business are too imprecise. Instead, there should be specific disclosure of *how* operations, financial condition or business would be affected *by what* specific risk.

8. In an introductory paragraph to the risk factors section, the issuer should not "hedge" against noncompliance by stating that there might be risks not considered material at the time that could become material. Or by making a blanket statement that there might be unidentified risks. The issuer must disclose all risks considered material at the time.

## .07  Glossaries and Defined Terms

Rule 421(b) specifies that the issuer "must avoid frequent reliance on glossaries or defined terms as the primary means of explaining information in the prospectus. Define terms in a glossary or other section of the prospectus only if the meaning is unclear from the context. Use a glossary only if it facilitates understanding of the disclosure."

Obviously, then, there are times when a glossary should be used. The bulletin suggests the following:

1. Terms used in a prospectus which are understood only by industry experts should be included in a glossary.

2. If the meanings of terms cannot be made clear from the context or explained concisely where they are first used, then the glossary is appropriate.

3. It is not necessary to use a glossary to define commonly understood abbreviations, like SEC, or acronyms, like NASDAQ.

4. A glossary should not be used to define terms that have been created solely for the purpose of the registration statement. In fact, with the exception of brand or trade names used to identify the type of security being offered, new terms should not be created.

Creating terms that exist only for use in a prospectus forces investors to learn a new vocabulary before they can begin to understand the disclosure. The issuer should eliminate over-reliance on defined terms as a primary means of explaining information in the prospectus, and instead, disclose material information in a clear, concise, and understandable manner.

## .09 Documents Incorporated by Reference

Some, but not all of the documents incorporated by reference into registration statements are subject to the plain English rule and amendments.

1. The information incorporated by reference in response to a general requirement need not comply with the plain English rule. For example, Item 12 on Form S-3 requires incorporation by reference of the issuer's recent Exchange Act reports in their entirety. The reports need not be rewritten.
2. However, any information incorporated by reference to satisfy a specific disclosure requirement must comply with the applicable plain English rule and amendments. For example, on Form S-3, if the filer incorporates by reference risk factors from a Form 10-K to satisfy Item 3, the risk factors must comply with Rule 421(d).

## .11 Post-Effective Amendments to Registration Statements

A post-effective amendment to a Form S-3 that, when first filed, was not subject to plain English will trigger the plain English requirements in two instances. A post-effective amendment must be rewritten to comply if:

1. It incorporates by reference audited financials that are more recent than those incorporated in any earlier post-effective amendment or the original registration statement.
2. Enough time has elapsed since the last post-effective amendment or the original registration statement that the issuer is required to post-effectively amend the prospectus under Section 10(a)(3) of the Securities Act of 1933.

## .13 Use of Legal Documents in Prospectus

Under Rule 421(b) of Regulation C, the issuer must avoid copying complex information directly from legal documents without any clear and concise explanation of the information. Language in the body of the prospectus should not be taken directly from the underlying indenture, shareholder agreements, rights plan, merger agreement, statute on dissenters rights, employment agreement, or similar document. The disclosure relating to such documents should be revised so that it is clear, concise, and understandable.

In the event that the issuer feels the language as it appears in the underlying legal documents is indispensable to a prospectus, it is necessary to:

1. Present it clearly, using bullet lists and concise sections and paragraphs.
2. Explain how that particular document affects investors.

## .15  Highly Technical Business Description in Plain English

Under the plain English rule, an issuer with a highly technical business should provide a brief, general description of the business with, if necessary, concrete examples to illustrate the description.

By comparing the following two descriptions of Computational Systems, Inc., it is obvious that it is possible to describe a tech-business effectively in plain English. The first example is from CSI's 1996 10-K, prior to the adoption of the plain English rules. The second is from the summary of a merger proxy that CSI filed during the company's participation in the Division's plain English pilot program:

1. *Computational Systems, Inc. 10-K*

   "The Company primarily designs, produces and markets an integrated family of advanced predictive maintenance products and services for use in large scale, continuous run manufacturing facilities. The Company's Reliability-Based Maintenance products and services help customers detect potentially disruptive conditions in the operation of their machinery before damage or complete mechanical failure occurs, thereby allowing maintenance to be scheduled at the most appropriate time."

2. *Computational Systems, Inc./Emerson Electric Company's merger proxy*

   "CSI's primary business is the design manufacture, and sale of a family of high-tech instruments that help companies determine when their industrial machines are in need of repair or adjustment. CSI also offers services to help its customers better manage the maintenance of their equipment. CSI's products and services help its customers keep their production lines running and maintain the quality of their products which may be adversely affected by an improperly functioning production line machine. CSI's customers are primarily large manufacturing, processing or power generating companies."

If the issuer must include technical terms that are understood only by industry experts, every effort must be made to explain these terms where they are first used. Where this is simply not possible, a glossary is acceptable.

¶35,017.15

In addition, technical terms and industry jargon are not appropriate for concise explanations.

## .17 Clarity, Not Brevity, Is the Goal

The goal of plain English is clarity, not brevity. Writing disclosure in plain English can sometimes actually increase the length of particular sections of a prospectus. The aim should be to reduce the length of a prospectus by writing concisely and eliminating redundancies—not by eliminating substance.

## .19 Electronic Filers Selected for Review

The Division of Corporation Finance has announced that, because issuers are required to file their registration statements electronically on EDGAR, the staff did not want them to send paper copies of their filings. However, in the plain English adopting release, if a registration statement that is subject to the new plain English rule is selected for review, the staff will need paper copies.

When issuers file their registration statements electronically on the EDGAR system, the document's layout is lost. Because the plain English rule is intended to enhance the readability of the prospectus through language *and design*, the staff needs to see the layout of the plain English sections as they are delivered to investors.

At present, the staff member assigned to a filing will call to request paper copies of the prospectus. The SEC is working to upgrade the EDGAR system to give issuers the option of filing an exact duplicate of the paper copy sent to investors, but this may not occur for some time.

## .21 Plain English and Acceleration Requests

The staff may ask the Commission to deny acceleration of a registration statement where the issuer has not made a good faith effort to comply with the plain English rule and amendments. The issuer must make a bona fide effort to make the prospectus reasonably concise, readable, and in compliance with the plain English requirements.

## .23 Cover Page Reminders

1.  If the cover page exceeds the one page limit imposed by the rule, much of the information included is probably too detailed. The information that is not required by Item 501 of Regulation S-K and other information that is not key to an investment decision should be moved off the cover page. More in-depth information should be in the summary.

    Superfluous information such as the par value of common stock, highly technical explanations of industry operations, and minute details about the mechanics of a possible merger obscure the information that is key to potential investors' decisions.

2. Using all capital letters, cascading margins, narrow margins and dense text all impede readability of the text on the cover page. Since requirements limit this page to information that is key to an investment decision, it is very important that it be readable and visually inviting. The layout must highlight the information required by Item 501 and encourage investors to read the prospectus.

3. Item 501(a)(5) of Regulation S-K requires the issuer to highlight the cross reference to the risk factors section by using prominent type or in another manner. In other words, the cross reference should be visually distinctive from the other text on the cover page. Highlighting this cross reference using bold-faced and italicized type is suggested. Placing the cross reference in all capital letters is not recommended.

## .25  Comments Relating to the Summary

1. *Like information* should be grouped together. For example, if in a summary the items that discuss how a transaction directly affects shareholders are mixed with information on other topics, a naive investor could very easily become confused. If the exchange ratio, the tax consequences for payments on fractional shares, discussions of regulatory matters, termination fees, conditions to the merger, and such are not organized in a logical order, even a sophisticated investor would be at a loss.

2. In the summary, the issuer should carefully consider and identify those aspects of an offering that are the *most significant* and determine how best to highlight them in clear, plain language. It is not necessary to explain at length technical steps a company must take, such as creating a merger subsidiary, directors' reasons for the merger, or the conflicts of interest that may result. This type of information would not be helpful for a shareholder making an investment decision.

3. The summary should not contain a lengthy description of the company's business and business strategy. Disclosure of this nature appears later in the prospectus. Detailed information is better suited for the body of the prospectus. If the issuer feels it important to highlight key aspects of the entity's business strategy, listing these in a bullet-point format, with one sentence per bullet point, is acceptable.

## .27  Sample Cautions for the Entire Prospectus

1. Long sentences make it difficult to understand on the first reading, particularly if there are embedded lists of information in paragraph form. Rather than including lists in paragraph form, they should be broken out, and each item marked with a bullet point, a number, or a letter.

¶35,017.27

2. Sentences containing parenthetical phrases disrupt the flow of information and make the sentences very long. As a result, investors may have to read them several times to understand the disclosure. Possible ways to eliminate parenthetical phrases are:

   a. If the information in the parenthetical phrase is part of the sentence, it may be set off by commas.

   b. If the parenthetical phrase does not fit as part of the sentence, it should be a separate sentence.

3. The use of footnotes should be avoided where possible. Some suggestions are:

   a. If the text in a footnote applies to an entire financial table, the footnoted material could be included in the narrative discussion that precedes the table.

   b. If a number of footnotes repeat the same text of a table, the information could be moved to the introductory paragraph.

   c. The footnoted material could be included in a column in the table.

4. A prospectus should be organized from the shareholders' perspectives. Information about the mechanics of a merger, for instance, is not important to investors. How the proposed transactions will affect their investments is important to them.

5. Redundancy should be consciously avoided. The only type of repetition that is appropriate in the prospectus would be:

   a. Introduction of topics on the cover page.

   b. Expansion of those topics in a summary fashion while summarizing other key aspects of the transaction in the summary.

   c. Discussion of those and the remaining topics in greater detail in the body of the prospectus.

6. Informative subheadings provide readers with helpful navigational cues. They should be descriptive and specific to a particular prospectus. If subheadings would work equally well in any other company's disclosure document, they are probably too vague to be helpful.

7. A prospectus should never be written from the perspective of someone who is already quite familiar with the transaction and the entities involved. For example, references to "certain circumstances," "certain matters," "certain amendments," "certain persons," and "certain extraordinary matters" would make sense to someone who is already familiar with these transactions. But, would the shareholders be? Probably not. The term "certain" should be replaced with a brief description of what makes the information qualify as "certain."

8. Legalese and industry jargon should not be used in a prospectus. Instead, concepts should be explained in concrete, everyday language. As always, any industry terms should be used in context so those potential investors who do not work in the industry can understand the disclosure.

¶35,017.27

# Chapter 36
## Derivatives

## CONTENTS

## ¶36,000   OVERVIEW

There is little doubt that Derivatives was the '90s buzz word in the areas of accounting, finance, banking, and investments. The SEC, the AICPA, the FASB, the GASB, the GAO, the FEI, the AIMR, the IASC, IOSCO, CBOT and myriad other worthy organizations all jumped into the fray to attempt to prevent another

Orange County, California-type debacle from occurring. The losses of Procter and Gamble, other large companies, and banks had raised concern, but the fiasco of a public body so obviously misusing derivatives—and being caught—called for drastic action. Despite numerous precautions taken by the accounting regulators, the problem has not been resolved. In testimony before Congress on February 9, 2005, the chief accountant for the SEC presented his rationale for a decision in December 2004 concerning suspected abuse by Federal National Mortgage Association (Fannie Mae) with respect to derivatives accounting. His report claimed that Fannie Mae had not complied in material respects with specific provisions of generally accepted accounting principles (GAAP). Highlighting the continuing difficulty of complying with existing reporting requirements for derivatives, the SEC notified Fannie Mae (the largest nonbank financial services company in the world) that its accounting for its hedging activities was not in compliance with FASB 133.

The Financial Accounting Standard Board's FASB 119, *Disclosures About Derivative Financial Instruments and Fair Value of Financial Instruments*, was a giant step in the right direction as far as disclosure was concerned, but it was not enough. After 10 years of wresting with the derivatives problem, the Board adopted FASB 133, *Accounting for Derivative Instruments and Hedging Activities*. FASB statement No. 133 supercedes FASBs 80, 105, and 119 and also amends FASBs 52 and 107.

Various private sector entities highlighted, pinpointed, and underlined problems associated with disclosures about these market risk sensitive instruments, as identified by users of financial reports. The Securities and Exchange Commission's study, preceding the release (in March, 1996) of their proposals for amendments to regulations governing disclosure information about derivatives and other financial instruments and the issuance in February, 1997 of amendments to SEC rules, took into consideration concerns by many organizations. For example, the Association for Investment Management and Research (AIMR), an organization of financial analysts, in a paper discussing financial reporting in the 1990s and on into the next century, noted that users are confounded by the complexity of financial instruments.

## ¶36,001    DERIVATIVE GUIDANCE AND FINE-TUNING AN ON-GOING PROJECT

As long as there are derivatives, there will be a continuing need for guidance and revisions of the rules. With FASB Statement No. 133, *Accounting for Derivatives and Hedging Activities*, on the books, there was, at least, a basis from which to work; however, that was only the beginning. The Board seems always to have several questions to be considered.

## ¶36,002    CLARIFICATION OF THE APPLICATION OF THE *SHORTCUT METHOD*

Based on the concerns raised by constituents, the Board added a project to its agenda to reconsider the disclosure requirements of Statement 133. In August 2006, the FASB staff had completed its research and was drafting materials for the Board to consider regarding application of the shortcut method in FASB Statement 133, *Accounting for Derivative Instruments and Hedging Activities.*

In February 2006, the Board had agreed to consider clarifying the existing guidance, which relates to the *shortcut method* described in paragraph 68 of the FASB 133.

A reporting entity may assume no ineffectiveness in a hedging relationship of interest rate risk involving a recognized interest-bearing asset or liability and an interest rate swap, if all of the conditions in paragraph 68 of Statement 133 are met. The achievement of "no ineffectiveness," as described in paragraph 68, is often referred to as the shortcut method. (In early 2006, approximately 40 restatements were blamed on improper application of this so-called shortcut method. Obviously, there was a need for guidance! )

Several practice issues had emerged relating to the interpretation of certain provisions of paragraph 68 that the staff believes should be clarified by the Board. The issues the staff believe need clarification relate primarily to the appropriateness of using the shortcut method in the following circumstances:

1.  The hedged item has a fair value that is not equal to its par value at the inception of the hedging relationship.
2.  The hedged item is subject to principal pay-downs prior to maturity.

The staff has completed its research and is currently drafting materials for the Board to consider before a decision is announced. It is important to remember that Board decisions become final only after a formal written ballot to issue a final Statement, Interpretation, or FSP. The Board actually has a number of projects related to derivatives being discussed and two have been finalized as the Standards below.

## ¶36,003    TWO STANDARDS AIMED AT SIMPLIFYING ACCOUNTING FOR DERIVATIVES

These two Standards are two more attempts to make less onerous some of the complicated accounting for derivatives. Both are amendments to FASB Standard No. 133, the much maligned initial reaction to the scandal resulting from Orange County, California's misuse of derivatives, and FASB 140,

*Accounting for Transfers and Servicing of Financial Assets and Extinguishments of Liabilities—a Replacement of FASB Statement 125.*

## .01 FASB 156 to Account for Separately Recognized Servicing Assets and Liabilities

The FASB issued Statement No. 156, *Accounting for Servicing of Financial Assets* in March 2006. The Standard, which is an amendment to FASB140, will simplify the accounting for servicing assets and liabilities, such as those common with mortgage securitization activities.

Specifically, the Standard addresses the recognition and measurement of separately recognized servicing assets and liabilities and provides an approach to simplify efforts to obtain hedge-like (offset) accounting.

The standard also:

1. Clarifies when an obligation to service financial assets should be separately recognized as a servicing asset or a servicing liability.
2. Requires that a separately recognized servicing asset or servicing liability be initially measured at fair value, if practicable.
3. Permits an entity with a separately recognized servicing asset or servicing liability to choose either of the following methods for subsequent measurement:
   a. Amortization Method
   b. Fair Value Method

FASB 156 permits a servicer that uses derivative financial instruments to offset risks on servicing to report both the derivative financial instrument and related servicing asset or liability by using a consistent measurement attribute – fair value.

The Board specifically designed this Statement to simplify and encourage more consistent accounting in the area. It is the latest step in a series of somewhat similar projects aimed at reducing complexity while providing an approach that allows hedge-like accounting without having to deal with the complexities of FASB 133.

The Statement is effective for all separately recognized servicing assets and liabilities acquired or issued after the beginning of an entity's fiscal year begun after September 15, 2006.

## .03 FASB 155 Simplifies Accounting for Hybrid Financial Instruments

The FASB issued a final standard in February 2006 that improves the financial reporting of certain hybrid financial instruments by requiring more consistent accounting that eliminates exemptions and provides a means to simplify the accounting for these instruments.

This standard, FASB 155, *Accounting for Hybrid Instruments,* also amends FASB Statements 133 and 140 and reflects constituent comments provided to the FASB in 2005.

Specifically, the standard allows financial instruments that have embedded derivatives to be accounted for as a whole (eliminating the need to bifurcate the derivative from its host) if the holder elects to account for the whole instrument on a fair value basis.

The standard also:

1. Clarifies which interest-only strips and principal-only strips are not subject to the requirements of Statement 133.
2. Establishes a requirement to evaluate interests in securitized financial assets to identify interests that are freestanding derivatives or that are hybrid financial instruments that contain an embedded derivative requiring bifurcation.
3. Clarifies that concentrations of credit risk in the form of subordination are not embedded derivatives.
4. Amends Statement 140 to eliminate the prohibition on a qualifying special-purpose entity (QSPE) from holding a derivative financial instrument that pertains to a beneficial interest other than another derivative financial instrument.

There are also several areas in which FASB 155 does not apply. It does not apply to hybrid instruments:

1. That are described in paragraph 8 of FASB Statement No. 107, *Disclosures about Fair Value of Financial Instruments,* which include insurance contracts as discussed in FASB Statements No. 60, *Accounting and Reporting by Insurance Enterprises,* and No. 97, *Accounting and Reporting by Insurance Enterprises for Certain Long-Duration Contracts and for Realized Gains and Losses from the Sale of Investments,* other than financial guarantees and investment contracts.
2. That are not financial instruments, such as nonfinancial instruments that require payments in a commodity, for example, gold.
3. That are not financial instruments, such as contracts that require the delivery of services.
4. That are not financial instruments, such as nonfinancial instruments that require volumetric production payments.

The FASB believes the standard improves financial reporting by reducing complexity through the elimination of unnecessary exemptions and by providing ways to make the overall accounting simpler.

¶36,003.03

The statement became effective for all financial instruments acquired or issued after the beginning of an entity's first fiscal year beginning after September 15, 2006.

## .05    Statement 155 Implementation Issue

At the October 25, 2006 FASB Board Meeting, as a result of concerns raised by constituents, the members Board decided to add yet another project on derivatives to the agenda. This particular project is to provide guidance on implementation issues related to the Statement above, FASB 155, *Accounting for Certain Hybrid Financial Instruments*. Specifically, this project will address circumstances in which a securitized interest in prepayable financial assets *would not be subject* to the conditions in paragraph 13(b) of FASB Statement No. 133, *Accounting for Derivative Instruments and Hedging Activities*.

The Board decided to:

1. Include a narrow scope exception for securitized interests that contain only an embedded derivative that is tied to the prepayment risk of the underlying prepayable financial assets. If a securitized interest contains any other terms that affect some or all of the cash flows or the value of other exchanges required by the contract in a manner similar to a derivative instrument and if those terms create an embedded derivative that requires bifurcation (ignoring the effects of the embedded call options in the underlying financial assets), that securitized interest would not meet the narrow scope exception and would therefore be evaluated pursuant to FASB Statement No. 133, *Accounting for Derivative Instruments and Hedging Activities*.

2. Have the guidance's effective date prior to the reporting deadline of periods ending December 31, 2006.

3. Address early adoption of FASB Statement No. 155, *Accounting for Certain Hybrid Financial Instruments*, in the following ways:

   a. For entities that early adopted Statement 155 and did not bifurcate embedded prepayment derivatives (consistent with the tentative decisions), no transition provisions are required. However, the Board's guidance will specifically address this scenario to ensure that there is no confusion over the possibility of restating prior financial statements.

   b. For entities that early adopted Statement 155, identified embedded derivatives that would otherwise be included in the proposed scope exception, and that elected to measure the entire hybrid instrument at fair value, the Board's guidance should be applied retrospectively. The company will be provided with the opportunity to elect any appropriate FASB Statement No. 115, *Accounting for Certain Investments in Debt and Equity Securities,* classification as part of that retrospective application. If the company elects a trading classification under Statement 115, no adjustment to the changes in fair value previously recorded in the income statement is required. However, if the company elected a classification of available-for-sale, the retrospective application would result in a reclassification from the income statement to accumulated other comprehensive income.

c. For entities that early adopted Statement 155 and identified and bifurcated embedded derivatives that would otherwise be included in the proposed scope exception, the Board's guidance should be applied retrospectively. This would result in the reversal of any changes in the fair value of the embedded derivative that were recorded in income during the prior interim period(s). The combined instrument should be recorded, both initially and subsequently, based on the Statement 115 classification previously elected for the host instrument.

The Board plans to issue the tentative guidance as a Statement 133 Implementation Issue with a 30-day public comment period; however, it's always important to remember that this was the thinking of the Board at the time. Nothing is official unless a Standard, an FSP, or an Interpretation has been issued.

## ¶36,005   FASB STATEMENT 133, ACCOUNTING FOR DERIVATIVE INSTRUMENTS AND HEDGING ACTIVITIES

The derivatives standard was adopted by a unanimous vote on June 1, 1998, after more than 10 years of painstaking effort by the FASB. Unquestionably, this Standard is one of the most far-reaching accounting standards yet produced. The hue and cry raised in every segment of the economy continues unabated.

The FASB repeatedly made it clear that they would not back down on certain requirements, regardless of "special interest" objections. The Board pointed out that trillions of dollars' worth of derivative transactions are occurring in the marketplace and they believe "investors have little, if any, information about them." The Board believed that the new Standard would give the investor further information about an entity so that they could make more knowledgeable decisions. However, they were not so naïve as to believe that Statement 133 would satisfy everyone, nor that it would not need further work, amendment, guidance and/or revision. And so it has been.

The U.S. Senate, the House of Representatives, the Federal Reserve, the American Bankers Association, and assorted others entered the fray over derivatives with very little success. On the other hand, the Board had modified some of the earlier positions in response to user requests, as in the Chicago Board of Trade's concern about some of the provisions relating to hedging.

One of the most important concessions was to the projected timing of the effective date. The Standard was to have become effective June 15, 1999. This meant that for calendar-year companies it would be effective January 1, 2000. Many segments had complained that the extra time and money being expended on trying to solve Y2K problems, coping with a new derivatives Standard of such proposed magnitude by December 15, 1998, was expecting too much.

FASB Statement 137, *Accounting for Derivative Instruments and Hedging Activities—Deferral of the Effective Date of FASB Statement 133*—delayed for a year the required application of FASB 133 to June 15, 2000. However, entities that had already issued interim or annual financial statements according to the requirements of Statement 133 could not return to their previous method of accounting for derivatives or hedging activities.

FASB 137 did not change any of the requirements; it merely postponed the inevitable to give the issuers additional time to cope with Y2K considerations and digest the ramifications of the new requirements.

The FASB also appointed a special task force to aid with implementation issues on derivatives. Among the comments received from users were many related to the complicated provisions of the proposed Standard—admittedly covering very complicated financial instruments. The Board agreed with the constituents that it should be prepared to provide assistance and guidance on a timely basis: thus, the task force. The task force continues to help in identifying implementation issues and recommending conclusions to the Board.

## .01   ED Modified Somewhat, Not Substantially

FASB Standard 133 retained most of the provisions that were issued in the ED of September, 1997. All derivatives are to be reported as assets or liabilities in financial statements at their fair value. New approaches to hedge accounting are outlined. As a result, more detailed, useful disclosures of derivatives, hedging activities, and related accounting practices should furnish the investor, creditor, and user with a better picture of an entity's true financial condition. In effect, the new derivative accounting practices should then reveal the economic realities of derivative transactions to the financial statement reader.

## .03   Hedge Accounting

Under certain conditions, the Standard permits management to designate a derivative as one of the following hedges—a fair value, cash flow, or foreign exchange hedge.

1. A *fair value hedge* is a hedge of the exposure to changes in the fair value of an asset or liability recognized on the balance sheet or of a firm commitment. The exposure to change must be attributable to a specific risk.

For this type of hedge, the gain or loss is recognized in current income. This amount is offset by the gain or loss in the fair value of the hedged item. The carrying amount is adjusted to reflect the fair value gain or loss. If the hedge is working as it is intended, the adjustment to the carrying amount of the hedged item recognized in income will equal the offsetting gain or loss on the hedging derivative and there will be no net effect on earnings. If the hedge, on the other hand, is not operating as it should, earnings will be affected to the extent that the hedge is ineffective. Assessment of effectiveness is required.

2. A *cash flow hedge* is a hedge of an exposure to variability in the cash flows of an asset or liability recognized on the balance sheet, or of a forecasted transaction, that is attributable to a particular risk. Forecasted transactions include forecasted sales and purchases for which no firm commitment has been made, and interest payments on variable rate debt reported as a liability.

   The effective part of a gain or loss on a derivative designated as a cash flow hedge is initially recognized in owners' equity as part of other comprehensive income and then in earnings in the same period in which the hedged forecasted transaction affects earnings. The ineffective aspect of the gain or loss is recognized in earnings.

3. A *foreign currency exposure hedge* is a hedge of the foreign currency exposure of:

   a. A firm commitment which is a foreign currency fair value hedge.

   b. An available-for-sale debt security, a foreign currency fair value hedge.

   c. A foreign currency-denominated forecasted transaction which is a foreign currency cash flow hedge.

   d. A net investment in a foreign operation.

   The gain or loss on a derivative or nonderivative financial instrument designated as a foreign currency hedge is accounted for depending upon its designations as a fair value or cash flow hedge in the same way as outlined above for those types of hedges.

   Thus, the gain or loss on a derivative financial instrument designated and qualifying as a foreign currency hedging instrument is to be accounted for as follows:

   a. The gain or loss on the hedging instrument in a hedge of a firm commitment is to be recognized in current earnings along with the loss or gain on the hedged firm commitment.

   b. The gain or loss on the hedging derivative in a hedge of an available-for-sale security is to be recognized in current earnings along with the loss or gain on the hedged available-for-sale security.

   c. In general, the effective aspect of the gain or loss on the hedging instrument in a hedge of a foreign-currency denominated forecasted transaction is to be reported as a component of other comprehensive income, outside of earnings. It is to be recognized in earnings in the same period or periods during which the hedged forecasted transaction affects earnings. The ineffective aspect of the gain or loss on the hedging instrument and any other remaining gain or loss on the hedging instrument is to be recognized in current earnings.

d. The foreign currency transaction gain or loss on the hedging instrument in a hedge of a net investment in a foreign operation is to be reported in other comprehensive income as part of the cumulative translation adjustment. The remainder of the gain or loss on the hedging instrument is to be recognized in current earnings.

## .05 Derivatives

A derivative is a financial instrument or other contract with several distinguishing characteristics:

1. It has one or more *underlyings* and one or more *notional amounts* or payment provisions or both. Those terms determine the amount of the settlement or settlements, and in some cases, whether or not a settlement is required.
2. It requires no initial net investment or one that is smaller than would be required for other types of contracts expected to have a similar response to changes in market factors.
3. The terms require or permit net settlement; it can readily be settled net by a means outside the contract, or it provides for delivery of an asset that puts the recipient in a position not substantially different from net settlement.

An "underlying" may be one of a number of variables that is applied to the notional amount to determine the cash flows or other exchanges required by the contract—a commodity price, a per-share price, an interest rate, a foreign exchange rate, or some other variable.

"Notional amount" refers to an amount of money, a number of shares, a number of bushels, pounds, or whatever can be dreamed up to create a more exotic derivative. A contract with these characteristics is a derivative instrument according to the Statement if, by the terms at its inception or upon the occurrence of a specified event, the entire contract meets the conditions delineated above.

FASB 133 specifically states that the following transactions do not constitute derivatives for the purpose of this Statement:

1. Regular security trades.
2. Normal purchases and sales.
3. Contingent consideration from a business combination.
4. Traditional life insurance contracts.

5. Traditional property and casualty contracts.
6. Most financial guarantee contracts.

The new Statement also points out that some contracts may be accounted for as derivatives by the holder but not by the user. These would include:

1. Contracts that are both indexed to the entity's own stock and classified in stockholders' equity on their balance sheets.
2. Contracts issued in connection with stock-based compensation arrangements covered in FASB 123, *Accounting for Stock-Based Compensation*.

## .07  How FASB 133 Affects Other Accounting Literature

FASB 133 supersedes and amends several other Statements. It supersedes:

1. FASB 80, *Accounting for Futures Contracts*.
2. FASB 105, *Disclosure of Information About Financial Instruments with Off-Balance-Sheet Risk and Financial Instruments with Concentrations of Credit Risk*.
3. FASB 119, *Disclosure About Derivative Financial Instruments and Fair Value of Financial Instruments*.

It amends:

1. FASB 52, *Foreign Currency Translation*, to permit special accounting for a hedge of a foreign currency forecasted transaction with a derivative.
2. FASB 107, *Disclosures About Fair Value of Financial Instruments*, to include in Statement 107 the disclosure provisions about concentrations of credit risk from FASB 105.

FASB 133 also nullifies or modifies the consensuses reached in a number of issued addressed by the Emerging Issues Task Force.

## .09  Application to Not-for-Profit Organizations

Since the Statement applies to all entities, not-for-profit organizations should recognize the change in fair value of all derivatives as a change in net assets in the period of change. In a fair value hedge, the changes in the fair value of the hedged item attributable to the risk being hedged also are recognized.

However, because of the format of their statement of financial performance, not-for-profit organizations may *not* apply special hedge accounting for derivatives used to hedge forecasted transactions. In addition, FASB 133 does not consider how a not-for-profit organization should determine the components of an operating measure if one is presented.

¶36,005.09

## .11  Another Amendment

The Financial Accounting Standards Board issued Statement 138, *Accounting for Certain Derivative Instruments and Certain Hedging Activities—an Amendment of FASB Statement 133* in June, 2000. The Statement addresses a limited number of issues causing implementation difficulties for a large number of entities getting ready to apply Statement 133.

The Board points out that FASB 133, *Accounting for Derivative Instruments and Hedging Activities*, establishes accounting and reporting standards for derivative instruments, including certain derivative instruments embedded in other contracts, (collectively referred to as derivatives) and for hedging activities. Because of difficulties in application and interpretations, the Statement amends FASB 133 so that:

1. The normal purchases and normal sales exception is expanded.
2. The specific risks that can be identified as the hedged risk are redefined so that in a hedge of interest rate risk, the risk of changes in a benchmark interest rate would be the hedged risk.
3. Recognized foreign-currency-denominated debt instruments may be the hedged item in fair value hedges or cash flow hedges.
4. Intercompany derivatives may be designated as the hedging instruments in cash flow hedges of foreign currency risk in the consolidated financial statements even if those intercompany derivatives are offset by unrelated third-party contracts on a net basis.

Certain Board decisions based on recommendations of the Derivatives Implementation Group (DIG) to clarify Statement 133 also have been incorporated in the Statement. The Statement 138 is the result of the Board's decision, after listening to its constituents, to address a limited number of issues using the following criteria:

1. Implementation difficulties would be eased for a large number of entities.
2. There would be no conflict with or modifications to the basic model of Statement 133.
3. There would be no delay in the effective date of Statement 133.

## ¶36,007   FASB Statement 149 Amends and Clarifies Guidance on Derivatives

The FASB issued Statement No. 149, *Amendment of Statement 133 on Derivative Instruments and Hedging Activities*, amending and clarifying accounting for derivatives, including certain derivative instruments embedded in other contracts, and for hedging activities under Statement 133 in April 2003.

The guidance amended Statement 133 for decisions made:

*   As part of the Derivatives Implementation Group process that effectively requires amendments to Statement 133.
*   In connection with other Board projects dealing with financial instruments.
*   Regarding implementation issues raised in relation to the application of the definition of a derivative. This was a major problem facing the FASB from the very beginning, particularly, in regard to the meaning of an underlying instrument and the characteristics of a derivative that contains financing components. The language now conforms to that used in the definition of an underlying in FASB Interpretation 45, *Guarantor's Accounting and Disclosure Requirements for Guarantees, Including Indirect Guarantees of Indebtedness of Others.*

The amendments set forth in FASB 149 improve financial reporting by requiring that contracts with comparable characteristics be accounted for similarly. It clarifies under what circumstances a contract with an initial net investment meets the characteristic of a derivative described in Statement 133. In addition, it clarifies *when* a derivative contains a financing component that calls for special reporting in the statement of cash flows.

Statement 149 also amends certain other existing pronouncements. Those changes result in more consistent reporting of contracts that are derivatives in their entirety or that contain embedded derivatives that warrant separate accounting.

## ¶36,009    TECHNICAL BULLETIN TO IMPROVE DISCLOSURES ABOUT DERIVATIVES

In an effort to improve disclosures about the risks associated with derivative contracts, the GASB issued accounting guidance in June 2003 that provides more consistent and comprehensive reporting by state and local governments. The Technical Bulletin, *Disclosure Requirements for Derivatives Not Presented at Fair Value on the Statement of Net Assets*, is designed to increase the public's understanding of the significance of derivatives to a government's net assets and to provide key information about the potential effects on future cash flows. It also provided the users of financial statements with better information about the risks assumed in derivative contracts. Derivatives are often used by governments as a means to potentially reduce borrowing costs. Although derivatives may support financing needs, the lower costs come with additional risks. The objectives and terms of derivative contracts, their risks, and the fair value of the contracts had generally not been specified in financial reports.

This Technical Bulletin is designed to increase the public's understanding of the significance of derivatives to a government's financial position and provide key information about their potential effects on future cash flows.

The GASB pointed out that even estimating the notional amounts of outstanding derivatives in this market is difficult based on information that has been readily available. Estimates of notional value in 2003 range from $200 billion to $400 billion. Under this guidance, state and local governments are *required* to disclose such information.

One GASB official agreed that its own research indicated that it often has been difficult to understand how governments have been accounting for derivatives. These disclosures should clear up the mystery surrounding the transactions. It should now be possible to see what a government has done, why it has done it, the fair value of the derivative, and the risks that have been assumed. Governments will be required to disclose information in their financial statements about risks that relate to credit, interest rates, basis, termination dates, rollovers and, market access.

While state and local governments use an array of increasingly complex derivative instruments to manage debt and investments, they may, at the same time, be assuming significant risks. Governments are expected to communicate those risks to financial statement users and the public. The proposed Technical Bulletin's purpose is to clarify existing accounting guidance so that more consistent disclosures can be made across all governments.

The GASB is aware of the fact that the market for derivative instruments has expanded for state and local governments, which find themselves in a dismal budgetary environment. Some derivative contracts may pose substantial risks; therefore, the Board's aim is to help officials better explain those risks in their financial statements.

This Technical Bulletin requires that governments disclose the derivative's:

- Objectives.
- Terms.
- Fair value.
- Risks.

The accounting guidance requires the governments to disclose in their financial statements what is faced in:

- Credit risk.
- Interest rate risk.
- Basis risk.
- Termination risk.

**¶36,009**

- Rollover risk.
- Market access risk.

This Technical Bulletin became effective for periods ending after June 15, 2003.

## ¶36,011  GASB Issues PV on Issues Related to Derivatives

The GASB issued a Preliminary Views (PV) document, *Accounting and Financial Reporting for Derivatives*, in April 2006, intended to improve the accounting and financial reporting of derivatives by state and local governments.

Derivatives are often-complex financial arrangements that governments are increasingly entering into. However, derivatives are rarely reported in the financial statements of governments and the public knows little about them or the risks associated with them.

The proposal would require that the fair value of derivatives be reported in the financial statements as well as the change in that fair value. If, however, a derivative is effectively hedging the risk it was created to address, then the annual changes in the derivative's fair value would be deferred and reported in a government's balance sheet. Deferral would continue until the derivative ends or ceases to be an effective hedge, at which time any remaining deferred credits or charges would be reported in investment income.

The GASB proposal details the characteristics of a hedge that qualifies for hedge accounting. It also lays out acceptable methods for determining if a hedge is effective.

## .01  GASB Invites Comments on the Derivates PV

Since the Governmental Accounting Standards Board (GASB) issued the Preliminary Views document to improve the accounting and financial reporting of derivatives by state and local governments, they have encouraged the active participation of all constituents in the process.

The GASB has been particularly interested in hearing from financial statement users, such as analysts, and governments that are participating in the derivatives market. The proposed changes could have a significant impact on the way state and local governments account for derivatives, thus, the Board wants to ensure that all interested parties have an opportunity to express their opinions.

# Chapter 37

# Consideration of Real Estate as an Asset

## CONTENTS

## ¶37,000  OVERVIEW

In the midst of a prolonged recession, with a moribund stock market, the residential real estate market continues to achieve record highs. In most areas, residential real estate is priced at levels not dreamed of as recently as two years ago when the recession began. Adjustable-rate loans are at historic lows; fixed-rate loans are near their lows. Builders put up homes as fast as they can—from custom-built mansions to starter condominium complexes. The appetite for residential real estate seems insatiable.

What does this mean to the tax preparer? It means that they can expect to have many more real estate transactions to address formally and even more informal client inquiries to consider.

## ¶37,001   INCOME-PRODUCING RENTAL PROPERTY

With a large segment of the population turning 18 between now and 2010, and considering leaving the nest, demand for rental housing will be on the increase. In most parts of the country, multifamily housing construction is barely keeping pace with demand, and vacancy rates are down countrywide. Fairly obviously, rental real estate income becomes an attractive consideration.

Rental income and expenses, and how to report them, is discussed in this section of the chapter. The discussion also covers casualty losses on rental property and the passive activity and at-risk rules.

### .01   Rental Income

The taxpayer must declare as income all remuneration received as rent. Rental income is *any* payment received for the use or occupation of property. If the taxpayer is a cash-basis taxpayer, all rental income should be reported for the year in which it is actually or constructively received.

In addition to amounts the taxpayer receives as normal rent payments, other amounts may be rental income:

1. *Advance rent* is any amount the taxpayer receives before the period that it covers. This, too, is included in rental income in the year the taxpayer receives it, regardless of the period covered or the method of accounting the taxpayer uses.

2. *Security deposits* are not included in income when received if the owner plans to return them to the tenants at the end of the lease. If, however, the taxpayer keeps part or all of the security deposit during any year because the tenant does not live up to the terms of the lease, then the amount the taxpayer keeps is included in income in that year. When a security deposit is to be used as a final payment of rent, it is considered *advance rent* and is include in income when received.

3. If the tenant pays to *cancel a lease*, the amount received is rent. The payment should be included in income in the year the taxpayer receives it, regardless of the method of accounting.

4. If the tenant pays for *expenses pertaining to the rental property*, the payments are rental income and the owner must include them in income. However, the taxpayer can deduct the expenses if they are deductible rental expenses.

5. When the taxpayer receives *property or services instead of money* as rent, the fair market value of the property or services must be included in rental income. If the services are provided at an agreed-on or specified price, that price is the fair market value, unless there is evidence to the contrary.

6. If the rental agreement gives the tenant the right to buy the rental property, the payments the taxpayer receives under the agreement are generally rental income. However, if the tenant exercises the right to buy the property, the payments received for the period *after the date of sale* are considered part of the selling price.

7. If owners rent property for fewer than 15 days during the tax year that they also use as their main home, the rent received is not included in income, nor is any rental expense deductible. However, the taxpayer can deduct the interest, taxes and casualty and theft losses that are allowed for nonrental property.

8. If the taxpayer owns a part interest in rental property, he or she must report the share of the rental income from the property.

## .03 Rental Expenses

Certain expenses of renting property ordinarily can be deducted from rental income if the taxpayer rents a condominium or cooperative apartment or part of the tax property, or if the taxpayer changes his or her property to rental use. The taxpayer generally deducts these rental expenses in the year the expenses are paid:

1. If the taxpayer retains property for rental purposes, it may be possible to deduct the ordinary and necessary expenses (including depreciation) for managing, conserving or maintaining the property while it is vacant. However, the taxpayer *cannot deduct any loss of rental income* for the period the property is vacant.

2. Ordinary and necessary expenses can be deducted for managing, conserving or maintaining rental property from the time it is made available for rent.

3. Depreciation on rental property begins when it is ready and available for rent.

4. When property that had been held for rental purposes is sold, the taxpayer can deduct the ordinary and necessary expenses for managing, conserving or maintaining the property until it is sold.

5. If the taxpayer sometimes uses the rental property for personal purposes, the expenses must be divided between rental and personal use. Also, the rental expense deductions may be limited.

6. An individual who owns part interest in rental property can deduct the part of the expenses he or she paid.

## .05 Differentiating Between Repairs and Improvements

Cost of *repairs* to rental property can be deducted. Although the cost of *improvements* cannot be deducted, they can be recovered by taking depreciation. Therefore, it is important to separate the costs of repairs and improvements and to keep accurate records. These records will be needed to know the cost of improvements when the taxpayer sells or depreciates the property.

A repair keeps the property in good operating condition. It does not materially add to the value of the property or substantially prolong its life. Repainting the property inside or out, fixing gutters or floors, fixing leaks, plastering and replacing broken windows are examples of repairs.

On the other hand, when the taxpayer makes repairs as part of an *extensive remodeling or restoration* of the property, the whole job is an improvement, which is an entirely different matter. An improvement adds to the value of property, prolongs its useful life or adapts it to new uses. When the taxpayer makes an improvement to property, the cost of the improvement must be capitalized. The capitalized cost can generally be depreciated as if the improvement were separate property.

## .07 Other Deductible and Non-Deductible Rental Expenses

Other expenses the taxpayer can deduct from the rental income include advertising, cleaning and maintenance services, utilities, fire and liability insurance, taxes, interest, commissions for the collection of rent, ordinary and necessary travel and transportation and the following expenses:

1. A taxpayer can deduct the rent paid on property that he or she then turned around and used for rental purposes (i.e., sublet). If the individual buys a leasehold for rental purposes, it is permissible to deduct an equal part of the cost each year over the term of the lease.

2. The taxpayer can deduct rent paid for equipment used for rental purposes. However, in some cases, *lease contracts* are actually *purchase contracts*. If this is the case, the taxpayer cannot deduct these payments but can recover the cost of purchased equipment through depreciation.

3. If an insurance premium is paid for more than one year in advance, each year the taxpayer can deduct the part of the premium payment that will apply to that year. The total premium cannot be deducted in the year it is paid.

4. Generally, the taxpayer *cannot deduct charges for local benefits* that increase the value of the property—such as charges for putting in streets, sidewalks or water and sewer systems. These charges are nondepreciable capital expenditures. They must be added to the basis of the property. The taxpayer can deduct local benefit taxes if they are for maintaining, repairing or paying interest charges for the benefits.

5. The taxpayer can deduct mortgage interest paid on rental property.

6. Certain expenses paid to obtain a mortgage on rental property cannot be deducted as interest. These expenses, which include mortgage commissions, abstract fees and recording fees, are capital expenses. However, the taxpayer can amortize them over the life of the mortgage.

## .09  Other Expenses Involving Points

The term "points" is often used to describe some of the charges paid by a borrower when he or she takes out a loan or a mortgage. These charges are also called loan origination fees, maximum loan charges or premium charges. If any of these charges (points) are solely for the use of money, they are *interest*.

Points paid when the taxpayer takes out a loan or mortgage result in original issue discount (OID). In general, the points (OID) are deductible as interest unless they must be capitalized. How the taxpayer figures the amount of points (OID) to deduct each year depends on whether or not the total OID, including the OID resulting from the points, is insignificant or *de minimis*. If the OID is not *de minimis*, the taxpayer must use the constant yield method to figure how much he or she can deduct.

In general, the OID is *de minimis* if it is less than one-fourth of 1 percent (.0025) of the stated redemption price at maturity (generally, the principal amount of the loan) multiplied by the number of full years from the date of original issue to maturity (the term of the loan).

If the OID is *de minimis*, the taxpayer can choose one of the following ways to figure the amount allowed for deduction each year:

1. On a constant yield basis over the term of the loan.
2. On a straight-line basis over the term of the loan.
3. In proportion to stated interest payments.
4. In full at maturity of the loan.

The preparer makes this choice by deducting the OID in a manner consistent with the method chosen on the timely filed tax return for the tax year in which the loan or mortgage is issued.

*The Constant Yield Method.*   If the OID is *not de minimis*, the taxpayer must use the constant yield method to figure how much he or she is allowed to deduct each year.

The CPA figures the taxpayer's deduction for the first year in the following manner by:

1. Determining the issue price of the loan. For example, if the taxpayer paid points on a loan, the points the taxpayer paid from the principal amount of the loan are subtracted to get the issue price.
2. Multiplying the issue price (the result in step 1) by the yield to maturity.
3. Subtracting any qualified stated interest payments from the result in step 2. This is the amount of OID the taxpayer can deduct in the first year.

To figure the deduction in any subsequent years, it is necessary to start with the *adjusted issue price*. To obtain the adjusted issue price, the CPA adds to the issue price any OID previously deducted and then follows steps 2 and 3.

*The yield to maturity* is shown in the information the taxpayer receives from the lender. If the taxpayer does not receive it, the tax advisor should consult the lender to obtain this information. In general, the yield to maturity is the discount rate that, when used in computing the present value of all principal and interest payments, produces an amount equal to the principal amount of the loan.

*Qualified stated interest* is stated interest that is unconditionally payable in cash or property (other than debt instruments of the issuer) at least annually at a single fixed rate.

**When the Loan or Mortgage Ends.**  If the taxpayer's loan or mortgage ends, the accountant may be able to deduct any remaining points (OID) in the tax year in which the loan or mortgage ends. A loan or mortgage may end due to a refinancing, prepayment, foreclosure, or similar event. However, if the refinancing is with the same lender, the remaining points (OID) generally are not deductible in the year in which the refinancing occurs, but they may be deductible over the term of the new mortgage or loan.

## .11  Travel Expenses

The taxpayer can deduct the ordinary and necessary expenses of traveling away from home if the primary purpose of the trip was to collect rental income or to manage, conserve or maintain the rental property. It is important to allocate the expenses properly between rental and nonrental activities.

It is also permissible to deduct ordinary and necessary local transportation expenses if they are incurred to collect rental income or to manage, conserve or maintain the rental property.

Generally, if taxpayers use a personal car, pickup truck or light van for rental activities, they can deduct the expenses by one of two methods: actual expenses or the standard mileage rate.

## .13  Tax Return Preparation

The taxpayer can deduct, as a rental expense, the part of tax return preparation fees paid to prepare that portion of the return pertaining to rental income. It is also possible to deduct, as a rental expense, any expense paid to resolve a tax underpayment related to the rental activities.

## .15  Condominiums and Cooperatives

If the taxpayer rents out a condominium or a cooperative apartment, special rules apply. Condominiums are treated differently from cooperatives.

¶37,001.11

*Condomuniums.*    If the individual owns a condominium, the property is considered a dwelling unit in a multiunit building. This also involves owning and being responsible for a share of the common elements of the structure, such as land, lobbies, elevators, and service areas. The taxpayer and the other condominium owners usually pay dues or assessments to a special corporation that is organized to take care of the common elements.

If the owner rents the condominium to others, the CPA can deduct depreciation, repairs, upkeep, dues, interest and taxes and assessments for the care of the common parts of the structure. It is not possible to deduct special assessments paid to a condominium management corporation for improvements. Taxpayers may, however, be able to recover a share of the cost of any improvement by taking depreciation. A condominium may be the ideal way to purchase rental property, as the price is usually lower than that for a single-family home and are often in ideal locations near schools, work places and public transportation.

Since condos are governed by a set of condominium documents, a homeowners association is expected to see that the rules set down in these documents are followed. It is extremely important before purchasing a condo unit for rental or other investment purposes to review these documents closely. Some condominium documents contain rather unusual and restrictive rules about rentals, for example. Therefore, it is wise to discover any objectionable details before incurring expenses, such as for a title search and loan application fees.

Contained in the condominium documents may be a stipulation that rentals are permitted only one time per year. This is probably very desirable for those who make their main home in the particular block of condominiums. Nor would it be a problem in an area where it is preferable to find a tenant for an annual rental, but a condo located in a popular resort area may be better offered as a "seasonal rental." Rents charged in the most popular seasons are typically much higher than at other times of the year. In such a case, the owner or investor should look carefully at the rental restriction rules.

Two other important details to check are the budget and the amount set aside for reserves by the homeowners association. If any special assessments are planned for the near future, it would be foolhardy to purchase a condominium and set a rental amount only to discover that out-of-pocket money will soon be assessed for a new roof.

Condominium budgets normally chart the useful remaining life of the major systems in the building and property.

*Cooperatives.*    If the taxpayer has a cooperative apartment that is rented to others, he or she can usually deduct as a rental expense all the maintenance fees paid to the cooperative housing corporation. However, a payment earmarked for a capital asset or improvement, or otherwise charged to the corporation's capital account cannot be deducted. For example, the taxpayer cannot deduct a payment used to pave a community parking lot, install a new roof, or pay the principal of the

¶37,001.15

corporation's mortgage. The payment must instead be added to the basis of their stock in the corporation.

The amount the taxpayer was assessed for capital items is treated as a capital cost. This cannot be more than the amount by which the taxpayer's payments to the corporation exceeded his or her share of the corporation's mortgage interest and real estate taxes.

The taxpayer's share of interest and taxes is the amount the corporation elected to allocate to him or her, if it reasonably reflects those expenses for the apartment. Otherwise, the share is figured by:

1. Dividing the number of taxpayer shares of stock by the total number of shares outstanding, including any shares held by the corporation.
2. Multiplying the corporation's deductible interest by the number the taxpayer figured in step 1. This is the taxpayer's share of the interest.
3. Multiplying the corporation's deductible taxes by the number the taxpayer figured in step 1. This is the taxpayer's share of the taxes.

In addition to the maintenance fees paid to the cooperative housing corporation, the taxpayer can deduct direct payments for repairs, upkeep and other rental expenses, including interest paid on a loan used to buy the stock in the corporation.

## .17   Property Changed to Rental Use

If the taxpayer changes his or her home or other property (or a part of it) to rental use at any time other than the beginning of the tax year, he or she must divide yearly expenses, such as depreciation, taxes and insurance, between rental use and personal use.

The taxpayer can deduct as rental expenses only the part of the expense that is for the part of the year the property was used or held for rental purposes. What cannot be deducted is depreciation or insurance for the part of the year the property was held for personal use. The home mortgage interest and real estate tax expenses, however, can be included as an itemized deduction for the part of the year the property was held for personal use.

## .19   Renting Part of a Property

If the taxpayer rents part of the property, certain expenses must be divided between the part of the property used for rental purposes and the part used for personal purposes, as though they were two separate pieces of property.

Expenses related to the part of the property used for rental purposes, such as home mortgage interest and real estate taxes, can be deducted as rental expenses. Expenses for the part used for personal purposes, subject to certain limitations, are deductible only if the deductions are itemized. A part of other expenses that normally are non-deductible personal expenses, such as expenses for electricity or painting the outside of the house, can also be deducted as rental expense. The taxpayer cannot deduct any part of the cost of the first phone line even if the tenants have unlimited use of it. The taxpayer does not have to divide the expenses that belong only to the rental part of the property.

If an expense is for both rental use and personal use, such as mortgage interest or heat for the entire house, the taxpayer must divide the expense between rental use and personal use. Any reasonable method for dividing the expense is permissible. It may be reasonable to divide the cost of some items (for example, water) based on the number of people using them. However, the two most common methods for dividing an expense are one based on the number of rooms in the home and one based on the square footage.

## .21 Personal Use of Dwelling Unit (Including Vacation Home)

If the taxpayer has any personal use of a dwelling unit (including vacation home) that is rented, the expenses must be divided between rental use and personal use.

If the taxpayer used the dwelling unit for personal purposes long enough during the year, it will be considered a "dwelling unit used as a home." If so, the taxpayer cannot deduct rental expenses that exceed rental income for that property. If the dwelling unit is not considered one used as a home, the taxpayer may deduct rental expenses that exceed rental income for that property subject to certain limits.

If the taxpayer uses the dwelling unit as a home and rents it fewer than 15 days during the year, no rent is included in income and no deduction is taken for rental expenses.

## .23 Definition of a Dwelling Unit

A dwelling unit can be a house, apartment, condominium, mobile home, boat, vacation home or similar property. It has basic living accommodations, such as sleeping space, a toilet and cooking facilities.

A dwelling unit *does not* include property used solely as a hotel, motel, inn or similar establishment. Property is used solely as a hotel, motel, inn or similar establishment if it is regularly available for occupancy by paying customers and is not used by an owner as a home during the year.

## .25 Dwelling Unit Used as Home

The tax treatment of rental income and expenses for a dwelling unit that the taxpayer also uses for personal purposes depends on whether the taxpayer uses it as a home. The taxpayer uses a dwelling unit as a home during the tax year if it is used for personal purposes more than the greater of:

1. 14 days or
2. 10 percent of the total days it is rented to others at a fair rental price.

If a dwelling unit is used for personal purposes on a day it is rented at a fair rental price, that day is not counted as a day of rental use in applying the 10 percent rule. Instead, it is considered a day of personal use in applying rules 1 and 2. This is moot if expenses are being divided between rental and personal use.

***Fair Rental Price.***    A fair rental price for property generally is an amount that a person who is not related to the taxpayer would be willing to pay. The rent charged is not a fair rental price if it is substantially less than the rents charged for other similar properties.

The following questions should be considered when comparing another property with the unit in question:

1. Is it used for the same purpose?
2. Is it approximately the same size?
3. Is it in approximately the same condition?
4. Does it have similar furnishings?
5. Is it in a similar location?

If any of the answers is no, the properties probably are not similar.

***Use as Main Home Before or After Renting.***    The days a taxpayer used the property as his or her main home before or after renting it or offering it for rent are not counted as days of personal use in either of the following circumstances:

1. The taxpayer rented or tried to rent the property for 12 or more consecutive months.
2. The taxpayer rented or tried to rent the property for a period of less than 12 consecutive months and the period ended because the property was sold or exchanged.

This special rule does not apply when dividing expenses between rental and personal use.

¶37,001.25

*Figuring Days of Personal Use.*    A day of personal use of a dwelling unit is any day it is used by any of the following persons:

1.  The taxpayer or any other person who has an interest in it, unless this individual rents it to another owner as his or her main home under a shared equity financing agreement (defined later).
2.  A member of the individual's family or a member of the family of any other person who has an interest in the property, unless the family member uses the dwelling unit as his or her main home and pays a fair rental price. "Family" includes only brothers and sisters, half-brothers and half-sisters, spouses, ancestors (parents, grandparents, great grandparents) and lineal descendants (children, grandchildren, great grandchildren).
3.  Anyone under an arrangement that lets the taxpayer use some other dwelling unit.
4.  Anyone at less than a fair rental price.

If the other person or member of the family in items 1 and 2 has more than one home, his or her main home is the one lived in most of the time.

*Shared Equity Financing Agreement.*    This is an agreement under which two or more persons acquire undivided interests for more than 50 years in an entire dwelling unit, including the land, and one or more of the co-owners is entitled to occupy the unit as his or her main home upon payment of rent to the other co-owner or owners.

*Donation of Use of Property.*    The taxpayer has used a dwelling unit for personal purposes if:

1.  The taxpayer donates the use of the unit to a charitable organization.
2.  The organization sells the use of the unit at a fund-raising event.
3.  The "purchaser" uses the unit.

*Days Used for Repairs and Maintenance.*    Any day that the taxpayer spends working substantially full time repairing and maintaining a property is not counted as a day of personal use. It is not counted as a day of personal use even if family members use the property for recreational purposes on the same day.

## .27   How to Divide Expenses

If a person uses a dwelling unit for both rental and personal purposes, expenses are divided between the rental use and the personal use based on the number of days used for each purpose. When dividing the expenses, following are the correct rules:

1. Any day that the unit is rented at a fair rental price is a day of rental use even if the taxpayer used the unit for personal purposes that day. This rule does not apply when determining whether the taxpayer used the unit as a home.
2. Any day that the unit is available for rent but not actually rented is not a day of rental use.

## .29   How to Figure Rental Income and Deductions

How the taxpayer figures the rental income and deductions depends on whether the dwelling unit was used as his or her home and, if used as a home, how many days the property was rented.

If the taxpayer does not use a dwelling unit as a home, all the rental income is reported and all the rental expenses are deducted.

If the taxpayer uses a dwelling unit as a home during the year, how the rental income and deductions are handled depends on how many days the unit was rented. If the owner uses it as a home and rents it fewer than 15 days during the year, none of the rental income is included in income, nor are any expenses declared as rental expenses.

On the other hand, if the taxpayer uses a dwelling unit as a home but rents it 15 days or more during the year, all of the rental income must be declared. If the taxpayer had a net profit from the rental property for the year (that is, if the taxpayer's rental income is more than the total of the rental expenses, including depreciation), all of the rental expenses may be deducted.

However, if there was a net loss, the taxpayer's deduction for certain rental expenses is limited.

**Limit on Deductions.**   If rental expenses are more than the rental income, the owner cannot use the excess expenses to offset income from other sources. The excess can be carried forward to the next year and treated as rental expenses for the same property. Expenses carried forward to the next year will be subject to any limits that apply then. The taxpayer can deduct the expenses carried over to a year only up to the amount of the rental income for that year, even if the property is not used as the taxpayer's home during that particular year.

## .31   Depreciation

The taxpayer recovers the cost in income-producing property through yearly tax deductions by *depreciating* the property; that is, by deducting some of the cost on his or her tax return each year.

Three basic factors determine how much depreciation the taxpayer can deduct:

1. The taxpayer's basis in the property.
2. The recovery period for the property.
3. The depreciation method used.

The taxpayer cannot simply deduct the mortgage, principal payments or the cost of furniture, fixtures and equipment as an expense.

The taxpayer can deduct depreciation only on the part of the property used for rental purposes. Depreciation reduces the basis for figuring gain or loss on a later sale or exchange. (For further information on depreciation, see Chapter 33; for figuring the basis of property, see Chapter 35.)

## .33 Casualties and Thefts

As a result of a casualty or theft, the taxpayer may have a loss related to property and be able to deduct the loss on his or her income tax return. Damage to, destruction of or loss of property is a *casualty* if it results from an identifiable event that is sudden, unexpected or unusual. The unlawful taking and removing of money or property with the intent to deprive the taxpayer of it is a *theft*.

When the taxpayer has a casualty to, or theft of, property and receives money, including insurance, that is more than the adjusted basis in the property, he or she generally must report the gain. However, under certain circumstances, it is possible to defer paying tax by choosing to postpone reporting the gain. To do this, the taxpayer must buy replacement property within two years after the close of the first tax year in which any part of the gain is realized. The cost of the replacement property must equal or exceed the net insurance or other payment received.

## .35 Limits on Rental Losses

Rental real estate activities are considered passive activities, and the amount of loss the taxpayer can deduct is limited. Generally, taxpayers cannot deduct losses from rental real estate activities unless they have income from other passive activities. However, they may be able to deduct rental losses without regard to whether they have income from other passive activities if they "materially" or "actively" participated in the rental activity.

Losses from passive activities are first subject to the at-risk rules. At-risk rules limit the amount of deductible losses from holding most real property placed in service after 1986. However, if rental losses are less than $25,000, and the taxpayer actively participated in the rental activity, the passive activity limits probably do not apply.

¶37,001.35

If the taxpayer used the rental property as a home during the year, the passive activity rules do not apply to that home. Instead, the CPA must follow the rules explained relating to personal use above.

***At-Risk Rules.***    The at-risk rules place a limit on the amount the CPA can deduct as losses from activities often described as tax shelters. Losses from holding real property (other than mineral property) placed in service before 1987 are not subject to the at-risk rules.

Generally, any loss from an activity subject to the at-risk rules is allowed only to the extent of the total amount the taxpayer has at risk in the activity at the end of the tax year. The taxpayer is considered "at risk" in an activity to the extent of cash and the adjusted basis of other property contributed to the activity and certain amounts borrowed for use in the activity.

***Passive Activity Limits.***    In general, all rental activities (except those relating to real estate professionals) are passive activities. For this purpose, a rental activity is an activity from which the taxpayer receives income mainly for the use of tangible property, rather than for services.

Deductions for losses from passive activities are limited. The taxpayer generally cannot offset income, other than passive income, with losses from passive activities. Nor can the taxpayer offset taxes on income, other than passive income, with credits resulting from passive activities. Any excess loss or credit is carried forward to the next tax year.

***Losses from Rental Real Estate Activities.***    If the taxpayer or spouse actively participated in a passive real estate rental activity, he or she can deduct up to $25,000 of loss associated with the activity from the nonpassive income. This special allowance is an exception to the general rule disallowing losses in excess of income from passive activities. Similarly, the accountant can offset credits from the activity against the tax on up to $25,000 of nonpassive income after taking into account any losses allowed under this exception.

If the taxpayer is married, filing a separate return, and lived apart from a spouse for the entire tax year, the special allowance cannot be more than $12,500. If the taxpayer lived with a spouse at any time during the year and is filing a separate return, he or she cannot use the special allowance to reduce the nonpassive income or tax on nonpassive income.

The maximum amount of the special allowance is reduced if the modified adjusted gross income is more than $100,000 ($50,000 if married filing separately).

If the modified adjusted gross income is $100,000 or less ($50,000 or less if married filing separately), the CPA can deduct the taxpayer's loss up to $25,000 ($12,500 if married filing separately). If the modified adjusted gross income is more than $100,000 (more than $50,000 if married filing separately), this special allowance is limited to 50 percent of the difference between $150,000 ($75,000 if married filing separately) and the modified adjusted gross income.

¶37,001.35

Generally, there is no relief from the passive activity loss limits if the modified adjusted gross income is $150,000 or more ($75,000 or more if married filing separately).

The taxpayer actively participated in a rental real estate activity if he or she (and the spouse) owned at least 10 percent of the rental property and made management decisions in a significant and bona fide sense. Management decisions include approving new tenants, deciding on rental terms and approving expenditures.

## ¶37,003  INVESTING IN RENTAL REAL ESTATE

Statistics published by the U.S. Census Bureau indicate that 75 percent of multifamily investors in rental residential real estate are over the age of 45. Of these, more than one-half own fewer than five units and earned approximately 31 percent of their income from ownership of rental properties.

Most real estate investors enter this activity in their upper-middle years because they are concerned about their retirement, have probably reached their highest potential earning power, have inherited money or real estate and have more discretionary funds available.

Four reasons are often advanced for considering real estate as an investment option:

1. *Cash flow*—It is possible in many parts of the country to have a cash flow return on real estate investment. After all of the previously listed expenses have been covered (e.g., mortgage, vacancy factor, repairs and property management) there can still be some money coming in while equity is being built up.

2. *Increase in equity*—As the mortgage is reduced and the equity increases, every mortgage payment gives the investor a greater sense of being a "man or woman of property."

3. *Appreciation*—It is within reason to expect a 4 percent appreciation level. Depending upon supply and demand and the escalation of costs, including the increased costs of construction, land and development costs, some periods will be more opportune than others. However, as long as the overall demand increases in relation to the availability of adequate housing, real estate investments will continue to appreciate.

   The average single-family home sold for $23,400 in 1970; in 2000, a similar average home sold for $169,000. An approximate 8 percent annual increase with little chance of a drastic drop in value is almost always a tempting investment. But remember, location, location, location is a prime consideration.

4. *Tax savings*—The IRS permits all but actual real estate dealers to depreciate their investment properties on Schedule E when filing annual tax

returns. Residential properties depreciate over 27.5 years; commercial properties, over 39 years.

Of course, the government gets a share with the sale of investment property. The investor is faced with a 20 percent capital gains tax on the increase in value of the property and the recapture of the depreciation. This cost can be deferred if the seller completes a 1031 tax-deferred exchange to trade up from property to property.

Regardless of the size of a real estate investment, it is possible to make a return, but as with *any* investment, it is important to research the market.

## ¶37,005  IMPORTANCE OF REAL ESTATE TO THE CLIENT

A client cannot expect that the tax preparer be an authority on real estate law and regulations. However, those handling tax preparation should understand that, for most of their clients, their homes are the single largest purchase and investment they will ever make. Therefore, the accountant is well-advised to credit the seriousness, consequence and priority of any questions clients ask about their residential real estate.

## ¶37,007  SELLING A HOME

This portion of the chapter explains the tax rules that apply in selling a main home. It does not cover the sale of rental property, second homes, or vacation homes.

If the taxpayer has a gain from the sale, the preparer may be able to exclude up to $250,000 of the gain from his or her income ($500,000 on a joint return in most cases). Any gain not excluded is taxable. It is not possible to deduct loss from the sale of a main home.

It is not necessary to report the sale of the main home on the tax return unless there is a gain, at least part of which is taxable.

### .01  The Main Home

The main home can be a house, houseboat, mobile home, cooperative apartment or condominium. To exclude gain under the rules, the person generally must have owned and lived in the property as the main home for at least two years during the five-year period ending on the date of sale.

If a person sells the land on which the main home is located, but not the house itself, the accountant cannot exclude any gain from the sale of the land.

If the taxpayer has more than one home, the preparer can exclude gain only from the sale of the main home. Gain from the sale of any other home must be included in income. If someone has two homes and lives in both of them, the main home is ordinarily the one lived in most of the time.

If the taxpayer uses only part of the property as the main home, the rules discussed in this chapter apply only to the gain or loss on the sale of *that part* of the property.

## .03  Rules for Sales

If the taxpayer sold the main home, as just noted, it may be possible to exclude any gain from income up to a limit of $250,000 ($500,000 on a joint return in most cases).

The main topics in this section include:

1. How to figure gain or loss.
2. Excluding gain from the sale of a home.
3. Ownership and use tests.
4. Special situations.
5. Reporting the gain.
6. Real estate and transfer taxes.


***How to Figure Gain or Loss.***    To figure the gain or loss on the sale of the main home, the CPA must know the selling price, the amount realized and the adjusted basis. The selling price is the total amount received for the home. It includes money, all notes, mortgages or other debts assumed by the buyer as part of the sale and the fair market value of any other property or any services received. The selling price of the home does not include amounts received for personal property sold with the home. Personal property is property that is not a permanent part of the home. Separately stated cash the taxpayer received for these items is not proceeds from the transaction.

The taxpayer may have to sell the home because of a job transfer. If the employer pays for a loss on the sale or for selling expenses, this is not include as part of the selling price.

*Option to Buy.*    If the taxpayer grants an option to buy his or her home and the option is exercised, then the amount received for the option is added to the selling price of the home. If the option is not exercised, the accountant must report the amount paid for the option as ordinary income in the year the option expires.

If the taxpayer can exclude the entire gain, the person responsible for closing the sale generally will not have to report it. The preparer will use sale documents and other records to figure the total amount received for the sale of the home.

*Gain or Loss?*   Selling expenses include commissions, advertising fees, legal fees and loan charges paid by the seller (such as loan placement fees or points). The amount realized is the selling price minus selling expenses.

While the taxpayer owned the home, he or she may have made adjustments (increases or decreases) to the basis. This adjusted basis is used to figure gain or loss on the sale of the home. (For information on how to figure the home's adjusted basis, see Chapter 35.)

To figure the gain or loss, the amount realized is compared to the adjusted basis. If the amount realized is more than the adjusted basis, the difference is a gain and, except for any part the CPA can exclude, is generally taxable. If the amount realized is less than the adjusted basis, the difference is a loss. A loss on the sale of the main home cannot be deducted.

If the taxpayer and spouse sell their jointly owned home and file a joint return, the gain or loss is figured as for one taxpayer. If the taxpayers file separate returns, each of them must figure their own gain or loss according to their ownership interest in the home. The ownership interest is determined by state law.

If the taxpayer and a joint owner other than a spouse sell their jointly owned home, each of them must figure their own gain or loss according to their ownership interest in the home. Each of them applies the rules discussed in this chapter on an individual basis.

If a person trades an old home for another home, the trade should be treated as a sale and a purchase.

*Foreclosure, Repossession and Abandonment.*   If the taxpayer's home was foreclosed on or repossessed, he or she has a sale. The CPA figures the gain or loss from the sale in the same way as gain or loss from any sale. But the amount of the gain or loss depends in part on whether the owner was personally liable for repaying the debt secured by the home. If the taxpayer *was not* personally liable, then the selling price includes the full amount of debt canceled by the foreclosure or repossession. If the taxpayer *was* personally liable for the amount of the debt, then the selling price includes the amount of canceled debt up to the home's fair market value. There may be ordinary income in addition to any gain or loss. If the canceled debt is more than the home's fair market value, the taxpayer has ordinary income equal to the difference. However, the income from cancellation of debt is not taxed if the cancellation is intended as a gift, or if they are insolvent or bankrupt.

Generally, the borrower will receive Form 1099-A, *Acquisition or Abandonment of Secured Property*, from his or her lender. This form will have the information the preparer needs to determine the amount of gain or loss and any ordinary income from cancellation of debt. If the debt is canceled, the borrower may receive Form 1099-C, *Cancellation of Debt.*

An owner who abandons a home may have ordinary income. If the abandoned home secures a debt for which the owner is personally liable and the debt is canceled, the taxpayer has ordinary income equal to the amount of canceled debt.

¶37,007.03

If the home is secured by a loan and the lender knows the home has been abandoned, the lender should send out Form 1099-A or Form 1099-C. If the home is later foreclosed on or repossessed, gain or loss is figured as explained in that discussion.

*Effects of Transfer.*    When the taxpayer transfers the home to his or her spouse, or to a former spouse in a divorce settlement, there is no gain or loss (unless the exception below applies). This is true even if the taxpayer receives cash or other consideration for the home. Therefore, the rules explained in this chapter do not apply. Nor do they apply if the individual owned the home jointly with a spouse and transfers his or her interest in the home to that spouse or a former spouse. There is no gain or loss.

Furthermore, a transfer of the home to the spouse, or former spouse incident to divorce, does not affect the basis of any new home they buy or build.

These transfer rules do not apply if the spouse or former spouse is a nonresident alien. In that case, the taxpayer will have a gain or loss.

***Excluding Gain from the Sale of a Home.***    An individual may qualify to exclude from income all or part of any gain from the sale of the main home. This means that, if the individual qualifies, he or she will not have to pay tax on the gain up to the limit described below. To qualify, the taxpayer must meet the ownership and use tests described later. The person can choose not to take the exclusion, but in that case must include in income the entire gain.

*Maximum Amount of Exclusion.*    The preparer can exclude the entire gain on the sale of the main home up to:

1. $250,000, or
2. $500,000 if all of the following are true:
   a. The owners are married and file a joint return for the year.
   b. Either the taxpayer or spouse meets the ownership test.
   c. Both the taxpayer and spouse meet the use test.
   d. During the two-year period ending on the date of the sale, neither the taxpayer nor spouse excluded gain from the sale of another home.

*Reduced Maximum Exclusion.*    *The accountant can claim an exclusion, but the maximum amount of gain that can be excluded will be reduced if either of the following is true:*

1. The seller did not meet the ownership and use tests, but sold the home because of:
   a. A change in place of employment.
   b. Health.

¶37,007.03

    c. Unforeseen circumstances, to the extent provided in regulations (as discussed below).

  2. The exclusion would have been disallowed because of the rule described later, except that the seller sold the home because of:

    a. A change in place of employment.

    b. Health.

    c. Unforeseen circumstances, to the extent provided in regulations (as discussed below).

The problem is the IRS has not issued regulations defining "unforeseen circumstances." Therefore, a person cannot claim an exclusion based on unforeseen circumstances until the IRS issues final regulations—or other appropriate guidance.

    *More than One Home Is Sold During a Two-Year Period.* The taxpayer cannot exclude gain on the sale of a home if, during the two-year period ending on the date of the sale, he or she sold another home at a gain and excluded all or part of that gain. If the gain cannot be excluded it must be included in income. However, the CPA can still claim an exclusion if the home was sold because of the reasons discussed above.

    *Ownership and Use Tests.* To claim the exclusion, the taxpayer must meet the ownership and use tests. This means that during the five-year period ending on the date of the sale, the taxpayer must have:

  1. Owned the home for at least two years (the ownership test).

  2. Lived in the home as the main home for at least two years (the use test).

If the person owned and lived in the property as the main home for less than two years, the CPA can still claim an exclusion in some cases. The maximum amount that can be excluded will be reduced depending on the length of time spent in the home.

    The required two years of ownership and use during the five-year period ending on the date of the sale do not have to be continuous. The owners meet the tests if they can show that they owned and lived in the property as their main home for either 24 full months or 730 days ($365 \times 2$) during the five-year period ending on the date of sale.

    Short temporary absences for vacations or other seasonal absences, even if the property is rented out during the absences, are counted as periods of use. The taxpayer can meet the ownership and use tests during different two-year periods. However, both tests must be met during the five-year period ending on the date of the sale.

**¶37,007.03**

If the owner sold stock in a cooperative housing corporation, the ownership and use tests are met if, during the five-year period ending on the date of sale, the taxpayer:

1. Owned the stock for at least two years.
2. Lived in the house or apartment that the stock entitles him or her to occupy as the main home for at least two years.

*Some Exceptions.*    There is an exception to the use test if, during the five-year period before the sale of the home:

1. The taxpayer becomes physically or mentally unable to care for him- or herself.
2. The taxpayer owned and lived in the home as the main home for a total of at least one year.

Under this exception, the taxpayer is considered to live in the home during any time that he or she owns the home and lives in a facility (including a nursing home) that is licensed by a state or political subdivision to care for persons in his or her condition. Anyone meeting this exception to the use test must still meet the two-out-of-five-year ownership test to claim the exclusion.

For the ownership and use tests, the preparer may be able to *add the time* owned and lived in a previous home to the time lived in the home on which the taxpayer wishes to exclude gain. This can be done if all or part of the gain on the sale of the previous home was postponed because of buying the home on which the taxpayer wishes to exclude gain.

For the ownership and use tests, the CPA adds the time the taxpayer owned and lived in a previous home that was destroyed or condemned to the time he or she owned and lived in the home on which the taxpayer wishes to exclude gain. This rule applies if any part of the basis of the home sold depended on the basis of the destroyed or condemned home. Otherwise, the taxpayer must have owned and lived in the same home for two of the five years before the sale to qualify for the exclusion.

*Rules Relating to Married Persons.*    If taxpayer and spouse file a joint return for the year of sale, the CPA can exclude gain if either spouse meets the ownership and use tests. If the taxpayer's spouse died before the date of sale, he or she is considered to have owned and lived in the property as the main home during any period of time when the spouse owned and lived in it as a main home.

If the home was transferred to the taxpayer by the spouse (or former spouse if the transfer was incident to divorce), he or she is considered to have owned it during any period of time when the spouse owned it.

The taxpayer is considered to have used property as the main home during any period when:

1. The taxpayer owned it, and
2. The spouse or former spouse is allowed to live in it under a divorce or separation instrument.

*Business Use or Rental of a Home.*    The CPA may be able to exclude the gain from the sale of a home that the taxpayer has used for business or to produce rental income if the ownership and use tests have been met.

If someone was entitled to take depreciation deductions because he or she used the home for business purposes or as rental property, the CPA cannot exclude the part of the gain equal to any depreciation allowed or allowable as a deduction for periods after May 6, 1997. If the accountant can show by adequate records or other evidence that the depreciation deduction allowed was less than the amount allowable, the amount that person cannot exclude is the smaller figure.

In the year of sale someone may have used part of a property as a home and part of it for business or to produce income. Examples are:

1. A working farm on which the house was located.
2. An apartment building in which the taxpayer lived in one unit and rented the others.
3. A store building with an upstairs apartment in which the taxpayer lived.
4. A home with a room used for business (home office) or to produce income.

If the taxpayer sells the entire property, the CPA should consider the transaction as the sale of two properties. The sale of the part of the property used for business or rental is reported differently from that used as the main home. To determine the different amounts to report, the CPA must divide the selling price, selling expenses and basis between the part of the property used for business or rental and the part used as a home. In the same way, if the owner qualifies to exclude any of the gain on the business or rental part of the home, the maximum exclusion is divided between that part of the property and the part used as a home.

The CPA generally can also exclude gain on the part of the home used for business or rental if the taxpayers owned and lived in that part of the home for at least two years during the five-year period ending on the date of the sale.

*Special Situations.*    The following situations may affect the taxpayer's exclusion:

1. The taxpayer cannot claim the exclusion if the expatriation tax applies. The expatriation tax applies to U.S. citizens who have renounced their

citizenship (and long-term residents who have ended their residency) if one of their principal purposes was to avoid U.S. taxes.

2.  If the home was destroyed or condemned, any gain (for example, because of insurance proceeds received) qualifies for the exclusion.

3.  Subject to the other rules in this chapter, the CPA can choose to exclude gain from the sale of a remainder interest in the taxpayer's home. If the preparer makes this choice, the owner cannot choose to exclude gain from the sale of any other interest in the home that he or she sells separately.

4.  The taxpayer cannot exclude gain from the sale of a remainder interest in the home to a related person. Related persons include brothers and sisters, half-brothers and half-sisters, spouse, ancestors (parents, grandparents, great grandparents), and lineal descendants (children, grandchildren, great grandchildren). Related persons also include certain corporations, partnerships, trusts, and exempt organizations.

*Reporting the Gain.*    It is not necessary to report the sale of the main home on the tax return unless:

1.  The taxpayer has a gain and does not qualify to exclude all of it.
2.  The taxpayer has a gain and chooses not to exclude it.

When the taxpayer has taxable gain on the sale of the main home that is not excluded, the entire gain realized in the transaction must be reported.

If the owner used the home for business or to produce rental income during the year of sale, the sale of the business or rental part (or the sale of the entire property if used entirely for business or rental in that year) must be reported.

*Installment Sale.*    Some sales are made under arrangements that provide for part or all of the selling price to be paid in a later year. These sales are called "installment sales." If the seller finances the buyer's purchase of the home, instead of having the buyer get a loan or mortgage from a bank, the sale is probably an installment sale. The CPA may be able to report the part of the gain the taxpayer cannot exclude on the installment basis.

*Seller-Financed Mortgages.*    If the taxpayer sells the home and holds a note, mortgage or other financial agreement, the payments receive generally consist of both interest and principal. The interest received as part of each payment must be reported separately as interest income. If the buyer of the home uses the property as a main or second home, the taxpayer must also report the name, address, and social security number (SSN) of the buyer to the Internal Revenue Service.

The buyer and seller must give each other their SSN. Failure to meet these requirements may result in a $50 penalty for each failure.

If either the seller or the buyer of the home is a non-resident or resident alien who does not have and is not eligible to get an SSN, the IRS will issue that person an ITIN. This is for tax use only. It does not entitle the holder to social security benefits or change the holder's employment or immigration status under U.S. law.

*Real Estate and Transfer Taxes.* The seller and the buyer must deduct the real estate taxes on the home for the year of sale according to the number of days in the real property tax year that each owned the home.

The seller is treated as paying the taxes up to, but not including, the date of sale and can declare these taxes as an itemized deduction in the year of sale. It does not matter what part of the taxes actually were paid.

The buyer is treated as paying the taxes beginning with the date of sale. If the buyer paid the seller's share of the taxes (or any delinquent taxes owed), the payment increases the selling price of the home. The buyer adds the amount paid to his or her basis in the property.

The taxpayer cannot deduct transfer taxes, stamp taxes and other incidental taxes and charges on the sale of a home as itemized deductions. However, if the taxpayer pays these amounts as the seller of the property, they are expenses of the sale and reduce the amount realized on the sale. If the taxpayer pays these amounts as the buyer, they are included in the cost basis of the property.

## ¶37,009 IT'S A REAL ESTATE MARKET

Those CPAs dealing with tax preparation can anticipate more and more questions from clients about the tax ramifications of their residential real estate dealings. We continue to have a positive house sales environment and will continue to have as long as we remain in a low mortgage rate environment. While it is true that most people have no tax obligation created by the sale of their primary residence, there are a number of issues related to basis, estate, second home, parents' home and business use that can crop up any day of the week.

¶37,009

# Chapter 38

## Saving for a Higher Education

## CONTENTS

## ¶38,000 OVERVIEW

Education-related tax breaks come in three varieties—deductions, credits, and income exclusions—each with its limitations and restrictions. Some can be used together; some are mutually exclusive. Some change incrementally each year; some the government changes arbitrarily. Some are federal; some are state.

¶38,000

Confused? Just imagine what the client is thinking . . . and join the club. Take the state-offered College 529 plans. With more than 40 plans sold nationwide by individual states, they include an ever-changing array of state tax implications, a wide range of fees, and everything from an average portfolio with conservative returns to high-risk mutual fund investments. It's a jungle out there.

Federally, the IRS delineates education-related adjustments to income. The guidelines are fairly clear. However, which to use, when and whether you can use multiple adjustments, is not. This is mostly because each individual and the circumstances are different. That is where the financial advisor earns his or her money.

There are dozens of Internet Web sites that compare and contrast many of these college plans, showing up-to-the minute changes and excellent definitions of each plan. As always, reader beware. Web sites are for educational purposes only and usually present one side of a discussion—it is important to check the credibility of the Web site and it authors.

## ¶38,003   EMPLOYER-PROVIDED EDUCATIONAL ASSISTANCE

Employers may provide their workers with as much as $5,250 a year in tax-free educational assistance benefits. This tax benefit now applies to graduate-level courses, as well as undergraduate courses.

## ¶38,005   QUALIFIED TUITION PROGRAMS (QTPS)

Many states now offer programs that allow individuals to prepay a student's tuition or contribute to a higher education savings account. These tax benefits related to such programs also apply to tuition prepayment programs offered by qualifying private educational institutions.

Beginning in 2004, a distribution from a QTP established and maintained by an eligible educational institution (generally, private colleges and universities) can be excluded from income if the amount distributed is less than or equal to the beneficiary's adjusted qualified education expenses.

Students receiving tax-free benefits from QTPs will also be allowed to claim the Hope or Lifetime Learning Credit or receive a tax-free distribution from a Coverdell Education Savings Account (ESA), as long as the same expenses are not used for more than one of these benefits.

Beginning in 2005, the amount of the Hope or lifetime learning credit is gradually reduced (phased out) if the modified adjusted gross income (MAGI) is between $43,000 and $53,000 and ($87,000 and $107,000 for a joint return). Individuals may not claim a credit if their MAGI is $53,000 or more ($107,000 or more for a joint return). This is an increase from the 2004 limits of $42,000 and $52,000 ($85,000 and $105,000 if filing a joint return). The amounts have been increased annually since the inception of the programs. It is more than likely that the amounts will continue to increase each year. However, the benefits to the lower income students in particular, have not kept pace with the rise in the cost of getting that degree.

Taxable distributions not used for qualified higher education expenses are generally subject to an additional 10 percent tax.

## .01  Distributions from State-Maintained QTPs

A distribution from a QTP established and maintained by a state (or an agency or instrumentality of the state) can be excluded from income if the amount distributed is less than or equal to the beneficiary's adjusted qualified education expenses. Previously, the beneficiary was required to pay tax on any earnings from a QTP unless the earnings were tax free under some other provision of the law.

## .03  QTPs Maintained by Educational Institutions

An individual can make contributions to a QTP established and maintained by one or more eligible educational institutions. Any earnings distributed before January 1, 2004, are taxable. Previously, contributions could be made only to a QTP established and maintained by a state (or an agency or instrumentality of the state).

## .05  Rollovers of QTPs to Family Members

For purposes of rollovers, and changes of designated beneficiaries, the definition of family members is expanded to include first cousins of the original beneficiary.

A qualifying family member may become a designated beneficiary, or an amount rolled over to a family member's QTP within 60 days of distribution, without tax consequences.

## .07  Rollovers of QTPs without Changing Beneficiary

Amounts in a QTP can be rolled over, tax free, to another QTP set up for the same beneficiary. However, the rollover of credits or other amounts from one QTP to another QTP for the benefit of the same beneficiary cannot apply to more than one transfer within any 12-month period.

## .09  Qualified Expenses

Calculation of the amount that is considered reasonable for room and board expenses has been changed. The dollar limits for qualifying room and board expenses for students living off-campus now reflect the qualifying educational institution's published "cost of attendance" amounts. The taxpayer must contact the educational institution for their qualified room and board costs.

## .11 Special Needs Beneficiaries

The definition of "qualified higher education expenses" has been expanded to include expenses of a special needs beneficiary that are necessary for that person's enrollment or attendance at an eligible institution.

## .13 Coordination with Coverdell ESAs

Someone can make contributions to QTPs and Coverdell ESAs (the new name for Education IRAs) in the same year for the same beneficiary. Previously, contributions could be made to only one program or the other.

## ¶38,007 COVERDELL ESAs (FORMERLY EDUCATION IRAs)

Coverdell Education Savings Accounts(ESAs)—formerly known as Education IRAs—do not give any immediate tax benefit, but they allow beneficiaries to accrue tax-free earnings for qualifying educational expenses. There have been numerous changes to ESAs, including:

- A decision of the U.S. Department of Education announced more favorable financial aid treatment in 2004, by not treating ESAs as the child's assets.
- Qualifying educational expenses now include certain elementary and secondary school costs.
- College students who use Coverdell ESA funds may also claim the Hope or Lifetime Learning Credits, as long as the credits are claimed for different expenses than those paid from the ESA funds.
- Although most beneficiaries must use up their ESA accounts before age 30 or transfer them to a qualified relative, there is no longer an age limit for special needs beneficiaries.

## .01 Contributions

The most an individual can contribute each year to a Coverdell ESA is $2,000. There is no limit to the number of Coverdell ESAs that can be established for one beneficiary. However, total contributions made to all Coverdell ESAs for any beneficiary in one tax year cannot be greater than $2,000.

In general, the designated beneficiary of a Coverdell ESA can receive tax free distributions to pay qualified education expenses. The distributions are tax free to the extent the amount of the distributions do not exceed the beneficiary's qualified education expenses. If a distribution does exceed the beneficiary's qualified education expenses, a portion of the distribution is taxable.

A beneficiary may have contributions made to both a Coverdell ESA and a state tuition program in the same year.

## .03 Qualified Expenses

The definition of qualified education expenses has been expanded to include elementary and secondary education expenses. Qualified elementary and secondary education expenses include expenses for:

- Tuition, fees, academic tutoring, special needs services in the case of a special needs beneficiary, books, supplies, and other equipment incurred in connection with enrollment or attendance as an elementary or secondary school student at a public, private, or religious school.

- Room and board, uniforms, transportation, and supplementary items and services (including extended day programs) that are required or provided by a public, private, or religious school in connection with such enrollment or attendance.

- The purchase of computer technology or equipment or Internet access and related services if such technology, equipment, or services are to be used by the beneficiary and the beneficiary's family during any of the years the beneficiary is in school (not including expenses for computer software designed for sports, games, or hobbies unless the software is predominantly educational in nature).

## .05 Special Needs Beneficiaries

The taxpayer can continue to make contributions to a Coverdell ESA for a special needs beneficiary after his or her 18th birthday. A person can also leave assets in a Coverdell ESA set up for a special needs beneficiary after the beneficiary reaches age 30.

## .07 Coordination with Hope and Lifetime Learning Credits

A person can claim the Hope or lifetime learning credit in the same year he or she takes a tax-free distribution from a Coverdell ESA, provided the distribution from the Coverdell ESA is not used for the same expenses for which the

¶38,007.07

credit is claimed. Previously, an individual could not claim the Hope or lifetime learning credit if he or she received a tax free withdrawal from a Coverdell ESA and did not waive the tax-free treatment of the withdrawal.

## .09 Coordination with Qualified Tuition Programs

The taxpayer can make contributions to Coverdell ESAs and qualified tuition programs in the same year for the same beneficiary. Previously, contributions could be made to only one program or the other.

## ¶38,009 DEDUCTION FOR HIGHER EDUCATION EXPENSES

Beginning in 2002, taxpayers might have been able to deduct qualified tuition and related expenses paid during the year for themselves, their spouse, or a dependent, even if they did not itemize deductions.

Qualified tuition and related expenses are tuition and fees required for enrollment or attendance at an eligible educational institution. They may be paid for the expenses of:

- The taxpayer.
- The taxpayer's spouse.
- A dependent for whom the taxpayer claims an exemption.

Student activity fees and fees for course-related books, supplies, and equipment are included in qualified tuition and related expenses only if the fees must be paid to the institution as a condition of enrollment or attendance.

An eligible educational institution is any college, university, vocational school, or other postsecondary educational institution eligible to participate in a student aid program administered by the Department of Education. This encompasses virtually all accredited, public, nonprofit, and proprietary (privately owned, profit-making) postsecondary institutions. (The particular educational institution should be able to tell the taxpayer if it is an eligible educational institution.)

A person must reduce qualified expenses by the amount of any tax-free educational assistance received. Tax-free educational assistance includes:

- Scholarship.
- Pell grants.
- Employer-provided educational assistance.
- Veterans' educational assistance.

- Any other nontaxable payments (other than gifts, bequests, or inheritances) received for education expenses.

Expenses that are not considered "qualified tuition and related expenses" include the cost of:

- Medical expenses (including student health fees).
- Insurance.
- Room and board.
- Transportation.
- Similar personal, living, or family expenses.

This is true even if the fee must be paid to the institution as a condition of enrollment or attendance.

Qualified tuition and related expenses generally do not include expenses that relate to any course of instruction or other education that involves sports, games, or hobbies, or any noncredit course. However, if the course of instruction or other education is part of the student's degree program, these expenses can qualify.

## .01   Maximum Deduction

For tax years beginning in 2002 and 2003, the taxpayer may be able to deduct as much as $3,000 paid for qualified tuition and related expenses as an adjustment to income. For 2004 and 2005, he or she may be able to deduct $4,000.

## .03   Income Limits

For tax years beginning in 2004 and 2005, the taxpayer may deduct as much as $4,000 of qualified tuition and related expenses if the MAGI is not more than $65,000 ($130,000 on a joint return). If the MAGI is more than $65,000 ($130,000 on a joint return) but not more than $80,000 ($160,000 on a joint return), the accountant may deduct up to $2,000 of qualified tuition and related expenses. If the MAGI is more than $80,000 ($160,000 on a joint return), the deduction cannot be taken.

For purposes of this deduction, the MAGI is the adjusted gross income shown on the taxpayer's income tax return plus any foreign earned income exclusion, foreign housing exclusion or deduction, exclusion of income for bona fide residents of American Samoa, and exclusion of income from Puerto Rico.

## .05 Coordination with Credits and Other Deductions

The taxpayer cannot deduct any amount for qualified tuition and related expenses for a year if:

- A Hope credit or lifetime learning credit is claimed with respect to expenses of the individual for whom the tuition and related expenses were paid.
- The expense can be deducted under any other provision of the law.

## .07 Coordination with Exclusions

The CPA must reduce the qualified tuition and related expenses by:

- Expenses used to figure the amount of interest on qualified U.S. savings bonds that the taxpayer excluded from income because it was used to pay qualified higher education expenses.
- Expenses used to figure the amount of any tax-free withdrawals from a Coverdell ESA.
- Expenses used to figure the portion of any distribution of earnings from a qualified tuition program a person excludes from income because the earnings were used to pay the beneficiary's qualified higher education expenses.

## .09 Limits on Eligibility

The student cannot claim the deduction for qualified tuition and related expenses if any of the following applies:

- Another taxpayer is entitled to claim an exemption for that individual as a dependent on his or her return. This is true even if the other taxpayer does not actually claim the exemption.
- The filing status is married filing separate return.
- The student is a nonresident alien and has not elected to be treated as a resident alien for the tax year.

## .11 Year of Deduction

Generally, the taxpayer can deduct only those expenses for a year that are in connection with enrollment at an institution of higher education during the same year. However, it is possible to deduct expenses paid in a year if they are for an academic period beginning within the year or during the first three months of the next year.

¶38,009.05

## .13   Student Name and ID Number

To take the deduction, the taxpayer must show on the income tax return the name and taxpayer identification number (usually the Social Security number) of the person for whom the expenses were paid.

## .15   Termination

This new deduction is not available for tax years beginning after 2005.

## ¶38,011   STUDENT LOAN INTEREST DEDUCTION

A taxpayer may be able to deduct up to $2,500 of the interest paid on a qualified student loan. And, if the student loan is canceled, it may not be necessary to include any amount in income. The deduction is not limited to government-sponsored loans, but does not apply to loans made by family members.

The amount of a student loan interest deduction will be phased out if the modified adjusted gross income is between $50,000 and $65,000 ($100,000 and $130,000 for a joint return). The individual will not be able to take a student loan interest deduction if the modified adjusted gross income is $65,000 or more ($130,000 or more for a joint return).

The deduction is claimed as an adjustment to income so it is not necessary to itemize deductions on Schedule A Form 1040.

The deduction cannot be claimed if:

- Another taxpayer claims an exemption for the individual as a dependent.
- The filing status is married filing separately.
- The individual is not legally obligated to make payments on the loan.

A qualified student loan is a loan taken out solely to pay qualified higher education expenses. The expenses must have been:

- For the recipient, his or her spouse, or a person who was the recipient's dependent when the loan was made.
- Paid or incurred within a reasonable time before or after the recipient took out the loan.
- For education furnished during an academic period when the recipient was an eligible student.

Qualified higher education expenses are the costs of attending an eligible educational institution, including graduate school. The costs of attendance are determined by the eligible educational institution and include tuition and fees, an allowance for room and board, and an allowance for books, supplies, transportation and miscellaneous expenses.

Costs incurred must be reduced by:

- Non-taxable employer—provided educational assistance.
- Non-taxable distributions from a Coverdell education savings account.
- Non-taxable distributions from a qualified tuition program (QTP).
- U.S. Savings Bond interest that is non–taxable because it is used to pay qualified higher education expenses.
- The non-taxable part of scholarships and fellowships.
- Veterans educational assistance.
- Any other non-taxable payments (other than gifts, bequests, or inheritances) received for educational expenses.

The student must have been enrolled in a degree, certificate, or other program leading to a recognized educational credential at an eligible educational institution and must have carried at least one half of a normal full–time work–load for the course of study being pursued.

## ¶38,013   TAX-EXEMPT BOND FINANCING FOR QUALIFIED PUBLIC EDUCATIONAL FACILITIES

Beginning in 2002, the private activities for which state and local tax-exempt bonds may be issued will be expanded to include providing qualified public educational facilities.

A qualified public educational facility is any school facility that is:

- Part of a public elementary school or a public secondary school, and
- Owned by a private, for-profit corporation under a public private partnership agreement with a state or local educational agency.

The issuer of the bond should be able to tell the taxpayer whether the bond is tax exempt or not.

## ¶ 38,015   EDUCATION SAVINGS BOND PROGRAM

Beginning in 2005, the amount of the interest exclusion for education savings bond will be phased out (gradually reduced) if the filing status is married filing jointly or qualifying widow(err) and the individual's modified adjusted gross income (MAGI) is between $91,850 and $121,850. The deduction cannot be taken if the MAGI is $121,850 or more. For 2004, the limits that applied were $89,750 and $119,750. For all other filing statuses, is interest exclusion is phased out if the MAGI is between $61,200 and $76,200. The deduction cannot be taken if the MAGI is $76,200 or more. For 2004, the limits that applied were $59,850 and $74,850. Here again, the limits that applied one year are increased the next year, but the figures are released very late in the year.

## ¶ 38,017 BUSINESS DEDUCTION FOR WORK-RELATED EDUCATION

Beginning in 2005:

- If the taxpayer drives a car to and from school and is qualified to deduct transportation expenses, the amount that can be deducted for miles driven from January 1, 2005, through August 31, 2005, was 40 cents per mile. The amount that could be deducted for miles driven from September 1, 2005, through December 31, 2005, was 48 cents per mile. This was up from 37 cents per mile in 2004, and these figures will all undoubtedly be up again for the 2007 tax season.
- If the adjusted gross income for 2005 is more than $145,950 ($72,975 if married filing separately), the itemized deductions may be limited. The deduction will start to phase out when modified AGI exceeds certain amounts.
- If $600 or more of interest was paid on a qualified student loan during the year, the taxpayer will receive a Form 1098e, *Student Loan Interest Statement*, from the financial institution, from a governmental unit (or any of its subsidiary agencies), from educational institutions, or any other person to whom the student loan interest of $600 or more was paid in the course of their trade or business.

## ¶ 38,019 EDUCATION-RELATED ADJUSTMENTS TO INCOME

Taxpayers do not have to itemize deductions on Schedule A to claim the three deductions described below. Each is an adjustment to income on the first page of either Form 1040 or 1040A. These deductions are not available on Form 1040EZ.

### .01 Tuition and Fees Deduction

Most taxpayers with adjusted gross incomes up to $65,000 ($130,000 on a joint return) may deduct up to $4,000 for tuition and fees paid to attend an accredited college, university, or vocational school. Married couples filing separately and individuals who may be claimed as a dependent may not take this deduction.

A taxpayer may not claim both this deduction and a tax credit for education expenses for the same student in one year. Qualifying expenses from a Coverdell ESA, a qualified tuition program, or an education savings bond must be reduced by any nontaxable earnings.

## .03 Student Loan Interest Deduction

Generally, personal interest, other than certain mortgage interest, is not deductible. However, if the modified adjusted gross income (MAGI) is less than $65,000 ($135,000 if filing a joint return), it may be possible to take a deduction for interest paid on a student loan (also known as an education loan) used for higher education. For most taxpayers, MAGI is the adjusted gross income as figured on their federal income tax return before subtracting any deduction for student loan interest. This deduction can reduce the amount of income subject to tax by up to $2,500 in 2005.

This deduction is now available to most taxpayers with incomes up to $65,000, with the deduction amount phasing out as income increases above $50,000. For married couples filing jointly, the phaseout range is from $100,000 to $130,000.

## .05 Tax-Free Scholarships

Although scholarships are usually taxable if they carry a future service requirement, tuition, books, and other equipment paid for by the National Health Service Corps Scholarship Program or the Armed Forces Health Professions Scholarship and Financial Assistance Program are no longer taxed. This benefit does not extend to room and board payments under these programs.

## .07 Deduction for Educator Expenses

Educators who worked at least 900 hours during the school year as a teacher, instructor, counselor, principal, or aide, may deduct up to $250 of qualified out-of-pocket expenses for books and classroom supplies purchased in 2005. It is taken as an adjustment to gross income, rather than as a miscellaneous itemized deduction. If the individual and his or her spouse file jointly and both are eligible educators, the maximum deduction is $500. However, neither spouse can deduct more than $250 of his or her qualified expenses. The deduction is available for those in public or private elementary or secondary schools (including kindergarten). Educators must reduce qualifying expenses by any nontaxable earnings received from Coverdell ESAs, qualified tuition programs, or educational savings bonds.

¶38,019.03

An eligible educator is one who, for the tax year, is a kindergarten through grade 12 teacher, instructor, counselor, principal, or aide, and who works at least 900 hours during a school year in a school that provides elementary or secondary education, as determined under state law.

Although the educator expenses provision was scheduled to expire after 2003, the Working Families Tax Relief Acto of 2004 extended it through 2005.

## .09 Qualified Expenses

Qualified expenses include ordinary and necessary expenses paid in connection with books, supplies, equipment (including computer equipment, software, and services), and other materials used in the classroom. An ordinary expense is one that is common and accepted in your educational field. A necessary expense is one that is helpful and appropriate for your profession as an educator. An expense does not have to be required to be considered necessary.

Qualified expenses do not include expenses for home schooling or for nonathletic supplies for courses in health or physical education.

Qualified expenses must be reduced by the following amounts: Tax-free interest on U.S. series EE and I savings bonds (Form 8815). Tax-free portion of a distribution from a qualified tuition program (QTP). Tax-free portion of a distribution from a Coverdell education savings account (ESA). Any reimbursements you received for these expenses that were not reported to you in box 1 of your Form W-2.

## ¶38,021  529 EDUCATION FUNDS

More than 40 states offer a variety of 529 plans that have been developed to help families save for college expenses. Many of those states offer 10 or 15 variations of plans within the state itself. Regardless, all plans adhere to 529 basic requirements and therefore the earnings are free of federal taxes. These funds are often exempt from state income taxes—but not always. More and more states are taxing earnings of their residents who save in 529s outside their home states. Although these plans are aimed mostly at parents, other relatives can participate in the saving of up to $100,000 a year without paying federal gift and estate taxes. The maximum permitted per beneficiary is up to $300,000 for some state plans.

## .01 Pitfalls to Watch For

Most of the 529 plans fall into one of two categories: either they are plans that financial professionals sell, or they are plans that are sold directly by the state. The majority of plans are sold by financial professionals, and this is no surprise, as it takes a diligent professional to sort through this can of worms.

However, in the states' favor, the costs and fees generated by using a financial advisor can offset any benefit earned by the fund. In addition, 529s purchased through financial professionals often have higher management and maintenance fees than plans purchased from the state, with another fee tacked on if the plan is used sooner than anticipated.

Conversely, with the assistance of a financial planner, the client has a better opportunity to make an informed decision. In addition, with recent rule changes, it is much easier to change from one state's plan to another's, without penalty.

Financial planners should advise clients not to make a 529 plan their sole college savings, but just one part of the portfolio.

It is important to remember that any particular plan's substantial fees and limited investment choices may make 529s less attractive. On the other hand, the federal financial aid formula classifies these savings plans as the *parents'* assets rather than the child's. Some of the vehicle's high fees are offset, because this same financial aid formula counts a child's assets more heavily than the parents' in calculating how much the family can afford to contribute toward his or her education.

## ¶38,023   PREPAID TUITION PLANS

Many states also offer a prepaid tuition plan that permits saving for college via a tax-advantaged investment account. Most prepaid plans are limited to state residents and are not marketed by financial firms, so their scope is not as wide as the 529 tuition provisions arrangements.

Prepaid tuition plans offer major tax benefits. Gains are tax free if they are being used for college tuition. Some states even allow for part of the contribution to be exempt from state income tax. The primary disadvantage is that, although some funds may be used outside of the home state, the funds may not go as far as intended. If a recipient attends a private school, or transfers in to a state university as an out-of-state resident, the funds may not stretch far enough to meet the student's needs. A prepaid tuition plan is just that—prepaid tuition; this money may not be used for housing expenses, books, or supplies. In addition, financial aid may be harder to qualify for, as often scholarships will be reduced based on the amount of money saved within the Prepaid Tuition Plan. Finally, many prepaid programs only have one window of time in which to invest every year.

# PART VII

## Tax Matters

# TAX MATTERS

# Chapter 39

# American Jobs Creation Act and Working Families Tax Relief Act

## CONTENTS

## ¶39,000 OVERVIEW

In October of 2004 President Bush signed two tax laws covering a wide range of issues. Most of the provisions take affect in 2005; a few were retroactive to earlier years, and others scheduled to take effect as late as 2008. Among the moving forces behind the American Jobs Creation Act of 2004 was the need felt by Congress to address certain aspects of the taxation of foreign subsidiaries of domestic corporations as well as to strengthen disincentives for the corporate tax shelter industry. The Working Families Tax Relief Act of 2004 makes a number of technical corrections to previous legislation, unifies a number of items dealing with children, and extends certain provisions that were scheduled to expire. The scope of the two new laws is vast and the purpose of this chapter is to draw attention to a number of their provisions having the most general significance. Many provisions in the new laws relate to highly specialized and technical issues and are beyond the scope of this general overview.

Two additional tax bills were signed into law in August 2005. Both deal with energy conservation and alternative fuels. The provisions of both are very specific and targeted to provide incentives through a number of energy related tax credits. A brief overview is provided at the end of the chapter.

## ¶39,001   BUSINESS TAXPAYERS, DEPRECIATION AND AMORTIZATION

### .01   Extension of Section 179 Expensing Until 2007

The use of the expanded Section 179 expensing election is extended for qualified property placed in service during years beginning after 2002 and before 2008. This provision allows taxpayers to continue immediately writing-off qualifying business property up to $100,000 (indexed for inflation: $105,000 for 2005 and $102,000 for 2004). The deduction is subject to the following limitations and conditions:

1.  If the taxpayer places more than $400,000 (indexed for inflation: $420,000 for 2005 and $410,000 for 2004) of qualified property in service during the year, the $100,000 is reduced dollar for dollar by the amount exceeding $400,000. (If $500,000 or more of qualified property is placed in service, the benefits of Section 179 are fully phased out.)
2.  Taxpayers may now file an amended return to revoke or change an earlier Section 179 election.
3.  The expensing election is now applicable to off-the-shelf computer software.
4.  The full expensing election is no longer available for sport utility vehicles (SUVs) with a gross weight exceeding 6,000 pounds; for these vehicles it is limited to $25,000.
5.  Existing rules concerning the kind of property eligible, the income limitations and the carryover of unused depreciation remain in effect as under prior law.

### .03   Sport Utility Vehicles

As noted earlier in the explanation of the extension of the Section 179 immediate expensing election, a limitation has been placed on SUVs with a gross weight between 6,000 and 14,000 pounds. Only $25,000—and not the full

$100,000 of expensing election—is available for these vehicles. This restriction does not apply to vehicles having a seating capacity of more than nine persons behind the driver's seat, those featuring a 6-foot interior cargo area, or ones possessing an enclosed driver compartment.

## .05  Leasehold Improvements for Nonresidential Business Property

A new 15-year straight-line MACRS depreciation (cost recovery) is mandated for leasehold improvements to the interior of nonresidential business real estate (Section 1250 property). Under the law being replaced, such improvements were depreciable over 39 years, so this is a significant decrease. There are several restrictions on the more rapid depreciation:

1. The improvement must be made to *leased* real estate but not including elevators or escalators, structural components that benefit a common area, general enlargements of a building, or improvements to the internal structural framework.
2. The lessee and lessor may not be related parties, which include members of a controlled group.
3. Improvements eligible are those made after October 22, 2004, and before January 1, 2006, and may be made by either the lessee or the lessor.
4. Depreciation is computed using MACRS straight-line method. To avoid this treatment, an election must be made to use the MACRS alternative depreciation method resulting in straight-line depreciation over a period of 39 years.

## .07  Deduction for Organization and Start-up Costs

An immediate deduction for both start-up and organization costs up to $5,000 is now available for new businesses. Amounts greater than $5,000 are to be amortized over 15 years (180 months). If a business incurs more than $50,000 of start-up or organization costs, the benefit of the $5,000 immediate write-off is phased out on a dollar-for-dollar basis. This change will primarily benefit small businesses and may actually slow down the deduction of these costs for larger businesses—requiring a 15-year rather than a 5-year amortization period.

## ¶39,003  DEDUCTION FOR INCOME FROM DOMESTIC PRODUCTION

In 1984 the beneficial provisions for U.S. exporters qualifying as domestic international sales corporations (DISCs) were replaced with a set of foreign sales corporation (FSC) rules. In 2000 the U.S. modified its treatment of foreign source income further by repealing FSC provisions and replacing them with rules governing extraterritorial income (ETI). In 2004, the American Jobs Creation Act repealed the EIT provisions as well. Each of these changes was prompted by allegations from the World Trade Organization (WTO) and others that the United States was engaging in banned export subsidies.

As a result, the 2004 Act dramatically alters the approach of the United States in encouraging exports. This is done by the introduction of a new deduction relating to U.S. production activities. New Internal Revenue Code (IRC) Section 199 allows a deduction equal to 9 percent (when fully phased in) of the lesser of either "qualified production activities income" or taxable income (determined without regard to this new deduction). This is a deduction without a comparable financial or economic cost to the taxpayer; no additional resources are used up in generating the deduction; in this sense it is analogous to the dividends received deduction for corporations or the statutory depletion allowance.

For 2005 and 2006 the deduction is 3 percent rather than 9, and for 2007 through 2009 it is increased to a 6 percent deduction. Not until 2010 is the full 9 percent deduction available. The key to understanding the benefit provided by this new deduction is found in explicating the meaning of *qualified production activities income*. This income is calculated as follows:

- Isolate a business' gross receipts from domestic production (that is, excluding international production revenue).
- From this gross revenue subtract the cost of goods sold which produced those gross receipts—which must be items produced, manufactured, grown, or extracted in the United States.
- From the resulting gross profit are deducted directly related costs or expenses (for example, sales commissions or bad debts arising from the qualified sales).
- Finally, a deduction is taken for a pro-rata portion of other expenses incurred by the company, although not directly related to its domestic production receipts.

Once the lesser of the qualified production activities income or taxable income is determined, a further limitation is placed on the deduction. It may not be greater than 50 percent of the company's W-2 wages for the year.

The kinds of businesses benefiting from this new deduction are diverse and include those generating domestic production revenue in the form of sales, leases, rentals, exchanges, or other dispositions from:

- Manufacturing taking place in the United States.
- Production taking place in the United States.
- Agriculture grown in the United States.
- Construction performed in the United States.
- Films (qualifying) produced in the United States.
- Electricity generated in the United States (does not apply to revenue from its transmission).

¶39,003

- Natural gas extracted in the United States (does not apply to revenue from its transmission).
- Potable water processed in the United States (does not apply to its distribution).
- Engineering performed in the U.S. for projects to be constructed in the United States.
- Architecture performed in the U.S. for construction to be erected in the United States.
- Natural resource extraction taking place in the United States.

Excluded from the benefits of this deduction are sales by domestic restaurants of food or beverages.

## .01 Illustration of Computing the Deduction

The following table shows how the domestic production deduction is calculated, breaking down totals into their qualified and nonqualified amounts.

|  | Domestic | Nonqualified | Total |
|---|---|---|---|
| Gross receipts | $1,500,000 | $1,000,000 | $2,500,000 |
| Cost of goods sold | 500,000 | 300,000 | 800,000 |
| Gross profit | 1,000,000 | 700,000 | 1,700,000 |
| Costs directly related to domestic production | 200,000 | – | 200,000 |
| Pro-rata nonrelated costs | 100,000 |  | 100,000 |
| All other costs | 200,000 | 400,000 | 600,000 |
| Net income | $500,000 | $300,000 | $800,000 |
| 2005-2006 deduction | × .03 |  |  |
|  | $15,000 |  |  |

If W-2 wages are $28,000, the deduction is limited to 50 percent of this amount or $14,000. Because the deduction is based on the percent of the lesser of the domestic production income or taxable income (excluding the deduction), it will generally be based on the domestic production income unless the company's other income produces a loss. In the above table, if the nonqualified net income had been a loss of $100,000, the company's taxable income would have been only $400,000 and the deduction limited to three percent of this amount or $12,000.

Qualifying production property is limited to:

- Tangible personal property.
- Any computer software.
- Any property described in IRS section 168(f)(4).

The benefits of this deduction are not limited to taxable C corporations but are extended to S Corporations, partnerships, LLCs, sole proprietorships (as a for AGI deduction), estates, or trusts. In applying the rules to pass-through or conduit entities (S corporations, partnerships, and so on) the applicable amounts required to calculate the deduction are passed through as separately stated items on the same basis as other items. Thus the appropriate amount of W-2 wages paid by an S corporation is reported to each shareholder so they may apply the 50 percent limit at the shareholder level. For sole proprietors the limitations on the deduction are applied by substituting "adjusted gross income" for "taxable income." It is not yet clear how the W-2 limit will impact sole proprietorships or partnerships in which only the owners are employed by the business and hence no W-2s are issued.

The beneficial provisions of the old law (FSC/ETI) are phased out as follows: for 2004 taxpayers can claim 100 percent of their FSC/ETI tax benefits; for 2005, 80 percent; for 2006, 60 percent.

The deduction is not limited to businesses that export goods and it is available to offset the alternative minimum tax as well as the regular income tax.

## .03   The *Gulf Opportunity Zone Act of 2005*

The Gulf Opportunity Zone Act of 2005, signed into law in December 2005, as well as regulations proposed by the IRS to clarify certain aspects of Internal Revenue Code section 199 make explicit certain provisions of the domestic production deduction. These clarifications and technical corrections are retroactive to correspond with the coverage of the original law. The proposed IRS regulations indicated that the W-2 wages that are used to determine the deduction limitation may be wages paid by an agent of the employer. This may thus include leased employees if they are common law employees of the taxpayer. However if the labor is subcontracted to another taxpayer, the W-2 wages of that employer would not be included. The W-2 wages are those paid to common law employees of the taxpayer claiming the deduction. Because sole proprietors, partners of a partnership and members of a limited liability company are not issued W-2s for their services, the deduction limit is restricted to common law employees who do receive W-2s.

## .05   Determining Domestic Production Gross Receipts

To avail itself of the domestic production deduction, the taxpayer must determine the portion of its total gross receipts that are "domestic production gross receipts." This is an important issue for manufacturers that produce part of their end product within the U.S. and part in another country. The determination must be made on an item-by-item basis rather than by product line or division revenue.

In its interim guidance to taxpayers, the IRS provides a safe harbor rule for gross receipts. If less than 5% of the taxpayer's gross receipts are attributable to production outside the U.S., the taxpayer may treat all gross receipts as domestic. The taxpayer must use a reasonable method for allocating gross revenue. In making its determination of "reasonableness" the IRS will take into consideration whether the taxpayer is using the most accurate information available to the taxpayer, the relationship between the gross receipts and the base chosen, the accuracy of the method chosen as compared with other possible methods, whether the method is used by the taxpayer for internal management or other business purposes, whether the method is used for other federal, state, or foreign income tax purposes, the time, burden, and cost of using various methods, and whether the taxpayer applies the method consistently from year to year.

A second safe harbor rule is also provided with respect to the requirement that the qualifying revenue must be from items manufactured, produced, grown or extracted in the U.S. Under this rule a taxpayer will be treated as manufacturing, producing, growing or extracting property in whole or in significant part within the U.S. if, in connection with the property, conversion costs (direct labor and related factory overhead) of the manufactured, produced, grown or extracted property are incurred by the taxpayer within the U.S. and the costs account for 20% or more of the total cost of goods sold of the property. An exception to this rule is made for packaging, repackaging, labeling and minor assembly operations, the cost of which should not be included in measuring the 20% of costs.

The Domestic Production Activities Deduction is computed and claimed using IRS form 8903. Owners of pass-through entities will receive information on form K-1 regarding the amount of domestic production income and the amount of related W-2 wages. If a taxpayer has domestic production income from more than one source, the amounts are to be combined and specific rules to be followed in determining the effect of the W-2 limitation.

The domestic production deduction is allocable to computations of Alternative Minimum Tax (AMT) as well as regular tax.

# ¶39,005  CREDIT EXTENSIONS

The following tax credits are extended through the end of 2005.

- Research credit.
- Welfare to work.
- Work opportunity.
- Renewable electricity production.

## ¶39,007 CORPORATIONS

### .01 Brother-Sister Controlled Group—New Modified Definition has Broader Reach

Pairs or groups of small C corporations owned and controlled by five or fewer shareholders have been subject to possible restriction on the use of separate tax brackets, separate exemptions for alternative minimum tax, and separate accumulated earnings credits. This provision of the tax law is intended to prevent corporations from manipulating the corporate graduated tax rates by operating in controlled groups.

The effect of the new law is to broaden the reach of the brother-sister rules. If five or fewer individuals (estates or trusts) own more than 50 percent of the combined voting power or more than 50 percent of the total value of two or more corporations' stock, they are now considered related even if the there is no 80 percent common ownership, as under prior law. This will mean that more corporations with overlapping ownership are required to share tax brackets, AMT exemptions and accumulated earnings retention limits. Pairs or groups of corporations with five or fewer shareholders (individuals, estates, or trusts) that had formerly escaped classification as a brother-sister controlled group by failing the 80 percent common ownership test should now retest their status using only the more than 50 percent common ownership test.

To illustrate this change, consider the following example.

|  | Corporation 1 | Corporation 2 | Identical |
|---|---|---|---|
| Shareholder A | 30% | 40% | 30% |
| Shareholder B | 40% | 30% | 30% |
| Shareholder C | 30% | 0% | 0% |
| Shareholder D | 0% | 30% | 0% |
| > 50% identical ownership test |  |  | 60% |
| 80% common ownership test | 70% | 70% |  |

Five or fewer individuals own corporations 1 and 2. In addition they share 60 percent identical ownership because Shareholders A and B each own at least 30 percent of both corporations. Under the new law the two corporations are part of a brother-sister controlled group. However, the two corporations fail the 80 percent common ownership test, which required the ownership of the individuals controlling greater than 50 percent of the stock to also own 80 percent or more of the two corporations. Under the old law the two corporations would have failed the 80 percent test and not been classified as brother-sister controlled corporations. The result: Tax planning that aimed to limit commonly owned corporations from being taxed as brother-sister corporations may no longer work. All such groups of interrelated corporations should now be reevaluated applying this less stringent test.

## .03  New Corporate Schedule M-3 Reconciliation

Separate from the Jobs Act, the IRS now requires C corporations with net assets in excess of $10 million to complete a new reconciliation schedule with their corporate tax returns. The schedule is an expansion of information provided on Schedule M-1 that reconciles financial statement (accounting or book) income to taxable income reported on page one of the tax return. M-3 is a detailed reconciliation of accounting income to tax return income. Its significance will impact corporations engaging in complex transactions resulting in wide spreads between book and tax income.

## .05  Charitable Donations of Computer Equipment and Technology

In addition to the regular rules regarding charitable contributions of C corporations, a special rule governs the deduction of computers and related technology to educational organizations, tax-exempt entities, public libraries, and certain private foundations. The amount of the deduction is equal to the corporate donor's basis in the property donated plus one-half of the ordinary income potential from the equipment's sale—but not to exceed twice the basis. In the case of inventory the limit amounts to one-half of the expected gross profit were the equipment sold but not more than twice its basis. The rule generally applies to gifts of inventory to be used for the exempt organization's exempt purpose. Thus, donations of computers held in inventory to an education institution must be used in the education process (not resold). This special provision had not been applicable for 2004 contributions but received retroactive extension for 2004 and also applies to corporate donations in 2005.

Generally, when a C corporation makes a noncash charitable contribution in excess of $5,000 it must obtain an appraisal; if the donation exceeds $500,000, the appraisal must be attached to the federal income tax return for the year. But this rule does not apply to donations of inventory or publicly traded securities.

## .07  S-Corporations: Maximum of 100 Shareholders

The number of shareholders allowed before an S Corporation loses its qualifying status is raised by the new law to 100 from the previous 75.

The qualifying types of shareholders remain the same—limiting ownership primarily to individuals. Family members may elect to be treated as one shareholder for purposes of determining the number of shareholders.

## .09  Foreign Tax Matters

Prior to a temporary change in law regarding the income of controlled foreign subsidiaries, such income was taxed only when received by the U.S. parent corporation. A provision of the new law is intended to encourage the repatriation of income from foreign subsidiaries by providing a one year window during which such payments can be offset by a special 85-percent dividends received deduction.

- A temporary 85-percent dividends received deduction is provided for dividends received by U.S. corporations in cash from controlled foreign subsidiaries.
- The amount of the eligible dividend is limited to $500 million.
- A dividend must be determined "extraordinary" which means it must exceed the amount of past dividends measured during a base period.
- The temporary period is generally 2004 or 2005. The law specifies the applicability of the deduction to either dividends received during the first tax year beginning on or after the date of the law's enactment (2005) or during the last tax year beginning before the date of enactment (2004).
- Eligibility for the deduction in contingent on the existence of a domestic reinvestment plan. This is the corporation's plan to invest the proceeds of the dividend in the United States.
- The temporary 85 percent dividends received deduction is taken in lieu of the normal dividends received deduction (70 percent, 80 percent, or 100 percent).
- The effective tax rate for the repatriated dividends is 5.25 percent (the 15 percent of the dividend that is taxable times the top corporate rate of 35 percent).

*Foreign Tax Credit.*   The limitation under prior law allowing no more than 90 percent of the Alternative Minimum Tax (AMT) to be offset by the foreign tax credit is repealed beginning in 2005. The new law also enables taxpayers to apply the exchange rate in effect when foreign taxes are paid, rather than the average exchange rate for the year, when translating the amount of foreign taxes paid into U.S. dollars. This is a tax election made by the taxpayer and is binding for subsequent tax years unless permission is granted by the IRS to revert to the average rate.

*Allocation of Interest on a Worldwide Basis.*   A change not taking effect until 2008 will allow a U.S. parent corporation and its subsidiaries to elect to use a worldwide basis for purposes of allocating interest expense between foreign source and U.S. source taxable income. The result will be to treat the parent and subsidiaries as if they were one corporation for purposes of allocating interest expense paid to third parties. Internal Revenue Code Section 864(f)(1) specifies that at worldwide affiliated group means a group consisting of the includible members of an affiliated group and all controlled foreign corporations in which such members in the aggregate meet the ownership requirements.

The worldwide allocation for domestic members of the worldwide affiliated group is to be made by subtracting the total interest expense of all foreign members of the affiliated group from the amount resulting from multiplying the total interest expense of the worldwide affiliated group by the ratio which the foreign assets of the worldwide affiliated group bears to all the assets of the affiliated group.

The allocation formula is:

[(Worldwide interest expense × Foreign assets) ÷ Worldwide assets] − Interest expense of all foreign corporations in affiliated group = Amount of interest used to compute the taxable income of the domestic members from sources outside the United States.

## .11 Deferred Compensation

*No Federal Income Tax Withholding or FICA or FUTA Tax on Statutory Stock Options.* *Statutory stock options* also known as *qualified stock options*—including incentive stock options (ISOs) and employee stock purchase plan (ESPP) options—generally have the benefit of deferring income for the employee receiving the option. The income is the spread between the option price and the fair market value of the underlying stock. When a qualified stock option is granted to an employee, the receipt or exercise of the option is not treated as a taxable event. Tax is due when the employee sells the stock realizing a capital gain. However, ordinary income is generated for the employee-recipient when there is a disposition of the option before the required holding period or employment provisions of the plan are met. Such a disposition is referred to as a "disqualifying disposition." Although such a disposition generates ordinary income for the employee and is reportable on their W-2, the IRS no longer requires withholding of federal income taxes or FICA or the payment of FUTA on the value of these options. This rule is effective for stock acquired pursuant to statutory options exercised after October 22, 2004.

*New Rules on Nonqualified Deferred Compensation Plans.* Nonqualified deferred compensation plans are those failing to meet the specific legal requirements of qualified deferred compensation plans (IRC Section 401). Such qualifications include, for example, strict antidiscrimination rules against favoring owners or highly compensated executives. Nonqualified plans generally allow a deduction by the employer of the deferred compensation only in the year the employee is required to recognize and pay tax on the amount deferred.

¶39,007.11

In contrast, qualified deferred compensation plans generally allow a current deduction for the employer as funds are set aside for employees, yet employees are not required to report these amounts in income until later received.

The goal of many nonqualified plans has been to mirror the benefits of qualified plans by creating a deferral of income to the employee through reliance on specific Internal Revenue Code sections. The new law establishes certain operational and design features for nonqualified plans. The result for plans failing to meet these new requirements will be immediate recognition of income deferred in the current and previous years plus interest and penalties.

Employers and employees with existing nonqualified plans should have them reviewed because the likelihood of noncompliance with the new law is great. For example, the new law allows distributions from nonqualified plans only under specific conditions:

- Separation from service.
- Disability of the employee.
- Death of the employee.
- A change in ownership or effective control of the corporation.
- Occurrence of an unforeseeable emergency.
- A specified time under the plan—specified at the time of the deferral.

These conditions, set out in new IRC Section 409A, have the effect of limiting the discretion the employer or employee may exercise in distributing the deferred compensation. Current plans allowing distributions under conditions other than these would therefore be in violation of the new law—resulting in the loss of deferral. In addition, the new law prohibits a plan from allowing an acceleration of benefits to an employee. Other specific plan requirements relate to performance based compensation and offshore property in trust.

One of the keys to the deferral of nonqualified deferred compensation has been a substantial risk of forfeiture of the compensation. Employees receiving deferred compensation were allowed to defer the income as long as its actual or constructive receipt was subject to a substantial risk of forfeiture. The new law defines *substantial risk of forfeiture* in this way: "The rights of a person to compensation are subject to a substantial risk of forfeiture if such person's rights to such compensation are conditioned upon the future performance of substantial services by any individual."

## .13   Donations to Charity

The donation of a patent or other intellectual property to a charitable organization is now limited to the smaller of its fair market value on the date of donation or the donor's basis. The donor is allowed to take an additional charitable deduction based on a specific percentage of income the donee receives with respect to the donated property. In addition, C corporations making donations of property other than cash, inventory, or publicly traded securities, must now obtain appraisals when the value of the charitable deduction exceeds $5,000.

## ¶39,009  PARTNERSHIPS

### .01  Built-in Loss Rules Tightened to Curb Abuse of Duplicate Loss Deductions

Contributions of property to partnerships by partners can produce built-in losses where the partner's basis of the property contributed exceeds its fair market value. The transfer of a partnership interest involving a substantial built-in loss (defined as basis exceeding fair market value by more than $250,000) now requires a mandatory IRC Section 743 basis adjustment reducing the property's basis to the partnership to its fair market value, thus preventing loss recognition when the property is sold.

The following discussions highlight rules for specific industries.

### .03  Agribusiness

*Income Averaging and AMT.*  Farmers are allowed income averaging using a three-year period to smooth out the tax consequences of profitable and unprofitable years. The income averaging rules for farmers have now been coordinated with the alternative minimum tax (AMT) rules preventing the beneficial effects of income averaging from producing a greater exposure to the AMT. This is accomplished by a separate computation of the regular tax without the benefits of averaging, and only the excess of the AMT over this tax, rather than over the tax computed using income averaging is charged. This provision was effective beginning in 2004.

*Involuntary Conversion Replacement Period.*  The replacement period for involuntary conversions resulting from forced sales of livestock has been extended from two years under prior law to four years. The rule prevents the necessity of recognizing realized gains caused by early, unplanned sales of livestock. The allowable causes of such involuntary conversions have also been expanded from soil or other environmental contamination to weather-related conditions, including droughts and floods. In addition, the replacement rules have been liberalized in certain cases to allow replacement of livestock with farm machinery and equipment or farm real estate.

## .05 Commercial Fishermen

The income averaging provisions previously available to farmers have now been extended to commercial fishermen. The averaging available allows spreading the income of more profitable years over less profitable years potentially reducing the marginal tax rates and resulting in an overall tax savings. The new rules apply only to fishermen engaged in the business of fishing. This provision is effective beginning in 2004.

## .07 Private Debt Collection Agencies

The IRS is now allowed to enlist the aid of private debt collection services (PDCs) in attempting to collect back taxes. Like the IRS, PDCs may offer installment payment plans to delinquent taxpayers.

## .09 Railroads

*Credit for Track Repair.* Small and mid-sized railroads (Class II and Class III) are the beneficiaries of a new tax credit to encourage track repair. The credit is equal to 50 percent of the amount expended on track repairs, up to a maximum of $3,500 per mile of track owned or leased by the railroad. The track repair expenditures eligible for the credit must be made between January 1, 2005, and December 31, 2007. The repairs included may be to track, roadbeds, bridges, and other related items. In addition to the railroads themselves, the credit is available to persons who transport property using the track facilities of Class II and III railroads. Class II railroads are those with annual operating revenue of up to $250 million but not less than $20 million, whereas Class III railroads have operating revenue of $20 million or less. Once earned, the credit may be carried forward as part of the general business credit for up to 20 years, offsetting taxes due on a dollar-for-dollar basis.

*Diesel Fuel Tax Reduction.* The 4.3 cents per gallon excise tax formerly imposed on diesel fuel used by trains is scheduled to be phased out and eventually eliminated. The phase-out period includes reductions to 3.3 cents per gallon for the first six months of 2005 and 2.3 cents for the last half of the year. Total phase-out will be completed by January 1, 2007.

## .11 REITs

For purposes of the rule limiting real estate investment trusts (REITs) to holding no more than 10 percent of the value of the outstanding securities of a single issuer, the definition of "straight debt" is modified, providing more flexibility than under prior law. The new law also provides a safe-harbor rule regarding the testing dates applied in determining whether 90 percent of a REIT's property is rented to unrelated persons.

## .13  Renewable Electric Energy Production

A credit is provided for the domestic production of electricity using three technologies: (1) wind energy, (2) closed-loop biomass, and (3) poultry waste. The date for these facilities to be placed in service to be eligible for the credit has been extended through 2005. For 2004 the amount of the credit was computed as the product of 1.8 cents multiplied by the kilowatt-hours of electricity sold by the taxpayer.

## .15  Restaurants

Improvements to restaurant buildings made after October 22, 2004, but before January 1, 2006, are eligible for special MACRS 15-year straight-line depreciation (formerly 39 years were required). This change applies to "qualified restaurant property," defined as improvements to a building (section 1250 property) if more than 50 percent of the building's square footage is used for serving and preparing meals for on-premise consumption by customers. The building being improved must have been in existence at least three years prior to the improvements being made. This provision is automatic and not elective; if a longer depreciation period is preferred, taxpayers may elect to use the MACRS alternative depreciation system which mandates straight-line depreciation over 39 years. Because the new law specifies improvements to a building, it excludes improvements to sidewalks or exterior signs, for example.

## .17  Tax Practitioners

The regulation of tax practitioners by the IRS is provided in IRS *Circular 230*. Its rules prescribe who may represent taxpayers before the IRS and the limits of appropriate conduct. Failure to comply can result in suspension of practice before the IRS. The new law adds to the list of enforcement sanctions, censure of tax advisors, and monetary penalties. The function of the additional enforcement tools is to discourage tax practitioners who are involved in the design or marketing of tax shelters.

## .19  Tax Shelter Advisors/Promoters

The new law defines a category of tax shelter advisors referred to as *material advisors* and stipulates strict reporting requirements regarding their tax shelter activities. A material advisor is defined as any person who provides, for remuneration, any material aid, assistance, or advice with respect to organizing, managing, promoting, selling, implementing, insuring, or carrying out any reportable transaction. A *reportable transaction* refers to a tax avoidance mechanism or tax shelter involving $50,000 in the case of an individual (natural person) or $250,000 in the case of a corporation or other taxpayer other than a natural person. Tax shelters are generally understood as transactions in which the tax benefits to the taxpayer during the first five years are twice the amount of the investment made.

In addition, material advisors are required to maintain a list identifying clients or customers to whom advice was provided regarding reportable (tax shelter) transactions.

## ¶39,011    INDIVIDUALS

### .01    Itemized Deduction for Sales Tax

The law now allows a potential deduction for state sales taxes incurred during the year in lieu of a deduction for state income taxes. Itemized deductions have previously included state income taxes, but not all states impose this tax. The new law allows taxpayers to choose to deduct either their sales taxes paid or state income taxes. The sales tax computation may be made either by saving receipts or by using an IRS-supplied table that relates sales tax to income. Local county and city sales taxes may be included, as well as the sales tax on certain large-ticket items such as automobiles.

### .03    Extension of Child Tax Credit of $1,000

The $1,000 credit allowed per qualifying child under age 17 is extended through 2009.

### .05    Uniform Definition of Child: "Qualifying Child"

Various provisions of the Internal Revenue Code dealing with children have been subsumed under a new uniform definition of a child. Previously different definitions of child were applied for different purposes. The new definition of a qualifying child applies, for example, to children in determining

1. The dependency exemption.
2. The child tax credit.
3. Head-of-household status.
4. Earned income credit.
5. The dependent care credit.

¶39,011

The tests for a qualifying child include:

- Relationship.
- Domicile.
- Age.

For the dependency exemption, for example, this streamlines the prior five-test determination:

- Relationship for qualifying child: daughter, son, stepdaughter, stepson, sister, brother, stepsister, stepbrother, half-sister, half-brother, or a descendent of one of these individuals (grandchild, niece, nephew). The relationship test is also met for an adopted child or an authorized foster child.
- The child is qualifying only if he or she had the same principal place of abode as the taxpayer for more than one-half of the taxable year.
- A qualifying child must be under age 19—unless he or she is a full-time student—in which case the child must be less than age 24. A disabled child, however, is exempt from the age requirement. The age requirement for the child tax credit remains at under age 17 and under age 13 for the dependent care credit.

The new rules incorporate the realities of many contemporary domestic relations. As a result, it was necessary to establish a number of tie-breaking rules in which a child might be considered a qualifying child by more than one adult in the household. These rules hold as follows:

- If more than one adult could otherwise claim a qualifying child, a parent trumps the other(s).
- If both parents are living apart and could claim the qualifying child, the one with whom the child lived the longer period during the year predominates. Should the child have lived with both parents for an *equal* period of time, the parent with the greater AGI is allowed to claim the qualifying child.
- If two nonparents could each claim the qualifying child, the one with the highest AGI prevails.

As a result of these changes, the law no longer automatically awards the exemption for a child of divorced parents to the custodial parent. The new law adds, as one test for claiming the exemption, the specific wording of the divorce decree awarding the exemption to the noncustodial parent. Without this wording the noncustodial parent may not claim the child; with the wording, the noncustodial parent is entitled to the exemption if the support, residency and other requirements of Internal Revenue Code Section 152(e)(1) are met.

¶39,011.05

This chart may help to simplify the new dependency rules.

|  | Qualifying Child | Qualifying Relative or Member of Household |
|---|---|---|
| Relationship | Son, daughter, stepson, stepdaughter, brother, sister, stepbrother, stepsister, half brother, half sister or a descendent of one of these, for example grandchildren, nephews, nieces, (not cousins), adopted child, foster child (with exceptions). Note:Because more than one taxpayer may qualify to claim a given child, tie breaking rules allow first priority to a parent, then to the parent with most days of custody for the year, then higher AGIs have priority over lower AGIs. | A relative need not be member of the household; a member of household need not be relative, but must live in the household for the entire year. In addition to the relatives listed under *qualifying child* are added: father, mother, stepfather, stepmother, uncle, aunt, son-in-law, daughter-in-law, father-in-law, mother-in-law, brother-in-law, sister-in-law, grandfather, grandmother—relationships formed by marriage continue after divorce (exception for ex-spouse one year rule). A cousin is not a relative and would have to qualify as member of household. |
| Age | Must be under age 19 or, if full time student, under age 24 (exception for disabled child). | Only important for child of taxpayer who must be under age 19 or under 24 if full-time student because the income requirement is waived (may earn any amount). A child over these ages may still qualify as relative or member of household but is subject to the income test. |
| Support | No specific support calculation —but must live in home of taxpayer claiming child as a dependent for more than half the year. For a taxpayer to claim the child it is not necessary to prove they provided more than half of the support. But if the child is self-supporting (where the | The taxpayer claiming the dependent must provide more than half of the support for the individual. Amounts earned by the individual but saved are not counted in determining support. Support includes payments for room and board, insurance, and capital goods used only by the dependent. |

| | | |
|---|---|---|
| | child supplies more than half of his or her own support) the child does not qualify. | |
| Domicile | Must have same principal place of abode as the taxpayer for more than half of the year. Temporary absences for education or illness do not count against the half year residency. | If not a relative, must live in the taxpayer's house for the entire year. |
| Joint return | A married qualifying child may not file a joint return with a spouse. An exception is made if the couple owes no tax, is not required to file a return, and is only filing to receive a refund of withheld taxes. | A married qualifying child may not file a joint return with a spouse. An exception is made if the couple owes no tax, is not required to file a return, and is only filing to receive a refund of withheld taxes. |
| Gross income | No gross income test—unless child is self-supporting, in which case he or she is not a qualifying child. See Support above. | May not exceed amount of personal exemption except for children under 19 or children who are full time students and under age 24. |
| Citizenship or residence | Must be U.S. citizen, U.S. resident, or a resident of Mexico or Canada for some part of the year.Exception for adopted child who need not meet the general rule above is his or her principal place of abodc is with a U.S. citizen. | Must be U.S. citizen, U.S. resident, or a resident of Mexico or Canada for some part of the year. Exception for adopted child who need not meet the general rule above if his or her principal place of abode is with a U.S. citizen. |

## .07  Donated Vehicles, Boats, and Airplanes

An individual who makes a charitable donation of a vehicle, boat, or airplane claiming the value to exceed $500 is now subject to restrictions depending on how the charity uses the asset. If the charity sells the asset to raise cash without using it in its operations, the donor's itemized charitable deduction is limited to the amount of proceeds received by the charity.

## .09  National Health Services Corps Loan Repayments

Healthcare professionals participating in the National Health Services Corps Loan Program receive educational loans that may be forgiven if the professionals provide medical services within specified geographical areas. Prior law required the loan repayments made on behalf of participants

¶39,011.09

(forgiveness of the loans) to be included in gross income; the new law excludes such repayments from gross income and from subjection to employment taxes.

## .11  Individuals Who Terminate Long-Term Residency or U.S. Citizenship

Individuals who terminate long-term residency or U.S. citizenship after June 3, 2004, are subject to new regulations aimed at thwarting evasion of U.S. taxes. Affected individuals are now subject to an alternative tax regime for 10 years following their termination of residency or relinquishment of citizenship. An exemption is provided for taxpayers whose average net income tax for the preceding five years was not greater than $124,000 and whose net worth does not exceed $2 million, or for certain dual-citizenship individuals. During the 10-year period subject taxpayers are required to file an annual return with the IRS even if they owe no federal income tax. Failure to comply with the annual return requirements subjects taxpayers to an annual $5,000 penalty.

## .13  Tax Deductibility of Interest on Home Mortgage

The Bankruptcy Abuse Prevention and Consumer Protection Act, signed into law on April 20, 2005 by President Bush, contains an income tax provision dealing with the deductibility of interest on home mortgages. Generally, the deduction is only limited if the acquisition debt exceeds $1 million for a personal residence (other limits apply to second mortgages and equity loans). The new law places a further limit on the deductibility of home mortgage interest if the mortgage exceeds the fair market value of the personal residence. The new rule stipulates that "in any case in which the extension of credit exceeds the fair market value (as defined under the Internal Revenue Code of 1986) of the dwelling, the interest on the portion of the credit extension that is greater than the fair market value of the dwelling is not tax deductible for federal income tax purposes."

Although this change may affect only a few taxpayers, those who will feel its pinch are homeowners in areas of the country that have recently seen home prices take off—those who are perhaps experiencing the warning signs of a housing bubble. Should prices in the hot housing markets reverse, highly leveraged property owners could find themselves "upside-down," owing more than their home is worth. The interest on the mortgage debt that exceeds their home's value will be nondeductible.

## ¶39,012  PENSION PROTECTION ACT OF 2006 TAX CHANGES FOR INDIVIDUALS

The Pension Protection Act of 2006 made a number of changes in the area of charitable giving. The changes are generally effective after August 17, 2006.

¶39,011.11

## .01  IRA Distributions to Charity

The law change provides taxpayers a new option for making charitable donations. The law change allows distributions directly from IRAs (regular or Roth) to a qualified charity. The amount distributed in this way is not taxed although no deduction is allowed for the donation either. The annual limit on direct IRA distributions to charity is $100,000. The use of this direct distribution can provide a tax savings to taxpayers whose itemized deductions are partially phased out or those for whom a taxable distribution would place them in a higher tax bracket. Also for taxpayers age 70 1/2 who are required to make annual distributions from their IRAs the option allows them to make the distribution directly to a charity. This option is available for 2006 and 2007.

## .03  Donations of Clothing and Household Goods

For donations of clothing and household goods with a value of less than $500 the new law places a floor on quality of what is donated. The new law provides that no deduction is allowed for a charitable contribution of clothing or household items unless these items are in good used condition or better. Further, the IRS is authorized to deny a deduction for certain items that by their nature have limited value including used socks and underwear.

## .05  Recordkeeping for Cash Contributions

The provision requires that in the case of a charitable contribution of money, regardless of the amount, the donor must maintain a cancelled check, bank record or receipt from the donee organization showing the name of the donee organization, the date of the contribution, and amount of the contribution.

## ¶39,013  TWO NEW TAX ACTS BECOME LAW

In response to higher oil prices, and with no immediate relief in sight, Congress passed two bills containing tax incentives promoting alternative fuels and energy savings for both individuals and businesses. *The Energy Tax Incentives Act of 2005* and the *Safe, Accountable, Flexible, Efficient Transportation Act of 2005* were both signed into law by President Bush on August 8, 2005. The new laws attack the problem of U.S. dependency on foreign oil through a number of mechanisms, most involving tax credits. Some of the more notable provisions include the following:

- A list of substances comprising alternative fuels is provided including: liquefied petroleum gas, compressed or liquefied natural gas, liquefied hydrogen, liquid fuels derived from coal, and liquid hydrocarbons derived from biomass.

- A tax credit is made available on the retail sale of alternative fuels of 50 cents per gallon.

- A tax credit for 30 percent of the cost of installing a clean-fuel vehicle refueling properties is available for costs incurred after 2005.

- Two new credits are provided to encourage investment in qualified advanced clean-coal projects.

- A 50 percent tax credit is provided for investment in qualified liquid fuel refineries. This applies to new refineries that meet the requirements of applicable environmental laws.

- For independent oil producers who are otherwise eligible for percentage depletion (rather than only cost depletion), the limitation on the amount of depletion deductible each year has been liberalized.

- Qualified hydropower production facilities are added to the list of qualified energy resources used to produce electricity, thereby becoming eligible for the renewable electricity production credit.

- In the area of motor vehicles, new credits are instituted to provide incentives for the production of qualified fuel cell motor vehicles, advanced lean burn technology motor vehicles, qualified hybrid motor vehicles, and new qualified alternative fuel motor vehicles.

- To increase the energy efficiency of personal residences, a new home-builder's credit is established for energy-efficient homes. A credit is provided, as well, for certain energy saving home improvements made by homeowners.

- For businesses, a 10 percent credit is allowed for certain types of energy properties, including solar equipment used to generate electricity that is used for heating or cooling the facilities of the business.

- The energy research credit is expanded.

## ¶39,015   END-OF-YEAR IRS CHANGES

### .01   Mileage Allowance

In response to higher crude oil prices, and consequently higher prices at the pump, the IRS increased the business mileage allowance from 37.5 in 2004 to 40.5 for the first eight months of 2005 and then to 48.5 cents a mile for the last four months of 2005. The 15 cents a mile allowed for medical travel and moving expense was also increased to 22 cents a mile for September 1 to December 31 of 2005. The 14 cents per mile allowed for providing services for charitable organizations is set by statute and has not been changed. It is up to Congress rather than the IRS to make any adjustment.

¶39,015

## .03   Accommodations for Hurricane Victims

In the aftermath of Hurricane Katrina, the IRS has announced certain accommodations for residents of the "presidentially declared" disaster areas of Louisiana (64 parishes), Mississippi (52 counties), Alabama (6 counties), and Florida (11 counties). In addition, the IRS announced that it would "work with" taxpayers living outside of these specific areas if their accountants or their books and records are (were) located within the disaster area. A special IRS phone number is provided for victims of Hurricane Katrina: 1-866-562-5227.

For most income tax returns (individual or business) for declared hurricane victims due on or after August 29, 2005, the due date has been extended to January 3, 2006. This would include individual 1040s with extensions until October 17, as well as corporations with returns having regular or extended due dates falling within that period. No special forms or permits are required to request this relief. For individuals, the third quarter estimated tax payment, due on September 15, 2005, is extended until January 3, 2006, for people in the Katrina disaster area. The due date for payroll tax deposits for business is also extended, but only until September 23, 2005, — if the deposit was originally due on or after August 29, 2005. For employers with qualified pension and profit sharing plans, the IRS and the Department of Labor's Employee Benefits Security Administration as well as the Pension Benefit Guarantee Corporation have combined to extend certain due dates for plan contributions and for filing form 5500.

## .05   Casualty Loss Provisions

Existing casualty loss rules apply to taxpayers located in the "presidentially declared" disaster area. Specifically, these rules allow taxpayers meeting certain threshold requirements to deduct casualty losses occurring in 2005 either on their 2005 income tax returns or on their 2004 returns. If the hurricane victim's 2004 return has already been filed, it may be amended to claim the value of any deduction, potentially resulting in a refund. In measuring the amount of a casualty loss, taxpayers must follow IRS calculation guidelines in terms of overall income limitations for individuals, and in terms of measuring the decrease in value of the affected property after factoring in any insurance reimbursement.

Before deciding between taking the deduction in 2004 or 2005, a determination should be made of the difference in income between the two years. Since the amount of a casualty loss for an individual is limited to the amount that exceeds 10 percent of adjusted gross income, any significant difference in the AGI from 2004 to 2005 may affect the benefit of the deduction. This difference should be weighted against the timing of the potential refund of 2004 taxes and the potential savings on the 2005 return. If filing an amended 2004 return is hindered by the loss of the taxpayer's copy of that return, a copy may be requested from the IRS at no cost by filing IRS Form 4506 and writing "Hurricane Katrina" in red at the top of the form. Special consideration may also be provided by the IRS to affected individuals who are contacted regarding the collection of past due taxes.

## .07 Leave Donation Program

To encourage donations to the hurricane relief efforts, the IRS has announced that employees may chose to donate vacation, sick, or personal leave. In exchange for this contribution, the employer will make a contribution of the cash value of the benefits the employees forgo to a qualified, tax-exempt organization providing relief for the Hurricane Katrina victims. The employer must make these cash payments before January 1, 2007. Employees will not be required to include the value of the donated leave in gross income, but employers will be allowed a deduction of the cash payments.

## .09 On-going Disaster Relief Provisions

In a related matter, organizations recently formed for the purpose of aiding in the hurricane relief efforts, and seeking tax-exempt status from the IRS will be accorded an expedited review and approval process. To benefit from this accommodation, the organization should write on the top of IRS Form 1023 "Disaster Relief, Hurricane Katrina." The IRS has indicated that its efforts to provide accommodations to individuals and businesses affected by Hurricane Katrina are on-going and that the IRS website may be consulted for any additional measures that may be provided in the future.

Generally, for individuals, contributions to tax-exempt charitable organizations are limited to 50 percent of the taxpayer's adjusted gross income. Any excess amount may be carried over for a period of up to five years. The new law removes the 50 percent limitation for all cash donations to a charitable organization for the period beginning on August 28, 2005, and ending on December 31, 2005. The provision also exempts those donations from the application of the phase-out of itemized deductions for high-AGI taxpayers. A taxpayer must elect to have contributions treated as qualified contributions under these provisions. This provision does not require a connection with Hurricane Katrina.

# Chapter 40

# Federal Bankruptcy—2005 Changes and Federal Tax Aspects

## CONTENTS

## ¶40,000 OVERVIEW

This chapter covers basic principles of bankruptcy and federal income tax aspects of a bankruptcy filing for corporations, partnerships, and for individuals. The discussion does not provide detailed coverage of the tax rules for complex corporate bankruptcy reorganizations or other highly technical and legal aspects of business and individual bankruptcy proceedings. Competent professional advice should be obtained for the highly complex bankruptcy law.

Bankruptcy proceedings begin with a decision by the attorney for the debtor regarding the appropriate "Chapter" under which a petition for bankruptcy is filed with the U.S. Bankruptcy Court. The filing of the petition produces a stop to the collection activities of the creditors (*automatic stay*) and creates a bankruptcy estate, consisting of all the assets of the person or business filing the bankruptcy petition.

## ¶40,001  TYPES OF BANKRUPTCIES

The various chapters by which bankruptcies are referred are chapters of the *Bankruptcy Code*, Title 11 of the U.S. Code. Chapter 7, for example, deals with bankruptcies requiring liquidation of the debtor's assets and satisfaction of liabilities with the proceeds. In such cases an individual's assets and debts are turned over to a *bankruptcy trustee* who, under the guidance of a plan of liquidation and with the supervision of the Bankruptcy Court judge, disposes of the assets and makes equitable payment to the creditors. In this most drastic form of bankruptcy, the debtor is generally allowed to exempt specific items based on federal or state law. These items vary in kind and value from state to state but often include the debtor's homestead and certain personal property. One function of such a proceeding, as in all bankruptcy matters, is to protect the debtor from further collection efforts by the creditors and to see that creditors are paid according to their rights under the law rather than in terms of their size or the aggressiveness of their collection efforts.

Bankruptcy cases originally filed under one chapter of the Bankruptcy Code may be converted to another chapter if there is a need to do so and the requirements for such conversion are met. Thus, a case originally filed under Chapter 7 may be converted to Chapter 11, 12, or 13. Chapter 11 bankruptcies are reorganizations of a debtor's financial affairs effected in such a way as to use the debtor's existing assets to generate revenue to pay the creditors—but not necessarily the original amounts owed nor in compliance with the original terms of the debts when incurred.

Corporations as well as individuals may file for bankruptcy protection under Chapter 11—for individuals it is sometimes referred to as the "rich man's bankruptcy." In the case of a corporation or other business, the daily operations of the business may be taken over by a bankruptcy trustee or in other cases left in the hands of the owners or management, referred to *debtor-in-possession*. Bankruptcies may be voluntary, in which case they are initiated by the debtor, or involuntary, in which case they are filed by a group of creditors. A case originally filed under Chapter 11 may be converted to Chapter 7.

Under whichever chapter of the Bankruptcy Code a petition for bankruptcy is filed, the process is overseen and under the jurisdiction of the U.S. Bankruptcy Court. In each case as well, a trustee carries out the necessary mechanics of the proceeding, and both the creditors' and debtor's rights regarding the bankruptcy are enforced.

Creditors' claims are categorized in a hierarchical scheme beginning with priority claims, listed here in descending priority order:

1. Payroll (trust fund) taxes.
2. Court-ordered child care and maintenance payments and administrative expenses of the bankruptcy estate.

3. Secured debt (creditor has lien against debtor's assets).
4. Unsecured debt, which is further subdivided.

Chapter 12 bankruptcies deal with the adjustments of debts of a family farmer with regular annual income. A case originally filed under Chapter 12 may be converted to Chapter 7. Like Chapter 11, Chapter 12 does not involve a liquidation of assets but rather the continuation of a business and structured payments of its debts. Under such a plan future earnings of the farmer are allocated for payment of debt in a manner overseen by the trustee and the court.

Chapter 13 bankruptcy is an adjustment of debts of an individual with regular income (wage earner, self-employed or retiree with pension or other regular income). Eligibility includes a limit on the amount of unsecured debt (that is not contingent or in dispute), which may not exceed $100,000. Like Chapters 11 and 12, future income is allocated, via a plan overseen by a trustee of the court, to the payment of debts over a specified period up to five years. If the debtor is self-employed, the business is the source of future income and is continued under the supervision of the court. A case originally filed under Chapter 13 may be converted to Chapter 7 for liquidation of the bankruptcy estate or Chapter 11 if unsecured debt exceeds $100,000.

For a number of years Congress has been aware of the increasing number of bankruptcy filings and specific abuses of the system, but not until 2005 was it able to complete a package of reforms that became law on April 20, 2005, when President Bush signed the Bankruptcy Abuse Prevention and Consumer Protection Act.

## ¶40,003    2005 BANKRUPTCY ABUSE PREVENTION AND CONSUMER PROTECTION ACT

The new law generally becomes effective on October 17, 2005, 180 days after its signing. Notable exceptions to the effective date are limits on the homestead exemption, which are effective immediately, and the requirement for audits of certain Chapter 7 and 13 cases, which does not begin until 18 months after the enactment (both discussed below). The new law is intended to fight abuses to the bankruptcy process, and it focuses attention on the intent and timing of transactions entered into by individual debtors before their filing for bankruptcy as well as abuses caused by the same debtors repeatedly filing for protection under the bankruptcy laws. As the amount of U.S. consumers' debt continues to increase, the changes in the law could impact significant numbers of debtors in the future.

At the bill's signing President Bush proclaimed, "Our bankruptcy laws are an important part of the safety net of America. They give those who cannot pay their debts a fresh start. Yet bankruptcy should always be a last resort in our legal system. If someone does not pay his or her debts, the rest of society ends up paying them. In recent years, too many people have abused the bankruptcy laws. They've walked away from debts even when they had the ability to repay them. This has made credit less affordable and less accessible, especially for low-income workers who already face financial obstacles. . . . By restoring integrity to the bankruptcy process, this law will make our financial system stronger and better. By making the system fairer for creditors and debtors, we will ensure that more Americans can get access to affordable credit." The majority of changes made by the law apply to individual rather than corporate debtors.

## .01  Mandatory Credit Counseling and Debtor Education

Under the new law, within 180 days prior to filing for bankruptcy protection, an individual debtor must receive credit and budget counseling from an approved (by the U.S. bankruptcy trustee) nonprofit credit counseling agency. Upon completion of the counseling, the debtor is required to file with the Bankruptcy Court a certificate from the credit counseling agency describing the services provided along with the debt management plan developed as the result of such counseling. This provision applies to Chapter 7, 11, 12, and 13 filings. A requirement for the approval of nonprofit credit counseling agencies is that they provide their services for a fee that is not contingent on the debtor's ability to pay. Exceptions are provided to these rules in the case of emergencies and for debtors who are incapacitated or disabled.

In the case of a Chapter 13 filing the court will not grant the discharge of debt until the debtor has completed a course in personal financial management as approved by the Bankruptcy Trustee.

## .03  Production of Tax Returns and Other Documents

Among new petition filing requirements for individual debtors seeking bankruptcy protection are the following:

- Recent pay stubs—"copies of all payment advices or other evidence of payment received within 60 days before the filing."
- A calculation of net monthly income remaining after essential expenses are paid—referred to as *current monthly income.*
- Evidence that the debtor was given an informational notice required by the new law.
- A calculation of reasonably anticipated increases in income or expenses during the 12-month period following the date of the filing of the petition.
- Current federal, state, and local income tax returns and, in the case of Chapter 13 filings, evidence that all applicable tax returns that were due

within the preceding four years were filed with the appropriate taxing body.

- A Chapter 13 plan will not be confirmed until the debtor certifies that all postpetition domestic support obligations (child support and maintenance) are current. Past due domestic support obligations owed directly to a family member are classified as *priority claims* and must be paid in full; such obligations paid to a government agency may be paid in less than the full amount due.

## .05  New Means Testing for Chapter 7 Bankruptcy

The individual debtor's "state median income" is now an important threshold for qualifying under Chapter 7. This is the median income in the debtor's state of residence as reflected in U.S. Census Bureau data. In the case of debtors whose income exceeds this amount, abuse of the bankruptcy system is presumed, and the trustee or any creditor may bring a motion to dismiss the bankruptcy proceeding. The calculation of the threshold involves a five-year (60-month) calculation that effectively compares the debtor's condition to that of a Chapter 13 filer.

The calculation of the debtor's income begins with a determination of one month's current gross income (for example, take-home pay) based on a look-back to the most recent six-month period. This income excludes Social Security Act payments and certain payments to victims of war crimes or payments to victims of international or domestic terrorism. From this income is subtracted 1/60 of the secured debt payments scheduled during the following 60 months. From this remainder is subtracted the equivalent of one month's priority debts (the total amount of priority payments due in the next five years, divided by 60).

The amount of monthly expenses allowed by the IRS in its offers-in-compromise and other delinquent tax payment negotiations (living expenses not including debt payments) is then subtracted, along with the monthly amount of certain other allowed expenses (for example: payments for the care of an elderly, chronically ill, or disabled household member). If the debtor's actual monthly expenses are less than the IRS allowance, the lower actual amount is used.

If the remainder (the *current monthly income*) is less than $100, the Chapter 7 case may go forward; there is no automatic presumption of abuse. If the current monthly (net) income is $100 or more per month (after above deductions), the debtor is presumed abusive and the case may be dismissed or, with the consent of the debtor, converted to a Chapter 11 or 13 bankruptcy. The new law provides that such Chapter 13 cases will generally involve a five-year debt payment plan and require annual financial statements to be prepared and filed with the U.S. Bankruptcy Court or trustee.

¶40,003.05

An exception to the above abuse presumption (current monthly income of more than $100) exists if the debtor's unsecured debt exceeds $24,000 and the remaining net income after deducting the items listed above is sufficient to pay 25 percent of this unsecured debt during a five-year period.

If the current monthly (net) income after allowed deductions is $150 or more, abuse is presumed unless the debtor has more than $36,000 of unsecured debt. And if the current monthly (net) income is $166.67 ($2,000 per year or, for five years, $10,000) then abuse is presumed unless the unsecured debt is greater than $39,998.40. The finding of abuse is a presumption and may be rebutted; but the presumption of abuse is grounds for the Court's dismissal of the bankruptcy case.

If the debtor's income is less than the state median, the Court may still determine abuse, but the creditors no longer have standing to file a motion for dismissal. Abuse can be alleged for a number of separate reasons, including previous recent bankruptcy filings, fraudulent asset conveyances, bad faith in presenting or failing to present documentation, or incurring debt for luxury items shortly before filing. Under prior law fraud was presumed if a debtor charged on a credit card luxury goods of $1,225 or more shortly before filing for bankruptcy; the new law reduces the presumption threshold to $500. A similar adjustment is made with cash advances from a credit card where the presumed fraud limit is reduced from $1,225 to $750.

The yardstick used for determining the debtor's income for testing against the state's median income is the National Standards and Local Standards issued by the IRS for the area in which the debtor lives. Allowed in the calculation of monthly expenses are amounts for health and disability insurance, as well as payments to a health savings account. In contrast to the otherwise Spartan levels of IRS sanctioned expenses, the new law also allows the debtor's monthly costs to include "actual expenses for each dependent child less than 18 years of age, not to exceed $1,500 per year per child, to attend a private or public elementary or secondary school."

Other expenses deductible in arriving at the current monthly income include:

- Certain additional home energy costs.
- Expenses of administering a Chapter 13 plan.
- Certain expenses for protection from family violence.
- 1/60 of all secured debt and priority debt due in the succeeding five years.

An exception is provided to the means test if the debtor is a disabled veteran if the debt "occurred primarily during a period during which he or she was on active duty or performing a homeland defense activity." No discharge is allowed under the new law of fraudulent taxes in Chapter 11 or 13 cases and certain student loans are also barred from discharge.

**¶40,003.05**

Median state income will be determined from U.S. Census Bureau data adjusted for increases in the Consumer Price Index (CPI). The data will reflect the size of the family unit. In a joint filing for bankruptcy, both spouses' income is included in the determination. It appears that the means test, applying U.S. Census Bureau data for gross annual income and Internal Revenue Service data for monthly allowed expenses—resulting in a net income—will require considerable coordination in applying the triggering thresholds for presumed abuse (such as the greater than $100 current monthly income). Either the allowed IRS expenses must be annualized and grossed-up to arrive at annual gross income, or the gross income will have to be converted to monthly net income by applying the IRS allowed deductions.

In addition to the formal means test applied to determine abuse on the part of the debtors, abuse and consequent dismissal of Chapter 7 cases may also result from a finding by the U.S. trustee, bankruptcy administrator, or Court that the debtor filed for bankruptcy in bad faith.

## .07  Extended Time Between Debt Discharges

Preempting the Biblical admonition to forgive our debtors every seven years, the new law, in the case of Chapter 7 bankruptcy filings, extends the period for new filings to eight years if the debtor has previously received a discharge of debt in a Chapter 7 or Chapter 11 case. (Prior law specified six years.) For debtors filing under Chapter 13, who had previously filed under Chapters 7, 11, or 12, the waiting period to file a new petition is now four years; if the previous filing was under Chapter 13, the waiting period is two years. Limited exceptions are provided.

## .09  Homestead Limitations

A controversial area of bankruptcy law is the state *homestead exemption*. This is the value of the debtor's equity in his or her personal residence, which amount varies greatly from one state to another. The state homestead exemption protects the debtor's interest in his or her personal residence from creditor claims. Although federal bankruptcy law generally allows state homestead exemptions for the debtor's state of residence, the new law places limits on the amount of the exemption in certain cases. Under the new law, if a debtor has increased the value of his or her home's equity—the amount qualifying for state homestead exemption—by more than $125,000 during the 1,215 days prior to the bankruptcy filing, the amount greater than $125,000 is excluded from the state exemption amount.

In addition, if the debtor has been convicted of a felony or owes a debt from the violation of federal or state securities laws or racketeering or fiduciary fraud or crimes or intentional torts causing serious bodily injury or death during the five years preceding the bankruptcy filing, a limit of $125,000 is placed on the amount of homestead exemption available to the debtor. An exception is made if the homestead is "reasonably necessary for the support of the debtor and any dependent of the debtor"—for example, a family farm.

## .11   Limitations on an Automatic Stay

To curb the abuse of frequent bankruptcy filings, through which abusers gain the benefit of the automatic stay from collections, the new law stipulates that for any Chapter 7, 11, or 13 case filed within one year of the dismissal of an earlier case, generally the automatic stay for the new filing will terminate after 30 days. An exception is provided if the debtor can establish that the new case is filed in good faith. If a second filing occurs within a one-year period, the automatic stay will not take affect at all.

## .13   Limitation on Items Available for Discharge

Certain items of debt—most notably income taxes but including debt induced by fraud, embezzlement, or breach of fiduciary duty—have traditionally been beyond the scope of discharge. The new law expands this list of items to include student loans, debt for certain luxury purchases and cash advances (described above), debt incurred in violation of securities fraud laws (this provision is effective retroactively to July 30, 2002—the effective date of the Sarbanes-Oxley Act) and certain homestead exemption amounts. In addition, to discourage debtors from shopping for the states with the largest exemptions, the new law specifies that the debtor's state of residence for exemption purposes is the state in which the debtor resided for the 730 days prior to filing.

## .15   Exclusion from Bankruptcy Estate Property

The assets in the bankruptcy estate are those that may be used to liquidate the debtor's liabilities. Certain items, like the amount of the homestead exemption, fall outside this category. To assets that may not be used for discharging debt, the new law adds amounts deposited to an educational retirement account more than 365 days prior to the bankruptcy filing. These amounts are set aside to pay for the education of a child or grandchild of the debtor. The amount contributed prior to the 365 days may not be more than $5,000.

## .17   Enhanced Disclosures Under an Open-End Credit Plan

Attacking the causes of consumer credit problems from the perspective of consumer education, the new law establishes a series of consumer warnings to appear on the consumer's bill. "In the case of an open end credit plan that requires a minimum monthly payment of not more than 4 percent of the balance on which finance charges are accruing, the following statement, located on the front of the billing statement, disclosed clearly and conspicuously: 'Minimum Payment Warning: Making only the minimum payment will increase the interest you pay and the time it takes to repay your balance. For example, making only the typical 2-percent minimum monthly payment on a balance of $1,000 at an interest rate of 17 percent would take 88 months to repay the balance in full. For an estimate of the time it would take to repay our balance, making only minimum payments, call this toll-free number: XXXXXX.' (the blank space to be filled in by the creditor.''

A similar minimum payment warning is also required for open-end credit plans that require a minimum monthly payment of more than 4 percent. In certain cases the toll-free number will be a number at the Federal Trade Commission.

## .19 Tax Deductibility of Interest on Home Mortgage

Deductibility of interest on a home mortgage is generally only limited if the acquisition debt exceeds $1 million. The new law places a further limit on deductibility of home mortgage interest if the mortgage exceeds the fair market value of the personal residence. The new rule stipulates that ''in any case in which the extension of credit exceeds the fair market value (as defined under the Internal Revenue Code of 1986) of the dwelling, the interest on the portion of the credit extension that is greater than the fair market value of the dwelling is not tax deductible for Federal income tax purposes.'' The new law modifies the Truth in Lending Act to include a requirement that advertisements relating to home mortgage lending include a warning that interest on the balance of the mortgage in excess of fair market value is not tax deductible.

Although this change may affect only a few taxpayers, those who will feel its pinch are homeowners in areas of the country that have recently seen home prices take off—those who are perhaps experiencing the warning signs of a housing bubble. Should prices in the hot housing markets reverse, highly leveraged property owners could find themselves ''upside-down,'' owing more than their home is worth. The interest on the mortgage debt that exceeds their home's value will be nondeductible.

## .21 Pro-Creditor Provisions

If the changes described so far are seen as negatives for debtors, the glass is definitely half-full for creditors. Sprinkled through the above changes limiting the abusive actions of debtors are pro-creditor provisions. Creditors have increased powers to move for the dismissal of a bankruptcy filing. The rules limiting the ability of debtors to repeatedly file for bankruptcy, thus enjoying the benefits of the automatic stay on collections, give more control to creditors. The antifraud provisions and the presumption of abuse by debtors whose income exceeds their state median income are further evidence of the benefits accruing to business from the new law.

## .23 New CPA Practice Area

Beginning 18 months after the enactment of the new bankruptcy provisions, 0.4 percent of individual Chapter 7 and 13 cases will be selected randomly for audit, as well as other cases "which reflect greater than average variances from the statistical norm of the district in which the schedules were filed." Such variances include higher income or greater expenses than the statistical norm for that district. The audits are to be conducted by Certified Public Accountants or Licensed Accountants. Specific auditing standards are to be developed for use in these audits. CPAs interested in more information about such work should contact the U.S. Attorney General's office, which has been directed to develop the applicable audit standards.

## ¶40,005 FEDERAL TAX ASPECTS OF BANKRUPTCY

Bankruptcy proceedings begin with the filing of a petition with the U.S. Bankruptcy Court. The filing of the petition creates a bankruptcy estate, which consists of all the assets (with certain exceptions) of the person filing the bankruptcy petition.

Note: A *person* in the tax law is an individual, a trust, estate, partnership, association, company, corporation, an officer or employee of a corporation, a member or employee of a partnership who is under a duty to surrender the property or rights to property to discharge the obligation.

Just as a separate taxpayer is created upon the death of a taxpayer, the taxpayer's estate, a separate taxable entity is created when a petition is filed by an individual under Chapter 7 or Chapter 11 of the Bankruptcy Code—the bankruptcy estate. The tax obligations of the person filing a bankruptcy petition, the debtor, vary depending on the bankruptcy chapter under which the petition is filed.

## .01 Individuals in Chapter 7 or Chapter 11 Proceedings

For an individual debtor who files for bankruptcy under Chapter 7 or Chapter 11 of the Bankruptcy Code, a separate estate is created consisting of property that belonged to the debtor before the filing date. This bankruptcy estate is a new taxable entity, completely separate from the debtor as an individual taxpayer. The estate, under a Chapter 7 proceeding, is represented by a trustee. The trustee is appointed by the U.S. Bankruptcy Court to administer the estate and liquidate the *nonexempt assets* of the debtor. In a Chapter 11 case either the debtor remains in control of the assets as a debtor-in-possession or the bankruptcy court will appoint a trustee who will take control of the assets.

## .03  The Bankruptcy Estate

The individual debtor must file income tax returns during the period of the bankruptcy proceedings; the income, deductions, or credits belonging to the separate bankruptcy estate should not be included. Also, the debts canceled because of bankruptcy should not be included in the debtor's income; as explained below, the bankruptcy estate must reduce certain losses, credits, and the basis in property, to the extent of these items by the amount of canceled debt. The debtor has the option of ending the tax year on the date before the bankruptcy petition is filed. This allows the tax due on the short-period return to be a claim on the bankruptcy estate.

If a bankruptcy case begins, but is later dismissed by the bankruptcy court, the estate is not treated as a separate entity and the debtor is treated as if the bankruptcy petitions had never been filed. When this occurs, the debtor files an amended return (Form 1040X) to replace any returns previously filed that should include items of income, deductions, or credits that were or would have been reported by the bankruptcy estate on its returns and were not reported on individual returns previously filed.

## .05  Transfer of Assets to the Estate

All of the debtor's legal and equitable interests initially become property of the estate, and certain property can subsequently become exempt from the estate. A transfer, other than by sale or exchange of an asset from the debtor to the bankruptcy estate, is not treated as a disposition for income tax purposes. This means that the transfer does not result in gain or loss, recapture of deductions or credits, or acceleration of income or deductions. The transfer of an installment obligation, for example, to the estate would not accelerate gain under the rules for reporting installment sales. When the bankruptcy estate is terminated, the debtor is treated the same as the estate was regarding any assets transferred back to the debtor.

The Bankruptcy Abuse prevention and Consumer Protection Act of 2005 added to the items included in the estate, in the case of Chapter 11 filings, all property that "the debtor acquires after the commencement of the case but before the case is closed, dismissed, or converted" as well as "earnings from services performed by the debtor after the commencement of the case but before the case is closed, dismissed, or converted."

¶40,005.05

The individual debtor cannot carry back any net operating loss or credit carryback from a year ending after the bankruptcy case has begun to any tax year ending before the case began. The estate, however, can carry the loss back to offset any prebankruptcy income.

## .07 Election to End the Tax Year

If an individual debtor has assets, other than those exempt from the bankruptcy estate, the debtor can choose to end his or her tax year on the day before the filing of the bankruptcy case. Then the tax year is divided into two short tax years of fewer than 12 months each. The first year ends on the day before the filing date, and the second year begins with the filing date and ends on the date the tax year normally ends. Once made this choice cannot be changed. Any income tax liability for the first short tax year becomes an allowable claim arising before bankruptcy against the bankruptcy estate. If the tax liability is not paid in the bankruptcy proceeding, the liability is not canceled because it can be collected from the debtor as an individual. If the debtor does not choose to end the tax year, then no part of his or her tax liability for the year in which bankruptcy proceedings began can be collected from the estate.

If married, the debtor's spouse can also join in the choice to end the tax year, only if the two file a joint return for the first short tax year. These choices must be made by the due date for filing the return for the first short tax year. Once the choice is made, it cannot be revoked for the first year, but the choice does not mean that they must file a joint return for the second short tax year.

If the debtor's spouse files for bankruptcy later in the same year, he or she can also choose to end his or her tax year, regardless of whether he or she joined in the choice to end the debtor's tax years. Because each of the two has a separate bankruptcy estate, one or the other of them can have three short tax years in the same calendar year. If the debtor's spouse had joined in his or her choice, or if the debtor had not made the choice to end his/her tax year, the debtor can join in his or her spouse's choice. But if the debtor had made an election and his or her spouse did not join in the election, the debtor cannot join in the spouse's later election. This is because the debtor and spouse, having different tax years, could not file a joint return for a year ending on the date before the spouse's filing of bankruptcy.

## .09 Employer Identification Number

The trustee or the debtor-in-possession must obtain an employer identification number (EIN) for a bankruptcy estate if the estate must file any form, statement, or document with the IRS. The trustee uses the EIN on any tax return filed for the bankruptcy estate including estimated tax returns. The Social

Security number of the individual debtor cannot be used as the EIN for the bankruptcy estate.

## .11  Determination of the Estate's Tax

The gross income of the bankruptcy estate includes any of the debtor's gross income to which the estate is entitled under the bankruptcy law. The estate's gross income also includes any income the estate is entitled to and receives or accrues after the beginning of the bankruptcy case. Gross income of the bankruptcy estate does not include amounts received or accrued by the debtor before the bankruptcy petition date.

The bankruptcy estate can deduct or take as a credit any expenses it pays or incurs, the same way that the debtor would have deducted or credited them had he or she continued in the same trade, business, or activity and actually paid or accrued the expenses. Allowable expenses include administrative expenses, such as attorney's fees and court costs.

The bankruptcy estate figures its taxable income the same way as individuals figure their taxable income. The estate can take one personal exemption and either individual itemized deductions, or the basic standard deduction for a married individual filing a separate return. The estate cannot take the higher standard deduction allowed for married persons filing separately who are 65 or older, or blind. The estate uses the rates for a married individual filing separately to figure the tax on its taxable income.

Bankruptcy law determines which of the debtor's assets become part of the bankruptcy estate. These assets are treated the same in the estate's hands as they were in the debtor's hands.

When the bankruptcy estate is terminated, any resulting transfer other than by sale or exchange of the estate's assets back to the debtor is not treated as a disposition. The transfer does not result in gain or loss, recapture of deductions or credits, or acceleration of income or deductions to the estate.

## .13  Determination of Tax—Corporations

A bankrupt corporation—or a receiver, bankruptcy trustee, or assignee having possession of, or holding title to, substantially all the property or business of the corporation—files a Form 1120 for the tax year. After the return is filed, the Internal Revenue Service can redetermine the tax liability shown on the return. When the administrative remedies with the Service have been exhausted, any remaining tax issues can be litigated either in the bankruptcy court or in the U.S. Tax Court.

The trustee of the bankruptcy estate can request a determination of any unpaid liability of the estate for the taxes incurred during the administration of the case by the filing of a tax return and a request for such a determination with

¶40,005.13

the IRS. Unless the return is fraudulent or contains a material misrepresentation, the trustee, the debtor, and any successor to the debtor are discharged from liability for the taxes upon payment of the taxes:

- As determined by the IRS.
- As determined by the bankruptcy court, after the completion of the IRS examination.
- As shown on the return if the IRS does not notify the trustee within 60 days after the request for the determination that the return has been selected for examination.
- As shown on the return, if the IRS does not complete the examination and notify the trustee of any tax due within 180 days after the request or any additional time permitted by the bankruptcy court.

To request a prompt determination of any unpaid tax liability of the estate, the trustee must file a written application for the determination with the IRS District Director for the district in which the bankruptcy case is pending. The application must be submitted in duplicated executed under the penalties of perjury. The trustee must submit with the application an exact copy of the return(s) filed by the trustee with the IRS for a completed tax period, and a statement of the name and location of the office where the return was filed. On the envelope must be written: *Do Not Open in Mail Room.*

The IRS examination agent will notify the trustee within 60 days from receipt of the application whether the return filed by the trustee has been selected for examination or has been accepted as filed. If the return is selected for examination, it will be examined as soon as possible. The examination function will notify the trustee of any tax due within 180 days from receipt of the application, or within any additional time permitted by the bankruptcy court.

## .15 Discharge of Unpaid Tax

Debts are divided into two categories: dischargeable and nondischargeable. *Dischargeable debts* are those that the debtor is no longer personally liable to pay after the bankruptcy proceedings are concluded. *Nondischargeable debts* are those that are not canceled because of the bankruptcy proceedings. The debtor remains personally liable for their payment.

There is no discharge for the individual debtor at the termination of a bankruptcy case for taxes for which no return, a late return, or a fraudulent return was filed. Claims against the debtor for other taxes predating the bankruptcy petition by more than three years can be discharged. If the IRS has a lien on the debtor property, the property can be seized to collect discharged tax debts.

If the debtor completes all payments under a Chapter 13 debt adjustment plan for an individual with regular income, the court can grant a discharge of debts, including priority debts (described above). If the debtor fails to complete all payments under the plan, the taxes are not discharged although the court can grant a discharge of other debts in limited circumstances.

If a debt is canceled or forgiven, other than as a gift or bequest, the debtor must include the canceled amount in gross income for tax purposes. A debt includes any indebtedness for which the debtor is liable or which attaches to property the debtor holds. However, a canceled debt should not be included in gross income if any of the following situations applies:

- The cancellation takes place in a bankruptcy case under the U.S. Bankruptcy Code.
- The cancellation takes place when the debtor is insolvent.
- The canceled debt is qualified farm debt incurred in operating a farm.
- The canceled debt is qualified real property business indebtedness, i.e.; debt connected with business real property.

If a cancellation of debt occurs in a Chapter 11 bankruptcy case, the bankruptcy exclusion takes precedence over the insolvency, qualified farm debt, or qualified real property business indebtedness exclusions. To the extent that the taxpayer is insolvent, the insolvency exclusion takes precedence over qualified term debt or qualified real property business indebtedness exclusions.

A bankruptcy case is a case under Chapter 11 of the U.S. Code, but only if the debtor is under the jurisdiction of the court and the cancellation of the debt is granted by the court or occurs as a result of a plan approved by the court. None of the debt canceled in a bankruptcy case is included in the debtor's gross income in the year canceled. Instead certain losses, credits, and basis of property must be reduced by the amount of excluded income, but not below zero. These losses, credits, and basis in property are called *tax attributes*.

A debtor is insolvent when and to the extent that his or her liabilities exceed the fair market value of the debtor's assets. The liabilities and the fair market value of assets are determined immediately before the cancellation of a debt to determine whether the debtor is insolvent and the amount by which he or she is insolvent. Gross income debt canceled when insolvent is excluded, but only up to the amount of the insolvency. The amount excluded must be used to reduce certain tax attributes.

## .17   Tax Attributes

Certain deduction and credit carryovers and elections that the debtor made in earlier years are taken over by the bankruptcy estate when the petition is filed. These include carryovers of deductions, losses, and credits, the debtor's method of accounting, and the basis and holding period of assets, referred to as tax attributes.

When the estate is terminated, the debtor assumes any remaining tax attributes that were taken over by the estate as well as any attributes arising during the administration of the estate. The bankruptcy estate's income tax returns are open upon written request for inspection by the individual debtor. The disclosure is necessary so that the debtor can properly figure the amount and nature of the tax attributes, if any, that the debtor must assume when the bankruptcy estate is terminated. In addition, the debtor's income tax returns for the year the bankruptcy case begins and for earlier years are open to inspection by or disclosure to the bankruptcy estate's trustee.

## .19 Reduction of Tax Attributes

If a debtor excludes canceled debt from income because it is canceled in a bankruptcy case or during insolvency, he or she must use the excluded amount to reduce certain tax attributes. Tax attributes include the basis of certain assets and the losses and credits listed below. By reducing these tax attributes, taxes on the canceled debt are in part postponed instead of being entirely forgiven. This prevents an excessive tax benefit arising from the debt cancellation.

If a separate bankruptcy estate was created, the trustee or debtor-in-possession must reduce the estate's attributes by the canceled debt, but not below zero.

The amount of canceled debt is used to reduce the tax attributes in the order listed below. However, the debtor can choose to use all or a part of the amount of canceled debt to first reduce the basis of depreciable property before reducing the other tax attributes.

Reduction of tax attributes is managed in the sequence described next.

*Net Operating Loss.*   NOLs are handled in this order:

1. Any net operating loss for the tax year in which the debt cancellation takes place.
2. Any net operating loss carryover to that tax year.

*General Business Credit Carryovers.*   Any carryovers to or from the tax year of the debt cancellation of amounts used to determine the general business credit are reduced.

*Minimum Tax Credit.*   Any minimum tax credit that is available at the beginning of the tax year following the tax year of the debt cancellation is reduced. This only applies to debt canceled in tax years beginning after 1993.

*Capital Losses.*   Any net capital loss for the tax year of the debt cancellation, and any capital loss carryover to that year are reduced.

*Basis.*    The basis (see the discussion below) of the debtor's property is reduced. This reduction applies to the basis of both depreciable and nondepreciable property.

*Passive Activity Loss and Credit Carryovers.*    Reduce any passive activity loss or credit carryover from the tax year of the debt cancellation. This applies to debt canceled in tax years beginning after 1993.

*Foreign Tax Credit.*    Any carryover to or from the tax year of the debt cancellation of an amount used to determine the foreign tax credit or the Puerto Rico and other possessions' tax credits is reduced.

Except for the credit carryovers, the tax attributes are reduced one dollar for each one dollar of canceled debt that is excluded from income. The credit carryovers are reduced by 33½ cents for each dollar of canceled debt that is excluded from income. The required reductions in tax attributes are to be made after figuring the tax for the year of the debt cancellation. In reducing net operating losses and capital losses, the loss for the tax year of the debt cancellation is reduced first, and then any loss carryover to that year in the order in which the carryovers are taken into account for the tax year of the debt cancellation.

In an individual bankruptcy under Chapter 7 (liquidation) or Chapter 11 (reorganization) of the U.S. Code, the required reduction of tax attributes must be made to the attributes of the bankruptcy estate, a separate taxable entity resulting from the filing of the case. Also, the trustee of the bankruptcy estate must make the choice of whether to reduce the basis of depreciable property first before reducing other tax attributes.

## .21 Basis Reduction

If any amount of the debt cancellation is used to reduce the basis of assets, the following rules apply to the extent indicated.

The reduction in basis is to be made at the beginning of the tax years following the tax year of the debt cancellation. The reduction applies to property held at that time.

*Bankruptcy and Insolvency Reduction Limit.*    The reduction in basis because of canceled debt in bankruptcy or in insolvency cannot be more than the total basis of property held immediately after the debt cancellation, minus the total liabilities immediately after the cancellation. This limit does not apply if an election is made to reduce basis before reducing other attributes.

*Exempt Property Under Chapter 11.*    If debt is canceled in a bankruptcy case under Chapter 11, no reduction is made in basis for property that the debtor treats as exempt property.

*Election to Reduce Basis First.*    The estate in the case of an individual bankruptcy under Chapter 7 or 11 can choose to reduce the basis or depreciable property before reducing any other tax attributes. This reduction of the basis of depreciable property cannot be more than the total basis of depreciable property held at the beginning of the tax year following the tax year of the debt cancellation.

Depreciable property means any property subject to depreciation, but only if a reduction of the basis will reduce the amount of depreciation or amortization otherwise allowable for the period immediately following the basis reduction. The debtor may choose to treat as depreciable property any real property that is stock in trade or is held primarily for sale to customers in the ordinary course of trade or business. The debtor must make this choice on the tax return for the tax year of the debt cancellation, and once the choice is made, he or she can only revoke it with IRS approval. If the debtor establishes reasonable cause, he or she can make the choice with an amended return or claim for refund or credit.

An election should be made to reduce the basis of depreciable property before reducing other tax attributes as well as the election to treat real property inventory as appreciable property. If any basis in property is reduced and is later sold or otherwise disposed of again, the part of the gain that is attributable to this basis reduction is taxable as ordinary income. The ordinary income part can be figured by treating the amount of the basis reduction as a depreciation deduction. A determination is made of what would have been straight-line depreciation as though there had been no basis reduction for debt cancellation.

## .23 Attribute Carryovers

The bankruptcy estate must treat its tax attributes the same way that the debtor would have treated them. These items must be determined as of the first day of the debtor's tax year in which the bankruptcy case begins. The bankruptcy estate gets the following tax attributes from the debtor.

1. Net operating carryovers.
2. Carryovers of excess charitable contributions.
3. Recovery of tax benefit items.
4. Credit carryovers.
5. Capital loss carryovers.
6. Basis, holding period, and character of assets.
7. Method of accounting.
8. Passive activity loss and credit carryovers.
9. Unused at-risk deductions.
10. Other tax attributes as provided in regulations.

¶40,005.23

Certain tax attributes of the estate must be reduced by any excluded income from cancellation of debt occurring in a bankruptcy proceeding. If the bankruptcy estate has any tax attributes at the time it is terminated, they are assumed by the debtor.

## .25  Bankruptcy Court Jurisdiction

The bankruptcy court has authority to determine the amount or legality of any tax imposed on the debtor for the estate, including any fine, penalty, or addition to the tax, whether or not the tax was previously assessed or paid.

The bankruptcy court does not have authority to determine the amount or legality of a tax, fine, penalty, or addition to taxes contested before and finally decided by a court administrative tribunal of competent jurisdiction before the date of filing the bankruptcy petition. Also, the bankruptcy court does not have authority to decide the right of the bankruptcy estate for a tax refund until the trustee of the estate properly requests the refund from the IRS and either the Service determined the refund or 120 days pass after the date of the request.

If the debtor has already claimed a refund or credit for an overpayment of taxes on a properly filed return or claim for refund, the trustee can rely on that claim. Otherwise, if the credit or refund was not claimed by the debtor, the trustee can make the request by filing the appropriate original or amended return or form with the District Director in the district in which the bankruptcy case is pending. For overpayment of taxes of the bankruptcy estate incurred during the administration of the case, the trustee can use a properly executed tax return form as a claim for refund or credit.

The IRS examination agent, if requested by the trustee or debtor-in-possession, examines the appropriate amended return, claim, or original return filed by the trustee on an expedited basis, and completes the examination and notify the trustee of its decision within 120 days from the date of filing of the claim.

## .27  Employment Tax

The trustee or debtor-in-possession in a Chapter 11 case must withhold income and Social Security taxes and file employment tax returns for any wages paid by the trustee or debtor, including wage claims paid as administrative expenses. Until these employment taxes are deposited as required by the IRS, they should be set apart in a separate bank account to ensure that funds are available to satisfy the liability. If the employment taxes are not paid as required, the trustee can be held personally liable for payment of the taxes.

The trustee has the duty to prepare and file Form W-2, "Wage and Tax Statement," in connection with wage claims paid by the trustee, regardless of whether the claims accrued before or during bankruptcy. If the debtor fails to prepare and file Form W-2 for wages paid before bankruptcy, the trustee should instruct the employees to file an IRS Form 4852, Substitute for Form W-2.

The debtor's income tax returns for the year the bankruptcy case begins and for earlier years are, upon written request, open to inspection by or disclosure to the trustee. If the bankruptcy case was not voluntary, disclosure cannot be made before the bankruptcy court has entered an order for relief, unless the court rules the disclosure is needed for determining whether relief should be ordered.

## .29 Statute of Limitations for Collection

In a Chapter 11 bankruptcy case, the period of limitations for collection of taxes—10 years after assessment—is suspended for the period during which the IRS is prohibited from assessing or collecting, plus 6 months thereafter.

## .31 Passive and At-Risk Activities

For bankruptcy cases beginning on or after November 9, 1992, passive activity carryover losses and credits and unused at-risk deductions are treated as tax attributes that the debtor passes to the bankruptcy estate and the estate passes back to the debtor when the estate terminates. Transfers to the debtor, other than by sale or exchange, of interests in passive or at-risk activities are treated as exchanges that are not taxable. These transfers include the return of exempt property to the debtor and the abandonment of estate property to the debtor. If a bankruptcy case begins before November 9, 1992, and ends on or after that date, the debtor and the trustee for an individual Chapter 7 case and the debtor-in-possession for a Chapter 11 case can elect to have these provisions apply. In a Chapter 7 case, the election is made jointly by the debtor and the trustee of the bankruptcy estate. In a Chapter 11 case, the election is incorporated in the bankruptcy plan.

The bankruptcy estate is allowed a deduction for administrative expenses and any fees or charges assessed to it. These expenses are deductible as itemized deductions subject to the 2 percent floor on the miscellaneous itemized deductions. Administrative expenses attributable to the conduct of a trade or business by the bankruptcy estate or the production of the estate's rents or royalties are deductible in arriving at adjusted gross income.

The expenses are subject to disallowance under other provisions of the Internal Revenue Code, such as disallowing certain capital expenditures, taxes, or expenses relating to tax-exempt interest. These expenses can only be deducted by the estate, never by the debtor.

If the administrative expenses of the bankruptcy estate are more than its gross income for the tax year, the excess amount can be carried back three years and forward seven years. The amounts can only be carried back or forward to a tax year of the estate, never to the debtor's tax year. The excess amount to be carried back or forward is treated like a net operating loss and must first be carried back to the earliest year possible.

The bankruptcy estate can change its accounting period tax year once without getting IRS approval. This allows the trustee of the estate to close the estate tax year early, before the expected termination of the estate. The trustee can then file a return for the first short tax year to a quick determination of the estates tax liability. If the bankruptcy estate itself has a net operating loss, separate from any losses passing to the estate from the debtor under the attribute carryover rules, the bankruptcy estate can carry the loss back not only to its own earlier tax years but also to the debtor's tax years before the year the bankruptcy case began. The estate can also carry back excess credits, such as the business credit, to the prebankruptcy years.

# Chapter 41

# Depreciation

## CONTENTS

## ¶41,000 OVERVIEW

Depreciation is an accounting and tax convention used to write-off the cost or other basis of long-lived assets, generally over more than one year. In the case of financial accounting, the purpose of depreciation is to match the expense of the assets against the revenue generated by their use on the income statement and to reflect wear and tear, age, deterioration, and obsolescence on the balance sheet. In the case of tax depreciation, it is a statutory method of expensing the basis of assets and is an integral part of the federal government's fiscal policy.

The Job Creation and Worker Assistance Act of 2002 and the Jobs and Growth Tax Relief Reconciliation Act of 2003 both made significant changes to first year bonus depreciation rules. The American Jobs Creation Act of 2004 extended some of these changes and modified others. These changes are detailed at the end of this Chapter.

## ¶41,001  TYPES OF PROPERTY

To determine if property may produce a depreciation deduction, the property must be classified as either tangible or intangible.

**Tangible property** is property that can be seen or touched. There are two main types of tangible property, real property, such as land, buildings, and generally anything built or constructed on land, growing on land, or attached to the land; and personal property including cars, trucks, machinery, furniture, equipment and anything that is not real property.

**Intangible property** is generally any property that has value but cannot be seen or touched. It includes items such as computer software, copyrights, franchises, patents, trademarks, and trade names. Generally, if the cost of intangible property is to be written off over a number of years the straight line method of amortization is used. It allows for the same amount of amortization each year.

In general, only the owner using the property for business or for producing income may claim depreciation or amortization.

Only property meeting all the following requirements may be depreciated.

1. It must be used in business or held to produce income.
2. It must be expected to last more than one year. In other words, it must have a useful life that extends substantially beyond the year it is placed in service.
3. It must be something that wears out, decays, gets used up, becomes obsolete, or loses its value from natural or economic causes.

## ¶41,003  WHAT CANNOT BE DEPRECIATED

Property placed in service and disposed of in the same year may not be depreciated.

### .01  Tangible Property

The following are types of tangible property that cannot be depreciated, even though they are used in business or held to produce income.

1. The cost of land may not be depreciated because land does not wear out, become obsolete, or get used up. The cost of land generally includes the

cost of clearing, grading, planting, and landscaping, because these expenses are all part of the cost of the land itself.

2. Inventory is any property held primarily for sale to customers in the ordinary course of business and may not be depreciated.

3. Generally, containers are part of inventory and cannot be depreciated.

4. Leased property may be depreciated only if the incidents of ownership for the property are retained. Leased property to use in business or for the production of income cannot be depreciated because the incidents of ownership are not retained. A lessor generally can depreciate its cost even if the lessee has agreed to preserve, replace, renew, and maintain the property. However, if the lease provides that the lessee is to maintain the property and return to the lessor the same property or its equivalent in value at the expiration of the lease in as good condition and value as when leased, the cost of the property may not be depreciated.

   "Incidents of ownership" include the legal title, the legal obligation to pay for it, the responsibility to pay its maintenance and operating expenses, the duty to pay any taxes and the risk of loss if the property is destroyed, condemned, or diminishes in value through obsolescence or exhaustion.

5. Generally, a deduction for depreciation may not be taken on a term interest in property created or acquired after July 27, 1989, for any period during which the remainder interest is held, directly or indirectly, by a person related to the owner.

## .03  Intangible Property

The depreciation of intangible property is referred to as amortization. Intangible assets, including goodwill and going-concern value, franchises (except sports franchises), trade names and trademarks, copyrights, patents, and covenants not to compete may be amortized over a 15-year period for tax purposes. This rule applies only to assets acquired in connection with the purchase of a business in the case of goodwill, covenants not to compete, copyrights, and patents. Note: for financial reporting purposes FASB No. 142 discontinued the amortization of goodwill. Other intangible assets may be amortizable if they have determinable lives.

## ¶41,005  WHEN DEPRECIATION BEGINS AND ENDS

Property may be depreciated when it is placed in service for use in a trade or business or for the production of income. It is no longer depreciable when the cost has been fully recovered or other basis or when it is retired from service, whichever happens first.

For depreciation purposes, property is placed in service when it is ready and available for a specific use, whether in a trade or business, for the production of income, a tax-exempt activity, or a personal activity. Even if the property is not being used, it is in service when it is ready and available for its specific use.

Property permanently withdrawn from use in trade or business or from use in the production of income is considered retired from service and is no longer depreciable. Property can be retired either when sold or exchanged, when it is abandoned or when it is destroyed.

## ¶41,007   Using the Section 179 Deduction

The Section 179 deduction is a means of recovering the cost of property through a current deduction rather than through depreciation. Section 179 of the Internal Revenue Code allows for the deduction of all or part of the cost of certain qualifying property in the year it is placed in service. This would be done instead of recovering the cost by taking depreciation deductions over a specified recovery period. However, there are limits on the amount that can be deducted in a year.

### .01   What Costs Can and Cannot Be Deducted

The Section 179 deduction may be used for the cost of qualifying property acquired for use in trade or business, but not for the cost of property held only for the production of income.

Only the cost of property acquired by purchase for use in business qualifies for the Section 179 deduction. The cost of property acquired from a related person or group may not qualify.

If an asset is purchased with cash and a trade-in, a Section 179 deduction can be claimed based only on the amount of cash paid. The Section 179 deduction does not include the adjusted basis of the trade-in used in the purchase.

### .03   Qualifying Property

Property qualifying for the Section 179 deduction is depreciable property and includes the following.

1. Tangible personal property.
2. Other tangible property (except buildings and their structural components) used as:
   a. An integral part of manufacturing, production, or extraction or of furnishing transportation, communications, electricity, gas, water, or sewage disposal services,

**¶41,007.01**

b. A research facility used in connection with any of the activities in above, or

c. A facility used in connection with any of the activities for the bulk storage of fungible commodities.

3. Single purpose agricultural (livestock) or horticultural structures.

4. Storage facilities (except buildings and their structural components) used in connection with distributing petroleum or any primary product of petroleum.

Generally, a Section 179 deduction may not be claimed based on the cost of leased property. However, a Section 179 deduction may be claimed based on the cost of the following:

1. Property manufactured or produced and leased to others.

2. Property purchased and leased to others if both of the following apply.

a. The term of the lease (including options to renew) is less than half of the property's class life.

b. For the first 12 months after the property is transferred to the lessee, the total business deductions allowed on the property (other than rent and reimbursed amounts) is more than 15% of the rental income from the property.

## .05  Partial Business Use

When property is used for both business and nonbusiness purposes, the Section 179 deduction may be used if the property is used more than 50% for business in the year it was placed in service. The part of the cost of the property that is for business use is the cost of the property multiplied by the percentage of business use. The result is the business cost.

## .07  Nonqualifying Property

Generally, the Section 179 deduction cannot be claimed on the cost of any of the following.

1. Property held only for the production of income.

2. Real property, including buildings and their structural components.

3. Property acquired from certain groups or persons.

4. Air conditioning or heating units.

5. Certain property used predominantly outside the U.S.

6. Property used predominantly to furnish lodging or in connection with the furnishing of lodging.

¶41,007.07

7. Property used by certain tax-exempt organizations.
8. Property used by governmental units.
9. Property used by foreign persons or entities.
10. Certain property leased to others by a noncorporate lessor.

## .09 Electing the Deduction

The Section 179 deduction is not automatic. An individual must elect to take a Section 179 deduction. For purposes of the Section 179 deduction, property is considered placed in service in the year it is first made ready and available for a specific use. This use can be in a trade or business, the production of income, a tax-exempt activity, or a personal activity. If property is placed in service in a use that does not qualify it for the Section 179 deduction, it cannot later qualify in another year even if it is changed to business use. Records must be kept that show the specific identification of each piece of qualifying Section 179 property. These records must show how the property was acquired, the person it was acquired from and when it was placed in service.

## .11 How to Figure the Deduction

The total cost a business can elect to deduct under Section 179 was increased to $108,000 for 2006. This maximum dollar limit applies to each taxpayer, not to each business. A taxpayer who is the owner of an interest(s) in a pass-through entity such as an S corporation, partnership or limited liability company, must aggregate pass-through section 179 amounts from these entities and subject them to the limitations at the taxpayer level. The full amount does not have to be claimed. A percentage of the business cost of qualifying property may be deducted under Section 179. Then it may be possible to depreciate any difference in the cost not deducted under Section 179. If more than one item of qualifying property is acquired and placed in service during the same year, it is possible to divide the deduction among the items in any way, as long as the total deduction is not more than the limits.

If there is only one item of qualifying property and it does not cost more than the dollar limit, the deduction is limited to the lesser of the following.

1. An individual's taxable income from trade or business.
2. The cost of the item.

The Section 179 deduction must be figured before figuring the depreciation deduction. The amount deducted under Section 179 must be subtracted from the business/investment cost of the qualifying property. The result is called the unadjusted basis and is the amount used to figure any depreciation deduction.

## .13   Deduction Limits

The Section 179 deduction cannot be more than the business cost of the qualifying property. In addition, the following limits must be applied to the Section 179 deduction.

1.  Maximum dollar limit. The total cost of Section 179 property that can be elected for deduction cannot be more than the amounts listed above.
2.  Investment limit. If the cost of the qualifying Section 179 property placed in service in a year is over $400,000 (indexed for inflation—$430,000 in 2006), the maximum dollar limit for each dollar over $400,000 ($430,000 in 2006) must be reduced (but not below zero). If the business cost of Section 179 property placed in service is $400,000 plus the maximum dollar limit, or more, a Section 179 deduction cannot be taken for more than the total, and cannot be carried over.
3.  Taxable income limit. The total cost that can be deducted each year is limited to the taxable income from the active conduct of any trade or business during the year. Generally, an individual is considered to be actively conducting a trade or business if he or she meaningfully participates in the management or operations of the trade or business.

## .15   Expanded Section 179 Deduction Extended Through 2007

Under section 179 of the Internal Revenue Code, it is possible to choose to recover all or part of the cost of certain qualifying property, up to a limit, by deducting it in the year placed in service. If the cost of qualifying section 179 property placed in service in a year is more than $400,000 (indexed for inflation), the dollar limit must be reduced dollar for dollar (but not below zero) by the amount of the cost over $400,000. Prior to 2003 the annual limit was $200,000 rather than $400,000. The use of the increased Section 179 expensing election was extended by the American Jobs Creation Act of 2004 for qualified property placed in service during years beginning after 2002 and before 2008. This provision allows taxpayers to continue immediately writing off qualifying business property up to $100,000 (indexed for inflation: $108,000 for 2006 and $105,000 for 2005). The deduction is subject to the following limitations and conditions:

1.  If the taxpayer places more than $400,000 (indexed for inflation: $430,000 for 2006, $420,000 for 2005 and $ 410,000 for 2004) of qualified property in service during the year, the $100,000 is reduced dollar for dollar by the amount exceeding $400,000. (If $500,000 or more of qualified property is placed in service, the benefits of Section 179 are fully phased out.)

¶41,007.15

2. Taxpayers may now file an amended return to revoke or change an earlier Section 179 election.

3. The expensing election is now applicable to off-the-shelf computer software.

4. The full expensing election is no longer available for sport utility vehicles (SUVs) with a gross weight exceeding 6,000 pounds; for these vehicles it is limited to $25,000.

5. Existing rules concerning the kind of property eligible, the income limitations, and the carryover of unused depreciation remain in effect as under prior law.

***Leasehold Improvements for Nonresidential Business Property.***    A new 15-year straight-line MACRS depreciation (cost recovery) is mandated for leasehold improvements to the interior of nonresidential business real estate (Section 1250 property). Under the law being replaced, such improvements were depreciable over 39 years, so this is a significant decrease. There are several restrictions on the more rapid depreciation:

1. The improvement must be made to *leased* real estate but not including elevators or escalators, structural components that benefit a common area, general enlargements of a building, or improvements to the internal structural framework.

2. The lessee and lessor may not be related parties, which include members of a controlled group.

3. Improvements eligible are those made after October 22, 2004 and before January 1, 2006, and may be made by either the lessee or the lessor.

4. Depreciation is computed using MACRS straight-line method. To avoid this treatment, an election must be made to use the MACRS alternative depreciation method resulting in straight-line depreciation over a period of 39 years.

***Increased Section 179 Expensing in Gulf Opportunity Zones***    The Gulf Opportunity Zone Act of 2005 increases the amount deductible under section 179 of the Internal Revenue Code from $100,000 to $200,000 for qualifying property acquired by certain victims of the 2005 hurricane season. The phase out of the deduction is also increased (by $600,000), beginning at $1 million (rather than $400,000) for qualified section 179 Gulf Opportunity Zone property. For 2006, this means the maximum amount of Section 179 depreciation is $208,000 and the limitation on the acquisition of qualified property before this amount is reduced is $1,030,000.

***Gulf Opportunity Zone Additional First Year Depreciation***    For MACRS property placed in service and used in the active conduct of a trade or business within the Gulf Opportunity Zone, unless the taxpayer elects out, an additional depreciation allowance of 50% of the cost of qualified property is available. To qualify the property must be acquired after August 28th, 2005 and placed in service before December 31, 2007 and must be MACRS property having a recovery period of 20 years or less. Specific exceptions apply including property used in a golf or country club, massage parlor or liquor store. This deduction also qualifies for AMT deduction.

*Partial Expensing for Demolition and Cleanup in Gulf Opportunity Zone*   Site cleanup and demolition related to property located in Gulf Opportunity Zone may qualify for a deduction of up to 50% of the cost for expenses otherwise required to be capitalized. Costs must be incurred after August 28, 2005 and before January 1, 2008.

## ¶41,009   THE MODIFIED ACCELERATED COST RECOVERY SYSTEM (MACRS)

The Modified Accelerated Cost Recovery System (MACRS) consists of two systems that determine how to depreciate property. The main system is called the General Depreciation System (GDS) and the second system is called the Alternative Depreciation System (ADS).

The main difference between the two systems is that ADS generally provides for a longer recovery period and uses only the straight line method of depreciation to figure a deduction. Unless specifically required by law to use ADS, GDS is generally used to figure a depreciation deduction.

Both systems simplify the way to figure the deduction by providing three preset conventions. These conventions determine the number of months for which depreciation may be claimed both in the year the property is placed in service, and in the year in which the property is disposed of. The conventions are as follows:

1.  Mid-month convention. Used for all nonresidential real property and residential rental property. The property is treated for tax purposes as if use began or ended in the middle of the month.

2.  Mid-quarter convention. Used if the basis of property placed in service during the last three months of the tax year is more than 40% of the total bases of all property placed in service for the entire year (excluding nonresidential real property, residential rental property, Sec. 179 property and property placed in service and disposed of in the same year). The property is treated for tax purposes as if use began or ended in the middle of the quarter.

3.  Half-year convention. Used for all other property. The property is treated for tax purposes as if use began or ended in the middle of the year.

MACRS provides four methods of figuring depreciation on property:

1. The 200% declining balance method over a GDS recovery period.
2. The 150% declining balance method over a GDS recovery period.
3. The straight line method over a GDS recovery period.
4. The straight line method over an ADS recovery period.

## .01  What to Depreciate Under MACRS

MACRS applies to most tangible depreciable property placed in service after 1986. MACRS must be used to depreciate all real property acquired before 1987 that has been changed from personal use to a business or income-producing use after 1986.

## .03  Knowing Which System to Use

Most tangible depreciable property falls within the *general* rule of MACRS, which is also called the General Depreciation System (GDS). Because GDS permits use of the declining balance method over a shorter recovery period, the deduction is greater in the earlier years.

However, there are specifications for the use of each system.

Both GDS and ADS have pre-established class lives for most property. Under GDS, most property is assigned to eight property classes based on these class lives. These property classes provide the number of years over which the cost of an item in a class may be recovered.

Some examples of this:

3-year property. Any race horse over 2 years old when placed in service. Any other horse over 12 years old when placed in service.

5-year property. Automobiles, taxis, buses, and trucks; computers and peripheral equipment; some office machinery; breeding cattle and dairy cattle.

However, ADS must be used for the following property:

1. Any tangible property used predominantly outside the U.S. during the year.
2. Any tax-exempt use property.
3. Any tax-exempt bond-financed property.
4. Any property used predominantly in a farming business and placed in service during any tax year in which the individual makes an election not to apply the uniform capitalization rules to certain farming costs.
5. Any imported property covered by an executive order of the President of the United States.

¶41,009.01

## .05   What Cannot Be Depreciated Under MACRS

MACRS cannot be used to depreciate the following property.

1. Intangible property.
2. Any motion picture film or video tape.
3. Any sound recording.
4. Certain real and personal property placed in service before 1987.

Any property that can be properly depreciated under a method of depreciation not based on a term of years may be excluded from MACRS.

***Property Placed in Service Before 1987.***   There are special rules that prevent the use of MACRS for property placed in service by anyone (for any purpose) before 1987 (before August 1, 1986, if MACRS was elected). These rules apply to both personal and real property. However, the rules for personal property are more restrictive. And although there are some exceptions to these rules, they do offer a basic guideline from which to work.

*Personal Property.*   MACRS may not be used for most personal property acquired after 1986 (after July 31, 1986, if MACRS was elected) if any of the following apply.

1. The individual or a relative owned or used the property in 1986.
2. The property was acquired from a person who owned it in 1986 and as part of the transaction the user of the property did not change.
3. The property was leased to a person (or someone related to this person) who owned or used the property in 1986.
4. The property was acquired in a transaction in which:
   a. The user of the property did not change, and
   b. The property was not MACRS property in the hands of the person from whom the individual acquired it because of (2) or (3).

*Real Property.*   MACRS may not be used for certain real property. This includes real property acquired after 1986 (after July 31, 1986, if MACRS was elected) if any of the following apply.

1. The individual or a relative owned the property in 1986.
2. The property was leased back to the person (or someone related to this person) who owned the property in 1986.
3. The property was acquired in a transaction in which some of the individual's gain or loss was not recognized. MACRS applies only to that part of the basis in the acquired property that represents cash paid or unlike

property given up. It does not apply to the substituted portion of the basis.

*Certain Nontaxable Transfers of Property.* MACRS does not apply to property involved in certain nontaxable transfers. This applies to property used before 1987 and transferred after 1986 to a corporation or partnership if its basis is determined by reference to the basis in the hands of the transferor or distributor. If MACRS was elected, it also applies to property used before August 1, 1986, and transferred after July 31, 1986, to a corporation or partnership if its basis is determined by reference to the basis in the hands of the transferor or distributor.

The nontaxable transfers covered by this rule include the following:

1. A distribution in complete liquidation of a subsidiary.
2. A transfer to a corporation controlled by the transferor.
3. An exchange of property solely for corporate stock or securities in a reorganization.
4. A contribution of property to a partnership in exchange for a partnership interest.
5. A partnership distribution of property to a partner.

## .07  Election to Exclude Property from MACRS

If property is depreciated under a method not based on a term of years, such as the unit-of-production method, that property may be excluded from MACRS.

## .09  Use of Standard Mileage Rate

If the standard mileage rate is used to figure a tax deduction for a business automobile, it is treated as having made an election to exclude the automobile from MACRS. However, the mileage rate is considered to include a depreciation component that reduces the vehicle's basis year by year. When the vehicle is sold or traded this reduced basis is used to compute any gain or loss.

## .11  How to Figure the Deduction

Once it is determined that the property may be depreciated under MACRS and whether it falls under GDS or ADS, the following information must be known about the property.

1. Its basis. Generally, this refers to the cost plus amounts paid for items such as sales tax, freight, installation, and testing.

2. Its property class and recovery period. This refers to the member of years over which the cost "basis" of the property is recovered.
3. The date it was placed in service. This refers to the date the item was actually first used—not when it was purchased.
4. Which convention to use—mid-month, mid-quarter, or half-year.
5. Which depreciation method to use:
   a. GDS or ADS
   b. Which class the property is in.
   c. What type of property it is.

## ¶41,011  DISPOSITIONS

A disposition is the permanent withdrawal of property from use in a trade or business or in the production of income. A withdrawal can be made by sale, exchange, retirement, abandonment, involuntary conversion, or destruction. Generally gain or loss on the disposition of property is recognized by a sale. However, nonrecognition rules may allow for postponement of some gain.

If property is disposed of before the end of its recovery period, it is called an early disposition. If that property is depreciated under MACRS, a depreciation deduction for the year of disposition is allowed. The depreciation deduction is determined for the year of disposition.

With the exception of gain on the disposition of residential rental and nonresidential real property, all gain on the disposition of property depreciated under MACRS is included in income as ordinary income, up to the amount of previously allowed depreciation deducted for the property. There is no recapture for residential rental and nonresidential real property.

## ¶41,013  GENERAL ASSET ACCOUNTS

It is possible to group separate properties into one or more general asset accounts. They then can be depreciated as a single item of property. Each account can include only property with similar characteristics, such as asset class and recovery period. Some property cannot be included in a general asset account. There are additional rules for passenger automobiles, disposing of property, converting property to personal use, and property that generates foreign source income.

Once a general asset account is established, the amount of depreciation for each account is achieved by using the depreciation method, recovery period, and convention that applies to the property in the account. For each general asset account, the depreciation allowance is recorded in a separate depreciation reserve account.

Property used in both a trade or business (or for the production of income) and in a personal activity in the year in which it was first placed in service may not be in a general asset account.

## .01 How to Group Property in General Asset Accounts

Each general asset account must include only property placed in service in the same year and that has the following in common:

1. Asset class.
2. Recovery period.
3. Depreciation method.
4. Convention.

The following rules also apply when establishing a general asset account.

1. No asset class. Property without an asset class, but with the same depreciation method, recovery period, and convention, placed in service in the same year, can be grouped into the same general asset account.
2. Mid-quarter convention. Property subject to the mid-quarter convention can only be grouped into a general asset account with property that is placed in service in the same quarter.
3. Mid-month convention. Property subject to the mid-month convention can only be grouped into a general asset account with property that is placed in service in the same month.
4. Passenger automobiles. Passenger automobiles subject to the limits on passenger automobile depreciation must be grouped into a separate general asset account.

## .03 Dispositions and Conversions

Property in a general asset account is considered disposed of when any of the following occurs:

1. It is permanently withdrawn from use in trade or business or from the production of income.
2. It is transferred to a supplies, scrap, or similar account.
3. It is sold, exchanged, retired, physically abandoned, or destroyed.

Note the following:

1.  The retirement of a structural component of real property is not a disposal.
2.  The unadjusted depreciable basis and the depreciation reserve of the general asset account are not affected by the disposition of property from the general asset account.
3.  Any property changed to personal use must be removed from the general asset account.

*Unadjusted Depreciable Basis.*    The unadjusted depreciable basis of an item of property in a general asset account is the same amount used to figure gain on the sale of the property, but it is figured without taking into account any depreciation taken in earlier years. The unadjusted depreciable basis of a general asset account is the total of the unadjusted depreciable bases of all of the property in the account.

*Adjusted Depreciable Basis.*    The adjusted depreciable basis of a general asset account is the unadjusted depreciable basis of the account minus any allowed or allowable depreciation based on the account.

*Disposition of Remaining Property.*    If all or the last item of property is disposed of in a general asset account, the adjusted depreciable basis of the general asset account can be recovered. Under this rule, the general asset account ends and the amount of gain or loss for the general asset account is figured by comparing the adjusted depreciable basis of the general asset account with the amount realized. If the amount realized is more than the adjusted depreciable basis, the difference is a gain. If it is less, the difference is a loss. If there is a gain, the amount that is subject to recapture as ordinary income is limited.

*Change to Personal Use.*    An item of property in a general asset account becomes ineligible for general asset account treatment if it is used in a personal activity. Once the property has been converted to personal use, it is removed from the general asset account as of the first day of the year in which the change in use occurs and make the appropriate adjustments are made.

# ¶41,017  COST SEGREGATION STUDIES

Cost segregation has become increasingly valuable, as depreciation write-off periods for commercial real estate have been repeatedly lengthened because of tax law changes. Initially, depreciable lives were lengthened from 15 to 18 years, then to 19 years, subsequently to 31.5 years, and finally, to 39 years for commercial property (or 27.5 years for residential property) as a result of the Revenue Reconciliation Act of 1993. Although a long-term depreciable life of 39 years is appropriate for assets such as buildings, it is not appropriate for assets that can be properly classified with shorter depreciable lives.

Examples of these include land improvements as outlined in asset class #00.3 under Revenue Procedure 87-56 and tangible personal property such as machinery/equipment, furniture and fixtures, as well as related components such as utilities, dedicated HVAC, and plumbing or electrical lines directly related to the particular type of machinery or equipment. Reclassification of assets as tangible personal property will result in depreciation periods of five or seven years, depending on the industry classification in which the business operates, whereas reclassification to land improvements will result in a depreciation period of 15 years. For example, businesses that are in the professional services or retail field would fall under asset class #57.0, Distributive Trade or Services, and be classified as tangible personal property with a depreciable life of five years.

## .01 Benefits of Cost Segregation Studies

Cost segregation studies (CSSs) have been an underused method of reducing current tax liabilities and improving the economic returns to owners of commercial properties. A *cost segregation study* is a total review of all costs associated with the acquisition or construction of a building. These studies require the use of tax experts and engineers who specialize in this area and are familiar with IRS requirements. These specialists can help to maximize the returns on commercial property investment and facilitate informed decisions that address the unique requirements of a specific piece of property. The purpose is to identify and classify the costs as either real or personal property so that the personal property items can be depreciated on an accelerated basis.

Thus, the time value of the property owner's money prevails. For example, if a property owner was able to carve out $100,000 of assets from a 39-year period to a five-year period, the difference in year one along would be an increase tax deduction (via depreciation) of $17,500 (39-year depreciation schedule approximately $2,500 versus $20,000 if under a five year life. The property owner will get the deduction over 39 years or $2,500 per year, whereas the cost segregation study will enable the complete write-off of the $100,000 asset in five years. The next best thing to not paying taxes is deferring the payment of taxes. Thus, the process identifies personal property assets that often get buried or grouped together within the real property asset.

It becomes obvious that many property owners can benefit from a cost segregation study. A CSS appears to be the answer for owners and investors who have been searching for ways to increase the current tax benefits from owning or investing in real estate. Both commercial and residential property can benefit from one, but in general, the more elaborate and costly the property, the greater the tax benefit.

¶41,017.01

## .03  Commercial Property Suitable for a CSS

Properties that readily lend themselves to the benefits of a cost segregation study, because they typically contain a significant amount of shorter-life assets, include:

- Apartments.
- Golf courses.
- Nursing homes.
- Parking lots.
- Hotels, motels, and casinos.
- Restaurants.
- Hospitals and medical facilities and offices.
- Warehouses and distribution centers.
- Manufacturing and industrial plants.
- Shopping centers.
- Senior living facilities.
- Grocery stores.
- Office and retail facilities.
- Car dealerships.
- Maintenance/service centers.
- Large distribution facilities.
- Data centers.
- Owner-occupied office buildings.
- For-profit health care and assisted living facilities.

Although almost every type of real estate can benefit from a CSS, certain types of property yield the highest tax saving benefits. Those properties include specialty-use buildings, such as medical facilities, manufacturing facilities, and high-end office buildings, to name a few. Warehouses and industrial properties tend to yield lower benefits, while residential garden apartments come some place between.

## .05  Property Eligible for Cost Segregation

Construction-related soft costs have historically been lumped together as part of real property. However, by performing a cost segregation study, these soft costs can be allocated on a pro-rata basis to various components as discovered within the cost segregation analysis. Some examples include architect/engineer fees, permits, capitalized interest, and the contractor's overhead and profit. The result is a faster write-off of costs previously included as real property. The amount of the benefits from performing a CSS will, of course, vary depending upon the type of property, the cost of the property, and the year it was placed in service. CSSs can be performed on the following:

- New buildings presently under construction.
- Purchases of existing properties.
- Existing buildings undergoing major renovation, remodeling, restoration, or expansion.
- Office/facility leasehold improvements and "fit-outs."
- Post-1986 real estate construction, building acquisitions or improvements where no cost segregation study was performed (even though the statute of limitations previously closed on the property construction/acquisition year).

In addition, IRS Revenue Procedure 2004-11 permits companies that have *claimed less than the allowable depreciation* to claim the omitted amount over a one -year period on a going-forward basis. Furthermore, the segregated components continue to be depreciated over shorter lives going forward. Savings derived from these studies flow directly to the bottom line in tax deferred savings and cash flow. This omitted amount, often referred to as the "catch-up deduction," is reported as a Section 481(a) adjustment that is an accounting method change and reported via Form 3115. (See *Brookshire Holdings*—a case that states that this is not an accounting method change.)

This filing procedure is an automatic approval by the IRS with no filing fees. It must be filed separately with the IRS in Washington, D.C., with a copy to be attached to the tax return of the entity that owns the real estate. The 3115 must be filed on the earlier of the due dates including extensions of the company's tax return or the date the company files its tax return.

## .07    Questions to Be Answered by the Client Before Undertaking a CSS

After considering these lists, some of the obvious questions for the CPA to ask the client include:

1. Do you have considerable depreciable real property?
2. Do you have a newly constructed building?
3. Have you recently purchased a building?
4. Are you planning a major renovation or expansion?
5. Have you purchased, constructed, or expanded real estate holdings any time after 1986?
6. Is the cost of the building at least $1,000,000?
7. Do you expect to retain your real estate holdings for at least the next three or four years?

A positive answer to any of these questions should indicate that the client could probably benefit from accelerating tax depreciation on their real estate holdings.

## .09    Legal Background for Cost Segregation Studies

Engineering-based cost segregation studies to classify depreciation have become an accepted standard approved by the IRS. Recent revenue rulings and procedures and a landmark court case make it possible to realize significant tax savings through accelerating the depreciation of real property costs. The Service has also published a *Cost Segregation Audit Techniques Guide (ATG)*, which gives very thorough instructions for conducting and/or scrutinizing a CSS. The IRS explains that the lack of consistency in cost segregation studies and the absence of bright-line tests for distinguishing property have both contributed to the difficulties related to cost segregation. The Service adds that the purpose of this ATG is to:

- Provide the basis for a better understanding of cost segregation studies.
- Provide a detailed outline and description of the examination steps that will facilitate the audit process.
- Minimize the burden on taxpayers, practitioners, and IRS examiners alike.

The *Hospital Corporation of America* (HCA) case, concluded in 1997, was a landmark case for taxpayers and owners of real estate. The decision was that property qualifying as tangible personal property under former investment tax credit (ITC) rules would also qualify in the same manner for purposes of tax depreciation. Thus, the accountant can use the guidance under the former ITC rules when determining whether property is depreciated as real property during a 39.5-year straight-line recovery period for commercial property and 27.5 years for residential property, or as personal property, usually over a five-year or seven-year, or 15-year life.

The HCA ruling effectively reinstated a form of component depreciation for certain building support systems, such as the electrical and plumbing systems that directly serve tangible personal property. Therefore, cost segregation methodologies previously used to allocate the cost of a building between structural components and ITC property can now be used for 1245 and 1250 property.

It cannot be overemphasized that the classification of assets is a factually intensive determination. Based on HCA, the recent *Action on Decisions* (AOD), and the *1999 Chief Counsel Advice Memorandum*, the use of cost segregation studies is expected to increase. The examiners are instructed by the IRS that they need to examine and evaluate a cost segregation study in light of the applicable statutes and judicial precedent established for a similar fact pattern. All of the cases are factually intensive and quite often the opinions of the courts conflict. Therefore, the examiner's ultimate determination generally cannot be based merely upon reading one case or considering one precedent. In addition to reading all the cases on point, the Service's position must be reviewed and followed. The examiner is also cautioned that he or she must also consider whether the IRS has acquiesced to a particular position or case. Keeping all of this in mind, it would be wise for those *conducting* a cost segregation study to be quite familiar with the contents of the Audit Techniques Guide.

## .11 Methodologies Used in Preparing Cost Segregation Studies

The following is a list of the methodologies described in the IRS Guide. Each approach is described in some detail. The attributes and potential drawbacks are also discussed.

The IRS notes that other methodologies may be used, but that most are merely derivatives of these:

- Detailed Engineering Approach from Actual Cost Records.
- Detailed Engineering Cost Estimate Approach.
- Survey or Letter Approach.
- Residual Estimation Approach.
- Sampling or Modeling Approach.
- "Rule of Thumb" Approach.

## .13 Detailed Engineering Approach from Actual Cost Records

The detailed engineering approach from actual cost records, or *detailed cost approach,* is the ideal approach for conducting a cost segregation study. It uses costs from contemporaneous construction and accounting records. In general, it is the most methodical and accurate approach, relying on solid documentation and minimal estimation. Construction-based documentation, such as blueprints, specifications, contracts, job reports, change orders, payment requests, and invoices, is used to determine unit costs. The use of actual cost records contributes to the overall accuracy of cost allocations, although issues may still arise as to the classification of specific assets. This approach is generally applied only to new construction, for which detailed cost records are available. But, ideally, the cost segregation study can begin before construction of a new building to take advantage of more tax planning.

For used or acquired property and for new projects for which original construction documents are not available, an alternative approach (e.g., the second approach, *detailed engineering cost estimate approach*) may be more appropriate.

The detailed cost approach typically includes the following activities:

1. Identify the specific project/assets that will be analyzed.
2. Obtain a complete listing of all project costs and substantiate the total project costs.
3. Inspect the facility to determine the nature of the project and its intended use.
4. Photograph specific property items for reference. Request previous site photographs that illustrate the construction progress as well as the condition of the property before the project began.
5. Review "as-built" blueprints, specifications, contracts, bid documents, contractor pay requests, and other construction documentation.
6. Identify and assign specific project items to property classes (e.g., land, land improvements, building, equipment, furniture and fixtures, and other items of tangible personal property).
7. Prepare quantitative "take-offs" for all materials and use payment records to compute unit costs.
8. Apply unit costs to each project component to determine its total cost. Reconcile total costs obtained from quantitative take-offs to total actual costs.
9. Allocate indirect costs, such as architectural fees, engineering fees, and permits, to appropriate assets.
10. Group project items with similar class lives and placed-in-service dates to compute depreciation.

The detailed cost approach is the most time consuming method and generally provides the most accurate cost allocations. The IRS explains that the discussion in each approach takes a closer look at the main components and attributes of each of the six methodologies discussed in the Guide. They point out to the examiners that these are the steps normally taken in the *preparation* of a cost segregation study. The examiners' responsibility is to review the steps taken in each study that comes before them, and evaluate the accuracy of that study.

## .15 Pros and Cons of Cost Segregation Studies

The resulting benefits of accelerated depreciation from a CSS can include:

- Eligibility to receive sales/use tax benefits.
- Property tax relief and other credits and incentives.
- Reduced current income taxes.
- Improved current cash flow.

- Improved internal rate of return on investment.
- Potential recapture of overpayments of sales tax (resulting from exemptions, which might have been overlooked prior to the segregation of assets).

As indicated earlier, a CSS is a systematic process of identifying and segregating the components of commercial property and associated costs according to their depreciable lives. Too often, all assets are lumped into a long-term depreciation account using a 39-year, straight-line method, thereby substantially reducing their current economic benefits. The CSS may identify between 5 and 50 percent of assets that qualify to depreciate over a 5, 7, or 15-year life.

A study accelerates tax deductions and the time-value of money generated by current tax savings. That tax deduction is worth significantly more today than it will be in the future. Although the savings from a cost segregation study vary depending on the type and cost of the property and the year placed in service, if expectations are realistic going into the undertaking, a CSS, usually results in considerable current tax savings,

## .17  Example of Savings Resulting from Study

Following is an example of a recent study completed by a company that specializes in conducting cost segregation studies with/for CPA firms.

For a 19-story office retail property acquired in 2004, containing approximately 300,000 square feet, located on a two-acre site at a cost basis of $35 million, a properly conducted CSS could provide an estimated benefit as follows:

- For years 2004–2007, additional tax depreciation of approximately $3.3 million in addition to what would have been received without a cost segregation study.
- For years 2004–2007, tax deferred savings (including both federal and state at a combined rate of 42 percent) of approximately $1.4 million.

## .19  Levels of Service Offered to CPAs

A company that specializes in these studies offers various service levels to CPA firms:

1. The company will cobrand or private label a service or study.
2. The company may partner with a CPA firm just to provide the engineer breakouts with the cost segregation engineer expertise. The CPA firm will complete the report to their client.

3. The CPA may refer the cost segregation company to his or her clients and the company will work directly with the CPA's clients.

Many CPA firms see the value added service as a way to provide unconventional services that competitors might not consider providing.

An active cost segregation company may also conduct educational (promotional) seminars and deal directly with end users of commercial real estate. They take into consideration the advantage of having the full compliment of professionals on their payroll to provide a turnkey service.

A relatively small number of CPA firms provide this service to their real estate clients. There are other firms whose particular niche is to partner with accounting firms to conduct these studies for CPAs and their clients. These companies often employ the non-CPA or engineer type professionals that have the background and training not only in the construction in commercial real estate, but the experience in reading, interpreting of blueprints along with the knowledge of estimating project costs in all construction divisions. Most of these professionals also have a working knowledge of the national industry average costing manuals.

## .21 Results Worth the Trouble

Even though the CSS is a relatively new procedure, it has generated millions of dollars in current federal and state income tax savings for owners of real estate. But it is not a quick-and-easy savings method. On the contrary, conducting the CSS can be fairly expensive, time consuming (four to six weeks) and complicated. Because of the nature of the study, it is obvious that a single CPA, even a tax expert, cannot expect to conduct a study without a team.

However, it is often the CPA who suggests consideration of a CSS to the client. A team for a study requires a tax expert with an intimate knowledge of the IRC, the relevant tax cases, and a network of resources to maximize the benefits for the accounting phase. The real estate/construction phase may include architects, structural experts, contractors, and/or engineers. As outlined above, even though a CSS may appear to be a complicated process, it is invariably worth the time, effort, and cost.

# Chapter 42

# Asset Valuation for Tax Purposes

## CONTENTS

## ¶42,000  OVERVIEW

Basis is the adjusted amount of an investment (equity) in property for tax purposes. The basis of property is used not only to figure depreciation but also amortization, depletion, and casualty losses. Further, it is also used to figure gain or loss on the sale or other disposition of property. It is important to keep accurate records of all items that affect the basis of property so that these computations can be made quickly and accurately.

This discussion is divided into three sections:

1. Cost Basis.
2. Adjusted Basis.
3. Basis Other Than Cost.

The basis of property bought is usually its cost. It may also be necessary to capitalize (add to basis) certain other costs related to buying or producing the property.

The original basis in property is adjusted (increased or decreased) by certain events. If improvements are made to the property, the basis is increased. If deductions are taken for depreciation or casualty losses, the basis is reduced.

Basis in some assets cannot be determined by cost. This includes property received as a gift or inheritance. It also applies to property received in a non-taxable exchange and in certain other circumstances.

# ¶42,001   Cost Basis of Assets

The basis of property bought is usually its cost. The cost is the amount paid in cash, debt obligations, other property, or services. Cost also includes amounts paid for the following items:

1. Sales tax.
2. Freight.
3. Installation and testing.
4. Excise taxes.
5. Legal and accounting fees (when they must be capitalized).
6. Revenue stamps.
7. Recording fees.
8. Real estate taxes (if assumed for the seller).

Certain other costs related to buying or producing property may have to be capitalized.

For property bought on any time-payment plan that charges little or no interest, the basis of that property is the stated purchase price, minus the amount considered to be unstated interest. There generally is unstated interest if the interest rate is less than the applicable federal rate. When a trade or business is purchased, this generally includes all assets used in the business operations, such as land, buildings, and machinery. The price is spread among the various assets, including any Section 197 intangibles such as goodwill.

## .01   Stocks and Bonds

The basis of stocks or bonds bought is generally the purchase price plus any costs of purchase, such as commissions and recording or transfer fees. If a person gets stocks or bonds other than by purchase, the basis is usually determined by the fair market value (FMV) or the previous owner's adjusted basis. Adjustments to the basis of stocks for certain events that occur after purchase will be necessary.

When it is possible to identify the shares of stock or the bonds sold, their basis is the cost or other basis of the particular shares of those stocks or the particular bonds. If someone buys and sells securities at various times in varying quantities, and no one can identify the shares sold, the basis of the securities is the basis of the securities acquired first.

For mutual fund shares acquired at different times and prices, it is appropriate to use an average basis.

## .03  Real Property

In a purchase of real property, certain fees and other expenses become part of the cost basis in the property.

If the purchaser pays the real estate taxes the seller owed on real property bought, and the seller did not reimburse the buyer, those taxes are part of the basis. The buyer cannot deduct them as taxes.

If a buyer reimburses the seller for taxes the seller paid, the buyer can usually deduct that amount as an expense in the year of purchase. That amount is not included in the basis of the property.

If the buyer did not reimburse the seller, the buyer must reduce the basis by the amount of those taxes.

***Settlement Costs.***    A buyer can include in the basis of property the settlement fees and closing costs that are for buying the property. A buyer cannot include fees and costs for getting a loan on the property. (A fee for buying property is a cost that must be paid even if the buyer bought the property for cash.)

The following items are some of the settlement fees or closing costs buyers *can* include in the basis of the property:

1. Abstract fees (abstract of title fees).
2. Charges for installing utility services.
3. Legal fees (including title search and preparation of the sales contract and deed).
4. Recording fees.
5. Surveys.
6. Transfer taxes.
7. Owner's title insurance.
8. Any amounts the seller owes that the buyer agrees to pay, such as back taxes or interest, recording or mortgage fees, charges for improvements or repairs, and sales commissions.

Settlement costs do not include amounts placed in escrow for the future payment of items such as taxes and insurance.

The following items are some settlement fees and closing costs a buyer *cannot* include in the basis of the property:

1.  Fire insurance premiums.
2.  Rent for occupancy of the property before closing.
3.  Charges for utilities or other services related to occupancy of the property before closing.
4.  Charges connected with getting a loan. The following are examples of these charges:
    a.  Points (discount points, loan origination fees).
    b.  Mortgage insurance premiums.
    c.  Loan assumption fees.
    d.  Cost of a credit report.
    e.  Fees for an appraisal required by a lender.
5.  Fees for refinancing a mortgage.

If these costs relate to business property, items (1) through (3) are deductible as business expenses. Items (4) and (5) must be capitalized as costs of getting a loan and can be deducted over the period of the loan.

***Points and Mortgages.***    If a buyer pays points to obtain a loan (including a mortgage, second mortgage, line of credit, or a home equity loan), the points are not added to the basis of the related property. Generally, a buyer can deduct the points over the term of the loan.

Special rules may apply to points the buyer and the seller pay when obtaining a mortgage on the purchase of a main home. If certain requirements are met, the buyer can deduct the points in full for the year in which they are paid. The basis of the home is reduced by any seller-paid points.

If a person buys property and assumes (or buys subject to) an existing mortgage on the property, the basis includes the amount the buyer pays for the property plus the amount to be paid on the mortgage.

If an individual builds property or has assets built, the expenses for this construction are part of the basis. Some of these expenses include the following items:

a.  The cost of land.
b.  The cost of labor and materials.
c.  Architect's fees.
d.  Building permit charges.
e.  Payments to contractors.
f.  Payments for rental equipment.
g.  Inspection fees.

¶42,001.03

In addition, if the owner of a business uses employees, material, and equipment to build an asset, the basis would also include the following costs:

1. Employee wages paid for the construction work.
2. Depreciation on equipment owned while it is used in the construction.
3. Operating and maintenance costs for equipment used in the construction.
4. The cost of business supplies and materials used in the construction.

These expenses may not be deducted. They must be capitalized; therefore, they are included in the asset's basis. On the other hand, it is necessary to reduce the basis by any work opportunity credit, welfare-to-work credit, Indian employment credit, or empowerment zone employment credit allowable on the wages paid in (1). The value of the owner's own labor, or any other labor not paid for, is not to be included in the basis of any property constructed.

## .05    Business Assets

If property is purchased to use in a business, the basis is usually its actual cost. If the owner constructs, creates, or otherwise produces property, the costs must be capitalized as the basis. In certain circumstances, the project may be subject to the uniform capitalization rules.

*Uniform Capitalization Rules.*    The uniform capitalization rules specify the costs added to basis in certain circumstances. Uniform capitalization rules must be used when any of the following applies to a trade, business, or any activity carried on for profit:

1. Production of real or tangible personal property for use in the business or activity.
2. Production of real or tangible personal property for sale to customers.
3. Acquisition of property for resale.

Property is produced when it is constructed, built, installed, manufactured, developed, improved, created, raised, or grown. Property produced for someone under a contract is treated as produced by that person up to the amount paid or costs incurred for the property.

Tangible personal property includes films, sound recordings, video tapes, books, or similar property.

Under the uniform capitalization rules, a person must capitalize all direct costs and an allocable part of most indirect costs incurred due to production or resale activities.

¶42,001.05

The following are not subject to the uniform capitalization rules:

1. Property someone produces that he or she does not use in trade, business, or activity conducted for profit.
2. Qualified creative expenses paid or incurred as a freelance (self-employed) writer, photographer, or artist that are otherwise deductible on the freelancer's tax return.
3. Property someone produced under a long-term contract, except for certain home construction contracts.
4. Research and experimental expenses allowable as a deduction under Section 174 of the Internal Revenue Code.
5. Costs for personal property acquired for resale if the current (or predecessor's) average annual gross receipts for the three previous tax years do not exceed $10 million.

*Intangible Assets.* Intangible assets include goodwill, patents, copyrights, trademarks, trade names, and franchises. The basis of an intangible asset is usually the cost to buy or create it.

The basis of a *patent* is the cost of development, such as research and experimental expenditures, drawings, working models, and attorneys' and governmental fees. If research and experimental expenditures are deducted as current business expenses, they cannot be included in the basis of the patent. The value of the inventor's time spent on an invention is not part of the basis.

For an author, the basis of a *copyright* will usually be the cost of getting the copyright plus copyright fees, attorneys' fees, clerical assistance, and the cost of plates that remain in the author's possession.

The value of the author's time, or any other person's time that was not paid for, is not included.

The purchase price of a *franchise, trademark,* or *trade name* is the basis unless the payments can be deducted as a business expense.

## .07   Allocating the Basis

When multiple assets are purchased for a lump sum, the amount paid is allocated among the assets received. This allocation is used to figure the basis for depreciation and gain or loss on a later disposition of any of these assets.

The buyer and the seller may agree to a specific allocation of the purchase price among the multiple assets in the sales contract of a lump-sum sale. If this allocation is based on the value of each asset, and the buyer and the seller have adverse tax interests, the allocation generally will be accepted.

*Acquistion of a Trade or Business.* In the acquisition of a trade or business, the purchase price is allocated to the various assets acquired. It is this Section that has been changed by the IRS.

**¶42,001.07**

For asset acquisitions occurring *after* January 5, 2000, the allocation must be made among the following assets in proportion to (but not more than) their fair market value (FMV) on the purchase date, in the following order:

1. Certificates of deposit, U.S. Government securities, foreign currency, and actively traded personal property, including stock and securities.
2. Accounts receivable, mortgages, and credit card receivables that arose in the ordinary course of business.
3. Property of a kind that would properly be included in inventory if on hand at the end of the tax year, and property held by the tax-payer primarily for sale to customers in the ordinary course of business.
4. All other assets except Section 197 intangibles, goodwill, and going concern value.
5. Section 197 intangibles, except goodwill, and going concern value.
6. Goodwill and going concern value (whether or not they qualify as Section 197 intangibles).

For asset acquisitions occurring *before* January 6, 2000, the allocation must be made among the following assets in proportion to (but not more than) their fair market value on the purchase date, in the following order:

1. Certificates of deposit, U.S. Government securities, foreign currency, and actively traded personal property, including stock and securities.
2. Accounts receivable, mortgages, and credit card receivables that arose in the ordinary course of business.
3. Property of a kind that would properly be included in inventory if on hand at the end of the tax year, and property held by the tax-payer primarily for sale to customers in the ordinary course of business.
4. All other assets except Section 197 intangibles, goodwill, and going concern value.
5. Section 197 intangibles, except goodwill and going concern value.
6. Section 197 intangibles in the nature of goodwill and going concern value.

The buyer and seller may enter into a written agreement as to the allocation of any consideration or the FMV of any of the assets. This agreement is binding on both parties unless the IRS determines the amounts are not appropriate.

Both the buyer and seller involved in the sale of business assets must report to the IRS the allocation of the sales price among Section 197 intangibles and the other business assets.

*Land and Buildings.* When a purchaser obtains buildings and the land on which they stand for a lump sum, the basis of the property is allocated among the land and the buildings to figure the depreciation allowable on the buildings.

¶42,001.07

The basis of each asset is obtained by multiplying the lump sum by a fraction. The numerator is the FMV of that asset, and the denominator is the FMV of the whole property at the time of purchase. If there is uncertainty about the FMV of the land and buildings, the basis can be allocated based on their assessed values for real estate tax purposes.

Demolition costs, and other losses incurred for the demolition of any building, are added to the basis of the land on which the demolished building was located. The costs may not be claimed as a current deduction.

A modification of a building will not be treated as a demolition if the following conditions are satisfied:

1.  75% or more of the existing external walls of the building are retained in place as internal or external walls.
2.  75% or more of the existing internal structural framework of the building is retained in place.

If the building is a certified historic structure, the modification must also be part of a certified rehabilitation.

If these conditions are met, the costs of the modifications are added to the basis of the building.

*Subdivided Lots.*   If a tract of land is purchased and subdivided, the basis for *each* lot must be determined. This is necessary because the gain or loss must be figured on the sale of each individual lot. As a result, the entire cost in the tract is not recovered until all of the lots have been sold.

To determine the basis of an individual lot, multiply the total cost of the tract by a fraction. The numerator is the FMV of the lot, and the denominator is the FMV of the entire tract.

If a developer sells subdivided lots before the development work is completed, it is possible (with IRS consent) to include, in the basis of the properties sold, an allocation of the estimated future cost for common improvements.

## ¶42,003   Adjusted Basis of Property

Before figuring gain or loss on a sale, exchange, or other disposition of property, or figuring allowable depreciation, depletion, or amortization, it is usually necessary to make certain adjustments to the basis of the property. The result of these adjustments to the basis is the adjusted basis.

### .01   Increases to Basis

The basis of any property is increased by all items properly added to a capital account. These include the cost of any improvements having a useful life of more than one year.

¶42,003.01

Rehabilitation expenses also increase basis. However, any rehabilitation credit allowed for these expenses must be subtracted before adding them to the basis. If any of the credit must be recaptured, the basis is increased by the recapture amount.

Separate accounts must be kept for additions or improvements to business property. Also, the basis of each modification is depreciated according to the depreciation rules that would apply to the underlying property, had they been placed in service at the same time as the addition or improvement.

The following items increase the basis of property:

1. The cost of extending utility service lines to the property.
2. Legal fees, such as the cost of defending and perfecting title.
3. Legal fees for obtaining a decrease in an assessment levied against property to pay for local improvements.
4. Zoning costs.
5. The capitalized value of a redeemable ground rent.

*Assessments for Local Improvements.*    The basis of property is increased by assessments for items such as paving roads and building ditches that increase the value of the property. They may not be deducted as taxes. However, charges for maintenance, repairs, or interest charges related to the improvements can be deducted as taxes.

*Deducting versus Capitalizing Costs.*    Costs that can be deducted as current expenses are not added to the basis. Amounts paid for incidental repairs or maintenance that are deductible as business expenses cannot be added to the basis. However, certain other costs can be either deducted or capitalized. If they are capitalized, they are included in the basis. If they are deducted, they are not included.

The costs that can be either deducted or capitalized include the following:

—Carrying charges, such as interest and taxes, that someone pays to own property, except those carrying charges that must be capitalized under the uniform capitalization rules (discussed earlier).

—Research and experimentation costs.

—Intangible drilling and development costs for oil, gas, and geothermal wells.

—Exploration costs for new mineral deposits.

—Mining development costs for a new mineral deposit.

—Costs of establishing, maintaining, or increasing the circulation of a newspaper or other periodical.

—Cost of removing architectural and transportation barriers for people with disabilities and the elderly. If someone claims the disabled access credit,

¶**42,003.01**

they must reduce the amount deducted or capitalize by the amount of the credit.

## .03  Decreases to Basis

The following items reduce the basis of property:

—Section 179 deductions.
—Deduction for clean-fuel vehicles and refueling property.
—Nontaxable corporate distributions.
—Deductions previously allowed (or allowable) for amortization, depreciation, and depletion.
—Exclusion of subsidies for energy conservation measures.
—Credit for qualified electric vehicles.
—Postponed gain from sale of home.
—Investment credit (part or all) taken.
—Casualty and theft losses and insurance reimbursements.
—Certain canceled debt excluded from income.
—Rebates received from a manufacturer or seller.
—Easements.
—Gas-guzzler tax (No longer applicable to limousines 10/01/05).
—Tax credit or refund for buying a diesel-powered highway vehicle.
—Adoption tax benefits.

A few of the more timely of these items are discussed below.

*Environmental Considerations.*   The basis is decreased in a car by the *gas-guzzler (fuel economy) tax* if the owner begins using the car within one year of the date of its first sale for ultimate use. This rule also applies to a subsequent owner who buys the car and begins using it not more than one year after the original sale. If the car is imported, the one-year period begins on the date of entry or withdrawal from the warehouse if that is later than the date of the first sale for ultimate use. If an income tax credit or refund has been received for a *diesel-powered highway vehicle* purchased before August 21, 1996, the basis is reduced by the credit or refund allowable.

If a deduction is taken for *clean-fuel vehicles or clean-fuel vehicle refueling property,* the basis is decreased by the amount of the deduction. Any subsidy received from a public utility company for the purchase or installation of an *energy conservation measure* for a dwelling unit can be excluded from gross income. The basis of the property for which the subsidy was received is reduced by the excluded amount.

*Depreciation.* The basis of property is decreased by the depreciation that was deducted, or could have been deducted, on tax returns under the method of depreciation chosen. If less depreciation was taken than could have been taken, the basis should be decreased by that amount. If no depreciation deduction was made, the basis is reduced by the full amount permitted. If more was deducted than should have been, the basis is decreased by the amount equal to the depreciation that should have been deducted, plus the part of the excess depreciation deducted that actually reduced the tax liability for the year. In decreasing the basis for depreciation, the amount deducted on the tax returns as depreciation, and any depreciation capitalized under the uniform capitalization rules, must be included.

## ¶42,005 BASIS OTHER THAN COST

There are many instances in which cost *cannot be used* as basis. In these cases, FMV or the adjusted basis of property may be used. Adjusted basis is discussed above; FMV is discussed in this section.

Fair market value (FMV) is the price at which property would change hands between a buyer and a seller, neither having to buy or sell, and both having reasonable knowledge of all necessary facts. Sales of similar property on or about the same date may be helpful in figuring the property's FMV.

### .01 Property Received for Services

If someone receives property for services, the property's FMV should be included in income. The amount included in income becomes the basis. If the services were performed for a price agreed upon beforehand, it will be accepted as the FMV of the property if there is no evidence to the contrary.

*Bargain Purchases.* A bargain purchase is a purchase of an item for less than its FMV. If, as compensation for services, someone purchases goods or other property at less than FMV, the difference between the purchase price and the property's FMV is included in income. The basis in the property is its FMV (the purchase price plus the amount included in income).

If the difference between the purchase price and the FMV represents a qualified employee discount, the difference should not be included in income. However, the basis in the property is still its FMV.

### .03 Taxable Exchanges

A taxable exchange is one in which the gain is taxable or the loss is deductible. A taxable gain or deductible loss is also known as a recognized gain or loss. If someone receives property in exchange for other property in a taxable exchange, the basis of the property received is usually its FMV at the time of the exchange. A taxable exchange occurs when a taxpayer receives cash or gets property not similar or related in use to the property exchanged.

## .05   Involuntary Conversions

If property is received as a result of an involuntary conversion, such as a casualty, theft, or condemnation, the basis of the replacement property is figured using the basis of the converted property.

If replacement property is similar or related in service or use to the converted property, the replacement property's basis is the old property's basis on the date of the conversion. However, the following adjustments should be made:

1.  Decrease the basis by the following:
    a.  Any loss recognized on the conversion.
    b.  Any money received that is not spent on similar property.
2.  Increase the basis by the following:
    a.  Any gain recognized on the conversion.
    b.  Any cost of acquiring the replacement property.

Money or property not similar or related in service or use to the converted property may be received. If the recipient buys replacement property similar or related in service or use to the converted property, the basis of the new property is its cost decreased by the gain not recognized on the conversion.

If more than one piece of replacement property is purchased, the basis is allocated among the properties based on their respective costs.

## .07   Nontaxable Exchanges

A nontaxable exchange is an exchange in which the recipient is not taxed on any gain and cannot deduct any loss. When property is received in a nontaxable exchange, its basis is usually the same as the basis of the property transferred. A nontaxable gain or loss is also known as an unrecognized gain or loss.

## .09   Like-Kind Exchanges

The exchange of property for the same kind of property is the most common type of nontaxable exchange. To qualify as a like-kind exchange, both the property transferred and the property received must be held by the transferor for business or investment purposes. There must also be an exchange of like-kind property.

The basis of the property received is the same as the basis of the property given up. Exchange expenses are generally closing costs. They may include such items as brokerage commissions, attorney fees, and deed preparation fees. They should be added to the basis of the like-kind property received.

***Related Persons.***    If a like-kind exchange takes place directly or indirectly between related persons and either party disposes of the property within two years after the exchange, the exchange no longer qualifies for like-kind exchange treatment. Each person must report any gain or loss not recognized on the original exchange. Each person reports it on the tax return filed for the year in which the later disposition occurs. If this rule applies, the basis of the property received in the original exchange will be its fair market value.

These rules generally do not apply to the following kinds of property dispositions:

1. Dispositions due to the death of either related person.
2. Involuntary conversions.
3. Dispositions in which neither the original exchange nor the subsequent disposition had as a main purpose the avoidance of federal income tax.

Generally, related persons are ancestors, lineal descendants, brothers and sisters (whole or half), and spouses. Other "related" persons may, for example, include two corporations, an individual and a corporation, a grantor and a fiduciary, or other business arrangements.

***Partially Nontaxable Exchange.***    A partially nontaxable exchange is an exchange in which someone receives unlike property or money in addition to like property. The basis of the property received is the same as the basis of the property given up, with the following adjustments:

1. Decrease the basis by the following amounts:
   a. Any money received.
   b. Any loss recognized on the exchange.
2. Increase the basis by the following amounts:
   a. Any additional costs incurred.
   b. Any gain recognized on the exchange.

If the other party to the exchange assumes the liabilities, the debt assumption is treated as money received in the exchange.

***Partial Business Use of Property.***    If someone has property used partly for business and partly for personal use, and exchanges it in a nontaxable exchange for property to be used wholly or partly in their business, the basis

¶42,005.09

of the property received is figured as if two properties had been exchanged. The first is an exchange of like-kind property. The second is personal-use property on which gain is recognized and loss is not recognized.

The adjusted basis in the property should first be figured as if someone transferred two separate properties. The adjusted basis of each part of the property is figured by taking into account any adjustments to basis. The depreciation taken or that could have taken is deducted from the adjusted basis of the business part. The amount realized for the property should then be figured and allocated to the business and nonbusiness parts of the property.

The business part of the property may be exchanged tax-free. However, any gain must be recognized from the exchange of the nonbusiness part. The taxpayer is deemed to have received, in exchange for the nonbusiness part, an amount equal to its FMV on the date of the exchange. The basis of the property acquired is the total basis of the property transferred (adjusted to the date of the exchange), increased by any gain recognized on the nonbusiness part.

If the nonbusiness part of the property transferred is the main home, it may be possible to exclude from income all or a portion of the gain on that part.

## .11    Property Transferred from a Spouse

The basis of property transferred to a spouse or transferred in trust for one's benefit by a spouse (or former spouse if the transfer is incident to divorce) is the same as the spouse's adjusted basis. However, the basis must be adjusted for any gain recognized by the spouse or former spouse on property transferred in trust. This rule applies only to a transfer of property in trust in which the liabilities assumed, plus the liabilities to which the property is subject, are more than the adjusted basis of the property transferred.

If the property transferred is a series E, series EE, or series I U.S. Savings Bond, the transferor must include in income the interest accrued to the date of transfer. The basis in the bond immediately after the transfer is equal to the transferor's basis increased by the interest income includable in the transferor's income. The transferor must, at the time of the transfer, turn over the records necessary to determine the adjusted basis and holding period of the property as of the date of transfer.

## .13    Inherited Property

The basis in property inherited from a decedent is generally one of the following:

1. The FMV of the property at the date of the individual's death.
2. The FMV on the alternate valuation date, if the personal representative for the estate chooses to use alternate valuation.

¶42,005.11

3. The value under the special-use valuation method for real property used in farming or other closely held business, if chosen for estate tax purposes.

4. The decedent's adjusted basis in land to the extent of the value that is excluded from the decedent's taxable estate as a qualified conservation easement.

If a federal estate tax return does not have to be filed, the basis in the inherited property is its appraised value at the date of death for state inheritance or transmission taxes.

*Appreciated Property.*   The above rule does not apply to appreciated property received from a decedent if a taxpayer or spouse originally gave the property to the decedent within one year before the decedent's death. The basis in this property is the same as the decedent's adjusted basis in the property immediately before his or her death, rather than its FMV.

Appreciated property is any property whose FMV on the day it was given to the decedent is more than its adjusted basis.

## .15  Community Property

In community property states (Arizona, California, Idaho, Louisiana, Nevada, New Mexico, Texas, Washington, and Wisconsin), husband and wife are each considered to own half the community property. When either spouse dies, the total value of the community property, even the part belonging to the surviving spouse, generally becomes the basis of the entire property.

For this rule to apply, at least half the value of the community property interest must be includable in the decedent's gross estate, whether or not the estate must file a return.

## .17  Farm or Closely Held Business

Under certain conditions, when a person dies, the executor or personal representative of that person's estate may choose to value the qualified real property on other than its FMV. In that case, the executor or personal representative values the qualified real property based on its use as a farm or its use in a closely held business. If the executor or personal representative chooses this method of valuation for estate tax purposes, that value is the basis of the property for the heirs. The qualified heirs should be able to get the necessary value from the executor or personal representative of the estate.

If a qualified heir received special-use valuation property, the basis in the property is the estate's or trust's basis in that property immediately before the distribution. The basis is increased by any gain recognized by the estate or trust because of post-death appreciation. Post-death appreciation is the property's

FMV on the date of distribution minus the property's FMV either on the date of the individual's death or the alternate valuation date. All FMVs should be figured without regard to the special-use valuation.

It is possible to elect to increase the basis in special-use valuation property if it becomes subject to the additional estate tax. This tax is assessed if, within ten years after the death of the decedent, the property is transferred to a person who is not a member of the family, or the property stops being used as a farm or in a closely held business.

## .19   Property Changed to Business or Rental Use

When property held for personal use is changed to business use or to produce rent, its basis for depreciation must be figured. An example of changing property held for personal use to business use would be renting out a former main home.

The basis for depreciation is the lesser of the following amounts:

1.  The FMV of the property on the date of the change.
2.  The adjusted basis on the date of the change.

If the property is later sold or disposed of, the basis of the property used will depend upon whether gain or loss occurred. The basis for figuring a gain is the adjusted basis when the property is sold. Figuring the basis for a loss starts with the smaller of the adjusted basis or the FMV of the property at the time of the change to business or rental use. This amount is then adjusted for the period after the change in the property's use to arrive at a basis for loss.

# Chapter 43

# Business Use of a Home

## CONTENTS

# ¶43,000 OVERVIEW

Now, with email and wireless connections—and with voice mail the industry standard—not only is it hard to tell where anyone is ... but also, the public perception of someone who works from home has gone from "hardly working" to "smart businessperson." The home office means that the client is not paying for an upscale office, a receptionist, a parking valet, or even a water cooler. The client is paying for time and product.

On airplanes now, the only limit to the work time is the life of the computer battery, and even this is no longer an issue, as many airlines offer electrical outlets on seat armrests. The home office has taken to the sky!

# ¶43,001 CLAIMING THE DEDUCTION

Claiming the deduction for business use of the home may include deductions involving a house, apartment, condominium, mobile home, or boat. As pointed out later it may include an unattached garage, studio, barn, or greenhouse; however, it does not include any part of the property used exclusively as a hotel or inn. In this chapter are:

1. The requirements for qualifying to deduct expenses for the business use of the home (including special rules for storing inventory or product samples).
2. Types of expenses that can be deducted.
3. How to figure the deduction (including depreciation of the home).
4. Special rules for day-care providers.
5. Deducting expenses for furniture and equipment used in the business.
6. Records that should be kept.

The rules in this chapter apply to individuals, trusts, estates, partnerships, and S corporations. They do not apply to corporations (other than S corporations). There are no special rules for the business use of a home by a partner or S corporation shareholder.

# ¶43,003 PRINCIPAL PLACE OF BUSINESS

Rules that went into effect in 1999 make it easier to claim a deduction for the business use of a home. Under these rules, many taxpayers may qualify to claim the deduction, even though they had never qualified before. The following information explains these rules.

Under these latest rules for deducting expenses for the business use of a home, it is easier for a home office to qualify as the principal place of business.

Under the old rules, a taxpayer had to consider the relative importance of the activities carried out at each business location when determining if a home was the principal place of business. The place where the taxpayer conducted the most important activities was the place where meetings were held with clients, customers, or patients, or the location where goods or services were delivered. Performing administrative or management duties in the home office was considered less important.

Before 1999, an outside salesperson's home office did not qualify as a principal place of business. The place where he or she met with customers to explain available products and take orders was considered more important than the home office where administrative duties were conducted. Beginning in 1999, however, a home office qualifies as a principal place of business for deducting expenses for the use of it:

1. If the home office is used exclusively for administration or management activities of a trade or business.
2. If the taxpayer has no other fixed location for conducting substantial administrative or management activities relating to a trade or business.

There are many activities that are administrative or managerial in nature. Some of these activities are:

1. Billing customers, clients, or patients.
2. Keeping books and records.
3. Ordering supplies.
4. Setting up appointments.
5. Forwarding orders or writing reports.

The following administrative or management activities performed at other locations will *not* disqualify a home office as a principal place of business:

1. When others conduct a taxpayer's administrative or management activities at locations other than the home.
2. The conduct of administrative or management activities at places that are not fixed locations of a business, such as in a car or a hotel room.
3. The taxpayer occasionally conducts minimal administrative or management activities at a fixed location outside of the home.
4. The taxpayer conducts substantial *non*administrative or *non*management business at a fixed location outside the home.
5. Suitable space to conduct administrative or management activities is available outside the home office, but a home office is used for those activities instead.

¶43,003

## ¶43,005  OTHER CRITERIA FOR DETERMINING PLACE OF BUSINESS

If the newer rules do not appear to cover the taxpayer's particular situation, the older rules may give an indication of other aspects when considering deductions for business use of the home.

It is permissible to have more than one business location, including a home, for a single trade or business. To qualify to deduct the expenses for the business use of a home, the home must be a principal place of business of that trade or business. To determine the principal place of business, all of the facts and circumstances must be considered. If, after considering the business locations, one cannot be identified as a principal place of business, then home office expenses cannot be deducted. The two primary factors to consider are:

1. The relative importance of the activities performed at each location.
2. The time spent at each location.

To determine whether a home is the principal place of business, the taxpayer must consider the relative importance of the activities carried out at each business location. The relative importance of the activities performed at each business location is determined by the basic characteristics of the business. If the business requires that meetings or conferences be held with clients or patients, or that goods or services be delivered to a customer, then the place where contacts are made must be given great weight in determining where the most important activities are performed.

If the relative importance of the activities does not clearly establish the principal place of business, such as when to deliver goods or services at both the office, in the home, and elsewhere, then the time spent at each location is important. Comparison should be made of the time spent on business at the home office with the time spent at other locations.

## ¶43,007  SEPARATE STRUCTURES

Expenses can be deducted for a separate free-standing structure, such as a studio, garage, or barn, if the structure is used exclusively and regularly for the business. The structure does not have to be the principal place of business, or a place where patients, clients or customers are met.

## ¶43,009  FIGURING THE DEDUCTION

Once it has been determined that the "home office" does qualify for a deduction, the next step is determining how much the taxpayer can deduct.

Certain expenses related to the business use of a home can be deducted, but deductions are limited by the following:

1. Percentage of the home used for business, i.e., the business percentage.
2. Deduction limit.

To find the *business percentage,* the taxpayer must compare the size of the part of the home used for business to the entire house. The resulting percentage is used to separate the business part of the expenses from the expenses for operating the entire home. Any reasonable method to determine the business percentage can be used. Two commonly used methods are:

1. Dividing the square foot area of the "business space" by the total area of the home.
2. Dividing the number of rooms used for business by the total number of rooms in the home. This method can be used if the rooms in the home are all about the same size.

## ¶43,011 DEDUCTION LIMIT

If gross income from the business use of a home equals or exceeds the total business expenses (including depreciation), all of the business expenses can be deducted. If the gross income from that use is less than the total business expenses, the deduction for certain expenses for the business use is limited. The deduction of otherwise nondeductible expenses, such as insurance, utilities, and depreciation (with depreciation taken last), allocable to business is limited to the gross income from the business use of the home minus the sum of the following:

1. The business part of expenses that could be deducted even if the home was not used for business (such as mortgage interest, real estate taxes, and casualty and theft losses).
2. The business expenses that relate to the business activity in the home (for example, salaries or supplies), but not to the use of the home itself.

A self-employed individual may not include in (2) above the deduction for half of the self-employment tax.

If deductions are greater than the current year's limit, it is possible to carry over the excess to the next year. Any carryover is subject to the gross income limit from the business use of the home for the next tax year. The amount carried over will be allowable only up to the taxpayer's gross income in the next tax year from the business in which the deduction arose whether the individual lives in that particular house or home during that year or not.

¶43,011

## ¶43,013 ASSORTED USE TESTS

To qualify under the *regular use test,* a specific area of the home must be used for business on a continuing basis. The regular-use test is not met if the business use of the area is only occasional, even if that area is not used for any other purpose.

To qualify under the *trade or business use* test requires that part of a home be used in connection with a trade or business. If part of the home is used for some other profit-seeking activity that is not a trade or business, a deduction cannot be taken for a business use.

A taxpayer who is an employee must qualify under the *convenience-of-the-employer* test. If an employer provides suitable work space for administrative management activities, this fact must be considered in determining whether this test is met. Even if expenses qualify for a deduction for the business use of a home, the deduction may be limited. If the employee's gross income from the business use of a home is less than the employee's total business expenses, the deduction for some of the expenses—utilities, insurance, depreciation, for example—is limited.

## ¶43,015 EXCLUSIVE USE

To qualify under the *exclusive use* test, a specific area of a home must be used only for a trade or business. The area used for business can be a room or other separately identifiable space. The space does not need to be marked off by a permanent partition. If the home area in question is used both for business and personal purposes, it does not meet the requirements of the exclusive use test rule.

The exclusive use test does not have to be met if space is used for the *storage of inventory or product samples,* or for a *day-care facility.* When part of a home is used for the storage of inventory or product samples, the following 5 tests must all be met:

1. The inventory or product samples are kept for use in a trade or business.
2. The trade or business is a wholesale or retail selling of products.
3. The home is the only fixed location of a trade or business.
4. The storage space must be used on a regular basis.
5. The space is an identifiably separate space suitable for storage.

## ¶43,017 PART-YEAR USE

Expenses for the business use of a home *may not* be incurred during any part of the year it was not being used for business purposes. Only those expenses

¶43,013

for the portion of the year in which it was actually used for business may be used in figuring the allowable deduction.

## ¶43,019  DAY-CARE FACILITY

If space in the home is used on a regular basis for providing day care, it may be possible to deduct the business expenses for that part of the home even though the same space is used for nonbusiness purposes. To qualify for this exception to the exclusive use rule, the following requirements must be met:

1.  The space must be used in the trade or business of providing day care for children, persons 65 or older, or persons who are physically or mentally unable to care for themselves.
2.  The taxpayer must have applied for, been granted or be exempt from having a license certification registration, or approval as a day-care center or as a family or group day-care home under state law. An individual does not meet this requirement if an application was rejected or license or other authorization was revoked.

If a part of the home is regularly used for day care, it is necessary to figure the percentage of that part which is used for day care, as explained above under *business percentage*. All the allocable expenses subject to the deduction limit, as explained earlier, may be deducted for that part used exclusively for day care. If the use of part of the home as a day-care facility is regular, but not exclusive, it is necessary to figure what part of available time it is actually used for business.

A room that is available for use throughout each business day and that is regularly used in the business is considered to be used for day care throughout each business day. It is not necessary to keep records to show the specific hours the area was used for business. The area may be used occasionally for personal reasons; however, a room used only occasionally for business does not qualify for the deduction.

To find that part of the available time the home is actually used for business, the total business-use time is compared to the total time that part of the home can be used for all purposes. The comparison may be based upon the hours of business use in a week with the number of hours in a week (168), or the hours of business use for the tax year with the number of hours in the tax year.

### .01  Meal Allowance

If food is provided for a day-care business, the expense is not included as a cost of using the home for business. It is a separate deduction on the tax-payer's Schedule C (Form 1040). The cost of food consumed by the taxpayer or his or her family may not be deducted. However, 100% of the cost of food consumed by the day-care recipients and generally only 50% of the cost of food consumed by employees can be deducted. However, 100% of the cost of food consumed by employees can be deducted if its value can be excluded from their wages as a de minimis fringe benefit. The value of meals provided to employees on business premises is generally de minimis if more than half of these employees are provided the meals for the taxpayer's convenience.

If cost of food for the day-care business is deducted, a separate record (with receipts) must be maintained of the family's food costs. Reimbursements received from a sponsor under the Child and Adult Food Care Program of the Department of Agriculture are taxable only to the extent they exceed expenses for food for eligible children. If reimbursements are more than expenses for food, the difference is shown as income in Part I of Schedule C. If food expenses are greater than the reimbursements, the difference is shown as an expense in Part V of Schedule C. Alternatively, day care providers may choose to use a standardized rate to claim the deduction for meals provided to children in their care instead of keeping detailed records and receipts of food purchased for use in their business. The rates follow the USDA Child and Adult Food Care Program.

## ¶43,021   Business Furniture and Equipment

Depreciation and Section 179 deductions may be used for furniture and equipment that an employee uses in his or her home for business or work. These deductions are available whether or not the individual qualifies to deduct expenses for the business use of a home. Following are explanations of the different rules for:

1. Listed property.
2. Property bought for business use.
3. Personal property converted to business use.

### .01   Listed Property

Special rules apply to certain types of property, called listed property, used in the home. Listed property includes any property of a type generally used for entertainment, recreation, and amusement (including photographic, phonographic, communication, and video recording equipment). But "listed property" also includes cell phones, computers and related equipment.

Listed property bought and placed in service since 1998 must be used more than 50% for business (including work as an employee) to be claimed as a Section 179 deduction or an accelerated depreciation deduction. If the business use of listed property is 50% or less, a Section 179 deduction cannot be taken and the property must be depreciated using the Alternate Depreciation System (ADS) (straight-line method). Listed property meets the more-than-50%-use test for any tax year if its qualified business use is more than 50% of its total use. Allocation among its various uses must be made for the use of any item of listed property used for more than one purpose during the tax year. The *percentage of investment use may not be used* as part of the percentage of qualified business use to meet the more-than-50%-use test. However, the taxpayer should use the combined total of business and investment use to figure the depreciation deduction for the property.

If an employee uses his or her own listed property (or listed rented property) for work as an employee, the property is business-use property only if both of the following requirements are met.

1. The use is for the convenience of the employer.
2. The use is required as a condition of employment.

"As a condition of employment" means that the use of the property is *necessary* for proper performance of work. Whether the use of the property is required for this purpose depends on all the facts and circumstances. The employer does not have to tell the employee specifically to have a computer for use in the home, nor is a statement by the employer to that effect sufficient.

If, in a year after placing an item of listed property in service, the taxpayer fails to meet the more-than-50%-use test for that item of property, he or she may be required to do both of the following.

1. Figure depreciation, beginning with the year the property is no longer used more than 50% for business, using the straight-line method.
2. Figure any excess depreciation and Section 179 deduction on the property and add it to:
   a. Gross income.
   b. The adjusted basis of the property.

It is not possible to take any depreciation of the Section 179 deduction for the use of listed property unless business/investment use can be proved with adequate records or sufficient evidence to support the individual's own statements. To meet the adequate records requirement, the taxpayer must maintain an account book, diary, log, statement of expense, trip sheet, or similar record or other documentary evidence that is sufficient to establish business/ investment use.

## .03  Property Bought for Business Use

The taxpayer who has bought certain property to use in his or her business can do any one of the following (subject to the limits discussed below).

¶43,021.03

1. Elect a Section 179 deduction for the full cost of the property.
2. Take part of the cost as a Section 179 deduction.
3. Depreciate the full cost of the property.

## .05  Section 179 Deduction

A Section 179 deduction can generally be claimed on depreciable tangible personal property bought for use in the active conduct of business. The taxpayer can choose how much (subject to the limit) of the cost to deduct under Section 179 and how much to depreciate. The Section 179 deduction can be spread over several items of property in any way selected as long as the total does not exceed the maximum allowable. However, the taxpayer cannot take a Section 179 deduction for the basis of the business part of the home.

## .07  Section 179 Deduction Limits

The Section 179 deduction cannot be more than the business cost of the qualifying property. In addition, the following limits apply when figuring a Section 179 deduction.

1. Maximum dollar limit.
2. Investment limit.
3. Taxable income limit.

If the cost of qualifying section 179 property placed in service in a year is more than $400,000 (indexed for inflation), the dollar limit must be reduced dollar for dollar (but not below zero) by the amount of the cost over $400,000. Prior to 2003, the annual limit was $200,000 rather than $400,000. The use of the increased Section 179 expensing election was extended by the American Jobs Creation Act of 2004 for qualified property placed in service during years beginning after 2002 and before 2008. This provision allows taxpayers to continue immediately writing off qualifying business property up to $100,000 (indexed for inflation: $108,000 for 2006; $105,000 for 2005 and $102,000 for 2004). The deduction is subject to the following further limitations and conditions:

1. If the taxpayer places more than $400,000 (indexed for inflation: $430,000 for 2006, $420,000 for 2005 and $ 410,000 for 2004) of qualified property in service during the year, the $100,000 is reduced dollar for dollar by the amount exceeding $400,000. (If $500,000 or more of qualified property is placed in service, the benefits of Section 179 are fully phased out.)
2. Taxpayers may now file an amended return to revoke or change an earlier Section 179 election.

¶43,021.05

3. The expensing election is now applicable to off-the-shelf computer software.

4. The full expensing election is no longer available for sport utility vehicles (SUVs) with a gross weight exceeding 6,000 pounds; for these vehicles it is limited to $25,000.

Existing rules concerning the kind of property eligible, the income limitations, and the carryover of unused depreciation remain in effect as under prior law.

The total cost that can be deducted each tax year is subject to the total *taxable income limit*. This is figured on the income from the active conduct of all trade or business activities, including wages, during the tax year. The taxable income for this purpose is figured in the usual way, but without regard to all of the following.

1. The Section 179 deduction.
2. The self-employment tax deduction.
3. Any net operating loss carryback or carryforward.

## ¶43,023   DEPRECIATION

Form 4562 is used to claim a deduction for depreciation. It does not include any costs deducted in Part I (Section 179 deduction).

Most business property used in a home office is either 5-year or 7-year property under MACRS.

- 5-year property includes computers and peripheral equipment, typewriters, calculators, adding machines, and copiers.
- 7-year property includes office furniture and equipment such as desks, files, and safes.

Under MACRS, the half-year convention is generally used, which allows deduction of a half-year of depreciation in the first year the property is used in the business. If more than 40% of the depreciable property was placed in service during the last 3 months of the tax year, the mid-quarter convention must be used instead of the half-year convention.

## ¶43,025   PERSONAL PROPERTY CONVERTED TO BUSINESS USE

If property is used in the home office that was used previously for personal purposes, a Section 179 deduction cannot be taken for the property, but it can be depreciated. The method of depreciation depends upon when the property was first used for personal purposes.

## ¶43,027 NEW ADDITIONAL FIRST-YEAR DEPRECIATION

For property acquired after May 5, 2003, and placed in service before January 1, 2005, taxpayers may take an additional 50-percent bonus first-year depreciation. This provision was added by the Jobs and Growth Tax Relief Reconciliation Act of 2003, increasing the 30-percent deduction allowed by the Job Creation and Worker Assistance Act of 2002. To qualify for this first-year depreciation, property must be new (original use).

# Chapter 44

# Limited Liability Companies

## CONTENTS

# ¶44,000  OVERVIEW

One of the most important decisions an accountant may advise a client about is the structure of a new business—the choice of entity. In the past, the analysis required a comparison of the advantages and disadvantages of a taxable corporation, an S corporation, a partnership, or a sole proprietorship. To this mix has been added the Limited liability company. A Limited liability company (LLC), if so elected, is taxed in the same manner as a partnership for federal income tax purposes. The advantage of an LLC over a partnership is the fact that the owners, referred to as members, are shielded from personal liability for the business' debts and liabilities. LLC members are liable only for their capital contributions.

A Limited liability company, therefore, offers the tax flexibility of a partnership with the personal liability protection of a corporation. It also provides options for management, allowing members either to participate directly in the management of the business or to designate certain members or nonmembers as managers.

In part, the demand for a new entity grew out of the restrictive nature of S corporations as vehicles for small business. These corporations were originally designed as a hybrid between a regular C (tax-paying) corporation and a partnership. However, in drafting the rules for S corporations, Congress limited the number of shareholders to 100 (originally 10), placed restrictions on classes of stock, prescribed the type of taxpayers who could own stock, controlled the relative amounts that can be distributed to shareholders, and introduced other restrictions and limitations as well as special taxes. The S corporation hybridization thus produced a very high-strung tax entity. In response, beginning with Wyoming in 1977, all 50 states have passed statutes creating LLCs as an alternative.

# ¶44,001  ADVANTAGES OF LLCs OVER S CORPORATIONS

LLCs offer many advantages over S corporations, sixteen of which are discussed below:

1. *Type of ownership.* Owners (members) may be individuals, partnerships, C corporations, S corporations, trusts or estates (there is no restriction on the type of tax entity that may own an interest). Whereas, only individuals, estates, S corporations owning 100 percent of their stock, and certain trusts may own S corporations. They may not be owned by C (taxable) Corporations or partnerships. In addition, only citizens or residents of the U.S. may own an S corporation.
2. *Number of owners.* There is no limit on the number of owners for an LLC. S corporations are limited to 100 shareholders; if they exceed that number, their status as an S corporation is terminated.

3. *Special allocations.* Like partnerships, LLCs are allowed to make special allocations of a member's share of income, deduction, gain, loss, or credit items, as long as such allocations have economic substance (are not done primarily for tax reasons). S corporations are allowed to allocate only separately stated items on a per-day, per-share basis.

4. *Basis adjustments.* Like partnerships, LLCs may elect to adjust the basis of assets to reflect changes in ownership. This election, which is not available to S corporations, allows new owners to benefit from additional depreciation deductions resulting from the appreciation of assets reflected in the purchase price.

5. *Basis from debt.* Members of an LLC, like partners in a partnership, are permitted to include in the calculation of their individual ownership basis (outside basis), their share of the LLC's debt. This may allow for the deduction of a loss that exceeds the basis of the assets contributed to the LLC by a member. S corporation shareholders include only the amount of debt personally loaned to the corporation in the calculation of their shareholder basis. Thus, S corporation shareholders may not use the S corporation's debt to allow deductions for losses generated by the S corporation.

6. *Special taxes.* LLCs are not subject to any special taxes. S corporations are subject to a built-in gains tax (Internal Revenue Code [IRC] sec. 1374) upon disposing of an appreciated asset held less than ten years (assuming the S corporation converted from a former C corporation).

7. *Partnership rules apply.* One of the greatest advantages of an LLC is that the rules of partnership taxation apply. Although LLCs are not covered by specific code sections in the Internal Revenue Code, their taxation is identical to partnerships, assuming they have elected to be treated in that manner.

8. *S corporation termination.* S corporations are subject to inadvertent termination of their tax status if they fail to comply with the ongoing eligibility requirements. Specifically, the election may be terminated by the IRS for having more than 100 shareholders, issuing more than one class of stock, having a foreign (nonresident, noncitizen) shareholder, having a corporate shareholder, or having a nonresident shareholder. LLCs are terminated in accordance with their controlling member agreements (analogous to a partnership agreement) or state law. The partnership rule that terminates a partnership when more than 50 percent of its ownership is sold, also applies to LLCs, however.

9. *Cash distributions to members.* LLCs offer more flexibility when it comes to distributions to members than do S corporations. LLCs place no limits on the amounts or timing of distributions to members. By contrast, S corporation distributions that are preferential or not based on shareholder

ownership percentages (pro rata) may be construed by the IRS as evidence of more than one class of stock.

10. *Fringe benefits*. Fringe benefits provided to LLC members may be treated as guaranteed payments, and are therefore deductible by the LLC. Such benefits include medical insurance, group-term life insurance, and similar items. In the case of S corporations, a deduction for fringe benefits is allowed only for those shareholders owning 2 percent or less of the company's stock.

11. *Transfer of appreciated assets*. The transfer of appreciated assets to an LLC may be accomplished without the recognition of gain. LLCs are not subject to the requirements of IRC section 351 that applies to S corporations. Shareholders of an S corporation failing to qualify under section 351 must recognize gain on the difference between the basis of assets they contribute and the fair market value of the stock they receive if the 80 percent control requirement of section 368(c) is not met. The section 351 requirement is ownership of at least 80 percent of the S corporation's stock by those transferring the assets.

12. *Transfer of liabilities*. The transfer of assets with related liabilities is generally not a problem for LLCs, as the liabilities adjust the basis of the LLC members' ownership interest (outside basis). In contrast, S corporation shareholders transferring assets with liabilities in excess of the basis of the assets will recognize a gain on the difference.

13. *Distribution of appreciated assets*. The distribution of appreciated assets to the members of an LLC generally does not produce gain for the LLC or its members. Corporations, including S corporations, however, are required to recognize the gain on appreciated property distributed to shareholders, although the gain is passed through to the S corporation shareholders (IRC sec. 311 and sec. 336).

14. *Former status*. S corporations that were formerly C corporations and have retained earnings and profits are subject to potential personal holding company income tax and risk termination of their S corporation elections if they generate a certain amount of passive income over a three-year period. LLCs have no such restrictions.

15. *Liquidation*. In contrast to S corporations, LLCs are not required to recognize gain on appreciated assets upon liquidation.

16. *Guaranteed payments*. Unique to partnerships and LLCs are payments from the partnership or LLC to a member for services or capital. The payments are deductible by the LLC and reportable as income by the member. In contrast to a member draw that has no tax result to the member, except to reduce his or her basis in the LLC interest, a guaranteed payment does not affect the member's basis. This is because distribution is cancelled out, as it is included in income. Guaranteed payments provide

flexibility in compensating LLC members. This provision is not available to S corporations.

## ¶44,003   DISADVANTAGES OF LLCs COMPARED TO S CORPORATIONS

The main disadvantages of LLCs as compared to S corporations follow:

- *Payroll taxes.* The S corporation's income taxed to its shareholders is not subject to self-employment Tax. Income earned by an LLC resulting from the efforts of its members is subject to self-employment tax. This provides an advantage to S corporation shareholders who may take part of the company's profits as salary, subject to Social Security, and part as S corporation distributions, which are *not* subject to self-employment or other payroll taxes.
- *Continuity of life.* The sale of S corporation stock does not dissolve the corporate entity (although the sale of more than 50 percent can result in revocation if the new majority owner affirmatively refuses to consent to election). Sale of more than 50 percent of an LLC interest dissolves the LLC (in accordance with partnership accounting rules and state law).
- *Untested waters.* Because state statutes regarding LLCs are not uniform and there is not yet a history of litigation and judicial rulings on their operation, some taxpayers have hesitated to use LLCs, especially in interstate commerce or when members are residents of different states. Third parties, such as banks may show reluctance to deal with an LLC until the legal status is more secure. As states adopt uniform LLC statutes and allow registration of foreign (from other states) LLCs, this problem should be resolved. Activities such as real estate holdings and exploitation of natural resources may use LLCs with little concern for these problems.
- *Family income splitting.* In attempts to split income among family members, the gift of the stock of an S corporation is more likely to be respected by the IRS than a similar gift of an LLC interest.

## ¶44,005   TERMINOLOGY

An understanding of LLCs can be aided by becoming familiar with the terms used to describe them. The following list of definitions will allow the accountant to better advise a client in choosing an entity that best represents the structure of a new business.

**articles of organization** The agreement forming the LLC and setting out its operating procedures.

**capital account** Each member has a capital account on the books of the LLC. To determine the value of a capital account, a member's capital sharing ratio is multiplied by the net asset value of the LLC (fair market value of assets less liabilities). This represents the amount a member would receive upon liquidation of the LLC.

**disregarded entity** The term applied by the IRS for one-member LLCs electing to be taxed as sole proprietorships.

**inside basis** The LLC's tax basis in its assets for depreciation purpose.

**K-1** The annual reporting form received by each member of the LLC (assuming the LLC has elected to be taxed as a partnership and not as a corporation).

**manager** Refers to a person who, alone or together with others, is vested with the continuing exclusive authority to make management decisions necessary to conduct the business for which the LLC was formed.

**members** The owners of an LLC are referred to as *members* rather than as partners or shareholders. Members may be assigned different roles in the organization with some handling management responsibilities and others serving only as investors.

**outside basis** The basis of an LLC member in his or her ownership position.

**profit and loss sharing ratios** Each member is assigned a percentage of the profits and losses of the LLC. The percentage may be changed by amending the operating agreement.

**separately stated items** The items of income, deduction, gain, loss, or credit that are allocated to each member in accordance with the operating agreement.

**single-member LLC** An LLC formed under state law with only one owner.

**special allocation** The operating agreement may specify that specific separately stated items be allocated in other than the profit and loss sharing ratios.

# ¶44,007 FORMATION OF AN LLC

A limited liability company is formed by the operation of state law. The first step is to draft *articles of organization* or a *certificate of formation*. This document, like articles of incorporation or a partnership agreement, sets out the basic ground rules for the organization. LLCs may be formed as new entities or they may emerge from the conversion or merger of already existing entities.

The articles of organization state the business purpose of the entity, its duration, the requirements for transfer of an interest, and the nature of management. In drafting the document, the goal is to maintain the limited legal liability of the owners while distinguishing the organization from a corporation. Until the "check the box" entity classification regulations promulgated by the IRS in 1996, there was significant concern and discussion regarding the avoidance of the following corporate characteristics: unlimited duration, free transferability of ownership interests, or centralization of management. The 1996 IRS rules allow LLCs to be taxed as partnerships or corporations at the election of the owners. The IRS developed Form 8832, *Entity Classification Election,* allowing taxpayers to check a box indicating what kind of taxable entity they elect to be. (IRS Regulations 301.7701-1–3.) The default for an LLC with two or more members is a partnership. For a single member LLC the default is a sole proprietorships. If the LLC wishes to be taxed as a corporation this form should be filed with the IRS within 75 days of the LLC's formation. If this deadline is passed, the IRS has provided relief, if the form is filed with the taxpayer's first tax return (see "Recent LLC Developments"). It is possible to change the election in a later year. All states also allow one-member LLCs that are described later.

## .01  Contribution of Assets

Contributions of property to an LLC (upon formation or later) generally result in no tax consequences to the contributing member or the LLC at the time of contribution. The LLC takes over the tax basis of the contributing member.

A member contributing appreciated property (fair market value in excess of tax basis), however, is allocated the precontribution gain or loss, to be recognized later when the property is sold. When the LLC sells the nondepreciable property, the built-in portion of the gain or loss is allocated first to the contributing partner before being allocated in accordance with the income and loss-sharing percentages of the articles of organization. For depreciable property, the Regulations (1.704-3) allow alternative methods of determining the precontribution gain. The assets are depreciated for book (capital account) and tax to reflect the differences in their basis.

---

## Illustration 45-1. Contribution of Assets

The articles of organization for the Fred-Bob Limited Liability Company call for all profits and losses to be allocated equally to the members, unless otherwise required by law. At the start of the company, Fred contributed 25 acres of land he had purchased for $25,000 ten years ago. At contribution the land is worth $100,000. Bob contributed cash of $100,000. The LLC uses the cash to develop a nine-hole golf course. Two years later, the golf course is completed and sold for $300,000. Each member receives $150,000 and the LLC is dissolved. How much gain is allocated to each member?

1. Total gain = $175,000 (sales price $300,000 minus basis $125,000)
2. Less: Fred's precontribution gain = $75,000 (fair market value of land $100,000 at contribution less basis $25,000)
3. Allocate balance of gain, $100,000 equally to Fred and Bob per articles of organization
4. Result = Fred's total gain is $125,000 and Bob's $50,000

## .03  Accounting Methods, Tax Year, and Elections of LLCs

The partnership accounting rules are applied to LLCs. A Limited liability company is allowed to use the cash method, accrual method, or a hybrid accounting method that clearly reflects its income. However, with the exception of small LLCs, if one or more of its members (owners) is a corporation required to use the accrual method, it must use the accrual method as well.

The tax year of an LLC is controlled by the partnership rules; it must use the year of its principle members. Generally, if the members are individuals, the LLC will have a calendar year. Exceptions are available for natural business years or business purpose.

Like partnerships, LLCs are allowed an election to step up the basis of a pro rata share of its property to reflect the purchase price a new member pays to buy the interest of an existing member. In the case of real estate investment, for example, this increases the depreciation deduction for the new member relative to the other members (see "Basis Step-Up Rules for Purchased LLC Interests").

Elections of other accounting methods such as inventory flow assumptions, depreciation method, and long-term contracts follow general tax rules set out in the Internal Revenue Code. An unincorporated business having two or more owners may elect to be taxed for federal income tax purposes as a corporation or as a partnership (Form 8832). Thus an LLC has the option of how it is taxed. Unless the LLC wishes to be taxed as a corporation the form is not filed.

Organization costs are amortized over 180 months except that upto $5,000 may qualify as an immediate deduction.

## .05  Allocation of Income, Deductions, Gain, Loss and Credits

For start-up businesses, the use of an LLC provides definite advantages over a taxable corporation or an S corporation. The LLC form allows special allocations of income, deductions, gains, losses, and credits tailored to the individual investors (subject to economic reality checks). In particular, this may be beneficial with businesses incurring significant initial R&D expenses. To the extent that these costs qualify, a loss produced by their deduction may be passed through to the members, offsetting their individual income.

## ¶44,009  ORDERING RULES FOR DEDUCTION OF LOSSES

A member's basis in the LLC is determined at the end of the tax year and includes all increases (including income) and decreases (including distributions)—*except losses*. The deductibility of losses is determined last. Losses are only deductible up to the amount of a member's basis. Losses are allocated to basis last (distributions and changes in liabilities have already been taken into account). This increases the chances of losses being disallowed (though they may be carried over to future years).

## ¶44,011  SEPARATELY STATED ITEMS

The separately stated items are those items of income or deduction, gain, loss, or credit that could affect the computation of one member's personal income tax differently from another member's. The list of separately stated items for LLCs is identical to that of partnerships or S corporations:

- Capital gains and losses—long term.
- Capital gains and losses—short term.
- IRC section 1231 gains and losses.
- Charitable contributions.
- Portfolio income (interest and dividends).
- Expenses related to portfolio income.
- Section 179 immediate expensing.
- Items specially allocated—specific items controlled by the operating agreement and differing from the profit or loss sharing ratios.
- Alternative Minimum Tax (AMT) preference items.
- Passive activity items—including rental income and expenses.
- Investment interest expense.
- Intangible drilling costs.
- Taxes paid to foreign countries.
- Tax-exempt income (increases member's basis).
- Nonbusiness and personal (nondeductible) items (decrease member's basis).

## ¶44,013  DISTRIBUTION OF ASSETS

Generally no gain or loss is recognized by the LLC or the member to whom assets are distributed. An exception occurs when the cash and marketable securities distribution is greater than the basis of the member in his or her

LLC membership interest. The property distributed to the member retains the same tax basis it had to the LLC. When an LLC is liquidated, each member must receive assets with a fair market value equal to the member's capital account. A member with a negative capital account is required to restore the balance to zero. If the articles of organization guarantee specific distributions upon liquidation, *regardless of the capital account balance,* the allocation will not have economic effect.

# ¶44,015 COMPLIANCE ISSUES

A multimember LLC must file IRS Form 1065 to report the LLC's income and the members' shares of income or loss as well as the members' shares of separately stated items. Single-member LLCs that have elected to be taxed as sole proprietorships report their activity on Schedule C of the owner's Form 1040. If Form 8832, *Entity Classification Election,* is being filed, it should be filed within 75 days of the formation of the entity. If this deadline is passed, it should be attached to the federal tax or information return of the entity for the taxable year for which the election is made (see "Recent LLC Developments").

# ¶44,017 CAPITAL ACCOUNT VERSUS BASIS

Members of LLCs are required to maintain a record of their ownership basis in the LLC (outside basis). This balance frequently differs from their capital account that is maintained on the LLC's books.

The member's basis in his or her ownership position is computed at least annually and consists of the prior year's ending basis *plus*:

- The basis of additional property contributed to the LLC during the year.
- Income (including tax exempt income) and gains (including capital gains) generated by the LLC and passed through to the member.
- Fair market value of services provided to the LLC in exchange for additional capital ownership.
- Any increase in the member's share of the LLC's liabilities.

*Minus*:

- Distributions from the LLC to the member.
- Losses and deductions (including nondeductible items) passed through to the member.
- The member's share of any reduction in the LLC's liabilities.

**¶44,015**

As with partnership accounting, the (book/accounting) capital accounts of the LLC members reflect the fair market value of their ownership interest in the LLC, whereas the basis in their LLC interest is used to compute gain or loss upon sale or other disposition of the interest.

A distribution (draw) cannot reduce the member's basis below zero. Therefore, a distribution in excess of basis produces a capital gain to the member. A reduction in a member's share of liabilities is treated as a distribution and has the same result as a cash distribution.

## ¶44,019   ASSETS CONTRIBUTED TO THE LLC

Assets contributed to an LLC by a member carry over the property's basis in the hands of the member. The holding period of capital and IRC section 1231 assets contributed continues the member's holding period as well. In the case of ordinary income property, such as inventory, the holding period for the LLC begins upon contribution. Capital gain property with a built-in loss (the basis exceeded the fair market value on the date of contribution) must be held by the LLC for five years before its sale will result in an ordinary loss.

The method and life used to depreciate property before its contribution carry over and are used by the LLC. No section 179 deduction is allowed on contributed property. If the property contributed was not used in a trade or business prior to its contribution, its basis for depreciation is the lower of its original cost or its fair market value on the date of contribution.

## ¶44,021   BASIS STEP-UP RULES FOR PURCHASED LLC INTERESTS

When an LLC interest is purchased, there is often a difference between the purchase price and the LLC's proportionate share of basis in its assets (inside basis). This is particularly common in real estate LLCs. An election is available to step-up (or down) the basis of the portion of the assets that represent the purchasing member's interest in those assets (IRC sections 754, 743, and 734). The assets are stepped-up to the new member's basis in the LLC. Depreciable assets are, thereby, stepped up to their fair market value, and depreciation deductions are increased *only with respect to the new member*. Additional accounting records are required to keep track of the depreciation for the new member as well as for the old, but if the difference between the old LLC basis and the purchase price of the LLC interest is significant, it can be worth the additional effort.

## ¶44,023   DEBT ALLOCATION—RECOURSE VERSUS NONRECOURSE

The amount of debt allocated to a member of an LLC affects his or her basis in that individual's ownership interest. The distinction between recourse and nonrecourse debt affects partnership accounting because general partners are personally liable for recourse debt. However, different rules apply to determine the amount of the debt allocated to a partner, depending upon whether it is recourse or nonrecourse debt.

Debt for which individual partners are personally responsible is recourse debt. In the case of recourse debt, the IRS prescribes a *constructive liquidation scenario,* which generally allocates an amount of debt to each partner that corresponds to his or her personal liability to the partnership were it to liquidate. See Illustration 45-2 below.

Debt for which no individual partner is personally liable is nonrecourse. Nonrecourse debt is allocated in stages depending upon the existence in the partnership (LLC) of minimum gain, precontribution gain and the wording of the operating agreement.

Because members of an LLC are protected from liability for the LLC's debt, all debt is nonrecourse, unless a member has agreed to be personally liable. Nonrecourse debt increases member basis but not necessarily the amount at-risk.

---

## Illustration 45-2: Nonrecourse Debt Allocation

Level 1:  Amount of nonrecourse debt

> }
> Sec. 704(b)   } = minimum gain
> } (allocate per agreement)

Level 2:  Fair market value of property on date of contribution

> }
> Sec. 704(c)   } = precontribution gain
> } (specific allocation)

Level 3:  Tax basis of property on date of contribution

> }
> } = allocation (based on
> } (profit sharing percent)

*Minimum gain.* If the amount of nonrecourse debt exceeded the fair market value of the assets on the date of contribution, a minimum gain was created. Calculation of the minimum gain assumes, hypothetically, that the lender is to foreclose on the property securing the debt (IRC sec. 704(b)).

If the property were foreclosed and the amount of LLC nonrecourse debt is in excess of the book basis (accounting/capital account basis/fair market value on date of contribution) of the property, the excess of the nonrecourse debt over the book basis is referred to as the minimum gain, and its allocation is in accordance with the LLC articles of organization.

If the property has been contributed to the LLC and the contributing member's tax basis in the property was less than the nonrecourse debt encumbering the property at the date of contribution, and less than its fair market value, an additional allocation of nonrecourse debt is made.

The amount of fair market value that was in excess of the contributing member's basis is allocated to that member. (This gain amount is the *built-in gain,* or *precontribution gain.*) (IRC sec. 704(c))

The balance of the nonrecourse debt (the amount up to the tax basis of the property when it was contributed) is allocated to the members using their profit sharing ratio.

# ¶44,025  AT-RISK LIMITS

LLCs are covered by the same restrictive limits as individuals, partnerships, and S corporations when it comes to the at-risk limits of IRC section 465. Losses passed through to the members by the LLC are deductible by the members only to the extent they *are* at economic risk of loss. The allocation of basis from LLC debt does not guarantee that a member will be able to deduct losses generated by the LLC. Unused losses may be carried forward by members and deducted later when the LLC generates income.

Planning can improve the ability of a member to deduct losses. An important step in this process involves the aggregation of at-risk activities. If a loss business and a profitable one operated by the LLC can be combined into one activity for at-risk purposes, the loss can offset the profit, and the net will be passed through to the members. If the two businesses are treated as separate activities, however, the profit will pass through separately to the member as well as the loss, and the loss may not be deductible.

# ¶44,027  LIMITED LIABILITY PARTNERSHIPS

In place of LLCs for professional services—doctors, dentists, attorneys, architects, accountants—states allow the formation of Limited Liability Partnerships. These afford general liability protection for a business in the same manner as professional corporations, but thus do not protect the individual owners from liability for their own malpractice or the malpractice of those whom they directly supervise. However, the limited liability generally extends protection to each individual owner against the malpractice of the other owners.

## .01 Tax Matters Partner

A Limited liability company electing to be taxed as a partnership files Form 1065 and is requested to name a *tax matters partner,* designated to deal with the IRS on behalf of the partnership. For purposes of naming a tax matters partner on behalf of a LLC, the IRS will allow only a member-manager of the LLC to be so named. In a partnership, only a general partner may serve as a tax matters partner.

## ¶44,029  ONE-MEMBER LLCS

All states allow the formation of one-member LLCs. These entities provide the owner with the personal liability protections of an LLC under state law but they are taxed either as a sole proprietor or a corporation for federal income tax purposes. The default of a one-member LLC is a sole proprietorship and if the owner desires corporate taxation, the owner makes this choice by filing IRS Form 8832 and checking the appropriate box. Form 8832 should be filed within 75 days of formation or be attached to the federal tax return of the entity (or individual) for the taxable year for which the election is made. If the owner does not elect to be taxed as a corporation the IRS refers to him or her as a *disregarded entity.* The owner completes 1040 form Schedule C (for a business) or Schedule E (for a real estate rental operation) and SE for other sole proprietorships.

In the past, sole proprietors seeking legal liability protection under state law were required to incorporate their business to gain this protection. As a result of forming a corporation, whether a taxable C corporation or a flow-through S corporation, the business incurs the additional accounting and paper-work required to file a federal income tax return for the business. In most cases this also requires quarterly payroll tax filing as well, for the owner's salary. The single-member LLC avoids the necessity of additional accounting and tax filing while providing the desired liability protection. Some states do impose an entity tax on single-member LLCs.

## ¶44,031  CONVERSION TO AN LLC

The owners of a corporation, including an S corporation, desiring to convert the corporation to an LLC are faced with the prospect of first liquidating the corporation and thereby incurring double taxation—first at the corporate level—and then on the distribution of assets to the shareholder. There is no direct reorganization statute that allows a tax-free conversion of a corporation to a LLC. By contrast, the conversion of a partnership or a sole proprietorship to an LLC is straightforward and can be accomplished without generating taxable income. However, state law may hold the members personally liable for the debts of the former entity.

# ¶44,033  RECENT LLC DEVELOPMENTS AND CAUTIONS

## .01  Members Can Avoid Liability for Unpaid Payroll Taxes

Businesses that find themselves strapped for cash sometimes hold back payments of withheld income, FICA, and Medicare taxes (trust fund taxes) to the IRS. This has always been a dangerous maneuver because the IRS has the authority to collect these taxes from the individual(s) involved in the decision to place other creditors ahead of the IRS (referred to as the "responsible person," IRC Section 6672). The result is referred to as the 100 percent penalty—the IRS collects up to 100 percent of the withheld payroll taxes from the responsible person. The responsible person has sometimes been the comptroller or the controlling shareholders of a small business. In addition, the IRS can collect withheld payroll taxes from the general partners of a partnership. However, in a recent Revenue Ruling (2004-41) the IRS indicated that it can not collect delinquent withheld payroll taxes from a member of an LLC—unless, of course, the member is also found to be a responsible person—the one with authority to withhold payment from the IRS. LLC members not directly involved in such decisions therefore receive protection not accorded the partners of a general partnership.

## .03  Built-in Loss Rules Tightened to Curb Abuse of Duplicate Loss Deductions

Contributions of property to partnerships by partners can produce built-in losses if the partner's basis of the property contributed exceeds its fair market value. The transfer of a partnership interest involving a substantial *built-in loss* (defined as basis exceeding fair market value by more than $250,000) now requires a mandatory IRC Section 743 basis adjustment reducing the property's basis to the partnership to its fair market value, thus preventing loss recognition when the property is sold.

## .05  AICPA Issues LLC Practice Bulletin

To aid practitioners in the preparation of financial statements for LLCs the AICPA issued Practice Bulletin 14, *Accounting and Reporting by Limited Liability Companies and Limited Liability Partnerships* in April, 1995. The bulletin addresses issues of disclosure and presentation. According to the AICPA, "A complete set of LLC financial statements should include a statement of financial position as of the end of the reporting period, a statement of operations for the period, a statement of cash flows for the period, and accompanying notes to the financial statements."

## .07 Form 8832 Entity Classification Election

The IRS has provided relief for LLCs that fail to file the Form 8832, *Entity Classification Election,* within 75 days of the entity's formation. IRS *Revenue Procedure 2002-59* specifies procedures for filing the form by the due date of the LLC's first federal income tax return (not including extensions). Owners failing to comply with government filing requirements risk personal liability for obligations of the LLC. If the LLC status is not properly maintained in accordance with state law, it may be disregarded by the IRS. Most states require an annual filing and fee. This is true of corporations as well.

Other cautions include:

- The at-risk loss rules apply to members of LLCs and may limit the deduction of losses by a member.
- The passive activity loss limits apply to members of LLCs and may limit the deduction of losses on passive rental activities.
- The Alternative Minimum Tax (AMT) adjustments and preferences generated by an LLC flow though to the individual members and are combined with their personal AMT items.
- The Internal Revenue Code contains rules defining tax shelters. If an LLC is classified as a tax shelter, specific restrictions apply, including the inability of the LLC to use the cash method of accounting.
- When an LLC interest is being sold, the kinds of assets held by the company should be analyzed. Although in general the sale will produce a capital gain to the seller, certain assets will convert part or all of the gain to ordinary income. The kinds of assets causing this result are referred to as *hot assets* and include unrealized receivables and inventory.

# Chapter 45

# Independent Contractor or Employee?

## CONTENTS

## ¶45,000 OVERVIEW

Whether a person is an employee or independent contractor has been an area of uncertainty for many years. In August 1996, during the 104th Congress, changing and strengthening the "safe harbor" provisions were enacted as part of the Small Business Jobs Protection Act. The changes allow small businesses to rely on previous IRS actions and determinations to avoid reclassification of independent contractors as employees. The legislation does, however, still leave open the key question of what exactly is an independent contractor.

To make the definition of an independent contractor as clear as possible under current law, the IRS issued a training manual for IRS personnel on the independent contractor issue; introduced procedures for facilitating rapid determinations and appeals; and reduced penalties where a business acts in good faith to classify its independent contractors.

## ¶45,001 Determining Who Is an Employee and Who Is an Independent Contractor

Before it is possible to treat payments made for services, it is necessary to know the business relationship that exists between the employer and the person performing the services. The person performing the services may be:

1. An independent contractor.
2. A common-law employee.
3. A statutory employee.
4. A statutory nonemployee.

These four categories are discussed below. A later section points out the differences between an independent contractor and an employee. If an individual who is not an employee under the common-law rules is employed by a business, generally it is not necessary to withhold Federal income tax from that individual's pay. However, in some cases the employer may be required to withhold under backup withholding requirements on these payments.

### .01 Independent Contractors

People such as lawyers, contractors, subcontractors, public stenographers, and auctioneers who follow an independent trade, business, or profession in which they offer their services to the public, are generally not employees. However, whether such people are employees or independent contractors depends on the facts in each case. The general rule is that an individual is an independent contractor if the person for whom the services are performed, has the right to control or direct *only the result* of the work and *not the means and methods* of accomplishing the result.

### .03 Common-Law Employees

Under common-law rules, anyone who performs services for an entity is an employee if the employer can control what will be done and how it will be done. This is so even when the employee is given freedom of action. What matters is that the employer has the right to control the details of the services performed.

If there is an employer-employee relationship, it makes no difference how it is labeled. The substance of the relationship, not the label, governs the worker's status. Nor does it matter whether the individual is employed full or part time.

For employment tax purposes, no distinction is made between classes of employees. Superintendents, managers, and other supervisory personnel are all employees. An officer of a corporation is generally an employee; however, an officer who performs no services or only minor services, and neither receives nor is entitled to receive any pay, is not considered an employee. A director of a corporation is not an employee with respect to services performed as a director.

It is generally necessary to withhold and pay income, Social Security, and Medicare taxes on wages paid to common-law employees. However, the wages of certain employees may be exempt from one or more of these taxes.

*Leased Employees.*    Under certain circumstances, a corporation furnishing workers to various professional people and firms is the employer of those workers for employment tax purposes. For example, a professional service corporation may provide the services of secretaries, nurses, and other similarly trained workers to its subscribers.

The service corporation enters into contracts with the subscribers under which the subscribers specify the services to be provided and the fee to be paid to the service corporation for each individual furnished. The service corporation has the right to control and direct the worker's services for the subscriber, including the right to discharge or reassign the worker. The service corporation hires the workers, controls the payment of their wages, provides them with unemployment insurance and other benefits, and is the employer for employment tax purposes.

## .05 Statutory Employees

If workers are independent contractors under the common law rules, such workers may nevertheless be treated as employees by statute ("statutory employees") for certain employment tax purposes if they fall within any one of the following four categories and meet the three conditions described under Social Security and Medicare taxes, below. The four categories are:

1.  A driver who distributes beverages (other than milk) or meat, vegetable, fruit, or bakery products, or one who picks up and delivers laundry or dry cleaning, if the driver is the entity's agent or is paid on commission.
2.  A full-time life insurance sales agent whose principal business activity is selling life insurance, annuity contracts, or both, primarily for one life insurance company.

3. An individual who works at home on materials or goods that are supplied and that must be returned to a business establishment, if the business also furnishes specifications for the work to be done.

4. A full-time traveling or city salesperson who works on the entity's behalf and turns in orders to the business from wholesalers, retailers, contractors, or operators of hotels, restaurants, or other similar establishments. The goods sold must be merchandise for resale or supplies for use in the buyer's business operation. The work performed must be the salesperson's principal business activity.

*Social Security and Medicare Taxes.* Social Security and Medicare taxes must be withheld from the wages of statutory employees if all three of the following conditions apply:

1. The service contract states or implies that substantially all the services are to be performed personally by them,

2. They do not have a substantial investment in the equipment and property used to perform the services (other than an investment in transportation facilities), and

3. The services are performed on a continuing basis for the same payer.

*The Federal Unemployment Tax Act (FUTA) and Income Tax.* For FUTA tax, the term employee means the same as it does for Social Security and Medicare taxes, except that it does not include statutory employees in categories 2 and 3 above. Thus, any individual who is an employee under category 1 or 4 is also an employee for FUTA tax purposes and subject to FUTA tax.

Income taxes are not to be withheld from the wages of statutory employees.

## .07  Statutory Nonemployees

There are two categories of statutory nonemployees: direct sellers and licensed real estate agents. They are treated as self-employed for all federal tax purposes, including income and employment taxes, if:

1. Substantially all payments for their services as direct sellers or real estate agents are directly related to sales or other output rather than to the number of hours worked.

2. Their services are performed under a written contract providing that they will not be treated as employees for federal tax purposes.

*Direct Sellers.*    Direct sellers include persons falling within any of these three groups:

1. Persons engaged in selling (or soliciting the sale of) consumer products in the home or place of business other than in a permanent retail establishment.
2. Persons engaged in selling (or soliciting the sale of) consumer products to any buyer on a buy-sell basis, a deposit-commission basis, or any similar basis prescribed by regulations, for resale in the home or at a place of business other than in a permanent retail establishment.
3. Persons engaged in the trade or business of delivering or distributing newspapers or shopping news (including any services directly related to such delivery or distribution).

Direct selling includes activities of individuals who attempt to increase direct sales activities of their direct sellers and who earn income based on the productivity of their direct sellers. Such activities include providing motivation and encouragement; imparting skills, knowledge or experience; and recruiting.

## ¶45,003  WORKER CLASSIFICATION

With the exception of statutory employees, work classification is based upon a common law standard for determining whether the worker is an independent contractor or employee. That standard essentially asks whether the business has the right to *direct and control the worker*. The courts have traditionally looked to a variety of evidentiary facts in applying this standard, and the IRS has adopted those facts to assist in classifying workers.

## ¶45,005  ACCOUNTANT'S CONCERN?

When conducting an audit, the auditor needs to assist taxpayers in identifying all of the evidence relative to their business relationships with workers. Many taxpayers may not be aware of what information is needed to make a correct determination of worker classification. Others have turned a blind eye. This is especially true of small business owners who may not be aware of the relief available under Section 530 of the Revenue Act of 1978, resulting from worker reclassification. An auditor's examination should actively consider Section 530 during an examination, including furnishing taxpayers with a summary of Section 530 at the beginning of an examination.

Essentially, an accountant's responsibility is similar to an IRS tax examiner's responsibility as set forth by the Treasury Department that states:

"The examiner has a responsibility to the taxpayer and to the government to determine the correct tax liability and to maintain a fair and impartial attitude in all matters relating to the examination. The fair and impartial attitude of an examiner aids in increasing voluntary compliance. An examiner must approach each examination with an objective point of view.''

# ¶45,007   Section 530 Relief Requirements

A business has been selected for an employment tax examination to determine whether certain workers were correctly treated as independent contractors. However, the employer will not owe employment taxes for those workers if the employer meets the relief requirements described below. If the employer does not meet these relief requirements, the IRS will need to determine whether the workers are, in fact, independent contractors or employees and whether employment taxes are actually owed for those workers.

To receive relief from paying employment taxes, three requirements must be met: reasonable basis, substantive consistency and reporting consistency.

## .01   Reasonable Basis

To establish a reasonable basis for not treating the workers as employees, an employer must show that:

1. It reasonably relied on a court case about federal taxes or a ruling issued by the IRS.
2. The business was audited by the IRS at a time when similar workers were treated as independent contractors and the IRS did not reclassify those workers as employees.
3. Workers were treated as independent contractors because that was how a significant segment of that particular industry treated similar workers.
4. The employer relied on some other reasonable basis—for example, on the advice of a business lawyer or accountant who knew the facts about the particular business and that industry.

The employer does not have a *reasonable basis* for treating the workers as independent contractors and therefore will not meet the relief requirements if his or her decision was not made on the basis of one of these criteria.

## .03   Substantive Consistency

In addition, the employer (and any predecessor business) must have treated the workers, and any similar workers, as independent contractors. If similar workers were treated as employees, this relief provision is not available.

¶45,007

## .05   Reporting Consistency

Form 1099-MISC must have been filed for each worker, unless the worker earned less than $600. Relief is not available for any year in which the required Forms 1099-MISC were not filed. If they were filed for some workers but not others, relief is not available for the workers for whom they were not filed.

## ¶45,009   THE DECISION: EMPLOYEE OR INDEPENDENT CONTRACTOR?

An employer must generally withhold income taxes, withhold and pay Social Security and Medicare taxes, and pay unemployment tax on wages paid to an *employee*. An employer does not generally have to withhold or pay any taxes on payments to *independent contractors*. This is the important distinction.

To determine whether an individual is an employee or an independent contractor under the common law, the relationship of the worker and the business must be examined. All evidence of control and independence must be considered. In any employee–independent contractor determination, all information that provides evidence of the degree of control and the degree of independence must be considered.

## ¶45,011   PRIMARY CATEGORIES

Officially termed the *worker classification issue,* the focus is centered on three main areas that the IRS has concluded are primary categories of evidence to draw a distinction between an employee and an independent contractor. The essence of the distinction is whether or not the employer has the right to direct and control the worker. The three areas are:

1. Behavioral control.
2. Financial control.
3. Relationship of the parties.

Those three areas provide evidence that substantiates the right to direct or control the details and means by which the worker performs the required services. Training is important in this context. Significant are such workplace developments as evaluation systems and concern for customer security in conjunction with business identification. All relevant information must be considered and weighed to determine whether a worker is an independent contractor or an employee.

Virtually every business will impose on workers, whether contractors or employees, some form of instruction. How else would a worker know what he or she is supposed to do, what duties to perform? This fact alone, however, is not sufficient evidence to determine a worker's status. As with every relevant fact, the problem is to determine whether the employer has retained the right to control the *details* of a worker's performance, or instead has given up the business's right to control those details. Accordingly, the weight of evidence in any case depends on the *degree* to which instructions apply with respect to *how the job gets done rather than to the end result.*

## .01 Behavioral Control

Behavioral control concerns whether there is a right to direct or control how the worker performs the specific task for which he or she is engaged. Instructions and training are the main factors in considering the degree of behavioral control.

An employee is generally subject to the business's instructions about when, where, and how to work. Following are types of instructions about how to do work:

1. When and where to do the work.
2. What tools or equipment to use.
3. What workers to hire or to assist with the work.
4. Where to purchase supplies and services.
5. What work must be performed by a specified individual.
6. What order or sequence to follow.

The degree of instruction depends on the scope of instructions, the extent to which the business retains the right to control the worker's compliance with the instructions, and the effect on the worker in the event of noncompliance. All these provide useful clues for identifying whether the business keeps control over the manner and means of work performance, or only over a particular product or service. The more detailed the instructions are that the worker is required to follow, the more control the business exerts over the worker, and the more likely the business retains the right to control the methods by which the worker performs the work. Absence of detail in instructions reflects less control.

Although the presence and extent of instructions is important in reaching a conclusion as to whether a business retains the right to direct and control the methods by which a worker performs a job, it is also important to consider the weight to be given those instructions if they are imposed by the business only in compliance with governmental or governing body regulations. If a business requires its workers to comply with established, municipal building codes related to construction, for example, the fact that such rules are imposed by the business should be given little weight in determining the worker's status. However, if the business develops more stringent guidelines for a worker in

¶45,011.01

addition to those imposed by a third party, more weight should be given to these instructions in determining whether the business has retained the right to control the worker.

The nature of a worker's occupation also affects the degree of direction and control necessary to determine worker status. Highly trained professionals such as doctors, accountants, lawyers, engineers, or computer specialists may require very little, if any, training and instruction on how to perform their services for a particular business. In fact, it may be impossible for the business to instruct the worker on how to perform the services because it may lack the essential knowledge and skills to do so. Generally, professional workers who are engaged in the pursuit of an independent trade, business, or profession in which they offer their services to the public are independent contractors, not employees. In analyzing the status of professional workers, evidence of control or autonomy with respect to the financial details of how the task is performed tends to be especially important, as does evidence concerning the relationship of the parties.

An employment relationship can also exist when the work can be done with a minimal amount of direction and control, such as work done by a store clerk, or gas station attendant. The absence of a *need* to control should not be confused with the absence of the *right* to control. The right to control as an incident of employment requires only such supervision as the nature of the work requires. The key fact to consider is whether the business retains the *right* to direct and control the worker, regardless of whether the business actually exercises that right.

Evaluation systems are used by virtually all businesses to monitor the quality of work performed by workers, whether independent contractors or employees. In analyzing whether a business's evaluation system provides evidence of the right to control work performance, or the absence of such a right, an auditor should look for evidence of how the evaluation system may influence the worker's behavior in performing the details of the job.

If an evaluation system measures compliance with performance standards concerning the details of how the work is to be performed, the system and its enforcement are evidence of control over the worker's behavior. However, not all businesses have developed formal performance standards or evaluation systems. This is especially true of smaller businesses.

Training is the established means of explaining detailed methods and procedures to be used in performing a task. Periodic or ongoing training provided by a business about procedures to be followed and methods to be used indicates that the business wants the services performed in a particular manner. This type of training is strong evidence of an employer-employee relationship.

## .03 Financial Control

Financial control concerns the facts which illustrate whether there is a *right* to direct or control how the worker's activities are conducted.

¶45,011.03

Factors to be considered are the business aspects of the worker's activities; significant investment, if any; unreimbursed expenses; services available to the relevant market; method of payment; and opportunity for profit or loss. These factors can be thought of as bearing on the issue of whether the recipient has the right to direct and control the means and details of the business aspects of how the worker performs services.

A significant investment is evidence that an independent contractor relationship may exist. It should be stressed that a significant investment is not necessary for an independent contractor. Some types of work simply do not require large expenditures. Even if large expenditures, such as costly equipment, are required, an independent contractor may rent the equipment needed at fair rental value. There are no precise dollar limits that must be met in order to have a significant investment. The size of the worker's investment and the risk borne by the worker are not diminished merely because the seller or lessor receives the benefit of the worker's services.

The extent to which a worker chooses to incur expenses and costs impacts his or her opportunity for profit or loss. This constitutes evidence that the worker has the right to direct and control the financial aspects of the business operations. Although not every independent contractor needs to make a significant investment, almost every independent contractor will incur an array of business expenses either in the form of direct expenditures or in the form of fees for pro rata portions of one or several expenses. Businesses often pay business or travel expenses for their employees. Independent contractors' expenses may also be reimbursed. An independent contractor can contract for direct reimbursement of certain expenses, or can seek to establish contract prices that will reimburse the contractor for these expenses. Attention should center on *unreimbursed* expenses, which better distinguish independent contractors and employees, inasmuch as independent contractors are more likely to have unreimbursed expenses. If expenses are unreimbursed, then the opportunity for profit or loss exists. Fixed ongoing costs that are incurred regardless of whether work is currently being performed are especially important. However, employees may also incur unreimbursed expenses in connection with the services they perform for their businesses. Relatively minor expenses incurred by a worker, or more significant expenses that are customarily borne by an employee in a particular line of business, would generally not indicate an independent contractor relationship.

An independent contractor is generally free to seek out business opportunities, as independent contractors' income depends on doing so successfully. As a result, independent contractors often advertise, maintain a visible business location, and are available to work for the relevant market. An independent contractor with special skills may be contacted by word of mouth and referrals without the need for advertising. An independent contractor who has negotiated a long-term contract may find advertising equally unnecessary, and may be unavailable to work for others for the duration of a contract. Other independent contractors may find that a visible business location does not generate sufficient business to justify the expense. Therefore, the absence of these activities is a neutral fact.

The method of payment can be helpful in determining whether the worker has the opportunity for profit or loss. A worker who is compensated on an hourly, daily, weekly, or similar basis is guaranteed a return for labor. This is generally evidence of an employer-employee relationship, even when the wage or salary is accompanied by a commission. In some lines of business, such as law, it is typical to pay independent contractors on an hourly basis. Performance of a task for a flat fee is generally evidence of an independent contractor relationship, especially if the worker incurs the expenses of performing the services. A commission-based worker can be either an independent contractor or employee. The worker's status will depend on the worker's ability to realize a profit or incur a loss as a result of services rendered.

The ability to realize a profit or incur a loss is probably the strongest evidence that a worker controls the business aspects of services rendered.

Also to be considered is whether the worker is free to make business decisions that affect his profit or loss. If the worker is making decisions that affect the bottom line, the worker likely has the ability to realize profit or loss. It is sometimes thought that because a worker can receive more money working longer hours or receive less money by working less, he has the ability to incur a profit or loss. This type of income variation, however, is also consistent with employer status and does not distinguish employees from independent contractors.

Not all financial control facts need be present for the worker to have the ability to realize profit or loss. For example, a worker who is paid on a straight commission basis, makes business decisions, and has unreimbursed business expenses, likely would have the ability to realize a profit or loss, even if the worker does not have a significant investment and does not market her services.

## .05  Relationship of the Parties

There are other facts that recent court decisions consider relevant in determining worker status. Most of these facts reflect how the worker and the business perceive the relationship to each other. It is much more difficult to link the facts in this category directly to the right to direct and control *how* work is to be performed than the categories discussed above. The relationship of the parties is important because it reflects the parties' *intent* concerning control. Courts often look at the intent of the parties because the intent is most often stated in their contractual relationship. A written agreement describing the worker as an independent contractor is viewed as evidence of the parties' intent that a worker is an independent contractor. However, a contractual designation, in and of itself, is not sufficient evidence for determining worker status. The facts and circumstances under which a worker performs services determine a worker's status. The *substance* of a relationship, not a label, governs the worker's status. The contract may be relevant in ascertaining methods of compensation, expenses that will be incurred, and rights and obligations of each party with respect to *how* work is to be performed. In addition, if it is difficult, if not impossible, to decide whether a worker is an independent contractor, the intent of the parties, as reflected in the contractual designation, is an effective way to resolve the issue.

Questions sometimes arise concerning whether a worker who creates a corporation through which to perform services can be an employee of a business that engages the corporation. If the corporate formalities are properly followed, and at least one nontax business purpose exists, the corporate form is generally recognized for both state law and federal law, including federal tax purposes. Disregarding the corporate entity is generally an extraordinary remedy, applied by most courts only in cases of clear abuse, so the worker will usually not be treated as an employee of the business, but as an employee of the corporation. (It should be noted that the fact that a worker receives payment for services from a business through the worker's corporation does not automatically require a finding of independent contractor status with respect to those services.)

*Employee Benefits.*    Providing a worker with employee benefits has traditionally been linked with employee status and, therefore, can be an important factor in deciding an independent contractor-employee relationship. If a worker receives employee benefits, such as paid vacation days, paid sick days, health insurance, life or disability insurance, or a pension, this constitutes some evidence of employee status. The evidence is strongest if the worker is provided with employee benefits under a tax-qualified retirement plan, 403(b) annuity, or cafeteria plan, because by statute, these benefits can be provided to employees only. If an individual is excluded from a benefit plan because the worker is not considered an employee by the business, this is relevant though not conclusive in determining the worker's status as an independent contractor. If the worker is excluded on some other grounds, the exclusion is irrelevant in determining whether the worker is an independent contractor or an employee. This is because none of these employee benefits is required to be provided to employees. Many workers whose status as bona fide employees is unquestioned receive no employee benefits, as there is no requirement that all workers be covered.

*Termination Rights.*    The circumstances under which a business or a worker can terminate their relationship have traditionally been considered useful evidence bearing on the status the parties intended the worker to have. However, in order to determine whether the facts are relevant to the worker's status, the impact of modern business practices and legal standards governing worker termination must be considered. A business's ability to terminate the work relationship at will, without penalty, provides a highly effective method to control the details of how work is performed, and indicates employee status. On the other hand, in the traditional independent contractor relationship, the business

¶45,011.05

could terminate the relationship only if the worker failed to provide the intended service, which indicates the parties' intent that the business does not have the right to control how the work was performed. In practice, businesses rarely have complete flexibility in discharging an employee. The business may be liable for pay in lieu of notice, severance pay, "golden parachutes," or other forms of compensation when it discharges an employee. In addition, the reasons for which a business can terminate an employee may be limited, whether by law, by contract, or by its own practices.

A worker's ability to terminate work at will was traditionally considered to illustrate that the worker merely provided labor and tended to indicate an employer-employee relationship. In contrast, if the worker terminated work, and the business could refuse payment or sue for nonperformance, this indicated the business's interest in receiving the contracted product or service, which tended to indicate an independent contractor relationship. In practice, however, independent contractors can enter into short-term contracts for which nonperformance remedies are inappropriate; or they may negotiate limits on their liability for nonperformance. Typical examples are professionals, such as doctors and attorneys, who can terminate their contractual relationship without penalty.

Businesses can successfully sue employees for substantial damages resulting from their failure to perform the services for which they were engaged. As a result, the presence or absence of limits on workers' ability to terminate the relationship, by themselves, no longer constitutes useful evidence in determining worker status. A business's ability to refuse payment for unsatisfactory work continues to be characteristic of an independent contractor relationship.

*Permanent/Indefinite Relationship.* The existence of a permanent relationship between the worker and the business is relevant evidence in determining whether there is an employer-employee relationship. If a business engages a worker with the expectation that the relationship will continue indefinitely, rather than for a specific project or period, it is a factor that is generally considered evidence of an intent to create an employment relationship.

A relationship that is created with the expectation that it will be indefinite should not be confused with a long-term relationship. A long-term relationship may exist between a business and either an independent contractor or an employee. The relationship between the business and an independent contractor can be long-term for several reasons:

1. The contract may be a long-term contract.
2. Contacts can be renewed regularly due to superior service, competitive costs, or lack of alternative service providers.

A business can also have a relationship with an employee that is long-term, but not indefinite. This could occur if temporary employment contracts are renewed, or if a long-term, but not indefinite, employment contract is entered into. As a result, a relationship that is long-term, but not indefinite, is a neutral fact that should be disregarded.

A temporary relationship is a neutral fact that should be disregarded. An independent contractor will typically have a temporary relationship with a business, but so too will employees engaged on a seasonal project, or on an "as needed" basis. The services performed by the worker, and the extent to which those services are a key aspect of the regular business of the company, are germane. In considering this, it should be remembered that the fact that a service is desirable, necessary, or even essential to a business does not mean that the service provider is an employee. The work of an attorney or paralegal is part of the regular business of a law firm. If a law firm hires an attorney or paralegal, it is likely that the law firm will present the work as its own. As a result, there is an increased probability that the law firm will direct or control the activities. However, further facts should be examined to see whether there is evidence of the *right* to direct or control before a conclusion is reached that these workers are employees. It is possible that the work performed is part of the principal business of the law firm, yet it has hired workers who are outside specialists and may be independent contractors.

## ¶45,013  CHECKLIST

The 20 factors indicating whether an individual is an employee or an independent contractor follow:

1. *Instructions.* An employee must comply with instructions about when, where, and how to work. Even if no instructions are given, the control factor is present if the employer *has the right* to control how the work results are achieved.

2. *Training.* An employee may be trained to perform services in a particular manner. Independent contractors ordinarily use their own methods and receive no training from the purchasers of their services.

3. *Integration.* An employee's services are usually integrated into the business operations because the services are important to the success or continuation of the business. This shows that the employee is subject to direction and control.

4. *Services Are Rendered Personally.* An employee renders services personally. This shows that the employer is interested in the methods as well as the results.

5. *Hiring Assistants.* An employee works for an employer who hires, supervises, and pays workers. An independent contractor can hire, supervise, and pay assistants under a contract that requires their contractor to provide materials and labor and to be responsible only for the result.

6. *Continuing Relationship.* An employee generally has a continuing relationship that may exist even if work is performed at recurring although irregular intervals.

7. *Set Hours of Work.* An employee usually has set hours of work established by an employer. Independent contractors generally can set their own work hours.

8. *Full-Time Required.* An employee may be required to work or be available full-time. This indicates control by the employer. An independent contractor can work when and for whom he or she chooses.

9. *Work Done on Premises.* An employee usually works on the premises of an employer, or works on a route or at a location designated by an employer.

10. *Order or Sequence Set.* An employee may be required to perform services in the order or sequence set by an employer. This shows that the employee is subject to direction and control, in contrast to the independent contractor who determines the order and sequence in which the work is performed.

11. *Reports.* An employee may be required to submit reports to an employer, which shows that the employer maintains a degree of control.

12. *Payments.* An employee generally is paid by the hour, week, or month. An independent contractor is usually paid by the job or on a straight commission. An independent contractor is paid by the job, which can include periodic payments based upon a percentage of job completed. Payment can be based on the number of hours needed to do the job times an hourly wage. The payment method should be determined before the job is undertaken.

13. *Expenses.* An employee's business and travel expenses are generally paid by an employer. This shows that the employee is subject to regulation and control.

14. *Tools and Materials.* An employee is normally furnished significant tools, materials, and other equipment by an employer.

15. *Investment.* An independent contractor has a significant investment in the facilities used in performing services for someone else.

16. *Profit or Loss Possibilities.* Independent contractors should be able to make a profit or a loss. Employees can not suffer a loss. Five circumstances show that a profit or loss is possible:
    - The independent contractor hires, directs, and pays assistants.
    - The independent contractor has his or her own office, equipment, materials, or facilities.
    - The independent contractor has continuing and recurring liabilities.
    - The independent contractor has agreed to perform specific jobs for prices agreed upon in advance.

¶45,013

- The independent contractor's services affect his or her own business reputation.
17. *Works for More than One Person or Firm.* An independent contractor is generally free to provide services to two or more unrelated persons or firms at the same time.
18. *Services Available to the Public.* Independent contractors make their services available to the general public by one or more of the following:
    - Having an office and assistants.
    - Having business signs.
    - Having a business license.
    - Listing their services in a business directory.
    - Advertising their services.
19. *Right to Fire.* An employee can be fired by an employer. An independent contractor cannot be fired as long as results are produced that meet the specifications of the contract.
20. *Right to Quit.* An employee can quit a job at any time without incurring liability. An independent contractor usually agrees to complete a specific job and is responsible for its satisfactory completion, or legally is obligated to make good for failure to complete it.

## ¶45,015   EMPHASIS ON CATEGORIES

Since the publication of the training manual for IRS personnel on worker classification, there has been less reliance upon the common law standard or the list of 20 factors. The three categories (behavioral control, financial control, and relationship of the parties) are relied upon more heavily for the determination. However, it is wise to consider all aspects of the arrangement. In fact, the IRS cautions, "In each case, it is very important to consider all the facts—no single fact provides the answer."

## ¶45,017   "ECONOMIC REALITY" TEST

The Department of Labor (DOL) published a fact sheet aimed at helping to solve the employee/independent contractor dilemma. It points out that employment relationship under the Fair Labor Standards Act (FLSA) must be distinguished from a strictly contractual one and may be somewhat different from standards used by other agencies. The sheet states, "Such a relationship must exist for any provision of the Act to apply to any person engaged in work, which may otherwise be subject to the Act." In the application of the FLSA, an employee, as distinguished from a person who is engaged in a business of his or her own, is one who, as a matter of economic reality, follows the usual path of an employee and is dependent on the business he or she serves. Thus, the employer-employee relationship under the FLSA is tested by "economic reality" rather than "technical concepts." It is *not* determined by the common law standards previously discussed.

As has become fairly evident through the years, even the U.S. Supreme Court has indicated on several occasions that the Court does not consider a single rule or test for determining whether an individual is an independent contractor or an employee for purposes of the FLSA, the IRS, state agencies, or any other path followed by a particular case. The Court has held that it is the *total activity or situation,* which controls the determination. Many of these factors are discussed above, but in summary, those the Court has considered significant are:

- The extent to which the services rendered provide an integral part of the principal's business.
- The permanency of the relationship.
- The amount of the alleged contractor's investment in facilities and equipment.
- The nature and degree of control by the principal party over the manner in which the work is performed.
- The worker's opportunities for profit and loss determined by the hiring party or the worker's own managerial skill.
- The amount of initiative, judgment, foresight, or skill in open market competition with others required for the success of the claimed independent contractor.
- The degree of independent business organization and operation.

Certain factors are considered immaterial in determining whether there is an employment relationship. Included among conditions considered to have *no* bearing on determinations as to whether there is an employment relationship or not are:

- The absence of a formal employment agreement.
- Whether an alleged independent contractor is licensed by a state or local governmental body.
- The time or mode of payment.
- The place where work is performed.

The last condition can pose problems. In these times of flexible hours and workplaces, people who perform work at their own home are often improperly considered to be independent contractors. The Act covers such homeworkers as employees and they are entitled to all benefits of the law if they meet those requirements that are material in the determination.

The employer is responsible for the following when it has been determined that an employer-employee relationship does exist and the employee is engaged in work that is subject to the FLSA:

- The employee must be paid at least the federal minimum wage.
- Usually, time and one-half must be paid for time worked over 40 hours per week.
- Child labor laws regulating the employment of minors under the age of 18 must be observed.
- Specific record-keeping requirements must be followed.

## ¶45,019   NEW PROCEDURES FOR PROCESSING EMPLOYMENT TAX CASES

It is not only the employer who considers the independent contractor/ employee situation a morass. At one point in the ongoing attempts to decipher the complex tax code tax lawyers, CPAs and corporate tax officers came up with a list of high priority suggestions for simplifing the tax situation: drop the minimum tax; standardize the rules on classifying workers as employees or independent contractors; clarify the eight tax incentives for education.

This addition to the Internal Revenue Code may not help in the worker classification process, but it does provide Tax Court review rights.

The Taxpayer Relief Act of 1997 (TRA'97) created Section 7436 of the Internal Revenue Code, which provides Tax Court review rights concerning certain employment tax determinations.

Code Notice 98-43 provides information about how taxpayers can petition for Tax Court review of employment tax determinations under the provision that became effective August 5, 1997. Attached to this notice as Exhibit 1 is a "Notice of Determination Concerning Worker Classification Under Section 7436."

With respect to taxpayers whose workers are the subject of an employment tax determination as to whether they are independent contractors, or, in fact, employees, the attached Notice of Determination addressed to a taxpayer will constitute the "determination" that is a prerequisite to invoking the Tax Court's jurisdiction.

The new Section of the Code contains the following provisions:

1. The Tax Court has the jurisdiction to review determinations by the IRS that workers are employees for purposes of Subtitle C of the Code.
2. And that the organization for which services are performed is not entitled to relief from employment taxes under Section 530 of the Revenue Act of 1978.
3. The determination must involve an actual controversy relating to independent contractor/employee status.

4. The determination is made as part of an examination of worker classification.

Section 7436 can be conducted pursuant to the Tax Court's simplified procedures for small tax cases set forth in the new Section of the Code and Rule 295 of the Tax Court's Rules of Practice and Procedure. Currently, taxpayers can elect, with the concurrence of the Tax Court, to use these simplified procedures if the amount of employment taxes placed in dispute resulting from workers being designated as independent contractors is $50,000 or less for each calendar quarter involved.

## .01 Issues to Which Section 7436 Applies

Section 7436(a) provides the Tax Court with jurisdiction to review the IRS's determinations that one or more individuals performing services for the taxpayer are employees of the taxpayer, not independent contractors, for purposes of Subtitle C of the Code, or that the taxpayer is not entitled to relief under Section 530 with respect to such individuals.

Thus, 7436(a) does not:

1. Provide the Tax Court with jurisdiction to determine any amount of employment tax or penalties.
2. Provide the Tax Court with jurisdiction to review other employment tax issues.
3. Apply to employment-related issues not arising under Subtitle C, such as the classification of individuals with respect to pension plan coverage or the proper treatment of individual income tax deductions.

Additionally, insofar as 7436(a) only confers jurisdiction upon the Tax Court to review determinations that are made by the IRS as part of an employment tax examination, other IRS determinations that are not made as part of an examination, including those that are made in the context of private letter rulings or Form SS-8, "Determination of Employee Work Status for Purposes of Federal Employment Taxes and Income Tax Withholding," are not subject to review by the Tax Court under this provision.

The IRS will issue a Notice of Determination only after the IRS has determined both that:

1. One or more individuals performing services for the taxpayer are employees for purposes of Subtitle C.
2. The taxpayer is not entitled to relief under Section 530. This will provide taxpayers with the opportunity to resolve both issues in one judicial determination.

¶45,019.01

## .03  Taxpayers Eligible to Seek Review

Section 7436(b) provides that a pleading seeking Tax Court review of the IRS's determination can be filed only by "the person for whom the services are performed." Thus, workers may not seek review of the IRS's determinations under these provisions. In addition, because there must be an actual controversy, review may not be sought by a third party who has not been determined by the IRS to be the employer.

# .05  Notice of Determination

The IRS will inform taxpayers of a determination by sending the taxpayer a Notice of Determination by certified or registered mail. The Notice of Determination will advise taxpayers of the opportunity to seek Tax Court review, and it provides information on how to do so. Attached to the notice will be a schedule showing each kind of tax with its proposed employment tax adjustment for the specific taxpayer by calendar quarter.

This schedule will be provided to enable the taxpayer to determine eligibility to elect use of the small tax case procedures under Section 7436(c). Currently, the small tax case procedures may be available if the amount of employment taxes in dispute is $50,000 or less for each calendar quarter involved.

In most cases, a taxpayer who receives a Notice of Determination will have previously received a "thirty-day letter," which the IRS sends to taxpayers in unagreed examination cases. The thirty-day letter lists the proposed employment tax adjustments to be made and describes the taxpayer's right either to agree to the proposed employment tax adjustments or, alternatively, to protest the proposed adjustments to the Appeals Division within thirty days of the date of the letter.

If the taxpayer does not respond to the thirty-day letter by agreeing to the proposed adjustments or, alternatively, by filing a protest with the Appeals Division, the taxpayer will receive, by certified or registered mail, a Notice of Determination. Under normal procedures, if the taxpayer does not respond to the thirty-day letter, the taxpayer should generally expect to receive the notice within sixty days after expiration of the thirty-day period beginning with the date on the thirty-day letter. If no notice is received during this period, the taxpayer may wish to contact the local Internal Revenue Service office to check on the status of the case.

If the taxpayer responds to the thirty-day letter by filing a protest with the Appeals Division (or if the case proceeds to Appeals by way of the employment tax early referral procedures), and the worker classification and Section 530 issues are not settled on an agreed basis in the Appeals Division, the taxpayer will then receive a Notice of Determination.

Taxpayers are encouraged to resolve cases in nondocketed status by requesting use of the early referral procedures in appropriate cases.

¶45,019.03

## .07 Prerequisite for Seeking Review

Because a Notice of Determination constitutes the IRS's determination of worker classification, it is a jurisdictional prerequisite for seeking Tax Court review of the IRS's determinations regarding classification of the worker as an independent contractor or an employee, and Section 530 issues (see above). Tax Court proceedings seeking review of these determinations can not begin prior to issuance of the notice.

## .09 Time of Filing

Section 7436(b)(2) provides that a taxpayer's petition for review must be filed with the Tax Court before the 91st day after the IRS mails its Notice of Determination to the taxpayer by certified or registered mail. If the taxpayer discusses the case with the IRS during the period before the 91st day following the mailing of the notice, the discussion will not extend the period in which the taxpayer may file a petition with the Tax Court.

A taxpayer who does not file a Tax Court petition within the allotted time retains the right to seek judicial review of the employment tax determinations by paying the tax and filing a claim for refund, as required by the Code. If the claim for refund is denied, the taxpayer may file a refund suit in district court or the Court of Federal Claims.

## .11 Appeals Jurisdiction

Cases docketed in the U.S. Tax Court will be referred by District Counsel to the Appeals Division of the IRS for consideration of settlement unless the Notice of Determination was issued by Appeals. Cases in which Appeals issued such a Notice of Determination may be referred to them unless District Counsel determines that there is little likelihood that a settlement of all or a part of the case can be achieved in a reasonable period of time. Appeals will have sole settlement authority over docketed cases referred to them until the case is returned to District Counsel.

## .13 Suspension of the Statute of Limitations

The ruling provides that the suspension of the limitations period for assessment in Section 6503(a) of the Code applies in the same manner as though a notice of deficiency had been issued. Thus, the mailing of the Notice of Determination by certified or registered mail will suspend the statute of limitations for assessment of taxes attributable to the worker classification and Section 530 issues. Generally, the statute of limitations for assessment of taxes attributable to these issues is suspended for the 90-day period during which the taxpayer can begin a suit in Tax Court, plus an additional 60 days thereafter.

¶45,019.13

Moreover, if the taxpayer does file a timely petition in the Tax Court, the statute of limitations for assessment of taxes attributable to the issues will be suspended during the Tax Court proceedings, and for 60 days after the decision becomes final.

## .15  Restrictions on Assessment

This same ruling provides that the restrictions on assessment in Section 6213 of the Code apply in the same manner as if a notice had been issued. Thus, the IRS is precluded from assessing the taxes prior to expiration of the 90-day period during which the taxpayer can file a timely Tax Court petition.

If he or she does file, this generally precludes the IRS from assessing the taxes until the decision of the Tax Court has become final. If the taxpayer does not file a timely Tax Court petition before the 91st day after the Notice of Determination was mailed, the employment taxes attributable to the workers described in the Notice of Determination can then be assessed.

## .17  Agreed Settlements

If the taxpayer wishes to settle the employment issues on an agreed basis before issuance of a Notice of Determination, the taxpayer must formally waive the restrictions on assessment. This will generally be accomplished by execution of an agreed settlement that contains the following language: "I understand that, by signing this agreement, I am waiving the restrictions on assessment provided in Sections 7436(d) and 6213(a) of the Internal Revenue Code of 1986."

The IRS will not assess employment taxes attributable to those issues unless either a Notice of Determination has been issued to the taxpayer and the 90-day period for filing a Tax Court petition has expired or, alternatively, the taxpayer has waived the restrictions on assessment.

If the IRS erroneously makes an assessment of taxes attributable to those issues without first either issuing a Notice of Determination or obtaining a waiver of restrictions on assessment, the taxpayer is entitled to an automatic abatement of the assessment. However, once any such procedural defects are corrected, the IRS can reassess the employment taxes to the same extent as if the abated assessment had not occurred.

Section 1454 of the Tax Relief Act (TRA) of 1997 was effective as of August 5, 1997. Thus, assessments that were made prior to the August 5, 1997 effective date of the Act are not subject to this legislation or the procedures discussed above. All employment tax examinations involving worker classification and/or Section 530 issues that were pending as of August 5, 1997 became subject to the legislation.

# Chapter 46
# Tip Income

## CONTENTS

## ¶46,000 OVERVIEW

What's the big deal? An estimated $9 billion a year in unreported, untaxed tip income, that's what. Reporting all tip income has always been required by law. When the significant extent to which taxpayers were ignoring the law became evident, the IRS stepped up the emphasis on the requirements for both employee and employer to report tip income.

Since the Tip Rate Determination/Education Program (TRD/EP), was introduced, voluntary compliance has significantly increased. In 1995, tip wages reported were $9.45 billion. For 2003, the amount exceeded $18 billion. By 2005, more than 15,000 employers had entered into tip agreements, representing nearly 47,000 individual establishments.

The Internal Revenue Service (IRS) points out that the TRD/EP has proven to be a winner for employers, employees, and the IRS. It reduces taxpayer burden and increases compliance. The Service hopes that more industries and employees will take advantage of the program.

## ¶46,001   SIMPLIFIED TIP REPORTING PROCEDURE

The Internal Revenue Service released formal guidance on additional tip reporting procedure in July 2006. The Attributed Tip Income Program (ATIP) expands the existing IRS tip reporting and education program by offering employers in the food and beverage industry another option for reporting tip income. ATIP reduces industry recordkeeping burdens, has simple enrollment requirements and promotes reporting tips on Federal income tax returns.

ATIP provides benefits to employers and employees similar to those offered under previous tip reporting agreements; however, it does not require employers to meet with the IRS to determine tip rates or eligibility. Employers are not required to sign an agreement with the IRS to participate. Like other tip reporting programs, participation by employers and their employees is voluntary.

Employers who participate in ATIP report the tip income of employees based on a formula that uses a percentage of gross receipts, which are generally attributed among employees based on the practices of the restaurant.

Both employers and employees should find this program beneficial at the same time that the IRS gains as a result of an increase in reported tip income.

Employers receive significant benefits by participating in ATIP as follows:

- The IRS will not initiate an "employer-only" 3121(q) examination during the period the employer participates in ATIP.
- Tip reporting is simplified and in many cases employers will not have to receive and process tip records from participating employees.
- Enrollment is simple. There are no one-on-one meetings with the IRS and no agreements to sign. Employers elect participation in ATIP by checking the designated box on Form 8027, Employer's Annual Information Return of Tip Income and Allocated Tips.

Participating employees are not required to keep a daily tip log or other tip records. They also benefit from ATIP because:

- The IRS will not initiate a tip examination during the period the employer and employee participate in ATIP.
- The improved income reporting procedures could help employees qualify for loans or other financing.
- Employees who work for a participating employer can easily elect to participate in ATIP by signing an agreement with their employer to have their tip income computed under the program and reported as wages.

The IRS also expects to benefit from the program by:

- Promoting tax compliance by both employers and employees with the Internal Revenue Code.
- Reducing disputes on audit.
- Reducing filing and recordkeeping burdens.

Some general requirements for participating restaurants:

- The employer annually elects to participate in ATIP and uses the pre-scribed methodology for reporting tips by filing Form 8027 and checks the ATIP participation box. Simplified filing is provided for small establishments not required to file Form 8027.
- Employer's establishment must have at least 20% of gross receipts as charged receipts that reflect a charged tip.
- At least 75% of tipped employees must agree to participate in the program.
- Employer reports attributed tips on Employees' Forms W-2 and pays taxes using the formula tip rate
- The formula tip rate is the charged tip rate minus two percent – the two percent takes into account a lower cash tip rate.
- The charged tip rate is based on information from the establishment's Form 8027.

ATIP is a three-year pilot program for food and beverage employers. Employers will participate on an annual basis. The first annual basis begins January 1, 2007. Details and requirements for participation for employers and employees are available in Revenue Procedure 2006-30.

## ¶46,003  TIP RATE DETERMINATION/EDUCATION PROGRAM

The TRD/EP was first promoted in the gaming industry (casino industry) in Las Vegas, Nevada, and has spread to the food and beverage industry. Other industries whose employees receive tips include beauty parlors, barber shops, nail salons, taxi companies, and pizza delivery establishments.

The Tip Rate Determination/Education Program created in 1993 is a national program used in all states. The employer has the option to enter into one of two arrangements under this program: the Tip Rate Determination Agreement (TRDA) or the Tip Reporting Alternative Commitment (TRAC) created in June 1995.

With the introduction of the new programs, four options became available for tip reporting:

1. Tip Rate Determination Agreement.
2. Tip Reporting Alternative Commitment.
3. The status quo—the old basic method following the requirements listed below without any "formal" agreement.
4. Examination of Tip Income Reporting.

Under the Tip Rate Determination/Education Program, the employer may enter into either the TRDA or TRAC arrangement. The IRS will assist applicants in understanding and meeting the requirements for participation. Many similarities exist between the two new alternatives, but there are some differences. Following is a descriptive list of the requirements for each, particularly in reference to the food and beverage industry:

## .01 TRDA

1. Requires the IRS to work with the establishment to arrive at a tip rate for the various restaurant occupations.
2. Requires the employee to enter into a Tipped Employee Participation Agreement (TEPA) with the employer.
3. Requires the employer to get 75 percent of the employees to sign TEPAs and report at or above the determined rate.
4. Provides that if employees fail to report at or above the determined rate, the employer will provide the names of those employees, their social security numbers, job classification, sales, hours worked, and amount of tips reported.
5. Has no specific education requirement relating to legal responsibility to report tips under the agreement.
6. Participation assures the employer that prior periods will not be examined during the period that the TRDA is in effect.
7. Results in the mailing of a notice and demand to employer for the employer's portion of FICA taxes on unreported tips determined for the six month period used to set the tip rate(s).

8. Prevents employer (only) assessments during the period that the agreement is in effect.

## .03 TRAC

1. Does not require that a tip rate be established, but it does require the employer to:
   a. Establish a procedure where a directly tipped employee is provided (no less than monthly) a written statement of charged tips attributed to the employee.
   b. Implement a procedure for the employee to verify or correct any statement of attributed tips.
   c. Adopt a method where an indirectly tipped employee reports his or her tips (no less than monthly). This could include a statement prepared by the employer and verified or corrected by the employee.
   d. Establish a procedure where a written statement is prepared and processed (no less than monthly) reflecting all cash tips attributable to sales of the directly tipped employee.
2. Does not require an agreement between the employee and the employer.
3. Affects all (100 percent) of the employees.
4. Includes a commitment by the employer to educate and reeducate quarterly all directly and indirectly tipped employees and new hires of their statutory requirement to report all tips to their employer.
5. Participation assures the employer that prior periods will not be examined during the period that the agreement is in effect.
6. Prevents employer (only) assessments during the period that the agreement is in effect.
7. Assures that employers comply with all tax reporting, filing, and payment obligations.
8. Requires employers to maintain and make available records to the IRS.
9. Emphasizes that employees earning $20 or more a month in tips must report them to the employer.

In return, the IRS generally will not perform a tip examination on employers complying with the TRAC guidelines. In contrast, an establishment whose employees underreport their tips could be liable for back FICA taxes.

The approach has helped lead to increased tip reporting, but the IRS believes there is still ample room for improvement. In the food and beverage sector alone, tip reporting jumped from $3.9 billion in 1993 to $9.45 billion in 1995 to more than $18 billion in 2003. However, estimates placed the amount of annual tips going to those same workers at $18 billion annually.

*TRAC Agreement Revised.* The IRS has been working cooperatively with the restaurant industry in response to industry concerns regarding some aspects of the TRAC program. In late 1999, the IRS took steps to reduce the administrative burdens of restaurant operators by making changes in the regulations:

1. The IRS will no longer revoke TRAC agreements in cases where employers make a good-faith effort at following the guidelines but employees still fail to report tips. Instead of pursuing the employers in such situations, the IRS will focus on the employees who are not in compliance with tip reporting.

2. Another change involves restaurants with locations in different IRS Districts. Under the new plan, the restaurant's headquarter operations will work directly with their local IRS office on TRAC issues. This streamlined approach will be simpler and more straightforward than the old system, where different locations of a company had to deal with different people in different IRS Districts.

The IRS has now extended TRD/EP to continue without a sunset date. With the indefinite extension of the tip program, the IRS will administer existing tip agreements without the need for employers to re-sign agreements.

## .05 Instituting the Program

To enter into one of the arrangements, an employer should submit an application letter to the area IRS Chief, Examination/Compliance Division, Attn: Tip Coordinator. The Tip Coordinator can provide a letter format as well as extensive information on the two separate arrangements.

All employers with establishments where tipping is customary should review their operations. Then, if it is determined that there is or has been an underreporting of tips, the employer should apply for one of the two arrangements under the TRD/EP. Employers currently with the TRDA in effect may revoke the arrangement and simultaneously enter into a TRAC.

The particular advantage to the employer who adopts one of these programs is that no subsequent tip examination is imposed as long as terms of the arrangement have been met and all tips have been reported.

## .07 Special Tip Reporting Rules for Large Restaurants

Large food or beverage establishments must meet the following criteria:

* Tipping is customary.
* Food or beverage is provided and consumed on the premises.
* In the preceding calendar year, the average number of hours worked by all employees on a typical business day was more than 80.

¶46,003.05

Establishments meeting the above criteria must satisfy additional tip reporting rules under the Internal Revenue Code section 6053(c)(4):

- Allocate tips if total tips reported by employees are less than 8 percent of gross receipts (excludes carry-out sales, receipts with a service charge added of more than 10 percent and state or local taxes).
- Report tip allocations on W-2 forms (for each employee who did not meet his or her share of the 8 percent).
- File Form 8027, *Employer's Annual Information Return of Tip Income and Allocated Tips*, to the IRS by the last day in February of the following year.

## ¶46,005  EMPLOYER TIP REPORTING ALTERNATIVE COMMITMENT PROGRAM (EMTRAC)

The IRS developed the EmTRAC Agreement program in response to employers in the food and beverage industry who expressed an interest in designing their own TRAC programs. These agreements are available to employers in this industry in which employees receive both cash and charged tips. The EmTRAC program retains many of the provisions of the TRAC agreement, including:

- The employer must establish an educational program that emphasizes that the law requires employees to report to their employer all of their cash and charged tips.
- Education must be furnished immediately for newly hired employees and quarterly for existing employees.
- The employer must establish tip reporting procedures under which a written or electronic statement is prepared and processed on a regular basis (no less than monthly), reflecting all tips for services attributable to each employee.

The employer may have one, or many places of business. For purposes of the program, each place of business is called an establishment. If an employer has more than one establishment, it can choose which establishments to include in its EmTRAC program.

### .01  Specific Requirements of the Program

The EmTRAC program provides an employer with considerable latitude in designing its educational program and tip reporting procedures, which the employer may combine. For example, a point-of-sale tip reporting system could meet both of these requirements, because the employee is reminded of the tip reporting requirement at the end of each sale and because the reporting occurs at the end of each sale.

The employer must agree:

- To comply with the requirements for filing all required federal tax returns and paying and depositing all federal taxes.
- To maintain the following records for at least four years after the April 14 following the calendar year to which the records relate:
  —Gross receipts subject to tipping.
  —Charge receipts showing charged tips.
- Upon the request of the IRS, to make the following quarterly totals available, by establishment, for statistical samplings of its establishments:
  —Gross receipts subject to tipping.
  —Charge receipts showing charged tips.
  —Total charged tips.
  —Total tips reported.

The IRS agrees:

- Not to initiate any tip examinations of the employer or an establishment included in the EmTRAC for any period for which the EmTRAC program is in effect, except in relation to a tip examination of one or more employees or former employees of the employer or an establishment.
- To base any section 3121(q) notice and demand issued to the employer or an establishment included in the EmTRAC and relating to any period during which the EmTRAC program is in effect solely on amounts reflected on:
  —Form 4137, *Social Security and Medicare Tax on Unreported Tip Income*, filed by an employee with his or her Form 1040, or
  —Form 885-T, *Adjustment of Social Security Tax on Tip Income Not Reported to Employer*, prepared at the conclusion of an employee tip examination.
- Not to evaluate the employer for compliance with the provisions of its EmTRAC program for the first two calendar quarters for which the EmTRAC program is effective.

Both parties agree that, for purposes of the EmTRAC program, a compliance review is not treated as an examination or an inspection of books of account or records, and an inspection of books of account or records pursuant to a tip examination is not an inspection of books or records for purposes of section 7605(b) of the Code, and is not a prior audit for purposes of section 530 of the Revenue Act of 1978.

The effective date of an EmTRAC program is the first day of the quarter beginning on or after the date the IRS signs an approval letter.

**¶46,005.01**

An employer may at any time terminate its EmTRAC program either completely or with respect to one or more establishments. The IRS may terminate its approval with respect to the EmTRAC program or a specific establishment or establishments, only if:

- The IRS determines that the employer or establishment(s) has failed to comply with the required provisions.
- The IRS pursues an administrative or judicial action relating to the employer, an establishment included in the EmTRAC, or any other related party to the employer's EmTRAC program.

Generally, any termination is effective the first day of the first calendar quarter after the terminating party notifies the other party in writing. If the employer has an existing TRAC agreement or TRDA covering one or more establishments included in the employer's EmTRAC program, the existing TRAC agreement or TRDA will terminate with respect to that establishment or those establishments upon the approval of the employer's EmTRAC program.

## .03   Procedures for Requesting Approval

The employer must request approval of its EmTRAC program. For this purpose, the Service has developed a pro forma letter that an employer must use to request approval of its EmTRAC program. The letter requests approval of the employer's EmTRAC program and states that the employer will comply with the provisions set forth in the letter and in the information above. A copy of the approval request letter can be obtained by mail by contacting the tip coordinator in any local IRS office or by calling (202) 622-5532.

## .05   Procedures for Approving Requests

After receiving the approval request letter, the IRS will review the employer's program. If the program meets the necessary requirements, the IRS will send the employer an approval letter specifying the effective date of the employer's EmTRAC program.

If the IRS determines that the employer's EmTRAC program fails to meet all the requirements, it will contact the employer and offer assistance in working out a program that will meet both the employer's needs and the IRS requirements.

Upon request to the local tip coordinator or the EmTRAC Coordinator, the IRS will assist any employer in establishing, maintaining, or improving its educational program or tip reporting procedures.

The Commissioner of Internal Revenue may terminate all EmTRAC programs at any time following a significant statutory change in the FICA taxation of tips.

In 2004, the Service announced an indefinite extension of the Tip Rate Determination and Education Program since by then, the program had helped in almost doubling the reporting of tip income. Now, the successful program will continue without a sunset date.

## .07   Wage Reduction under "Tip Credit" Rule

The Fair Labor Standards Act (FLSA), also commonly known as the federal wage and hour law, provides directives for employers on how much to pay their employees for both regular and overtime hours. The act requires employers to pay employees who are not otherwise exempt as follows:

- Regular wages must be paid at least the federal minimum wage of $5.15 an hour or the state minimum wage, whichever is higher.
- Overtime wages must be paid at one and one-half the regular rate of pay for each hour worked exceeding 40 hours a week.

One benefit under the FLSA is that restaurant owners are allowed to pay tipped employees less than the federal minimum wage as long as the difference is made up from tips. This wage reduction is known as a "tip credit." Restaurant owners may pay tipped employees a reduced federal minimum wage rate of $2.13, which may vary by state. However, this approach increases an employer's responsibilities when dealing with tipped employees:

- Tipped employees must be informed in writing that they are paid a reduced rate. Otherwise, the employer may be liable to pay them the full minimum wage rate.
- If hourly wages plus tips don't equal minimum wage for regular or overtime hours, the employer must make up the difference.
- Because not all states follow the federal law, the employer should check with the particular state's Department of Labor for rules on both minimum wage requirements and maximum tip credit amounts.

## ¶46,007   IRS AND GAMING INDUSTRY PARTNER ON VOLUNTARY TIP COMPLIANCE AGREEMENTS

In December 2003, the IRS announced it was expanding the new tip compliance agreement nationwide to the gaming industry. The agency encourages gaming industry employers to participate in the voluntary agreement and urges employees whose income includes tips to learn the benefits of participation. The program is designed to promote compliance by the gaming industry employers and employees with the provisions of the Internal Revenue Code relating to tip income and to reduce disputes and legal battles.

For employers, the agreement substantially reduces the record-keeping and reporting burden; for employees, the improved income reporting procedures could potentially make them eligible for higher Social Security, other pension, Medicare, unemployment, and workman's compensation benefits. This could also help qualify them when applying for loans or other financial arrangements.

The voluntary compliance process allows a gaming industry employer, employees, and the IRS to work together to determine tip rates for tipped employees in specified occupational categories. The process consists of several steps:

- The employer and the IRS sign a Gaming Industry Tip Compliance Agreement(GITCA). This incorporates tip rates specific to that employer's establishment and prescribes a threshold level of participation by the employer's employees.
- The employer recruits his employees to voluntarily participate.
- Participating employees must then report their tip income to their employer at or above the established tip rates, unless their tip logs can substantiate a lesser amount.
- The employer withholds income tax from the employees and reports income on the employees' Form W-2 based on the rates or the substantiated lesser amount.

An executed Gaming Industry Tip Compliance Agreement usually supersedes all existing tip compliance agreements between an employer and the Service. An employer under any gaming industry tip compliance agreement, including a Tip Rate Determination Agreement, may request to change to a Gaming Industry Tip Compliance Agreement.

The usual Gaming Industry Tip Compliance Agreements is for a term of three years. For new properties and for properties that do not have a prior agreement with the Service, however, the initial term of the agreement may be for a shorter period. As long as tips are reported at, or above, the established tip rate, the compliance agreement generally prevents the IRS from auditing the employee's tip Income. In addition, as long as the employer meets certain commitments, the IRS will not assert a liability against the employer with respect to tip income of participating employees while the agreement is in effect. The agreement may be renewed every three years. The result is a reduction of compliance burdens for the employer and enforcement burdens for the Service.

The agreement establishes tip rates that generally depend upon the particular casino, the specific job, the work shift, and the outlet worked for all eligible employees of gaming establishments in specified occupational categories in which tipping is customary. Housekeeping employees are not included in the program.

Representatives of the gaming industry, including employees, provided significant input into the development of this agreement. All employers

¶46,007

operating a gaming establishment may participate in the Gaming Tip Compliance Agreement. Either the IRS or an employer may initiate participation.

### .01  Indian Tribal Gaming

The Office of Indian Tribal Governments, under the Tax Exempt and Governmental Entities Operating Division (TEGE), serves as the coordinating office for all federal tax administration needs with Indian tribal governments, which includes tax administration in connection with Indian tribal gaming.

There are 566 federally recognized tribes across the country. There are 310 gaming facilities within these tribal units, approximately 65 percent of which have occupations where significant tipping occurs. The remaining 35 percent consist principally of bingo or video lottery terminals, and do not lend themselves to having tipped employees.

Between entities where agreements are in place, and entities where compliance actions are currently underway, tip reporting compliance is being addressed with nearly 90 percent of the applicable customer base. The IRS expects to reach 100 percent and will then focus primarily on maintaining compliance in the tip reporting area.

### ¶46,009  BASIC RULES RELATING TO TIP INCOME REPORTING

The following discussion concerns how tip income is taxed and how it should be reported to the IRS on the federal income tax return. The employees of food and beverage companies are the main subjects of this review; the record keeping rules and other information also apply to other workers who receive tips.

As pointed out earlier, all tips that are received by employees are taxable income and are subject to federal income taxes. Employees must include in gross income all tips received directly from customers, and tips from charge customers paid to the employer, who must pay them to the employee. In addition, cash tips of $20 or more that an employee receives in a month while working for any one employer are subject to withholding of income tax, social security retirement tax, and Medicare tax. The employee should report tips to the employer in order to determine the correct amount of these taxes.

Tips and other pay are used to determine the amount of social security benefits that an employee receives when he or she retires, becomes disabled, or dies. Noncash tips are not counted as wages for social security purposes. Future Social Security Administration (SSA) benefits can be figured correctly only if the SSA has the correct information. To make sure that an employee has received credit for all his or her earnings, the employee should request a statement of earnings from the SSA at least every other year. The SSA will send the person a statement that should be carefully checked to be sure it includes all of the employee's earnings.

Every large food and beverage business must report to the IRS any tips allocated to the employees. Generally, tips must be allocated to be paid by employees when the total tips reported to an employer by employees are less than 8 percent of the establishment's food and beverage sales of that employee. This necessitates the employer and employees keeping accurate records of the employee's tip income.

## .01  Daily Tip Record

The employee must keep a daily tip record so he or she can:

1. Report tips accurately to the employer.
2. Report tips accurately on a tax return.
3. Prove tip income if the taxpayer's return is ever questioned.

There are two ways to keep a daily tip record:

1. The employee can keep a daily "tip diary."
2. The employee should keep copies of documents that show the tips, such as restaurant bills and credit card charge slips.

The employee can start record keeping by writing his or her name, the employer's name, and the name of the business if it is different from the employer's name. Each workday, the employee should write and date the following information in a tip diary.

1. Cash tips received directly from customers or other employees.
2. Tips from credit card charge customers that the employer pays the employee.
3. The value of any noncash tips received, such as tickets, passes, or other items of value.
4. The amount of tips the employee paid out to other employees through tip pools, tip splitting, or other arrangements, and the names of the employees to whom tips were paid.

## .03  Reporting Tips to the Employer

The employee must report tips to the employer so that:

1. The employer can withhold federal income tax, social security taxes, and Medicare taxes.
2. The employer can report the correct amount of the employee's earnings to the Social Security Administration. This will affect the employee's

benefits when the employee retires or becomes disabled, or the family's benefits upon the employee's death.

## .05 What Tips to Report

Only cash, check, or credit card tips should be reported to the employer. If the total tips for any one month from any one job are less than $20, they should not be reported to the employer. The value of any noncash tips, such as tickets or passes, is not reported to the employer because the employee does not have to pay social security and Medicare taxes on these tips. The employee will, however, report them on his or her individual tax return. The following information should be written on the report to be given to the employer:

1. Name, address, and social security number.
2. The employer's name, address, and business name if it is different from the employer's name.
3. The month, or the dates of any shorter period, in which the tips are received.
4. The total amount of tips the employee received.

The employee must sign and date the report and give it to the employer. The employee should keep a copy of the report for his or her personal records. The report is to be completed each month and given to the employer by the tenth of the next month.

## .07 Employer Records for Tip Allocation

Large food and beverage establishments are required to report certain additional information about tips to the IRS. To make sure that employees are reporting tips correctly, employers must keep records to verify amounts reported by employees. Certain employers must allocate tips if the percentage of tips reported by employees falls below a required minimum percentage of gross sales. To allocate tips means to assign an additional amount as tips to each employee whose reported tips are below the required percentage. The rules apply to premises in which:

1. Food and beverages are provided for consumption on the premises.
2. Tipping is customary.
3. The employer normally employed more than ten people on a typical business day during the preceding calendar year.

Tip allocation rules do not apply to food and beverage establishments where tipping is not customary such as:

1. A cafeteria or fast food restaurant.
2. A restaurant that adds a service charge of 10 percent or more to 95 percent or more of its food and beverage sales.
3. Food and beverage establishments located outside the United States.

The rules apply only if the total amount of tips reported by all tipped employees to the employer is less than 8 percent, or some lower acceptable percentage of the establishment's total food or beverage sales, with some adjustments. If reported tips total less than 8 percent of total sales, the employer must allocate the difference between 8 percent of total sales, or some lower acceptable percentage approved by the IRS, and the amount of tips reported by all tipped employees. The employer will exclude carryout sales, state and local taxes, and sales with a service charge of 10 percent or more when figuring total sales.

Usually, the employer will allocate to all affected employees their share of tips every payroll period. However, the employer should not withhold any taxes from the allocated amount. No allocation will be made to the employee if the employee reports tips at least equal to the employee's share of 8 percent of the establishment's total food and beverage sales.

## .09 Penalty for Not Reporting Tips

If the employee does not report tips to his or her employer as required, the employee can be subject to a penalty equal to 50 percent of the social security and Medicare taxes owed. The penalty amount is in addition to the taxes owed. The penalty can be avoided if the employee can show reasonable cause for not reporting the tips to the employer. A statement should be attached to the tax return explaining why the tips were not reported to the employer. If an employee's regular pay is not enough for the employer to withhold all the taxes owed on the regular pay plus reported tips, the employee can give the employer money to pay the rest of the taxes, up to the close of the calendar year.

If the employee does not give the employer enough money, the employer will apply the regular pay and any money given by the employee in the following order:

1. All taxes on the employee's regular pay.
2. Social security and Medicare taxes on the reported tips.
3. Federal, state, and local income taxes on the reported tips.

Any taxes that remain unpaid can be collected by the employer from the employee's next paycheck. If withholding taxes remain uncollected at the end of the year, the employee must make an estimated tax payment. To report these taxes, a return must be filed even if the employee would not otherwise have to file. If the employer could not collect all the social security and Medicare taxes owed on the tips reported to the employer, the uncollected taxes must be shown by the employer on a Form W-2. The employee must then also report these uncollected taxes on his or her return.

## ¶46,011  TIP RATES

Depending on the Occupational Category and the employer's business practices, tips can be *measured* in different ways.

1. *Actual tips* generally apply to Employees in Occupational Categories (O.C.) where pooling of tips is common. The tips are pooled during a shift and the total is split among the employees of the O.C. who worked the shift.
2. *Tip rates* generally apply to employees in O.C. where pooling of tips is not common. The rate may be a percentage of sales, a dollar amount, or other accurate basis of measurement per hour or shift, a dollar amount per drink served, a dollar amount per working hour, or other accurate measurement.

## .01  Methods for Determining Tip Rates

The employer will determine tip rates for the O.C. based on information available to the employer, historical information provided by the IRS representative, and generally accepted accounting principles (GAAP). The rates will specify whether the tips are received as a percentage of sales, a dollar amount per hour or shift, a dollar amount per drink served, a dollar amount per dealing hour in a casino, or on another basis.

## .03  Initial Tip Rate

The initial tip rate for each O.C. is shown where pool and split tips methods are used by the employees.

## ¶46,013  ANNUAL REVIEW

The employer will review annually, on a calender year basis, changes in the tip rates assigned to its O.C. In connection with the review, the employer can review its O.C. The initial rates for each O.C. will apply to the first full calendar year of the review.

## .01  Employer Submission

If the employer believes that a revision of one or more rates or O.C. is appropriate, the employer will submit proposed revisions to the IRS representative by September 30. If the employer fails to submit a proposed rate revision by September 30 of the taxable year, the employee will be treated as having submitted the rate in effect for the current year.

## .03  Internal Revenue Service Review

The IRS representative will review the proposed rates and notify the employer in writing of the approval or disapproval by November 30. If the IRS representative does not approve one or more proposed rates, the existing rate or rates will be continued until no later than the last day of the following February.

The effective date of revised rates and O.C. will become effective on the later of January 1 of the calendar year, or on the first day of the month following the date the employer and the IRS representative agree upon a revised rate. The IRS representative can examine a participating employee's tip income for any period if an employee reports tips at a rate less than the tip rate for the employee's occupational category.

These amounts must be an additional tax on the employee's tax return. The employee may have uncollected taxes if his or her regular pay was not enough for the employer to withhold all the taxes the taxpayer owed, but did not give the employer enough money to pay the rest of the taxes. The employee must report these uncollected taxes on a return.

## ¶46,015  ALLOCATED TIPS

Allocated tips are tips that the employer assigned to an employee in addition to the tips the employee reported to the employer for the year. The employer will have done this only if the employee worked in a restaurant, cocktail lounge, or similar business that must allocate tips to employees, and the reported tips were less than the employee's share of 8 percent of food and drink sales. If allocated tips are shown on a return, and if social security and Medicare taxes were not withheld from the allocated tips, these taxes must be reported as additional tax on a return.

## .01  Allocation Formula

The allocation can be done either under a formula agreed to by both the employer and the employees or, if they cannot reach an agreement, under a formula prescribed by IRS regulations. The allocation formula in the regulations

¶46,015.01

provides that tip allocations are made only to directly tipped employees. If tips are received directly from customers, the employees are directly tipped employees, even if the tips are turned over to a tip pool. Waiters, waitresses, and bartenders are usually considered directly tipped employees. If tips are not normally received directly from customers, the employee is an indirectly tipped employee. Examples are busboys, service bartenders, and cooks. If an employee receives tips both directly and indirectly through tip splitting or tip pooling, the employee is treated as a directly tipped employee.

If customers of the establishment tip less than 8 percent on average, either the employee or a majority of the directly tipped employees can petition to have the allocation percentage reduced from 8 percent. This petition is made to the IRS representative for the IRS district in which the establishment is located. The percentage cannot be reduced below 2 percent.

A fee is required to have the IRS consider a petition to lower the tip allocation percentage. The fee must be paid by check or money order made out to the Internal Revenue Service. (The user fee amount for 2005 is $275; the IRS representative in the taxpayer's area will know if this amount has changed.)

The employees' petition to lower the allocation percentage must be in writing, and must contain enough information to allow the IRS representative to estimate with reasonable accuracy the establishment's actual tip rate. This information might include the changed tip rate, type of establishment, menu prices, location, hours of operation, amount of self-service required, and whether the customer receives the check from the server or pays the server for the meal. If the employer possesses any relevant information, the employer must provide it to the district upon request of the employees or the IRS representative.

The employees' petition must be consented to by more than one-half of the directly tipped employees working for the establishment at the time the petition is filed. If the petition covers more than one establishment, it must be consented to by more than one-half of the total number of directly tipped employees of the covered establishments. The petition must state the total number of directly tipped employees of the establishment(s) and the number of directly tipped employees consenting to the petition.

The petition may cover two or more establishments if the employees have made a good faith determination that the tip wages are essentially the same and if the establishments are:

1. Owned by the same employer.
2. Essentially the same type of business.
3. In the same Internal Revenue Service region.

A petition that covers two or more establishments must include the names and locations of the establishments and must be sent to the IRS representative for the district in which the greatest number of covered establishments are located. If there is an equal number of covered establishments in two or more districts, the employees can choose which district to petition. Employees who file a petition must promptly notify their employer of the petition. The employer must then promptly furnish the IRS representative with an annual information return form showing the tip income and allocated tips filed for the establishment for the three immediately preceding calendar years.

The employer will report the amount of tips allocated to employees on the employees' Form W-2 separately from wages and reported tips. The employer bases withholding only on wages and reported tips. The employer should not withhold income, social security, and Medicare taxes from the allocated amount. Any incorrectly withheld taxes should be refunded to the employee by the employer.

If an employee leaves a job before the end of the calendar year and requests an early Form W-2, the employer does not have to include a tip allocation on the Form W-2. However, the employer can show the actual allocated amount if it is known, or show an estimated allocation. In January of the following year, the employer must provide Form W-2 if the early Form W-2 showed no allocation and the employer later determined that an allocation was required, or if the estimated allocation shown was wrong by more than 5 percent of the actual allocation.

If an employee does not have adequate records for his or her actual tips, the employee must include the allocated tips shown on the Form W-2 as additional tip income on the tax return. If the employee has records, allocated tips should not be shown on the employee's return. Additional tip income is included only if those records show more tips received than the amount reported to the employer.

## ¶46,017   SUPREME COURT RULING ON "AGGREGATE METHOD"

In 2002, a 6-3 ruling by the Supreme Court upheld a move by federal tax collectors to force employers to pay the 7.65 percent Social Security tax on all income received by their workers, including tips. The dispute originally arose over the method used to calculate the total tip income, specifically in restaurants.

At some previous time, restaurant owners had been told that they could rely on reports from their servers and bartenders. However, tips were being notoriously underreported as was pointed out in the first paragraph of this chapter.

In the early 1990s, the IRS decided to survey credit card slips to calculate how much waiters and waitresses were actually receiving in tips. From this information, the Service would use the average tip to estimate the total of tips. For example, if customers on average added a 15 percent tip on their credit cards, the IRS would assume that customers tipped 15 percent on all of the restaurant's income, including cash payments. The owner could be assessed back taxes based on this amount.

The restaurant industry objected strenuously, claiming that customers who pay in cash often leave lower tips and that some leave no tip whatsoever. However, the Supreme Court Justices discounted such complaints and upheld the estimates based on credit card receipts as a reasonable way to assess the taxes owed by a restaurant.

In the specific instance, the IRS estimated the tips for 1992 as $368,374, not the $220,845 that the servers had reported. The IRS sent the owner an $11,286 bill for back taxes for 1992 to cover his share of the employee Social Security taxes, known officially as the Federal Insurance Contribution Act (FICA) taxes.

## .01    Steps Toward a Decision

A Circuit Court of Appeals judge had then ruled the IRS was not empowered to "slap an employer" with back tax assessments based on "rough and somewhat inflated estimates." However, the U.S. Solicitor General appealed the issue to the Supreme Court. It was pointed out that the amount of reported tips to the IRS rose from $8.5 billion in 1994 to $14.3 billion in 1999 after the tax agency pressed for better compliance. This demonstrated rather graphically that tip income had been greatly underreported.

There is no question but that the restaurant owners can challenge the accuracy of their tax assessments. However, the majority opinion of the Supreme Court stated that their objections do not "show the aggregate estimate method is an unreasonable way of ascertaining unpaid FICA taxes for which the employer is indisputably liable."

## .03    Reaction to the Decision

Leaders of the National Restaurant Association, which represents 200,000 eating establishments, denounced the decision and said they would take their fight to Congress. They feel that the ruling may affect all employers, like hotels, casinos and taxi companies whose employees receive tips.

An IRS lawyer stressed that the "aggregate estimate" method (the term given to this system of determining tax owed) has not been widely used so far. Moreover, it was emphasized that it is brought into the picture only when it appears restaurants are underpaying their taxes.

Understandably, the Commissioner for the IRS favored the Supreme Court decision and feels that it upholds the IRS's ability to make sure all Americans pay a fair share of taxes. The IRS plans to continue working cooperatively with the restaurant industry and other industries where tips are common.

With the 6-3 decision in the books, the IRS does not anticipate any particular change in the manner of determining and collecting the taxes on tip income.

¶46,017.01

# Appendices

Appendices

# Appendix A
# Financial Planning Tables

The following tables, involving the effects of interest factors, are useful in various forms of future business planning.

## SIMPLE INTEREST TABLE

| Number of Years | 3% | 4% | 5% | 6% | 7% | 8% | 9% | 10% |
|---|---|---|---|---|---|---|---|---|
| | | | | **Interest Rate** | | | | |
| 1 | 1.03 | 1.04 | 1.05 | 1.06 | 1.07 | 1.08 | 1.09 | 1.10 |
| 2 | 1.06 | 1.08 | 1.10 | 1.12 | 1.14 | 1.16 | 1.18 | 1.20 |
| 3 | 1.09 | 1.12 | 1.15 | 1.18 | 1.21 | 1.24 | 1.27 | 1.30 |
| 4 | 1.12 | 1.16 | 1.20 | 1.24 | 1.28 | 1.32 | 1.36 | 1.40 |
| 5 | 1.15 | 1.20 | 1.25 | 1.30 | 1.35 | 1.40 | 1.45 | 1.50 |
| 6 | 1.18 | 1.24 | 1.30 | 1.36 | 1.42 | 1.48 | 1.54 | 1.60 |
| 7 | 1.21 | 1.28 | 1.35 | 1.42 | 1.49 | 1.56 | 1.63 | 1.70 |
| 8 | 1.24 | 1.32 | 1.40 | 1.48 | 1.56 | 1.64 | 1.72 | 1.80 |
| 9 | 1.27 | 1.36 | 1.45 | 1.54 | 1.63 | 1.72 | 1.81 | 1.90 |
| 10 | 1.30 | 1.40 | 1.50 | 1.60 | 1.70 | 1.80 | 1.90 | 2.00 |
| 11 | 1.33 | 1.44 | 1.55 | 1.66 | 1.77 | 1.88 | 1.99 | 2.10 |
| 12 | 1.36 | 1.48 | 1.60 | 1.72 | 1.84 | 1.96 | 2.08 | 2.20 |
| 13 | 1.39 | 1.52 | 1.65 | 1.78 | 1.91 | 2.04 | 2.17 | 2.30 |
| 14 | 1.42 | 1.56 | 1.70 | 1.84 | 1.98 | 2.12 | 2.26 | 2.40 |
| 15 | 1.45 | 1.60 | 1.75 | 1.90 | 2.05 | 2.20 | 2.35 | 2.50 |
| 16 | 1.48 | 1.64 | 1.80 | 1.96 | 2.12 | 2.28 | 2.44 | 2.60 |
| 17 | 1.51 | 1.68 | 1.85 | 2.02 | 2.19 | 2.36 | 2.53 | 2.70 |
| 18 | 1.54 | 1.72 | 1.90 | 2.08 | 2.26 | 2.44 | 2.62 | 2.80 |
| 19 | 1.57 | 1.76 | 1.95 | 2.14 | 2.33 | 2.52 | 2.71 | 2.90 |
| 20 | 1.60 | 1.80 | 2.00 | 2.20 | 2.40 | 2.60 | 2.80 | 3.00 |
| 21 | 1.63 | 1.84 | 2.05 | 2.26 | 2.47 | 2.68 | 2.89 | 3.10 |
| 22 | 1.66 | 1.88 | 2.10 | 2.32 | 2.54 | 2.76 | 2.98 | 3.20 |
| 23 | 1.69 | 1.92 | 2.15 | 2.38 | 2.61 | 2.84 | 3.07 | 3.30 |
| 24 | 1.72 | 1.96 | 2.20 | 2.44 | 2.68 | 2.92 | 3.16 | 3.40 |
| 25 | 1.75 | 2.00 | 2.25 | 2.50 | 2.75 | 3.00 | 3.25 | 3.50 |
| 26 | 1.78 | 2.04 | 2.30 | 2.56 | 2.82 | 3.08 | 3.34 | 3.60 |
| 27 | 1.81 | 2.08 | 2.35 | 2.62 | 2.89 | 3.16 | 3.43 | 3.70 |
| 28 | 1.84 | 2.12 | 2.40 | 2.68 | 2.96 | 3.24 | 3.52 | 3.80 |
| 29 | 1.87 | 2.16 | 2.45 | 2.74 | 3.03 | 3.32 | 3.61 | 3.90 |
| 30 | 1.90 | 2.20 | 2.50 | 2.80 | 3.10 | 3.40 | 3.70 | 4.00 |
| 31 | 1.93 | 2.24 | 2.55 | 2.86 | 3.17 | 3.48 | 3.79 | 4.10 |
| 32 | 1.96 | 2.28 | 2.60 | 2.92 | 3.24 | 3.56 | 3.88 | 4.20 |
| 33 | 1.99 | 2.32 | 2.65 | 2.98 | 3.31 | 3.64 | 3.97 | 4.30 |
| 34 | 2.02 | 2.36 | 2.70 | 3.04 | 3.38 | 3.72 | 4.06 | 4.40 |
| 35 | 2.05 | 2.40 | 2.75 | 3.10 | 3.45 | 3.80 | 4.15 | 4.50 |
| 36 | 2.08 | 2.44 | 2.80 | 3.16 | 3.52 | 3.88 | 4.24 | 4.60 |
| 37 | 2.11 | 2.48 | 2.85 | 3.22 | 3.59 | 3.96 | 4.33 | 4.70 |
| 38 | 2.14 | 2.52 | 2.90 | 3.28 | 3.66 | 4.04 | 4.42 | 4.80 |
| 39 | 2.17 | 2.56 | 2.95 | 3.34 | 3.73 | 4.12 | 4.51 | 4.90 |
| 40 | 2.20 | 2.60 | 3.00 | 3.40 | 3.80 | 4.20 | 4.60 | 5.00 |

**Appendix A**

## COMPOUND INTEREST TABLE

Example of use of this table:
Find how much $1,000 now in bank will grow to in 14 years at 6% interest.
From table 14 years at 6%                    2.2609
Value in 14 years of $1,000                  $2,260.9

| Number of Years | 6% | 6 1/2% | 7% | 7 1/2% | 8% | 8 1/2% | 9% | 9 1/2% |
|---|---|---|---|---|---|---|---|---|
| 1 | 1.0600 | 1.0650 | 1.0700 | 1.0750 | 1.0800 | 1.0850 | 1.0900 | 1.0950 |
| 2 | 1.1236 | 1.1342 | 1.1449 | 1.1556 | 1.1664 | 1.1772 | 1.1881 | 1.1990 |
| 3 | 1.1910 | 1.2079 | 1.2250 | 1.2422 | 1.2597 | 1.2772 | 1.2950 | 1.3129 |
| 4 | 1.2624 | 1.2864 | 1.3107 | 1.3354 | 1.3604 | 1.3858 | 1.4115 | 1.4376 |
| 5 | 1.3332 | 1.3700 | 1.4025 | 1.4356 | 1.4693 | 1.5036 | 1.5386 | 1.5742 |
| 6 | 1.4135 | 1.4591 | 1.5007 | 1.5433 | 1.5868 | 1.6314 | 1.6771 | 1.7237 |
| 7 | 1.5030 | 1.5539 | 1.6057 | 1.6590 | 1.7138 | 1.7701 | 1.8230 | 1.8875 |
| 8 | 1.5938 | 1.6549 | 1.7181 | 1.7834 | 1.8509 | 1.9206 | 1.9925 | 2.0668 |
| 9 | 1.6894 | 1.7625 | 1.8384 | 1.9172 | 1.9990 | 2.0838 | 2.1718 | 2.2632 |
| 10 | 1.7908 | 1.8771 | 1.9671 | 2.0610 | 2.1589 | 2.2609 | 2.3673 | 2.4782 |
| 11 | 1.8982 | 1.9991 | 2.1048 | 2.2156 | 2.3316 | 2.4531 | 2.5804 | 2.7136 |
| 12 | 2.0121 | 2.1290 | 2.2521 | 2.3817 | 2.5181 | 2.6616 | 2.8126 | 2.9714 |
| 13 | 2.1329 | 2.2674 | 2.4098 | 2.5604 | 2.7196 | 2.8879 | 3.0658 | 3.2537 |
| 14 | 2.2609 | 2.4148 | 2.5785 | 2.7524 | 2.9371 | 3.1334 | 3.3417 | 3.5628 |
| 15 | 2.3965 | 2.5718 | 2.7590 | 2.9588 | 3.1721 | 3.3997 | 3.6424 | 3.9013 |
| 16 | 2.5403 | 2.7390 | 2.9521 | 3.1807 | 3.4259 | 3.6887 | 3.9703 | 4.2719 |
| 17 | 2.6927 | 2.9170 | 3.1588 | 3.4193 | 3.7000 | 4.0022 | 4.3276 | 4.6777 |
| 18 | 2.8543 | 3.1066 | 3.3799 | 3.6758 | 3.9960 | 4.3424 | 4.7171 | 5.1221 |
| 19 | 3.0255 | 3.3085 | 3.6165 | 3.9514 | 4.3157 | 4.7115 | 5.1416 | 5.6087 |
| 20 | 3.2075 | 3.5236 | 3.8696 | 4.2478 | 4.6609 | 5.1120 | 5.6044 | 6.1416 |
| 21 | 3.3995 | 3.7526 | 4.1405 | 4.5664 | 5.0338 | 5.5465 | 6.1088 | 6.7250 |
| 22 | 3.6035 | 3.9966 | 4.4304 | 4.9089 | 5.4365 | 6.0180 | 6.6586 | 7.3639 |
| 23 | 3.8197 | 4.2563 | 4.7405 | 5.2770 | 5.8714 | 6.5295 | 7.2578 | 8.0635 |
| 24 | 4.0489 | 4.5330 | 5.0723 | 5.6728 | 6.3411 | 7.0845 | 7.9110 | 8.8295 |
| 25 | 4.2918 | 4.8276 | 5.4274 | 6.0983 | 6.8484 | 7.6867 | 8.6230 | 9.6683 |
| 26 | 4.5493 | 5.1414 | 5.8073 | 6.5557 | 7.3963 | 8.3401 | 9.3991 | 10.5868 |
| 27 | 4.8223 | 5.4756 | 6.2138 | 7.0473 | 7.9880 | 9.0490 | 10.2450 | 11.5926 |
| 28 | 5.1116 | 5.8316 | 6.6488 | 7.5759 | 8.6271 | 9.8182 | 11.1671 | 12.6939 |
| 29 | 5.4183 | 6.2106 | 7.1142 | 8.1441 | 9.3172 | 10.6527 | 12.1721 | 13.8998 |
| 30 | 5.7434 | 6.6143 | 7.6122 | 8.7549 | 10.5582 | 11.5582 | 13.2676 | 15.2203 |
| 31 | 6.0881 | 7.0442 | 8.1451 | 9.4115 | 10.8676 | 12.5407 | 14.4617 | 16.6662 |
| 32 | 6.4533 | 7.5021 | 8.7152 | 10.1174 | 11.7370 | 13.6066 | 15.7633 | 18.2495 |
| 33 | 6.8408 | 7.9898 | 9.3253 | 10.8762 | 12.6760 | 14.7632 | 17.1820 | 19.9832 |
| 34 | 7.2510 | 8.5091 | 9.9781 | 11.6919 | 13.6901 | 16.0181 | 18.7284 | 21.8816 |
| 35 | 7.6860 | 9.0622 | 10.6765 | 12.5688 | 14.7853 | 17.3796 | 20.4139 | 23.9604 |
| 36 | 8.1479 | 9.6513 | 11.4239 | 13.5115 | 15.9681 | 18.8569 | 22.2512 | 26.2366 |
| 37 | 8.6360 | 10.2786 | 12.2236 | 14.5249 | 17.2456 | 20.4597 | 24.2538 | 28.7291 |
| 38 | 9.1542 | 10.9467 | 13.0792 | 15.6142 | 18.6252 | 22.1988 | 26.4366 | 31.4583 |
| 39 | 9.7035 | 11.6582 | 13.9948 | 16.7853 | 20.1152 | 24.0857 | 28.8159 | 34.4469 |
| 40 | 10.2857 | 12.4160 | 14.9744 | 18.0442 | 21.7245 | 26.1330 | 31.4094 | 37.7193 |

**Appendix A**

## Compound Interest Table (*Cont'd*)

| Number of Years | 6% | 6 1/2% | 7% | 7 1/2% | 8% | 8 1/2% | 9% | 9 1/2% |
|---|---|---|---|---|---|---|---|---|
| 1 | 1.1000 | 1.1100 | 1.1200 | 1.1300 | 1.1400 | 1.1500 | 1.1600 | 1.1700 |
| 2 | 1.2100 | 1.2321 | 1.2544 | 1.2769 | 1.2996 | 1.3225 | 1.3456 | 1.3689 |
| 3 | 1.3310 | 1.3576 | 1.4049 | 1.4428 | 1.4815 | 1.5208 | 1.5608 | 1.6016 |
| 4 | 1.4647 | 1.5180 | 1.5735 | 1.6304 | 1.6389 | 1.7490 | 1.8106 | 1.8738 |
| 5 | 1.6105 | 1.6350 | 1.7623 | 1.8424 | 1.9254 | 2.0113 | 2.1003 | 2.1924 |
| 6 | 1.7715 | 1.8704 | 1.9738 | 2.0819 | 2.1949 | 2.3130 | 2.4363 | 2.5651 |
| 7 | 1.9487 | 2.0761 | 2.2106 | 2.3526 | 2.5022 | 2.6600 | 2.8262 | 3.0012 |
| 8 | 2.1435 | 2.3045 | 2.4759 | 2.6584 | 2.8525 | 3.0590 | 3.2784 | 3.5114 |
| 9 | 2.3579 | 2.5580 | 2.7730 | 3.0040 | 3.2519 | 3.5178 | 3.8029 | 4.1084 |
| 10 | 2.5937 | 2.8394 | 3.1058 | 3.3945 | 3.7072 | 4.0455 | 4.4114 | 4.8068 |
| 11 | 2.8531 | 3.1517 | 3.4785 | 3.8358 | 4.2262 | 4.6523 | 5.1172 | 5.6239 |
| 12 | 3.1384 | 3.4984 | 3.8959 | 4.3345 | 4.8179 | 5.3502 | 5.9360 | 6.5800 |
| 13 | 3.4522 | 3.8832 | 4.3634 | 4.8980 | 5.4924 | 6.1527 | 6.8857 | 7.6986 |
| 14 | 3.7974 | 4.3104 | 4.8871 | 5.5347 | 6.2613 | 7.0757 | 7.9875 | 9.0074 |
| 15 | 4.1772 | 4.7845 | 5.4735 | 6.2542 | 7.1379 | 8.1370 | 9.2655 | 10.5387 |
| 16 | 4.5949 | 5.3108 | 6.1303 | 7.0673 | 8.1372 | 9.3576 | 10.7480 | 12.3303 |
| 17 | 5.0544 | 5.8950 | 6.8660 | 7.9860 | 9.2764 | 10.7612 | 12.4676 | 14.4264 |
| 18 | 5.5599 | 6.5435 | 7.6899 | 9.0242 | 10.5751 | 12.3754 | 14.4625 | 16.8789 |
| 19 | 6.1159 | 7.2633 | 8.6127 | 10.1974 | 12.0556 | 14.2317 | 16.7765 | 19.7483 |
| 20 | 6.7274 | 8.0623 | 9.6462 | 11.5230 | 13.7434 | 16.3665 | 19.4607 | 23.1055 |
| 21 | 7.4002 | 8.9491 | 10.8038 | 13.0210 | 15.6675 | 18.8215 | 22.5744 | 27.0335 |
| 22 | 8.1402 | 9.9335 | 12.1003 | 14.7138 | 17.8610 | 21.6447 | 26.1883 | 31.6292 |
| 23 | 8.9543 | 11.0262 | 13.5523 | 16.6266 | 20.3615 | 24.8914 | 30.3762 | 37.0062 |
| 24 | 9.8497 | 12.2391 | 15.1786 | 18.7880 | 23.2122 | 28.6251 | 35.2364 | 43.2972 |
| 25 | 10.8347 | 13.5854 | 17.0000 | 21.2305 | 26.4619 | 32.9189 | 40.8742 | 50.6578 |
| 26 | 11.9181 | 15.0793 | 19.0400 | 23.9905 | 30.1665 | 37.8567 | 47.4141 | 59.2696 |
| 27 | 13.1099 | 16.7386 | 21.3248 | 27.1092 | 34.3899 | 43.5353 | 55.0003 | 69.3454 |
| 28 | 14.4209 | 18.5799 | 23.8838 | 30.6334 | 39.2044 | 50.0656 | 63.8004 | 81.1342 |
| 29 | 15.8630 | 20.6236 | 26.7499 | 34.6158 | 44.6931 | 57.5754 | 74.0085 | 94.9270 |
| 30 | 17.4494 | 22.8922 | 29.9599 | 39.1158 | 50.9501 | 66.2117 | 85.84981 | 11.0646 |
| 31 | 19.1943 | 25.4104 | 33.5551 | 44.2009 | 58.0831 | 76.1435 | 99.58581 | 29.9456 |
| 32 | 21.1137 | 28.2055 | 37.5817 | 49.9470 | 66.2148 | 87.5650 | 115.51951 | 52.0363 |
| 33 | 23.2251 | 31.3082 | 42.0915 | 56.4402 | 75.4849 | 100.6998 | 134.0027 | 177.8825 |
| 34 | 25.5476 | 34.7521 | 47.1425 | 63.7774 | 86.0527 | 115.8048 | 155.4431 | 208.1226 |
| 35 | 28.1024 | 38.5748 | 52.7996 | 72.0685 | 98.1001 | 133.1755 | 180.3140 | 243.5034 |
| 36 | 30.9128 | 42.8180 | 59.1355 | 81.4374 | 111.8342 | 153.1518 | 209.1643 | 284.8990 |
| 37 | 34.0039 | 47.5280 | 66.2318 | 92.0242 | 127.4909 | 176.1246 | 242.6306 | 333.3319 |
| 38 | 37.4048 | 52.7561 | 74.1796 | 103.9874 | 145.3397 | 202.5433 | 281.4515 | 389.9983 |
| 39 | 41.1447 | 58.5593 | 83.0812 | 117.5057 | 165.6872 | 232.9248 | 326.4837 | 456.2980 |
| 40 | 45.2592 | 65.0008 | 93.0509 | 132.7815 | 188.8835 | 267.8635 | 378.7211 | 533.8687 |

**Appendix A**

## Compound Interest Table (*Cont'd*)

| Number of Years | 18% | 19% | 20% | 21% | 22% | 23% | 24% | 25% |
|---|---|---|---|---|---|---|---|---|
| 1 | 1.1800 | 1.1900 | 1.2000 | 1.2100 | 1.2200 | 1.2300 | 1.2400 | 1.2500 |
| 2 | 1.3924 | 1.4161 | 1.4400 | 1.4641 | 1.4884 | 1.5129 | 1.5376 | 1.5625 |
| 3 | 1.6430 | 1.6851 | 1.7280 | 1.7715 | 1.8158 | 1.8608 | 1.9066 | 1.9531 |
| 4 | 1.9387 | 2.0053 | 2.0736 | 2.1435 | 2.2153 | 2.2888 | 2.3642 | 2.4414 |
| 5 | 2.2877 | 2.3863 | 2.4883 | 2.5937 | 2.7027 | 2.8153 | 2.9316 | 3.0517 |
| 6 | 2.6995 | 2.8397 | 2.9859 | 3.1384 | 3.2973 | 3.4628 | 3.6352 | 3.8146 |
| 7 | 3.1854 | 3.3793 | 3.5831 | 3.7974 | 4.0227 | 4.2592 | 4.5076 | 4.7683 |
| 8 | 3.7588 | 4.0213 | 4.2998 | 4.5949 | 4.9077 | 5.2389 | 5.5895 | 5.9604 |
| 9 | 4.4354 | 4.7854 | 5.1597 | 5.5599 | 5.9874 | 6.4438 | 6.9309 | 7.4505 |
| 10 | 5.2338 | 5.6946 | 6.1917 | 6.7274 | 7.3046 | 7.9259 | 8.5944 | 9.3132 |
| 11 | 6.1759 | 6.7766 | 7.4300 | 8.1402 | 8.9116 | 9.7489 | 10.6570 | 11.6415 |
| 12 | 7.2875 | 8.0642 | 8.9161 | 9.8497 | 10.8722 | 11.9911 | 13.2147 | 14.5519 |
| 13 | 8.5993 | 9.5964 | 10.6993 | 11.9181 | 13.2641 | 14.7491 | 16.3863 | 18.1898 |
| 14 | 10.1472 | 11.4197 | 12.8391 | 14.4209 | 16.1822 | 18.1414 | 20.3190 | 22.7373 |
| 15 | 11.9737 | 13.5895 | 15.4070 | 17.4494 | 19.7422 | 22.3139 | 25.1956 | 28.4217 |
| 16 | 14.1290 | 16.1715 | 18.4884 | 21.1137 | 24.0855 | 27.4461 | 31.2425 | 35.5271 |
| 17 | 16.6722 | 19.2441 | 22.1861 | 25.5476 | 29.3844 | 33.7587 | 38.7408 | 44.4089 |
| 18 | 19.6732 | 22.9005 | 26.6233 | 30.9126 | 35.8489 | 41.5233 | 48.0385 | 55.5111 |
| 19 | 23.2144 | 27.2516 | 31.9479 | 37.4043 | 43.7357 | 51.0736 | 59.5678 | 69.3889 |
| 20 | 27.3930 | 32.4294 | 38.3375 | 45.2592 | 53.3576 | 62.8206 | 73.8641 | 86.7361 |
| 21 | 32.3237 | 38.5910 | 46.0051 | 54.7636 | 65.0963 | 77.2693 | 91.5915 | 108.4202 |
| 22 | 38.1420 | 45.9233 | 56.2061 | 66.2640 | 79.4175 | 95.0413 | 113.5735 | 135.5252 |
| 23 | 45.0076 | 54.6487 | 66.2473 | 80.1795 | 96.8893 | 116.9008 | 140.8311 | 169.4065 |
| 24 | 53.1090 | 65.0319 | 79.4968 | 97.0172 | 118.2050 | 143.7880 | 174.6306 | 211.7582 |
| 25 | 62.6686 | 77.3880 | 95.3962 | 117.3908 | 144.2101 | 176.8592 | 216.5419 | 264.6977 |
| 26 | 73.9488 | 92.0918 | 114.4754 | 142.0429 | 175.9363 | 217.5368 | 268.5120 | 330.8722 |
| 27 | 87.2597 | 109.5892 | 137.3705 | 171.8719 | 214.6423 | 267.5703 | 332.9549 | 413.5903 |
| 28 | 102.9665 | 130.4112 | 164.8446 | 207.9650 | 261.8636 | 329.1115 | 412.8641 | 516.9878 |
| 29 | 121.5005 | 155.1893 | 197.8135 | 251.6377 | 319.4736 | 404.8072 | 511.9515 | 646.2348 |
| 30 | 143.3708 | 184.6753 | 237.3763 | 304.4816 | 389.7578 | 497.9128 | 634.8199 | 807.7935 |
| 31 | 169.1773 | 219.7636 | 284.8515 | 368.4227 | 475.5046 | 612.4328 | 787.1767 | 1009.7419 |
| 32 | 199.6292 | 261.5187 | 341.8218 | 445.7915 | 580.1156 | 753.2923 | 976.0991 | 1262.1774 |
| 33 | 235.5625 | 311.2072 | 410.1862 | 539.4077 | 707.7410 | 926.5496 | 1210.3629 | 1577.7218 |
| 34 | 277.9638 | 370.3366 | 492.2235 | 652.6834 | 863.4441 | 1139.6560 | 1500.8500 | 1972.1522 |
| 35 | 327.9972 | 440.7006 | 590.6682 | 789.7469 | 1053.4018 | 1401.7769 | 1861.0540 | 2465.1903 |
| 36 | 387.0368 | 524.4337 | 708.8018 | 955.5938 | 1285.1502 | 1724.1855 | 2307.7069 | 3081.4879 |
| 37 | 456.7034 | 624.0761 | 850.5622 | 1156.2685 | 1567.8833 | 2120.7482 | 2861.5586 | 3851.8598 |
| 38 | 538.9100 | 742.6505 | 1020.6746 | 1399.0849 | 1912.8176 | 2608.5203 | 3548.3302 | 4814.8248 |
| 39 | 635.9138 | 883.7542 | 1224.8096 | 1692.8927 | 2333.6375 | 3208.4800 | 4399.9295 | 6018.5310 |
| 40 | 750.3783 | 1051.6675 | 1469.7715 | 2048.4002 | 2847.0377 | 3946.4304 | 5455.9126 | 7523.1638 |

**Appendix A**

## PERIODIC DEPOSIT TABLE

Example of use of this table:
  How much is $1,000 a year invested at 6% worth in 20 years?
  At 6% for 20 years, the figure is          38.993
  For $1,000 a year, the amount is      $38,993

| Number of Years | 6% | 7% | 8% | 9% | 10% | 11% | 12% | 13% |
|---|---|---|---|---|---|---|---|---|
| 1 | 1.060 | 1.070 | 1.080 | 1.090 | 1.100 | 1.110 | 1.120 | 1.130 |
| 2 | 2.183 | 2.215 | 2.246 | 2.278 | 2.310 | 2.342 | 2.374 | 2.407 |
| 3 | 3.375 | 3.440 | 3.506 | 3.573 | 3.641 | 3.710 | 3.779 | 3.850 |
| 4 | 4.637 | 4.751 | 4.867 | 4.985 | 5.105 | 5.228 | 5.353 | 5.480 |
| 5 | 5.975 | 6.153 | 6.336 | 6.523 | 6.716 | 6.913 | 7.115 | 7.323 |
| 6 | 7.394 | 7.654 | 7.923 | 8.200 | 8.487 | 8.783 | 9.089 | 9.405 |
| 7 | 8.897 | 9.260 | 9.637 | 10.028 | 10.436 | 10.859 | 11.300 | 11.757 |
| 8 | 10.491 | 10.978 | 11.488 | 12.021 | 12.579 | 13.164 | 13.776 | 14.416 |
| 9 | 12.181 | 12.816 | 13.487 | 14.193 | 14.937 | 15.722 | 16.549 | 17.420 |
| 10 | 13.972 | 14.784 | 15.645 | 16.560 | 17.531 | 18.561 | 19.655 | 20.814 |
| 11 | 15.870 | 16.888 | 17.977 | 19.141 | 20.384 | 21.713 | 23.133 | 24.650 |
| 12 | 17.882 | 19.141 | 20.495 | 21.953 | 23.523 | 25.212 | 27.029 | 28.985 |
| 13 | 20.015 | 21.550 | 23.215 | 25.019 | 26.975 | 29.095 | 31.393 | 33.883 |
| 14 | 22.276 | 24.129 | 26.152 | 28.361 | 30.772 | 33.405 | 36.280 | 39.417 |
| 15 | 24.673 | 26.888 | 29.324 | 32.003 | 34.950 | 38.190 | 41.753 | 45.672 |
| 16 | 27.213 | 29.840 | 32.750 | 35.974 | 39.545 | 43.501 | 47.884 | 52.739 |
| 17 | 29.906 | 32.999 | 36.450 | 40.301 | 44.599 | 49.396 | 54.750 | 60.725 |
| 18 | 32.760 | 36.379 | 40.446 | 45.018 | 50.159 | 55.939 | 62.440 | 69.749 |
| 19 | 3$.786 | 39.995 | 44.762 | 50.160 | 56.275 | 63.203 | 71.052 | 79.947 |
| 20 | 38.993 | 43.865 | 49.423 | 55.765 | 63.002 | 71.265 | 80.699 | 91.470 |
| 21 | 42.392 | 48.006 | 54.457 | 61.873 | 70.403 | 80.214 | 91.503 | 104.491 |
| 22 | 45.996 | 52.436 | 59.893 | 68.532 | 78.543 | 90.148 | 103.603 | 119.205 |
| 23 | 49.816 | 57.177 | 65.765 | 75.790 | 87.497 | 101.174 | 117.155 | 135.831 |
| 24 | 53.865 | 62.249 | 72.106 | 83.701 | 97.347 | 113.413 | 132.334 | 154.620 |
| 25 | 58.156 | 67.676 | 78.954 | 92.324 | 108.182 | 126.999 | 149.334 | 175.850 |
| 26 | 62.706 | 73.484 | 86.351 | 101.723 | 120.100 | 142.079 | 168.374 | 199.841 |
| 27 | 67.528 | 79.698 | 94.339 | 111.968 | 133.210 | 158.817 | 189.699 | 226.950 |
| 28 | 72.640 | 86.347 | 102.966 | 123.135 | 147.631 | 177.397 | 213.583 | 257.583 |
| 29 | 78.058 | 93.461 | 112.283 | 135.308 | 163.494 | 198.021 | 240.333 | 292.199 |
| 30 | 83.802 | 101.073 | 122.346 | 148.575 | 180.943 | 220.913 | 270.293 | 331.315 |
| 31 | 89.890 | 109.218 | 133.214 | 163.037 | 200.138 | 246.324 | 303.848 | 375.516 |
| 32 | 96.343 | 117.933 | 144.951 | 178.800 | 221.252 | 274.529 | 341.429 | 425.463 |
| 33 | 103.184 | 127.259 | 157.627 | 195.982 | 244.477 | 305.837 | 383.521 | 481.903 |
| 34 | 110.435 | 137.237 | 171.317 | 214.711 | 270.024 | 340.590 | 430.663 | 545.681 |
| 35 | 118.121 | 147.913 | 186.102 | 235.125 | 298.127 | 379.164 | 483.463 | 617.749 |
| 36 | 126.268 | 159.337 | 202.070 | 257.376 | 329.039 | 421.982 | 542.599 | 699.187 |
| 37 | 134.904 | 171.561 | 219.316 | 281.630 | 363.043 | 469.511 | 608.831 | 791.211 |
| 38 | 144.058 | 184.640 | 237.941 | 308.066 | 400.448 | 522.267 | 683.010 | 895.198 |
| 39 | 153.762 | 198.635 | 258.057 | 336.882 | 441.593 | 580.826 | 766.091 | 1012.704 |
| 40 | 164.048 | 213.610 | 279.781 | 368.292 | 486.852 | 645.827 | 859.142 | 1145.486 |

**Appendix A**

## COMPOUND DISCOUNT TABLE

This table shows the present or discounted value of $1 due at a given future time. For example, assume property which will revert to a lessor in 10 years will then be worth $1,000. The present value of this reversion, computed at an assumed rate of 4% on the investment, is found by finding the factor on the 10-year line in the 4% column. The factor .6756 is multiplied by 1000 to obtain the answer of $675.60.

| Years | 4% | 4-1/2% | 5% | 5-1/2% | 6% | 6-1/2% | 7% | 7-1/2% | 8% | 9% | 10% | 11% |
|---|---|---|---|---|---|---|---|---|---|---|---|---|
| 1 | 0.9615 | 0.9569 | 0.9524 | 0.9479 | 0.9434 | 0.9390 | 0.9346 | 0.9302 | 0.9259 | 0.9174 | 0.9091 | 0.9009 |
| 2 | .9246 | .9157 | .9070 | .8985 | .8900 | .8817 | .8734 | .8653 | .8573 | .8417 | .8264 | .8116 |
| 3 | .8890 | .8763 | .8638 | .8516 | .8396 | .8278 | .8163 | .8050 | .7938 | .7722 | .7513 | .7312 |
| 4 | .8548 | .8386 | .8277 | .8072 | .7921 | .7773 | .7629 | .7488 | .7350 | .7084 | .6830 | .6587 |
| 5 | .8219 | .8025 | .7835 | .7651 | .7473 | .7299 | .7130 | .6966 | .6806 | .6499 | .6209 | .5935 |
| 6 | .7903 | .7679 | .7462 | .7252 | .7050 | .6853 | .6663 | .6480 | .6302 | .5963 | .5645 | .5346 |
| 7 | .7599 | .7343 | .7107 | .6874 | .6651 | .6435 | .6227 | .6027 | .5835 | .5470 | .5132 | .4816 |
| 8 | .7307 | .7032 | .6768 | .6516 | .6274 | .6042 | .5820 | .5607 | .5403 | .5019 | .4665 | .4339 |
| 9 | .7026 | .6729 | .6446 | .6176 | .5919 | .5673 | .5439 | .5216 | .5002 | .4604 | .4241 | .3909 |
| 10 | .6756 | .6439 | .6139 | .5854 | .5584 | .5327 | .5083 | .4852 | .4632 | .4224 | .3855 | .3522 |
| 11 | .6496 | .6162 | .5847 | .5549 | .5268 | .5002 | .4751 | .4514 | .4289 | .3875 | .3505 | .3173 |
| 12 | .6246 | .5897 | .5568 | .5260 | .4970 | .4697 | .4440 | .4199 | .3971 | .3555 | .3186 | .2858 |
| 13 | .6006 | .5643 | .5303 | .4986 | .4688 | .4410 | .4150 | .3906 | .3677 | .3262 | .2897 | .2575 |
| 14 | .5775 | .5400 | .5051 | .4726 | .4423 | .4141 | .3878 | .3633 | .3405 | .2992 | .2633 | .2320 |
| 15 | .5553 | .5167 | .4810 | .4479 | .4173 | .3888 | .3624 | .3380 | .3152 | .2745 | .2394 | .2090 |
| 16 | .5339 | .4945 | .4581 | .4246 | .3936 | .3651 | .3387 | .3144 | .2919 | .2519 | .2176 | .1883 |
| 17 | .5134 | .4732 | .4363 | .4024 | .3714 | .3428 | .3166 | .2924 | .2703 | .2311 | .1978 | .1696 |
| 18 | .4936 | .4528 | .4155 | .3815 | .3503 | .3219 | .2959 | .2720 | .2502 | .2120 | .1799 | .1528 |
| 19 | .4746 | .4333 | .3957 | .3616 | .3305 | .3022 | .2765 | .2531 | .2317 | .1945 | .1635 | .1377 |
| 20 | .4564 | .4146 | .3769 | .3427 | .3118 | .2838 | .2584 | .2354 | .2145 | .1784 | .1486 | .1240 |
| 21 | .4388 | .3968 | .3589 | .3249 | .2942 | .2665 | .2415 | .2190 | .1987 | .1637 | .1351 | .1117 |
| 22 | .4220 | .3797 | .3418 | .3079 | .2775 | .2502 | .2257 | .2037 | .1839 | .1502 | .1228 | .1007 |
| 23 | .4057 | .3633 | .3256 | .2919 | .2618 | .2349 | .2109 | .1895 | .1703 | .1378 | .1117 | .0907 |
| 24 | .3901 | .3477 | .3101 | .2766 | .2470 | .2206 | .1971 | .1763 | .1577 | .1264 | .1015 | .0817 |
| 25 | .3751 | .3327 | .2953 | .2622 | .2330 | .2071 | .1842 | .1640 | .1460 | .1160 | .0923 | .0736 |
| 26 | .3607 | .3184 | .2812 | .2486 | .2198 | .1945 | .1722 | .1525 | .1352 | .1064 | .0829 | .0663 |
| 27 | .3468 | .3047 | .2678 | .2356 | .2074 | .1826 | .1609 | .1419 | .1252 | .0976 | .0763 | .0597 |
| 28 | .3335 | .2916 | .2551 | .2233 | .1956 | .1715 | .1504 | .1320 | .1159 | .0895 | .0693 | .0538 |

**Appendix A**

Compound Interest Table (Cont'd)

| Years | 4% | 4-1/2% | 5% | 5-1/2% | 6% | 6-1/2% | 7% | 7-1/2% | 8% | 9% | 10% | 11% |
|---|---|---|---|---|---|---|---|---|---|---|---|---|
| 29 | 0.3207 | 0.2790 | 0.2429 | 0.2117 | 0.1846 | 0.1610 | 0.1406 | 0.1228 | 0.1073 | 0.0822 | 0.0630 | 0.0485 |
| 30 | .3083 | .2670 | .2314 | .2006 | .1741 | .1512 | .1314 | .1142 | .0994 | .0754 | .0573 | .0437 |
| 31 | .2965 | .2555 | .2204 | .1902 | .1643 | .1420 | .1228 | .1063 | .0920 | .0691 | .0521 | .0394 |
| 32 | .2851 | .2445 | .2099 | .1803 | .1550 | .1333 | .1147 | .0988 | .0852 | .0634 | .0474 | .0354 |
| 33 | .2741 | .2340 | .1999 | .1709 | .1462 | .1251 | .1072 | .0919 | .0789 | .0582 | .0431 | .0319 |
| 34 | .2636 | .2239 | .1904 | .1620 | .1379 | .1175 | .1002 | .0855 | .0730 | .0534 | .0391 | .0288 |
| 35 | .2534 | .2142 | .1813 | .1535 | .1301 | .1103 | .0937 | .0796 | .0676 | .0490 | .0356 | .0259 |
| 36 | .2437 | .2050 | .1727 | .1455 | .1227 | .1036 | .0875 | .0740 | .0626 | .0449 | .0323 | .0234 |
| 37 | .2343 | .1962 | .1644 | .1379 | .1158 | .0973 | .0818 | .0688 | .0580 | .0412 | .0294 | .0210 |
| 38 | .2253 | .1878 | .1566 | .1307 | .1092 | .0914 | .0765 | .0640 | .0537 | .0378 | .0267 | .0189 |
| 39 | .2166 | .1797 | .1491 | .1239 | .1031 | .0858 | .0715 | .0596 | .0497 | .0347 | .0243 | .0171 |
| 40 | .2083 | .1719 | .1420 | .1175 | .0972 | .0805 | .0668 | .0554 | .0460 | .0318 | .0221 | .0154 |
| 41 | .2003 | .1645 | .1353 | .1113 | .0917 | .0756 | .0624 | .0515 | .0426 | .0292 | .0201 | .0139 |
| 42 | .1926 | .1574 | .1288 | .1055 | .0865 | .0710 | .0583 | .0480 | .0395 | .0268 | .0183 | .0125 |
| 43 | .1852 | .1507 | .1227 | .1000 | .0816 | .0667 | .0545 | .0446 | .0365 | .0246 | .0166 | .0112 |
| 44 | .1780 | .1442 | .1169 | .0948 | .0770 | .0626 | .0509 | .0415 | .0338 | .0225 | .0151 | .0101 |
| 45 | .1712 | .1380 | .1113 | .0899 | .0726 | .0588 | .0476 | .0386 | .0313 | .0207 | .0137 | .0091 |
| 46 | .1646 | .1320 | .1060 | .0852 | .0685 | .0552 | .0445 | .0359 | .0290 | .0190 | .0125 | .0082 |
| 47 | .1583 | .1263 | .1009 | .0807 | .0647 | .0518 | .0416 | .0334 | .0269 | .0174 | .0113 | .0074 |
| 48 | .1522 | .1209 | .0961 | .0765 | .0610 | .0487 | .0389 | .0311 | .0249 | .0160 | .0103 | .0067 |
| 49 | .1463 | .1157 | .0916 | .0725 | .0575 | .0457 | .0363 | .0289 | .0230 | .0147 | .0094 | .0060 |
| 50 | .1407 | .1107 | .0872 | .0688 | .0543 | .0429 | .0339 | .0269 | .0213 | .0134 | .0085 | .0054 |
| 51 | .1353 | .1059 | .0831 | .0652 | .0512 | .0403 | .0317 | .0250 | .0197 | .0123 | .0077 | .00488 |
| 52 | .1301 | .1014 | .0791 | .0618 | .0483 | .0378 | .0297 | .0233 | .0183 | .0113 | .0070 | .00440 |
| 53 | .1251 | .0970 | .0753 | .0586 | .0456 | .0355 | .0277 | .0216 | .0169 | .0104 | .0064 | .00396 |
| 54 | .1203 | .0928 | .0717 | .0555 | .0430 | .0333 | .0259 | .0201 | .0157 | .0095 | .0058 | .00357 |
| 55 | .1157 | .0888 | .0683 | .0526 | .0406 | .0313 | .0242 | .0187 | .0145 | .0087 | .0053 | .00322 |
| 56 | .1112 | .0850 | .0651 | .0499 | .0383 | .0294 | .0226 | .0174 | .0134 | .0080 | .0048 | .00290 |
| 57 | .1069 | .0814 | .0620 | .0473 | .0361 | .0276 | .0211 | .0162 | .0124 | .0073 | .0044 | .00261 |
| 58 | .1028 | .0778 | .0590 | .0448 | .0341 | .0259 | .0198 | .0151 | .0115 | .0067 | .0040 | .00235 |
| 59 | .0989 | .0745 | .0562 | .0425 | .0321 | .0243 | .0185 | .0140 | .0107 | .0062 | .0036 | .00212 |
| 60 | .0951 | .0713 | .0535 | .0403 | .0303 | .0229 | .0173 | .0130 | .0099 | .0057 | .0033 | .00191 |

Appendix A

## PRESENT WORTH TABLE — SINGLE FUTURE PAYMENT

Example of use of this table:
  Find how much $10,000 payable in 12 years is worth now at an interest rate of 6%.
  From table for 12 years 6%                                                       .4970
  Present value of $10,000 in 12 years (10,000×.4970)                              $4,970

| Number of Years | Interest Rate 6% | 7% | 8% | 9% | 10% | 11% | 12% | 13% |
|---|---|---|---|---|---|---|---|---|
| 1 | 0.9434 | 0.9346 | 0.9259 | 0.9174 | 0.9091 | 0.9009 | 0.8929 | 0.8850 |
| 2 | 0.8900 | 0.8734 | 0.8573 | 0.8417 | 0.8264 | 0.8116 | 0.7972 | 0.7831 |
| 3 | 0.8396 | 0.8163 | 0.7938 | 0.7722 | 0.7513 | 0.7312 | 0.7118 | 0.6931 |
| 4 | 0.7921 | 0.7629 | 0.7350 | 0.7084 | 0.6830 | 0.6587 | 0.6355 | 0.6133 |
| 5 | 0.7473 | 0.7130 | 0.6806 | 0.6499 | 0.6209 | 0.5935 | 0.5674 | 0.5428 |
| 6 | 0.7050 | 0.6663 | 0.6302 | 0.5963 | 0.5645 | 0.5346 | 0.5066 | 0.4803 |
| 7 | 0.6651 | 0.6227 | 0.5835 | 0.5470 | 0.5132 | 0.4816 | 0.4523 | 0.4251 |
| 8 | 0.6274 | 0.5820 | 0.5403 | 0.5019 | 0.4665 | 0.4339 | 0.4039 | 0.3762 |
| 9 | 0.5919 | 0.5439 | 0.5002 | 0.4604 | 0.4241 | 0.3909 | 0.3606 | 0.3329 |
| 10 | 0.5584 | 0.5083 | 0.4632 | 0.4224 | 0.3855 | 0.3522 | 0.3220 | 0.2946 |
| 11 | 0.5268 | 0.4751 | 0.4289 | 0.3875 | 0.3505 | 0.3173 | 0.2875 | 0.2607 |
| 12 | 0.4970 | 0.4440 | 0.3971 | 0.3555 | 0.3186 | 0.2858 | 0.2567 | 0.2307 |
| 13 | 0.4688 | 0.4150 | 0.3677 | 0.3262 | 0.2897 | 0.2575 | 0.2292 | 0.2042 |
| 14 | 0.4423 | 0.3878 | 0.3405 | 0.2992 | 0.2633 | 0.2320 | 0.2046 | 0.1807 |
| 15 | 0.4173 | 0.3624 | 0.3152 | 0.2745 | 0.2394 | 0.2090 | 0.1827 | 0.1599 |
| 16 | 0.3936 | 0.3387 | 0.2919 | 0.2519 | 0.2176 | 0.1883 | 0.1631 | 0.1415 |
| 17 | 0.3714 | 0.3166 | 0.2703 | 0.2311 | 0.1978 | 0.1696 | 0.1456 | 0.1252 |
| 18 | 0.3503 | 0.2959 | 0.2502 | 0.2120 | 0.1799 | 0.1528 | 0.1300 | 0.1108 |
| 19 | 0.3305 | 0.2765 | 0.2317 | 0.1945 | 0.1635 | 0.1377 | 0.1161 | 0.0981 |
| 20 | 0.3118 | 0.2584 | 0.2145 | 0.1784 | 0.1486 | 0.1240 | 0.1037 | 0.0868 |
| 21 | 0.2942 | 0.2415 | 0.1987 | 0.1637 | 0.1351 | 0.1117 | 0.0926 | 0.0768 |
| 22 | 0.2775 | 0.2257 | 0.1839 | 0.1502 | 0.1228 | 0.1007 | 0.0826 | 0.0680 |
| 23 | 0.2618 | 0.2109 | 0.1703 | 0.1378 | 0.1117 | 0.0907 | 0.0738 | 0.0601 |
| 24 | 0.2470 | 0.1971 | 0.1577 | 0.1264 | 0.1015 | 0.0817 | 0.0660 | 0.0532 |
| 25 | 0.2330 | 0.1842 | 0.1460 | 0.1160 | 0.0923 | 0.0736 | 0.0588 | 0.0471 |
| 26 | 0.2198 | 0.1722 | 0.1352 | 0.1064 | 0.0829 | 0.0663 | 0.0525 | 0.0417 |
| 27 | 0.2074 | 0.1609 | 0.1252 | 0.0976 | 0.0763 | 0.0597 | 0.0470 | 0.0369 |
| 28 | 0.1956 | 0.1504 | 0.1159 | 0.0895 | 0.0693 | 0.0538 | 0.0420 | 0.0326 |
| 29 | 0.1846 | 0.1406 | 0.1073 | 0.0822 | 0.0630 | 0.0485 | 0.0374 | 0.0289 |
| 30 | 0.1741 | 0.1314 | 0.0994 | 0.0754 | 0.0573 | 0.0437 | 0.0334 | 0.0256 |
| 31 | 0.1643 | 0.1228 | 0.0920 | 0.0691 | 0.0521 | 0.0394 | 0.0298 | 0.0226 |
| 32 | 0.1550 | 0.1147 | 0.0852 | 0.0634 | 0.0474 | 0.0354 | 0.0266 | 0.0200 |
| 33 | 0.1462 | 0.1072 | 0.0789 | 0.0582 | 0.0431 | 0.0319 | 0.0238 | 0.0177 |
| 34 | 0.1379 | 0.1002 | 0.0730 | 0.0534 | 0.0391 | 0.0288 | 0.0212 | 0.0157 |
| 35 | 0.1301 | 0.0937 | 0.0676 | 0.0490 | 0.0356 | 0.0259 | 0.0189 | 0.0139 |
| 36 | 0.1227 | 0.0875 | 0.0626 | 0.0449 | 0.0323 | 0.0234 | 0.0169 | 0.0123 |
| 37 | 0.1158 | 0.0818 | 0.0580 | 0.0412 | 0.0294 | 0.0210 | 0.0151 | 0.0109 |
| 38 | 0.1092 | 0.0765 | 0.0536 | 0.0378 | 0.0267 | 0.0189 | 0.0135 | 0.0096 |
| 39 | 0.1031 | 0.0715 | 0.0497 | 0.0347 | 0.0243 | 0.0171 | 0.0120 | 0.0085 |
| 40 | 0.0972 | 0.0668 | 0.0460 | 0.0318 | 0.0221 | 0.0154 | 0.0107 | 0.0075 |

**Appendix A**

## PRESENT WORTH TABLE—PERIODIC FUTURE PAYMENT

Example of use of this table:
  To find the cost now of $1,000 of income per year for 20 years at 7%.
  From table for 20 years at 7%                        10.5940
  Cost of $1,000 per year ($1,000×10.5940)             $10,594

| Number of Years | 6% | 7% | 8% | 9% | 10% | 11% | 12% | 13% |
|---|---|---|---|---|---|---|---|---|
| 1 | 0.9434 | 0.9346 | 0.9259 | 0.9174 | 0.9091 | 0.9009 | 0.8929 | 0.8850 |
| 2 | 1.8334 | 1.8080 | 1.7833 | 1.7591 | 1.7355 | 1.7125 | 1.6901 | 1.6681 |
| 3 | 2.6730 | 2.6243 | 2.5771 | 2.5313 | 2.4869 | 2.4437 | 2.4018 | 2.3612 |
| 4 | 3.4651 | 3.3872 | 3.3121 | 3.2397 | 3.1699 | 3.1024 | 3.0373 | 2.9745 |
| 5 | 4.2124 | 4.1002 | 3.9927 | 3.8897 | 3.7908 | 3.6959 | 3.6048 | 3.5172 |
| 6 | 4.9173 | 4.7665 | 4.6229 | 4.4859 | 4.3553 | 4.2305 | 4.1114 | 3.9975 |
| 7 | 5.5824 | 5.3893 | 5.2064 | 5.0330 | 4.8684 | 4.7122 | 4.5638 | 4.4226 |
| 8 | 6.2098 | 5.9713 | 5.7466 | 5.5348 | 5.3349 | 5.1461 | 4.9676 | 4.7988 |
| 9 | 6.8017 | 6.5152 | 6.2469 | 5.9952 | 5.7590 | 5.5370 | 5.3282 | 5.1317 |
| 10 | 7.3601 | 7.0236 | 6.7101 | 6.4177 | 6.1446 | 5.8892 | 5.6502 | 5.4262 |
| 11 | 7.8869 | 7.4987 | 7.1390 | 6.8052 | 6.4951 | 6.2065 | 5.9377 | 5.6869 |
| 12 | 8.3838 | 7.9427 | 7.$361 | 7.1607 | 6.8137 | 6.4924 | 6.1944 | 5.9176 |
| 13 | 8.8527 | 8.3577 | 7.9038 | 7.4869 | 7.1034 | 6.7499 | 6.4235 | 6.1218 |
| 14 | 9.2950 | 8.7455 | 8.2442 | 7.7862 | 7.3667 | 6.9819 | 6.6282 | 6.3025 |
| 15 | 9.7122 | 9.1079 | 8.5595 | 8.0607 | 7.6061 | 7.1909 | 6.8109 | 6.4624 |
| 16 | 10.1059 | 9.4466 | 8.8514 | 8.3126 | 7.8237 | 7.3792 | 6.9740 | 6.6039 |
| 17 | 10.4773 | 9.7632 | 9.1216 | 8.5436 | 8.0216 | 7.5488 | 7.1196 | 6.7291 |
| 18 | 10.8276 | 10.0591 | 9.3719 | 8.7556 | 8.2014 | 7.7016 | 7.2497 | 6.8399 |
| 19 | 11.1581 | 10.3356 | 9.6036 | 8.9501 | 8.3649 | 7.8393 | 7.3658 | 6.9380 |
| 20 | 11.4699 | 10.5940 | 9.8181 | 9.1285 | 8.5136 | 7.9633 | 7.4694 | 7.0248 |
| 21 | 11.7641 | 10.8355 | 10.0168 | 9.2922 | 8.6487 | 8.0751 | 7.5620 | 7.1016 |
| 22 | 12.0416 | 11.0612 | 10.2007 | 9.4424 | 8.7715 | 8.1757 | 7.6446 | 7.1695 |
| 23 | 12.3034 | 11.2722 | 10.3711 | 9.5802 | 8.8832 | 8.2664 | 7.7184 | 7.2297 |
| 24 | 12.5504 | 11.4693 | 10.5288 | 9.7066 | 8.9847 | 8.3481 | 7.7843 | 7.2829 |
| 25 | 12.7834 | 11.6536 | 10.6748 | 9.8226 | 9.0770 | 8.4217 | 7.8431 | 7.3299 |
| 26 | 13.0032 | 11.8258 | 10.8100 | 9.9290 | 9.1609 | 8.4881 | 7.8957 | 7.3717 |
| 27 | 13.2105 | 11.9867 | 10.9352 | 10.0266 | 9.2372 | 8.5478 | 7.9426 | 7.4086 |
| 28 | 13.4062 | 12.1371 | 11.0511 | 10.1161 | 9.3066 | 8.6016 | 7.9844 | 7.4412 |
| 29 | 13.5907 | 12.2777 | 11.1584 | 10.1983 | 9.3696 | 8.6501 | 8.0218 | 7.4701 |
| 30 | 13.7648 | 12.4090 | 11.2578 | 10.2737 | 9.4269 | 8.6938 | 8.0552 | 7.4957 |
| 31 | 13.9291 | 12.5318 | 11.3498 | 10.3428 | 9.4790 | 8.7331 | 8.0850 | 7.5183 |
| 32 | 14.0840 | 12.6466 | 11.4350 | 10.4062 | 9.5264 | 8.7686 | 8.1116 | 7.5383 |
| 33 | 14.2302 | 12.7538 | 11.5139 | 10.4644 | 9.5694 | 8.8005 | 8.1354 | 7.5560 |
| 34 | 14.3681 | 12.8540 | 11.5869 | 10.5178 | 9.6086 | 8.8293 | 8.1566 | 7.5717 |
| 35 | 14.4982 | 12.9477 | 11.6546 | 10.5668 | 9.6442 | 8.8552 | 8.1755 | 7.5856 |
| 36 | 14.6210 | 13.0352 | 11.7172 | 10.6118 | 9.6765 | 8.8786 | 8.1924 | 7.5979 |
| 37 | 14.7368 | 13.1170 | 11.7752 | 10.6530 | 9.7059 | 8.8996 | 8.2075 | 7.6087 |
| 38 | 14.8460 | 13.1935 | 11.8289 | 10.6908 | 9.7327 | 8.9186 | 8.2210 | 7.6183 |
| 39 | 14.9491 | 13.2649 | 11.8786 | 10.7255 | 9.7569 | 8.9357 | 8.2330 | 7.6268 |
| 40 | 15.0463 | 13.3317 | 11.9246 | 10.7574 | 9.7791 | 8.9511 | 8.2438 | 7.6344 |

**Appendix A**

# Appendix B
## Index to Journal Entries

### INDEX TO JOURNAL ENTRIES EXAMPLES
*References Are to Journal Entry Numbers*

**Appendix B**

**Appendix B**

**Appendix B**

## SAMPLE JOURNAL ENTRIES

OPENING INVESTMENT—Sole Proprietorship:
[1]

| | | |
|---|---:|---:|
| Cash | 5,000 | |
| Building (fair value) | 45,000 | |
| A. Able, Net Worth | | 50,000 |

OPENING INVESTMENT—Partnership:
[2]

| | | |
|---|---:|---:|
| Cash | 30,000 | |
| Inventory | 30,000 | |
| B. Baker (50%), Capital | | 30,000 |
| C. Charles (50%), Capital | | 30,000 |

PARTNERSHIP INVESTMENT—with Goodwill:
[3]

| | | |
|---|---:|---:|
| Building (fair value) | 45,000 | |
| Goodwill | 15,000 | |
| A. Able (50%), Capital | | 60,000 |

Able contributes building for ½ share
of partnership.

PARTNERSHIP INVESTMENT—Skill, no funds:
[4]

| | | |
|---|---:|---:|
| A. Able, Capital | 3,000 | |
| B. Baker, Capital | 3,000 | |
| C. Charles, Capital | 6,000 | |
| D. Dog, Capital | | 12,000 |

**Appendix B**

Dog gets 10% of partnership
for the skill he'll contribute.
Ratios will now be:

| | | |
|---|---|---|
| Able | (25% less 10%) | 22.5% |
| Baker | (   same   ) | 22.5% |
| Charles | (50% less 10%) | 45.0% |
| Dog | (as granted) | 10.0% |
| | | 100.0% |

## PARTNERSHIP INCORPORATES:
[5]

| | | |
|---|---|---|
| Cash | 30,000 | |
| Inventory—Raw Material | 30,000 | |
| Building (fair value) | 45,000 | |
| Capital Stock (par $10; 10,000 | | 100,000 |
| shares issued; 100,000 auth.) | | |
| Additional Paid-in Capital | | 5,000 |

Shares issued: A. 2250; B. 2250;
C. 4500; D. 1,000. Note that partnership goodwill
is not carried over to corporation.

## CORPORATE INVESTMENT—with Goodwill:
[6]

| | | |
|---|---|---|
| Machinery & Equipment (fair value) | 9,000 | |
| Goodwill | 1,000 | |
| Capital Stock (1,000 shares) | | 10,000 |

Issuing 1,000 shares to E. Easy
@ $10 par for machinery contributed.

## CORPORATION MONTHLY ENTRIES—The
corporation records all entries into the general
ledger *through* summary entries made in the general
journal from the books and sources of original entry:

[7] *Summary of Purchase Journal,* where all vendor
invoices are entered:

| | | |
|---|---|---|
| Purchases—Raw Material | 10,000 | |
| Shop Supplies | 2,000 | |
| Office Supplies | 1,000 | |
| Office Equipment | 3,000 | |
| Utilities | 1,000 | |
| Freight Out | 2,000 | |
| Advertising | 1,000 | |
| Accounts Payable | | 20,000 |

[8] *Summary of Cash Disbursement, Regular Cash A/C:*

| | | |
|---|---|---|
| Cash—Payroll A/C | 13,000 | |
| Petty Cash | 200 | |
| Accounts Payable | 14,500 | |

## Appendix B

| Federal Tax Deposits Made | 5,100 | |
| Bank Charges | 2 | |
| Cash—Regular A/C | | 32,602 |
| Cash Discounts Taken | | 200 |

[9]  *Summary of Cash Disbursement, Payroll A/C:*

| Direct Labor—Shop | 12,500 | |
| Indirect Labor—Shop | 1,500 | |
| Salaries—Sales Dept. | 2,000 | |
| Salaries—G & A | 4,000 | |
| Cash—Payroll A/C (net pay) | | 13,000 |
| W/H Tax Pay—Federal | | 4,400 |
| FICA Tax Withheld | | 1,200 |
| SUI & Disability W/H | | 300 |
| State Income Taxes W/H | | 600 |
| Savings Bonds W/H | | 500 |

[10]  *Summary of Sales Book:*

| Accounts Receivable | 35,000 | |
| Sales Returns & Allowances | 500 | |
| Sales—Product L | | 18,000 |
| Sales—Product M | | 16,600 |
| Sales Taxes Payable | | 900 |

[11]  *Summary of Cash Receipts Book:*

| Cash—Regular A/C | 30,500 | |
| Cash Discounts Allowed | 500 | |
| Accounts Receivable | | 30,000 |
| Machinery and Equipment | | 1,000 |

[12]  *Summary of Petty Cash Box:*

| Postage | 40 | |
| Entertainment | 60 | |
| Travel Expense | 30 | |
| Misc. Expense | 20 | |
| Petty Cash | | 150 |

[13]  *General Journal Entries during month:*

| Depreciation—M & E | 10 | |
| Machinery and Equipment | 400 | |
| Gain on Sale of Machinery | | 410 |

To correct entry from cash receipts:

| Basis | $ 600 | |
| Deprec. | 10 (1/60th) | |
| | 590 | |
| S.P. | 1000 | |
| Gain | $ 410 | |

**Appendix B**

[14]

| | | |
|---|---|---|
| Depr.—Bldg (1/40×45,000×1/12) | 94 | |
| Depr.—M&E (1/5×8,400×1/12) | 140 | |
| Depr.—OE (1/5×3,000×1/12) | 50 | |
| Amortization (1/40×1,000×1/12) | 2 | |
|     Accum Depr.—Bldg | | 94 |
|     Accum Depr.—M&E | | 140 |
|     Accum Depr.—OE | | 50 |
|     Goodwill | | 2 |

[15]

| | | |
|---|---|---|
| Real Estate Taxes | 300 | |
|     Accrued Taxes—RE | | 300 |
| 1/12th of estimated $3,600 for yr | | |

[16]

| | | |
|---|---|---|
| Direct Labor (3125) | 2,500 | |
| Indirect Labor (375) | 300 | |
| Salaries—Selling (500) | 400 | |
| Salaries—G & A (1000) | 800 | |
|     Accrued Salaries (5000) | | 4,000 |
| To accrue 4/5 of last payroll in month. | | |

[17]

| | | |
|---|---|---|
| W/H Tax Payable—Federal | 3,300 | |
| FICA Tax Withheld | 900 | |
| FICA Tax Expense—employer | 900 | |
|     Federal Tax Deposits Made | | 5,100 |
| FICA Tax Expense—employer | 300 | |
| SUI & DISAB Expense | 600 | |
| FUI Expense | 100 | |
|     Accrued Taxes—Payroll | | 1,000 |

To zero deposit account against withholding
accounts and to book employer FICA
expense and estimated unemployment
tax for month.

[18]

| | | |
|---|---|---|
| Overhead | 6,106 | |
|     Depr.—Bldg (60% of 94) | | 56 |
|     Depr.—M&E (all) | | 140 |
|     Indirect Labor (all) | | 1,800 |
|     Payroll Tax Exp (70% of 1900) | | 1,330 |
|     Shop supplies (all considered used) | | 2,000 |

## Appendix B

| | |
|---|---|
| Utilities (60% of 1000) | 600 |
| Taxes—RE (60% of 300) | 180 |

To allocate expenses to overhead.
Taxes based on payroll proportion.
Other allocations based on space occupied.

[19]

| | | |
|---|---|---|
| Inventory—Raw Materials | (15,000) | |
| Inventory—Work in Process | none | |
| Inventory—Finished Goods | 15,369 | |
| Cost of Production—Inventory Change | | 369 |

To increase or (decrease) inventory
accounts to reflect new month-end inventory
as follows:

*Raw Material:*

| | | |
|---|---|---|
| Opening Inventory | $ | 30,000 |
| Purchases | | 10,000 |
| Less used in production | | (25,000) |
| Closing inventory | | 15,000 |
| To adjust opening | $ | (15,000) |

*Finished Goods:*

| | | |
|---|---|---|
| Materials used (above) | $ | 25,000 |
| Direct labor costs | | 15,000 |
| Overhead costs | | 6,106 |
| 3 units produced | | 46,106 |
| 1 unit unsold (1/3) | $ | 15,369 |

(none at hand at beginning)
No work in process this month.

(The entries through here are all related with respect to the dollars shown. From here on, they are independent with respect to each CAPITAL HEADING, but related within the headed area.)

CUSTOMER'S CHECK BOUNCES
[20]

| | | |
|---|---|---|
| Accounts Receivable (Mr. A.) | 100 | |
| Cash (Disbursements) | | 100 |

To record bank charge for
Mr. A's check return—insufficient funds.

[21]

| | | |
|---|---|---|
| Cash (Receipts) | 100 | |
| Accounts Receivable (Mr. A.) | | 100 |

For re-deposit of above, per customer's instructions.

**Appendix B**

**NOTES RECEIVABLE DISCOUNTED**
[22]

| | | |
|---|---|---|
| Cash | 9,900 | |
| Interest Expense | 250 | |
| Notes receivable Discounted | | 10,000 |
| Interest Income | | 150 |

For proceeds from customer note discounted,
due 90 days @ 6%, discount rate 10%.

[23]

| | | |
|---|---|---|
| Notes Receivable Discounted | 10,000 | |
| Notes Receivable | | 10,000 |

To offset. Customer note paid, per bank notice.

**FIRST-YEAR DEPRECIATION**
[24]

| | | |
|---|---|---|
| Depreciation Expense—M & E | 2,000 | |
| Accumulated Depr—M & E | | 2,000 |

For maximum first-year depreciation
taken on 6/30 purchase of extruder.
See next entry for regular deprec.

[25]

| | | |
|---|---|---|
| Depreciation—M & E | 400 | |
| Accumulated Depr—M & E | | 400 |

To take straight-line on above:

| | |
|---|---|
| Cost | $ 10,000 |
| Less 1st yr. Depr | (2,000) |
| S/L basis | 8,000 |
| Over 10 yrs—per yr | $    800 |
| Six months this yr (no salvage value). | $    400 |

**TAX LOSS CARRYBACK**
[26]

| | | |
|---|---|---|
| FIT Refund and Interest Receivable | 106,000 | |
| Income Tax (Current Yr. Income Statement) | | 100,000 |
| Interest Income | | 6,000 |

To set up receivable for carryback tax refund
due, plus interest.

**SUBCHAPTER S EQUITY ENTRIES**

End of Year 1:

[27]

| | | |
|---|---|---|
| Net income for Current Year | 30,000 | |
| Undistributed Earnings—Post-Election | | 30,000 |

To close year's net income into new Sub-S
undistributed earnings Equity account.

# Appendix B

[28]

| | | |
|---|---|---|
| Retained Earnings | 55,000 | |
|     Retained Earnings—Pre-Election | | 55,000 |

To retitle opening retained earnings
account and keep it separate from earnings
after Sub-S election.

[29]

| | | |
|---|---|---|
| Post-Election Dividends | 10,000 | |
|     Cash | | 10,000 |

For cash distributions made of current
earnings. (NOTE: State law may require a
*formal* declaration of a dividend for
corporations. If this is true, and there
is no such declaration, this must be treated
as a *loan receivable* from stockholders.)

## INSTALLMENT SALES METHOD

[30]

| | | |
|---|---|---|
| Accounts Receivable | 1,000 | |
|     Cost of Installment Sale | | 700 |
|     Deferred Gross Profit on Installment Sales | | 300 |

For original sale. (GP% is 30%)

[31]

| | | |
|---|---|---|
| Cash | 300 | |
|     Accounts Receivable | | 300 |

For payment on account.

[32]

| | | |
|---|---|---|
| Deferred Gross Profit on Installment Sales | 90 | |
|     Realized Gross Profit | | 90 |

To amortize 30% of above collection to
realized income.

## VOIDING YOUR OWN CHECK (Issued in a prior period)

[33]

| | | |
|---|---|---|
| Cash (Ck # 1601) | 1,500 | |
|     Rent Expense | | 1,500 |

To void check # 1601 (last month).
Check reported lost. Payment stopped. Replaced
with this month's
check # 1752. (See CD book)

**Appendix B**

INVESTMENT TAX CREDIT—THE DEFERRAL METHOD

[34]

| | | |
|---|---|---|
| Taxes Payable | 7,000 | |
| Deferred Investment Tax Credits | | 7,000 |

To set up investment tax credit under
the deferred method. *Note:* The tax expense
for this year on the income statement does
*not* reflect the use of this credit.

Year 2:

[35]

| | | |
|---|---|---|
| Deferred Investment Tax Credits | 700 | |
| Income Tax Expense | | 700 |

To amortize 1/10th, based on 10-year
life of asset to which applicable.

ACCUMULATED PREFERRED STOCK DIVIDENDS

[36]

| | | |
|---|---|---|
| Dividends (Income Statement) | 30,000 | |
| Dividends Payable (Liability) | | 30,000 |

To accrue this year's commitment, 6%
of $500,000. *Note:* There was no "only
as earned" provision attached to this issue.

DIVIDEND DECLARATION—COMMON STOCK

[37]

| | | |
|---|---|---|
| Retained Earnings | 100,000 | |
| Common Stock Extra Dividend Declared—(show in Equity Section) | | 100,000 |

To segregate common stock extra
dividend from accumulated earnings (until
paid), 10¢ per share, 1,000,000 shares.

PAYMENT OF ABOVE TWO DIVIDENDS

[38]

| | | |
|---|---|---|
| Dividends Payable | 30,000 | |
| Common Stock Extra Dividend Declared | 100,000 | |
| Cash | | 130,000 |

For payment of dividends.

APPROPRIATION OF RETAINED EARNINGS

[39]

| | | |
|---|---|---|
| Retained Earnings | 50,000 | |
| Reserve Appropriation for Inventory Declines (Equity Section) | | 50,000 |

**Appendix B**

To set aside retained earnings for possible
inventory losses—per Board resolution.

[40]

| | | |
|---|---|---|
| Retained Earnings—(1/1 opening) | 150,000 | |
| Accounts Payable (XYZ Co.) | | 150,000 |

To record prior year billing error made by
supplier, XYZ Co., on invoice #_____, dated
12/10. Error not discovered by XYZ until
after closing of our books and issuance of
statements. Error is considered material
enough to treat as prior period adjustment.
Item was not in inventory at 12/31.

## STOCK DIVIDEND
Usually:

[41]

| | | |
|---|---|---|
| Retained Earnings (at market) | 45,000 | |
| Common Stock (par $10, 3,000 shares) | | 30,000 |
| Additional Paid-in Capital | | 15,000 |

For 3% stock dividend distributed on 100,000
shares—3,000 shares issued. Market value $15
at dividend date.

Sometimes:

[42]

| | | |
|---|---|---|
| Additional Paid-in Capital | 30,000 | |
| Common Stock (par $10, 3,000 shares) | | 30,000 |

For non-taxable distribution out of Paid-in
Capital.

## SPLIT-UP EFFECTED IN THE FORM OF A STOCK DIVIDEND
[43]

| | | |
|---|---|---|
| Retained Earnings (at par) | 1,000,000 | |
| Common Stock (par $10, 100,000 shs) | | 1,000,000 |

For split in the form of a stock dividend
(to conform with state law). One share
issued for each share outstanding.
100,000 shares at par of $10.

## STOCK SPLIT-UP
[44]

| | | |
|---|---|---|
| Common Stock (100,000 shares @ $10.) | memo | |
| Common Stock (200,000 shares @ $5.) | | memo |

**Appendix B**

Memo entry only. To record stock split-up by showing change in par value and in number of shares outstanding. One share issued for each outstanding. Par changed from $10 to $5.

## STOCK OPTIONS FOR EMPLOYEES AS COMPENSATION

### PARTNERSHIP WITHDRAWALS
[45]

| | | |
|---|---:|---:|
| S. Stone, Withdrawals | 15,000 | |
| T. Times, Withdrawals | 5,000 | |
| Cash | | 20,000 |
| For cash withdrawals. | | |

### PARTNERSHIP PROFIT ENTRY
[46]

| | | |
|---|---:|---:|
| Net Income—P & L a/c | 100,000 | |
| S. Stone, Capital (50%) | | 50,000 |
| T. Times, Capital (50%) | | 50,000 |
| To split profit as follows: | | |
| Per P & L closing account | $ 80,000 | |
| Add back above included in P & L account | 20,000 | |
| Profit to distribute | $ 100,000 | |

[47]

| | | |
|---|---:|---:|
| S. Stone, Capital | 15,000 | |
| T. Times, Capital | 5,000 | |
| S. Stone, Withdrawals | | 15,000 |
| T. Times, Withdrawals | | 5,000 |
| To close withdrawal accounts to capital accounts. | | |

### IMPUTED INTEREST (ON NOTES RECEIVABLE)
[48]

| | | |
|---|---:|---:|
| Notes Receivable (Supplier A—6 yrs) | 1,000,000 | |
| Cash | | 1,000,000 |
| For loan made to supplier. Received non-interest bearing note, due 6 yrs. | | |

[49]

| | | |
|---|---:|---:|
| Cost of Merchandise (from supplier A) | 370,000 | |
| Unamortized Discount on Notes Receiv. | | 370,000 |
| To charge imputed interest of 8% on above note, due in 6 years, to cost of merchandise bought from A. | | |

## Appendix B

Year 2:

[50]

| | | |
|---|---|---|
| Unamortized Discount on Notes Receiv. | 50,000 | |
|    Interest Income | | 50,000 |

To amortize this year's applicable imputed
interest on note.

## BOND DISCOUNT, PREMIUM AND ISSUE COSTS

[51]

| | | |
|---|---|---|
| Cash | 2,025,000 | |
| Unamortized Bond Issue Costs | 15,000 | |
|    Bonds Payable (8%, 10 yrs) | | 2,000,000 |
|    Unamortized Premium on Bonds | | 40,000 |

To set up face value of bonds, issue costs and
net cash proceeds received.

Year 2:

[52]

| | | |
|---|---|---|
| Unamortized Premium on Bonds | 4,000* | |
|    Unamortized Bond Issue Cost | | 1,500* |
|    Interest Expense (difference) | | 2,500 |

To set up approximate amortization.
(*Should actually be based on present values.)

[53]

| | | |
|---|---|---|
| Interest Expense | 160,000 | |
|    Cash | | 160,000 |

To record actual payment of bond interest.
8% of $2,000,000.

## FEDERAL INCOME TAX – INTERIMS – AND EXTRAORDINARY ITEM

[54]

| | | |
|---|---|---|
| Income Tax (on continuing operations) | 350,000 | |
|    Extraordinary Loss (tax effect) | | 50,000 |
|    Taxes Payable | | 300,000 |

To set up FIT at end of First Quarter
based on full year's 50% rate and to
segregate tax applicable to extraordinary item.

*Statement should show:*

| | |
|---|---|
| Net from continuing operations | $ 700,000 |
| Less FIT | (350,000) |
| | 350,000 |
| Extraordinary loss | |
|    (net of $50,000 tax effect) | 50,000 |
| Net Income | $ 300,000 |

**Appendix B**

CAPITALIZING A LEASE (LESSEE)
    At contracting:
[55]

| | | |
|---|---:|---:|
| Capitalized Leases | 1,920,000 | |
| Long-Term Lease Liability | | 3,600,000 |
| Unamortized Discount on Lease | | (1,680,000) |

To capitalize lease of $25,000 per month
for 12 years @ 12% imputed interest
rate. Estimated life of asset is 15 years.
Present value used, since fair value is
higher at $2,000,000.

(*Note:* The two credit items shown are
*netted* and shown as *one net liability* on
the balance sheet. The liability (at present value)
should always equal the asset value, also at
present value. Future lease payments are broken
out, effectively, into principal and interest.)

Month-end 1:

[56]

| | | |
|---|---:|---:|
| Long-Term Lease Liability | 25,000 | |
| Cash | | 25,000 |

First payment on lease.

[57]

| | | |
|---|---:|---:|
| Interest Expense | 18,950 | |
| Unamortized Discount on Lease | | 18,950 |

For one month's interest.
1% of $3,600,000 less $1,680,000, less
initial payment on signing of contract
of $25,000 (*entry not shown*) or $1,895,000.

[58]

| | | |
|---|---:|---:|
| Depreciation Expense | 10,667 | |
| Accumulated Depr of Capitalized Lease | | 10,667 |

One month: $1,920,000 \times 1/5 \times 1/12$

CASH SURRENDER VALUE – OFFICER LIFE INSURANCE
[59]

| | | |
|---|---:|---:|
| Officer Life Insurance – expense | 1,500 | |
| Cash | | 1,500 |

For payment of premium. *Note:* Expense is
not deductible for tax purpose and is a
*permanent* difference.

**Appendix B**

[60]

| | | |
|---|---|---|
| Cash Surrender Value-Officer Life Ins. | 1,045 | |
|     Officer Life Ins. Expense | | 1,045 |
| To reflect increase in C.S.V. for year | | |

[61]

| | | |
|---|---|---|
| Cash | 5,000 | |
|     Loans Against Officer Life Insurance | | 5,000 |
|     (Displayed against the asset "C.S.V.") | | |
| To record loan against life policy. | | |
| No intent to repay within the next year. | | |

STANDARD COST VARIANCES

[62]

| | | |
|---|---|---|
| Purchases—Raw Mat (at stand) | 200 | |
|     Accounts Payable—actual | | 188 |
|     Variance—material price | | 12 |

[63]

| | | |
|---|---|---|
| Direct Labor—at standard | 50 | |
| Variance—Direct Labor rate | 10 | |
|     Payroll—actual direct labor | | 58 |
|     Variance—Labor Time | | 2 |

[64]

| | | |
|---|---|---|
| Overhead—at Standard | 75 | |
| Variance—overhead | 15 | |
|     Overhead itemized actual accounts | | 90 |

*Adjusting Inventories:*

[65]

| | | |
|---|---|---|
| Inventory—Raw Materials at standard | 100 | |
| Finished Goods—at standard | 75 | |
|     Cost of Production—at standard | | 175 |
| To adjust inventory accounts to reflect | | |
| end-of-month on-hand figures at standards. | | |

[66]

| | | |
|---|---|---|
| Variance—material price | xx | |
| Variance—labor time | xx | |
|     Variance—direct labor rate | | xx |
|     Variance—overhead | | xx |
|     Contra Inventory Asset a/c (variances | | xx |
|         to offset standard and reflect cost) | | |

**Appendix B**

To pull out of variance accounts that portion
which is applicable to inventory, in order to keep
an isolated contra account, which in offset to the
"standard" asset account, reflects approximate
cost. The portion is based on an overall ratio of
variances to production and inventory figures (at
standard). (If normal, apply to cost of sales for
interims.)

ADJUSTING INVENTORY FOR SAMPLING RESULTS
[67]

| | | | |
|---|---|---|---|
| Cost of Sales | | 50,000 | |
|   Inventory | | | 50,000 |

To reduce inventory by $50,000 based
on sampling results:

| | | |
|---|---|---|
| Inventory per computer run | $1,000,000 | |
| Estimated calculated inventory | | |
| per sample | 950,000 | |
|   Reduction this year | $50,000 | |

Year 2:

[68]

| | | |
|---|---|---|
| Inventory | 10,000 | |
|   Cost of Sales | | 10,000 |

To adjust inventory to actual based on actual
physical count of entire inventory. Last year-end
sample error proved to be 4%, not 5%.

ADJUSTING CLOSING INVENTORY FROM CLIENTS STANDARD
COST TO AUDITOR'S DETERMINED (AND CLIENT AGREED)
ACTUAL COST, AND TO REFLECT PHYSICAL INVENTORY VS.
BOOK INVENTORY DIFFERENCES
[69]

| | | |
|---|---|---|
| Inventory—Finished Goods (Standard) | 25,000 | |
|   Cost of Sales | | 25,000 |

To adjust general ledger inventory (at
standard) to actual physical inventory
count, priced out at standard. Actual is
$25,000 more.

[70]

| | | |
|---|---|---|
| Cost of Sales | 80,000 | |
|     Inventory—Finished Goods (Asset | | 80,000 |
|       Contra Cost account) | | |

To set up a contra account reducing asset
account, which is at standard costs, effectively to
audited actual cost or market, whichever lower.

# Appendix B

Year 2: (End of Year)
[71]

| Inventory—Finished Goods (Asset Contra Cost account) | 50,000 | |
| Cost of Sales | | 50,000 |

To reduce the contra account to the new year-end difference between the "standard" asset account and the actual cost determined for this new year-end inventory.

PARTNERSHIP DISSOLUTION:

*Balance Sheet*

| Cash | $ 20,000 |
| Assets other | 35,000 |
| Liabilities | (25,000) |
| A Capital (50%) | (20,000) |
| B Capital (30%) | (14,000) |
| C Capital (20%) | 4,000 |
| | -0- |

[72]

| Cash | 15,000 | |
| Assets other | | 15,000 |

For sale of some assets at book value.

[73]

| A Capital ($\frac{5}{8}$) | 2,500 | |
| B Capital ($\frac{3}{8}$) | 1,500 | |
| C Capital | | 4,000 |

C cannot put in his overdraw—to apportion his deficit.

[74]

| Liabilities | 25,000 | |
| Cash | | 25,000 |

To pay liabilities

[75]

| Cash | 10,000 | |
| Loss on Sale of Assets other | 10,000 | |
| Assets other | | 20,000 |
| A Capital ($\frac{5}{8}$) | 6,250 | |
| B Capital ($\frac{3}{8}$) | 3,750 | |
| Loss on Sale of Assets other | | 10,000 |

Selling remaining assets and apportioning loss

**Appendix B**

[76]

| | | |
|---|---|---|
| A Capital (remaining balance) | 11,250 | |
| B Capital (remaining balance) | 8,750 | |
|    Cash | | 20,000 |

To distribute remaining cash and zero
capital accounts.

NOTE THE SHARING OF C'S DEFICIT AND
OF THE LOSS ON ASSET SALE *BEFORE*
DISTRIBUTING REMAINING CASH.

MARKETABLE SECURITIES

*Shown as Current Assets:*
[77]

| | | |
|---|---|---|
| Unrealized Loss—to P & L | 1,500 | |
|    Valuation Allowance—Current | | 1,500 |

To write down 100 U.S. Steel:

| | |
|---|---|
| Cost 1/1 | $10,000 |
| Market 12/31 | 8,500 |
| Unrealized Loss | $1,500 |

Year 2:

[78]

| | | |
|---|---|---|
| Cash | 4,500 | |
| Realized Loss—P & L | 500 | |
|    Marketable Securities—Current | | 5,000 |

| | |
|---|---|
| Sold 50 @ 90 | $4,500 |
| Cost 50 @ 90 | 5,000 |
|    Realized Loss | $ 500 |

[79]

| | | |
|---|---|---|
| Valuation Allowance—Current | 1,250 | |
|    Valuation Adjustment—Current (P&L Gain) | | 1,250* |

To adjust valuation allowance a/c
(current) for remaining securities
left in portfolio:

| | |
|---|---|
| 50 US Steel—cost 100 | $5,000 |
| Market, this year end—95 | 4,750 |
|    Bal. should be | 250 Cr. |
| Balance in valuation a/c | 1,500 Cr. |
|    Debit valuation a/c | $1,250 Dr. |

*Note: Unrealized *gains* are called
"valuation adjustments." Unrealized
losses are called "unrealized losses."

**Appendix B**

*Shown as Noncurrent Asset:*

[80]

| | | |
|---|---|---|
| Unrealized Noncurrent Loss (Equity section) | 1,000 | |
|    Valuation Allowance—Noncurrent | | 1,000 |

To write down 100 shares GM from cost of 60 to
market value at 12/31 of 50.

Year 2:

[81]

| | | |
|---|---|---|
| Cash | 2,900 | |
| Realized Loss—P & L | 100 | |
|    Marketable Securities—Noncurrent | | 3,000 |

| | |
|---|---|
| Sold 50 GM @ 58 | $2,900 |
| Cost 50 GM @ 60 | 3,000 |
|    Realized loss | $ 100 |

[82]

| | | |
|---|---|---|
| Valuation Allowance—Noncurrent | 1,000 | |
|    Unrealized Noncurrent Loss (Equity Section) | | 1,000 |

To adjust valuation allowance a/c
(Noncurrent) as follows:

| | |
|---|---|
| Cost 50 GM @ 60 | $ 3,000 |
| Market now @ 65 | N/A |
|    (Higher than cost) | |
| Valuation a/c should be | -0- |
|    (Because market is higher | |
|    than cost) | |
| Balance in valuation a/c | 1,000 Cr. |
|    Debit to correct | $1,000 Dr. |

TREASURY STOCK
   Purchase of:

[83]

| | | |
|---|---|---|
| Treasury Stock—at Cost | 125,000 | |
|    Cash | | 125,000 |

Purchase of 1,000 shares @ 125
market. Par value $50.
No intent to cancel the stock.

Sale of:

[84]

| | | |
|---|---|---|
| Cash | 140,000 | |
|    Treasury Stock—at Cost | | 125,000 |
|    Additional Paid—in Capital | | 15,000 |

For sale of treasury stock @ 140.

**Appendix B**

APPRAISAL WRITE-UPS

[85]

| | | |
|---|---|---|
| Building | 350,000 | |
| Appraisal Capital (Equity Section) | | 350,000 |

To raise building from cost of $400,000 to
appraised value of $750,000 per requirement
of the lending institution.

Year 2:

[86]

| | | |
|---|---|---|
| Depreciation—Building | 21,667 | |
| Accumulated Depreciation—Building | | 21,667 |

To depreciate based on appraised value:
(400,000 for 40 years; 350,000 for 30 yrs)
Building was 10 years old at appraisal.

FOREIGN CURRENCY EXCHANGE

[87]

| | | |
|---|---|---|
| Unrealized Loss (balance sheet) | 10,000 | |
| Accts Payable—Foreign | | 10,000 |

To adjust liabilities payable in Swiss Francs
to US Dollars at 12/31:

| | |
|---|---|
| Exchange rate at 12/31.40 | $40,000 |
| Booked at (100,000 frs).30 | 30,000 |
| More dollars owed | $10,000 |

[88]

| | | |
|---|---|---|
| Deferred Taxes | 5,000* | |
| Unrealized Loss | | 5,000* |

To show deferred tax effect (50% rate
times $10,000 above)
*Less Foreign or Domestic Dividend
Credits, if Applicable

Year 2:

[89]

| | | |
|---|---|---|
| Accounts Payable—Foreign | 20,000 | |
| Cash | | 19,000 |
| Realized gain (Books, not Tax) | | 1,000 |

For payment of 50,000 Swiss Francs at
exchange rate of .38

[90]

| | | |
|---|---|---|
| Accounts Payable—Foreign | 500 | |
| Balance Sheet | | 500 |

**Appendix B**

To restate liability at year-end:

| | |
|---|---:|
| 50,000 Frs @ .39 | $19,500 |
| Booked to last yr. | 20,000 |
| (Gain) | $ (500) |

[91]

| | | |
|---|---:|---:|
| Taxes Payable | 2,000 | |
| Income Tax Expense | 500 | |
| Deferred Taxes | | 2,500 |

To transfer to actual taxes payable
(from deferred) that portion applying
to the payment of $19,000. Original debt
in dollars was $15,000. 50% tax rate on
$4,000 or $2,000, plus $500—to offset
2,500 booked to last 12/31.

[92]

| | | |
|---|---:|---:|
| Income Tax Expenses | 250 | |
| Deferred Taxes | | 250 |

To adjust deferred taxes to equal 1/2 of 4,500
(19,500 liability now, less original liability of
15,000) for $2,250 tax deferral.

THE EQUITY METHOD
[93]

| | | |
|---|---:|---:|
| Investment—Oleo Co. | 275,000 | |
| Cash | | 275,000 |

Purchase of 25% of Oleo's stock, at cost
(25,000 shares @ $11).

[94]

| | | |
|---|---:|---:|
| Investment—Oleo Co. | 40,000 | |
| Deferred Good Will in Oleo | | 40,000 |

To set up additional underlying equity in
Oleo Co. at date of acquisition—to
write-off over 40 years.

[95]

| | | |
|---|---:|---:|
| Cash | 5,000 | |
| Investment—Oleo Co. | | 5,000 |

For receipt of 20¢ per share cash
dividend from Oleo.

[96]

| | | |
|---|---:|---:|
| Investment—Oleo Co. | 27,500 | |
| Income from Equity Share of Undistributed | | |
| Earnings of Oleo continuing operations | | 25,000 |
| Income from Equity Share of Undistributed | | |
| Extraordinary Item of Oleo | | 2,500 |

**Appendix B**

To pick up 25% of the following reported
Oleo annual figures:
   Net income after taxes, but
      before Extraordinary item $100,000
   Extraordinary Income (net)      10,000
   Total net income reported     $110,000

[97]

| | | |
|---|---|---|
| Income Tax Expense—Regular | 12,500* | |
| Income Tax Expense—Extra Item | 1,250* | |
|    Deferred Taxes | | 13,750* |

To set up 50% of above income as accrued
taxes. Expectation is that Oleo will
continue paying dividends.
*Dividend Tax Credit, if any, should reduce
these Amounts

[98]

| | | |
|---|---|---|
| Deferred Taxes | 2,500* | |
|    Income Taxes Payable | | 2,500* |

To set up actual liability for tax on
cash dividends received.
*Dividend Tax Credit, if any, should reduce
these Amounts

CONSOLIDATION

*Trial Balances*
*Now-at*
*12/31*-End of Year

| | A Co. | B Co. | Fair Value Excess at Acquisition |
|---|---|---|---|
| Cash | 10,000 | 6,000 | |
| A/R | 20,000 | 10,000 | |
| Inventory | 30,000 | 5,000 | |
| Equip | 50,000 | 30,000 | 5,000 |
| Investment Cost | 40,000 | | |
| Liabilities | (30,000) | (5,000) | (1,000) |
| Common Stock | (20,000) | (10,000)* | |
| Retained Earnings | (50,000) | (20,000)* | |
| Sales | (80,000) | (40,000) | |
| Costs of Sale | 20,000 | 14,000 | |
| Expenses | 10,000 | 10,000 | |
| | -0- | -0- | |
| | (Parent) | (Sub) | |

*Unchanged from opening balances.

*At year-end there were $5,000 intercompany receivables/*
payables. The parent had sold $5,000 worth of product

# Appendix B

to the subsidiary. The inventory of the subsidiary
was $1,000 over the parent's cost.

Consolidating Entries:

[99]

| | | |
|---|---|---|
| Excess Paid over Book Value | 10,000 | |
| Investment Cost | | 10,000 |

To reduce investment cost to that of the
subsidiary's equity at time of purchase
(unchanged at 12/31).

[100]

| | | |
|---|---|---|
| Equipment | 5,000 | |
| Liabilities | | 1,000 |
| Excess Paid over Book Value | | 4,000 |

To reflect fair value corrections at time of
consolidation for the combination of current
year-end trial balances.

[101]

| | | |
|---|---|---|
| B Co. Equity | 30,000 | |
| Investment Cost | | 30,000 |
| Sales | 5,000 | |
| Costs of Sale | | 5,000 |
| Costs of Sale | 1,000 | |
| Inventory | | 1,000 |
| Liabilities | 5,000 | |
| Accounts Receivable | | 5,000 |
| Excess paid over book value (expense) | 150 | |
| Goodwill | | 150 |

To eliminate intercompany dealings, debt,
investment, and to amortize goodwill.

Consolidated figures will then be:

| | |
|---|---|
| Cash | 16,000 |
| A/R | 25,000 |
| Inventories | 34,000 |
| Equipment | 85,000 |
| Investment cost | — |
| Goodwill | 5,850 |
| Liabilities | (31,000) |
| Common Stock | (20,000) (Opening) |
| Ret. Earnings | (50,000) (Opening) |
| Sales | (115,000) |
| Cost of sales | 30,000 |
| Expenses | 20,150 |
| | -0- |

**Appendix B**

The year's consolidated net income (before provision for income taxes) is $64,850.

## PURCHASE METHOD OF BUSINESS COMBINATION
[102]

| | | |
|---|---:|---:|
| Accounts Receivable (present value) | 50,000 | |
| Inventory (current cost or market, lowest) | 40,000 | |
| Building (fair value) | 110,000 | |
| Equipment (fair value) | 30,000 | |
| Investments, non-current securities-market | 5,000 | |
| Goodwill | 16,200 | |
|    Accounts Payable—(present value) | | 25,000 |
|    Long-term Debt—(face value) | | 30,000 |
|    Unamortized discount on long-term debt | | |
|      (to reflect present value) | | (3,800) |
|    Common Stock (Par $10; 10,000 shares) | | 100,000 |
|    Additional Paid-in Capital | | 100,000 |

To reflect, by the purchase method, the purchase of Diablo Company assets and liabilities for 10,000 shares of common stock; total purchase price of contract $200,000 based on market price of stock at date of consummation of $20 per share (1/1).

[103]

| | | |
|---|---:|---:|
| Amortization of Goodwill (1/40) | 405 | |
|    Goodwill | | 405 |
| Unamortized discount on long-term debt | 760 | |
|    Discount Income (approx 1/5th) | | 760* |

To amortize pertinent Diablo items, first yearend. Goodwill on straight-line basis—40 years.
*Should be calculated present value computation.

## POOLING METHOD OF BUSINESS COMBINATION
[104]

| | | |
|---|---:|---:|
| Inventory | 43,000 | |
| Cash | 5,000 | |
| Accounts Receivable | 60,000 | |
|    Reserve for Doubtful Accounts | | 7,000 |
| Building | 75,000 | |
|    Accumulated Depreciation—Building | | 15,000 |
| Equipment | 100,000 | |
|    Accumulated Depreciation—Building | | 60,000 |
| Investments—non-current securities | 4,000 | |
|    Accounts Payable | | 25,500 |
|    Long-Term Debt | | 30,000 |
|    Common Stock (10,000 shs @ par $10) | | 100,000 |
|    Additional Paid-in Capital | | 49,500 |

# Appendix B

To reflect the pooling of Diablo items, per *their book value* on date of consummation.

FUND ACCOUNTING
 Initial transactions:
[105]

| | | |
|---|---|---|
| Cash | 100,000 | |
|   Dues Income | | 100,000 |

For initial membership dues received.

[106]

| | | |
|---|---|---|
| Building | 50,000 | |
|   Mortgage Payable | | 40,000 |
|   Cash | | 10,000 |

Purchase of building for cash and mortgage.

[107]

| | | |
|---|---|---|
| Interest Expense | 2,400 | |
| Mortgage Payable | 2,000 | |
|   Cash | | 4,400 |

For first payment on mortgage.

[108]

| | | |
|---|---|---|
| Net income (100,000 less 2,400) | 97,600 | |
|   Current Fund Balance | | 97,600 |

To close year's income

[109]

| | | |
|---|---|---|
| Mortgage Payable | 38,000 | |
| Current Fund Balance | 12,000 | |
|   Building | | 50,000 |

To transfer building and mortgage to plant fund.

Plant Fund Entry:
[110]

| | | |
|---|---|---|
| Building | 50,000 | |
|   Mortgage Payable | | 38,000 |
|   Plant Fund Balance | | 12,000 |

To set up building in plant fund.
Note that interest expense is to be borne by the current fund every year as a current operating expense used in the calculation of required dues from members. Also, the principal sum-payments against mortgage are to come out of

**Appendix B**

current fund assets, with no interfund debt to be set up, until such time as a special drive is held for plant fund donations for improvements and expansion.

## MUNICIPAL ACCOUNTING—CURRENT OPERATING FUND

*To book the budget:*

[111]

| | | |
|---|---|---|
| Estimated Revenues | 600,000 | |
| Appropriations | | 590,000 |
| Fund Balance | | 10,000 |

*Actual year's transactions:*

[112]

| | | |
|---|---|---|
| Encumbrances | 575,000 | |
| Reserve for Encumbrances | | 575,000 |
| To enter contracts and purchase orders issued. | | |

[113]

| | | |
|---|---|---|
| Expenditures—itemized (not here) | 515,000 | |
| Vouchers Payable | | 515,000 |
| Reserve for Encumbrances | 503,000 | |
| Encumbrances | | 503,000 |

To enter actual invoices for deliveries received and service contracts performed and to reverse applicable encumbrances.

[114]

| | | |
|---|---|---|
| Taxes Receivable—Current | 570,000 | |
| Revenues | | 541,500 |
| Estimated Current Uncollectible Taxes | | 28,500 |

To enter actual tax levy and to estimate uncollectibles at 5%.

[115]

| | | |
|---|---|---|
| Cash | 55,000 | |
| Revenues | | 55,000 |

For cash received from licenses, fees, fines and other sources.

[116]

| | | |
|---|---|---|
| Cash | 549,500 | |
| Estimated Current Uncollectible Taxes | 8,000 | |
| Taxes Receivable | | 549,500 |
| Revenues | | 8,000 |

For actual taxes collected for this year.

## Appendix B

*To close out budget accounts:*
[117]

| | | |
|---|---|---|
| Revenues | 604,500 | |
| Appropriations | 590,000 | |
| Estimated Revenue | | 600,000 |
| Expenditures | | 515,000 |
| Encumbrances | | 72,000 |
| Fund Balance | | 7,500 |

To zero budget accounts and adjust fund balance.

## DISCS—DEEMED DISTRIBUTIONS (Parent's Books)

*1975—under old law*
[118]

| | | |
|---|---|---|
| DISC Dividends Receivable (previously taxed) | 110,000 | |
| Deemed Distribution from DISC (income) | | 110,000 |

To pick up 1/2 of DISC's net of $220,000.

*1976—under the new law*
[119]

| | | |
|---|---|---|
| DISC Dividends Receivable (previously taxed) | 189,375 | |
| Deemed Distribution from DISC (income) | | 189,375 |

As follows:
Facts:

| | |
|---|---|
| Gross export receipts average for 1972–1975 | $1,100,000 |
| Gross exportreceipts—1976 | $1,300,000 |
| Net DISC income–1976 only | $250,000 |

Since the 1976 net income is over $150,000, the graduated relief in the 1976 law does not apply, and the calculation is:

| | |
|---|---|
| 67% of 1,100,000 = 670,000 | |
| 670,000÷1,300,000 = 51.5% | |
| 51.5%×250,000 = | $128,750 |
| 250,000–128,750 = 121,250 | |
| 121,250×50% = | 60,625 |
| Total Deemed Distributions | $189,375 |

[120]

| | | |
|---|---|---|
| Capitalization of Interest Costs | | |
| Qualifying Asset | 10,000 | |
| Accrued Interest | | 10,000 |

[121]

| | | |
|---|---|---|
| Employee Compensation | 50,000 | |
| Accrued Vacation | | 50,000 |

**Appendix B**

# Appendix C
## Tax Terminology

**A**

**accountant's report**   When used regarding financial statements, a document in which an independent public or certified public accountant indicates the scope of the audit (or examination) which has been made and sets forth an opinion regarding the financial statements taken as a whole, or an assertion to the effect that an overall opinion cannot be expressed. When an overall opinion cannot be expressed, the reasons must be stated.

**accounting method**   A set of rules used to determine when and how income and expenses are reported. Examples are accrual, cash and hybrid.

**adjusted issue price**   The issue price increased by any amount of discount deducted before repurchase, or, in the case of convertible obligations, decreased by any amount of premium included in gross income before repurchase.

**adverse party**   Any person having a substantial beneficial interest in the trust which would be adversely affected by the exercise or nonexercise of the authority which he/she possesses regarding the trust.

**affiliate**   An affiliate of, or a person affiliated with, a specific person is one who directly or indirectly, through one or more intermediaries, controls, or is controlled by, or is under common control with, the person specified. (See person below)

**affiliated group**   One or more chains of includable corporations connected through stock ownership with a common parent corporation which is an includable corporation. (See includable corporation below). The ownership of stock of any corporation means the common parent possesses at least 80 percent of the total voting power of the stock of such corporation and has a value equal to at least 80 percent of the total value of the stock of that corporation.

**agent**   A person authorized by another, the principal, to act on behalf of the principal. An employee may be an agent of his or her employer.

**alien A**   foreigner is an alien who has filed his/her declaration of intention to become a citizen, but who has not yet been admitted to citizenship by a final order of a naturalization court.

**allowed or allowable**   When an business asset is sold or disposed of, its basis is computed (or recomputed) by recognizing the amount of depreciation allowed or allowable. Allowed refers to the amount of depreciation reported for the asset on the entity's tax return (whether correctly computed or not). Allowable refers to the amount of depreciation that should have been taken if the depreciation had been computed correctly. If the proper amount of depreciation is reported each year on the tax return, then the amount allowed will be the same as the amount allowable. If the two amounts are not the same, then the greater amount for each year is used in computing the basis of the asset disposed of.

**amount**   When used regarding securities, the principal amount if relating to evidences of indebtedness the number of shares if relating to shares, and the number of units if relating to any other kind of security.

**amount loaned**   The amount received by the borrower.

**annual accounting period**   The annual period, calendar year or fiscal year, on the basis of which the taxpayer regularly computes his/her income in keeping the books.

**annual compensation**   Includes an employee's average regular annual compensation, or such average compensation over the last five years, or such employee's last annual compensation if reasonably similar to his or her average regular annual compensation for the five preceding years.

**annuity contract**   A contract which may be payable in installments during the life of the annuitant only.

**applicable installment obligation**   Any obligation which arises from the disposition of personal property under the installment method by a person who regularly sells or otherwise disposes of personal property of the same type on the installment plan. The disposition of real property under the installment method which is held by the taxpayer for sale to customers in the ordinary course of the taxpayer's trade or business, or the disposition of real property under the installment method which is property used in the taxpayer's trade or business, or property held for the production of rental income, but only if the sale price of such property exceeds $150,000.

**arm's length transaction**   A transaction entered into by unrelated parties each acting for his or her own self interest.

**assignment of income**   Who is the taxpayer? You put money in a certificate of deposit at the bank. The certificate will come due and pay interest in a year. Three days before the interest is to be paid to you, you give the CD to your child who is in a lower tax bracket. You have attempted to assign your income to someone else and it won't fly. Similarly if you asked that your paycheck be made out to your child who is in a lower tax bracket.

**associate**   Indicates a relationship with any person, and means 1) any corporation or organization of which such person is an officer or partner or is directly or indirectly the beneficial owner of 10 percent or more of any class of equity securities, 2) any trust or other estate in which such person has a substantial beneficial interest or for which such person serves as trustee or in a similar fiduciary capacity, and 3) any relative or spouse of such person, or any relative of such spouse, who has the same home as such person or who is a director or officer of the registrant or any of its parents or subsidiaries.

# B

**balance**   With respect to a reserve account or a guaranteed employment account, the amount standing to the credit of the account as of the computation date.

**bank holding company**   A person who is engaged, either directly or indirectly, primarily in the business of owning securities of one or more banks for the purpose, and with the effect, of exercising control. (See person below)

**basis of obligation**   The basis of an installment obligation is the excess of the face value of the obligation over an amount equal to the income which would be returnable were the obligation satisfied in full.

**below-market loan**   Any demand loan for which the interest is payable on the loan at a rate less than the applicable Federal rate, or in the case of a term loan (see term loan below) the amount loaned exceeds the present value of all payments due under the loan.

**bond**   Any bond, debenture, note, or certificate or other evidence of indebtedness, but does not include any obligation which constitutes stock in trade of the taxpayer or any such obligation of a kind which would properly be included in the inventory of the taxpayer if on hand at the close of the taxable year, or any obligation held by the taxpayer primarily for sale to customers in the ordinary course of trade or business.

**brother-sister corporations**   Two or more corporations owned by five or fewer individuals having at least a 50% common ownership. The result is a sharing of the tax brackets and other tax items.

# C

**C corporation**   With respect to any taxable year, a corporation which is not an S corporation for such year.

**calendar year**   A period of 12 months ending on December 31. A tax-payer who has not established a fiscal year must make his/her tax return on the basis of a calendar year.

**capital asset**   Property held by a taxpayer, whether or not connected with a trade or business. The term does not include stock in trade of the taxpayer or other property of a kind which would properly be included in the inventory of the taxpayer if on hand at the close of the taxable year, or property held for sale to customers in the ordinary course of a trade or business.

**capital expenditure**   Any cost of a type that is properly chargeable to a capital account under general Federal income tax principles. Whether an expenditure is a capital expenditure is determined at the time the expenditure is paid with respect to the property. Future changes in law do not affect whether an expenditure is a capital expenditure. Capital expenditures do not include expenditures for items of current operating expense that are not properly chargeable to a capital account–so called working capital items.

**capital gain**   The excess of the gains from sales or exchanges of capital assets over the losses from sales or exchanges.

**carrier**   An express carrier, sleeping car carrier, or rail carrier providing transportation.

**casualty loss**   When a taxpayer suffers a loss to property resulting from an earthquake, tornado, hurricanes, volcanoes, fires, hail or other sudden and unexpected disaster special tax rules may allow a deduction for loss of value.

**charitable contribution**   A contribution or gift to or for the use of a corporation, trust, community chest, fund, or foundation operated exclusively for religious, charitable, scientific, literary, or educational purposes, or to foster national or international amateur sports competition if no part of its activities involves the provision of athletic facilities or equipment. A contribution or gift is deductible only if it is used within the United States or any of its possessions.

**charter**   Articles of incorporation, declarations of trust, articles of association or partnership, or any similar instrument affecting, either with or without filing with any governmental agency, the organization or creation of an incorporated or unincorporated person (see person below).

**child**   Son, stepson, daughter, stepdaughter, adopted son, adopted daughter, or for taxable years after December 31, 1958, a child who is a member of an individual's household if the child was placed with the individual by an authorized placement agency for legal adoption pursuant to a formal application filed by the individual with the agency.

**child care facility**   Any tangible property which qualifies as a child care center primarily for children of employees of the employer, except that the term does not include any property not of a character subject to depreciation, or located outside the United States.

**citizen**   Every person born or naturalized in the United States and subject to its jurisdiction.

**claim of right**   In a dispute – if you have been paid but you might have to refund part of the money back, it is still income to you and the later repayment will be a deduction.

**collapsible corporation**   A corporation formed or availed of principally by the manufacture, construction, or production of property, for the purchase of property which is in the hands of the corporation, or for the holding of stock in a corporation so formed or availed of with a view to the sale or exchange of stock by its share-holders. The term includes distribution to its shareholders, before the realization by the corporation manufacturing, constructing, producing, or purchasing the property of 2/3 of the taxable income to be derived from such property, and by the realization by such shareholders of gain attributable to such property.

**common equity**   Any class of common stock or an equivalent interest including, but not limited to a unit of beneficial interest in a trust or a limited partnership interest.

**common trust fund**   A fund maintained by a bank exclusively for the collective investment and reinvestment of moneys contributed thereto by the bank in its capacity as a trustee, executor, administrator, or guardian, or as a custodian of accounts which the Secretary determines are established pursuant to a State law, and which bank has established that it has duties and responsibilities similar to the duties and responsibilities of a trustee or guardian.

**company**   Corporations, associations, and joint-stock companies.

**complete liquidation**   (See distribution below)

**computation date**   The date, occurring at least once each calendar year and within 27 weeks prior to the effective date of new rates of contributions, as of which such dates are computed.

**constructive dividend**   A dividend attributed to the owner of a corporation (usually as the result of an IRS audit) based on personal use by the shareholder of company assets without adequate compensation to the corporation. A constructive dividend may also arise from a non-arm's length transaction between the shareholder of a closely held corporation and the corporation.

**constructive receipt**   A doctrine applicable to cash basis tax payers requiring the inclusion in income of cash not actually received by the taxpayer, but for which there was no significant restriction on the taxpayer receiving the cash. An example would be declining the receipt of a payment due to the taxpayer for services performed and requesting the payment be remitted after the tax year-end.

**constructive sale price**   An article sold at retail, sold on consignment, or sold otherwise than through an arm's length transaction at less than the fair market price.

**contributions**   Payments required by a State law to be made into an unemploy-ment fund by any person on account of having individuals in his/her employ, to the extent that such payments are made without being deducted or deductible from the remuneration of the employed individuals.

**control**   The ownership of stock possessing at least 80% of the total combined voting power of all classes of stock entitled to vote and at least 80% of the total number of shares of all other classes of stock of the corporation.

**controlled foreign corporation**   Any foreign corporation if more than 50% of the total combined voting power of all classes of stock of such corporation entitled to vote, or the total value of the stock of such corporation, is owned, directly or indirectly, by and for a foreign corporation, foreign partnership, foreign trust, or foreign estate shall be considered as being owned proportionately by its share-holders, partners, or beneficiaries.

**controlled group of corporations**   One or more chains of corporations connected through stock ownership with a common parent corporation if stock possessing at least 80% of the total combined voting power of all classes of stock entitled to vote or at least 80% of the total value of shares of all classes of stock of each of the corporations, and the common parent corporation is owned by one or more of the other corporations.

**convertible obligation**   An obligation which is convertible into the stock of the issuing corporation, or a corporation which, at the time the obligation is issued or repurchased, is in control of (see control above) or controlled by the issuing corporation.

**cooperative bank**   An institution without capital stock organized and operated for mutual purposes and without profit, which is subject by law to supervision and examination by State or Federal authority having supervision over such institutions.

**cooperative housing corporation**   A corporation having one and only one class of stock outstanding, each of the stockholders of which is entitled, solely by reason of ownership of stock in the corporation, to occupy for dwelling purposes a house, or an apartment in a building, owned or leased by the cooperative housing corporation. No stockholder of the housing corporation is entitled to receive any distribution that is not out of earnings and profits of the corporation except on a complete or partial liquidation of the corporation.

**corporate acquisition indebtedness**   Any obligation evidenced by a bond, debenture, note, or certificate or other evidence of indebtedness issued by a corporation to provide consideration for the acquisition of stock in another corporation; or the acquisition of the assets of another corporation in accordance with a plan under which at least two-thirds in value of all the assets (excluding money) is used in trades and businesses carried on by the corporation.

**corporation**   Includes associations, joint-stock companies, and insurance companies.

**currency swap contract**   A contract involving different currencies between two or more parties to exchange periodic interim payments on or prior to maturity of the contract. The swap principal amount is an amount of two different currencies which, under the terms of the currency swap contract, is used to determine the periodic interim payments in each currency and which is exchanged upon maturity of the contract.

# D

**date of original issue**   The date on which the issue was first issued to the public, or the date on which the debt instrument was sold by the issuer. In the case of any debt instrument which is publicly offered, it is the date on which the debt instrument was issued in a sale or exchange.

**debt instrument**   A bond, debenture, note, or certificate or other evidence of indebtedness.

**deficiency**   The amount by which the tax imposed exceeds the sum of the amount shown as the tax by the taxpayer upon his/her return, if a return was made by the taxpayer and an amount indicated as the tax. Deficiency includes the amounts previously assessed or collected without assessment as a deficiency over the amount of rebates.

**deficiency dividends**  The amount of dividends paid by the corporation on or after the date of the determination (see determination below), before filing claims which would have been includable in the computation of the deduction for dividends paid for the taxable year with respect to which the liability for personal holding company tax exists, if distributed during such taxable year. No dividends are considered as deficiency dividends unless distributed within 90 days after the determination.

**deficiency dividend deduction**  No deduction is allowed unless the claim therefore is filed within 120 days after the determination.

**demand loan**  Any loan which is payable in full at any time on the demand of the lender.

**dependent**  Any of the following individuals over half of whose support for the calendar year in which the taxable year of the taxpayer begins was received from the taxpayer or treated as received from the taxpayer:

1. A son or daughter of the taxpayer, or a descendant of either.
2. A stepson or stepdaughter of the taxpayer.
3. A brother, sister, stepbrother, or stepsister of the taxpayer.
4. The father or mother of the taxpayer, or an ancestor of either.
5. A stepfather or stepmother of the taxpayer.
6. A son or daughter of a brother or sister of the taxpayer.
7. A brother or sister of the father or mother of the taxpayer.
8. A son-in-law, daughter-in-law, father-in-law, mother-in-law, brother-in-law, sister-in-law, of the taxpayer.
9. An individual, other than an individual who at any time during the taxable year was the spouse, who, for the taxable year of the taxpayer, has as his/her principal place of abode the home of the taxpayer and is a member of the taxpayer's household.

**depositary share**  A security, evidenced by an American Depositary Receipt, that represents a foreign security or a multiple of or fraction thereof deposited with a depositary.

**determination**  A decision by the Tax Court or a judgment, decree, or other order by any court of competent jurisdiction, which has become final.

**development stage company**  A company which is devoting substantially all its efforts to establishing a new business and either of the following conditions exists:

1. Planned principal operations have not commenced.
2. Planned principal operations have commenced, but there has been no significant revenue therefrom.

**distiller**  Any person who produces distilled spirits from any source or substance.

**distribution**  A distribution is treated as in complete liquidation of a corporation, if the distribution is one of a series of distributions in redemption of all of the stock of the corporation pursuant to a plan.

**dividend**  Any distribution of property made by a corporation to its shareholders out of earnings and profits of the taxable year, or from the most recently accumulated earnings and profits, computed at the close of the taxable year, without regard to the amount of earnings and profits at the time the distribution was made.

**domestic**  When applied to a corporation or partnership, created or organized in the United States or under the laws of the United States or of any State.

**domestic building and loan association**  A domestic building and loan association, a domestic savings and loan association, or a federal savings and loan association.

## E

**earned income**  Wages, salaries, or professional fees, and other amounts received as compensation for personal services rendered by an individual to a corporation which represent a distribution of earnings or profits rather than a reasonable allowance as compensation for the personal services actually rendered. Earned income includes net earnings from self-employment to the extent such net earnings constitute compensation for personal services actually rendered.

**earnings and profits (E & P)**  A calculation, for tax purposes, of the amount available for paying dividends. A corporation's earnings and profits is derived from its income adjusted for resources that were not taxable, but which are available for the payment of dividends and for expenses or deductions that did not expend resources. Earnings and profits are segregated between current earnings and profits and accumulated earnings and profits.

**educational organization**  An organization which normally maintains a regular faculty and curriculum and normally has regularly organized body of students in attendance at the place where its educational activities are carried on.

**employee**  Any officer of a corporation; any individual who, under the usual common law rules applicable to determining the employer-employee relation-ship, has the status of an employee; any individual who performs services for remuneration for any person as an agent-driver engaged in distributing products; a full-time life insurance salesperson; a home worker performing work; a traveling or city salesperson.

**employee stock purchase plan**  A plan which provides that options are to be granted only to employees of the employer corporation, or of its parent or subsidiary corporation, to purchase stock in any such corporation; and such plan is approved by the stockholders of the granting corporation within 12 months before or after the plan is adopted.  Under the terms of the plan, no employee can be granted an option if the employee, immediately after the option is granted, owns stock amounting to 5% or more of the total combined voting power or value of all classes of stock of the employee corporation or of its parent or subsidiary corporation. Under the plan, options are to be granted to all employees of any corporation whose employees are granted any of such options by reason of their employment by such corporation, except employees who have been employed less than 2 years, or employees whose customary employment is 20 hours or less per week, or employees whose customary employment is for not more than 5 months in any calendar year.

**employee v. independent contractor**  Many tax issues depend on whether someone is self-employed (an independent contractor) or an employee. Among the issues are whether the employer is required to withhold and remit Social Security and federal and state income taxes. Also at issue are fringe benefits such as retirement coverage.

**employer**  With respect to any calendar year, any person who during any calendar quarter in the calendar year or the preceding calendar year, paid wages of $1500 or more, or on each of some 20 days during the calendar year or during the preceding calendar year (each day being in a different calendar week) employed at least one individual in employment for some portions of the day.

**employment**  Any service of whatever nature performed by an employee for the person employing him or her, irrespective of the citizenship or residence of either within the United States; or any service in connection with an American vessel or American aircraft under a contract of service which is entered into within the United States or during the performance of which and while the employee is employed on and in connection with such vessel or aircraft when outside the United States. The term also includes any service of whatever nature performed outside the United States by a citizen or resident of the United States as an employee of an American employer, or if it is service, regardless of where or by whom performed, which is designated as employment or recognized as equivalent to employment under an agreement entered into under the Social Security Act.

**endowment contract**  A contract with an insurance company which depends in part on the life expectancy of the insured, which may be payable in full during the insured's life.

**energy property**  Property that is described in at least one of 6 categories:

1.  Alternative energy property.
2.  Solar or wind energy property.
3.  Specifically defined energy property.
4.  Recycling equipment.
5.  Shale oil Equipment.
6.  Equipment for producing natural gas from geopressured grime.

Property is not energy property unless depreciation or amortization is allowable and the property has an estimated useful life of 3 years or more from the time when the property is placed in service.

**enrolled actuary**  A person who is enrolled by the Joint Board for the Enrollment of Actuaries.

**enrolled agent**  A tax professional, often a former IRS employee, who has passed an examination given by the IRS and is thereby qualified to represent taxpayers before the IRS on audit and collection matters.

**equity security**  Any stock or similar security, or any security convertible, with or without consideration, into such a security, or carrying any warrant or right to subscribe to or purchase such security, or any such warrant or right.

**exchanged basis property**  Property having a basis determined in whole or in part by reference to other property held at any time by the person for whom the basis is determined.

**executor**  The administrator of the decedent, or, if there is none appointed, qualified, and acting within the United States, then any person in actual or constructive possession of any property of the decedent.

# F

**farm**  Includes stock, dairy, poultry, fruit and truck farms; also plantations, ranches, and all land used for farming operations.

**farmer**  All individuals, partnerships, or corporations that cultivate, operate, or manage farms for gain or profit, either as owners or tenants.

**fiduciary**  A guardian, trustee, executor, administrator, receiver, conservator, or any person acting in any fiduciary capacity for any person.

**fifty-percent-owned person**  A person approximately 50% of whose outstanding voting shares is owned by the specified person either directly or indirectly through one or more intermediaries (see person).

**financial statements**  Include all notes to the statements and all related schedules.

**fiscal year**  An accounting period of 12 months ending on the last day of any month other than December; the 52–53 week annual accounting period, if such period has been elected by the taxpayer. A fiscal year is recognized only if it is established as the annual accounting period of the taxpayer and only if the books of the taxpayer are kept in accordance with such fiscal year.

**foreign**  A corporation or partnership which is not domestic or which is domestic but which is operating in a state different from the one in which it was formed.

**foreign currency contract**  A contract which requires delivery of, or settlement of, and depends on the value of, a foreign currency which is a currency in which positions are also traded through regulated futures contracts. The contract is traded in the interbank market, and is entered into at arm's length at a price determined by reference to the price in the interbank market.

**foreign earned income**  The amount received by any individual from sources within a foreign country or countries which constitutes earned income attributable to services performed by such individual. Amounts received are considered to be received in the taxable year in which the services to which the amounts are attributable are performed.

**foreign estate (foreign trust)**    An estate or trust, as the case may be, the income of which comes from sources without the United States which are not materially connected with the conduct of a trade or business within the United States.

**foreign insurer or reinsurer**    One who is a non-resident alien individual, or a foreign partnership, or a foreign corporation. The term includes a nonresident alien individual, foreign partnership, or foreign corporation which will become bound by an obligation of the nature of an indemnity bond. The term does not include a foreign government, or municipal or other corporation exercising the taxing power.

**foreign investment company**    Any foreign corporation which is registered under the Investment Company Act of 1940, as amended, either as a management company or as a unit investment trust, or is engaged primarily in the business of investing, reinvesting, or trading in securities, commodities, or any interest in property, including a futures or forward contract or option.

**FSC (foreign sales corporation)**    Any corporation which was created or organized under the laws of any foreign country, or under the laws applicable to any possession of the United States, has no more than 25 shareholders at any time during the taxable year, does not have any preferred stock outstanding at any time during the taxable year, and during the taxable year maintains an office located outside the United States in a foreign country, or in any possession of the United States. The term FSC does not include any corporation which was created or organized under the laws of any foreign country unless there is in effect between such country and the United States a bilateral or multilateral agreement, or an income tax treaty which contains an exchange of information program to which the FSC is subject.

**foreign trading gross receipts**    The gross receipts of any FSC which are from the sale, exchange, or other disposition of export property, from the lease or rental of export property for use by the lessee outside the United States, or for services which are related and subsidiary to any sale, exchange, lease, or rental of export property by such corporation.

**forgiveness of debt**    Having a loan or other debt forgiven or erased is the same as receiving income and paying off the debt. If someone loans you money and you are later not required to pay back the entire amount, the forgiven amount is income. Unless a specific tax provision makes the forgiven income non-taxable it must be reported as income.

**foundation manager**    With respect to any private foundation, an officer, director, or trustee of a foundation responsible for any act, or failure to act, and for the employees of the foundation having authority or responsibility, and for their failure to act.

# G

**general partner (see partner)**    The person or persons responsible under state law for directing the management of the business and affairs of a partnership that are subject of a roll-up transaction (see roll-up transaction) including, but not limited to, a general partner(s), board of directors, board of trustees, or other person(s) having a fiduciary duty to such partnership.

**general power of appointment**    The power which is exercisable in favor of the decedent, his/her estate, his/her creditors, or the creditors of the estate.

**generation-skipping transfer**    A taxable distribution, a taxable termination, and a direct skip. The term does not include any transfer to the extent the property transferred was subject to a prior tax imposed; and such transfers do not have the effect of avoiding tax.

**gift**    The lifetime transfer of something of value from one taxpayer to another with no strings attached, giving rise to a potential gift tax. An annual gift tax exclusion applies to gifts below the annual threshold (indexed for inflation) permitting gifts without incurring a gift tax.

**gift loan**    Any below-market loan where the forgoing of interest is in the nature of a gift (see below-market loan).

**gross income**    All income derived from whatever source; income realized in any form, whether in money, property, or services; income realized in the form of services, meals, accommodations, stock, or other property, as well as in cash. Gross income, however, is not limited to the items enumerated.

**H**

**head of household**    An individual is considered a head of household if, and only if, such individual is not married at the close of his/her taxable year, is not a surviving spouse, (see surviving spouse), maintains as his or her home a household that constitutes, for more than one-half of such taxable year, the principal place of abode of a dependent relative. However, an unmarried child, grandchild, stepchild, or adopted child need not be a dependent. In addition, if the taxpayer maintains a separate home for his or her parent or parents, head of household status may be claimed if at least one of the parents is a dependent.

**holder**    Any individual whose efforts created property held; any other individual who has acquired an interest in such property in exchange for consideration in money or money's worth paid to such creator of the invention covered by the patent, if such individual is neither the employer of the creator, nor related to the creator.

**hot assets**    Assets such as inventory and accounts receivable that normally produce ordinary income. In the context of a partnership distribution, for example, taxpayers may attempt to achieve beneficial capital gains treatment for the receipt of assets otherwise producing ordinary income.

**housing expenses**    The reasonable expenses paid or incurred during the taxable year by or on behalf of an individual for housing in a foreign country for the individual, spouse and dependants.

# I

**includable corporation**   Any corporation except those exempt from taxation, foreign corporations, insurance companies subject to taxation, regulated investment companies, and real estate investment trusts subject to tax.

**income recognition**   Dividends are included in income on the ex-dividend date; interest is accrued on a daily basis. Dividends declared on short positions existing on the record date are recorded on the ex-dividend date and included as an expense of the period.

**income tax return preparer**   Any person who prepares for compensation, or who employs one or more persons to prepare for compensation, any return of tax or any claim for refund of tax. The preparation of a substantial portion of a return or claim for refund is treated as if it were the preparation of such return or claim for refund. A person is not an income tax return preparer merely because such person furnishes typing, reproducing, or other mechanical assistance, or prepares a return or claim for refund of the employer, or of an officer or employee of the employer, by whom the person is regularly and continuously employed.

**Indian tribal government**   A governing body of a tribe, band, pueblo, community, village, or a group of native American Indians, or Alaska Native.

**individual retirement account**   A trust created or organized in the United States for the exclusive benefit of an individual or his/her beneficiaries, but only if the written governing instrument creating the trust meets the following requirements:

1. The trustee is a bank, or such other person who demonstrates that the manner in which such other person will administer the trust will be consistent with the requirements of this section.
2. No part of the trust funds will be invested in life insurance contracts.
3. The interest of the individual in the balance of the account is non-forefeitable.
4. The assets of the trust will not be commingled with other property except in a common trust fund or common investment fund.

**individual retirement annuity**   An annuity contract, or an endowment contract issued by an insurance company which meets the following requirements:

1. The contract is not transferable by the owner.
2. Under the contract, the premiums are not fixed.
3. Any refund of premiums will be applied before the close of the calendar year following the year of the refund toward the payment of future premiums or the purchase of additional benefits.
4. The entire interest of the owner is nonforfeitable.

**influencing legislation**  Any attempt to have an effect on legislation by trying to impact the opinions of the general public or any segment thereof through communication with any member or employee of a legislative body, or with any government official or employee who may participate in the formulation of the legislation. It does not include any communication with a government official or employee other than one whose principal purpose is to affect legislation.

**insurance company**  A company whose primary and predominant business activity during the taxable year is the issuing of insurance or annuity contracts, or the reinsuring of risks underwritten by insurance companies. It is the character of the business actually done in the taxable year which determines whether a company is taxable as an insurance company. Insurance companies include both stock and mutual companies, as well as mutual benefit insurance companies. A voluntary unincorporated association of employees, including an association formed for the purpose of relieving sick and aged members, and the dependants of deceased members, is an insurance company.

**installment sale**  A sale where the proceeds will be received over two or more accounting periods. The amount of income to be reported each year is based on a computation of the gross profit percent from the original sale times the amount received each year to determine the amount of income to be reported. So the basis of what is sold is spread over the periods during which the payments are to be received.

**interest**  Return on any obligation issued in registered form, or of a type issued to the public, but does not include any obligation with a maturity (at issue) of not more than 1 year which is held by a corporation.

**international organization**  A public international organization entitled to the privileges, exemptions, and immunities as an international organization under the International Organizations Immunities Act.

**investment in the contract**  As of the annuity starting date, the aggregate amount of premiums or other consideration paid for the contract, minus the aggregate amount received under the contract before such date, to the extent that such amount was excludable from gross income under prior income tax laws.

**itemized deductions**  Those allowable other than the deductions allowable in arriving at adjusted gross income and the deduction for personal exemptions.

# J

**joint return**  A single return made jointly by a husband and wife.

# L

**life insurance contract**  An endowment contract which is not ordinarily payable in full during the life of the insured.

**like-kind exchange**  An exchange of assets under the rules of IRC 1031 wherein the basis of the respective assets exchanged is adjusted rather than currently recognizing income resulting from the transaction.

**limited liability company (LLC)**  An entity created by state law for conducting business. Like a corporation an LLC provides legal protection to the owners (referred to as members) but like a partnership it provides flexability in organization.

**limited liability partnership (LLP)**  An entity created by state law for the operation of a professional organization (such as a group of doctors or accountants). It provides protection for is owners from the malpractice of other owners but not against an owner's own malpractice.

**lobbying expenditures**  Amounts spent for the purpose of influencing legislation (see Influencing Legislation).

**long-term capital gain**  A gain from the sale or exchange of a capital asset held for more than 1 year, if and to the extent such gain is taken into account in computing gross income.

**long-term capital loss**  A loss from the sale or exchange of a capital asset held for more than 1 year, if and to the extent that such loss is taken into account in computing taxable income.

**long-term contract**  A building, installation, construction or manufacturing contract (see manufacturing contract) which is not completed within the taxable year in which it is initiated.

**lowest price**  Determined without requiring that any given percentage of sales be made at that price, and without including any fixed amount to which the purchaser has a right as a result of contractual arrangements existing at the time of the sale.

**majority-owned subsidiary company**  A corporation, stock of which represents in the aggregate more than 50% of the total combined voting power of all classes of stock of such corporation entitled to vote, is owned wholly by a registered holding company, or partly by such registered holding company and partly by one or more majority-owned subsidiary companies, or by one or more majority-owned subsidiary companies of the registered holding company.

**managing underwriter**  An underwriter(s) who, by contract or otherwise, deals with the registrant, organizes the selling effort, receives some benefit, directly or indirectly, in which all other underwriters similarly situated do not share in proportion to their respective interests in the underwriting, or represents any other underwriters in such matters as maintaining the records of the distribution, arranging the allotments of securities offered, or arranging for appropriate stabilization activities, if any.

**manufacturing contract**  A long-term contract which involves the manufacture of unique items of a type which is not normally carried in the finished goods inventory of the taxpayer, or of items which normally require more than 12 calendar months to complete regardless of the duration of the actual contract.

**material**  Information required for those matters about which an average prudent investor ought reasonably to be informed.

**mathematical or clerical error:**

1. An error in addition, subtraction, multiplication, or division shown on any return.
2. An incorrect use of any table provided by the IRS with respect to any return, if such incorrect use is apparent from the existence of other information on the return.
3. An entry on a return of an item which is inconsistent with another entry of the same or another item on the return.
4. An omission of information which is required to be supplied to substantiate an entry on the return.
5. An entry on a return of a deduction or credit in amount which exceeds a statutory limit, if such limit is expressed as a specified monetary amount, or as a percentage, ratio, or fraction, and if the items entering into the application of such limit appear on the return.

**member**    The owner of a limited liability company.

**municipal bond**    Any obligation issued by a government or political subdivision thereof, if the interest on such obligation is excludable from gross income. It does not include such an obligation if it is sold or otherwise disposed of by the taxpayer within 30 days after the date of its acquisition.

**N**

**net capital gain**    The excess of the net long-term capital gain for the taxable year over the net short-term capital loss for that year.

**net capital loss**    For corporations, the excess of the losses from sales or exchanges of capital assets only to the extent of gains from such sales or exchanges. For taxpayers other than a corporation, losses from sales or exchanges of capital assets are allowable only to the extent of the gains from such sales or exchanges, plus the lower of $3,000 ($1,500 in the case of a married individual filing a separate return), or the excess of such losses over such gains.

**net earnings from self-employment**    The gross income derived by an individual from any trade or business carried on by such individual, less the deductions allowed which are attributable to such trade or business.

**net long-term capital gain**    The excess of long-term capital gains for the taxable year over the long-term capital losses for such year.

**net long-term capital loss**    The excess of long-term capital losses for the taxable year over the long-term capital gains for such year.

**net operating loss**    The excess of the deductions allowed over the gross income. In the case of a taxpayer other than a corporation, the amount deductible on account of losses from sales or exchanges of capital assets cannot exceed the amount includable on account of gains from sales or exchanges of capital assets.

**net short-term capital gain**   The excess of short-term capital gains for the taxable year over the short-term capital losses for such year.

**net short-term capital loss**   The excess of short-term capital losses for the taxable year over the short-term capital gains for such year.

**nonadverse party**   Any person who is not an adverse party (see adverse party, above).

**nonrecognition transaction**   Any disposition of property in a transaction in which gain or loss is not recognized in whole or in part.

**notional principal contract**   A contract that provides for the payment of amounts by one party to another at specified intervals calculated by reference to a specified index upon a notional principal amount in exchange for a specified consideration or a promise to pay similar amounts.

## O

**obligation**   Any bond, debenture, note, certificate, or other evidence of indebtedness.

**operating foundation**   Any private foundation which makes distributions directly for the conduct of the activities constituting the purpose or function for which the foundation is organized and operated, equal to substantially all of the lesser of its adjusted net income, or its minimum investment return.

**option**   The right or privilege of an individual to purchase stock from a corporation by virtue of an offer of the corporation continuing for a stated period of time, whether or not irrevocable, to sell such stock at a price determined under an option price, or price paid under the option. Option Price means the consideration in money or property which, pursuant to the terms of the option, is the price at which the stock subject to the option is purchased. The individual owning the option is under no obligation to purchase, and the right or privilege must be evidenced in writing. While no particular form of words is necessary, the written option should express, among other things, an offer to sell at the option price and the period of time during which the offer will remain open. The individual who has the right or privilege is the optionee and the corporation offering to sell stock under such an arrangement is referred to as the optionor.

**organizational expenditures**   Any expenditure which is incident to the creation of a corporation, chargeable to capital accounts, and is of a character which, if expended incident to the creation of a corporation having a limited life, would be amortizable over such life.

**overpayment**   Any payment of an Internal Revenue tax which is assessed or collected after the expiration of the period of limitation properly applicable thereto.

**owner-employee**   An owner of a proprietorship, or, in the case of a partnership, a partner who owns either more than 10% of the capital interest, or more than 10% of the profits interest, of the partnership.

## P

**paid or incurred (paid or accrued)**   Defined according to the method of accounting upon the basis of which the taxable income is computed. Paid refers to cash basis while incurred applies to accrual basis.

**parent**   Of a specified person, (see person) is an affiliate controlling such person directly, or indirectly, through one or more intermediaries.

**parent corporation**   Any corporation, other than the employer corporation, in an unbroken chain of corporations ending with the employer corporation if each of the corporations other than the employer corporation owns stock possessing 50% or more of the total combined voting power of all classes of stock in one of the other corporations in the chain.

**partially pooled account**   A part of an unemployment fund in which all contributions thereto are mingled and undivided. Compensation from this part is payable only to individuals to whom compensation would be payable from a reserve account or from a guaranteed employment account but for the exhaustion or termination of such reserve account or of a guaranteed employment account. (See pooled fund.)

**partner**   An owner  member of a partnership.

**partner's interest, liquidation thereof**   The termination of a partner's entire interest in a partnership by means of a distribution, or a series of distributions, to the partner by the partnership. A series of distributions means distributions whether they are made in one year or in more than one year. Where a partner's interest is to be liquidated by a series of distributions, the interest will not beconsidered as liquidated until the final distribution has been made. One which is not in liquidation of a partner's entire interest is a current distribution. Current distributions, therefore, include those in partial liquidation of a partner's interest, and those of the partner's distributive share.

**partnership**   A syndicate, pool, group, joint venture or other unincorporated organization through or by means of which any business, financial operation, or venture is carried on, and is not a corporation, trust, or estate.

**partnership agreement**   Includes the original agreement and any modifications thereof agreed to by all the partners or adopted in any other manner provided by the partnership agreement. The agreements or modifications can be oral or written.

**payroll period**   A time frame for which a payment of wages is ordinarily made to the employee by the employer. The term miscellaneous payroll period means one other than a daily, weekly, biweekly, semimonthly, monthly, quarterly, semiannual, or annual period.

**pension plan contracts**   Any contract entered into with trusts which at the time the contracts were entered into were deemed to be trusts and exempt from tax. Includes contracts entered into with trusts which were individual retirement ac-counts, or under contracts entered into with individual retirement annuities.

**person**   Includes an individual, a trust, estate, partnership, association, company, or corporation, an officer or employee of a corporation or a member or employee of a partnership, who is under a duty to surrender the property or rights to property to discharge the obligation. The term also includes an officer or employee of the United States, of the District of Columbia, or of any agency or instrumentality who is under a duty to discharge the obligation.

**personal holding company**   Any corporation if at least 60% of its adjusted ordinary gross income for the taxable year is personal holding company income, and at any time during the last half of the taxable year more than 50% in value of its outstanding stock is owned, directly or indirectly, by or for not more than 5 individuals. To meet the gross income requirement, it is necessary that at least 80% of the total gross income of the corporation for the taxable year be personal holding company income (see personal holding company income).

**personal holding company income**   The portion of the adjusted ordinary gross income which consists of dividends, interest, royalties (other than mineral, oil, or gas royalties or copyright royalties), and annuities.

**political organization**   A party, committee, association, fund, or other organization, whether or not incorporated, organized and operated primarily for the purpose of directly or indirectly accepting contributions or making expenditures for an exempt function activity. A political organization can be a committee or other group which accepts contributions or makes expenditures for the purpose of promoting the nomination of an individual for an elective public office in a primary election, or in a meeting or caucus of a political party:

1.  exempt function activity. Includes all activities that are directly related to and support the process of influencing or attempting to influence the selection, nomination, election, or appointment of any individual to public office, or office in a political organization.

2.  segregated fund. A fund which is established and maintained by a political organization or an individual separate from the assets of the organization or the personal assets of the individual. The amounts in the fund must be for use only for an exempt function, or for an activity necessary to fulfill an exempt function. A segregated fund established and maintained by an individual may qualify as a political organization.

**pooled fund**   An unemployment fund or any part thereof other than a reserve account (see reserve account) or a guaranteed employment account, into which the total contributions of persons contributing thereto are payable, in which all contributions are mingled and undivided, and from which compensation is payable to all eligible individuals.

**predecessor**   A person from whom another person acquired the major portion of the business and assets in a single succession, or in a series of related successions. In each of these successions the acquiring person received the major portion of the business and assets of the acquired.

**previously filed or reported**   Previously filed with, or reported in, a definitive proxy statement or information statement, or in a registration statement under the Securities Act of 1933.

**principal holder of equity securities**   Used regarding a registrant or other person named in a particular statement or report, a holder of record or a known beneficial owner of more than 10 percent of any class of equity securities of the registrant or other person, respectively, as of the date of the related balance sheet filed.

**principal underwriter**   An underwriter in privity of contract with the issuer of the securities as to which he or she is underwriter.

**promoter**   Any person who, acting alone or in conjunction with others, directly or indirectly, takes initiative in founding and organizing the business or enterprise of an issuer. Any person who in so doing received in consideration of services or property, or both services and property, 10 percent or more of any class of securities of the issuer or 10 percent or more of the proceeds from the sale of any class of securities. However, a person who receives such securities or proceeds with or solely as underwriting commissions or solely in consideration of property will not be deemed a promoter within the meaning of this paragraph if such person does not otherwise take part in founding and organizing the enterprise.

**property used in the trade or business**   That property used in a trade or business of a character which is subject to an allowance for depreciation, held for more than 1 year, and real property used in a trade or business, held for more than 1 year, and which is not a copyright, a literary work, musical, artistic composition, or similar property. Also not included in the definition is property of a kind which would properly be includable in the inventory of the taxpayer if on hand at the close of the taxable year, nor property held by the taxpayer primarily for sale to customers in the ordinary course of the trade or business.

# Q

**qualified assets**   The nature of any investments and other assets maintained, or required to be maintained, by applicable legal instruments in respect of outstanding face-amount certificates. If the nature of the qualifying assets and amount thereof is not subject to the provisions of the Investment Company Act of 1940, a statement to that effect should be made.

**qualified individual**   An individual whose tax home is in a foreign country and who is a citizen of the United States and establishes that he/she has been a bona fide resident of a foreign country (or countries) for an uninterrupted period which includes an entire taxable year, or a citizen or resident of the United States and who, during any period of 12 consecutive months, is present in a foreign country (or countries) during at least 330 full days in such period.

**qualified pension, profit-sharing, stock bonus plans and annuity plans**   Compensation is paid under a deferred payment plan, and bond purchase plan. The plan is a definite written program and arrangement which is communicated to the employees and which is established and maintained by an employer.

In the case of a pension plan, to provide for the livelihood of the employees or their beneficiaries after the retirement of such employees through the benefits determined without regard to profits.

In the case of a profit-sharing plan, to enable employees or their beneficiaries to participate in the profits of the employer's trade or business, or in the profits of an affiliated employer who is entitled to deduct any contributions to the plan pursuant to a definite formula for allocating the contributions and for distributing the funds accumulated under the plan.

In the case of a stock bonus plan, to provide employees or their beneficiaries benefits similar to those of profit-sharing plans, except that such benefits are distributable in stock of the employer, and that the contributions by the employer are not necessarily dependent upon profits.

**R**

**real estate investment trust (REIT)**   A corporation, trust, or association which meets the following conditions:

1.  Is managed by one or more trustees or directors. A trustee means a person who holds legal title to the property of the real estate investment trust, and has such rights and powers as will meet the requirement of centralization of management. The trustee must have continuing exclusive authority over the management of the trust, the conduct of its affairs, and the disposition of the trust property.
2.  Has beneficial ownership which is evidenced by transferable shares or by transferable certificates of beneficial interest and must be held by more than 100 persons determined without reference to any rules of attribution.
3.  In case of a taxable year beginning before October 5, 1976, does not hold any property, other than foreclosure property, primarily for sale to customers in the ordinary course of its trade or business.
4.  Is neither a financial institution, nor an insurance company.
5.  Beneficial ownership of the REIT is held by 100 or more persons.
6.  The REIT would not be a personal holding company if all of its gross income constituted personal holding company income.

**realized v. recognized**   Income or a loss is realized when a transaction takes place. But not all income is taxable, so only taxable income is also recognized (reported to the IRS). Likewise not all losses are deductible, for example, losses on the sale of personal use personal property are not deductible. In this case a loss can be realized in a transaction (you sell your car) but not recognized (you don't report it to the IRS).

**recomputed basis**   With respect to any property, its adjusted basis recomputed by adding to it all adjustments reflected on account of deductions allowed or allowable to the taxpayer or to any other person for depreciation or amortization.

**recovery**   Regarding the recovery of tax benefit items, gross income does not include income attributable to the recovery during the taxable year of any amount deducted in any prior taxable year to the extent such amount did not reduce the amount of tax imposed.

**recovery exclusion**    Regarding a bad debt, prior tax, or delinquency amount, it is the amount determined in accordance with regulations of the deductions or credits allowed, on account of such bad debt, prior tax, or delinquency amount, which did not result in a reduction of the taxpayer's tax under corresponding provisions of prior income tax laws.

**registrant**    The issuers of the securities for which an application, a registration statement, or a report is filed.

**related parties**    All affiliates of an enterprise, including its management and their immediate families, its principal owners and their immediate families, its investments accounted for by the equity method, beneficial employee trusts that are managed by the management of the enterprise, and any party that may, or does, deal with the enterprise and has ownership of, control over, or can significantly influence the management or operating policies of another party, to the extent that an arm's-length transaction may not be achieved.

**reorganization, a party to**    Includes a corporation resulting from a reorganization, and both corporations in a transaction qualifying as a reorganization where one corporation acquires stock or properties of another corporation. A corporation remains a party to the reorganization although it transfers all or part of the assets acquired as a controlled subsidiary. A corporation controlling an acquiring corporation is a party to the reorganization when the stock of the controlling corporation is used in the acquisition of properties.

**repurchase premium**    the excess of the repurchase price paid or incurred to repurchase the obligation over its adjusted issue price (see adjusted issue price).

**restricted securities**    Investment securities which cannot be offered for public sale without first being registered under the Securities Act of 1933.

**return**    Any return, statement, schedule, or list, and any supplement thereto, filed with respect to any tax imposed by the law.

**return of capital**    You sell a car that cost $4000 for $4500. The first $4,000 is return of your original investment (capital) and is not taxed – only the $500 additional would be taxable. You always get to recover your investment before you have to start paying tax on a transaction.

**roll-up transaction**    Any transaction or series of transactions that, directly or indirectly, through acquisition or otherwise, involve the combination or reorganization of one or more partnerships and the offer or sale of securities by a successor entity, whether newly formed or previously existing, to one or more limited partners of the partnerships to be combined or reorganized.

**rules and regulations**    All needful rules and regulations approved by the Commissioner for the enforcement of the Code. Includes all rules and regulations necessary by reason of the alterations of the law in relation to Internal Revenue.

# S

**S corporation**   Regarding any taxable year, a small business corporation for which an election is in effect for such year (see small business corporation).

**section 1245 property**   Any property, other than livestock, which is or has been property of a character subject to an allowance for depreciation or subject to an allowance for amortization and is personal property, or other property if such property is tangible, but not including a building or its structural components.

**section 1250 property**   Any real property, other than Section 1245 property, which is or has been property of a character subject to an allowance for depreciation.

**self-employment income**   The net earnings from self-employment derived by an individual during any taxable year, except if such net earnings for the taxable year are less than $400.

**sham transaction**   A transaction done only to save taxes with no business purpose.

**share**   A unit of stock in a corporation, or unit of interest in an unincorporated person. short-term capital gain A gain from the sale or exchange of a capital asset held for not more than 1 year, if and to the extent such gain is taken into account incomputing gross income.

**short-term capital loss**   A loss from the sale or exchange of a capital asset held for not more than 1 year, if and to the extent that such loss is taken into account in computing gross income.

**short tax year**   A tax year of less than twelve months either in the first or last year of a corporation's operation (or other tax entity) or resulting from a change in year-end.

**significant subsidiary**   A subsidiary, including its subsidiaries, which meets any of the following conditions:

1. The registrant's and its other subsidiaries' investments in and advances to the subsidiary exceed 10 percent of the total assets of the registrant and its subsidiaries consolidated as of the end of the most recently completed fiscal year for a proposed business combination to be accounted for as a pooling-of-interests. This condition is also met when the number of common shares exchanged by the registrant exceeds 10 percent of its total common shares outstanding at the date the combination is initiated.

2. The registrant's and its other subsidiaries' proportionate share of the total assets, after intercompany, eliminations, of the subsidiary exceeds 10 percent of the total assets of the registrant and its subsidiaries consolidated as of the end of the most recently completed fiscal year.

3. The registrant's and its other subsidiaries' equity in the income from continuing operations before income taxes, extraordinary items and cumulative effect of a change in accounting principle of the subsidiary exceeds 10 percent of such income of the registrant and its subsidiaries consolidated for the most recently completed fiscal year.

**small business corporation**    A domestic corporation which is not an ineligible corporation, e.g., a member of an affiliated group, and which does not have more than 75 shareholders, does not have as a shareholder a person, other than an estate or trust, who is not an individual, and does not have a nonresident alien as a shareholder.

**standard deduction**    The sum of the basic standard deduction and the additional standard deduction.

**step transaction**    You want to buy a car for cash in the amount of $36,000. The dealer informs you that he will have to report the receipt of that much cash to the IRS (payments of $10,000 or more in cash must be reported). So you decide to buy the car by giving the dealer $9,000 down, then the next day an additional $9,000 and so on until the car is paid for. The step transaction doctrine requires the dealer to collapse these individual transactions into one $36,000 transaction.

**straight debt**    Any written unconditional promise to pay on demand or on a specified date a sum certain in money if the interest rate and interest payment dates are not contingent on profits or the borrower's discretion, not convertible into stock, and the creditor is an individual, an estate, or a trust.

**substance over form**    The owner of a small business (corporation) writes himself a check and calls it a loan (so it will not be taxable income to him) – but there is no note, no interest rate, no collateral, no time when due – it is really a dividend and he must pay tax. The form of a transaction is how it is characterized or outwardly structured. The form of a transaction might be a sale because the parties filled out a form that says Bill of Sale. The substance of a transaction is what is actually occurring and may be different from the form. What is structured like a sale might actually be a bribe or a gift or a dividend, depending on the specific circumstances. The idea is that the IRS can "look behind" a transaction to see what its real nature or affect is.

**subsidiary corporation** (see parent corporation.)

**substituted basis property**    Property which is transferred basis property, or exchanged basis property.

**summarized financial information**    The presentation of summarized information as to the assets, liabilities and results of operations of the entity for which the information is required.

**support**    Includes food, shelter, clothing, medical and dental care, education, etc. The amount of an item of support will be the amount of expense incurred by the one furnishing such item. If the item of support furnished an individual is in the form of property or lodging, it is necessary to measure the amount of such item of support in terms of its fair market value.

**surviving spouse**    A taxpayer whose spouse died during either of his/her two taxable years immediately preceding the taxable year, and who maintains as his/her home a household which constitutes for the taxable year the principal place of abode as a member of such household.

**T**

**tax benefit rule**   If you deduct an item in one year and receive a refund in a later year ( e.g. insurance) the refund is taxable to the extent you received a benefit in the year of deduction.

**tax court**   The United States Tax Court.

**tax-exempt obligation**   Any obligation if the interest on such obligation is not includable in gross income.

**tax shelter**   In general a transaction where the amount paid will result in deductions greater than the amount paid is potentially a tax shelter. Such transactions are scrutinized by the IRS and their use is subject to restrictions.

**taxable gifts**   The total amount of gifts made during the calendar year, less the deductions provided.

**taxable income**   Gross income minus the deductions allowed, other than the standard deduction (see standard deduction). For individuals who do not itemize deductions for the taxable year, it is adjusted gross income, minus the standard deduction, and the deductions for personal exemptions.

**taxable transportation**   Transportation by air which begins and ends in the United States or in the 225-mile zone. The term 225-mile zone means that portion of Canada and Mexico which is not more than 225 miles from the nearest point in the continental United States. The term Continental United States means the District of Columbia and the States other than Alaska and Hawaii.

**taxable year**   The taxpayer's annual accounting period if it is a calendar year or a fiscal year, or the calendar year if the taxpayer keeps no books or has no accounting period. (See annual accounting period and calendar year.)

**term loan**   Any loan which is not a demand loan (see demand loan).

**tips**   Wages received while performing services which constitute employment, and included in a written statement furnished to the employer.

**totally held subsidiary**   A subsidiary substantially all of whose outstanding equity securities are owned by its parent and/or the parent's other totally held subsidiaries, and which is not indebted, in an amount which is material in relation to the particular subsidiary, excepting indebtedness incurred in the ordinary course of business which is not overdue and which matures within 1 year from the date of its creation whether evidenced by securities or not. Indebtedness of a subsidiary which is secured by its parent by guarantee, pledge, assignment, or otherwise, is excluded.

**tract of real property**   A single piece of real property, except that two or more pieces of real property should be considered a tract if at any time they were contiguous in the hands of the taxpayer, or if they would be contiguous except for the imposition of a road, street, railroad, stream, or similar property.

**trade or business**   Includes the performance of personal services within the United States at any time within the taxable year. Includes the performance of the functions of a public office.

**transferred basis property** Property having a basis determined in whole or in part by reference to the basis in the hands of the donor, grantor, or other transferor.

**trust As used in the** Internal Revenue Code, an arrangement created either by a will or by an inter vivos declaration whereby trustees take title to property for the purpose of protecting or conserving it for the beneficiaries under the ordinary rules applied in chancery or probate courts. Usually the beneficiaries of such a trust do no more than accept the benefits thereof and are not the voluntary planners or creators of the trust arrangement.

## U

**undistributed foreign personal holding company income** The taxable income of a foreign personal holding company.

**undistributed personal holding company income** The amount which is subject to the personal holding company tax.

**united states property** Any property which is a tangible property located in the United States, stock of a domestic corporation, an obligation of a United States-resident, or any right to the use in the United States of a patent or copyright, an invention, model, or design (whether or not patented).

**unrealized receivables** Any rights, contractual or otherwise, to payments for goods delivered, or to be delivered, to the extent that such payment would be treated as received for property other than a capital asset. Includes services rendered, or to be rendered, to the extent that income arising from such right to payment was not previously includable in income under the method of accounting employed. The basis for unrealized receivables includes all costs or expenses attributable thereto paid or accrued, but not previously taken into account under the method of accounting employed.

**unrecognized gain** Any position held by the taxpayer as of the close of the taxable year, the amount of gain which would be taken into account with respect to such position if such position were sold on the last business day of such taxable year at its fair market value.

## V

**valuation of assets** The balance sheets of registered investment companies, other than issuers of face-amount certificates, which reflect all investments at value, with the aggregate cost of each category of investment and of the total investments reported shown parenthetically.

**voting shares** The sum of all rights, other than as affected by events of default, to vote for election of directors; the sum of all interests in an unincorporated person (see person).

# W

**wages**   All remuneration for services performed by an employee for an employer, including the cash value of all remuneration, including benefits.

**welfare benefits fund**   Any fund which is part of a plan of an employer, and through which the employer provides welfare benefits to employees or their beneficiaries.

**wherewithal to pay**   This general doctrine says that before someone should be asked to pay taxes on a transaction, they should have received the cash to do so. An example is an installment sale. An individual who sells some property, say a house, and is to receive payments over a number of years, is not required to report (recognize) the income from the sale until the payments are actually received. Contrast this with ordinary business accrual accounting where a business would credit sales and debit a note receivable. There all the income is recorded in the year of sale.

**wholly owned subsidiary**   A subsidiary substantially all of whose outstanding voting shares (see voting shares) are owned by its parent and/or the parent's other wholly owned subsidiaries.

# Y

**year** Any 12 consecutive months.

# Appendix D
## Investment Vocabulary

Any language has a core vocabulary of about 700 words—English, French or Russian—it doesn't matter which one. In addition, all professions have vocabularies of similar size. What we hope to accomplish here is to give basic definitions of words that crop up in most media treatments of securities and investment. While this is not an exhaustive vocabulary, nor are these complete definitions, they are most certainly working definitions of the most common words. They will help the CPA/PFS get through almost any article or conversation without feeling hopelessly confused and left out by the nomenclature of the discussion.

## A

**account** The formal relationship between a securities entity and a client wherein the client buys and sells securities.

**account executive** The person responsible for executing your securities transactions.

**account statement** Monthly written record of a securities client's positions and transactions.

**across the board** Activity in the stock market where seemingly everything goes up or everything goes down in tandem.

**acquisition** One company buying out another.

**active market** Large trading volume for a period of time in either a specific security or in investment vehicles per se.

**against the box** Short sale of a security that the holder owns with a long position already.

**American Depository Receipt (ADR)**   U.S. versions of foreign stocks traded domestically, mitigating against relying upon foreign exchanges to invest in their securities.

**American Depository Share (ADS)**   Shares that make up an ADR and are the underlying security of that ADR.

**American Stock Exchange (AMEX)**   Stock exchange in New York that is second only to the New York Stock Exchange (NYSE) in volume. It largely specializes in small and middle capitalization stocks, options, bonds and some over-the-counter (OTC) issues.

**annual meeting**   Annual recounting of a company's activities held in a public place with management, directors, shareholders, and the press.

**Annual Percentage Rate (APR)**   Simple annual percentage expression of the costs of a loan to consumers that must be disclosed per the Truth In Lending Act.

**annual report**   Annual accounting in print of all the activities of a company required by the SEC.

**annual return**   Pre-tax and expense figure resulting from total income and gain or loss being combined to create one total return figure for the year.

**annualize**   Conversion of a return to an annual basis.

**appreciation**   Increase in value of a security.

**asset**   Something of measurable value.

**asset allocation**   Determining the percentage of funds invested between cash, stock and bonds.

**B**

**back-ended load**   A vanishing deferred sales charge common in mutual funds and annuities that enables investors to have their entire investment working for them at the onset of their investment.

**balanced mutual fund**   Asset allocation fund that has a blend of stocks, bonds and cash—usually, consistent with a conservative investment pattern.

**basis**   Cost of a security including all expenses related to the acquisition of that security.

**bear market**   Market in which prices go down for an extended period of time.

**bid and offer**   The prices at which people are willing to buy (bid) and sell (offer) securities to someone else.

**big board**   Slang name for the New York Stock Exchange.

**block**   Large number of securities.

**blue chip**   Stock of a household-name company that has done very well over an extended number of years.

**bond**   A debt security obligating the issuer to pay the holder interest for some period of time.

**bond rating**   A measurement of a bond issuer's ability to pay its bondholders their interest and principal.

**Appendix D**

**bottom**  Lowest point of something (stock, market, yield) at some measured time (day, quarter, year).

**bottom-up**  Micro to macro look at a subject.

**breakpoint**  Mutual fund dollar commitment that results in a lower sales fee.

**breakup value**  Market value of the parts of a company separated from its whole.

**broker**  Same as account executive; colloquial rather than official term.

**brokered CD**  Certificates of deposit (CDs) sold at brokerages rather than at the bank and having the same characteristics as bank CDs.

**budget**  Estimate of cash flow and expenses.

**bull market**  Market in which prices go up for an extended period of time.

**business cycle**  Recurring periods of expansion and recession in the economy.

**buy**  Make an investment.

**buy and hold**  Long-term investment.

**buyer's market**  A market in which investment in securities predominates.

**buying on margin**  Investing in securities on credit.

**buyout**  Take over the control of a company.

## C

**call feature**  Bond issuer's ability to claim back a bond before it matures as stated in the schedule of redemption for that bond.

**call option**  Opportunity to buy a certain amount of a security at a certain price for a certain amount of time.

**callable**  The ability of an issuer to redeem securities before their stated maturity.

**called**  Security is redeemed prior to maturity.

**capital gain**  Profit realized on sale of a security.

**capital gains distribution**  Distribution of profit, usually in December, from a mutual fund's successful trading.

**capital loss**  Loss realized on sale of a security.

**capital markets**  Markets where stocks and bonds are traded, both public and private.

**capitalization**  The value of a company based on its total stock shares multiplied by the price of the stock.

**cash**  Currency.

**cash dividend**  Dividend paid out to shareholders in cash.

**cash equivalent**  Securities so safe and liquid that they are just removed from being cash.

**central bank**  A country's bank; in the U.S., the Federal Reserve System.

**certificate of deposit (CD)**  Interest-paying debt instrument issued by banks.

**certified financial planner (CFP)**  Financial planner who has completed the program of the Institute of Certified Financial Planners.

**certified public accountant (CPA)**    Accountant who has completed the program required to obtain certification in the state in which he or she works as an accountant.

**chairman of the board**    Highest ranking officer in a corporation, who presides over board meetings.

**charitable remainder trust**    Trust that is irrevocable and that gives money to a charity, generates an income for life to the grantor, and creates tax benefits for the grantor.

**chief executive officer (CEO)**    Actual manager of a company, as opposed to a ceremonial title, responsible for its day-to-day operation.

**chief financial officer (CFO)**    Person who controls the purse strings of a company.

**churning**    Excessive trading in a brokerage account.

**closed-end mutual fund**    Mutual fund with a finite number of shares traded on a stock exchange.

**common stock**    An equity security of a public company.

**company**    A business.

**compliance department**    Entity set up to see that securities activities are in accordance with the law.

**confirmation**    Paper slip used to inform clients in writing of a securities transaction.

**constant dollar plan**    Dollar cost averaging.

**contrarian**    Person who does the opposite of what he or she perceives everyone else is doing.

**controlling interest**    Enough shares to control a company.

**convertible securities**    Securities that can be converted from one security into another; usually from a bond into stock.

**cornering a market**    Illegally gaining control of a security.

**corporate bond**    Bond issued by a company.

**corporation**    Chartered legal company.

**correction**    Downward price adjustment in a security or market.

**cost basis**    Acquisition price of a security.

**coupon**    Rate of return on a bond as expressed by a percentage of the face value of the bond.

**crash**    Extraordinary drop in stock prices, usually in one day.

**credit rating**    A measurement of an entity's ability to pay its creditors.

**credit risk**    Chance that a debt will not be repaid.

**custodial account**    Account created for a minor.

**custodian**    Entity that holds securities for another entity, such as a bank holding securities for a mutual fund.

**cyclical stock**    Stock whose price reflects the state of the economy.

**D**

**debt instrument**    Written document that is issued to cover a debt.

**debt security**    Security that is issued to cover a debt.

**debt service**   Loan payments.

**defined benefit pension plan**   Pension plan that pays a specific amount to a participant after a given employment tenure for the life of that participant.

**defined contribution pension plan**   Pension plan in which there is a specific contribution allowed and the ultimate benefits are dependent upon the investment results of the plan.

**delisting**   Removal of a security from an exchange.

**denomination**   Face value of some financial instrument stated in currency.

**derivative**   Security whose value is based on the value of some other security.

**devaluation**   Lowering the value of a currency relative to the value of some other currency.

**disclosure**   Positive and negative information required by the SEC for determination of an investment decision.

**discount bond**   Bond selling at below its par value.

**discount broker**   Brokerage that charges commissions below the full-service brokerage commissions.

**discounting the news**   Price fluctuations based on anticipated news about a company.

**discount rate**   The rate the Federal Reserve charges member banks for loans secured by various acceptable securities.

**discretionary account**   Account in which trades may be made without first consulting with the client.

**discretionary income**   Income left over after all obligations have been met.

**disintermediation**   Taking funds out of a bank.

**disposable income**   Income left over after all government tax obligations have been met.

**diversification**   Spreading risk by investing in multiple types of investment.

**dividend**   Earnings distribution.

**dividend investment plan**   Reinvesting stock dividends in that company's stock to add more stock to a position on a regular basis.

**dollar cost averaging**   Securities investment of a given amount of money at a given time interval for an indefinite period, where volatility is lessened because of the time factor.

**downside risk**   Estimate as to how low the value of an investment can go.

**downtick**   Trade at lower price than previous one.

**down trend**   Security moving downward in price.

**dumping**   Selling large amounts of stock regardless of the price offered.

**E**

**early withdrawal penalty**   Fee paid to terminate a time deposit contract, usually with bank CDs.

**earned income**   Income actively earned.

**earnings momentum**   Accelerated earnings that tend to provoke upward price movement in stocks.

**earnings per share**   Post-tax, post-bond and preferred stock payment amount of earnings expressed on a per-share basis.

**Employee Retirement Income Security Act (ERISA)**   Private pension and benefit plans law enacted in 1974.

**employee stock ownership plan (ESOP)**   Stock purchase plan set up for the employees of a company to buy their company's stock.

**encumbered**   Owned by one party but another party has a justified claim for ownership.

**endorse**   Transfer ownership.

**entrepreneur**   Risk-oriented investor.

**equity**   Ownership.

**equivalent taxable yield**   Adjustment made to compare tax-exempt yields on an equivalent basis to taxable ones.

**estate**   What a person owns at death.

**estate planning**   Orderly addressing of the documentation and tax planning for the disposition of an estate.

**Eurodollar**   Dollars in banks in Europe.

**event risk**   Risk that something will happen to cause a lower rating of a security and a subsequent decline in price.

**excess reserves**   Reserves of money above Federal Reserve requirement by a member bank.

**exchange rate**   Price one currency can be bought at with another currency.

**ex-dividend**   Time between declaration and payment of a dividend.

**execution**   Consummate a trade.

**executor/executrix**   Administrator of an estate.

**exercise**   Utilize right to do something by contract, usually, with options or futures.

**expense ratio**   A mutual fund's operating expenses expressed as a percentage of the fund's assets that are used to pay expenses plus its 12b-1 fees divided by the fund's net asset value.

**F**

**face value**   Stated denomination of a security on the certificate of that security.

**family of funds**   List of funds managed by the same company.

**favorable trade balance**   Occurs when you export more than you import.

**federal deficit**   Shortfall of revenue relative to expenses of the federal government.

**Federal Deposit Insurance Corporation (FDIC)**   Federal agency that insures bank deposits.

**federal funds**   Commercial bank deposits at the Federal Reserve Bank.

**federal funds rate**   Bank-to-bank loan rates charged on excess deposits at the Federal Reserve.

**Federal Open Market Committee (FOMC)**   Federal Reserve committee that sets government short-term monetary policy.
**Federal Reserve Banks**   Group of banks making up the Federal Reserve System.
**Federal Reserve Board (FRB)**   Board that governs the Federal Reserve.
**Federal Reserve System**   Regulator of U.S. monetary policy and banking system.
**fiduciary**   Entity responsible for another's assets.
**fill**   Complete a customer's order.
**Financial Accounting Standards Board (FASB)**   Establishes and interprets accounting terms and rules.
**financial markets**   The total of the different markets of all types.
**financial planner**   Person who analyzes clients' financial circumstances and prepares a plan for them to realize their goals.
**financial pyramid**   Graphic representation of investments going from least (base) to most (peak) speculative investments.
**financial statement**   Written financial record including balance sheet and income statement.
**financial supermarket**   A large number of financial products sold at one company.
**fiscal year**   A 365-day accounting period.
**fixed annuity**   An annuity that guarantees a specific rate of return.
**fixed cost**   Cost that remains the same regardless of outside sales effects.
**fixed income investment**   A security whose payout rate is set.
**fixed rate**   Loan or security whose interest rate does not change.
**flat**   Bonds trading without interest payment accruing.
**flight to quality**   Rush to high-grade securities in difficult times.
**floating rate**   Loan or security whose interest rate changes.
**floor broker**   Agent who acts for clients of a member firm on an exchange floor.
**floor trader**   Trader who acts for him- or herself on an exchange floor.
**forecasting**   Predicting the future.
**foreclosure**   Seizure of property.
**foreign exchange**   Payments between countries.
**forward**   Buy or sell contract for a commodity.
**401(K) plan**   Elective pre-tax contributions to a qualified tax-deferred retirement plan.
**fraud**   Illegal detrimental behavior to obtain advantage.
**front-ended load**   Up-front mutual fund sales charge.
**full-service brokerage**   A financial supermarket where many financial products are available.
**fully invested**   Asset allocation involving no cash but only stocks and bonds.
**fully valued**   Stock prices at exactly what a company's earnings justify.
**fundamental analysis**   Determination of the price movement of a stock based on earnings expectations as suggested by balance sheet and income statement data.
**futures contract**   A buy or sell agreement for a specific amount of a product at a specific price for a specific time.
**futures exchanges**   Markets where future contracts are traded.

**Appendix D**

## G

**general obligation (GO) bond**   Municipal bond backed by the full faith and credit of its issuer.

**general partner**   Managing partner of a limited partnership with theoretically limitless liability.

**going long**   Purchasing a security.

**going private**   Removing a company from public ownership by buying up all its stock.

**going public**   Making a public sale of a company.

**going short**   Selling a security that is not owned by the seller.

**gold fixing**   Setting of the cash (spot) price of one ounce of gold.

**gold mutual fund**   Mutual fund made up primarily of gold and other mining shares.

**gold standard**   Monetary system whereby currency is convertible to bullion on demand.

**goldbug**   Someone who believes in the appreciation potential of gold.

**golden handcuffs**   Incentives to keep a person from leaving a company.

**golden parachute**   Corporate takeover protection for a key employee.

**good faith deposit**   Earnest money for a securities trade.

**government securities**   Securities issued by the U.S. government and its agencies.

**grandfather clause**   Exemption from a new rule by virtue of prior involvement.

**green shoe**   Provision to issue additional shares of an underwriting if demand is strong enough.

## H

**hard dollar fee**   Payment in cash for services.

**high-yield bond**   Bonds rated BB or lower.

**holding period**   Amount of time an owner has held an asset.

**hot issue**   New stock issue everyone wants because these stocks tend to go up sharply in price.

**hot stock**   Stock that is trading large relative volume and often is going up sharply in price.

**hypothecation**   Using securities as loan collateral.

## I

**illiquid**   Cannot be immediately converted to cash.

**in-the-money option**   Option where the underlying security is trading at a price that would be advantageous to exercise the option.

**inactive security**   Illiquid security owing to scarcity of trading activity for any reason.

**income tax**   Tax on income imposed by country, state or city.

**indemnify**   Agree to pay for loss.

**Appendix D**

**index**   Compilation of statistics (economy) or prices (securities) as a measurement standard.

**index fund**   Fund made up of the constituents of a securities index.

**index option**   Put or call on an index.

**individual retirement account (IRA)**   Personally created retirement account subject to various regulations that are often altered and amended over the years.

**individual retirement account rollover (IRA Rollover)**   Lump sum distribution deposited into an IRA account to avoid current tax consequences.

**inflation**   Increase in prices caused by excessive demand for limited supply of goods and services.

**inflation rate**   Rate of increase in prices of goods and services attributable to excessive demand and limited supply.

**initial public offering (IPO)**   New stock issue that is publicly traded for the first time.

**inside information**   Significant corporate information that has not yet been made public.

**insider**   Person who has access to inside information about a company.

**insolvent**   Unable to pay obligations.

**institution**   Bank, mutual fund, pension fund, corporation, insurance company, college or union.

**insurance**   Contract to reimburse for a loss.

**insured account**   Accountant at a financial entity with government or private insurance coverage.

**interest sensitive**   Reacts to upward or downward movement of rates.

**intermediate term**   In stocks or bonds, a year or more.

**intermediation**   Putting money on deposit at a bank.

**inverted yield curve**   Yield curve where short-term rates are higher than long-term rates.

**investment banker**   Firm that intermediates as broker between issue and buyers.

**investment company**   Entity that manages mutual funds.

**investment grade**   Bonds rated BBB or better.

**investment history**   Pattern of investment practice through time.

**investment income**   Income from securities.

**investment strategy**   Asset allocation plan.

**Investor Relations Department**   Corporate office responsible for addressing investor needs.

**irrevocable trust**   A trust in which the beneficiary must agree to any changes in, or the termination of, that trust.

**issuer**   Entity that issues and promotes sale of its securities.

# J

**joint account**   Account opened and owned by two or more people.

**joint venture**   Two or more parties in contract on a project together.

**jumbo certificate of deposit (jumbo CD)**    Usually, a certificate of $100,000 or more.

**junk bond**    Bond rated BB or lower.

**K**

**Keogh plan**    Type of tax-deferred pension plan.

**kicker**    Usually, equity partnership in a bond deal to enhance appeal of the bond.

**kiddie tax**    Tax filed for children's accounts as they generate taxable income or gains.

**know your customer**    Obligation on the part of the broker to determine client suitability.

**L**

**labor intensive**    Industry that requires a high number of workers.

**ladder**    Succession of fixed income maturities set up to diversify risks associated with timing or reinvestment.

**last sale**    Most recent sale of a security in a trading period.

**last trading day**    Last day a futures contract can settle.

**late tape**    Heavy trading volume that causes the tape to lag behind transactions.

**lay off**    Usually, risk reduction.

**leader**    Stock or group of stocks that leads an advance or decline, usually in volume activity.

**leverage**    Borrowing.

**leveraged buyout**    Takeover relying on borrowed funds.

**liability**    Claim on assets.

**lien**    Creditor's claim against an asset.

**limit order**    Order to buy or sell at a specific price or better than the current market level.

**limit price**    Price set in a limit order.

**limited partnership**    Investors who have invested in a partnership, but who do not have liability beyond their investment for losses.

**liquid asset**    Asset that can immediately be converted to cash.

**liquidity**    Measurement of an asset's convertibility to cash.

**listed security**    Security traded on a recognized U.S. exchange.

**listing requirements**    Standards for inclusion on a given exchange.

**load**    Mutual fund sales charge.

**loan**    Borrowing of an asset by one entity from another entity.

**loan value**    Value of collateral.

**long bond**    The U.S. 30-Year Treasury Bond.

**long position**    Owning a security.

**long term**    Holding period of more than six months for a security.

**long-term debt**    Debt issued for more than one year.

**Appendix D**

**loophole**   Way to legally, but not always ethically, get around a rule or law.

**lump sum distribution**   Cashing out an entire vehicle for one payment.

# M

**macroeconomics**   National economic view and study.

**maintenance fee**   Brokerage account fee to cover costs of services and generate revenue for the brokerage.

**make a market**   Willing to buy or sell a given security at its current price.

**managed account**   Discretionary account where a manager allocates the asset for a fee.

**management**   The organizational structure of a company.

**management fee**   Comprises internal fees of a mutual fund established to cover costs of services and generate revenue for the fund.

**managing underwriter**   Lead underwriter of an offering.

**manipulation**   False appearance of price movement, volume or any kind of activity in a security.

**margin**   Borrowing capability of a security.

**margin account**   An account set up to facilitate margin trades if the customer so desires.

**margin agreement**   Mutual agreement between brokerage and client regarding margin activity rules.

**mark to the market**   Timely adjusted price of a security.

**market**   Public area to buy and sell.

**market analysis**   Study of different markets in order to project the future behavior of one particular market.

**market capitalization**   Value of a company as determined by outstanding shares of its stock multiplied by the stock's current price.

**market letter**   Research publication directed toward market projections.

**market maker**   Person who will buy and sell at current prices of a security.

**market order**   Order to buy or sell at current prices.

**market price**   Most recent price of a security.

**market research**   Research to evaluate a market for a product.

**market risk**   Risk attached to a market as a whole, as reflected in any one security.

**market share**   The part of a market that a given security or product makes up.

**market timing**   Buying or selling of securities based on a perception of what the market as a whole may do.

**market tone**   Psychological status of a market.

**market value**   Security's value based on current price.

**marketability**   Liquidity.

**marketable security**   Liquid security.

**marketing**   Selling.

**marketplace**   Market.

**mature economy**   Economy of a major nation that is in its later stages of growth.

**Appendix D**

**maturity date**   Date on which a security comes due for payment to the holder.

**medium term**   Intermediate-term maturity of a note.

**medium-term notes (MTNs)**   Notes of 2-to-10-year duration that often pay monthly.

**member bank**   A Federal Reserve Bank.

**member firm**   Firm that has a seat on an exchange.

**merchant bank**   Bank that facilitates investment activities.

**merger**   The joining of two or more companies.

**microeconomics**   Study of primary units of an economy.

**missing the market**   Failure to execute an order in a timely fashion that is to the client's disadvantage.

**momentum**   Rate of flow, price, or volume of a security.

**monetary policy**   Money supply policy set by the Federal Reserve.

**money center bank**   Bank located in one of the major financial centers of the world.

**money market**   Trading market for short-term debt securities.

**money market fund**   Open-ended mutual fund made up of short-term debt securities.

**money supply**   Cash or cash deposits in the economy.

**monopoly**   Control of something to the extent that competition is precluded.

**mortgage-backed security**   A security issued with mortgages as its backing.

**mortgage pool**   Collection of similar mortgage into one lot.

**most active list**   Highest volume of traded shares on a per day basis.

**moving average**   Trend analysis of a security price using a preset period of time as a scale.

**multinational corporation**   Domestic company with at least one foreign branch established to operate as a foreign subsidiary.

**municipal bond**   Bond issued without federal tax consequence by a nonfederal government entity.

**municipal bond insurance**   Private insurance for municipal debt bought by the issuer for the benefit of the bondholder to cover interrupted payments in default or ultimately to pay off defaulted principle payments.

**mutual fund**   Pooled money managed by an investment company for the benefit of shareholders invested in stocks, bonds, cash or other securities.

**mutual fund custodian**   Bank where mutual fund assets are deposited for safety reasons.


N

**narrow market**   Illiquid and low-volume market.

**narrowing the spread**   Reducing the gap between the bid and offer on a security.

**National Association of Securities Dealers (NASD)**   Regulators of OTC securities dealers.


**Appendix D**

**National Association of Securities Dealers Automated Quotation System (NAS-DAQ)**  A price quotation system for OTC securities.

**national bank**  Bank with a U.S. charter.

**national debt**  Money owed by the U.S. government.

**nationalization**  Government takeover of a company.

**negative cash flow**  Spending in excess of income.

**negotiable**  Transferable.

**net asset value (NAV)**  Bid price of a mutual fund established daily after the close by adding the value of the fund's assets, subtracting its liabilities and dividing by the number of shares outstanding.

**net change**  Change in price of a security from one day to the next.

**net current assets**  Working capital.

**net earnings**  Net income.

**net proceeds**  Amount left from a transaction after all costs have been subtracted.

**net sales**  Sales less all costs after they have been subtracted.

**net transaction**  Securities trade with no fees attached.

**net worth**  Amount left in assets after all liabilities have been removed by subtraction.

**new account page**  Form filled out by broker to fulfill know-your-client regulations.

**New York Stock Exchange (NYSE)**  Oldest and largest U.S. securities exchange.

**niche**  Area of a company's business that distinguishes it from other companies of its type.

**Nikkei Stock Exchange**  Tokyo stock exchange.

**no-load fund**  Mutual fund with no front-end sales charge.

**non-callable**  Bond or preferred stock that cannot be redeemed at the option of the issuer.

**non-public information**  Information of a significant nature that will affect the current price of a company's securities once it becomes public.

**note**  Usually, intermediate-term debt issues.

**not rated**  Security unrated by any type of rating service, often simply by choice, and neither a positive nor a negative event.

**O**

**offer**  Asked buy price.

**offering price**  Price per share for an IPO or secondary offering.

**offset transaction**  Closing trade to eliminate a position.

**one-decision stock**  A buy-and-hold stock.

**144A bonds**  Junk-debt private placements of low issuer cost.

**open-end management company**  Mutual fund sales company that sells open-ended funds.

**open-end mutual fund**  Mutual fund with an unlimited number of shares issued through a management company.

**opening trade**   Establishes a position.

**operations department**   Department in a brokerage firm that handles customer-related clerical functions.

**option**   Opportunity to buy or sell a certain number of securities at a certain price for a certain amount of time.

**option agreement**   Account document required to activate an option trading account for a client.

**Options Clearing Corporation (OCC)**   Corporation dealing in customer-related clerical functions that manages options exchanges.

**option writer**   Entity that sells options.

**order**   Request for a securities transaction.

**order ticket**   Form with request for a securities transaction written on it.

**ordinary income**   Earned income.

**organizational chart**   Company employment positions chart.

**original cost**   All costs bundled together to determine price for an asset acquisition.

**originator**   Investment banker.

**OTC** See **over the counter**.

**other income**   Not normal income.

**out of favor**   Currently unpopular with analysts and investors for performance reasons.

**out-of-the-money option**   Options whose price does not warrant exercising the option at current levels.

**overbought**   Unnaturally high price for a security.

**overhanging supply**   Excessive quantity of securities available awaiting price to sell opportunity.

**overheating**   Excessive economic expansion.

**oversold**   Unnaturally low price for a security.

**oversubscribed**   Banking issue with demand in excess of the available supply.

**over the counter (OTC)**   Securities not traded on an organized exchange.

**overvalued**   Unnaturally high price for a security from a price/earnings standpoint.


**P**


**paper gain**   Unrealized gain, as no transaction has been made to take the gain.

**paper loss**   Unrealized loss, as no transaction has been made to take the loss.

**par**   Face value.

**parent**   Company that owns other companies.

**partnership**   Two or more people in business together.

**passive income**   Income from investments deemed by the IRS to be passive investments.

**passive loss**   Losses from investments deemed by the IRS to be passive investments.


**Appendix D**

**pass-through security**  Security that is a packaged income product that passes through the income to the security's holders.

**payment date**  Income payment date to security holder.

**pay up**  To pay above the currently perceived value of a security on the belief that the security will trade still higher.

**penny stocks**  Usually, stocks that trade at less than $10 per share are OTC and are quite speculative.

**pension fund**  Retired workers' retirement fund.

**physical commodity**  The underlying tangible item upon which a futures contract is based.

**pink sheets**  Listing of thousands of OTC stocks, their current bid/offer prices and who trades them.

**pledging**  Surrendering collateral as security for a loan or other obligation.

**plow back**  Usually with aggressive growth stocks, to retain rather than distribute earnings.

**point**  One percent, as it relates to debt securities; one dollar, as it relates to stocks.

**poison pill**  Securities transaction that is activated by hostile takeover to make a company both less attractive and less susceptible to takeover.

**portfolio**  All securities assets held.

**portfolio manager**  Professional securities manager.

**portfolio theory**  Risk/reward approach to evaluating securities.

**position**  Security holding.

**position building**  Accumulating a security holding.

**power of attorney (POA)**  Permission to act for another in a brokerage relationship.

**preferred stock**  Nonvoting, income producing dividend-oriented stock.

**premium**  Payment above norm.

**premium bond**  Bond priced above par.

**premium income**  Option-writing income.

**prepayment**  Debt payoff before maturity or due date has arrived.

**prerefunding**  Replacing one bond with another before the first is due by using proceeds of the replacement bond to pay it off.

**present value**  Future income measured in today's dollars.

**price/earnings ratio (P/E)**  Price of a stock divided by its most recent annual earnings.

**price range**  Usually, the 52-week high/low price of a security.

**price support**  Usually, government support levels for commodities prices.

**pricey**  Too high an offer price or too low a bid price.

**primary dealer**  Entities that can deal directly with the Federal Reserve to buy government securities.

**primary issue**  New issue of securities.

**primary market**  New-issue market.

**prime rate**  Rate banks charge their most creditworthy customers.

**principal**  Total amount invested (including all costs of acquisition) in a security.

**Appendix D**

**principal amount**    Face amount of a bond.

**probate**    Process by which a will is administered through court system with executor.

**producer price index (PPI)**    Wholesale price index calculated once per month.

**profit**    Selling price minus purchase price, if to the advantage of the seller.

**profit center**    Area of a company that on its own is expected to make money.

**profit sharing**    Corporate plan to distribute some of its profits internally to employees.

**profit taking**    Usually, sharp responses to broad-based selling by traders who made some money, often quickly, on a security, industry group or even a market.

**program trading**    Buying and selling by computer-driven price-monitoring schemes.

**progressive tax**    Tax system under which the more one makes, the more taxes one pays.

**projection**    Prediction.

**pro rata**    Proportionate share.

**prospectus**    SEC-required informational publication on securities offered for sale.

**proxy**    Vote designation.

**proxy fight**    Usually, takeover-related vote designation battle.

**proxy statement**    SEC-required informational publication on securities vote.

**Prudent Man Rule**    State-by-state determination of fiduciary rules.

**publicly held**    Shares owned by the public.

**public ownership**    Shares owned by the public.

**purchasing power**    Margin credit line at a brokerage.

**pure play**    Security that is without any diversification from its stated industry group.

**put option**    Opportunity to sell a certain amount of a security at a certain price for a certain amount of time.

**pyramid**    Leverage.


**Q**

**qualified annuity**    Annuity purchased in a qualified plan.

**qualified plan**    Tax-deferred retirement plan.

**quantitative analysis**    Numbers-related analysis that depends on statistical interpretation of price movement.


**R**

**raider**    Investor oriented toward takeover and new management.

**rally**    Upward movement of securities prices, especially after a decline.

**random walk**    The notion that the past is no indication of the future as securities respond only to the random-pattern current events, and these are in no way predictable.

**Appendix D**

**range**  High/low quotes on a security over some given period of time.

**rate of return**  Measurement of performance.

**rating**  Credit ranking assessing default risk to debt and investment grade to equity as assigned by rating agencies.

**Real Estate Investment Trust (REIT)**  Usually, publicly traded packaged real estate portfolio.

**real rate of return**  Inflation-adjusted return.

**rebate**  Purchase inducement by refund.

**recession**  Usually, two quarters in a row of downside economic activity.

**recovery**  Upward economic or market movement after a decline.

**redemption**  Payoff of a debt security.

**refinancing**  Refunding a debt issue by issuing another.

**regional bank**  Local bank.

**regional stock exchange**  A local exchange that for a non-New York market.

**registered representative**  Broker.

**regressive tax**  Tax system under which the more one makes, the fewer taxes one pays.

**regulated investment company**  Mutual fund that conforms to IRS regulations under Regulation M.

**reinsurance**  Insurance company risk diversification.

**reinvestment**  Returning dividends into the original investment to grow or compound at the rate of return of the investment itself.

**relative strength**  Price movement comparing one security to another.

**reorganization**  Redoing a firm under bankruptcy laws.

**rescind**  Cancel.

**research and development (R&D)**  Creating and preparing for sale a product.

**research department**  Security analysis area of a securities-oriented company.

**retail deposit notes (RTNs)**  Monthly pay senior-debt notes of 5 to 20 years with 2 to 5 years of call protection that are bank issued and FDIC insured.

**retail investor**  Person who invests.

**return**  Profit or loss on an investment.

**return on equity (ROE)**  Percent earnings based on price of a stock.

**reversal**  Change of direction in a security price or market.

**rich**  Security that is overpriced relative to past history, other stocks in its group or the market.

**right of survivorship**  Ability to take title of something when an owner dies.

**risk**  Downside potential.

**risk adverse**  Avoids risk.

**risk-free return**  Usually, short-term U.S. Treasury Bill returns.

**riskless transaction**  Transaction in which the maker cannot lose money.

**risk premium**  Total return potential minus a risk-free return.

**rollover**  Investment transfer from one investment to another.

**run**  Usually, a rapid rising price.

**S**

**salary reduction plan**   Tax-deferred retirement plan so named because the contributions are pre-tax.

**sale**   Completed transaction.

**sales charge**   Fee paid for securities purchase.

**sales literature**   Marketing material.

**sales load**   Mutual fund sales charge.

**savings bank**   Retail bank.

**savings bond**   U.S. government bonds in $10,000 or smaller denominations; typically used for a child's savings plans.

**screening**   Computer scanning for securities of a given parameter.

**seasonal**   Securities that go up or down in some relationship to the time of year.

**seat**   Euphemism for securities exchange membership.

**secondary**   Public distribution of existing shares in a publicly traded company.

**secondary market**   Post-original-issue markets.

**secondary stock**   Small- or middle-capitalization stock.

**sector**   Stock group.

**sector fund**   Mutual fund of stock group.

**secured debt**   Debt with collateral attached.

**securities analyst**   Securities prognosticator.

**Securities and Exchange Commission (SEC)**   Public protection agency that regulates the securities industry.

**Securities Industry Association (SIA)**   Securities industry lobby.

**Securities Investor Protection Corporation (SIPC)**   Corporations that insure customer accounts against non-market-related brokerage losses, such as default of the house.

**security**   Investment instrument.

**security ratings**   Investment and/or credit evaluation of companies.

**sell off**   Dumping securities with the premise that they will go lower in price sooner than they will rise.

**sell out**   Usually, to cover a margin debit, liquidation of a position or an account.

**sell short**   Selling a security not owned, with the theory in mind that it will go lower in price and can be bought to close the position at a profit on a later date.

**seller's market**   Demand exceeds supply.

**selling climax**   Usually, market bottom induced by a drop in volume and price.

**selling group**   Underwriters who market an issue to the public.

**sentiment indicators**   Gauge of public investor confidence.

**settle**   Pay.

**settlement date**   Payment date for a securities purchase.

**shakeout**   Elimination of secondary-level competition in an industry.

**share**   Usually, equity unit of ownership of a security.

**shareholder**   Owner of shares.

**share repurchase plan**   Corporate stock buyback.

**Appendix D**

**shelf registration**   Two-year window of opportunity to issue a public offering.

**shop**   Retail brokerage office.

**short covering**   Buying shares to close out a short position.

**short position**   Shares sold short and not yet covered.

**short squeeze**   Rising securities prices go up so far and so fast that many short-sellers, particularly those who sell on margin, are forced to cover because of the magnitude of their losses.

**short term**   One year or less.

**short-term debt**   Paper maturing in one year or less.

**short-term gain or loss**   Gain or loss realized in six months or less.

**simple interest**   Stated rate of interest divided by principal invested.

**simplified employee pension (SEP) plan**   Plan combining aspects of an IRA and a 401(K).

**single-premium deferred annuity**   Lump sum payment annuity that earns without tax consequences until distributions begin.

**single-premium life insurance**   Lump sum payment whole life insurance.

**Small Business Administration (SBA)**   Federal loan agency established to help start up businesses of risk.

**small-capitalization stocks**   Stocks of companies with less than $500 million capitalization that are often, because of their size, more volatile than large-capitalization stocks ($1 billion or more, often quite a bit more).

**small investor**   Usually, the stock odd-lot and modest mutual fund investor who does not have significantly large investments.

**soft currency**   Usually, currency of an economy that has no hard assets to back up that currency and thus lacks liquidity in the currency exchange markets.

**soft dollars**   Commission fees paid to a brokerage.

**soft landing**   Slow but not collapsing economy.

**soft market**   One in which supply exceeds demand.

**soft spot**   Weak stock in a group or weak group in a market.

**solvency**   Ability to pay debt obligations.

**sovereign risk**   Political risk.

**specialist**   Exchange market maker.

**speculation**   Assumption of significant risk for unusually significant return.

**spin-off**   Company that is removed from another company and becomes independent.

**split**   Dividing shares without influencing capitalization with the idea that a stock will be more attractive to investors if it is at a lower price.

**spread**   Difference between bid and offer.

**squeeze**   Forced short-sale-position closing due to sharply rising prices.

**stabilization**   Leveling.

**staggered maturity**   Reinvestment risk reduction in bond portfolios by laddered maturities.

**stagnation**   Arrested or declining economic growth.

**Appendix D**

**Standard and Poor's Index (S&P 500)**   Widely held bundle of 500 stocks that is the generally accepted index of U.S. stock performance.

**standard deviation**   Margin of error in a calculation.

**start-up**   New business.

**state bank**   State-chartered rather than federally chartered bank.

**statement**   Client's written periodic account record.

**staying power**   Pain tolerance in a declining market.

**stock**   Equity ownership of shares.

**stock average**   Standard of market measurement to gauge market performance.

**stock buyback**   Corporation buys its own stock for an assortment of purposes.

**stock certificate**   Piece of paper that represents equity ownership shares.

**stock dividend**   A share rather than cash dividend.

**stock exchange**   Organized securities trading place.

**stock index**   Standard of market measurement to gauge market performance.

**stock market**   Usually, Dow Jones Industrial Averages; or, an exchange where securities are traded.

**stock option**   Opportunity to buy or sell a given amount of stock for a given amount of time at a given level of price.

**stock purchase plan**   Internal corporate buying plan for employees.

**stock symbol**   Series of letters to identify companies, usually, one to three letters for listed stocks and four to five letters for OTC stocks.

**stockholder**   Entity that owns shares.

**stockholder of record**   Owner of a share on a given day.

**strategic buyout**   Buyout with what is perceived as an organized plan and purpose.

**street**   Wall Street.

**street name**   Brokerage term for collective positions of customers' securities held by their securities firm for safekeeping and convenience in the name of the firm.

**strip**   Zero coupon treasury security.

**subject**   Quote on a security that can be changed and is therefore not firm.

**suitability rules**   Know-your-client requirements related especially to higher-risk securities.

**support level**   Area in which a declining security price is expected to stabilize.

**suspended trading**   Trading halt generated by some announcement of significance or important information.

**swap**   One security is replaced with another.

**syndicate**   Underwriting group.

**syndicate manager**   Underwriting manager.

**synergy**   The notion that the sum of the various parts of a corporate merger will somehow exceed their separate values.

**synthetic**   Artificially created securities.

**systematic investment**   Dollar cost averaging of mutual funds by contracted agreement with the fund family.

**systematic risk**   Market risk.

**Appendix D**

**T**

**take a position**   Long or short position in a security.

**takeover**   Assumed control of a corporation.

**taking delivery**   Getting a security certificate in hand and assuming possession of it.

**tangible asset**   Real asset, such as collectibles, real estate or other physically formed property.

**target**   Takeover candidate.

**target price**   Stated price goal of an investor at which he or she might want to sell.

**tax basis**   Total cost basis of an investment.

**tax bracket**   Maximum rate of tax on a given income.

**tax credit**   Dollar-for-dollar offset of income tax liability with a credit.

**tax deferred**   Tax liability postponed but not avoided until effective possession has been secured.

**tax-exempt security**   Usually, municipal bond whose interest is not taxable federally or by the state or city in which the issuer is located.

**tax planning**   Systematic and orderly look at a tax situation with the design of reducing tax liability to a minimum.

**tax selling**   Usually, generating losses at year-end to utilize as an offset against gains.

**taxable equivalent yield**   Taxable yield that nets the same to a bondholder as a tax-free municipal bond would.

**taxable income**   Total income remaining at the bottom line of the tax form after all credits and deductions.

**technical analysis**   Price and volume indicators used as a predictor of future securities performance.

**technical rally**   Usually, a bounce-up of prices in a downtrend perceived as being based upon technical factors.

# Appendix E
# The Going Concern Concept

The concept that financial statements are prepared on the basis of a "going concern" is one of the basics relating to financial accounting. There is an underlying presumption in the standards set for financial accounting that a business, once started, will continue functioning and operating. For example, the use of historical costs for building and property, which are currently more valuable, presupposes that the *use* of that property will generate more advantages than would present disposition. Deferrals to future periods through systematic allocations also indicate a presumption of longevity.

This presumption of continuance as a going concern is never stated by the independent auditor—never worded in his or her own opinion. On the *contrary*, it is when there appears to be danger of the firm's *not* being able to continue as a going concern that the auditor makes the assertion that "the statements have been prepared on the basis of a going concern," and that he or she is *unable* to express an opinion because of major uncertainties, then described. Therefore, the actual use of the terminology, "going concern," in the auditor's opinion indicates trouble.

Two types of problems may dictate against an entity's continuation as a going concern:

1. Operational uncertainties which may present two different types of situations giving cause for concern:
   a. Progressive deterioration of a firm's financial stability resulting from changing markets, outmoded or inefficient plant and facilities, inept management. This, in turn, leads to declining earnings or actual losses,

reduced cash balances and eventually an inability to meet current liabilities. Such uncertainties may result in gradual deterioration or, less frequently, in a very sudden turnaround of a previously profitable firm.

b. A start-up business that may never get off the ground. This is the enterprise that begins with high hopes but has not yet met with success nor achieved a solid financial footing. In the event of even a minor setback at this juncture, the firm's continuation may be open to question particularly in relation to the liquidity of its assets. What assets it has are probably tied up in inventories, specialized plant and equipment and deferred charges.

2. External difficulties beyond the control of an entity. These may be as a result of governmental controls, natural disasters such as earthquakes or floods, mandatory product recalls or devastating lawsuits. Any of these or other potential catastrophes could drain an entity beyond its financial capacity to recover.

Following is a random listing of factors which could be indicative of *possible* failure to continue as a going concern:

1. Inability to satisfy obligations on due dates.
2. Inability to perform contractual obligations.
3. Inability to meet substantial loan covenants.
4. A substantial deficit.
5. A series of continued losses.
6. The presence of major contingencies which could lead to heavy losses.
7. Catastrophes which have rendered the business inoperable.
8. Negative cash flows from operations.
9. Adverse key financial ratios.
10. Denial of usual trade credit from suppliers.
11. Necessity of finding new sources of financing.
12. Loss of key personnel.
13. Loss of a principal customer.
14. Work stoppage and labor disputes.

**Appendix E**

# Appendix F
# Guidelines for Interim Reporting

Guidelines for interim reporting by publicly traded companies have been established by the AICPA (and the SEC). For those private companies which do not bear the same responsibility for full and adequate disclosure to public shareholders, the guideline for public disclosure should be studied and followed, where feasible and relevant, for possible selfprotection against insurgent parties, since adherence to standards would probably be more defensible than nonadherence.

Following are the standards for determining applicable information and the appropriate guidelines for minimum disclosure:

1. Results should be based on the same principles and practices used for the latest annual statements (subject to the modifications below).
2. Revenue should be recognized as earned for the interim on the same basis as for the full year. Losses should be recognized as incurred or when becoming evident.
3. Costs may be classified as:
   a. Those associated with revenue (cost of goods sold);
   b. All other costs expenses based on:
      1. Those actually incurred, or
      2. Those allocated, based on: time expired, or benefits received, or other period activity.

4. Costs or losses (including extraordinary times) should not be deferred or apportioned unless they would be at year end. Advertised costs may be apportioned in relation to sales for interims.

5. With respect to inventory and cost of sales:
   a. LIFO basis should not be liquidated if expected to be replaced later, but should be based on expected replacement factor;
   b. Inventory losses should not be deferred because of cost or market rule; and conversely, later periods should then reflect gains on market price recoveries. Inventory losses should be reflected if resulting from permanent declines in market value in the interim period in which they occur; recoveries of such losses would be gains in a later interim period. If a change in inventory value is temporary, no recognition is given.
   c. With standard costs, variances which are expected to be absorbed by year end should be deferred for the interim, not expensed. Unplanned purchase price or volume variance, not expected to turn around, is to be absorbed during the period;
   d. The estimated gross profit method may be used, but must be disclosed.

6. The seasonal nature of activities should be disclosed, preferably including additional 12-month-to-date information with prior comparative figures.

7. Income taxes:
   a. Effective yearly tax rate (including year-end applicable tax-planned advantages) should be applied to interim taxable income;
   b. Extraordinary items applicable to the interim period should be shown separately net of applicable tax and the effect of the tax not applied to the tax on ordinary net income.

8. Extraordinary and unusual items including the effects of segment disposals should be disclosed separately, net of tax, for the interim period in which they occur, and they should not be apportioned over the year.

9. Contingencies should be disclosed the same as for the annual report.

10. Changes in accounting practices or principles from those allowed in prior periods should be disclosed and, where possible, those changes should be made in the first period of the year.

11. Retroactive restatement and/or prior period adjustments are required under the same rules applying to annual statements.

12. The effect of a change in an accounting estimate, including a change in the estimated effective annual tax rate, should be accounted for in the period in which the change in estimate is made. No restatement of previously reported interim information should be made for changes in estimates, but the effect on earnings of a change in estimate made in a current interim period should be reported in the current and subsequent interim periods, if material in relation to any period presented, and

should continue to be reported in interim financial information of the subsequent year, for as many periods as necessary to avoid misleading comparisons.

## MINIMUM DATA TO BE REPORTED ON INTERIM STATEMENTS

1. Sales or gross revenues, provisions for income taxes, extraordinary items (including related tax), cumulative effect of changes in accounting principles or practices, and net income;
2. Primary and fully diluted earnings per share data for each period presented;
3. Seasonal revenue, costs and expenses;
4. Disposal of business segments and extraordinary items, as well as unusual or infrequent items;
5. Contingencies;
6. Changes in estimates, changes in accounting principles or practices;
7. Significant changes in balance sheet items;
8. Significant changes in tax provisions;
9. Current year-to-date, or the last 12 months, with comparative data for prior periods;
10. In the absence of a separate fourth-quarter report, special fourth-quarter adjustments and extraordinary, infrequent or unusual items which occurred during that fourth quarter should be disclosed in a note to the annual financial statement;
11. Though not required, condensed balance sheet data and funds flow data are suggested to provide better understanding of the interim report.
12. If a fourth quarter is not presented, any material adjustment to that quarter must be commented upon in the annual report.

Interim reports are usually prepared by management and issued with that clear stipulation.

Accounting firms which issue reports for interim periods are to be guided by auditing standards set for "Reports on a Limited Review of Interim Financial Information" in Section 722 of Statements on Auditing Standards, April, 1981.

## ACCOUNTING CHANGES IN INTERIM STATEMENTS

FASB 3, *Reporting Accounting Changes in Interim Financial Statements* amended APB Opinion No. 28, *Interim Financial Reporting* with respect to reporting an accounting change in interim financial reports that have a *cumulative effect*.

The following disclosures of accounting changes that have cumulative effects on income from continuing operations, net income, and related per share amounts for the interim period in which the change is made must be included in interim reports:

1. In the interim period in which the new accounting principle is adopted, disclosure should explain the nature and justification for the change.
2. Disclosure should be made of the effect of the change in the interim period in which the change is made.
3. The effect of the change for each pre-change interim period of that fiscal year should be disclosed.
4. The cumulative effect of the change should be shown on retained earnings at the beginning of that fiscal year, if the change is made in other than the first interim period of the company's fiscal year.
5. In the interim period in which a change is made, disclosure must include amounts computed on a *pro forma* basis for the interim period in which the change is made and for any interim periods of prior fiscal years for which financial information is being presented.
6. In financial reports for a subsequent interim period of the fiscal year in which a new principle is adopted, disclosure must include the effect of the change on income from continuing operations, net income, and related per share amounts for the post-change interim period.

# Appendix G

## Reporting Cash Payments of Over $10,000

Often smugglers and drug dealers use large cash payments to "launder" money from illegal activities. Laundering means converting "dirty" money or illegally gained money to "clean" money. Congress passed the Tax Reform Act of 1984 and the Anti-Drug Abuse Act of 1988 requiring the payment of certain cash payments of over $10,000 to be reported to the Internal Revenue Service. Any person in a trade or business who receives more than $10,000 in a single transaction or in related transactions must report the transaction to the IRS. The government can often trace the laundered money through payments that are reported. Compliance with the law provides valuable information that can stop those who evade taxes and those who profit from the drug trade and other criminal activities.

A "person" includes an individual, a company, a corporation, a partnership, an association, a trust, or an estate. A report does not have to be filed if the entire transaction, including the receipt of cash, takes place outside of:

1. The 50 states.
2. The District of Columbia.
3. Puerto Rico.
4. A possession or territory of the United States.

However, a report must be filed if the transaction, including the receipt of cash, occurs in Puerto Rico or a possession or territory of the United States and the person is subject to the Internal Revenue Code.

A transaction occurs when:

1. Goods, services, or property are sold.
2. Property is rented.
3. Cash is exchanged for other cash.
4. A contribution is made to a trust or escrow account.
5. A loan is made or repaid.
6. Cash is converted to a negotiable instrument such as a check or bond.

Payments to be reported include:

1. A sum over $10,000.
2. Installment payments that cause the total cash received within one year of the initial payment to total more than $10,000.
3. Other previously unreportable payments that cause the total cash received within a 12-month period to total more than $10,000.
4. Those received in the course of a trade or business.
5. Those received from the same buyer or agent.
6. Those received in a single transaction or in related transactions.

## A DESIGNATED REPORTING TRANSACTION

A designated reporting transaction is the retail sale of any of the following:

1. A consumer durable, such as an automobile or boat. A consumer durable is property other than land or buildings that is suitable for personal use and can reasonably be expected to last at least one year under ordinary usage.
2. Has a sales price of more than $10,000.
3. Tangible property.
4. A "collectible," including works of art, rugs, antiques, gems, stamps, coins.
5. Travel or entertainment, if the total sales price of all items sold for the same trip or entertainment event in one transaction, or related transactions, is more than $10,000. The sales price of items such as air fare, hotel rooms, and admission tickets are all included.

## RETAIL SALES

The term "retail sales" means any sale made in the course of a trade or business that consists mainly of making sales to ultimate consumers. Thus, if

**Appendix G**

a business consists mainly of making sales to ultimate consumers, all sales made in the course of that business are retail sales. This includes sales of items that will also be resold.

## DEFINITION OF CASH

In this context, cash is considered to be:

1.  The coins and currency of the U.S. and any other recognized country.
2.  Cashier's checks, bank drafts, traveler's checks, and money orders received if they have a face value of $10,000 or less and were received in:
    a.  A designated reporting transaction.
    b.  Any transaction in which the receiver knows the payer is trying to avoid the reporting of the transaction.

A check drawn on an individual's personal account is not considered cash; however, a cashier's check, even when labeled a "treasurer's check" or "bank check," is considered cash.

## EXCEPTIONS TO DEFINITION OF CASH

A cashier's check, bank draft, traveler's check, or money order received in a designated transaction is not treated as cash if:

1.  It is the proceeds from a bank loan. As proof that it is proceeds from a bank loan, a copy of the loan document, a written statement or lien instructions from the bank, or similar proof are acceptable as evidence,
2.  If received in payment on a promissory note or an installment sales contract, including a lease that is considered a sale for federal tax purposes. This exception applies if:
    a.  The receiver uses similar notes or contracts in other sales to ultimate consumers in the ordinary course of trade or business.
    b.  Total payments for the sale are received on or before the 60th day after the sale, and are 50% or less of the purchase price.
3.  For certain down payment plans in payment for a consumer durable or collectible, or for travel and entertainment, and *all three* of the following statements are true:
    a.  It was received under a payment plan requiring one or more down payments, and payment of the remainder before receipt of goods or service.

**Appendix G**

b. It was received more than 60 days before final payment was due.

c. Similar payment plans are used in the normal course of the trade or business.

## TAXPAYER IDENTIFICATION NUMBER (TIN)

The receiver must furnish the correct TIN of the person or persons from whom the cash is received. If the transaction is conducted on behalf of another person or persons, the receiver must furnish the TIN of that person or persons. There are three types of TINs:

1. The TIN for an individual, including a sole proprietor, is the individual's social security number (SSN).
2. The TIN for a nonresident alien individual who needs a TIN, but is not eligible to get an SSN, is an IRS individual taxpayer identification number (ITIN). An ITIN has nine digits, similar to an SSN.
3. The TIN for other persons, including corporations, partnerships, and estates, is the employer identification number.

A nonresident alien individual or a foreign organization does not have to have a TIN, and so a TIN does not have to be furnished for them, if *all* the following are true:

1. The individual or organization does not have income effectively connected with the conduct of a trade or business in the United States, or an office or place of business or a fiscal or paying agent in the United States, at any time during the year.
2. The individual or organization does not file a federal tax return.
3. In the case of a nonresident alien individual, the individual has not chosen to file a joint federal income tax return with a spouse who is a U.S. citizen or resident.

## RELATED TRANSACTIONS

Any transaction between a buyer, or an agent of the buyer, and a seller that occurs within a 24-hour period are related transactions. If a person receives over $10,000 in cash during two or more transactions with one buyer in a 24-hour period, he or she must treat the transactions as one transaction and report the payments. For example, if two products are sold for $6,000 each to the same customer in one day, and the customer pays the seller in cash, they are related transactions. Because they total $12,000, they must be reported.

**Appendix G**

Transactions can be related if they are more than 24 hours apart if the person knows, or has reason to know, that each is one of a series of connected transactions. For example, a travel agent receives $8,000 from a client in cash for a trip. Two days later, the same client pays the agent $3,000 more in cash to include another person on the trip. These are related transactions and must be reported.

When a person receives $10,000 or less in cash, the person may voluntarily report the payment if the transaction appears to be suspicious. A transaction is suspicious if it appears that a person is trying to cause the receiver not to report, or is trying to cause a false or incomplete report, or if there is a sign of possible illegal activity.

The amount received and when it was received determines when it must be reported to the IRS. Generally, a report must be filed within 15 days after receiving payment. If the first payment is not more than $10,000, the seller must add the first payment and any later payments made within one year of the first payment. When the total cash payments are more than $10,000, the buyer must file within 15 days. After a report is filed, a new count of cash payments received from that buyer within a 12-month period must be reported to the IRS within 15 days of the payment that causes the additional payments to total more than $10,000. The report can be filed in the seller's local IRS office.

A written statement must be given to each person named on the report to the IRS. The statement must show the name and address of the person who receives the payment, the name and telephone number of a contact person, and the total amount of reportable cash received from the person during the year. It must state that the information is being reported to the IRS. The statement must be sent to the buyer by January 31 of the year after the year in which the seller receives the cash that caused the information to be filed with the IRS. The individual making the report must keep a copy of every report filed for five years.

## PENALTIES

There are civil penalties for failure to:

1. File a correct report by the date it is due.
2. Provide the required statement to those named in the report.
3. If the person receiving the cash payment intentionally disregards the requirement to file a correct form by the date it is due, the penalty is the larger of:
   a. $25,000.
   b. The amount of cash the person received and was required to report, up to $100,000.

**Appendix G**

There are criminal penalties for:

1. Willful failure to file a report.
2. Willfully filing a false or fraudulent report.
3. Stopping or trying to stop a report from being filed.
4. Setting up, helping to set up, or trying to set up a transaction in a way that would make it seem unnecessary to file a report.

Interference with or prevention of the filing of a report as well as actual willful failure to file sa report may result in a substantial fine, imprisonment, or both. The fine can be up to $250,000 ($500,000 for corporations). An individual may also be sentenced to up to five years in prison. Both a fine and a prison sentence may be imposed.

The penalties for failure to file can also apply to any person, including a payer, who attempts to interfere with or prevent the seller, or business, from filing a correct report. This includes any attempt to *structure* the transaction in a way that would make it seem unnecessary to file a report by breaking up a large cash transaction into small cash transactions.

**Appendix G**

# Appendix H
# Goodwill

Goodwill is an intangible asset that represents the advantage or benefits acquired in a business in excess of the value of the other assets. Goodwill can be internally generated as a result of earnings, or it can be purchased as part of the cost of acquiring a group of assets in the purchase of another business. Goodwill is an intangible asset because it is difficult to determine its value directly, despite it being associated with aspects of a business, such as its value as a going concern, skilled employees, expected continued customer patronage, name or reputation, effective management, and future expected profits. For both financial accounting and tax accounting, goodwill is recognized only when there is a purchase of another business. Thus, no accounting or tax recognition is given to internally generated goodwill.

In the acquisition of a business, the purchase price is compared with the fair market values of the identifiable tangible and intangible assets acquired, and the difference is assigned to goodwill if the purchase price exceeds the values of the individual assets, or badwill, if the value of the assets exceeds the purchase price. The underlying assets in a business purchase must be individually assigned a fair value at the date of acquisition; this normally requires an appraisal of the tangible and intangible assets purchased (excluding goodwill).

For accountants who have been practicing for more than a decade, that period has seen a complete reversal of position on the amortization of goodwill by the IRS, Congress, and the FASB. Internal Revenue Code (IRC) sec. 197 was enacted as part of the *Revenue Reconciliation Act of 1993* allowing business intangibles, including goodwill, acquired after August 10, 1993 to be amortized over a 15-year period. Before that, any amortized goodwill was strictly nondeductible.

The FASB in 2002 issued FASB 142, *Goodwill and Other Intangible Assets* effective for fiscal years beginning after December 15, 2001, putting a halt to the amortization of goodwill for financial reporting purposes. The result for corporate tax returns is that whereas the amortization of goodwill was formerly an M-1 item that was deductible for book purposes but not for tax purposes, it is now an M-1 item that is deductible for tax purposes but not for financial reporting.

The fundamental reasoning of the Board in issuing FASB 142 was to make the amortization of intangibles dependent upon their measurable lives or their benefits to the business. It addresses acquired intangible assets but leaves the former coverage of internally developed intangibles as directed in APB Opinion No. 17, *Intangible Assets*. The FASB concluded that the benefits of goodwill are too indeterminable to be assigned a definite life, and hence are not subject to amortization.

## TAX TREATMENT OF GOODWILL

IRC sec. 1060 sets out the method for allocating the purchase price of an ongoing business to its assets. The IRS requires Form 8594, *Asset Acquisition Statement Under Section 1060*, to be filed by both the buyer and seller. This form records the allocation of the purchase price to various classes of assets, including goodwill. This requirement applies regardless of the form of the business (sole proprietorship, partnership, LLC, C Corporation, S Corporation, or trust). The form is attached to the first tax return filed following the sale-purchase.

IRS Form 8594 requires dividing the acquired assets into classes:

- Class I assets include cash and cash equivalents.
- Class II assets include publicly traded stocks and securities (but not the stock of the target company), certificates of deposit, U.S. government securities and foreign currency.
- Class III assets include accounts receivable and other debt assets that the taxpayer marks-to-market at least annually for federal income tax purposes.
- Class IV assets include inventory or stock in trade of the purchased business, or other assets held for sale to customers in the ordinary course of business.
- Class V assets are all assets not included in another class, including class VI.
- Class VI assets are all IRC sec. 197 intangibles except goodwill and going concern value. IRC sec. 197 assets include workforce in place, business books and records, customer-based intangibles, licenses, permits,

**Appendix H**

covenants not to compete, franchises, interest in land, certain computer software, interests under leases of tangible property, certain separately acquired interests in patents or copyrights, professional sports franchises and certain transaction costs. The basis of intangible assets is the cost to buy or create them, including legal fees to defend them when applicable.

- Class VII assets are goodwill and going concern value (whether or not the goodwill or going concern value qualified as sec. 197 intangibles).

The IRS requires the residual method for allocating the sales price of the purchased assets. Based on the fair market value of the assets purchased, the residual method allocates the sales price beginning with Class I assets and working up the classes to Class VI. Any remaining balance after the allocation to all other assets may be allocated to Class VII, goodwill and going concern value.

The fair market value (to be assigned to assets in Classes I-VI) is the price at which property would change hands between a buyer and a seller, neither under a compulsion to buy or sell, and both having reasonable knowledge of all relevant facts.

Amortization is a ratable deduction for the cost of certain intangible property over the period specified by law, 15 years, in the case of sec. 197 intangibles, including goodwill and going concern value. Intangibles are amortized on a straight-line basis, by the month in the year of acquisition and annually thereafter.

If the acquisition of an ongoing corporation is accomplished through the purchase of its stock, consideration should be given to an IRC sec. 338 election, treating the deal as an asset purchase for tax purposes.

## FINANCIAL REPORTING TREATMENT OF GOODWILL

For financial reporting, although amortization of goodwill is no longer allowed, identifiable reductions in the value of goodwill are subject to write-downs if the asset becomes impaired. Specific rules are provided by FASB 121 for determining when impairment has occurred.

FASB 142 provides that goodwill shall be tested for impairment at least annually and at the same time of the year each time, though it may be done anytime during the year. Impairment is the condition that exists when the carrying amount of goodwill exceeds its "implied fair value." The use of the term *implied fair value* indicates that the value of goodwill cannot be measured directly but is always a residual amount. The testing for impairment of goodwill is done in two steps. First, the fair value of the business, or reporting unit, is compared with its carrying amount, including goodwill. As long as the fair value of the business exceeds its carrying amount, there is no impairment and no further measures are required.

**Appendix H**

If, as a result of comparing the fair value of a company with its carrying amount, the fair value is less than the carrying amount, then the second step of the process requires determining the extent to which goodwill has been impaired. The second step involves comparing the carrying amount of the goodwill with the implied fair value of the goodwill. If this test discloses an amount that the carrying amount exceeds the implied fair value, that amount is a recognizable impairment. The loss from the impairment of goodwill is reported on the income statement as a separate line item before the subtotal *income from continuing operations*. An exception is made if the impairment is identified with a discontinued operation, in which case the loss is reported net of tax in the subtotal for results of discontinued operations.

In addition to the annual testing for impairment of goodwill, specific events are identified by FASB 142 that would more likely than not reduce the fair value of a business below its carrying value. Included among these events are an adverse action or assessment by a regulator, a loss of key personnel, or unanticipated competition. A write-down of goodwill due to an impairment loss is never reversed if conditions improve.

# Appendix I
## Foreign Currency Translations

## FASB Statement 52, *Foreign Currency Translations*

FASB 52 covers accounting for the translation of foreign currency statements and the gain and loss on foreign currency transactions. Foreign currency transactions and financial statements of foreign entities include branches, subsidiaries, partnerships and joint ventures, which are consolidated, combined, or reported under the equity method in financial statements prepared in accordance with U.S. generally accepted financial principles.

*Why is translation necessary?* It is not arithmetically possible to combine, add, or subtract measurements expressed in different currencies. It is necessary, therefore, to translate assets, liabilities, revenues, expenses, gains, and losses that are measured or denominated in a foreign currency.

### Definitions

An understanding of this rather complex accounting rule can be aided by becoming familiar with the terms used in the Statement. The following list of definitions will enable the accountant to apply the accounting procedures and methods outlined below.

*Attribute*—For accounting purposes, the quantifiable element of an item.

*Conversion*—Exchanging one currency for another.

*Currency Exchange Rate*—The rate at which one unit of a currency can be exchanged or converted into another currency. For purposes of translation of financial statements, the current exchange rate is the rate at the end of the period covered by the financial statements, or the dates of recognition in the statements for revenues, expenses, gains and losses.

*Currency Swap*—An exchange between enterprises of the currencies of two different countries with a binding commitment to reverse the exchange of the two currencies at the same rate of exchange on a specified future date.

*Current Rate Method*—All assets and liabilities are translated at the exchange rate in effect on the balance sheet date. Capital accounts are translated at *historical exchange rates.*

*Discount or Premium on a Forward Contract*—The foreign currency amount of a contract multiplied by the difference between the contracted forward rate and the spot rate at the date of inception of the contract.

*Economic Environment*—The nature of the business climate in which an entity *primarily* generates and expends cash.

*Entity*—In this instance, a party to a transaction which produces a monetary asset or liability denominated in a currency other than its functional currency.

*Exchange Rate*—The ratio between a unit of one currency and the amount of another currency for which that unit can be exchanged at a particular time. The appropriate exchange rate for the translation of income statement accounts is the rate for the date on which those elements are recognized during the period.

*Foreign Currency*—A currency other than the functional currency of the entity being referred to. For example, the dollar could be a foreign currency for a foreign entity. Composites of currencies, such as the Special Drawing Rights (SDRs), used to set prices or denominate amounts of loans, etc., have the characteristics of foreign currency for purposes of applying Statement 52.

*Foreign Currency Transaction*—A transaction in which the terms are denominated in a currency other than an entity's functional currency. Foreign currency transactions arise when an enterprise buys or sells goods or services on credit at prices which are denominated in foreign currency; when an entity borrows or lends funds and the amounts payable or receivable are denominated in foreign currency; acquires or disposes of assets, or incurs or settles liabilities denominated in a foreign currency.

*Foreign Currency Translation*—Amounts that are expressed in the reporting currency of an enterprise that are denominated in a foreign currency. An example is the translation of the financial statements of a U.S. company from the foreign currency to U.S. dollars.

In the translation of balance sheets, the assets and liabilities are translated at the *current exchange rate*, e.g., rate at the balance sheet date. Income statement items are translated at the *weighted-average exchange rate* for the year.

There are two steps in translating the foreign country's financial statements into U.S. reporting requirements:

1. Conform the foreign country's financial statements to GAAP.
2. Convert the foreign currency into U.S. dollars, the reporting currency.

**Appendix I**

*Foreign Entity*—An operation (subsidiary, division, branch, joint venture, etc.) whose financial statements are prepared in a currency other than the currency of the reporting enterprise. The financial statements are combined and accounted for on the equity basis in the financial statements of the reporting enterprise.

*Foreign Exchange Contract*—An agreement to exchange, at a specified future date, currencies of different countries at a specified rate, which is the *forward rate*.

*Functional Currency*—The currency of the primary economic environment in which an entity operates; that is, the currency of the environment in which an entity primarily generates and expends cash.

*Hedging*—An effort by management to minimize the effect of exchange rate fluctuations on reported income, either directly by entering into an exchange contract to buy or sell one currency for another, or indirectly by managing exposed net assets or liabilities' positions by borrowing or billing in dollars rather than the local currency. An agreement to exchange different currencies at a specified future date and at a specified rate is referred to as *the forward rate*.

*Highly Inflationary Economy*—Economies of countries in which the *cumulative* local inflation rate over a three-year period exceeds approximately 100 per cent, or more.

*Historical Exchange Rate*—A rate, other than the current or a forward rate, at which a foreign transaction took place.

*Inflation*—Not defined by specific reference to a commonly quoted economic index. Management can select an appropriate method for measuring inflation. An annual inflation rate of about 20% for three consecutive years would result in a cumulative rate of about 100%.

*Intercompany Balance*—The foreign currency transactions of the parent, the subsidiary, or both. An intercompany account denominated in the local foreign currency is a foreign currency transaction of the parent. An intercompany account denominated in dollars is a foreign currency transaction of a foreign entity whose functional currency is a currency *other than* the U.S. dollar.

*Local Currency*—The currency of a particular country.

*Measurement*—Measurement is the process of measuring transactions denominated in a unit of currency (e.g., purchases payable in British pounds).

*Remeasurement*—Measurement of the functional currency financial statement amounts in other than the currency in which the transactions are denominated.

*Reporting Currency*—The currency used by an enterprise in the preparation of its financial statements.

*Reporting Enterprise*—An entity or group whose financial statements are being referenced. In Statement 52, those financial statements reflect a) the financial statements of one or more foreign operations by combination, consolidation, or equity accounting; b) foreign currency transactions; c) both a) and b).

**Appendix I**

*Self-Contained Operations*—Operations which are integrated with the local economic environment, and other operations which are primarily a direct or integral component or extension of a parent company's operations.

*Speculative Contracts*—A contract that is intended to produce an investment gain (not to hedge a foreign currency exposure).

*Spot Rate*—An exchange for *immediate delivery* of the currencies exchanged.

*Transaction Date*—The date at which a transaction, such as a purchase of merchandise or services, is recorded in accounting records in conformity with GAAP. A long-term commitment may have more than one transaction date; for example, the due date of each progress payment under a construction contract is an *anticipated transaction date* credited to shareholders' equity.

*Transaction Gain or Loss*—Gains or losses from a change in exchange rates between the functional currency and the currency in which a foreign transaction is denominated.

*Translation Adjustment*—Translation adjustments translate financial statements from the entity's functional currency into the reporting currency. The amount necessary to balance the financial statements after completing the translation process. The amount is charged or credited to shareholder's equity.

*Unit of Measure*—The currency in which assets, liabilities, revenues, expenses, gains and losses are measured.

*Weighted Average Rates*—Determined on a monthly basis by an arithmetic average of daily closing rates, and on a quarterly and an annual basis by an arithmetic average of average monthly rates.

## Discussion of FASB Statement 52

Statement 52 applies to the financial reports of most companies with foreign operations. The essential requirements of the Statements are:

1. Transaction adjustments arising from consolidating a foreign operation which do not affect cash flows are *not* included in net income. Adjustments should be disclosed separately and accumulated in a separate classification of the equity section of the balance sheet.
2. Exchange rate changes on a foreign operation which directly affect the parent's cash flows must be included in net income.
3. Hedges of foreign exchange risks are accounted for as hedges without regard to their form.
4. Transaction gains and losses result from exchange rate changes on transactions denominated in currencies other than the functional currency.
5. The balance sheet translation uses the exchange rate prevailing as of the date of the balance sheet.

**Appendix I**

6. The exchange rate used for revenues, expenses, gains and losses is the rate on the date those items are recognized.

7. Upon sale (or liquidation) of an investment in a foreign entity, the amount accumulated in the equity component is removed and reported as a gain (or loss) on the disposal of the entity.

8. Intercompany transactions of a long-term investment nature are not included in net income.

9. Financial statements for fiscal years before the effective date of this Statement may be restated. If restatements are provided, they must conform to requirements of the Statement.

10. The financial statements of a foreign entity in a highly inflationary economy must be remeasured as if the functional currency were the reporting currency. A "highly inflationary economy" is defined in the Statement to be an economy that has had a cumulative inflation rate of 100%, or more, over a three-year period.

11. If material change in an exchange rate has occurred between year-end and the audit report date, the change should be reported as a subsequent event.

*Background.*    The rapid expansion of international business activities of U.S. companies and dramatic changes in the world monetary system created the need to reconsider the accounting and reporting for foreign currency translation. In considering this topic, the FASB issued FASB Statement 52, which related to the following four areas:

1. Foreign currency transactions including buying or selling on credit goods or services whose prices are denominated in a foreign currency; i.e., currency other than the currency of the reporting entity's country.

2. Being a party to an unperformed foreign exchange contract.

3. Borrowing or lending funds denominated in a foreign currency.

4. For other reasons, acquiring assets or incurring liabilities denominated in foreign currency.

Statement 52 also applies to a foreign enterprise which reports in its currency in conformity with U.S. generally accepted accounting principles. For example, a French subsidiary of a U.S. parent should translate the foreign currency financial statements of its Italian subsidiary in accordance with Statement 52. The objective of translation is to measure and express in dollars, and in conformity with U.S. generally accepted accounting principles, the assets, liabilities, revenues, or expenses that are measured or denominated in foreign currency. In achieving this objective, translation should remeasure these amounts in dollars without changing accounting principles. For example, if an asset was originally measured in a

**Appendix I**

foreign currency under the historical cost concept, translation should remeasure the carrying amount of the asset in dollars at historical cost, not replacement cost or market value.

The most common foreign currency transactions result from the import or export of goods or services, foreign borrowing or lending, and forward exchange contracts. Import or export transactions can be viewed as being composed of two elements—a sale or purchase and the settlement of the related receivable or payable. Changes in the exchange rate, which occur between the time of sale or purchase and the settlement of the receivable or payable, should not affect the measurement of revenues from exports or the cost of imported goods or services.

Foreign currency statements should be translated based on the exchange rate at the end of the reporting year. Translation gains and losses are presented in the stockholders' equity section. Also important is the accounting treatment of gains and losses resulting from transactions denominated in a foreign currency. These are shown in the current year's income statement.

Because of the proliferation of multinational companies, expanding international trade, business involvement with foreign subsidiaries, and joint ventures, FASB 52 was established, in effect, by popular demand. The stated aims of Statement 52 are to (a) provide information that is generally compatible with the expected effects of a rate change on an enterprise's cash flows and equity, and (b) reflect in consolidated statements the financial results and relationships of the individual consolidated entities as measured in their functional currencies, whether the U.S. dollar or a specified foreign currency, in conformity with U.S. generally accepted accounting principles.

The method adopted to achieve these aims is termed the *functional currency approach* which is the currency of the primary economic environment in which the entity carries on its business; in substance, where it generates and expends cash. The Statement permits a multiple measurement basis in consolidated financial statements (depending upon the country in which the subsidiary operates) because business enterprises made up of a multinational enterprise operate and generate cash flows in diverse economic environments, each with its own functional currency. When an enterprise operates in several of these environments, the results of business transactions are measured in the functional currency of the particular environment. "Measured in the functional currency" has the specific meaning that gains and losses comprising income are determined only in relation to accounts denominated in the functional currency.

Mechanically, the functional currency approach calls for eventual translation of all functional currency assets and liabilities into dollars at the current exchange rate. Under Statement 52, use of the current rate for all accounts resolves both the economically compatible results and operating margins distortions. In the past, these distortions came about with the translation of nonmonetary accounts at historical rates. The volatility of earnings distortions is alleviated by recording the translation adjustments directly into shareholders' equity.

**Appendix I**

The functional currency approach presumes the following:

1. Many business enterprises operate and generate cash flows in a number of different countries (different economic environments).
2. Each of these operations can usually be identified as operating in a single economic environment: the local environment or the parent company's environment. The currency of the principal economic environment becomes the functional currency for those operations.
3. The enterprise may be committed to a long-term position in a specific economic environment and have no plans to liquidate that position in the foreseeable future.

Because measurements are made in multiple functional currencies, decisions relating to the choice of the functional currency of a specific foreign operation will in all likelihood have a significant effect upon reported income. Even though the management of the business enterprise is entitled to a degree of latitude in its weighing of specific facts, the thinking behind adoption of this Statement is that the functional currency is to be determined based on the true nature of the enterprise and not upon some arbitrary selection which management feels might be of particular advantage to the reporting entity.

*Determining the Functional Currency.* Multinational companies are involved with foreign business interests either through transactions or investments in foreign entities operating in a number of different economic environments. Each of these endeavors may be associated with one primary economic environment whose currency then becomes the functional currency for that operation. On the other hand, in a foreign country where the economic and/or political environment is so unstable that a highly inflationary economy is likely, it may be deemed wise to carry on the enterprise with the dollar as the functional currency. If the operations in situations of this nature are remeasured on a dollar basis, further erosion of nonmonetary accounts may be avoided.

When there is a reasonably stable economic situation, the national environment of each operation should be considered as the primary economic environment of the particular operation since national sovereignty is a primary consideration in relation to currency control.

Industry practice, on the other hand, may in some instances be instrumental in the determination of a primary economic environment and functional currency. If it is an industry-wide practice that pricing or other transaction attributes are calculated in a specific currency, such as prices set in dollars on a worldwide basis, that fact may be more of a determinant than local currency considerations.

**Appendix I**

The actual decisions in determining a functional currency depend to a large extent upon the operating policy adopted by the reporting company. Two broad classes of foreign operations are to be considered:

1. Those in which a foreign currency is the functional currency. This designation will have been made after receiving the facts and determining that this particular aspect of foreign business operations is largely autonomous and confined to a specific foreign economic environment. That is, ordinary operations are not dependent upon the economic environment of the parent company's functional currency, nor does the foreign operation primarily generate or expend the parent's functional currency.

2. When the workaday business of the foreign operation is deemed to be in actuality just an extension of the parent company's operation and dependent upon the economic environment of the parent company, the dollar may be designated as the functional currency. In substance, most transactions can reasonably be in dollars, thus obviating the need for foreign currency translation.

One of the objectives of Statement 52 is to provide information that is generally compatible with the expected economic effects of a rate change on an enterprise's cash flow and equity in a readily understood manner. If a foreign operation's policy is to convert available funds into dollars for current or near-term distribution to the parent, selection of a dollar functional currency may be expedient.

Therefore, reporting for investments expected to be of short-term duration, such as construction or development joint ventures, the dollar should probably be designated the functional currency. If the nature of an investment changes over a period of time, future redetermination of the appropriate functional currency may become necessary. Such redetermination is permissible only when, in actual fact, significant changes in economic facts and/or circumstances have occurred. The operative functional currency cannot be redetermined merely because management has "changed its collective mind." It becomes evident that functional currency determination should be carefully considered with the decision weighted in favor of the long-term picture rather than short-term expectations.

In the event that redetermination is necessary, three procedures should be kept in mind:

1. When the functional currency has been changed, Statement 52 provides that the prior year's financial statement need not be restated for a change in functional currency.

2. When the functional currency change is from the local currency to the dollar, historical costs and exchange rates are to be determined from translated dollar amounts immediately prior to the change.

**Appendix I**

3. When the functional currency change is from the dollar to the local currency, nonmonetary assets are to be translated at current exchange rates, charging the initial translation adjustment to equity similar to that produced when Statement 52 was adopted.

*Translation.* Translation is the process of converting financial statements expressed in one unit of currency to a different unit of currency (the reporting currency). In short, translation as used in Statement 52 is the restatement into the reporting currency (the U.S. dollar) of any/all foreign currency financial statements utilized in preparing the consolidated financial statements of the U.S. parent company.

Thus, the focus for the preparation and subsequent translation of the financial statements of individual components of an organization is, as previously stated, to:

1. Provide information that is generally compatible with the expected economic effects of a rate change on the enterprise's cash flows and equity, and

2. Reflect in consolidated statements the financial results and relationships of the individual consolidated entities as measured in their functional currencies in conformity with U.S. generally accepted accounting principles.

Measurement is the process of stating the monetary value of transactions denominated in a particular unit of currency (e.g., purchases payable in British pounds). These transactions may also be figured in a unit of currency other than that in which they are denominated. This process then becomes remeasurement and is accomplished by assuming that an exchange of currencies will occur at the exchange rate in effect at the time of the remeasurement. As is evident, should the exchange rate fluctuate between the date of the original transaction and the date of the exchange, a foreign exchange gain or loss will result. The gains or losses so recorded vary little from other trading activities and are, therefore, included in income.

It is important to note that while translations were formerly based on the premise that financial statements of a U.S. enterprise should be measured in a single unit of currency—the U.S. dollar—translation was under FASB 80, *Accounting for Futures Contracts*, a one-step process that included both remeasurement and reporting in dollars. In the newer context of the functional approach, multiple units of measure are permitted so that remeasurement is required only when (1) the accounts of an entity are maintained in a currency other than its own functional currency, or (2) an enterprise is invoiced in a transaction which produces a monetary asset or liability not denominated in its functional currency.

**Appendix I**

The subsequent translation to dollars under FASB 52 is the second step of a two-step process necessary to prepare U.S. dollar financial statements.

*Foreign Currency Transactions.*Foreign currency transactions are those denominated in a currency other than the entity's functional currency. These transactions include:

1. Buying or selling goods priced in a currency other than the entity's functional currency.
2. Borrowing or lending funds (including intercompany balances) denominated in a different currency.
3. Engaging in an unperformed forward exchange contract.

As becomes evident, companies with foreign subsidiaries can readily become engaged in foreign currency transactions which must be considered when financial statements are prepared. But, in addition, companies which have no foreign branches may also in the everyday course of business become involved in foreign currency transactions.

Regardless of whether the company is entirely domestic-based or not at the transaction date, each resulting asset, liability, revenue, expense, gain, or loss not already denominated in the entity's functional currency must be so measured and recorded. At the close of each subsequent accounting period, all unsettled monetary balances are to be remeasured using the exchange rates in effect on the balance-sheet date. Gains and losses from remeasuring or settling foreign currency transactions are accounted for as current income.

**Appendix I**

# Index

*All references are to paragraph (¶) numbers.*

*All references are to paragraph (¶) numbers.*

*All references are to paragraph (¶) numbers.*

**CHE**

*All references are to paragraph (¶) numbers.*

*All references are to paragraph (¶) numbers.*

*All references are to paragraph (¶) numbers.*

*All references are to paragraph (¶) numbers.*

*All references are to paragraph (¶) numbers.*

*All references are to paragraph (¶) numbers.*

*All references are to paragraph (¶) numbers.*

**IAS**

*All references are to paragraph (¶) numbers.*

*All references are to paragraph (¶) numbers.*

**Operating segments**–continued
. defined . . . 5001.11
. disclosures for . . . 5003.01; 20,005.09
. economic characteristics of . . . 5011.07
. for Internet portion of business . . . 19,019.05–
.07
. quantitative thresholds for separate reporting
of . . . 5001.15

**Organization and start-up costs,
deducting** . . . 39,001.07

**Organization for Economic Cooperation and
Development Anti-Bribery Convention,
implementation of** . . . 23,003.25

**Other disclosures (accounting policies and
notes)** . . . 1003

## P

**Partnerships**
. built-in loss rules for . . . 39,009.01
. change in tax year of . . . 15,039.15; 15,039.21

**Payroll fraud** . . . 23,019.25

**PCAOB Auditing Standard No. 1,
References in Auditors' Reports to Standards
of the Public Company Accounting Oversight
Board, use of PCAOB standards in
engagements under** . . . 27,015.01

**PCAOB Auditing Standard No. 2, An Audit of
Internal Control Over Financial Reporting
Performed in Conjunction with an Audit of
Financial Statements**
. assessment of internal controls in . . . 23,000
. disclosures and expectations of management
in . . . 27,015.03

**PCAOB Auditing Standard No. 3, Audit
Documentation, responsibility for record
preparation and retention in** . . . 27,015.05–.07

**PCAOB Auditing Standard No. 4, Rules on
Auditor Independence and Tax Services,
ethics and independence rules
in** . . . 27,015.09

**Pension and Other Postretirement Plans, FASB
Statement No. 158** . . . 6001

**Pension information, disclosure of** . . . 6015.01

**Pension Protection Act of 2006**
. charitable giving changes . . . 39,012
mandates for transparency in Exempt
Organizations . . . 10,003.15–10,003.19

**Personal Financial Specialist, investment
counseling by.** *See* Financial planning by CPA

**Personal Financial Specialist
credential** . . . 28,029
. experience requirement for . . . 28,029.05
. knowledge about equities and debt of . . . 29,000
. points for . . . 28,029.01
. reaccreditation for . . . 28,029.03

**Personal service corporation, change in tax year
of** . . . 15,039.19; 15,039.21

**Plain English Disclosure rule** . . . 35,000–
35,017.27
. amendments affecting . . . 35,017.11
. cautions for using . . . 35,017.27

**Plain English Disclosure rule**–continued
. comment letters received for . . . 35,013
. compliance with . . . 35,009.01; 35,017.21
. costs for preparing documents
using . . . 35,015
. cover pages under . . . 35,017.23
. documents subject to . . . 35,017.09
. glossaries and defined terms for . . . 35,017.07
. guidance for . . . 35,017–35,017.27
. investor protection intended by . . . 35,001
. legal documents filed with prospectuses that
use . . . 35,009.05; 35,017.13
. length of prospectus using . . . 35,017.17
. pilot program using . . . 35,005
. prospectuses simplified using . . . 35,003;
35,011.01–.09
. risk descriptions under . . . 35,017.01–.05
. SEC adoption of . . . 35,000; 35,007–35,009.05
. summary for . . . 35,017.25
. for technical terminology . . . 35,009.03;
35,017.15

**Pooling-of-interest method prohibited for
business combinations** . . . 6043.01;
10,009.05

**Portfolio management of
investments** . . . 28,023.03–.07

**Potpourri projects of FASB** . . . 6019

**Power of attorney for representing
client** . . . 18,030
. Form 56 required for . . . 18,030.13
. revoking . . . 18,030.15
. situations not requiring . . . 18,030.07

**Practice before the IRS** . . . 18,000–18,030
. authorization for . . . 18,007
. defined . . . 18,005
. enrollment for . . . 18,009
. enrollment renewal for . . . 18,027
. recognized representatives for . . . 18,007
. regulations for . . . 18,003

**Practice Bulletin 14, Accounting and Reporting
by Limited Liability Companies and Limited
Liability Partnership, disclosure and
presentation addressed in** . . . 44,033.05

**Preferred stock, types of** . . . 3001.03

**Prepaid tuition plans** . . . 38,023

**Present value, computing and
applying** . . . 1037

**Presidentially declared disaster areas, tax relief
for** . . . 39,015.03

**Principal residence, sale of.** *See* Main home

**Principles-based accounting standards, study
of** . . . 6019.01

**Prior period adjustments** . . . 3005

**Production budget**
. adjusting . . . 14,005.01
. goods in process investigated
for . . . 14,009.05
. preparing . . . 14,005.03
. to smooth out fluctuations for optimal productive
capacity . . . 14,005

**Production costs**
. determining . . . 14,005.03
. elements of . . . 13,009.05

*All references are to paragraph (¶) numbers.*

*All references are to paragraph (¶) numbers.*

*All references are to paragraph (¶) numbers.*

*All references are to paragraph (¶) numbers.*

*All references are to paragraph (¶) numbers.*